VIVA
TRAVEL GUIDES

Chile

1st Edition
April 2010

Santiago - Middle Chile - Norte Grande - Norte Chico -
The Lake District - Chiloé - Carretera Austral -
Patagonia - Argentine Patagonia - Tierra del Fuego -
Antarctica - Pacific Islands

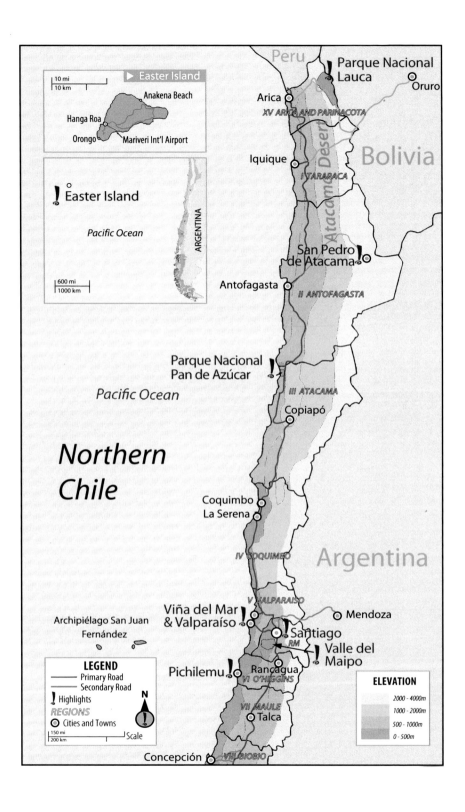

Easter Island

10 mi
10 km

Anakena Beach

Hanga Roa

Orongo

Mariveri Int'l Airport

Easter Island

Pacific Ocean

ARGENTINA

600 mi
1000 km

Peru

Parque Nacional
Lauca

Oruro

Arica

XV ARICA AND PARINACOTA

Atacama Desert

Iquique

I TARAPACA

Bolivia

San Pedro
de Atacama

Antofagasta

II ANTOFAGASTA

Parque Nacional
Pan de Azúcar

III ATACAMA

Pacific Ocean

Copiapó

*Northern
Chile*

Coquimbo
La Serena

IV COQUIMBO

Argentina

V VALPARAÍSO

Archipiélago San Juan
Fernández

Viña del Mar
& Valparaíso

Mendoza

Santiago
RM

Valle del
Maipo

Pichilemu

Rancagua

VI O'HIGGINS

LEGEND

Primary Road
Secondary Road

Highlights

REGIONS

Cities and Towns

150 mi
200 km

Scale

N

VII MAULE

Talca

ELEVATION

2000 - 4000m
1000 - 2000m
500 - 1000m
0 - 500m

Concepción

VIII BIOBÍO

ELEVATION

2000 - 4000m
1000 - 2000m
500 - 1000m
0 - 500m

Easter Island

Pacific Ocean

Argentina

600 mi
1000 km

Antarctica

Concepción

VIII BIOBIO

IX LA ARAUCANIA

Temuco
Pucón

Valdivia

XIV LOS RÍOS

X LOS LAGOS
Puerto Montt

Ancud

Chiloé
Island

Carretera Austral

Southern
Chile

Coyhaique

XI AYSEN

Pacific Ocean

Villa O'Higgins

Parque Nacional
Los Glaciares

El Calafate

Atlantic Ocean

Parque Nacional
Torres del Paine

Puerto Natales

XII MAGALLANES

Porveni

Punta Arenas

Ushuaia

LEGEND
——— Primary Road
——— Secondary Road
❗ Highlights
REGIONS
◉ Cities and towns
150 mi
200 km

N

Scale

▲ Torres del Paine National Park - Chilean Patagonia

Named for the 3,000-meter (10,000 ft) rock formations that tower over the region, Torres del Paine is an outdoor enthusiast's paradise with countless opportunities for climbing, hiking and trekking. As part of the UNESCO Biosphere Reserve, the park is blessed with mega-fauna like guanacos (pictured), rhea (relatives of ostriches) and condors. With beautiful lakes, rivers, forests and mountains, the scenery is unparalleled anywhere on the planet.

▲ Pucón - The Lake District

Surrounded by crystal clear lakes and towering volcanoes, Pucón offers easy access to outdoor adventure activities like skiing, snowboarding, hiking, trekking, climbing, horseback riding, fishing and whitewater rafting. After a day of adventure, relax in the myriad of natural hot springs or treat yourself to a luxury spa.

▲ Easter Island (Rapa Nui) - Pacific Islands

Famed for its mysterious Moai sculptures, this volcanic island boasts captivating sacred sites and extraordinary festivals. Easter Island has enough activities to keep you occupied for days: wander the grasslands on bike or horseback in search of ruins, or dive, snorkel and surf in the Pacific.

▲ San Pedro de Atacama - Norte Grande

The landscape here is so strange that it can sometimes feel like you've stepped into another dimension. Although set in the driest desert in the world, San Pedro de Atacama has way more than just sand. A visit here includes the chance to explore a volcano, geysers, canyons and endless stars above.

▼ Valparaíso & Viña del Mar

Affectionately known as Valpo, Valparaíso's beautiful architecture helped it become a UNESCO World Heritage site in 2003. The city's famous bohemian vibe dominates the bars, cafés and restaurants. Viña del Mar is the place to be seen by affluent Chileans and is one of the country's hottest beach resorts.

▲ Antarctica

Access the white continent on a cruise departing from Ushuaia, Argentina or Punta Arenas, Chile. Remote and surreal, Antarctica teems with wildlife, including penguins, seals and whales. Budget 10 - 20 days and a big roll of cash.

▲ Lauca National Park - Norte Grande

Parque Nacional Lauca is one of Chile's, and indeed the world's, most extraordinary national parks. These snowy, pre-Andean volcanoes, vast highlands and lush wetlands are complemented by amazing wildlife, including vicuñas, vizcachas and condors. This is the perfect place to relax and get in touch with nature.

▼ Pan de Azúcar National Park

At Pan de Azúcar it can be hard to tell where the beach ends and the desert begins. Birdwatchers, beach bums and sightseers alike will love this amazing national park. The area is known for its white sand beaches and colorful sunsets over sky-high ocean cliffs. Keep an eye out for guanacos and don't forget your binoculars.

▲ Santiago

Chile's capital city, Santiago, is a major cultural center where you can spend days visiting museums, parks, open markets, theaters, restaurants, dance clubs and bars. Sandwiched between mountain ranges, smack dab in the middle of the country, Santiago also makes a great jumping off point to Chile's other famous destinations.

▲ Glacier National Park - Argentine Patagonia

In Parque Nacional Los Glaciares you'll find hundreds of glaciers, treacherous peaks, forests, flatlands and glacial waterways. A variety of activities are possible in the park–a UNESCO World Heritage Site–including trekking and fishing. Summit some of the most challenging climbs in the world like Mt. Torre and Fitz Roy, or leisurely gaze at the Perito Moreno Glacier's crumbling walls.

▼ Carretera Austral - Northern Patagonia

This legendary scenic highway serves Chile's expansive and sparsely populated Aisén and Los Lagos regions. Beginning in Puerto Montt and ending in Villa O'Higgins, the journey covers 1,247 kilometers (775 mi). Travel by bike, car or motorcycle to Parque Nacional Hornopirén and Coyhaique. All but the most adventurous should steer clear of Volcán Chaitén, as it continues its massive eruptions.

▲ Maipo Valley - Wine Country

For a hint of old world sophistication, come to Valle del Maipo—home to 20 world-class wineries. The broad geography allows for a particularly broad variety of wines. Tours and tastings can be found at every scale, from well-known vineyards like Concha y Toro to family-owned micro-wineries.

▼ Chiloé - Northern Patagonia

If there is anyplace that can be described as quaint, it is Chiloé. This island in the south of Chile has wonderful seaside drives, lovely little fishing villages, and lots of island charm. Be sure to check out the fantastic wooden churches between meals of freshly caught seafood.

▲ Pichilemu - Surf Haven

Picilemu, with its soft, charcoal black sandy shores, is regarded as being one of the best surf spots in the world. Punta Lobo's half-mile-long-left gets waves up to 20 ft (6 m) high. This coastal town also offers lush forests, historical attractions and a thriving nightlife, making it much more than just a place to hit the waves.

RECOMMENDED ITINERARIES

Because of its shape, Chile is a difficult country to travel extensively. Be aware that any itinerary will involve days in transit. Air travel within the country will speed things up, but will increase costs tremendously. If you're only going for a week, it's best to focus on a specific area.

The Whirlwind

Chile from top to bottom in two weeks:

Day 1: Arrive in Santiago and settle in. Hit the Mercado Central for a taste of Chile's culinary variety, then ascend Cerro San Cristobal or Cerro Santa Lucia for a panoramic view of the city.

Days 2-4: Fly to Calama, then make your way to San Pedro de Atacama by rental car or bus. Spend a few days enjoying the strange beauty of the world's driest desert.

Day 5: Fly to Punta Arenas.

Days 6-10: From Punta Arenas, head north to Puerto Natales and spend the next four days touring and hiking Torres del Paine National Park.

Days 11-13: Fly back to Santiago, then hop a bus to the coast to spend a few days in Viña del Mar and Valparaíso. On the way back to Santiago, make a circuit through Isla Negra to tour the home of Pablo Neruda, then Pomaire, famous for its cheap, handmade ceramics.*

Day 14: Return to Santiago.

You can substitute Days 11-13 with a stop in Pucón (flights between Punta Arenas and Santiago usually stop there) for some adventure in the Lake District, including volcano treks, horseback excursions, rafting, natural hot springs, zip-lining through the canopy and more lakes and waterfalls than you can shake a stick at."

San Pedro de Atacama, Laguna de Chaxa

Santiago Skyline

Santiago and the Central Valley

With Patagonia in the south and the Atacama Desert in the north, it can be tempting to jet away from Santiago as soon as possible. But the leisurely beach towns and world-famous vineyards of the Central Valley hold pleasures all their own.

In one week:

Day 1: Arrive in Santiago. Follow suggestions for day one in The Whirlwind itinerary.

Days 2-3: Arrange tours of the vineyards in the Colchagua Valley, like Clos Apalta, Casa Silva and Montes.

Days 4-6: Head to Viña del Mar to walk the boardwalk, lay out on the beach, and take a dip in the Pacific. Then take a trip down the coast to Valparaíso for a day or two of wandering among the graffiti-covered buildings that twist up the hillsides, and stay for some of the best nightlife in Chile.

Day 7: Return to Santiago.

In two weeks:

Day 1: Fly into Santiago.

Days 2-3: The Vineyards. Follow suggestions for days 2-3 in the one-week itinerary.

Day 4-6: For a taste of Argentina's offerings as well as a ride through the Andes on a road shaped like ribbon candy, take a bus to the tranquil town of Mendoza, just across the border.

Days 7-10: Viña del Mar and Valparaíso. See days 4-6 in the one-week itinerary.

Day 11: From Valparaíso, take a trip to Isla Negra, home of the Nobel-winning poet Pablo Neruda, and, working your way back to Santiago, visit Pomaire, famous for its cheap, handmade pottery.

Days 12-14: Santiago. Follow suggestions for day one in The Whirlwind itinerary, but add a few more stops, like Barrio Bellavista (for a raucous night out) and the artisan market Santa Lucía.

To the End of the World

Patagonia's foreboding terrain, combined with the often-frigid temperatures, make it the ideal place for adventurers to test their mettle.

In one week:

Day 1: From Santiago, fly to Punta Arenas.

Day 2: Take a bus north to Puerto Natales, your gateway to Torres del Paine National Park.

Day 3: Bus tour through the park. You'll want to do more, but you only have a week.

Day 4: Bus to El Calafate, Argentina.

Day 5: Take a boat to the face of the Perito Moreno glacier.*

Days 6-7: Return to Puerto Natales, then travel to Punta Arenas to catch a flight back to Santiago.

Alternatively, skip Perito Moreno and spend three days properly enjoying Torres del Paine. Either way, the distances involved make one week a very rushed Patagonian experience.

To the End of the World

One-Week Itinerary

Torres del Paine

Paine Horns and Lake Pehoé

In two weeks:

Days 1-2: Same as one-week itinerary.

Days 3-5: Torres del Paine. You'll want at least two days in Torres del Paine, and up to 10 if you plan to hike the famous W or Circuit trails.

Day 6: Take a bus across the Argentine border to El Calafate.

Day 7: Boat trip to the face of the Perito Moreno glacier.

Days 8-10: Head even farther north to El Chaltén for a day or two hiking around Mt. Fitz Roy.

Day 11: Back to El Calafate for a flight to Ushuaia.*

Day 12: Enjoy being in the southernmost city in the world.

Days 13-14: Flight back to Punta Arenas, then back to Santiago.

If your thirst for southern exposure is still unquenched in Ushuaia, and if time and spirit allow, take a ferry to Puerto Williams and, finally, to the desolate Parque Nacional Cabo de Hornos—congratulations, you can officially go no farther south without being in Antarctica.

The Carretera Austral

This 1,247-kilometer (775 mi) dirt road that begins just south of Puerto Montt and ends in Villa O'Higgins in Northern Patagonia, passes through vast stretches of un-populated and thickly forested terrain. It's a famous challenge for bicyclists and motorists; this is the truly pioneering way to see Patagonia. You can start in Puerto Montt, or skip it and start in Chaitén, as the trip between the two involves many ferry crossings, which can be expensive.

In two weeks:

Day 1: Fly into Santiago. Check out the city.

Day 2: Fly to Puerto Montt, pick up your rental car, and lay in supplies. Lunch on great seafood at Anselmó Market and take in a few sights before catching the night ferry to Chaitén.*

Day 3: Have your camera ready to catch Volcán Chaitén in action as the ship nears Chaitén port. Head directly to Termas El Amarillo for a good soak in the hot

Priceless view from the Carretera Austral

Massive Volcano Eruption of Volcán Chaitén

springs and a night's stay, or rest at Puerto Cárdenas on the shores of Lago Yelcho.

Day 4-5: To Futaleufú, east off the Carretera Austral, to kayak or raft the turquoise waters of this world-class river.

Day 6: Back on the Carretera Austral, south to Puyuhuapi. Hike to the hanging glacier in Parque Nacional Queulat. Close out the day relaxing at Termas de Puyuhuapi hot spring resort on an island in the fjord.

Day 7-8: To Coyhaique to stock up on supplies and cash. Visit one of the three nearby nature reserves. Or, if you can spare an extra day, take a cruise from Puerto Chacabuco to Laguna San Rafael. On the last evening in Coyhaique, drive down to Villa Cerro Castillo.

Day 9: In the morning, horseback ride into Reserva Nacional Cerro Castillo. Drive down to Río Tranquilo.

Day 10: In Río Tranquilo´s morning light, take a boat tour to the marble caves dotting Lago General Carrera. In the afternoon, head out on the Bahía Explorador road to visit Glaciar Los Exploradores. An extra day here can be spent hiking the glacier.

Day 11: A day's fishing at Puerto Bertrand's trout-rich lake, or rafting on the Río Baker.

Day 12: Drive along the south shore of Lago General Carrera to Chile Chico. Spend the day visiting the wildlife and rock paintings in Reserva Nacional Jeínemeni.**

Day 13: Take the ferry from Chile Chico to Puerto Ibáñez on the lake's north shore, then continue to Coyhaique. Return your rental car.

Day 14: Fly back to Santiago.

Transportation to and from Chaitén can be disrupted at any time by Volcán Chaitén, which is active and extremely unstable. Overnight stays are restricted to people arriving on late ferries or catching one the next day.

**If you can plan a third week, you can reach the end of the road at Villa O'Higgins, stopping along the way at Cochrane and Caleta Tortel. And if you happen to have yet another week to spare, hang onto the car and take the ferry from Puerto Chacabuco to Quellón on Isla Chiloé and make your way back to Puerto Montt. Drop off your rental car car there and fly back to Santiago.*

V!VA TRAVEL GUIDES

Chile

About this Book

At V!VA, we believe that you shouldn't have to settle
for an outdated guidebook. You can rest assured that in your hands
is the most up-to-date guidebook available on Chile because:

-- The final research for this book was completed on February 1, 2010.
-- Each entry is "time stamped" with the date it was last updated
-- V!VA's hyper-efficient web-to-book publishing process brings books to press
   in days or weeks, not months or years like our competitors
-- V!VA's country guides are updated at least once per year.

When you buy a V!VA Guide, here's what you're getting:

-- The expertise of professional travel writers, local experts and real travelers in-country bringing
   you first-hand, unbiased recommendations to make the most out of your trip
-- The wisdom of editors who actually live in Latin America, not New York, Melbourne, or London like
   other guidebook companies
-- Advice on how to escape the overly-trodden gringo trail, meet locals and understand the culture
-- The knowledge you'll need to travel responsibly while getting more for your money

V!VA Boot Camps

Many of the contributors to this book were students at V!VA's Santiago, Chile Boot Camp.
Join V!VA at an upcoming Travel Writers Boot Camp and learn all you need to become a
guidebook writer.

Santiago, Chile bootcamp

Buenos Aires, Argentina
bootcamp

Cuernavaca, Mexico
bootcamp

Antigua, Guatemala
bootcamp

Join us at the next Boot Camp:
Costa Rica September 27 - October 1, 2010
find out more at www.vivatravelguides.com/bootcamp/

V!VA Travel Guides Chile.

ISBN-10: 0-9791264-7-9

ISBN-13: 978-0-9791264-7-5

◊ Cover Design: Jason Halberstadt, 2009 ◊
◊ Cover Photo: Luciano Stabel, "Puerto Varas 11 - Llanquihue 1," 2008 ◊
◊ Cover Photo: Rustyn Mesdag, "Port Lockroy, Antarctica," 2008 ◊
◊ Color Insert Photos: Jason Halberstadt, "guanaco posing, "Pucón," "Penguin," "Santiago Catedral," "Glacier," torres sky," and "Torres," 2008 ◊

CONTENTS

INTRO & INFO

Middle Chile   124

INTRO & INFO

INTRO & INFO

ABOUT THE WRITERS

Upon re-declaring her independence at age 29, **Lorraine Caputo** packed her trusty Rocinante (so her knapsack's called) and began traipsing throughout the Americas, from Alaska to Tierra del Fuego. Her work has been published in a wide variety of publications in the U.S., Canada and Latin America. As the lead writer, Lorraine spent many months hiking and hitching through the depths of Chile, specifically The Lake District, and Northern and Southern Patagonia.

This native Ohioan and University of Cincinnati graduate left the world of sports journalism to sign on full time with V!VA in 2008. **Chris Hughes** has resided in South America for more than a year, exploring Chile, Argentina and Ecuador in the process. A seasoned traveler, he has also visited other Latin American destinations such as Colombia, Puerto Rico and Brazil, as well as Europe. For this book, Chris worked on the Norte Grande and Norte Chico chapters.

Noleen Turner originally hails from Northern Ireland but has lived in Chile for two years, where she likes the weather and food much better! She holds degrees from the University of Glasgow and University of Ulster and previously worked for five years producing corporate publications and two years as an editor. When she's not scouring Santiago hotspots for V!VA, Noleen can be found composing folk songs that no one wants to listen to and cycling around the city.

Lauren Yero is a young but compulsive traveler who has trekked across four continents in search of the the magnificent and the unique. After finishing an undergraduate degree in literature and philosophy, she came to work for V!VA, writing up the coastal area of Middle Chile—and in the process added quite a few *Chilenismos* to her Spanish. A self-proclaimed global citizen, for the time being she calls Portland, Oregon, her home-sweet-home.

Originally from the United States, **Rustyn Mesdag** has been living in Patagonia for five years, working as a guide for Erratic Rock Guide Service in and around Torres del Paine. He is also their office carpenter and our Patagonia expert, but his true love is climbing waterfall ice around the world. Rustyn lives in Puerto Natales with his wife and two sons, and for the past four years has published the English-language travel newspaper for Southern Chile.

Kevin Funk is a native of the Pennsylvania Dutch heartland city of York, and a graduate of the University of Pittsburgh with degrees in political science and journalism. When not writing political commentary about U.S. foreign policy, Kevin indulges his wanderlust—especially in Latin America, and his home-away-from-home, the wondrously unique and criminally underappreciated port city of Valparaíso, Chile. Kevin wrote the Chiloé section of this book.

OUR CONTRIBUTORS:

Zenan Delaney, Julian Soames, and Tiago Braga contributed Easter Island coverage; Shanie Matthews wrote up Puerto Varas, and Jon Santiago wrote the Puerto Williams section. Additionally: Alison Isaac, Carrie Murphy, Dr. Crit Minster, Dag Olav Norem, Daniel Arredondo, Daniel T. Johnson, David Vincent, Erin Hellend, Heather Poyhonen (and the Black Sheep Patagonia); Karin Malonek, Kelley Coyner, Mariana Cotlear, Nick Rosen, Peter Anderson, Rick Segreda, Tammy Portnoy, Tom Ravenscroft, Will Gray, and Lamas Hostal.

INTRO & INFO

ABOUT THE EDITORS

INTRO & INFO

Paula Newton is V!VA's operations expert. With an MBA and a background in New Media, Paula is the Editor-in-Chief and the organizing force behind the team. With an insatiable thirst for off-the-beaten-track travel, Paula has traveled extensively, especially in Europe and Asia, and has explored more than 30 countries. She currently lives in Quito.

Andrea Davoust joined V!VA after over two years of working and living out of a suitcase in Eastern Europe and various African countries. Before that, she studied political science and international relations in Paris, and earned a degree in journalism in Scotland. As the resident Frenchwoman, Andrea brings her expertise of France, Europe and the African continent. Andrea was the managing editor of this first edition.

Margaret Rode hails from Chicago where she received BA degrees in English Literature and Spanish from North Park University. Her pins in the map include, but are not limited to: a train-traipse through Europe and southern Sweden, volunteering in the Dominican Republic and on Ecuador's coast, and a roadtrip across the U.S. Her most recent explorations include Colombia, Peru, Bolivia, and Ecuador.

Karen Nagy is a staff editor/writer at V!VA. She studied travel writing and learned the joys of Mediterranean island-hopping in Greece, and went on to receive BA degrees in Journalism and International Studies from the University of Oregon. After living in Argentina in 2007, she was eager to make a South American base-camp for herself once again in Quito.

Michelle Lillie is a staff editor/writer at V!VA. She holds a BA and MA in International Relations from Loyola University Chicago, and brings to V!VA some substantial globe-trotting experience. Michelle has not only traversed Europe, Asia, North Africa, Central and South America, but has also lived in Italy, Thailand and China. Michelle currently resides in Quito, Ecuador.

Rachel Anderson is currently a staff editor/writer at V!VA. Midwestern born and bred, she earned a BA in Psychology and a minor in Eastern Religion from Gustavus Adolphus College. Her life's varied landscape includes studying psychiatry in Fiji and unleashing her inner Inca as a volunteer in Cusco, Peru. Before V!VA, Rachel studied copywriting at an advertising school in Minneapolis, Minnesota.

MANY THANKS TO:

Emma Mueller, Joanne Sykes, Kyle Adams and Mark Samcoe—V!VA's intern superheroes; Maribel Jarrin and Fernanda Ureña (map-maker extraordinaires); Rigoberto Pinto and Cristian Avila, the programming masterminds who keep www.vivatravelguides.com running smoothly and are always willing to lend a hand to the not-so-computer-savvy staff; and to the whole Metamorf team for their support.

Additional thanks to Nelia & Vincent, Stéphanie & Simon, Trevor, the biking geologists Olivier & Caroline, Javier, Yvonne & Felipe, Hank & Erik, Elisabeth—plus Sebastian & Marisol & the hundreds of Chileans who taught us about the culture, history & beauty of their country through *cueca* and poetry, sharing wine & *maté*

Join VIVA on Facebook. Fan "VIVA Travel Guides Chile."

About VIVA Travel Guides

We began VIVA Travel Guides back in 2007 because we simply wanted a better travel guide to our home country of Ecuador. All the guidebooks at the time were years out of date and weren't nearly as helpful as they should have been to real travelers. We knew we could do better.

We asked the question: "What would the travel guidebook look like if it was invented today from the ground up in the era of Google, Facebook, Wikipedia and nearly ubiquitous Internet connectivity?"

We concluded that the key to creating a superior guide is a knowledgeable community of travelers, on-the-ground professional travel writers, local experts and street-smart editors, all collaborating together on the web and working toward the goal of creating the most helpful, up-to-date guide available anywhere.

INTRO & INFO

Continuously Updated
Traveler reports come in daily via the web and we take advantage of highly efficient 'web to book' technology and modern digital printing to speed the latest travel intelligence to the printed page in record time. We update our books at least once per year—more often than any other major publisher. We even print the date that each piece of information in the book was last updated so that you can make informed decisions about every detail of your trip.

A Better Way to Build a Guidebook
We're convinced we make a better guidebook. It's a more costly, painstaking way to make a guidebook, but we think it's worth it, because you're be able to get more out of your trip to Chile. There are many ways that you can get involved in making VIVA Travel Guides even better.

Help other travelers by writing a review
Did you love a place? Will you never return? Every destination in this guidebook is listed on our website with space for user ratings and reviews. Share your experiences, help out other travelers and let the world know what you think.

Make corrections and suggestions
Prices rise, good places go bad, and bad places go out of business. If you find something that needs to be updated or improved in this book, please let us know. Report any inaccuracies at www.vivatravelguides.com/corrections and we'll incorporate them into our information within a few days. As a small token of our thanks for correcting an error or submitting a suggestion we'll send you a coupon for 50 percent off any of our E-books or 20 percent off any of our printed books.

Make your reservations at www.vivatravelguides.com
You can support VIVA's mission by reserving your hotels and flights at www.vivatravelguides.com. When you buy from our website, we get a commission, which we reinvest in making our guides a better resource for travelers. Find the best price on flights at www.vivatravelguides.com/flights and efficiently reserve your hotels and hostels at www.vivatravelguides.com/hotels.

We sincerely hope you enjoy this book, and your trip to Chile even more.

Happy Trails,

Jason Halberstadt
Founder, VIVA Travel Guides

REGIONAL SUMMARIES

Santiago, p.72

Santiago, smack in the middle of Chile, is a modern city with a European feel and is the place where most visitors begin their trip. Frequent earthquakes have gradually claimed most of the colonial buildings, and Santiago lacks the 24-hour party reputation of other Latin American capitals, so a couple of days should be sufficient to see all the main attractions. The Museo Chileno de Arte Precolombina shouldn't be missed, as it features 3,000 pieces of Pre-Columbian art from over 1,000 Latin American cultures. On a clear day, the high Cerro San Cristobal provides fine views over both the city and the Andes. Head up to the summit on the funicular railway and enjoy a picnic in the park at the top. Clear days are rare in Santiago, but try to catch a sunset from the top of the cerro, when the thick layer of haze burns a deep orange. Check out Barrio Bellavista, Santiago's Latin Quartergets particularly lively on Thursday, Friday and Saturday nights when Chileans and foreigners pour into the restaurants, bars, cafés and 'salsatecas' that line the narrow streets. Santiago's Old-World feel and the proliferation of modern conveniences, such as high-quality hotels and restaurants, make the city a good base for exploring the nearby regions. Day or overnight trips to the wine country to the south, the beaches to the west, and the Andean ski resorts to the east can easily be arranged in the capital. See "Around Santiago" for more information about these day trips.

Middle Chile, p.124

Middle Chile is the country's most densely populated region, but with the forbidding desert in the north and the harsh Patagonian terrain in the south, most of the population lives to the just-right center. This is the location of the capital, Santiago, as well as the spirited and grungy Valparaíso and the beach resort Viña del Mar. Chile's world-famous wines, now rivaling those of France—and at a fraction of the price—are produced here in the Central Valley. Although deserts, mountains and glaciers beckon, don't be too quick to rush away from this area; there is plenty to see and do. Take a tour of the historic port city Valparaíso, a UNESCO World Heritage Site. Visit the Mercado Central in Santiago for a fresh seafood plate, then ride one of the almost vertical *ascensores* (funicular railways) to the top of one of the cerros surrounding the city—Cerro San Cristobal or Cerro Santa Lucia. Take a day trip to Sewell, the city of stairs. Ski or snowboard the legendary Andes mountains. Go camping in Reserva Nacional Río Los Cipreses, close to Rancagua. Enjoy a day out with a real Chilean cowboy at the Puro Caballo Ranch (www.purocaballo.cl) about one hour from Santiago. Go tour a few of the vineyards in the Central Valley to taste their world-renowned wines.

Norte Grande, p.181

As you move north, the sun-baked hills and gentle valleys of the Norte Chico gradually give way to the more desolate plains of the Atacama desert, and the beginning of the Norte Grande. On the eastern edge of the country, the desert climbs up into the Altiplano highlands, where salt flats and lakes spread out far into the distance, eventually spilling over into Bolivia and Argentina. As a whole, the area takes up nearly a quarter of the country's landmass, yet contains less than five percent of its inhabitants, a testimony to the aridity of the land. Apart from the Lake District, the Norte Grande is the most visited area of Chile. Most people opt to visit via tour, as the vast and inhospitable landscape makes independent travel difficult. In the Atacama desert, you can take a trip out to the nitrate ghost towns of Humberstone and Santa Laura, which are easy to reach from the coastal town of Iquique. Another of the desert's highlights are the immense geoglyphs carved into the sides of the gaping ravines by long-departed indigenous tribes. The vast, steaming El Tatio Geysers just south of San Pedro de Atacama are also worth a visit. Up in the highlands of the northern Altiplano, head to one of the national parks on the border of Bolivia, such as Parque Nacional Lacuna and Parque Nacional Volcán Isluga, where mineral baths and shimmering blue lakes are surrounded by miles of empty salt flats.

Norte Chico, p.242

The Norte Chico stretches about 500 kilometers north from the Santiago region and is characterized by long, parched hills. The dry terrain is punctuated occasionally by lush valleys, based around rivers that flow down from the Andes toward the ocean. This is where Chile's national drink Pisco comes from; the region has prospered mainly due to the huge reserves of gold and silver that were discovered by the Incas and are still being mined today. The coast is a definite highlight, with beaches that are considered among the best in Chile, although few have been developed for tourism like those closer to Santiago. The sandy bays and turquoise waters make a relaxing getaway for those who want to chill out and do nothing for a few days. Perhaps the main attraction of this region, though, is La Serena, one of Chile's oldest cities and, with its colonial architecture and seaside setting, arguably its most attractive. It makes a great base for exploring some of the nearby beaches, as well as the inland scenery. Parque Nacional Nevado Tres Cruces is another great spot to visit, with its vibrant green lakes, misty volcanoes, and abundant wildlife. It's easy to get to from Copiapó, but is surprisingly seldom visited by tourists – which makes it all the more pleasant for those who do visit.

The Lake District, p.268

The Lake District is Chile's most visited area, and it's easy to see why. The region, filled with placid lakes, white-water rivers, forests and cloud-shrouded volcanoes, contains several national parks and reserves, including the Parque Nacional Vicente Pérez Rosales, the oldest in the country. Good roads and public transportation mean that it's easy to travel around the district. Despite the fact that thousands of tourists pour into the region each year, the many hiking trails are not crowded and you could easily walk for days without seeing another person. Kayaking, rafting and climbing are also becoming increasingly popular as the tourist infrastructure improves, and there are many good bases to choose from. One of the most popular is Pucón, a small tourist town on the shores of Lago Villarrica. It's a laid-back place, with plenty of opportunities for meeting up with other travelers.

Chiloé, p.374

Chiloé consists of nearly 100 islands just off the coast of the Carretera Austral, of which only 30 or so are inhabited. Modern development is slowly starting to filter through to the islands from the mainland, but people still live in traditional stilt-raised houses on the shore, and almost every corner has a historic wooden church or chapel. The main island is also called Chiloé. At 200 by 75 kilometers, it is the second largest island in South America, after Tierra del Fuego. Parque Nacional de Chiloé, on the west coast, is the reason for most people's visit here. It is very accessible and has numerous hiking trails that meander through the dense coastal rainforest and rolling sand dunes. Castro, the island's capital, makes a good base for exploring the park as it is close by and tours can be arranged in the town. Other visitors stay at Ancud, a lively little fishing town in the north, which is always bustling with activity and certainly worth a visit, even if you don't spend the night there. Boats go to all of the inhabited islands, although schedules vary widely. Isla Quinchao and Isla Lemuy are just off the mainland and accessible by bus. You can see everything in a day, but many people choose to stay a few more just to relax and enjoy the slow pace of life.

The Carretera Austral and Northern Patagonia, p.391

Considering its proximity to the Lake District, the Carretera Austral (Southern Highway) and the Chilean part of Southern Patagonia receive surprisingly few visitors—a lot of people simply skip over the area on their way down to Tierra del Fuego. The climate starts to get harsher around here, with strong winds, freezing cold nights and barren terrain—a landscape immortalised by novelist Bruce Chatwin's book *In Patagonia*. One interesting spot on the Carreterra Austral is Villa O'Higgins, a tiny hamlet in the south that owes its popularity mainly to the fact that it marks the end of the Carretera, the narrow dirt road from which this region takes its name. The 1,240-kilometer (770-mi) road is a famous challenge for bicyclists and, in recent years, has become increasingly popular with motorists who want a more independent Patagonian experience. The drive down the final 100 kilometers of the road boasts some amazing scenery, as does the town itself, set on the edge of Lago O'Higgins.

Southern Patagonia and Tierra del Fuego, p.450

In Southern Patagonia, the "land of fire," icy channels and fjords rend the land, fraying it into thousands of islands. Ragged, glacier-frosted mountains stab into the cold blue sky. To the east, the earth relaxes into pampas and steppes. Guanaco (lama) and ñanadú (lesser rhea) wade through stiff, golden grasses, and rose flamingos feed in icy lagoons. Wind-sheared trees permanently stoop to one side. A long gash across the southern tip of the continent connects the Atlantic and Pacific Oceans. Here, penguins and other seabirds nest on islets. Further toward the "End of the World" looms Tierra del Fuego, Isla Navarino and finally the frozen continent of Antarctica. Chile's Southern Patagonia and Tierra del Fuego is a region of castle-like fairy tales, granite spire mountains, glistening ice fields and virgin forests. This is where, in the days of the explorers, sailors battled their way around Cape Horn (Cabo de Hornos) through Drake's Passage and the Straits of Magellan (Estrecho de Magallanes). The winds across the Patagonia plains, whistling around the farthest reaches of the Andes, are a notorious challenge for bicyclists and hikers. It is a land of 150,000 people, two million sheep, and half a million penguins. No road connects Chile's Northern Patagonia with its Southern counterpart. Some day, perhaps, the Carretera Austral will find a way here, but in the meantime, the only way to arrive by land is to enter Argentina and exit again into Chile. The famous Navimag Canales Patagónicos ferry plows through the icy channels along the Pacific coast, from Puerto Montt to Puerto Natales. Get ready to join the ranks of the indigenous peoples, explorers and colonizers and strike your claim in this wild land.

Pacific Islands, p.558

Chile's offshore assets are as alluring as the mainland. Each year, thousands of tourists board the five-hour flight to Easter Island, now one of the most popular travel destinations for overseas visitors. Located thousands of miles from the mainland, the island is famous for its Moai sculptures and ancient cultural celebrations. The Juan Fernández Islands were used as the basis for *Robinson Crusoe*, Daniel Defoe's classic novel of island survival. Tourism has never really taken off here, despite the fact that it is much closer to the mainland than Easter Island. The islands are beautiful—if your thirst is for the road less-traveled, they don't get much less-traveled than this.

Introduction

Wedged between the Andes and the Pacific Ocean, the best known fact about Chile is its wholly improbable shape. Stretching 4,000 km (2,500 mi) south from the base of Peru right to the tip of the continent, it has almost three times as much coastline as its neighbour, yet only half the total landmass. As you might expect of such a country, Chile features huge extremes in its landscape. The very north of the country is occupied by the world's driest desert, some parts of which have never felt a drop of rain, while deep in the south, the famous ice fields of Tierra del Fuego stretch out into the distance like giant floating boulders. In between, more hospitable terrain greets visitors; palm-fringed sandy beaches and well-developed ski-resorts can be reached in a couple of hours from Santiago and further south, the Lake District and Patagonia both feature world-class hiking. On your way down, you can stay in a comfortable hacienda in the midst of Wine Country.

In comparison to Chile's natural wonders, its cities are something of a disappointment. Santiago certainly doesn't have the 24-hour party reputation of other Latin capitals, and its buildings are mainly modern; frequent earthquakes have gradually claimed most of the colonial buildings here, which have since been replaced with more stable, but unattractive, concrete structures. However, they do tend to be clean and safe, with all the modern conveniences (and prices) of a European city, and are good jumping-off points for exploring the back country. Also more reminiscent of Europe than Latin America is Chile's transport system.

The best time to visit Chile depends on which areas you are planning to visit. You can visit Northern Chile all year round, although rain falls in January and February, which can occasionally make road travel difficult. Santiago and the central region is best September to April, when the smog (in Santiago) is minimal and skies are blue. Chileans take their holidays in January and February, so the beaches can get very crowded at this time. Ski resorts are open between June and September. For Patagonia and the Lake District, October to April is a good time – it can rain at any time of year, and falls more the south you go.

Geography

Chile is the longest country in the world, north to south, covering the equivalent of the distance from Norway to Morocco, or New York to Los Angeles. It stretches along 4,300 kilometer (2672 mi) of the South American continent, between the Pacific Ocean and the high ranges of the Andes mountains, encompassing a huge variety of climates and eco-systems.

To the north lies the parched plateau of the Atacama Desert, which is the driest in the world and contains minerals like copper. The central region, which has a Mediterranean climate, is the most populated and is where the majority of wine production is concentrated. Southern Chile is a more temperate land of forests, pastures, lakes and volcanoes, with an Alpine climate that often brings winter snows. While the southern coast is cut into a myriad of fjords, inlets, islands and peninsulas, the wild reaches of Chilean Patagonia are home to glaciers and ice fields.

Also under Chilean sovereignty are Easter Island (Rapa Nui) and Isla Sala y Gómez in the Pacific. Chile has a claim to a wedge of Antarctica, which overlaps with Argentine and British claims, but all have been frozen under the Antarctic treaty. Updated: Mar 04, 2009.

Flora

The elongated body of Chile stretches from the dry and hot Atacama Desert in the north, to the clear blue water of the Lake District, to the icy depths of Patagonia, and contains a huge diversity of animal and plant life in these varied terrains.

Scientists estimate that Chile has between 5,000 and 6,000 species of flora, including the largest number of endemic plants on earth. Due to its isolation from its neighboring countries (by desert, ocean and mountain), Chile's flora has adapted to a range of unique habitats and conditions. To the north, close to the Peruvian border, the arid Atacama Desert blocks any migration of species into the country, and what vegetation there is clusters near the coastal areas. Even in these dry lands, cacti are able to carve out an existence in extraordinary ways, for example by absorbing moisture from the ocean fog.

Native flora dominates most of central Chile, whose shrubs are able to conserve water during the dry season. Chile's national flower, the red bell-shaped Copihue, can be found in the central valley and southern parts of Chile, and as a climbing plant, can reach up to ten meters high above shrubs and trees.

The climate in the south of Chile has encouraged the growth of one of the largest temperate rainforests in the world. The Southern Valdivian, Magellanic and Araucaria forests are home to evergreens and bamboo like plants, pine trees and shrubbery, and the famous "Monkey puzzle" tree.

The Juan Fernández Islands and Easter Island have over 209 native species between them.

National Flower

There are a number of myths concerning the origins of the Copihue, or "long sigh" as the Chilean national flower is known. These stories are nearly all concerned with love, war or bloodshed. One interesting legend says that when the Mapuche were fighting the Spanish, native warriors were forced to leave their families alone for months on end. As legend goes, when the war moved closer to Mapuche land, the wives of the warriors climbed the highest trees they could find to see if there were any survivors. Confronted only by smoke and death, they climbed down weeping, wetting the leaves as they did so. Magically, a blood flower was born of their tears, which was then kept to renubd them of the many indigenous men who lost their lives.

Chilean officials granted the Copihue legal protection in 1977, making picking the flower a crime. It continues to represent the spirit of the Chilean people, both past and present. Updated: May 11, 2009.

Fauna

Living among the plants are a fascinating array of Chilean animals and birds. Due to its many unique habitats, the country has a number of endemic species, of which a full third cannot be found anywhere else on earth. These rare species include the Moustached Turca, a bird found only in Chile's Mediterranean woodlands, the Long-tailed Chinchilla, and the Juan Fernandez Fur Seal.

Llamas and alpacas are common in Chile, particularly in the Altiplano. The northern coast has a variety of bird and marine life, including sea lions and Bottle-nosed Dolphins. Three species of flamingo can also be found in Chile's lakes, including the gregarious Pink Flamingo in the Atacama Desert.

Magellanic Penguins

The southern part of Chile is a great place to view Magellanic Penguins, the vivacious South American birds. The Magellanic Penguin is distinguished from the Humboldt and African Penguins by the two bands that cross its front, one a wide black strip under the chin and the other a horseshoe shape on the stomach. The penguins are naturally shy and nest in deep burrows. The penguins often hide, but keep quiet when visitors approach, as they will quickly come waddling out.

If you time it right, the penguins, some of the only black and white breeds you will see outside Antarctica, can be observed running between the beach and their nests.

The 60-centimeter tall animals feed on a diet of squid and small fish. It is very easy to spend a good two hours just watching the amusing antics of these loveable birds.

The best time to see penguins is during the breeding season from late September to early February, when adults spend much of their time on the beach constructing the nesting sites. It takes five to six weeks for the eggs to hatch; spotting chicks is rare as they usually hide out in the burrow for a month or so before taking their first icy plunge into the sea sometime around April.

Condors are most common in the central valley, while elsewhere, in the Andes, the puma is known to prowl, along with its endangered cousins, the Andean cat and jaguar.

Penguins in Patagonia draw thousands of tourists each year to witness their smart and dignified gatherings. To see these beloved black and white birds, head to Punta Arenas, where two Magellanic Penguin colonies can be found near town: you can reach the Otway Sound colony by car, but need to catch a ferry to Isla Magdalena to see the other group.

Patagonia's largest land vertebrate, the guanaco, a type of wild llama, can be found in Torres del Paine. Guanaco's can exceed speeds of around 30 miles per hour, running faster than any other Patagonian animal, except the puma. If you fail to spot one of these animals, listen for their distinctive greeting, which at times can be confused for a turkey gobble.

The Nandú, a large flightless bird, also inhabits both parts of southern Chile and the highland regions. This ostrich-like bird can run exceptionally fast and is able to hide its neck and head under its full body of feathers in order to blend inconspicuously into its environment. Updated: May 11, 2009.

National Parks

Chile has an extensive holding of protected areas, from the desert of the north to the icy waters of the Straits of Magellan and the sultry waters of the Pacific Ocean.

The country's Sistema Nacional de Áreas Silvestres Protegidas del Estado (SNAPSE – National System of State-Protected Wildlife Areas) includes 31 national parks (parque nacional, PN), 48 national reserves (reserva nacional, RN), 15 natural monuments (monumento natural, MN) and three nature sanctuaries (santuario de la naturaleza), plus Parque Marino Francisco Coloane, a marine reserve in the Estrecho de Magallanes. Other protected areas are being developed, including one near Valdivia and another marine reserve near Caleta Tortel.

The governmental agency Corporación Nacional Forestal (Conaf) is responsible for the administration of SNAPSE areas. Conaf

Photo by Dag Olav

also manages forests, waterways, and other natural resources. The national office in Santiago has park maps and other publications, and dispenses mountaineering and trekking information Monday - Thursday, 9:30 a.m. - 5:30 p.m., Friday 9:30 a.m. - 4:30 p.m. Av. Bulnes 285, Tel: 56-663-0000, E-mail: consulta@conaf.cl, URL: www.conaf.cl.

A few of the PNs have their own websites, in Spanish and English, with more information about the natural history, activities and services: PN Conguillío (www.conguillio.cl), PN Puyehue (www.parquepuyehue.cl), and PN Torres del Paine (www.torresdelpaine.com). The capital of each political region has an office that handles the affairs of that region's reserves. Brochures, maps and other information can be obtained from them.

Conaf accepts volunteers with training or experience in conservation, national parks and related fields. Apply with the national office, or if you know with which park you would like to volunteer, contact the Conaf office of that region or the specific park.

In 1907, Chile created its first protected wildlife area, RN Malleco (IX Región), the first such park in South America, the third in all the Americas and the ninth in the world. The SNAPSE areas extend from PN Lauca, in the far north on the Bolivian border, to PN Cabo de Hornos just north of Antarctica. In the far Pacific Ocean are PN Archipiélago Juan Fernández and Rapa Nui (Easter Island).

The largest entity is PN Bernardo O'Higgins (XI–XII Región), which includes the Campo de Hielo Sur and covers over 3.5 million hectares, an area larger than Belgium. The smallest reserve is the 4.5 hectare MN Isla Cachagua, near Zapallar (V Región). Much of southern Chile is safeguarded as SNAPSE: including over 40 percent of the territory in XI Región de Aysen and over 50 percent of XII Región de Magallanes. The most popular of Chile's national parks are PN Villarrica, near Pucón (IX Región), the cruise to the Campo de Hielo Norte glaciers of PN Laguna San Rafael (XI Región) and PN Torres del Paine (XII Región), the trekkers' paradise near Puerto Natales in the Southern Patagonia. Updated: Jul 07, 2009.

Climate

Unlike most South American countries, Chile has four distinct seasons: winter (June to August), spring (September to November), summer (December to February), and autumn (March to May). Generalizing the country's overall climate can be tricky, as it varies significantly across the long and narrow land. Basically, the weather there is Mediterranean climate through the central area, with wider temperature brackets in the southern and northern areas.

Temperatures range throughout the year from highs of 30°C (86°F) to lows of -1°C (30°F). Rainfall is most abundant in the central and southern areas, during autumn and winter months (May is the wettest). Wind, rain and snow are dependable daily occurrences in Tierra del Fuego and Chilean Patagonia. Summers in Santiago and beyond are hot but pleasant, as humidity is low, and winter around the country is perfect for outdoor adventures such as snowboarding and skiing. Updated: Jul 06, 2009.

History

Chile has a long history of rugged isolation. The indigenous people who settled there had to adapt to some of the harshest conditions on Earth. Most famously, the Yaghan people in the deep south routinely went around naked even as the wind whipped the snow around them: they hunted sea lions in freezing water with stone knives.

In other parts of Chile, men and women adapted to deserts, rocky islands and snow-capped mountains. The climate made the people tough: the Mapuche people fought off the Inca Empire and then fought the Spanish so viciously and for so long that the conquest of the Mapuche took 300 years.

The first Europeans to visit this formidable land were defeated as much by the conditions as the people who lived there. As for the Yaghan, they started to die off when missionaries introduced them to clothing, which trapped moisture and germs and created an environment to which their bodies were not accustumed.

EARLY EXPLORERS

The first Europeans to see Chile were Ferdinand Magellan and his expedition, which sailed past after discovering the Strait of Magellan in 1520. In 1535, conquistador Diego de Almagro led a large force of Spanish mercenaries and native auxiliaries south from Peru, but harsh conditions and fierce natives meant they turned back empty-handed.

In 1540, Pedro de Valdivia, a veteran of the conquest of the Inca Empire, once again invaded the area and founded the city of Santiago. Santiago was plagued by Mapuche attacks—Valdivia himself was killed during a Mapuche raid, but the city managed to survive.

THE COLONIAL ERA
Chile remained a backwater of the Spanish Empire during the colonial era. It did not have the mineral wealth of Peru to the north or the vast grazing lands of Argentina to the east, and was difficult to reach. The fertile valleys proved good for agriculture, and the waters off the coast were rich with fish, so the colony was largely self-supporting. Chile has great mineral wealth, and mining has always been an important industry.

INDEPENDENCE
In September of 1810, Chile joined most of the rest of Latin America in rebelling against Spain, then ruled indirectly by Napoleon. Fighting was intermittent until 1817, when local patriot Bernardo O'Higgins was joined by a force of Argentines led by Jose de San Martin. Together, they were able to finally drive the Spanish from Chile. O'Higgins became the new nation's first president.

A NEW REPUBLIC
Chile remained a quiet backwater from its independence until the latter part of the 19th century, when it began to expand. A massive new offensive against the resilient Mapuche finally opened up the south and the north, Chile was victorious in the 1879–1883 War of the Pacific, gaining lands rich in nitrates and cutting Bolivia off from the Pacific. After the War of the Pacific, Chile began a brief period of great affluence.

CIVIL WAR
The wealth was not to last long, however. Conflicts between President Jose Manuel Balmaceda and Congress over Balmaceda's unchecked spending on new social programs deteriorated into a civil war in 1891. The war only lasted a few months, but thousands of Chileans were killed. Balmaceda was defeated and took refuge in the Embassy of Argentina, where he committed suicide. The war was a costly one for Chile and set its development back.

EARLY 20TH CENTURY
Chile was torn by strife in the first half of the 20th century, and went through a series of governments in a short time. Post-Russian Revolution, Marxist groups appeared and fascists tried to get their country to emulate Mussolini's Italy. A growing middle class mitigated the crises and provided some stability, although very few Chileans could agree on how their country should be run.

By the 1950s, elections were taking place and transitions of power were generally peaceful. From 1964 to 1970 Chile was ruled by moderate Eduardo Frei Montalvo, who managed to annoy liberals, who felt he was too conservative, and conservatives, who felt he was too liberal. Trouble was certainly brewing.

ALLENDE
In 1970, Chileans elected Salvador Allende, a former Senator and well-known Socialist. He immediately began a radical program of socializing Chile's economy and cultivated close ties to the USSR and Fidel Castro's Cuba. His economic reforms mostly failed and by 1973 the economy was in a major crisis. On September 11, 1973 Allende was removed and a coup d'etat led by several high-ranking military officials. As soldiers invaded the Presidential palace,

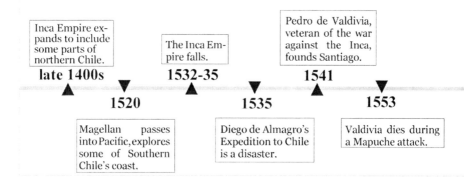

Inca Empire expands to include some parts of northern Chile.		The Inca Empire falls.		Pedro de Valdivia, veteran of the war against the Inca, founds Santiago.	
late 1400s	1520	1532-35	1535	1541	1553
	Magellan passes into Pacific, explores some of Southern Chile's coast.		Diego de Almagro's Expedition to Chile is a disaster.		Valdivia dies during a Mapuche attack.

Allende took his own life. After the dust settled, career military officer General Augusto Pinochet assumed control of the nation.

PINOCHET AND OPERATION CONDOR

Allende still had his supporters despite his poor handling of the economy. Leftist Marxist groups such as the MIR (Revolutionary Left Movement) had been carrying out urban guerrilla attacks, trying to destabilize the government. As one of his first acts, Pinochet ordered the arrest of thousands of leftists, communists and suspected insurgents. The stadium in Santiago was for a time used to hold these suspected enemies of the state.

Within a month, Pinochet had authorized the "Caravan of Death," a group of army officers who traveled by helicopter to different cities executing the most likely insurgent leaders: as many as 100 jailed civilians may have been executed by these officers without any sort of trial.

Sadly, the "Caravan of Death" was only the first ugly incident in a long war waged by the government of Chile on its own citizens. Pinochet and his inner circle were determined to stamp out the MIR and other Marxist groups by whatever means necessary. Thousands were tortured, imprisoned and murdered for nothing more than mentioning they didn't like the government. During Pinochet's dictatorship, which lasted until 1990, it is estimated that some 6,000 Chilean citizens were executed by the government and countless more detained and tortured.

Pinochet was also the architect behind "Operation Condor," which was a collaborative effort of several South American governments to help one another round up and eliminate suspected insurgents. Chile teamed with Argentina, Brazil, Uruguay, Paraguay and Bolivia to root out and murder one another's problem citizens. The campaign was very effective: by the late 1970s, the MIR and other Marxist groups were all but neutralized in the southern cone of South America. But the torture and death continued.

Pinochet left the Presidency in 1990, although he kept his status as a senator and army officer, mostly to escape prosecution for human rights abuses. International courts tried to bring him to trial between 2002-2006, but he died before anything could come of it.

THE MODERN ERA

Since Pinochet, Chile's democracy has been stable, aided no doubt by a strong economy based on the industries of mining, wine, fishing and tourism. The biggest issue facing Chile currently is what to do with former army officers suspected of horrible human rights violations in the 1970s and 1980s. Some, like Manuel Contreras (former head of the DINA, Chile's secret police) have been convicted of kidnapping and assassination.

Much like the people of Argentina, the people of Chile are torn between thinking that the past should be put behind them and confronting it in public courtrooms.

Chileans elected their first woman president, Michelle Bachelet Jeria, of the Socialist Party in 2006. Bachelet is remarkable for many reasons, not least of which is the fact that she was one of the thousands of young Chileans who were detained and tortured during the Pinochet regime.

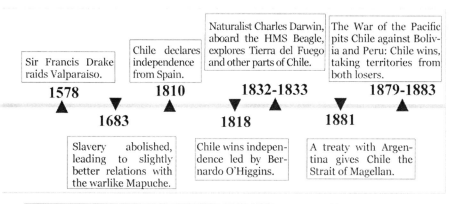

1578		1810		1832-1833		1879-1883
Sir Francis Drake raids Valparaiso.		Chile declares independence from Spain.		Naturalist Charles Darwin, aboard the HMS Beagle, explores Tierra del Fuego and other parts of Chile.		The War of the Pacific pits Chile against Bolivia and Peru: Chile wins, taking territories from both losers.

1683		1818		1881
Slavery abolished, leading to slightly better relations with the warlike Mapuche.		Chile wins independence led by Bernardo O'Higgins.		A treaty with Argentina gives Chile the Strait of Magellan.

Fortunately, she survived in time to go into exile: her father, an army officer who resisted Pinochet's power grab, died in prison. During her time in office, she made steady gains in social programs aimed at helping the poorest Chileans. Updated: Dec 14, 2009.

Politics

Politics in Chile is conducted via a presidential representative democratic republic. There are three branches of governance: executive power is controlled by the government; legislative power is exercised by the government and the two chambers of the National Congress; and the judicial branch is independent. The president, both the head of state and the head of government, is elected by popular vote for a four-year term and immediate re-election is not allowed. The Palacio de la Moneda in Santiago is the official seat of the president.

In the early 1970s the country had attracted world attention by electing Marxist Salvador Allende, the first democratically elected socialist president in the Americas. Allende envisaged total socio-economic reform under a plan named *La Vía Chilena al Socialism*, (the Chilean Path to Socialism), including nationalization of major industries, government administration of healthcare and land seizure and re-distribution.

Allende's bold socialist policies generated fear in certain circles and, in 1973, he was overthrown by a U.S.-backed coup d'état. For the next 30 years Chile was again in the spotlight, but as a notorious example of modern-day authoritarianism. Democratic government was

re-established in March 1990, after General Augusto Pinochet peacefully stepped down (though he remained Commander-in-Chief of the Chilean Army until 1998).

Pinochet's brutal dictatorship had been responsible for the death, torture and disappearance of thousands of people. Despite at least 300 criminal charges pending against him for human rights violations, tax evasion and embezzlement, a judge ruled Pinochet medically unfit to stand trial in 2004 and he died two years later, at the age of 91.

Economic reforms carried out by the Pinochet government are credited by some as being the grounds for the investment and growth in of the 1990s, which successive governments have built on.

Chile's outgoing president, Michelle Bachelet, a separated mother of three and an open agnostic, assumed presidential duties in 2006. The campaign platform of the center-left politician was one of continued free-market policies combined with an increase in social benefits.

In December of 2009, right-wing billionaire Sebastian Piñera won the national election's opening round. He will go heard-to-head against former president and center-left candidate Eduardo Frei (1994-2000) in the election's second round in Janurary, 2010.
For further reading, try *Politics in Chile: Socialism, Authoritarianism and Market Democracy* by Lois Hect Oppenheim, Westview Press 2007. Updated: Dec 14, 2009.

Conflict between President Jose Manuel Balmaceda and Congress bring about Chilean Civil War; thousands die before Balmaceda loses.	Moderate President Eduardo Frei Montalvo is unable to halt polarization of the nation between liberals and conservatives.	Augusto Pinochet and other military leaders depose Allende, who commits suicide. Then "The Caravan of Death" travels through Chile: Army officers kill up to 100 political prisoners, some of whom had voluntarily turned themselves in.
1891	**1964-1970**	**1973**
▲	▲	▲
1924	**1970**	**1970s-1980s**
General Luis Altamirano stages a coup against civilian government: years of chaos follow.	Socialist Salvador Allende elected: he socializes economy and cultivates close ties to communist nations, earning the enmity of Washington and the Chilean elite.	Up to 3,000 Chilean are murdered and man more are tortured by secu rity forces in the name o counter-terrorism.

Mapuche People

The Mapuche people are the largest indigenous group in Chile, comprising 10 percent of the population. The name Mapuche is derived from the Mapudungun words "Che" (people) and "Mapu" (of the land). The majority of Mapuche people live in either the Araucania Region, from the Bío Bío River to the Chiloé Island, or in Santiago and its surrounding areas. There are also approximately 300,000 Mapuche living in Argentina.

Once a large and prosperous ethnic group that occupied the entire Central Valley zone in Chile, the Mapuche people have dwindled; an estimated 200,000 people are left that can still speak the native language of Mapudungun. Historically, the Mapuche had an agriculture-based economy. With the loss of their land, the people turned to metal working. Many now rely on making and selling silver jewelry for monetary support.

Over 300 years of successful resistance against the Spanish and the Inca Empire has left these people with both a legacy of strength and determination, but the Mapuche are equally poverty stricken and marginalized by Chilean society. One of the reasons the Mapuche were able to successfully avoid the powerful Spanish was their lack of a traditional political system, which left the invading army confused by their fragmented system of authority. The Mapuche continue with this way of life, living not in contained villages but rather spread out with their families.

Today the battle is not with Spanish conquistadores, but rather the Chilean government and the large timber and hydroelectric multinational companies that threaten their land and way of life. Violent clashes with the police have led to protests and arbitrary arrests.

Four different international bodies, including the United Nations, have requested that Chile review its criminal justice policy toward indigenous people. Yet, the Mapuche people in Chile still live in social and political isolation with little access to education or health care. Updated: Jul 07, 2009.

Economy

Chile has a tremendously strong economic reputation, both in Latin America and within the greater global economic community. Over the past decade, by building up a market-oriented fiscal system which is heavily focused on financial institutions and foreign trade, the Chilean government has successfully created a stable and fruitful economy.

Chile's economy is very reliant on the copper trade. This natural resource provides an impressive third of all government revenue; fruit, fish products, paper and pulp, chemicals, and wine round out the rest. Exports as a whole account for 40 percent of the country's $69.1 billion Gross Domestic Product (as of 2008).

To meet it's own demand for oil (and its by-products), chemicals, electrical and telecommunications equipment, industrial

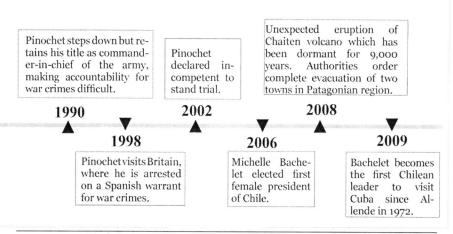

Pinochet steps down but retains his title as commander-in-chief of the army, making accountability for war crimes difficult.

Pinochet declared incompetent to stand trial.

Unexpected eruption of Chaiten volcano which has been dormant for 9,000 years. Authorities order complete evacuation of two towns in Patagonian region.

1990   **2002**   **2008**

1998   **2006**   **2009**

Pinochet visits Britain, where he is arrested on a Spanish warrant for war crimes.

Michelle Bachelet elected first female president of Chile.

Bachelet becomes the first Chilean leader to visit Cuba since Allende in 1972.

Augusto Pinochet

Chile's current status as one of Latin America's strongest economic performers owes much to the policies of its 30th president, Augusto Pinochet, who ruled from 1973 to 1990. But Pinochet's improvements have been justly over-shadowed by a ruthless 17-year regime during which countless opponents and their families disappeared.

Born Augusto José Ramón Pinochet Ugarte in Valparaíso in 1915, Pinochet studied in a military academy and rose quickly through the ranks of the army. He came to power violently in a CIA-backed military coup, overthrowing Marxist president Salvador Allende in September, 1973, one month after Allende had appointed him commander-in-chief of the army. Governing as the head of a military junta, Pinochet quickly consolidated power, assuming the presidency in December, 1974. He broke up Congress and suspended the constitution, banned political parties, arrested dissidents, muzzled the media and hiked military spending. Around 3,000 people were killed, tens of thousands tortured, and many jailed or forced into exile. In an effort to revamp the nation's economy, Pinochet instituted a series of free-market reforms, including privatization and the elimination of trade barriers. While this helped to stabilize the country, Pinochet's cuts to social spending resulted in widespread inequality.

Pinochet remained in office through the recession-filled 1980s, sworn in under a dubiously approved new constitution. He also survived an assassination attempt. Facing intense opposition at home and from abroad, he legalized political parties. In 1988 his attempt to stay in office eight more years was rejected by voters in a referendum, and by 1989 he had lost the country's first democratic election in 19 years. Pinochet left office but stayed on as military general and a senator, which gave him lifetime immunity from criminal prosecution. Attempts to prosecute Pinochet and his security forces for their alleged human rights violations were repeatedly quashed. The former president claimed his actions had been necessary to strengthen the country and protect it from the threat of communism.

Pinochet's final years were marked by judicial wrangling. In 2000, he was indicted for a series of 1973 executions. These charges were dismissed when a medical report revealed that the former general was suffering from dementia and memory loss. Pinochet then gave up his senate post—a 2000 constitutional amendment allows for an ex-president to receive immunity from prosecution and a guaranteed allowance in exchange for giving up a seat in the senate; however, an appeals court soon stripped him of his immunity. In 2004, the Supreme Court overturned its decision, claiming Pinochet was in good enough health to stand trial. Allegations also arose that a U.S. bank had helped Pinochet hoard millions of dollars, and he was indicted on charges of tax evasion and placed under house arrest.

The legal tug-o-war continued as a sequestered Pinochet continued to oppose efforts to bring him before a judge. More indictments piled on for kidnappings, tortures, and assassinations. In 2006, on his 91st birthday, Pinochet admitted political responsibility for his actions. On December 10th of that year he died from complications after a heart attack. He was never tried for the more than 300 charges of human rights violations and embezzlement charges filed against him. Updated: Jun 24, 2009.

machinery, motor vehicles, and natural gas, Chile imports mainly from the U.S., China, Brazil and Argentina. Currently these imports do not outweigh Chile's exports and the country is operating with a trade surplus.

PAST

For most of the 20th century Chile's economy suffered under the military dictatorship. Under the Pinochet regime, economic policy was heavily inspired by the so-called "Chicago Boys" and followed a path of heavy liberalization and consolidation of the free market; poverty jumped dramatically too. However, following the overthrow of Pinochet in the 90s, the Chilean economy thrived. Patricio Aylwin's democratically elected government inspired impressive growth rates and introduced much-needed economic reforms; during this time the GDP averaged a staggering eight percent yearly growth. In 1999, the bubble burst. Following low export earnings and unwise monetary policies put into place to control mounting deficits, the country fell into a moderate recession.

Chile quickly bounced back and by the end of 1999 the fiscal situation was already beginning to improve. Since then, the country's GDP has grown at a steady rate each year and Chile has continued to build its reputation as a solid economic force through government efficiency, high-quality education, reliable infrastructure and high workforce productivity.

A commitment to building a strong and stable economy has lead to (among other things) the 2004 implementation of a free trade agreement with the U.S., an active example of their belief in trade liberalization.

PRESENT
While Chile has had its economic ups and downs, the country has the strongest economy in Latin America, boasting the highest nominal GDP per capita. The World Bank considers Chile to have simple and solid regulations for conducting business with strong protection over property rights—they rank Chile 33rd in the world with the Ease of Doing Business Index. A few quick facts concerning Chile's economy:

-Chile's main industries are wood and wood products, textiles, iron, steel, transport equipment, cement, fish processing, copper and other minerals.

-Chile produces 15,100 barrels of oil per day, but consumes 253,000.

-Chile's GDP per capita is $163,915 (as of 2007, World Bank).

Chile's strong economy is not without its problems. In January 2009, the external debt reached an estimated $64.57 billion and the rich/poor divide continues to increase disproportionately.

What's more, the county's great dependence on a few natural resources (copper in particular, whose overall value dropped last year) and a lack of natural gas and oil, means that it remains vulnerable to fluctuations in global economic conditions. Updated: Jul 06, 2009.

Population
The population of Chile is over 16 million (July 2008 estimate), with an annual growth rate of 0.97 percent. This rate is one of the lowest in Latin America, just behind Uruguay and Cuba. The population, however, is expected to reach 20 million by 2025.

Chile's present-day population is made up mostly of white and mestizo Chileans (30 percent and 65 percent, respectively), mixed descendants from European and indigenous Indian cultures. There is a relatively homogenous national and ethnic identity, referred to as "Chilenidad". Chilean Europeans came mainly from Spain, specifically Basque and Castilian areas. Additionally, there are the descendents of French, Italian, Irish, English, Swiss, Croatian and most significantly, German immigrants. A noteworthy German migration took place in 1848, filling up the provinces of Valdivia, Llanquihue and Osorno, and creating a German-Chilean community. Indigenous people make up 4.6 percent of Chile's population; the Mapuches, who live in the south, are the largest group (85 percent), though smaller populations of Aymara, Atacameño, Rapa Nui and Kawaskhar peoples inhabit the country as well. Updated: Mar 24, 2009.

Language
Almost all Chileans speak Spanish, the country's official language. Their dialect, however, is not typically Latino, and is similar to Canary Islands Spanish—both speak with aspirated "s" sounds and do not finish pronouncing the word completely. For example, a phrase such as "Estoy cansado" (I'm tired) actually sounds like "Toy cansow." Because of this difficult dialect, Chile is not the easiest place for novices to learn the language (Chileans, in fact, often claim to speak Castellano, or Castillian Spanish, rather than Español).

What's more, Chileans use a great deal of slang, referred to as Chilenismos. There are a fare share of slang dictionaries, translating from Chilean to English and Chilean to Spanish, as many immigrants and Spanish-speaking travelers have a lot of trouble with the Mapuche-infused lingo. For insight into the colloquial, try How to survive in the Chilean Jungle by John Brennan and Alvaro Taboada. Some examples of Chilenismo slang include:

-*Pololo*: boyfriend or fiance.
-*Al tiro*: immediately.
-*Po*: the ever-popular slang word used for emphasis. *Sí po* is the most popular way to say yes and *no po* is more popular than just no. There's

also *ya po*, which means hurry or that's enough and *po solo* can be used throughout sentences whenever you need an emphasis.

-Cachai: a word added to many sentences/words/syllables meaning, "ya know?" It can also serve as the Spanish *conoces*.

Cachai is derivative of a Chilean verb tense slang which seems to come from the formal vosotros form (used in predominately in Spain, though also in Argentina). This tense is used for the singular *tú* (you), and ads an -ai where the –er, -ar, and –ir ending normally would be: *Me gustai* means "I like you," and *Cantai?* translates to "Do you sing?" Another popular manifestation of this is *Queri?* for *Quieres?* (Do you want?).

In addition to Spanish, there are several tribal languages spoken in Chile; Mapudungun (used between the Itata and Tolten rivers), and Aymara (in the northern mountains) are the two most common. Chilean Quechua, Rapa Nui lan (on Easter Island), and Huilliche/Chesungun are also among the indigenous languages. Updated: Jul 02, 2009.

Religion

The most widely practiced religion in pre-colonial Chile was of the largest indigenous population, the Mapuche. Theirs was an animistic faith, centered around a priestess. As in all of Latin America, a forced conversion to Catholicism was not 100 percent complete, and elements of Mapuche beliefs persist to the present, mostly in rural communities. Still, 70 percent of Chileans are Catholic, but a growing body of Protestant Evangelicals now make up 15 percent of the population, with small groups of practicing Jews, Muslims, Mormons, New Agers, Hindus, Buddhists, atheists and agnostics. Updated: Jul 23, 2008.

Culture

Undoubtedly one of the sexiest cultures in South American, Chile has money, art, literature, music, dance, and a 96 percent literacy rate. Culture in Chile is no hidden gem, rather, it is a commodity shared by the rest of the world, those who love Pablo Neruda, Chilean wine and summers skiing in the Andes. The incredible thing i that while seemingly more worldly than other Latino countries, Chilean culture is distinctly Chilean.

To say that culture in this country is well-defined suggests both bad and good. Chileans enjoy being Chilean, and can seem both proud and detached when it comes to their culture. They have had little influence outside of their country, and whether this was built by the dictatorship, land-shape isolation or simply by choice, it remains a reality today. The Chilean people keep to themselves, are quiet, restrained and unamused by travelers passing in and out.

In addition to the repressive Pinochet regime, Chileans have been influenced by a once tough-ruling Catholic church and conservative conformity. With a lack of diversity in religious and ethnic terms, minor amounts of racism and prejudices among the conservative classes are present internally in Chile, and sometimes projected outwardly to foreigners.

This isn't to say that gringos will be unwelcome or that Chileans are a rigid people. Rather, it is evidence of the greater cultural divide. There are those who have stuck with this conservative mindset, others who have completely rebelled, and a majority middle ground that is progressive and peace-seeking.

In some ways Chile's pride and self-preservation is an impressive strength. Coming from years of Pinochet censorship and repression, Chileans emerged proud of their beauty and heritage. Chileans are also extremely family focused, although the families are not exceptionally large. They have cut poverty in half in the last 15 years. Whether it concerns politics, education, film, literature, or setting fashion-forward trends, the culture here is rich and ready to be explored. Updated: Jun 25, 2009.

Art

Chile is an unmatched force in the arts. The country boasts rich architecture, painting and sculpture, as well as literature, with such heavyweights as Pablo Neruda and Isabel Allende. Against such oppressive odds as devastating earthquakes and the Pinochet dictatorship, Chilean art has fought an arduous battle for its current position as a rescuer and preserver of history and tradition, and as a platform for progress in contemporary culture.

ARCHITECTURE

Although Chile is not known for its modern-day architecture, its colonial era treasures are worth noting. To name but a few, the Catedral Metropolitana de Santiago, the Iglesia San Francisco and the World Heritage mansions in Valparaiso have withstood the ravages of time and natural disasters. Historically, Chilean towns were set up with a center square, town hall and church. There are a few ancient examples but other towns were rebuilt in the 19th century after having been destroyed by earthquakes and similar disasters.

PAINTING AND SCULPTURE

Chileans have a special place in their culture for traditional 19th century paintings by the likes of Juan Francisco González, Alberto Valenzuela Llanos and Pablo Burchard, but it is contemporary art from the 1900s and onwards that gives Chile domestic and international recognition. Roberto Matta was one of Chile's most celebrated artists, a leader in the Surrealist movement as well as abstract expressionism of the 1940s. Some of Matta's works can bee seen at the Museo de Artes Visuals (Museum of Visual Arts) in Santiago.

POST-PINOCHET ART

Finally free from a dictatorship which exiled and even murdered some of its most talented contributors, the Chilean artistic community is flourishing. Contemporary art does not look to the past and point fingers, rather, it offers views of a more positive future. Artists tend to focus on issues of economy, religion and identity, with art that playfully mocks consumerism and the free market, and addresses subjects which are no longer off-limits, such as gender, poverty and sexuality.

As part of this desire to inspire positive growth and change, new forms of creative art have emerged throughout Chile. Mixed media, found art and various artistic ecological movements are growing in popularity. The new forms inspire a mix of traditional and modern ideas, such as evoking ancient Chilean civilizations, identities and attitudes.

Present-day artists involved in the modern movements include: Zinnia Ramírez, Leo Moya, Norma Ramírez, Carlos Montes de Oca and Andres Vio. Their works are displayed internationally, and also are frequently shown in Chilean museums. Updated: Jul 06, 2009.

Music

Chile's musical scene is not only historic, but diverse, not just entertaining, but expressive. With traditional indigenous roots, what has developed over the span of Chilean history is a culturally rich musical timeline that is documented by the introduction of uniquely Andean instruments, sounds, movements and styles. To the musical world, Chile has contributed several trumpets, rattles, drums (including the caja chayera, the makawa and the kultrun), and flutes (the kena, siku and tarka). These instruments create a base and background for movements that range from the folkloric days of the payadores to today's modern Chilean Rock scene.

TRADITION

Traditional Chilean music is undeniably rooted in religious heritage, as music and dance were part of both aboriginal and Roman Catholic festivals. Mestizo and Creole music also made their way into this rhythmic form of expression. Spanish-derived poetic forms such as romance, the villancico and the décima combined with guitar accompaniment to create the verso and the tonada, classic songs of Chile. Also essential to Chile's musical culture was the cueca, a national dance and song style derived from the Peruvian zamacueca and influenced by African, Spanish and Arab-Andalucían traditions. The cueca is performed by brass bands or panpipe ensembles and is accompanied by guitars or accordions, depending on the region. As expected from folkloric music, the cueca narrates daily life and historical events; it pays tribute to popular figures, records struggles and misfortunes, and glorifies conquests.

LA NUEVA CANCIÓN CHILENA

From the cueca sprang Chile's most popular movement, and arguably its greatest musical contribution, La Nueva Canción Chilena, or The New Chilean Song. This mid-1960s revitalization of traditional native and folk music quickly became associated with political activism, reformation and the Popular Unity government. The movement spoke out on social injustices and the necessary reforms, and many musicians had to flee into exile as a result. Singer Victor Jara was killed in 1973 as a result of his involvement with the movement. Other artists active in the movement have included Violeta Parra, her daughters Isabel and Angel Parra, and the ensembles Inti-llimani and Qualiapaún.

Although the mix of ancient rhythms and contemporary peace-seeking lyrics ultimately was banned by the oppressive Pinochet regime, Nueva Canción music went into underground circulation throughout the 1970s and 1980s. What's more, the children of the persecuted musicians have now come into their own in

INTRO & INFO

the music scene and are the face the Armada Chilena, a present-day musical movement presenting contemporary versions of the former protest songs. Artists involved in this scene include: DJ Ricardo Villalobos, DJ Luciano, Alejandro Vivanco, Pier Bucci, Cuti Aste, Bitman and Roban, Claude Roubillie and the Electrodomesticos. Updated: Sep 24, 2008.

Museums

Santiago is museum-central. The Museo Histórico Nacional, formerly the Supreme Court and Congress, has something for everyone, while the Museo de Arte Precolombino showcases the Chilean and Andean past. The busy Museo de Santiago reveals the city's history through art, clothing, photos and maps, and children will love the popular new Museo Interactivo Mirador, with its many hands-on exhibits and interactive activities. Don't miss the paintings, sculptures and international exhibitions of the Museo Nacional de Bellas Artes, which shares space with the Museo de Arte Contemporaneo.

In northern Chile, Arica's clifftop Museo Histórico y de Armas is a tribute to the War of the Pacific, and the Museo Ferroviario de Arica will fascinate train enthusiasts. Nearly 400,000 regional artifacts, as well as gold and mummies, fill the Museo Gustavo le Paige in San Pedro de Atacama. In Vicuña, the museum of Nobel Prize-winning poet Gabriela Mistral contains memorabilia from her life.

To learn about Chile's independence, visit Talca's Museo O'Higginiano y Bellas Artes de Talca. Pablo Neruda is the focus of several museums in Chile, including Valparaíso's La Sebastiana and Isla Negra–chock-a-block with nautical gadgetry. Villarrica's Museo Arqueológico Municipal and Museo de Leandro Penchulef richly detail the area's immigrant and indigenous history, and Temuco's Museo Nacional Ferroviario Pablo Neruda is an excellent tribute to both the late poet and Chile's railroad history.

There are many museums in and around Valdivia, like the Museo de Arte Contemporáneo and the Cervezaría de Kuntsmann and Museo de la Cerveza, where you can learn about Chilean brewing history while enjoying a beer. In Hanga Roa on Easter Island, Museum Sebastián Englert's artifacts attempt to unravel the mystery of Rapa Nui. The museums in Punta Arenas are highly regarded; learn about the life in Patagonia in years past at the Museo Regional de Magallanes. Other museums are dedicated to naval, military and brewing history. For a comprehensive history of Tierra del Fuego, visit the

Museo Provincial Fernando Cordero Rusque in Porvenir. Updated: Jun 25, 2009.

Dance, Theater and Comedy

Theater and dance are deeply rooted in Chilean culture, with many existing companies dating back to the 19th century. Although the Pinochet dictatorship threatened the future of creative arts, its oppressive rule actually ushered in an inventive, contemporary movement, with performers using artistic expression as a vehicle for political criticism and reform. Since the return of democracy, the Chilean performance arts scene has blossomed, with dozens of companies, old and new, thriving in Santiago, as well as other culturally rich cities like Valparaíso and Viña del Mar.

The cueca, Chile's national dance, is said to be based in 19th century peasant folklore. This lively courtship dance, inspired by the mating ritual between a rooster and a hen, begins with a man approaching a woman, and follows his persistent attempts to capture her elusive attention. The couple engage in flirtatious, intimate (but never touching) choreography, twirling handkerchiefs and stomping their feet to music, which traditionally involves a guitar, harp, piano and two singers. Initially simple and straightforward, the dance picks up speed and complexity through the use of handclapping and percussion.

Live cueca dances can be found throughout Chile. One of the best times to witness, and participate, in live cueca is during fiestas patrias, Chile's national holiday. Starting on September 18, this multi-day celebration has a variety of performances of traditional dance and music; cueca performances can be found in every major city during this time. In June, head to the Apaza Valley for the Concurso Nacional de Cueca, the region's annual festival celebrating the national dance.

For fans of classical dance, Chile has a variety of reputable ballet companies. In Santiago, head to Teatro Municipal (Agustinas 794, Tel: 56-2-463-1000, URL: www.municipal.cl), a beautifully elegant 19th-century building that hosts a variety of classical music, opera and dance performances. The theater is home to The Santiago Ballet, but a variety of other national ballet companies travel to the venue for performances. Another dance company worth checking out is the University of Chile's Ballet Folklorico Antumapu (Av. Libertador Bernardo O'Higgins 1058, Oficina 240, Tel: 56-2-978-1014, URL: www.balletantumapu.uchile.cl).

Isabel Allende

The Chilean-American novelist Isabel Allende Llona is probably the best-known and most successful female Latin American literary figure alive. Her books, among which are the best-selling *House of Spirits* (published in 1982) and *City of the Beasts* (2002), have been translated into 30 languages and have sold over 51 million copies worldwide. Describing herself as a "proud feminist," Isabel Allende has based many of her novels and short stories on her personal experience as a woman, creating independent-minded, adventurous heroines, like in *Daughter of Fortune* (1999).

Her characters are also participants in the history of their times, like the Trueba family of *The House of Spirits*, whose destiny unfolds against the backdrop of intense moments in Chilean history. *The House of Spirits*, set during the agrarian reform of her uncle Salvador Allende's presidency, is indeed her most political work, although it also weaves in fantastic elements, in the tradition of Latin American "magical realism." The manuscript for that novel grew from a letter which Isabel started writing to her beloved 99-year-old grandfather when she learned that he was dying. Indeed, her best writing is born of deep love and acute suffering, like *Paula*, the moving memoir of her childhood and years in exile, written in the form of a letter to her daughter Paula, who lay in hospital in a coma (and later died).

Isabel Allende's life makes for interesting reading. Born in 1942 in Peru (her father was a diplomat), young Isabel attended private schools in Lebanon and Chile and grew up to be a TV personality and magazine journalist, then married in 1962 and went on to work for the United Nations' Food and Agricultural Organization. The 1973 coup against Salvador Allende forced her to flee to Venezuela, where she lived for 13 years, working as a columnist. She met her second husband on a visit to the U.S. in 1988 and, having obtained American citizenship in 2003, now lives in California, where she teaches literature and writes. Updated: Feb 16, 2009.

Chile has a thriving and diverse theater scene. Santiago is the main hub, with dozens of theaters offering an array of performances from classical to contemporary. The Teatro Municipal (see above) often hosts international operatic groups. For a slightly more contemporary feel, check out the University of Chile's Teatro Nacional (Sala Antonio Varas, Tel: 56-2-324 9780, URL: www.tnch.uchile.cl), which puts on a variety of productions. A hip new modern theater gaining popularity is Matucana 100 (Estación, Tel: 56-2-682-4502, E-mail: matucana100@m100.cl, URL: www.m100.cl).

Chile's most spectacular display of theatrical prowess occurs throughout January during Santiago's Teatro a Mil (www.stgoamil.cl), the country's annual summer festival devoted to celebrating and promoting performance arts.

Since its inception in 1995, the festival has grown to include over 40 acts from 30 different countries, with international and Chilean acts performing side-by-side at over 15 venues throughout Santiago. With performances scattered throughout the city—both indoors and outdoors—the festival aims to make theater fun, accessible and cheap (the name Teatro a Mil means Theater of 1,000 pesos). It's definitely worth checking out.

Northeast of Santiago, on the central coast, picturesque beach town Viña del Mar hosts touring groups of classical music and theater in its Teatro Municipal (Plaza Vergara, Tel: 56-3-268-8466). The bohemian port town Valparaíso also has a Teatro Municipal (Uruguay 410, Tel: 56-32-225-7480.) Located off the main Plaza O'Higgins, this theater offers ballet, theater and opera.

Comedy is harder to find, but the larger cities have a few options. In Santiago, check out Teatro Circus Ok (Av. Providencia 1176, Tel: 56-2-2368105, E-mail: circus@cocolegrand.cl, URL: www.cocolegrand.cl), a comedy and music theater run by Chilean's own "King of Comedy," the legendary Coco Le Grand. Updated: Mar 02, 2009.

Cinema

The history of Chilean filmmaking, like Chilean history in general, can be divided into two separate periods: BC and AC, or Before-Coup and After-Coup. Chilean cinema went through cycles of productivity and decline from the early 20th century until the 1960s, and there had been several attempts to create a Chilean film industry to rival those in Argentina, Mexico and Brazil. Chile actually had a substantial film industry by Latin American standards throughout the 1920s, which came to a halt with the coming of sound. The technology needed to make films with sound in Chile was cost prohibitive, and distributors inundated the market with products from Hollywood, Spain, Mexico and Argentina.

In the 1940s and 1950s some new Chilean cinema emerged in co-productions with Argentina, thanks to new funding from the state. In the 1960s the newly-elected socialist Christian Democrats helped sponsor a new generation of filmmakers, as well as film festivals and journals. With the election of Socialist president Salvador Allende, local filmmaking was seen as a way to promote the Popular Unity Front. From 1967 onwards, numerous politically and artistically ambitious films were made, many of them openly promoting the progressive politics of these parties. Once the military coup lead by Augosto Pinochet removed Allende from office, Pinochet actively persecuted and exiled almost all of the country's filmmakers and put an end to state-supported filmmaking. Much of pre-1973 Chilean cinema was destroyed, either intentionally or through neglect.

For the remainder of the 1970s there was little filmmaking inside Chile, but a uniquely Chilean cinema was developed abroad by writers and directors who had relocated to countries such as France, the Soviet Union, Mexico, Nicaragua and the United States. Many of the films addressed Chile's climate of political oppression, either overtly or covertly. The most famous was a three-hour documentary, "The Battle of Chile" by Pablo Guzman, which chronicled the rise and fall of Allende's Popular Unity Front coalition, including the Pinochet coup. Much of the film's footage was smuggled out of the country by the film crew as they sought refugee status abroad.

The most successful exile however, has been Raoul Ruiz, a prolific artist whose work encompasses everything from experimental avant-garde to mainstream French cinema, with stars such as Catherine Deneuve. The most famous Chilean director is Alejandro Jodorowsky, whose surrealist efforts, such as "El Topo," are considered influential classics of cinematic magic realism.

Ironically, it was in 1977, during the Pinochet period of severe repression, that national Chilean cinema experienced a high-water mark of success, with "Julio Comienza en Julio" (Julio begins in July), by Silvio Caiozzi, one of the few filmmakers who chose to stay. Widely considered the greatest Chilean film ever made, this historical film, set at the close of the 19th century, has been praised as a subversive critique of the upper classes and of totalitarianism. In 1988, civil liberties and state support for the arts were restored after Pinochet lost his bid for the presidency to the left-of-center Patricio Aylwyn. A new Chilean cinema emerged, one more creatively bold and politically inquisitive.

Among the new directors to gain international recognition was Sergio M. Castilla, whose films include the surreal political allegory "Gentile Alloute" and "Gringuito," a "Candide"-like account of post-Pinochet Chile through the eyes of a nine-year-old. Andres Wood, who began by making short films that caught the attention of film festivals around the world, scored the largest box office success in Chile's history with "Machuca," a powerful account of events leading up to the 1973 coup as experienced by two boys from divergent class and racial backgrounds.Updated: Sep 29, 2008.

Literature

Chilean writers are among the best in all of Latin America. In fact, they've won two of the four Nobel prizes for literature awarded to Latin Americans (awarded to Chileans Pablo Neruda and Gabriela Mistral, Colombian Gabriel Garcia Marquez and Guatemalan Miguel Angel Asturias).

Gabriela Mistral (1889-1957), whose real name was Lucila de María del Perpetuo Socorro Godoy Alcayata, was more than a talented poet: she was also a diplomat, feminist and educator. Her poems deal with Latin America, love, betrayal and loss. She won the Nobel Prize for Literature in 1945. She is still well-known in Chile although not as much elsewhere.

Pablo Neruda (1904-1973), another poet, is better-known than Mistral. Unlike Mistral, Neruda is considered more of a world poet than simply a Chilean one: Gabriel García Marquez once called him "The greatest 20th century poet in any language." After receiving his Nobel Prize, he was invited to read his poetry at Chile's national stadium: 70,000 attended. His poetry is hard to define, but it's visceral, elegant and often erotic or romantic. Even more famous than either Mistral or

Neruda is **Isabel Allende**, niece of former President Salvador Allende. She exploded onto the literary scene with *La Casa de los Espiritus* (*The House of the Spirits*) in 1982 and never looked back. Although her later novels are not as literary as *The House of the Spirits*, there is no denying her broad appeal: she sells millions of novels in several languages.

Luis Sepulveda is a major novelist who scored an international hit with his 1992 classic *The Old Man Who Read Love Stories*. He writes novels and short stories and his new works are eagerly awaited by an appreciative Chilean public. His *The Story of a Seagull and the Cat Who Taught Her to Fly* is a children's book beloved around the world.

Roberto Bolaño, who died young in 2003, is widely considered one of Chile's best modern writers: his novels are often mysteries or detective tales, yet literary. Marcela Serrano is a highly regarded young writer whose works are mostly about women and their relationships with one another. Updated: Jun 24, 2009.

Holidays and Festivals

Chile has a wealth of year-round religious, historic, and cultural festivities:

January 1: Año Nuevo, or New Year's Day, often celebrated outdoors.

March or April: Semana Santa, or Holy Week, including Palm Sunday (Domingo de Ramos), Good Friday (Viernes Sanato), and Easter (Pascua de Resurrección) is arguably the most important religious holiday in predominantly Catholic South America. Semana Santa is celebrated from Palm Sunday to Easter Sunday with religious ceremonies and processions taking place in churches and throughout the streets. Participants sometimes carry large wooden crosses or walk the streets on their knees in order to pay homage to their Catholic faith.

First Sunday after Easter: Cuasimodo, or Correr a Cristo (Run to Christ). Primarily celebrated in Santiago, this day-long celebration begins with a mass and continues with a procession of the parish priest in a decorated carriage. Townspeople follow him on cart, bike or foot, move through the city, shouting and stopping along the way to enjoy food, drink and music in honor of el Rey, Christ the King. The celebration stems from colonial times when priests would deliver the

Eucharist to the elderly and ill who could not attend mass on Easter.

May 1: Día de los Trabajadores, or Labor Day.

May 21: Día de las Glorias Navales, or Navy Day, commemorates the epic Battle of Iquique between Chile and Peru in 1879, with speeches, parades, celebrations and festivities. Specifically honoring captain Arturo Prat Chacón, who is considered Chile's greatest military hero, el día de las Glorias Navales is celebrated nationally throughout the country.

June 29: Feast of San Pedro and San Pablo.

August 15: Asunción de la Virgen / assumption.

First Monday in September: Day of National Unity. Replacing a previous holiday that celebrated the military coup which brought dictator Augusto Pinchet to power, this rather recent celebration (introduced by the government in 1999) is a public holiday also called Reconciliation Day.

September 18: Fiestas Patrias, or National Independence Day. Celebrating the country's independence from Spain in the early 1800s, the holiday typically includes dancing, drinking, and eating traditional Chilean foods. There are also parades, music and nearly every home is decorated in the colors of the national flag: red, blue and white.

September 19: Día de las Glorias del Ejército, or Armed Forces Day. Immediately following the country's independence day, Chileans celebrate their Armed Forces with a parade, or Parada Militar, in which troops from all branches form up in Santiago's second largest park, Parque O'Higgins. Smaller parades throughout cities and towns, as well as government air displays, round out the festivities.

October 12: Día de la Raza, Día del Descubrimiento de Dos Mundos, or Columbus Day, is a celebration of Hispanic heritage in Latin America. Songs, dances and costumes honor the discovery of the New World, as well as *mestizaja*, or the mingling of races.

November 1: Todos los Santos (All Saint's Day).

December 8: Immaculate Conception.

December 25: Navidad, or Christmas, is celebrated in summer, as Chile is located in the southern hemisphere and December presents warmer temperatures and longer days. Just as the rest of the world, good Chilean children are visited by Viejito Pascuero (Old Man Christmas), and given toys and other gifts from his reindeer-drawn sled. These gifts are opened close to midnight on Christmas Eve and enjoyed all Christmas Day.

Typical Chilean foods are prepared, such as Pan de Pascua, a special sweet fruitcake dessert, and Cola de Mono, a traditional drink made from milk, coffee, liquor, cinnamon, and sugar. Updated: Feb 17, 2009.

Social and Environmental Issues

INCOME INEQUALITY

Chile is widely hailed as one of South America's economic success stories. Strong economic growth has reduced poverty over the past couple of decades, yet income is still divided extremely unequally. The wealthiest 10 percent of the population take the lion's share of national income—over 40 percent—while the poorer 10 percent receive a mere one percent of the income, making Chile the second most unequal society in South America after Brazil.

Another rift in society is marked by access to pure drinking water, a normal feature of daily life for 99 percent of urban Chileans, but only for half of those living in rural areas.

POLLUTION

Chile's main environmental problems are the pollution of its air, water and land, and deforestation. Pollution from industry and transportation is especially acute in urban centers, where the population has doubled over the last 30 years.

Air Pollution

Santiago—choking in bus and truck diesel fumes and home to half of the country's industry—was ranked the second most polluted city in Latin America after Mexico City by Science magazine a few years ago.

Because Santiago sits in a basin between the coastal range and the Andean crests, smog engulfs the city during most of the dry winter months. Attempts at imposing alternative driving days for private vehicles have made little difference, and the congested public transportation system contributes to unpleasant levels of noise pollution.

A different form of air pollution affecting Chile's southernmost parts is the increased ultraviolet radiation caused by the hole in the ozone layer above the Antarctica. The main effect on humans is a higher risk of skin cancer, so travelers to Patagonia and Antarctica should wear high-factor sun block, especially during the Antarctic spring, from September to December.

Water and Land Pollution

While Chile has made the best of its natural resources, turning itself into a leading exporter of fish, fresh fruit and copper, it has done so without much regard for conservation, so the country's rivers and lakes are contaminated by sewage of domestic, agricultural and industrial origin. For instance, it is estimated that only 70 percent of waste water is treated in Santiago, and the Mapocho river, which runs across the capital, is terribly contaminated; a number of new wastewater processing plants are now under construction.

The central valley may be a bread basket but at a price: fruit growers use copious amounts of fertilizers and pesticides, which filter through to the water table. Salmon farming operations, also a booming sector in the Lake District and in Patagonia, disperse salmon waste, antibiotics and other contaminants into streams, while fish escaping from commercial farms are said to colonize rivers and supplant native species.

The mining sector, one of Chile's leading industries, is one of the worst offenders. While copper smelters spew away, gold mines use cyanide which is extremely toxic for humans, livestock and wildlife. Large Canadian- and U.S.-owned mining corporations are increasingly seeing their operations under heavy fire from environmental activists. The mining industry also happens to be a greedy one in terms of energy needs, which indirectly puts a heavy strain on Chilean natural resources.

Endesa, Chile's largest utility company, has plans to invest massively in hydroelectricity and has been constructing power stations to take advantage of the rivers rushing down from the Andes, a reliable way to deal with the country's regular power shortages.

However, plans to build dams on the Río Bío Bío and Río Futaleufú have already led to raging battles with indigenous activists, who point out that the dams would run afoul of indigenous laws. Another plan, the ambitious HydroAysen project, which requires damming two of Patagonia's most pristine rivers, the Pascua and the Baker, would flood rare temperate rainforests and some of Patagonia's best ranching lands. The proposed 2000-kilometer (1,243 mi), high-voltage transmission line north toward Santiago would also clear-cut beautiful forested areas.

Conservation groups are campaigning against the damming projects, arguing that they pose a considerable threat to the million-dollar tourism industry, which needs the area's white waters and pristine parks to attract visitors. Find out more by visiting the site of Futafriends, which aims to preserve the Futaleufú valley from environmental damage: www.futafriends.org.

DEFORESTATION
Forests cover roughly 20 percent of Chile's surface, but excessive logging and the resulting soil erosion are a severe problem. Also, the figures (15 million hectares of forested lands) do not reflect the fact that native trees are being replaced by commercial plantations of eucalyptus and Monterey pine. Many parts of Chile are bathed in a dry, Mediterranean climate and are susceptible to forest fire outbreaks, so take extra caution when lighting a camping stove or fire within a park.

Threatened areas are often home to Chile's most fragile wildlife. Chilean animal species considered endangered include the South Andean Huemul (a type of white-tailed deer), the Tundra Peregrine Falcon, the Puna Rhea (an ostrich-like flightless bird), the Chilean Woodstar (the smallest bird in Chile, of the hummingbird family), the Ruddy-headed Goose and the Green Sea Turtle. Also threatened are four types of freshwater fish and more than 200 plant species. Updated: Jul 06, 2009.

Chile by Numbers
Independence: September 18, 1810.

Area: 756,626 sq km / 292,058 sq miles.

Length of the territory: 4,329 km (2,690 mi); average width: 180 km (112 mi); coastline: 4,500 km (2,796 mi).

Population: 16.6 million (as of July 2009)

People: White and mixed European and Amerindian descent 95.4%, Mapuche 4%, other indigenous groups 0.6%. The indigenous community is comprised of the following groups: Mapuche (87%), Aymara (7%), Atacamenos (3%), Quechua, Rapa Nui, Colla, Alacalufe and Yamana.

Religions: Roman Catholic 70%, Evangelical 15.%, other Christian churches 2%, other religions (including Jews and Muslims) 4.5%, and atheists/indifferent 8.3%.

Life expectancy: 76 years.

Literacy rate: 96%.

GDP: $181.5 billion (2008 estimate).

Annual growth: 4% (2008 estimate).

GDP composition by sector: agriculture: 5%; industry: 50%; services: 45%.
Unemployment: 7.3% (February 2008).

Currency: Peso. Exchange rate December, 2009: 499 Chilean pesos to 1 U.S. Dollar. Updated: Dec 16, 2009.

Additional Basic Facts
Official Name: Republic of Chile.

Capital: Santiago.

Languages: Spanish (official), Mapudungun, German, English.

Government: Republic. Chief of state and head of government: President Michelle Bachelet (inaugurated March 11, 2006). A new president will be elected in early 2010.

Agriculture: grapes, apples, pears, onions, wheat, corn, oats, peaches, garlic, asparagus, beans, beef, poultry, wool, fish, timber. Main Industries: copper, other minerals, foodstuffs, fish processing, iron and steel, wood and wood products, transport equipment, cement, textiles.

Main exports: copper, fish, fruits, paper and pulp, chemicals, wine.

Provinces: 13 Administrative regions: Aisen del General Carlos Ibanez del Campo, Antofagasta, Araucania, Atacama, Bio-Bio, Coquimbo, Libertador General Bernardo O'Higgins, Los Lagos, Magallanes y de la

Antarctica Chilena, Maule, Region Metropolitana (Santiago), Tarapaca, Valparaiso.

Mainland Time: GMT minus 4 (GMT-3 from second Sunday in October to second Sunday in March). Easter Island Time: GMT minus 6 (GMT- 5 from second Sunday in Oct to second Sunday in March).

Electricity: 220 Volts AC 50 Hz. 3-pin plugs are used. Updated: Jul 02, 2009.

Foreign Embassies in Chile

Argentina
Santiago: Vicuña Mackenna 41, Tel: 56-2-5822606 / 2608, Fax: 56- 2-2226853, E-mail: consuladosantiago@embargentina.cl, URL: www.embargentina.cl

Antofagasta: Blanco Encalda 933, Tel: 56-5-5220441 / 0440, Fax: 56-5-5378707, E-mail: cantofagasta@embargentina.cl.

Concepción: O'Higgins N 420, Oficina N 82, Tel: 56-4-1230257 / 2521459, Fax: 56-4-1521462, E-mail: cconcepcion@embargenina.cl,cconc2@entelchile.net

Valparaíso: Cochrane 867, Office 204, Tel: 56-3-22217419 / 13691 / 58165, Fax: 56-3-222-17419, E-mail: cvalparaiso@embargentina.cl

Puerto Montt: Calle Pedro Montt 160. 6th floor, Tel: 56-6-5253996, Fax: 56-6-5282878, E-mail: cpmontt@embargentina.cl

Punta Arenas: 21 de Mayo 1878, Tel: 56-6-1261912 / 1532, Fax: 56-6-1261264, E-mail: cparenas@embargentina.cl

Australia
Santiago: Isidora Goyenechea 3621, 13th floor, Las Condes, Tel: 2-550-3500, Fax: 2-331-5960, E-mail: consular.santiago@dfat.gov.au, URL: www.chile.embassy.gov.au

Belgium
Santiago: Edificio Forum, Av. Providencia 2653, Office 1103, Providencia, Tel: 56-2-2321070, Fax: 56-2-2321073, E-mail: Santiago@diplobel.org, URL:www.diplomatie.be

Bolivia
Santiago: Av. Santa María 2796, Providencia, Tel: 56-2-6581280 / 2328180, Fax: 56-2-6581284, E-mail: colivian-santiago@consuladodebolivia.cl, URL: www.consuladobolivia.cl

Brazil
Santiago: Enrique Mac-Iver 225, 15th floor, Tel: 56-2-8205800, Fax: 56-2-441 9197, E-mail: consbraschile@consbraschile.cl, URL: www.consuladodebrasil.cl

Canada
Santiago: Nueva Tajamar 481, World Trade Center, Torre Norte, 12th floor, Tel: 56-2-6523800, Fax: 56-2-6523912, E-mail: stago@international.gc.ca, URL: www.canadainternational.gc.ca/chile-chil

Colombia
Santiago: Av. Presidente Errazuriz 3943, Las Condes, Tel: 56-2-2061999 / 2061314, E-mail: esantiag@cancilleria.gov.co, URL: www.embajadaenchile.gov.co

Costa Rica
Santiago: Zurich 255, Office 85, Las Condes, Tel: 56-2-3341600, E-mail: info@costarica.cl, URL: www.costarica.cl

Cuba
Santiago: Av. Los Leones 1346, Providencia, Tel: 56-2-3679738 / 3679739, Fax: 56-2-3679745, URL: www.embacuba.cl

Czech Republic
Santiago: Av. El Golf 254, Las Condes, Tel: 56-2-2321066 / 2311910, Fax: 56-2-2320707, E-mail: santiago@embassy.mzv.cz, URL: www.czechembassy.org/wwwo/?amb=68

Denmark
Santiago:Jacques Cazotte 5531,Casilla 19002, Correo 19, Vitacura, Tel: 56-2-9415100, Fax: 56-2-2181736, E-mail: sclamb@um.dk, URL:www.ambsantiago.um.dk

Ecuador
Santiago: Av. Providencia 1979 esq. Pedro de Valdivia, 5th floor, Tel: 56-2-2312015 /2315073, Fax: 56-2-2325833, E-mail: embajaecuador@adsl.tie.cl, URL: www.embajadaecuador.cl

El Salvador
Santiago: Calle Coronel 2330, 5th floor, Office 51, Providencia, Tel: 56- 2-2338324 / 2338332 /2316370, E-mail: embasalva@adsl.tie.cl URL: www.rree.gob.sv/embajadas/chile.nsf

Finland
Santiago: Alcántara 200, office 201, Las Condes, Tel: 56-2-2634917, E-mail: sanomat.snt@formin.fi URL: www.finland.cl

France
Santiago: Condell 65, Providencia, Tel: 56-2-4708000, Fax: 56-2-4708050, E-mail: consulat.santiago@diplomatie.gouv.fr, URL: www.france.cl

Germany
Santiago: Las Hualtatas 5677, Vitacura, Casilla 220, Tel: 56-2-4632500, Fax: 56-2-4632525, URL: www.santiago.diplo.de

Greece
Santiago: Jorge Sexto 306, Las Condes, Tel: 56-2-2127900, Fax: 56-2-2128048, E-mail: embassygr@grecia.cl, URL: www.greekembassy.cl

Guatemala
Santiago: Zurich, 255, office 55, Las Condes, Tel: 56-2-5864430 / 5864431, E-mail: embajada@guatemala.cl, URL: www.guatemala.cl

India
Santiago: Triana 871, Providencia, Tel: 56-2-2352005 / 2352633, Fax: 56-2-2359607 / 2641312, E-mail: info@embajadaindia.cl, URL: www.embajadaindia.cl

Israel
Santiago: San Sebastián 2812, 5th floor, Las Condes, Tel: 56-2-7500500, Fax: 56-2-7500555, E-mail: info@santiago.mfa.gov.il, URL: http://santiago.mfa.gov.il

Italy
Santiago: Clemente Fabres 1050, Providencia, Tel: 56-2-4708400, Fax: 56-2-2232467, E-mail: info.santiago@esteri.it, URL: www.ambsantiago.esteri.it

Mexico
Santiago: Félix de Amesti 128, Las Condes, Tel: 56-2-5838400, Fax: 56-2-5838484, URL: www.emexico.cl

Netherlands
Santiago: Av. Apoquindo 3500, 13th floor, Las Condes, Tel: 56-2-7569200, Fax: 56-2-7569226, E-mail: stg@minbuza.nl, URL: www.holanda-paisesbajos.cl

New Zealand
Santiago: El Golf 99, Office 703, Las Condes, Tel: 56-2-2909800, Fax: 56-2-4580940, E-mail: embajada@nzembassy.cl, URL: www.nzembassy.cl

Norway
Santiago: San Sebastián 2839, Office 509, Las Condes, Tel: 56-2-2342888, Fax: 56-2-2342201, E-mail: emb.santiago@mfa.no, URL: www.noruega.cl

Peru
Santiago: Bucarest 162, Providencia, Tel: 56-2-2318020 / 2322095, Fax: 56-2-3341272, URL: www.conpersantiago.cl

Poland
Santiago: Mar del Plata 2055, Providencia, Tel: 56-2-2041213 / 2690212 Fax: 56-2-2049332, E-mail: embchile@entelchile.net, URL: www.poland.cl

South Africa
Santiago: Av. 11 de Septiembre 2353, 17th floor, Providencia, Tel: 56-2-2312862, E-mail: info.chile@foreign.gov.za, URL: www.embajada-sudafrica.cl

Spain
Santiago: Av. Andres Bello, 1895. Providencia, Tel: 56-2-2352754 / 2352755, Fax: 56-2-2361547 / 2351049, E-mail: emb.santiagodechile@mae.es

Sweden
Santiago: Av. 11 de Septiembre 2353, 4th floor, Providencia, Tel: 56-2-9401700, Fax: 56-2-9401730, E-mail: ambassaden.santiago-de-chile@foreign.ministry.se, URL: www.embajadasuecia.cl

Switzerland
Santiago: Américo Vespucio Sur 100, 14th floor, Las Condes, Tel: 2-263-4211, Fax: 2-263-4094, E-mail: san.vertretung@eda.admin.ch, URL: www.eda.admin.ch/santiago

U.K.
Santiago: Av. El Bosque Norte 0125, Las Condes, Tel: 56-2-3704100, Fax: 56-2-3704160, E-mail: embsan@britemb.cl, URL: www.britemb.cl

USA
Santiago: Av. Andrés Bello 2800, Las Condes, Tel: 56-2-3303000, Fax: 56-2-3303710, URL: www.usembassy.cl

Uruguay
Santiago: Av. Pedro de Valdivia 711, Providencia, Tel: 56-2-2047988 / 2744066, Fax: 56-2-2047772, E-mail: urusgo@uruguay.cl, URL: www.uruguay.cl. Updated: Jul 02, 2009.

Before You Go

Chile has a well-developed tourist infrastructure, making it an easily accessible country for travelers. When packing, don't forget that the seasons in Chile are opposite of those in the northern hemisphere. Also, bring a small first aid kit with any medicine you take on a regular basis, plus some anti-diarrhea pills, aspirin, insect repellent, band-aids and sunscreen. Most of these items are easily available throughout Chile; however, it is best to bring them from home than to risk not finding what you want. Updated: Jun 25, 2009.

Insurance

Taking out a travel insurance policy is an essential precaution for all tourists who plan to travel to Chile, or anywhere in South America for that matter. As there are a great deal of different insurers offering a wide variety of products, it is worth spending some time to research the policy that is most suitable for your trip. Before you do though, check to see if you already have coverage, as some credit and bank cards provide basic travel insurance.

Travel insurances policies cover a wide range of potential problems, including cancellation of transportation, delays, hijacking, the loss or theft of valuables and legal expenses. The most important part of any policy is the medical provision. The costs of medical treatment for serious injuries can quickly mount up. Find out both how much your insurance will pay for necessary emergency expenses and if your policy includes helicopter rescue and emergency evacuation, should you need to return home, or be flown to the U.S. for serious medical attention. Most policies (and hospitals in Chile) will demand that you pay for your medical treatment up front (usually in cash). If you have to pay cash at a hospital, make sure that you get receipts for any medical care you receive, as you will need to provide copies when making your claim. Before you leave home, make sure that the policy you chose covers all the activities that you intend on doing, or think that you might try; activities such as climbing, trekking and skiing may be considered adventurous activities and thus not covered under a basic policy.

Although medical coverage is extremely important, most travel insurance claims relate to lost or stolen items. If you intend on taking expensive belongings such as cameras, laptops or iPods to Chile, there is a chance that they could be stolen or damaged. Purchase a policy that offers an appropriate level of protection to cover all the items you intend to take on your trip, or consider leaving any extremely expensive items at home. If you are robbed while in Chile, report the incident to the police within 24 hours. Make sure to obtain a copy of the report, as your insurance company may demand this (along with the item's receipt) when you make your claim.

Basic travel insurance policies may not include any provision for the loss or theft of valuables and, in general, the more money you are willing to spend, the greater the level of protection you will have. If you purchase a more comprehensive policy, the deductibles will be smaller, single item limits will be higher, there may be coverage for cash and the cost of reissuing passports. Check the details very closely to make sure that you are happy with the level of coverage your policy provides.

Note: Be sure to bring your insurer's 24-hour emergency contact number and a copy of your policy number with you. It is also a good idea to keep your insurance details in an E-mail account so you can access them where ever you are, even if someone steals your bags. Insurance companies also recommend taking written records of any medical conditions and proper names of any medication you are taking, plus a prescription for it, just in case. Updated: Apr 22, 2009.

Getting To and Away From Chile

Chile is easily accessed by plane, with many international airlines offering flights into Santiago. It's not the cheapest destination as flights can get costly. If you're trip includes other countries as well as Chile, consider flying in somewhere else first to cut costs. Traveling between Chile and other countries in South America can be done by air or land, depending on your priorities. Air is faster and more reliable, but buses will allow you to take in the truly breathtaking scenery. From cliff-hugging coastal roads to ribbon-like climbs through the Andes, land transport in Chile is better than most South American countries, but still obviously slower than flying. Updated: Jul 02, 2009.

BY PLANE

Many travelers choose to fly into Chile, and there is a plethora of flights linking the airports of Santiago and Concepción with the rest of South America. Santiago has the main entry and departure points for intercontinental flights. From North America: Santiago can

Getting To and Away From Chile   35

INTRO & INFO

be reached from New York and Miami directly on American Airlines and Chile's LAN; from Atlanta on Delta; and from Toronto on Air Canada. LAN also flies to Auckland, with connections throughout Oceania.

From Europe: Iberia and LAN fly directly between Santiago and Madrid, and Air France offers direct service from Paris. Direct flights are often significantly more expensive than flights with layovers in countries like Panama, Argentina and Brazil, unless booked far in advance. Travelers should shop around, since round-trip tickets from North America, Europe or Oceania can often be had for under $1,000 if booked well ahead. Updated: Apr 13, 2009.

DEPARTURE TAX
The departure tax (not to be confused with the reciprocity fee changed upon arrival to the airport in Santiago) may or may not be included in the price of your airplane ticket. Check with your airline's representative. If the fee was not included in your ticket, expect to pay about $30. Cash and credit cards are accepted forms of payment. Updated: Feb 24, 2009.

BY LAND
There are a number of ways for travelers to enter Chile by land. Long-range buses link Santiago to the major cities in South America, though the cross-continental journeys are painfully long. Crossing from Peru, the only open route is the one between Tacna and Arica, which is well-traveled. From Bolivia, the easiest route with public transport is along the paved La Paz-Arica highway.

There are a number of bus routes linking Chile and Argentina; among those of particular interest to visitors are the ones linking Calama with Salta in the north, Santiago with Mendoza, Osorno in the Lakes District with Bariloche, and Punta Arenas with Río Gallegos in Patagonia. Twice-daily train service links Tacna and Arica, and three trains per week connect Calama with Uyuni, Bolivia. See Border Crossings for details on arriving by private vehicle.Updated: Jul 06, 2009.

BORDER CROSSINGS
Chile shares a few border crossings with its northern neighbors, Peru and Bolivia, and a great number with Argentina. Chile's only legal crossing with Peru is between Tacna and Arica. Between Bolivia and Chile, the main crossing is along the La Paz-Arica highway, though lesser-used crossings exist along the

Iquique-Colchane road, as well as at Portezuelo del Cajón. Well over a dozen official border crossings exist on the frontier with Argentina, but many of these are difficult to access.

Popular Andean crossings include Paso de Jama (between Calama and Jujuy), Paso Colchane (between Iquique and Oruro), Los Libertadores (between Santiago and Mendoza), Paso de Mamuil Malal on the road from San Martín de los Andes to Temuco, Paso Cardenal Samoré (between Osorno and Bariloche), as well as the bus and ferry link between Puerto Montt and Bariloche. In Patagonia, main crossings include the one between Puerto Natales and Río Turbio, the crossing along the Punta Arenas-Río Gallegos highway, and the post between the two Tierra del Fuego towns of Porvenir and Río Grande. Other crossings can be made in summer, but passes are frequently closed during the winter. Severe storms will close even the major passes, so travelers should check ahead.

Passengers on public transport can expect to have their bags searched and sometimes X-rayed at the busiest crossings, so film should be kept separate. Travelers bringing vehicles into Chile will be required to purchase insurance and fill out a Relaciones de Pasajeros document at the border. Drivers will also be expected to provide the registration documents and, if the car is rented, a notarized document attesting to the rental agreement. Border officials may also ask drivers for a carnet de passages or libreta de pasos por aduana, but travelers are advised to check with their national automobile club before departing. Whether traveling by car or bus, passengers will need to go through customs and immigration on both sides of the border.Note on customs: Be aware of very strict restrictions on the entry of meat, dairy, fruits and vegetable products. Chile fines heavily for possession of these items if they are not declared. Lists of forbidden items are posted and bags are frequently searched. If in doubt while filling in immigration forms, check the box that you do have such products and it is less likely you will be fined. Updated: Jul 07, 2009.

BY BOAT
It is much easier to arrange boat travel within Chile than it is to enter the country by boat. A few cruise liners depart from San Diego, Fort Lauderdale or Rio de Janeiro with Valparaíso as a final destination. These are usually expensive multi-week affairs, but last-minute deals do occasionally pop up. Quicker and more

economical is the short but scenic boat journey from Ushuaia in Argentina to the Puerto Williams. The journey, which is much easier in the summer than in the winter, passes through some of Tierra del Fuego's most beautiful landscapes. It is easy to arrange a charter or passage on a yacht or commercial boat between the two towns, and Victory Cruises has daily departures costing $120 one-way. Travelers will usually be responsible for paying a $10 port tax. Cheaper, more regular ferry service might begin soon. Updated: Apr 13, 2009.

Visa Information

It is necessary for all travelers entering Chile to present a passport which is valid for six months beyond the date of arrival. Upon entrance, all visitors must show the aforementioned valid passport and one of the following: return ticket to country of origin or residence, a credit card, or sufficient funds to purchase return ticket, and if so required, a visa (within valid passport). Additionally, travelers with passports from the U.S., Canada, Mexico and Australia must pay a reciprocity tax upon entering the Santiago airport and before passing through Customs, if entering overland. The fee must be paid in U.S. Dollars (cash) and it is valid until the passport expires (for American and Canadian passport holders) or for three months (for Mexican and Australian passport holders). The fees are follows: US—$100, Canada—$132, Mexico—$32, Australia—$61.

Citizens with the following passports are not required to obtain a visa for entrance into Chile for stays up to 90 days: British, Australian, Canadian, U.S.A., E.U. (with the exception of nationals of Greece, who can stay up to 60 days and of Romania, who can stay for 30 days). Nationals not referred to here are advised to contact a local Chilean embassy to verify visa requirements. Those visitors who are not required to obtain visas will receive a Chilean tourist card upon arrival in the country issued free of charge. It is essential for travelers to carry this tourist card while they're in the country.

If you plan to stay for more than 90 days, depending on your purpose, a visa may be required. If you are obtaining a visa, all applications require the following: a valid passport, evidence of sufficient funds to cover stay, a return or onward ticket. Student visa applications specifically require: a letter of acceptance from the institution you will be studying at, a letter of confirmation that the school and courses are government approved, a letter of police

clearance, a doctor's health certificate, and three passport-sized photos. Issuing a visa usually takes between 24-hours and seven days; be sure to leave adequate time. From the date of issue, tourist visas are valid for up to 90 days, and student visas are valid for up to one year. Note that it is illegal to work in Chile under either a tourist or student visa. Also be aware that visa and passport requirements are subject to change at any time. It is recommended that you check with your embassy or consulate for verification. Updated: Jun 22, 2009.

Getting Around Chile

BY PLANE

Due to the length of the country and distances between its attractions, many visitors to Chile choose to travel on domestic flights in order to save time. Flights are a particularly popular option for travelers who arrive in Santiago and plan to visit the far north or Patagonia. The two main carriers in Chile are LAN and Sky Airlines, which link all the major cities in the country. Fares on most routes from Santiago start at under $200 one-way. In Patagonia, where transportation is thin on the ground, local flights are a speedy alternative to long waits and circuitous bus and ferry routes, and a handful of small regional air carriers and private air charters compete with the major airlines. One destination that virtually requires a flight is Easter Island, and LAN has several departures each week from Santiago. Be forewarned however, that the tickets don't come cheap—they start at $500. Domestic tickets are subject to a small departure tax, but this is usually included in the ticket price; be sure to ask when booking. Updated: Apr 15, 2009.

BY BOAT

Chile hugs the Pacific, so it is not surprising that boats play an important role in the country's travel infrastructure. This is especially true in Patagonia, where it can be nearly impossible to travel around without setting foot on the deck of a ferry. Many routes only run a few days each week, and the boats often travel slowly, but you will usually be compensated with some wonderful views. Ferry travel is not very expensive; the price depends on the company and the route, but you can usually count on a basic ticket costing about $2-3 for every hour of the trip. There are multiple classes of service on longer journeys, and prices rise according to the level of comfort. Ferries will also carry bicycles and automobiles for an extra charge. Charter and tour boats also serve

Ecotourism

Once thought to be the least sustainable country in the world because of its exploitation of natural resources, Chile is slowly becoming more aware of the importance of protecting its environment.

Ecotourism in Chile seeks to conserve the natural areas and raise environmental awareness. A number of natural reserves work to provide activities that respect nature and show visitors unique flora and fauna. For example, Pan de Azucar, a national park in the Atacama region notable for historical and archaeological richness, is working on how to better sustain its maritime eco-systems by collecting samples. Like many national parks and reserves in the country, Pan de Azucar has a camping area, eco-lodges, mini-market and restaurant to facilitate responsible tourism.

Eco-tours are becoming popular in Chile. Adventure Life Journeys prides itself on small-group travel and exploration of local cultures and landscapes, while Amerika Venture undertakes ecological studies of various environments and also documentary production.

Environmental education is also becoming more important in Chile, thanks to various campaigns by the Agricultural Ministry, dating as far back as 1965. Hoping to raise awareness about the threat of forest fires, a campaign, dubbed "Forestín," used the image of the puma to alert the public to the danger of fires not only to Chile's flora but also to its fauna. This image later changed in 1976 to a Coipo, a type of beaver, to depict an animal that lived in the trees. The campaign became so successful that the Coipo became the national symbol of the protection of forest resources and is today used in schools to educate Chilean children.

Corporación Nacional Forestal (Conaf), the governing body of all national parks, promotes sustainable forest management. It offers services to various groups of visitors based on the effects of tourism on wildlife and how they can be more responsible. Updated: Jul 07, 2009.

some routes, providing greater comfort at a higher cost. During the winter, ferry service is sometimes suspended, and charters will be your only option. Updated: Apr 15, 2009.

BY TRAIN

Chile's rail network has shrunk from its heyday a century ago, but it is still possible to travel several routes by train. The Empresa de Ferrocarriles del Estado (www.efe.cl) operates Chile's passenger trains and offers several departures each day from Santiago to Chillán and Talca, and more frequent trains to San Fernando. There are also rail lines linking Constitución with Talca, Hualqui with Mercado, Concepción with Lomas Coloradas and Victoria with Temuco. EFE changes its routes frequently; until recently you could travel from Santiago as far as Puerto Montt. The line from Santiago to Temuco is usually in operation during the summer but not during the winter. With that in mind, it is best checking with EFE before you make your plans. When the domestic trains do run, they cost a little more than buses, but are relatively comfortable and efficient. Updated: Apr 15, 2009.

BY BUS

Chile has some of the most comfortable buses on the continent, which is a blessing because journeys can be painfully long. There are a number of bus lines, the most prominent of which are TurBus (www.turbus.com) and Pullman Bus (www.pullman.cl). They both cover the entire country, offering online booking and multiple classes of buses. Classes in Chile range from standard coaches to premium luxury buses with seats that fold down into beds (coche cama).

Bus tickets are generally good value and only need to be booked more than a day in advance during holidays or for long-distance routes. Few routes however, service national parks and other wilderness areas. One alternative for travelers, albeit a pricey one, is to take a hop-on/hop-off bus trip. Pachamama by Bus (www.pachamamabybus.com) and ChileXperience (www.chilexperience.com) offer services to touristy areas. Passengers buy a ticket for a certain number of days or a certain route and are free to get off the bus wherever they'd like and board again when the next bus passes through. Updated: Apr 15, 2009.

BY TAXI

Taxis are an easy way to get around Chile's cities and towns. They are metered and the rates are displayed on the window in most places. Major cities and towns that see a lot of tourists tend to have the priciest cabs, and there is typically a surcharge tacked on to the fare at night and on Sundays. In a few of the smaller cities, taxis are not metered and you will have to negotiate a fare with the driver before you depart; if you can, ask a local about the going rate for your trip. This is also the case when you charter a cab or take a trip outside town. Many cities also have shared taxis called colectivos which function in much the same way as buses, with fixed routes and fares. Colectivos are often faster than buses, but are marginally more expensive and can be quite cramped. They can usually be hailed on the street or at designated stops, and they have their routes and fares prominently displayed. In a few places in the north, they also provide intercity transportation. Updated: Apr 20, 2009.

BY CAR

Driving can be a pleasant and efficient way of getting around the country. Drivers are generally more conscientious than elsewhere in South America, and the main highways are in good condition. That said, renting a car is quite expensive, especially because many destinations are on unpaved roads and only accessible with a costly 4x4 vehicle. Rental costs are frequently higher in the Lake District and Patagonia, and there are significant surcharges for one-way rentals. Members of the Automobile Club of Chile (www.automovilclub.cl) may be eligible for a rental discount. One alternative to renting is buying a car and then re-selling it at the end of a trip, but you should be mindful of inspection dates and tax responsibilities. You can also drive into Chile (see the Border Crossings section). However you get your hands on a set of wheels, remember that driving is on the right, speed limits are strictly enforced, and an international license can make dealing with the police and rental agencies much easier. Nighttime driving is to be avoided. Finally, driving in Santiago is restricted on especially smoggy days. Updated: Apr 20, 2009.

BY HITCHHIKING

Hitchhiking is not recommended in Chile. While Chile is one of the safest and easiest countries on the continent in which to hitch a ride, there are risks inherent in getting into a vehicle with a stranger, and the danger is only heightened for women and those traveling alone. That said, many travelers do decide to hitchhike rather than wait for infrequent public transportation, especially in the extreme south. If you choose to hitch, take precautions; travel in pairs and let someone know about your itinerary. If you're going to be off the main highways, dress and pack as if you'll be spending a lot of time standing by the side of the road. It is easiest to get a lift on the main highways, especially the Pan-American, or at truck service centers around major cities. Waiting times can be long in rural areas, especially in the desert and south of Puerto Montt. Updated: Apr 20, 2009.

BY BICYCLE

Chile is a great destination for cyclists. In addition to getting a lot of exercise, you can enjoy the country at your own pace and easily escape from the tourist trail. The logistics of traveling by bicycle are relatively simple, too. Bicycles can be rented in any tourist town or main city, and they can also be carried on buses, trains, planes and boats. This makes it easy to take in the diversity of Chile's landscapes while cycling. You should use a bike with wide tires, for gripping steep or unpaved roads, and carry a lot of water. A mounted mirror can help you see cars on narrow roads, and Chilean law (as well as common sense) requires the use of a helmet. It is a good idea to stay off the roads after dark, and morning is often the best time to ride, since the heat and wind will usually not have kicked up yet. Finally, while most Chilean towns have a bike shop, it's still smart to carry spare parts and tools. Updated: Apr 15, 2009.

Chile Tours

Chile tours range from trekking through the Patagonia, to relaxing at a wine-tasting or hitting the beach. Santiago city tours feature fine restaurants, museums and monuments as well as excellent day-trips to beaches and Andean ski-resorts. Chilean wine-country tours are offered throughout the rolling Andes region and can include lodging at traditional haciendas, ranches. Chile adventure tours, especially in the rustic terrain of the Norther Altiplano, Tierra del Fuego, Patagonia and the Lake District are incredibly popular with travelers who love the rush of adrenaline. Tours of Easter Island can give the traveler a glimpse of past cultures with its famous Moai sculptures. The following are a few companies that can help you get started booking a tour:

ChileQuest International Tour Operator

Santiago: Lira 441 Suite 65, Tel: 56-2-6279042 Fax: 56-2 6650408, E-mail: info@chilequest.com, URL: http://www.ChileQuest.com, Updated: Dec 07, 2006.

Chip Travel

Santiago: Av. Santa Maria 227, Of. 11, Recoleta. Tel: 56-2-7375649, E-mail: info@chiptravel.cl, URL: www.chiptravel.cl. Updated: Aug 6, 2009.

Ecotours

Santiago: Guillermo Franke 2298, Av Bustamante 130, E-mail: info@ecotours.cl, URL: www.ecotours.cl. Updated: Dec 07, 2006.

Santiago Adventures

Santiago: Coyancura 2270 Of. 801, Tel: 56-2-4150667, E-mail: bpearson@santiagoadventures.com, URL: www.santiagoadventures.com. Updated: Dec 07, 2006.

WINE TOURS

As Chilean wines have matured into worldly nectars, winemakers have also caught on the touristic potential and more valleys are setting up tours. If you want to swill *vinos tintos* and *blancos*, sniff out the fruity and woody aromas, learn to tell your cabernet from your merlot, and your sauvignon from your chardonnay, just head out to the valleys of Casablanca, Colchaga, Maule or Maipo.

Most wine routes (*ruta del vino*) will take you through several bodegas over the course of a day or two, with vineyard visits, stops at the wine cellars and of course wine tasting, sometimes with a meal. Guides can explain the fermentation and maturation process in Spanish and often in EnglishPrices depend on the length of the tour (which can range from three hours to 12 days) and on whether the wines are premiums. A typical day-long tour organized by a Santiago operator, with transportation and meals included, will cost between $100 and $200, but you can also arrange directly with wine producers' associations or, if you have your own car, drop in independent wineries.

Wine valleys can be visited any time of the year because of their mild climate, but if you go in the austral fall, from February to April, you have better chances of catching harvest festivals, during which wine-tastings are organized. For more info, see www.rutadelvino.cl, www.colchaguavalley.cl or www.casablancavalley.cl. Updated: Mar 30, 2009.

TOURS IN THE LAKE DISTRICT

The Lake District is a great destination for outdoors activities like hiking, fishing,

canopying, horseback riding, kayaking and rafting—just to name a few. Adventure seekers should head to Pucón or Puerto Varas where you'll be met with a wide array of tour operators ready show you the ropes.

Although certain activities can be done independently, more technical and potentially dangerous activities like whitewater sports or volcano ascents should be done with a guide (and Chile officials may require one). In addition to adventure sports, you can also go on cultural tours to local Mapuche villages. As an example, a two-day horseback ride in the Cochamó valley can start at $114, a day of canyoning at $64, and an ascent of Volcán Villarica around $70. Updated: Jun 29, 2009.

PATAGONIA TOURS IN CHILE

Stunning scenery and wildlife abound in the Chilean section of Patagonia. From the sub-Antarctic Isla Grande de Tierra del Fuego, across the Beagle Channel to Puerto Williams, and the Fjords of Fuegia, Chilean Patagonia is characterized by rugged mountain chains, islands within inland seas, and a network of massive glaciers and ice fields spread across pristine forests. The most popular traveler spot is Torres del Paine, which can be accessed from nearby Puerto Natales. The region offers a variety of adventure and nature tours, including hiking and trekking, climbing, horseback riding, kayaking, and birdwatching. Tours can be organized in Puerto Natales and Punto Arenas, or across the border in Ushuaia. Updated: Dec 13, 2006.

TOURS ON EASTER ISLAND

Travelers who want to take a tour on Easter Island can either make their arrangements on the mainland or on the island itself in Hanga Roa. Keep in mind however, that tour operators based in the mainland are likely to be more expensive, unless you are with a larger group. At the same time, mainland agencies can be very helpful in arranging car rentals, transfers or hotel reservations.

Tour packages range from a day to week-long endeavors. Longer tours will take visitors through fascinating archaeological sites like the Orongo ceremonial ruins or the lines of Moai. If history's not your thing, you can also go volcano trekking or scuba diving. Tour prices determine the level of luxury, but most are pretty high, especially since the majority do not include airfare, which is usually about $800 from Santiago. If booked locally, a simple four-day tour with transportation, meals, accommodation, bilingual guide and entrance to the national park starts at $285 per person; a seven-day tour should be in the $800-$900 range. Updated: Jul 01, 2009.

OTHER TOUR TYPES

Although tours to Patagonia, Easter Island and the Lake District are top picks among tourists, Chile's spectacular diversity offers an enormous array of tour options and destinations. Bold travelers can brave the beauty and mystique of the world's driest desert, the Atacama. Within this rainless wonder lies Reserva Nacional Los Flamencos, where tours visit the lunar-landscaped Valley of the Moon. Tours to salt flats and nearby abandoned mining towns can also be arranged. Amid the altiplano is the Parque Nacional Lauca, whose name means "aquatic grass." Here travelers can tour a variety of lagoons and lakes while watching llamas and vicuñas frolic across the landscape. If you're wanting to cover large areas, bicycle and mountain-biking tours spanning the Andes, Patagonia and the Pacific are popular choices; those seeking a less active mode of transportation can try one of the train ride excursions. For more information, check out our section on mountain biking (p.43) or traveling by train (p.37).Updated: Jun 25, 2009.

PRE-ARRANGED / ORGANIZED TOURS

Chile has a very good tourism infrastructure. Whether it's outdoor adventure or city siteseeing, Chile provides it all, and all manners of doing it too! Many travelers choose to set up tours once they get to their destination. This is a less-expensive option, though also less-stable, as tours can fill up, or run on a schedule that doesn't fit yours. For these reasons, many travelers choose to pre-arrange tours with companies that offer organized packages. To set it all up beforehand is a fairly simple task in Chile, as almost all tour companies provide online services which can be booked from home or elsewhere on the road. You're best bet is to get online and research what it is you want to do, when you want to do it, and how you want it done; it's all out there. A hint of advice, check out Tucan Travel or GAP Adventures Worldwide, two of the leading organized tour companies that service South America. Updated: Jun 26, 2009.

Sport and Recreation in Chile

Chile's impressively extreme landscape is an outdoor lover's paradise, offering endless opportunities for activities as diverse as the landscape itself. Travelers could spend a lifetime exploring Chile's natural playground, from four-wheeling through the Atacama Desert to kitesurfing down the Pacific coastline to world-famous fly fishing in Patagonia. Snow bunnies flock to Central Chile, whose high-quality slopes and beautiful landscape offer arguably the best skiing and snowboarding in the South America.

Just outside Santiago lie an array of reputable resorts such as Valle Nevado, La Parva and El Colorado, with many more dotting the Andes. Resorts further south offer lower altitude skiing on volcanic slopes. Try the Antillanca Ski Center, whose name means "jewel of the sun" in the Mapuche language. Just south of Osorno, this ski resort allows skiers to whip through the forests of the Casablanca volcano. Southern Chile's unspoiled landscape and pristine lakes, rivers and fjords offer spectacular opportunities for fly-fishing. Cast a line at Coyhaique, a remote Patagonian village famed to be one of the world's best destinations for first class fly-fishing. Organized fishing tours and vacation lodges cover all of Patagonia and the Lake District.

Chile's amazing waters provide much more than fishing. Eco-friendly sports such as rafting and kayaking are popular in Patagonia. The surging class V whitewaters of the Futaleufu and Bio-Bio rivers are internationally famous. Exhilarating, but less extreme, trips can be made down Central Chile's class III/IV Maipo, Teno and Claro rivers. Chile's rugged landscape will not disappoint climbers. Popular volcano summits include high-altitude Parinacota in the far north, as well as the less extreme (though still difficult) peaks of Villarrica and Osorno in Central Chile. Climbers can test their mountaineering skills with the demanding Mts. Tupungato and Ojos del Salado. Ice climbers can "pick" from a variety of snow-capped mountains; El Plomo, La Paloma and El Altar are popular climbs that are easily accessible from Santiago.

For entertaining (but less extreme) activities, Chile offers plenty of options. Leisurelovers can soak in thermal baths at Termas de Colina or Termas Geométricas. Travelers can also enjoy scenic views while camping in one of the many national parks scattered throughout the country. The gorgeous Torres del Paine in Patagonia offers a variety of campgrounds along its beautiful waters, including Lago Puhoé and Río Serrano.

FÚTBOL FEVER

As with most Latin American counties, futbol (soccer) reigns supreme; its popularity transcends all ages and socioeconomic classes.

Although the teams are not as internationally popular as those of its Argentine and Brazilian neighbors, Chile shares their passion and intense pride for the game. Travelers can watch matches of all levels, from local city parks to national stadiums.

Chile's national team—nicknamed "La Roja" (the Red One)—has appeared in seven World Cup tournaments, including a third-place showing in the 1962 World Cup, hosted by Santiago's massive stadium Estadio Nacional de Chile. To football fans' delight, Copa Chile, the country's national championship, returned in 2008 after being cancelled in 2000. An international game between Peru and Chile is an electrifying experience, as the countries' passionate rivalry dates back to the fight for Bolivia's sea border in the War of the Pacific (also see our "Pisco controversy" box). For a taste of national fútbol fever, check out a heated match between rivals La U (Club de Fútbol Universidad de Chile) and Colo-Colo (Corporación Club Social y Deportivo Colo-Colo). Updated: Jun 02, 2009.

Adventure Travel

The combination of well-developed tourism industry and diverse geography means Chile has a wide range of adventure travel opportunities to offer adrenaline junkies.
There's skiing in the winter, as well as parachuting, paragliding and kayaking, when the weather's right. There are a number of rivers in southern Chile which are great spots to go rafting, while beaches along the Pacific coast are ideal for windsurfing. Be sure to get in touch with tour operators and guides who can help you organize your quest for adventure. Updated: Mar 24, 2009.

HIKING

The phenomenal diversity of landscapes, climates, and flora and fauna in each region makes Chile a very popular trekking destination. While there's ample terrain to explore with glaciers, hot springs, forests and volcanoes, trails outside of national parks and reserves often lack signage and are not well maintained. Chile offers countless day and multi-day excursions to suit every hiker, from the greenest to the most expert. On overnight or lengthy trips, you can bunk down in everything from campgrounds to refugios, trail huts and even five-star lodges.

It's possible to hike most of Chile year-round, though you may find yourself mired in snow and mud in winter. The most popular trails can get crowded in the high season, so you might want to plan your trekking around those times. However, avoid veering off the beaten path alone just for the sake of getting away, particularly if you are a novice hiker. Stick to the marked trails or hire a local guide. Chile will soon be home to the world's longest network of trails, with 8,500 kilometers (5,282 mi) of paths spanning the length of the country, from the Peruvian border to Cape Horn. This massive undertaking, initiated by the independent foundation Sendero de Chile, aims to connect existing trails by 2010 and to promote ecology and rural culture.

Norte
The northern altiplano features otherworldly landscapes to explore, including the striking Atacama desert, the Valle de la Luna—one of the most desolate places on earth the Valle de la Muerte with its curious rock formations, and the geyser fields of El Tatio. Legging it along the coast, you'll find yourself enveloped in morning fog, surrounded by cacti, Bulbous, Centenarian llareta plants, and, further south, Cinnamon Trees in Parque Nacional Fray Jorge. Near Copiapó, Parque Nacional Nevado Tres Cruces and Ojos del Salado—the highest active volcano in Chile, (6,893 m / 22,615 ft) offer good hikes and sights.

Central Valley
Go coastal and trek in soaring temperatures, or head east of Santiago and ascend the highest peaks in the Andean Cordillera. The river valley of Cajón del Maipo is only an hour and a half away from the capital, while the commanding El Morado stands 5,060 meters (16,596 ft) above sea level in a national reserve filled with hummingbirds, Cometocino and thrushes. Parque Nacional La Campana, situated between Santiago and Valparaíso is a rising star, and worth visiting before its trails become over-run. The Altos de Lircay, a national reserve featuring a swarm of rivers, gorges and archaeological sites, is also worth a trip.

The Lake District
The Lake District in southern Chile has a wealth of hiking trails. In Parque Nacional Nahuelbuta you will find the bizarre araucaria, or monkey-puzzle tree. Parque Pumalin has plenty of meandering paths through the rainforest, where many newly developed trails lead to awesome viewpoints. El Monumento Natural Cerro Ñielol, the country's only protected forest within an urban center, Temuco, has many hiking trails worth exploring. The large number of unmaintained

trails in the region, combined with rapid forest growth, means that footpaths tend to disappear over several years.

Southern Patagonia and Tierra del Fuego

There are a mind-boggling number of hikes in Patagonia, from the five-day circuit to Los Dientes de Navarino to the trails crisscrossing Tierra del Fuego. The most acclaimed trekking destination in Chile is Parque Nacional Torres del Paine. Its network of trails is set against a backdrop of majestic glaciers, turquoise lakes, and of course, the three famous basalt spires known as "cuernos." Because of the park's popularity, its main path, the "W," is swamped by hikers in the summer months, but you can always walk along secondary trails to escape the crowds.

Pacific Islands

Parque Nacional Rapa Nui on Easter Island offers pristine hiking to those who can afford the trip out. Thousands of kilometers from the mainland, the island is home to spellbinding greenery and archaeological mysteries. The islands comprising Archipiélago Juan Fernández belong to a national park and UNESCO world biosphere reserve and are another remote hiking destination blessed with a unique eco-system. Updated: Jul 01, 2009.

RAFTING AND KAYAKING

Chile is a great destination for whitewater sports, attracting enthusiasts from around the world. Whether you are interested in rafting or kayaking, Chile offers first-class spots.

Packing List

Swimsuit, tennis shoes or sandals with secure ankle straps, T-shirt (quick-drying material is best), easy-dry shorts or running tights, safety strap if wearing glasses and waterproof cameras are all recommended. Don't forget a waterproof bag for anything you want to keep dry during your trip and a change of clothes for the trip back.

Central Region

There are some good rafting options right around Santiago. The Cajón del Maipo is a popular destination. The course is full of obstacles and major class III and IV rapids. Río Claro, located within the Radal Siete Tazas National Reserve and easily reachable from Curicó via Molina, also attracts whitewater experts from near and far, but more for its waterfalls than its rapids. The challenge is

to raft down the waterfalls and live to tell the tale—no easy feat! For this reason, Rio Claro is reserved to the professional.

Southern Region

There are many lagoons and lakes for kayaking in Southern Chile. Río Bío Bío is considered one of the world's classic whitewater runs. With its steep canyons and deep class V rapids, it challenges even the best. Tours can be taken from Concepción. Trancura River, located near Pucón, is a good place for both beginners and experts. With class III and IV rapids, the river produces great waves and is set amid beautiful scenery.

Northern Patagonia

In Northern Patagonia, Río Futaleufú is an internationally renowned site. Winding between landscapes that are dominated by snow-dusted volcanoes and dense rainforest, it boasts one class IV-V rapid after the other. Tours can be taken from the nearby town of Chaitén. Espolon River precedes the Futaleufú. Its warm turquoise water and numerous class II-III rapids make it an ideal kayak school and teaching river.

Southern Patagonia

Serrano River is located in the remote and beautiful Torres del Paine National Park. The swift but calm rapids only reach a class I, perfect both for the beginner and sightseer to take in the awesome scenery. Updated: May 19, 2009.

CLIMBING

Chile's diverse climate and geology mean a variety of year-round rock, alpine and ice climbing opportunities in various conditions, from tough high-altitude rock climbs in the northern altiplano, year-round glacier ascents in the Central Valley, and moderate ascents on volcanoes in the Lake District and Patagonia. If you plan to climb border peaks, Torres del Paine and Volcán Osorno, you must receive permission from Dirección de Fronteras y Limites (www.difrol.cl). Contact them well in advance by submitting a climbing resumé with emergency contacts. Also, register with rescue service Cuerpo de Socorro Andino (www.socorroandino.cl) before embarking on your own climb. Let them know your destination and when you plan to begin and end your ascent. Give yourself an adequate amount of time to acclimatize before attempting the higher altitude climbs. Federación de Andinismo (www.feach.cl) is a great climbing resource, they offer information, advice, as well as guided expeditions, and training courses in Santiago.

Norte

Northern Chile is primarily a rock climbing destination. You can find well-known routes at Toconoa, Socaire Creek and La Pampilla. Cerro Guane Guane has tricky mixed climbing. Popular border climbs include Volcán Licancábur, Payachatas and Cerro Ojos del Salado—just shy of being South America's highest peak. Thunderstorms are common during the summer months. Many climbing companies have policies whereby you'll be refunded a portion of your climbing fees if your hike is canceled due to poor weather conditions.

Central Valley

Chile's best ice climbing routes are found in the Central Valley. The capital is an excellent city for climbers, as it has a number of indoor walls and there are countless places to climb nearby, including Yerba Loca, which has been known to have upwards of 50 waterfalls, and which can be climbed from June to September. Other ice climbing close to Santiago happens on the waterfalls of Loma Larga and Cerro Plomo. Around 30 kilometers (18.6 mi) from Santiago, Cajon del Maipo and has a wealth of rock climbing destinations, including Piedra Rommel, whose routes are ideal for training and can be tested year-round, and Hitchcock, a newer location with stark sandstone walls. In the vicinity, El Morado's mixed terrain attracts advanced climbers—Colgante del Morado, a hanging glacier, can be climbed any month of the year. Cerro Aparejo, with it's near-perfect triangular peak and treacherous rock is another popular alpine climbing spot. Build up experience at Las Palestras, and Las Chilcas—just a short drive from the capital—has lengthy, obstacle-laden routes.

Lake District and Patagonia

Río Petrohué, in the Lake District, is a popular canyoning location. Volcanes Osorno and Villaricca in Patagonia have the region's best developed infrastructure, as they are the biggest focus of guided climbs. Conical Osorno has ice caves and technical climbing. Reaching Villarrica's lava-spitting crater requires a strenuous day-long climb. Termas de Chillan is suitable for climbers of varied skill levels. The famous Torres del Paine is a challenge, and the colossal cliffs on Lago Todos Los Santos have attractive climbing routes. Updated: Jul 01, 2009.

MOUNTAIN BIKING AND CYCLING

Chile is a bonanza for cyclists and mountain bikers. You can pedal lakeside loops and through backcountry villages, or rattle your frame rocketing down volcanic slopes. Cycling congested city streets will test your tolerance for stress and air pollution, but in rural Chile, beyond the reach of public transportation, biking is an unhurried way to take in the country's extremes of climate and geography. Single tracks criss-cross mountains and valleys, and a number of inviting long-distance routes stretch latitudinally, including the Pan-American highway, Carretera Austral and Sendero de Chile. Biking the entire length of Chile is becoming the trek to boast about, and, if you have the means, the Pacific Islands' steep, meandering trails make for challenging, secluded riding. Biking in Chile is best done October to March (spring-summer), though in some parts you can cruise year-round.

If you're flying to Chile, break your bike down and bring it as checked luggage. In-country you can put it on buses without being charged, but, you'll pay a fee when traveling by ferry. If you're planning a long-distance biking trip, gear up before arriving, as items such as racks and touring panniers are costly in Chile. Those seeking vertical descents will need a solid front suspension to withstand the rugged, bone-rattling backroads. Chile has no shortage of repair shops, but you should still carry your own kit for emergencies. When renting, check the bike thoroughly before setting out.

Norte

You can bike both easy and expert trails in the windy altiplano all year, but beware of heavy rain and even hail in December and January. The sun is scorching, water is scarce and towns are an anomaly in the Atacama desert, so bring as much water as you can when riding. Bring a filter or water treatment tablets if you're planning to stay in small villages, where bottled water isn't always available. In addition to battling the elements, you'll be faced with the challenge of high altitude. Be sure to acclimatize before hitting the road. Popular trips in the north include the Quebrada del Diablo (Devil's Gorge) near San Pedro de Atacama—a scribble of looping single tracks, and the vast, flat Atacama desert. A unique option is to bike a path that follows an old railroad line from La Ligua to Ovalle, on which you pass through five tunnels.

Central Valley

Winter and spring are the best seasons to bike here, where riding is less rigorous than in the north. During the summer, ride early or late to beat the heat, or head up into the Andes. Well over half of Chile's population lives in the central valley (70 percent), so it's harder to get away from the masses. However, there are day rides aplenty, many within striking distance of Santiago, and even within the city. Cerro San Cristóbal, the hot springs at El Plomo and Valle Nevado, which has a mountain biking lift during the summer months, are popular destinations. Less taxing day rides can be made around coastal resorts.

Lake District and Patagonia

In the Lake District, biking is a more relaxed affair. You'll have the lakes and volcanoes nearly all to yourself. The weather is generally mild in the Lake district. Near Pucón, on Lake Villarrica, you can ride through villages to the waterfalls of Los Ojos del Caburga. There's more vivid scenery at the Cuevas Volcánicas and on Volcán Casablanca. The extremely popular Carretera Austral begins in Puerto Montt and unfolds over 1000 km (621 mi) of mostly gravel—and some paved—road down to Villa O'Higgins in northern Patagonia. The weather is full of surprises in Patagonia. Hop ferries between the islands on the Carretera, and cycle around lakes like Llanquihae, or grind it out up Volcán Osorno, before zooming down its side. Updated: Jun 19, 2009.

HORSEBACK RIDING

Chile provides a range of excellent riding opportunities. Experience beautiful terrains on horseback, from the arid and dusty Atacama Desert to the wild Andean central valleys to the dramatic landscape of Patagonia. The incredible Andean scenery will lure you with its colorful canyons, not to mention the chance to see condors. Many tour companies offer treks with local cattle herders and guides. This is a great way to learn more about the lifestyle of people living in remote areas. A number of stables in Chile rent horses. The perfect horse for a long trek however, is the sturdy Chilean Criollo that adapts well to different weather conditions.

Rules of Riding

Stable standards, ethics and horse-care policies vary tremendously in Chile. Horse owners and trainers change regularly, which means that training and care also changes. When considering a horse for hire, follow these basic rules:

If a horse appears ill, lame or abused, RE-FUSE to ride it. Change horses or leave.

If you cannot control the horse or do not feel safe, it's best to change horses or to not ride.

If you are on a trail when a problem arises, do not hesitate to dismount.

If the tack (saddle and bridle) looks ill-fitted, old, cracked or damaged, ask to have it changed, or a fall could ruin your entire trip. Check the tack adjustments before getting on the horse. Is the girth band tight? Are the reins and stirrup leathers in good condition?

Most importantly, take the time to set your stirrups for the right length. Stirrups that are too short will hurt your knees and can be dangerous, the same with stirrups that are too long. Western saddles are recommended as they are safer going up and down steep terrain and are generally more comfortable for long rides.

Where to Ride

Among the many places to ride in Chile, the Atacama Desert is a rustic place to begin. With a little imagination you could easily feel like you were on the set of a western movie. Tours in the Atacama region offer expeditions to volcanoes, stark lava fields and huge rolling dunes. The Lake District has stunning scenery and some tours combine horse riding here with other activities such as rafting or kayaking. Torres del Paine National Park is hard to beat in terms of beauty and interest. The park has many attractions perfect to explore on horseback, such as the Towers Rock Formation and the emerald colored Lake Nordenskjold.

When to Ride

The geography of Chile offers a variety of climates, meaning that you can ride year round. The Atacama Desert is known to be hot and dry, where as rain is common in the Lake District. It's best to check weather conditions with your chosen trek group before you start your expedition. Updated: May 11, 2009.

BIRDWATCHING

Chile, with its wide variety of ecological zones and climates, is a birdwatching hotspot. And how could it not be? On one side, you've got the mighty Pacific Ocean, rich feeding ground for sea birds of all sorts. On the other side, you have the majestic Andes Mountains, home to the condor as well as hundreds of other bird species. In between, you've got rivers, valleys, rainforests and even a desert. Most birders with limited travel time head down to Patagonia, Chile's frigid deep south. Patagonia is home to many fascinating bird species, most notably the Ñandu, a large, flightless ostrich-like bird that roams the Patagonian plains. On the coast, there are Magellanic Penguins and many sea birds including gulls, albatrosses, herons, egrets, petrels and shearwaters. The Patagonian mountains are home to condors, eagles, falcons and more.

Central Chile has mountains, valleys and long stretches of virgin coast, all of which are fantastic for birding. Along the coast there are numerous species, including: plovers, oystercatchers, snipes, ducks, swans, grebes, tyrants, and rails. Some of the rarer birds sometimes spotted include the endemic Seaside Cinclodes or the Warbling Doradito. A litte further inland is La Campana National Park, only about two hours from Santiago and home to six endemic species including the Moustached Turca, White-throated and Dusky Tapaculos, Dusky-tailed Canastero, Chilean Mockingbird and Chilean Tinamou. Other species include the Striped Woodpecker, Giant Hummingbird and Chilean Pigeon. The nutrient-rich Humboldt current passes by Valparaiso, feeding millions of sea birds: many birders take coastal boat rides to see them.

The lake district is well known for birding. The coveted birds to glimpse include the Magellanic Woodpecker and the Andean Condor, but there are dozens more: the Austral Pygmy Owl, White-browed Ground Tyrant and the Black-chested Buzzard Eagle. The Rio Cruces Nature Reserve is home to many terns, gulls, herons and tyrants, where Puyehue National Park has many species, such as the Magellanic Woodpecker.

Dry and cool, northern Chile is home to a large percentage of the nation's endemic birds. Look for the Chilean Woodstar, White-throated Earth-creeper, Slender-billed Finch and Tamarugo Conebill. There are also seabirds, owls, tyrants, plovers, finches, woodpeckers and the famous Diademed Sandpiper-Plover. Birders will want to pack carefully; a true birding tour will go from the sea to the heights of the Andes. In Chile you can go from a sunny, humid coastal forest to a snowy mountain pass in a couple of hours, so dress accordingly.

There are many reputable tour agencies that specialize in birdwatching, so look around to find a tour that can provide an experienced guide. Updated: May 20, 2009.

SKIING AND SNOWBOARDING

Chile's resorts are regarded as the best in South America and offer every type of skiing, from classic Alpine skiing and snowboarding to cross-country and backcountry skiing. Ski centers dot the mountains from just outside of Santiago to the remote Punta Arenas area. The majority of resorts are equipped with modern chairlifts, rental shops, lodges, and are staffed by international ski instructors and ski patrollers. A few hills also have snow-making equipment. It's possible to both dine and spend the night on some slopes or in close proximity to the base. The bigger central resorts are pricier, and lift tickets are usually cheapest mid-week. If you're in Chile exclusively to ski or ride it's best to bring your own gear. However, it's also easy to rent or buy equipment when you arrive.

Where to Ski

Resorts in central Chile are characterized by their high elevations, and are composed of craggy, expansive, treeless trails, reminiscent of the Alps. Southern resorts are often perched on the slopes of volcanoes, with attractive ridges and half pipes formed by lava flows. In general, to access truly challenging slopes, you have to hike up or traverse. The season usually runs from mid-May into October, though in central Chile the season often begins late and ends early. At those resorts, snow is dry and light, with some runs machine groomed. To the south, the snow is wetter and heavier, the weather more erratic, and trails less maintained. There you can also hit the slopes earlier, and lifts have been known to operate until late October.

Safety

Be aware that avalanches are common in the central Andes. The snow pack in the south is more stable but the weather is worse. If skiing or snowboarding in the backcountry, contact mountain rescue services to leave details of where you're going and when you're coming back. Altitude sickness is a factor in the higher elevation resorts, so acclimatize first and take it easy. Check individual ski resort websites and andesweb.cl for snow conditions, number of lifts operating, and weather reports.

Central Valley

A short drive from the capital brings you to five major resorts: Farellones, El Colorado, La Parva, Valle Nevado. Farellones, Chile's first ski resort, is highly popular among Santiaguinos. There are numerous intermediate runs at El Colorado, some bona fide black diamonds, and plenty of areas for bump skiing. La Parva has a luxurious chalet village and vibrant nightlife. It's more suitable for intermediate and advanced skiers and snowboarders. Valle Nevado, site of the 1993 Pan-American winter games, has a self-contained village on its slopes and ultra-modern infrastructure—including 41 lifts and a snowboard park and half-pipe. It, along with La Parva and Valle Nevado are accessible by a multiple-resort ticket.

Chile's premier resort, Portillo, is northeast of the capital, near the Argentine border and Mendoza. It is so highly regarded for its powder and steep slopes, where downhill speed records have been set, that Olympic ski teams from the U.S. and Germany now train there. Chapa Verde, near Rancagua, is a less frequented and cheaper alternative to the bigger hills. There's a variety of terrain and some of the best out of bounds skiing in Chile. Lagunillas, in Cajón del Maipo, is a small not-for-profit ski center, with modest infrastructure, average snow pack and fantastic views.

The Lake District
Some resorts in the south are close to hot springs, which makes for great après-ski relaxation. Termas de Chillán is the largest and arguably the best resort in the south. It has trails for all skill levels, a snowboard park and half-pipe, and allows for heli opportunities. Trails in Parque Nacional Villarrica are set on the lower slopes of an active volcano. Many runs remain closed throughout the year, but it's a good spot for novices, and there's something to be said for ripping down a smoking volcano. Antillanca, east of Osorno on Volcán Casablanca, and Las Araucarias on Volcán Llaima have captivating vistas and a few un-challenging trails, with a couple of slow lifts and limited services.

Patagonia
Patagonia is home to out-of-the-way hills like Cerro El Fraile, Corralco, the Los Arenales Ski Center, and Cerro Mirador in the Reserva Nacional Magallanes. These inexpensive resorts offer prime views, and are perfect for those starting out on four or two edges. Updated: Jul 01, 2009.

SURFING AND KITE SURFING IN CHILE
With its consistently powerful surf, world-class swells and minimal chances of shark attacks, Chile is a great destination to ride the waves. There are ideal spots in the northern and central regions. It is possible to surf practically all year round, but April to October is generally thought to be the best period. During this season, the waves are at their most reliable, the water is as warm as it will get all year and the weather is still good. June to August can be a more difficult time since north winds whip up huge swells.

Wetsuits
Because of the cold current coming down from the north, the temperature of the water is very cold, fluctuating from 10 to 20 °C. As a rule of thumb, the further south you go in Chile, the colder the water gets. A 3 to 4 mm wet suit is therefore a definite must to help maintain the body's temperature and increase buoyancy. Booties, hoods and gloves are also highly recommended. All can be easily picked up from surf shops, either to rent or buy.

Northern Chile
Arica, in Northern Chile, is considered to have some of the most consistent surfing in the world. For world-class surfers like Shane Dorian, Arica is the place to go. Two rounds of the world surfing and bodyboard circuit and one round of the big wave surfing circuit are held in this area. It's ideal for all levels of

Photo by Kyle Adams

surfing, featuring great beginner waves all year round. Iquique is also well worth a visit; Playa Cavancha is its most popular beach, with some useful surf breaks along its rocky northern parts. Las Machas in the Atacama region is an exposed beach perfect for kite surfers. As a broad, unshaded beach, the swell can be very strong, reaching five or six feet.

Central Region

The Central Region offers quite a variety of surfing destinations that are close to Santiago. However, you may find the water in this region more polluted than other areas in Chile, because of the popularity of beaches like Valparaíso and Viña del Mar. Pichilemu is undoubtedly the Chilean capital of surf and the main destination for surfers looking for quality waves. Beaches La Puntilla, El Infiernillo and Punta Lobos have the best waves. The region has also produced a couple of Chile's most talented surfers, Ramon Navarro and Diego Medina, who won the Billabong XXL Paddle Award. Thanks to its long waves and beautiful setting, Pichilemu is a must on any surfer's map. Lessons and boards are readily available along the beach, and accommodation is easily found. It's a good idea to avoid Pichilemu in February when the town gets overridden by Chileans taking their summer beach break here. Reñaca is also a popular beach in this region. Home to many surf championships over the years, Reñaca has a chilled vibe and some wonderful waves. It is easily accessible from Valparaíso, Viña del Mar or Santiago.

Southern Region

In the south, Boca-Lebu, two kilometers (1.2 mi) from the city of Lebu, is a good place to practice surfing and body boarding. Updated: Jul 01, 2009.

Studying Spanish in Chile

Chile is a popular place to study Spanish. Its diverse landscape allows students to actively travel during their studies, and Chileans' friendly attitude toward foreigners makes it a great place to not only learn but also practice the language. Chilean Spanish is known for its speed and slang, infused with idioms that even South Americans struggle to understand. For practical reasons, many travelers end up studying at a language school in order to better communicate during their stay. There are lots of options out there to suit travelers' time schedules, interests and levels of proficiency. Santiago undoubtedly has the most options in terms of schools. The modern city gives

students loads of opportunities to practice their Spanish without having to sacrifice basic comforts from home, and its central location makes it easy to plan side trips to the north or south. Amerispan (www.amerispan.com) has one-on-one and group courses in Santiago, including customized courses for business executives. Spanish Abroad (www.spanishabroad.com) offers individual, group, or combined courses, and can tailor courses for medical and business professionals. Active students can sign up for the Spanish and Ski Program, offered from June to September. This program combines language study with twice-weekly outings to the Andes (transportation included). Escuela Bellavista (www.escuelabellavista.com) hosts a variety of combined culture-and-language programs, including Spanish and Wine, Spanish and Ski, and weekend hiking and biking excursions. Other Santiago-based schools include BridgeChile (www.bridgechile.com) and TANDEM International (www.tandem-schools.com).

If you prefer to study outside of Santiago, check out Contact Chile (www.contactchile.cl), which offers a variety of courses in schools scattered throughout the country, including Valparaíso, Iquique, Puerto Varas, Talca and Puerto Montt. Languages in Action (www.languagesinaction.com) offers courses in Pucon and Viña del Mar, and Escuela Bellavista (listed above) offers combined studies in Santiago and Viña del Mar. Updated: Mar 12, 2009.

CHILE SPANISH SCHOOLS

Be aware when thinking about studying Spanish in Chile that what's known as Castellano chileno is not what you may have learned in high school. Spanish in Chile has been influenced by many Mapudungun and Quechua words (like gua-gua for baby instead of bebe). Also, Chilenos tend to use a lot of slang (poto for buttocks) and eat the s on the end of words, so there may be a lot of "otra vez, por favor?" ("One more time, please?") when speaking with the fast-talking natives. You might want to check out a guide for slang first (joeskitchen.com/chile/culture/slang.htm). Test your Spanish level at ABC Spanish School's website (spanish-schools.com.ar) to see what level you would place in their Santiago school.

If you don't have a lot of time to devote to school, invest $260, take the Crash Course —six classes a day for five days—and don't miss out on the school activities, like visiting Pablo Neruda's houses. Smack in the middle of Chile's Lake District, the Pucón Center of Languages and Culture (www.languagepucon.com) really emphasizes learning Spanish through immersing yourself in the culture, i.e. getting out there and conversing with people, like the woman selling homegrown vegetables. A prime example is one of the mixed learning programs the Pucón Center offers; the 10-week Spanish and work program has you spending two weeks in Spanish classes and two months working on a horse farm ($1,052 with meals and housing included). Updated: Apr 24, 2008.

Volunteering in Chile

Chile provides a great base for volunteers to explore and contribute to the land and its people, from the country's arid Atacama to the Andes to the sunny Pacific to the southern tip's sprawling, glaciated Patagonia. Volunteer opportunities in Chile are as varied as the landscape itself.

Volunteer teaching positions are popular and plentiful, especially in rural communities where educational funding and resources are limited. As a volunteer teacher, you can help children participate and succeed in the global economy. While Chile boasts a superior economy to some of its Latin American neighbors, there's still a large gap between the rich and poor. There are a host of community-based projects, including mentoring street children, building and restoring houses for rural families, and promoting self-sufficiency sustainability to indigenous groups like the Mapuche in Patagonia.

Chile has a variety of animal and nature conservation projects, particularly in Tierra del Fuego. Volunteers can build and restore hiking trails at Torres del Paine National Park or help protect endangered Patagonian species such as the Humboldt penguin. There are tons of non-profits and volunteer programs to suit just about any interest or passion. While some organizations provide a small stipend for volunteer workers, others charge a fee that goes to housing, meals and the organization itself. Some projects require a certain level of education or an intermediate level of Spanish. However, many simply ask for an open mind and energetic spirit.

While there are literally hundreds of options out there, below is a starting list of projects based in Chile. Additionally, international programs such as United Planet (www.

unitedplanet.org), Bridge Volunteers (www.bridgevolunteers.org) and Projects Abroad (www.projects-abroad.org) offer a variety of volunteer projects throughout Chile.

VEGlobal (Voluntarios de la Esperanza) (http://voluntariosesperanza.org). This non-profit is dedicated to ending the cycles of poverty and abuse that still dominate much of Santiago. There are a variety of opportunities in assisting with education, literacy, art and athletics.

English Opens Doors (EOD)(www.centrodevoluntarios.cl). Developed by the Chilean Ministry of Education, EOD allows volunteers to teach English part or full-time. The program also encourages volunteers to initiate self-directed activities such as art classes, creative writing courses or recreational sports promoting physical health and positive teamwork. The program offers online Spanish courses to its volunteers.

Patagonia Volunteer (www.patagoniavolunteer.org). Developed by the MAPU Association to help improve the social and environmental struggles in Patagonia, Patagonia Volunteer hosts a variety of conservation and community-based projects, including educating the community on ways to protect its land, as well as promoting human rights for Patagonian natives, whose lives and work have been exploited by large corporations. Updated: Mar 03, 2009.

Working in Chile

While on a tourist visa, foreigners are not allowed to accept paid work in Chile, however, there have been circumstance (usually in the case of an international artist) when a temporary work permit has been issued. The easiest way to find paid work in Chile is by teaching English, especially in the bigger cities like Santiago or the Valparaiso-Viña del Mar area. A TEFL or CELTA certificate is desired, but for many of these jobs it is not a requirement. As a private English tutor, it's acceptable to charge anywhere from $10 to $20 an hour. Speaking Spanish opens up many job opportunities in Chile, but remember that the Chilean Ministry of Foreign Affairs requires at least 85 percent of each company (with over twenty-five people) to be Chilean nationals.

Chile also offers a "retirement and periodic income visa" which allows expats to work, retire, invest or start a business within the country. This is one of the easiest visas for expats to obtain and is preferable to a work visa because your immigration status will not change even if your occupation status does.

Nationals of Australia, New Zealand, Canada, United States and the United Kingdom can stay in Chile for up to three months without a visa. In order to work in Chile a work permit or visa is necessary, but is easy to obtain while in the country. Australia and New Zealand have a working holiday agreement with Chile where citizens can apply to work temporarily, part-time or full-time in Chile. A politically stable country with one of the strongest economies in Latin America makes Chile a good place to find work abroad. Updated: Mar 24, 2009.

Living in Chile

If you decide to move to Chile, you will not be alone in the expatriate sphere. Chile is a popular choice for many reasons: political and economic stability, quality of living, varied and beautiful landscapes, not to mention great wine and cuisine. For these reasons, the country is not cheap compared to the rest of South America. That said, health care, public transport, restaurants and most of the main grocery shops are reasonably priced and cheaper than many Western countries.

LIVING EXPENSES

For a one-bedroom apartment in Santiago, expect to pay between $260 and $420/month, and for a two-bedroom apartment, $390 to $670/month. Homestays are cheaper, ranging from $200 to $325/ month, and often include meals. For apartment listings, check out the local newspapers, such as The Santiago Times or El Mercurio.

VISAS

If you are planning on staying in Chile for longer than 90 days, you must secure a one-year renewable work or temporary resident visa within 30 days of arrival. See our visa section (p.36) for more information. Each person living in Chile is also required to carry an identity card. You can obtain one from the Chilean Passport Bureau for a small fee, and you must carry it with you at all times. Updated: May 11, 2009.

Chile Lodging

There is wide range of accommodation options across Chile, catering to travelers on a tight budget as well as for those with more cash. There are plenty of camping facilities as well as youth hostels and a growing network of backpackers' hostels. Rooms costs more in Santiago than elsewhere in the country. In more out of the way places you can take advantage of hospedajes (a room in a local's house) as well as refugios (rustic shelters) in national parks.

Cabañas, chalet-style cabins, also exist in resort areas, again covering the full range from self-catering or full board deluxe. It is important to account for the peak holiday season in Chile, roughly December through February and Easter, when accommodation prices can rocket and rooms may be hard to come by without a prior reservation. During the low season you can always try to negotiate a discount on the advertised rate.

HOSTELS

There are heaps of hostels in the capital, and no shortage of options in resort towns like Viña del Mar. The farther south you go, toward remote areas of Patagonia, the less choice you will find, but budget accommodation is nonetheless available. In general, you can score a dorm bed in Chile for about $10. Springing for your own quarters will set you back about $20, on the low end. Hostels are typically well situated, with day and nighttime attractions, transit, and amenities within walking distance. While many hostels offer the expected facilities (breakfast, laundry, Internet), some even deliver WiFi, tours, and BBQ. Occasionally you'll encounter added frills like pinball machines and foosball tables. Although quality has improved, dingy digs and erratic shower temperatures still exist. Don't be too quick to judge a hostel by its weathered exterior. Some of the best places to stay happen to be in historical buildings.

HOTELS

If you can, it's always best to take a look before committing yourself to a hotel room in Chile as the one-to-five-star rating is more a measure of amenities than décor and up-keep. In high season digs can be in short supply, so pre-booking and risking a not-so-great room may be preferable to no room at all. Rooms are usually en-suite with a shower and hot water, but standards vary. Expect to pay about $40 for mid-range and $70 or upwards for high-end hotels. In Santiago there are various large chain hotels as well as luxury boutique hotels. Away from the city there are some fantastic hacienda lodgings and lake resorts which also organize horseback riding, rafting, fishing and hiking excursions. Check the Chilean National Hotel Association for more info (www.hotelga.cl).

Culinary Vocabulary

DRINKS
Agua : water
Agua de hierba / infusión de hierba /
té de hierba: herb tea
Batido: milkshake
Bebida: drink
Cedrón: lemon verbena
Cerveza: beer
Chopp: beer on tap
Gaseosas: carbonated soft drinks
Hielo: ice
Jugo natural: freshly squeezed juice
Leche: milk
Licuado: drink made from fruit blended
with water
Manzanilla: chamomile
Té negro: black tea
Vino tinto / blanco : red / white wine

FRUIT AND VEGGIES
Aceitunas: olives
Ají: hot pepper
Berenjena: eggplant
Ciruela: plum
Durazno: peach
Ensalada: salad
Fruta: fruit
Frutilla: strawberry
Lechuga: lettuce
Legumbres or verduras: vegetables
Lentejas: lentils
Maíz: corn
Manzana: apple
Naranja: orange
Palta: avocado
Pera: pear
Piña: pineapple
Sandía: watermelon
Zanahoria: carrot
Zapallo: squash

MEAT, FISH AND EGGS
Almejas, machas: clams
Atún: tuna
Bife: steak
Calamares: squid
Camarones: shrimps
Cangrejo: crab
Carne: meat

Cerdo: pork
Ceviche: cold seafood marinated
in lemon juice
Chicharrones: (usually pork) rinds
Cholgas, choritos: mussels
Chuleta: chops
Churrasco: barbecued meat
Cordero: lamb
Corvina: sea bass
Huevos: eggs
Huevos revueltos: scrambled eggs
Jamón: ham
Mariscos: shellfish
Ostiones: scallops
Ostras: oysters
Pavo: turkey
Pescado: fish
Pulpo: octopus
Tocino: bacon

ON THE SIDE
Arroz: rice
Avena: oats or oatmeal
Azúcar: sugar
Helado: ice cream
Mantequilla: butter
Mermelada: jam
Pan: bread
Pan tostado: toast
Papas: potatoes
Papas fritas: French fries
Pastel: cake
Pimienta: pepper
Pollo (or ave): chicken
Queso: cheese
Sal: salt
Sopa: soup

ORDERING
A la plancha: grilled with a bit of butter
Al vapor: steamed
Chifa: Chinese food
Comedor: cheap eatery
(la) cuenta: the bill
Fuente de soda: eatery without
an alcohol license
Plato fuerte: main course
Postre: dessert
Updated: Mar 02, 2009.

CAMPING
Official campsites can be expensive in Chile, whether they are of modest facilities or part of fancy holiday resorts, but all are usually well kept. Campsites in the national parks can be pretty basic and tend to be more expensive in the south than in the north of the country. In some parks wild camping is possible, although it is wise to seek permission from any landowner first. Refugios, basic stone huts with bed space and gas stoves, are found in more remote locations, but you should contact the

The Pisco Controversy

A veritable war is now being fought between Peru and Chile over the rights to claim Pisco as their respective national drink. While Peru claims its historic origin, Chile was the first to expand its production and create a massive export market. Chileans argue that foreign taste buds recognize their product as the authentic version. Peruvians counter that the Chilean version, which allows additives and is yellow in color as opposed to clear, is not authentic because it deviates from the traditional method of production. The Pisco battle is not likely to be settled anytime soon. In the meantime perhaps each side could try to kick back, and have a strong Pisco Sour—made with Pisco from their origin of choice.

Ingredients: 2 oz. Pisco; ¾ oz. lime juice; ½ oz. simple syrup (granulated sugar melted in water); 1 egg white; 3 oz. ice or enough to fill a cocktail shaker; a few dashes of Angostura bitters.

First make the simple syrup, then blend together Pisco, lime juice, simple syrup, and egg white with ice. Take an old-fashioned or highball glass, dip the rim in egg white and then sugar. Strain the drink into the glass and sprinkle with a few drops of Angostura bitters. *Salud!* Updated: Jun 29, 2009.

park ranger stations before relying on this option. You may also be able to camp on some beaches; check with the local police first. Turistel publishes a camping guide listing sites, facilities, opening times. URL: www.turistel.cl.

HOSPEDAJES, RESIDENCIALES AND CASAS DE FAMILIA

The distinction between these three types is not always obvious, and doesn't necessarily matter as long as keeping to your budget is your priority. Hospedajes are usually cheaper versions of residenciales and both provide simple rooms either as part of the main house of a private home or in an extension at the back.

Some of the more expensive residenciales are in impressive well-maintained houses while others can be dark and dank. It can be hit or miss with the quality so ask to see the room first. Casas de familia (or casas familiares) as the name suggests, offer rooms in a family's home and are pretty much along the same lines as the others. Family members may tout their open rooms in bus stations, and you can save money by catching a ride with them Updated: Jun 05, 2009.

Food and Drink

Thanks to the country's 4,000-kilometer- (2,485-mi) long shoreline and fertile farmland, Chilean cuisine boasts an extraordinarily wide selection of seafood and fresh produce. The blend of native staples like corn, potatoes and beans with European influences, notably Spanish and German cuisine, has produced a very varied gastronomy. While it may not be particularly spicy or refined, it will keep budget and mid-range travelers alike satisfied, especially those with a sweet tooth.

MEALS

Breakfast (*desayuno*) is usually a simple affair, with coffee or tea accompanying bread rolls or toast with jam, cheese or avocado. Lunch (*almuerzo*), eaten around 1 or 2 p.m., is the heartiest meal of the day and can be had for cheap in a comedor offering a set meal (*menú del día*).

Such meals usually consist of a *cazuela*, a thickish broth made from meat, usually chicken or beef, cooked with vegetables (often potato or pumpkin), then a main a dish of meat with veggies, followed by dessert. A snack similar to English tea and deceptively called *once* (eleven) is sometimes served in the late afternoon. Dinner (*cena*) is a family occasion, pretty similar to lunch in terms of dishes, and eaten around 9 p.m.

SEAFOOD

Abalones, razor clams, mussels, spider crabs, oysters, octopus, conger eels, salmon, corbinas and sole are among the wealth of marisco to be found up and down Chile. Fish is fried or cooked in a thick chowder (caldillo). Shellfish are often prepared raw in a delicious cold marinade of lemon juice, spiced with cilantro, and known as ceviche. You can also try curanto, the typical dish of island of Chiloé, also available throughout most of the southern coast and on Easter Island. It is a kind of stew with shellfish, pork, potatoes, potato bread and other vegetables all cooked together, traditionally in a hole in the ground, now more commonly in a pressure cooker. If you are lucky enough to visit Easter Island, you can sample lobster (langosta) among other seafood dishes.

MEAT
Vegetarians will have a hard time finding satisfying meals, although some restaurants in Santiago or touristy areas may serve meat-free dishes like omelets or pizzas. It is best to always ask about any form of animal protein in the dish before ordering, because the word *carne* usually means beef and will not be understood as including pork or chicken.

SNACKS
The most popular snack in Chile is the empanada, a fried or baked turnover filled with pino, a mixture of meat, onions, raisins, olives, hard-boiled eggs and shortening, or cheese. Sweet empanadas, filled with apples, can also be had just about everywhere. Other ubiquitous snacks are *humitas* (similar to Mexican tamales), a Native American cornmeal dish cooked in corn husks, which can be sweet or savory, and *sopaipilla*, a flour and pumpkin fried tortilla. Various sorts of breads, like sliced loaves or marraqueta buns, are sold in the many bakeries (*panaderías*). In restaurants, a basket of bread will sometimes be accompanied by *pebre*, a spicy sauce made with tomato, hot pepper, onion and cilantro.

VEGETABLES AND FRUIT
Staple veggies include tomatoes (the main ingredient of the basic *ensalada chilena*), beans (*porotos*), squash, lentils, eggplant, lettuce and lots of potatoes. Travelers will also be familiar with most of the fruits grown in the temperate climate of Chile: apples, pears, oranges, peaches, plums, watermelon, bananas and the like. These are great eaten as such (and washed carefully of course) but also as freshly squeezed juices (*jugo natural* or *exprimido*). If the juice is being prepared in front of you, you may want to check they are not heavy-handed with sugar, as is often the case.

DESSERTS
Anyone with a sugar craving is sure to be satisfied with Chilean desserts, as cookies (*golosinas*) and cakes (*pasteles*) abound. Alfajores are cookies glazed with sugar or chocolate and sometimes stuffed with manjar, a paste of caramelized condensed milk (also

known as *dulce de leche*)—the overly sweet paste can also be eaten in its pure form.

Another typical dessert worth trying is *mote con huesillos*, a soupy mixture of syrup, dried peaches and cooked wheat. Pumpkin *sopaipillas* can also be eaten as a sweet treat. Finally, if your calorie-meter has not exploded yet, you can indulge in a solid strudel while visiting the German-influenced Lake District.

DRINKS
Water comes sparkling (*con gas*) or still (*sin gas*); you will usually be asked which you prefer. Soft drinks can be found everywhere and you will notice that carbonated drinks like Coca-Cola can be purchased in every conceivable size, from half-liter to gallon. Freshly squeezed and industrial fruit juices, coffee, black tea and herbal infusions (usually chamomile, or *manzanilla*) are largely available, though lovers of real java will be disappointed, since caffeine usually comes in the form of instant Nescafe. Ask for *café negro* (black) or *café cortado* (with milk); you may also be able to get a cappuccino in the touristy areas. Imported yerba mate, the bitter, stimulating Argentine infusion, is easy to find, especially in Patagonia.

In the alcohol department, there are some local beers, the most common being Cristal and Escudo, both lagers, but wine is the star beverage. Once considered cheap, fruity tipples, Chilean wines have greatly improved in quality. There are excellent reds to be sampled, with cabernet sauvignon and merlot dominating among vino tinto, and some whites made from sauvignon blanc also fare pretty well (see below for more information on Chilean wines).

Pisco, a spirit distilled from grapes and similar to brandy, is also a favorite Chilean drink. It is often sipped for *aperitivo* as pisco sour, a cocktail made with lemon or lime juice, egg white, syrup and bitter, but some clubbers knock back piscolas, pisco mixed with Coca-Cola. Another hard liquor you may find is *chicha*, made from fermented *maize* or fruit, usually apples or grapes, and drunk during National Day celebrations. Updated: Feb 20, 2009.

Chilean Wine
Along with its Argentine neighbor, Chile is the leading wine-producing nation of South America. Although its viticulture has a history stretching back 500 years, Chile used to

be mostly known for cheap, fruity reds and only in the past couple of decades has wine quality improved tremendously.

Wine grapes were introduced in the early 1500s by the Catholic missionaries who followed in the steps of the Spanish Conquistadores and needed the drink for sacramental purposes. The País grape took so well to the Chilean climate that vineyards were quickly planted throughout the country, from the Limarí Valley in the north to Bío-Bío Valley in the south, and wine consumption spread well beyond religious celebrations.

Indeed, thanks to its mild climate, Chile is the New World's natural home for wine; long daytime hours of Mediterranean-like sunshine, plus nights cooled by the Andean air help maintain acidity levels in the ripening fruit. Springtime frost is rare, as is rain during the February to May harvest season.
In the mid-19th century, wealthy Chilean landowners introduced noble varieties from France, such as cabernet sauvignon, merlot and malbec. Then the phylloxera pest devastated European vineyards and sent desperate French winemakers to South America in search of better conditions, bringing with them experience and techniques. With such favorable conditions, no wonder that Chile had over 40,000 hectares of vineyards producing some 275 million liters by the beginning of the 20th century.

High taxes, state protectionism and restrictive regulations held back the progress of the wine industry until a new turn in the 1980s. A whole revitalization process saw Chile propel itself into the premium market and to the position of fifth largest wine exporter in the world, its main markets being the U.K. and the U.S.

Again, foreign influence proved decisive, as winemakers such as Miguel Torres of Spain brought in new techniques which boosted quality. Imported oak barrels and stainless steel tanks replaced the traditional rauli beechwood ones that gave the alcohol an unpleasant taste. Joint-ventures between Old World and New World wineries created new brands, like the Almaviva produced by Château Mouton Rothschild and Concha y Toro. Chile's signature grape, Carménère, also appeared at that time. The ancient red Bordeaux grape, thought to be extinct, had in fact arrived in Chile before the phylloxera crisis. It matures into a deep

crimson wine with berries aromas. Good Carménère include Concha y Toro's Terrunyo and De Martino's Single Vineyard.

Yet the most distinctive Chilean wine is the one made from the cabernet sauvignon grape, which is planted in roughly one third of the country's 118,000 hectares of vineyards. It is known for making easy drinking wines with soft tannins and flavors of green bell pepper, mint and eucalyptus. Try Perez Cruz's Reserva, Grande Reserve by Los Vascos or Concha y Toro's Terrunyo. If you want to stray from red, which accounts for the three quarters of Chilean wine production, dip your lips in Casas del Bosque's Sauvignon Blanc or Miguel Torres Santa Digna Reserve Sauvignon Blanc.

Nearly all regions in Chile grow wine, but the most accessible valleys for wine tours are Maipo, the country's oldest wine region, Casablanca, with large plantings of white varieties, Colchagua, where organic viticulture is developing, and Maule, whose geographical diversity makes great wine. Updated: Jul 06, 2009.

Shopping

The shopping selection in Chile is large and varies from local markets filled with Lapis Lazuli jewelry and Alpaca sweaters to sprawling malls and department stores full of imported and expensive international goods. Bargaining for prices at markets and small stores in Chile is rare and more hostile than in other Latin American countries. Many vendors consider bargaining impolite and are insulted by extremely low offers, seeing it as the equivalent of saying their product is defective. While a little bargaining may be appropriate at markets and street stalls, it is inappropriate at malls and department stores. Below is a list of shopping types and locations in Chile.

ARTISAN MARKETS

Traditional Chilean handicrafts made of wood, silver, leather, as well as other local and regional crafts can be found in artisan markets throughout the country. In Santiago, browse the 180 plus artisan stalls at Pueblito Los Dominicos, (open daily, except Monday, 10:30 a.m.-7 p.m.) located at Av. Apoquindo 9085 or the outdoor shopping area at Patio Bellavista (Pio Nono 55, Tel: 56-2-7774582, URL: http://www.patiobellavista.cl). Artesanias de Chile run by the Chilean Crafts Foundation, is a non-profit which is not surprisingly concerned with

Special Artisan Markets

Markets are a great way to get a whiff and taste of Chilean life, and none so much as specialized markets.

Mercado Central is a major draw in Chile's capital city, Santiago. The initial smell is perhaps a little overwhelming, as dozens of stalls of locals selling fish attempt to entice both foreigners and residents alike. Good lunch options can be found at the many restaurants within the market. Open 6 a.m. – 4 p.m. Sunday to Thursday and 6 a.m. – 6 p.m. on Saturday.

Mercado Franklin, the largest flea market in Chile, can be found at and around Bio-Bio Street in Santiago. Specializing in precious antiques, furniture, private copies of music and software, the market is open Saturdays and Sundays, 9 a.m.–mid-afternoon.

Pueblo Los Dominicos is built on the grounds of a Dominican monastery and exhibits the works of over 200 artisans. Ceramics, knitwear and jewellery can all be found here, among other crafts. There are also many café bars in which to spend a few hours. Open daily from 10 a.m. – 7 p.m., Av. Apoquindo 9085, Las Condes, Santiago. Updated: Apr 30, 2009.

preserving traditional crafts of Chile. Open Monday to Saturday from 10 a.m. to 7 p.m. (Av. Bellavista 0357, Tel: 56-2-7779429, URL: http://www.artesaniasdechile.cl).

OTHER MARKETS
Known as ferias, street markets sell anything from fresh produce and fish to clothes, furniture and antiques. The days and times of most ferias vary, but with so many options any day of the week you are guaranteed to find at least one open.

La Vega Central, one of Santiago's oldest and biggest fruit and vegetable markets, is the place to go for the best produce in the city. The market opens daily around dawn and closes in the afternoon between 4 and 6 p.m. From the Cal y Canto subway stop, cross the Mapocho River and walk one block north. Mercado Central is a good stop for fish and seafood, but go early for the freshest catch of the day, as the merchants sell out quickly. Located opposite Parque Venezuela on Av. Ismael Valdes Vergara and Av. 21 de Mayo.

Santiago is home to Bio-Bio, also known as Mercado Franklin, the largest *persa* (flea market) in Chile. Bio-Bio is filled with antiques, furniture, old books and music. Located off the Franklin Metro Station on Bio-Bio, open weekends only.

MALLS
Air conditioned (and heated) malls complete with designer clothing stores, food courts and movie theaters have sprung up in major cities in Chile. Parque Arauco is an American-style mall complete with a park, swimming pool and bowling alley, as well as

hundreds of stores selling everything from local items to imported goods, (open Monday to Saturday from 10 a.m. to 9 p.m and Sunday from 11 a.m. to 9 p.m. Av. Presidente Kennedy 5413, Vitacura, Santiago, Tel: 56-2-2990500, URL:www.parquearauco.cl.)

Alto Las Condes is a more upscale alternative, located on the same street. Las Condes is open daily 10 a.m. – 10 p.m. (Av. Kennedy 9001). Other malls in Santiago include Mall Panorámico (open Monday-Saturday 10 a.m. – 9 p.m. and Sunday 11 a.m. – 9 p.m., Av. 11 de Septiembre 2155) and Mall del Centro (Open daily from 10 a.m. to 9 p.m. located in Rosas on the corner of 21 de Mayo). Updated: Jun 25, 2009.

BARGAINING IN CHILE
While it still exists, bargaining is not nearly as common, or as widely accepted, in Chile as it is in its northern Andean neighbors. Lodging accommodations and organized tours typically have set prices that are rarely open to negotiation, especially during peak seasons. However, it is possible to bargain a bit during the off-season, as many places will ease up in order to secure a sale. Travelers can also try practicing their bargaining skills in smaller villages off the tourist track where eager-to-sell street vendors and shop owners are more open to negotiations.

Maps
There is a large variety of Chilean maps, ranging from area specific, to those that encompass every route through Chile. Bothtypes of maps are readily available and can be purchased

before leaving on your trip at most major book retailers, as well as online stores such as Amazon.com. One you have landed in Chile, the National Tourist Service (SERNATUR) gives out free maps and tourist information. Every region has SERNATUR offices, generally located in the center of the city.

A SERNATUR counter is located in the Arturo Merino Benitez International Airport in Santiago. (Tel: 56-2-6019320, Open Monday to Sunday from 8:15 a.m. to 8 p.m.) Another SERNATUR office in Santiago can be found in the Manuel Montt metro station located on Calle Providencia 1550. (Tel: 56-2-7318336 / 7318337, open Monday to Friday, from 9 a.m. to 6 p.m., and Saturday 9 a.m. to 2 p.m.). Buy specialty maps for hiking and other outdoor activities prior to entering Chile as the maps from SERNATUR are not always comprehensive. Updated: Jun 25, 2009.

Health and Safety

Although most visits to Chile are trouble-free, travelers should still take a few basic precautions. Make sure medications are clearly labeled in their original containers, do not carry syringes or needles (unless you have a doctor's letter stating their medical importance) and make sure to keep proper documentation of any unusual medication. If you wear glasses or contacts, it's a good idea to bring copies of your prescription.

Traveler's health insurance is always recommended, especially if your regular health insurance does not cover medical expenses and emergency evacuation abroad.

For the most part, Chile is free from major diseases that demand a vaccination, as it is part of temperate South America (as opposed to tropical). No vaccinations are required to enter the country. It is strongly recommended, however, that you receive vaccinations for rabies, hepatitis B, and tuberculosis if you are traveling here. It is also recommended that travelers are up to date on their hepatitis A and typhoid boosters.

If you are coming to Chile from a tropical area, there's a chance that you will be asked to present verification that you have been vaccinated for yellow fever, as it is endemic in some areas—something to keep in mind before leaving on an extended or multi-country trip. Additionally, tourists should be aware that in 2007 the World Health Organization verified reports of dengue fever in parts of Chile. Covering up and using insect repellent is always a good idea to minimize exposure.

To remain healthy while in Chile, take common-sense precautions such as washing your hands frequently, washing fresh fruit and vegetables, drinking only bottled water (though Chilean tap water is said to be drinkable in all places other than San Pedro de Atacama), and eating healthy. See below for Minor and Major Health Problems. Updated: Mar 24, 2009.

Minor Health Problems

While Chile is considered a relatively safe and healthy country preparation and prevention are essential. There is always the possibility of developing a minor health problem, especially

Bargaining Basics

When bargaining, it's wise to follow a few basic rules. Typically the vendor will state an initial price. If he or she doesn´t, simply ask by saying "cuanto?" Once an initial price is set, offer half to two-thirds of that amount, then work from there. To ask for the lowest price a vendor will accept, ask "el último?"

Before making a purchase, browse multiple stalls selling similar items to get a feel for the item's relative quality and value. It's easier to gauge a good deal once you have a general idea of what's out there.

Also, it's wise to buy in bulk; many vendors offer special discounts to those purchasing multiple items from them. For better bargains, venture out from tourist-populated centers and corners. Less-visited stalls on the outskirts are often more eager to make a sale.

Finally, don't pass up a coveted item for the sake of a dollar. In Chile, excessive bargaining over small price differences might be seen as rude or disrespectful. That dollar will probably mean a lot more to the stall holder or vendor than to you, and you might later regret turning down a precious item. It's best to think beyond monetary terms and assess the item's personal or emotional value. Updated: Mar 02, 2009.

in rural or remote areas. Below is a list of common illnesses which can be contracted while traveling throughout Chile. Heed your doctor's advice above all and come prepared.

ALTITUDE SICKNESS

Though not as high as neighboring Andean countries, some of Chile's tallest points reach an altitude that may induce sickness among travelers. When visiting these areas, it is important to rest the first few days and drink plenty of bottled water. Avoid alcohol and sleeping pills. Should you feel a severe headache, drowsiness, confusion, dry cough, and/or breathlessness, the first course of action is to hydrate yourself with water and rest as much as possible. If the symptoms continue past five days, you may want to move to a lower altitude.

Anyone planning to hike, ski, or snowboard at high altitudes should acclimatize for a few days before undertaking any physical exertion. Note that altitude sickness, locally called *soroche* or *puna*, can come on suddenly if you experience an abrupt change of altitude.

SUNBURN/HEAT EXHAUSTION

The ozone layer is especially thin at the bottom of the world. This means that even at low altitudes in Chile, sunburns are entirely possible. Travelers should take proper precautions to protect themselves from ultraviolet radiation, and note that they will burn faster here than in Europe or the U.S. From September to November, travelers to Patagonia are to be aware of "red alert" days, when fair-skinned visitors can burn within 10 minutes of sun exposure.

To protect yourself, apply sunscreen with at least an SPF of 30 every few hours you are outside. If you get severe sunburn, treat it with a cream and stay out of the sun for a while. To avoid overheating, wear a hat and sunglasses and drink lots of water. Overweight people are more susceptible to sun stroke. The symptoms of heat exhaustion are profuse sweating, weakness, exhaustion, muscle cramps, rapid pulse and vomiting. If you experience heat stroke, go to a cool, shaded area until your body temperature normalizes and drink lots of water. If the symptoms continue, consult a doctor.

MOTION SICKNESS

Even the hardiest of travelers can be hit by motion sickness on the buses throughout this long and narrow land. Sit near the front of the bus or stay above deck on any boats you may take, and focus on the horizon. If you are prone to motion sickness, eat light, non-greasy food before traveling and avoid drinking too much, particularly alcohol. Over-the-counter medications such as Dramamine can prevent it; in Chile, go to a pharmacy and ask for Mareol, a liquid medicine similar to Dramamine. If you know that you commonly suffer from severe motion sickness, you may want to get a prescription for something stronger for your travels, such as a medicinal patch.

TRAVELER'S DIARRHEA

This is probably the most common disease for travelers. There is no vaccine to protect you from traveler's diarrhea; it is avoided by eating sensibly. Contrary to popular belief, it is usually transmitted by food, not contaminated water. To best prevent traveler's diarrhea, eat only steaming hot foods that have been cooked all the way through in clean establishments. Avoid raw lettuce and fruit that cannot be peeled, like strawberries. Vegetables are usually safer than meat. An inexpensive vegetable wash can be purchased at any supermarket and is a good way to ensure clean fruit and vegetables if you are cooking your own meals.

Make sure any milk you drink has been boiled. Avoid ice cream that could have melted and been refrozen, such as anything for sale in the street. Helado de paila does not contain milk and is safer. If you do get diarrhea, the best way to remedy it is to let it run its course while staying hydrated with clear soups, lemon tea, Gatorade and soda that has gone flat. Bananas are also a good source of potassium and help stop diarrhea. If you need to travel and can't afford to let the illness run its course, any pharmacy will give you something that will make you comfortable enough for a bus trip. If the diarrhea persists for more than five days, see a doctor. Updated: Feb 25, 2009.

Major Health Problems

DENGUE FEVER

As Chile is not a tropical area, there is not much threat for mosquito-carried diseases. In 2007 however, there were reports that a small breakout had occurred on Easter Island. Officials said the disease was contained and would not spread to the mainland but it is still good to be aware of the possibility. To reduce your risk of infection, cover up with clothes and wear the proper insect repellent.

DYSENTERY

This digestive illness is the far more serious version of traveler's diarrhea. It involves mucus and blood in one's feces, and is contracted most

INTRO & INFO

often from drinking, or eating foods washed with untreated and unsanitary water. This water carries micro-organisms, or parasites, which destroy the intestinal lining and cause bacterial infections in the system. Symptoms of dysentery include excessive bowel movements and vomiting. The best way to remedy dysentery is by oral rehydration therapy given in proper medical facilities.

HANTAVIRUS

The Hantavirus is a disease carried and spread by rats and mice; it is passed through their bites, feces, and urine, either via direct contact or air contamination. Since 1993, there have been 188 reported cases of the Hantavirus in Chile, mainly in rural, forested, or poorly ventilated areas. The only times you may potentially be in contact with the virus is if you are camping or for some reason exploring a cellar. Symptoms of the disease include the onset of a flu and fever, as well as muscle and head pain, nausea, vomiting, and serious stomach pain. Symptoms may worsen, causing difficulty breathing and heart and circulation problems. If you show all or some of these symptoms go directly to the nearest clinic or hospital and do not forget to mention that you may have had contact with rats.

HEPATITIS A

Hepatitis A is a severe and infectious disease of the liver, caused by the ingestion of fecal matter, even microscopic amounts. If you are planning to live in Chile for more than six months or work in a hospital, it may a good idea to get a vaccination against hepatitis (a hepatitis vaccination is not considered necessary, though still is recommended, for short-term travelers). The disease usually lasts for a couple of weeks, though it does not lead to chronic infection.

RABIES

There are stray dogs throughout Chile that are usually harmless. However, many home-owners train guard dogs to attack trespassers. On long hikes in rural areas, always carry a walking stick to defend yourself if a dog starts to attack. If you are attacked by a dog and were not vaccinated before your trip, rabies vaccinations are readily available in Santiago and other major cities. Be sure to see a doctor immediately if you believe you were infected.

TYPHOID

From the 1970s to the 1990s, Chile suffered from epidemics of typhoid which spread throughout the land. This disease is caused by ingesting food or water contaminated with feces, and symptoms include dangerously high fever, profuse sweating, and severe, but non-bloody, diarrhea. While cases of typhoid have significantly dropped in Chile in recent years, it is still important to be cautious. Wash your hands as frequently as possible, and try your best to eat food from restaurants with good reputations. Oral or injectable vaccinations are recommended by the World Health Organization, and should be taken before travel if you are planning to be in South America for an extended period of time (six months or more). The injection needs a booster every three years.

YELLOW FEVER

This mosquito-borne disease is endemic to many parts of South America, though not in Chile. Talk to your doctor before taking the vaccine, as it is not recommended for people with certain allergies, pregnant women and other special cases. The vaccine is good for 10 years. If you plan to visit any of the endemic areas (mostly tropical places), before traveling to Chile, you will most likely need to show proof of vaccination at some point. Updated: May 29, 2009.

Safety

Although most visits to this Chile are trouble-free, you should still be aware of potential risks.

EARTHQUAKES

Chile is in one of the most active earthquake regions in the world. While visiting, it is more than likely you will experience at least one small tremor (temblor), or even a minor earthquake (terremotos). Major earthquakes only occur every 10 or 20 years. The smaller scale activity usually causes no damage, and almost all modern buildings in Chile have been built with reinforced steel to meet earthquake-resistance requirements. If you do happen to be in Chile when an earthquake strikes, remain calm and stay indoors. Move to the strongest, most reinforced area of the room, usually a door frame or bathroom, and stay clear from windows and cabinets. Note: Since 2007 there has been recurring seismic activity in Aysén, in the far south of Chile. If you plan to visit this area, keep an eye on the press for government warnings and check the website www.onemi.cl (in Spanish) for more information.

MINEFIELDS

Aside from earthquakes, visitors to Chile ought to be aware of the presence of minefields at the border territories of Tarapacá and

Antofagasta, in the north, near Peru and Bolivia, as well as in Magallanes and the Chilean Antarctic. Remember that border crossing should be made only at authorized locations, and although most minefields are marked, signs may have shifted, become obstructed or been vandalized. These border areas are still considered somewhat dangerous, and check with local authorities before traveling here.

DEMONSTRATIONS

If you intend on being in Chile on March 27th, you should be aware that this is the Day of the Combatant, and is consequently celebrated as such. Most action is seen in urban areas such as Santiago, Conception, Temuco and Antofagasta where in recent years there have been numberous energized demonstrations including reports of violence clashes between police and protesters.

CRIME

When it comes to personal safety, Chile is a relatively good destination. Crime rates are low, although Santiago, Valparaíso, and other major cities can be dangerous at night. Remain particularly alert to crime while in Plaza de Armas, Mercado Central, and areas of Las Condes, Vitacura, Providencia, Suecia, and Bellavista in Santiago, and at the port and adjoining tourist areas in Valaparaiso. Public transport, including, taxis, the Metro, and the bus terminals, are also hotspots for scams and petty theft. When traveling in large cities, take the same precautions as you would take in cities back home. While there have been few violent crimes against foreigners, visitors are far more susceptible to pick-pocketing and personal item theft. Look out especially for cameras, purses and backpacks. As long as you take common sense precautions, keeping track of your belongings, traveling without expensive jewelry or other flashy items, and not drawing lots of attention, you should be free from problems.

If theft does occur, be sure to report it to the local police and your nearest embassy or consulate. Note, that while overseas, ultimate resolution falls under Chilean jurisdiction. You can find out more about the Chilean legal system at www.ministeriopublico.cl. For emergency help in Chile, dial the following:

Ambulance (*samu*) — 131

Fire Department (*bomberos*)—132

Police Department (*carabineros*)—133
Updated: Jul 06, 2009.

Hospitals

Chile has extremely high medical standards at relatively low prices. Clean, well-equipped hospitals and qualified doctors (often bilingual) should not be too hard to find, especially in the capital city, Santiago. Private hospitals (clínicas) receive more funding and therefore tend to offer better services than public hospitals. Additionally, they may be more willing to your work with you concerning payment, which will depend on your medical insurance from home or traveler's insurance abroad. Below are a few hospital suggestions, all based in Santiago. Updated: Mar 24,2009.

Clínica Alemana

Av. Vitacura 5951, Vitacura, Tel: 56-2-2129700 / 2101111, Ambulance Tel: 56-2-2101010

Clínica Universidad Católica

Lira 40, Santiago Centro, Tel: 56-2-6334122, Ambulance Tel: 56-2-6332051, Metro Station: Universidad Católica

Clínica Indisa

Av. Santa Maria 1810, Providencia, Tel: 56-2-3625555, Metro Station: Pedro de Valdivia

Doctors

Finding a doctor in Chile should not be an issue, as there are walk-in clinics and 24-hour services in most major cities. The quality is generally high in urban areas such as Santiago, though this may not be the case in more remote areas. Whether at a small local clinic or a larger office in the city, expect to pay for medical services in cash, regardless of your health or traveler's insurance plan. This may mean you have to keep all the documentation from your visit and dealing with your insurance once you are home. Note that most medicines are available over-the-counter at pharmacies throughout the country. If your ailment isn't severe, it may serve as a speedy solution to consult a pharmacist before heading to the doctor. Below is a list of English-speaking doctors in Santiago.

Dr. Philippa Moore

Apoquindo 3990, Office 605, Las Condes, Tel: 56-2-2070747 / 6866735, Fax: 56-2-2070609, Metro Station Alcantara, E-mail: moore@med.puc.cl

Dr. Eduardo Alñcantara

Clínica Las Condes, Calle el Puente 2082, La Dehesa, Tel: 56-2-2071067

Dr. Gail Grossman
Apoquindo 3990, Office 704 Las Condes, Tel: 56-2-2071067, Metro Station: Alcantara. Updated: Jul 01, 2009.

Pharmacies

Pharmacies in Chile are a great resource for travelers, as most pharmacists are well-informed and many medicines are sold over-the-counter at low cost. While it is inappropriate to abuse this system, it is helpful to know that many drugs which require prescriptions in other countries do not require them in Chile. Pharmaceuticals do not have directions on the box, so be sure to ask the pharmacist for complete and detailed instructions. Most pharmacies in Chile belong to three networks: Cruz Verde, Farmacias Ahumada, and SalcoBrand. The pharmacies listed below are located in Santiago and have English-speaking pharmacists. They are open 24-hours.

Farmacia Ahumada Downtown
Av. Portugal 155, Santiago Centro,
Metro Station: Universidad Católica
Tel: 56-2-2224000,

Farmacia Ahumada
Av. Las Condes 8590, Las Condes,
Tel: 56-2-2224000

Farmacia AhumadaLa Reina
Aguas Claras 1680, La Reina,
Tel: 56-2-222-4000

Farmacia Ahumada Vitacura
Av. Vitacura 6277, Vitacura,
Tel: 56-2-2224000

Farmacias Brand
Santa Blanca and José Alcalde Délano,
Lo Barnechea, Tel: 56-2-2418171,
Updated: Jul 01, 2009.

Communications and Media

Chile has enjoyed freedom of the press since the 2001 Press Freedom Act got rid of the censorship placed on the media during Pinochet's regime. Now the newspapers, radio and TV openly criticize the government and provide fairly balanced news reports of national and international events, and discuss controversial topics as well.

NEWSPAPER

Almost all print media is owned by either the Edwards family media group (the conservative daily El Mercurio) or the Copesa group (the daily national La Tercera). Other national daily newspapers include Las Ultimas Noticias and La Segunda. La Nacion is owned by the government and reflects government policies. A popular tabloid is La Cuarta but it's written in Chilean slang and almost impossible for foreigners to read. El Diario Financiero covers all the business news. La Hora is a free newspaper handed out at metro stations. The Santiago Times reproduces major news stories in English and is available online at www.santiagotimes.cl.

CHIP, (Chile Information Project) is run by local expats, exchange students andwriters for the Santiago Times and the Patagonia Times (http://www.patagoniatimes.cl). It's a Chile English-language network of radio, newspapers, magazines and tour operators and has lots of good info for tourists and expats (http://www.chipsites.com/public).

ONLINE

Chile is well and truly in the age of the world wide web. Many homes and businesses have Internet connection. Communication by e-mail is very common and it's possible to book tours and hostels via the Internet. Most hotels have Internet facilities for guests, but expect to pay for the service in some hotels. Online shopping is becoming more common with the larger supermarkets and department stores now offering this option. In Santiago, you can access free WiFi in many metro stations.

RADIO

Radio is very popular in Chile. From the music-based Radio Horizonte to the news-based Radio Cooperativa, a wide variety of radio stations are broadcast throughout the country. Two of the most popular radio stations in the Santiago area are Radio Cooperativa 93.3 FM, which plays news and sports, and Radio Carolina 99.3FM, which plays popular music.

TV

Eighty-seven percent of Chilean households own at least one color TV set. Local channels, in Spanish language, include Canal 13, Chilevision, Megavision, La Red and TV Universidad Catolicá de Chile (run by the Universidad Catolicá) and the state-owned National TV of Chile. Programs include international and local news, chat shows, movies, documentaries and soap operas. Cable TV is available in many hotels and hostels, and shows a range of international channels in English language. Updated: Jun 18, 2009.

Mail/Packages

Chile's national post office is called Correos de Chile (www.correos.cl). You can find several post offices in cities and at least one in most towns. Correos de Chile provides regular mail services, registered post, parcel delivery and courier services to both national and international destinations. Most post offices are open Monday to Friday (9 a.m. – 6 p.m.) and on Saturday (9 a.m. – 12:30 p.m.). Post office service can be painfully slow and there is usually a line. Avoid going at lunchtime. You can see a list of post offices online at www.correos. cl. Follow the links for Puntos de Servicios and choose the Sucursales option followed by the region you are interested in. Chile's postal service is reliable but slow. International mail is usually sent by airl but can take two or more weeks to reach overseas destinations. You can pay an extra fee to have mail sent by express service. Expect to pay around $0.50 to send a postcard or letter to a Chilean destination, and $0.75 to send one overseas.

When posting parcels from Chile to your home country, consider the mail regulations for your own country. For example, liquids and food may be rejected and either held in customs or sent back to Chile. The cost of mailing parcels varies according to weight and destination. Alternatively, you can use an express courier service to send mail. Fed Ex (www.fedex.cl) and DHL (www.dhl.cl), both have offices in Santiago although these services are considerably more expensive than regular mail. Updated: Jun 18, 2009.

Telephones/Calling Cards

Almost all hotels and hostels have facilities for making local and international telephone calls, but rates vary. Check before calling home. You can easily find public telephones at newsstands and in shops and markets in most towns and cities. Public telephones take 100 peso coins. They are fine for making local calls, but international calls are either barred or charged at very high rates. Most towns and cities have centros de llamadas (call centers) and Internet cafés, which you can use for local and international telephone calls. Here you can make calls from a private booth or in some cases make VoIP calls, for example via Skype. The cost of international calls depends on the destination and is calculated by the minute. Expect to pay around $0.40 per minute to call the U.S. from Chile.

A cheaper option is to buy an international calling card from a newsstand. These prepaid phone cards come charged with calling credit

and you can use them to make local and international calls to and from any phone. Updated: Jun 18, 2009.

Telephone Calls

Making telephone calls can be a complicated and exhausting process in Chile because the dialing codes change depending on whether you are using a landline or cell phone. Follow these simple instructions and you should be fine.

LOCAL LANDLINE CALLS

To make a local call from a landline, dial the area code + telephone number. So, if you are in Santiago and want to call a local number from a landline, simply dial 2 + telephone number.

CELL PHONE TO CELL PHONE

The number 7, 8 or 9 prefixes all cell phone numbers. If you want to make a call to a local cell phone from a local cell phone, you need to dial the prefix + telephone number (for example, 9 + telephone number).

CELL PHONE TO LANDLINE

To call a landline from a local cell phone you need to dial 0 + area code + telephone number. For example a call to Santiago would be 0 + 2 + telephone number.

OUTSIDE CHILE TO LANDLINE/CELL PHONE

If you want to call a Chilean cell phone from overseas, you need to dial the international access code + country code + prefix + telephone number. The international access code for the U.S. and Canada is (011), and (00) for the U.K. So. If you want to call a Chilean phone from the U.K. dial 00 + 56 + 9 + telephone number).

INTERNATIONAL CALLS TO CHILE

The international dialing code for Chile is 56. To place an international call to Chile, dial the international access code + country code + area code + telephone number. The international access code for the U.S. and Canada is (011), and (00) for the U.K. For example, if you want to call Santiago from England, you need to dial 00 + 56 + 2 + number.

INTERNATIONAL CALLS FROM CHILE

When making an overseas phone call you must dial the operator code + 0 + country code (of the destination you are calling) + area code + telephone number. Operator codes are three-digit numbers. The most widely used are:
Entel (123)
Movistar (181)
Telefonica (188)
VTR (111)

For example, to call New York in the U.S. using Entel, you need to dial 123 + 0 + 1 + 212 + telephone number. Updated: Jun 18, 2009.

Cell Phones

Cell phones are common in Chile and there is network coverage in most of the country.

TRAVELING WITH YOUR OWN CELL PHONE

Chile has international roaming coverage and you should be able to make international calls from your cell phone in most areas. Coverage is good in large cities but can be limited in rural areas. Your service provider will be able to advise you on call rates. Petty theft of cell phones is not uncommon, so take care in big cities, especially at night.

PREPAID CELL PHONES

Prepaid cell phones are quite cheap and it's worth investing in one if you plan to be in Chile for some time. You can buy a prepaid cell phone in department stores such as Paris or Falabella and in most malls. There are three service providers: Movistar, Entel PCS and Claro, all of which are reliable. You can't make international calls with a prepaid cell phone for the first three months, but you can receive them. Check to be sure that the phone is GSM enabled before buying. You can load credit onto your prepaid cell phone at most pharmacies and in many metro stations. The cost of calls and SMS varies between service providers and calls across local networks are more expensive than network to network. Updated: Jun 18, 2009.

Internet

Most hotels and hostels have Internet connection and an increasing number have WiFi. Internet connection is usually free in hostels but hotels tend to charge to use the service.

You can easily find Internet cafés in towns and cities. Expect to pay around $0.30 for 10 minutes, $0.90 for 30 minutes and $1.25 for 60 minutes. Many Internet cafés are equipped with headphones and microphones to enable VoIP calls. You can also use the Internet in centros de llamadas (call centers). Many metro stations in Santiago have free WiFi connection and it's common to see people surfing the net with their laptops. Several coffee shops in the capital offer free WiFi too. Updated: Jun 18, 2009.

Money and Costs

The currency of Chile is the Chilean Peso (CH$). Unless otherwise indicated, **all prices in this book are given in US$**.

At the time of writing in October 2009, $1 USD = 547.800 CLP. Chilean bank notes are available in denominations of CH$20,000, 10,000, 5,000, 2,000, and 1,000. Coins are available in denominations of CH$500, 100, 50, 10, 5 and 1 (although the smaller coins are less common). A 10 percent tip is customary in all restaurants and bars. The tip is usually not included in the bill but if you want to check, ask, 'la propina esta includio?' Carry small change to leave for tips. Carry notes in small denominations especially when taking a taxi, as it's not uncommon for taxi drivers to be without change.

Chile is one of the most expensive countries in Latin America, but still cheaper than Europe, North America and Australia. Backpackers can live comfortably on US$30 per day. This should cover food and drink in budget restaurants, hostel accommodation, entry into a tourist attraction and public transport. If you want to stay in a mid-range hotel, eat and drink in decent restaurants and take the occasional taxi, budget for around US$110 per day.

SAMPLE COSTS

Metro ticket (one way): CH$400
Bottled water: CH$390
Bar of soap: CH$450
Toothpaste: CH$500
Bottle of shampoo: CH$1,900
Bottle of wine: from CH$1,800
Soft drink / coffee in a café: CH$1,000
Draft beer in a bar: CH$1,500
Glass of wine in a bar: CH$1,200
Lunch in a budget restaurant: CH$3,000
Men's haircut: CH$7,000
Woman's haircut: CH$12,000
Updated: Jun 18, 2009.

BANKS

Banks are open from 9 a.m. until 2 p.m. Monday to Friday. Bank customers have preferential treatment with separate lines and more bank tellers, while non-customers have to wait patiently. Go before lunchtime or you will have to wait in a long line for more than an hour.

In general, bank tellers only speak Spanish. If you don't have a Chilean RUT card (national identity card) you will need your passport as a form of ID for most transactions. If you are cashing a check, don't be surprised if the staff asks to make a photocopy of your passport and take a fingerprint. In order to open a bank account in Chile you must have a residency visa and a salary of at least $1,600 paid into your account monthly.

INTRO & INFO

ATMs in Chile are called Redbancs or cajero automático. Most accept Maestro, Cirrus, Visa and Mastercards. The maximum withdrawal is $200,000 Chilean pesos per day (about $345). Foreigners are charged around $7 per withdrawal depending on the exchange rates. Credit cards are accepted in many restaurants, shops and supermarkets but only with a passport as proof of identity. Updated: Jun 18, 2009.

CREDIT CARDS

Credit cards (Visa, Mastercard, Dinners Club and American Express) are accepted in many restaurants, hotels, bars and tour agencies, especially in bigger towns and cities. However, it's always a good idea to ask first. You can pay by credit card in big department stores such as Falabella, Paris and Ripley, but you will need your passport for ID. You can use ATMs for a cash advance from credit cards, but remember you will be charged a fee. Updated: Jun 18, 2009.

TRAVELER'S CHECKS

You can exchange traveler's checks in the bigger cities and towns at any casa de cambio (exchange house). It's worth shopping around to get the best exchange rate. Outside of Santiago, it's a good idea to carry traveler's checks in U.S. dollars as you can sometimes get better exchange rates and some vendors don't want to buy other currencies. Casas de cambio are open Monday to Saturday 9 a.m. – 7 p.m. and Sunday 9 a.m. – 2 p.m. Updated: Jun 18, 2009.

WIRING MONEY

If you want to wire money from Chile to an international bank account or vice versa, you need a Chilean bank account, which you can only obtain with a residency visa and proof of a monthly salary that will be paid into your account. It's much easier to use Western Union. There are branches in all the big cities and towns, and a transfer usually takes 24 – 48 hours. Alternatively, make a cash transfer by PayPal, but remember this can take three to five working days. Updated: Jun 18, 2009.

Dress and Etiquette in Chile

Chileans are very polite and courteous. Greet people with a warm *buenos días* (morning) or *buenos tardes* (afternoon and evening). Greetings between men and women, or women only, involve a kiss on the right cheek; between men, a handshake is customary. Try to introduce or greet people by their formal title; if unknown, señor or señora is fine. First-name exchanges should be reserved for friends and family.

HOW TO DRESS

Chileans tend to dress more formally than Europeans or North Americans. It's probably best to dress conservatively while learning the area's dress code. Typically, urban areas are more formal and fashion-conscious; to avoid standing out, wear clean, sleek clothes. Business workers should always dress in formal attire. For other daily interactions, business casual is the norm. In rural and coastal regions, the dress code tends to be more relaxed. Be aware that shorts should only be worn inside resorts.

FOOD MANNERS

Table manners are more formal in Chile than in other Latin American countries. Always use silverware and keep elbows up while eating. Women sit down before men. When dining out, travelers may notice that servers are not as service-oriented as in their home country. This is customary and shouldn't be taken personally. Remember to always ask for the bill, as it will never be automatically brought to the table.

At restaurants, a 10 percent tip is appropriate. Also, it's polite to tip the grocery bagger at the market; $0.75 to $1 should be fine. Side note: In Chile, lunch is the most important meal of the day. Dinner tends to be quite late, and is typically served between 9 and 10 p.m. Many dinner restaurants don't open until 8 p.m. Curb hunger Chilean-style: drink onces—a local mid-afternoon tea.

VISITING SOMEONE IN THEIR HOME

When visiting someone's home, it's polite to bring a small gift, such as chocolate, sweets or wine. Big gifts are overwhelming and may pressure the host to return the favor. Wine should be poured with the right hand, and is never drunk until the host has made a toast. During the toast, always make direct eye contact—it's rude not to. If you are staying with your host for an extended period of time, help out with groceries and chores. A memento from your hometown, like a keychain or book, is a kind gesture. Be respectful of utility costs. Stick to short showers and avoid excessive electrical use. To cut costs on phone bills, use prepaid cards or rent/purchase a cell phone. Updated: Feb 20, 2009.

Officialdom and Business

Passports are required for nearly all travelers entering Chile; the only exceptions are citizens from select South American countries: Argentina, Brazil, Uruguay, and Paraguay.

Citizens from all North American and most European nations do not need advance visas. However, nationalities that must obtain a visa prior to arrival include Indians, Jamaicans, Koreans, Poles, Russians, and Thais.

Chile grants 90-day permits on tourist cards; keep this card because it must be presented upon departure. Extensions can be made in 90-day increments by contacting Departamento de Extranjería (Moneda 1342, Santiago Centro, Tel: 56-2-6725320). Plan ahead, as these require a $100 charge and often take days to process. Some travelers find it easier to simply hop across the border and re-enter. Missing tourist cards can be reported and/or replaced by contacting Policía Internacional (General Borgoño 1052, Independencia, Santiago, Tel: 56-2-7371292).

In general, public officials are very honest and helpful, even to foreigners. However, do not attempt to bribe them; this is extremely disrespectful and may result in a harsher punishment. Most penalties are on par with Western countries, except drug possession, which is considered a serious crime and has strict penalties. The general police, or carabineros, wear green uniforms. They can demand documentation at any time, so always carry your passport (or a copy). The national emergency number to reach the police is 133. Members of the Chilean military take themselves very seriously and should be given the upmost respect. Don't photograph military personnel, as this could lead to film confiscation or even jail time!

In business settings—as with most settings—Chileans are very polite; formalities are common and expected. Men should always remove their hats before entering any office. Greet others with pleasantries such as buenas dias (morning) or buenas tardes (afternoon and evening). Handshakes are standard between men. Men and women often kiss on the right cheek, but a simple handshake is a safe default in formal settings. Chileans have a strong work ethic, often working six days a week. Always be punctual—even if they sometimes aren't. Before entering a business negotiation, Chileans like to build rapport and exchange pleasantries. It's best to cushion business deals with kind words and to be open to compromise. Updated: Mar 12, 2009.

Responsible Tourism

In recent years Chile has experienced an influx of tourism, largely due to its friendly attitude and wealth of natural diversity. Tourism offers many benefits: it creates employment opportunities, stimulates the economy, and increases intercultural awareness and understanding. However, Chile has struggled to regulate and organize its rapidly growing travel industry, causing threats to its native lands and culture.

There are many ways travelers can reduce their ecological footprint and support local business. Don't litter in the streets and be efficient with water and electrical use. Promote and protect national parks and heritage sites simply by expressing interest in them and paying the entrance fee, as this money goes directly to their maintenance. When visiting parks or camping, don't leave a trash trail—always pick up and dispose of any garbage. Support the Chilean food industry by avoiding international chains, dining at local restaurants and buying national produce.

Travelers can support the nation's hospitality business by staying in locally owned and operated accommodations. There are many clean and comfortable options available, and V!VA Travel Guides usually mentions whether a particular lodging is run by locals or foreigners. You can support local culture by purchasing the markets' arts and handicrafts. Be respectful and sensitive when visiting rural areas populated by indigenous people, such as the Mapuche of Southern Chile. Don't stare or take their photograph simply because they look unique or different.

You can also promote Chilean culture and business by booking trips through locally run tour operators and organizations. Latin Trails (E-mail: info@traveltochile.net URL: www.latintrails.com) has an extensive list of eco-friendly tour operators and conservation projects in Chile. Cascada Expediciones (www.cascada.travel/index.php) specializes in sustainable tourism and offers a range of adventurous and culturally rich trips throughout Chile.

SouthWorld Aventours (Doctor M. Barros Borgoño, 349, Providencia, Santiago, Tel: 56-2-2352066, E-mail: info@swachile.com, URL:www.swachile.com) supports responsible travel by arranging eco-friendly adventure activities and organizing fair trade tours that give travelers in-depth insight into local culture and politics both past and present.

Patagonia has experienced rapid growth in tourism, but needs improved infrastructure in order to protect its fragile fjords and forests.

Futa Friends (www.futafriends.org) strives to protect the natural beauty of the Futaleufu Valley and River by educating locals on the economic and social benefits of protecting the area, as well as urging government to stop mining and building dams that destroy the free-flowing river. You can donate or participate in FutaFestival, which raises money for the local cause by hosting live music and competitions of eco-friendly sports such as rafting and kayaking. Updated: Mar 13, 2009.

Photography Tips

Any budding photographer or serious amateur will have a field day traveling around Chile with a camera at hand. The scenery is absolutely stunning, so you won't be able to help snapping away at those spectacular mountain vistas. Besides the famous landmarks like the peaks of Torres del Paine, Chilean nature provides beautiful opportunities in the macro world, so do not forget to take close-ups of ferns, dew drops or other patterns when hiking through forests. If in luck when wildlife-watching, you may also be able to take home good shots of penguins, whales, condors or vicuñas. No doubt you will also be photographing lively arts and crafts markets or colorful houses, like the cabins on stilts on the island of Chiloé. In short, the photo ops are endless, so come prepared.

BASIC EQUIPMENT

If using a silver-film camera, bring lots of rolls of film, some slow (100 ISO) for bright sun and some faster (200 or 400 ISO) for lower light conditions. Although there are Fuji and Kodak shops around Chile that process and selling old-fashioned film, it may be harder to obtain (or may be expired) in remote areas, especially slide film. If using digital, bring an ample supply of memory cards. Unless you are carrying a laptop and can download your pictures regularly, you don't want to have to restrain yourself for lack of space. More memory allows you to shoot in higher resolution (wouldn't it be a shame to be forced to cram those once-in-a-lifetime memories into tiny, low-res files?) and for another, you will lose fewer photos if a card is lost or stolen. Doing back-ups of your most meaningful shots in an online storage space is not a bad idea either.

SERIOUS AMATEUR EQUIPMENT

If you want to bring home more than just basic holiday snaps of you and your friends, you may want to invest in a little extra equipment which will greatly improve your shots. The simplest is a UV filter, which eliminates haze and produces sharper pictures, while a polarizer reduces glare and improves contrast. Both can be useful in places with very bright light, like the sunny northern coast or in the Atacama Desert. A lot heavier to haul around, but useful if you are going to shoot in windy places, is a tripod. It is also necessary to support a long telephoto lens if you plan a wildlife photo safari. Needless to say, keep an eye on all that gear. Chile is relatively crime-free, but expensive items may prove tempting if you leave them lying about.

PROTECTING YOUR GEAR

Climate conditions vary widely between regions in Chile, so you need to protect your equipment against its worst enemies: sand and humidity. It is best to always store your camera in its bag when at the beach or anywhere rainy—anywhere along the Carretera Austral, for instance. Also watch out for dust, like in the Atacama Desert, when changing lenses or memory cards, moves best performed indoors and quickly! If you travel south to Patagonia, you may find yourself taking photos in very cold conditions. Try not to expose your camera to brutal changes in temperature: you are better off brushing a little snow off a cold camera than tucking it under the warmth of your coat, which risks creating condensation on your lens.

HANDLING THE LIGHT

Of course, weather conditions also impact heavily on light conditions—an essential aspect of landscape photography. As a rule of thumb, the light most conducive to quality shots is early morning or late afternoon light. Also remember that the light changes all the time in Patagonia. So if you see a beautiful scene, don't think twice about it, shoot it. Don't wait to "catch it on the way back" or until you stop for a picnic. By then, the clouds will have rolled in, the wind will have ruffled the surface of the lake or the light will have disappeared—and you will have lost the shot.

PORTRAITS AND SENSITIVE SUBJECTS

When taking photos of people, unless they just happen to be present in a street scene, it is basic courtesy to ask permission, especially with indigenous people, who tend to be camera-shy. Also avoid taking photos of navy ships or army buildings, it could get you into trouble. Last but not least, do not look at Chile merely through the viewfinder, focusing only on finding something to photograph. Traveling and bringing home great memories is first and foremost about living beautiful experiences. Updated: Jul 01, 2009.

Travel Tips

WHEN TO GO

The summer months of December to February are usually considered the best time to travel to southern Chile as the temperatures are the warmest. Since this is the busy tourist season though, prices will increase, sometimes even double. October, November, March and April have lower temperatures and fewer tourists, making these months a good time to visit Chile.

BEFORE YOUR TRIP

Make sure to register with your country's embassy and submit your itinerary. As a precaution, the embassy will send E-mails informing travelers of various dangers and annoyances that occur in the country. It's recommended to see your health care provider about four to six weeks before your trip in order to have enough time for any vaccines to take effect. No vaccines are obligatory for Chile, but it is a good idea to be up to date on routine shots like polio, rabies, MMR (measles, mumps, rubella) and DPT (diphtheria, pertussis, tetanus).

DRINKING WATER

Even if the water is safe to drink in various regions of Chile, it will still be different from the water your body is used to drinking. Just in case, it's good to stick to drinking only bottled or carbonated (bubbly) drinks in cans or bottles. Avoid tap water, fountain drinks, and ice cubes. If you purchase fresh fruits and vegetables, wash them with bottled water before eating.

MONEY

Daily spending money should be carried in a different and more accessible pocket or bag than the rest of your trip money. As a back up to cash, Visa, Mastercard, American Express or Diner's Club are accepted at most locations that take credit cards. Traveler's checks can be difficult to cash in Chile. Carry a separate folder or scan the following information into your E-mail account: a copy of your passport, the numbers of your credit cards, traveler's checks, bank accounts, airplane tickets, and emergency contacts. Remember an additional 10 percent for service will be added to restaurant and bar tabs; the I.V.A. (Value Added Tax) is 19 percent and normally is included in the price of purchase.

BUSINESS HOURS

Private businesses and government offices are open Monday to Friday from 8:30 a.m. to 6 p.m. with a two hour lunch break from noon to 2 p.m. Banks are generally open Monday to Friday from 9 a.m. until 2 p.m. and closed on weekends. Shopping malls are open weekdays from 10 a.m. to 9 p.m. and weekends, from 9 a.m. to 2 p.m. Supermarkets are open Monday to Sunday from 9 a.m. to 11 p.m. Updated: Apr 02, 2009.

Women Travelers

Chileans are known for their warm and welcoming attitude. The country has seen an influx of women travelers, especially those traveling solo or on gender-exclusive trips. Whether alone or with others, women should feel fairly safe during their trip, but should heed certain precautions and tips.

Chilean men do embody a sense of machismo, though their displays are more subdued, and less vocal, than their Argentine counterparts. Chilean men tend to ogle, or stare intensely. Although leering rarely poses any real threat, some women find it uncomfortable or creepy. While walking down the street, women may hear piropos—comments, whistling, kissy noises and catcalls—ranging from innocent to obscene. Again, this is more annoying than dangerous. Usually, the best option is ignore them; reactions often elicit more remarks. However, occasionally women may feel the need to react, especially if the comments appear disrespectful or rude.

When traveling in Chile, women should walk with confidence and assurance—even if feigned. Travelers looking lost or confused can appear vulnerable, making them easy targets for crime. In general, women should dress conservatively to detract attention and reduce flirtatious come-ons. Wearing a wedding band often helps ward off men, as does carrying pictures of your significant other (real or invented) in your purse. Women should exercise caution when using transportation. If taking a taxi at night, make sure it's registered or marked. Hitchhiking is not recommended. Longer trips along the Pan-American route can be taken by bus or train. Women traveling solo often prefer buses, which have reserved seats and locked storage for luggage.

Women with wanderlust should check out www.womentraveltips.com or www.journeywoman.com. Designed by—and for—globetrotting females, these websites are excellent resources for further travel tips and advice. Books worth buying include:

Wanderlust and Lipstick: The Essential Guide For Women Traveling Solo by Beth Whitman.

A Journey of One's Own: Uncommon Advice for the Independent Woman Traveler by Thalia Zepatos.

Gutsy Women: More Travel Tips and Wisdom for the Road by Marybeth Bond. Updated: Feb 20, 2009.

Gay Chile

In general, "machista" attitudes toward gender and sexuality are conservative throughout Latin America, but there are latitudes of freedom and tolerance among various nations, and Chile stands out as having a more visible gay subculture than most, especially in its capital, Santiago.

This is not to say that Chile has caught up with Europe and North America. In the 18 years since democracy was restored to Chile, homosexuality has been decriminalized, but it is still regarded with suspicion by most Chileans. However, as with other Latin states, HIV and AIDS in the 1980s forced the public and the government to acknowledge male homosexuality. In the 1990s the Internet and a globalized economy, with the resultant cross-pollination of cultures, helped liberalize attitudes among the younger generation.

Along the way, initially in response to the AIDS crisis, more gay men and lesbians have braved coming out and mobilizing for gay rights. Groups like "Moviemento Unificado de Minorías Sexuales," or MUMS have lobbied for civil rights and fought prejudices against gay individuals. A hugely popular TV soap opera, "Machos," about the lives of seven brothers, broke ground when the producers had one of the siblings come out of the closet. In 2006, Chile's congress introduced legislation legalizing same-sex civil unions, a measure supported by center-left president, Michelle Bachelet, but it met with strong resistance from the Catholic church and conservative groups. A similar bill was reintroduced and is still pending.

Santiago has no less than nine gay (male) bars, three lesbian bars, 10 gay discos and three saunas. The most prominent gay media is a periodical named "Opus Gay," a cheeky reference to the conservative Catholic group, "Opus Dei," which unsuccessfully sued for trademark infringement. Its website, www.opusgay.cl, along with http://santiago.queercity.info and www.puntogay.cl offer a more comprehensive overview of gay life in Chile. However, the unwary Net surfer should be forewarned that the domain name, www.chilegay.com has been purchased by a conservative protestant church, and one will be redirected to its evangelical homepage. Updated: Jul 06, 2009.

Senior Travelers Chile

Chile's diverse landscape—from the mystery of Patagonia and awe of Easter Island to the glaciated wilderness in Patagonia—attracts a lot of senior travelers. While visiting Chile, senior travelers should feel safe and supported. Chileans are very considerate and respectful toward both local and foreign senior citizens, and the nation's government has been a progressive world leader in the promotion and protection of senior citizens' rights, implementing initiatives such as The National Service for Older People (SENAMA, www.senama.cl) which helps develop, promote and finance organizations dedicated to the needs and rights of the elderly.

Older travelers should be particularly cautious if traveling to Santiago during the winter (June, July and August), when the city's smog can reach dangerously high levels, causing authorities to place the city on emergency status to restrict emissions. Seniors (particularly those with respiratory problems) should avoid downtown during this time. Older travelers are eligible for senior discounts at various museums, national parks and attractions; be sure to ask about special offers, as they are not always openly advertised. Senior travelers can save by joining organizations such as AARP (www.aarp.org), which offers a number of discounts on hotels, airfare and car rentals for travelers aged 50 and older.

Several tour operators cater specifically to seniors and organize group tours to popular destinations throughout Chile. Travelers aged 55 and older can check out Elderhostel (www.elderhostel.org), which offers culturally educational tours to Chile's diverse array of regions, including the Andes, Atacama Desert, Pacific Coast and Patagonia. Elder-Treks (www.eldertreks.com) specializes in adventurous and off-the-beaten-track trips for travelers aged 50 and up. Travelers can search by destination, activity level and activity type—ranging from mild (photography, arts/culture) to wild (diving, kayaking and hiking). Updated: Mar 12, 2009.

Disabled Travelers

As with many Latin American countries, Chile's infrastructure for disabled accessibility is patchy at best. However, the country is striving to improve its system. The law now requires all new buildings (restaurants, hotels, etc.) to provide disabled access, and various existing buildings have added lifts. It's best to call ahead and ask before making a reservation. Also, many national parks, cruises and ferries have discounts or free upgrades for disabled visitors; be sure to ask when making a reservation.

The narrow, crumbling and poorly maintained pavements that dominate Chilean streets will prove difficult and frustrating for disabled travelers. While annoying and inconvenient, navigating the streets shouldn't be too dangerous. Chileans are very courteous toward those with disabilities, often helping them cross the street or stopping their car to wait. In attempts to streamline the chaotic transportation system in Santiago, the government launched Transantiago (www.transantiago.cl) in 2007, placing emphasis on making public transport more accessible to those with impaired mobility. Although the idea and its intentions were good, execution has been disorganized, resulting in harsh criticism.

As part of Transantiago's initiative, the Metro (www.metrosantiago.cl) has invested in making new lines wheelchair-accessible, and has refitted various existing lines. As of now, Lines 5, 4 and the extensions of 2 and 5 have the proper equipment. The line to Maipú and the extension of Line 1 (until Plaza Los Dominicos) will include wheelchair accessibility in the future. In addition to buses, Tixi Service (URL: www.tixi.cl, Tel: 56-2-4813235) offers wheelchair-accessible transportation services around Santiago.

There are several travel agencies that cater to disabled travelers in Chile. Accessible Journeys (www.disabilitytravel.com) offers group tours to Chile and Argentina, and provides custom-designed travel tips and planning to ensure a safe and comfortable trip. Access-Able Travel (http://www.access-able.com) offers guided trips, travel advice and directories of tour operators offering services for a wide range of physical and development disabilities. Run by a family in Valparaiso, Chile, AMAPI Expeditions (www.amapiexpeditions.com, Tel: 56-3-2815886), provides custom-designed á la carte tours to Chile and Argentina. With years of experience in physical therapy and tourism, the staff at AMAPI is detail-oriented and thorough, helping disabled adventure-seekers realize their travel dreams. For further information

and advice on disability travel, check out the Society for Accessible Travel and Hospitality (www.sath.org). Updated: Mar 09, 2009.

Traveling with Children

Chileans simply adore children, whose well-received popularity makes Chile a very safe and family-friendly country to explore. Many accommodations have playgrounds, swimming pools and organized kids' activities. Staying in suites is often cheaper than booking multiple rooms, since most places charge by the number of beds, not people. Suites normally have a pull-out couch, and additional cots can often be requested at little or no charge.

Chile poses few health and food risks for children. However, if traveling to the south, load up on sun-block; the lack of ozone can be dangerous on delicate skin. When walking down the street, children are often curiously attracted to stray dogs; hold their hands or keep an eye on them in order to avoid illness or injury from interaction. Toilet paper, hand sanitizer and wet wipes are hard to find in certain areas, making them an invaluable investment to stock up on before arrival.Food tends to be more bland here than in other Latin American countries; cooking and dining out should be safe. And although children's menus are virtually nonexistent, restaurant meal portions are very generous, making it easy, and economical, to split a main course between two people. Most restaurants are understanding and will happily give you extra utensils.

Chile's sprawling geography requires a lot of travel time between excursions, so be sure to bring lots of games and books to occupy children's fleeting attention spans. Trains have space for moving around, but long-distance buses can be cramped and rarely offer discounts for children. Local buses do not charge for children, but paying customers get first priority with seating. However, Chileans often offer their seat to children anyway—another testament to the country's warm attitude toward families. Domestic flights offer extensive discounts for children under 12, so be sure to ask when buying tickets. Also, remember to ask for family or child discounts on sightseeing excursions, as many companies offer, but don't openly advertise, these options. Updated: Mar 13, 2009.

Tips for Budget Travelers

Chile is one of the more expensive countries in South America and, although it will take more effort to keep your bank balance in check, this impressive country still has a lot to offer the budget traveler. Take tips from the locals; eat where they eat (but always keep in mind your own health and safety), buy groceries where they shop. Avoid expensive beach or ski resorts. Make friends to share with and just enjoy the simpler things in life.

SECURITY TIPS

If you are staying in hostels and shared dorm rooms, make sure you take your own padlocks, either for securing your backpack or your assigned locker. You could even take a chain and lock to fasten your bag to your bed, in case there are no safe storage. Watch out for pickpockets on busy buses and, for long distance journeys, always take your bag on to the bus if you can.

TOUR TIPS

Traveling on your own can bump up the cost of everything, so try to link up with other travelers, and take advantage of group discounts. A good place to get free tour information is from Sernatur (URL: www.sernatur.cl) the country's official tourist office. You can pick up free booklets, in English and Spanish, with info on accommodation, restaurants, activities and maps.

LODGING TIPS

Hospedajes or residenciales are the cheapest sleeping options. Camping is also available, especially inside the national parks, but campsite prices vary, depending on the facilities, so always check. Dorm rooms in hostels are handy, especially if you're traveling alone. Before booking, ask if there is free Internet, a washing machine, space to hang hand-washing and a common room for meeting other travelers. If you do end up staying in a hotel, opt for shared bath and make sure breakfast is included, to minimize the cost.

FOOD TIPS

Try out the food at street stalls or stop by the mercado central, an all round great place to stock up on fresh fruit, have a cheap meal and take in the market atmosphere. You can fill up on tasty but cheap empanadas (savory filled pastries) or humitas (savory or sweet steamed corn wrapped in corn husks) and go for the almuerzo (set lunch). Pisco (a type of grape brandy), a staple of bars in Chile, is cheaper and better than the beer.

TRANSPORT TIPS

Local buses, known as micros, although often packed-full, will take you right across

town for next to nothing. Also, getting yourself a good map and walking is a great way to save money and see more. Overnight buses are a cheap way to travel long distances and save on lodging. But, remember your supplies: warm clothing and blanket (to combat the A/C), ear plugs, eye-mask, snacks and toilet paper! You might also check on last minute flight deals and so avoid the backache. Updated: Jun 26, 2009.

Tips for Mid-Range Travelers

As a mid-ranger traveler you will definitely feel comfortable in Chile. With more spending power, you can sample the excellent local wines, stay in significantly better lodging and get more out of the organized tours.

SECURITY TIPS

Staying in better accommodation and taking organized tours, you are less of a target than budget travelers, but it is still advisable to take care of your belongings, lock your luggage if taking the bus and be sure to ask about the hotel safe.

TOUR TIPS

Take advantage of the many tours offered across Chile and relax knowing everything is taken care of, from the airport transfer (therefore saving you the hassle of negotiating with the taxi drivers) to the reservations at the country ranch where you're staying while wine-tasting, skiing, or trekking through Patagonia.

LODGING TIPS

Mid-range accommodation options are definitely a lot more exciting and offer significantly more value for your pennies. Away from the cities, do not miss the lovely haciendas and resorts—the stuff great memories are made of.

FOOD TIPS

Chileans know what good food is and there are a lot of excellent restaurants, especially in the cities. You will find the full range of cuisines, local and international, to suit all palates. For lunch, food courts in shopping malls are handy for good clean fare. In the evening, the restaurants in upmarket hotels are often a nice change from your usual à la carte and often afford great views. You will be pleased to know that you will also not need to go without your cappuccino or latte, as good coffee shops abound.

TRANSPORTATION TIPS

You can avoid the crowded buses and take the metro, or even better, just hop straight into one of the many taxis, known as colectivos, which are still very reasonably priced. For long journeys, the executive buses are quite comfortable or, for more civilized way to travel, take one of the many well-maintained trains out south of Santiago. Updated: Jul 01, 2009.

Tips for Luxury Travelers

As a top end traveler you can really take in so much more of the country and in a shorter amount of time. Chile is made for those who have no spending worries and there is no shortage of luxury hotels in jaw-dropping locations or high-end restaurants in which to sample the very best cuisine that Chile has to offer.

SECURITY TIPS

Luxury travelers need not worry too much about security, although as when traveling anywhere, and even at home, it is always advisable to take care of your possessions and not leave expensive items temptingly out on show. Upper-end hotel rooms will typically have safe boxes and transport organized by tour agencies. Your hotel should also be secure.

TOUR TIPS

If you don't want the hassle of planning your own itinerary, there are plenty of tour operators in Chile and online that can take care of every last details for you, even making sure that the up-market hotels of Torres del Paine, which are often full-booked in high season, have champagne on ice waiting for you.

LODGING TIPS

Not only will you find the usual top-end international chain hotels to suit your needs in the cities, the lakes, mountains, desert and ski destinations are home to some wonderfully luxurious boutique hotels and all-inclusive resorts with first class service and surroundings.

FOOD TIPS

With more to offer than just menu of the day and market stalls, high cuisine is sought by locals as well as tourists, driving up the quality and variety of fine food restaurants in Chile. You will also find some great delicatessens in the cities as well as large department stores with grocery sections. Be sure to visit the wine regions for some truly excellent cooking.

TRANSPORT TIPS

Traveling in luxury means you do not have to deal with the usual threats of have your blackberry stolen on the dangerously overloaded bus or having to check every time the coach stops that no one is running off with

your luggage from the storage space below. You can easily rent a car, which your hotel or tour agency can arrange for you, or even better, hire a car and a driver for the day. For cross-country travel take an internal flight. Updated: Jun 26, 2009.

Suggested Reading

Exile, social and political turmoil are common themes in Chilean literature. Pinochet's dictatorship often lurks in literary plots and character backgrounds, and magic realism is a widely practiced genre in Chilean literature. Below is a list of Chilean writers and their most notable work:

• Culled from her five books, *Selected Poems of Gabriela Mistral*, University of New Mexico Press, 2003, is a generous anthology of and great introduction to the beloved poet's free-verse. Sharp translations expose powerful poems whose themes range from the Chilean landscape to grief and loss.

• Pablo Neruda's *The Essential Neruda: Selected Poems*, City Lights Publishers, 2004, is a high-quality introduction to the acclaimed poet, with contributing translations from renowned poets and scholars. This definitive collection includes the Nobel Prize-winning poet's most essential works: love poems, historical epics, and political manifestos.

• Isabela Allende's best-selling debut novel, *The House of the Spirits*, Knopf, 1985, made her a literary star. Described as "extraordinary, astonishing and mesmerizing," the book makes use of magic realism, telling the story of a family whose members toil and endure through tumultuous times.

• Exiled during the Pinochet years, award-winning writer Luis Sepúlveda's *The Old Man Who Read Love Stories*, Harvest Books, 1995, is an endearing morality tale set in Amazonian Ecuador, while *The Story of a Seagull and the Cat Who Taught Her to Fly*, Scholastic Paperbacks, 2006, which has sold more than a million copies worldwide, deals with life, death, and following your true calling.

• Roberto Bolaño's *The Savage Detectives*, Picador, 2008, was perceived to be a masterpiece, until the English publication of the epic *2666*, Picador, 2009, arrived. Published posthumously, Bolaños haunting, voluminous story of violence, death and dislocation is considered a landmark novel, and wound up on year-end best-of lists and landed

Suggested Reading

several top fiction awards.

• The dramatic plot of Marcela Serrano's Antigua and My Life Before, Anchor, 2001 is suffused with political and feminist struggles. Serrano's first English-translated book follows—out-of-sequence—the lives of two women who've been friends since grade school.

• José Donoso, who spent the Pinochet years in exile, was a member of the Latin American literary boom of the 1960s and 1970s. His novel *Curfew*, Grove Press, 1994, explores sexuality and psychology in his homeland while displaying his trademark touches of black humor and magic realism.

• Antonio Skármeta's *Burning Patience* (widely available as The Postman, W.W. Norton and Co., 2008) was the inspiration for the Oscar-nominated Italian film Il Postino. Skármeta spent the Pinochet years in Argentina and Germany, and his passionate tale—set before the dictatorship—follows the friendship between a fictional postman and Pablo Neruda.

There have been many books written by non-Chilean authors that cover Chile's history, politics, environment. The books listed below are but two of the many engaging reads:

• Pamela Constable and Arturo Valenzuela's *A Nation of Enemies: Chile under Pinochet*, W. W. Norton and Co., 1993, is a meticulously documented deliberation on the 1973 coup, Pinochet's rule, and the transition to democracy.

• Jürgen Rottmann, one of the pre-eminent biologists in Chile, wrote *Bosques de Chile: Chile's Woodlands*, IGES, 1988. Published in Spanish and English, and filled with photos, this book is an in-depth study of Chile's forests. Updated: Jul 02, 2009.

)))))

Get these other guidebooks before your trip!

Santiago

 638 m 4,837,295 2

Photo by Peter Anderson

Slap-bang in the middle of Chile, Santiago is a modern city with a European feel, and is the place where most visitors begin their trip. It's not a particularly attractive city, since frequent earthquakes have gradually claimed most of the colonial buildings here.

Santiago also lacks the 24-hour party reputation of other Latin American capitals, so a couple of days should be sufficient to see all the main attractions before heading out into the countryside.

Despite its flaws, Santiago's European flavor and the proliferation of modern conveniences, such as high-quality hotels and restaurants, make the city a good base for exploring the nearby regions. Day or overnight trips to the wine country to the south, the beaches to the west, and the Andean ski resorts to the east can easily be arranged in the capital. See "Around Santiago" (p.118) for more information about these trips.

History

Santiago was founded on February 12, 1541, by Spanish explorer and conquistador Pedro de Valdivia. The region had been explored before, but found to be harsh, unforgiving, and full of warlike natives, so settlement was slow in coming. During the early years, settlers faced the dangers of starvation, earthquakes and floods as well as regular raids by the natives.

The city survived, however, and flourished during the colonial era. Some of the city's most interesting architecture dates from the Spanish colonial period. The city, which was answerable to the Viceroy of Peru in Lima, had an economy based on livestock and agriculture, although later mining would become important.

Highlights

The Plaza de Armas (p.81), Santiago's official center, is always buzzing with life. Schoolchildren, families, workmen on their lunch-break, and tourists all come here to soak up the atmosphere and watch the world go by.

Chile's most impressive museum, **The Museo Chileno de Arte Precolombina (p.81)**, features 3,000 pieces of Pre-columbian art from more than 1,000 Latin American cultures, all laid out in a manageable and interesting display.

On a clear day, the high **Cerro San Cristóbal (p.95)** gives fine views over both the city and the Andes. Head up to the summit on the funicular railway and enjoy a picnic in the park at the top. Or, as clear days are rare in Santiago, make the summit at dusk to watch the golden-orange glow of the sun setting on the hazy city.

Santiago's Latin Quarter, **Barrio Bellavista (p.93)**, gets particularly lively on Thursday, Friday and Saturday nights when Chileans and foreigners pour into the restaurants, bars, cafes and 'salsatecas' that line the narrow streets. Updated: Dec 01, 2008.

After France invaded Spain in 1808, Santiago became the center of the Chilean independence movement. Different governors tried to discourage dissent, but once the movement had begun it was impossible to stop. After the royalists lost the decisive Battle of Chacabuco in 1817 not far from Santiago, Chilean Independence became a fact and Santiago was named the capital.

The city was well-managed as it grew, with places set aside for parks and universities. During the early Republican years, Chile earned a reputation as a relatively stable place and Santiago became a magnet for political refugees from other South American countries.

At the end of the nineteenth century, the country experienced an economic boom due to nitrate mining. The newly-wealthy Chileans built buildings with their money, and some fine Santiago architecture dates from this period.

In the twentieth century the city industrialized, and factory work attracted men and women from all over the nation and abroad, causing the city to swell. It would eventually become one of the most important commercial, industrial and transportation hubs of South America.

For a long time, Chile retained its reputation as a relatively peaceful, safe place to live: exceptions include the War of the Pacific (1879-1884) and the 1891 civil war under President Balmaceda. This image of a peaceful nation was shattered on September 11, 1973, when President Salvador Allende was ousted by a military coup led by General Augusto Pinochet. Allende himself barricaded himself in the Presidential Palace to fight off the soldiers and eventually killed himself rather than relinquish power peacefully.

In the ensuing years, Pinochet relentlessly pursued "insurgents," real and imaginary at home and abroad. Thousands of innocent Chilean citizens were arrested and many of them were executed without any judicial process and Santiago suffered disproportionately. With the end of the Pinochet regime and military rule, peace has returned to Santiago, although it still struggles to cope with the recent past.

When to Go
You can visit Santiago at any time of the year. Summers (November to February) are hot and dry with average temperatures of 30°C (86° F). February is the hottest month and it can get pretty sticky in the city.

Winter (June to August) has average temperatures of 13°C (55°F) and more rain. The mornings are cold, and at night temperatures drop close to freezing. This is a good time to head to the mountains, about one hour from Santiago, for winter sports.

National holidays are celebrated on September 18, *Fiestas Patrias* (Independence Day) and September 19, *Día de las Glorias del Ejército* (Army Day). Updated: Nov 03, 2008.

Getting To and Away From Santiago
BY AIR
The main airport in Santiago is Arturo Merino Benítez International Airport (Tel: 56-2-6901752), in Pudahuel, about 14 kilometers

northeast of Santiago, which services major airports all over the world. Check schedules at URL: www.aeropuertosantiago.cl.

From the airport, you can get a taxi to the city center for around $30. A much cheaper option ($3) is to take one of the buses, which stop just outside the airport and can take you into the center. To get to the airport from the city, take the metro to La Moneda or Pajaritos on Line 1 and then take the bus from there. Buses depart every 15 minutes throughout the day.

BY BUS
There are five bus stations in Santiago with services to both the north and south and to other countries in South America. The price of longer journeys is determined by the type of seat you request: *clásico* (classic), *semi-cama* (semi-reclining seat), *cama ejecutivo* (fully-reclining seat) or premium. Bus services are generally very good.

Terminal Santiago is on Avenida Bernardo O'Higgins (Alameda) 385, Barrio Brazil. Tel: 56-2-3761755, URL: www.terminaldebuses-santiago.cl. International departures leave here to both the north and south. The closest metro station is Pila del Ganso, Line 1.

Terminal San Borja is on San Borja 184, barrio Brazil. Tel: 56-2-7760645, URL: www.terminalsanborja.cl. Buses from here go to the north and central zone. The closest metro station is Estación Central, Line 1.

Terminal Los Héroes is on Calle Tucapel Jiménez 21. Tel: 56-2-4200099. Buses go to the north and south. The closest metro station is Los Heroes, Line 1.

Terminal Alameda is on Avenida Bernardo O'Higgins 3750, Barrio Brazil. Tel: 56-2-2707500. This is a private station that TurBus and Pullman use for national and international departures. The closest metro station is Universidad de Santiago, Line 1.

Estación Pajaritos is on Calle General Bonilla 5600, Barrio Brazil. Tel: 56-2-503468. This serves as a sub-station for Turbus and Pullman for national and international departures. The closest metro station is Pajaritos, Line 1.

BY TRAIN
Train services in Chile are limited. The only long-distance train services from Santiago run south to Chillán or Temuco. Bus

SANTIAGO

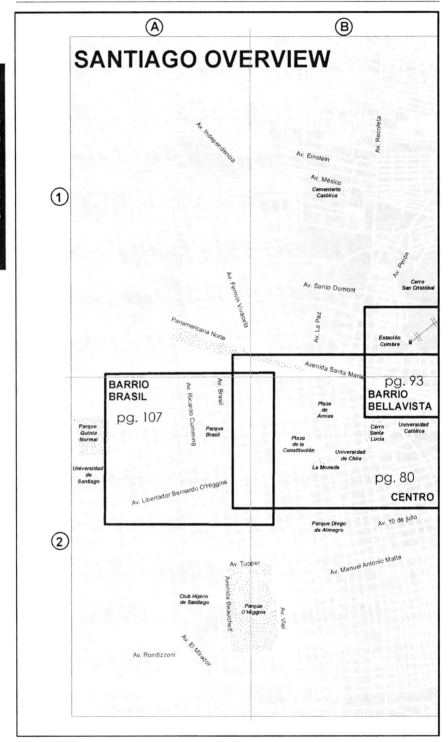

Ⓐ Ⓑ

SANTIAGO OVERVIEW

Av. Independencia

Av. Einstein

Av. México
Cementerio
Católica

Av. Recoleta

①

Av. Fermín Vivaceta

Av. Perón

Cerro
San Cristóbal

Av. Santo Dumont

Av. La Paz

Panamericana Norte

Estación
Cumbre

Avenida Santa María

**BARRIO
BRASIL**

pg. 107

Av. Ricardo Cumming

Av. Brasil

Parque
Brasil

Plaza
de
Armas

pg. 93
**BARRIO
BELLAVISTA**

Cerro
Santa
Lucía

Universidad
Católica

Parque
Quinta
Normal

Plaza
de la
Constitución

Universidad
de Chile

Universidad
de
Santiago

La Moneda

Av. Libertador Bernardo O'Higgins

pg. 80

CENTRO

Parque Diego
de Almagro

Av. 10 de julio

②

Av. Tupper

Av. Manuel Antonio Matta

Club Hípico
de Santiago

Avenida Beauchef

Parque
O'Higgins

Av. Viel

Av. El Mirador

Av. Rondizzoni

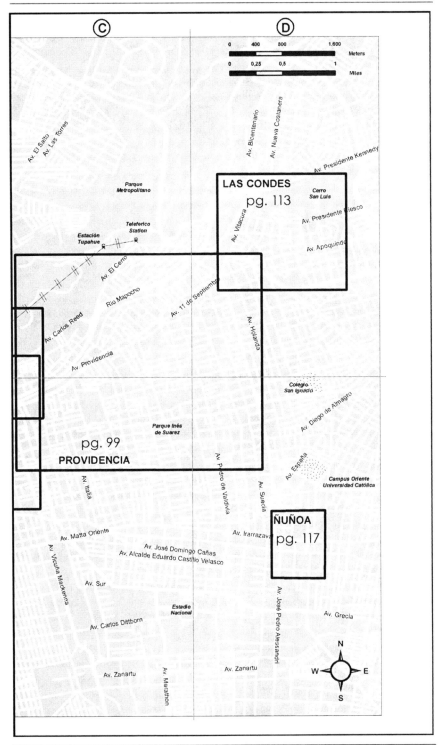

connections are necesary to go farther south. Trains depart from **Estación Central**, Avenida Bernardo O'Higgins (Alameda) 3170, Barrio Brazil.

You can find more information on train services at URL: www.efe.cl or by calling Tel: 56-2-3768500.

BY CAR

Santiago is halfway along Ruta 5, a north-south highway that can take you all the way from one end of Chile to the other. Take Ruta 5 north to get to La Serena (5-6 hours), Antofagasta (15 hours) and Arica (23 hours). Take Ruta 5 south to get to Rancagua (1 hour), Chillán (4-5 hours), Valdivia (9-10 hours) and Puerto Montt (12 hours). To get to the coast, take Ruta 68 to Valparaíso and Viña del Mar (1.5 hours). To get to Punta Arenas and the far south, you need to cross into Argentina.

The major highways around Santiago charge a toll via an electronic device called TAG, which you can buy from most service stations. A daily pass costs around $9.

The speed limit on highways is 120 kmph, on secondary roads 80 kmph and in cities 60 kmph. Updated: Jul 07, 2009.

Getting Around

Santiago is very easy to get around. Buses and the metro system are run by Transantiago, URL: www.transantiago.cl. Buy a rechargeable BIP card from any metro station ($2.30) to swipe on your way onto the metro or a bus.

Each bus ride costs $0.76. Service is frequent during the day, but less reliable at night. Subway fares vary between $0.76 during off-peak and $0.84 for rush hours. The metro operates from 6:30 a.m. to 11 p.m. Monday – Friday, 6:30 a.m. to 11 p.m. Saturdays and Sundays and holidays 8:30 a.m. to 10:30 a.m. You can get subway maps and travel information at the subway stations.

It's very easy to find yellow and black taxis on the street. They are relatively cheap for short distance journeys; fares start at $0.50.

Alternatively, take a *colectivo* taxi, which runs on a fixed route. These are black cars with a destination sign on the roof. Private taxis can be booked from hotels or hostels. Updated: Jul 07, 2009.

Safety

Santiago is generally a safe city. Some pickpocketing occurs in the city center and at popular tourist spots. Be sensible: keep valuables in your bag, don't flash expensive cameras, jewelry or cash, take care of your belongings at street cafes or restaurants. Many restaurants provide security clips to attach your bag to your chair. Use them!

Stay away from city parks and the *costañera* (river sidewalk) at night. There have been some reports of tourists being mugged both in the city center and at Plaza Italia at night. Updated: Nov 13, 2008.

Services

TOURISM

The main tourist office, **Servicio Nacional de Turismo** (SERNATUR), is located at Avenida Providencia 1550. Tel: 56-2-7318336 / 8337, URL: www.sernatur.cl. The office is a few minutes' walk from the Manuel Montt metro station. Open Monday – Friday, 9 a.m. – 6 p.m. and Saturday 9 a.m. – 2 p.m. The staff speaks Spanish and English and can provide information on tours and lodgings.

MONEY

Banks are open Monday – Friday from 9 a.m. – 2 p.m. Avoid going at lunchtime, unless you like waiting in line for two hours.

There are hundreds of ATMs throughout the city that accept Visa, Mastercard and Maestro. ATMs marked Red Banc accept international cards. They only dispense Chilean pesos.

Calle Huérfanos, just off Plaza de Armas is full of *Casas de Cambio* (money exchange offices). They are open Monday – Saturday, 9 a.m. – 6 p.m. Shop around to get the best rates.

KEEPING IN TOUCH

Postal services are run by Correos Chile, URL: www.corroes.cl. There are several branches throughout the city, but here are a few in Providencia:

Mall Panoramico, Av. 11 Septiembre 2092

Plaza Pedro de Valdivia, Pedro de Valdivia 1781

Tobalaba, Luis Thayer Ojeda 0146.

The post office is open Monday – Friday 9 a.m. – 6 p.m., and Saturday 10 a.m. – 2 p.m. There are several Internet cafes and international call offices in the main tourist areas and at metro stations. Most have facilities for Skype calls. Updated: Nov 13, 2008.

MEDICAL
There are pharmacies on almost every street corner. Many seem to work on commission and the staff will try to sell you expensive name brand drugs. Ask for *remedio generico* (generic drugs), which are manufactured by local companies and cost a quarter of the price.

SHOPPING
Santiago is one of the most expensive cities in South America. International clothing brands, CDs, electronics and cosmetics are all readily available, although they are imported, so expect to pay at least what you'd pay at home, perhaps more. If you want to save money, buy local products and brands.

For local shopping, you can go about anywhere in the city. Spend the afternoon haggling with local shop owners and boutiques along the streets of the Bellavista neighborhood, especially in the artisan fair.

The fish and seafood at Mercado Central attract hordes of tourists, for obvious reasons: the hustle of the market fascinates newcomers and you can sample local cuisine before scooting off to another site.

In Santiago, look to buy jewelry, carvings and ornaments made of *lapis lazuli*, a semiprecious stone only found in Chile and Afghanistan. You can also buy Mapuche silver jewelry. Several jewelry stores are in Patio Bellavista and along Avenida Santa Maria.

Most supermarkets have a fairly good range of wine and pisco priced from $3 to $25. If you're looking for something special, try El Mundo del Vino.

Avoid buying books. There's a hefty government tax on books and they are incredibly expensive throughout the country. Updated: Nov 03, 2008.

Things to See and Do
Metropolitan Park is the place to go if you want a zoology lesson, a stroll through the green or a visit to one of the many attractions in the vicinity. The National Zoo, which features about 150 different species, lies on the outskirts of the park, close to the Funicular. The Funicular is a tram that totes you to the top of Cerro San Cristobal, a tall hill frequented by Chileans and tourists alike. If you hope to see a panoramic view of the city from atop the *cerros*, head to Metropolitan Park early to beat the onset of Santiago's daily smog.

Santiago's many museums will satiate the appetite of all aviation enthusiasts, history buffs, poetry fans and art aficionados. For a few pesos you can tiptoe around one of the houses of the Nobel-prize poet Pablo Neruda or gawk at the 70,000 exhibits on display at The National Historical Museum (p.84).

Santiago also serves as a good base for exploring nearby areas. Outdoorsy folks should venture outside of the city to check out the hiking, rafting and fishing opportunities in Cajón del Maipo. The ski resorts that surround the capital are great for fans of fresh powder.

You can also set up a private or shared wine tour with companies that shuttle you to some of the most popular red-wine vineyards. One-day trips will take you to quaint Valparaíso (p.127), to the beach resort of Viña del Mar or to the pottery capital of the area, Pomaire. Updated: Jun 29, 2009.

Studying Spanish
Santiago is an outstanding place to take Spanish classes. The city houses several schools, and the high teaching quality makes selecting one difficult; try a sample lesson before you make up your mind. The programs are geared toward beginners and backpackers with limited time and money, so schools tend to be quite flexible, particularly the smaller ones. Updated: Oct 30, 2008.

Escuela Bellavista
Escuela Bellavista Spanish School has a friendly and welcoming ambiance. Its youthful, yet experienced teaching staff will help you work on your language skills, ensuring that you speak only Spanish in class, including during your break times with the other students, thus maximizing your learning opportunities.

The school offers both one-on-one and group classes; the former are more expensive. Salsa classes, a variety of weekend trips and free Internet use are some of the other benefits associated with studying here. Ca. del Arzobispo 0605, Bellavista. Closest metro:

Salvador. Tel: 56-2-7323443 / 7895869, E-mail: info@escuelabellavista.cl, URL: www.escuelabellavista.cl. Updated: Jul 02, 2009.

Woodward Chile

Woodward offers group Spanish classes in blocks of 10, 20, 25 or 50 hours. Students can set their own timetable and decide how many hours they want to study per week. Classes run between 10 a.m. and 6 p.m. Prices vary depending on the number of hours booked, but are cheaper in the winter. Check the website for the latest deals. The school is government approved; there is free Internet for students, a BBQ area and terrace, and school officials frequently organize social events. Staff can also arrange homestays. Av. Apoquindo 4248, Barrio Brazil. Closest metro: Escuela Militar. Tel: 56-2-4812240, E-mail: info@woodward.cl, URL: www.spanish.cl. Updated: Oct 30, 2008.

Escuela Newen

Escuela Newen is a few minutes from the Bellas Artes Museum. The school is small, the staff friendly, and the standard of teaching excellent. The teachers speak only Spanish with students. Ismael Valdés Vergara 514 Depto B-22, Santiago Centro. Closest metro: Bella Artes. Tel: 56-2-6385687, E-mail: info@escuelanewen.cl, URL: www.escuelanewen.cl. Updated: Oct 30, 2008.

Volunteering

It can be difficult to find information about volunteering opportunities in Santiago. When you do find an organization, many want to charge you for your volunteer services. The rationale behind these schemes is that you are paying for the company's organizational skills (i.e. securing a placement) and their contacts. Be careful and check out the validity of any organizations offering volunteer positions. Ask for references and if they have legal charity status or are recognized by the Chilean government.

Volunteers often work with the poor and disadvantaged. Most positions involve teaching English, working with youth programs or working in orphanages and hospitals. Updated: Oct 30, 2008.

Cactus Language

Cactus Language school offers a unique opportunity to learn Spanish in Santiago and volunteer at the same time. The program lasts 2 – 12 weeks. The last four weeks are spent volunteering with a local project. Students have 20 lessons a week and the school organizes social events. Accommodation is provided with a host family during school time and in a shared apartment during the volunteer placement. URL: www.cactuslanguage.com. Updated: Jun 30, 2009.

WorldTeach

Volunteers for WorldTeach become English instructors. There are two programs available: Chile Ministry or Chile DuocUC. Volunteers teach at either primary/secondary public or semi-public schools. The Chile DuocUC program runs for a year. Volunteers teach at a Chilean post-secondary institute, similar to a community college in the US.

Volunteers must be native English speakers and have a Bachelor's degree. Teaching qualifications are not required. Departures are in early February (Chile DuocUC Year), mid-March (Chile Ministry Year) and mid-July (Chile Ministry Semester). All programs finish by mid-December. URL: www.worldteach.org/programs/chile_year. Updated: Oct 30, 2008.

VE Global

VE Global has legal NGO status in Chile and, unlike many organizations, doesn't charge volunteers a fee. Volunteers carry out rewarding work with Santiago's underprivileged children in orphanages, schools and community centers. They develop and implement educational programs and spend time building relationships with the children.

Volunteers must be over 18 years old and speak either English or Spanish. Volunteers can work full time (40 hours per week) or part time (at least three or five hours per week). Full-time volunteers must commit to a period of three months, but it's possible to stay for 12 months or longer. Potential volunteers must complete an application form and interview and provide letters of recommendation. Carabineros de Chile 33, Depto. 42, Santiago Centro. Tel: 56-2-7179937, E-mail: info@ve-global.org, URL: www.voluntariosesperanza.org. Updated: Apr 24, 2009.

Tours

There are a lot of tour operators in Santiago that offer both city tours and day trips. Most tours pick you up at your hotel and drop you off there afterward. Generally, tour guides are bilingual, speaking Spanish and English. If you are short on time, try one of the hop-on, hop-off city bus tours. Day tours to vineyards and neighboring Valparaíso and Viña del Mar are fairly expensive; it's much cheaper to arrange day trips yourself. Updated: Oct 30, 2008.

Santiagovision
(PRICE: $24 adults, $6 children under 12) Santiagovision provides a hop-on, hop-off city bus that focuses on Santiago's historical areas. Stops include Palacio de la Moneda, Iglesia San Francisco, Cerro Santa Lucia, Ricardo Lyon, Alonso de Cordova, Cerro San Cristobal, Palacio de Bellas Artes, Plaza de Armas and Estación Mapocho. Independencia 1630, Barrio Ñuñoa. Tel: 56-2-7353998, E-mail: info@santiagovision.cl, URL: www.santiagovision.cl. Updated: Jul 07, 2009.

Turistik
(PRICE: $30 adults, $10 children) Turistik operates hop-on, hop-off city tours to the most popular tourist spots on open-top double decker buses. Bus tours operate every day, 9:30 a.m. – 6:30 p.m. except Christmas Day and New Year's Day. You get one free child-entry per adult ticket purchased. The circuit lasts about two hours, so if you don't have much time, you can still get a glimpse of the major sights. Commentary in English and Spanish.

The bus tour picks up/sets down at the following locations approximately every half hour: Plaza de Armas: Calle Monjitas 821; Mercado Central: Calle Puente 889; Plaza de la Constitucion: Calle Teatinos 254; Santa Lucia: Av. Libertador Bernardo O'Higgins 406; Providencia: Calle Lota 2229; El Golf: Av. Vitacura 2841; Parque Arauco: TURISTIK bus stand at Boulevard de Parque Arauco; Alonso de Cordova: Av. Alonso de Cordova 3107; Sheraton Hotel: front of building; Bellavista: Av. Bellavista 112; and Museo Nacional de Bellas Artes: front of building. Tel: 56-2-2990600, URL: www.turistik.cl. Updated: Oct 30, 2008.

CHIP Travel
Also known as the Chile Information Project, CHIP Travel isn't your typical city site service. The company takes topics they are earnestly interested in, such as literature, history, golf, biking and of course, Chilean wine, and creates interesting and comprehensive tours. Check out the Bike and Wine combo tour, which maps an awe-inspiring route through the valley. You'll see amazing vistas back-dropped with the majestic Andes and sample a wine tasting at a family-owned vineyard (Price: two people:

$150; three – five people: $140; five or more: $120. Prices are per person. Includes private transport to and from hotel, English-speaking guide, lunch, all necessary bike equipment, vineyard visits and wine tasting).

Another worthy CHIP tour is the Human Rights Walking Tour. This service is the only one in Santiago that explores the 17-year Pinochet dictatorship and its dramatic consequences. You can do a full- or half-day trip that tours the city, its harrowing history and present-day culture (Half-day: $70 per person, full-day: $180 per person). Av. Santa Maria 227, Of. 11, Recoleta. Tel: 56-2-7375649, E-mail: info@chiptravel.cl.com, URL: www.chiptravel.cl. Updated: Aug 6, 2009.

Fueguinos
Fueguinos operates one-day trekking tours in Chile's central zone for small groups. Destinations include Cajón del Maipo in the Andes Mountains (with a stop at the El Morado National Monument and San Francisco Glacier), Parque Nacional La Campana and Isla Negra. The company also arranges customized group tours.

Tours depart from your hotel between 7 a.m. and 7:30 a.m. and return to Santiago at 8 or 9 p.m. At $100, the price is a bit steep, but it does include transport, a bilingual guide, tickets to national parks, breakfast, lunch and a snack. Tel: 56-2-737325, URL: www.fueguinos.cl. Updated: Oct 29, 2008.

TurisTour
TurisTour offers city tours of Santiago, including a walking tour. The city tour focuses on the historical part of the city and doesn't have as many stops as other providers. TurisTour does, however, offer a number of day trips from Santiago, including trips to Valparaíso, Viña del Mar, Isla Negra and the ski resorts. They also operate a number of wine tours. All tours pick up at your hotel and have bilingual tour guides. Tel: 56-2-4880444 E-mail: reservas@turistour.cl, URL: www.turistour.cl. Updated: Oct 29, 2008.

Lodging
Inexpensive digs are not hard to come by in Santiago's barrios. However, dishing out an extra few dollars will get you more comfortable and safer options.

Santiago's center provides a plethora of accommodations. Younger travelers and the young-at-heart should head to Barrio

Bellavista and Barrio Brazil for hostels filled with people who tend to get a little rowdy. Travelers on a budget should know that in the center of the city you can find a bed for pennies or a better room with a kitchen, continental breakfast and decent bath for an extra $15 or so. Higher-end accommodations lie to the east. In neighborhoods like Providencia and Las Condes, chic hotels, ranging from $130 to over $200 a night, are abundant.

Skiers hoping to find an economical place to stay before hitting the slopes will have to settle for a tiny room or allow time for a short stint on the metro before taking one of the ski buses that leave from ski rental shops in Providencia.

Many hostels offer discounts for larger groups, students with ISIC cards and those staying extended periods. Some mid-range hotels charge taxes, so be sure to ask about final prices.

Those staying for longer than a few weeks may want to rent a room or stay with a local family. Santiago's periodicals *El Mercurio* and *El Rastro* give listings for apartments, rooms and family residences. Notice boards at the tourist office may also provide leads. Updated: Jun 27, 2008.

Restaurants

In general, Chilean food tends to be simple, but Santiago boasts some of the best seafood, national, international and vegetarian dishes in Chile. Those looking for a romantic dinner won't be disappointed by the capital's selection of fine foods. At the same time, cafes provide affordable, local meals for about $6.

A meal-of-the-day usually comes with a main dish such as fried fish, a side such as rice, plus a beverage and small dessert. At night, instead of eating Italian or Mexican, opt for Chile's light specialty, *once*, served at most cafes in Santiago. (*Once* consists of a sandwich or bread, a type of cake, and coffee or tea.)

Groovy jazz, live music and laid-back atmospheres add to your meal experience in the restaurants around Barrio Bellavista and Barrio Brazil. Many *locales* with live music charge an entrance fee and require reservations on Friday and Saturday nights.

On the east end of town, elegant restaurants accompany expensive hotels. In Providencia and Las Condes neighborhoods, the high-end restaurants offer top-notch Italian cuisine, fish and seafood. Don't underestimate some restaurants' classy air, either. At one hot spot you can sample delicious duck from atop a revolving 16th floor. The eastern sections of town also have French, Thai, Chinese and contemporary restaurants. For those with less tolerant stomachs, many of Chile's sit-down franchises, such as Tip y Tap, Buffalo and Cuernavaca, offer standard sandwiches for reasonable prices, such as a large beef sandwich with French fries and a pint of Escudo, a national beer. McDonalds, Burger King and other fast-food restaurants are also available in most commercial areas. Updated: Apr 20, 2009.

Nightlife

Travelers generally find whatever type of entertainment they're looking for amid the nightlife in Santiago. There are plenty of hole-in-the-wall bars with live music by unknown local musicians, an abundance of packed dance floors offering over-played pop beats in Barrio Bellavista or laid-back watering holes in the bohemian neighborhood of Ñuñoa. Updated: Mar 10, 2009.

Santiago Centro

Barrio Santiago Centro is the historical part of the city and is full of tourist attractions, including Cerro Santa Lucia, National Library, Plaza de la Constitución, La Moneda, Plaza de Armas, Museo Precolombino, Palacio de la Real Audiencia, Catedral Metropolitana and Museo Histórico Nacional. The area is easy to navigate and it's possible to explore it in one day. Tourists are well catered to, and it's easy to find hotels and restaurants. Foodies will love the Mercado Central (fish market) and La Vega (fruit and vegetable market).

If you have a bit more time to spend in the city center, you'll notice that despite the historical buildings and impressive plazas, this is the home of the working class. You can find some department stores and there's Mall de Centro on Puente 689, but with numerous discount stores and market stalls, Santiago Centro is more of a bargain hunters' shopping paradise than Rodeo Drive.

Adventurous explorers might be tempted to try a coffee in one of the infamous Cafes con piernas (coffee shops with waitresses in miniskirts). Some are touristy and fairly wholesome, something like Hooter's. Others, identifiable only by their blackened windows and low thumping music, are little more than strip clubs that serve coffee.

Santiago Centro is a good base if you want to make a whistle-stop tour of the city. However, it can be a bit scary after dark and tourists should be careful with their belongings. If you plan to stay in Santiago for a few days, it's probably better to stay in Bella Vista or Providencia where the nightlife is better. Updated: Apr 20, 2009.

Things to See and Do

Museo Chileno de Arte Precolumbino

This museum, specializing in pre-Columbian Chile, is one of the country's best. Located in an elegant white building in the center of Santiago, the museum is a journey through time. It displays a range of ceramics, textiles, artwork, and eating and drinking vessels of the ancient inhabitants of Chile and Central and South America that date back some 4,500 years before the arrival of Columbus. Highlights include the Chinchorroc mummies and ceremonial tablets. The museum is closed on Mondays. Bandera 361. Closest Metro: Plaza de Armas. Tel: 56-2-6887348, URL: www.precolombino.cl. Open 9 a.m. – 6 p.m. Closed Monday. Updated: Jul 07, 2009.

Mercado Central

A major fixture in Chilean society, the Mercado Central may be touristy, but rest assured that the tourists are visiting for good reason. Located in a lovely steel art nouveau building, it has much more ambiance than many markets in Latin America.

The major product sold in this market is seafood, in particular fresh fish. The aisles are lined and piled with stacks of fish, filleted fish and whole fish, big fish and small fish...a veritable Dr. Seussian display of fish. The many restaurants in and nearby the market allow visitors to sample what they see. Mercado Central is a great place to take a sense-assaulting morning stroll, then catch lunch before heading off to another site in Santiago. Ismael Valdes Vergara and Av. 21 de Mayo. Open 7 a.m. – 3 p.m. Updated: Jul 07, 2009.

V!VA ONLINE REVIEW
MERCADO CENTRAL

Very wonderful—it was oozing with authenticity!

June 16, 2009

Plaza de Armas

The Plaza de Armas dates back to 1541 when Pedro de Valdivia founded Santiago. The square was used as an army training ground, with a protected area in the middle that was used to store arms. The Spanish later built important religious and civic buildings in the surrounding area, including the Cathedral Metropolitana (1745), Municipalidad de Santiago (1785), the Palacio de la Real Audiencia (1804) and the Correo Central (1882). The plaza has been badly damaged several times by earthquakes and was last remodeled in 1999.

Today, the Plaza de Armas is a big draw for tourists who want to soak up the sun as well as some of Santiago's past and current culture. There are several sidewalk cafes and the area attracts artists and street entertainers. Plaza de Armas 444. Updated: Nov 13, 2008.

Palacio de la Moneda

The Palacio de la Moneda was originally the National Mint of Chile. Designed by Italian architect Joaquin Toesca at the end of the 18th century, it's now viewed as one of the best examples of neoclassical architecture in Latin America, and easily ranks as one of the most beautiful buildings in the city.

La Moneda served as the official presidential residence from 1846 until 1958. On 11 September 1973, Pinochet's troops bombed the palace until President Allende surrendered and committed suicide. The palace was almost destroyed by fire and was rebuilt during Pinochet's military dictatorship. Today, Palacio de la Moneda is used as presidential offices. Tourists can enter the courtyard that runs through the middle of the building. On alternate days, there is a changing of the guard ceremony at 10 a.m. Ca. Morandé 130/Av. Bernardo O'Higgins (Alameda)/Ca. Teatinos. Closest Metro: La Moneda. Tel: 56-2-6904000, Updated: Oct 17, 2008.

Catedral Metropolitana

The Cathedral Metropolitana, also known as the Catedral de Santiago, sits on the west side of the Plaza de Armas and stretches for almost a block. There have been five cathedrals on the site, but the previous structures were destroyed by earthquakes. The present building was begun in 1745 and completed in 1780. The work was overseen by Joaquin Toesca, the same architect who designed Palacio de La Moneda. Throughout the years the cathedral has undergone continuous

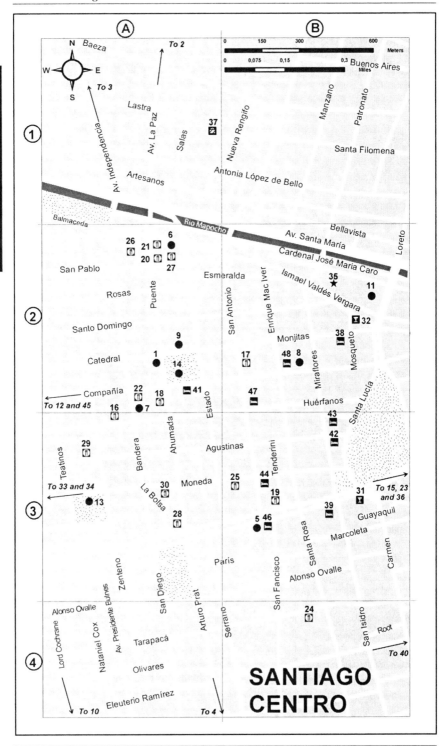

Activities ●

1 Catedral Metropolitana A2
2 Cementerio General A1
3 Hipódromo A1
4 Iglesia de los Sacramentinos A4
5 Iglesia, Convento y Museo de San
   Francisco B3
6 Mercado Central A2
7 Museo de Arte Precolombino A2
8 Museo de Santiago B2
9 Museo Histórico Nacional A2
10 Palacio Cousiño A4
11 Palacio de Bellas Artes / Museo de Bellas
   Artes/ Centro de Arte Contemporáneo B2
12 Palacio de la Alhambra A2
13 Palacio de la Moneda A3
14 Plaza de Armas A2
15 Plaza Italia B3

Eating 🍴

16 Bar Nacional A3
17 Big Planet B2
18 Bravíssimo A2
19 Da Dino B3
20 Doña Camila A2
21 Donde Augusto A2
22 El Rápido A2
23 Japón B3
24 La Habana Vieja B4
25 La Naturista B3
26 La Piojera A2

27 Richard - El Rey del Mar A2
28 Schopdog A3
29 Subway A3
30 Unión Bar A3

Nightlife 🍸

31 777 B3
32 El Túnel B2
33 Laberinto A3
34 La Chimenea A3

Services ★

35 Escuela Newen A2
36 VE Global B3

Shopping 🛍

37 La Vega Central A1

Sleeping 🛏

38 Andes Hostel B2
39 Caesar Business Hotel B3
40 Eco Hostel B4
41 Hostal Plaza de Armas A2
42 Hostal Santa Lucía B3
43 Hotel Carlton House B3
44 Hotel Galerías B3
45 Hotel Panamericano A2
46 Hotel Plaza San Francisco B3
47 Santa Lucía Hotel B2
48 Santiago Apartments B2

SANTIAGO

work and refurbishments. The two towers were only added in the late 19th century. The ornate façade now features intricate baroque and classical designs and the interior is beautifully decorated. It's worth a quick look if you are in the area. Plaza de Armas. Updated: Nov 13, 2008.

Cementerio General

Cementerio General, Santiago's most famous cemetery, was established in 1820 by Bernardo O'Higgins. All of Chile's Presidents are buried in here, except for Gabriel González Videla and Augusto Pinochet. One of the most visited graves is that of former President Salvador Allende. He was originally buried in Viña del Mar, but in the 1990s his body was exhumed and he was given a ceremonial burial in Cementerio General. The cemetery also has a memorial to the thousands who "disappeared" under Pinochet's regime.

The cemetery covers an area of more than 85 hectares in downton Recoleta. The lovely landscaped gardens are filled with numerous sculptures and ostentatious mausoleums.

Photo by Kyle Adams

Av. La Paz and Profesor Alberto Zañartu 951. Closest metro: Cerro Blanco. Tel: 56-2-7379469. Updated: Oct 30, 2008.

Iglesia, Convento y Museo de San Francisco

(ADMISSION: $1) This church is one of the oldest buildings in Chile, built between 1586 and 1628. However, due to earthquakes, it has been restored several times throughout the years. There is a museum on-site that covers the history of the church—interesting, but probably only for die-hard church historians. Most people will find a walk through the church satisfactory. Av. Bernardo O'Higgins. Tel: 56-2-6383238. Open Tuesday – Saturday, 10 a.m. – 1 p.m.; Sundays 3 – 6 p.m.; holidays 10 a.m.– 2 p.m. Updated: May 30, 2007.

Museo Histórico Nacional

(ADMISSION: $0.80 adults, $0.50 children under 18; free Sunday and holidays) This site, originally constructed in 1807, is a must-see. Although it has been remodeled some, the original splendor is still very visible. At one time, when the Spaniards still ruled Chile, the Palacio was the site of the Supreme Court. Later, the first Chilean congressional session was held here following the country's independence. Today, the Palacio holds the National History Museum, with over 70,000 artifacts. The museum also has a comprehensive exhibit on the history of Chile. Plaza de Armas 951. Tel: 56-2-6381411. Open 10 a.m. – 5:30 p.m. Closed Monday. Updated: May 10, 2007.

Palacio de Bellas Artes / Museo de Arte Contemporáneo

(ADMISSION: $1.20) Founded in 1880, The Museo Nacional de Bellas Artes (National Fine Arts Museum) is an essential stop for art-lovers. It's housed in the Palacio de Bellas Artes, which was designed by Emilio Jéquier in the style of Paris's Petit Palais. Neoclassical, with art nouveau features, it was declared a national monument in 1976. The museum has a permanent collection of paintings and sculptures by European and Chilean artists and regularly hosts exhibits by contemporary international artists.

The Museo de Arte Contemporáneo, on the other side of the building, is run by the art faculty of the Universidad de Chile. It holds a collection of modern photography, sculpture, and web art displays.

If you only have time to visit one museum or art gallery, go to Bellas Artes. Parque Forestal, Casilla 3209. Tel: 56-2-6330655, URL: www.dibam.cl/bellas_artes. Open 10 a.m. – 7 p.m. Closed Monday. Updated: Jul 07, 2009.

Museo de Santiago

(ADMISSION: $1 adults, $0.40 children; free Sundays) The Museo de Santiago is located just off the Plaza de Armas in Casa Colorada, an 18th century colonial mansion. The house, now a national monument, was built in 1769 and is one of the few remaining examples of a pre-colonial home in the city. Inside, the museum exhibits a collection of ceramics, letters, costumes, carriages, photos, maps and models that chart the history of Santiago from pre-Columbian times to the establishment of the Republic.

Some of the displays look a bit like school art projects, but if you're interested in the history of the city it's worth checking out. The museum is generally packed with tourists and school children. Ca. Merced 680. Closest Metro: Plaza de Armas. Tel: 56-2-6330723, URL: www.munistgo.cl/colorada/p1.htm. Open Tuesday through Friday, 10 a.m. – 6 a.m.; Saturday 10 a.m. – 5 a.m.; Sunday 11 a.m. – 2 a.m.; closed Monday. Updated: Nov 13, 2008.

Iglesia de los Sacramentinos

The huge Iglesia de los Sacramentinos (The Church of the Blessed Sacrament) overlooks Parque Diego de Almagro and makes for a good photo opportunity. Work started on the Roman Byzantine basilica in 1912 under the command of architect Ricardo Larrain Bravo and was completed in 1931. The church was declared a national monument in 1991. Iglesia de los Sacramentinos is a copy of the Sacre Coéur, but lacks the splendid location of its Parisian rival. Corner of Arturo Prat and Santa Isabel. Closest Metro: Santa Isabel, URL: www.sacramentinos.cl. Updated: Oct 30, 2008.

Plaza Italia

Plaza Italia is literally the center of downtown Santiago. It's a meeting point for people from all over the city and is where Santiaguinos gather to support national sporting events or make political protests. The plaza is quite inappropriately named, since it's actually not a plaza but more of a huge road junction with very little pedestrian access. The only reason a tourist would come here is to cross the river to get to the bars and restaurants in Bellavista. Closest metro: Baquedano. Updated: Jul 08, 2009.

Palacio de la Alhambra

Palacio de la Alhambra is a Moorish style palace designed and built by Manuel Aldunate between 1860 and 1862. Like most of Santiago's architecture from this period, it was heavily influenced by European style. In this case, the original Palacio de la Alhambra in Granada provided inspiration, right down to the complete replica of the lion water fountain.

The palace was at various times used as a family home and a fortress, but is currently the headquarters of the National Society of Fine Arts. It was declared a national monument in 1973 and hosts regular fine art exhibitions. Ca. Compañía 1340. Closest metro: Santa Ana or Plaza de Armas. Tel: 56-2-6980875. URL: www.snba.cl, Updated: Oct 30, 2008.

Palacio Cousiño

(ADMISSION: $4, with guided tour in English) Palacio Cousiño was built between 1870 and 1878 by French architect Paul Lathoud. It was originally the family home of Santiago's richest family, the Cousiño-Goyenecheas, who made their fortune from coal and silver mines and the Cousiño-Macul Vineyard, which they still own.

In 1940, the property and all its fabulous contents were bought by the city of Santiago. It was then used as a residence for famous visitors to the city. In 1968, a fire destroyed most of the second floor, but the rest of the palace remains perfectly intact. It was opened as a museum in 1977 and declared a national monument in 1981.

The palace has a ballroom, music room, reception room, dining room, great hall, weapons room, picture gallery and the first elevators in Chile. It's filled with the finest handcrafted furniture, most of which was imported from Europe. Ca. Dieciocho 438. Closest metro: Toesca. Tel: 56-2-6985063, URL: www.palaciocousino.co.cl. Open Tuesday to Friday, 9:30 a.m. – 1:30 p.m. and 2:30 p.m. – 5:30 p.m.; Saturdays and Sundays 9:30 a.m. – 1:30 p.m. Closed Monday. Updated: Oct 30, 2008.

Museo Interactivo Mirador

(ADMISSION: $6 adults, $4 children; for an extra $3 you can also visit the main aquarium in Santiago) The Museo Interactivo Mirador (MIM), or The Children's Interactive Museum of Science, opened in 2000 and quickly became Chile's busiest museum. The exhibition rooms include Earth, Mind and Brain, Energy, Light, Try Yourself, Liquids, Perception and Electromagnetism. Children are encouraged to touch, feel and experiment with the exhibits. There are two entrances to the museum, one at Punta Arenas 6711 and the other at Calle Sebastopol 90. Get the metro to Mirador, Line 5. From there you can get a *colectivo*, or shared taxi, to the museum. Tel: 56-2-2807800, URL: www.mim.cl. Open Monday 9:30 a.m. – 1 p.m.; Tuesday to Sunday 9:30 a.m. – 6:30 p.m. Updated: Jul 07, 2009.

Hipódromo

Founded in 1904, the Hipódromo is the other horse racing track in Santiago. Live racing takes place on Saturdays and Thursdays. Located in Independencia, it isn't as romantic a location as Club Hípico, but many punters prefer the dirt track. Av. Hipódromo 1715. Tel: 56-2-2709237, URL: www.hipodromo.cl. Updated: Oct 30, 2008.

Shopping

La Vega Central

La Vega is one of Santiago's biggest and oldest fruit and vegetable markets. It's housed inside two huge warehouses: Grande and Pequeña. Head for Grande, since it has a bigger selection of food. Here you'll find the best fruit and vegetables in the city. The market is busy and crowded, so be careful with your wallet. There are also a number of cheap cafes inside. They aren't pretty, but are definitely worth a try. You can eat a tasty traditional Chilean lunch for around $3. Metro to Puente Cal and Canto and across the river. Open 9 a.m. – 5 p.m. Updated: Nov 13, 2008.

Avenida Providencia and Avenida 11 de Septiembre

If you can't face the crowds in the mall, take the metro to Los Leones. Avenidas Providencia and 11 de Septiembre are home to department stores, such as Falabella and Paris, and small but funky shopping malls including Drugstore and Mall Panoramico. There are several independent stores for clothes, household goods, shoes and electronics. You can buy virtually everything you might need within a two-block area. Closest metro: Los Leones. Open 10 a.m. – 7 p.m. Closed Sunday. Updated: Nov 03, 2008.

Persa Bío Bío

Everyday things are sold at Persa Bío Bío, like furniture, clothes, electrical goods, household items, CDs, bikes, construction tools and antiques. It's in a fairly run down neighborhood and there is a higher chance of being pickpocketed, but a visit to Bío Bío will give you an opportunity to see the real Santiago. Closest metro: Franklin. Open Hours 10 a.m. – 6 p.m. Updated: Nov 13, 2008.

Lodging

The hotels in the downtown area cater primarily to business travelers who have meetings in one of the many office buildings in the neighborhood. Most of the hotels are upscale and offer modern facilities and services; it is not uncommon to find rooftop pools, on-site restaurants, business centers and highly trained professional staff. Leisure travelers will enjoy the extras at these hotels if they have the budget. A few lower-priced options, such as hostels, can be found with a little effort. Staying near the Plaza de Armas is very convenient for history- and museum-lovers. Updated: Apr 20, 2009.

BUDGET

Eco Hostel

(ROOMS: $11 – 33, includes breakfast) This hostel prides itself on being eco-friendly, evidenced primarily by its recycling system. The hostel offers both private and communal rooms. Luggage storage, Internet use and a laundry service, along with reliable hot water, make life easier for the weary backpacker. Helpful English-, German- and Spanish-speaking staff offer tourist information and guided tour services. If you're looking to be sociable and meet other travelers, this is a good place to be. Each week, the hostel holds a BBQ for their guests. General Jofre 349b. Tel: 56-5-2226833, E-mail: info@ecohostel.cl, URL: www.ecohostel.cl. Updated: Jul 10, 2008.

Hostal Santa Lucia

(ROOMS: $14 and up) Hostal Santa Lucia is right in the heart of the city, just a stone's throw away from Cerro Santa Lucia and also within easy reach of Barrios Brazil, Lastarria and Santiago Centro. This cozy hostel caters to all backpackers' needs and has a living room and terrace with spectacular views. Staff is really helpful and will advise you on everything from sightseeing to the best restaurants and bars in town. Breakfast and Internet are

included. Av. Santa Lucia 168. Closest metro: Santa Ana. Tel: 56-2-6648478, E-mail: info@ hostalsantalucia.cl, URL: www.hostalsantalucia.cl. Updated: Apr 21, 2009.

Hostel Plaza de Armas

(ROOMS: $15 and up) Centrally located in the historic Plaza de Armas, as the name indicates, this hostel occupies the sixth floor and has great views of the activity below. The design of the common areas is very posh with wood floors, high ceilings and glass balcony doors. There are dorms and private rooms; all include a full breakfast. There is a washer/dryer, a fully equipped kitchen, free Internet access and lockers available (outside the rooms). The only downside is that the open floor plan—none of the rooms have individual ceilings—may cause a lot of noise issues. Compañia 960, apt. 607. Tel: 56-2-6714436, E-mail: hostel@plazadearmashostel.com, URL: www.plazadearmashostel.com. Updated: Jan 06, 2009.

Andes Hostel

(ROOMS: $17 and up) Andes Hostel is trying really hard to be the coolest hostel in Santiago—and doing a pretty good job of it. The hostel is modern and funky and has a living room, terrace, bar, pool table, pinball machine and free Internet. The atmosphere is friendly and travelers are encouraged to join in with the weekly BBQs and parties. If you can drag yourself away from the hostel, Bella Artes and Lastarria are within walking distance. Monjitas 506. Closest metro: Bellas Artes. Tel: 56-2-6329990, URL: www.andeshostel.com. Updated: Apr 20, 2009.

MID-RANGE

Hotel Carlton House

(ROOMS: $42 single, $51 double; apartment for one person $55, apartment for two – four people $63) Hotel Carlton House is a three-star hotel-cum-restaurant right in the center of town. There are single and double rooms available as well as self-catering apartments. All rooms have private bathrooms, security box, telephone and cable TV. Business travelers can also use the conference facilities. The staff will help you arrange city tours, airport transfers and advise you on good places to eat. The décor is a bit old-fashioned, but rooms are comfortable and clean. Máximo Humbser 574. Closest metro: Santa Lucia. Tel: 56-2-6383130, URL: www.hotelcarlton.cl. Updated: Apr 21, 2009.

Santa Lucia Hotel

(ROOMS: $54 single, $63 double) Just one block from the Plaza de Armas, the Santa Lucia is a two-star tourist hotel on the fourth floor of an office building. It is excellent value for money and perfect for budget travelers who can't face staying in a hostel. Continental breakfast is included in the price but is only served until 9:30 a.m. The reception staff speaks English and is very friendly. San Antonio 327. Closest metro: Plaza de Armas, Tel: 56-2-6398201, URL: www.hotelsantalucia.cl. Updated: Apr 21, 2009.

Santiago Apartments

(ROOMS: $60, one-/two-person apartment; $70 three-/four-person apartment) Santiago Apartments provide self-catering apartments for one to four people, offering a cheap alternative to a hotel. Apartments are clean and comfortable and have one bedroom, a kitchen, living/dining area and bathroom. All are equipped with WiFi, cable TV, microwave and fridge. There's also laundry and maid services, and 24-hour security at the front door. The apartments are comfortable for two people but can be a bit cramped with four. Merced 691, Closest metro: Bellas Artes / Santa Lucia. Tel: 56-2-6399454, E-mail: departamentos@adsl.tie.cl, URL: www.santiagodepartamentos.cl. Updated: Apr 21, 2009.

Caesar Business Hotel

(ROOMS: $110 double) Santiago's version of the Caesar Hotel is a four-star modern tower block close to Cerro Santa Lucia. While it doesn't have too much in the way of personality, the Caesar is modern, clean and comfortable. The hotel has a gym, outdoor swimming pool (only open in summer), restaurant, bar and meeting rooms. Rooms have private bathrooms, satellite TVs, minibars and hairdryers. The price includes a buffet breakfast, but you have to pay extra for Internet and WiFi. The Caesar is a good choice for business travelers, couples and those who want to spend a little more for a few home comforts. Alameda Libertador Bernardo O'Higgins 632. Closest metro: Santa Lucia. Tel: 56-2-5956622, URL: www.caesarbusiness.com. Updated: Apr 21, 2009.

Hotel Panamericano

(ROOMS: $90 single, $120 double) Hotel Panamericano, just a few blocks from La Moneda in downtown Santiago, has 145 bedrooms equipped with LCD cable TVs, minibars, private bathrooms, security boxes, telephones and hairdryers, as well as free Internet access. There's also a restaurant that serves a $10 daily set lunch menu. If you can stretch your budget a little bit further there are much better hotels available nearby. Teatinos 320. Closest metro: La Moneda. Tel: 56-2-6723060, E-mail: contacto@hotelamericano.cl, URL: www.hotelpanamericano.cl. Updated: Apr 21, 2009.

HIGH-END

Majestic Hotel

(ROOMS: singles from $100, doubles from $110) The Majestic Hotel is part of the Best Western group and offers upper-range accommodation a few minutes from the city center. Rooms have private bathrooms and cable TV and are comfortable but not luxurious. The hotel has a very good Indian restaurant and a small outdoor swimming pool and garden. There's a buffet breakfast and guests can use the Internet in the reception area. There's no elevator so it isn't suitable for people with physical disabilities. Santa Domingo 1526. Tel: 56-2-6909400, URL: www.hotelmajestic.cl. Updated: Apr 21, 2009.

Hotel Plaza San Francisco

(ROOMS: $125 single, $135 double; special offers available online) Hotel Plaza San Francisco is a luxurious hotel close to Cerro Santa Lucia and Santiago Centro. The hotel has an award-winning *haute* cuisine restaurant, bar, gym, swimming pool, sauna, spa and business center. Helpful staff can arrange tours and airport transfers. Rooms have recently been refurbished and come with private bathrooms, cable TVs and safes. This hotel is a good value and is perfect for business travelers, or those on a romantic break or family holiday. WiFi costs extra. Alameda 816. Closest metro: Santa Lucia. Tel: 56-2-3604445, URL: www.plazasanfrancisco.cl. Updated: Apr 21, 2009.

Hotel Galerias

(ROOMS: $132 single, $143 double; special offers available online) Hotel Galerias is a four-star modern hotel located in the financial district of Santiago Centro. You'll recognize it by the fake Easter Island statues at the front door. Despite the slightly tacky entrance, the hotel has plenty to offer, with a restaurant, bar, nightclub, outdoor swimming pool and spa. Rooms are spacious and include private bathrooms, minibars, safes, hairdryers and cable TVs. The price includes a continental breakfast but guests are charged for Internet access. Staff is friendly and will help you arrange tours and airport pick-ups. San Antonio 65. Closest metro: Santa Lucia. Tel: 56-2-4707400, URL: www.hotelgalerias.cl. Updated: Apr 21, 2009.

Restaurants

At first impression, the restaurants in Santiago Centro appear to be nothing more than a collection of greasy spoons shoveling out French fries, *completos* (hotdogs) and beer. There are plenty of these so-called 'restaurants' serving up heart attacks on a plate as the daily lunch special. However, on closer investigation, you'll find that Santiago Centro is also home to a few culinary wonders.

Don't miss the local fish and seafood market, Mercado Central, which is heaving with tourist-friendly restaurants. Another well-kept secret is La Vega, the local fruit and vegetable market. Restaurants here are basic, and cater to locals rather than tourists, but you can eat some of the best traditional Chilean food for as little as $4. For fine dining you'll have to look a bit harder, but there are some quality restaurants, especially on Merced. For people-watching, you can't beat the slightly overpriced eateries around the Plaza de Armas. Updated: Apr 20, 2009.

Starlight Coffee

When you are looking for a good cup of coffee in the downtown area of Santiago, check out Starlight Coffee. The warm, artsy interior with its designer lighting invites you to grab a barstool and relax, while table seating is offered just outside. The menu lists seemingly every type of coffee imaginable, including a house blend. The cafe offers a small selection of pastries, sandwiches and salads. Even non-coffee drinkers will enjoy the tea or hot chocolate—perhaps with a decadent American-style chocolate-filled doughnut. Starlight is a great alternative to the crowded Starbucks. Tenderini 143. Tel: 56-2-3909707. Open Monday – Friday 7 a.m. – 9 p.m. Saturday 9 a.m. – 7 p.m. Updated: Jan 06, 2009.

Bravissimo

If you can stand the day-glow green and yellow décor and the painfully slow service, Bravissimo is a good place to get a fix of all things sweet and sugary. The restaurant has a very tempting range of ice creams, cakes and desserts. They also serve pretty tasty salads and sandwiches. There are seats available on the street, if you like to people-watch, or inside, if you prefer the shade. Ahumada 311. Closest metro: Plaza de Armas. Tel: 56-2-4665077, URL: www.bravissimo.cl. Updated: Jul 01, 2009.

El Rapido

(ENTREE: $2 and up) Right next to the Museo Pre-Columbino, El Rapido is a fast-food bar that serves up delicious empanadas and hot sandwiches at low prices. There's no seating area, but you can eat at the breakfast bar or take the food to go. Meat-lovers should try the *pino* empanadas, filled with beef, onions, olives and egg, while vegetarians should stick to the cheese empanadas. Bandera 371. Closest metro: Plaza de Armas. Updated: Apr 21, 2009.

Big Planet

(EMPANADA: $2 and up) Big Planet is a fast-food joint that specializes in tasty empanadas named after planets. There are over 20 flavors to choose from, including: prawns and cheese, crab and cheese, meat, seafood, cheese and pineapple, cheese and tomato, chicken and cheese. This is a great place to make a pit stop and fill up while sightseeing. Delivery service is available so you can have empanadas delivered directly to your hostel. San Antonio 431. Closest metro: Plaza de Armas. Open Monday – Friday 10 a.m. – 8:30 p.m. and Saturday 11 a.m. – 3 p.m. Tel: 56-2-639 8475. Updated: Jun 18, 2009.

Subway

(ENTREES: $4 – 7) South America is littered with fast-food restaurants, including most of the American franchises, such as McDonald's and Burger King. Santiago's branch of the popular sandwich chain, Subway, is on Plaza Constitucion, right on the tourist trail, and after seeing the familiar logo you may find it hard to resist grabbing a footlong. The prices are in line with Western countries, thus expensive for South America, but if you feel like you deserve a bready treat, this is the place to go. Agustinas 1235 (On Plaza de la Constitucion). Open 8 a.m – 9 p.m. Updated: Jun 10, 2009.

Schopdog

(SANDWICHES: $5) Schopdog is the Chilean version of Burger King, but without the plastic. It's a chain of 1950's American-themed diners that serves up generous servings of rock 'n' roll with Chilean fast food. Choose from hot sandwiches, completos, empanadas or *chorrillana*, a huge plate of French fries with steak, fried egg and fried onions. The bar serves soft drinks and beer. Ahumada 37. Closest metro: Universidad de Chile, URL: www.schopdog.cl. Updated: Apr 21, 2009.

La Piojera

(ENTREES: $5 and up) Just a few steps from Mercado Central, La Piojera (the flea) is one of the most infamous bars in Santiago. It's been around for almost 100 years and got its name when a local nobleman left the place in disgust, saying it was full of fleas. La Piojera is still a dive, and serves mediocre Chilean food, but people come here in droves for the lively atmosphere and impromptu sing-a-longs. Don't leave without trying a *ter-remoto*, a mixture of sweet white wine and ice cream. This is not the safest area in the city, so you're better off visiting the bar during the day. Aillavilú 1030. Closest metro: Puente Cal y Canto, URL: www.lapiojera.cl. Updated: Apr 21, 2009.

Unión Bar

(ENTREES: $6 and up) The Unión Bar is an old-fashioned, old man's bar in downtown Santiago which provides a glimpse of the real Santiago. Union is usually packed with locals playing dominos and catching up on gossip. Service is slow, but you'll be too busy people-watching to be bothered by time. Try the *arrollado* (spicy pork) or *lomito* (beef) sandwich washed down with a Schop beer. Closed Sunday afternoons. Nueva York 11. Closest metro: Universidad de Chile. Tel: 56-2-696 1821. Updated: Apr 21, 2009.

Richard—El Rey del Mar

(ENTREES: $7 and up) Richard, the self-appointed King of Fish, has been serving up fresh and tasty seafood dishes for years. Situated in a corner of Mercado Central, Richard's is a firm favorite among locals who want to enjoy good food without paying tourist prices. Seating is available on the ground floor and on a first-floor terrace that has great views of the market. Don't take a seat above the kitchen as it gets very warm, especially in the summer. Mercado Central. Closest metro: Puente Cal y Canto. Updated: Apr 21, 2009.

Bar Nacional

(ENTREES: $7 – 11; SANDWICHES: $3 – 4) This diner-style establishment is extremely popular with locals who come for its reliably good food and to watch soccer matches. There are two dining areas: one at street level, with a bar; and a smaller room downstairs. A page of the leather-bound menu is in English for easy ordering. The wait-staff is attentive, without being bothersome, and they don't mind if you remain at the table after your meal. If you want a drink, try the Ponche Vino y Chirimoya, a tasty wine and fruit mixture. Huérfanos 1151. Tel: 56-2-6965986. Updated: Jan 06, 2009.

Da Dino

(PIZZA: $7 – 15) Serving up delicious pizza, Da Dino is guaranteed to put a smile on even the weariest traveler's face. The restaurant cooks each pizza to order, and each slice is loaded with fresh toppings. Service is efficient, but this place is always busy at lunchtime so be prepared to wait a bit while sipping your soft drink or beer. Avenida Bernardo O'Higgins 737. Closest metro: Santa Lucia. Tel: 56-2-6381833. Updated: Apr 21, 2009.

Donde Augusto

(ENTREES: $8 and up) Donde Augusto is the biggest tourist trap in Mercado Central, but it's a trap you may be happy to stay in for a couple of hours. The restaurant offers a good range of fish, seafood and meat dishes accompanied by rice, salads and/or French fries. Service can be slow, but the food is worth the wait and the staff is more attentive if they think they are going to get a big tip. If you have spare cash, try the giant spider crab, a Chilean speciality that costs $100. Mercado Central. Closest metro: Puente Cal y Canto. Updated: Apr 21, 2009.

La Naturista

(ENTREES: $10) Since Chilean cuisine usually involves meat or fish, finding good vegetarian food can be a struggle. La Naturista is one of the rare places providing cheap and tasty veggie salads, pastas and snacks. But it isn't anything to write home about, and hardcore vegeterians can probably cook more imaginative meals themselves. As La Naturista caters to the work crowd, this place is very busy at lunchtime. Closed on Sundays. Moneda 846. Closest metro: Universidad de Chile / Santa Lucia. Tel: 56-2-3905940. Updated: Apr 21, 2009.

Doña Camila

(ENTREES: $10 – 12) You can't visit Chile without trying the fish. Locals buy and eat their favorite seafood at the Mercado Central, where it's easy to feel overwhelmed by the many dining options. Doña Camila is one choice that will not disappoint. The eatery is clean, friendly, bright and inviting. Waiters are knowledgeable about wines, but be sure to verify costs as the drink prices are not on the menu. Mercado Central Local 80 Ismael Valdés Vergara 960. Tel: 56-2-6967657. Updated: Jun 10, 2008. Updated: Nov 13, 2008.

Japón

(ENTREES: $15 – 60) Established in 1978, Japón is Santiago's original Japanese restaurant. The menu includes a mouthwatering range of sushi, sashimi, tempura and gyoza. You can sit at a private table but it's better to try for a seat at the bar and watch the Japanese chef go to work. Service is good and the waiters will advise you on the best drinks to accompany your meal. Japón is expensive but not overpriced, and the food is prepared with high quality ingredients. It's perfect for a celebration or a romantic night out. Barón Pierre de Coubertin (Ex Marcoleta) 39. Closest metro: Baquedano. Tel: 56-2-2224517. Updated: Apr 21, 2009.

La Habana Vieja

(ENTREE: $20 and up; COVER: $3.50) La Habana Vieja is a lively Cuban restaurant with traditional Cuban music and dancing. The menu includes favorites like *frijoles negros* (black beans), *ropa vieja* (beef cooked in Creole sauce) and *lechon asado* (spit-roast pork), as well as a range of appetizers and salads. There's a full bar that serves some seriously strong rum cocktails to get you into a dancing mood. Live music on the weekends. Reservations are recommended. Tarapacá 755. Closest metro: Santa Lucia. Tel: (56-2) 638 5284, E-mail: info@lahabanavieja.cl, URL: www.lahabanavieja.cl. Open Tuesday through Thursday 7:30 p.m. – 1 a.m.; Friday and Saturday 7:30 p.m. – 3 a.m. Updated: Jun 18, 2009.

Nightlife

La Chimenea

La Chimena is a cool, trendy little place tucked into a quiet back alley and conveniently located near Palacio la Moneda. The distinctive bar has a small stage for impressive local acts to jam most evenings. Relax with a Pisco sour and revel in the fact that you are in a pure Chilean bar while the rest of the gringos congregate at some cookie-cutter Irish pub. Closed Sundays. Principe de Gales 90. Tel: 56-2-6970131 / 6979935, URL: www.lachimenea.cl. Updated: Apr 22, 2009.

777

This is probably not the most comfortable place to drink for gringos over 25. It is truly a youthful scene where beer crates double as seats and the majority of the college-aged patrons don red-streaked hair or heavy metal T-shirts. But the beer is cheap, so if you're feeling carefree swing in for a few cold ones. Alameda 777. Updated: Apr 22, 2009.

El Tunel

Miss the 1970s? Out of nostalgia or because you weren't born yet? Either way, El Tunel provides the blast from the past you've been craving. The disc jockeys spin classics from more than 30 years ago for club-goers who want to try out their disco moves. Sometimes a few songs from the 1980s are mixed in to appease those sporting Flock of Seagulls haircuts. Santo Domingo 439. Updated: Apr 22, 2009.

Laberinto

(COVER: $15) A crowd of Santiago's hippest and stylish often gathers at this club in Ñuñoa. Laberinto has several dance floors with varying sounds such as indie, rock, techno or house music. While it is the cool place to be, entrance is not cheap. Vicuña Mackenna 915. Updated: Apr 22, 2009.

Barrio Lastarria

Barrio Lastarria is a bohemian and historical quarter close to downtown Santiago. Think historical buildings, theaters, art galleries, funky shops and lively cafes and restaurants. The neighborhood is very small and can easily be covered in a few hours. Most spots of interest can be found along Calles Merced, Monjitas and José Victorino Lastarria (a pedestrian area that has a flea market from Thursday to Saturday). Updated: Jul 07, 2009.

Things to See and Do

Museo de Artes Visuales (MAVI)

(ADMISSION: $2 adults, $1 children; includes entrance to the Museo Arqueológico; Free Sunday) The Museo de Artes Visuales (MAVI) opened in 2001. The permanent collection has more than 1,400 examples of modern Chilean art by more than 400 artists. The work includes paintings, sculptures, engravings, photography and drawings from the 1960s onwards. There are also regular exhibitions by major Chilean artists.

Guided tours are available from Tuesday to Friday, but you must contact the museum in advance. Alternatively, tours run for the general public on Saturdays at 4 p.m. Open 10:30 a.m. – 6:30 p.m. Closed

Activities ●
1 Cerro Santa Lucía A2
2 Museo Arqueológico B1
3 Museo de Artes Visuales (see 2)

Eating 🍽
4 Café Subté B1
5 Don Victorino B1
6 El Diablito B1
7 Les Assassins B1
8 Living de Té B1
9 Squadritto B2

Shopping 🛍
10 Feria de Santa Lucía A2

Sleeping 🛏
11 Hotel Foresta A1
12 Hotel Montecarlo Santiago A2
13 Lastarria Tourist Apartments B2
14 Suites and Apartments Barrio
     Lastarria B2
15 Windsor Suites Hotel A2

Monday. José Victorino Lastarria 307, Plaza Mulato Gil de Castro,.Closest metro: Universidad Católica / Bellas Artes. Tel: 56-2-6383502, URL: www.mavi.cl, E-mail: educación@mavi.cl. Updated: Nov 13, 2008.

Museo Arqueológico (MAS)
(ADMISSION: $2; free Sunday; free with admission to MAVI) The Museo Arqueológico (MAS) is located next to the Museo de Artes Visuales (MAVI) in Barrio Lastarria. The museum has a collection of textiles, ceramics, jewelry, indigenous carvings and everyday artifacts from the pre-Columbian era. Highlights include the Chinchorro mummy and the tablets used by religious leaders to sniff hallucinogenic drugs. The museum is small and everything can easily be seen in under an

hour. Open 10:30 a.m. – 6:30 p.m. Closed Monday. José Victorino Lastarria 307. Closest metro: Bellas Artes or Universidad Católica. Tel: 56-2-6383502, URL: www.mavi.cl. Updated: Nov 13, 2008.

Cerro Santa Lucía
Cerro Santa Lucía is a national monument and one of Santiago's main tourist attractions. Legend goes that the Spanish conquistador Pedro de Valdivia founded Santiago at the bottom of the hill in 1541 and used the view from the top to plan the layout of the city.

In the late 1800s, Benjamín Vicuña Mackenna, Mayor of Santiago, began to transform the hillside to make it an attraction for high society. He built elaborate fountains, lookout points and gardens, which are all connected by a labyrinth of stairways.

Tourists go to Cerro Santa Lucia to enjoy the pleasant gardens and the panoramic view of the city. The best views are after a rainstorm. Av. Bernardo O'Higgins (Alameda) 499. Open 9 a.m. – 7 p.m. Updated: Nov 13, 2008.

Shopping

Feria Santa Lucia

Head to Feria Santa Lucia for souvenirs such as T-shirts, leather and wool goods, jewelry and wooden handcrafted items. The market items are cheaper than the tourist shops in Patio Bellavista, but prices are fixed and are more or less the same on each stall. Open 10 a.m. – 8 p.m. Closed Sunday. Cerro Santa Lucia. Updated: Nov 13, 2008.

Lodging

Barrio Lastarria is a small and mostly residential area, so the accommodation options are limited. If you absolutely must stay in Barrio Lastarria, the best choice is probably one of the self-catering apartments, which are available for both a single night or longer stays. There are plenty of hostels and hotels in nearby Bellas Artes, too. Updated: Jun 18, 2009.

Hotel Foresta

(ROOMS: $20 – 40) Don't let the dingy lobby of Hotel Foresta scare you; it is a great budget lodging option in Santiago. The rooms are fairly spacious and clean, while the odd mismatched antique furniture is endearing rather than tacky. The staff is also friendly and very accommodating. On the roof you'll find a restaurant and bar that offer a stunning view of the surrounding area. All rooms have private bathrooms. Victoria Subercaseaux 353. Tel: 56-2-6396261/4862. Updated: May 08, 2007.

Suites and Apartments Barrio Lastarria

(ROOMS: $60 and up, not including taxes) Suites and Apartments Barrio Lastarria has 280 self-catering apartments that sleep on

e to three people. Apartments are small but modern and tastefully decorated. A typical apartment has a living room/kitchen, bedroom and bathroom.

They are also equipped with WiFi, LCD flat-screen cable TVs, hairdryers, irons and ironing boards, and stereo systems. Parking spaces are available and there is 24-hour security/reception staff. José Victorino Lastarria 70. Closest metro: Universidad Católica. Tel: 56-2-2181263, Cell: 56-9-8782813, E-mail: contacto@suites-apartments.cl, URL: www.suites-apartments.cl. Updated: Jun 18, 2009.

Lastarria Tourist Apartments

(ROOMS: $60, not including tax) Located inside a restored historical building, Lastarria Tourist Apartments provide modern, stylish self-catering apartments for one to six people. They come with fully equipped kitchens, WiFi, safety deposit boxes, irons and ironing boards. There is also a laundry room in the building. It's possible to rent the apartments for longer stays. Talk directly to staff to negotiate cheaper rates. José Victorino Lastarria 43. Closest metro: Universidad Católica, Tel: 56-2-6383230 / 56-2-6393132, E-mail: contacto@apartmentsantiago.cl, URL: www.apartmentsantiago.cl. Updated: Jun 18, 2009.

Hotel Montecarlo Santiago

(ROOMS: $65 and up) Hotel Montecarlo is a budget hotel situated close to Cerro Santa Lucia. Rooms come with private bathrooms, hair dryers, TVs and safety deposit boxes. Continental breakfast is included in the price and the hotel has a restaurant and 24-hour room service. Internet is available but costs extra. The best thing about Hotel Montecarlo is its central location. Ask for a room with a view of the hill. Victoria Subercaseaux 209. Closest metro: Universidad Católica. Tel: 56-2-6339905, URL: www.hotelmontecarlo.cl. Updated: Jun 18, 2009.

Windsor Suites Hotel

(ROOMS: $80 double) Windsor Suites Hotel is strategically positioned between Providencia and Santiago Centro and is close to all the major tourist attractions. The hotel isn't much to look at from the outside, and rooms are a bit old-fashioned, but they are clean and come with private bathroom, hair dryer, cable TV and telephone. A buffet breakfast is included in the price but guests have to pay extra for Internet or WiFi connections. There's a restaurant on-site and lots of cafes and bars nearby. Victoria Subercasaeux 65. Closest metro: Universidad Católica, Tel: 56-2-4693100, E-mail: reservas@hotelwindsor.cl, URL: www.hotelwindsor.cl. Updated: Apr 21, 2009.

Restaurants

Although it only covers a few streets, Barrio Lastarria has several funky coffee shops and restaurants. Most are located on Calle Merced and Calle José Victorino Lastarria. Many restaurants here have outdoor seating. Generally the restaurants cater to the residential and student populations and are reasonably priced, while still managing to have decent quality food. Updated: Jun 18, 2009.

Living de Te

Living de Te is a cute little teahouse that serves up English tea, real coffee, hot chocolate, fresh fruit juice, sandwiches, salads and delicious cream cakes. Open every day, it's a good spot for lunch or a snack. It's pretty busy at lunchtime, so get there before 1 p.m. if you want to avoid the rush. Merced 297. Closest metro: Bellas Artes / Universidad Católica. Tel: 56-2-6396253. Updated: Apr 21, 2009.

Cafe Subté

There's no better way to start a day's sightseeing than breakfast in Cafe Subté. This bright little coffee shop is a few minutes from Museo Bellas Artes and serves freshly squeezed fruit juice, toast with marmalade or avocado, and ham and cheese toasties. At lunchtime they serve a range of healthy salads and sandwiches--followed by a milkshake, cookies or sticky cake, if that's your style. Staff is friendly and used to dealing with Spanglish-speaking tourists. Monjitas 374 - 376. Closest metro: Bellas Artes. Tel: 56-2-6386077. Updated: Apr 22, 2009.

El Diablito

El Diablito (the little devil) is a funky restaurant that looks a bit like a schizophrenic's treasure trove of antique odds and ends. It attracts a young and trendy crowd that comes for the late night drinking—to tunes from the 80s and 90s—as much as for the traditional Chilean food. A set menu is available at lunchtime for under $6. Alternatively, try the house speciality, *Carne a la diabla* (devil's meat). Ca. Merced 336,. Closest metro: Bellas Artes / Universidad Católica. Tel: 56-2-6383512. Updated: Apr 21, 2009.

Les Assassins

(ENTREE: $15) Les Assassins is a popular French bistro that has been serving up tasty treats, including French onion soup, coq au vin, beef bourguignon and crème brûlée, since 1965. The restaurant is tiny, but the atmosphere will transport you thousands of miles away to a cafe in the City of Light. Prices are reasonable given the high quality of the food, and the service is good, making the place a good bet for a romantic meal. Closed Sundays. Merced 297. Closest metro: Bellas Artes. Tel: 56-2-6384280. Updated: Apr 21, 2009.

Don Victorino

(ENTREES: $15 – 25) Don Victorino, along a quiet street in cozy Bellavista, is one of your best choices in Santiago. Dishes are varied and many, the interior is classic yet colorful, and service is friendly. Start with a pisco sour at the bar, then proceed into the patio to enjoy a plate of jambalaya or spicy seafood risotto. Don Victorino is so pleasant that you will always find room for a dessert just to stay a bit longer. José Victorino Lastarria 138. Tel: 56-2-6395263, Fax: 639 5263. Updated: Jul 01, 2009.

Squadritto

(ENTREE: $30 and up) White table cloths, real napkins, polished silverware, fresh flowers and elegant surroundings all set the scene for the fine dining experience in Squadritto. This smart restaurant serves up a range of Italian dishes—including cannelloni, risotto, gnocchi, meat and fish—but it's *haute* cuisine so don't expect any pasta bow ties. The food is delicious but portions are a bit small. Service is efficient and there's a good wine list. On Sundays the restaurant is only open for lunch. Bookings are recommended. Rosal 332. Closest metro: Universidad Católica. Tel: 56-2-6322121. Updated: Apr 22, 2009.

Barrio Bellavista

During the day, tourists pass through Bellavista on their way to the the zoo, Cerro San Cristobal and La Chascona (the Santiago home of Pablo Neruda). The area packs in plenty of restaurants and cafes, with enough sights and stores to fill a tourist's daylight hours. At night, the streets are lined with cheap plastic tables full of young Chileans and foreigners knocking back beers, rum and pisco before hitting the nearby dance floors. The barrio, the gay center of the capital, has some of the most consistently rowdy nightlife in Santiago. This is not the place to go for

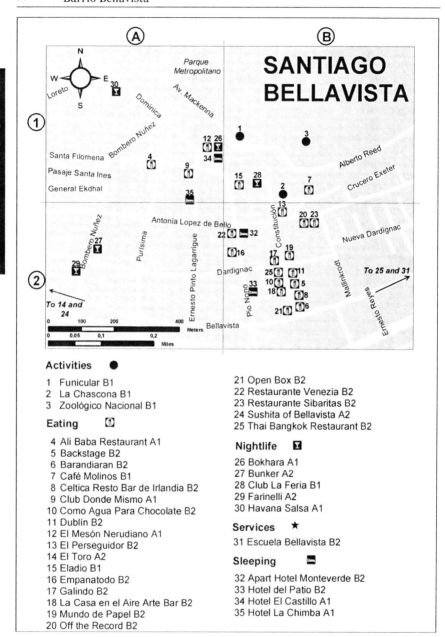

Activities ●

1 Funicular B1
2 La Chascona B1
3 Zoológico Nacional B1

Eating

4 Ali Baba Restaurant A1
5 Backstage B2
6 Barandiaran B2
7 Café Molinos B1
8 Celtica Resto Bar de Irlandia B2
9 Club Donde Mismo A1
10 Como Agua Para Chocolate B2
11 Dublín B2
12 El Mesón Nerudiano A1
13 El Perseguidor B2
14 El Toro A2
15 Eladio B1
16 Empanatodo B2
17 Galindo B2
18 La Casa en el Aire Arte Bar B2
19 Mundo de Papel B2
20 Off the Record B2

21 Open Box B2
22 Restaurante Venezia B2
23 Restaurante Sibaritas B2
24 Sushita of Bellavista A2
25 Thai Bangkok Restaurant B2

Nightlife

26 Bokhara A1
27 Bunker A2
28 Club La Feria B1
29 Farinelli A2
30 Havana Salsa A1

Services ★

31 Escuela Bellavista B2

Sleeping

32 Apart Hotel Monteverde B2
33 Hotel del Patio B2
34 Hotel El Castillo A1
35 Hotel La Chimba A1

a few quiet beers before bed. The nightclubs and discos that spring to life in the evenings blast reggaeton, techno, salsa, rock and hip hop into the wee hours of the morning. If you plan to stay through the night, it's best to keep your wits about you and your eyes on your wallet. Avoid crossing the bridges to Providencia after dark unless you're in a large group, as there can be security issues; taxis are a wise choice. There are many craft shops and stalls in the area which remain open into the evening, selling the famous blue lapis lazuli stones and Chilean copper. Updated: Jul 07, 2009.

Things to See and Do

Zoológico Nacional

(ADMISSION: $4 adults, $2.60 seniors, $2 children) The Zoológico Nacional of Santiago features more than 150 animal species. The park spans 4.8 hectares at the base of Cerro San Cristobal, just beyond the Funicular. The "Zoocine," a small indoor movie theater, is entertaining for the kids. The trails are in a bit of disrepair, so be sure to wear comfortable walking shoes. Allow roughly two hours to explore the entire park. Open 10 a.m. – 5 p.m. Closed Monday. Ca. Pio Nono (The zoo has multiple entrances. The main entrance is Calle Pio Nono, just above the Funicular.) Tel: 56-2-7301331, URL: www.parquemet.cl. Updated: Jun 17, 2008.

Funicular

(PRICE: $2.50 two-way; $1.50 one-way) On a clear day, the view from the top of Cerro San Cristóbal is spectacular, providing the best view of the stunning contrast between Santiago and its surrounding mountains. The hill is a popular ride for bikers on nice days, though the steep incline makes for a strenuous trip. Perhaps the easiest—and most novel—way to summit the hill is to take the Funicular (vertical train ride), which is a cable-pulled trolley that picks up at Pio Nono and takes visitors to the top, where the Virgen de la Immaculada stands waiting with open arms.

Head up at sunset for a particularly spectacular experience. The more athletic may prefer to hike back down the hill—there are marked trails for this purpose. The Funicular also makes a stop at the zoo, for those who want to spend the day in the area. Open Tuesday – Sunday 10 a.m. – 8 p.m., Monday 1 p.m. – 8 p.m. Pio Nono 445, URL: www.funicular.cl. Updated: Nov 13, 2008.

La Chascona

(ADMISSION: $7) Museo Casa La Chascona is the former home of Chile's Nobel Prize-winning poet, Pablo Neruda. La Chascona means "uncombed" and is a reference to the unruly hair of Matilde Urrutia, his secret lover at the time and later his third wife.

Built in 1953, and mostly designed by the poet, the house is a bizarre structure filled with strange and wonderful things, including Neruda's enormous collection of books. Guided tours in English, French and German cost $7. Tours in Spanish cost $5. You must make reservations before visiting. Open 10 a.m. – 6 p.m. Closed Monday. Fernando Márquez de La Plata 0192. Closest metro: Baquedano. Tel: 56-2-7778741, URL: www.fundacionneruda.org. Updated: Nov 13, 2008.

Santuario Immaculada Concepción

Just below the statue of the Virgen de la Immaculada Concepción, on Cerro San Cristobal, is a wide amphitheater. This is Santuario Immaculada Concepción, an open-air church, set in the lovely gardens of Parque Metropoliano. The area offers great views of the city and an opportunity to say a quick prayer, if so inclined. You can join in on Catholic mass services on Sunday mornings and on religious festivals. Updated: Jul 07, 2009.

Shopping

Bellavista Street Fair and

Patio Bellavista

There are a number of artisan market stalls along Calle Pio Nono and in Patio Bellavista. This is a quick and easy place to buy some souvenirs. The 30-plus booths have a diverse range of high quality goods: custom made boots of any style (they take a week to complete), jewelry made from the Chilean stone Lapiz lazuli, handmade guitars, clothing, art and candles. Be sure to bring cash, since only a few of the vendors accept credit cards. Note, however, that the fair is one of the main tourist thoroughfares and prices are hiked up. Open 10 a.m. to about 10 p.m., though closing time varies. Ca. Pio Nono. Closest metro: Bellavista. Updated: Oct 17, 2008.

Lodging

Accommodations in the vibrant and lively Barrio Bellavista are as varied and eclectic as the writers, artists and backpackers who inhabit them. Many of the hostels are a bit run down, but they do offer the standard budget options available in most of Chile. The bohemian vibe is very strong in Barrio Bellavista, making this the barrio in Santiago to have a wild night out. With the raucous nightlife, many hostels serve no other purpose than to provide a bed to stumble into after the bars close. Updated: Jun 26, 2009.

La Chimba Hostel

(ROOMS: $13 – $32, includes light breakfast) La Chimba Hostel offers a safe and cozy refuge for backpackers. Come to this clean and friendly place for a good night's rest; the beds are remarkably comfortable by hostel standards. Staff members speak English, though some better than others, and will often join guests for a movie in the common room. Because it's in Bellavista, expect to hear the sounds of music and revelry from surrounding venues on the weekend. Ernesto Pinto Lagarrigue 262. Closest metro: Baquedano (Cross over the river and follow Pio Nono to Antonia Lopez de Bello, where you'll take a left. Go one block to Ernesto Pino Lagarrigue and take a right. The hostel will be on your left.) Tel: 56-2-7358978, E-mail: info@lachimba.com, URL: www.lachimba.com. Updated: Mar 16, 2009.

Hotel Castilla

(ROOMS: $25 single, $40 double; includes breakfast) Although the building, which dates from the 1920s, is well maintained, Hotel Castilla is gloomy inside. The beds are tired and have seen better days. The staff are not quick to help, but warm up with some coaxing. Castilla's biggest draw is its great location at the base of Cerro San Cristobal, near the zoo and steps away from countless bars and restaurants. It is one of cheapest options in terms of a private room and bath within Barrio Bellavista. The hotel also doubles as a by-the-hour motel. Pio Nono 420. Tel: 56-2-7350243, URL: www.moteles.cl/stg01/scl1.htm. Updated: Jun 11, 2008.

Apart Hotel Monteverde

(ROOMS: $39 – 53, includes breakfast, parking, taxes) Located crawling distance from the bars and clubs of Barrio Bellavista, Apart Hotel Monteverde does not look very inviting from the outside (or from the reception area for that matter), but the rooms are actually quite comfortable. The hotel is nice and clean, and long-term stay options are available. The staff is helpful, but does not assist with excursions. Pio Nono 193. Tel: 56-2-7773607, Fax: 2-737-0341, E-mail: aparthotelmonteverde@terra.cl, URL: www.aparthotelmonteverde.cl. Updated: Jun 11, 2008.

Hotel del Patio

(ROOMS: $110 – 165, includes WiFi and breakfast) A remodeled 19th-century mansion, the Hotel del Patio is a modern, chic place to spend the night. It has spacious rooms, wood floors, and comfortable beds. The friendly English-speaking staff is available to assist with travel excursions, particularly mountain adventures. The hotel is located within an indoor shopping complex full of artisan wares, restaurants and a rooftop patio that's perfect for soaking up views of the Andes. Prices here are a bit high due to the luxurious ambiance. Pio Nono 61. Tel: 56-2-7327571, E-mail: info@hoteldelpatio.cl, URL: www.hoteldelpatio.cl. Updated: Jul 01, 2009.

Restaurants

Barrio Bellavista has many moderately priced restaurants that are worth the money. Within the barrio you can find a variety of traditional Chilean restaurants, as well as some of Santiago's best ethnic restaurants. Most of the area's eateries can be found on the parallel streets Constitución and Pio Nono, including the trendy Patio Bellavista, which runs between the two. Start by walking down these streets to check out menus, prices and clientele if you can't make up your mind. Be warned: Bellavista has a reputation for being popular among tourists. Waiters pace like predators in front of their restaurants and will hassle you as you try to make up your mind. Updated: Nov 13, 2008.

Empana Todos

This very small, primarily carry-out establishment (with counter service and bar stool seating), is a great place for a quick meal or snack. The menu is restricted to empanadas and some sushi, but the options are by no means limited. The large menu board above the counter is arranged in a unique, order-friendly grid, with more than 30 different combinations of empanada fillings. The simple, fresh ingredients—including cheeses, different types of meat and vegetables—and the low prices will make you want to try them all. Pio Nono 153. Tel: 56-2-7382709. Updated: Jan 06, 2009.

Mundo de Papel

(SANDWICHES: $5) For the literary-minded traveler, check out this cafe whose slogan reads, "Books and coffee of the world." The open, light-filled cafe serves salads, sandwiches, soups and crêpes. Fresh-squeezed seasonal fruit juice is available, as well as a decent selection of teas and coffee. The attentive staff will often sit and read alongside customers when business slows down. Book recommendations are posted on the bulletin board for browsers. Sit outside on the sunlit patio or downstairs with a book from the well-stocked bookshelves. Constitución 166. Tel: 56-2-7350411, E-mail: sanmartin.christian@gmail.com, URL: www.mundodepapel.cl. Updated: Jul 07, 2009.

El Perseguidor
(COVER: $2 – 5) Those looking for live jazz and a good meal in the Bellavista area should head to El Perseguidor. El Perseguidor (named for Julio Cortázar's story on the life of jazz musician Charlie Parker) features upscale artisan appetizers and traditional Chilean dishes with a bit of flare. Reservations are necessary on Friday and Saturday. Visit the website for details on individual performers. If El Perseguidor is full, however, and you still need your jazz fix, head to Club de Jazz de Santiago —the other hotspot for live jazz— located near Plaza Ñuñoa. Antonia Lopez de Bello 0126. Tel: 56-2-7776763. Updated: Jun 02, 2008.

El Toro
(ENTREES: $5 – 10) For standard Chilean fare, the locals head to El Toro. This swanky restaurant and bar is decorated with red pleather, disco lights and walls covered in guests' handwritten comments. The covered outdoor area, complete with paper tablecloths and crayons, is great for kids. Smoking is permitted both indoors out, and the service is impeccable. Loreto 33. Tel: 56-2-7375937. Updated: Jun 11, 2008.

Ali Baba Restaurant
(ENTREES: $5 – 10) This small, family-run restaurant provides a taste of Palestine in an intimate and romantic ambience. The cuisine is Arabian, with house-specialty lamb and vegetarian dishes. The ceilings are made to mimic a desert tent, with light, billowy fabric, and a variety of Middle Eastern decorations adorn the walls. The service is warm and welcoming, and the staff is accommodating and helpful. The menu has descriptions in Spanish and English for those not familiar with the dishes. Santa Filomena 102. Tel: 56-2-7327036, URL: www.restaurantalibaba.cl. Updated: Jul 04, 2008.

Galindo
(ENTREES: $8 – 15) Galindo is a traditional Chilean restaurant located in touristy Bellavista. The décor is basic, but what the restaurant lacks in style it makes up for in taste and a lively atmosphere. The menu offers a wide selection of delicious meats, seafood, salads, sandwiches and snacks. The bar serves a variety of beers and hard liquor; the wine list is limited.

Galindo is open from 12 p.m. to 2 a.m. It's busy at lunchtime and in the evening, but if you don't mind waiting they can usually find somewhere to squeeze you in. Reservations are accepted via E-mail or telephone. Dardignac 098 on the corner of Constitución, Barrio Bellavista, Santiago. Tel: 56-2-7770116, E-mail: reservas@galindo.cl, URL: www.galindo.cl. Updated: Mar 23, 2009.

Barandiaran
(ENTREES: $9 – 11) While Barandiaran offers some Chilean dishes, Chile's northern neighbor Peru is the restaurant's heart and soul. Voted by El Mercurio in 2006 as the best new restaurant and best value in Santiago, this clean, rustic spot is the place to go if you crave some traditional Peruvian delicacies. They also maintain a bar stocked with every drink under the sun. The outdoor seating is good for people-watching and non-smokers. Lunch is only served on Sundays. Meals are mid-range, compared to the surrounding eateries. Constitución 40 Local 52, Patio Bellavista. Tel: 2-737-0725, URL: www.barandiaran.cl. Updated: Jun 11, 2008.

Club Donde Mismo
Pop into Club Donde Mismo for cheap Chilean/Peruvian food and a full bar. The place is unpretentious and clean, the food is decent, and the service is efficient. The lunch menu provides several filling options and, in the evening, the venue hosts karaoke. Ernesto Pinto Lagarrigue 284. Tel: 56-2-7771068, E-mail: clubdondemismo@gmail.com. Updated: Nov 13, 2008.

Dublin
(ENTREES: $10 – 15) Part of the fancy Patio Bellavista food court, although accessible from outside, the Dublin pub offers a variety of beers, (not including Guinness), in a mock-Irish setting. The music hails from the United Kingdom, but is not really Irish, and the food, a selection of bar snacks, sandwiches, mains and curries, are not remotely Irish. That said, it is a pleasant enough place to while away an evening and toss back a few beers. Constitución 58. Tel: 56-2-7300526. Updated: Jun 11, 2008.

Openbox
Openbox is an outdoor sushi heaven. The seating area is a great place to people-watch (especially on the weekends). Openbox's bar, also located outside, is fully stocked and offers well-priced drink specials in the evenings. There are heat lamps to help with the cold. Constitución 40, Local 75, Patio Bellavista. Tel: 56-2-7621316. Updated: Jun 11, 2008.

Backstage
(ENTREES: $10 – 15) Backstage is the Chilean equivalent of the Hard Rock Cafe, except it offers a much bigger menu. The food ranges from North American specialties to standard Chilean

meals, including some Asian dishes. The drink list is just as extensive. Prices can be slightly higher than neighboring restaurants. There is ample seating and a non-smoking section. Backstage offers live music on Thursdays, Fridays, and Saturdays (sometimes Wednesdays as well). Check out their website to see who's playing when. Constitución 40 Local 57, URL: www.backstagechile.com. Updated: Jun 11, 2008.

La Casa en el Aire Arte Bar

La Casa en el Aire, named after a song by Colombian singer Rafael Escalona, is a small restaurant within the Patio Bellavista shopping area. Its Colombian and Chilean dishes are tasty and the prices are very reasonable. Their house cocktail of grenadine, sugar cane liquor, fresh orange juice and secret ingredients is worth a try. Fresh squeezed juices like pineapple and papaya are also available. The tea-and-pastry breakfast a great deal, especially if you have it in their inviting outdoor area. Constitución 40 Local 56. Tel: 56-2-735-6680, URL: www.lacasaenelaire.cl. Updated: Jun 11, 2008.

Celtica Resto Bar de Irlandia

A good place to start a night of partying, Celtica is a small, unassuming restaurant with many hard alcohol options. The menu also offers Italian and Chilean dishes, though prices are a bit high for the quality of the ambiance. There is an outdoor seating area, giving non-smokers a chance to breathe some fresh air. Constitución 40 Local 55. Updated: Jun 11, 2008.

Restaurant Venezia

Despite its prominent sign, complete with a picture of a gondola, Restaurant Venezia is not a typical Italian restaurant. Alongside pasta and seafood selections, the menu includes many local dishes such as *lomo a lo pobre* (steak with French fries and a fried egg). The establishment is popular with locals, many of whom gather around the full bar. The cloth napkins seem a bit out of place amid the shabby silverware and condiments in plastic bottles. There is a separate dining room in back which allows smoking, but both spaces have similar furnishings, a casual atmosphere and quick service. Pío Nono 200. Tel: 56-2-7370900. Updated: Jan 06, 2009.

Sushita of Bellavista

This Santiago restaurant chain is the Japanese sister of the Italian eatery, Sorrentinos. The sushi isn't of the highest quality, though, and tastes as if it was made off-premises. The interior décor is clean, but not overly inviting. Beer and wine are available. Loreto 26. Tel: 56-2-7351191, URL: www.sushita.cl. Updated: Jun 11, 2008.

Eladio

(ENTREES: $15 – 30) If you're looking for a classy but affordable way to spend your evening, Eladio is an excellent choice. Located centrally within the Bellavista neighborhood, Eladio features traditional entrees and steaks (try the *bife a lo pobre*) in a comfortable but elegant atmosphere. Show up after 9 p.m. if you want to dine with the locals. With its wide selection of Chilean wine, excellent service and leisurely atmosphere, you're sure to leave Eladio feeling full and satisfied. Pío Nono 251. Tel: 56-2-7775083.

Cafe Molinos

Cafe Molinos, a quiet spot to have lunch, is just off the main Bellavista drag on Calle Arzobispo. The cafe offers an ample *menu del dia* (a set lunch menu that changes daily), which includes soup or salad, a generously portioned entrée, and dessert or coffee. The atmosphere is welcoming and the service is friendly, but you may face problems if you come with a large group, as seating is limited. Try the *pastel de papas*, if available. Calle Arzobispo and Bellavista. Updated: Nov 13, 2008.

Thai Bangkok Restaurant

(ENTREES: $20 – 30) Thai Bangkok is one of the best spots in Chile to have Thai food. The chef, Cshi, has a talent for mixing unique spices and flavors to create wonderful dishes. The chicken coconut soup is especially good. Thai Bangkok's ambiance is modern, simple and exquisitely clean. The owner speaks English and is very helpful. Service can be slow during popular dining hours, but prices are very reasonable, especially considering the location. Lunch is only offered on Sundays. Constitución 92. Tel: 56-2-7326930, E-mail: bangkokrestaurant@tie.cl, URL: www.restaurantbangkok.cl. Updated: Jun 11, 2008.

V!VA ONLINE REVIEW
THAI BANGKOK RESTAURANT

This restaurant really surprised me—some of the best Thai food I ever had, good service and relaxing atmosphere. Highly recommended!

December 25, 2008

Off the Record

(ENTREES: $20 – 40) If you're looking for a hangout spot that satisfies your cultural needs, Off the Record is a good option.

Chilean artists, filmmakers and writers take the stage every Monday for performances, screenings and debates, and live bands play every Friday and Saturday. The décor is kitschy with a literary flare (Bukowski's poetry makes an appearance on the menu), and the atmosphere is laid-back. Food is moderately priced and ranges from traditional Chilean entrees to pizzas, sandwiches, and vegetarian dishes. A full bar is also available. Antonia López de Bello 0155. Tel: 56-2-7777710, URL: www.offtherecord.cl.

Como Agua Para Chocolate

(ENTREES: $20 – 25) Named after Mexican novelist Laura Esquivel's famous book, *Like Water for Chocolate*, this restaurant has flirty flair. The décor has a fun Mexican feel, with bright colors, lots of beautiful wood and even a bed turned into a table. Most of the selections on the menu are said to be an aphrodisiac. You could find a cheaper meal elsewhere, but Como Agua has a unique worth the higher cost. Constitución 88. Tel: 56-2-7778740. Updated: Apr 22, 2009.

Restaurant Sibaritas

(ENTREES: $25) For a classy night on the town, begin your evening at Sibaritas Restaurant. This gourmet establishment features international cuisine in an elegant, but not stuffy, atmosphere. Sibaritas has a beautifully plated chef's menu, an extensive selection of wine and a fixed *degustación* menu (for sampling multiple items). Although it's not cheap, Sibaritas is high on the list of top restaurants in Santiago for many foodies. Mallinkrodt 184. Tel: 56-2-7771470, E-mail: sibaritasbellavista@gmail.com, URL: www.sibaritas.cl. Updated: Jun 02, 2008.

Nightlife

CLUBS

Maestra Vida

(COVER: varies, but usually about $6) Salseros looking to get their salsa fix while in Santiago should try out Maestra Vida, located on the busy Pío Nono strip. DJs play primarily salsa music (with a bit of traditional Cueca and Vallenato thrown in as the night progresses), and the local crowd is glad to show newcomers the ropes. The dance floor is small and packed on the weekends, but there are plenty of tables and chairs where you can have a drink when you need to take a breather from dancing. Live music on Wednesdays and Thursdays. Updated: Nov 13, 2008.

Bunker !

(COVER: $8) Bunker is a the hotspot for travelers looking to find the gay scene in Santiago. The club's disc jockey bounces head-pounding beats off the walls of the renovated theater. Don't worry about being late because the dancing lasts until the early-morning hours, especially on weekends when the place really fills up. Bombero Nuñez 159. Tel: 56-2-7371716, URL: www.bunker.cl. Closed Sunday and Monday. Updated: Apr 20, 2009.

Bokhara

Bokhara is another lively disco, and popular part of Santiago's gay scene. It regularly features drag shows, and the service is generally friendly. Pío Nono 430. Tel: 56-2-7321050. Updated: Apr 22, 2009.

Club La Feria

(COVER: $10) Club La Feria is a typical disco, with disc jockeys that scramble electronic beats into the early morning hours. The place fancies itself as trendy, so do not wear sneakers. Guys in too tight T-shirts and ripped jeans spend the evening attempting to court well-dressed girls on the dance floor. Constitución 275. Tel: 56-2-7358433, E-mail: laferia@clublaferia.cl, URL: www.laferia.cl. Updated: Apr 22, 2009.

Havana Salsa

This might be about as close to Cuba as a traveler from the United States can legally get. The Havana-themed décor culminates in a dance floor where veteran and amateur salsa dancers congregate. The club often has impressive live shows, so check ahead. Dominica 142. Tel: 56-2-7775829. Updated: Apr 22, 2009.

Farinelli

At Farinelli, waiters serve drinks in G-strings for the gay crowd, which also hosts ensemble drag shows. Should you go there and find that the service is not exactly to your taste, try one of the good ice creams instead. Bombero Nuñez 68. Updated: Apr 22, 2009.

Providencia

Providencia doesn't have historical buildings to rival Santiago Centro, posh boutiques like Vitacura or the bohemian attitude of Bellas Artes. Nevertheless, the barrio is a good option as your base camp in Santiago. Providencia is much safer than downtown Santiago, cheaper than Vitacura and not as touristy as Bellas Artes or Bella Vista. It's much easier to book a hostel, and all the tourist attractions are still within easy reach by metro or bus.

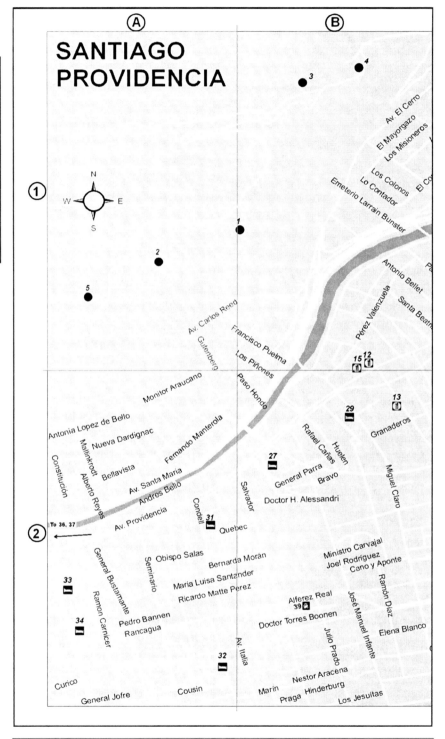

SANTIAGO

SANTIAGO

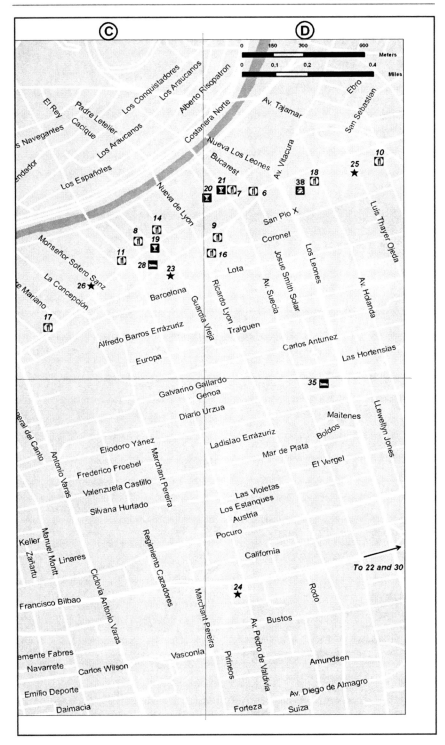

Activities ●
1 Jardin Botánico Mapulemu B1
2 Parque Metropolitano A1
3 Piscinas Tupahue and Antilén B1
4 Teleférico B1
5 Virgen de la Immaculada Concepciòn A1

Eating ▢
6 Delhi Darbar D1
7 Domino D1
8 El Huerto C1
9 El Popular D1
10 Elkika Ilmenau D1
11 Gatsby C1
12 Liguria B1
13 Los Cuates B2
14 Los Insaciables C1
15 Normandie B1
16 Oh! Salad Garden D1
17 PhoneBox Pub C1
18 Rishtedar D1

Nightlife ▣
19 Bar Subterráneo C1
20 Boomerang D1

21 Brannigan´s D1
22 Oz D2

Services ★
23 Post Office C1
24 Post Office D2
25 Post Office D1
26 SENATUR C1

Sleeping ▭
27 Ají Hostel B2
28 Apart Hotel La Fayette C1
29 Atacama Hostel B2
30 Casa Club la Reina D2
31 Casa Condell A2
32 El Patio Suizo A2
33 Footsteps Backpackers A2
34 Hostal Casa Grande A2
35 Hostal Don Alfredo D2
36 Hotel de Ciudad de Vitoria A2
37 NewenKara Hostel A2

Shoppping ▣
38 Tatoo "Los Leones" D1
39 Tatoo "Salvador" B2

Most activity revolves around Avenidas Providencia and 11 de Septiembre with their lively mix of shops, bars, restaurants, office buildings and apartments. For shopping, head to the malls and department stores close to Metro Los Leones. For food and drink, wander along the main avenues and side streets from Metro Los Leones to Metro Manuel Montt. You'll discover countless restaurants catering to the office crowd and offering cheap set-price lunch deals. The main nightlife can be found along Avenida Suecia, Paseo Orrego Luco and around Metro Manuel Montt (but take care on Avenida Suecia at night). Providencia is a bit of a ghost town on the weekends, as the workers abandon the streets for home. though you can still find some life around Avenida Manuel Montt. Updated: Apr 20, 2009.

Shopping

Tatoo Adventure Gear

This major outdoor equipment distributor is a top source for brand-name sportswear, trekking and camping gear, biking accessories and more. Tatoo's two Santiago stores, Los Leones and Salvador, also stock guidebooks and maps, provide information on mountaineering courses and seminars, and offer tips on everything from the best routes to climb to buying the perfect hiking boot. URL: http://cl.tatoo. ws/home. Los Leones store: Monday to Friday 10:30 a.m. – 8 p.m., Saturday 10:30 a.m. – 7 p.m., Av. Los Leones 81. Tel: 56-2-9460008, E-mail: losleones@ tatoo.ws. Salvador store: weekdays from 9 a.m – 6 p.m., Dr. Torres Boonen 686. Tel: 56-2-2040006 / 2749308, E-mail: providencia@tatoo.ws. Updated: Oct 31, 2009.

Things to See and Do

Virgen de la Immaculada Concepción
The Virgen de la Immaculada Concepción is a 14-meter high statue of the Virgin Mary that sits atop Santiago's highest hill, Cerro San Cristobal. The gleaming white statue with outstretched arms is visible from most parts of the city, especially when illumintated at night. Although it can't compete with Rio de Janeiro's Christ the Redeemer, it is, nevertheless, an impressive sight. Wear comfortable shoes for the climb. Cerro San Cristobal, Parque Metropolitano, Pío Nono 450, Barrio Bellavista. Closest metro: Baquedano. URL: www. parquemetropolitano.cl; Open 8 a.m. – 7 p.m. Updated: Jul 07, 2009.

Teleférico
(PRICE: $3 roundtrip) The Teleférico is a cable-car ride that runs from downtown Providencia to the top of Santiago's highest hill,

Cerro San Cristóbal. The ride takes about 20 minutes and on a clear day provides great views of Parque Metropolitano and the city.

The Teleferico runs Monday – Tuesday from 2:30 p.m. to 7 p.m., Wednesday – Friday 12:30 p.m. to 7 p.m. and Saturdays, Sundays and holidays 10:30 a.m. – 7:30 p.m. Av. Pedro de Valdivia Norte/Av. El Cerro. Closest metro: Pedro de Valdivia. Tel: 56-2-7376669, URL: www.funicular.cl/en/teleferico/index.htm. Updated: Oct 29, 2008.

Piscinas Tupahue and Antilén

(ADMISSION: $9; $10 on weekends) If the hot city is too much to bear, cool off in the huge outdoor swimming pools in Parque Metropolitano. Set on the slopes of Cerro San Cristóbal and surrounded by trees and gardens, Piscinas Tupahue and Antilén provide great views of the city. There is ample space where you can sunbathe, and kiosks sell drinks and snacks. The pools are very busy in the summer, especially during the school holidays in January and February. Interior Parque Metropolitano, Closest metro: Baquedano. Tel: 56-2-7776666, URL: www.parquemetropolitano.cl, Open 10 a.m. – 7 p.m. Closed Monday. Updated: Oct 29, 2008.

Jardín Botánico Mapulemu

Set in Parque Metropolitano, Jardín Botánico Mapulemu covers an area of about four hectares and has more than 80 species of native plants and trees. There is also a waterfall, duck pond and medicinal plant garden. The sculpted gardens offer great views of the city and are a peaceful spot to recover after climbing Cerro San Cristobal. Interior Parque Metropolitano, Closest metro: Pedro de Valdivia. URL: www.parquemetropolitano.cl, Open 9 a.m. – 5:30 p.m. Updated: Jul 07, 2009.

Parque Metropolitano

Covering 728 hectares, Parque Metropolitano is one of the largest parks in Chile. It is spread over several hills, including Cerros San Cristóbal, Chacarillas, Gemelos and Pirámide. The summit at Cerro San Cristóbal is 860 meters above sea level and crowned with a 14-meter-high statue of the Virgen de la Immaculada Concepcion.

The park also has walking and bicycle trails, two outdoor swimming pools, picnic and BBQ areas, botanical gardens, children's play areas, a chapel and restaurants. The easiest way to get to the top is to use the Teleférico cable car or the Funicular. Parque Metropolitano is by far the loveliest park in the city and should

not be missed. Open 8 a.m. – 7 a.m. Pío Nono 450. Closest metro: Baquedano. Tel: 56-2-7301331, URL: www.parquemetropolitano.cl. Updated: Nov 13, 2008.

Lodging

Providencia is has lodging options for every budget, from five-star hotels to budget hostels and apart-hotels. Places located along the main avenues (Providencia and 11 de Septiembre) tend to be more expensive, but if you're willing to walk a couple of blocks from the metro station you can find several good-value hotels. The standard of accommodation is fairly high with even the cheapest hostel offering a clean and comfortable bed for the night. Many of the cheaper hotels are located in the sprawling residential area of Providencia and can be a bit difficult to find on foot. You might want to consider booking a room in advance or at least have an idea of where you are going. Updated: Apr 20, 2009.

Atacama Hostel

(ROOMS: $10 and up, includes breakfast) With its central location (one block from Metro Manuel Montt) and laid-back atmosphere, Atacama Hostel is a great choice if you want to enjoy Providencia's nightlife and meet other travelers. From the welcome beer handed to you on arrival to the regular BBQ nights, the friendly staff goes out of their way to make sure you feel at home. Atacama has all the usual comforts: a cozy lounge, terrace, Internet, laundry service and bike rental. Dorm rooms are a bit cramped, however. Roman Diaz 130, Closest metro: Manuel Montt. Tel: 56-2-2642012, E-mail: info@atacamahostel.cl / atacamahostel@hotmail.com, URL: www.atacamahostel.cl. Updated: Apr 20, 2009.

NewenKara Hostel !

(ROOMS: $13 and up) NewenKara Hostel is located on a quiet street in the heart of residential Providencia, just a five-minute walk from Metro Manuel Montt and the bars and restaurants of Avenida Providencia. Set in a 20th-century house with whitewashed walls and wooden floors, the hostel is bright and airy. NewenKara is favored by long-staying guests for its shared kitchen, lounge and garden, all of which are spotlessly clean. Staff is friendly and, with only nine bedrooms, this place has more of a personal feel than some of its bigger competitors. Double and family rooms are a bit sparsely decorated however, and could do with a set of drawers. Price includes free breakfast and WiFi. Calle La Sierra 1441, Closest metro: Manuel Montt.

SANTIAGO

Tel: 56-2-7107604, E-mail: info@newen-karahostel.cl, URL: www.newenkarahostel.cl. Updated: Apr 20, 2009.

Ají Hostel (previously Chilli Hostel)

(ROOMS: $13 – 42; 10 percent discounts for stays longer than five days, and for groups of more than five people) Only a block from busy Providencia, this converted 1930s house is a surprisingly tranquil hostel. Paintings by local artists decorate the walls, and the original staircase and large wooden doors give the place a classic, dignified atmosphere. The spacious kitchen, comfortable common area and light-filled patio are big draws for any guests.

But it is the owners' eagerness to create a sense of community among their guests that leads many to pick Ají. On various days the hostel has different promotions, like free pisco sours on Mondays, free pasta dinners on Wednesdays and an at-cost BBQ on Fridays. Triana 863, Closest metro: Salvador.

Follow Av. Providencia one block to Av. Eliodoro Yañez. Turn right onto Triana and follow the street around until you see the red Ají Hostel on your right. Tel: 56-2-2364401, E-mail: info@ajihostel.cl, URL: www.ajihostel.cl. Updated: Apr 20, 2009.

Footsteps Backpackers !

(ROOMS: $16, shared dorm, includes breakfast) The best thing about Footsteps hostel is its location. Just a few minutes from Metro Baquedano, it's within walking distance of Bellavista, Parque Metropolitano, Museo de Bellas Artes, Lastarria and Cerro Santa Lucia. With all these attractions on your doorstep it's unlikely you'll spend much time in the hostel. If you do though, there's plenty to keep you entertained, like the pool table, Playstation, book exchange and free Internet. Almirante Simpson 50, Closest metro: Baquedano. Tel: 56-2-6347807, E-mail: footsteps@footsteps.cl, URL: www.footsteps.cl. Updated: Apr 20, 2009.

Casa Condell

(ROOMS: $17 single without breakfast; $22 with breakfast) With only seven rooms, Casa Condell really is a home away from home. The guesthouse is set in a period house on a quiet residential street in Providencia but is still within walking distance of the center of Providencia, Bella Vista and downtown Santiago. Rooms are simple but elegant and have wooden floors. There

is a communal living area, kitchen and terrace. The huge breakfast is a good start to the day and it's worth every cent of the $5 surcharge. Casa Condell is a good bet if you fancy a quiet hideaway. Avenida Condell 114, Closest metro: Salvador / Baquedano. E-mail: max@casacondell.com, URL: www.casacondell.cl. Updated: Apr 17, 2009.

Casa Club la Reina

(ROOMS: $24 per person; includes breakfast) This hostel is located in a quiet residential sector, close to buses, supermarkets, banks and restaurants. Axel Munthe 7710-La Reina. Tel: 56-2-8818463, Fax: 056-2-8818463, E-mail: casaclublareina@hotmail.com, URL: www.casaclublareina.blogspot.com. Updated: May 26, 2009.

Hostal Casa Grande

(ROOMS: Single with shared bathroom from $20; double from $34; triple from $44; quadruple from $60) On a street just off Plaza Italia, Hostal Casa Grande is in the heart of Santiago and is a short distance from all the tourist attractions. The hostel is a spacious period house with wooden floors, high ceilings and bright bedrooms. There's also a communal kitchen, living room and garden. With 16 bedrooms it can get a bit crowded sometimes, but there's always someone to talk to. Breakfast and WiFi are included in the price. Avenida Vicuña Mackenna 90, Closest metro: Baquedano / Parque Bustamente. Tel: 56-2-2227347, URL: www.hostalcasagrande.cl. Updated: Apr 20, 2009.

El Patio Suizo

(ROOMS: Single room with shared bathroom from $30; double from $40) El Patio Suizo is a cozy B&B run by a Swiss family. There are single, double and triple rooms available with shared or private bathrooms. Rooms are comfortable and very clean. There's also a garden with hammocks and a BBQ area. This place attracts a more mature crowd—think late twenties and up instead of the college crew—and is a good choice for couples and families. The price includes breakfast and free Internet. Staff is helpful and speaks Spanish, English and German. Avenida Condell 847, Closest metro: Parque Bustamente. Tel: 56-2-4740634, E-mail: info@patiosuizo.com, URL: www.patiosuizo.com. Updated: Apr 20, 2009.

Hostal Don Alfredo

(ROOMS: $36 single, $40 double/triple, $60 quadruple) Hostal Don Alfredo is never going to be your first choice—it's too far away from the metro and Providencia's nightlife. However, if you find yourself stuck with nowhere to stay it really isn't a bad third or fourth option. More of a budget hotel than a hostel, Don Alfredo provides single, double, triple and quadruple rooms with either shared or private bathrooms. Rooms are a bit old-fashioned but comfortable and many are equipped with cable TV. Alberto Henckel 2360, Closest metro: Pedro de Valdivia. Tel: 56-2-2055929 / 2699135, E-mail: info@hostaldonalfredo.cl, URL: www.hostaldonalfredo.cl. Updated: Apr 20, 2009.

Hotel de Ciudad de Vitoria

(ROOMS: $69 – 130, includes taxes, breakfast and WiFi) Hidden within a nondescript office building, Ciudad de Vitoria is a quaint boutique hotel that should not be passed up because of its camouflage. This comfortable establishment, complete with frilly curtains and flowered sofas, is warm and welcoming. The hotel has a friendly and accommodating staff, some of whom are bilingual. Hotel Ciudad de Vitoria is also well located amid the impressive architecture of Providencia, the metro and local hangouts. The price is reasonable compared to other hotels in the area. Monjitas 527, Edificio Galaxy Center. Tel: 56-2-6333150, Fax: 56-2-6333270, E-mail: info@ciudaddevitoria.com, URL: www.ciudaddevitoria.cl. Updated: Jun 11, 2008.

Apart Hotel La Fayette

(ROOMS: $70, includes breakfast and WiFi) Right in the center of Providencia, Apart Hotel La Fayette is a great option if you prefer self-catering or just want to avoid backpackers. Each modern apartment is 30 square meters (98 square feet) and can sleep up to four people. The apartments have a bedroom, kitchen-living area (including cable TV, fridge, table, chairs and sofa-bed), bathroom and terrace. There's also underground parking and a small gym. Avenida 11 de Septiembre 2040, Closest metro: Pedro de Valdivia. Tel: 56- 2-2344433, URL: www.lafayette.cl. Updated: Apr 20, 2009.

Restaurants

Avenidas Providencia and 11 Septiembre, and their side streets are lined with restaurants, cafes and fast-food joints to suit all budgets and tastes. You can choose from traditional Chilean food, Italian, Japanese, Chinese, Peruvian, American and Mexican. Most establishments here cater to hungry office workers and many offer a set lunch menu that includes starter, main course, dessert and drink for under $10. Bear in mind that, with a fast turnover, service doesn't always come with a smile; in most cases you get what you pay for. For a good bargain lunch, head to Avenida Suecia and the restaurants around Metro Los Leones. If you fancy something a bit more upmarket, try the restaurants on Metro Manuel Montt and on Avenida Manuel Montt. Many eateries in Providencia are closed on Sundays. Updated: Apr 20, 2009.

Domino

(HOTDOGS: $3) You can't leave Chile without trying a *completo*, the Chilean-style hotdog, and there's no better place to try one than Domino. Opened in 1952, Domino sandwich bar has built up a small empire and now has outlets throughout the city. Sandwiches are packed with taste and calories. Forget the diet and try an *italiano completo* topped with lashings of mashed avocado and mayonnaise. The seating area is very small and at lunchtime you might have to eat standing at the bar. Avenida Providencia 2304, corner of Avenida Suecia, Closest metro: Los Leones. URL: www.domino.cl. Updated: Apr 20, 2009.

Oh! Salad Garden

(SALADS: $3 – 6) Oh! Salad Garden is a favorite among the work crowd with hundreds descending on it for lunch. This is fast food done the healthy way. You can get a range of soups, salads and sandwiches and meal deal combos. The food is generally fresh and tasty—the only criticism is that they're a bit heavy-handed with the lettuce. If you aren't a fan, telling the server "no quiero lechuga" should do the trick. Only soft drinks are served. Ricardo Lyon 190, Closest Metro: Los Leones. Tel: 56-2-2442787. Updated: Apr 20, 2009.

El Popular

(SANDWICHES: $6) El Popular is a sandwich bar located just beside Metro Los Leones and is a good place to stop if you need a quick snack. The tiny restaurant has space for about four people inside but there is a seating area outside. It can get pretty noisy, though, with the traffic from busy Avenida 11 de Septiembre. The menu includes a range of freshly made *completos* (hotdogs), hot sandwiches, French fries, beer and soft drinks. Try the *chacarero* (beef/chicken with tomato, green beans and green chili) or their special French fries coated in *merquen* (chili). Avenida 11 de Septiembre 2236. Tel: 56-2-3353208. Updated: Apr 20, 2009.

SANTIAGO

Elkika Ilmenau

(SANDWICHES: $6 and up) Elkika is a popular German restaurant located beside Metro Tobalaba. The restaurant offers a range of main courses, salads and snacks, but is really famous for the huge sandwiches. You can get steak, pork or chicken sandwiches piled high with vegetables, salads and spices. They're a bit overgenerous with the mayo, so if you're not a fan make sure you say so. Elkika has seating inside but try to get a table outside. Since it gets very busy at lunchtime, service can be a bit slow. Hernando de Aguirre 47. Tel: 56-2-2310260. Closed Sundays. Updated: Apr 20, 2009.

Rishtedar

(ENTREES: $6 – 8) Bright, colorful and modern, the Rishtedar Indian restaurant caters to a young, professional clientele. The cuisine is mainly styled after Goa in southern India, and includes a selection of vegetarian dishes. Their colorful basmati rice, served with cinnamon bark, is elegant but is definitely single-portion sized. The selection of beer and wine is limited, but kulfi lovers will enjoy their mixed almond and pistachi kulfi. Holanda 160. Tel: 56-2-2313257, URL: www.rishtedar. com. Updated: Jul 06, 2009.

El Huerto

(ENTREES: $7 – 10) El Huerto is well known in Santiago for its natural vegetarian food. If you are looking for a delicious but healthy meal during your time in Santiago, this is the place to go. The menu changes every week, which adds to the restaurant's attraction, so there is always something new and exciting to try at El Huerto. Orrego Luco 54. Tel: 56-2-2332690. Updated: Mar 24, 2008.

PhoneBox Pub

(ENTREES: $8 and up) Although hidden away in Galeria El Patio off Avenida Providencia, the PhoneBox Pub is easily recognizable by the red phone box at the main entrance. This is a traditional pub with excellent service and delicious food. It serves up traditional pub grub favorites like fish 'n' chips, chicken curry and steak and kidney pie in generous portions.

You can also get traditional Chilean food for about half the price. For $10 you can also get a set lunch menu (served from 1 p.m. to 3 p.m.) that includes starter, main course, dessert and alcoholic or non-alcoholic drink. This place gets really busy at night. Avenida

Providencia 1652, Galería El Patio, Closest metro: Pedro de Valdivia. Tel: 56-2-2359972. Updated: Apr 20, 2009.

Normandie

(ENTREES: $8 – 12) Located right on Avenida Providencia, Normandie is an old-fashioned French bistro with wooden tables, checked tablecloths and a traditional bar. The menu includes a range of salads, sandwiches, crepes and fish and meat dishes, although many people just come here to drink. At night the atmosphere is lively and it's a good place to meet old friends or make new ones. There are separate smoking and non-smoking sections. Avenida Providencia 1234, Closest Metro: Manuel Montt. Tel: 56-2-236 3011, URL: www.normandie1234.cl. Updated: Apr 20, 2009.

Delhi Darbar

(ENTREES: $9) The stylish, minimalist Delhi Darbar offers a range of typical Indian cuisine. Sometimes the food can be a bit salty, which is common in Chile. Accompaniments are good and traditional breads are served hot. Their lunchtime executive menu is reasonably priced and a full range of drinks are available. 11 Septiembre 2345. Tel: 56-2-3218102. Updated: Jul 06, 2009.

Los Insaciables

(ENTREES: $10 and up) Los Insaciables is a decent Italian restaurant just off Avenida Providencia that serves up healthy portions of pasta, pizza and salad. The best thing about this place is the incredible 'all you can eat' pizza deal. The deal is available for $9, Monday through Friday from 1 p.m. to 3:30 p.m., and includes countless slices of thin-crust pizza (meat and vegetable options) and a soft drink. Outside these hours you have to pay $11. There's indoor seating and tables on the street. The bar only serves soft drinks and beer. Andés de Fuenzalida 40, Closest Metro: Los Leones. Tel: 56-2-2323668, URL: www. losinsaciables.cl. Updated: Apr 20, 2009.

Los Cuates !

(ENTREES: $12 and up) Owned by a Mexican-Chilean couple, Los Cuates serves up authentic Mexican food in comfortable surroundings. The menu includes tacos, enchiladas, fajitas and burritos and a long list of tequilas and beers. Because it gets busy on weekends, service can be slow but the food is worth the wait. There are smoking and non-smoking sections. Avenida Manuel Montt 235, Closest metro: Manuel Montt. Tel: 56-2-2642376, URL: www.restaurant-loscuates.cl. Updated: Apr 20, 2009.

Liguria

(ENTREES: $12 – 18) When celebrities come to Santiago they head to Liguria for traditional Chilean food in unpretentious surroundings. The atmosphere is lively, the bar fully stocked and you can easily find yourself abandoning other plans and staying there for hours. The menu changes daily but you can expect a selection of tasty meat, pasta and seafood dishes all served up by efficient waiters. Liguria is very busy at lunchtime and at night. Make sure you are there by 1 pm for lunch and 8 pm for evening meals, otherwise you'll have to wait for a table and the choice of available dishes becomes limited. Avenida Providencia 1373, Closest metro: Manuel Montt. Tel: 56-2-2357914, URL: www. liguria.cl. Updated: Apr 20, 2009.

Gatsby

(BUFFET: $14) Gatsby (named after F. Scott Fitzgerald's *The Great Gatsby*) is an all-you can-eat buffet restaurant. For $14 you get to work your way through a range of starters, salads, main courses, desserts and soft drinks. There are also sandwiches, crepes and a huge range of cakes on the regular menu. No alcohol is served. Gatsby gets very busy at lunchtime. Avenida Providencia 1984, Closest metro: Pedro de Valdivia. Tel: 56-2-4817879, URL: www.gatsby.cl. Updated: Apr 20, 2009.

Nightlife

Bar Subterraneo

(COVER: $5) Subterraneo, located in Providencia, provides guests with some of the city's better disc jockey's - DJ Suau's freestyle beats tend to draw a crowd. A strong Caipiriña will cost approximately $5, though beers can be had for $2.50. The bar also has a sushi menu for those that need a bit of raw fish. Paseo Orrego Luco 46, E-mail: contacto@subterraneo.cl, URL: www.subterraneo. cl. Updated: Apr 22, 2009.

Boomerang

Locals and foreigners alike mix together at this popular spot in Providencia. The dance music is loud, but there are also pool tables to distract drinkers or tired dancers. The drinks are not overpriced and the menu offers some good bar food to reenergize yourself during breaks from the dance floor. General Holley 2285. Tel: 56-2-3345457. Updated: Apr 22, 2009.

Brannigan's

(ENTREES: $18) Brannigan's is a little more up-scale and not exactly the place to lose control. Still, this swanky corner pub in Providencia is a fine place to listen to some music while being able to maintain a conversation with the person across from you. Av. Suecia 35. Updated: Apr 22, 2009.

Oz

(COVER: $20) This is a high-priced option for those looking for a place to dance into the early morning. Chileans with a lot of style and money populate this techno club in Providencia. Admission is approximately $20. Bilbao 477. Updated: Apr 22, 2009.

Barrio Brazil

Bohemian Barrio Brazil is a favorite haunt of students and musicians. The area has great nightlife, good restaurants, a host of museums, and was declared a conservation area by local authorities for the abundance of beautiful old buildings, some predating the early 1900s. Many of the streets are still cobbled, which makes for a romantic ambiance. An insight into the well-to-do society of early 20th century Santiago, Barrio Brazil is a beautiful part of the city, and is worth the visit.

Life in the barrio is centered around Plaza Brazil. During the day, you'll find children playing amid the sculptures by Federica Matta (daughter of Roberto Matta, a famous Chilean painter). Night transforms the plaza into a meeting point for young people before they go partying in the clubs and bars. The plaza is a short walk from Metro station Cumming (green line).

On and around the streets Ricardo Cumming and Av. Brazil you'll find a wide choice of bars, cafes and restaurants to suit most tastes. Along Calle Concha y Toro (a short distance from Metro station República on line 1, the red line) you'll discover Zully, a trendy bar and restaurant that draws a crowd for its fancy cocktails.

Culture lovers will find good theaters a few blocks from Metro station República (red line), such as Teatro Palomera. Av. Matucana, near Metro station Quinta Normal (green line), holds The Centro Cultural Matucana 100, a renowned visual art gallery and performing arts venue, along with the Biblioteca de Santiago, the city's main library.
Quinta Normal, Santiago's oldest park, founded as a botanical garden in 1830, has it all: Museo de Historia Natural, Museo de Ciencia y Technolgia, Pabellon Gay,

SANTIAGO

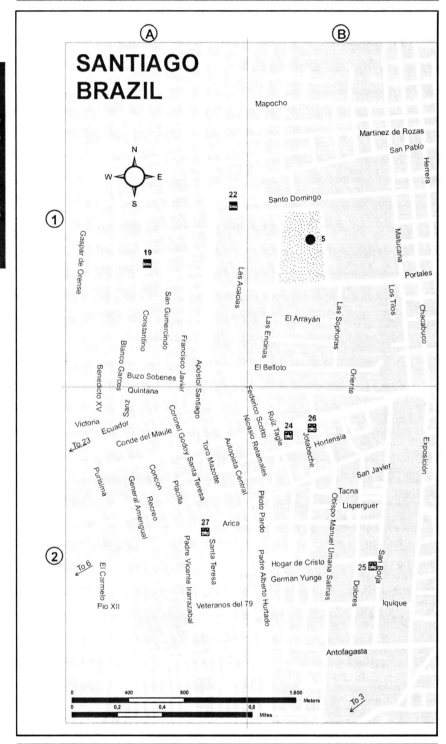

SANTIAGO

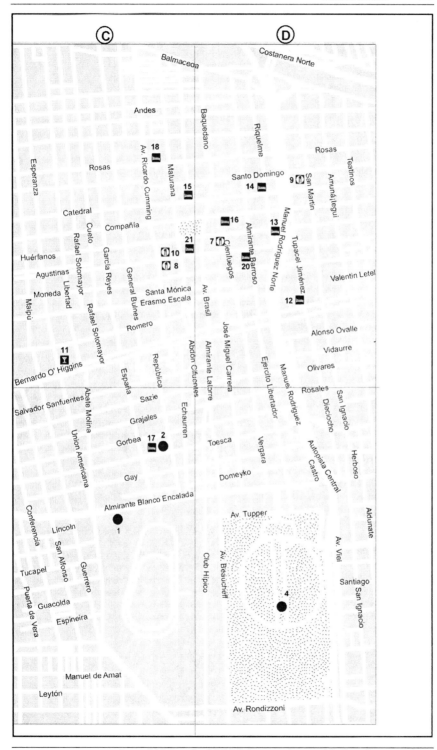

SANTIAGO

Activities ●		Sleeping ◼
1 Club Hípico C2		12 Che Lagarto Santiago D1
2 Museo de la Solidaridad Salvador		13 Chilestay Apartments D1
Allende C2		14 El Moai Viajero D1
3 National Aeronautic Museum B2		15 Happy House Hostel C1
4 Parque O´Higgins D2		16 Hostal Americano D1
5 Parque Quinta Normal B1		17 Hostal de Sammy C2
6 Templo Votivo de Maipu A2		18 Hostal Rio Amazonas C1
		19 Hostel Plaza de Armas A1
Eating 🍴		20 Hotel Tokyo D1
		21 La Casa Roja C1
7 Las Vacas Gordas D1		22 Majestic Hotel A1
8 Los Vikingos C1		
9 Majestic D1		Transportation 🚌
10 Ocean Pacific C1		
		23 Bus Estación Pajaritos A2
Nightlife 🍷		24 Bus Terminal Alameda B2
		25 Bus Terminal San Borja B2
11 Blondie C1		26 Bus Terminal Santiago B2
		27 Estación Central A2

Centro Cultural Municipal, Museo Infantil, the Centro de Extensión Balmaceda, Museo de Arte Contempeoráneo, Parque Museo Ferroviario, along with a sports center and Metro Station Quinta Normal (green line). Around the park area you'll find the Museo Artequin and the Basilica Lourdes. A block away from the park on Escuela Normal is the Museo Pedagologico Gabriella Mistral, named after the famous Chilean writer.

The city's main railway station, Metro Estación Central (red line), constructed in 1897, boasts an Art Nouveau glass roof. Around the central station are many market stalls and importers, which makes a good stop for the budget shopper. The metro is an easy way to get around the area, but taxis are necessary after the metro stops running at 10:30 p.m. (10 p.m. on Sundays). Updated: Jul 07, 2009.

Things to See and Do

Club Hípico
Opened in 1870, Club Hípico was Santiago's first horseback riding club. The original building, inspired by the Long Champs Riding Club in France, was destroyed in a fire in 1892. It was subsequently rebuilt and reopened in 1923. In its heyday, Club Hípico was considered the playground of the elite. It now attracts a more working class crowd and it is still the most popular spot to watch horse racing in Santiago.
The club also has bars and restaurants, a picnic area and landscaped gardens. Go on Monday or Friday if you want to catch live races. The website has up-to-date race schedules. Av.

Blanco Encalada 2540. Closest metro: Parque O'Higgins. Tel: 56-2-6939600, URL: www.clubhipico.cl, Open 9 a.m. – 6:30 p.m. Closed Saturday and Sunday. Updated: Jul 07, 2009.

Museo de la Solidaridad
Salvador Allende
(ADMISSION: $1.20; free Sundays) The Museo de la Solidaridad Salvador Allende was founded in the early 1970s, but was forced underground during Pinochet's dictatorship. Now run by the Salvador Allende Foundation, the museum commemorates the life and political career of the deposed socialist President. Many of the artworks were created by artists around the world in support of Allende's socialist regime. Others were created in protest of Pinochet's coup, Allende's subsequent suicide and the dictatorship that followed.

Whether you love or hate Allende's political policies, the museum offers a kitsch collection of art that dates from the 1960s to 1980s. This isn't a must-see, but a good stop on a rainy day, or if you have time to kill in Santiago. Av. República 475. Closest metro: Metro República. URL: www.mssa.cl. Open 10 a.m. – 6 p.m. Closed Monday. Updated: Oct 29, 2008.

National Aeronautic Museum
(ADMISSION: Free; donations encouraged) At this indoor/outdoor museum, plane buffs can discover the history of Chilean aviation. The museum holdings range from Chile's very first plane, right through to an example of the jets used in Pinochet's 1973 military coupe. You'll

find some of the larger planes exhibited in pleasant gardens at the front of the building. The museum also has a small exhibit for space endeavors. Camino a Melipilla 5000. Tel: 56-2-4353030, E-mail: museo@dgac.cl, URL: www.museoaeronautico.cl. Open 10 a.m. – 5:30 p.m. Updated: Jun 10, 2008.

Parque O'Higgins !

Parque O'Higgins, named after Chile's liberator, Bernardo O'Higgins, covers an area of 77 hectares and is Santiago's second largest park. It used to be the playground for the rich, but is now popular with the working class, especially on the weekends and holidays. There is plenty of green space where you can walk, cycle and picnic. There's also a public pool, skate park, tennis courts and a football field. Other attractions at Parque O'Higgins include: the amusement park Fantasilandia; Arena Santiago, which hosts musical events; Museo del Huaso, Chile's cowboy museum, and El Pueblito, a small street with restaurants and shops that sell artisan goods.

The best time to visit is during the national holidays on September 18 and 19. At this time, the park has a number of *fondas* (traditional parties with food, drink, live music and dancing). On September 19, the military performs an impressive parade at Campos de Marte. Av. Via Norte Sur. Closest metro: Parque O'Higgins. Tel: 56-2-7318336, Open 9 a.m. – 7 p.m. Updated: Oct 30, 2008.

Parque Quinta Normal

Quinta Normal is one of Santiago's most popular parks, covering an area of 40 hectares in the west part of the city. It has several walkways, a small boating lake, a skate park and go-karts to rent. It's also home to four museums, including the Natural History Museum, Artequin Museum (that features reproductions of world-famous paintings), Science and Technology Museum and Railway Museum. The park and museums are a bit run down and underfunded. There are much nicer parks in the city and Quinta Normal is worth going to if you have run out of ways to entertain the kids. Matucana 520. Closest metro: Quinta Normal. Open 9 a.m. – 7 p.m. Updated: Oct 29, 2008.

Templo Votivo de Maipú

Templo Votivo de Maipú, built between 1944 and 1974, is a huge Catholic temple erected on a historical site that dates back to the early 1800s. Bernardo O'Higgins commissioned a church dedicated the Virgen del Carmen to commemorate Chile's success in the Maipú battlefields and the country's progression toward independence. O'Higgins relied on public donations and the construction was never really finished. Today you can still see the ruins of the original, ill-fated church. Av. 5 de Abril and Ca. Carmen 1750. Updated: Jul 01, 2009.

Lodging

Barrio Brazil has many budget hotels and hostels, all of which are well located in terms of transportation and tourism. The beauty of this barrio is that the hotels can be cheaper than the hostels, meaning better service and a quieter stay for less money. Check them out before you book a hostel in the area. The barrio also has many motels; these are normally rented on an hourly basis by courting couples and lovers. Some do welcome overnight visitors and are cheaper than you might think. However, you should note that motels can present a different noise problem than what you find in hostels.

Hostal de Sammy

(ROOMS: $10 – 16, includes breakfast) Named after the owner's late pet dog, this place is a backpacker's dream. The hostel, set in a huge house in Santiago, has a kitchen that serves breakfast every morning, a dining room, a living room with a TV, DVD player and video game system, a game room with a pool and ping pong table, and a laundry room which residents can use for free.

There are single, double, and dorm rooms available. Guests who plan to stay more than six days can recieve a discount. Monthly rates are also available. Toesca 2335. Tel: 56-2-6898772, URL: www.hostaldesammy.com. Updated: May 08, 2007.

Che Lagarto Santiago

(ROOMS: $12 and up; promotions available online) Che Lagarto Santiago is one of a chain of hostels located throughout South America. If you want cheap, no-frills accommodation and a chance to meet with other like-minded backpackers, this will be right up your alley. Most beds are in small, shared dorms with shared bathrooms, but there is free Internet, WiFi, breakfast, dinner promos and tours. Che Lagarto is close to the main bus station (Los Heroes), and the airport bus stop is just five minutes up the street. Tucapel

Jimenez 24. Closest metro: Los Heroes. Tel: 56-2-6691493, URL: www.chelagarto. com. Updated: Apr 20, 2009.

La Casa Roja

(ROOMS: $12 shared dorm; $36 double with private bathroom) This hostel is an old, big,red building that is probably one of the largest in Santiago. If you're looking for a place with a pool and bar, it's perfect. They even have a cricket pitch. Dorms are white with some colorful wood work and old but elegant wood furnishings. Communal areas are welcoming, though the kitchen makes for a chaotic place when the hostel is full. Ample Internet access and WiFi are provided. Tourism info and services, including tours, can be found at the reception. Communal and private double dorms are available. Augustinas 2113. Tel: 56-2-6964241, E-mail: info@ lacasaroja.tie.cl, URL: www.lacasaroja.cl. Updated: Jun 04, 2008.

El Moai Viajero

(ROOMS: $15 and up) Set inside a pretty colonial house, El Moai Viajero is just minutes away from historical downtown and the bars and restaurants of Barrio Brazil. With its chilled-out atmosphere, El Moai Viajero is a welcoming home away from home for a few days. The hostel has private rooms and shared dorms that sleep up to six. Facilities include a kitchen and dining room, living room, garden and BBQ area. Breakfast and free WiFi are included. Staff can also arrange Spanish lessons. Riquelme 536 (between Catedral and Santa Domingo). Closest metro: Santa Ana. Tel: 56-2-6990229, E-mail: info@ elmoaiviajerohostel.cl / reservas@elmoaivi-ajerohostel.cl, URL: www.moaiviajerohostel. cl. Updated: Apr 21, 2009.

Happy House Hostel

(ROOMS: $18 and up, includes breakfast) With its sleek modern touches and Victorian buildings, the Happy House Hostel has a more upscale feel than most other backpacker haunts. The hostel offers both private and dorm rooms, some of which have their own bathrooms. Discounts are available for longer stays. There is an entertainment room, living room, kitchen, and laundry room on-site. Happy House is a bit more expensive than other hostels, but if you want a place with ambiance, this is a wonderful option. Catedral 2207. Tel: 56-2-6884849, E-mail: info@happyhouse.cl, URL: www.happy-househostel.cl. Updated: May 08, 2007.

Hostal Rio Amazonas

(ROOMS: $25, single with bathroom; $36 double with bathroom) This typical single-story Chilean building's streetfront doesn't give an overpowering impression, but features a seemingly endless and widening hallway. The hallway leads to a light and airy cafe and a bar that stays open until midnight. Dorm or double rooms are available, which are lightly furnished and functional. The staff is welcoming and informative. You'll find an extensive information library on hand at reception. A short walk from Metro station Cumming (green line), this hostel is well positioned and can arrange airport transfers. Rosas 2234, E-mail: reservas@hostalrioamazonas.cl, URL: www. hostalrioamazonas.cl/english. Updated: Jun 04, 2008.

Hostal Americano

(ROOMS: $26 and up) More of a B&B than a hostel, Hostal Americano offers single, double, triple and quadruple rooms and is a favorite among travelers in their mid-20s to 30s. It's one metro stop from the Plaza de Armas and for a few dollars you can get a taxi to the bars and restaurants of Barrio Brazil. Breakfast and WiFi are included and there's a shared kitchen, living room and garden with BBQ area to relax in. Compañia de Jesús 1906. Closest metro: Santa Ana. Tel: 56-2-6981025, E-mail: hostal@hostalamericano.cl, URL: www.hosta-lamericano.cl. Updated: Apr 21, 2009.

Hotel Tokyo

(ROOMS: $50, double with bathroom) Hotel Tokyo is an elegant townhouse with a touch of Tokyo. Rooms have a delicate floral décor, and there is a a pleasant garden and ample covered parking. A great choice for couples on a budget, this hotel is also well located for public transport, near metro station Los Heroes. Almirante Barroso 160. Tel: 56-2-6984500, E-mail: info@hoteltokyo.cl, URL: www.hotel-tokyo.cl. Updated: Jun 04, 2008.

Chilestay Apartments

(ROOMS: $60, one-bedroom apartment; $90, two-bedroom apartment) Chilestay Apartments has one- and two-bedroom self-catering apartments available for longer stays. The modern apartments are a great option for families or those who are just tired of hotels. They are fully furnished and come with TV, WiFi and a portable phone. The apartments are located on a quiet street a couple of blocks from Santa Ana metro station, but are still close to plenty of restaurants. There is a guard at the door providing 24-hour security. The minimum stay is two nights. 1685 Huerfanos. Closest metro: Santa Ana, Tel: 1-(415)-578-3183, URL: www. chilestay.com. Updated: Apr 21, 2009.

Restaurants

Barrio Brazil has some of the best restaurants, cafes and fashionably styled bars in Santiago. The variety is second to none, with themed and specialty restaurants, such as Mexican, Peruvian, Chinese and the local favorite, Sushi. Most are located around Plaza Brazil and toward Av. Liberator Bernardo O'Higgins, on and around the main streets Av. Brazil and Ricardo Cumming. Prices range from cheap to expensive, making the barrio a suitable place for every budget.

Los Vikingos

(ENTREES: $5 – 10) If you're looking to try the local food in a fun place, then this is a must. A Viking long-boat, flaming torches, shields and weapons adorn the entrance and interior of this Medieval-themed restaurant that claims to dish out "Barbarian Flavors." The wine list is short, but the service is good. Specialties here are the meat dishes, Pernil, steak and ribs, but they also have a good selection of seafood. The Chilean stews (*calderas*) are also recommended. Sopaipillas and mini empanadas give the bread basket a touch of Chile. Ricardo Cumming 174. Tel: 56-2-6972413. Updated: Jun 04, 2008.

Las Vacas Gordas

(ENTREES: under $10) Las Vacas Gordas makes meat their forte using a flame and charcoal grill. Chorizo comes in sizes up to half a kilo. Las Vacas Gordas (the fat cows) is also known for its king prawn and oyster dishes. It's a popular eatery, marked by a starkly lit and bland interior. If you are looking for style above all, then this isn't for you. But, if you want whopping steaks and simple, reasonably priced food, then you'll love it. It's a restaurant that locals recommend, and reservations are a must. Cienfuegos 280. Tel: 56-2-6736962 / 6971066. Updated: Jun 03, 2008.

V!VA ONLINE REVIEW
LAS VACAS GORDAS

Great atmosphere with the open grill, see your great steaks cooked in front of you!

August 18, 2008

Ocean Pacific

(ENTREES: $10 – 16, includes wine) This ocean-themed restaurant won't disappoint seafood lovers. Ocean Pacific is well known locally and specializes in typical Chilean dishes. It has themed dining areas, such as the torpedo-inspired Comedor El Torpedero. Nautical nuts will delight in the adjoining souvenir shop. The menu has pictures of the dishes, which are helpful for non-Spanish speakers. The non-seafood menu is admirable as well, with several decent meat dishes. Service is good and the staff are accommodating. Ricardo Cumming 221, Santiago. Tel: 56-2-6972413. Updated: Jun 04, 2008.

Majestic

(ENTREES: $15 – 25) Majestic is by far the best Indian restaurant in Santiago. In fact, you'll have to book one week in advance if you want to eat there. The Indian chef specializes in curries and tandoori cuisine and the menu includes vegetarian and vegan options. The food isn't cheap, but is well worth the price. The staff is friendly and provide excellent service. Open daily for lunch and dinner, closed Sunday. Santo Domingo 1526. Tel: 56-2-6909400, Fax: 56-2-6974051, E-mail: hotelmajestic@hotelmajestic.cl, URL: www. hotelmajestic.cl. Updated: Jun 04, 2008.

Blondie

(COVER: $7) Blondie draws hip and youthful bar-seekers to its four-floor dance club and can pack in as many as 2,000 dancers. Each level features different genres of music, but the main floor draws the most people. Sometimes the club features live concerts by local musicians. Alameda 2879. Tel: 56-2-6817793. URL: www.blondie.cl. Updated: May 18, 2009.

Las Condes

Las Condes, in Santiago Oriente or East Santiago, is one of the most modern and stylish of all Santiago's neighborhoods. This upmarket location covers an area of 99.4 square kilometers (61.7 sq. mi) and is home to Santiago's business and financial district. The wide tree-lined avenues of Isidora Goyenechea, El Bosque Norte and Apoquindo are filled with steel and glass skyscrapers and five star hotels, though the quieter side streets host modern apartment blocks.

This area doesn't offer much by the way of history, but it does present an interesting glimpse into how the middle class live, work and play. Updated: Jun 04, 2008.

SANTIAGO

Shopping

Parque Arauco

Parque Arauco is a huge shopping mall with several major brand stores and a food court. It also has a multiplex cinema, bowling alley, iceskating rink and boulevard with several restaurants and bars. The closest metro stop is Escuela Militar. From there you can walk about 20 minutes, take a taxi for around $2 or get the bus from Avenida Apoquindo. Av. Kennedy 5413. Tel: 56-2-2990500, URL: www.parquearauco.cl, Open 11 a.m. – 9 p.m. Updated: Nov 03, 2008.

Alto Las Condes

Alto Las Condes is the most upmarket mall in Santiago, with several chain stores and boutiques. It also has a foodcourt and cinema. The closest metro stop is Escuela Militar. From there you can get the bus to Avenida Apoquindo. Av. Presidente Kennedy 9001. Tel: 56-2-2996965, URL: www.cencosud-shopping.cl/altolascondes/index.php. Open 10 a.m. – 10 p.m. Updated: Nov 03, 2008.

Mall Sport

Mall Sport is a bit out of the way, but it's the best bet if you want to buy sportswear or equipment. The mall is dedicated to all things sporting, including snow, equestrian, camping, surfing, biking and sailing gear. It's also a good place to take the kids for a few hours, since it has an artificial wave pool to practice surfing, a rock-climbing wall, a skate park and an iceskating rink. Av. Las Condes 13541, URL: www.mallsport.cl. Open 10 a.m. – 9 p.m. Updated: Nov 03, 2008.

Pueblo Los Dominicos

Pueblo Los Dominicos is the place to buy artisan goods. The craft village has more than 150 workshops that sell ceramics, furniture, paintings, sculptures, jewelry, leather goods and clothes. It also has several cafe-bars and live entertainment. It's a great place to spend a few hours. The metro line is currently being extended to serve Pueblo Los Dominicos, but for now you'll have to make do with the bus. Use the journey planner at www.transantiagoinforma.cl to plan your route. Av. Apoquindo 9085, URL: www.pueblito-losdominicos.com, Open 11 a.m. – 8 p.m. Closed Mondays. Updated: Jul 08, 2009.

Alonso de Cordova

Avenida Alonso de Cordova is the most exclusive shopping street in Santiago. It's home to world-famous designer brands and several stylish boutiques. This classy avenue also has several restaurants. If you like fashion, it's a great place to spend a few hours browsing. There is no metro station close by so you'll have to get a micro bus. Use the journey planner at www.transantiagoinforma.cl. Avenida Alonso de Cordova, Vitacura. Hours vary. Closed Sunday.

Lodging

If you're looking for cheap hotels in Las Condes, forget it. Hotels here cater only to the mid and upper end of the market. Here you can find all the usual international suspects (Holiday Inn, Mariott, Hyatt and Raddison) located on the main avenues. There are some cheaper, independent hotels on the side streets, but they can be difficult to find. Ask a local to point you in the right direction. If you prefer to stay with the tried and tested brand, shop around. Good deals are available online. Updated: Jun 04, 2008.

Leonardo da Vinci

(ROOMS: $130 and up) If you want to stay in Las Condes, and your hotel budget won't stretch to the five star rivals, you could do worse than the Hotel Leonardo da Vinci. Tucked off the busy Av. Apoquindo, this comfortable hotel offers all the amenities for a lower price. The décor is traditional, but the rooms are large and equipped with cable TVs, minibars, safes and free WiFi. The friendly staff will go out of their way to help you. Malaga 194, Closest metro: Alcantara. Tel: 56-2-3745800, Fax: 56-2-3745834, E-mail: reservas@hotelleonardo-davinci.cl, URL: www.hotelleonardodavinci.cl, Updated: Jun 05, 2008.

Holiday Inn Express

(ROOMS: $140 and up) The Holiday Inn Express-Las Condes is a perfect resting place for the weary business traveler. Although the hotel doesn't have much personality, its proximity to the heart of Santiago's business district makes it a smart choice. The large and functional rooms are equipped with a desk, Internet and cable TV. There is also a gym and sauna. The buffet breakfast is included in the price, as well as a coffee bar that serves beer. The hotel doesn't have a restaurant but it's close to several restaurants and bars. The reception staff can also order food from three local restaurants as late as 1 a.m.

The helpful staff speaks Spanish, English and Portuguese and can arrange anything from airport transfers to getting your

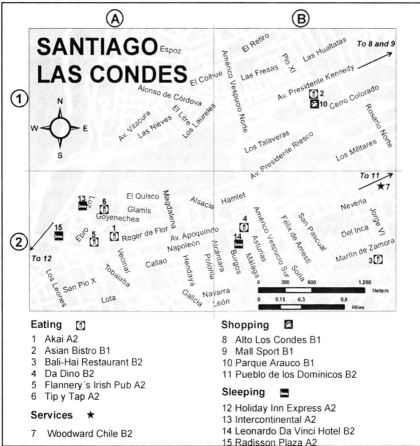

Eating 🍽

1 Akai A2
2 Asian Bistro B1
3 Bali-Hai Restaurant B2
4 Da Dino B2
5 Flannery's Irish Pub A2
6 Tip y Tap A2

Services ★

7 Woodward Chile B2

Shopping ◪

8 Alto Los Condes B1
9 Mall Sport B1
10 Parque Arauco B1
11 Pueblo de los Dominicos B2

Sleeping 🛏

12 Holiday Inn Express A2
13 Intercontinental A2
14 Leonardo Da Vinci Hotel B2
15 Radisson Plaza A2

laundry done. Av. Vitacura 2929, Closest metro: Tobalaba. Tel: 56-2-4996000, Fax: 56-2-4996200, E-mail: reservas@talbot.cl, URL: www.holidayinn.cl. Updated: Mar 12, 2009.

Intercontinental

(ROOMS: $170 and up) From the moment the concierge, dressed head to toe in black dress jacket and top hat, welcomes you to the Intercontinental Hotel, you know you've entered a classy joint. The luxurious reception area somewhat outshines the traditionally decorated rooms, but they do come equipped with everything you would expect from a five-star hotel. The facilities include two restaurants (Italian and international), a bar with live music, 24-hour gym, heated pool, sauna, business center and gift shop. The hotel has several meeting rooms. Room service is available 24 hours. Don't miss the great view of Santiago from the hotel pool.The Intercontinental is located in the center of Santiago's business district, close to several restaurants and a five minute taxi ride from the designer boutiques of Vitacura. Av. Vitacura 2885, Closest metro: Tobalaba. Tel: 56-2-3942000, Fax: 56-2-3942075, E-mail: santiago@interconti.cl, URL: www.intercontisantiago.com. Updated: Jun 04, 2008.

Radisson Plaza

(ROOMS: $170 and up) Located in the World Trade Center, this four star hotel is right in the heart of Santiago's business and financial district, but still a stone's throw away from the more relaxed Providencia. The Radisson is more like a small village with on-site restaurants and bar, spa, swimming pool, beauty salon, florist and gift shop. For those arriving by helicopter, there's even a heliport.

It's a great option for both business travelers and anyone who wants to splurge for a few days. Great deals are available if you book online. Av. Vitacura 2610, Closest metro: Tobalaba (5 mins by taxi or 15 mins walk from Tobalaba). Tel: 56-2-2036000, Fax: 56-2-2036001, E-mail: radisson@radisson.cl, URL: www.radisson.com/santiagocl. Updated: Jun 05, 2008.

Restaurants

Despite being Santiago's most exclusive area, Las Condes has restaurants to suit every budget. There are several fine dining establishments for the wealthy, especially around Isidora Goyenechea. Look a little deeper and you'll find more affordable places catering to the thousands of hungry office workers. Restaurants in Las Condes tend to be crowded at lunchtime (1 – 3 p.m.) and many either close or sit empty in the afternoon. Those serving alcohol pick up again when the offices close. Many restaurants have terraces for al fresco dining and serve real coffee. Updated: Jun 04, 2008.

Akai

(SUSHI: $5 – 10) It can be hard to find good sushi in Santiago, but Akai delivers some of the tastiest and freshest sushi around, at a very reasonable price. Make sure you pay in cash, as the prices double if you pay by credit card. Akai is open for lunch from 1 – 3 p.m., and dinner from 7 – 11:15 p.m. The work crowd invades about 1 p.m. so make sure you get there early to avoid waiting for a table. There are smoking and non-smoking areas, and a terrace for al fresco dining. No alcohol is served. Carmencita 106. Tel: 56-2-2315878, URL: www.akaisushi.cl. Updated: Jun 05, 2008.

Asian Bistro

The Asian Bistro offers an ambitious range of Chinese, Thai and Japanese food in a bright, modern restaurant with mirrored walls and glass staircase. The menu includes wantons, tempura, spring rolls, sushi, Thai curries, duck, seafood and meat dishes. The food, though slightly overpriced, is good and served in large portions. The restaurant has smoking and non-smoking areas and a terrace. If you want peace and quiet, then check it out in the late afternoon, as lunchtimes and evenings are pretty busy. Av. Kennedy 5413/Boulevard Parque Arauco, local 373. Tel: 56-2-2201430. Updated: Jun 04, 2008.

Da Dino

(PIZZA: $7 – 15) Da Dino might be a little out of your way, but its well worth the journey to experience the best pizza in town. It's unlikely you'll be able to manage more than two or three of these slices, which is just as well, as the place isn't cheap. Be warned: you may find yourself dreaming about the pizza for weeks afterward. The restaurant also serves hot sandwiches, snacks, main courses and a delicious range of desserts, but the bar only serves beer. Av. Apoquindo 4228. Updated: Jun 05, 2008.

Tip y Tap

(ENTREES: $10 and up) Opened in 1975 with the mission of creating the best sandwiches in Santiago, Tip y Tap does not disappoint. Try the delicious Hamburguesa or Ave. Tip y Tap (a huge, hot chicken sandwich filled with lettuce, tomato, avocado, red peppers, melted cheese and ketchup). The restaurant also offers salads, desserts, a kid's menu, more expensive meat and fish dishes and a wide selection of alcoholic and non-alcoholic drinks. Tip y Tap attracts the usual work crowd, but is also a place to meet friends and relax. The staff is friendly and the service is excellent. Isidora Goyenechea 2922. Tel: 56-2-3343302. Updated: Jun 04, 2008.

Bali-Hai Restaurant

(ENTREES: about $30) Styling itself as the "unique Easter Island Restaurant in Latin America," this place offers dinner with a dance show. Dances are from different parts of Chile, including Chiloé and of course, Easter Island. Food is Chilean and Polynesian themed, offering options for a variety of palates, including vegetarian. There is a set menu for $30, which is a cut down version of the main menu. For this price you can expect pre-dinner drink, starter, main and dessert. Once the performance is over, the dance floor clears and patrons are free to get up and strut their stuff. The clientele is mainly Chileans and Latin American tourists. Open from 8.30 p.m. Monday through Saturday. Av. Colón 5146. Tel: 56-2-2288273 / 2294235, URL: www.balihai.cl. Updated: Jul 01, 2009.

Flannery's Irish Pub

(ENTREES: $8 – 11) In general, Irish pubs abroad are tourist traps, and Flannery's is no exception. This is not all bad, however. The bar food is good, there is Guinness and, if Chilean football is not your cup of tea, it is a good place to find a game from the United States or Europe. Encomenderos 83. Tel: 56-2-2336675. Updated: Apr 22, 2009.

Barrio Ñuñoa

The middle-class residential area of Ñuñoa is home to the national football stadium, Estadio Nacional, and to Santiago's only mosque, Al-Salam. Most of the business takes place along Irarrázaval Avenue, which stretches across the entire barrio. The main reason to come to Ñuñoa is for the rich nightlife. The action is concentrated in Plaza Ñuñoa, which is full of bars with live music, restaurants and fast-food joints. Don't miss Club de Jazz (www.clubdejazz.cl), which famously hosted Louis Armstrong. If rock is more your thing, then head to Batuta (www.batuta.cl). Plaza Ñuñoa isn't covered by the metro network. To get there, take the metro to Irarrazaval and take a bus (eastbound) to the plaza. Updated: Jun 18, 2009.

Things to See and Do

Parque por la Paz Villa Grimaldi

This park is a place of great historical importance in Chile. Once a symbol of independence, the founding fathers of Chile came here to draw up ideas for freedom from Spain. In the late 1800s and mid 1900s it was used as a meeting place for intellectuals, artists and politicians. Then, during Pinochet's 1973 military coup, Villa Grimaldi was turned into a detention, torture and death camp. It is the only preserved detention center in Latin America.

In the early 1980s, attempts were made to demolish the estate and hide the evidence, but human rights groups intervened and saved the grounds. The park is worth a visit if you want to understand Chile's turbulent recent history. Jose Arrieta 8401. URL: www.villagrimaldicorp.cl/eng/index_eng.htm. Updated: Dec 09, 2008.

Restaurants

Fuente Suiza

(SANDWICHES: $4 and up) Fuente Suiza is an old-fashioned family restaurant that probably hasn't changed much since it opened in 1954. But when the food tastes this good, why change the recipe? The restaurant serves up delicious homemade empanadas and huge sandwiches washed down with beer or soft drinks. It's a great place to sink your teeth into one of Chile's sloppy *churrasco italianos* (a big greasy sliced-beef sandwich topped with tomato, avocado, and mayo). It gets busy at lunchtime and in the evening, but is surprisingly large inside and, if

Eating

1 Blue Pub B1
2 Fuente Suiza B1
3 La Tecla B2

Nightlife

4 Club de Jazz A2
5 HBH Brewery A1
6 Laberinto A1
7 Las Lanzas B1

SANTIAGO

you're willing to wait a short while, the friendly staff will find somewhere to squeeze you in. Av. Irarrázaval 3361, URL: www.fuentesuiza. cl. Updated: Jun 18, 2009.

Blue Pub

(ENTREES: $15 and up) The Blue Pub is a cute little bistro that serves up salads and pastas at lunchtime and a range of tablas, empanadas and sushi at night. The tasty snacks are all accompanied by happy hour cocktails (usually lasting all night) and live music. It's a popular spot with locals and a good choice for a night out, especially if you want to get off the well-beaten tourist track of Bellavista and Providencia. 19 de Abril 3526. Tel: 56-2-2237132, URL: www. pubblue.cl. Updated: Jun 18, 2009.

La Tecla

(ENTREES: $18 and up) One block from Plaza Ñuñoa, La Tecla ("the keyboard") is easy to spot. Just look for the pink period house with a gaudy piano keyboard painted over most of the exterior walls. The keyboard theme continues inside, with the bar designed to look like a piano key. Don't let this put you off, though. The restaurant is famous for two things: delicious homemade pancakes with savory and sweet fillings, and the local celebrities who hang out there. Whether you'll be able to recognize them or not after a few shots at the bar is anyone's guess. Doctor Johow 320. Tel: 56-2-2743603 / 4751673. Updated: Jun 18, 2009.

Nightlife

Las Lanzas

This is a popular spot among locals to find a cheap drink in Ñuñoa. It is in full bloom during the summer months when patrons spill out into the street. Head here to mix with the hip Chileans and to avoid the tourists in the bars or clubs of Bellavista. Trucco 25. Tel: 56-2-2255589. Updated: Apr 20, 2009.

HBH Brewery

A popular spot among local students, young professionals and beer snobs, this microbrewery offers its own highly-rated dark (*negro*) and light (*rubia*) beers, as well as a wide selection of bottled brews for picky drinkers. The atmosphere is laidback and there is generally good music to accompany a glass of suds. Av. Irarrázaval 3176. Tel: 56-2-2043075. Updated: May 18, 2009.

Club de Jazz

(COVER: $5; $3 for students) Club de Jazz is a nice spot to relax and listen to live jazz music in Ñuñoa. The atmosphere is relaxed and the drink service is quick. The bar often has international musicians who jam in the small, intimate, and usually packed, space. Local jazz artists also put on a pretty good show at this club. There is a nice open-air garden at the bar, too. Plan on live music on Thursdays, Fridays and Saturdays. Av. José Pedro Alessandri 85. Updated: Apr 22, 2009.

AROUND SANTIAGO

Santiago is surrounded by a bevy of activities that offer a little something for everyone. You can try some of the best wine in the whole of Chile (which puts it pretty high on the list of best wine in the world) on a day-trip from Santiago, such as at the nation's most famous winery, Viña Concha y Toro. After an afternoon of wine tasting, spend the next day on an outdoor adventure. Depending on the season, there are great rafting, hiking and horse riding choices. During the winter season, Chile boasts world-class skiing. Portillo earns high marks from all visitors and La Parva claims to be the most exclusive in the area, but there are cheaper options available for backpackers and those on a budget. Updated: Jun 29, 2009.

VINEYARDS

South of Santiago, the endless sprawling suburbs gradually melt away to reveal Chile's most fertile region; orchards, vineyards and pastures make up a blanket of greens, yellows and browns as far as the eye can see. Sip your way through the Ruta del Vino, where vineyards produce what is arguably the best red wine in South America. Nearly all vineyards offer tours and tastings of their vintages, which you can then buy at knockdown prices. Many of the larger estates also offer accommodation, often in traditional haciendas.

If you visit in March, you'll see the grapes being harvested and pressed. It is possible to take an all-inclusive tour to a vineyard Santiago, which can be a good idea if you're short on time or Spanish skills. Otherwise, it's far cheaper to organize transport yourself, as the vineyards themselves don't charge. Two of the best vineyards are Viña Concha y Toro, one of the oldest in the country, and Viña Santa Inés. Both offer tours in English. Updated: Jul 07, 2009.

Viña Concha y Toro

Viña Concha y Toro is the largest and best-known winery in Chile. The grapevines here originally came from France when local politician and businessman Don Melchor Concha y Toro planted the Bordeaux product on these beautiful grounds in Pirque. The tour includes a couple of glasses of wine, a viewing of "El Diablo" and you get to keep your glass at the end of the tour. Be sure to call in advance to reserve a spot. Av. Virginia Subercaseaux 210, Pirque. Tel: 56-2-4765269, URL: www.conchaytoro.com.

Viña Santa Rita

Viña Santa Rita is located in the village of Alto Jahuel, south of Santiago. The vineyard was founded in 1880 by Domingo Fernández Concha, and today produces some of the best wines in the nation. There is a fine restaurant and museum on-site as well, which are both included in the tour. Reservations can be made by filling out an online form. Camino Padre Hurtado 0695. Tel: 56-2-3622594, URL: www.santarita.cl.

Viña Santa Carolina

Viña Santa Carolina is especially nice for those that do not have much time to stray from the capital but still want to visit a winery. It's located in the neighborhood of Macul, just a 15 minute walk from Metro Rodrigo de Araya (Línea 5). The vineyards themselves are located in the valleys of Cachapoal, Colchagua, and Casablanca. Rodrigo de Araya 1431, Macul, Santiago. Tel: 56-2-4503000, URL: www.santacarolina.com.

Viña Undurraga

This winery was founded in 1885 by Francisco Undurraga. It is located approximately 30 kilometers (18 mi) southwest of Santiago on old Melipilla Highway between Talagante and Peñaflor. Camino a Melipilla Km 34. Tel: 56-2-3722850, URL: www.undurraga.cl.

Viña Cousiño Macul

Viña Cousiño Macul is located within the city limits of Santiago in the southeastern neighborhood of Peñalolén, and is one of the nation's oldest wineries.

By subway, take Línea 4 to the Quilín stop and walk for about 30 minutes east on Quilin Avenue, or take a taxi. Av. Quilín 7100. Tel: 56-2-3514135, URL: www.cousinomacul.cl, E-mail: info@cousinomacul.cl.

Viña De Martino

Viña De Martino was founded in 1934 by Pietro De Martino and is located only 50 kilometers (31 mi) from Santiago in beautiful Isla del Maipo (between the Andes and the Pacific Ocean). Tours begin in the wine shop where a bilingual guide explains aging, bottling and other aspects of wine making. The tour then moves into the tasting room. Manuel Rodríguez 229, Isla de Maipo. Tel: 56-2-8192959 / 2062, Fax: 56-2-8192986, URL: www.demartino.cl. Updated: Jul 07, 2009.

SKIING

Portillo has a reputation for the best international skiing in Chile. The United States, Italian and Austrian Olympic teams come to these hills, next to the alpine lake Laguna del Inca and near the Argentine border, for summer training. The slopes range in altitude from 2,590 – 3,310 meters (8,497 – 10,859 ft), with the longest run at 3,200 meters (1.9 mi). Valle Nevado, La Parva and El Colorado are also popular destinations, and all welcome snowboarders as well.

The ski and snowboard season runs from June until late September or early October. Be sure to check your intended resort's website for up-to-date weather conditions. Most of the resorts have equipment shops that rent gear. Companies also generally offer shuttles between the capital and the resort, though prices vary.

Portillo

World-class skiing is synonymous with Portillo, so it is no surprise the U.S., Italian and Austrian Olympic teams flock to this beautiful and exclusive spot for summer training. Former U.S. women's national team member and Olympic gold medalist Picabo Street once claimed that Hotel Portillo was the most inspirational resort in the world. There is also heli-skiing for adventurous souls in search of unspoiled powder ($295 per person first run, $165 following runs), while ski and snowboard novices can find sufficiently mild trails. The slopes are well groomed, though the expert terrain is left with its natural ice pack.

Hotel Portillo offers a variety of room options, from the luxurious ($1,200 – 5,300 per person, per week) to dorm-style. Prices depend on the season, and include seven nights of lodging, four meals per day, lift tickets and access to fitness and entertainment facilities. For those less interested in style, stay in Hotel

Portillo's Octagon Lodge ($890 – 1,390 per person, per week) that offers four bunks and a private bathroom in each room, or the Inca Lodge ($590 – 900), which is popular among backpackers less than 30 years old. Rooms are small, and the bathroom is communal, but it is the cheapest way to stay in Portillo. Tel: 56-2-2630606, URL: www.skiportillo.com, E-mail: info@skiportillo.com.

It is also possible to find cheaper accommodation approximately 70 kilometers (43 mi) to the west in the city of Los Andes.The scenic, two-hour drive from Santiago to Portillo can be arranged through Portillo Tours and Travel. Tel: 56-2-2630606 or toll free from U.S. 1-800-829-5325, E-mail: traslados@skiportillo.com. Updated: Jun 27, 2009.

Lagunillas
The cozy ski resort of Lagunillas has slopes that range from 2,220 to 2,580 meters (7,283 – 8,464 ft) in altitude. The resort is located less than 70 kilometers (43 mi) from the capital in San José de Maipo. The best part about this resort is that its prices tend to pale in comparison to the more popular resorts such as Portillo—and that cheaper price does not necessarily mean a cheaper experience. There are four lifts and 13 runs at this locale. Check the website for up-to-date seasonal rates. Tel: 56-9-8253578, URL: www.skilagunillas.cl.

Valle Nevado
Valle Nevado is conveniently located 60 kilometers (37 mi) from Santiago at 3,025 meters (9,924 ft) and is in the middle of spectacular Andean landscapes. The powder is perfect for snowboarders and skiers, and the resort also offers heliskiing for those who need to push the limit. Avenida Vitacura 5250 office No. 304, Vitacura, Santiago. Tel: 56-2-4777000, Fax: 56-2-4777734, URL: www.vallenevado.com.

La Parva
La Parva bills itself as the most exclusive and family-oriented resort near Santiago. It is suspended high on a mountainside less than 50 kilometers (31 mi) from the capital.There are more than 1,000 houses and condominiums in this small town, which can accommodate as many as 7,000 people during the high season. There are also a few choice restaurants in the area. Isidora Goyenechea 2939, office No. 303, Las Condes, Santiago. Tel: 56-2-4310420, URL: www.skilaparva.cl.

El Colorado
El Colorado has 22 different slopes for skiers and snowboards of any level. There are 18 lifts that go as high 3,333 meters (10,935 feet) above sea level. If you are truly new to skiing, nearby Farellones is probably the better, tamer option. Apoquindo 4900, office No. 47, Santiago. Tel: 56-2-2463344, www.elcolorado.cl.

Farellones
This ski town is located only 32 kilometers (19 mi) from Santiago and is an easy day-trip with some nice slopes. It has the distinction of being the nation's first ski resort and is generally much cheaper than other options. Because of its price and lower hills, it's a draw for beginners and snowtubers. Tel: 56-2-3211149, URL: www.farellones-ski.com. Updated: Apr 22, 2009.

HIKING
Being so close to the Andes, Santiago offers some decent hiking options just outside the city. Portillo, along with numerous ski resorts, offers travelers fine hiking oportunities when it is not ski season. The Cajón del Maipo area, in particular San Alfonso, is a good hiking destination. Another fine place to hike is Parque Nacional La Campana, where there are views of the Andes on one side and the ocean on the other—Sector Granizo is the most popular trail. Updated: Apr 20, 2009.

HORSEBACK RIDING
The best options for horseback riding around Santiago are in the Central Valley. Riding has long been part of the culture here and there are plenty of pastures, peaks and rivers for wannabe cowboys or cowgirls to explore. Guided trips generally last from several days to a week. Plan to be riding approximately six hours per day. One-day riding trips can often be negotiated in a matter of moments—Conaf can help you find a guide. Updated: Jul 01, 2009.

RAFTING
The Cajón del Maipo area is a popular spot for rafters looking for some action near the capital. The top destinations in the country are found on the Río Futaleufú and the Río Bío Bío, first-class destinations which attract top rafters from around the world. Updated: Apr 28, 2009.

CAJÓN DEL MAIPO
It is hard to believe this stretch of heaven for adventure-seekers is located just southeast of bustling Santiago. Cajón del Maipo is a magnificent river valley created by the

Río Maipo in the shadows of the Andes. In just a weekend, you can easily get your fill of mountain biking, paragliding, horseback riding, rafting or hiking.

The mouth of the Cajón at Las Vizcachas is located 25 kilometers (15 mi) from the capital. The area is green with orchards and vineyards, while locals line the roads selling homemade treats and fruits. Push onward another 25 kilometers (15 mi) to reach a small town called San José de Maipo. The little town, cluttered with one-story adobe homes, was founded in 1791 after the discovery of silver in the area. It is also the final opportunity for drivers to refuel on gasoline. There are no banks or ATMs in the town, so bring all the money you might need from Santiago.

Lodging

Tuti Cuanti
Tuti Cuanti doubles as a restaurant and hotel in San José. The food is good and the rooms are well-kept. The restaurant/hostel is located one half block from the main plaza at Comercio 19881. Tel: 56-2-8612547, URL: www.tuticuanti.cl.

Los Castaños
This beautifully remodeled Italian-style country home is at Camino al Volcán 30846 in San Alfonso. There are only four rooms here, with a total capacity for eight guests, so be sure to call ahead for reservations. Tel: 56-2-8614241.

Cascadas de la Animas
(CAMPING: about $15/person) Cascadas de la Animas offers camping and cabins on the river's edge in San Alfonso. A nice, though slightly pricey, restaurant is situated on the grounds, and guests can sign up for a number of activities including rafting, horseback riding, ziplining, and mountain biking. Camino al Volcán 31087. Tel: 56-2-8611303, URL: www.cascadadelasanimas.cl.

San José at Parque del Río
Camping can be found in San José at Parque del Río (Del Río 20.071) for approximately $4 per person. Tel: 56-8-2558342 / 56-9-5052503.

San Alonso's La Bella Durmiente
San Alonso's La Bella Durmiente offers cabins and has a restaurant open Tuesday – Sunday. Los Maitenes 107. Tel: 56-2-8611525, URL: www.labelladurmiente.cl.

Donde Tío Pepe in El Manzano
Donde Tío Pepe in El Manzano offers traditional Pastel de Choclo baked in clay dishes, served all year around. Camino al Volcán 12.305. Tel: 56-2-8711129, URL: www.dondetiopepe.net.

Getting To and Away From Cajón del Maipo
White and blue Cajón del Maipo buses depart four times daily from a little terminal near the metro outside Parque O'Higgins in Santiago. Buses go as far as El Volcán. Tursmontaña services Baños Morales from Plaza Italia, but call ahead to reserve a seat (Tel: 56-2-8500555). Departures are scheduled for the early-morning hours. You can also rent a car and make the journey with a couple of friends, but be warned that weekend traffic is awful. It is best to leave around 8 a.m. and return before 3 p.m. or wait until nightfall. Updated: Apr 27, 2009.

Things to See and Do

Pirque
Pirque, on the outskirts of the Cajón, offers the kind of small-town charm that's impossible to find in Santiago. Most famously, the town is home to Viña Concha y Toro, Chile's largest winery. Pirque is also a nice place to find quality leather goods on weekends. Take Línea 5 on the metro to Bellavista de La Florida, then transfer to metro bus 74 or 80 at Paradero 14 on Av. Vicuña Mackenna outside the station. Updated: Apr 27, 2009.

Reserva Nacional Río Clarillo
Continue 23 kilometers (14 mi) southeast from Pirque to find the 13,000-hectare Reserva Nacional Río Clarillo. This tributary canyon of the Cajón boasts a beautiful river, forest and wildlife, including the endangered Chilean iguana. Hiking and picnicking are popular activities here. Take Línea 5 on the metro to Bellavista de La Florida, then transfer to metro bus 74 or 80 at Paradero 14 on Av. Vicuña Mackenna outside the station. Updated: Jul 01, 2009.

San Alfonso
Located 15 kilometers (9 mi) past San José, San Alfonso is a fantastic place to clear your head. The area also offers excellent rafting, kayaking, horseback riding and breathtaking views of the Andes. To avoid large crowds, the best time to visit is on weekdays or in the off-season. Updated: Apr 28, 2009.

Termas de Colina

(CAMPING: $10 adults, $5 children; HOSTEL: $30) Termas Valle de Colina is a nature reserve situated about 45 kilometers (28 mi) from Santiago in the scenic Cajón del Maipo, close to the small town of Colina. The resort is famous for its nine natural hot springs that are infused with minerals and supposedly able to cure a number of ailments.

There are camping facilities, a hostel, a bar and a restaurant on-site. Other activities include trekking and horseback riding. There is no public transport to the reserve. Take a bus to Baños Morales and then a taxi for the remaining 12 kilometers (7 mi). Fundo El Volcán, sector Termas Valle de Colina. Tel: 56-2-2396797, E-mail: contacto@termasvalledecolina.cl, URL: www.termasvalledecolina.cl. Open 24 hours. Updated: Jul 07, 2009.

Monumento Natural El Morado

(ADMISSION: $3) Located approximately 90 kilometers (55 mi) from Santiago, Monumento Natural El Morado is a scenic park with views of the San Francisco glacier and Cerro El Morado. The park is only about 3,000 hectares, but it contains the gleaming Laguna El Morado, and the hot springs of Baños Morales. Closed May – September. Updated: Apr 27, 2009.

Las Vizcachas

There is a shrine to the folk saint Difunta Correa located past the Carabineros police station at Las Vizcachas. Also, interestingly, there is a drive-in movie theater nearby called the Autocine. Updated: Apr 27, 2009.

La Obra

La Obra used to be a stop on the military railroad that once climbed from Puente Alto to El Volcán. Located approximately 800 meters (0.5 mi) from Las Vizcachas, Estación La Obra is now a national monument. Updated: Apr 27, 2009.

El Manzano

El Manzano is a scenic area with a variety of streams where outdoorsmen can cast a line to do a little fishing. There are also some decent trails for hiking and horseback riding, as well as several campsites and the Italian restaurant Trattoria Calypso located at Camino al Volcán 5247. Updated: Apr 27, 2009.

Guayacán

Several kilometers north of San José is the town of Guayacán, named after a tree with distinctive streaks in its bark. You can find picnic tables, restaurants and cafes in this little town. Updated: Apr 27, 2009.

El Melocotón

Located approximately 5 kilometers (3 mi) south of San José is El Melocotón. It is known throughout the country as the site of Pinochet's riverfront home. Updated: Apr 28, 2009.

CAJÓN DEL MAPOCHO

Cajón del Mapocho is the name of a somewhat vague area that covers Sanctuarios de la Naturaleza Yerba Loca and El Arrayan. Although it is sometimes used as a general name for the four ski resorts closest to Santiago, Chileans more often refer to the resorts by their individual names.

Things to See and Do

Sanctuario de la Naturaleza Yerba Loca

(ADMISSION: $4 adults, $2 children) Sanctuario de la Naturaleza Yerba Loca is a 39,000-hectare nature reserve about one hour from downtown Santiago. It's run by Conaf (National Forestry Corporation) and has trekking paths that take in several glaciers, including La Paloma and El Altar, and also has a campsite with picnic and BBQ areas. More adventurous types can try their hand at mountaineering, ice climbing and horseback riding. If you're really lucky you might catch sight of some condors and eagles. Stick to the marked paths for safety and conservation reasons. There is an information office at the entrance to the reserve and the campsite is 4 kilometers (2.5 mi) further along a dirt road. The best time to go is in summer (December to March).

There is no public transport directly to the Sanctuary. You can take a bus to the Farellones ski center and get off at the entrance. A better option is to take a *colectivo* (shared) taxi from Plaza San Enrique (Lo Barnechea). Camino a Farellones (Km 26, curva 15). Tel: 56-2-3280300. Open 9 a.m. – 5 p.m. Updated: Jul 07, 2009.

Sanctuario de la Naturaleza El Arrayán

(ADMISSION: $4 adults, $3 children) The El Arrayán nature reserve is less than an hour from downtown Santiago in the Cajón del Mapocho. The reserve offers activities such as trekking, fly-fishing, mountaineering, cycling and horse-riding, and there's plenty of spectacular scenery if you just want to enjoy the view. Picnic and BBQ areas available. Camping is not permitted. There is no public transport directly to the sanctuary. Take a *colectivo* (shared) taxi from Plaza San Enrique (Lo Barnechea). Camino El Cajón 21000, Lo Barnechea. Tel: 56-2-3216524, URL: www.santuariodelanaturaleza.cl. Open 9 a.m. – 8 p.m. Updated: Jul 07, 2009.

POMAIRE

 243m   10,000   2

Pomaire is a breezy, old-world town located 50 kilometers (31 mi) southwest of Santiago and was originally created in the 18th century by the Spanish in an attempt to control the native population. The village is known primarily for its skilled potters, and the majority of Pomaire's modern inhabitants devote themselves to perfecting this craft. The town has one long street lined with the shops of local craftsmen selling their handiworks. Bowls, pots and other Chilean kitchenware are molded from brown and white clay in front of curious pedestrians. Potters take Mondays off, so do not expect to see much action in the town on those days. Although cuisine takes a backseat to pottery, the restaurants do serve some of the best traditional food in Chile. La Greda (Manuel Rodriguez 251) offers food hot off the grill for about $5.

Getting To and Away From Pomaire

From Santiago, hop on a bus to Melipilla (leaving every 15 minutes) at the Terminal San Borja, located behind Estación Central. Ask the driver to stop at Pomaire, and you will be dropped along the highway. It is a half-hour walk to the village or an easy ride on one of the *colectivos* that head toward the center. Head back toward the highway to catch a bus back to the capital. Updated: Apr 23, 2009.

)))))

SANTIAGO

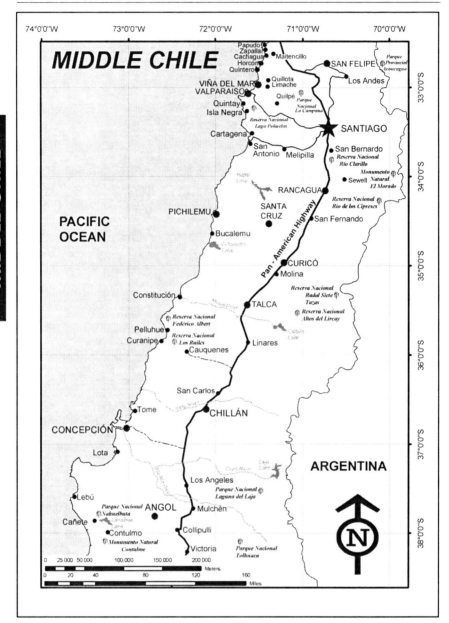

Middle Chile

All too often, tourists come to Chile armed with a checklist of the major hotspots (the desert in the north and the lakes and forests of the south) and ignore Middle Chile. By doing so, they miss out on some of the most important places, historically and culturally, of Chile.

Stretching from coast to *cordillera*, Middle Chile has many sandy beaches, with the popular resorts of Viña del Mar and Pichilemu, rich farmland and towering mountains. It is *huaso* (cowboy) country, with weather-beaten cowboys tending the land, competing

Highlights

The Landscape
The central part of Chile is dotted with lively coastal towns, rich farmland and wine valleys at the foot of the Andes.

Valparaíso
Bohemian **Valparaíso (p.127)**, a UNESCO Heritage Site, is built haphazardly on 16 volcanoes and is one of the most interesting cities in the country, with multi-colored facades and great views of the gritty port.

Wineries
Valle de Cachapoal (p.126), near Rancagua (80 km south of Santiago), has around 14 wineries. **Valle de Colchagua (p.126)** (130 km south of Santiago) has over 20 wineries and hosts a March wine festival. **Valle de Maule (p.163)** (roughly 240 km south of Santiago) is Chile's largest wine valley. Half of the wine exported from Chile each year is produced here.

Ski Resorts
High up in the spectacular Andean range are several world-class ski resorts. **Portillo (p.154)** and **El Colorado** are among the most popular with tourists due to their proximity to Santiago. All of the ski centers in the region have on-site accommodation and provide lessons for beginners. More adventurous types can arrange for heli-skiing. Updated: Jun 22, 2009.

National Reserves
Hike the canyons and valleys of **Altos del Lircay (p.167)** and **Río de los Cipreses (p.158)**, and pay a visit to the waterfalls of **Radal Siete Tazas (p.163)**. Updated: October 5, 2009.

in rodeos and dancing the *cueca* (national dance of Chile). Middle Chile is also wine country, with numerous vineyards and wine tours. The area also hosts several ski centers, including, Valle Nevado, El Colorado, La Parva, Farellones, Lagunillas and Las Araucarias. See www.chileanski.com for more details.

Those interested in history will find two UNESCO World Heritage sites to explore: the historic city of Valparaíso (p.127) and the abandoned mining city of Sewell (p.158). Other places worth visiting in the region are Rancagua, Talca and Chillán. Rancagua

(87 km south of Santiago) is famous for its hot springs, Las Termas de Cauquenes, its national park, Reserva Nacional Río Los Cipreses, and the Chapa Verde ski resort. You can take day trips to all these attractions from Rancagua (p.155)

Talca is a historic city about 250 kilometers (155 mi) south of Santiago (p.164). It has recently undergone a mini-renovation and now offers several good restaurants and a casino. Talca, surrounded by the Maule Valley, is a vale of rich farmland, vineyards and hot springs. Stop by here for a day with an authentic Chilean cowboy, a wine tour and a relaxing bath in the hotsprings just as nature intended.

Chillán (about 400 km south of Santiago) is a hotspot for outdoor activities (p.168). Here you can try skiing, rafting, hiking and climbing. Updated: Jul 08, 2009.

History
The Mapuche were the original inhabitants of Middle Chile. They had no written language, but some artifacts remain that give insight into their lifestyle. They were hunters, gatherers and farmers that lived in small family groups and villages.

Middle Chile was invaded first by the Inca Empire in the late 1400s, but the Mapuche managed to maintain control of the region. The Spanish arrived in the 1530s, bringing with them advanced weaponry and disease. The Spanish founded many cities, including Chillán (1580), Talca (1742) and Rancagua (1743).

The Chilean war of independence, led by Bernardo O'Higgins, was fought from 1810 to 1826. Chile's liberator was born in Chillán and many important battles were fought between the Spanish conquistadors and the native Chileans in the area. Several battles took place in and around Rancagua, including The Disaster of Rancagua (1814), which saw Chilean forces defeated by the Spanish.

Eventually the Chileans managed to gain independence from Spain. Bernardo O'Higgins famously signed Chile's declaration of independence in Talca in 1818. Updated: Jun 22, 2009.

When to Go
There's plenty to enjoy in Middle Chile year round. The area has a Mediterranean-style climate. If you're looking for time on the beach, it's best to go in summer (December to

February). Bear in mind that Viña del Mar is particularly busy during this period, especially on New Year's Eve, which is a spectacular occasion in Viña del Mar and Valparaíso. The Viña del Mar festival also takes place during February and attracts thousands of tourists.

If you want to go camping and hiking, it's best to go in autumn (March to May) or spring (September to November), when the temperatures are warm and pleasant. March is harvest time in the vineyards and is a good time to take a wine tour. To make the most of the ski season, go in the winter, from July to mid-September. Updated: Jun 22, 2009.

Safety
Cities in Middle Chile are generally safe, but like anywhere, opportunistic theft occurs. Take care of your personal belongings and beware of pickpockets, especially in Viña del Mar and Valparaíso in the summer season when the streets are crowded with tourists. Carry your bag on your chest. It's not uncommon for thieves to rummage through your bag while you are waiting to cross a road. Women should not walk alone in the cities at night. Avoid the beach town of Cartagena, as it is full of drunken holidaymakers, often fighting in the streets at night. Updated: Jun 19, 2009.

Tours
These operators are specialists in the region:

TurisTour (www.turistour.cl) operates tours of Viña del Mar, Valparaíso, the Casablanca wine valley and Isla Negra. Tel: 56-32-2381056.

Santiago Adventures (www.santiagoadventures.com) has horse-riding, wine tours, hiking and ski tours, lasting one to ten days. Tel: 56-2-2442750 or in the U.S., 1-802-904-6798.

City Discovery (www.city-discovery.com) organizes day trips to Viña del Mar, Valparaíso and vineyards around the Santiago area. Tel: 1-866-988-8687 from the U.S.

VTS (www.vts.cl) has day tours to the abandoned mining village and UNESCO World Heritage Site, Sewell. Tours depart Santiago and Rancagua. Tel: 56-72-210290.

Altue (www.altue.com) is Chilean run and has a good reputation. The company offers trekking, horseback riding, skiing and wine-tours. Tel: 56-2-2351519. Altue can also organize personalized tours.

Train enthusiasts will love the wine tours offered by **Tren del Vino** (www.trendelvino.com). The tour, by steam train, stops off at vineyards in Valle de Colchagua and Valle de Cachapoal and transport is by steam train. Tours depart from Santiago and last one day. There are only three or four per month so check ahead. Tel: 56-2-4707403.

For something completely different, visit the **Gillmore vineyard** in Tabonko (URL: www.tabonko.cl), close to Talca. Here you can indulge in some alternative wine therapy—spa treatments, not drinking. Updated: Jun 22, 2009.

Lodging
Middle Chile has accommodation to suit all budgets. Most hostels and hotels are in the bigger cities and towns, along the coast and in ski resorts. Viña del Mar and Valparaíso have lodging to suit all budgets. Summer (December to February) is the peak period and prices increase with demand. New Year's Eve is particularly busy so, if you plan to visit during the holidays, book in advance. Generally, accommodation in the ski resorts is quite expensive. You can choose from hotels, B&Bs and self-catering apartments. Log on to www.chileanski.com for a full list of prices. The cities of Rancagua, Talca and Chillán have a modest range of hostels and budget hotels. Updated: Jun 24, 2009.

Valparaíso and The Central Coast
The Central Coast is a rare thing: both a popular tourist destination and an incredibly authentic Chilean experience. The capital of the region, Valparaíso, known lovingly as "Valpo" and Chile's main port, is a rich labyrinth of brightly colored, expertly graffitied houses that climb the steep *cerros* surrounding the bay. Instead of being planned, the city was allowed to grow like a coral reef—maybe one of the best descriptions of a place that really must be experienced on foot, at a leisurely pace.

Valparaíso was named Chile's Arts Capital in 2003, owing to its growing community of students, artists, writers and immigrants, and its historic center is a UNESCO World Heritage Site. Just north along the coastal highway (a beautiful drive in itself) is the more cleancut beach town of Viña del Mar, where both Chileans and tourists go to relax for the day or weekend in the sun and sand. Viña del Mar is a common destination for Chilean students, who stay at the beachfront hotels for the summer concerts held there (some of which are fondly remembered years later, à la Woodstock). Viña is the glitz to Valpo's grit; both are truly Chilean, but in very different ways—fitting for a country that considers itself a land of contrasts. Updated: Jul 02, 2009.

VALPARAÍSO

 24 m   282,000   32

Lovers of right angles beware: when you enter Valparaíso, you're entering a labyrinth that defies all structural reason. Streets twist whimsically as though they have a mind of their own. The willing traveler can explore road mazes among candy-colored buildings and graffiti-covered walls. The best way to approach the city is to take a walk with no particular destination; your inner photographer will love you for it.

The city consists of two distinct parts: the 45 hills, or cerros, and the streets that run along the coastline. These two areas couldn't be more different. Wandering through the cerros can make you feel as though you're the last person in the city, with only stray dogs and intricate graffiti to keep you company.

Down by the waterfront, however, speeding *micros* and *colectivos* flood the streets, and locals fill the sidewalks. Down here, you'll find all the city's practicalities—grocery stores, pharmacies, banks, tourism offices—but you have to look hard for the same otherworldly charm you'll find up in the hills.

The city's architecture, which ranges from British colonial houses to impressive Yugoslavian palaces, is a testament to Valparaíso's diverse sociological history. The region was originally inhabited by a tribe of native fisherman called the Changos. In 1536 a ship of Spanish explorers arrived and renamed the valley Valparaíso, becoming the first of a long line of Europeans to make their home along the bay.

The young city was devastated by earthquakes and pirates. The legendary Sir Francis Drake, for instance, sacked the city in 1577 on his hunt for Spanish gold. But, by the 19th century, Valparaíso had become one of the most important ports in the Pacific Ocean, known by many as "The Jewel of the Pacific." With economic prosperity came intellectual prosperity. Valparaíso became the first city in Chile to open a public library and a women's secondary school, the first to have a telegraph and telephone service, and the first city in Latin America to establish a stock exchange and volunteer fire department. As the city's accolades poured in, so did European immigrants—from Germany, England, Italy and France.

This prosperity came to a halt, however, when a massive earthquake and subsequent fire in 1906 killed over 20,000 city residents. The disaster, followed by the opening of the Panama Canal in 1914, caused the city to fall into an economic despair from which it has yet to fully recover.

Valparaíso was recently rediscovered by a wave of young, moneyed artists from Europe and Santiago, who literally gave the city a new face by covering walls and buildings with elaborate graffiti murals and reinvigorating the arts in Valparaíso. In 2003, UNESCO recognized the cultural significance of the city by naming its historic center a World Heritage site, placing it among Prague, Venice and the Great Wall of China. Updated: Aug 01, 2008.

When to Go

Though many towns in this region are seasonal, Valparaíso is a functional port town year round—restaurants, cafes and bars stay open through the winter, and many accommodations have lower prices in the off-season. The weather in Valparaíso is moderate, though winter nights get chilly and most places don't have central heating.

Walking around the hills in winter can be enchanting, as you'll have the twisting streets and stairways all to yourself. If you're planning on heading to the beaches at nearby Viña del Mar, however, you'll want to come in the summer months; January and February bring crowded beaches, but the weather is sunny and warm. Updated: Sep 21, 2008.

V!VA ONLINE REVIEW
VALPARAÍSO

The ocean, the hills, the people, the atmosphere, the poetry, the sunshine, everything is wonderful.

September 20, 2008

MIDDLE CHILE

Photo by Teca Mota

Getting To and Away From Valparaíso

Most people will be arriving in Valparaíso from Santiago, which is 112 kilometeres (70 mi) away. By bus, the trip takes about one and a half hours. The main bus companies leave Santiago every 15 minutes from the terminal at metro station Universidad de Santiago. Try to get a direct bus if you can. If you are driving from Santiago, take Ruta 68. There are also roads that connect Valparaíso to the coastal towns of San Antonio, Laguna Verde, Quintay, Cartagena, and Isla Negra.

Buses leave Valparaíso several times daily for northern destinations, but as these leave less frequently than those to Santiago, you should stop by the station or call individual bus lines to get specific times. Updated: Sep 21, 2008.

Getting Around

Valparaíso, like much of Chile, has very good regional transport (which includes readily available micros and colectivos that will take you to and from the bus station) to nearby Viña del Mar, and even up the cerros if the elevators are closed and you don't feel like walking. There are also designated colectivos for nearby towns that are inaccessible by bus (like Quintay); buses run every 30 minutes to San Antonio, Isla Negra, and Cartagena. An above ground

Metro system (with an underground section that goes through downtown Viña del Mar) also links Valparaíso with towns as far northeast as Limache, from which you can access Parque Nacional La Campana. Updated: Sep 21, 2008.

Safety

Valparaíso has a reputation for being one of the most dangerous cities in Chile. While it's true that there's a large economic disparity, if you're careful, aware of your surroundings and are discreet with your belongings, you likely won't have a problem. Locals will warn you not to go into the old historic part of town alone (between Plaza Sotomayor and Cerro Artilleria), and to never go at night. Though their cautionary words may be a bit exaggerated, you probably shouldn't choose a hostel or hotel located in this section, as there are many accommodation options available in other parts of town.

One thing that hostellers should be aware of is a trend that's recently arrived in Valparaíso: a person posing as a potential guest will ask to see an occupied room, and when the hostel staff isn't looking, will snatch whatever's in sight and stick it in their bag. It's therefore best in Valparaíso, as in any town, to keep your valuables locked up and to put all of your belongings in your pack when you go out for the day. Updated: Sep 21, 2008.

Services
Most services—including banks, money exchange offices, travel agencies, postal services, Internet and telephone cafes, and pharmacies—can be found on Calle Esmerelda, at the base of Cerro Concepción. You'll find a Cinema just east of Plaza Victoria on Avenida Independencia, and there are several supermarkets near Plaza Victoria as well on Avenida Pedro Montt. The Puerto Deportivo at Muelle Barón offers a variety of diving courses and water sport equipment for rent. And, if you're spending some time in the hostel or going for a drive, the radio station La Radioneta (URL: www.laradioneta.cl) plays an eclectic selection of music and interviews by local artists. Updated: Sep 21, 2008.

Shopping
Though shopping isn't the primary reason to come to Valparaíso, there are some worthwhile outdoor markets and small artisan shops around town, as well as lots of independent art galleries up on Cerro Alegre and Cerro Concepción that sell contemporary Chilean artwork. The **Antique Feria** on Saturdays in Plaza O'Higgins is the most popular antiques market in town and is a good place to wander around on a Saturday morning; there are several little *artesanía* stores as you walk up Almirante Montt toward Cerro Concepción. At the few small markets—there's one by the port, for example, and another by the Naval museum—they sell tourist favorites like alpaca gloves and sweaters, lapis lazuli jewelry, and Indio *Pícaro* statues (pick one up and you're in for a surprise). Updated: Jul 01, 2009.

Neighborhoods

CERRO ARTILLERIA
Described by locals as a place of decadent beauty, Cerro Artilleria begins in the old quarter of Valparaíso and has the Chilean Naval Museum and the Antigua Escuela Naval. From the top of Cerro Artilleria, there's a magnificent view of Valparaíso and the harbor, and on a clear day, you can see all the way to Aconcagua, the highest peak in the Americas. A string of vendors along the perimeter of the museum sell typical Chilean handicrafts like cheap alpaca sweaters and lapis lazuli jewelry. There are a few restaurants and places to stay in this area, but it isn't safe for lone travelers at night. Take the Artilleria ascensor to get to the top of the hill rather than taking the stairs. Updated: Nov 02, 2008.

CERRO SANTO DOMINGO
Cerro Santo Dominco is located in the heart of the historic center of Valparaíso, for which the city was named a Cultural World Heritage site by UNESCO. This part of town was the first piece of land developed by Spanish explorers. They built a small square and church where a community of indigenous people called the Changos had lived. The unassuming Iglesia La Matríz that stands in the historic Plaza Matríz is the oldest in the city (the current building dates back to 1842, but the original church was built in this plaza in 1559).

At the foot of this cerro is the Port Market, where you can find fresh produce downstairs and cheap but delicious seafood lunches upstairs. A walk around this part of the city can be rewarding, but is slightly more dangerous for tourists, so take extra precautions when you take out your camera and which streets you decide to turn down. There are several accommodation options here, but those unfamiliar with the city would do best not to walk around this area at night. Updated: Nov 02, 2008.

CERRO ALEGRE
Cerro Alegre is a quiet, cheerful hill full of upper-class colorful English houses and gardens, many of which have been converted into small hotels and hostels. William Bateman, a well-to-do Englishman, was the first to build a house on this hill, and as fellow English immigrants began to follow his lead, the face of Cerro Alegre as a colorful place to live began to take shape. On this hill and the neighboring Cerro Concepción, you'll find many of the city's independent art galleries and top-quality artisan shops. This hill has a more moneyed feel than many of the others, so don't be surprised if you turn the corner to find a Colonial-style mansion or Yugoslavian palace. You'll also notice that the surroundings take on a decidedly meditative turn with ashtanga yoga studios dotted along the streets, Tibetan prayer flags hung in every other doorway, and the Om symbol painted prominently across doors and walls. Updated: Nov 02, 2008.

CERRO PANTEÓN AND CERRO CÁRCEL
Cerro Panteón and Cerro Cárcel, two isolated hills visible from one another, are historical remnants of old Valparaíso. Cerro Panteón has the illustrious dead of the city in three different cemeteries. The regal Cementerio Número 1 was the first Catholic cemetery in the city, and is next to the Cementerio de Disidentes, the more modest cemetery for the city's important Protestant families. The

MIDDLE CHILE

MIDDLE CHILE

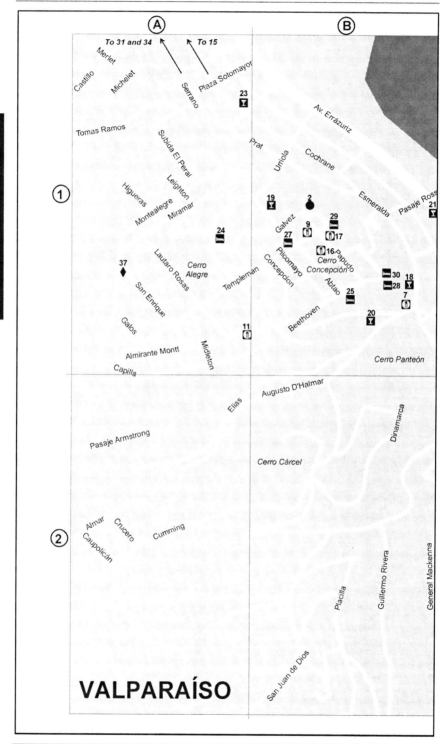

VALPARAÍSO

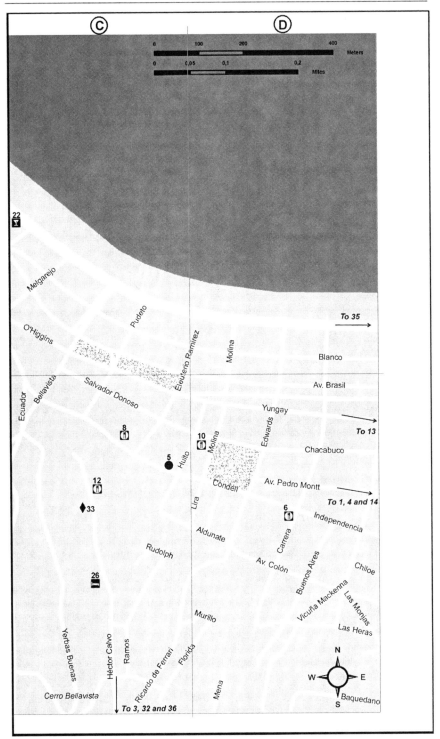

MIDDLE CHILE

MIDDLE CHILE

Activities ●

1 Antiques and Book Market D2
2 Casa Mirador de Lukas B1
3 La Sebastiana C2
4 Mercado Puerto D2
5 Museo de Historia Natural C2

Eating

6 Bambú D2
7 Café del Poeta B1
8 Casino Social J Cruz C2
9 Color Café B1
10 Empanadas Famosas de Adali D2
11 Epif Café A1
12 Gato Tuerto C2
13 La Otra Cocina D2
14 Marisquería Maribel D2
15 Porto Viejo A1
16 Restaurant La Concepción B1
17 Turri B1

Nightlife

18 El Cinzano B1
19 El Gremio B1

20 El Ritual B1
21 Hache Havana B1
22 La Piedra Feliz C1
23 Valparaíso Eterno A1

Sleeping

24 Casa Aventura A1
25 Gagliardo House B1
26 Hostal Caracol C2
27 Hostal Pilcomayo B1
28 Hotel Brighton B1
29 Hotel Gervasoni B1
30 Hotel Manoir Atkinson B1
31 Loft La Matriz A1
32 Puerto Natura C2

Tours ◆

33 Fundación Valparaíso C2
34 Héctor Medina A1
35 Puerto Deportivo D1
36 Tourism and Culture Information C2
37 Valparaíso Expediciones A1

names on the headstones give visitors an idea of Valparaíso's international origins in Germany, England and Italy.

A stone's throw from Cerro Panteón is Cerro Cárcel, where you'll find the ex-prison, roofless and full of local art. The prison ceased operating as a penitentiary in 1999, has recently become one of the most vibrant venues for Valparaíso artists. The open courtyards are full of sculpture, history, and (of course) graffiti, and on weekends you can catch local theater performances in the large black box theater. The government is now considering commissioning a project to convert the structure into a modern cultural center and performance venue for visiting artists.

If you're staying up in the hills, walk along Avenida Alemania to get some gorgeous views on your way to the ex-Cárcel and the cemeteries. Updated: Jul 07, 2009.

CERRO BARÓN

The hill was named after Ambrosio O'Higgins, Barón de Vallenary. This mostly residential cerro near Muelle Barón has some lovely walks, but is outside the part of town visited by most tourists, and you won't find much in the way of accommodation or restaurants. The nearby Ascensor Polanco on Cerro Polanco is the most famous of the city's elevators and is definitely worth a visit.

If you're feeling adventurous, take a walk down the Paseo Muelle Barón and look to your right for a small opening in a chain-link fence. In a few steps, you'll find yourself in an abandoned, burnt-out train station with two ghostly trains covered in graffiti, awaiting a departure that will never come. Nearby you'll also find several markets, including the sizable antique feria on Saturdays in Plaza O'Higgins and the frenetic Wednesday and Saturday farmer's markets (on Av. Argentina near the National Congress building). Updated: Jul 07, 2009.

CERRO CONCEPCIÓN

Many visitors to Valparaíso choose to stay on Cerro Concepción, and for good reason. This hill has the widest variety of accommodation in the city and is historically, architecturally, and culturally ripe for exploring. Don't be put off by the graffiti that covers the walls, stairs and doorways of this part of the city, the area is quite safe. Artists who have relocated here have taken it on themselves literally to paint the town, so think of it as artistic expression rather than vandalism. On this hill, you'll find evidence of the wealthy European influence that began in the 1800s. English immigrants were later joined by Germans and French, who built large, colorful houses in the style of their mother countries and a Lutheran and an Anglican church within shouting distance from each other. Updated: Nov 02, 2008.

CERRO BELLAVISTA

Though less well-known than some of Valparaíso's other cerros, Bellavista is home to quite a few of the city's cultural iconographies, as well as several good hotels and hostels. Neruda himself chose the view at the top of Bellavista for his house, La Sebastiana, which is now a museum open to the public. The Museo a Cielo Abierto (a series of vibrant murals painted on the walls of the winding streets between Ferrari and Héctor Calvo) is perhaps the most obvious affirmation of the phrase "graffiti is not a crime" that you'll find stenciled around the city. To get a comprehensive sense of what this part of Valparaíso offers in the way of museums, cafes, and accommodation, contact Ruta Bellavista. The project, started by the non-profit Fundación Valparaíso, offers free tours of the area, leaving from the Teatro Mauri every Saturday starting at noon. Updated: Nov 02, 2008.

Things to See and Do

Perhaps the most popular thing to do in Valparaíso is simply to explore the streets on foot. The city wears its history and culture on its sleeve, so if you pick the right path (and there are many guides available for walking tours of the city), you're sure to find something interesting—a prison-turned-cultural park, or a farmer's market that never seems to end. The city offers more traditional activities, as well. In Valparaíso you'll find several museums, a lively harbor and a small multitude of art galleries scattered through the hills. There are the nearby beaches of Viña del Mar for a day in the sun. Updated: Jul 08, 2009.

Museo a Cielo Abierto

(ADMISSION: Free) Though marketed as the centerpiece of Valparaíso's visual art obsession, the Museo a Cielo Abierto is more typical of Valparaíso artwork than quintessential. The "museum" isn't really one at all, but rather a series of impressive, brilliantly colored paintings commissioned for the walls of Cerro Bellavista. The 17 giant murals, painted by art students and Chilean artists like Roberto Mata, are definitely worth a look, but don't think that the city's visual stimulation ends here. There are equally stunning graffiti murals all through the city's hills.

You can stop at the nearby Fundación Valparaíso for a map of the area and of the different murals. The Espíritu Santo elevator, which is off of Plaza Victoria, will take you up Cerro Bellavista and leave you right in the middle of the Museo a Cielo Abierto. For a map of the various murals, stop by the Fundación Valparaíso on calle Hector Calvo Cofre. Updated: Aug 01, 2008.

Museo de Historia Natural de Valparaíso

(ADMISSION: $1.20) This small museum, located inside the imposing Palacio Lyon, is the second oldest in Chile. It was first established in 1878 by Don Eduardo de la Barra. Inside you'll find a comprehensive—though somewhat disparate—history of the earth and its inhabitants, with the story of Pangea and tectonic plate activity next to a room full of meticulously categorized shells. The museum is great for kids with its dynamic, colorful, and clearly explained displays, though older visitors may feel a bit like they've returned to middle school science class. All displays are in Spanish. Open from: Tuesday – Friday: 10 a.m. – 1 p.m. and 2 a.m. – 6 p.m. (though closes at 2 p.m. on Sat, Sun, and holidays). Condell 1546, Casilla 3208. Tel: 56-32-257441 / 450405, Fax: 56-32-220846, E-mail: mhnv@entelchile.net. Updated: Aug 01, 2008.

Casa Mirador de Lukas

(ADMISSION: $2, or $1 if you buy something from the cafe) This small gallery has an upper-crust air to it, with its dainty out-

Photo by Millvoj Sherrington

door cafe and beautiful vista. Inside you'll find several rooms devoted to the artwork of the beloved Valparaíso-raised cartoonist and painter Renzo Antonio Giovanni Pecchenino Raggi (aka Lukas). A walk through these small, sunlit salas will have you giggling to yourself at the always playful, sometimes poignant, comics. Many deal with places that tourists have visited such as Rapa Nui, Viña del Mar or Valpo. The museum also devotes itself to keeping a rotating exposition of local artists whose work is for sale in an upstairs gallery. Casa Mirador is immediately to the right once you exit the Cerro Concepción elevator. Open 10:30 a.m. – 6 p.m. Closed Mondays. Paseo Gervasoni 448. Tel: 56-32-221344 / 225281, Fax: 56-2-221344, E-mail: osman.r@lukas.tie.cl / Lukas. cafeteria@gmail.com, URL: www.lukas.cl. Updated: Aug 01, 2008.

La Sebastiana

(ADMISSION: $5, students and seniors $2) La Sebastiana is a perfect testament to Nobel prize-winning poet Pablo Neruda's love for objects and gives lovers of Neruda special insight into his poetry. Handpicked items from around the world fill this house, which was shared with two friends and partially designed by all three. Unlike in La Chascona or Neruda's Isla Negra home, visitors to La Sebastiana are not forced to take a guided tour. Instead, a written guide (available in multiple languages) leads visitors through each room, providing facts and snippets of Neruda's life—including the recipe for his original cocktail, the *Coquetelón*. From Plaza Victoria, take the Espíritu Santo elevator up Cerro Bellavista. Turn right from the exit and then left at Hector Calvo heading up the hill. The road will change to Ferrari, and you'll see the museum on the right. Open March – December: 10 a.m. – 6 p.m.; January – February: 10:30 a.m. – 6:50 p.m. Closed Mondays. Ferrari 692 Av. Alemania. Tel: 56-32-256606, Fax: 56-32-233759, E-mail: lasebastiana-neruda@entelchile.net, URL: www.lasebastiana-neruda.cl, Updated: Aug 04, 2008.

Feria de Verduras

On Wednesdays and Saturdays, a huge outdoor farmer's market of fruits and vegetables opens early in the morning to sell all kinds of local produce dirt-cheap. Here you can get a kilo of kiwi or a big chunk of sweet potato for next to nothing. But the long walk down the colorful gauntlet full of vendors asking you to try their oranges or olives or sweet dried fruits is enjoyable on its own. Be careful with your camera or handbag when strolling through the market as it is a notorious place for petty theft. The market is a short walk from the bus station toward the Congreso Nacional. From the center of town, you can catch a micro or colectivo toward the congress building. The market stretches along Av. Argentina for several blocks near the National Congress building and is only open Wednesdays and Saturdays from morning 'til dusk. Updated: Aug 01, 2008.

Mercado Puerto

In a time-worn building at the heart of Valparaíso's Old Town is the city market. Here you'll find a smattering of produce; vendors sell basic fruits and vegetables alongside some more exotic selections such as papaya and sweet cucumber. Don't come to this market expecting the sensory overload characteristic of many marketplaces, however. The building that houses the mercado is scheduled for renovation in the course of 2009, and many of the vendors no longer hawk their wares here. On the second floor of the market, you'll find a concentrated bunch of *marisquerías* (seafood restaurants) whose wait staff will quite literally fight for your business. Corner of Cochrane and San Martín. Updated: Aug 01, 2008.

Plaza O'Higgins Antiques and Book Market

One of Neruda's favorite pastimes was to pick through the antiques at the weekend markets scattered around Valparaíso. On Saturdays, Plaza O'Higgins has perhaps the most popular antique market in town, where you can find everything from chandeliers and phonographs to retro pin-ups and manual camera parts that aren't excessively cheap but are mostly high quality. There are packs of old men playing chess and *Briscas* at the tables around the plaza, and there are places to sit and take coffee or have a snack. Open Saturdays from morning 'til dusk. Plaza O'Higgins at calle Victoria and Uruguay. Updated: Jul 31, 2008.

Parque Cultural Ex-Cárcel

(ADMISSION: Free) The ex-prison on top of Cerro Cárcel is perhaps one of the most emblematic sites in the city. Only recently did the space shift from being a place of confinement to being one of liberal expression and literal openness. In 1999, the prison permanently opened its cells and closed its doors in order to reopen as a public park and art museum a few years

Valparaíso Walking Tour

Although many Chileans associate Valparaíso with trash-lined alleys and opportunistic thieves, visitors will be pleasantly surprised to find a slice of gritty bohemianism in two of the downtown's adjacent cerros (hills), Alegre and Concepción.

The central location of the hills makes them an appropriate jumping off point for exploring the area. Yet, the funky, cafe-lined streets of Cerros Alegre and Concepción are a destination in and of themselves and demand at least an afternoon of meandering through their snaking thoroughfares and hidden walkways.

Food and drink are readily available, as are quirky artisan wares. There are postcard-worthy views of the bay from the sector's several miradores (overlooks). And, in spite of the ever-increasing number of hostels catering to backpackers, Cerros Alegre and Concepción remain stubbornly Chilean, even as they accommodate the influx of camera-wielding foreigners.

The heart of Cerros Alegre and Concepción can be reached quickly (if not effortlessly) by foot, climbing Almirante Montt, which originates in the Plaza Anibal Pinto, or Urriola, several blocks closer to the city's port. Those looking to avoid a serious calf workout can make use of Valparaíso's iconic acensores (inclines), or catch a colectivo (shared taxi) at Anibal Pinto. Detailed maps are available at tourist kiosks both in Anibal Pinto and the port. Updated: Apr 24, 2008.

later. The graffiti murals covering this park are brilliant (even by Valparaíso standards), plays are performed each weekend in the large black box theater, and at any given time, you'll find children playing soccer, locals going for a run in the main area, or acrobats taking workshops in a tucked-away corner. The history of the space is fascinating, and tours, which are irregularly available, are often given by artists and ex-inmates. The future of the cultural park, however, currently lies in limbo—a project has been proposed to convert the space into an official cultural center and theater. Either take the Reina Victoria elevator or follow calle Cumming up the hill from Plaza Amibal Pinto. Open Mon-Fri 9 a.m. – 7 p.m. (Open until 11 a.m. Sat – Sun). Tel: 56-32-258567. Updated: Aug 01, 2008.

Muelle Prat

A walk down to Prat Harbor gives you a sense of what makes the city of Valparaíso tick: huge barges with cargo from around the world move to and fro, and hordes of small fishing boats putter through the frigid water. Boat rides around the harbor are quite cheap—a thousand pesos ($2) per person if the boat is full of paying passengers. There is a small vendor's market that stretches along the harbor selling typical Chilean handicrafts and touristy merchandise. Be advised, however, not to bring children down to the harbor when a big ship has just come into port, as the returning sailors often attract company that isn't exactly family-friendly. Near Plaza Sotomayor. Muelle

Prat is a short walk from the center of town, but you can also take the metro to Estación Puerto. Updated: Aug 01, 2008.

Bicentennial Walking Tours

Though some like the idea of letting the city take them where it will, others find the thought of getting lost in Valparaíso's twists and turns a bit unnerving. Visitors who prefer structured wandering, take heart: you can pick up a very comprehensive reading guide to excellent walking routes through the city, complete with cues for when to look out for a particularly spectacular view. You can purchase guides at the Fundación Valparaíso or online. The Fundación Valparaíso has offices in a brightly colored building on Cerro Bellavista. Take the stairs up from Plaza Ecuador and follow Hector Calvo, or take the Espiritu Santo elevator up Cerro Bellavista. Fundación Valparaíso, Hector Calvo Cofre 205, Cerro Bellavista. Tel: 56-32-593156, Fax: 56-32-593142, URL: www.fundacionvalparaiso.org or www.senderobicentenario.cl. Updated: Jul 31, 2008.

Tours

Puerto Deportivo

If you want to go diving, take a windsurfing class, kayak around the bay, or try your hand at sailing, this is definitely the place to go. Puerto Deportivo, on Paseo Muelle Baron, was the first public nautical center to be established in Chile. They have a small but highly qualified staff and an excellent website where you can check the costs and times of various activities. Cost varies greatly based on the activity. Muelle Baron. Tel: 56-32-2592852, E-mail: info@puertodeportivo.cl, URL: www.puertodeportivo.cl. Updated: Jul 29, 2008.

Valparaíso Expediciones

Valparaíso Expediciones is an innovative agency which offers bicycle tours along ancestral roads in the valleys and along the Pacific Ocean, as well heritage research in collaboration with architects, archaeologists and historians from two universities. The idea of the tours, which include stops in museums and vineyards, is to help discover and maintain the heritage of the Aconcagua Valley. Montealegre 416-B, Cerro Alegre. Tel: 56-32-2492499, E-mail: info@valparaiso expediciones.cl, URL: www.valparaisoexpediciones.cl. Updated: Jul 01, 2009.

Discover Valparaíso

For something a bit different from your run-of-the-mill tour, check out Discover Valparaíso. This one-man tour operator, a former French journalist, offers private tours of Valparaíso, Viña del Mar, the Concón dunes, Isla Negra, and the Casablanca vineyards, among others. Tours are offered in English, French, or Spanish. Tel: 56-09-81724441 / 56-9-81724441, E-mail: visiter.valparaiso@gmail.com, URL: visit-chile.over-blog.com. Updated: Jul 01, 2009.

Hector Medina

Hector's Travel Service offers tours to the following destinations: Chile North (Calama, San Pedro de Atacama and surrounding areas); Central Valley (Santiago, Valparaíso, Viña del Mar, Coastal Cities, Country villages, Wineries, etc.); Chile South (Patagonia, Puerto Montt, Puerto Chacabuco, San Rafael Lagoon, Patagonia cruises, Punta Arenas.) Guides speak English, Spanish, French, German, Portuguese. Levarte 1442, Edificio 12, office B. Tel: 56-09-89002248, E-mail: hectortourservice@gmail.com, URL: sites.google.com/site/privatetourguidechile. Updated: Jul 07, 2009.

Tourism & Culture Information Center

Next door to Pablo Neruda's home, La Sebastiana, on top of Cerro Bellavista, is the Centro de Información Touristica y Cultural. This tourist center has four computers with Internet, information about tours and activities in the area, and helpful staff, most of whom speak English. Though it's out of the way for travelers staying near the port or on Cerro Concepción or Cerro Alegre, the office is in a less stressful environment than some of the more centrally located tourism offices. The tourism center keeps the same hours as La Sebastiana. Ferrari 692, next to La Sebastiana. Tel: 56-32-2256606 / 2233759. Updated: Nov 01, 2008.

La Fundación Valparaíso

The still young Fundación Valparaíso, established in 1998 by a North American poet smitten with the city, is a non-profit organization that's been working over the past few years to build up the tourism infrastructure of Valparaíso. So far, their work has included bringing jazz and film festivals to Valparaíso, mapping out a series of historical walking tours, and developing plans for preservation and restoration of the city. The foundation's building is located on Cerro Bellavista, where you'll also find cultural and tourist info, some tasteful artisan shops (with really unique, artsy postcards) and a restaurant, Gato Tuerto, that serves Southeast Asian food. Hector Calvo Cofre 205. Tel: 56-32-593156, Fax: 56-32-593142. URL: www.fundacionvalparaiso.org. Updated: Nov 01, 2008.

Lodging

Valparaíso is brimming with places to stay, ranging from dirt-cheap to full-on luxury, but you'd be wise to do your research in advance, as there are some real gems to be found among the hills for the treasure seeker. Many accommodation options are located along the winding passages of Cerro Constitución and Cerro Alegre, where you'll also find many of the city's private art galleries and stylish cafes. The hotels and hostels on Cerro Bellavista provide another option for travelers. Remain close to the bus station only if you must—the life and charm of the city lie in its port and its rambling hills. Updated: May 28, 2009.

Hostal Pilcomayo

(ROOMS: $9) This backpacker's hostel is rough around the edges, but it's an easy place to throw your pack after a long day. Dishes pile up in the shared kitchen and there's a

Valparaíso

single bathroom shared by all, but Pilcomayo is not without its charms. The dorms and private rooms are clean, there's a cafe downstairs (with a Sunday brunch), and the light-filled passageway gives the place a warm and welcoming feel. Also, the hostel's prime location on top of Cerro Concepción places it on many travelers' lists. Pilcomayo 491, Cerro Concepción. Tel: 56-32-2251075, E-mail: hostalpilcomayo@yahoo.es, URL: hostalpilcomayo.cl. Updated: Jul 29, 2008.

Hostal Caracol

(ROOMS: $15) Hostal Caracol embodies the charm of the city of Valparaíso: inviting, colorful and one of a kind. Stowed away in a converted turn-of-the-century house high in the hills of the city and close to Neruda's La Sebastiana, this hostel is perfect for the traveler looking for a place that feels like home. The secluded, sunlit patio, comfortable beds and elegant architecture make Caracol an excellent place to rest your head. But it's the knowledgeable, welcoming staff that makes it the kind of place you'd go out of your way to visit again. Highly recommended. Calle 3 between Av. D and Av. Central, Isla Colon. Updated: May 14, 2009.

Casa Aventura !

(ROOMS: $15 – 56) Casa Aventura has become a hotspot in Valparaíso. Tucked inside an alley leading into the labyrinth-like hills of Valparaíso, this place has developed quite a following. The hostel, run by a Chilean-German couple, is located in a converted century-old house. Its relatively small size makes it easy to get to know fellow travelers, and you'll hear backpackers up and down the country recommending Casa Aventura's hearty breakfast. Book in advance, as the hostel fills up, particularly in high season. From the bus station, take a bus to "Aduana" and get off at the Shell gas station. Go three blocks up Calle Urriola to your left, then left at Pasaje Galvez. The door tucked away to your left, halfway up the stairs, is Casa Aventura. Pasaje Galvez 11, Cerro Concepción. Tel: 56-32-2755963, E-mail: info@casaventura.cl, URL: www.casaventura.cl. Updated: Jul 01, 2009.

Loft La Matriz

(ROOMS: $40 – 60) In a renovated building built in 1879, just in front of La Matriz Church and within walking distance of main attractions and public transport, this loft-style hotel has huge, comfortable rooms with private shower, kitchenette, WiFi and a washing machine. Reservations are necessary. Santo Domingo 30. Tel: 56-32-2497908, E-mail: info@visitvalparaiso.info, URL: www.visitvalparaiso.info. Updated: Jul 08, 2009.

Gagliardo House

(ROOMS: $50 – 100) A cheerful and inviting B&B, Gagliardo House is run by a man who takes pride in his establishment—and it shows. Rooms are immaculate, each with private bathroom, TV and a small refrigerator. The B&B sits on a quiet street atop Cerro Concepción, across from the Lutheran church and near many of the area's cafes and interesting walks. The ample breakfast, included in the price, consists of ham and cheese, bread, juice, coffee and tea. Beethoven 322. Tel: 56-32-2459476, E-mail: info@gagliardohouse.cl, URL: www.gagliardohouse.cl. Updated: May 18, 2009.

Hotel Brighton

(ROOMS: $60 – 80) Situated in a quaint house perched on the hillside of Cerro Concepción, Hotel Brighton has a distinctly British feel. Rooms, which vary in price based on the quality of the view, have small private bathrooms and very small TVs. The hotel is prettily decorated and everything—down to the carefully arranged sitting room—feels prim and proper. Breakfast is included in the price of the room, and you'll find the well-known (but somewhat pricey) Brighton cafe downstairs. Every Friday and Saturday starting at 11 p.m., Brighton also hosts live jazz, tangos, and boleros with a cover charge. Paseo Atkinson 151-153. Tel: 56-32-2223513, Fax: 56-32-2598802, E-mail: hotelbrighton@vtr.net, URL: www.brighton.cl. Updated: Jul 29, 2008.

Puerto Natura !

(ROOMS: $60 – 130) The Puerto Natura hotel and spa is for travelers who like luxury without the pomp and circumstance. A night's stay in one of these carefully designed rooms will be enough to convince any visitor how much the hotel's owner and his wife genuinely care about the wellbeing of their guests. The hotel, which also doubles as a holistic spa, offers a 15 percent discount on the spa's restorative therapies, including Reiki sessions, yoga classes and medicinal herb baths. There's also an extensive garden with avocado and peach trees and a light-filled terrace with a view that rivals that from Neruda's La Sebastiana house a few blocks higher. Hector Calvo 850. Tel: 56-32-2224405 / 2112730, E-mail: patricio@puertonatura.cl, URL: www.puertonatura.cl. Updated: Jul 08, 2009.

MIDDLE CHILE

Hotel Gervasoni

(ROOMS: $120 – 300) Gervasoni is a stately hotel housed in an impeccably restored 19th-century Victorian mansion that overlooks the port (all but two rooms have a harbor view). With thick, wooden banisters and stained-glass windows, this hotel has more personality than most luxury hotels, and its location atop Cerro Concepción, right next to the ascensor, couldn't be more desirable. Private bathrooms with low ceilings are located (strangely enough) down a spiral staircase in each room. Paseo Gervasoni 1. Tel: 56-32-2239236 / 8-9004033, E-mail: reserves@hotelgervasoni.com, URL: www.hotelgervasoni.com. Updated: Jul 30, 2008.

Hotel Manoir Atkinson

(ROOMS: $150 – 215) The Manoir Atkinson is a small hotel with seven carefully decorated rooms (one is an upstairs suite) in a renovated colonial mansion. Rooms with a view cost more, but the view isn't spectacular enough to merit paying extra (try Hotel Brighton's cafe next door for an excellent harbor view). This hotel is perfect for visitors looking for a quiet stay that is both comfortable and elegant. Manoir Atkinson also has an ample sitting and dining area downstairs with antique furniture and an upright piano. Paseo Atkinson 165. Tel: 56-32-2351313, E-mail: info@hotelatkinson.cl, URL: www.hotelatkinson.cl. Updated: Jul 29, 2009.

Restaurants

Marisquería Maribel

(SET MENU: $4 – 6) On the second floor of the Mercado in Old Town is Marisquería Maribel, one of the many seafood restaurants to choose from in this old building. Stop by for lunch and you'll get a selection of fixed menus to choose from, though drinks are not included. The piping hot empanadas here are particularly delicious, as is the *pipeño* (very sweet and dry white wine produced in the region). The friendly and very accommodating staff is sure to appreciate your business at this competitive location. Mercado Puerto, second floor, Local 80. Updated: Aug 01, 2008.

Bambú

(PRICES: $5 – 10) Bambú is situated in what used to be someone's private dining room, and is an excellent vegetarian option for those travelers whose stomachs can't take another *lomo a lo pobre* (beef with a fried egg on top). There are typically two set menus to choose from, as well as a long list of other veggie dishes on the menu, including tofu entrees, salads, fresh seasonal juices and sweets. Food is hearty and well priced, and the atmosphere is very familiar. The restaurant also has a number of local products for sale, such as large jars of wildflower honey and whole-wheat vegan cookies. Open Mon to Sat 10:30 a.m. – 6:30 p.m.; Sundays during summer and on holidays. Independencia 1790. Tel: 56-32-2234216, URL: www.bambuvegetariano.cl. Updated: Aug 01, 2008.

Color Cafe

(ENTREES: $6 – 8) With the motto "a place of encounters," Color Cafe is an enchanting place to spend the afternoon. The walls are covered with words of wisdom, maps, artwork and dozens of other curiosities. For lunch and dinner, there is a fixed menu, which always includes a vegetarian option. The price includes an appetizer, soup, main course, and dessert. The cafe also has a very respectable list of loose teas, as well as coffee, fresh juices, alcoholic beverages and sweets. An absolutely charming experience. Papudo 526. Tel: 56-32-2226687. Updated: Aug 01, 2008.

Cafe Del Poeta

(PRICES: $6-9) There's something for everybody at Cafe Del Poeta, which is why you'll see people around the tables of this little cafe at all hours of the day. Serving everything from breakfast to traditional Chilean options to Asian dishes in a classy but relaxed atmosphere, this is a place that can please everyone. Although there is no real specialty, the food here is very good. The outdoor patio extending into Plaza Anibal Pinto makes for a pleasant place to break from a busy day with a *menu del día*, an ice cream or an omelet. Plaza Anibal Pinto 1181. Tel: 56-32-228897. Updated: Mar 09, 2009.

Casino Social J Cruz

(ENTREES: $10 – 15) In the mid-20th century, laborers coming back from work at the harbor wanted to eat something delicious, filling, cheap and fast—and they wanted lots and lots of it. The result is the *chorrillana*: a mountain of French fries, eggs, grilled onions and beef. Though you'll find a variety of chorrillanas across the city—some with colorful additions like sausage or tomato—the birthplace of the dish is a tiny restaurant called Casino Social J Cruz ("Jota Cruz"). The Casino Social serves only drinks and chorrillanas, and the walls are covered with hand-written messages from previous visitors. Open Monday-Thursday and Sunday 12 a.m. – 2 a.m., Friday and Saturday: 12 a.m. – 6:30 a.m. Condell 1466. Tel: 56-32- 211225. Updated: Aug 01, 2008.

Cafe Turri

(ENTREES: $11 – 15) Internationally known Cafe Turri has received mixed reviews. Some say the upper-crust dishes (*terrine de foie gras*, steak tartare and duck confit, to name a few) are the best in the city but that the service is poor; others say the staff is quite friendly, but the food is nothing to write home about. Cafe Turri, at the top of ascensor Constitución, has a large outdoor patio with a perfect view of the city, and it offers a unique, classy option for diners to try for themselves. Calle Templeman 147.Tel: 56-32-2365307, URL: www.cafeturri.cl. Updated: Aug 01, 2008.

La Otra Cocina

(DINNER: $15 – 20) A lesser-known restaurant near Plaza Victoria, La Otra Cocina turns into a lively, welcoming place to have dinner late in the evening. Grilled fish and meats are paired with delectable sauces.Prices aren't cheap, but the quality of the food is worth a few extra bucks. Locals show up after 9 p.m. for wine and *entradas* (appetizers), and entertaining street musicians stop in to sing popular Valparaíso favorites to the dining public. Av. Francia (corner with Yungay) 2250. Tel: 56-32-220839. Updated: Aug 01, 2008.

Restaurant La Concepción

(ENTREES: $20 – 50) Restaurant La Concepción offers international cuisine in a restored *patrimonio* home, originally built in 1880, where diners sit among gardens or in front of the open fireplace and can overlook the port of Valparaíso and Viña. The restaurant is owned and run by a North American expat, and serves Mediterranean dishes embellished with international touches. The menu, which uses local and organic ingredients, is dominated by seafood, like deep-sea fish and coastal shellfish. The wine list includes more than 50 kinds of Chilean wine, including an elite selection of old vintage wines. Papudo 541, Cerro Concepción. Tel: 56-32-2498192, E-mail: restaurantlaconcepción@yahoo.com. Updated: Jul 07, 2009.

Empanadas Famosas de Adali

Even before Valparaíso became popular, Empanadas Famosas was famous for its cheesy empanadas (fried or oven-baked). Order at the take-out counter in the small front room or can sit at a table in the back with a beer while you wait for your empanada *frita* (all fried empanadas are made to order). The shrimp and cheese empanada is especially delectable. Mon – Fri 10 a.m. – 6:30 p.m., Sat, Sun, and Holidays: 10 a.m. – 2:30 p.m. Salvador Donoso 1381. Tel: 56-32-2227497. Updated: Aug 01, 2008.

Sibaritico

This sandwich shop may be tiny, but the gigantic Italiano sandwiches they serve here defy imagination. Think of the Italian flag atop a piping hot sausage: red salsa, green guacamole and creamy white *aioli* (garlic mayonnaise sauce). Businessmen line up for these giant Italianos at lunchtime, and a younger crowd takes over at night. The sandwiches are cheap, and you'll be hard-pressed to finish a whole one. Closed Sunday. Open Mon and Tue 12:30 p.m. – 4 p.m. and 6 p.m. – 11 p.m., Wed – Sat 12:30 p.m. – 4 p.m. and 6 p.m. – 7 a.m. Libertad 50. Tel: 56-32-2993876. Updated: Aug 01, 2008.

Gato Tuerto

The Gato Tuerto (one-eyed cat) is located inside Fundación Valparaíso's newly constructed home on Cerro Bellavista. Serving an interesting mix of Southeast Asian cuisine (from Indian to Indonesian to Thai), the restaurant does a good job of combining classy dishes with a casual atmosphere. The food is filling (though it's not the best bang-for-your-buck in town), and it provides a convenient dining option if you're on your way down the hill from La Sebastiana. Hector Calvo Jofre 205, Local 1. Tel: 56-32-2220867, E-mail: gatotuerto@gmail.com URL: www.gatotuerto.cl. Updated: Dec 29, 2008.

Epif Cafe Vegetariano

Epif Cafe fills the vegetarian niche missing in many Chilean towns. Salads, 100 percent natural juices, soy burgers and guac dishes will satisfy the omnivore's palate as well as the vegetarian's. Some of the staff speak English and there is free WiFi. The atmosphere is relaxed and friendly, and they serve a decent cup of coffee. It's well worth the climb for an all-around satisfying experience. Open Tuesday – Thursday: 7 p.m. – 1 a.m., Friday – Saturday: 8 p.m. – 2 a.m., Sunday: 6 p.m. – 11 p.m. Ca. Dr. Grossi 268. Tel: 56-32-2595630, E-mail: info@epif.cl, URL: www.epif.cl. Updated: Aug 01, 2008.

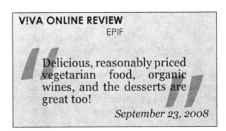

V!VA ONLINE REVIEW

EPIF

"Delicious, reasonably priced vegetarian food, organic wines, and the desserts are great too!"

September 23, 2008

Porto Viejo

Next to the Puerto Mercado is Porto Viejo, a casual seafood restaurant with excellent food and a familiar atmosphere. On the menu you'll find an extensive list of shellfish, BBQ and fish, as well as several house specials like *pulpo a la gallego* (octopus prepared with paprika, rock salt and olive oil). The restaurant, with its big sepia photos of old Valparaíso, fills with a good mix of locals and tourists at midday. It's a great place to watch a soccer match with a few appetizers, a beer, or an impressively large milkshake. Valdivia 154 corner with Cochrane 99. Tel: 56-32-2212709, E-mail: contacto@portoviejo.cl, URL: www.portoviejo.cl. Updated: Aug 01, 2008.

Nightlife

El Ritual

(PRICES: $3 – 7) Offbeat café by day, laidback bar by night, El Ritual is the kind of place to start off your evening. At the base of Cerro Concepción, El Ritual is situated in the middle of plenty of bars and live music venues. Art and sculpture by local artists give the place a tasteful flair, and domestic beer is priced at less than $2. The food, which is served into the night, is mostly cheese or meat plates and specialty pizzas. There are plenty of veggie options, and milkshakes. Almirante Montt 48. Tel: 56-32-252610. Updated: Aug 06, 2008.

Valparaíso Eterno

(PRICES: $5 and up) What used to be a three-story, late-night venue for live music and salsa changed hands in the last few years and now occupies only one floor. Around 11 p.m. at the end of the week, local musicians play in the dimly lit upstairs bar, and the music of Victor Jarra, Joan Baez and Violeta Parra captivates the crowd. This venue was once a place where artists and intellectuals came to express political dissent through music, and the bar still retains an air of subversive intimacy. Come with a song you'd like to hear; performers often put the audience on the spot for requests. Almirante Señoret 150. Tel: 56-32-228374. Updated: Aug 05, 2008.

La Piedra Feliz

(WEEKEND COVER: $12) On Errazuriz, down by the water, this diverse live music venue and three-story club (four-stories if you include the Subterráneo bar where dance hall, punk and new-wave DJs alternate nights) brings in all types of people during the week with tango and salsa classes, live blues and jazz, flamenco, and boleros. The dances are performed in a series of large, wood-floor rooms. On Fridays and Saturdays, the cover charge is high, and drinks and food aren't terribly cheap, but there's a happy hour Monday to Friday until 11 p.m. Closed Sunday. Entrance at both Errazuriz 1054 and Blanco 1067. Tel: 56-32-2256788, E-mail: info@lapiedrafeliz.cl, URL: www.lapiedrafeliz.cl. Updated: Jul 01, 2009.

Bar El Gremio

A night at El Gremio feels like going to a relaxed house party—probably because the bar sits inside a posh two-story townhouse off of a quiet backstreet. Inside, the bar is pleasantly lit, with mismatched yet chic couches and chairs. Morrissey plays on the sound system, and an upstairs room is available for private parties. Drinks are moderately priced, food specials like sushi are often available, and clientele tend to be twenty-something Chileans who err on the yuppie side. Galvez 173, Cerro Concepción. Tel: 56-32-2228394, E-mail: restaurant@gremio.cl. Updated: Aug 05, 2008.

Ache Havana

Next to La Piedra Feliz is Ache Havana, a strictly salsa venue with lively Cuban music and a warm Cuban feel. The club is open Tuesday through Saturday, and *salseros* show up on any given night for good dancing and good rum. Check the website for events, which range from live music and salsa classes to Cuban film festivals. The cover charge includes a drink. Av. Errazuriz 1042. Tel: 56-32-2450187, E-mail: info@achehavana.cl, URL: www.achehavana.cl. Updated: Aug 05, 2008.

El Cinzano

When you come to Bar Cinzano, you're in for a night steeped in *vino arreglado* (cheap wine mixed with better-quality wine, sugar or liquor) and joyful nostalgia. The food in this century-old bar is typical Chilean fare dominated by flavorful *parrilladas* (BBQ) and potatoes, but the real attraction is in the evening—10 p.m. at the earliest, Wednesday through Saturday—when an ancient trio of musicians takes the stage, just as they've done for decades, to play old tango tunes for a rapt audience. Diners will often join in singing the chorus of "Valparaíso Eterno" or will take a partner and tango across the small dining area. This legendary Valpo experience is not to be missed. Open Monday – Thursday 9 p.m. – 2 a.m., Friday – Saturday 9:30 p.m. – 5 a.m. Plaza Aníbal Pinto 1182. Tel: 56-32-2213043, E-mail: barcinzano@gmail.com, URL: www.barcinzano.cl. Updated: Aug 06, 2008.

QUINTAY

Quintay is a tiny, mostly residential beach town hidden among wooded seaside hills about 40 minutes south of Valparaíso. Since this tiny dot on the map is only accessible by private vehicle or by colectivo, you won't find any big tourism offices or moneyed hotels. Unlike its more developed neighbors, Quintay is a relaxed but shabby beach community—homes and small local businesses are connected by dirt roads that radiate from the playground, which is the town's central plaza. On your way into town, colectivos will drop you at this plaza, and this is the best place to find a ride back to Valparaíso.

At the entrance to town, you'll see a plaque with a nice map of Quintay's services and a list of helpful contact information. If you're looking to stay in Quintay, there are a few restaurants down by the water, and a several small accommodation options scattered around town. On Calle Jorge Montt, a road leading out to the sea, you'll find **Carcola**, a small lodge and restaurant. Further inland on this same road, there is a small artisan shop and ecotourism center where you can get information on renting kayaks and guided tours to Ballenera (Tel: 56-89-55137 / 9-238279, URL: http://etnoquintay.com). Updated: Nov 02, 2008.

ISLA NEGRA !

(ADMISSION: $6, seniors and students $3) Tour guides at Pablo Neruda's Isla Negra home will claim that, of his many houses, this was the place that most embodied the poet's spirit. Isla Negra is not on an island at all, but instead a house perched on the edge of the Pacific coastline. The house, which overlooks the sea that so fascinated and frightened the poet, is almost absurdly full of nautical paraphernalia—including an expansive collection of giant ship's figureheads, countless antique navigational instruments, and Neruda's very own sailboat (which he never took out to sea alone).

The house was constructed by members of the Isla Negra community, so it feels much more rustic than his Santiago or Valparaíso homes. The house can only be visited on a tour and it can feel a bit rushed, but the guides are knowledgeable and can field any questions about the poet's life. Open from 10 a.m. – 6 p.m. Closed Mondays. Tel: 56-35-461284.

The town of Isla Negra is itself very small, with a little beach, a few restaurants, and some tourist shops. The cafe inside the museum is notoriously overpriced, so walk into town a bit to find more reasonable food options. On a nice day, try **El Rincón de Florencia**—a pleasant mid-range cafe with an outdoor dining area and a mostly seafood set menu.

Buses leave frequently from the Valparaíso terminal to Isla Negra and surrounding towns, making a final stop at the large port city of San Antonio. Let the bus driver know you'll be getting off at Isla Negra and the bus will drop you along the main road. Updated: Nov 02, 2008.

CARTAGENA

Cartagena, advertised as the "*Capital del adulto mayor*" (Senior Citizen Capital) was once a beach resort for the moneyed elite. But what was once a trendy beach getaway for Chile's jet-setting upper crust is now a town of ruins and crumbling fortunes. The absence of new development and of a tourism office betrays the fact that the city hasn't grown in decades, and the locals living and working here are fairly reserved and almost cold, like they've all seen better days.

The town has two beaches, the tiny Playa Chica, which is clean and lined with a walkway leading to restaurants and shops, and the Playa Grande, which extends the neighboring towns along the coast. Though it's a fairly safe town most of the year, in the summer, the town is flooded with a rougher breed of drug-toting tourists from Santiago and it becomes exponentially more dangerous.

There is no shortage of accommodation here, though much of it is unpublicized and hard to find in guidebooks or on the Internet. *Residenciales* seem to be in every other house in the hills and near the beach. **Residencial San Fernando** (Av. Cartagena 60. Tel: 56-8 -9096000), for instance, is cheap, clean and near the central plaza, though the rooms are bare-bones and hot water isn't available 24-hours. **Casa Blanca Hotel** is a fancier option, situated in a captivating old Spanish-style compound and has 24-hour reception and rooms with pretty views.

In terms of food, **Restaurant La Ola** (Av. La Marina 102. Tel: 56-35-452678, www.laolacartagena.cl) serves pricier dishes, but since the food is average, it's clear that you're paying for the fantastic view. It is also next to a set of relatively new cabins. For a cheaper option, try some of the restaurants along the terraza with lunch menus that feature fresh Chilean seafood dishes. **Clariso Odilia Reyes Delgado** (Av. Cartagena 190. Tel: 56-35-21095) near the central plaza offers inexpensive food and is a good place to take an *once*. Updated: Jul 07, 2009.

SAN ANTONIO

A grimy seaside town that publicizes its poetic underbelly, San Antonio is Chile's largest and most important port. Since it is south of more popular tourist destinations like Isla Negra, San Antonio is often skipped over by non-Chilean tourists. For most of the year, the city consists primarily of locals going about their business and it is relatively safe. In the summer, however, Santiago vacationers arrive and the city becomes more dangerous. That said, San Antonio is a great stop for those who want to see more of Chile than the parts typically outlined in the guidebooks. The city of San Antonio is doing a good job of helping tourists get to know the area. Stop by the tourism office near San Antonio's Plaza de Armas when you arrive; they'll give you a packet with excellent information about places to visit in the city.

The city is sorely lacking a decent selection of cheap accommodation. It tends to be limited to mid-to-high end hotels and cabins. **Bello Horizonte** (Av. Antonio Nuñez de Fonseca, 3865; Tel: 56-35-219115) has mid-range cabañas on a hill north of the San Antonio city center, which is inconvenient for those wishing to access the center, but the atmosphere is far more peaceful. **Residencial Tú y Yo** (Blanco Encalada, 289; Tel: 56-35-211189), which has a cheery restaurant attached, is two blocks from the tourism office and is, for the most part, the most economical option you'll find in town, at $18 per night. Shared and private bathrooms are available, and rooms with a patio and view come at a bit higher price.

In terms of food, there are, of course, plenty of restaurants serving fresh, cheap seafood by the harbor. You can also find some fancier options with nice overlooks. **Restoran Logroño** (21 de Mayo, 274; Tel/Fax: 56-35-233621, E-mail: logrono@restorantlogrono.cl, URL: www.restoranlogrono.cl) has pricier dishes in a classy upstairs dining area on a hill. **Cafe Literario La Negra** (Av. Barros

Luco, 104; Tel: 56-35-210607), just down the street, has tasty sandwiches and fresh juices for a good price in a slightly gaudy but nonetheless comfortable atmosphere. Both restaurants have WiFi access.

There are a few services in town. The **tourism office** (21 de Mayo, 05; Tel: 56-3-5231858, E-mail: oftursanantonio@gmail.com, URL: www.sanantonio.cl) is just off the Plaza de Armas. There are several banks around the perimeter of the plaza and there is a hospital just south of the plaza on 21 de Mayo. On Calle Centenario you will find a currency exchange office, postal services, and phone centers. There are several Internet cafes just off Centenario on Lauro Barros. **Tur Bus** and **Pullman** have multiple offices around the city, the most central of which is on Centenario and Susini. Updated: Jul 08, 2009.

PARQUE NACIONAL LA CAMPANA

 400 – 2,222m   33

(ENTRANCE FEE: $2.70, children $1) Occupying 8,000 hectares (80 square kilometers) in the middle of the coastal mountain range, Parque Nacional La Campana is one of the central zone's definitive areas. Created in 1967 and named a UNESCO World Biosphere Reserve in 1984, the park is home to one of Chile's last remaining palm forests and the imposing Cerro La Campana, one of the most-climbed peaks in Chile. The park lies 60 kilometers (37 mi) east of Viña del Mar and 112 kilometers (70 mi) northwest of Santiago, where the forests of southern Chile spill into the the desert brush of the north. The park has three sectors: Ocoa, Granizo and Cajón Grande; each is connected by trails that meet in the center at the Portezuelo Ocoa.

Parque Nacional La Campana has a Mediterranean climate, and receives coastal mists and fog. Summers are scorching, while winters are rainy. The park is flush with flora and fauna—there are more than 300 different plant and 50 bird species. Srubland vegetation and *roble* (oak) forest are predominant, while *patagua* (a type of evergreeen) and *quillay* (soap bark tree) thrive in the park's arid summers. Deciduous forests, cacti and shrubbery flourish at higher elevations. The park's star flora are the slow-growing Chilean palms, which often top out at 30 meters (98 ft) and live to be 1,000 years old. The trees feature tiny coconut-like fruits and bulgy trunks that can measure a meter or more in diameter. Thanks to a reforestation program and protection efforts, this species of palm has bounced back from an overexploited past in which it was all but wiped out. The palm is favored for its sap, used to make *miel de palma*. It is not unusual to come across burnt-out, discarded ovens in the park, once used to boil the tree's sap. The park is home to foxes, wildcats, a variety of rodents such as vizcachas and chinchillas, skunks, and legions of birds. Finches, mockingbirds, tapaculos, owls and giant hummingbirds are just a few of the many species that make La Campana a prime birding destination.

Trekking is the park's most popular activity. The giant network of linked hiking trails makes for endless exploring and rewards visitors with ocean and Andes views. Hiking Cerro La Campana will test even the most tried hikers and granite rock climbing is possible below the summit. Biking and horseback are also available.

Parque Nacional La Campana is open year-round, and spring is the best time to visit. Park rangers sometimes have maps and books on flora, fauna and conservation. Tour operators offer hiking trips from October to April. The best are **El Caminante** (Tel: 56-71-1970096, turismocaminante@ trekkingchile.com, www.trekkingchile.com) and **Altué Active Travel** (Tel: 56-2-2351519, www.altue.com).

OCOA

Encompassing about 5440 hectares, northern Ocoa is home to the world's most southerly palm groves and is popular with birders and hikers. Sendero El Amasijo begins two kilometers (1.2 mi) past the sector entrance, and climbs up through palm forest to the Portezuelo de Granizo—good views on clear days—where it forks into Sendero Los Robles, which descends south to Cajón Grande, and Sendero Los Peumos, which heads west to Granizo. Starting from Ocoa and finishing via either leg takes the better part of a day. Bring plenty of drinking water. A four-hour round trip on Sendero La Cascada gets you to and from Salto de la Cortadera, a 30-meter (98-ft) waterfall that swells during spring runoff. Hummingbirds are a common sight in spring and summer.

GRANIZO

Lush 972-hectare Granizo is a trekker's utopia. Sendero Los Peumos runs from the entrance to the Portezuelo Ocoa, and has the sector's best survey of the flora and fauna. Hiking Sendero Andinista leads to Cerro La Campana's 1880-meter (6168-ft) summit, where Charles Darwin stood in 1834. The view from the top stretches to the Pacific, the Andes and Santiago. To say the hike is arduous is an understatement. Normally an eight-hour roundtrip, it brings a swift change in elevation: a rise of 1455 meters (4773 ft) in just seven kilometers (4 mi). Most of the hike is shaded, and the trail passes through three natural springs with potable water—the last, *la mina*, is an abandoned mine site with drive-in campground. Above the springs, at around 1500 meters (4,921 ft), are two commemorative markings: one honoring Darwin, the other remembering climbers who died in an 1868 landslide. Adjacent to Granizo, 1,588-hectare Cajón Grande features an oak forest-filled canyon, El Plateau and La Poza del Coipo, a freshwater pond.

Lodging

Camping is the park's only accommodation option. Each sector has a number of tent campsites. Backcountry camping requires the permission of Conaf. Lodging outside the park can be found in Olmué, Limache, Villa Alemana, and Viña del Mar. In Olmué, try **Hosteria el Copihué** (Diego Portales 2203, Tel: 56-33-441-544) or **Residencial Sarmiento** (Blanco Encalada 4647. Tel: 56-33-441-263).

Getting To and Away From Parque Nacional La Campana

Granizo and Cajón Grande are accessible via Olmué, a kilometer southwest of the park. Buses run from Viña del Mar and and Santiago through Limache to Olmué. You can also reach Granizo from Valparaíso, which is 60 kilometers (37 mi) to the east, by hopping on Limache-bound buses that run along Errázuriz. Direct access to Ocoa is tricky. Most northbound buses from Santiago drop you off at Hijuelas and from there you must hitchhike or walk the remaining 12 kilometers (7 mi) to the entrance, or grab a taxi. If you have your own transportation, take Ruta 5 Norte from Santiago, turning at kilometer 100 and following the road for 12.5 kilometers (8 mi) until you hit the Ocoa entrance. If you are Olmué-bounded, you can either take Ruta 5 Norte followed by Ruta 60, or drive Ruta 5 Norte and Til-Til. Updated: Jul 07, 2009.

VIÑA DEL MAR

 33 m   294,500   32

Covering an area of 2.359/km² (6.1/sq mi) Viña is the fourth largest city in Chile. It is also one of the country's most popular tourist destinations, not least because it is just 110 kilometers (68 mi) from Santiago and can easily be reached by bus within two hours.

Viña is characterized by its arc-shaped beach with views of neighboring Valparaíso and Reñaca. It is a modern city with wide avenues and boulevards, plazas and holiday apartments fighting for a view of the Pacific Ocean. It is also known as the "garden city" because of the large number of parks and palm trees along the sidewalks.

Viña was founded in 1874 by engineer Jose Francisco Vergara and the name was inspired by the local vineyards. During the 1800s, several earthquakes destroyed the old part of the city. As a result, only a few historical buildings remain today. These are mostly situated along Avenida Libertad, Calle Quillota and Quinta Vergara.

During the 1980s, Viña's economy suffered as the world economy took a downturn. Many factories closed and the government of General Pinochet failed to resolve the unemployment crisis. The city is fighting back, however, and tourism is now the backbone of the economy.

Viña enjoys a mild climate all year long. Most people go there for the sun and the attractive beach, although few Chileans swim, as they find the water too cold. In the summer, the beach and the surrounding bars and restaurants are packed with both Chilean and international tourists.

Viña is also home to a popular casino and hosts the Festival Internacional de la Canción, an international song-writing contest that attracts thousands of tourists each February.

Other highlights include the Fonck Museum, which has a large number of pre-Columbian artifacts; Quinta Vergera, a city park; Palacio Rioja, a turn of the century mansion turned museum; and Palacio Carrasco, an historic building now used as the city library and for art exhibitions. Viña has a wide range of hotels and restaurants to suit every budget. There are literally hotels on every street

corner, from five-star hotel to budget hostel. Restaurants are mostly found on Avenida San Martin, Mexico Square, Avenida Valparaíso and Viña Square. You can find traditional Chilean food, fine seafood, Italian, Mexican and Japanese cuisine, and Argentine steak houses. Fast-food chains are found along Avenida San Martin . There are several bars along the same street and on the corner of Avenida Valparaíso and Von Schroeders. Large shopping malls, cinemas and supermarkets can be found on Avenida 15 Norte.

Viña is a pleasant city to pass a few days, but more importantly, it is the gateway to more beautiful beaches on the central coast. Updated: Apr 02, 2009.

When to Go
Viña enjoys sunny summers and mild winters. The temperatures range from 22ºC (72ºF) to 10ºC (50ºF), so it's possible to visit all year round.

The city swells with tourists during the summer season, between December and February. February's Festival Internacional de la Canción attracts thousands of tourists, so if you don't like crowds avoid Viña at this time.

The winter season, from June to August, is quiet and there are fewer tourists. Hotel prices are also considerably lower in the winter, but it does get pretty cold at night.

Independence Day, on the 18th of September, is a national holiday and the biggest celebration of the year. Viña holds many *fondas* or parties with traditional music and dance, and lots of food and drink.

The best months to go are probably March and November, as the weather is still warm enough for the beach and the crowds are less stifling.

New Year's Eve is a huge celebration in Viña, with thousands descending on the beach to drink champagne and watch the spectacular fireworks display. Although hotels get booked up early and prices triple, it is a truly memorable way to ring in the New Year. Updated: Jul 10, 2008.

Getting To and Away From Viña del Mar
Buses run every 15 minutes between Viña and Santiago. There is no need to book in advance. The main bus station in Santiago,

Terminal Alameda, is at metro station Universidad de Santiago, on metro line 1. Alternatively, take metro line 1 to Pajaritos and use the small bus station, which is a lot less crowded. **Pullman** and **Turbus** operate services to Viña from both stations. A return ticket between Santiago and Viña costs around $12 and the journey takes about 1 hour 40 minutes. In the high season and after New Year, it can be difficult to get a seat on Sunday evening departures for Santiago.

Buses run from Viña to the south of Chile and to Mendoza, Argentina. You can't book online, so ask at the bus terminal (Av. Valparaíso 1055. Tel: 56-32-2752000 / 2093.) for schedules.

If driving from Santiago or the south, use Highway 68, through Agua Santa. If driving from Argentina, take Highway 60 via Quillota and Concón. Updated: Jul 10, 2008.

Getting Around

Viña is not a large city. If you are reasonably fit, it is easy to get around by foot. Viña also has a good network of local buses or *micros* that run around the city and to neighboring Valparaíso, Renaca and Concón. All the buses have a destination sign. You can catch them on the main street and boulevards.

You can find taxis on most street corners, but they are the most expensive in the entire country. If you must take a taxi, try to get a *colectivo*. Colectivos run on fixed routes and are much cheaper than private taxis. You can board them at bus stops. They are black and you can recognize them by the sign on top advertising their route.

Viña's train system, or *metro*, runs from Valparaíso to Viña, Quilpue, Villa Alemana and Limache. The metro stations are located along Avenida Alvarez and Avenida Vianna.

There are plenty of car hire companies as well. Try **Hertz** on Quillota 766, (Tel: 56-2-2381020) or **Automovil Club de Chile** on 1 Norte 901 (Tel:56-2-2460060). Updated: Jul 07, 2009.

Safety

Viña del Mar is generally a safe city, but opportunistic theft does occur. Carry your backpack on your chest. It is not uncommon for thieves to target tourists waiting at traffic lights or at a busy road junction. They will open your rucksack and help themselves to whatever they can get hold of. Beware of the tricksters

operating along the beachfront. These infamous group of women, usually gypsies, will approach you with the pretense of wanting a light for their cigarette. They will proceed to tell your fortune, offer you prayers and steal your money. Updated: Jul 10, 2008.

Services

TOURISM

The **Tourist Information Center** is on Marina Avenue at Libertad Bridge Corner (just off Plaza JF Vergara). It only provides information about Viña.

Sernatur, Calle Valparaiso 507 (Tel: (56-32)-2684117 E-mail: infovalparaiso@sernatur.cl), provides regional tourist advice for the Valparaíso region.

MONEY

There are a number of banks located on Plaza Jose Francisco Vergara that will exchange American dollars and traveler's checks.

KEEPING IN TOUCH

Most hotels provide free Internet but there are also several cybercafes located throughout the city. There are numerous pharmacies, especially on the main avenues. The **post office** is located beside the Tourist Information Office.

MEDICAL

There are several hospitals including **Clínica Miraflores** on Los Fresnos 276. Tel: 56-32-670897 and **Clinica Reñaca**, Anabaena 336. Tel: 56-32-658000. Updated: Jul 31, 2008.

Things to See and Do

The main reason people go to Viña del Mar is to enjoy the sun and the beach, but the food is also worthwhile. Viña has excellent restaurants offering international cuisine including Mexican, Italian, Japanese and Argentine.

Viña is also home to several parks, including Quita Vergera and the National Botanical Gardens. If history is your thing, you can visit a number of national historic buildings and museums. including the Fonk Museum, Museo Palacio Rioja and Palacio Carrasco. The Municipal Theater also hosts classical, popular and folk music concerts all year long. If baking in the sun is not your thing, take a walk from the *Reloj de flores*, or flower clock, opposite Caleta Abarca beach, and walk around the coast past Wolf Castle and Ross Castle, cross the Casino Bridge, past the Casino and along the beach until you come

MIDDLE CHILE

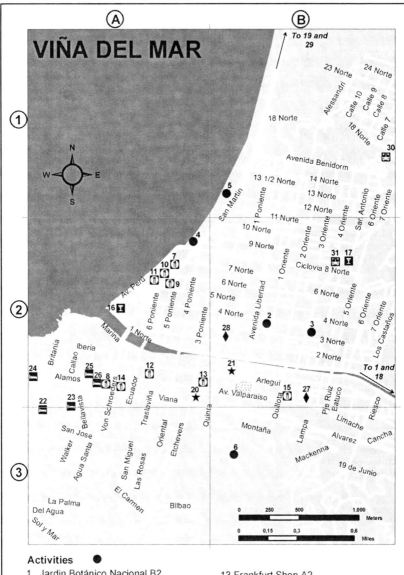

Activities ●

1 Jardín Botánico Nacional B2
2 Museo Francisco Fonck B2
3 Museo Palacio Rioja B2
4 Playa Acapulco A2
5 Playa El Sol B2
6 Quinta Vergara B3

Eating 🍴

7 Café Dolce Amaro A2
8 Café Journal A2
9 Ciao A2
10 Cuernavaca A2
11 Delicias del Mar A2
12 Doner-Kabab A2

13 Frankfurt Shop A2
14 Jardín del Profeta A2
15 San Isidro B2

Nightlife ♍

16 Casino A2
17 Scratch B2

Services ★

18 Clínica Miraflores B2
19 Clínica Reñaca B1
20 Sernatur A2
21 Tourist Information Center B2

Support VIVA! Reserve your hotels or hostels at vivatravelguides.com/hotels/

Sleeping 🛏	Tours ♦
22 Casa del Sol A3	27 Agencia de Turismo B2
23 Che Lagarto A2	28 Excursiones TurisTour B2
24 Hostal Reloj de Flores A2	29 Turismo Bravo B1
25 Hostal Vista Hermosa A2	**Transportation** 🚌
26 Hotel Rokamar A2	30 Automóvil Club de Chile B1
	31 Hertz B2

MIDDLE CHILE

to Vergara Pier. Continue along the beach to the artisan market and children's amusement area. In the high summer there is usually street entertainment in the form of music and street theater. On the way back stop for some food or drink on the bustling Avenida San Martin, which is parallel to the beach.

If that sounds like too much work, you can get a tour of the city by traditional horse and carriage. Tours depart from Avenida Peru. Updated: Jul 10, 2008.

Museo Palacio Rioja

(ADMISSION: $1) Museo Palacio Rioja is a French neoclassical mansion, once the home of rich Spanish banker Fernando Rioja. The ornate house was built between 1906 and 1910. It features Corinthian style columns, a grand double staircase and stone carvings. The original gardens spread over four blocks.

The building was declared a national monument in 1985. Today, Museo Palacio Rioja houses an environmental museum, meeting rooms and a cinema. Most people come here to get a glimpse into the grandeur of the original house and how the rich residents of Viña del Mar lived in the early 1900s. According to local hearsay, there is even a resident ghost wandering about the place. Open Tues-Sun 10 a.m. – 1:30 p.m. and 3 p.m. – 5:30 p.m. Closed Mondays and holidays. Calle Quillota 214 (between 3 and 4 Norte), Vergara Quarter. Tel: 56-32-883322. Updated: Jul 10, 2008.

Quinta Vergara

Quinta Vergara, originally the estate of the prosperous Vergara family, is a public park in the center of Viña del Mar. It features several acres of lovely landscaped gardens, as well as the Palacio Vergera, which was rebuilt after the 1906 earthquake. Palacio Vergara is now the Museo Municipal de Bellas Artes. Quinta Vergara also has an amphitheater that hosts the Festival Internacional de la Cancion. The entrance to the park is on Avenida Errazuriz. Quinta Vergara open daily, 7 a.m. to 7 p.m. Palacio Vergara open Tue-Sun 10 a.m. – 2 p.m. and 3 p.m. – 6 p.m. Calle Errázuriz 596. Updated: Jul 10, 2008.

Jardin Botánico Nacional

(ADMISSION: adults $2, children $1) Chile's national botanical garden covers an area of 40 hectares and is home to over 3,000 native and exotic plants species. The park is a great place to enjoy a relaxing walk and picnic. The gardens were badly damaged by wildfires a few years ago, so barbecues and open fires are strictly forbidden. Jardin Botánico Nacional is on the outskirts of town. To get there, take bus number 20 from Avenida Vianna and get off at the bus terminal in El Salto. Cross the El Olivar bridge and walk for 10 minutes. The gardens are on your left. Casilla Postal 488, Camino El Olivar s/n - El Salto. Tel: 56-32-2672566, URL: www.jardin-botanico.cl. Updated: Jul 07, 2009.

Museo de Archaeología e História Francisco Fonck

(ADMISSION: $4) You won't be able to miss this small museum with its striking moai (Easter Island statue) standing guard outside. The museum documents the lives of the early Chilean peoples from the Norte Grande region, though displays of jewelry, artifacts and pottery. There are also collections from the Moche, Chimú and Nasca cultures of Peru. A separate section holds items from Easter Island, with explanations of how moais were made, and how magic was engraved into the stones. Allow 45 minutes to see everything. Open Monday – Saturday 10 a.m. to 7 p.m., Sunday until 2 p.m. Av. 4 Norte 784, URL: www.museofonck.cl.

Casino

(GAME ROOM ENTRANCE: $6) The casino in Viña was opened in 1930 and is the oldest and most popular in the country. The impressive building is set among lovely gardens. The casino features 1,500 gaming machines and 90 game tables. The casino also has a bar, a nightclub and three restaurants. In 2002, a posh hotel was built onto the original building in the same style. You can enter the casino bar and slot machines room for free but you need to pay for the games room. Be warned, this place is very smoky. Open 24 hrs. Av. San Martín 199. Tel: 56-32-846100, URL: www.casino.cl. Updated: Jul 15, 2008.

Beaches

Vacationers from around South America and the world flock to Viña beaches during summer (late December to late March). Put on a bathing suit and soak up rays on one of the many Viña beaches, or walk or take a bus to Reñaca (3 miles way) and Concón for more beautiful beaches.

In Viña, possibly the most popular beach is Playa Acapulco (8 Norte and Av. San Martín), where there's ample room and plenty of craft stands to browse. Check out the animal sculptures people mold from only sand and water. Children of all ages can rent a bike cart and pedal around the area.

Playa El Sol is only a few blocks away (11 to 14 Norte with Av. San Martín), and has a lot more room to lay your beach towel. There are also shaded tables where you can enjoy a fresh juice. There's a park near Playa El Sol where children can go on small amusement rides or ride horses.

Playa Caleta Abarca is next to the Sheraton Hotel near the Clock of Flowers off of Avenida Marina. The strip of white sand offers a nice view of Valparaíso and Reñaca. Go up the stairs and walk around the gardens by the hotel. Updated: Jul 07, 2009.

Tours

Many of the tour operators don't have offices in Viña, so apart from the two operators in the bus station, they can be a little hard to find on the street. You can get information about local tour operators from Sernatur or from the Tourist Information Center on Plaza JF Vergara, Freefone: 800-800-830. You can also book tours through most hotels.

There is a wide range of tours available, including city tours of Viña and Valparaíso, trips to local vineyards, horse riding and trips up the coast to neighboring beaches. In summer, tours are in high demand, so you'll need to book excursions two or three days in advance. Updated: Jul 08, 2009.

Agencia de Turismo

Agencia de Turismo, located in the bus station, is government approved. The agency runs a city tour of Viña, Valparaíso and Renaca which costs $20. It also offers a tour of Isla Negra and a local vineyard for $60. Prices don't include entrance fees or lunch. Tour guides speak English and buses have air-conditioning. Buses depart from the station or pick you up from your hotel. Agencia de Turismo also offers good deals with local hotels and apartments. Av. Valparaíso 1055. Tel: 56-32-2714924, E-mail: reservas@vinadelmar.cl. Updated: Jul 10, 2008.

Excursiones TurisTour

Although based in Santiago, TurisTour offers a number of tours of Viña del Mar and the surrounding area. A half-day tour of Viña and Valparaíso costs $30. The company also offers a tour of the Casablanca wine valley (half day $50, full day $60). For $80, you can get a full-day tour to the Casablanca wine valley, Isla Negra and Casa Museo Pablo Neruda. Staff are bilingual and tours pick you up from your hotel. All major credit cards are accepted. Book by phone. Rio Itata 9632. Tel: 56-32-2381056, E-mail: excursions@turistour.cl, URL: www.turistour.cl. Updated: Jul 10, 2008.

Turismo Brava

Turismo Brava operates much more interesting tours than many of its rivals. The Viña del Mar city tour ends with a coastal drive to neighboring Reñaca and Concón. There is a day tour to Maintencillo, Cachagua, Zapallar and Papudo. The tour operator also offers horseback riding tours across Ritoque Beach, including a moonlight ride that ends with snacks, singing and dancing around a campfire. There is also a vineyard tour, which includes a traditional horse show and a tour of Isla Negra with a stop at Pablo Neruda's house. Turismo Brava can arrange airport transfers. Av. Concón - Renaca 41, Concón. Tel: 56-32-2813439, E-mail: ventas@turismobravo.cl, URL: www.turismobravo.cl. Updated: Jul 07, 2009.

Lodging

As Chile's tourist capital, it's not surprising that Viña offers a huge range of accommodation. Options include five-star hotels, private apartments, B&Bs and hostels. In the summer season, the city is packed, be sure to book ahead. Prices triple around New Year's Eve and it can be near impossible to find a bed. Many hotels charge foreigners 19 percent for local taxes. Make sure to check if this is included in the price before you book. Updated: Jul 08, 2009.

Che Lagarto
(ROOMS: $10 – 20) Che Lagarto is one of the cheapest hostels in Viña del Mar. With 70 beds, it is also one of the best places to go if you want to meet up with other travelers. The hostel is set in a beautiful old house with high ceilings and wooden floors. There is a large garden that is perfect for sunbathing and BBQs. There is also a bar that hosts parties or themed dinners every night. Breakfast is included and the hostel has free WiFi. The dorm rooms are crowded with bunk beds and there isn't much room for personal belongings. If you pay in Chilean pesos instead of dollars, they will try to charge you the 19 percent local tax. 131 Diego Portales (off Calle Chaigneau). E-mail: vinadelmar@chelagarto.com, URL: www.chelagarto.com. Updated: Jul 07, 2009.

Hostal Vista Hermosa
(ROOMS: $20) Hostal Vista Hermosa is set in a lovely old house at the bottom of Cerro Castillo. There is a big kitchen and terrace area. The living room is welcoming and has a large comfy leather sofa and grand staircase. This is a perfect spot for those looking for a quiet getaway. During the school term, the hostel is home to several students. The rooms (all private) are a bit old-fashioned, but are clean and spacious and come with bathroom and TV. Vista Hermosa 26. Tel: 56-32-666820, E-mail: info@vistahermosa26.cl, URL: www.vistahermosa26.cl Updated: Jul 11, 2008.

Hostal Reloj de Flores
(ROOMS: $20 – 40) Hostal Reloj de Flores is a comfortable hostel five minutes from Caleta Abarca beach. There is a big communal kitchen and living room with free Internet and stereo. The bedrooms are cozy and have cable TV. If you are lucky, you might get one with a terrace and sea views. During the year, the hostel houses several students, but don't let this put you off. The hostel is clean and very quiet. Los Baños 70 (between Chaigneux and Roma). Tel: 56-32-2485242, E-mail: ninfar@gmail.com. Updated: Jul 01, 2009.

Hotel Rokamar
(ROOMS: $30 – 40) Hotel Rokamar is a budget hotel in downtown Viña, about four blocks from the beach and the restaurants of Avenida San Martin. The lovely old building dates from the early 1900s. The décor is a bit dated but rooms are clean and come with private bathroom, cable TV and phone. Breakfast is included in the price but there is no bar or restaurant. The atmosphere is good and there is a real sense of relaxed enjoyment. The staff are friendly. Viana 107 (corner of Esquina Von Schroeders). Tel: 56-32-690019, Fax: 56-32-695398, E-mail: hotelrokamar@entelchile.net, URL: www.hotelrokamar.cl. Updated: Jul 11, 2008.

Casa del Sol
(ROOMS: $44) Casa del Sol is a beautiful guesthouse just one block from Caleta Abarca beach. With high ceilings, wooden floors, period features and pretty rooms, this place is an oasis of calm. The garden features a BBQ area and two sun terraces. All rooms come with private bathroom and are decorated in a rustic style. There is a large communal kitchen and living room area. Breakfast is included and Internet access is free. Collectivos and buses run from the front door to the city center. Pasejo Romero 375. Tel: 56-32-2485242, E-mail: ninfar@gmail.com, URL: www.bbcasadelsol.com. Updated: Jul 11, 2008.

Hotel Marina del Rey
(ROOMS: $110 – 160) Hotel Marina del Rey is a four-star hotel in downtown Viña, about five blocks from the beach, casino and restaurants. The décor is traditional but the hotel offers all the comfort and reliability you expect from a Best Western. It has a restaurant and bar, and breakfast is included. It's a good choice for travelers with a bit more cash. There's nothing exciting about Marina del Rey, but there's nothing wrong with it either. Ecuador 299. Tel: 56 -32-2383000, Fax: 56-32-2383001, E-mail: info@marinadelrey.cl, URL: www.marinadelrey.cl. Updated: Jul 10, 2008.

Sheraton Miramar
(ROOMS: $200 and up) Built on rocks overlooking Caleta Abarca Beach, the five-star Miramar is one of Viña's newest hotels. Everything about it screams luxury, from the heavy paneled doors to the glass elevators. All 142 rooms have sea views, a sun terrace and all the utilities you would expect. The outdoor pool, terrace, restaurants and bar all have beautiful views. Av. Marina 15. Tel: 56-32-2388600, Fax: 56-32-2388799, URL: www.sheraton.com/vinadelmar. Updated: Jul 02, 2009.

Restaurants
Viña prides itself on the variety and quality of restaurants in town. Most are on Avenida San Martín, Avenida Valparaíso and Plaza JF Vergara. San Martín is the main tourist thoroughfare and the restaurants are not cheap. You are spoiled with choices by a large number of Chilean, seafood, Italian, Argentine,

MIDDLE CHILE

Japanese and Mexican restaurants as well as fast-food chains. If you are on a tight budget, go along Avenida Valparaíso and on the corner of Valparaíso and Von Schroeders to find cheap bars selling snacks in addition to drinks. Updated: Jul 08, 2009.

San Isidro

San Isidro has cheap Chilean fast food. With plastic tables and chairs, the décor is basic. The friendly staff serve up everything from fried eggs on toast, to *completos*—Chilean hotdogs. San Isidro also offers *chorrillana*, a traditional dish of fries piled high with beef, pork sausage, fried egg and fried onion. The food, while not exactly healthy, is very tasty.

The best thing about San Isidro is its location, across the road from the main bus station. Open 8:30a.m. – 11p.m., it is a great place to fill up before or after a long bus journey. Av. Valparaíso 948. Updated: Jul 15, 2008.

Doner-Kabab

This little hole-in-the-wall joint, inconspicuously wedged between two neighboring tiendas, is easy to miss. But find it, and your taste buds will be rewarded with delicious shawarmas and yummy Middle Eastern pastries. Select from chicken, beef, mixed or vegetarian shawarmas, and choose a sauce (garlic or cilantro) to top it off. These shawarmas are of the particularly messy variety, so the most casual of dress is mandatory (unless, of course, you like to wear your food). Value is good, and so is the service. Traslaviña 161. Tel: 56-2-46-5846. Updated: Dec 19, 2007.

Cuernavaca

Cuernavaca is a cheesy Mexican-themed restaurant and bar. The wooden décor and open fire make it a cozy place, but the music is a constant mix-tape that ranges from Peter Andre to Madonna and Metallica. The menu features a tasty range of fajitas, enchiladas, burritos, tacos, chimichanga and quesadillas. The bar offers a huge cocktail list as well as wine and beer. It's a good place to go

with friends. Av. San Martín 501. Tel: 56-32-739084, URL: www.cuernavacarestaurant.cl. Updated: Jul 15, 2008.

Cafe Dolce Amaro

This bistro serves a tempting range of seafood appetizers, tapas, meat and seafood dishes, salads, sandwiches and desserts. The bar offers a wide selection of cocktails, beer and pisco, and real coffee. During the week, the set lunch menu includes a starter, main dish, dessert and drink for a reasonable price. The bistro also exhibits paintings and craft works. Try to get the comfy leather sofa on the terrace. Av. San Martín 581. Updated: Jul 15, 2008.

Jardín del Profeta

Jardín del Profeta offers tasty vegetarian cuisine at very cheap prices. You can choose from a delicious range of vegetarian burgers, pasta dishes, pizza, tortillas, empanadas, quiche, sandwiches and main dishes. The restaurant has a relaxed vibe, but is a bit sparsely decorated and could do with a bit more furniture. The place is non-smoking and doesn't serve alcohol. Viana 99. Tel: 56-32-695886, E-mail: jardindelprofeta@gmail.com. Updated: Jul 15, 2008.

Delicias del Mar

This family-run restaurant serves an interesting variety of fish and seafood dishes. The menu is based on original recipes served by the owners' grandmother in the Basque country. Service is first class and the helpful waiters are happy to recommend a dish if you can't make up your mind. The food isn't cheap but is very good. The owner obviously likes Marilyn Monroe because there are over 200 photographs of the legend displayed in the restaurant. The kitsch photos contrast with the posh white tablecloths and polished silverware. Av. San Martín 495. Tel: 56-32-290837, URL: www.deliciasdelmar.com. Updated: Jul 15, 2008.

Cafe Journal

Cafe Journal mainly caters to a cool college crowd, though it also tends to attract swarms of *gringos* (hence its nickname Cafe Gringo). Locals and foreigners alike congregate here for cold beers and hard drinks (be warned—your *piscola* is more pisco than cola!), in a fun, funky atmosphere. Every available surface of the restaurant is covered in risqué magazine cutouts and posters, further adding to the venue's hip factor. The place is huge—two stories, with indoor and outdoor seating, as well as several dance floors. Food options include empanadas, pizzas, salads, and sandwiches, and there's a never-ending drink menu. Prices aren't exactly low, but aren't bad for expensive Viña del Mar, and the friendly bilingual staff works hard to ensure your satisfaction. Agua Santa 4-10. Tel: 563-2-266-6654, URL: www.cafejournal.cl. Updated: Dec 19, 2007.

Frankfurt Schop !

Frankfurt Schop is on a first-floor terrace that hosts a number of similar eating and watering holes. The menu offers a range of burgers, *completos*, fries and sandwiches. There is also a full bar. The décor is basic. Plastic tables and chairs line the terrace and the inside has traditional wooden furniture. The food is served in generous helpings and the evening atmosphere is quite nice. Av. Valparaíso 553. Tel: 56-32-979685. Updated: Jul 15, 2008.

Ciao

Ciao boasts over 20 specialty pizzas and an ample drink menu. The never-ending special of two medium pizzas for the price of one and the two-for-one drink menu make Ciao an affordable dinner spot. If you're looking for healthier food, order a salad, salmon empanada or fresh-squeezed juice. Chat with friends on the couches, and warm up around the wood stove or one of the tall heaters placed between leafy plants and stylish tables. Overall, the atmosphere is great and the service is excellent. 5 Norte, 164 (between 1 Poniente and Av. San Martín). Tel: 56-32-2696569. Updated: Aug 08, 2008.

Nightlife

Scratch

Scratch is a huge nightclub with capacity for 1,200 people, usually a friendly mix of locals and tourists. There are three bars and a VIP area. The DJ plays a mixture of techno, cheesy pop hits and Latino music. Chileans like to party late so don't get there before 12 a.m. The music stops at 5 a.m. The dress code is casual and jeans are fine. Girls should bring a supply of toilet paper for the bathroom. Ca. Quillota 898. Tel: 56-32-381381, E-mail: info@scratch.cl, URL: www.scratch.cl. Updated: Jul 15, 2008.

QUINTERO

Quintero is a beach town that rests on a peninsula about 50 kilometers (68 mi) north of Viña del Mar. It was "discovered" by the Spanish Captain Don Alonso de Quintero on his way back from a voyage to Peru. He was so impressed by the beauty of the landscape that he named the area "Bahia de Quintero" or Quintero Bay in honor of himself.

Quintero is popular for its beaches (there are about 20 to choose from), water sports and fishing. It can get very crowded in the summer and is best enjoyed off-peak.

Some argue that the best beach is Playa Loncura. There are lots of tourist restaurants and beach houses so it's a good place to base yourself while exploring the area. Another popular beach is Playa el Durazno. It's good for swimming and there are lots of bars and restaurants nearby. Playa Ritoque, a 12-kilometer (7.5-mi) beach is most popular with surfers but it is more remote. Playa las Cañitas, although small, has a lovely view and there is very good diving. Avoid noisy Playa Albatros, located beside a huge air force base.

According to local folklore, La Cueva del Pirata, or the Pirate's Cave, in the north of Quintero, was used as a hideout by pirates including Francis Drake and Joris Spilpergen. It's also rumored to be the site of buried treasure. You can't swim there but it offers stunning views of the coast. Another great viewpoint is Cerro de la Cruz, also known as Cerro Centinela (Sentry Hill), located in the southwest.

For a cheap sleep try **Hotel Monaco** on Avenida 21 de Mayo (Tel: 56-32-930939), **Cabanas Rocas del Pirata** on Baquedano 10 (Tel: 56-9-4328111 or www.cabanas-quintero.com) or **Dunas Hostal** on Playa Ritoque (Tel: 56-99-0511748 / 9-0511748 or E-mail: info@dunashostel.com).

For a quick snack try **Empanadas Pamela** (470 Av. 21 De Mayo) or **Patto's Shop** (2164 Av. 21 De Mayo). For a treat, try some tradition Chilean food at **La Cocina de TEUH** on Francisco Bilbao 147. Updated: Aug 26, 2008.

Getting To and Away From Quintero

BY CAR

Driving from Santiago: Take route 5 Norte until Nogales. Then take route F-20 until you come

MIDDLE CHILE

to routes F-30-E and F-210. Head south at this junction.

From Viña del Mar or Valparaíso: Head north for routes F-30-E and F-210.

From Mendoza: Take routes 60, 5 Norte, F30--E and F-210.

BY BUS

From Santiago: Take a bus from Estacion Central.

From Viña del Mar: Buses depart from Plazas Sucre (just off Av. Valparaíso) and Parroquia (close to the entrance of Quinta Vergera) every 30 – 40 minutes. Final departures take occur up to 9 p.m. in summer, 7 p.m. in winter.

From Valparaíso: Quintero-bound buses can be found along Avenida Errázuriz. Updated: Aug 26, 2008.

HORCÓN

Horcón is a small fishing town based around a sheltered bay, 44 kilometers (27 mi) north of Viña del Mar and 163 kilometers (101 mi) from Santiago. The pretty town is perched atop lush rolling hills that meet the Pacific Ocean. The area is very beautiful and very green.

In the 1960s Horcón was something of a hippy hangout. Today it has evolved into an artisan center, with several craftspeople making and selling handmade goods in the town. During the week, it's a sleepy town, but it comes alive at weekends when people come to buy fresh fish and seafood, visit the craft fair and eat in the local restaurants.

There are several beautiful beaches in Horcón, including Playa Cau-Cau, Playa Larga, Playa El Claron, Playa Los Agatas, Playa Luna, Playa Los Tebos and Playa La Caleta de los Pescadores. Playa Luna is a nudist beach.

Activities in the area include lazing on the beach, swimming, fishing, diving and paragliding. There is plenty of accommodation and good restaurants serving the day's catch.

For cheap lodgings try **Cabañas Horcón** (Ca. Principal 267. Tel: 56-32-2794613, URL: www.cabanashorcon.cl), or **Cabañas Nena** on Los Aromos (Tel: 56-32-2794062).

For great seafood try **Caballo de Mar** on Playa Cau-Cau (Tel: 56-32-2796138). For traditional Chilean food at reasonable prices try **Restaurant Horcon-Museo** (Av. Costanera 73. Tel: 56-32-2794540). Updated: Jul 07, 2009.

Getting To and Away From Horcón

See Getting To and Away From Quintero (p. 151), just stay on all routes until Horcón. Updated: Aug 26, 2008.

MAITENCILLO

Maitencillo is 180 kilometers (112 mi) northwest of Santiago on the central west coast. The town stretches for 4 kilometers (2.4 mi) around the beautifully rugged coast, which is a mixture of rocky headlands, tranquil white beaches, steep cliffs and hills filled with pine and eucalyptus trees. The town is not overdeveloped and has a rustic charm but still enough bars and restaurants to keep you entertained at night.

There are seven beaches to choose from, including Playa Grande, Playa Chica, Playa Aguas Blancas, Playa La Caleta, Playa Los Pinos, Playa Los Pocitos and Playa El Abanico. Playa Aguas Blancas, which stretches for almost 5 kilometers (3.1 mi), is the most popular. It has big waves and is popular for surfing and body boarding. During the summer season there is a tourist information hut on Playa El Abanico with information about lodgings, restaurants and events. Updated: Oct 24, 2008.

Getting To and Away From Maitencillo

See Getting To and Away From Quintero (p.151), just stay on all routes until Maitencillo. Updated: Aug 26, 2008.

Things to See and Do

The main activities in Maitencillo are paragliding, body boarding and surfing. You can also fish or hike along the coast. The area is also rich in wildlife. If you are lucky, you might even see a Humboldt penguin. Updated: Oct 24, 2008.

CACHAGUA

One of many coastal resort villages, Cachagua is best known for its community of penguins. Between 1,000 and 2,000 Magellanic and Humboldt penguins inhabit the protected Monumento Natural Isla Cachagua (Isla de los Pingüinos), a desolate rock off the west end of the beach. Surfers flock to Cachagua's waves, where there is good fishing and horseback riding. Restaurants front the town's beach, while a more secluded stretch of sand, Playa las Cujas, is just a short hike away. The town has scores of second homes, but lacks lodging for tourists. Look for a place to stay 10 kilometers to the south in Maitencillo or in Zapallar. Updated: Jul 02, 2009.

Getting To and Away From Cachagua

See Getting To and Away From Quintero (p.151), just stay on all routes until Cachagua. Updated: Aug 26, 2008.

ZAPALLAR

At one time, rich Chileans spent their vacations in Viña del Mar. Then the crowds descended and spoiled everything. The rich grabbed their designer suitcases, jumped in their cars and traveled around 125 kilometers north in search of something better. They found Zapallar, or "place of pumpkins," and quickly transformed it from a sleepy fishing town into one of the most exclusive beach resorts in Chile. Zapallar's stunning golden bay is sheltered by lush, tree-covered hills, which are dotted with luxurious holiday homes, many of them old mansions. It's a quiet town, with fewer than 6,000 full-time residents, and quaint little streets to wander along if you fancy a break from the beach.

It's possible to do a range of water sports in Zapallar, and the path around the bay makes a lovely walk. Climb over the rocks to Isla Seca, or "dry island," which is actually a peninsula and not an island! It's not a good idea to swim here though, as the sea is rough. If you're feeling a bit more energetic, climb Cerro Higuera, a 692-meter high hill, for incredible coastal views.

There isn't much by way of cheap accommodation in Zapallar but **Residencial La Terraza on Del Alcalde** 142 is a budget hotel (Tel: 56-0-711409). If you have a bit more money and a car, try the stylish **Hotel Isla Seca** (Camino Costero Ruta F-30-E 31. Tel: 56-33-741224). **Chiringuito Restaurant** at the Caleta is famous for seafood (Tel: 56-32-741024). Or go to the fish market **Caleta Zapallar**, buy produce straight from the sea and cook it at home. Updated: Aug 27, 2008.

PAPUDO

Papudo is a fishing town 115 kilometers (71.5 mi) north of Viña del Mar and five kilometers north of Zapallar. Legend has it that the Spanish first landed on the shores of Papudo in 1536. The area was then inhabited by the Chango tribe, whose leader Chief Carande had a double chin (*papada* in Spanish) and so the Spanish called the area Papudo.

The area once described by Pedro de Valdivia as the "paradise of God" has undergone tourist development, and although some say it's not quite as pretty as it used to be, it's still beautiful and worth visiting.

There are several golden beaches where you can relax or enjoy water sports. Playa Grande, in the north of Papudo, is popular with body boarders and surfers. Playa Chica is quieter and good for swimming and water sports. In good weather, you can take a fishing trip or hire horses and ride across the beach. The area is home to an impressive array of wildlife, including penguins, otters, sea lions and dolphins.

If you get bored of the beach, visit Iglesia Nuestra Senora de Las Mercedes, a pretty neo-colonial church completed in 1918. Alternatively, take a walk along Avenida Costanera Glorias Navales for great views of all the beaches in Papudo. Another tourist attraction is the fish market, Caleta de Pescadores.

For cheap lodgings try **Il Gabiano** (Chorrillos 183. Tel: 56-3-3790155, URL: www.ilgabbiano.cl), **Hotel Carande** (Chorrillos 89. Tel: 56-3-3791105, URL: www.hotel-carande.cl) or **Cabañas Los Arrayanes** on Baquedano 333 (Tel: 56-3-3790138).

For fish and seafood **Il Gabiano** has an attached restaurant, or check out **Donde Pablo** on Avenida Glorias Navales (Tel: 56-3-3791942). Updated: Jul 27, 2009.

Getting To and Away From Papudo

See Getting To and Away From Quintero (p.151), just stay on all routes until Papudo. Updated: Aug 26, 2008.

Aconcagua Valley

The Aconcagua Valley offers fantastic wine tours. The narrow valley has drastic slopes and is home to the Río Aconcagua, which stems from Cerro Aconcagua. Highway 60 stretches along the valley, across the Andes to Mendoza, Argentina, and offers breathtaking views along the way. The region offers some of the best skiing in the world at Portillo. Updated: Jul 01, 2009.

SAN FELIPE

 636 m   54,200   53

San Felipe, on the Aconcagua River, was founded in 1740 as San Felipe El Real. The town is ideally located in the heart of a valley that most famously produces excellent, ripened grapes and world-renowned wines (due to its ideal micro-climate). In the past, the area was copper and gold mining land. This Andean town is a semi-bustling trade center thanks to its relatively close proximity to Mendoza, Argentina.

San Felipe boasts a pleasant Plaza de Armas, which is usually full of laid-back locals and vendors. The highlight of the plaza is without a doubt the artisan market where visitors can purchase local handicrafts, souvenirs or homemade snacks such as sweet popcorn. The **Museo Histórico de Aconcagua** (Av. Riquelme) displays regional artifacts. The **Catedral de San Felipe** stands on the northern side of the plaza, while another important church in the city is **Iglesia y Claustro del Buen Pastor** (Av. Yungay between San Martín and O'Higgins). Or, if religious architecture is too serious during a vacation, you can check out live bands and art exhibits at the Teatro Municipal, on the western edge of the Plaza de Armas.

San Felipe does not offer very many choices for accommodations. A backpacker's best bet is the clean **Hotel Reinares** (Carlos Condell 75), where a comfortable bed costs approximately $11. **Hosteria San Felipe** (Ca. Merced 204) is a hospitable option; staff is friendly and quick with advice at **Residencial Aldo's** (Salinas 67). **Club Social San Felipe** is a hip place to spend the night out after some Asian food at **Restaurante Sheng Fa** (Ca. Portus 156) or find Arabic and traditional Chilean dishes at **Club Árabe** (Prat 124).

San Felipe's **Terminal de Buses** is located on Avenida Yungay between San Martín and Freire. Buses run to and from Santiago every 20 minutes from various companies. Numerous buses run to and from Viña del Mar, as well as east toward Los Andes and onward to the Argentine border. Updated: Jul 01, 2009.

LOS ANDES

This Chilean town was founded in 1791 as "Santa Rosa de Los Andes" by Ambrosio O'Higgins, the father of famous Chilean liberator Bernardo O'Higgins. The city lies at the crossroads of Route 57 from Santiago and Route 60, which runs from Viña del Mar. Much like nearby San Felipe, the microclimate here is conducive to the production of high-quality grapes and tremendous wines. The well-tended and shaded Plaza del Armas is the center of Los Andes urban life. The Gobernación Provincial, which served as the provincial governor's residence until 1964, is on the northern edge of the plaza. Government offices are now located around its central patio.

While checking out the sights in Los Andes, head toward the **Museo Arqueológico de Los Andes** (Santa Teresa 398. Tel: 56-34-420115, $2, Tuesday – Sunday 10 a.m. – 6 p.m.) to learn a bit about the local history. Stone tools, pottery and other items are showcased. There are some interesting Mapuche artifacts as well. Nearby **Museo Antiguo Monasterio del Espíritu Santo de Los Andes** (Santa Teresa 389) is a popular pilgrimage site for the faithful. You can also see **the mural A la Hermandad Chileno-Argentina**, by artist Gregorio de la Fuente, at the judicial offices in the former waiting room of the Estación Ferrocarril Transandino.

There are several accommodation options for travelers. **Plaza Hotel** (Esmeralda 367) has simple rooms with TVs and phones, and a continental breakfast included. Expect to pay $56 for a single or $64 for a double room. **Hotel Olicar's** (Papudo 385) clean single rooms ($26) are great for budget travelers.

After securing a place to rest, head out to one of the town's restaurants. Fresh spaghetti and other scrumptious Italian meals are served at **Círculo Italiano** (Esmeralda 246). Other good options are **El Guatón** (Av. Santa Teresa 240), for regional cuisine, or the fancy **La Table de France** (Camino Internacional, Km 3. Tel: 56-34-406319) which starts lunches off with a delicious onion soup. Updated: Jun 30, 2009.

PORTILLO

Portillo, a beautiful and exclusive spot next to the alpine lake Laguna del Inca and near the Argentine border, is synonymous with world-class skiing. So it is no surprise that the U.S., Italian and Austrian Olympic teams flock here for summer training. Former U.S. women's national team member and Olympic gold medalist Picabo Street once claimed Hotel Portillo—at an altitude of 2,850 meters (9,350 ft)—was the most inspirational resort on the roof of the world. There is also heli-skiing for adventurous souls in search of unspoiled powder ($295 per person first run, $165 following runs), while ski and snowboard novices can also find sufficient trails. Altitudes range from 2,590 meters to 3,310 meters, the longest run being 3,200 meters. The slopes are well groomed, though the expert terrain is left with its natural ice pack.

Hotel Portillo offers room options that range from the luxurious ($1,200 – $5,300 per person, per week) to dorm-style, and prices, which depend on low or high season, include seven nights of lodging, four meals per day, lift tickets and access to fitness and entertainment facilities. Those less interested in style can stay in **Hotel Portillo's Octagon Lodge** ($890 – $1,390 per person, per week), that offers four bunks and a private bathroom in each room, or the **Inca Lodge** ($590 – $900), which is popular among backpackers under 30. Rooms are small and the bathroom is communal but the lodge is the cheapest place to stay in Portillo (Tel: 56-263-0606, URL: www.skiportillo.com, E-mail: info@skiportillo.com).

It is also possible to find cheaper accommodation 70 kilometers (43 mi) to the west, in the city of Los Andes. The scenic, two-hour drive from Santiago to Portillo can be arranged through **Portillo Tours and Travel** (Tel: 56-22-630606 or toll free from U.S. 1-800-829-5325, E-mail: traslados@skiportillo.com). Updated: Jun 30, 2009.

Southern Heartland

The majority of Chilean wine comes from this area south of Santiago, encompassing Region V (Valparaíso), Region VI (Rancagua), Region VII (Maule) and Region VIII (Bío Bío). The climate is perfect for vast orchards and vineyards, and surfers can find great breaks along the coastline. The cordillera south of Rancagua has some great hiking, but is routinely overlooked in favor of the better-known parks further south. Updated: Jul 01, 2009.

RANCAGUA

 518m   229,065   72

The agricultural town of Rancagua does little to distinguish itself from others in the Central Valley with the exception of modern malls and department stores found along Paseo Independencia. Government has also kept its local historic buildings well maintained. The town is ideal as a hub to explore surrounding

attractions such as the Chapa Verde Ski Resort, Reserva Nacional Río los Cipreses and the hot springs at Termas de Cauquenes.

The Plaza de los Heroés is named in memory of Bernardo O'Higgins and his patriot soldiers who fought against the Royalists in 1814. Although the battle was lost, O'Higgins returned to the city four years later. There is now a statue in the center of the plaza memorializing him.

A room can be easily found a few blocks from the train and bus stations, and there is an array of options for hungry tourists. Updated: Jan 25, 2009.

When to Go

By far the biggest show in town is the Campeonato Nacional de Rodeo, which takes place annually in early fall (late March to early April). Book ahead if you are planning to stay here around this engrossing *huaso* (cowboy) festival. Celebrations marking Chile's independence occur in September, and the Encuentro Criollo folklore festival in November. The lifts at nearby Chapa Verde are open from mid-June to mid-October and draw skiers and snowboarders looking to avoid the crush on the central region's more popular slopes. Updated: Jul 02, 2009.

Getting To and Away From Rancagua

BY TRAIN
From Santiago, the 45-minute train ride ($9) drops passengers off on Avenida Estacion, a short walk from the center of town. Trains run hourly from the capital to Rancagua.

Trains north to Santiago also run hourly. It is also possible to travel to San Fernando, Talca, Curico and many other cities by rail from Rancagua, though some routes require connections.

BY BUS
Buses run to and from the terminal at Salinas 1165, which is slightly north of the train terminal, and is serviced by an array of companies. Tickets to and from Santiago cost $6.50. Prices to other destinations from Rancagua vary depending on distance and class of bus. Updated: Jan 25, 2009.

Getting Around

Taxis and buses are plentiful around Rancagua. Be sure to check that your cab driver turns on his meter. Buses often stop wherever a prospective passenger flags down the driver, so don't be shy about waving your arms. Car rental is available at Weber **Rentacar** (Membrillar 40, office No. 2, 72-226005). Updated: Jan 25, 2009.

Safety

There are very few dangers in Rancagua besides the occasional pickpocket, so just practice common sense. Updated: Jul 02, 2009.

Services

You can find ATMs at several banks on Paseo Independencia, including **Banco Estado** (Independencia 666). Some banks will cash traveler's checks, or go to **Afex** on Campos 363 to exchange U.S. dollars. Most hotels have WiFi access, and though Internet cafes are scarce it is possible to get online at **Ciber Space** (Alcazar 376). The **hospital** is found on Av. Libertador Bernardo O'Higgins between Asorga and Campos. The post office is at Campos 322. Updated: Jan 25, 2009.

Things to See and Do

Rancagua has fairly modern malls and department stores if you need to shop, while the Plaza de los Heroés and Iglesia Catedral are worth a quick visit. However, the town better serves as a base for other activities in Lago Rapel, El Teniente, the Chapa Verde Ski Resort, Reserva Nacional Rio los Cipreses and the hot springs at Termas de Cauquenes. Updated: Jun 29, 2009.

Museo Regional de Rancagua

(ADMISSION: $1) The Museo Regional de Rancagua occupies a beautiful, single-story 18th-century colonial house. Inside, several rooms show off a décor synonymous with urban colonial style. Also on display are documents from the independence movement. Estado 685. Tel/fax: 56-72-221524 URL: www.museorancagua. cl Tuesday – Friday 10 a.m. – 6 p.m., Saturday – Sunday 9 a.m. – 1 p.m. Updated: Apr 15, 2009.

Iglesia Catedral

The highlight of the Plaza de los Heroés is the imposing, canary-yellow Iglesia Catedral. The church, which was originally built in 1775, received its Doric columns and double tower when it was rebuilt in 1861 after sustaining considerable damage during a battle between patriot soldiers and Royalist forces. Updated: Jan 29, 2009.

Plaza de los Héroes

Named in honor of the town's patriot soldiers led by Bernardo O'Higgins, the Plaza de los Héroes is the center of Rancagua. Cafes offering ice cream line the east side of the square. Browse for handicrafts, jewelry, used books and hand-knit sweaters at the small market adjacent to Iglesia Catedral or find a bench to people-watch in the shade. Updated: Apr 15, 2009.

The Rancagua Rodeo

Chilean rodeo's practice is largely concentrated in the rural central valley, but come late March, Rancagua draws crowds from all over to its national rodeo championship. Declared Chile's national sport in 1962, rodeo is believed to have begun in the 16th century. At that time, loss of livestock was frequent, so Governor García Hurtado de Mendoza decreed that cattle be brought to the Plaza de las Armas in Santiago annually in order for the animals to be branded and organized. Dates of the event changed, but the practice remained, and, over the years, cowboys (*huasos*) became expert at driving cattle.

In the 17th century, the sport became more regulated and took place on a rectangular track. Riders had to separate a calf from a herd and guide it unassisted. Awards went to the most skilled. In the late 1800s, the crescent track, or *medialuna*, was adopted and continues to be used today. Now the goal is for a team of two cowboys on horseback to pin the calf against the cushioned corral wall in three different spots, known as *quinchas*. The padding softens the blow the calf receives from being slammed into the wall, and each calf participates in a rodeo only once in its lifetime. Regulations are strict-- only Chilean horses are used and cowboys must wear traditional ponchos and wide, flat-brimmed hats (*chupallas*).

Rancagua has hosted the Campeonato Naciónal de Rodeo since the mid-20th century. The three-day event caps a six-month series of eliminatorial regional tournaments, and has all the trappings of a country fair: meat, drink, tack, traditional song and dance. The rodeo is held in La Medialuna, which holds 12,000 spectators. Teams (*colleras*) dig in their spurs and go all out in hopes of earning the maximum 13 points. The site www.caballoyrodeo.cl has information in Spanish on all things Chilean rodeo. Updated: Jul 03, 2009.

Lodging

Rancagua has several hotels withing walking distance of the bus and train stations. Most hotels are within walking distance of the Plaza de los Héroes. Updated: Jun 29, 2009.

Hotel España

(ROOMS: $24 – 45) The cleanliness, 24-hour hot water and hospitable staff have made Hotel España a leader among backpackers in Rancagua, so it fills up fast. The rooms are set around an interior patio in this antique, colonial-style building. San Martín 367. Tel: 56-72-230141, E-mail: noraberriosf@latinmail.com. Updated: Jan 19, 2009.

Hotel Aguila Real

(ROOMS: $40 – 92) The Aguila Real serves as a mid-range option for those interested in more than a comfortable bed. The hotel boasts 50 rooms, each with a private bathroom, cable TV, telephone and Internet access. There is also a pool, table tennis area and a conference room. Av. Brasil 1045. Tel: 56-72-223002, E-mail: hotelaguilareal@terra.cl. Updated: Jul 06, 2009.

Restaurants

Rancagua restaurants are full of typical Chilean foods, such as roast chicken, while Paseo Independencia is stocked with numerous fuentes de soda, like Reina Victoria (Independencia 667) that serves set lunches and ice cream. Updated: Jun 29, 2009.

Snack Paris

(SNACKS: $2, ENTREES: $3.50 – 5.50) Grab some shade at one of Snack Paris' umbrella-covered tables and people watch as locals stroll and bike through Plaza de los Héroes. You can enjoy an ice cream or fresh juice for $2, or order a burger off the grill, accompanied with French fries. 301 Plaza de los Héroes. Updated: Apr 21, 2009.

La Carpa

(ENTREES: $3.50 – 36.50) At La Carpa groups can score traditional Chilean dishes for up to four people. Order up the Especial 3-4 Personas to be served a healthy mix of *vacuno*, *chuletas*, *pollo*, *costillar* and *papas cocidas* for approximately $30. Monday – Saturday 12 p.m. – 10 p.m., closed Sunday. 801 José Berardo Cuevas. Updated: Apr 17, 2009.

La Pica de Sancho

This small but friendly cafe is an ideal place to grab an early-morning breakfast or late-afternoon lunch. Locals scurry in and out in the morning, while regular bar flys nurse their beers throughout the afternoon. There is no official menu, but the restaurant rotates traditional chicken, pork and beef dishes served along with salad, bread and a side of rice. Monday – Saturday 9 a.m. – 5 p.m. Estado 135. Updated: Jun 27, 2009.

AROUND RANCAGUA
CHAPA VERDE

Once a private resort, Chapa Verde Ski Resort is now a place where you can hit the slopes (and it's only 58 km / 36 mi east of Rancagua). It was originally built for employees by Codelco, the government-owned copper corporation that runs nearby mines called El Teniente, but is now open to the public July to September. There are more than seven square kilometers of terrain with 22 trails that range in difficulty from beginner to advanced. There are no hotels, but it is possible to check with the ski area administration for information on private home rentals.

Chapa Verde can be accessed by private car, though it is necessary to call the ski club for a permit, or by way of **Bus El Teniente,** located at Av. Miguel Ramírez 665, Rancagua (departures July through September weekdays at 9 a.m., weekends at 8 a.m. and 9:30 a.m., return daily at 4:30 p.m.). Ski equipment is available for rent for $26 or full snowboard gear for $28. Lift tickets ($30 adult or $15.50 children) are sold at Chapa Verde's central office at Av. Miguel Ramírez 665. Tel: 56-72-217651 E-mail: info@chapaverde.cl; URL: www.chapaverde.cl. Updated: Apr 15, 2009.

TERMAS DE CAUQUENES

Perched high above the Río Cachapoal and surrounded by the Andean foothills, Termas de Cauquenes is arguably the most beautiful hot springs resort in Chile. The water comes out in antique marble tubs and hits temperatures between 42 – 47°C (107 – 118°F) degrees. It contains magnesium, potassium and lithium, as well as other minerals. It is not necessary to stay overnight at the hotel to enjoy the body-healing baths. Take a dip on a half-hour pass for $6.50 in the marble tubs or use the outdoor pool for $5.50. Buses run from Rancaugua's Mercado Municipal daily at 8:30 a.m. and 2 p.m., and return to Rancagua at 11 a.m. and 5 p.m. Tel: 56-72-899010, URL: www.termasdecauquenes.cl. Updated: Apr 15, 2009.

SEWELL

Dubbed "the city of stairways," Sewell lies 55 kilometers northeast of Rancagua (85 km south of Santiago) at an altitude of 2,600 meters. It was home to numerous families from the El Teniente copper mines between 1905 and 1975. The town's unique architecture was built to handle the high-altitude climate and the copper mining families. URL: www.sewell.cl. Updated: Apr 15, 2009.

Reserva Nacional Río de los Cipreses

(ADMISSION: $3) Roughly 15 kilometers down the road from the Termas de Cauquenes are 36 square kilometers of protected land called the Reserva Nacional Río Los Cipreses. Take three or four days to thoroughly enjoy some multi-day hiking, horseback riding or to catch a glimpse of a condor, fox or burrowing parrot. The reserva also features the canyon of the Río de los Cipreses, with altitudes ranging from 900 to 4,900 meters. Camping there costs $8. Monday – Sunday, 8:30 a.m. – 6 p.m. Updated: Feb 11, 2009.

SAN FERNANDO

San Fernando, 339 meters above sea level, has been the capital of the province of Colchagua since 1840. The area produces large amounts of fruit—the cherries are especially delicious. It is also boasts good wine and a plethora of traditional vineyards.

Buses run from the terminal at the corner of Avenida Manso de Velasco and Rancagua. Once in San Fernando, find **Hotel Marcano** (Manuel Rodriguez 968. Tel: 56-72-714759) or for a more basic room with a TV and phone try nearby **Hotel España** (Manuel Rodriguez 959. Tel: 56-72-711098). Nearby **Hotel Casa Silva** (Hijuela Norte. Tel: 56-72-913091, Fax: 56-72-717491, URL: www.casasilva.cl) caters to a more exclusive crowd—evidenced by the polo pitch on its grounds. After checking in, walk a few blocks to Manuel Rodriguez 815 to grab a sandwich or drink at **Cafe Roma** or a fill up on a *pollo asado* at **Club Social** (Manuel Rodriguez 787).

A long, leisurely walk along the narrow streets is one of the highlights of this town set in the hilly Central Valley. Manuel Rodriguez is filled with shops and snack bars. The Neo-Gothic **Iglesia de San Francisco** also shows off its 32-meter-high tower. San Fernando has a second Gothic church called the **Capilla San Juan de Dios** on the corner of Negrete and Avenida Manso de Velasco. Visit the Museo Casa Patronal de Lircunlauta at the corner of Jimenez and Avenida Manso de Velasco to see an art or photo exhibition ($0.40, Tuesday – Friday 9 a.m. – 1 p.m., 3 p.m. – 7 p.m., Saturday – Sunday 10 a.m. – 1 p.m., 4 p.m. –6 p.m.).

If you need a bit more excitement, arrange a trip to the rapids with **Mundo Aventura Rafting** (Manuel Rodriguez 430. Tel: 56-72-721733). Another highlight is the popular **Termas del Flaco**, though the thermal baths are actually 107 kilometers east of San Fernando. Updated: Mar 09, 2009.

Hacienda Los Lingues

This estate, 18 kilometers (11 mi) from San Fernando, was originally given as a gift to the first mayor of Santiago in 1599, and the same family has retained the rights to it over the years. The family's European tastes are reflected throughout the hacienda, especially in the English Room and the French Room. Los Linques is decorated with family pictures and religious iconography - a break from traditional hotels. The property also features beautiful gardens, elegant wines and stables. Due to the hacienda's high rates, visitors generally opt for a day tour of the grounds ($80/person), though sometimes promotions are offered on the website. The tour generally includes a welcome cocktail, lunch and a horse show. E-mail: informaciones@loslingues.com, URL: www.loslingues.cl. Updated: Apr 22, 2009.

SANTA CRUZ

 165m   33,900   72

Situated in the middle of wine-making country, Santa Cruz owes much of its success and popularity among tourists to former arms dealer Carlos Cardoen. He owns the magnificent, swanky Hotel Santa Cruz Plaza, which overlooks the Plaza de Armas. Cardoen has also donated countless items to the Museo de Colchagua, the largest private museum in Chile, which showcases artifacts from different cultures around the world.

The vineyards of Viu Manent are another popular draw for visitors, though they are located slightly north of Santa Cruz on the Carretera del Vino. There is an on-site restaurant, however it is more cost-effective to head back to Santa Cruz and select one of the many restaurants along the Plaza de Armas. The Vendimia Hotel is a nearby alternative to the high-priced Hotel Santa Cruz Plaza. Updated: Apr 23, 2009.

When to Go

The summer months, January and February in particular, are the best time to visit Santa Cruz and venture into its surrounding vineyards. Wine connoisseurs should show up in early March for the Fiesta de Vendimia (Grape Harvest Festival), which is held on Plaza de Armas. Updated: Apr 23, 2009.

Getting To and Away From Santa Cruz

The bus terminal is at Rafael Casanova 478, roughly four blocks from the Plaza de Armas. **Buses Nilahue** and a variety of others run to and from the terminal every half hour. There is easy access to San Fernando, Rancagua, Pichilemu, Lolol, El Huique and Santiago. Expect to pay about $7 for a bus to the capital. Updated: Feb 28, 2009.

Getting Around

Strolling on foot is the preferred mode of transportation in Santa Cruz since it is a relatively small place. Still, taxis are available. Updated: Feb 28, 2009.

Safety

Santa Cruz is a safe place, with locals and tourists alike routinely walking around and enjoying late evenings along the main plaza. Updated: Apr 23, 2009.

Services

Calle Rafael Casanova runs from the bus terminal (Rafael Casanova 478) east four blocks to a helpful **Sernatur** kiosk located in a mini bell-tower. Its friendly staff is quick to give out useful town information. There are several pharmacies and banks with ATMs located along the streets that surround Plaza de Armas. Updated: Jul 02, 2009.

Things to See and Do

Museo de Colchagua

(ADMISSION: $5) It is easy to spend hours here, in Chile's largest private museum. It has artifacts from a variety of different cultures from around the world. The Pavilion of Arms is of particular interest and possibly one of the most important weapon collections in the country. It showcases pre-Columbian, African and European weapons that date from the Middle Ages until World War II.

There is also a collection of firearms, swords and symbols of the German Third Reich. Open 10 a.m. – 7 p.m. (summer), 6 p.m.

(winter), closed Mondays. Av. Errázuriz 145. Tel: 56-72-821050, E-mail: museocol@entelchile.net, URL: www.museocolchagua.cl. Updated: Apr 23, 2009.

Viu Manent Vineyards

(PRICE: $20) Don't miss the beautiful vineyards surrounding Santa Cruz. The vineyards at Viu Manent are slightly north of the town itself on the Carretera del Vino. Tour the grounds, then sample some wine and grab lunch at the on-site restaurant. Its cuisine features a menu inspired by Don Miguel Viu García's Spanish recipe book. The food bears Catalan and French influences and each recipe revives ingredients of the Viu family gastronomic legacy. Tel: 56-72-823179, URL: www.viumanent.cl. Updated: Apr 23, 2009.

Lodging

Vendimia Hotel

(ROOMS: $115) The Vendinia Hotel is perfect for those who want to be close to the action but not entirely in it. Four blocks from the center of town and three from the Museo de Colchagua, this quiet hotel is clean and well-kept with private bathrooms, WiFi access, cable TV, library and a swimming pool. Ismael Valdez 92. Tel: 56-72-822464, E-mail: reservas@hotelvendimia.com, URL: www.hotelvendimia.com. Updated: Apr 23, 2009.

Hotel Santa Cruz Plaza

(ROOMS: $246 – 665) This colonial-style hotel features 113 rooms, including 14 suites as well as a presidential suite, overlooking the Plaza de Armas and the hotel's interior park. Chances are, if you have to ask how much a room costs, you can't afford it. All rooms have cable TV, WiFi, mini-bar, magnetic door locks and air conditioning. Advance bookings are recommended. Plaza de Armas 286. Tel: 56-72-822529, E-mail: reservas@hacp.cl, URL: www.hotelsantacruzplaza.cl. Updated: Apr 23, 2009.

Restaurants

Club Social

(ENTREES: $11 – 20) Conveniently situated on the northern end of the plaza, Club Social is a great place to grab lunch after visiting the Museo de Colchagua. Club Social combines traditional Chilean meals with friendly, quality service. The wait staff goes out of its way to make customers feel comfortable. Try the fried *pejerreyes* and salad. Plaza de Armas 178. Updated: Apr 23, 2009.

MIDDLE CHILE

Licanrray

Licanrray is one of numerous restaurants along the western side of the Plaza de Armas. It serves basic but familiar and delicious Chilean dishes such as lomo de pobre. It is an economical choice if you want to fill up for a few dollars. Plaza de Armas 130-A. Updated: Apr 23, 2009.

PICHILEMU

 36m   12,300   72

Agustín Ross Edwards envisioned a European-style resort town when he developed architectural projects in Pichilemu in the second half of the 19th century. However, the modern version has strayed far from Edwards' ideal. Pichilemu is overrun with surfers seeking the perfect wave and beach bums lounging for hours on the soft, charcoal-colored sand while soaking up the sun.

Chile's first casino was on Avenida Agustín Ross in a storied, 19th-century building—though now it is no longer in use and is in a sad state of disrepair. The run-down building clashes with the town's now bustling streets full of empanada restaurants, budget-priced hostels, and throngs of backpackers. Next to the now-abandoned casino is the well-tended Parque Ross lined with Phoenix palms on the hill overlooking the beach.

Pichilemu is filled with areas to set up camp for those with a tent. There are also cabañas on every corner and locals often hawk rooms to travelers fresh off the bus at the terminal.

There are more than enough food options in Pichilemu. Anibal Pinto is lined with cheap options such as pizza and empanada restaurants—do yourself a favor and sample at least one offering from La Casa de las Empanadas (260-B Anibal Pinto). Updated: Apr 29, 2009.

When to Go

Chileans and tourists alike populate Pichilemu during the summer months; January and February are the most popular months. Expect to pay higher rates at hostels during the high season. Pichilemu weather is warm during the day and can be a bit cool after the sun sets. The town also

has a decent nightlife. The bars on Anibal Pinto can be lively and there are frequent impromptu beach parties during the high season. Updated: Apr 29, 2009.

Getting To and Away From Pichilemu

The bus terminal is inconveniently located on the outskirts of town on Calle Millaco, between Calle Comercio and J. Errazuriz. Simply walk toward the ocean and you'll be in town within five minutes. **Pullman del Sur**, **Buses Nilahue** and a few other companies offer routine service from Pichilemu with buses leaving as often as every 10 minutes during high season. Expect to pay $9 to get back to Santiago. Buses also run to Rancagua, San Fernando, Santa Cruz, Talca, Curíco and Chillán. Updated: Apr 29, 2009.

Getting Around

Walking is the most common form of transportation in Pichilemu since it is a fairly small town. However, taxis are easy to track down, as are horse-pulled carriages that operate as taxis. Pichilemu has no local bus service. Updated: Apr 29, 2009.

Safety

Pichilemu is a relatively safe and laid-back town. People routinely stroll along the beach and streets in the early morning without problems—still, it is wise to be vigilant. Updated: Apr 29, 2009.

Services

TOURISM

You can pick up a town map at the **Municipalidad de Pichilemu** near the bus terminal at Angel Gaete 365.

MONEY

Banco Estado on the corner of Federico Errazuriz and J.J. Prieto (Av. Agustin Ross also converges here) has a currency exchange, 24-hour ATM and cashes traveler's checks.

KEEPING IN TOUCH

Make international calls or surf the web at **Surf Net Plus** at 105 Anibal Pinto.

MEDICAL

There is a medical emergency center on the corner of Valderrama and J. Errazuriz, close to Parque Ross. For over-the-counter assistance, visit **Postoverde** on 246-A Anibal Pinto. Updated: Apr 29, 2009.

Things to See and Do

K-Nopy

(PRICE: $5) This zip line over the beach will take you soaring 350 meters over the heads of fellow beach bums. If you're not in the mood to zip, put down a towel on the beach to watch other brave souls glide overhead while you work on a tan. Main beach along Ca. Costanera. Updated: Apr 29, 2009.

Lobos del Pacifico Escuela de Surf

Those hippies in old surfing movies were telling the truth. Surfing can be more than a sport—it can be a spiritual experience. And there is no better place than Pichilemu to put that theory to the test. Head toward Lobos del Pacifico Escuela de Surf to rent a board, a wetsuit and purchase a lesson from a surfing veteran. A two-hour lesson complete with gear and board costs $20. Or if you are already a pro, rent the board and wetsuit for the entire day for $13. Av. Costanera 720. Tel: 56-9-5062127, E-mail: lobosdelpacifico@hotmail.com, URL: www.lobosdelpacifico.cl. Updated: Apr 29, 2009.

Lodging

Surf Hostal

(ROOMS: $16 – 66) Dutchman Marcel Janssen opened this pleasant hostel across the street from Playa Infiernillo, away from the noise and crowds and a 10-minute walk to popular restaurants on Anibal Pinto. Each room is equipped with feathered pillows, a private bathroom with 24-hour hot water and shower heads with fantastic water pressure - a rarity in South America. There is WiFi for those with laptops. Guests are also welcome to use the Internet in Janssen's across-the-street restaurant El Puente Holandes, where hostel patrons also are served a complimentary breakfast. 164 Eugenio Diaz Lira. Tel: 56-72-842350, E-mail: marceljanssen75@hotmail.com, URL: www.surfhostal.com. Updated: Jul 07, 2009.

Hotel Chile España

(ROOMS: $25 – 33) Hotel Chile España is a popular spot among backpackers due in large part to its close proximity to the vast number of restaurants and bars that clutter nearby Anibal Pinto. The hostel is also a two-minute walk downhill to the beach. Rooms are simple but clean with private bathrooms, and the hostel has a computer with Internet access. 255 Ortúzar. Tel: 56-72-841314, E-mail: hotelchilespana@terra.cl. Updated: Apr 30, 2009.

Restaurants

100% Pizza

(SLICE: $1, PIZZA: $10) Despite the name 100% Percent Pizza, this restaurant also has empanadas for $1.50. But pizza is its specialty. Grab a slice of cheese pizza, add toppings for a bit more, or order an entire pizza for just $10. 277 Anibal Pinto. Updated: Apr 29, 2009.

La Casa de las Empanadas

(EMPANADAS: $1.80 – $2.75) This is where Pichilemu locals beeline for cheap, savory meals. The restaurant is so popular in town that several other empanada shops are relatively empty while diners pack La Casa de las Empanadas. Customers receive numbered tickets and wait for an empanada stuffed with their choice of cheese, chicken, mushrooms or an array of other options. 260-B Anibal Pinto. Updated: Apr 29, 2009.

Puente Holandes

(ENTREES: $2.75 - 15) Dutchman Marcel Janssen, who also owns the well-kept Surf Hostal directly across the street, built this intimate restaurant. The patio overlooks the ocean, allowing patrons to eat only a few steps from Playa Infiernillo. The view is tough to beat and service is friendly. The food, however, is unremarkable. The plate of *ravioli loco*, eight medium-sized pieces of ravioli covered with a spinach sauce, is served with bread. A cheese empanada can be had for under three bucks, the salmon for $8. Guests of the Surf Hostal receive a 10 percent discount on meals and drinks. 167 Eugenio Diaz Lira. Tel: 56-72-842350, E-mail: marceljanssen75@hotmail.com, URL: www.surfhostal.com. Updated: Jul 01, 2009.

CURICÓ

218m	123,800	75

The Plaza de Armas is the pride of Curicó—without a doubt one of loveliest central plazas in Chile. The town is also close to several decent wineries, and it is a short bus ride to Radal Siete Tazas and Lago Vichuquén.

Curicó has its fair share of reasonably priced accommodation with a variety of residencias around town, as well as more upscale options. Quaint restaurants, ice cream shops and cafes are scattered about Curicó, so simply take your pick. Updated: Jul 07, 2009.

When to Go

Curicó is a beautiful town that is best visited in the summer season, when it is much more pleasant to see the waterfalls of Reserva Nacional Radal Siete Tazas and the wildlife at Lago Vichuquén. Plus, it's always nicer to meander through the town on a warm afternoon. Updated: Feb 10, 2009.

Getting To and Away From Curicó

The bus terminal is located on the corner of Avenida Camilo and Carmen and is three blocks north of the Plaza de Armas. **Buses Hernández** head to Radal Siete National Park during the high season. **Buses Díaz** take passengers daily on the two-hour ride to Lago Vichuquén at 3:20 p.m. There are several other companies running routes to Pichilemu, San Fernando and Temuco. Pullman can take you back to Santiago.

Trains pull into the station four blocks west of the plaza at Calle Prat. Eight trains run daily north to Santiago and Rancagua, while there is service south to Talca and Chillán. Updated: Feb 10, 2009.

Getting Around

Curicó is a small town and most things can easily be reached with a short walk. The Plaza de Armas is five blocks from the train, and bus stations are less than 10 minutes away on foot. There are enough taxis available for those who decide to wander further. Updated: Feb 26, 2009.

Safety

Curicó, like many towns in Middle Chile, is a relatively safe place. Locals and tourists enjoying a slower pace of life, especially around the Plaza de Armas. Updated: Feb 10, 2009.

Services

It's difficult to miss the pharmacy **Cruz Verde** upon arrival to town, which is located at the bus terminal, along with several ATMs. The hospital is at Chacabuco 121 (Tel: 56-75-206206). The post office is opposite the Plaza de Armas at Carmen 556 and is right next to the Municipalidad. Two minutes down the road is **Multiservices Condell** at Carmen 491, which offers Internet access, fax and photocopies. And there is a **Forex** at Carmen 497 to exchange cash and travelers' checks. On the corner of Yungay and Estado, opposite the Plaza de Armas, is a **Banco de Chile**. Updated: Feb 26, 2009.

Things to See and Do

Curicó is not full of activities, but what attractions it does have are worth seeing. The area also counts natural beauties like Cerro Carlos Condel and the waterfalls of Radal Siete Tazas. Updated: Feb 26, 2009.

Cerro Carlos Condell

This 100-meter high hill on the eastern side of town offers decent views. There is also a picnic area. And while here, do not forget to check out the interesting statue of the Virgen la Concepción. Updated: Jul 03, 2009.

Plaza de Armas

The Plaza de Armas is a must-see as it is one of the best central plazas in the country with its towering Canary Island palm trees planted throughout the square. Residents of the "Big Easy" will feel at home with on the northern side of the plaza where there is a green, wrought-iron bandstand configured in typical New Orleans style. There is also a neat fountain dispersing water into a small pond. Updated: Jul 03, 2009.

Lodging

Due to the fruit and wine trade, many people go into town on business, so the lodging scene tends to cater to those more willing and able to pay for creature comforts. Still, Curicó has a little bit of everything: unembellished guesthouses that fill up quickly, run-of-the-mill hostels that consider room cleaning to be more than just a flip of the mattress, and the recently renovated upscale spots. Ramshackle hotels tend to be surprisingly quiet, clean and charming on the inside, so check out a couple before you decide. Updated: Jul 02, 2009.

Residencial Rahue

(ROOMS: $10) Residencial Rahue is a solid option for cash-strapped backpackers. This place has comfortable, brightly painted rooms which are well-kept and relatively quiet. There are shared and private bathrooms. Peña 410. Tel: 56-75-312378. Updated: Apr 15, 2009.

Residencial Maipu

(ROOMS: $11) Being close to the bus terminal, Residencial Maipu is an ideal spot for those who only want to walk a short distance to catch an early ride out of town or a close place to check out after a late arrival. The hotel is nothing spectacular but it is a cheap place to rest for the night. Maipu 570. Updated: Apr 15, 2009.

Hotel Turismo

(ROOMS: $60 – 90) Hotel Turismo is a favorite of businessmen and other visitors with a comfortable budget. The hotel was recently renovated and has a lounge area with a fireplace, on-site restaurant, laundry service and and Internet room. The rooms are spacious, with private bathrooms, air conditioning, electronic safes, and cable TVs. Carmen 727. Tel: 56-75-543440, E-mail: recepcion@hotelturismocurico.cl, URL: www.hotelturismocurico.cl. Updated: Apr 15, 2009.

Restaurants

There is an abundance of restaurants, ice cream shops and cafes scattered about Curicó, so simply take your pick. Updated: Feb 10, 2009.

La Guindaleera

(ENTREES: $3) This unassuming restaurant does nothing to distinguish itself on the outside—in fact there's a decent chance you will stroll past it on the way to the Plaza de Armas. But that would be a mistake. La Guindaleera serves up some tasty dishes at very reasonable prices. Try the pollo asado, a large portion of tender, juicy chicken served with French fries and a side of *ají*. Prat 599-B. Updated: Mar 30, 2009.

Terruño Express

(SET LUNCH: $5.50) This hotspot gives its customers the opportunity to chow down and, for those with a laptop, plug in to the world of WiFi. Chow down on a set lunch of meat or chicken, rice and vegetables while surfing the Internet. Yungay 615. Updated: Feb 10, 2009.

Al Cafe

(ENTREE: $8.50 – 12.50) Al Cafe is a bit costlier than its competitors but its *almuerzos* are top notch. Receive a starter, well-prepared entrée and dessert, as well as a coffee or water. Set dinners are a bit more extravagant and come with a glass of wine. The fish and seafood are particularly good, as are the ham rolls. The restaurant has indoor and outdoor tables, and is actually an extension of Hotel Turismo. Carmen 727. Tel: 56-75-310552, Monday – Sunday 8 a.m. – 10 p.m. Updated: Apr 15, 2009.

AROUND CURICÓ

The land around Curicó is much more interesting than the city itself. Lakes and parks dot the area and there are plenty of trails for horseback riding, hiking and enjoying the wildlife. Updated: Jul 07, 2009.

Radal Siete Tazas

(ADMISSION: $5) Siete Tazas (literally "Seven Teacups") is a magnificent sight. The blue water of the Río Claro cascades down black basalt rock into a sequence of pools. These can be reached after a five-minute walk on a marked trail. The trail eventually leads to nearby Salto de la Leona, a waterfall that plunges 55 meters down a gorge into the Río Claro. Follow the trail to the river itself where people nap and sunbathe on large rocks or jump into the water to cool off.

Siete Tazas can be reached from Curicó on Buses Hernández (next to the train station) and across from the bus station. For approximately $1, buses that leave every 10 minutes take passengers to its terminal in Molina, where it is necessary to purchase another ticket ($2) for a different bus to finish the bumpy, two-hour ride down a gravel road to the waterfalls. Updated: Apr 15, 2009.

Lago Vichuquén

Hordes of water sports enthusiasts flock to Lago Vichuquén to splash around its blue waters surrounded by deep-green pine trees. Just four kilometers after the village of Vichuquén, the lake is only a short distance from the Pacific. It tends to attract an upper-class crowd—it is common for Santiago's elite to own a lakeshore villa with its own little private beach.

Find high-end accommodation at **Hotel Marina Vichuquén** (Tel: 56-75-400265), which offers guests and non-guests mountain bikes, horseback riding and its water sports facilities. Check the hotel's website for updated room rates (www.marinavichuquen.cl). There are also various camping options, such as **Camping Vichuquén** beyond Aquelarre. Updated: Mar 09, 2009.

Wine Tours

The Maule Region is the main producer of wine in the country, thanks to its optimum conditions of soil and climate. **La Ruta del Vino Valles de Curicó** (office inside Hotel Turismo on Carmen 727, URL: www.rvvc.cl) represents a union of 16 vineyards, promotes the traditions of the valley and organizes guided tours. Altacima, Las Pitras, Correa Albano, Casa Donoso, Miguel Torres and Valdivieso are some of the vineyards that visitors get to see along the route. Updated: Mar 01, 2009.

MIDDLE CHILE

TALCA

 102m   209,323   71

Talca claims a central role in the Chilean independence movement. National hero Bernardo O'Higgins lived here as a child and the nation's declaration of independence was signed here in 1818. Artifacts and documents from the movement can be viewed at Museo O'Higginiano y Bellas Artes de Talca. Also, the town sits in the heart of wine country and is adept at handling the influx of tourists in search of the perfect glass. Other highlights of the town include the Mercado Central and the Reserva Nacional Altos de Lircay, which is one hour away by bus. Updated: Apr 17, 2009.

When to Go

During Talca's four-month dry season (November to March), temperatures hit the mid- to high 20°C (80°F) and most grape picking takes place in the countless vineyards in the Valle del Maule; wine tours are possible year-round. Outside of summer, milder, more temperate weather prevails. The nightlife rocks a little harder from March through December, when classes at the city's numerous universities are in full swing. Trekking the neighboring Altos de Lircay is best done outside of winter. Updated: Jul 02, 2009.

Getting To and Away From Talca

The **bus terminal** (Tel: 56-71-243270) is at 12 Oriente and 2 Sur, the **train terminal** one block further east at 11 Oriente 1150. Trains run to and from Santiago, Curicó and Constitucíon. The daily train to and from Constitucíon is not recommended since it takes around two hours longer than the bus, and it is basically a rickety school bus on railroad tracks, and occasionally there are fallen trees on the tracks. There are a cluster of buses at the terminal, including **Pullman del Sur**, which offer service to Santiago, Curicó, Temuco and Constitucíon among other places. Updated: Apr 17, 2009.

Getting Around

Talca has a glut of taxis and buses. At the bus or train stations, you will find cabbies waiting to offer a ride, in case 10 blocks to the Plaza de Armas seems too far to walk. Updated: Apr 17, 2009.

Safety

There are few dangers in Talca besides the occasional pickpocket. Practice good common sense. Updated: Feb 17, 2009.

Services

TOURISM

Head to the **Sernatur** (Tel: 71-226-940) at 1 Poniente 1281 to pick up a map of Talca and gather other pertinent information.

MONEY

Banco Santander is at 1 Sur and 4 Oriente. Exchange cash at **AFEX**, **Moneygram** at 1 Sur 898. Updated: Feb 20, 2009.

MEDICAL

The **hospital** is several blocks north of the bus and train terminals on 1 Norte. Pharmacies can be found at multiple destinations along 1 Sur. **Farmacias Ahumada** has one store at 1 Sur 1501 and another at 1 Sur 1191.

SHOPPING

Galeria Maule, a shopping center, on 1 Sur between 7 Oriente and 6 Oriente has ATMs and a **Power Net** store with Internet access.

Things to See and Do

Talca has a typical Plaza de Armas; a neo-Gothic Cathedral stands on its northwest corner. Don't mioss the Mercado Central. It has almost any handicraft, fruit or vegetable you might need, and its interior is lined with quaint cafes and restaurants. **Museo O'Higginiano** showcases the Chilean independence movement, while **Museo Bomberil Benito Riquelme** (2 Sur 1160, admission: free) is a firefighter museum. Updated: Apr 17, 2009.

Museo O'Higginiano y Bellas Artes

(ADMISSION: $0.50 children, $1 adults) The museum is a very important feature of both Talca and Chile. It is where liberator Bernardo O'Higgins lived as a child and eventually signed the declaration of Chilean independence in 1818. The building is now home to historical documents, sculptures, coins, photographs and 19th-century furniture. Open Saturday – Sunday 11 a.m. – 2 p.m., Tuesday – Friday, 9 a.m. – 1 p.m. and 2 p.m. – 6 p.m. 1 Norte 875, E-mail: museodetalca@gmail.com, URL: www.museodetalca.cl. Updated: Apr 17, 2009.

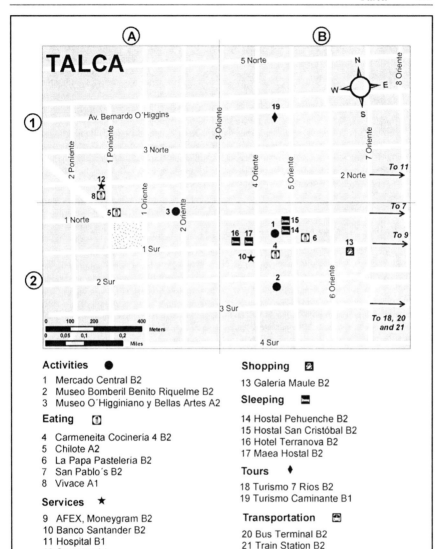

Activities ●
1 Mercado Central B2
2 Museo Bomberil Benito Riquelme B2
3 Museo O´Higginiano y Bellas Artes A2

Eating 🍴
4 Carmeneita Cocineria 4 B2
5 Chilote A2
6 La Papa Pasteleria B2
7 San Pablo´s B2
8 Vivace A1

Services ★
9 AFEX, Moneygram B2
10 Banco Santander B2
11 Hospital B1
12 Sernatur A1

Shopping
13 Galeria Maule B2

Sleeping
14 Hostal Pehuenche B2
15 Hostal San Cristóbal B2
16 Hotel Terranova B2
17 Maea Hostal B2

Tours ◆
18 Turismo 7 Ríos B2
19 Turismo Caminante B1

Transportation
20 Bus Terminal B2
21 Train Station B2

Mercado Central
Talca boasts one of the best markets in Middle Chile. On the Mercado Central (1 Sur between 5 Oriente and 4 Oriente), locals hawk a wide assortment of knick-knacks, handicrafts, fruit, veggies, meat, second-hand books and clothes. The interior of the market is lined with various cafés. Some have outdoor tables where you can sip coffee or tea and people-watch. Updated: Apr 17, 2009.

Wineries
Wine connoisseurs will be delighted: 15 wineries are open to the public near Talca. Winery and vineyard tours form the Ruta del Vino del Maule—additional information is available at the Sernatur in Talca. Since most are not open to walk-in visitors, it is necessary to make prior arrangements. Contact the Ruta del Vino del Maule at Villa Cultural Huiquilemu (Tel: 56-73-246460, URL: www.valledelmaule.cl).

Viña Balduzzi in San Javier is a place you should visit. Tours ($5) of its bodegas take guests through the wine-making process and include tastings. And, not surprisingly, there is the chance to purchase wines - a nice option since most are produced for export. With its 200 acres of vineyards and charming grounds, which feature a chapel and park full of trees such as the American oak, European oak, Imalaya's cedro, Libano's cedro and araucaria, Viña Balduzzi is the romantic's image of a Central Valley winery. Av. Balmaceda 1189, San Javier, Monday - Saturday 9 a.m.-6 p.m. Tel: 56-73-322138, URL: www.balduzzi.cl.

Viñas Calina is closer to Talca and is in business with California-based Kendall-Jackson. The wine is top-shelf and produced with state-of-the-art technology. Tours cost $7. Fundo El Maitén, Camino Las Rastras. Tel: 56-71-263126, www.calina.com.

Casa Donoso's focus is fine cabernet sauvignon, merlot and chardonnay, and since the place has been upgraded, it boasts a restaurant and guesthouse. This is the closest winery to the center of Talca. Tours, which include wine tasting ($5), are available from 10 a.m. to 6 p.m. Monday to Saturday. Reservations are necessary for Casa Donoso's restaurant which has good food and, as one would assume, a nice selection of wine. Tel: 56-71-242506, URL: www.casadonoso.com. Updated: Apr 21, 2009.

Villa Cultural Huilquilemu

(ADMISSION: $1) The Villa Cultural Huilquilemu is a magnificently restored house now open to the public under the guise of a museum. Originally built in 1850, the house has long corridors, wooden ceilings and beautiful gardens with sequoia, araucarias and oak trees. The Universidad Católica del Maule, which administers the villa, has added religious and folk art, statues and a library in honor of regional writers such as Neruda and Pablo de Rokha. There is also a restaurant. Huilquilemu is 10 kilometers east of Talca. To get there, take any micro going toward San Clemente. Buses leave from the terminal every 15 minutes ($1, 15 min). Open Tuesday – Friday, 9 a.m. – 1 p.m. and 3 p.m. – 6:30 p.m., Saturday 12-6 p.m. E-mail: huilquilemu@huala.ucm.cl. Updated: Apr 21, 2009.

Tours

Turismo Caminante is a fantastic source of information on trails, trekking, kayaking and horse rides. It has information not only on the area surrounding Talca, but on the whole of Chile. Casilla 143. Tel: 56-71-1970097, URL: www.trekkingchile.com, E-mail: turismocaminante@hotmail.com.

Kayakers should head to **Turismo 7 Ríos** to get equipment and information on the Maule, Corel and Lircay rivers which have rapids from class III to V. 1 Norte. Tel: 56-71-210611. Updated: Feb 20, 2009.

Lodging

There are a range of accommodation options along 1 Sur and 1 Norte in Talca.

Hostal Pehuenche

(ROOMS: $14 – 27) This hostel is one of the more affordable places for those on a budget. Service is friendly and the staff speaks some English. The owner offers well-kept single rooms with a shared bathroom or with a private bathroom. Rooms have air conditioning and cable TV. 5 Oriente 1184 apartment. 6. Tel: 56-71-217749, E-mail: hostalpehuenche@tie.cl. Updated: Apr 17, 2009.

Maea Hostal

(ROOMS: $17 – 48) This hostel is another good budget option. The service is friendly and the rooms are clean. Rooms have cable TV, WiFi, and all prices include breakfast. 1 Sur 1080. Tel: 56-71-210910, E-mail: monica_sota_101@hotmail.com. Updated: Apr 17, 2009.

Hostal San Cristobal

(ROOMS: $29 – 31) This hostel is clean, though dark, and offers double rooms, including breakfast, with shared bathrooms. Hostal San Cristobal shares a building with Hostal Pehuenche, but it is not quite as nice as its neighbor. 5 Oriente 1184, Depto. 3. Updated: Apr 17, 2009.

Hotel Terranova

(ROOMS: $40 – 50) Located several blocks from the Plaza de Armas, Hotel Terranova has all the amenities a traveler might need, though it is a little costly. There are rooms for four available. Rooms have telephones, cable TVs and private bathrooms. Breakfast is included, and there is an Internet room and restaurant. 1 Sur 1026. Tel: 56-71-239603, E-mail: hotelterranova@entelchile.net. Updated: Apr 17, 2009.

Restaurants

Talca is jammed with typical *fuentes de sodas*, as well as restaurants that offer a quick and cheap empanada. But the town also features Vivace and Chilote, a pair of restaurants that offer a break from the ordinary. Updated: Apr 22, 2009.

San Pablo's

(EMPANADAS: $1) San Pablo's advertises the best empanadas in town, and, although the food is just adequate, the price is right for an empanada joint. There are also donuts, pies and other pastries. 1 Norte 1322. Updated: Apr 21, 2009.

Carmeneita Cocineria 4

(ENTREES: $1 – 6) Smack dab in the middle of Mercado Central, this cozy restaurant is a nice place to take a break from shopping. Choose between set breakfasts or lunches—depending on the time of the day—or sip on a coffee or tea before delving back into the market. 1 Sur between 5 Oriente and 4 Oriente. Updated: Apr 21, 2009.

Vivace ♪

(DRINKS: $3, ENTREES: $9 and up) After one bite of Vivace's ravioli you'll know why the restaurant is considered to be one of the best in town. A portion of *antipasto* is big enough to feed four people, and there is an impressive selection of wines. You can also just sit at the bar and enjoy a pisco sour. Monday – Saturday, 12 p.m. – 3 p.m. and 8 p.m. – 12 a.m. Isidoro del Solar 50. Tel: 56-71-238227, E-mail: vivacerestaurante@turismomaule.cl / restaurantvivace@hotmail.com. Updated: Apr 21, 2009.

Chilote

(ENTREES: $5 – 12) Conveniently located on the corner of the Plaza de Armas, Chilote specializes in fish and seafood, and it has fairly reasonable prices. The salmon with the sauce of the day cost $8 and you can sample a dish of *lenguado* for $12. Monday – Saturday 10:30 a.m. – 12 a.m. 1 Norte 711, E-mail: reschilote@hotmail.com. Updated: Apr 21, 2009.

La Papa Pastelería

Upon arriving in Talca, walk toward the plaza and cool off along the way with an ice cream or freshly squeezed juice at La Papa Pastelería. Talca has a plethora of helado options, but the treats here are arguably the best. Choose from the wide variety of flavors—sample the *frambuesa* (raspberry). A double scoop cone costs $1. There is also a selection of pastries and cakes. 5 Oriente 1106. Updated: Apr 17, 2009.

AROUND TALCA
RESERVA NACIONAL ALTOS DEL LIRCAY

(ADMISSION: $3) The Altos del Lircay, just 6 kilometers past the mountain village of Vilches, is an amazing sight in the central cordillera. The native forest is still intact here, and in the distance there are great views of mountains and volcanoes. Hikers will be in heaven thanks to the multiple backcountry hiking options; there are plenty of canyons, valleys and summits in the 12,163 hectares of forested wilderness. Near the entrance is an information center that gives out info on the park's flora and fauna, and the indigenous people who still reside in the area and still grind grain at the Piedras Tacitas.

The best time to visit is before winter sets in and there is a risk of heavy snowfall, so try to pass through between October to May.

There are campgrounds near the entrance of the park where **Conaf** charges roughly $15 per campsite, and there also are several private campsites along the dusty road just before the entrance. It is not necessary to use the existing campsites because you can camp in the wild, especially on multi-day hikes. However, it is not permitted to start a campfire due to the risk of wildfires. There are several stores near the entrance where you can purchase supplies, but items are generally overpriced so buy necessary items from the stores in Talca.

Getting To and Away From Reserva Nacional Altos de Lircay

Buses to and from Altos del Lircay leave from the bus terminal in Talca, 67 kilometers northwest of the reserve. Most of the road is paved, though the final 27 kilometers are not, and vehicles kick up constant dust during the summer dry period. Updated: Apr 22, 2009.

CONSTITUCIÓN

Constitución is a small port town in the mouth of the Río Maule. It has charcoal-colored sand beaches, though it pales in comparison to much better coastal towns such as Pichilemu or the quiet beaches to the south. Smelly whiffs from the town's cellulose plant, located several hundred meters near the public beach, do not improve the ambience.

The Plaza de Armas is a pleasant place to spend some time. From there, it is a 20-minute walk along Freire, past the eyesore that is the cellulose plant, to the beach where several huge rock formations jut out of the sea. The most famous is Piedra de la Iglesia, which resembles a huge stone church and serves as a resting place for local birds. There is also a quaint, early-morning market on Calle Infante where you can find deals on fruits, vegetables and handicrafts.

If you are unable to find cheap accommodation in Constitución, you are not looking. Odds are locals will begin to hound you the first moment off the bus or train to stay at their *residencial*. Don't feel obliged to take that first option because there are plenty of places located along Freire and Prieto.

A good, affordable option is **Casa Particular** (Ca. Pinto 159. Tel: 56-71-671857). There are no signs to make the place stand out, so simply ring the bell and Senora Morelia—the friendly woman who owns the operation—will answer and usher you to a room. A clean dorm with a shared bathroom cost $6. Add a few dollars and she'll cook breakfast, too. For $8 a night head to **Residencial Lopez** (Freire 153, 71-671183). Rooms are clean, though dark, and the bathroom is shared.

A string of restaurants along the beach offer about the same options of fish or empanadas. **Pipa Grill** (MacIver 1340, Tel: 56-71-673003) offers good fish for about $5. Closer to the Plaza de Armas, **La Rica Cochina** (Freire 267) is a typical fuente de soda with completos, Italianos and sandwiches. Nothing costs more than $4 on the menu.

Tourists can pick up town information at the kiosk in the Plaza de Armas. The pharmacy **Cruz Verde** is located at Freire 644, while **Banco de Chile** (Freire 500) can exchange currency or travelers checks, and has ATMs. The bus and train terminals are opposite one another a few blocks northeast of the plaza along the river on Calle Rosas.

There is a daily train ($2) that rides more like a slow school bus on rails and is about a four-hour ride to and from Talca. A better, faster option is a bus. **Pullman del Sur**, **Pullmann Contimar** and **Buses Santa Olga** all operate from the terminal and head toward Talca, Santiago and Santa Olga. Updated: Feb 10, 2009.

CHILLÁN

 124 m   170,000   42

Chillán is known throughout Chile as the birthplace of liberator Bernardo O'Higgins. On a not so positive note, it is also famous for the earthquakes that have battered the town during the course of its history—which long ago ravished most of Chillán's colonial appeal. Still, the town is worth a visit and is more than just a starting point for the nearby Termas de Chillán.

The Feria de Chillán is an impressive sight, especially on Saturdays when the hustle and bustle in the street can reach a fever pitch. The open-air market has on display all the fresh fruits and vegetables desired. A bit of bartering can net decent deals on jewelry, handicrafts and paintings from local artists here, too.

Another great sight is the Escuela México, which was donated to the city by the Mexican government in the wake of the 1939 earthquake, and displays gorgeous murals in honor of both Mexican and Chilean history. Museo San Francisco memorializes the Franciscans who came to convert locals, and the Catedral is supposedly immune to the destruction brought about by earthquakes.

Chillán offers a good variety of dining options with great local dishes found in Mercado Central or Casino Cuerpo de Bomberos, though there are more extravagant options too. Updated: Mar 01, 2009.

When to Go
If you want to stroll the Feria de Chillán then it is more enjoyable during the summer months. Termas de Chillán has a great three-hour hike to the peak of the mountain, as well as excellent rock climbing, nature trails and mountain biking during the summer months. However, from mid-June until mid-October, the slopes at Termas de Chillán open and offer magnificent skiing. Updated: Apr 27, 2009.

Getting To and Away From Chillán
Trains arrive from Santiago, Concepción and Temuco—check www.efe.cl for times—five blocks east of the plaza near the old bus station on Av. Brasil (Tel: 56-42-222424).

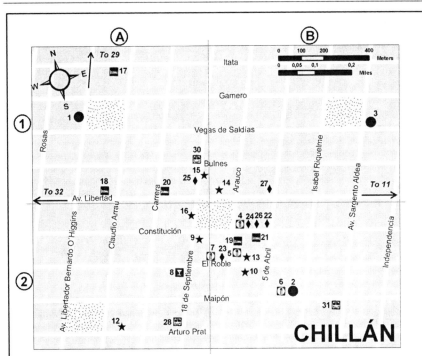

CHILLÁN

Activities ●
1 Escuela México A1
2 Feria de Chillán B2
3 Museo San Francisco B1

Eating
4 Centro Español B2
5 Fuente Alemana B2
6 Mercado Central B2
7 Vegetariano Arcoiris B2

Nightlife
8 Casino Cuerpo de Bomberos A2

Services ★
9   Banco Estado A2
10 Casa de Cambio B2
11 Hospital B1
12 Lava-Matic A2
13 Planet Internet Café B2
14 Post Office B1
15 Sernatur A1
16 Tourism Office A2

Sleeping
17 Casa Sonia Segui A1
18 Hostal Canadá A1
19 Hotel Cordillera B2
20 Hotel Javiera Carrera A1
21 Las Terrazas B2

Tours ◆
22 Agencia Aérea de Turismo y Viajes Albatour B2
23 Agencia de Viajes Alto Nivel B2
24 Agencia de Viajes Lathina Chile B2
25 Centro Tour A1
26 Jb Turismo Internacional B2
27 Munditur B1

Transportation
28 Larrana Rent a Car A2
29 Long-Distance Bus Terminal A1
30 Renta-car A1
31 Terminal Rural B2
32 Train Station A1

MIDDLE CHILE

Almost all long-distance buses stop at Terminal María Teresa (O'Higgins 010. Tel: 56-42-272149) on the northern edge of Chillán. The usual suspects all operate from here: **Tur Bus**, **InterSur**, **Nilahue** and more compete to take locals and travelers to destinations such as Angol, Los Angeles, Puerto Montt, Santiago, Talca and Valdivia. The regional and local buses use the more central Terminal Rural at Maipón 890. Updated: Apr 27, 2009.

Getting Around

From the bus and train terminals, it is easy enough to walk almost anywhere in town. Alternatively, you can catch a taxi or bus.

You can find cars to rent at **Renta-car**, (18 de Septiembre 380. Tel: 56-42-212243), **Ecarent** (Estación de Ferrocarriles, Local 3. Tel: 56-42-229262) or **Larrana Rent a Car** (18 de Septiembre 870. Tel: 56-42-210112) if a trip to Termas de Chillán or another out-of-town attraction is on the agenda. Updated: Apr 27, 2009.

Safety

Chillán does not have too many problems with crime. Be alert, watch out for pickpockets, do not to flash wealth—basically practice common sense. Updated: Apr 27, 2009.

Services

TOURISM

The main **tourism office** (18 de Septiembre 590. Tel: 56-42-433459) is in the Municipalidad in the Plaza de Armas. **Sernatur** also provides tourist information (18 de Septiembre 455. Tel: 56-42-223272, E-mail: info chillan@sernatur.cl) and there is a tourism office at the train station (Tel: 56-42-244837) as well.

MONEY

One of the town's numerous ATMs is located at **Banco Estado** (Constitución 500). Exchange money at the **Casa de Cambio** in Caracol Primavera, local 10 (El Roble 655), or at Constitución 550, local 15 (Tel: 56-42-238638).

KEEPING IN TOUCH

The **post office** is near the Plaza de Armas at Libertad 505. Get on the Internet at **Planet Internet Cafe** (Arauco 683, 2nd floor).

MEDICAL

Hospital Herminia Martin (Tel: 42-212345) is east of the plaza on the corner of Argentina and Francisco Ramírez.

LAUNDRY

The **Lava-Matic** (Arturo Prat 357-B) gets clothes clean quickly. Updated: Jul 07, 2009.

Things to See and Do

Chillán is home to a series of important and impressive sights. The Catedral de Chillán has nine giant arches and stands alongside a giant cross built to memorialize the citizens killed in the 1939 earthquake. In the wake of the devastation caused by that event, Chillán received the beautiful Escuela México as a gift from the Mexican government, complete with murals from two of Mexico's most prestigious artists. The Museo San Francisco houses artifacts from Franciscan missionaries who tried to convert local Mapuche. And the open-air market is one of the best in the region. Updated: Apr 24, 2009.

Museo San Francisco

There is an abundance of furniture, military and religious objects on display at this museum from the Franciscan missionaries who arrived in 1585 and tried to convert the Mapuche. There are also letters from Bernardo O'Higgins on display. Open Tuesday – Sunday 9 a.m. – 1 p.m. and 3 p.m. – 6 p.m. Closed Mondays. Sargento Aldea 265. Tel: 56-42-211634. Updated: Apr 24, 2009.

Catedral

Now the focus point of the Plaza Bernardo O'Higgins, this supposedly earthquake-resistant cathedral was built between 1941 and 1961. It has nine rising arches which allow a vast amount of sunlight to enter the church. Next to the cathedral is a 36-meter-high concrete cross erected in honor of those killed in the devastating 1939 earthquake. Updated: Apr 24, 2009.

Feria de Chillán

This open-air market offers all the fresh produce you could desire. Most of the action is within the streets of Isabel Riquelme, Arturo Prat, Maipón and 5 de Abril, though it does overflow into surrounding streets as well. There are also a wealth of handicrafts and paintings on sale. The market is open every day, but it is best to visit on a Saturday when it is at its liveliest. Plaza de la Merced (southeast of the Plaza de Armas). Open 9 a.m. – 6 p.m. Updated: Apr 24, 2009.

Escuela México

(ADMISSION: by donation) After Chillán endured a devastating earthquake in 1939, the Mexican government donated money to build Escuela México. However, the generosity did not stop there. Pablo Neruda directed two famous Mexican artists—David Alfaro Siqueiros and Xavier Guerrero—to decorate the main staircase and library with murals to honor both Mexican and Chilean history. O'Higgins 250. Open Monday – Friday 10 a.m. – 1 p.m. and 3 p.m. – 6:30 p.m., Saturday – Sunday 10 a.m. – 6 p.m. Updated: Apr 24, 2009.

Tours

One of the most respected tour agencies is **Centro Tour** (18 de Septiembre 486. Tel: 56-42-221306). Line up a trek with guides here, some of whom speak English. Other reliable tour operators are **Jb Turismo Internacional** (Mall Patio Las Terrazas, Constitución 664, office 308. Tel: 56-42-210744) and **Munditur** (Av. Libertad 691-A. Tel: 56-42-224857).

Lodging

Chillán has a lot of good options for accommodation. Budget travelers will have no problem finding a cheap bed to crash on, while upper- and mid-range hotels are scattered about town. Updated: Apr 24, 2009.

Casa Sonia Segui

(ROOMS: $9) This hostel is a popular choice in Chillán among backpackers. Solo travelers might have to share a room when the place is full but it is a great opportunity to make new friends. And there is a fully equipped kitchen if you're in the mood to cook. Itata 288. Tel: 56-42-214879. Updated: Apr 24, 2009.

Hostal Canadá

(ROOMS: $9 – 25) Hostal Canadá is probably the best budget option in Chillán. For $9 per person, guests can enjoy clean rooms with comfortable beds, and showers with consistently hot water. The rooftop terrace is an excellent place to meet other travelers. Libertad 269. Tel: 56-42-234515, E-mail: hostalcanada@hotmail.com. Updated: Apr 24, 2009.

Hotel Javiera Carrera

(ROOMS: $24 – 30) The showers are a bit on the small side, but the simple rooms are decently sized, with clean sheets and a comfortable pillow. The staff is friendly and helpful. Carrera 481. Tel: 56-42-244360, E-mail: hotel.javiera.carrera@terra.cl. Updated: Apr 24, 2009.

Hotel Cordillera

(ROOMS: $40 – 65) This family-run establishment is near the busy city center at the southeast corner of the Plaza de Armas. Hotel Cordillera's rooms are well-kept and have cable TV, telephone and private bathrooms with hot water. Arauco 619. Tel: 56-42-215211, Fax: 56-42-211198, E-mail: hotelcordilla@hotelcordilla.cl, URL: www.hotelcordillera.cl. Updated: Apr 24, 2009.

Las Terrazas

(ROOMS: $70 – 80) Las Terrazas is a solid mid-range option, which caters more to businessmen and families. It is on the fifth floor of a modern office building and operates a business center across the street. Constitución 664, 5th floor. Tel: 56-42-227000, Fax: 42-227001, URL: www.lasterrazas.cl. Updated: Apr 24, 2009.

Restaurants

There are a lot of cheap dining options in Chillán. Head to the Roble Mall if you are in need of a fast-food fix. For a more local flavor look no further than the simple Chilean cuisine found at Mercado Central. There are good vegetarian options and pleasant cafes. Updated: Mar 01, 2009.

Casino Cuerpo de Bomberos

(DISHES: $2 and up) This is a surprisingly good second option for local cuisine if the hustle and bustle of the Mercado Central proves to be too much. The fire station serves simple, inexpensive dishes. El Roble and 18 de Septiembre. Tel: 56-42-222233. Updated: Apr 24, 2009.

Mercado Central

(DISHES: $5 – 10) The true flavors of a town are often found in the eateries that dot its central market and Chillán's revitalized Mercado Central definitely is no exception. Try the popular seafood stew before indulging in something more filling from one of the butcher shops. Monday – Saturday 8 a.m. – 6 p.m. Maipón between 5 de Abril and Isabel Riquelme. Updated: Apr 24, 2009.

Vegetariano Arcoiris

(ROOMS: $6 – 10) This vegetarian option has more than bunny food—though the greens here are worth a taste. Arcoiris has an all-you-can-eat-buffet, sandwiches, over-sized omelets and fresh juices. Monday – Friday 8:30 a.m. – 9:30 p.m., Saturday 8:30 a.m. – 4:30 p.m. El Roble 525. Tel: 56-42-227549. Updated: Apr 24, 2009.

Centro Español

(ENTREES: $6 – 12) Centro Español is a more upscale choice near the plaza, with elegantly dressed waiters eager to serve the chef's latest tasty creation. The paella is an excellent and very popular choice. Monday – Saturday 12 p.m. – 4 p.m. and 8 p.m. – 12 a.m. Arauco 555. Tel: 56-42-216212. Updated: Apr 24, 2009.

Fuente Alemana

Breakfast and lunch at Fuente Alemana will fill you up at a reasonable price—the chicken with rice is $4—but the best reason to dine at Fuente Alemana is the real coffee. And while the blend might not win any awards, it's definitely a welcome change from the usual bland instant coffee served at most restaurants. The restaurant also has outdoor tables to enjoy nice days. Arauco 661. Tel: 56-42-212720. Updated: Apr 24, 2009.

AROUND CHILLÁN
TERMAS DE CHILLÁN

Termas de Chillán is a poor man's Portillo or Valle Nevado. The slopes of the 3,122-meter (10,243-ft) Volcán Chillán might not draw international ski teams, but the area generally receives greater snowfall than the more famous mountains to the north and the skiing is still fantastic. The hill boasts 28 runs for all levels of experience, a snowboard park, and an international and certified ski school staff. The ski area also has dogsledding opportunities, as well as the luxurious Hotel Termas de Chillán on its grounds—where you can expect to pay around a minimum of $1,000 for a weeklong stay. Ski season is best enjoyed mid-June to mid-October.

Termas de Chillán is not just a paradise for skiers, though winter is the perfect time to enjoy the slopes, nine open-air steam baths, mud baths and spa center. During the summer months Termas de Chillán offers nice hikes with beautiful views of the Andes, mountain biking, golf, paintball, rock climbing on an artificial rock wall, tennis, rappelling and equestrian classes. Tel:56-42-434200, E-mail: info@termaschillan.cl, URL: www.termaschillan.cl. Updated: Jul 01, 2009.

VALLE HERMOSO

(ADMISSION: $4) These public thermal baths are just a bus ride away from Chillán, shortly before Valle Las Trancas. There is a campsite here which is a fantastic budget option during the summer, since it costs $15 per campsite. It is also possible to find and purchase supplies in this area. Be sure to let the bus driver know where you want to go so that he lets you out. Updated: Apr 24, 2009.

PARQUE MONUMENTAL BERNARDO O'HIGGINS

(ADMISSION: Free) Take the short bus ride south along Av. O'Higgins to visit this manicured park built in tribute to the famous Chilean liberator. The 60-meter-long tiled mural that depicts O'Higgins' life is an impressive, though faded, sight. O'Higgins mother and sister are buried at a nearby chapel (open 8 a.m. – 8 p.m.). Within the park, the Centro Histórico y Cultural is open for tours (10 a.m. – 6 p.m. weekdays except Monday, and 10 a.m. – 1 p.m. Saturday). Updated: Apr 27, 2009.

Valle Las Trancas

Several kilometers before the entrance to Las Termas there is a small mountain village with a group of more affordable cabins, restaurants, and bars that often feature live music. And while your room won't be directly next to the slopes, the cash savings will be considerable.

Las Cabras (Km 72) is a relatively new set of modern cabins. Rooms have private bathrooms, central heating, fully equipped kitchens complete with microwaves, living rooms, terraces and cable TVs. There is also laundry and maid service. A cabin for 1-2 people costs $73 per night during the low season and $100 during the high season. Las Cabras has room options for up to eight people; an eight-person cabin in the high season costs $185.

Hotel Robledal, set in the woods, is a quiet option off the main highway next to the Río Renegado. The comfortable rooms are a great place to rest up for another day of skiing. Rooms and suites cost between $37 and $370 per person depending on the season. Tel: 56-42-432030, URL: www.hotelrobledal.cl.

Hotel Parador Jamón, Pan y Vino (Km 74) offers hotel and cabin accommodations for about $80 per person per night, as well as an on-site swimming pool. Though the rooms are acceptable, the best reason to visit is the restaurant—the eager staff serves traditional Chilean dishes so skiers can refuel after a long day on the slopes. Tel: 56-42-432-100, URL: www.paradorjamonpanyvino.cl.

Linea Azul operates bus service from Chillán to Valle Las Trancas, as well as to the Termas, year-round ($4). Tel: 42-211192. Updated: Apr 27, 2009.

CONCEPCIÓN

 12m   220,607   41

Founded in 1550, Concepción is a series of metropolitan areas (an agglomeration, if you want to be specific) that has grown to be the second-largest in Chile, behind Santiago. It is also one of the country's most important areas due to its many universities and commercial activities such as the local agricultural, hydroelectric and coal industries. Unfortunately, the industrial sprawl of bland, soul-less buildings scattered throughout the city, does little to enhance Concepción's image.

Catastrophic events—Mapuche raids against the Spanish, earthquakes—have also taken their toll on the appearance of the city. Coal mining in the nearby town of Lota helped spur Concepción's growth, and now the town hopes to exploit its past to attract tourists.

Concepción has a decent amount to offer visitors during the day. Most popular is perhaps the Galería de la Historia, though Jorge González Camarena's Mexican mural at Casa del Arte is also an impressive sight. The Plaza de la Independencia, Catedral de la Santísima Concepción, Parque Ecuador and Museo Haulpén are worth visiting too. Updated: Apr 28, 2009.

When to Go

A popular time to visit Concepción is during the Fiesta de la Primavera, which celebrates the founding of the city. The universities organize this week-long event in early October. Due to their being many universities in the area, the nightlife is at its best when school is in session and the students are out and about. Updated: Apr 28, 2009.

Getting To and Away From Concepción

Concepción's Aeropuerto Carriel Sur is on the outskirts of the city. There is service by **LAN** to and from Santiago's airport.

Most long-distance buses arrive at Terminal de Buses Collao (Tegaulda 860) near the highway where it is easy to find a colectivo or taxi to advance downtown. **Tur Bus**, **Sol del Sur** and various other companies have numerous buses daily to Santiago (expect to pay about $10), as well as farther north. **Cruz del Sur** moves southward to Temuco, Valdiva and Puerto Montt. There is also service to Los Angeles, Angol, Saltos del Laja, Lota, Arauco and more.

EFE runs trains from Barrio Estación north and south. The six-hour ride to Santiago costs $20. It's about the same cost to travel southbound to Temuco. Updated: Mar 03, 2009.

Getting Around

Concepción has its fair share of micros that run from the bus station along San Martin to the town's center. There are more micros constantly filling the streets along O'Higgins. These offer cheap rides at about $0.50 per ride. Taxis are easy to flag down, and there are several places to rent a car in the city, including the ever-reliable option of **Hertz** (Prat 241. Tel: 41-230341). Updated: Apr 28, 2009.

Safety

As far as South American cities are concerned, Concepción is a relatively safe place. Still, it is not immune to big-city problems, so be sure to watch for pickpockets and not flash wealth. Also, be careful while swimming in the Bío Bío River during the summer months because underwater currents can be unexpectedly strong and suck swimmers beneath the surface. Updated: Apr 28, 2009.

Services

Tourist information is readily available at the **Sernatur** (Aníbal Pinto 460. Tel: 56-41-741337) or at **Conaf** (Barros Arana 215. Tel: 56-41-624000). The **hospital** (Tel: 56-41-208500) is north of the plaza at San Martin and Lautaro, while the **post office** is at O'Higgins 779. Also on O'Higgins near the plaza is a cluster of banks with ATMs. Change money at **Varex** at O'Higgins 537. Internet cafes are numerous—one is **Double Click** at Chacabuco 707. Updated: Mar 03, 2009.

Things to See and Do

Concepción has plenty of places where you can find live music and good nightlife. Most visitors spend their days checking the Galería de la Historia to learn about the city's past or at the Casa del Arte to see Jorge González Camarena's Mexican mural. The Plaza de la Independencia, Catedral de la Santísima Concepción, Parque Ecuador and Museo Haulpén are also popular attractions. Updated: Mar 03, 2009.

MIDDLE CHILE

MIDDLE CHILE

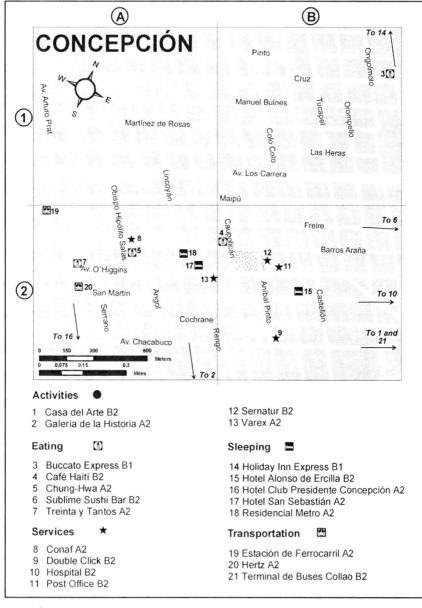

Activities ●

1 Casa del Arte B2
2 Galería de la Historia A2

Eating 🍴

3 Buccato Express B1
4 Café Haití B2
5 Chung-Hwa A2
6 Sublime Sushi Bar B2
7 Treinta y Tantos A2

Services ★

8 Conaf A2
9 Double Click B2
10 Hospital B2
11 Post Office B2

12 Sernatur B2
13 Varex A2

Sleeping 🛏

14 Holiday Inn Express B1
15 Hotel Alonso de Ercilla B2
16 Hotel Club Presidente Concepción A2
17 Hotel San Sebastián A2
18 Residencial Metro A2

Transportation 🚌

19 Estación de Ferrocarril A2
20 Hertz A2
21 Terminal de Buses Collao B2

Galería de la Historia

The Galería de la Historia tells the tale of Concepción's history through impressive dioramas. There are rotating displays of local artwork in the art gallery. Open Monday 3 p.m. – 6:30 p.m., Tuesday – Friday 10 a.m. – 1:30 p.m. and 3 p.m. – 6:30 p.m., Saturday – Sunday 10 a.m. – 2 p.m. and 3 p.m. – 7 p.m. Hospicio 25, Parque Ecuador. Tel:

56-41-2853756, Fax: 56-41-2853759, E-mail: galeriahistoriaconcepcion@gmail.com, URL: www.galeriadelahistoriadeconcepcion.cl. Updated: Apr 28, 2009.

Casa del Arte

(ADMISSION: Free) Mexican artist Jorge González Camarena's huge mural "La Presencia de América Latina" is a must-see at the Casa del

Arte. There are also landscapes and portraits on display at this art museum located on campus at Universidad de Concepción. Tuesday – Friday 10 a.m. – 6 p.m., Saturday 10 a.m. – 4 p.m., Sunday 10 a.m. – 1 p.m. Chacabuco and Larenas. Updated: Apr 28, 2009.

Antigua Estación de Ferrocarril

The train sation is noteworthy because of modernist architect Luis Herreros' columns on the façade. Another appealing feature in the station is Gregorio de la Fuente's striking mural Latidos y Rutas de Concepción, which depicts historical scenes and natural disasters that have ravaged the city over time. Av. Arturo Prat 501 corner Barros Arana, opposite Plaza España. Updated: Apr 28, 2009.

Lodging

Concepción is stocked with nice hotels that have plenty of amenities (Hotel Alonso de Ercilla, Hotel Club Presidente Concepción and Holiday Inn Express). The bad news for backpackers, or visitors on a tight budget, is that all those nice hotels are expensive. However, there are a few deals to be found. Updated: Apr 29, 2009.

Residencial Metro

(ROOMS: $11 – 20) The rooms are clean, simple and cheap at the Residencial Metro so it is no surprise it attracts many backpackers. A good-sized breakfast is included in the price, and the hotel is conveniently situated near the plaza and Mercado Central. Barros Arana 464. Tel: 56-41-225306. Updated: Apr 28, 2009.

Hotel San Sebastián

(ROOMS: $27 – 43) Budget accommodation is not widely available in Concepción, but Hotel San Sebastián offers the wallet some relief. This family-run establishment is clean and centrally located. Rengo 463. Tel:56-41-956719. Updated: Apr 28, 2009.

Hotel Alonso de Ercilla

(ROOMS: $53 – 115) Hotel Alonso de Ercilla is a good mid-range option for travelers who want to be within several blocks of the plaza, theaters and local culture. The hotel has impressive wood furnishings, a helpful staff and serves decent breakfasts, which are included. Rooms have cable TVs, phones for direct international calls, an Internet room, WiFi and there is a 24-hour cafeteria on-site. Colo Colo 334. Tel: 56-41-2227984, URL: www.hotelalonsodeercilla.cl. Updated: Apr 28, 2009.

Hotel Club Presidente Concepción

(ROOMS: $100) There is a lot to like about Hotel Club Presidente Concepción. It is in a nice part of town close to the city center, surrounded by a wealth of good restaurants and several bars where guests can have a drink or two. The hotel's 36 rooms each have cable TV, air conditioning, a safety box and telephone. Book ahead because the hotel can fill up fast. Pedro de Valdivia 721. Tel: 56-41-2339090, E-mail: infocc@presidente.cl, URL: www.presidente.cl. Updated: Apr 28, 2009.

Holiday Inn Express

(ROOMS: $115) The amenities found in any typical Holiday Inn in Kansas or Ohio are replicated at Concepción's branch of the famous hotel chain. It has a pool, Jacuzzi, gym and parking. Rooms are very clean and equipped with cable TV, coffeemakers and towels. San Andrés 38. Tel: 56-41-481484, E-mail: reservas.chile@talbot.cl, URL: www.hiexpress.com. Updated: Apr 28, 2009.

Restaurants

From cheap eats to pricey concoctions, Concepción has it all, stocked with cafés, *fuentes de soda* and classy restaurants galore. Updated: Apr 28, 2009.

Buccato Express

(ENTREES: $5 –10) Buccato Express offers a wide range of options. Dine on traditional Chilean dishes, order a regular hamburger, or the soup and sandwich. There is outdoor seating for warm and sunny afternoons. Paicavi 1221. Tel: 56-41-2250288. Updated: Apr 28, 2009.

Chung-Hwa

(ENTREES: $5 – 11) This restaurant is where locals head when they're craving authentic Chinese cuisine. Most entrées are fairly priced and the service is speedy and friendly. Open noon – 11:30 p.m. Barros Arana 262. Tel: 56-41-229539. Updated: Apr 28, 2009.

Sublime Sushi Bar

(DINNER: $15) Sushi Bar is a mid-range restaurant for the visitor in need of something a little more upscale than the usual *fuente de soda* on the streets of Concepción. It is cozy spot to wine and dine a date. Freire 1633. Tel: 56-41-2794194. Updated: Apr 28, 2009.

Cafe Haiti

Enjoy one of the best cups of coffee or tea in town at Cafe Haiti. The café has seating upstairs so patrons can relax with a drink and

MIDDLE CHILE

observe others scurrying through the plaza. Monday – Saturday 8 a.m. – 10 p.m., Sunday 9 a.m. – 8:30 p.m. Caupolicán 511, Local 7. Updated: Apr 28, 2009.

Treinta y Tantos

A favorite of local students in Barrio Estación, Treinta y Tantos dishes out delicious and cheap empanadas. As the name of the place suggests, there are more than 30 types of empanadas to choose from. Do not arrive too early because the eatery does not open until 6 p.m., but stays open until 2 a.m. Monday through Saturday (closed Sundays). It is also a nice place to knock back a few drinks before some late-night dancing. Prat 404, Updated: Apr 28, 2009.

AROUND CONCEPCIÓN
LOTA

This former coal mining town is an easy daytrip from Concepción. Although it is one of Chile's poorer cities it is beginning to tap into the tourism industry. There are modern hotels, a casino, and visits to the coal mine with an ex-miner as a guide. Those curious to experience a miner's life can see the 820-meter shaft of Chiflón del Diablo ($7.30) or head 1,500 meters (4,921.5 ft) below surface and ride on a mine train in the Pique Carlos ($11). Near the exit from the tunnels there is a museum with mining equipment and tools. In the church on the town's plaza there is a statue of the Virgin carved out of coal. A bit to the west is pleasant Parque de Lota, which has a garden, colonial homes and a museum.

Getting To and Away From Lota

Buses J. Ewert, near the Concepción train station, provides reliable daily service to and from Lota. Los Carrera and Tucapel. Updated: Apr 29, 2009.

CAÑETE

Above Río Tucapel, 92 kilometers (57 mi) south of Lota, the agricultural town of Cañete was the site of a famous battle between the indigenous and the Spanish in the 16th century. Today it continues to be a Mapuche stronghold. Meander to the northern end of the main street to visit Fuerte Tucapel, the remains of the town's fortifications, and find the best views of the river valley. Slightly south of the town, there is an exhibition of indigenous funerary customs, musical instruments, jewelry and weapons at the Museo Mapuche de Cañete. Updated: Apr 29, 2009.

Cañete Mapuche Museum

From the road you'll see a white circular building where more than 1,200 artifacts and an art gallery are housed. As you enter the car park, you'll discover a *ruca* (traditional Mapuche house) and many other ancient tools, all set in gardens of native plants used by the Mapuche. The ruca is also a shop and cafe, which serves traditional snack foods and sells local arts and crafts. Open Monday – Friday 9:30 a.m. – 6 p.m., Saturday – Sunday, 11 a.m. – 7 p.m. To get there, drive south out of town along the road to Contulmo and you'll see the museum on the right. Tel: 56-41-611-093, E-mail: museomapuche@terra.cl, URL: www.museomapuchecanete.cl. Updated: Jun 25, 2009.

PARQUE NACIONAL LAGUNA DEL LAJA

(ADMISSION: $2) This amazing landscape was named for the lake that formed after the 1972 eruption of Volcán Antuco, when the lava flow dammed Río Laja. The volcano, which stands 2,985 meters high, is the park's chief attraction.

Pick up information at the **Conaf** hut, or about 1 km beyond at the **Centro de Informaciones** at Chacay, which holds talks and shows videos about the park. There is an easy hiking path nearby which leads to the Salto las Chilcas and Salto del Torbellino waterfalls. East of the information center along the road through the park, you'll find a ski center. The center is open from June to October so that skiers can hit the slopes of the volcano. During the winter, the 50-bed **Refugio Digeder** (O'Higgins 740, Office 23. Tel: 56-41-2226797) is open at the Volcán Antuco ski area. It offers meals and rents equipment. For reservations, contact the refugio.

The road turns into a dirt path along the southern shore of the lake and continues to Paso Pichachén and the Argentine border. Take a walk along here for breathtaking views of the mountains of Sierra Velluda.

Accommodation in the park is limited. **Cabañas y Camping Lagunillas** (Tel: 56-43-321086) is a campsite with running water, showers and electricity. It costs $12 per site. There are a few cabins ($50/person) which sleep up to six people and have kitchen facilities as well. You can find a restaurant on the banks of Río Laja. There is a nice and affordable hostel called **Hostería El Bosque** five kilometers from the park entrance in Abanico, 12 kilometers from the lake. The place has nice grounds and a small swimming pool. Lodging only costs $7 a person with an option to upgrade to full board. Tel: 56-43-372719.

To get to the park take public transportation from Los Angeles Terminal Rural (Villagrán 501) on **ERS,** which offers five daily buses (three on Sundays) to Abanico (2 hours, $3). There is no public transportation from El Abanico so it is a five-kilometer uphill hike to the park entrance and an additional 6km to the park office—bring water to stay hydrated. Updated: Apr 29, 2009.

LOS ANGELES

Los Angeles is an unspectacular agricultural town without any true must-see places. The sights like the Museo de la Alta Frontera, which has Mapuche silver, or the Salto del Laja, close to the highway, are worth a glance if you have the time. The highlight of Los Angeles is 20 kilometers north at El Rincón. The riverside location, in a beautiful, quiet setting, makes it an ideal place to relax for several days. Updated: Jun 29, 2009.

When to Go

Los Angeles probably is not worth a visit itself, though it is a good base for exploring to Parque Nacional Laguna del Laja and spectacular Volcán Antuco, or to the upper portion of Río Bío Bío. Updated: Jul 07, 2009.

Getting To and Away From Los Angeles

Terminal Santa María (Av. Sor Vicenta 2051) ,northeast of the center of town, is the destination for long-distance buses arriving in Los Angeles. There are numerous companies serving the terminal, such as **Tur Bus, Tas Cho-apa, Condor** and **Jota Be**, which take passengers to Angol, Concepción (which is also the bus to Saltos del Laja), Santiago, Puerto Montt and Temuco. A typical trip to Santiago cost approximately $15 and takes eight hours. Terminal Santa Rita (Villagrán 501) has buses that travel to the villages of Abanico and Antuco. Updated: Apr 29, 2009.

Getting Around

From the terminal you can take a bus, and once in town it is easy to walk almost anywhere. Taxis are easy to flag down. You can also hop on a colectivo or rent a car from **Interbruna** (Caupolicán 350). Updated: Jun 29, 2009.

Safety

Los Angeles is is by no means an overwhelmingly dangerous place, so you should be fine practicing standard safety precautions. Take a little extra care at night, especially if walking alone. Updated: Apr 29, 2009.

Services

Town information can be found at the Sernatur (Caupolicán 450, office 6, 3rd floor). Send postcards or other mail from the post office near the Plaza de Armas at Caupolicán 464. The hospital (Tel: 56-43-409600) is at Ricardo Vicuña 147. Lavajet does laundry at Valdiva 516. Updated: Apr 29, 2009.

Things to See and Do

Los Angeles is known for El Rincón (20 km north), where you can stop for several days of peace and quiet. The Museo de la Alta Frontera has an outstanding collection of Mapuche silver. The waterfall Salto del Laja is close to the highway and is worth checking out you are in the area. Updated: May 19, 2009.

Museo de la Alta Frontera

(ADMISSION: Free) The Museo de la Alta Frontera has a fascinating and astonishing collection of traditional Mapuche silver ornaments and jewelry. The museum has 600 pieces in its collection, though the display rotates. Try to visit the museum in January or February when you might see a local Mapuche woman modeling the items. Open from 8 a.m. – 1:45 p.m., 3 p.m. – 6:30 p.m. Closed Saturdays and Sundays. Colón 195. Tel: 56-43-409400. Updated: May 16, 2009.

Salto del Laja

At Salto del Laja, Río Laja emerges from the Andes and tumbles more than 50 meters (164 ft) down a cliff before making its way 40 kilometers (25 mi) west to the Río Bío Bío at La Laja. The cascade is near the highway and you can stop to see it. Updated: Jul 01, 2009.

Tours

Interbruna Turismo Ltda. (Caupolicán 350. Tel: 56-43-313812) has a helpful staff with English speakers. A highly recommended adventure tourism agency is **Fundo Curanilahue** (Tel: 56-43-1872819,

Fax: 56-43-1972829) located six kilometers north of Salto de Laja-Camino Chillancito. Updated: Jun 27, 2009.

Lodging

Los Angeles has several nice residenciales around town, but, unfortunately, few options for the traveler on a tight budget.

Hotel Océano

(ROOMS: $13 – 25) Be sure to book ahead for a stay at this popular hotel. Océano is a favorite among backpackers for its relatively inexpensive, bright rooms, which are always clean. Bathrooms are shared or private. Colo Colo 327. Tel: 56-43-342432, E-mail: hoteloceanola@hotmail.com. Updated: May 19, 2009.

Hotel Don Lucho

(ROOMS: $40 – 50) Hotel Don Lucho's building dates back to the early 1900s. Rooms are clean and well kept, and breakfast is included in the price. Lautaro 579. Tel: 56-43-321643. Updated: May 19, 2009.

Hotel Mariscal Alcázar

(ROOMS: $75 – 140) Located just off the plaza, the high-end Hotel Mariscal Alcázar features 60 rooms with air conditioning, cable TVs, telephones, WiFi and room service. There are singles and doubles, and rooms on the upper floors have views of the plaza. There is a restaurant on-site. Lautaro 385. Tel: 56- 43-311725, URL: www.hotelalcazar.cl. Updated: May 19, 2009.

Restaurants

Los Angeles has a decent amount of dining options for any budget, including good Italian and seafood.

Cielo, Mar y Tierra

(SET MENU: $5) Cielo Mar y Tierra's patio is a pleasant, relaxed place for relatively inexpensive lunch specials. The restaurant's offerings of fresh seafood and pasta dishes are worth a try. Rengo 378. Tel: 56-43-340336. Updated: May 19, 2009.

Club de la Unión

(MEALS: $5 – 9) Club de la Unión serves up great *almuerzos* and typical Chilean dinners. The chicken at lunch is well prepared, the *pastel de choclo* is a treat, and the service is excellent. The restaurant's staff is friendly and helpful. Some of the staff speaks limited English. Colón 261. Tel: 56-43-322218. Updated: May 19, 2009.

Julio's Pizza

(ENTREES: $5 – 9) This place is a haven for pizza lovers. Julio's serves up homemade pizza loaded with toppings, and has hearty pasta dishes as well for those not in the mood for a slice of pie. Monday – Sunday 10 a.m. – midnight. Colón 452. Tel: 56-43-314530. Updated: May 19, 2009.

AROUND LOS ANGELES

El Rincón

(ROOMS: $26 – 50) El Rincón is in the heart of the southern Chilean Central Valley. There are beautiful gardens, wooded grounds and fruit trees. The hotel is a fantastic place to relax and forget the rest of the world for several days. Breakfast and dinner are extra. Ruta 5, Km 494. Tel: 56-99-4415019, E-mail: wlohmar@yahoo.com, URL: www.elrinconchile.cl. Updated: May 18, 2009.

ANGOL

 79 m   50,000   42

Angol is the last stop before Temuco, which is referred to as the gateway to the Lake District. The town has a bustling and attractive Plaza de Armas. On the southern edge of the plaza is a red-brick cathedral with a tower. Five blocks northwest of the plaza, on the corner of Covadonga and Vergara, is the region's oldest church, the **Iglesia de San Buenaventura**. It is worth the walk to see the cream-and-pink building with a yellow wooden tower.

Angol hosts one of Chile's largest festivals, with a folk song theme and extravagant prizes, during the second week of January. The town is also the most logical base for a visit to Parque Nacional Nahuelbuta.

Accommodation can be found at **Residencial Olimpia** (Caupolicán 625. Tel: 56-45-711162) where the rooms are a bit small but a single costs approximately $10. **Hotel Millaray** (Prat 420. Tel: 56-45-711-570) is more costly, at around $25 per night, but it is a convenient two-minute walk to the Plaza de Armas.

After you settle into a room, head to **Sparlotto Pizza** (Lautaro 418) for a filling slice of pizza or to the garden area of **Josánhaecha** (Caupolicán 579) for snacks and meals.

Terminal Rodoviario, on José Luis Osorio, is where long-distance buses run to and from

Angol. The company **Bus Angol** has tours of Parque Nacional Nahuelbuta during the summer season. **Jota Be** has daily buses to Los Angeles and Concepción. And **Tur Bus** runs to Santiago, as well as to all larger destinations along the Panamericana. In Angol, you can find the **tourism office** at Bonilla and O'Higgins. Updated: Mar 09, 2009.

CONTULMO

Nestled beside the beautiful Lake Lanalhue, this village of 2,500 is a slice of rural life. German immigrants settled in the town in 1884 and founded the first German school in Chile here in 1893. The old wooden houses fill the town, and you can practice water sports on the lake. Contulmo is also one of only two places in Chile where the albino strawberry is grown, so if you're visiting in the summer, try the white berries. Updated: Jul 06, 2009.

Dungunwe Museum

(ADMISSION: By donation) This small museum half a block from the main square is dedicated to the first German immigrants who settled in Chile in the 1800s. The museum has exhibits with their clothes, utensils, tools and arms, as well as Mapuche artifacts. There is a collection of old photographs depicting the life of the settler in 19th-century Chile. Open 3 p.m. – 9 p.m. Ca. Los Notros. URL: www.contulmo.cl. Updated: Jul 22, 2008.

Hosteria Playa Tranquila

(ROOMS: $65) On the shore of Lake Lanalhue, this large red wooden building is a great homey getaway. The hotel's lakeside position and three hectares of land means you can step out onto a nice beach surrounded by native flora. For those who just want to be pampered, the hotel has a restaurant and room service. The children's area ensures that parents can escape, too. Tel: 56-9-6497204 / 5, URL: playatranquila@ hotmail.com. Updated: Jul 22, 2008.

AROUND ANGOL
PARQUE NACIONAL NAHUELBUTA

(ADMISSION: $3.50) A dusty dirt road connects Angol to the entrance of Parque Nacional Nahuelbuta (December – March 8 a.m. – 9 p.m., April – November 8 a.m. – 6 p.m.), 35 kilometers west (21.7 mi). The park was created in 1939 to conserve the dwindling population of araucaria trees in the coastal mountains. Some in the park have reached nearly 50 meters in height, two meters in diameter and are almost 1,000 years old. You might catch a glimpse of park wildlife such as pumas, foxes, deer or woodpeckers. Find all the information about flora and fauna at the information center approximately 5 kilometers west along the road from the park's entrance.

An easy trail near Pehuenco goes through the forest, passing sporadic springs until it reaches Cerro Piedra del Aguila, which offers fabulous views of the Andes. Toward the southeast you can see volcanoes such as Antuco, Villarrica, Lanín and, on a clear day, Osorno over the southern horizon. At 1,400 meters (4,593 ft) above sea level, Cerro Anay has excellent views of the surroundings. Many believe it is the best peak to view the park.

There is no public transportation to the park in the winter, but in summer Buses Nahuelbuta and Buses Angol make the trip from Angol's Terminal Rural (Ilabaca 422). Buses Angol also operates tours in the summer; you can arrange a tour at Angol's tourist office, at the fork of Bonilla and O'Higgins. Buses drop passengers off at El Cruce, which is an hour's walk to the entrance of the park. It is also possible to drive to the park but remember from June to September there will be snow and a 4x4 is necessary.

There are a couple of camping areas in the park where it costs roughly $9 per night to set up tent. Pehuenco is 5 kilometers from the park entrance, near the park's headquarters. Pehuenco has 11 campsites complete with picnic tables, bathrooms and cold showers. The other campsite, Coimallín is 5 kilometers north of Pehuenc, has no facilities at all, so it is more for the seasoned camper. Remember to bring enough food and water for the trip because there is nowhere to purchase supplies in the park. Updated: Apr 29, 2009.

!!!!!

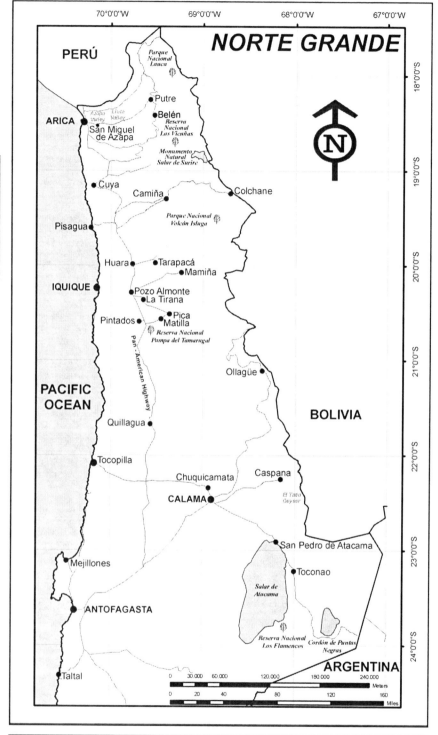

Norte Grande

As you move north, the sun-baked hills and gentle valleys of the Norte Chico gradually give way to the more desolate plains of the Atacama desert, marking the beginning of the Norte Grande. On the eastern edge of the country, the desert climbs up into the altiplano highlands, where salt flats and lakes reach as far as Bolivia and Argentina.

Norte Grande takes up nearly a quarter of the country's landmass, yet accounts for less than five percent of its inhabitants—testimony to the land's aridity. Apart from the Lake District, Norte Grande is one of the most visited areas of Chile. Most people opt for a group tour, as the vast and inhospitable landscape makes independent travel difficult.

The Norte Grande region can be divided into three major areas: the Atacama Desert in the middle, the Pacific beaches to the east, and the Altiplano to the west. Although the Atacama contains many well-preserved ruins, most visitors stick to Norte Grande's highlands and beaches.

History

Before the arrival of the Spanish, the Chinchorro and Chango cultures roamed this land and found ways to adapt to the harsh, extremely dry desert environment. Living off of wild game and subsistence agriculture, the Chinchorro and the Chango people were able to survive through the arrival of the Spanish. Given the intense dryness of the Atacama, remnants of these civilizations have been well preserved: ancient fortresses, geoglyphs and mummies can all be easily visited. When the Spanish arrived, the barren landscape didn't seem worth the struggle against local indigenous forces. Although technically part of Bolivia and Peru, many areas of the Norte Grande remained under indigenous rule. It wasn't until the *Guerra del Pacífico* (War of the Pacific, 1879 – 1884) that Chile—committed to supporting the many Chileans laboring in Bolivian mines—was able to claim the region.

In the early 20th century, copious amounts of nitrate were discovered in the ground and the region suddenly became immensely important. Entire towns sprouted up around mines in the desert. However, most of these towns have since been abandoned, as nitrate was quickly upstaged by more modern European fertilizers. The sudden

change in the market took a drastic toll on Chile, resulting in the loss of enormous amounts of money and countless jobs.

Deliverance came in the form of that pinkish, ductile metal known as copper. Today, copper continues to be one of Chile's most important natural resources, with export sales contributing a large part to the economy. Updated: Jul 07, 2009.

When to Go

July and August are the busiest months in Norte Grande, so prices tend to rise for guides, accommodation and tour agencies. If you plan to visit during these vacation months, consider reserving tours and hotel rooms in advance.

The region is also quite busy in January and February when hordes of Chileans head north to spend their summer vacations at the beach. Again, you may want to book in advance during this time. Beware that between December and February heavy rains wreak havoc on roads and it gets much colder in the Altiplano. Updated: Jul 02, 2009.

Highlights

Head to the **beaches of Iquique (p.209)** and **Arica (p.183)** to catch some surf—or maybe just some rays. Thrill-seekers can try **paragliding (p.218)** along the hilly pacific coast.

Get out your moon boots and spend hours wandering the mystical maze of sand dunes, strange rock formations and odd crunchy surfaces in the **Valle de la Luna (p.235)**.

In the Atacama desert, take a trip out to the nitrate ghost towns of **Humberstone (p.221)** and **Santa Laura (p.221)**.

Another of the desert's highlights are the immense geoglyphs carved into the side of the vast ravines by long-departed indigenous tribes. The vast, steaming **Geisers del Tatio (p.236)** are worth a visit.

Parque Nacional Lauca (p.202) and **Parque Nacional Volcán Isluga (p.222)** provide endless opportunities for exploration and adventure, with geysers, volcanoes, salt flats and gorgeous mountain lakes. Updated: Jul 07, 2009.

NORTE GRANDE

Safety

When traveling through the Norte Grande take care to keep your money hidden and avoid toting around expensive items that may catch a curious eye. Use cabs in areas that are less populated. Overall, use a little common sense and you'll be fine.

Mother Nature is probably your biggest threat in the Norte Grande. The sun is very powerful, so always carry sunscreen with a high SPF. The Atacama is the driest desert in the world, so be sure to stay hydrated. Finally, when exploring the highlands, make sure that you have the proper equipment that will protect you from the elements. It might be helpful to travel with a local guide that knows the territory. Updated: Jul 02, 2009.

Things to See and Do

The Norte Grande is the second most popular tourist destination in Chile for good reason. The beaches to the west are great for sunbathing, paragliding or surfing. And, with two national parks (Parque Nacional Lauca and Parque Nacional Volcán Isluga) and a number of national reserves (Reserva Nacional Pampade Tamarugal, Reserva Nacional los Flamencos, and Reserva Nacional las Vicuñas), you'll never run out of sights to see or trails to trek.

Visit markets, museums, churches, observatories and indigenous ruins or go on an adventure and try to hike a volcano. Visitors should also check out the ancient geoglyphs, the Geisers del Tatio and the Valle de la Luna. Updated: Jul 07, 2009.

Tours

Traveling with a guide in the Norte Grande can help ensure your safety while allowing you to see and discover places you might not have otherwise been aware of. Guided tours are especially recommended for travelers interested in high-risk adventure sports, as safety can be an issue.

When searching for a tour agency, start your search in conveniently located cities. For excursions to Parque Nacional Lauca, Reserva Nacional Las Vicuñas or Parque Nacional Volcán Isluga, head to Arica or Putre—Putre being the cheaper option. Iquique is a good starting point for day tours around the city, as well as trips to Pica, Pisagua, Mamiña or nearby geoglyph sites. Finally, San Pedro de Atacama is loaded with tourist agencies ready to guide visitors to the Geisers del Tatio, the Termas de Puritama, the Salar de Atacama, and other nearby lakes, mountains, salt flats and volcanoes. Updated: Jul 07, 2009.

Lodging

With so many national parks and reserves, a tent, sleeping bag and pillow are all you need for a good night's sleep in the Norte Grande. There are also plenty of accommodation options available, catering to a wide range of budgets. Towns and cities close to national parks and popular hiking areas are likely to have the most budget options for backpackers, while those looking for a little more comfort and indulgence should stick to bigger cities like Arica or Iquique. In more rural areas, hospedajes or refugios are usually a good bet.

Rock Art

Geoglyphs, petroglyphs, petrographs: These three terms are used to describe artwork done by prehistoric societies, and although they may be used interchangeably, distinctions do exist.

Geoglyphs are gigantic drawings made on the sides of hills. These drawings have only been found in the following areas: Arizona (United States), Nasca (Peru) and Northern Chile from Arica to Iquique. Techniques varied, but principally consisted of designs being scraped into the earth. In some environments, like Nasca, the morning dew was sufficient to keep the form of the design intact for centuries. In other instances, like the Atacama Desert, urine was used. Some artists added rocks to outline the figure for heightened distinction.

Petroglyphs are rock (petro) carvings (glyphs), or stones engraved with geometric, anthropomorphic and animal pictures. Petrographs, also called pictographs, are paintings done on rocks, usually inside caves or in protected recesses. Both these techniques are common throughout the Americas and other parts of the world. Updated: Jun 24, 2009.

ARICA

 38 m   186,000   58

Arica is a major port in the extreme north of the country. Nicknamed the City of Eternal Spring, it has a pleasant climate year-round. Arica rests on the border of both Peru and Bolivia, so it is often the first (or last) Chilean town travelers' visit. This vibrant yet laid-back city is a nice place to pass a few days.

The desert coastal land around Arica has been inhabited for over 11,000 years. The first people here were the Chinchorro who lived in fishing hamlets and developed primitive, yet elaborate methods to mummify their dead. The Camanchacos were another early indigenous tribe in the region. These initial settlers created tremendous geoglyphs across the landscape. A prime place to see them is in the Valle de Azapa and the Museo de San Miguel de Azapa, which has mummies, pottery and weavings. From the 4th to the 9th century, Arica was dominated by the Tiwanaku Empire, then regional lords took over until the Inca conquest in 1473.

The Spaniards arrived in 1536. They named this area of small fishing villages Arica, which in Aymara means "New Door". Some historical linguists say it may be interpreted as "a narrow access to the Altiplano," in reocognition of the role of this natural harbor had in pre-Columbian commerce. Lucas Martínez Vegaso founded San Marcos de Arica on April 25, 1541. The town quickly became the principal port for the shipment of Potosí's silver to the coffers of the Spanish crown—and a favorite target for pirates Sir Francis Drake, Thomas Cavendish, Richard Hawkins, Joris van Spilbergen and William Daumpier, among others. Major churches and treasure storehouses were connected beneath the city by tunnels to help locals escape pirate raids.

With Latin America's independence from Spain, Arica came under the jurisdiction of Peru. An 8.5 earthquake and the 7–10m (23–39 ft) tsunami that followed destroyed most of the city in 1868. Alexandre Gustave Eiffel was contracted to design some of the new buildings, including the Customs House and the Municipalidad. His cathedral successfully survived a second tidal wave in 1877, which reached a height of 14 meters (45 ft).

In the struggle to control nitrate and other reserves, Chile invaded Bolivian and Peruvian territories in 1879, thus provoking the Guerra del Pacífico. Several decisive skirmishes were fought in Arica, including a naval battle and the capture of El Morro, a major defensive point of the port. The territory as far north as Tacna then reverted to Chile. The Peruvian army unsuccessfully attempted to regain control of the city in 1891. Later, the Peace and Friendship Pact of 1904 between Bolivia and Chile allowed the landlocked Andean nation to have access to the Arica seaport, and the Arica-La Paz railroad began operations in 1913. Arica continues to serve as Bolivia's main export harbor. Since October 8, 2007, the city has been the capital of Chile's new Region XV, or Región de Arica y Parinacota.

As a result of the city's complex history, Arica's present popuation is an ethnic mix of Altiplano indigenous, descendents of African slaves on olive plantations in the Azapa valley, and migrants from the Chincha and Ica regions of now-Southern Peru. Holiday celebrations in Arica feature Afro-Peruvian and Aymara dances and music, as well as the Chilean cueca. The cuisine also has a multi-national flavor.

The city and its region claim several world records: the shortest and highest altitude railroads (the Arica-Tacna and Arica-La Paz lines), the oldest mummies, and the highest non-navigable lake (Chungará). It is fascinating to explore the hidden corners of Arica, from the geoglyphs of the Azapa and Lluta Valleys to the heights of El Morro, the architecture of Eiffel and the railroad, tracing this city's past accomplishments and savoring its present. Arica has many fine beaches and some of the most challenging waves in the world. Birdwatching is excellent all along the coast, especially at the mouth of the Río Lluta and at Caleta de Camarones, which Humboldt Penguins call home. Updated: Nov 08, 2008.

When to Go

Rain rarely falls on Arica. Temperatures average 18°C (65°F) and nights are cool. During most of the year, clouds form during the dark hours, but burn off by noon.

During the summer months there are free movies, volleyball tournaments, concerts and other events at Chinchorro and La Lisera beaches and on Plaza Baquedano in town.

NORTE GRANDE

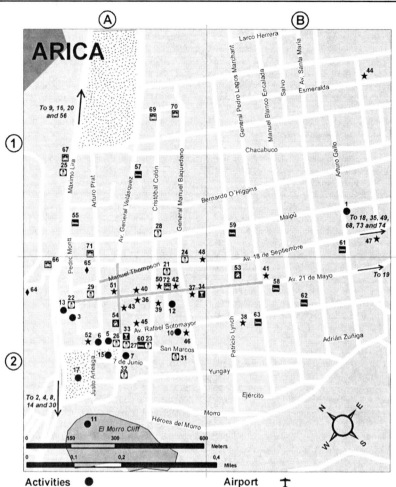

Activities ●

1   Amauta Sub B1
2   Arica en Vuelo A2
3   Casa de la Cultura A2
4   El Laucho, Playas La Lisera, Brava &
    Arenillas Negras A2
5   El Roto A2
6   Gobernación de Arica A2
7   Iglesia San Marcos de Arica A2
8   Isla del Alacrán A2
9   Magic Chile Surf School A1
10 Mercado Central A2
11 Morro de Arica A2
12 Museo del Mar A2
13 Museo Ferroviario A2
14 Parapente Arica A2
15 Parque Colón A2
16 Playas Chinchorro & Las Machas A1
17 Plaza de Armas A2
18 Poblado Artesanal B1
19 Yamabushi Adventure B2

Airport ✈

20 Aeropuerto Internacional de
    Chacalluta A1

Eating ⬦

21 Café Latino A2
22 El Andén A2
23 El Molino Viejo A2
24 Express Lider A2
25 Fish Markets A1
26 Govindas A2
27 Heladeria Cafetería La Fontana A2
28 Mercado Colón A1
29 Pizzaiola A2
30 Restaurante Maracuyá A2
31 Restaurante Mi Casa A2
32 Terra Amata A2

Nightlife ⬥

33 Scala Club A2
34 Vieja Habana Salsateca A2

Services ★

35 Automóvil Club de Chile B1
36 Banco del Estado A2
37 BBVA A2
38 Bolivian Consulate B2
39 Cambio Yanulaque A2
40 Casa de Cambio Moreno A2
41 Centro de Llamadas Sin Fronteras B2
42 Chile Express A2
43 Ciber Tux A2
44 Conaf B1
45 Cyber Pub A2
46 Dirección de Turismo A2
47 Hospital Dr. Juan Noé B1
48 La Moderna A2
49 Peruvian Consulate B1
50 Santander (ATM) A2
51 Scotiabank A2
52 Sernatur A2

Shopping 🛍

53 Casa de los Deportes B2
54 Gringo Surf shop A2

Sleeping 🛏

55 Hotel Arica A1
56 Hotel Bahía A1
57 Hotel El Paso A1
58 Hotel Huanta-Jaya B2
59 Hotel Lynch B1
60 Hotel Plaza Colón A2
61 Lamas Hostel B1
62 Residencias Don Luis B2
63 Residencias Real B2

Tours ♦

64 Mata Rangi A2
65 Raíces Andinas A2

Transportation 🚉

66 Arica - Tacna Train Station A2
67 Arica - La Paz Train Station A1
68 Avis B1
69 Budget A1
70 Hertz A1
71 LAN A1
72 Skyline A2
73 Terminal Rodoviario Nacional B1
74 Trans Paloma B1

NORTE GRANDE

HOLIDAYS AND FESTIVALS

January—Carnaval Andino Intichallampi
February—Andean carnaval with the Fuerza del Sol ceremonies
May—Fiesta de la Cruz de Mayo (Feast of the May Cross)
August—World Surfing Championship
September 18–19—Fiestas Patrias, marking Chile's independence. Updated: Jul 06, 2009.

Getting To and Away From Arica

BY BUS

Buses leave from Terminal Rodoviario Nacional to Chilean destinations (Av. Diego Portales 948. Tel: 56-58-241390). The terminal's services include phone, luggage storage, cafés, restrooms, money exchange and ATM (MasterCard, Cirrus, Visa, Plus, American Express). Passengers must pay a $0.20 boarding pass fee at the departure gate kiosk.

To Iquique: More than two dozen companies, including **Pullman Santa Rosa**, **Carmelita**, **Pullman Bus** and **TurBus** run frequent trips to the city ($12 – 15, 4.5 hours).

To Antofagasta: TurBus, **Pullman Bus** and a dozen other companies ($24 – 27, 9 – 10 hours) offer trips to the city.

To Calama: TurBus, **Pullman** and others ($24, 9 hours).

To Santiago: Carmelita (8 a.m.), **Pullman Bus** (9 a.m., 10:30 a.m., 2 p.m., 6 p.m.), **TurBus** and others ($62 – 66, 28 – 30 hours).

There are also buses to Valparaíso ($60 – 68, 24 hours), Coquimbo ($52, 20 hours) and other points between Arica and Santiago.

Purchase tickets to international destinations at the national terminal. Check to see from which depot the bus will depart.

Salta, Argentina, by way of Calama:
Pullman Bus (Monday, Tuesday, Saturday 9:30 p.m. ($76, 1 day / 1 night).
To Rio de Janeiro, São Paulo and Porto Alegre, Brazil: by way of Santiago, with **Chilebus**.

The international bus terminal is next door to the national depot. See Chile-Peru Border Crossings (p.194) and Chile-Bolivia Border Crossings (p.195) for more information. Transportation for villages closer to Arica leave from different points in the city.

To Valle de Azapa: Colectivo taxis leave from the corner of Chacabuco and Lynch (6 a.m. – 11 p.m., $1.90, 20 minutes).

To Valle de Lluta: Minibuses leave from Chacabuco 974-976 (Monday – Friday, four morning departures: 6 – 11 a.m., four afternoon depatures: 1 – 8 p.m., last back 10:30 p.m.; Saturday and Sunday 7 a.m., 8 a.m., four afternoon departures 12:30 – 7:30 p.m., last back 9:45 p.m, $4).

To Putre: Gutiérrez from Panadería Seria, Tucapel and Esteban Ríos; Monday, Wednesday, Friday 7 a.m. ($6, 3 hours), **Trans Paloma** (Germán Riesgo 2071. Tel: 56-58-222710; daily 7 a.m., $6, 3 hours).

To Belén: Trans Paloma (Tuesday, Friday 7 a.m., $6.60).

Trans Paloma also has services to Codpa, Tignamar, Socoroma, Zapahuira, Chapiquiña and other villages in the Precordillera de Belén.

BY TRAIN
The only train service from Arica runs to Tacna, Peru. It makes no stops between the two cities. **See Chile-Peru Border Crossings for full details.** There are plans to reopen the Arica-La Paz line again, with service as far as Villa Industrial. To keep up with the progress, visit: www.efe.cl.

BY AIR
Arica's airport, **Aeropuerto Internacional de Chacalluta**, is on the road to the Peruvian border (Km 18.5 Panamericana Norte s/n. Tel: 56-58-211116). **Lan** (Monday – Friday 9 a.m. – 1 p.m., 4 – 7 p.m., Saturday 9:30 a.m. – 1 p.m. Prat 391. Tel: 56-58-251641, URL: www.lan.com) and **Skyline** (Monday – Friday 9 a.m. – 1:30 p.m., 4 – 7 p.m.; Saturday 9:30 a.m. – 1 p.m. 21 de Mayo 356. Tel: 56-58-251816) have daily direct flights to Iquique (40 minutes) and twice daily to Santiago (2.5 hours). Updated: Oct 29, 2008.

Getting Around
Minibuses frequently run within the city and to surrounding areas. Many pass by 18 de Septiembre, including those for the national and international bus terminals ($0.70). Colectivo taxis have yellow license plates and run on set routes that are announced on a roof sign ($1). Routes 8, 10 and 11, or any that say "Avenida Santa María," go past the terminals. Radiotaxis, or the normal cab, have orange plates. They can be flagged down on the street or called ahead for $2.10. Many major car rental agencies operate in Arica: **Budget** (Colón 996. Tel: 56-58-259911, Fax: 56-58-258918, E-mail:

reservas@budget.cl, URL: www.budget.cl), **Hertz** (Baquedano 999. Tel: 56-58-231487), and **Avis** (Guillermo Sánchez 660, Tel: 56-58-228051). Updated: Oct 29, 2008.

Safety
Arica is prone to tsunamis. If one occurs while you are visiting, head for higher ground. Evacuation routes are posted throughout town; follow the instructions given by officials.

Many of the city's beaches are not suitable for swimming due to rocks or dangerous currents. Beware of jellyfish, especially on the southern beaches. Updated: Oct 29, 2008.

Services
TOURISM
Sernatur (Servicio Nacional de Turismo) has information on the entire Arica-Painacota and Tarapacá regions, as well as other parts of Chile (Monday – Friday 8:30 a.m. – 5:30 p.m. San Marcos 101. Tel: 56-58-252054, E-mail: infoarica@senatur.cl). The city has its own tourism office, **Dirección de Turismo** (Monday – Friday 8:30 a.m. – 5:30 p.m. Sotomayor 352. Tel: 56-58-206245 / 47, E-mail: aricaturistica@gmail.com, URL: www.municipalidaddearica.cl).

Other useful contacts in Arica are:

Conaf (Corporación Nacional Forestal, national park office)—Monday – Friday 8:30 a.m. – 5:30 p.m. Vicuña Mackenna 820. Tel: 56-58-201206 / 25-0750, URL: www.conaf.cl.

Carabineros (police)—Tel: 133 (emergency)

Automóvil Club de Chile—18 de Septiembre 1360, Tel: 25-4293)

Bolivian Consulate—Monday – Friday 9:30 a.m. – 2 p.m. Lynch 298. Tel: 58-3390.

Peruvian Consulate—18 de Septiembre 1554. Tel: 56-58-231020.

These nations also have consulates in Arica:
Austria—Sotomayor 169. Tel: 56-58-231274
Brazil—Las Margaritas 717
Denmark—General Lagos 559-571. Tel: 56-58-25-2234
Ecuador—LaTorre 565, office 404, 4th floor. Tel: 56-58-257086
Germany—Arturo Prat 391, 10th floor, office 101. Tel: 56-58-254663

Hungary—Tucapel 50
Italy—Chacabuco and San Martín
Norway—Blanco Encalada
Spain—Santa María 2660. Tel: 56-58-224655
Uruguay—21 de Mayo 345, office 45, Tel: 56-58-256686

MONEY

The pedestrian street 21 de Mayo is the financial heart of the city, with branches for all major banks present. Besides offering ATMs, most also change U.S. dollars and euros during business hours (Monday – Friday 9 a.m. – 2 p.m.):

Scotiabank (2 de Mayo 187)—ATM: MasterCard, Cirrus, Visa, Plus

Banco del Estado (2 de Mayo 228-238)—24-hour ATM: MasterCard, Cirrus

BBVA (21 de Mayo 402)—ATM: MasterCard, Cirrus, Visa, Plus
Santander (several along 21 de Mayo; ATM at 21 de Mayo 345)—ATM: Visa, Plus, MasterCard, Cirrus, American Express

Several exchange houses are also along this stretch, including Casa de Cambio

Walking Tour of Arica

The historical center of Arica is on Bolognesi, between San Marcos and 7 de Junio, near the base of El Morro. This area was destroyed by tidal waves in 1868 and 1877. Many of the buildings are from the late 19th century.

On Bolognesi, Iglesia San Marcos de Arica looks like a church from a model train set. This all-metal, neo-Gothic church (open daily 8 a.m. – 6 p.m.) was designed by the French architect-engineer Alexandre Gustave Eiffel (of Eiffel Tower fame). Arica's original temple, constructed of adobe with a straw roof, was swept away by the 1868 tsunami. At the time, the parts of the present church were in a warehouse in Ancón. In 1870, the Peruvian government ordered that it be erected in Arica. It was officially consecrated in 1876.

From Iglesia San Marcos, steps lead down to Parque Colón. This broad palm-tree-lined plaza has benches beneath bougainvillea trellices. The park is laid out in terraces leading to a fountain where birds and squirrels congregate. The final level of the plaza has a bust of Christopher Columbus.

The terraces of Parque Colón flow down to the newer part of the Plaza de Armas. A statue of Benjamín Vicuña Mackenna overlooks the sweeping space with evenly planted palms and a low fountain. This plaza is a favorite for families and skateboarders.

To the north of Parque Colón there is a small park honoring both the 100 years of peace since the Guerra del Pacífico and the Ariqueños who died during that war. A statue, El Roto, is dedicated to the "Genuine Expression of the Chilean Race."

The red metal, white-trimmed Gobernación de Arica is an Eiffel creation dating from 1876. It sits at the corner of Prat and San Marcos.

North on Calle Montt is another Eiffel building: the ex-Aduana, constructed between 1871 and 1874. Built from brick and quarried stone, it served as the customs headquarters until 1977 and is now the Casa de la Cultura, with rotating art galleries. Occasional theater, concerts and dance shows are performed in the amphitheater in front (Monday – Friday 8:30 a.m. – 5:30 p.m., Saturday, Sunday 10 a.m. – 4 p.m).

In the green space to the north there is a steam engine that was used on the Arica-La Paz rail line.

Finish your tour with a ceviche or seafood empanada in the fish market along the west side of the Arica-La Paz train station. Try La Chipola, which makes good *empanadas de jaiba-queso* (crab and cheese pies). Updated: Jul 06, 2009.

NORTE GRANDE

Moreno which changes U.S. dollars, euros, soles, bolivianos and pesos (daily 9 a.m. – 2:30 p.m., 4:30 – 9:30 p.m. 21 de Mayo 217). A few doors up there is a shopping gallery with several other exchange houses. **Cambio Yanulaque** changes American Express traveler's checks, but has poor rates (Monday – Friday 8 a.m. – 1:30 p.m., 4 – 8 p.m., Colón 388). **Chilexpress** is the major Western Union agent and pays transfers in pesos or dollars (Monday – Friday 9 a.m. – 7:30 p.m., Saturday 10 a.m. – 1 p.m. 21 de Mayo 335, URL: www.chileexpress.cl).

KEEPING IN TOUCH

Phone offices and Internet cafés are common in Arica's downtown area. Most are closed on Sunday. The more expensive ones are on the 21 de Mayo pedestrian mall. Internet averages $0.80 per hour. A few dependable ones are:

Ciber Tux (Monday – Saturday 10 a.m. – midnight. Bolognesi 370)—Sells snacks and refreshments; smoking allowed; children not permitted.
Cyber Pub (Monday – Friday 9 a.m. – 11 p.m., Saturday, Sunday, holidays 10 a.m. – 11 p.m. Sotomayor 275)—Has sandwiches and full bar; one of the few cafés open Sundays.

Centro de Llamadas Sin Fronteras charges $0.20 per minute for calls to the U.S., Canada and most European countries (Monday – Saturday 9 a.m. – 6 p.m. 21 de Mayo 601).

The post office, **Correos de Chile**, is in the Servicios Públicos building at the corner of Emilio Castro and Prat (Monday – Friday 8:30 a.m. – 2 p.m., 3:30 – 6:30 p.m., Saturday 9 a.m. – 12:30 p.m.).

MEDICAL

Arica's main health facility is **Hospital Dr. Juan Noé** (18 de Septiembre 1000, Tel: 56-58-230259). Many pharmacies are found along the pedestrian section of 21 de Mayo.

LAUNDRY

La Moderna charges $3.60 per kilo to wash, dry and iron clothes (Monday – Friday 9:30 a.m. – 2 p.m., 4:30 – 9 p.m., Saturday 9:30 a.m. – 2 p.m. 18 de Septiembre 457).

SHOPPING

The pedestrian malls (*paseos peatonales*) Bolognesi and Thompson are lined with small kiosks selling clothing, jewelry, woodworks, musical instruments and other crafts, as well as toys, books and CDs. The **Feria**

Internacional Máximo Lira next to the Arica-Tacna train station specializes in Peruvian and Bolivian woolens and artesanía. **Casa de Desportes El Gallo** stocks sleeping bags, insulation pads and some camping gear, but no tents (Monday – Friday 9:30 a.m. – 2 p.m., 5 – 9:30 p.m., Saturday 9:30 a.m. – 2 p.m., 6 – 9:30 p.m. Lynch 450, Tel: 56-58-232062). Updated: Jul 06, 2009.

Things to See and Do

Many travelers use Arica only as a watering hole, as a brief stop on the way to other destinations in the country, or to wait there a day before re-entering Peru or Bolivia. That being said, it does feature some attractions. Surfers know this is one of the best places to catch some challenging waves. On the beaches to the north and south of the city you can practice different sports, birdwatch or just work on your tan. Arica is also home to museums and buildings designed by Gustave Eiffel. The Valleys of Azapa and Lluta are not only major agricultural areas, but also have many geoglyphs and other reminders of long-ago civilizations. Updated: Jul 06, 2009.

El Morro de Arica and Museo Histórico y de Armas

(ADMISSION: $1.20, children $0.60) Arica's landmark, El Morro, is a thick cliff that rises up at the south edge of downtown. Since the founding of this Spanish port, El Morro has played a role in its defense. Its most important moment came in 1880, when it protected Peru from invading Chilean troops. The bluff offers a commanding view of the harbor; here you will find the Cristo de la Concordia monument, which commemorates the 1929 peace treaty between Chile and Peru. The Museo Histórico y de Armas, set in the trenches of a once-great fortress, features photos, arms and personal items from the Guerra del Pacífico, with discussions on the battles and background of the war. The museum also has armaments from more modern times, such as World War II. To get there, take the footpath that begins at the end of Colón. To drive up, follow Sotomayor. A cab, with half-hour wait, costs $10. No minibuses or collective taxis go up. (Open daily 8 a.m. – 8 p.m.). Updated: Oct 29, 2008.

Museo del Mar

(ADMISSION: Adults, $2, Children, $1) Museo del Mar's glass cases have more than one thousand varieties of caracoles. Don Nicolás has spent 50 years gathering what is said to be the largest such collection in Chile.

Most of the shells come from the Indo-Pacific Oceans; there are also some from the Caribbean and Mediterranean. Museo del Mar also has a small gift shop with postcards of prime specimens. Monday – Saturday 11 a.m. – 7 p.m. Sangara 315. URL: www.museodelmardearica.cl. Updated: Oct 29, 2008.

Museo Ferroviario

Museo Ferroviario de Arica is a must for train buffs—and for those who have never had a chance to learn about the railroad. Located inside a former train station, the museum displays items used by the Ferrocarril Arica-La Paz (FCALP) during its 82 years of operation. Everything is here, from generations of adding machines and telephones to forging tools and conductor caps. The open-air section has a 1906 Shunting locomotive, a crane and other implements. Steam engine 3317, made by the German firm Esslingen and used from 1927 to 1967, sits in the small park in front of the station. The guard, Bernardo Oliva, can show you around the museum. The station is also home to El Andén, an upscale restaurant. Monday – Friday 9 a.m. – 1 p.m, Arica-La Paz Train Station, 21 de Mayo 51. Tel: 56-58-232692. Updated: Oct 29, 2008.

Surfing in Arica

Arica is high on the list of surfing hotspots, and one of the southernmost places to practice on South America's Pacific Coast. The El Gringo and El Buey waves off Isla del Alacrán are world-famous challenges, for experts only. Other places to surf, bodyboard and windsurf are Playa El Chinchorro to the north and Playa La Lisera to the south. Every August an international surfing competition is held at Alacrán.

Several shops in downtown Arica can help you suit up, like **Gringo Surf** shop (Paseo Bolognesi 440. Tel: 56-58-252125, URL: www.gringosurfshop.cl). **El Gringo Coffee,** at the far end of Isla del Alacrán, rents and sells boards. **Magic Chile Surf School** is staffed by bilingual teachers and rents boards (Ginebra 3857, Playa Chinchorro. Tel: 56-58-311120. E-mail: surfcamp.magicchile@gmail.com, URL: www.surfschool.cl). Note, the water along this coast is cold, so a wetsuit is necessary. Updated: Jul 06, 2009.

Poblado Artesanal

Poblado Artesanal is a living and working artisan village on the south side of Arica. Founded in 1979, this brainchild of José Raúl Naranjo Menenses has white-washed huts with straw roofs. Painters, ceramicists (many using pre-Columbian designs), weavers and stone carvers all have workshops here where their creations may be purchased (daily 9:30 a.m. – 1:30 p.m., 3:30 – 8 p.m.). Poblado Artesanal also has an amphitheater, exhibit hall, gardens and restaurant. The church, a reproduction of one found in Parinacota, a village in the heart of Parque Nacional Lauca, has mass Sundays at 11 a.m. Collective taxis "U", 2, 8, 13, 18 and 23 ($1) and city buses 2, 7, 8, 9, 12, 14 and 16 pass the Poblado Artesanal. Hualles 2825. Tel: 56-58-228584 / 1290, E-mail: pobladoartesanal@gmail.com. Updated: Nov 08, 2008.

Isla del Alacrán

Isla del Alacrán, or Scorpion Island, was once an important source of fish and guano for indigenous tribes. In the 17th and 18th centuries the Spanish maintained a fort on the island to protect the royal storehouse (overflowing with Potosí silver and port) from pirate attacks. The fort was destroyed by the 1868 tsunami, but its ruins remain and can be explored. In 1964 the isle officially became ex-Isla del Alacrán when local officials built a causeway that connected it with the mainland, causing a decrease in birds using it for resting and nesting grounds. Even so, Alacrán is still a good place to observe birds and explore tidal pools. It is also one of Chile's most popular places to surf; the formidable El Gringo and El Buey waves draw competitors from around the world every August.

It is safest to visit the island during daylight hours. To get to the island, walk five minutes south on Avenida Comandante San Martín to the causeway that leads to the island. Café El Gringo, on the island's west end, rents boards and serves snacks as well as drinks. Updated: Nov 08, 2008.

Northern Beaches and the Desembocadura de Lluta

There are several beaches for swimming and surfing to the north of Arica. The 2km **El Chinchorro** is the best place to catch a wave or to take a dip. Along the waterfront boardwalk, families can rent tandem bicycles. An old pier juts out across the platinum-blue sea and, though a sign warns to stay off, many sneak on to drop a fishing line. Playa Chinchorro has restaurants, hotels and a surfing shop.

At **Playa Las Machas**, the USS Wateree, a Civil War-era ship that formed part of the U.S. South Pacific fleet. The August 13, 1868,

NORTE GRANDE

tsunami washed the original ship three kilometers (1.8 miles) inland. Since it was still intact, the ship served as a hospital and later as a first-class hotel. The 1877 tidal wave ripped it apart and hauled it off the shore. Its fate, then, was to be used for target practice during the Guerra del Pacífico, before being dismantled. Today, only the boilers remain.

Playa Las Machas is a broad, unshaded beach and the sea is strong. Swimming is inadvisable. Free camping is allowed across from the carabineros base. A family provides bath services ($0.25) and has a small shop.

A half-hour walk north leads to the Desembocadura de Lluta, or the mouth of the Lluta River. This estuary is a protected area conserving an important biodiversity zone. It is also a birdwatchers paradise, with North American birds resting here on their yearly migrations and many resident sea and shore birds, including gulls, plovers, herons, ducks and coots.

To reach Chinchorro, take a collective taxi with a green "U" sign from Calle Lynch ($1) or a number 12 or 14 minibus from 18 de Septiembre ($0.70). Some bay boat tours go to the beaches. Updated: Oct 29, 2008.

Southern Beaches

South of Isla del Alacrán a chain of beaches drapes the coast south of Arica and have a different character than the northern chain of beaches. Here, ancient lava flows have created rocky shores with stretches of black sand called *balnearios*. Many birds can be observed between these beaches, which are also great for soaking up sun, playing volleyball and observing tidal pools.

El Laucho (1.5 km/ 1 mi south of Arica) has a pleasant terraced boardwalk, several restaurants and discos.

Playa La Lisera (2 km/ 1.2 mi from Arica) is named for its abundance of lisa fish. The circular bay is almost completely enclosed, forming a tranquil pool. This beach is frequented by families. A multi-level malecón with gardens runs along La Lisera.

Playa Brava is a rocky cove perfect for birding and tidal-pooling.

Playa Arenillas Negras, a long stretch of ebony sand washed by harsh currents, is three kilometers (1.8 mi) south of the city. This beach ends with the lookout point

Mirador Abilio Gutiérrez Porta. Another six kilometers or so further, beyond the point, is Playa Corazones. A 20-minute walk from this southernmost beach leads to Cueva de Azota, which has ancient rock paintings.

The beaches can be reached via a paved foot and biking path. Most of them have signage indicating that they are not suitable for swimming. El Laucho and La Lisera have lifeguards (in season). Beware of jellyfish.

Playa Arenillas Negras is a rather popular campground in summer. The city provides portable bath facilities. Some daring folks go sand-boarding on the dunes along the road. Updated: Jul 06, 2009.

Other Adventure Sports

Out in the desert, up on the hills and under the waves, thrill seekers have plenty of ways to get their adrenaline pumping.

Paragliding, or parapente, is one way to get a unique view of the geoglyphs in the valleys around Arica. Try outfitters **Arica en Vuelo** (CC Parque Colón, local 44-45. Tel: 56-58-252064, E-mail: gargola2002chile@yahoo.com) or **Parapente Arica** (Punta del Este 603, La Lisera. Tel: 56-58-250081, E-mail: raulgliders@hotmail.com).

Scuba diving will give you a view of the world under Arica's waves and let you scope out sunken ships. Recommended dive shops are **Amauta Sub** (Maipú 1001. Tel: 56-58-205440 / 255501, E-mail: amawtasub@hotmail.com) and **Arica Scuba** (Tel: 58-9-2131252 / 58-8-4975028, E-mail: aricascuba@gmail.com, URL: www.aricascuba.com).

Yamabushi Adventure offers rappelling in the mountains east of the city (Ignacio Vergara 589. Tel: 58-8-6235964, E-mail: lambertvanbattenburg@yahoo.es). Updated: Jul 06, 2009.

Bay Tours

Several companies leaving from the Muelle Pesquero offer boating tours ($2 to $24 per person) around the beautiful bay. The more basic trips, which last an hour, take their passengers to fishing grounds and other areas important to Arica's economy, past nearby beaches and to habitats of birds and sea lions. Longer sojourns are three to four hours long and take more time to explore the coastal and sea fauna, including colonies of Humboldt penguins. Updated: Nov 08, 2008.

Tours

Many of the tour operators who offer excursions to Parque Nacional Lauca, Reserva Nacional Las Vicuñas, Salar de Surire and other areas are concentrated along Paseo Peatonal Bolognesi and Thompson. This makes comparing prices and trips convenient. To get a cheaper price, you may have to wait a few days for the company to gather a group for your destinations. At the Muelle Pesquero in the port there are agencies that offer boating tours of the bay. Updated: Oct 18, 2008.

Mata Rangi

Mata Rangi is the one company that offers tours of Arica's bay with a focus on birdwatching. The basic one-hour tour visits bird colonies of Inca tern, boobies, cormorant, gulls, pelican, elegant tern and black-crowned night herons, as well as sea lions. The four-hour Pingüinos en el Desierto excursion (daily at 10 a.m.) goes down the coast to a Humboldt penguin colony, observing other birds and sea lions along the way. The outing ends with a picnic on the beach north of Corazones. The guide speaks Spanish; the captain speaks Spanish and English. Mata Rangi also has a tasty restaurant that specializes in seafood. Bay tour: $24 for one person, $10 per additional person. Penguin tour: two people ($80) to six people ($160). Máximo Lira 501, Muelle Pesquero. Tel: 56-9-682-5005, E-mail: turismomarino@gmail.com, URL: www.turismomarino.com. Updated: Oct 29, 2008.

Raices Andinas

One recommended tour operators in Arica, Raices Andinas takes groups of up to six people to Parque Nacional Lauca: four-day trip visits Reserva Nacional Las Vicuñas and Laguna Salar Surire before swinging down to Colchane, Parque Nacional Isluga, Giant of Atacama and Humberstone. Tours of five to nine days can also be arranged. All trips include lodging, food, transport, entrance fees and guide (English or French-speaking upon request at no extra charge). It is best to contact Raices Andinas by e-mail, since the office has irregular hours. Paseo Thompson, local 21. Tel: 56-58-233305 / Skype: raicesandinas, E-mail: info@raicesandinas.com, URL: www.raicesandinas.com / www.chilephotos.com. Updated: Oct 29, 2008.

Lodging

The diversity of hotels in Arica is as broad as its visitors: everyone from international businesspeople to families on vacation to backpacker will find a place to fit their needs. Cheaper lodging is in the center of town, along Sotomayor, Baquedano and Maipú streets. Camping is another option for backpackers with gear, especially during the summer months. Playa Las Machas has all-year sites; camping is also permitted at Playa La Lisera. In Villa Frontera, six kilometers (3.6 mi) north of Arica, near Playa Las Machas are several campgrounds. Senatur tourism office has a complete list of these. Updated: Oct 24, 2008.

Hotel Lynch

(ROOMS: $6 – 16) From the outside, the three-story Hotel Lynch looks rather non-descript, but the inside is like a beach resort. Rooms on the top floor share clean, bleach-scented bathrooms. On the other floors there are rooms with private bath and cable TV. Umbrella-shaded tables line the patio. Lynch 589. Tel: 56-58-231581. Updated: Nov 03, 2008.

Residencias Real

(ROOMS: $8 –$20) Residencias Real is one of the least expensive hostels in Arica. Its rooms are clean, large and amply furnished with nice touches like built-in shelves for stowing luggage, cable TV and a reading lamp. Even though the rooms are decked with two or three beds, the lone travelers are welcome. All rooms share common baths with hot water upon request. Rooms in the back on the second floor are airy and light. These share a small balcony patio. Sotomayor 578. Tel: 56-58-253359. Updated: May 29, 2009.

V!VA ONLINE REVIEW
RESIDENCIAS REAL

Good for backpackers. An excellent, cheap place. The owner is very friendly and helpful. Comfortable beds!

May 27, 2009

Residencias Don Luis

(ROOMS: $10 – 20) Painted on the yellow wall of Residencias Don Luis is a sign that reads "$10 per person, private bath, kitchen, living room with DVD and the latest movies". It sounds like a budget traveler's dream—until you enter. A musty smell fills the reception. Despite the sign's listed price, rooms are $20 with private bath and single or double bed. Upstairs rooms have partitions and missing window panes covered with thin boards. The staircase carpeting is threadbare. Better bargains can be found in Arica. Sotomayor 757. Tel: 56-58-252668. Updated: Nov 03, 2008.

Lamas Hostal

(ROOMS: $13 – 26, BEDS: $8) Lamas Hostel is a hostel/guesthouse located in downtown Arica near the Arica hospital and business area of the city, on the corner of Gallo and Sotomayor, and is one block south of pedestrian street 21 Mayo. Lamas hostel has 22 rooms with private bathroom, cable TV, and WiFi. Other services include payphone, fax, photocopier and a working business area with desk and computer. There is a cafeteria with soft drinks and snacks, all at affordable prices. There are entrances at both Gallo 281 and Sotomayor 884. Arturo Gallo 281. Tel: 56-5-8253461, Fax: 56-58-253461, E-mail: lamashostal@hotmail.com, URL: www.lamashostal.webs.com. Updated: Jun 30, 2009.

Hotel Bahía

(ROOMS: $15 – 110) On the beach between downtown Arica and Playa Chinchorro, Hotel Bahía has Mediterranean-style architecture set in a palm-shaded estate. All 16 of its rooms have sea views and a balcony (or patio, if you're on the first floor). The simply furnished rooms are spacious with common or private bath. Hotel Bahía also provides excursions to Parque Nacional Lauca, as well as mountain biking, horseback riding and birdwatching. It is a half-kilometer (0.3 mi) from the bus terminals and the train station. Av. Luis Berotta Porcel 2031. Tel: 56-58-260676, E-mail: info@bahiahotel.cl / latinor@entelchile.net, URL: www.bahia-hotel.cl. Updated: Nov 03, 2008.

Hostal Huanta-Jaya

(ROOMS: $16 – 32) Huanta-Jaya doesn't offer much beyond a place to lay your head, though everything is very neat and the staff is friendly. All rooms have sufficient space, good beds and baths with hot water. However, the price doesn't include breakfast; you can ask for hot water to prepare your own food in the dining room. The hostel is a half-block from the pedestrian portion of 21 de Mayo and away from car traffic. 21 de Mayo 660. Tel: 56-58-314605, E-mail: hostal.huanta.jaya@gmail.com. Updated: Nov 03, 2008.

Hotel Plaza Colón

(ROOMS: $37 – 53) Hotel Plaza Colón, a pink and blue five-story building with white balconies, is a half-block from Eiffel's church. This three-star hostel will suit the more discerning tourist or businessperson. All 31 rooms come with a balcony and are well decorated. The clean baths have both tub and shower. There's a small seating area for breakfast, or you can have your meal in the fifth-floor restaurant with great views of El Morro and the bay. The hotel features ramps and an elevator for less-mobile guests. San Marcos 261. Tel: 56-58231244 / 254424, E-mail: hotel_plaza_colon@entelchile.net, URL: www.hotelplaza-colon.cl. Updated: Jul 06, 2009.

Hotel El Paso

(ROOMS: $83 – 165) Opened in 1962 for the World Cup, Hotel El Paso is a four-star retreat set on three hectares of gardens overflowing with palms, hibiscus and bougainvillea. The hotel has tennis and volleyball courts, as well as swimming pools. The newer wings of bungalows have suites with larger bathrooms, sitting areas and patios. The hotel is between the Universidad de Tarapacá and Casino de Arica. Av. General Veláquez 1109. Tel: 56-58-230808, Fax: 23-1965, E-mail: reservashotel@hotelelpaso.cl, URL: www.hotelelpaso.cl. Updated: Nov 03, 2008.

Hotel Arica

(ROOMS: $170 – 340) Between Playa El Laucho and Playa La Lisera, Hotel Arica is much more than the city's most exclusive hotel. It is also a resort with a spa, two swimming pools (one for adults and one for children), tennis courts and mini-golf. This is a place to have fun in the sun. It isn't all rest and relaxation here, though, as Hotel Arica also provides complete convention facilities. Standard rooms have all the staples: minibar, cable TV and private bath. Superior rooms have a sitting area and balcony with sea view. Península, the hotel's restaurant, has a commanding view of El Morro. The cabañas provide more secluded accommodations. Av. Comandante San Martín 599. Tel: 56-58-254540, Fax: 56-58-231133, E-mail: reservas@hotelarica.cl, URL: www.panamericanahoteles.cl. Updated: Nov 03, 2008.

Restaurants

After months in Peru or Bolivia, be prepared for the sticker shock of Chile. The lunch special (usually served 1 – 3 p.m.) costs $2.40 – 4.20 for a simple two-course meal (soup and main) and $4.20 – 20 for a more elaborate affair (drinks rarely included). À la carte is much more expensive. Seafood is the thing to try and often makes an appearance on even the cheaper eateries' daily specials. Some local delicacies are empanadas de jaiba-queso and *sopa marinera* (seafood soup). The nightlife in Arica continues until the early morning hours, with many bars staying open until the roosters crow.

If you're eating on a budget, look for the cheaper diners around and inside the market areas. Some allow you to order only the *plato fondo* (main dish). The old mercado central is at Sotomayo 340 and the larger Mercado Colón at Calle Colón and Maipú. Express Líder supermarket, at 18 de Septiembre and Baquedano, is open Monday – Saturday 9 a.m. – 10:30 p.m. Fish markets are on Máximo Lira, next to the Arica-La Paz train station, and on the muelle pesquero.

Beware of establishments that write a suggested tip on the bill. Not only is this considered crass by Chilean standards, it is also illegal. Tips are purely voluntary. Updated: Oct 24, 2008.

Restaurant Mi Casa
(MEALS: $3.20 – 3.60) Restaurant Mi Casa is a pleasant surprise among the budget dining scene in Arica. Set in an older home, Mi Casa features rooms off a long corridor. With golden-colored walls and clothed tables, the ambiance, plus the smart service and excellent food, are qualities you might expect to see in upscale bistros rather than in a place for the budget-conscious. Monday – Saturday 12:30 – 6:30 p.m. San Marcos 370. Tel: 56-58-317099. Updated: Jul 06, 2009

Pizzaiola
(PIZZA: $6 – 10) Whether you're coming for the daily lunch special or a menu item, Pizzaiola is a good place to have a relaxed meal while watching the world go by. There are 21 varieties of pizza–the smallest is large enough for one starving person or two with more moderate appetites. Happy hour is celebrated with imported beer. Pizzaiola is one of the few restaurants on the 21 de Mayo mall that is open Sundays. Breakfast $2.60 – 4.20, lunch special $5 – 5.60. daily 9 a.m. – 11:30 p.m. 21 de Mayo 174. Tel: 56-58-256881. Updated: Nov 03, 2008.

El Andén
(LUNCH: $7 – 8) This fine dining restaurant is on the platform of the old Arica-La Paz station, allowing diners to eat while waiting for the train to come in. Supreme Chilean dishes from land and sea grace the menu. The gastronomic journey begins with a tray of appetizers, the next stop is the main course and the meal ends with a tray of desserts. Drinks, whether aperitifs, wine or other, are extra. The patio dining area features a steam engine, handcarts and other remnants of the rail line. Daily 1 p.m. – 3 p.m. 21 de Mayo 51, Arica-La Paz Train Station. Tel: 58-7-8132192. Updated: Nov 03, 2008.

El Molino Viejo
(ENTREES: $7 – 12) The interior of El Molino Viejo recreates the feeling of an old mill-turned-restaurant, but with a touch of class. Pine-paneled walls, a long counter and a large table dominate the front space. The sunny back room has more intimate arrangements. This bistro is a favorite with Ariqueño businesspeople, for the quick service and generous portions. The three-course daily lunch menu includes a drink ($4.60). El Molino is open also for mid-morning breakfasts or early dinners. Monday – Friday 10:30 a.m. – 4 p.m., Saturday 10:30 a.m. – 5 p.m. San Marco 285. Updated: Nov 03, 2008.

Terra Amata
(ENTREES: $11.40 – 20) The blue and white Mediterranean-looking building that spirals like a seashell beneath El Morro is Terra Amata, one of Arica's finest restaurants. Its large windows flood the restaurant with sun during the day and provide a view of the harbor at night. The menu features novo-Chilean dishes, including lamb and seafood, which come with a selection of sauces. Desserts like Boa Boa—seasonal fruits flambéed in orange liqueur served over cinnamon ice cream—are a perfect ending. Lunch special $10 – 18. Monday – Saturday 1 – 3:30 p.m., 8:30 p.m. – 1 a.m. Yungay 201. Tel: 56-58-259057, E-mail: terraamata_arica@utr.net. Updated: Jul 06, 2009.

V!VA ONLINE REVIEW
TERRA AMATA

Very good dinner, good meal, excellent service, good value!!

May 11, 2009

Café Latino
Café Latino is one of four cheap eateries in a row next to the Express Líder supermarket. Like its neighbors (one of which specializes in Chinese food), Café Latino

is a step above a shack. The menu always includes several choices of down-home Chilean food hot from the kitchen and the option to order a one- to three-course meal. On Sundays there's a soup made of clams, mussels and other seafood. Daily from 9 a.m. – 9 p.m. 18 de Septiembre 431. Tel: 56-58-254615. Updated: Nov 03, 2008.

Heladería-Cafetería La Fontana

Finding a cup of real coffee can be difficult in Arica. Everyone seems to serve instant and charge a premium price. Heladería-Cafetería La Fontana, though, serves espresso and other machine-made java. The strong, hot *"expres"* comes with a wafer cookie and sparkling water. Try a bowl of one of the two dozen flavors of homemade ice cream, including the intriguing *cocha* (toasted wheat) and *malta con huevo* (malt drink with egg). Ice cream $2.40 – 3, coffee and other drinks $1 – 2. Monday – Friday 9:30 a.m. – 7 p.m., Saturday 11 a.m. – 2:30 p.m. Bolognesi 320. Updated: Nov 03, 2008.

Govindas

Introducing Arica to the vegetarian lifestyle, this simple, two-room diner serves up a delicious, Indian-style three-course lunch, including salad, soup and main course with a drink. The furnishings are creative recyclings: old phone cable spools turned into tables and chairs. Service is friendly and relaxed. Govindas also is a yoga ashram where travelers can work out kinks and stress. Govindas devotees sell whole-grain bread along 21 de Mayo. San Marcos 200. Tel: 56-8-3283937 / 9-9064402, E-mail: danisthapriyada@hotmail.com / yoga_arica@hotmail.com, URL: www.larevoluciondelacuchara.org. Updated: Nov 03, 2008.

Restaurant Maracuyá

In an old beach house between Arica and Playa El Laucho you'll find one of the city's most prestigious bistros, Restaurant Maracuyá. There are ocean views from the dining halls and even better ones from the verandas. Maracuyá's menu specializes in international- and national-style preparations of the finest fish and seafood. Four-course meals with wine or other drinks and after-dinner coffee cost $22 – 32. Daily 12:30 – 4 p.m., 8:30 p.m. – 1 a.m. Av. Comandante San Martín 0321. Tel: 56-58-227600, E-mail: reserves@restaurantmaracuya.cl, URL: www.restaurantmaracuya.cl. Updated: Jul 06, 2009.

Nightlife

Scala Club

Scala Club is a classy old place that doubles as a karaoke bar. The anteroom has couches and overstuffed chairs in dim corners. The century-old carved wood bar, decked with wine and martini glasses, stocks the finest liquors. People sing along to videos played on a giant screen in the main hall. The playlist isn't only latino hits—plenty of English ones make the grade, too. Monday – Saturday 5 p.m. – 5 a.m. Bolognesi 367. Tel: 56-58-230416 / 233837. Updated: Nov 03, 2008.

Vieja Habana Salsoteca

(DRINKS: $2 – 4) This salsateca takes it name from Cuban son rhythms that helped giver birth to the dance nearly a century ago. Son, cumbia, reggaetón and tropical dance music has a home here. This is *the* place in Arica to to dance the night away. Friday, Saturday and holidays midnight – 4:30 a.m. 21 de Mayo 487. Tel: 56-58-231674 / 9-849-1236. Updated: Oct 24, 2008.

Border Crossing to Peru

The only official border crossing between Chile and Peru is between Arica and Tacna.

BY BUS

The border road is called Chacalluta on the Chile side and Santa Rosa in Peru. It is about a kilometer (0.6 mi) between the two posts. Border hours are Sunday – Thursday 8 a.m. – 8 p.m. (Chilean time), Friday and Saturday 24 hours. Buses pause at each border post to go through immigration and customs procedures. Change money in Peru as there are more curreny exchanges and the rates are better.

Buses to the Peru border depart from the international terminal on Avenida Diego Portales, next to the national rodoviario. *Busetas* (minibuses) leave from the left side of the terminal (daily 7 a.m. – 9 p.m., $3, 1.5 hours). *Colectivos* (shared taxis) leave from the right side of the terminal (daily 7 a.m. – 9 p.m., $6, 1 hour).

BY TRAIN

From Arica, an *autovagón* (rail bus) leaves at 9 a.m. and 7 p.m. for Tacna, Peru. Tickets can be bought the same day; however, you're better off buying them in advance. Sales are Monday – Saturday 10 a.m. – noon, 4 – 6 p.m. The fare Monday – Friday is $2.40, on Saturday and holidays, the price is $3.20 (1 hour 15 minutes). Immigration and customs procedures are performed at the train station in both countries. Arica's train station is located along the sea front (Máximo Lira 791, Tel: 56-58-231115). In Tacna the station is at Avenida Gregorio Albarracín 412 (Tel: 56-58-247126). Updated: Jun 29,2009

Border Crossing to Bolivia

In winter, Chile and Bolivia are on the same time; in the summer, Bolivia is one hour behind. About a half-dozen companies have buses that depart from Arica's international terminal on Avenida Diego Portales, next to the national rodoviario, heading to La Paz and other Bolivian cities. International buses from Iquique involve a transfer in Arica (for La Paz) or in Calama (for Oruro and Uyuni).

To Visvirí: The road to the Visvirí border goes by Painacota. The highway is accessible all year. The border is open 8 a.m. – 8 p.m. Buses leave Tuesday and Friday 7 a.m. ($14).

To Chungará / Tambo Quemado: This is the major route to La Paz. Most companies leave between 8 and 10:30 a.m. and midnight to 2 a.m. ($12 – 18, 8 hours). Buses stop at the respective border posts. Some companies continue to Oruro ($14), Cochabamba ($18) and Santa Cruz ($24). The border post is open daily 8 a.m. – 8 p.m.

Other crossings accessible from Arica do not have public transportation. However, you may cross them in a private vehicle. They include Colchane-Pisiga (paved; daily 8 a.m. – 8 p.m.), Apochete de Irpa or Cancoso (you will need a *salvoconducto* from the Policía Internacional in Iquique; gravel road; daily 8 a.m. –8 p.m.). Updated: Jul 02, 2009.

AROUND ARICA
VALLE DE AZAPA

Valle de Azapa lies east of Arica, along the banks of the Río San José. This is the most renowned olive-producing region of Chile, with groves dating back to the 17th century. In recent decades, farmers here have also started growing tomatoes and tropical fruits like mangos, *maracuyás* (passion fruit) and *guayabas* (guava). Humans have lived in this river valley for many millennia. The Chinchorro people left behind some of

the oldest known mummies, which can be seen in the Museo San Miguel de Azapa. Indigenous geoglyphs and petroglyphs still decorate the hillsides. The Museo Arqueológico's website has an excellent map of the valley's archaeological sites.

Two roads head into the Valle de Azapa. Ruta A-27 is the more direct road to the Museo Arqueológico and the village of San Miguel de Azapa. It runs along the north side of the Río San José. Cerro Chuño is at the very beginning of this road, to the distant left. The most notable works are of a man wearing a loincloth and feathers.

A few kilometers south of Rotonda M. Castillo (Las Gredas and Av. 18 de Septiembre), off the Pan-American Highway (Ruta 5), the Camino a Cerro Sombrero (Ruta A-33 or Ruta Arquelógica) passes at the feet of numerous hills displaying ancient artistry. Fourteen panels of geometric, anthropomorphic and zoomorphic rock designs are scraped and chipped into mountain rock on the southern edge of the river valley. All the archaeological sites are marked with tall white obelisks.

Cerro Sombrero, the first sight along A-33 , shows a human herding a group of llamas. These drawings date from the Cultura Arica period (1000 – 1400 AD). Golfing enthusiasts wanting to try their hand at a course composed entirely of sand may stop for a round at the **Club de Golf Río Lluta**, an 18-hole, Par 72 course (Camino Cerro Sombrero, Tel: 56-58-223377 / 22-6935, E-mail: valentincubillos@hotmail.com).

On Atoca hill you can see another caravan of llamas with a guide and two dancers, presumably representing the traders connecting the coast and highlands. After Atoca, there is a road heading south at the foot of Cerro Sombrero, home to the greatest concentration of geoglyphs from the Cultura Arica era, including a stylized puma and other animals. An excellent view of these designs can be seen from Túmulos de San Miguel, approximately one kilometer further down A-33. This site is also called Alto Ramírez for the cultural phase from which these date (400 BC – 400 AD). The side road leading up to the hilltop gazebo passes by a quadrangular sun drawn on another hillock.

On Ruta A-33 there are signaled turnoffs for a second Zona Túmulos (burial sites; 2 km / 1.2 mi) and Púkara San Lorenzo (another 2 km / 1.2 mi). This púkara city dates back to the Tiwanaku period (300-1100 AD), a time of great pan-Andean integration.

From the Túmulos-Púkara turnoff, Ruta A-33 turns northward, going through Las Maitas village and crossing Río San José before joining with Ruta A-27, just before the **Museo Arqueológico San Miguel de Azapa (**ENTRANCE FEE: adults $2, children 6 – 17 years old $1). The museum has excellent chronological displays that take you from the first human settlements 10,000 years ago to the colonial olive plantation that once thrived on these grounds. On exhibition are the oldest mummies yet uncovered and very fine weaving from later periods. Another series of galleries explain the Aymara culture. The museum has free guidebooks in six languages. At the end of the museum road is a private hummingbird farm (irregular hours, entry by donation). March – December daily 10 a.m. – 6 p.m., January – February daily 9 a.m. – 8 p.m., closed January 1, May 1, September 18, December 25. Tel: 56-58-205555, Fax: 56-58-205552, E-mail: museo@uta.cl, URL: www.uta.cl/masma.

A half-kilometer (0.3 mi) east on A-27 is the village of San Miguel de Azapa (12 km / 7.2 mi from Arica). Its 17th-century church, at the end of Calle los Misioneros, was one of the first erected in the region. The cemetery dates back to pre-Columbian times. San Miguel celebrates its patron saint, Archangel Saint Michael, on September 29.

Ruta A-27 winds into the Precordillera foothills to the Sendero de la Virgen de las Peñas near Livircar. Her feast day is observed the first week of October and again on December 8.

Lodging and dining opportunities are slim in the Valle de Azapa. **Hotel del Valle**, near Arica, is the only place to stay (Camino Azapa 3221, Tel: 56-58-241296, Fax, 56-58-241328, E-mail: hoteldelvalle@ nemhparx.cl). There are no hotels in San Miguel. Most restaurants are located either at the beginning of Ruta A-33 near Cerro Sombrero (**Los Hornitos** and **Rancho don Floro**) or in San Miguel de Azapa. Don't forget to pick up some olives and other produce from the local farmers.

Single men traveling in Valle de Azapa may be warned by locals about the Novia de Azapa, a legendary bride phantom searching for her lost groom. Updated: Jul 06, 2009.

Getting To and Away From- Valle de Azapa

Rutas A-27 and A-33 are the main access roads to the valley. Side roads connect them at Cerro Sombrero and near the museum. A half-kilometer (0.3 mi) past San Miguel village is another road that goes to Poconchile in the Valle de Lluta.

Colectivo taxis leave from the corner of Chacabuco and Lynch in Arica (daily 6 a.m. – 11 p.m., $1.90, 20 minutes). These collective cabs usually take A-27 directly to the museum, which means you will miss out on seeing the geoglyphs. If you are into doing a bit of walking, catch a cherry-red buseta with a sign reading "Cerro Sombrero" from Avenida 18 de Septiembre in Arica ($0.60). Be sure to tell the driver you want to go to the geoglifos. From where the bus route ends it is a six-kilometer (3.6 mi) walk to the museum. Updated: Jun 24, 2009.

VALLE DE LLUTA

Valle de Lluta is one of the breadbaskets of northern Chile. Farmers here grow corn, alfalfa, *haba* (fava bean), onion and other crops

The main road through the valley is Ruta CH-11, located about 10 kilometers (6 mi) north of Arica on Ruta 5 (the Pan-American Highway). This major highway winds along the Río Lluta, across the river valley into the Precordillera (foothills), to Putre and Parque Nacional Lauca and the Chungará / Tambo Quemado border crossing into Bolivia. The road follows the old Arica-La Paz rail line.

There are two large panels of geoglyphs along the south side of the highway, between Kms 13 and 15. The first group of figures portrays an eagle, a dove and llamas. The second set represents humans.

Eco-Truly, near the hamlet of Linderos (Km 29), is an ecological retreat run by the Hare Krishna. The centerpiece is the high, egg-shaped temple where meditation and yoga classes are held. Eco-Truly has several smaller huts of similar design where guests may stay ($12 per person, including breakfast). Camping is also allowed ($4 per person). Eco-Truly also has a vegetarian restaurant ($3 – 5 per meal), organic farm, anti-stress therapy sessions and ecotours of the grounds (Tel: 56-8-3532350 / 9-342-7123, E-mail:

info@ecotruly-arica.org / tierradorada@
hotmail.com, URL: www.ecotruly-arica.org
/ www.yogainbound.org).

Poconchile, a colonial village, sits at
Kilometer 37 (altitude: 598 m / 1,944 ft,
population: 6,090). The town's Iglesia
San Jerónimo is a national monument.
Founded in 1605, the white-washed church
was rebuilt in the 19th Century with twin
wooden bell towers. Also of interest in Poconchile is its stone and wood railroad station. Villagers celebrate San Jerónimo on
October 30 and San José on March 19.

There are several lookouts over the Valley of
Lluta and the Andean foothills a few kilometers past Poconchile. Los Molinos (altitude:
850 m / 2,763 ft) is at Kilometer 52 and has
an 18th century adobe church with wood
campaniles. The surrounding countryside
provides hiking and birdwatching opportunities. Updated: Jun 22, 2009.

Getting To and Away From Valle de Lluta

Minibuses leave Arica from Chacabuco 974-
976 (Monday – Friday four departures, 6 –
11 a.m., four afternoon departures 1 – 8 p.m.,
last back 10:30 p.m.; Saturday and Sunday
7 a.m., 8 a.m., four afternoon buses 12:30 –
7:30 p.m., last back 9:45 p.m., $4).

Alternately, you can take any bus going to Putre
or the Chile-Bolivian border; all pass through
Valle del Lluta. Updated: Jun 19, 2009.

PRECORDILLERA DE BELÉN

East of Arica the land suddenly rises up to
the foothills of the soaring Andean mountains. At an altitude of over 3,000 meters
(9,750 ft), the Precordillera de Belén lies at
the base of the range. A chain of scattered
villages—from Putre to Codpa—stretches
across the plains. The landscape is desolate
for miles between, with pre-Incan fortresses,
and roaming rhea and vicuña.

Ruta CH-11, the international highway to
La Paz, passes through the Valle de Lluta
before climbing into the Precordillera. **Pukará de Copaquilla,** a pre-Incan fortress
from the 12th century, is at Km 90. The fortress has a double wall of volcanic rock surrounding some 400 round structures with
stone floors, which were perhaps corrals or
defensive parapets. Another important set

of ruins is **Tambo de Zapahuira,** from the
Inca period (around 1470 AD). The ruins are
located at Km 111 on Ruta CH-11, near the
crossroads with Ruta A-35.

This tambo was a principal rest stop along
the coast-highland route. It has two types
of stone buildings: rectangular, which were
administrative offices, and round, which
were for lodging.

A *camino del Inca,* or stone road used
by pre-Inca and Inca traders, connects
Zapahuira with Socorama (population:
132, altitude: 3,250 m / 1,0563 ft). This
pre-Columbian hamlet was later used by
Spanish merchants as they traveled the
Arica-Potosí route. The adobe church,
built in 1560, has an adobe and stone
altar, four silver-crowned statues and four
paintings of the Cuzqueña School. From
Ruta CH-11, Socorama is nine kilometers
(5.4 mi) north of Zapahuira, then five kilometers (3 mi) off the main highway.

From Zapahuira, the unpaved Ruta A-35
heads south to the small Aymara pueblos
of the Precordillera de Belén. After seven
kilometers (4.2 mi), a two-kilometer
(1.2-mi) side road arrives at **Portezuelo
de Murmuntani** where many women
weave.

The first village on Ruta A-35 is **Chapi-
guiña,** 17 kilometers (10.5 mi) into the
hills. **Belén,** 17 kilometers (10.5 mi) further on, is the main settlement of the foot-
hill region. This cobblestone village was
founded by the Spaniards in 1625. It was
a major stop on the Potosí -Azapa-Arica
trek. Two churches face its plaza: Iglesia
Nuestra Señora de Belén, the smaller and
older one, and Iglesia Nuestra Señora del
Carmen, built in the 18th century, which
has a Baroque façade. Within the sanctuary are over 20 saintly statues and a carved
wooden altar screen. Not too far from the
town is another pre-Hispanic fortress, the
Pukará de Belén. The next two hamlets
down A-35, **Lupica** and **Saxamar,** also
have pukarás associated with them.

Ticnamar (also spelled Tignamar), 20 kilometers (12 mi) from Belén, is the next town of
note, famous for its woolen artesanía and religious festivals, which include Carnaval, Cruz de
Mayo, Corpus Christi, San Juan and Día de los
Difuntos. Its fiesta patronal, commemorating
the Virgin, is August 15. The original pueblo,

NORTE GRANDE

Ticnamar Viejo, is close by and still preserves its adobe and straw church. Beyond Ticnamar Viejo, a track goes to Termas de Chitune.

Ruta A-35 winds south to Timar, Ofragia and Guañacagua, before arriving at **Codpa**. On the banks of the Río Vítor, this oasis town grows guava and other tropical fruits. However, Codpa is most famous for its wine (*vino pintatani*) and wine festival, held at the end of March and beginning of April.

Codpa was a missionary center during the colonial period. The church, built in 1668, has two side chapels and a polychrome, wooden altar screen. During the celebration of its patron saint on November 11, San Martín de Tours rides a donkey through the streets.

Most of the villages in the precordillera have no hostels. Ask about staying with a family or be prepared to camp. In Portezuela de Murmuntani, visitors may be able to stay at the school or the *sede social* (community center). In Ticnamar, lodging is available with families. Conditions are very basic. If staying in thatch-roofed huts, beware of the *vinchuca* (assassin bug) which carries Chagas disease. Make sure to use a bug net during your stay. Updated: Jul 08, 2009.

Getting To and Away From Precordillera de Belén

If you are driving, take extra fuel, food and water, as villages are spread far apart and gas and other services are scarce.

Transporte de Paloma (Germán Riesgo 2071, Arica, Tel: 56-58-222710) goes to the Precordilerra villages, departing Arica Tuesday and Friday at 7 a.m. Fares are: Zapahuira $5, Murmitane $5.60, Chapiquiña $6, Belén $6.60. The bus returns the same day, departing from Belén at about 1:30 p.m. Separate services go Ticnamar ($6) by way of Codpa (Tuesday and Friday 7 a.m., return 4 p.m.) and to Socorama ($6).

If you have time, it's worthwhile to spend several days in the region. Take the bus to one village, then walk from one to another, catching the bus as it passes through. Updated: Jun 20, 2009.

HOLIDAYS AND FIESTAS
The villages of the Precordillera de Belén celebrate agricultural and religious events. Come for the traditional dances and songs, and drinking and feasting of the Aymara people. Updated: Jun 20, 2009.

Month	Event
February	**Fiesta de Carnavales**—all communities
March-April	**Semana Santa** (Easter week, moveable feast) and **Vendimia** (wine harvest)—Codpa
May	3—**Cruz de Mayo**—all communities
June	24 - **San Juan Bautista** - Ticnamar
July	15, 16—**Corpus Christi** (moveable feast) - Ticnamar; **Virgen del Carmen**—Socorama, Belén; 25—**Santiago** (patron saint) - Belén, Pontezuelo de Murmuntani
August	25—**Asunción de la Virgen**—Ticnamar; 30—**Santa Rosa**—Ticnamar
October	3, 4—**San Francisco de Asís** - Belén, Socorama; 1st week—**Siembra de la Papa** (potato planting festival)—Socorama, Belén, Ticnamar
November	1—**Todos los Santos** (All Saints Day)—all villages; 2—**Día de los Difuntos** (Day of the Dead)—Belén; 11—**San Martín de Tours** (patron saint)—Codpa; 21—**Presentación de la Virgen**—Zapahuira

PUTRE

 3,500 m 2,800 058

Tucked away in the Altiplano, among the rugged Andean landscape, is Putre, a large village whose indigenous refer to the mountains as *mallkus*, or sacred hills. Volcán Tarapacá casts its shadow over the pre-Inca terraces, now used for cultivating alfalfa and oregano. Although Putre existed long before the Spaniards came, officially this town was founded in 1580. It was an important missionary post and rest stop for mule trains hauling silver from Potosí to Arica.

Putre means the "whisper of the waters" in Aymara. Its landscape is laced with streams trickling down off the Andean heights and pooling across the high plains.

Putre's cobblestone streets are lined with buildings of typical colonial-altiplano architecture. Many of the squat stone-adobe homes were rebuilt in the 18th and 19th centuries, using the carved stone portals of the original buildings. Throughout town, colorful murals depict local history and legends. There is a multi-level plaza in the center of town with an adobe church dating from 1670. Its single, broad nave is lined with old, hand-carved statues of the saints.

The town preserves much of its indigenous heritage. Many families still speak Aymara at home; school subjects are taught in both Aymara and *castellano* (Spanish). Alpaca sweaters, shawls, ponchos and other woolens are produced by several *talleres* (workshops). Restaurants dish up food made from quinoa, llaita, and alpaca. The Feria Regional Andina (Feran), an agriculturual-artisan fair takes place in October. Putreños also celebrate a number of religious festivals.

Putre is a convenient place to acclimatize to the altitude before visiting Parque Nacional Lauca, Reserva Nacional Olas Vicuñas and Monumento Natural Salar de Surire. Tours to these preserves are much cheaper from Putre than from Arica or other cities. Near town there are pictographs and hot springs. The village has hostels and restaurants, as well as most services. Updated: Jun 20, 2009.

When to Go

Because it is in a valley, Putre's weather is pretty much the same all year round. Days can get up to 22°C (72°F). Nights are cold, dipping to 0°C (32°F) or below. December-March is the Altiplano's winter. January and February are the chilliest and rainiest; at higher altitudes it snows.

HOLIDAYS AND FIESTAS

The major celebration in Putre is the movable feast of Cristo Rey in October. The pre-Lenten Carnaval Andino con la Fuerza del Sol in February is another important feast, in which indigenous and Christian traditions mesh. August 15 is the feast day of the Virgen de Asunta. October has the Feria Regional Andina. The first week of November Putreños dance Pachallampe, a ritual for the potato planting. Updated: Jun 20, 2009.

> ### V!VA ONLINE REVIEW
> PUTRE
> *Breathtaking... quite literally! Not only are the views of the surrounding Nevados de Putre spectacular, but the altitude really takes your breath away. My favorite place in Chile by far!*
> March 26, 2009

Getting To and Away From Putre

Putre is 145 kilometers (87 mi) from Arica. Gas is sometimes available at a shop on Calle Canto, near Baquedano. Look for the sign that reads "Here Fuel." Buses leave from either Calle Baquedano or near the plaza.

To Arica: **Paloma** (daily 2 p.m., $6), **Gutiérrez** (Monday, Wednesday, Friday 5 p.m., $6).

To the Precordillera de Belén: The municipality has contracted a weekly bus service to and from Ticnamar in the Precordillera de Belén. It passes through all the villages along that route, arriving in Putre about 10 a.m. Wednesday and leaving that same afternoon for Ticnamar. The service, however, appears to be irregular. Check with the municipalidad for more information. Also, you can ask the driver of the bus to notify you when he arrives in town or at the **Kukulí** store (Baquedano 301). The same transport company runs a Tuesday route to Socorama.

To Bolivia: **Cali Tours** (Baquedano 399, Tel: 56-8-5180960, E-mail: cali_tours@hotmail.com, URL: www.calitours.cl) is the local contact for buses to Tambo Quemado border crossing into Bolivia. Arrange fares with it. Otherwise, go up to the crossroads and

NORTE GRANDE

wait for the bus to pass at about 11 a.m. Buses for Visvirí border, going by way of Parinacota, run on Tuesday and Friday. Updated: Jun 24, 2009.

Getting Around

There are no formal services for getting around town. The crossroads to the main highway is four kilometers (2.4 mi) uphill—quite a hike if weighted down with a backpack. Try to hitch a ride early in the morning from the shops along Baquedano, or ask a local tour agency for a lift ($4). Updated: Jun 20, 2009.

Safety

Keep in mind that Putre is at a higher altitude. Take it slow and easy, especially if you are hiking in the parks. When staying outside of town, use a mosquito net to protect against the *vincucha* bug, which carries Chagas disease. Updated: Jun 20, 2009.

Services

TOURISM

The **tourism information office** isn't very helpful, but it does have a good map of the city (Monday – Thursday 8 a.m. – 1 p.m., 2:30 – 7 p.m., Friday 8 a.m. – 2 p.m. On the Calle Prat side of the main plaza). **Conaf** provides information on Parque Nacional Lauca and other area reserves (Monday – Friday 8 a.m. – 1 p.m., 2:30 – 5:30 p.m. Teniente del Campo, between Latorre and O'Higgins). The **carabinero post** is on the corner of Riquelme and Condell streets. Information about Putre's history and festivals can be found at: http://pueblo-de-putre.blogspot.com.

MONEY

Banco del Estado exchanges U.S. dollars and euros. Its ATM accepts MasterCard and Cirrus and is accessible only during business hours (Monday – Friday 9 a.m. – 2 p.m.).

KEEPING IN TOUCH

There are only two Internet cafés in town. The better one is **Tecnicom**, charging $0.80 per hour; it also has international phone service starting at $0.60 per minute (daily 9 a.m. – 10 p.m. Canto, between Latorre and Riquelme). There is another café on the corner of Lynch and Baquedano. The **Centro de Llamadas** , on the Prat side of the plaza, has irregular hours. **Correos de Chile** is on Carrera, between Baquedano and O'Higgins.

MEDICAL

Putreños rely on the **Consultorio General Rural Putre**, which has an ambulance (Baquedano 261). Putre has no pharmacy. The general stores have basic medicine. For anything heavy duty, try the health post. Updated: Jun 20, 2009.

SHOPPING

There are several artisan shops around the plaza selling locally made alpaca sweaters, scarves, shawls, *ruandas* (ponchos) and other goods. Some also have run-of-the-mill souvenirs and post cards. Most close for lunch between noon and 3 p.m. Taller de Artesanía Demonstrativo has a large selection of alpaca, sheep and llama wool items, all of which arel made on-site (Ca. Carrera 521, Tel: 56-8-5044985). Artesanías Chungará specializes in woolens, ceramics, wood and cactus carvings, and alpaca leatherwear (Carrera 401, Tel: 56-8-9555111). Updated: Jun 24, 2009.

Things to See and Do

Most travelers come to Putre only as a stopover on their way to Parque Nacional Lauca. But the village offers short hikes to help you acclimatize. Enjoy walks to ancient indigenous rock paintings, to viewpoints outside of town, or stroll through the narrow streets to check out the colorful murals illustrating local legends. Finish off a day of hiking with a soak in **Termas Jurasi**, located outside the village. Updated: Jun 20, 2009.

Pictografías de Vilacaurani

For millennia indigenous peoples have lived and traveled along trails between the Altiplano and the coast. Wherever they went, they left behind artwork. These *pinturas rupestres* served to help guide journeyers or were created for religious reasons. The Pictografías de Vilacaurani, west of Putré, has rock overhang with a large panel decorated with humans, animals, geometric shapes and other designs, the age and significance of which are unknown. From the plaza, walk west toward Chakana. Two hundred meters (650 ft) before the inn, take the road to the right. Keep to the right at each intersection. It is about a 2 – 3 hour walk. Maps are available at Tour Andino. This trip can also be done on horseback. Updated: Jun 20, 2009.

Mirador

One way to get yourself ready to trek in Parque Nacional Lauca is to take a hike up to the *mirador*, or lookout point just northeast

NORTE GRANDE

of the town center. Follow Calle Prat eastward, past Calle Maipú to the trail entrance. From atop you'll have tremendous views of the whitewashed village on the plain below. Volcán Tarapacá is behind Putre, where other volcanoes stud the Altiplano horizon. Updated: Jun 30, 2009.

Tours

All tour operators in Putre are conveniently located on Calle Baquedano. Excursions to Parque Nacional Lauca are much cheaper to do from here than from Arica. Expect to pay about $40 – 70 per person. Likewise, trips to Reserva Nacional Las Vicuñas and Parque Nacional Volcán Isluga are less expensive. A few of the agencies in town are listed below.

Tour Andino (Daily 8:30 a.m. – 1 p.m., 2:30 – 7 p.m. Baquedano 360, Tel: 56-9-0110702, E-mail: jiron@tourandino.com, URL: www.tourandino.com)—Also does village market visits, the Precordillera de Belén circuit and mountain climbing. Guides are local Aymara.

Cali Tours (Baquedano 399, Tel: 56-8-5180960, E-mail: cali_tours@hotmail.com, URL: www.calitours.cl)—Also does four- to seven-day treks across the altiplano.

Alto Andino (Baquedano 299, Tel: 56-9-2826195, E-mail: altoandino@yahoo.com, URL: www.birdingaltoandino.com)—Resident naturalist and Alaska native Barbara Knapton leads birdwatching and nature tours of the region, including a five-day / four-night expedition through a variety of habitats from the coast to the altiplano wetlands. Reservations are required. Updated: Jun 20, 2009.

Lodging

Hotels in Putre are mostly family-owned affairs, providing basic yet comfortable rooms with all the necessities for the cold nights at this altitude: hot showers and thick blankets. A few of the more modern hotels have heating. Most hostels are on Baquedano, making the search for a room a bit easier for the oxygen-deprived visitor arriving here. A few are on the outskirts of town, providing a quieter retreat. Updated: Jun 20, 2009.

Hostal Cali

(ROOMS: $10 – 16) Hostal Cali is one of Putre's cheaper hotels. It has a sparse feeling, with rooms along a narrow back patio which doubles as a parking lot at night. Rooms are comfortably furnished for two or more

people. All bathrooms have on-demand hot water—just ask doña Yolanda to light the heater. Common baths are very clean and breakfast is available on request. Depending on availability, Hostal Cali may be able to help you out with Internet and gasoline. Guests may use the kitchen. Baquedano 399. Tel: 56-8-5361242, E-mail: hostal_cali@hotmail.com, URL: www.calitours.cl.Updated: Jun 20, 2009.

Chakana Mountain Lodge

(ROOMS: $16 – 72) In Aymara, Chakana means Southern Cross, the constellation that holds the guiding star for this hemisphere. Chakana Mountain Lodge is such a star for journeyers to Putre, leading them to a warm welcome, cozy rooms and good food. Located at the outskirts of town, about a 10-minute walk from the plaza, this ecolodge has both cabins and a four-bed dorm. To keep guests warm on cold nights, heaters and feather comforters are provided. The kitchen/dining room is a sunny space where tea is served at any hour. Marisol and George speak English, French, German and Spanish, and are very knowledgeable about the area. Chakana is a member of Fair Chile, a network of ecologically sound businesses. From the plaza, follow Carrera toward the military base at the outskirts of town. Turn right and after 50 meters, take a left. Further down is a road that goes directly to Chakana (750 meters).Casilla 154, Arica. Tel: 56-9-7459519, E-mail: info@la-chakana.com, URL: www.la-chakana.com. Updated: Jun 24, 2009.

Kukuli

(ROOMS: $26 – 44) A relatively new kid on the Baquedano block, Kukuli is already the most popular resting stop for tour groups, and for good reason, it seems. The cozy single and double rooms are tastefully decorated. Each has a private bathroom with 24-hour hot water. It is difficult to get a room here, so reservations are recommended. Baquedano 351. Tel: 56-9-1614709. Updated: Jun 23, 2009.

Restaurants

Restaurants in Putre specialize in typical Altiplano dishes using local ingredients like quinoa and *llaita*, a freshwater algae. While in town, be sure to try the trout and salmon fresh from the highland streams. A real culinary adventure is alpaca meat, frequently featured on pizza. The town is also known for its cheeses. You can stock up for treks in Parque Nacional Lauca at the several general stores

NORTE GRANDE

in town. **Panadería Sandercito** is the only bakery (Ca. Lynch, between O'Higgins and Latorre). Updated: Jun 23, 2009.

Kuchu Marka

(LUNCH: $4) Kuchu Marka means "corner of the village" in Aymara. This restaurant is a charming nook on Putre's main street. On chilly nights, a fire crackles in the chimney. Kuchu Marka's menu features traditional Aymara cooking with ingredients from the Altiplano such as alpaca and trout. The tourist menu offers four-course meals. Vegetarians have several choices, such as an omelet made of llaita and goat cheese. The menu of the day is a three-course affair. Dinner $8. Open daily noon – 3 p.m., 6 p.m. – 9:30 p.m. Baquedano 351. Tel: 56-9-0114007. Updated: Jun 23, 2009.

Rosamel

(ENTREES: $6) This popular, simple eatery on the corner of the plaza is warm and homey. The portions are absolutely huge. Lunch is a four-course affair, which includes appetizer and dessert ($5). Although you'll leave stuffed, your wallet won't be much thinner. Rosamel is the one of the least expensive diners in town. Open daily 7 a.m. – 8:30 p.m. Corner of Latorre and Carrera. Updated: Jun 23, 2009.

Cantaverdi

(ENTREES: $6) The rough-painted walls hung with Guayasamín prints, the cloth-draped ceiling, the fireplace and the heavy wooden furniture give Cantaverdi a cozy feeling. The menu is an eclectic mix of highland foods, like alpaca and salmon, and non-traditional meats, such as seafood and beef. Pizzas hot out of the oven come in a variety of combos, including the intriguing Potreña with local cheese, alpaca meat, Azapa olives and quinoa. Vegetarians have a few options on the menu. Starting at 11 a.m., a four-course lunch is served ($5). Monday – Saturday 9 a.m. – midnight. Canto 339. Updated: Jun 25, 2009.

PARQUE NACIONAL LAUCA

Parque Nacional (PN) Lauca is one of Chile's most impressive and beautiful national parks. Snowy volcanoes embrace dry Altiplano plains where ñandú and vicuña roam, and its many wetlands are filled with birds. The park's Aymara name, Lawquia, means aquatic grasses.

The park, originally founded as a forest reserve in 1965 and upgraded to a national park in 1970, covers 137,883 hectares. Altitudes range from 3,200 meters (10,400 ft) to 6,342 meters (20,612 ft). The highest peaks are **Parinacota** (6,342 m / 20,612 ft), **Pomerape** (6,282 m / 20,417 ft) and **Guallatire** (6,060 m / 19,695 ft).

The park has two distinct ecosystems: the Precordillera (3,200 – 3,800 m / 10,400 – 12,350 ft altitude) and the Altiplano (over 3,800 m / 12,350 ft). The precordillera is characterized by cacti and scrub vegetation. Guanaco, llama, puma and foxes roam the Andean foothills. The Altiplano has dry plains awash with wetlands. Two major rivers flow through it: the Lauca, which empties into Salar de Coipasa in Bolivia, and the Vizcachani, a tributary of the Lauca. The largest wetland is near the Parinacota village, and others surround Laguna de Cotacotani.

Lago Chungará is one of the highest lakes in the world. Flora include the tuna; llareta, a hard, green, moss-like plant that grows in cushions; *queñoa de altura*; the stiff golden grass, *paja brava*; and *chachacoma*, a low bush. Vicuña, alpaca and vizcacha—a small rodent once prized for its fur—are denizens of the plains, as are the ñandú, *perdiz de puna* and condor.

The lakes, lagoons and wetlands provide homes and nesting grounds for a variety of birds including flamingo and duck. In total, about 140 endemic, resident and migratory bird species can be found in PN Lauca.

When you visit the park, be sure to bring warm clothing, as weather conditions change quickly. Have a parka, heavy jacket, sweater, hat, and gloves to protect yourself from freezing temperatures. Use a high-factor sunscreen and sunglasses. Much of the park is at over 4,500 meters (14,625 ft). Take time to acclimatize, and descend if you exhibit signs of altitude sickness. During the winter months (January – March) roads may be impassable. Check with Conaf in Putre and at the ranger stations within the park about road and trail conditions.

Conaf in Arica and in Putre have good, self-guiding pamphlets of the trails at Las Cuevas, Lago Chungará and the Parinacota wetlands. These free brochures are only available in Spanish. There is no park entrance fee. You may camp at the Chungará ranger station. Lodging is also offered in Parinacota, where there is a basic shop. Bring all the food that you will need. In

Putre you can find hostels, general stores, restaurants and most basic services. Updated: Jul 07, 2009.

Getting To and Away From Parque Nacional Lauca

Getting to Parque Nacional Lauca is easy. The paved Ruta CH-11, connecting Arica with La Paz, passes through the heart of the park (53 km / 32 mi). Tours will take you to the major attractions, and are cheaper from Putre than from Arica or Iquique. If driving, be sure to have a full tank of gas. It is best to fill up in Arica, as the shop in Putre often runs out.

You can also reach the park via public transportation from Arica:

To Putre: **Gutiérrez** (from Panadería Seria, Tucapel and Esteban Ríos; Monday, Wednesday, Friday 7 a.m., $6, 3 hours), **Trans Paloma** (Germán Riesgo 2071. Tel: 56-58-22-2710; daily 7 a.m., $6, 3 hours).

To Chungará / Tambo Quemado: Buses leave from Arica's international bus terminal (Av. Diego Portales s/n) and travel along Ruta CH-11. The highway is well-paved and often used by trucks. The road passes through PN Lauca to the border post at the end of Lago Chungará. Most companies leave from Arica between 8 and 10:30 a.m. and midnight and 2 a.m. ($12 – 18, 8 hours).

To Parinacota / Visvirí: The road to the Visvirí border goes by way of Parinacota. The highway is passable all year— **Trans Paloma** (Tuesday, Friday 11 a.m., return next day 9 a.m., $11 / $14). Updated: Jun 23, 2009.

Things to See and Do

For many, the major attractions are the vistas and the wildlife, but there are also ruins and Aymara villages worth visiting. **Las Cuevas** has wetlands and

archaeological remains. **Parinacota**, an indigenous-colonial village famous for its church and weaving, is a convenient starting point for hiking to Ciénagasa de Parinacota and climbing Guane Guane. Easily accessible **Lago Chungará** is a birdwatcher's paradise. There are interpretive trails at these three sites. A longer trail that can be walked or driven goes from the Chucuyo settlement to Laguna Cotacotani. Updated: Jun 25, 2009.

Termas de Jurasi

According to a local myth, a young Inca princess stayed eternally young thanks to the special waters of Termas de Jurasi. Years later, she fell in love and married. Her husband noticed how she stayed youthful while neighbors faded with age. One day he stealthily followed her to the warm pools and discovered her secret. He, too, began to immerse himself on the sly. One day the princess caught him at the hot springs and yelled, *"Jurasi, jurasi, jurasi!"* (which in Aymara means, boil, boil, boil). The waters bubbled up and her husband suffered a horrible death.

However, you won't have to worry about any such curse these days. What better way to relax after a day of hiking in Parque Nacional than to soak in its 50 – 53°C (122 – 127°F) mineral waters? One pool is open-air and the other is in a cabaña. There are also mud baths. The hot springs are 10 kilometers (6 mi) east of Putre, just off Ruta CH-11 ($2, 9 a.m. – 5 p.m.). Updated: Jun 24, 2009.

Las Cuevas

There's a 1.3-kilometer (0.8-mi) path from Las Cuevas' ranger station that passes through bofedales (wetlands) where you can observe vizcacha, Brown pintail, Andean gulls, condors, foxes and vicuña. The trail passes by caves that were used by hunters and traders in the Late Archaic Period (6000 – 4000 BC). The four-kilometer (2.4 mi) Sendero Chacu Las Cuevas heads to a stone corral used by Aymara and Inca to capture vicuñas.

Las Cuevas is eight kilometers (4.8 mi) from the western entry to the park and 45 kilometers (27 mi) from the east entry at the Bolivian border Tambo Quemado. Tours stop at this site. Las Cuevas has a ranger station, tourist information office, souvenir shop and restrooms. No camping is allowed.

Near the trail head there is a *baño termal* or hot spring, with 70°C (158°F) water. The roofed pools of Termas de Chiriguaya are on Ruta A-35, approximately 30 minutes from the Las Cuevas turn-off. Updated: Jun 25, 2009.

Parinacota

Parinacota is 20 kilometers (12 mi) east of Las Cuevas. This tiny indigenous-colonial village, long a rest stop for indigenous and later Spanish travelers, was declared a national monument. Its name derives from the Aymara word Parinaquita, meaning Lagoon of Flamingos. Parinacota, at 4,392m, is the starting point to Ciénagasa de Parinacota (the flamingo bogs) and many come to climb Cerro Guane Guane.

Parinacota is a hamlet of white-washed homes, backdropped by the twin volcanoes of Payachatas: Parinacota (which, according to local lore, is San Miguel Arcángel) and Pomerape (or María Isabel, says the legend). The town's 17th-century church, Iglesia de la Natividad, is made of adobe and thatched with paja brava. The temple's interior walls are painted with frescoes. Among the church's treasures are hand-carved saints.

High-quality alpaca sweaters, shawls and other wool apparel are produced here and sold at a community shop across from the church. Prices are much lower here than in Arica and other cities. Don Leonel Terán's **Albergue Uta Kala** and other families lodge guests ($6 – 8 per person). A small store has very basic supplies.

Parinacota is right in the center of Parque Nacional Lauca, 28 kilometers (17 mi) from the west entrance. Updated: Jun 25, 2009.

Ciénagasa de Parinacota

Ciénagas de Parinacota, also called Bofedales de Parinacota, is a major wetland on the northern Chilean altiplano. The principal flora are paja brava and evergreen mosses like llareta. Alpaca, llama and other animals water at the lagoons, and a variety of ducks, flamingos and other birds rest here. A three-kilometer (1.8 mi) interpretive trail begins in the village of Parinacota and winds through the wetlands to Lagunilla Pillacota, where Giant coot and several species of ducks nest. At Bofedal de Uncaliri there is a small stone and thatch chapel and a smaller series of bogs where the Río Lauca begins. Frequent miradores allow excellent wildlife viewing. Updated: Jun 25, 2009.

Cerro Guane Guane

Cerro Guane Guane is one of the several volcanoes that you can see from the village of Parinacota. This 5,097-meter (3,058 ft) tall mountain is an easy all-day hike from the pueblo below. Once atop the hill, you'll be rewarded with views of volcanoes and lagoons strewn across the high-altitude plains. On the peak there is a ceremonial site where ancient Aymara celebrated religious rites.

To get here, follow the signed path from town, consult with locals, or hire a guide in town. Check with Conaf about weather and trail conditions before embarking on this hike or any others. Updated: Jun 25, 2009

Lagunas de Cotacotani

Lagunas de Cotacotani is a mosaic of turquoise-blue lakes scattered across the Altiplano northeast of Parinacota. The landscape is shadowed by the Payachatas and covered in a field of lava. Lago Cotacotani, fed by Lago Chungará, is the centerpiece of the group and one of Parque Nacional Lauca's largest lakes. Cotacotani is also a major bird habitat.

To get here, take the Sendero Chucuyo-Cotacotani that begins from the hamlet Chucuyo on Ruta CH-11 near the turn-off for Parinacota. There is also a road that heads to the lagoons. Updated: Jun 25, 2009.

Lago Chungará

At the east end of Parque Nacional Lauca, Lago Chungará is the park's largest lake, covering 21.5 square kilometers (8.3 square mi). Its deepest point is 37 meters (120 ft). At an altitude of 4,517 meters (14,680 ft), Lago Chungará is the world's highest non-navigable lake.

Chungará is a major bird habitat, home to coots, ducks, pintails, teals, cormorants and flamingos, among others. Vicuña graze on the shores, and other common mammals are mice and vizcacha. Lago Chungará's blue waters reflect Volcán Parinacota's snow-glazed peak (6,342 m / 20,612 ft). The nevados Quimsachatas and Quisiquine, to the east, are both over 6,000 meters (19,500 ft) high. A 30-minute interpretive trail with five observation points leads you through an important part of the wetlands. The path begins at the viewpoint along the main road (Ruta CH-11). Nearby there is a roadside hotel dating from the Inca period.

Lago Chungará is near the far east end of Parque Nacional Lauca, along Ruta CH-11, 37 kilometers (22.5 mi) from the western entry near Putre and 12 kilometers (7.5 mi) from the eastern entry, Tambo Quemado, on the Bolivian border.

The lake is the only place in the park where you can camp. Sites here have stone wall wind breaks. There is also a refuge with an equipped kitchen (Chileans $7, foreigners $19, per person per night). The ranger station has an information office, bathrooms and a souvenir stand.

When hiking around the lake do not stray from the trail; the ground is delicate and many of the plant species are endangered. Conaf has a good, free pamphlet of the hike, available only in Spanish. Updated: Jun 25, 2009.

RESERVA NACIONAL LAS VICUÑAS

Reserva Nacional (RN) Las Vicuñas, founded in 1983, is a 209,131-hectare preserve designed to protect vicuña. Not only will you see these star residents, but puma, alpaca, and armadillo also live in the park. Keep an eye on the sky and plains for condor and hawk. The reserve is also flush with many endemic species of flora.

The altiplano steppe in RN Las Vicuñas ranges from 4,300 to 5,600 meters (13,975-18,200 ft) in altitude. The highest peaks and volcanoes are Puquintica (5,780 m / 18,785 ft), Aritinca (5,990 m / 19,468 ft), Salle (5,403 m / 17,560 ft), Belén (5,260 m / 17,095 ft) and Anocariri (5,050 m / 16,413 ft). The main waterways are Río Lauca and Guallatire, and Laguna Paquisa and Guallatire.

The climate is dry, with only 260 millimeters (10.25 in) of precipitation per year. It rains in summer, snows in the winter, and daytime temperatures range from 8°C to 15°C (46 – 59°F). At night it gets quite nippy, -5° to -15°C (10 – 21°F).

Park activities include birdwatching, hiking, fishing and climbing. You can also visit the many Aymara villages throughout the reserve. Feast days are celebrated with small musical bands playing traditional instruments. Apachetas, stone altars built

as offerings near the road or atop tombs, scatter the landscape. There are pre-Hispanic sanctuaries on the highest heights.

The reserve's headquarters are in Guallatire. **Casa de Hospedaje Guallatire** has hot water showers (per person: $10 common bath, $12 private bath).

Entry into the reserve is free. Be sure to take it easy and watch for signs of altitude sickness. The sun is strong; use sunglasses and sunscreen. Bring plenty of warm clothing, including hat and gloves. Updated: Jun 25, 2009

Getting To and Away From Reserva Nacional Las Vicuñas

The only way to visit Reserva Nacional Las Vicuñas is via tour or in a private or rented vehicle. From Parque Nacional Lauca, Ruta A-235 turns off Ruta CH-11 just east of Las Cuevas. Another signed turn-off is near the east end of Lago Chungtará, heading to Guallatire. This is a dirt road often used by trucks.

During the rainy season (December – February) high-clearance vehicles with four-wheel drive or chains are recommended. Bring extra gasoline (for at least 500 kilometers / 300 miles), as there are no stations along the way. Check tires, brakes and other mechanics before setting out. Updated: Jun 23, 2009.

MONUMENTO NATURAL SALAR DE SURIRE

Established in 1983, Monumento Natural Salar de Surire is an 11,298-hectare reserve that includes a massive salt flat and many wetlands. Flamingos nest here—all three major species can be seen—and other birds such as avocet, duck and the park's namesake, Suri, can also be found within the reserve. The plains are covered with tola and paja brava and are inhabited by vicuña, llama and alpaca.

From the eastern end of Monumento Natural Salar de Surire you will find Aguas Termales de Polloquere. The pools of blue waters are lined in white. Picnic tables and two campsites (without latrines) line the shores.

The climate here is very dry. Summer rains and winter snows amount only to 250 millimeters (less than 10 in) per year. In winter temperatures reach 5°C (41°F) during the day and

NORTE GRANDE

-15°C (5°F) at night. Summer temperatures range from -5°C – 5°C (23 – 41°F). Avoid hard physical activities at this high altitude.

There is a carabinero post on the northwest side of the salar, near the salt mining operations. The Conaf ranger station, on the shores of Salar de Surire, has lodging. Make reservations with Conaf in Arica (Monday – Friday 8:30 a.m. – 5:30 p.m. Vicuña Mackenna 820, Tel: 56-58-201206 / 25-0750, URL: www.conaf.cl) or in Putre (Monday – Friday 8 a.m. – 1 p.m., 2:30 – 5:30 p.m. Teniente del Campo, between Latorre and O'Higgins). Updated: Jun 25, 2009.

Getting To and Away From Monumento Natural Salar de Surire

The only way to visit Monumento Natural Salar de Surire is by tour or in a private or rented vehicle. From Reserva Nacional Las Vicuñas, continue along Ruta A-235. The salar can also be reached from Colchane, through Parque Nacional Volcán Isluga (79 km / 48 mi, 2 hours).

From the coast, take A-31, a poor dirt road that begins 30 kilometers (18 miles) south of Arica, off the Pan-American Highway (Ruta CH-11). Check with carabineros or Conaf about the condition of A-31 before setting off. There are other backroads to Salar de Surire, but maps of this part of Chile are extremely poor. From the Salar de Surire ranger station there's a new road that heads to Parcohaylla (13 km / 8 mi; camping) and then across desolate plains inhabited only by the occasional ñandú or vicuña.

The road becomes narrow and steep in parts. Twenty-two kilometers (13.5 mi) after Parcohaylla there is an unmarked crossroads; go left. After 42 kilometers (25.5 mi) you'll come to A-35, which goes to Codpa on the edge of the Precordillera de Belén and to Arica.

No matter which route you take, ask carabinero posts and Conaf about road conditions. During the rainy season (December – February) high-clearance vehicles with four-wheel drive or chains are recommended. Bring extra gasoline (for at least 500 kilometers / 300 miles), as there are no stations along the way. Updated: Jun 25, 2009.

PISAGUA

 Sea level 260 57

In Aymara, Pisagua is known as *Pisa Wayña*, Scarcity of Water. Pisagua is a small fishing village with less than 300 residents. However, it was once the third most important port in Chile, during its nitrate mining days from 1880 to 1920. Now, little remains of its six wharves. Evidence of its rich past still remains. A blue and white clock tower, raised in 1881 to commemorate Chile's victory in the Guerra del Pacífico, sits on a cliff high above town. The fire station on Avenida Prat and the Teatro Municipal around Plaza Santa María were both built from imported Oregon pine—the station in 1888 and the classic European style theater, five years after the war. The Teatro, whose ceiling mural represents the four performance arts and was painted by Sixto Rojas, was once the cultural center, hosting operas, comedies and concerts. Mannequins dressed in period clothing now fill the box seats, awaiting some future performance. Visitors can take a peak at the back stage.

Next door to the theater is Iglesia de San Pedro, which has an unusual oblong nave and a dark green ceiling covered in stars. Only one of its towers remains. (Keys to the theater and church can be requested at the two-story blue house to the left of the **Club Deportivo Pisagaua** on Av. Prat). The old train depot behind the police station is another reminder of the town's golden age.

In the 20th century, the nitrate boom fizzled and Pisagua became better known for its innocuous-looking peach building trimmed in rose: Colonia Penal, the town jail. Constructed in 1910, it was here that social and political prisoners were tortured and executed. The jail was used for three major internments. The first occurred in 1942, during the height of the Second World War. Then, from 1947 to 1948, President Gabriel González Videla rounded up communists and others opposing his regime. Poet Pablo Neruda managed to escape this dragnet and with his opus Canto General exposed the Pisagua nightmare to the world. The final internment occurred after the 1973 coup d'etat. There's evidence also indicating that homosexuals were detained here in 1941 during the government of Aguirre Cerda. At some counts, Pisagua has been a concentration camp 11 times. For a short period in the 1990s the jail was renovated into a hotel.

Along the road into town there is a monument that pays tribute to an 1879 battle fought here and, far below, a thin band of surf carves the beach.

More vestiges of Pisagua's history lie near a side road at Km 40. Below the road, near the railroad depot, remain the ruins of the six detention centers of the Pinochet dictatorship. The first of several graveyards appears on the left. White crosses honor those who fell during the attack on Playa Blanca. A monument commemorates this Guerra del Pacífico sea-to-land assault, said to be the model for World War II's Normandy invasion. In 1990 a mass grave of those killed from 1973 – 1974 was found. Several memorials now grace the site and every October 29 the town holds memorial ceremonies to honor the dead.

Every June 28 – 29 Pisagua fetes San Pedro, the patron saint of those who go to sea. The town's dark times are depicted on a mural near Plaza Santa María. Signs around the town allow a self-guided historical tour.

Despite its dark past, Pisagua does have some brighter wonders for visitors to enjoy: playas Guata and Blanca north of the hamlet are full of birds and there is a sea lion colony at Punta Pinchalo south of town, where you can also find archaeological remains of the Chinchorro culture (3000 BC).

Services are pretty sparse in Pisagua, though it does have a carabinero and health post. The town has two lodging options: **Hostal La Roca** (Tel: 56-57-731502, E-mail: viejopisagua2@hotmail.com; single $20, double $28) and **La Picada de Don Gato** (Tel: 56-57-731511, E-mail: dongato@chilesat.net; $10 per person, private bath). **Camping Pisagua** is on Playa Blanca. **Don Gato** is the only restaurant in town, though there is a general store and locals sometimes sell empanadas out of their homes. Updated: Jul 07, 2009.

Getting To and Away From Pisagua

Pisagua is 183 kilometers (114 mi) south of Arica and 168 kilometers (104 mi) north of Iquique. Take Ruta 5 (Pan-American Highway) to Ruta A-40.

Without a private vehicle, it is difficult to get to Pisagua. **OC Travel** in Iquique is the only agency to offer tours to the village

(Serrano 389, oficina 407, Tel: 56-57-3260 / 56-57-3263, E-mail: info@octravel.cl, URL: www.octravel.cl).

A buseta departs from Iquique's Terminal Internacional Rodoviario (Av. Prat and Lynch, Tel: 56-57-416315) Monday and Friday at 5 p.m.; it departs Pisagua for Iquique the same days at 7 a.m. During the summer, a daily service is contracted; ask at Iquique's municipality and with **Sernatur** for details.

Hacienda Tiliviche and the British cemetery are on the Pan-American Highway, 10 kilometers (6 miles) north of the A-40 turn-off. The **Geoglifos de Tiliviche** are across the road. From here, a poor dirt road goes to Pisagua Viejo, which was destroyed by a mid-19th century earthquake. Updated: Jun 29, 2009.

HUARA

 1,103 m 958 ☎ 057

In 2005, Huara was heavily damaged by an earthquake. However, back in the glory days of nitrate mining, Huara was known as *the* place for miners to come for some R&R. They weren't allowed to take women into the camps, so they would come to visit the *casas de citas* (house of dates) in town. It is said that every other house in this town was a "recreational" center where men could see women. Locals sometimes refer to Huara as "Pueblo Anciano," as many of the young people have left to seek fortunes elsewhere.

Huara also has a religious past. In 1908 the Catholic Redentorista order arrived here and established a school to educate villagers and local miners. Later the Franciscans took over this work. One of the most famous to preach and participate in this effort was San Alberto Hurtado, canonized in 2005.

Huara's Parroquía Santísimo Redentor is a simple chapel. Like other towns in the region, Huara celebrates pre-Lenten carnival with Aymara flourishes (movable feast: February-March). The town's patron saint, the Virgen del Perpetuo Socorro, is celebrated on June 27, and August 5 is the feast of Santísimo Redentor. Another reason to drop into Huara is to visit the Botica Libertad, once one of the most important pharmacies on the plains and now a museum (Arturo Prat N°180). The railroad station is a national monument.

Chumbeques

The chumbeque is a square cookie sandwich made from three thin, flaky shortbread cookies layered with fruit jam, a confection created by Kaupolin Koo Kau, an immigrant from Canton, China, and Petronila Bustillos Sandoval of the Valle de Pica, in 1920. Chumbeques were inspired by desserts from Koo's hometown and *alfajores* (sponge cakes filled with toffee) in Pica. The traditional chumbeque filling is lemon (*limón*), though these days other flavors have been used, such as mango, papaya, passion fruit (*maracuyá*), guava (*guayaba*), orange, caramel (*manjar*) and chocolate.

The modern-day Rey del Chumbeque (King of Chumbeque) is Koo's grandson, Arturo E. Mejía. He continues his grandfather's tradition at the Fábrica de Chumbeques M. Koo (Monday – Saturday 8:30 a.m. – 10 p.m., Sunday 8:30 a.m. – 5 p.m. Ramírez 795. Tel: 56-57-412532, E-mail: elreydelchumbeque@hotmail.com). Chumbeques are only available in Iquique, a secret for visitors to this port to discover when they stop by "La Esquina de Buen Sabor." Updated: Jun 30, 2009.

If you want to spend the night, stay at **Hostería La Chinita** (Donato Zanelli 12) or at **Residencial Manuelito**. Both lodgings have restaurants. Stands along the roadside sell mangoes, oranges and other fruits grown in the pampas. To learn more about what Huara has to offer, visit: www.municipalidaddehuara.cl.

Near the turnoff for Huara is A-55, which passes El Gigante de Atacama, Tarapacá, Colchane and Parque Nacional Volcán Isluga before crossing into Bolivia. There are a few interesting stops worth making along the highway north of Huara. Just past the village, **Cerro Aura** has a series of geoglyphs. The road goes through the Zapiga Sector of Reserva National Pampa de Tamarugal.

The ex-oficina **Dolores** is almost 40 kilometers (24 mi) north of Huara, about six kilometers (3.6 mi) south of the Pisagua turnoff. This nitrate mine operated up until 1960, but had its peak from 1880 to 1930. Located two kilometers (1.2 mi) off the main highway, the former town is now in ruins. One of the most important land battles of the Guerra del Pacífico, la Batalla de Dolores, occurred here on the three hills surrounding a vital water well. On November 29, 1879, 6000 Chilean forces confronted a combined Peruvian-Bolivian army of 11,000. The monument has explanations (in Spanish) detailing the historic battle. Updated: Jul 02, 2009.

El Gigante de Atacama

On the side of Cerro Unitas, a mosaic-eyed man with upraised hands stares out across the arid plain. Was this a tribute to a ruler or to an extraterrestrial god? We may never know who the Gigante de Atacama represents, but such geoglyphs are common in this region of northern Chile. The Gigante is considered to be the largest in the world, 86 meters (280 ft) tall; if his crown is included, he measures 115 meters (374 ft). There are a staff and trumpet to the sides of the figure. To the right, there are two circles, one of which may have pointed travelers to a nearby water source. It was created about 900 AD. The designs were created by scraping the design into the earth, then covering it with caliche (nitrate-laden soil) so it would gleam in the sun. To hold the alkaline caliche in place, it was mixed with an acid—in this case, uric acid.

El Gigante de Atacama is on the north side of the A-55. To get to the Gigante de Atacama from Iquique with public transportation, you must first take any bus heading northward. Km 11 of Ruta A-55. The turnoff for A-55 is on the Pan-American highway at Huara. Updated: Jul 01, 2009.

Getting To and Away From Huara

Huara is on the west side of Ruta 5 (the Pan-American Highway), 26 kilometers (15.6 mi) north of Humberstone and Ruta A-16 for Iquique. To get to Huara from Iquique with public transportation, take any bus heading to Arica ($8). Some tours include Huara and other sites along Ruta 5 on their itinerary. Updated: Jul 01, 2009.

Border Crossings to Argentina

There are three ways to cross from San Pedro de Atacama into Argentina. The best option is to cross at Paso de Jama, located approximately 165 kilometers (102 mi) southeast of town and reached via a road through the Salar de Tara. This part is also a sector of the Reserva Nacional de los Flamencos.

Paso de Sico, slightly more than 200 kilometers (124 mi) south of San Pedro, is another alternative, which can be reached via a road that runs through Toconao and Socaire.

The third option is located at Paso de Socompa, which can be reached via a very bumpy road from Pan de Azúcar. Argentina, unlike Bolivia, does not require citizens of the United States to purchase a tourist visa before they enter. Updated: Jul 07, 2009.

IQUIQUE

 1m   238,950   57

From the desert plains of the pampas the land suddenly drops toward a port on a narrow line of coast. Here you'll find Iquique—capital of Chile's I Región Tarapacá, a city that stretches for as far as the eye can see to the north and south.

For at least nine millennia, indigenous people lived along this coast, harvesting guano to fertilize the fields in the pampa oasis. They built villages in nearby valleys and at the numerous hot springs. Unfortunately, little is known about these people. They may have been part of the Chinchorros, but they are generally known as Changos. By the 19th century they were wiped out by diseases brought by the Europeans and general mistreatment.

Within a few years after the conquest of the Inca Empire, Iquique became Spain's most important ports. It was a tempting target for pirates, like Sir Francis Drake, who sacked the city in 1579. A more peaceful ship, the HMS Beagle, docked in port on July 12, 1835, with naturalist Charles Darwin aboard.

After the colonies' independence from Spain, Bolivia was granted lands along the Pacific coast to the Río Loa. However, the administration fell largely into the hands of the Peruvians. But the majority of the inhabitants were from neither of those countries: They were Chileans who came as contract workers for the oficinas, the nitrate mines and other international ventures.

Control of the *oro blanco*, as nitrate was called, caused a rift between Peru and Chile, sparking the Guerra del Pacífico (1878 – 1879). The war's major naval battle was fought in Iquique harbor on May 21, 1879. Two ships went down, the Chilean Esmeraldas and the Peruvian Independencia, and Chile's great naval commander, Arturo Prat, was killed. Boat tours now visit the exact spot where the Esmeraldas sank.

After the War of the Pacific, the British established many nitrate mining companies on the pampas. They built family mansions in the port area, where the climate was much more agreeable. Other immigrants flocked to the area, setting up social clubs like the Casino Español, the Club Protectora for Chilean high society and Hrvatski Dom for the Croatians. Chinese also arrived to work in the mines. However, most of the workers in those harsh lands were Aymara, coming from the Altiplano of Chile, Bolivia and Peru.

During the late 19th century, then President José Manuel Balmaceda began nationalizing industries, including the British-owned mines. Moneyed forces and elements of the provincial government opposed this action. In 1891, a miners' strike and a naval revolt broke out and the city became a war zone once more.

During this time, labor conditions grew more intolerable. Workers and their families arrived en masse to Iquique to air their grievances and take shelter in the Escuela de Santa María. On December 21, 1907, the military opened fire, killing between 500 and 3,000 people, becoming one of modern Chile's greatest massacres.

Iquique's history is reflected in its architecture, though much of the original town was destroyed in the earthquakes and resultant tsunamis of 1868 and 1878. The ex-Aduana, built in 1871, is one of the oldest buildings. The prisoners taken during the naval Battle of Iquique were held here. Like in other cities in Latin America, Gustave Eiffel is said to have left his mark in Iquique: the design of the Torre Reloj is attributed to him. The splendid mansions of families who owned nitrate mines line Paseo Baquedano. The railroad station, on Sotomayor and Vivar, was once the depot for the trains to the mining camps; it is now houses government offices.

There is also a monument commemorating the 1907 strikers. Escuela Santa María, across from the Mercado Centenario

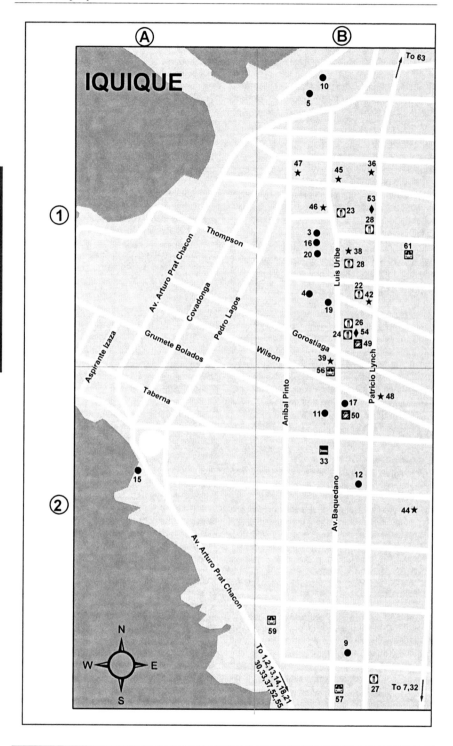

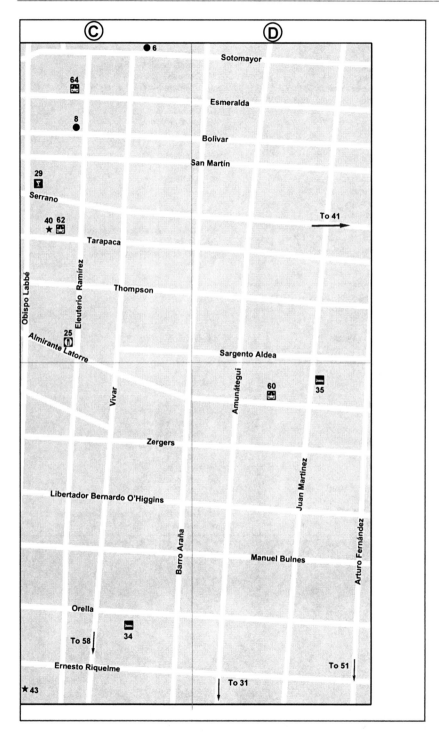

Activities ●

1 Arturo Prat Monument B2
2 Beaches B2
3 Casino Español B1
4 Club Protectora B1
5 Edificio de la Aduana B1
6 Ex-Estación de Ferrocarriles C1
7 Fly Iquique B2
8 Iglesia Catedral C1
9 Museo Histórico Militar Tarapacá B2
10 Museo Naval de Iquique B1
11 Museo Regional B2
12 Palacio Astoreca B2
13 Parque Temático Cavancha B2
14 Paseo Costanera B2
15 Playa Bellavista A2
16 Plaza Prat B1
17 Sala de Arte Casa Collahuasi B2
18 Santuario de Lourdes B2
19 Teatro Municipal B1
20 Torre del Reloj B1
21 Vertical Rent and Tour B2

Eating 🍴

22 Boccados B1
23 Café Split B1
24 Capuccino Pizza B1
25 Fábrica de Chumbeques M. C1
26 Hrvatski Dom B1
27 Restaurant El Tercer Ojito B2
28 Salón de Té y Cafetería Vizzio B1

Nightlife 🍸

29 Club Democrático C1
30 New Mango's Club B2

Sleeping ▬

31 Backpackers Hostel D2
32 Hostal North House B2
33 Hotel de la Plaza B2
34 Hotel Terrado Suites C2
35 Residencial El Turista D2

Services ★

36 Afex B1
37 Automóvil Club de Chile B2
38 Banco de Chile B1
39 Correos B1
40 Chilexpress C1
41 Hospital D1
42 Mundo Click B1
43 Lavarrápido C2
44 Police B2
45 Scotiabank B1
46 Santander B1
47 Sernatur B1
48 Thrifty B2

Shopping

49 Galería Turística Artesanal B1
50 Marka Sawuri B2
51 Mall de las Américas D2

Tours ♦

52 Peninsula Travel Service B2
53 O.C. Travel B1
54 Turismo Lirima B1

Transportation 🚍

55 Aeropuerto Internacional
    "Diego Aracena" B2
56 Aeropuerto Tarapacá kiosk B2
57 Arrendamos Bicicletas B2
58 Avis C2
59 Hertz B2
60 Kenny Bus D2
61 Lan B1
62 Sky Airline C1
63 Terminal Internacional Rodoviario B1
64 TurBus C1

Photo by Eszter Sára Kóspál

An Introduction to Iquique's Beaches

A chain of pale beaches drape southward along Iquique's coast. Starting in the city's center, at Calle O'Higgins and Avenida Prat, **Bellavista** is a broad band of sand trimmed with ragged rock. Although most of the beach is not safe for swimming, adventuresome surfers take turns here. Paseo Costanera Parque Balmaceda is a sail-roofed promenade along Avenida Prat, connecting Bellavista with the city's most popular beach, **Playa Cavancha**, on the north edge of Península Cavancha and the Club Náutico. **Playa Buque** is on the south side of the peninsula. There are good places to picnic in the many nooks in the rock heaps and, at low tide, pools large enough for swimming. Locals often fish at this beach.

Continuing along Avenida Prat, Parque Las Americas flies all of the flags of Latin America. Next on the coast, **Playa Brava** is a several-kilometer-long, pale beige beach perfect for sunbathing, building sandcastles and flying kites. An expansive promenade paralleling it has a skateboard and mountain bike tracks, as well as a large playground. Further on, **Primer Piedra's** rocky shore is perfect for picnicking, fishing or checking out tidal pools. Expensive mansions hug the shore.

To get to the last of Iquique's beaches, **Playa Huaquique**, you must turn back inland toward the avenue. This beach is most popular among surfers and is suitable for all levels of expertise. The long strand of sand is also good for beach sports, sunbathing and fishing, though not for swimming. A lot of shore and seabirds also hang out here. To get to Playa Huaquique, take any bus marked "Huaquique" ($0.80). It is almost 10 kilometers (6 mi) from there to Playa Bellavista. You can spend the day wandering from one beach to another. Most of the beaches are marked not safe for swimming, though in summer some have lifeguards on duty. Updated: Jun 30, 2009.

NORTE GRANDE

(Latorre, between Barros Arana and Amunategui), has murals on its walls depicting the story of the massacre. Cementerio Número Dos and the mass grave in which the massacre victims were buried lie within the walls of Cementerio Número Tres. On the outside of this graveyard are memorial plaques to the victims of the Pinochet dictatorship.

Iquique has become a prime destination for both national and foreign travelers. Its year-round sunny skies and warm temperatures draw many the town's Playa Cavancha and other fine beaches. The waves here are among some of the most famous in the world. Visitors also head outside of the city to see the geoglyphs and rusting saltpeter mines, soak in the hot springs of Mamiña and Pica, and take in the religious fervor of villages like La Tirana and Tarapacá.

Iquique has the Zofri, a *zona franca* (free trade zone). People come from as far away as Paraguay to go shopping here, and Chileans come from all over the country to purchase used cars. As part of the Corredor Internacional shipping highway to Oruro, Bolivia, the importance of this port city continues to grow. Updated: Jul 07, 2009.

When to Go

During the summer (December – March), the weather is hot during the day and brisk at night. The rest of the year is more pleasant. Nights tend to be cold, though, between June and September.

HOLIDAYS AND FIESTAS

Iquique is a popular destination in the summer (December – March), for Fiestas Patrias in September, and during other national holidays. During these times things in Iquique tend to get a bit crowded and pricey. During these months the city hosts a variety of arts festivals. In January, keep an ear out for the Festival de Tunas y Estudiantes, a competition of university *tunas*, or mediaeval-era troubadour troupes. In February the Festival del Teatro, the Encuentro de Danza América and the big Festival de Iquique feature internationally known musicians.

The pre-Lenten Carnaval de Iquique is marked in February or March. During Semana Santa (March – April), Iquiqueños climb the bluff behind town to the Estaciones de la Cruz (Stations of the Cross) to seek forgiveness for last year's sins. Don't miss the fishermen's tipping of the hat to San Pedro on June 29 out at Cavancha Peninsula. May 21 is also a big holiday here,

The Ghosts of Iquique

The pampas have their share of legends. Uncounted thousands died crossing the arid plains, hoping to find work in the mines. Many more died laboring there. In the highlands there are tales of phantom hitchhikers—drivers will not pick up anyone unless the hitcher is at a town or rest stop. Truckers keep a bottle of urine handy to dispel any spirits still lost in the barren salt lands. And in Pisagua, where so many were tortured and executed, people speak of moans overheard after dark. Ghosts of the past are also said to wander Iquique. Guards at the Palacio Astoreca say they hear and see things at night, and there are rumors of screams heard in and around Escuela Santa María, especially on December 21. Updated: Jun 30, 2009.

commemorating the decisive naval battle of the Guerra del Pacífico and the death of Commander Arturo Prat. Music, cueca dancing, tours and other events pay tribute to that heroic Chilean victory. Updated: Jun 29, 2009.

Getting To and Away From Iquique

BY BUS

Most long-distance buses depart from the Terminal Internacional Rodoviario, whose facilities include bathrooms, showers, phone, Internet, snack shops and luggage storage (Av. Prat and Lynch, Tel: 56-57-416315). Other buses include: **TurBus** (Esmeralda 594), **Kenny Bus** (La Torre 944) and **Cuevas y González** (Sargento Aldea 850).

Many companies have offices around Mercado Centenario. **Pullman Bus**, **Carmelita**, **Ramos Cholete**, **TurBus** (ticket office only), **Zambrano**, **Cruz del Norte**, **Santa Angela** and **Chacón** are on Barros Arana. **Santa Rosa** and **Ormeño** are on Sargento Aldea.

To Arica: $15, 5 hours—**Santa Rosa** (every 3.5 – 4 hours 7:20 a.m. – 1:45 a.m.). Also Cuevas y González. Only morning buses to Arica leave from the Rodoviario; afternoon runs depart from individual bus depots.

To Calama: $20, 5 – 6 hours—**Pullman Bus** (3:45 p.m., 11 p.m.), **Kenny Bus** (5 p.m., 10:30 p.m., $24-40). Also **TurBus**.

To San Pedro de Atacama: Go to Calama first, and take a bus from there.

To Santiago and points between: 25 hours—**TurBus** (hourly 10 a.m. – 9 p.m., $75-134 depending on level of service), **Pullman** (9 a.m., 11:45 a.m., 5:30 p.m., 8 p.m., $56-80), **Flota Barrios** (8:45 a.m.,

$60), **Carmelita** (8 a.m., 2 p.m., 5 p.m., $64), **Zambrano** (4 p.m., 7 p.m., $66). Also **San Andrés**.

To Antofagasta: 6 hours—**TurBus** (same bus as to Santiago, $30 – 48), **Pullman** (direct 3:30 p.m., 11 p.m., $20).

To Tocopilla: TurBus (Santiago schedule, $14 – 32, 4 hours). For Antofagasta and Tocopilla you can also take any Santiago-bound bus that is taking the coastal (not inland) route.

To Santa Laura and Humberstone: Santa Angela ($3.80) or any bus or colectivo going to Pozo Almonte, La Tirana or Pica.
To Huara: Take any bus heading to Arica, $8.
To Pozo Almonte: Chacón ($3.80). Also yellow colectivos from Sargento Aldana (daily 7 a.m. – 9 p.m., last return 8:45 p.m., $4).

To Mamiña: Santa Angela (daily 8 a.m., return 6 p.m., $7 one way), **Cruz del Norte** (Monday – Saturday 8 a.m., 4 p.m., return 8 a.m., 6 p.m, Sunday 8 a.m., return 6 p.m., $7.50).

To La Tirana / Pica: Several companies along the 900-block of Barros Aldana run this route 8 a.m. – 9 p.m., including Santa Angela and Chacón ($5 / $5.50). Colectivo taxis leave from Sargento Aldana and Amantegui ($7 / 8).

To Peru and Bolivia: International buses from Iquique going to Peru and La Paz, Bolivia, involve a transfer in Arica. On those services to Uyuni or Oruro, Bolivia, passengers must change in Calama.

To La Paz: Cuevas y González (daily 1:30 a.m., by way of Arica, $30, 14 hours).

BY AIR
Aeropuerto Internacional Diego Aracena is 40 kilometers (24 mi) south of the city (Tel: 56-57-420349 / 410787). For

a taxi to the airport, contact **Aeropuerto Tarapacá**. Monday – Saturday 6:30 a.m. – midnight. Kisosk at the corner of Baquedano and Wilson, Tel: 56-57-419004, Fax: 56-57-415916, E-mail: taxistarapaca@tie.cl (private taxi $20, shared taxi $10).

LAN (Monday – Friday 8:45 a.m. – 2 p.m., 3:45 – 6:30 p.m., Saturday 9:30 a.m. – 1 p.m. Tarapacá 465, Tel: 600-526-2000, URL: www.lan.com)—flights to **Arica** (one flight daily, $63 round trip), **Santiago** (5 daily, $127 – 193), **Antofagasta** (once daily, $63 round trip), and also to **Santa Cruz** and **La Paz**, Bolivia. One-way flights are more expensive than round-trip ones.

Sky Airline (Monday – Friday 9 a.m. – 2 p.m., 4 – 7 p.m., Saturday 10 a.m. – 1 p.m. Tarapacá 530, Tel: 56-57-415013, URL: www.skyairline.cl)—flights to **Santiago** (by way of Antofagasta or Copiapó, Saturday direct—3 days per week, 2 flights on weekends, $150 – 314), **Arica** (Daily $48 – 70), **Arequipa**, Perú (Wednesday, Friday, Sunday). Updated: Jun 29, 2009.

Getting Around

Micros, or urban minibuses, operate within the city and go up to Alto Hospicio (until 10 p.m., $0.80 – 1). Colectivos are shared taxis that run set routes ($1). You can phone ahead for a taxi or flag one down on the street ($2.50 and up).

Bicycles are another way to zip around the city and to the beaches. Centrally located **Arrendamos Bicicletas** (Baquedano 1440, Tel: 56-57-417599, E-mail: paseandoenbici@gmail.com) provides chains, locks and helmets with its rentals (1.5 hours $4, five hours $7, eight hours $12, plus $20 security deposit).

Some places around Iquique are easier to reach in a rented car; try **Thrifty** (Lynch 898, Tel: 56-57-472612), **Avis** (M. Rodríguez 722-730, Tel: 56-57-4330; airport Tel: 56-57407049), or **Hertz** (Aníbal Pinto 1303, Tel: 56-57-510432; airport Tel: 56-57-410924). Updated: Jun 27, 2009.

Safety

Beware of pickpocketers on the beach and at the bus terminals. After dark, take special care around the market and port. When at the beach, pay attention to signed warnings. Most beaches are marked off limits for swimming due to rocks and heavy surf. Heavy weather sometimes causes beaches to close down to water sports. Updated: Jun 27, 2009.

Services

TOURISM

Sernatur, the tourism office for Tarapacá Region, has maps but scarce information. It is now developing a tourism route along the pre-Inca stone roads in the altiplano, to be part of the nation-wide Sendero de Chile (Monday – Friday 9 a.m. – 5 p.m., Saturday 10 a.m. – 2 p.m. Pinto 436, Tel: 56-57-419241, E-mail: infoiquique@sernatur.cl.)

The city's tourism office, **Dirección de Turismo y Cultura**, has better information about the city, including a map with descriptions of attractions. During the high season the office has kiosks on Plaza Prat and at Playa Cavancha (Monday – Friday 8 a.m. – 5 p.m. Edificio Ex-Aduana, piso 2, Tel: 56-57-514799, Fax: 56-57-514765, E-mail: turismo.iquique@gmail.com, URL: www.municipioiquique.com).

Conaf, the national park service, has its main office in Reserva Nacional Pampa de Tamarugal (Carretera Panamericana Norte Ruta A-5, Km 1787, Tel: 56-57-751055).

Other useful websites are: www.iquique.com and www.iquiqueonline.cl.

Additional services in the city are: **Carabineros** (O'Higgins 427, Tel: 55-7040, Emergency 133), and **Automóvil Club de Chile** (Av. Héroes de la Concepción 2855, Tel: 52-7333).

Several nations have consulates in Iquique:

Bolivia—Gorostiaga 215, 3rd floor, apartment E, Tel: 56-57-414506, E-mail: colivianiquique@entelchile.net
Holland—Tarapacá 123, Tel: 56-57-393110
Italy—Serrano 447, Tel: 56-57-421588
Paraguay—San Martín 385; Patricio Lynch, office 104, 4th floor Tel: 56-57-419040
Peru—Zegers 570, Tel: 56-57-411466
Spain—Oficina Mapocho, Sitio 48 F; Casilla 1522, Correo ZOFRI, Tel: 56-57-413016
Sweden and Norway—Zegers 249, Tel: 56-57-411584

MONEY

Most banks are open between 8 a.m. and 2 or 4 p.m. The following, located near Plaza Prat, exchange U.S. dollars and euros, and have ATMs that accept Visa, Plus, MasterCard and Cirrus: **Banco de Chile** (Baquedano, 600 block, on Plaza Prat), **BBVA** (Plaza Prat 594), **Santander** (Uribe 525), **Scotiabank** (Uribe and Serrano; its ATM also accepts American Express).

NORTE GRANDE

Casas de cambio exchange most major Western currencies and Japanese yen, as well as American Express traveler's checks (at a slightly lower rate): **Afex** (Monday – Friday 8:30 a.m. – 5 p.m., Saturday 10 a.m. – 1 p.m. Lynch 467A, Tel: 56-57-414324), **Cambios Guiñazú** (Monday – Friday 8:30 a.m. – 6 p.m, Saturday 9:30 a.m. – 1 p.m.). Other exchange houses are in the mall at Lynch and Tarapacá.

Chilexpress is a Western Union agent that wires in U.S. dollars or Chilean pesos (Monday – Friday 9 a.m. – 7 p.m., Saturday 10 a.m. – 1 p.m. Tarapacá 520).

KEEPING IN TOUCH

The **post office** is where you can drop a letter to the gang back home (Monday – Friday 9 a.m. – 2 p.m., 3:30 p.m. – 7 p.m., Saturday 9 a.m. – 12:30 p.m. Bolívar 485). **Entel** provides national and international phone service at several locations throughout the downtown area (Gorostiaga 287, Diego Portales 840, Tarapacá 472).

Internet access can be found all over the city and even the smaller cafés have Skype. They charge $0.80 – 1 per hour. Many are closed on Sunday. A good choice any day of the week is **Mundo Click** (Monday – Friday 9 a.m. – 2 a.m., Saturday 11 a.m. – 2 a.m., Sunday 1 p.m. – 2a.m. La Torre 370, Tel: 56-57-413774; $0.80 per hour).

MEDICAL

The regional medical center is **Hospital Dr. Ernesto Torres Galdames** (Av. Héroes de la Concepción 502, Tel: 56-57-405700). In the downtown area, there are several pharmacies on the 700 and 800 block of Vivar and the 600 block of Tarapacá. The local newspaper, *La Estrella de Iquique*, lists the day's farmacia de turno, the drugstore that'll be open throughout the night.

LAUNDRY

Lavarrápido charges $3 per kilo for washing and drying, with same-day service, even on Saturday, if dropped off early in the morning (Monday – Friday 9 a.m. – 1 p.m., 4 – 8 p.m., Saturday 9 a.m. – 2 p.m. Labbé 1446, Tel: 56-57-344727).

SHOPPING

Along Paseo Baquedano, near Plaza Prat, street stalls sell artisan wares, antiques, books and other wares. **Galería Turística Artesanal** is a mini-mall of artisan stands selling everything from handmade crafts to kitschy souvenirs (Gorostiaga 301). **Marka Sawuri**, a cooperative of Aymara women from Chile's Altiplano, sells fine shawls, *ruandas* (ponchos) and clothing. All are handmade from alpaca (Sunday – Friday 10 a.m. – 2 p.m., 3 – 7 p.m. Baquedano 958, Tel: 56-57-519594, E-mail: contactos@markasawuri.cl, URL: www.markasawuri.cl).

Megashoppers have a few places in Iquique where they can flex their muscles. **Mall de las Américas** is a typical U.S.-style shopping center, replete with movie theaters and a food court (daily 11 a.m. – 9 p.m. Av. Héroes de la Concepción near Playa Cavancha. URL: www.zofri.com). The big game, however, is out at the **Zona Franca de Iquique**, simply known as Zofri (on north side of town, beyond Av. Barranquilla, Tel: 56-57-515600).

This free-trade zone draws shoppers from all corners of Latin America and the world. Any import item can be purchased here, including electronics and motorcycle parts. Balfer specializes in camping gear. To get to Zofri, take a black and yellow colectivo taxi with a Zofri sign in its window ($1). Monday – Saturday 11 a.m. – 9 p.m., open Sundays in summer. Zofri Mall, Módulo 2032, Tel: 56-57-419006 / 414669, E-mail: balferiq@balfer.cl. Updated: Jun 29, 2009.

Things to See and Do

Iquique has many beautiful old mansions to visit, as well as museums that provide a window into the city's history. Most attractions are located around Plaza Prat and along Paseo Baquedano. Other interesting buildings include the ex-Estación de Ferrocarriles (Sotomayor and Vivar) and the Iglesia Catedral (Bolívar and Ramírez).

Ocean explorations are also popular, whether above the waves in a one-hour boat tour of the bay (from the Muelle de Pasajeros on Av. Prat; adults $4, teens $2, under 12 free, minimum 10 passengers), or scuba diving. Iquique is one of the hottest spots to surf, and paragliding is becoming a popular adventure sport.

Iquique is a good base for day trips out to the nitrate mining towns of Humberstone and Santa Laura (take the Tren Pampino from Pozo Almonte train station). The hot springs at Pica and Mamiña, the Reserva Nacional Pampas de Tamarugal and the numerous geoglyphs are all nearby, as is the Gigante de Atacama. Updated: Jun 30, 2009.

Museo Regional

(ADMISSION: Donations accepted) Museo Regional's many galleries lead you through the history of the Iquique region. Most of the rooms trace the development of the indigenous cultures, beginning with the Chinchorros who lived along this coast around 4000 – 2000 BC. A special attraction of the museum is the mummies from this epoch. The rise and influence of the Tiwanaku Empire and Inca conquest are also discussed, as are modern Aymara traditions. Other rooms cover the nitrate mine era, with a collection of tokens that the different companies issued to their workers in lieu of the national money. Explanations are only in Spanish. Monday – Friday 9 a.m. – 5:30 p.m., weekends and holidays 10 a.m. – 5 p.m. Baquedano 951. Tel: 56-57-413278. Updated: Jul 02, 2009.

Museo Naval de Iquique and The Edificio de la Aduana

(ADMISSION: $0.40, children: free) The Museo Naval de Iquique is on the south side of the old Aduana building. Dedicated to one of the most important sea battles of the Guerra del Pacífico, maps and dioramas recount the blow-by-blow action of May 21, 1879. Exhibits also include artifacts of the two sunken ships, the Esmeralda the Independencia. Monday – Friday 10 a.m. – 11:30 a.m., 2 – 4 p.m., Sotomayor and Baquedano.

Around the corner, in the main part of the ex-Aduana, are displays about Iquique's history. A supplemental collection of big guns and anchors are at the Naval Base near the bus terminal. Tuesday – Friday 10 a.m. – 1 p.m., 4 – 8 p.m. Saturday 10 a.m. – 1 p.m., closed Sunday and Monday. Updated: Jun 29, 2009.

Plaza Prat

The neo-Gothic Torre del Reloj is located in the plaza's center. The clock tower was designed by French architect Eduardo de Lapeyrouse and built in 1877. The tower was inaugurated just months before the naval battle that forever changed the city. The gazebo next to the tower is a fun place to hang out and people watch. Hrvatski Dom, the social club of Iquique's immigrant Croatian community, is on the northeast corner of the plaza (Club Croata, Plaza Prat 310, Tel: 56-57-764162).

Next door, the Casino Español (Plaza Prat 584 Tel: 56-57-333911) is popular with the resident Spanish community. Designed in 1903 by Miguel Retornano, the building has spectacularly rich Moorish styling. Interior murals depict scenes from Spanish history. Some were painted by Sixto Rojas, who survived the Escuela Santa María massacre.

Chilean's elite enjoy retreating to the Club Protectora on the plaza's southwest corner. Beside the Protectora, the Teatro Municipal, built in 1889 from Oregon pine, has a neo-Classic façade featuring four female figures representing each season. Tours are available. (Daily 8 a.m. – 5 p.m. Entry: adults $2, students and retirees $1. Thompson 269, corner of Baquedano, Tel: 56-57-544734, E-mail: teatromunicipal@yahoo.es).

Paseo Baquedano

Paseo Baquedano is a pedestrian street lined with family casonas built during the nitrate mine heyday (1880-1920). Many are built of Oregon pine imported from the U.S. and Canada. These mansions are of Georgian-style architecture, characterized by slender columns, wood balustrades and balconies. Wrought-iron street lanterns run down the center of the flagstone street. Take a leisurely stroll down the wooden plank sidewalks, stopping into the many museums, artisan galleries and sidewalk cafés.

Calle Zeger (900 block of Baquedano) has a plaza with fountains and bstract marble sculptures by Hernán Puelma (2005) give a modern touch to this length of the paseo. Along this stretch, the **Sala de Arte Casa Collahuasi** hosts art exhibits, free movies and other cultural events (Tuesday – Friday 11 a.m. – 7 p.m., Saturday 10 a.m. – 2 p.m. Baquedano 930). The Aymara women's cooperative, **Marka Sawuri**, is a few doors down. On the other side of the street, the **Museo Regional** has an impressive collection of ancient indigenous artifacts (Monday – Friday 9 a.m. – 5:30 p.m., weekends and holidays 10 a.m. – 5 p.m. Baquedano 951. Entry by donation). On the next corner, O'Higgins, the Palacio Astoreca is furnished with luxurious period furniture.

Museo Histórico Militar Tarapacá is dedicated to the Guerra del Pacífico, with maps of the battles, as well as armaments, photos and soldiers' personal effects (Monday – Friday 10 a.m. – 1:15 p.m., 4:15 – 7 p.m., Wednesday 10 a.m. – 1:30 p.m. Baquedano 1396. Entry by donation). Just after this museum, Baquedano merges with Avenida Prat, near the Paseo Costanera Parque Balmaceda, between Playas Bellavista and Cavancha. At this intersection there is a giant monument dedicated to the hero of the Guerra del Pacífico, Arturo Prat. Updated: Jul 02, 2009.

Palacio Astoreca

This impressive Georgian-style pine mansion was designed and built by Manuel Ritornano for the Astoreca family. They never lived here, though, as they moved to Valparaíso after patriarch Juan Higinio Astoreca's death. The Palacio is a museum exhibiting furniture from different periods (neo-French Renaissance, faux Louis XIV-XVI, neo-Classical and Art Nouveau), much of it made of mahogany. An incredible three-panel, stained glass skylight crowns the front hall. There are temporary art exhibits on the second floor, plus two rooms with permanent collections of seashells. O'Higgins 350, and Baquedano. Tel: 56-57-425600. Monday – Friday 10 a.m., 4 p.m., Saturday 10 a.m., Monday – Friday 1 p.m., 7 p.m., Saturday 1 p.m., closed Sundays. Updated: Jun 29, 2009.

Playa Cavancha

The biggest beach scene in Iquique is at Playa Cavancha. Everyone heads out its several kilometers of pale gray sand to lie in the sun or to surf in the brisk water. This perfectly crescent-shaped beach has much to offer.

From Avenida Prat to the sea there is a long wooden walkway lined with food and souvenir stalls, Casino Iquique, and Aventura Yacaré, an aquarium and mini-zoo featuring the *yacaré* to the north (Tuesday – Sunday 9 a.m. – 9 p.m.).

A short walk up the grassy park between the avenue and beach will bring you to Parque Temático Cavancha, where sea lions give free shows in El Colegio de los Lobos (Friday 11:30 a.m., Saturday 12:30 p.m. and 4:30 p.m. Tel: 56-57-544857 / 8-929-4160, E-mail: p.villegas.f@gmail.com). The parks' corrals are home to alpaca and llama. Along the promenade there are pools with waterfalls cascading off man-made rocks.

Playa Cavancha is classified as a beginner surfer's beach, though do beware of the rocks. There are many upscale hotels and restaurants on Península Cavancha as well as the small Santuario de Lourdes whose altar screen is a replica of the Lourdes caves in France.

Playa Cavancha is about a 15-minute walk from Iquique's town center. *Micro* (city bus) No. 10 leaves from Tarapacá and Martínez downtown to go to Playas Brava, Cavancha and Huaquique ($0.80). Updated: Jun 30, 2009.

Surfing

Iquique is internationally renowned for its surfing. Every year the city hosts the Juegos Panamericanos de Surf at the beginning of November (www.panamericansurf.com). In the interim, you can get in shape by hitting the local beaches. Beginners should aim for El Faro or Cavancha. Both of these have left- and right-wave action. Huaquique (which sounds eerily like Waikiki) has five-point waves.

The water is chilly in this part of Chile, so a wetsuit is highly recommended. To find out about surf conditions in Iquique, consult http://magicseaweed.com/Iquique-Surf-Report/421 or www.surfline.com. Some surfers consider action to be better up the coast at Arica.

Some hostels, like Backpackers (p.219), rent boards and have instructors. **Vertical Rent and Tour** rents surfing equipment and gives lessons (Av. Arturo Prat 580, Tel: 56-57-376034, E-mail: rent@verticalst.cl, URL: www.verticalst.cl).

To get to Playa Huaquique, take any bus marked "Huaquique" ($0.80). Micro No. 10 leaves from Tarapacá and Martínez downtown to go to Playas Brava, Cavancha and Huaquique ($0.80).Updated: Jun 30, 2009.

Paragliding in Iquique

Strap on wings and go soaring above the bay of Iquique. Paragliding (*parapentismo*) gives flyers a bird's eye view of the nitrate flats and geoglyphs decorating the landscape. The take-off point is at Alto Hospicio. Beginners can go in tandem flights with a pro, or take courses to learn to leap solo. Several agencies specialize in paragliding: **Fly Iquique** (Labbé 1518, Tel: 56-57-427008 / 432373, E-mail: Miguel.flyiquique@gmail.com) and **Escuela Profesional de Parapente**. For information about parapentismo in Iquique, visit www.parapenteiquique.cl. Updated: Jun 30, 2009.

Tours

O.C. Travel

O.C. Travel has one of the most extensive lists of tours in the Iquique region, including all-day trips to Pica and the salt mines ($36 per person), and the Mamiña hot springs ($40). This is the only agency that offers trips to Pisagua (Monday and Wednesday $44). Half-day excursions to Salar Grande and the South Coast ($24 per person)are available, as well as a historic tour of the bay ($9) and a cultural city tour ($24).

O.C. Travel works primarily with senior citizen groups, with set days for excursions, but it also accepts the lone traveler. O.C. also arranges paragliding and scuba adventures, and multi-day trips to the Altiplano. Monday – Friday 8:30 a.m. – 2 p.m., 4 – 7 p.m., Serrano 389, office 407. Tel: 56-57-3260 / 56-57-3263, E-mail: info@octravel.cl, URL: www.octravel.cl. Updated: Jun 29, 2009.

Turismo Lirima

Turismo Lirima offers all-day tours to sites in and around Iquique. The Oasis de Pica tour visits Santa Laura and Humberstone, Pozo Almonte, Reserva Nacional Pampa de Tamarugal, Pica and other hotspots along this route, which happens to be decked with geoglyphs ($34 per person). The costera tour goes along the southern coast, stopping at archaeological sites like Salar Grande and several beaches. Day tours include guide, transport, lunch, snack and park fees. The agency coordinates sole travelers into groups. Lirima also has multi-day excursions to Lauca and the other parks in the Altiplano. Galería Turística Artesanal, Gorostiaga 301. Tel: 56-57391384, E-mail: turismolirima@hotmail.com. Updated: Jul 02, 2009.

Peninsula Travel Service

Peninsula Travel Service offers tours of Iquique city, the ex-Salitrera route (Humberstone and Oficina Santa Laura), the hot springs at Pica, and visits down the coast to see cave paintings. Prices for excursions are slightly higher in the summer season. Ask about student and child discounts. Manuel Antonio Matta 2757, Apt. 2602, Cavancha. Tel: 33-1938, E-mail: contacto@peninsula-turismo.cl, URL: www.peninsulaturismo.cl. Updated: Jun 29, 2009.

Lodging

Iquique has accommodation to fit almost all budget levels. The city has several international chain hotels, like Radisson and Holiday Inn, and even has marina hotels for those arriving in on their own yacht. Budget travelers should know that, in general, rooms with shared baths cost up to $16 per person and those with private bath

start at $24. Many cheap and low-mid-range hostels are located near the market. Some are dives, while others are OK. Hotel prices begin to rise at the end of October and remain high through March. Also expect to pay more during national holidays. Updated: Jun 29, 2009.

Residencial El Turista

(ROOMS: $10) Residencial El Turista is one of the nicer inexpensive hotels in the market area. The multi-level hotel is like a giant labyrinth and is full of travelers, long-term guests and Latin Americans on shopping expeditions to the Zofri. The place can be quite noisy at times, but the staff is friendly and accommodating, helping their guests negotiate the intricacies of the city. Hot water is available in the morning and evening in each of its 16 showers. Martínez 857. Tel: 56-57-422245, Fax: 56-57-474238. Updated: Jun 30, 2009.

Backpackers Hostel

(ROOMS: $12 – 28) Popular and busy is the best way to describe Backpackers Hostel. Located just a block from Cavancha Beach, this is the preferred destination for budget travelers. Like other Hosteling International entries, Backpackers is equipped with common areas, a kitchen and BBQ area. It also has some extras, like a billiards room. The hostel rents bikes, as well as surf and body boards that they sometimes use to teach surfing to guests. The rooftop has a wonderful ocean view. The hostel will pick you up at the bus station for free. Amunategui 2075. Tel: 56-57-320223. Updated: Jun 30, 2009.

Hostal North House

(ROOMS: $14 – 36) Close to the beach, Hostal North House is in a well-kept, nearly century-old house. Natural wood gleams throughout the spacious rooms, available for solo travelers, couples and groups. All accommodations come with private bath and cable TV. The hostel also offers paragliding flights and lessons. Labbé 1518. Tel: 56-57-427008 / 8-6698519, E-mail: Miguel.flyiquique@gmail.com. Updated: Jun 30, 2009.

Hotel de la Plaza

(ROOMS: $22– 36) Hotel de la Plaza is located in one of the nitrate-era mansions on the Baquedano pedestrian mall. Here, travelers can sample the luxury of that by-gone time. A new back addition has several floors of shining guest rooms set around a patio. All accommodations include private, hot-water bath and cable TV. Hotel de la Plaza is in the heart of the city, just four and a half blocks from the sea. Baquedano 1025. Tel: 56-57-417172. Updated: Jun 30, 2009.

Hotel Terrado Suites

(ROOMS: $113 – 289) Hotel Terrado Suites is a high-rise hotel on the Cavancha Peninsula. The lobby is laid in three-color marble, and common areas and a patio with swimming pools line the seafront. Executive rooms have views over the city and superior suites have balconies over Playa Cavancha. The Suite Royal is the most exclusive accommodation here. Guests receive the five-star treatment, with a free spa session and a welcome drink upon arrival. You can arrive by car or yacht—Terrado has both a garage and a marina. Los Rieles 126, Península de Cavancha. Tel: 56-57-437755, E-mail: reservassuites@terrado.cl, URL: www.terrado.cl. Updated: Jun 30, 2009.

Restaurants

As can be expected in an ocean-side city, seafood is a big item on Iquiqueño menus. Empanadas made of crab and shrimp make a delicious and cheap quick meal. While in Iquique, try a *chumbeque* (p.208), a local treat. Iquique's central market, Mercado Centenario, sells produce and other products, and has inexpensive restaurants (Sargento Aldana, between Amunategui and Barros Arana). Two supermarkets are also in the downtown area: **Rossi** (Tarapacá 579) and **Palmira** (M. Rodríguez 964 and Vivar 786). Updated: Jun 29, 2009.

Salón de Té y Cafetería Vizzio

Salón de Té y Cafetería Vizzio is a popular getaway from the bustle of the city. Its broad windows, polished woodwork and mirrored walls make this a great people-watching spot. Coffee and tea are served. Food items include sandwiches and desserts (from $4.40). Monday – Saturday 8:30 a.m. – 10:30 p.m. Tarapacá 400. Tel: 56-57-325869. Updated: Jun 30, 2009.

Boccados

(LUNCH: $2) Boccados, on a narrow side street just up from Paseo Baquedano, is actually a family who has opened up its home to provide one of Iquique's most affordable restaurants. The couch and chairs are pushed to the walls, and tables are set in the former parlor and two other rooms. Every day people crowd in to enjoy the two-plate *colación* (special) of delicious,

traditional Chilean fare dished up by the family. Breakfast starts at $1.10. Monday – Friday 9 a.m. – 5 p.m., weekends 10 a.m. – 5 p.m. Latorre 362. Updated: Jun 30, 2009.

Capuccino Pizza

(ENTREES: $4 – 10) Capuccino Pizza is in one of the old mansions lining Paseo Baquedano. This bistro has a lot more on its menu than pizza, serving up three-course lunch specials, seafood empanadas and sandwiches—just the thing to hit the spot during your sightseeing tour. Capuccino's sidewalk café is a great place to sit and check out the street scene. The daily lunch special is $6. Monday – Saturday 9 a.m. – 1 a.m., Sunday noon – 1 a.m. Baquedano 796-798. Tel: 56-57-416528. Updated: Jun 30, 2009.

Restaurant El Tercer Ojito

(ENTREES: $9.80 – 15) It's pretty hard to find a place catering to vegetarians in Iquique, but El Tercer Ojito's owner Cristina Burchardi (granddaughter of painter Pablo Burchardi) has created a wondrous menu of gourmet-styled vegetarian foods. Seafood dishes also grace the menu. The back courtyard patio is a quiet place to enjoy your meal. The lunch is $7 (not including drink). Tuesday – Sunday 12:30 – 5 p.m., 7:30 – 10 p.m. Lynch 1420-A. Tel: 56-57-426517 / 41-3847, E-mail: contacto@eltercerojito.cl, URL: www.eltercerojito.cl. Updated: Jun 30, 2009.

Café Split

(LUNCH: $6.60) Despite its real name, everyone knows this place as Club Croatia. Still serving as the Hrvatski Dom—the home of Iquique's Croatian community, it is also an upscale restaurant. The daily lunch runs from 1 – 4:30 p.m and includes a three-course meal that comes with soda or wine, tea or coffee, and dessert. After 4:30, the café becomes a pub, serving only sandwiches, juices, coffee and drinks. Monday – Friday 9 a.m. – 2 a.m., Saturday 10:30 a.m. – 4 a.m. Plaza Prat 310. Tel: 56-57-764162, E-mail: ctmconcesionaria@gmail.com. Updated: Jun 30, 2009.

Club Democrático

(COVER: $2 and up) It's not a glitzy place, but on Friday and Saturday nights Club Democrático fills up with people coming to hear the club's live jazz. Club Democrático also features Andean music and *nuevo canto* (modern folk music). Doors open at about 9 p.m. and shows begin around 11 p.m. The neighborhood is a bit sketchy after dark, so don't carry valuables and consider taking a taxi. Labbé 466-470. Updated: Jun 30, 2009.

New Mango's Club
(ENTREES: $6.40 – 10.40) Salsa reigns supreme at New Mango's Club on Friday and Saturday nights. A DJ spins from 10 p.m. until the band takes the stage at 1:30 a.m.—then the place really picks up. Take a break from the dance floor at one of the many tables or booths, gazing out the long window into the night sea while having a cocktail with friends. Mango's isn't just a place to dance until dawn—it also serves lunch specials ($7.60), à la carte dinners and pizzas. Tuesday – Sunday 12:30 – 4 p.m., 8 p.m. – 4 a.m. (to 5 a.m. Friday and Saturday). Av. Arturo Prat 1727. Tel: 56-57-437507 / 450737, E-mail: chefhhernandez@chile.com. Updated: Jun 30, 2009.

AROUND IQUIQUE
HUMBERSTONE
Salitrera Humberstone was one of the most famous and largest nitrate mines in northern Chile. Founded in 1872 by the Peruvian Nitrate Company, by 1889 it had a population of over 3,000. It later changed its name to Salitrera La Palma in 1894, and again in 1934 to Humberstone, in honor of Santiago Humberstone who had developed the Shanks method of refining nitrate ore. By 1940, over 3,700 workers labored here.

Humberstone was declared a Monumento Nacional in 1971 and a UNESCO World Heritage of Humanity Site in 2005 (URL: www.museodelsalitre.cl). Chilean poet Pablo Neruda came to the region in the 1940s, and documented the horrendous work and living conditions through his poetry, most notably in *Canto General.*

Humberstone gives an inside look into the mine. The main street into the compound is lined with the higher-ranking employees' spacious homes. The plaza has a market (with artisan and souvenir stalls), church and hotel. On the north side there is an 800-seat theater that hosted European operas and Hollywood movies. To the west, the former general store is now a museum with exhibits of the daily life of miners and the 1907 Escuela Santa María Massacre.

Southeast of the plaza you'll find the block that used to be home for single male miners. Several men lived in each of these claustrophobic rooms, measuring only five by four meters (16 x 13 ft). A common bathhouse was used by the residents of the 62 rooms of each street. Behind this complex were the married workers' homes and their shared outhouses.

Administrators, the doctor and other upper echelon staff of the Humberstone lived around another plaza, just below the hill where the refinement plant was. These spacious homes had all the amenities. On the north side, the oldest building, the Casa Administrativa (1883), had lodging, a library, billiards parlor and game room, reflecting the typical colonial British architecture of the era, with a broad veranda.

A path leads up to a hill to the mechanical heart of Humberstone. The field is strewn with abandoned machines. Inside the refinery, signs explain nitrate processing. Beyond are the barren fields where miners scraped the ore from the earth's surface. Another trail leads up to the top of the waste ore pile. From atop you can see the entire Humberstone compound and a modern-day nitrate mine to the south.

Getting To and Away From Humberstone
Humberstone lies at the junction of Ruta 5 (Pan-American Highway) and Ruta A-16, which goes to Iquique (47 km / 29 mi). To get to Humberstone from Iquique, take the **Santa Angela** bus ($3.80), or take any bus or colectivo going to Pozo Almonte (Adults: $2; children under 12: $1.) Tickets include the entrance fee to Oficina Santa Laura (see below). Updated: Jul 01, 2009.

OFICINA SANTA LAURA
Oficina Santa Laura was another one of the many mines on the wind-blasted plains near Iquique. Founded in 1872 by William Wendell, it was acquired by the Peruvian government in 1878. After Chile's victory in the Guerra del Pacífico, the mine was turned over to the London Nitrate Co., Ltd. By 1921 Santa Laura was producing 3,500 tons of nitrate per month and four tons of iodine. It continued to operate until 1960. All that remains today is the Rancho de Empleados, with a museum displaying miscellaneous items found in the camp. In a shed there is a well-preserved Shanks plant with signs explaining the refinement process.

NORTE GRANDE

Oficina Santa Laura is about 1.5 kilometers (1 mi) west of Humberstone, on Ruta A-40. It is about a 25-minute walk between the two. Updated: Jul 06, 2009.

PARQUE NACIONAL VOLCÁN ISLUGA

(ADMISSION: free) Just north of Colchane is Parque Nacional (PN) Volcán Isluga, a 174,744-hectare park founded in 1967. The land rolls from an altitude of 2,100 meters (6,825 ft) to 5,400 meters (17,550 ft). The highest peaks are Quimsachata (5,400 m / 17,550 ft), Tatajachura (5,252 m / 18,382 ft) and Latarani (5,207 m / 19,923 ft). The park's namesake, Volcán Isluga (5,218 m / 16,959 ft), has permanent snows and fumeroles steaming into the blue sky. The most important river is Río Arabilla, whose headwaters are on the southern slopes of the Quimsachatas. The river changes it name several times during its course, to Río Islaga and finally Río Sitani. Lagunas Parinacota and Arabilla are important bird habitats.

Parque Nacional Volcán Isluga has two ecosystems: the Precordillera and the Altiplano. In the Precordillera zone (3,000 – 3,900 m/ 9,750 - 12,675 ft) zone, the principal flora are cacti and low-lying plants. Park animals include foxes and llamas. In the Altiplano, Indian fig, *llareta* and *paja brava* grow (over 4,000 m/13,000 ft). Vicuña, alpaca and vizcacha live on these high-altitude plains.

Birds at Bofedal Isluga include heron, while Río Islauga and Río Todos los Santos are home to geese, and along these rivers you also can spot ducks. The park protects many threatened species, including puma, gato colorado, taruca and guanaco. Endangered birds include the condor and different varieties of flamingos.

Isluga is divided into three sectors. The ranger station is at sector Enquelga, 10 kilometers (6 mi) from the park's northern entrance. Sector Poblado de Isluga is at the south end of the preserve, near Colchane. Both of these sectors have information and environmental education centers. The third sector is Laguna Arabilla. At Aguas Calientes, two kilometers (1.2 mi) south of the Enquelga guardería, there is a campsite for two tents and a fire pit at the side of two natural hot spring pools. The park has no restaurants; the nearest food facilities are in Colchane, the southern gateway town to the park. There are lodging options there, also.

Photography and wildlife observation are just two of the activities you enjoy while in PN Volcán Isluga. Archaeological sites like Pukará de Isluga, Cementerio Aymará Usamaya, the towns Chok and Cholloy, and the Chullpas de Sitani are tucked into the landscape. You may also visit Aymara villages and learn about indigenous culture.

The park has two trails:

Laguna Arabilla (Distance: 600 m/1,950 ft, difficulty: medium, duration: 30 min)— Five stations (miradores) take you through different ecological niches to the shores of Laguna Arabilla, where flamingos and other birds are found in abundance.

Pukará de Isluga (Distance: 3 km/1.8 mi, difficulty: medium-hard, duration: 2 - 2.5 hours)—This stone path off the Enquelga-Colchrane road goes to the top of a hill with great views of the Altiplano and volcanoes. Do not attempt this hike if you are affected by the altitude.

Take it easy and watch for signs of altitude sickness. The sun is strong; use sunglasses and sunscreen. Bring plenty of warm clothing, including hat and gloves. The park receives only 50 – 250 millimeters (2 – 10 in) of precipitation per year, mostly December-March. Temperatures average between 10ºC (50ºF) and -5ºC (23ºF). Updated: Jun 25, 2009.

Getting To and Away From Parque Nacional Volcán Isluga

To get to Parque Nacional Volcán Isluga from Iquique, take Ruta A-16 to Humberstone at the junction with Ruta 5. Turn north, toward Huara (26 km/16 mi), to the paved Ruta A-55. This goes northwest to Colchane (180 km/108 mi, 6 hours). The total distance is 250 kilometers (150 mi).

To get to the park from Arica, go south to Huara and follow Ruta A-55 (total distance: 250 km/150 mi, 5.5 hours). It is 15 kilometers from Colchane to the Sector Enquelga guardería There are buses from Iquique to Colchane. If driving, bring extra gasoline and check tires and brakes before setting out. Updated: Jun 25, 2009.

MAMIÑA

 2,750m 500 057

From Pozo Almonte, a road cuts across the pampa, entering the multi-colored Andean foothills. The road ends at Mamiña, a small village perched above a fertile valley. This desert oasis has long been known for its hot springs. The Inca and other indigenous people came here to restore their health. Legend says the Inca ruler's daughter, Ñusta Huillas, was going blind. He called his wisest advisors to come and demanded that they heal her. Searching high and low for an answer, the wise ones heard about hot springs that lay south of Cusco. The Inca rushed his daughter there and witnessed her sight restored. He called the place *Mamilla*, an Aymara word meaning "girl of my eyes."

These days, the village's cobblestone streets are lined with stone houses thatched with straw. Iglesia San Marcos, built in 1632, is a typical Andean church with two wooden bell towers. Outside the hamlet there are Inca-era ruins. The population, largely Aymara and Quechua, preserves many of their traditions. Every June solstice, they observe Inti Raymi. The Catholics also have celebrations, including Semana Santa (Easter Week) and Nuestra Señora del Rosario (first Sunday in October).

Like the Inca before them, most visitors come to Mamiña for its hot springs. One pool, **Ipla**, has 45°C (113°F) waters. The other, **El Tambo**, reaches 57°C (135°F). Mud baths are also part of the complex. Open all year, these mineral waters are said to be good for respiratory distresses, rheumatism, back problems and other ailments.

Mamiña has several lodging options. If you want to stay at the hot springs, try **Hotel Termas La Coruna** (Termas de Mamiña s/n, Tel: 56-57-420645, E-mail: termas24@hotmail.com) or **Hotel Termas de Mamiña** (Tel: 56-57-380677, E-mail: reserves@termasdemamina.cl, URL: www.termasdemamina.cl). In the village there are a few basic hotels and restaurants.

Just south of Mamiña, on Ruta A-629, is **Macaya**, another village with hot springs, petroglyphs and a campsite. Updated: Jun 29, 2009.

Getting To and Away From Mamiña

The turn-off for A-65, which goes to Mamiña (73 km/44 mi) is just north of Pozo Almonte, at Km 1808.75 of the Pan-American Highway. Getting to La Mamiña from Iquique on public transportation is easy. Two companies go there daily: **Santa Angela** (daily 8 a.m., return 6 p.m., $7 one way), and **Cruz del Norte** (Monday – Saturday 8 a.m., 4 p.m., return 8 a.m., 6 p.m, Sunday 8 a.m., return 6 p.m., $7.50). Updated: Jun 29, 2009.

LA TIRANA

 995m 560 57

The small village of La Tirana is best known for its Feast of the *Virgen del Carmen*, one of the most important festivals in Chile. Every year over 80,000 faithful congregate from July 12 to 18. Dances with pre-Hispanic roots are part of the celebration.

Iglesia de La Tirana faces the plaza and has paintings of the Inca princess who, according to legend, gave birth to the town. Next door, a museum displays offerings made to the Virgin. Museo José Manuel Balmaceda is a general store whose displays reveal daily family life from years past. Sector La Tirana of Reserva Nacional Pampa de Tamarugal is just outside of town. Pica, which is further up the main road, has hot springs. The road to Pica is nine kilometers (5.4 mi) south of Pozo Almonte. La Tiran is at Km 11.

From Iquique, buses heading to Pica pass by La Tirana. Several companies along the 900 block of Barros Aldana run this route from 8 a.m. to 9 p.m.

If you camp at the nearby Los Pintados de La Tirana, you'll hear the salty soil contracting in the cold night. The sound is said to be the masses marching across the plains. Updated: Jun 29, 2009.

RESERVA NATURAL PAMPA DEL TAMARUGAL

(ADMISSION: free) La Pampa de Tamarugal stretches across the arid lands of Chile's north, from Quebrada de Tana to María Elena. Across these sterile plains there are vestiges of ruined civilizations: rock

NORTE GRANDE

paintings by ancient peoples and abandoned potassium nitrate mining towns. This is an absolute desert, with 250 clear days per year. Lows reach -5 to -12°C (23 to 54°F) and highs soar to between 36 and 40°C (97 to 104°F). The soil is burdened with salt and the only moisture comes from the mists that drift up from the Pacific Ocean. Few things can live in such an environment.

One plant that does grow is the endemic tamarugo, which, when the Spanish arrived, covered the plain. By the mid-20th century, the tree, prized for its wood, had been all but wiped out. In 1987, the Reserva Natural (RN) Pampa Del Tamarugal was created to protect the last tamarugo and to reforest the region.

The tamarugo is perfectly adapted to this desert. Its canopy captures mist and its long taproot reaches to the brackish ground water deep beneath the surface. Aside from its precious wood, the tamarugo also produces a pod with eight to 10 protein-rich seeds, which are used mostly as cattle feed.

Lizards and snakes proliferate in the Pampa de Tamarugal. Foxes and quique are the resident carnivorous mammals. Rodents, owls and hawks also find refuge here.

The 100,650 hectares of RN Pampa de Tamarugal are divided into three sectors. Near Huara, 17,650-hectare Zapiga runs along Ruta 5, north of the Iquique turn-off. There are no offices or services there.

Sector Los Pintados, amid the Salar de Pintados salt flats, is the largest, conserving 79,289 hectares of forestlands, of which 2,500 hectares are tamarugo. The park administration and regional Conaf offices are in this part of the reserve. There are campsites and a refuge as well. Within the reserve is Los Pintados, the largest panel of geoglyphs in the world. There are over 900 drawings of humans, animals and geometric designs across approximately four kilometers (2.4 mi) of hillside (Km 1766 Pan-American Highway / Ruta 5, 80 km/48 mi south of Pozo Almonte).

The smallest sector of the reserve, La Tirana, is only 5,225 hectares. It is off the Pan-American Highway, near the village of the same name. Updated: Jun 29, 2009.

Getting To and Away From Reserva Natural Pampa Del Tamarugal

Any bus going between Arica and Iquique passes by the Zapiga Sector of the reserve. For Sector Los Pintados, where the ranger station and Conaf offices are, take any bus heading south on the Pan-American Highway (Ruta 5). You can reach Sector La Tirana via the village of the same name. Updated: Jun 25, 2009.

PICA

 2,731 m   1,700   57

At first glance, Pica appears to be a mirage, then it slowly reveals itself as an oasis of lush fruit groves. The town is famous for its limes, which are used to concoct the nation's favorite drink—pisco sour. Arguably the most popular recreational activity among locals is slowly sipping a freshly squeezed juice on the Plaza de Armas.

Pica's highlights include the impressive hot springs at **Cocha Resbaladero** ($2, Monday – Sunday 8 a.m. – 8 p.m.), which is about a 2-kilometer walk north of town. Soak in the lagoon-like pool that is said to have magical healing powers. The 19th-century Iglesia de San Andrés, located at the Plaza de Armas, is also worth a look.

Hotel Los Emilios is a favorite place to stay among tourists. There are only seven rooms, none of which has air conditioning, but this B&B makes guests feel at home. Breakfast is included and there is an on-site pool, restaurant and laundry service ($20, Lord Cochrane 213. Tel: 56-57-741126). **Camping Miraflores** (corner Calle Miraflores, Tel: 56-57-741338) has campsites for approximately $2 per site.

Food options in Pica are limited, but **Mía Pappa** (Balmaceda 118), near the town center, has a nice patio shaded by citrus trees. **Los Naranjos** (Barboza 200. Tel: 56-57-741318) is a favorite among locals for its cheap prices and traditional meat- and fish-based dishes.

Pica has a small **tourism office** in the Municipalidad on the main square (Monday – Friday, 8:30 a.m. – 1 p.m. and 3 – 7 p.m.). There are a few international calling centers and a post office on Avenida O'Higgins.

NORTE GRANDE

The town is served by buses and tours from Iquique. La Tirana is approximately 40 kilometers from Pica. Updated: Apr 23, 2009.

TOCOPILLA

 Sea level 25,000 55

Tocopilla is a port town that exports fish, flour and ores, among other products. Unless you want a snapshot of its ugly thermoelectric plant, there aren't many reasons to go out of your way for a visit. The trip on Ruta 1 from Iquique to Tocopilla actually does offer some great scenery, though traffic can be a bit heavy along the narrow highway.

In town, the Torre Reloj located on the corner of Prat and Baquedano is moderately interesting, as is the Playa El Salitre—a beach where you can relax and get a tan. However, resist the urge to take a dip, as the water is highly contaminated.

Hotel Atenas, located at 21 de Mayo 1448, is a nice place and its 20 rooms are equipped with a refrigerator and cable TV. A single room costs approximately $30, a double $35 (Tel: 56-55-813650). **Hotel Croacia** (Bolívar 1332. Tel: 56-55-810332) is a cheaper option, with clean bathrooms. Rooms cost approximately $20 per night.

Club de la Unión (Prat 1354. Tel: 56-55-813198) without a doubt serves the best traditional lunch and dinners in Tocopilla for a decent price ($4-8). **Lucciano's Pizza**, four blocks north of the plaza on 21 de Mayo, has good slices of pie.

To get to Tocopilla, take one of the buses that run daily between Antofagasta and Iquique. For those in rental cars, remember this is the last stop for gas until Iquique. Updated: Jul 07, 2009.

CALAMA

 2,250 m 150,000 55

Calama is all about copper: Even the church has a copper-gilded roof, a shining example of the metal's influence on the town. The city is a major residential area for the huge copper mine to the north of Chuquicamata. Calama was also once an important stop on the Oruro-Antofagasta railroad in the late 1800s.

The city is primarily used as a place to collect oneself or withdraw money before a trip to San Pedro de Atacama (as there are no ATMs or banks there). Cheap accommodation is scarce; however, there is a nice selection of eateries in town. Updated: Jun 29, 2009.

When to Go
Calama tends to be pretty quiet and unchanging. However, every year on March 23 the town unleashes an impressive display of fireworks to commemorate the return of Chilean troops from the War of the Pacific. Updated: May 11, 2009.

NORTE GRANDE

Photo by Ester Sára Köspál

NORTE GRANDE

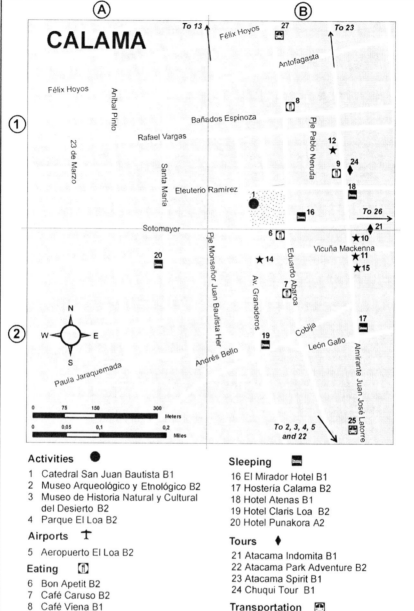

Activities ●

1 Catedral San Juan Bautista B1
2 Museo Arqueológico y Etnológico B2
3 Museo de Historia Natural y Cultural del Desierto B2
4 Parque El Loa B2

Airports ✝

5 Aeropuerto El Loa B2

Eating 🍴

6 Bon Apetit B2
7 Café Caruso B2
8 Café Viena B1
9 Mercado Central B1

Services ★

10 Bolivian Embassy B2
11 Corporación de Cultura y Turismo B2
12 Currency Exchange B1
13 Hospital Carlos Cisterna A1
14 Post Office B2
15 Tourism Office B2

Sleeping 🛏

16 El Mirador Hotel B1
17 Hostería Calama B2
18 Hotel Atenas B1
19 Hotel Claris Loa B2
20 Hotel Punakora A2

Tours ◆

21 Atacama Indomita B1
22 Atacama Park Adventure B2
23 Atacama Spirit B1
24 Chuqui Tour B1

Transportation 🚌

25 Hertz B2
26 Train Station B1
27 Tur Buses and Buses Atacama B1

Getting To and Away From Calama

Calama does not have a central terminal, so where you are dropped off in town depends on where that particular company's office is located. The popular **Tur Bus**—which runs service to and from Santiago, La Serena, Iquique, Arica and Antofagasta—has a relatively new terminal, but it is more than a kilometer north of town. Expect to shell out approximately $3 – 4 for a cab ride to the city center.

Trains to and from Boliva operate from the station three blocks east of the plaza. You must show your passport when purchasing tickets. Also, if needed, you can obtain a visa from the Bolivian Embassy (Latorre 1395. Tel: 56-55-341976). Note that citizens of the United States need a visa to enter Bolivia; it can be obtained at the border with proper documentation.

Flights to Calama land at Aeropuerto El Loa, which is approximately 5 kilometers from town. Updated: May 11, 2009.

Getting Around

You will have little problem finding a taxi in Calama. Cab drivers are even willing to transport people all the way to San Pedro de Atacama, but be sure to negotiate a fee before the ride (approximately $30 – 40) otherwise you will probably get overcharged. There are also colectivos, or you can rent a car from **Hertz** (Latorre 1510. Tel: 56-55-341380). Updated: May 11, 2009.

Safety

You should be pretty safe during the day, but the town becomes a little more dangerous after the sun sets; take taxis and use common sense. Updated: May 11, 2009.

Services

TOURISM

The Corporacion de Cultura y Turismo (Latorre 1689. Tel: 56-55-531707, URL: www.calamacultural.cl) has maps and other information. It is open Monday to Friday 8 a.m. – 1 p.m. and 2 – 6 p.m., and Saturday 9 a.m. – 1 p.m.

MONEY

Calle Sotomayor has a glut of ATMs and banks, and the currency exchange **Tokori Tour** is at Latorre 2018.

KEEPING IN TOUCH

Send mail from the post office at Vicuña Mackenna 2167. There is an international call center with Internet access on the corner of Sotomayor and Vivar (Tel: 55-314515).

MEDICAL

Hospital Carlos Cisterna is at Av. Granaderos (Tel: 56-55-342347).

Things to See and Do

Museo Arqueológico y Etnológico

(ADMISSION: Less than $1) Located in the well-trimmed Parque El Loa, this natural history museum has exhibits displaying local culture and has dioramas to emphasize the area's pre-Columbian history (Tuesday – Friday 10 a.m. – 1 p.m. and 3 – 7:30 p.m., Saturday – Sunday 3 – 7:30 p.m.. Tel: 56-55-316400). Updated: May 12, 2009.

Museo de Historia Natural y Cultural del Desierto

Located within the Museo Arqueológico y Etnológico, the Museo de Historia Natural y Cultural de Desierto del Atacama focuses on local paleontology and ecology. There are interesting displays of flora, fauna and pre-Columbian items from the region, and there is a room dedicated to the history of mining. Tuesday – Friday 10 a.m. – 1 p.m. and 3 – 7:30 p.m., Saturday – Sunday 3 – 7:30 p.m.,Av. Bernardo O'higgins s/n Interior del Parque El Loa. Tel: 56-55-349103, URL: www.museodecalama.cl. Updated: May 12, 2009.

Catedral San Juan Bautista

Not even the church is immune from the constant reminder of the importance of copper in Calama. The Catedral San Juan Bautista, located on the main square, can be easily spotted due to its shimmering roof constructed of the valuable metal. Updated: May 12, 2009.

Parque El Loa

Parque El Loa has a riverside swimming pool and a replica of Chiu Chiu's famous church. The Museo Arqueológico y Etnológico is also located in the park, and there is some interesting flora. The park is on the south side of Av. O'Higgins (10 a.m. – 8 p.m.). Updated: May 12, 2009.

Tours

Calama itself is rather unremarkable, but if you are looking for tour operators in town, check out reliable agencies such as

Chuqui Tour (see below), **Atacama Spirit** (Riquelme 4326, Fax: 56-55-365151), **Atacama Indomita** (Sotomayor 1971. Tel: 56-55-361102) or **Atacama Park Adventure** (Camino Aeropuerto 1392. Tel: 56-55-447700). One of the best adventure tour agencies is **Keps** (Sotomayor 1812. Tel: 56-55-318983). Updated: Jul 01, 2009.

Chuquitour
With over 20 years of tour experience, Chuquitour offers a wide range of tours in the area surrounding Calama. Organized trips include visits to local archeological sites/ruins, Atacama's numerous lagoons and saltflats, the majestic Valle de la Luna, and the world-famous Geisers del Tatio. Those looking to venture off the tourist trail can try one of Chuquitour's unique visits to nearby indigenous villages, learning about the tiny pueblos' agriculture, crafts and daily local culture. Chuquitour can accommodate large groups. Latorre 1512. Tel: 56-55-340190, Fax: 56-55-362570 URL: www.chuquitour.cl. Updated: Jul 01, 2009.

Lodging
When it comes to accommodation, Calama can be expensive; most hotels are either mid-range or high-end. That being said, there are a few budget options as well.

Hotel Claris Loa
(ROOMS: $8 – 15) Do not come here looking for fancy accommodations. The rooms are very basic, but the prices are perfect if you are on a budget. Av. Granaderos 1631. Tel: 56-55-311939. Updated: May 12, 2009.

Hotel Atenas
(ROOMS: $12 – 28) Atenas is conveniently located on the main street, with easy access to restaurants and entertainment. Rooms are not terribly spacious, but there are little to no problems with street noise—often a rarity at hotels this centrally positioned. There are rooms with shared and private bathrooms, and the hotel has a kitchen for guests to use. Ramírez 1961. Updated: May 12, 2009.

Hotel El Mirador
(ROOMS: $40 – 58) El Mirador Hotel is in an old English colonial-style home built at the end of the 19th century. The hotel has 15 rooms, a lounge with a fireplace and is decorated with a collection of antique photographs from the region. Rooms have WiFi, private bathrooms and room service.

Sotomayor 2064. Tel: 56-55-340329, E-mail: contacto@hotelmirador.cl, URL: www.hotelmirador.cl. Updated: May 12, 2009.

Hotel Punakora
(ROOMS: $55 – 65) Punakora is a well-run hotel on a quiet street. Its 26 rooms come with cable TV, private bathroom and a refrigerator. There is also an on-site restaurant. Santa María 1640. Tel: 56-55-344955. Updated: May 12, 2009.

Hostería Calama
(ROOMS: $55 – 90) This is arguably the best place to stay in town, but be prepared shell out some cash. The hotel has a game room, Internet room, pool, gym and transfer service to the airport. Rooms are heated and have desks, refrigerators, private bath and cable TV. Latorre 1521. Tel: 56-55-341511, E-mail: hcalama@tie.cl, URL: www.hosteriacalama.cl. Updated: May 12, 2009.

Restaurants
Calama has a good selection of restaurants and, to the delight of backpackers passing through, many of them happen to decent cuisine at budget prices. One cheap choice is the always authentic cocinerías in the Mercado Central. Updated: May 12, 2009.

Mercado Central
(MEALS: $2 – 4) The cocinerías in this typical central market serve up fast and filling food. Here you will find plenty of meat and fish served with rice. Since the prices are low and the food (while not extraordinary) is filling, the market is a favorite eating place among locals. Latorre between Vargas and Ramírez. Updated: May 12, 2009.

Café Viena
(SET MEAL: $3) Hungry gringos and locals alike head to this restaurant for cheap food and hearty portions. The salads are nice starters and the sandwiches are excellent compared to what usually is available in South America. Wash the meal down with a fresh-squeezed juice or sip on some coffee. Abaroa 2023. Tel: 56-55-341771. Updated: May 12, 2009.

Bon Apetit
(ENTREES: $4 – 8) This is *the* spot in Calama if you need a real shot of caffeine—you won't find any instant coffee here. There are set lunches or deliciously sweet pastries on the menu, as well. Sotomayor 2129. Tel: 55-434600. Updated: May 12, 2009.

Café Caruso
(ENTREES: $7 – 13) Café Caruso is a nice place to relax with a cup of coffee or tea and gaze at the old photos of Calama that decorate the restaurant. The food is good and almost anything on the menu goes well with a glass of wine. Avaroa 1702. Tel: 56-55-364872. Updated: May 12, 2009.

AROUND CALAMA
CHUQUICAMATA
Chuquicamata is one of the largest open-pit copper mines in the world and is located just 16 kilometers (10 mi) north of Calama. The huge chasm that seems to reach the core of the earth produces more than 600,000 tons of copper annually. There are massive trucks with wheels almost four meters high hauling the ore from the crater's floor. Chile's government-owned copper corporation Codelco runs this site, as well as a nearby town with its own school, hospital and movie theater for employee families. The plan is to eventually move to Calama to allow for more excavation.

Colectivos run from Calama's main square to Chuquicamata (20 minutes, $1.50). Calama's tourist office can make a reservation for a tour through Codelco, which also has a booking office at the corner of Tocopilla and Carrera (Monday – Friday 8:30 – 11:30 a.m. and 3 – 5 p.m. Tel: 55-327469). Tours generally last an hour and a half. Be sure to book in advance during the high season in January and February. Updated: May 12, 2009.

CHUG CHUG
Chug Chug has 300 geoglyphs spread over a hillside 50 kilometers (31 mi) west of Chuquicamata. There are circles, human faces and geometric designs, some of which date back to the Tiwanaku culture from 1000 AD. To get here, follow the paved highway toward Tocopilla for 20 kilometers (12.4 mi), then follow the sign for Chug Chug north down a dirt road. Updated: Apr 09, 2009.

SAN PEDRO DE ATACAMA

 2,400 m   5,000   55

Thanks to the numerous spectacular sights near and around San Pedro de Atacama, this small desert town has transformed into a tourist haven. Chile's largest salt flat—home to flamingos—geyser fields, and beautiful landscapes and rock formations, are all just a short trip away.

However, the charm of San Pedro's narrow dirt streets and adobe houses is beginning to fade as overpriced hotels continue to spring up and try to take advantage of travelers. Still, the highlights of the town far outweigh the annoyances created by the tourism industry. It's a spectacular place for learning how to sand-surf, speeding down dunes on a mountain bike, or ascending a volcano. The hot springs at **Termas de Puritama (p.235)** soothe, the **Salar de Atacama (p.236)** is an incredible sight and the **Geisers del Tatio (p.236)** should not be missed. In town, the **Museo Gustavo le Paige (p.231)** has an extensive display of local artifacts and Iglesia de San Pedro at the Plaza de Armas is a welcoming Andean church.

There is plenty of accommodation available, particularly for budget travelers willing to share a room. However, as is common with tourist towns, San Pedro has its share of overpriced trendy hotels that aren't always worth the price. There is no shortage of restaurants in San Pedro de Atacama and the prices are relatively affordable even at nicer locations. A lot of establishments attract guests with decently priced meals, happy hour specials and late-night live music. Updated: Jul 08, 2009.

When to Go
No matter the season, expect typical desert weather conditions in San Pedro de Atacama. In the winter, temperatures hover around 22°C (71.6°F) during the day but drop to around 4°C (39.2°F) once the sun goes down. Bring shorts, T-shirts and sunblock for afternoons, but have warmer clothes on hand for cold nights. The town celebrates several festivals, including Fiesta de Nuestra Señora de la Candelaria in early February, Carnaval, Fiesta de San Pedro y San Pablo on June 29 and the traditional religious festival of Fiesta de Santa Rosa de Lima on August 30. Updated: May 05, 2009.

Getting To and Away From San Pedro de Atacama
Several bus companies operate between San Pedro de Atacama and Calama. There are usually 10 – 15 connections per day from Calama with **Tur Bus** or **Buses Atacama** (Abaroa 2105-B. Tel: 56-55-314757).

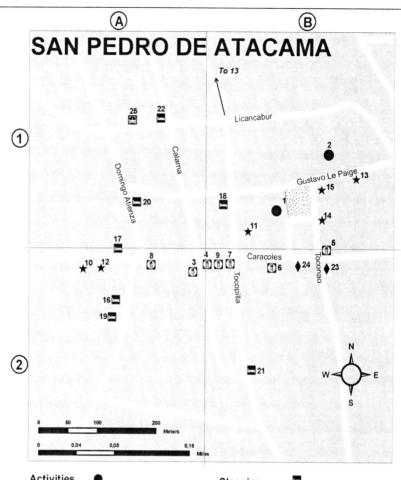

SAN PEDRO DE ATACAMA

Activities ●

1 Iglesia de San Pedro B1
2 Museo Gustavo Le Paige B1

Eating 🏠

3 Blanco A2
4 Café Adobe B2
5 Café Export B2
6 Café Tierra B2
7 Casa de Piedra B2
8 La Casona A2
9 Milagro B2

Services ★

10 ATM A2
11 Café Etnico B1
12 Entel A2
13 Post Office B1
14 Posta Médica B1
15 Tourism Office B1

Sleeping ▄

16 Casa Adobe A2
17 Hostal Don Raúl A2
18 Hostal Florida B1
19 Hostal Inti and Killa A2
20 Hostal Katarpe A1
21 Hostal La Ruca B2
22 Hostal Sonchek A1

Tours ◆

23 Atacama Connection B2
24 Vulcano Expeditions B2

Transportation 🚌

25 Tur Bus A1

Tur Bus departs San Pedro from from Licancábur 11 (Tel: 56-55-851549), running
service to Calama, Arica, Antofagasta and
Santiago.

To Santiago: (major stops made in between, $55 – 70 to the capital)—8:51 a.m.,
2:21 p.m., 4:46 p.m., 6:35 p.m., 7:30 p.m.

To Calama: ($5 – 7)—8:51 a.m., 10:30 a.m.,
1:00 p.m., 2:20 p.m., 4:46 p.m., 5:50 p.m.,
6:35 p.m., 7:30 p.m., 8:45 p.m.

To Arica: 8:45 p.m.
Updated: May 05, 2009.

Getting Around
Traveling on foot is the easiest—and most
common—way to explore the town. If you
prefer to explore on wheels, head to a tour
operator and rent a bike—just be sure to request a map. Updated: May 05, 2009.

Safety
San Pedro de Atacama is a safe desert oasis.
You can stroll along the town's streets late at
night or early in the morning without problem.
Common sense and a standard level of vigilance
should suffice. Updated: May 05, 2009.

Services
TOURISM
The **tourism office** is located at the corner
of Toconao and Gustavo le Paige (Tel: 56-55-
851420). Monday to Friday 9:30 a.m. – 1 p.m.
and 3 – 7 p.m., and Saturday 10 a.m. – 2 p.m.

MONEY
The town has two ATMs, though they often run
out of cash. It's best to be safe and bring enough
money from Calama or Antofagasta. One of the
ATMs is located in a handicrafts store without
an address, next to 119 Caracoles. The other
ATM is on Gustavo Le Paige, two minutes from
the Plaza de Armas. Many establishments take
credit cards, but not all, so bring plenty of cash
to be safe. Money can be exchanged near the
post office at **Casa de Cambio.**

MEDICAL
Posta Médica is the local medical clinic, located on Toconao along the Plaza de Armas.

KEEPING IN TOUCH
The post office is at Toconoa 423 and the
international calling center **Entel** at Caracoles 259-C. You can send e-mails from
Café Etnico (Tocopilla 423).

LAUNDRY
Viento Norte (Vilama 432-B) does laundry, but you are probably better off checking to see if your hostel has service first.
Updated: May 05, 2009.

Things to See and Do
San Pedro de Atacama will keep visitors busy
throughout the duration of their stay. The
Museo Gustavo le Paige is definitely a place
to spend some time, with its interesting relics
and artifacts. Iglesia de San Pedro at the Plaza
de Armas is a nice sight. That being said, adventure activities are athe main draw here.
Active pursuits include sand-surfing, biking,
and volcano ascensions. Tours of Geisers del
Tatio, Termas de Puritama and Salar de Atacama are popular (and worthwhile) options
as well. Updated: May 05, 2009.

Iglesia San Pedro
Built in 1744, Iglesia San Pedro rests on the
western edge of the Plaza de Armas and is
one of the most interesting Andean churches
in the region. The bell tower was added in the
late 19th century. Updated: May 17, 2009.

Museo Gustavo le Paige
(ADMISSION: $4) Taking a tour of the
Museo Gustavo le Paige is a must while visiting San Pedro de Atacama. Belgian Jesuit
priest Gustavo Le Paige, who arrived in town
in 1955, collected artifacts of great archaeological value while visiting pre-historic cemeteries and places inhabited by indigenous
people. By 1957, he helped open the area's
first museum (in his house), setting up exhibits of numerous pre-Hispanic ceramics,
textiles, metals and mummies. The museum
now contains more than 380,000 regional
artifacts. The Treasure Room is particularly
impressive, displaying crafts made from
gold. Monday – Friday 9 a.m. – 12 p.m. and
2 – 6 p.m., Saturday – Sunday, 10 a.m. – 12
p.m. and 2 – 6 p.m., Gustavo Le Paige 380.
Tel: 55-851002. Updated: Jul 07, 2009.

Tours
San Pedro de Atacama has many tour operators—all eagerly competing for your tourist
dollars. Shop around and see what's available before making a final decision.

Atacama Connection
Atacama Connection is one of the more
established tour operators in San Pedro de
Atacama. The company offers excursions
to the salt deserts, lagoons, mountains and
valleys in the surrounding area. Corner of

NORTE GRANDE

Caracoles and Toconao. Tel: 56-55-851421, E-mail: atacamaconnection@entelchile. net, URL: www.atacamaconnection.com. Updated: May 07, 2009.

Vulcano Expeditions

Vulcano Expeditions specializes in active excursions and adventure sports. Their knowledgeable guides can take you on a variety of adventures, including sand-surfing, biking, horseback riding, and volcano treks. They also offer tours of the Geisers del Tatio, Termas de Puritama and Salar de Atacama. Caracoles 329B. Tel: 56-55-851023, E-mail: vulcanochile@terra.cl, URL: www.vulcanochile.com. Updated: May 07, 2009.

Lodging

There is a wide range of accommodations for travelers. For those on a budget, there are a few campsites near the village, and the town has numerous hostels—though the lone traveler will most likely have to share a room during the summer high season. A handful of high-end hotels have recently sprung up to cater to those with thicker walltets. Updated: May 05, 2009.

Hostal Monypan

(ROOMS: $8 per person) The low prices at Monypan draw large numbers of students and twentysomethings. The best part of the hostel is the smell of fresh-baked bread that often wafts in from the nearby bakery. The hostel has double, triple and quadruple rooms with shared bathrooms, hot water, and there is a shared kitchen to whip up cheap meals. Lasana 687. Tel: 56-55-851246, E-mail: hostalmonypan@sanpedroatacama. com. Updated: May 06, 2009.

Cabañas Candelaria

(ROOMS: $8 – 11) Cabañas Candelaria is a fantastic budget option on the outskirts of San Pedro. The owners are a friendly couple who will introduce you to their dog, Pon-Pon, and set you up in a comfortable bed in a dorm-style room. There is an on-site kitchen, shared showers with (very) hot water, and a nice outdoor area with picnic tables where you can chat with fellow travelers. It is a 10-minute stroll to the Plaza de Armas. If you're traveling in a group, you can try to bargain down the price. Ca. Candelaria 170. Tel: Tel: 56-55-851284, E-mail: caba.candelaria@hot-mail.com. Updated: May 06, 2009.

Hostal Mamatierra

(ROOMS: $9 — 19) Hostal Mamatierra is a quaint and relatively quiet place to relax between desert adventures. The owner is usually there to welcome you, and she is very helpful at directing guests to the best restaurants in town. The hostel has 10 rooms—four with private bathroom. There is 24-hour hot water, a kitchen and laundry service. There is also a store nearby where you can pick up some ingredients to cook dinner. Pachamama 615. Tel: 56-55-851418, E-mail: hostalmamatierra@sanpedroatacama.com. Updated: May 06, 2009.

Casa Adobe

(ROOMS: $10 per person) Casa Adobe is a small and cozy hotel built from adobe and other local materials. It has 14 rooms, each with private bath and 24-hour hot water. The outside terraces with tables are great for sitting and talking to other guests. Domingo Atienza 582. Tel: 56-55-851249, E-mail: casadobe@sanpedroatacama.com. Updated: May 06, 2009.

Hostal La Ruca

(ROOMS: $10 and up) Hostal La Ruca is a relatively new addition to the budget accommodation scene in San Pedro de Atacama. It caters to backpackers in need of a cheap (but good) night's rest. The beds are clean, the pillows are comfortable, the showers have hot water and the bar in the courtyard helps attract a lively crowd. They provide free Internet service for 10 minutes. Toconao 513. Tel: 56-55-851568, E-mail: laruca@sanpedroatacama.com. Updated: May 06, 2009.

Hostal Sonchek

(ROOMS: $11 and up) This hostel is full of character, and has adobe walls and a thatch roof. There is a small courtyard that guests enter through the kitchen. It is a good budget option for backpackers in need of a cheap bed. Calama 370. Tel: 56-55-851112. Updated: May 06, 2009.

Hotel Katarpe

(ROOMS: $12 and up) This is a nicer option for travelers who want to avoid being crammed into a dorm room with travelers who snore all night or stumble in at all hours. Katarpe is very clean and a great pick for singles. Domingo Atienza s/n. Tel: 56-55-851011. Updated: May 06, 2009.

Hotel Florida

(ROOMS: $20 per person) There are no singles available here, so expect to share your room. The hostel is a nice spot to meet other backpackers, since it tends to draw a younger crowd. Each of the 12 rooms can fit up to four people, and all have shared bathrooms. Amenities include 24-hour hot water, safe boxes, laundry service and a kitchen. The staff also organizes BBQs on Fridays and often organizes sand-boarding exhibitions on nights with a full moon. Tocopilla 406. Tel: 56-55-851021, E-mail: hostalflorida@sanpedroatacama.com. Updated: May 06, 2009.

Hostal Inti and Killa

(ROOMS: $53 – 78) Hostal Inti and Killa is a former house that was restored and furnished to cater to travelers' needs. Rooms are clean, spacious and decorated with warm colors that give off a welcoming vibe. The 24-hour hot water in all private bathrooms is nice, too. There are no TVs here because the hostel wants guests to get out and enjoy the surrounding landscape. Domingo Atienza 294. Tel: 56-55-852114, E-mail: intikilla@sanpedroatacama.com, URL: www.intikilla.cl. Updated: May 05, 2009.

Hotel Don Raúl

(ROOMS: $55 – 65) Come here for a pleasant mid-range option. Hotel Don Raúl has 33 well-kept rooms with private bathrooms and comfortable beds. There is satellite TV, a cafeteria and Internet. The staff is glad to arrange tours and can provide tourist information. There are also cabins that fit four people for $120 per night. Caracoles 130-Casilla No. 14. Tel: 56-55-851138, E-mail: info@donraul.cl, URL: www.donraul.cl. Updated: May 06, 2009.

Restaurants

The tourism boom in San Pedro de Atacama has stiffened competition between restaurants, which has kept prices relatively low—even in places that would naturally charge more because of their location on a main street. A lot of restaurants attract diners not just with their menus, but also with their entertainment and drink specials. Updated: May 07, 2009.

Café Tierra

(ENTREES: $4 – 9) Tierra is the natural choice (literally) for a meal in San Pedro de Atacama. The restaurant uses only natural wheat flour to prepare its empanadas, pizza and pastries. The crepes are excellent, the omelets are decent-sized, and yogurt and fruit accompany the breakfasts. The owner has a good collection of books in case you want to read while you eat healthy. Caracoles 271. Tel: 56-55-851585, E-mail: cafetierrasanpedro@ yahoo.com. Updated: May 06, 2009.

Café Adobe

(ENTREES: $4 – 10) Café Adobe is the perfect spot to grab an early breakfast or a late night drink. There are at least three different set meals per day, and the restaurant's large wooden picnic tables are continually filled with travelers and locals throughout the evening. The outdoor patio has a fire every night to keep patrons warm while they sip a coffee or toss back a beer. Caracoles 211. Tel: 56-55-851132, E-mail: cafeadobe@san-pedroatacama.com, URL: www.cafeadobe. cl. Updated: May 07, 2009.

Milagro

(ENTREES: $6 – 17) Chic Milagro is great place to enjoy wine and conversation. The restaurant serves set breakfasts, is better known for its dinner menu. The *tres carnes al plato* is an excellent dish of grilled steak, chicken and pork. The chocolate truffles are a nice treat to finish off the meal. Caracoles 241. Tel: 55-851515, E-mail: milagro@san-pedroatacama.com, URL: www.milagro.cl. Updated: May 07, 2009.

Casa de Piedra

(ENTREES: $7 – 10) The restaurant's occasional live local music and friendly service help this restaurant stand out on a street with no shortage of eateries. Casa de Piedra specializes in meats and international cuisine (the parrilladas are recommended). The restaurant is open for both lunch and dinner. Caracoles 225. Tel: 56-55-851271, E-mail: casadepiedra@san-pedroatacama.com, URL: www.restaurantcas-adepiedra.cl. Updated: May 07, 2009.

La Casona

(ENTREES: $7 – 14) La Casona is a perfect place for an inexpensive meal and is probably the best bang for your buck in San Pedro. The recently remodeled restaurant has a large dining room which usually features live music from local bands. There are some fine puddings here, and the food is filling. Caracoles 195. Tel: 56-55-851004, E-mail: lacaso-naspa@yahoo.com. Updated: May 07, 2009.

Café Export

Tired travelers head here for a jolt of caffeine to wake up after early-morning treks to the geysers. There are also good sandwiches, and the patio is a nice place to lunch with friends. Caracoles and Toconao. Updated: May 06, 2009.

Blanco

Blanco is new to the city's restaurant scene. The atmosphere is pleasant, but the real reason to visit is for the food. The menu features recipes inspired from Blanco's owners' various trips around the globe. The three-pepper seasoned Easter Island tuna is delicious and the fresh pasta is a good choice. However, budget travelers beware: meals can cost as much as $50 per person depending on the bottle of wine. Open seven days a week from 6 p.m. Make reservations in advance. Caracoles and Calama. Tel: 56-55-851939, E-mail: blancorestaurant@san-pedroatacama.com. Updated: May 07, 2009.

Border Crossing to Bolivia

There are a couple of ways to cross into Bolivia from San Pedro de Atacama. The southern option is located approximately 45 kilometers (28 mi) east at Hito Cajones where a bumpy road leads toward Paseo de Jama at La Cruz. There is no public transportation along this route, and hitchhiking is not reccommended, for hikers run risk of being stranded without help for days—especially once on the Bolivian side of the border.

The northern route passes through Ollagüe via the Salar de Ollagüe (3,695 m). Do not under any circumstances decide to take your car for a spin on the inviting soft salt beside the road, otherwise the weight of the car will crack the ground and you will fall through. Also, be prepared to bring a thick blanket because the border crossing is closed overnight and the desert temperatures drop as the sun sets. United States citizens can purchase the necessary visa for entry into Bolivia at the consulate in San Pedro de Atacama. Updated: Jul 07, 2009.

Border Crossing to Argentina

There are three crossings into Argentina from San Pedro de Atacama. The best is the northernmost, which crosses at Paso de Jama, approximately 165 kilometers (102.5 mi) southeast of town and reached via a road through the Salar de Tara. This part is also a sector of the Reserva Nacional de los Flamencos.

Paso de Sico, slightly more than 200 kilometers (124.2 mi) south of San Pedro, is another alternative, which you can reach via a road that runs through Toconao and Socaire.

The third option is further south at Paso de Socompa, which is reached via a very bumpy road from Pan de Azúcar. Unlike Bolivia, Argentina does not require citizens of the United States to purchase a tourist visa to enter. Updated: Jun 29, 2009.

AROUND SAN PEDRO DE ATACAMA

Pukará de Quitor

The ruins of Pukará de Quitor are all that remain of a 12th-century fortress originally built on a steep hillside on the Río San Pedro. Indigenous forces attempted to repel Pedro de Valdivia's conquest but succumbed to the attack and lost the battle in 1540. The site's close proximity to town—only 3 kilometers (1.8 mi) north along Calle Tocopilla and then the river—make it an easy excursion to reach on foot or by bike. Updated: May 07, 2009.

Photo by Catherine Eames

Photo by Rafael Gómez Carrera

Tambo de Catarpe

Travel an additional 4 kilometers (2.5 mi) past Pukará de Quitor and you'll find the ruins of Catarpe. Although it's an interesting place on its own, the smaller ruins tend to pale in comparison to the closer (and much larger) ruins of Pukará de Quitor. Updated: May 07, 2009.

Termas de Puritama

(ENTRANCE: $8) These volcanic hot springs are approximately 28 kilometers (17.4 mi) from San Pedro de Atacama. Hidden in a small canyon, these falls and pools of hot water, produced by the Río Puritama, reach 30°C (86°F). Hotel Explora is in charge of administration of the springs. Bring a towel. Updated: May 19, 2009.

Reserva Nacional Los Flamencos

(ADMISSION: $4, children: $1) The Reserva Nacional Los Flamencos extends over 73,986 hectares (180 acres) which are divided into seven separate sectors. With a broad palette of attractions—lagoons, mountains, rock formations, archaeological sites, and flora and fauna—the reserve offers a little something for everyone to enjoy in the park. Horseback riding, birdwatching and photography are popular activities any time of the year. There are also hiking trails of varying lengths in the Valle de la Luna (900 m/0.5 mi), Salar Tara (8 km/5 mi) and other sectors.

The desert temperatures can change dramatically depending on the time of day, so be prepared with appropriate clothing as well as sunscreen. Many people rent 4WD vehicles and make the drive from San Pedro de Atacama to the reserve. The same can be done from Calama. Otherwise, enlist with a tour operator and roll down on their bus—breakfast is usually included, but be prepared to depart very early. Updated: Jul 07, 2009.

Valle de la Luna

One look from atop an enormous sand dune, and it's no mystery how the Valle de la Luna (Valley of the Moon) got its name. Watching the sun set behind a lunar landscape of hills that hover over a shimmering valley is one of the most unforgettable sights in Chile. At sunset the area is full of tour groups eager to view the spectacular colors the disappearing sun gives off. Tours usually cost $6 – 10. Be sure to bring enough sunscreen and water. Camping is prohibited.

Laguna Chaxa

(ADMISSION: $4) Just 25 kilometers (15.5 mi) from San Pedro de Atacama, Laguna Chaxa is an easily accessible flamingo breeding

NORTE GRANDE

site. Birdwatchers can observe three different species—Chilean, Andean and James—at this salt lake. The best time to visit is at sunrise, which coincides with feeding time.

Lagunas Miscanti and Miñiques
The excursion to these lakes ($4) from San Pedro de Atacama is a bit long, but well worth it once you arrive at the lakes and their backdrop of barren volcanoes. Laguna Miscanti, the smaller of the two lakes, is a breeding ground for the Andean flamingo.

Salar de Tara and Salar de Pujsa
Salar de Tara features both permanent and seasonal lakes, the main one being Laguna Tara. The area provides a habitat for various endangered and vulnerable species such as the Andean Goose, Andean Gull and Horned Coot. It is also possible to see the culpeo fox in the area. Salar de Pujsa is further south along the road.

Geisers del Tatio
A trip to the world-famous Geisers del Tatio, the world's highest geothermal field (4,300 m/14,100 ft above sea level) is a once-in-a-lifetime experience. Just watch your step—some of the ground is too thin to support the weight of an adult; obey the signs and your guide if you're on a tour. Most tour buses leave at 4 a.m. for a two-hour ride to the site. You can observe the steaming, bubbling and spurting geysers from 6 to 8 a.m. Pools of water on the ground reflect sunlight in a million different directions. Dress in layers, though: It will be freezing cold you feel when you wake up, but by the time you are back in the bus for the ride home it will be very warm. Also, be sure to bring a bathing suit, since most tour companies stop at a thermal pool owned by Hotel Explora.

A trip with a tour operator is the most popular way to visit the Geisers del Tatio. Others travelers can rent a car , but be sure to follow the buses to the geysers because it is difficult to navigate the road alone. The benefit of going on your own is that most tour companies leave the site by 8 a.m., giving you ample time to enjoy the surroundings in relative peace after they leave. Updated: May 07, 2009.

TOCONAO

 2,414 m   750   55

Toconao is a tiny traditional Andean village 40 kilometers (24.8 mi) south of San Pedro de Atacama. This colonial town was constructed

out of liparita volcanic stone. Most of the inhabitants here work in agriculture or use the volcanic stone to make handicrafts.

On the perimeter of town you'll find orchards full of fruit trees, herbs and flowers. The **Quebrada de Jere** (Tel: 56-55-852010) is worth a visit, as is a stroll to view Toconao's unique homes. **Iglesia de San Lucas**, with its separate bell tower, was erected in 1750. There are also a few artisan shops selling llama-wool ponchos and gloves, along with various handicrafts. To the east of town there is a narrow yellow sandy canyon, **Valle de Jeria**, with a crystalline stream, fruit trees and palms.

For lodging, try **Residencial y Restaurant Valle de Toconao** (Lascar 236. Tel: 56-55-852009). It's on the small side, but a single bed only costs $7. The on-site restaurant also serves local dishes for less than $5. To get here, use **Buses Atacama 2000** or **Frontera**; both companies have daily service to and from Toconao. Updated: May 13, 2009.

MEJILLONES

 4 m   7,850 55

The small port town of Mejillones, 60 kilometers (37.2 mi) north of , is flanked by the Pacific Ocean and the Atacama Desert. The desert town serves mainly as a beach resort for Antofagasta inhabitants in need an escape.

You can find nice accommodation with excellent views of the ocean at **Hotel Mejillones** (Manuel Montt 86. Tel: 56-55-621590, E-mail: reservas@hotelmejillones.cl). The hotel has 24 rooms, each equipped with cable TV and private bathrooms. The on-site restaurant has a waterfront view and serves incredible seafood from 6 to 11 p.m. **Bar Costa del Sol**, also on the premises, serves quick and filling empanadas, drinks and has live music.

Residencial Elisabeth (Alte Latorre 440. Tel: 56-55-621568) is a budget option with simple rooms and shared bathrooms. **Restaurante Juanito** (Las Heras 241) serves filling and cheap meals—a lot of roasted chicken and rice.

The main street, Avenida San Martín, is home to the uninspiring **Museo de Mejillones** (Tel: 56-55-621289). The museum is free and open Tuesday to Friday 10 a.m. – 2 p.m. and 3 – 6 p.m., Saturday 10 a.m. – 2 p.m. and 3 – 5 p.m., and Sunday 10 a.m. – 2 p.m. The **hospital** is on Bernardo O'Higgins, and **tourist information** can be found a block east of the plaza.

Buses to and from Antofagasta stop in Mejillones. Taxi colectivos also serve the town. Updated: May 13, 2009.

ANTOFAGASTA

 275 m   300,000   55

If your time in Chile is limited, there are more interesting places to see in the north of the country than Antofagasta. That being said, the city does have a few sights and is a good place to fill up on essential supplies or find decent banks and ATMs. Antofagasta was a Bolivian city until 1879, when it was annexed during the War of the Pacific. These days, the city is a flourishing as export center for the mines in the region. The downtown area is compact, with several older buildings, while the coastal avenue is more modern and spread out.

The city has a distinctly European flavor thanks to former British residents who built the Torre Reloj, a replica of Britain's Big Ben. The Museo Regional and the Católica del Norte have some interesting items on display, and there are good views of the city from Ruinas de Huanchaca. Antofagasta has a mix of budget and high-end accommodation, but little in the mid-range.

As expected from a city by the sea, there is delicious (and fresh) seafood in Antofagasta; you can also get good steak and chicken. Updated: May 12, 2009.

When to Go

A good time to stop through town is on February 14 when the town celebrates the anniversary of its founding with fireworks at the Balneario Municipal near the southern end of Avenida Grecia. Now matter when you visit, prepare for the desert weather: bring warm clothes for evenings and light clothes for afternoons. Updated: May 12, 2009.

Getting To and Away From Antofagasta

A wide range of bus companies connect numerous cities to and from Antofagasta. Most companies have their own terminals close to downtown. In addition, there is a central terminal at Argentina 1155 where companies such as **Libac** and **Ramos Cholele** operate.

Tur Bus (Latorre 2751. Tel: 56-55-264487) and **Pullman Bus** (Latorre 2805. Tel: 56-55-268838) service Arica, Calama, Iquique, Santiago and Tocopilla. **LAN** (Prat 445) has multiple daily flights to Santiago, Calama, La Serena and Iquique. Updated: May 12, 2009.

Getting Around

Taxis are plentiful in Antofagasta and are the quickest option from the Aeropuerto Cerro Moreno, 25 kilometers (15.5 mi) north of the city. There are several local buses and you can rent a car at **Avis** (Tel: 56-55-221073) located at Balmaceda 2556, or **Hertz** (Tel: 56-55-269043) at Balmaceda 2492. Updated: May 12, 2009.

Safety

Although Antofagasta is not a terribly dangerous place, there are some shady streets—especially at night. It is best to play it safe and take a cab after dark. Updated: Apr 16, 2009.

Services

The **Sernatur** office near the plaza at Prat 384 has tourist information. It is open Monday to Friday 8:30 a.m. – 5:30 p.m. **Conaf** (Av. Argentina 2510) has information on regional attractions. There are banks and ATMs all along the central square and main commercial streets like Prat and Washington. You can exchange cash at **Ancla** (Baquedano 524). **Entel** (Condell 2451) has Internet and long-distance calls, and the **post office** is at Washington 2623. The regional **hospital** (Tel: 56-55-269009) is at Avenida Argentina 1962. Updated: May 12, 2009.

Things to See and Do

Antofagasta is not a spectacular destination for tourists, but there are a few fun places to visit.

Museo Regional

(ADMISSION: $1) The Museo Regional, located in the former Aduana (customs building) was originally built in Mejillones but disassembled and moved piece by piece to Antofagasta in 1888. The museum has natural history items on display. Artifacts also include items from the nitrate era. Tuesday – Friday 9 a.m. – 5 p.m., Saturday – Sunday 11 a.m. – 2 p.m., Balmaceda 2786 and Bolívar 188. Tel: 56-55-227016, URL: www.dibam.cl/sdm_m_antofagasta. Updated: May 12, 2009.

Ruinas de Huanchaca

Perched on the hillside at the southern end of Avenida Argentina, these ruins were once the foundation of a 19th-century British-Bolivian silver refinery. To get here, take colectivo 3 from downtown

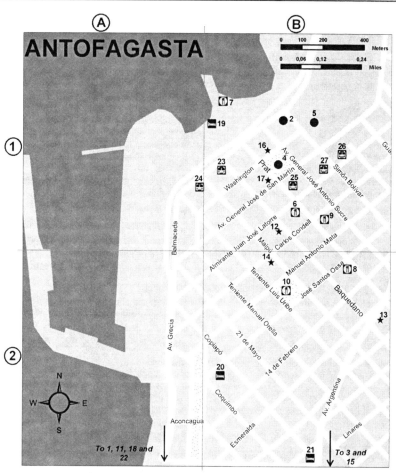

ANTOFAGASTA

Activities ●

1　Católica del Norte A2
2　Museo Regional B1
3　Ruinas de Huanchaca B2
4　Torre Reloj B1
5　Train Station B1

Eating

6　Café del Centro B1
7　Club de Yates B1
8　Don Pollo B2
9　El Arriero B1
10　Mercado Central B2
11　Picadillo A2

Services ★

12　Ancla B1
13　Conaf B2
14　Entel B2
15　Hospital B2

16　Post Office B1
17　Sernatur B1

Sleeping ⌂

18　Holiday Inn Express A2
19　Hotel Antofagasta B1
20　Hotel Brasil B2
21　Hotel Isla Capri B2
22　Radisson Hotel Antofagasta A2

Transportation

23　Avis B1
24　Hertz A1
25　LAN B1
26　Pullman Bus B1
27　Tur Bus B1

and ask to be dropped off at the Minas de Plata to take in some spectacular views of the city. Updated: May 12, 2009.

Torre Reloj
No, you have not just been teleported to London: you are looking at Torre Reloj, erected in Antofagasta by British residents in 1910. Plaza Colón. Updated: May 12, 2009.

Estación de Ferrocarril
This dark green train station, which was once a stop on the Antofagasta-La Paz railway, has been restored, though it is not open to the public. Its main floor dates from 1887 and the upper floor from 1900. Freight trains now run through here, and it is possible to catch a glimpse of some older rail cars through the fence. Bolívar. Updated: May 12, 2009.

Lodging
There are some decent cheap options in Antofagasta, as well as some higher end places, but there's not much in the middle, so plan on either roughing it in a hostel or spending between $70 and $100 for typical American chain hotel. Updated: May 13,2009

Hotel Isla Capri
(ROOMS: $10 and up) This is a budget option for backpackers who want to be near the university. Its single and double rooms are basic but well-kept and have comfortable beds. The staff also serves breakfast before sunrise for travelers in a hurry to get out of town. Copiapó 1208. Tel: 56-55-263703. Updated: May 13, 2009.

Hotel Brasil
(ROOMS: $11 – 20) The rooms at Hotel Brasil are plain but spacious and have cable TV. The lack of flash keeps the price down. A double room with a shared bathroom is a reasonable $17. JS Ossa 1978. Tel: 56-55-267268. Updated: May 13, 2009.

Radisson Hotel Antofagasta
(ROOMS: $70 and up) The Radisson, located on the main coastal avenue, is a typical chain hotel that caters to businesspeople. There is a pool, gym and business center in the hotel, while the rooms—all with private bathroom—are fully furnished with WiFi, telephone, coffee maker, cable TV and a mini-bar. Ejercito 01151. Tel: 56-55-350400, URL: www.radisson.com/antofagastacl. Updated: May 13, 2009.

Holiday Inn Express
(ROOMS: $90 and up) The Holiday Inn Express is a decent option for the businessperson and has all the amenities anyone would need, including a relaxing Jacuzzi. Grecia 1490. Tel: 56-55-228888, URL: www.chile-hotels.com/holianto.htm. Updated: May 13, 2009.

Hotel Antofagasta
(ROOMS: $200 and up) There is no debate about where to find the best hotel in Antofagasta: Nestled near the port with a fantastic view of the bay, Hotel Antofagasta is a chain hotel with a top-shelf bar—complete with a piano—and pool. The rooms, some with ocean views, are completely furnished, with large, private bathrooms. Balmaceda 2575. Tel: 56-55-228811, URL: www.hotelantofagasta.cl. Updated: May 13, 2009.

Restaurants
Antofagasta's unique position between the desert and the sea provides a gorgeous backdrop for its many restaurants scattered about town. Elegant seaside restaurants serving seafood, sushi and steak are popular and plentiful. For those on a tighter budget, there are several smaller joints around the Mercado Central (Plaza Sotomayor) serving cheap, but tasty local cuisine. Updated: Jul 01, 2009.

Café del Centro
(ENTREES $3 – 6) This simple café is a nice place to enjoy a cup of coffee and people watch during the late afternoon or early evening. There are sandwiches and pastries on the menu in case you're craving a snack to accompany your caffeine kick. Prat 490. Updated: May 13, 2009.

Don Pollo
(ENTREES: $3 – 5) The menu at Don Pollo is not complex: chicken, chicken and more chicken. The tender white meat may be the only thing available here, but it is some of the best rotisserie chicken in Chile. Ossa 2594. Updated: May 13, 2009.

Club de Yates
(ENTREES: $7 – 20) Club de Yates is a bit uppity, but the nice views of the port go well with a plate of oysters or fish. Prices are higher than most other restaurants, but diners are paying for atmosphere, as well as food and good service. It is a good idea to call ahead for reservations. Balmaceda 2705. Tel: 56-55-284116. Updated: May 13, 2009.

El Arriero
(ENTREES: $7 – 13) Go straight to El Arriero for a fantastic steak or a good-sized portion of meat off the grill. The menu is packed with traditional dishes from Spain's Basque

NORTE GRANDE

country along with a decent selection of wine. The restaurant has hams hanging from the walls and there is usually someone playing piano late evenings. Condell 2644. Tel: 56-55-264371. Updated: May 13, 2009.

Picadillo
This oceanside restaurant has it all: live music, fantastic service and perfect plates of sushi. There are also some pretty good desserts here, so save room. Making reservations is a good idea since the place can get crowded—especially on weekends. Av. Grecia 1000. Tel: 56-55-247503, E-mail: contacto@picadillo.cl, URL: www.picadillo.cl. Updated: Jul 01, 2009.

AROUND ANTOFAGASTA
MONUMENTO NATURAL LA PORTADA

The temperamental Pacific Ocean has pounded and eroded this gigantic rock formation into a natural arch. Situated on top of a volcanic base, this monument is the main attraction of a 31-hectare piece of protected land 25 kilometers (15.5 mi) north of Antofagasta. Pack a lunch and enjoy a meal on the area picnic tables. To get here, take micro 15 from Terminal Pesquero to the junction at La Portada, then walk 3 kilometers (1.8 mi) west. Updated: May 13, 2009.

JUAN LÓPEZ

Slightly north of La Portada is a paved road that heads west to the charming beach village of Juan López. The beach has soft, gray sand and the water is relatively warm compared to other spots in Chile. Updated: May 13, 2009.

MANO DE DESIERTO

A huge, 11-meter-high (36-ft) granite hand emerges from the sand with its fingers stretched toward the sky at the junction of Ruta 28 and Panamericana, 75 kilometers (46.6) south of Antofagasta. This attraction was built in 1992 by sculptor Mario Irarrázaval. Updated: May 13, 2009.

OBSERVATORIO CERRO PARANAL

Observatorio Cerro Paranal has four 8.2-meter (26.9-ft) telescopes and is one of the highest-powered in the world. It is located approximately 120 kilometers (74.6 mi) south of Antofagasta on Cerro Paranal at 2,664 meters (8740.2 ft) above sea level. You have to schedule visits in advance, and will need to arrange your own transportation—check the observatory's website for more information (www.eso.org/public). Updated: May 13, 2009.

TALTAL

 33 m 10,000 55

The small fishing town of Taltal, snuggled at the base of the coastal mountains, is the only stop of relative significance on the trip from Chañaral to Antofagasta. The town was once a key nitrate port, but is now a simple fishing village with some interesting buildings and a few well-tended plazas.

At the center of the town, monuments to the nitrate era stand on **Plaza Arturo Prat**. The **Iglesia San Francisco Javier**, dating back to 1897, is here as well. Take a peek at the former houses and offices of the **Taltal Railway Company** and the old locomotive that rests at the corner of Prat and O'Higgins. The **Museo de Taltal** on Prat has an archaeological collection from the region.

Club Social Taltal serves delicious fresh seafood. It is located at Torreblanca 162. **Las Anclas**, located on the corner of Esmeralda and Martínez has great seafood, too.

Hotel San Martín (Martínez 279. Tel: 56-55-611088) has simple single rooms for as little as $10. **Hostería del Taltal** (Esmeralda 671. Tel: 56-55-611173) offers accommodation near the sea; rates run approximately $35 per night and include breakfast. Rooms are spotless and the beds are comfortable. Taltal is found easily enough if you are driving. Follow the sign pointing to a road that leads 25 kilometers (15.5 mi) west off the Panamericana. Several bus companies, including **Tur Bus**, offer service to Taltal, as well as onward to Antofagasta and Chañaral. Updated: Jul 06, 2009.

!!!!!

Norte Chico

The region of Norte Chico—or "Little North"—bridges the gap between the fertile heartland and the vast deserts of Norte Grande, which stretch across the borders into Peru and Bolivia. While its name makes the region sound like the far north's little sibling, Norte Chico holds its own. La Serena (p.252), the slender nation's third oldest city, boasts some of the best beaches in the entire country. This area is also home to Chile's national drink 'Pisco', and the amazing *desierto florido* (a simultaneous flowering of many desert plants) that occurs, though rarely, in the seemingly barren land around Vallenar (p.251). While you're in the area, don't miss Bahía wildlife. Although it's easy to reach from the city of Copiapó, the park is surprisingly seldom visited by tourists—which makes it all the more pleasant for those who do visit. Updated: Dec 01, 2006.

History

Mining, more than agriculture, defines Norte Chico. The Incas originally mined gold here before the Spaniards arrived. The 19th century brought a silver rush, and railways, roads, and mining towns along with it. The discovery of copper later on brought more wealth into the region. From the 1840s to the 1870s, Norte Chico was the largest copper producing area in the world. Updated: Apr 30, 2009.

When to Go

Most visitors head to La Serena in the summer, so avoid this time if you can to sidestep the rush and inflated prices. A perfect time to see the region is during the *desierto florido* between late July and September, though it is impossible to predict whether or not the flowers will appear. Reserva Nacional Pingüino de Humboldt, Parque Nacional Nevado Tres Cruces or Ojos del Salado are enjoyable year-round. Updated: Apr 30, 2009.

Safety

Norte Chico is one of the safest regions in Chile. Most of its towns are relatively small, so big-city problems are absent. There are ample opportunities to camp throughout the region, but be aware that occasional theft does occur if possessions are left unguarded. Updated: Apr 30, 2009.

Things to See and Do

Norte Chico has plenty of opportunities for nature-lovers. Try a trip to the unbelievably green Laguna Verde or Ojos del Salado (p.250) near the Argentine border, or visit the white beaches and clear waters at Bahía Inglesa near Caldera (p.244). Updated: Apr 30, 2009.

Tours

A lot of the tour operators in the region are based in Copiapó. Guides—some knowledgeable, others not so much— are eager to escort tourists to all the popular destinations in Norte Chico. Bahía Inglesa, Ojos del Salado, Laguna Verde and Nevado Tres Cruces are among the most frequently visited. Updated: Apr 30, 2009.

Lodging

Outdoor-types will find a wealth of fantastic camping opportunities along beaches, in national parks and in reserves.

Highlights

Take a walk around **La Serena (p.252)**, Chile's third-oldest city, home to beautiful beaches and churches.

Witness the rare **desierto florido** in the desert around **Vallenar (p.251)**.

Wander off the beaten path to the snow-capped volcanoes of **Parque Nacional Nevado Tres Cruces (p.250)**.

Try a **pisco sour**, the nation's favorite drink, in the **Elqui Valley (p.258)**.

Check out the dolphins, sea otters, sea lions and penguins at **Reserva Natural Pingüino de Humboldt (p.252)**. Updated: Apr 30, 2009.

Inglesa (p.246), Parque Nacional Nevado Tres Cruces (p.250), Laguna Verde, Ojos del Salado and the Reserva Nacional Pingüino de Humboldt (p.252).

The Norte Chico stretches 500 kilometers (310 mi) north from the Santiago region. The geography is characterized by long, parched hills, punctuated occasionally by lush valleys. This is semi-arid territory, with little vegetation, and it marks the transition between the fertile heartland and the bone-dry deserts in Norte Grande. Not everything is parched here. The Choapa, Limarí, Copiapó, Elqui and Huasco rivers flow from the Andes to the coast, irrigating the surrounding land. Here, beautiful green farmlands rife with olives and apricots follow the rivers through the dry, brown hills.

The coast is a highlight, with beaches that are considered among the best in Chile, although few have been developed like those closer to Santiago. Their sandy bays and turquoise waters make a relaxing getaway for those looking to live easy for a few days.

Perhaps the biggest draw in this region is La Serena. Arguably Chile's most attractive city, with its colonial architecture and seaside setting, La Serena makes a great base for exploring some of the nearby beaches, or for taking hikes inland.

Parque Nacional Nevado Tres Cruces is another great spot to visit, with its emerald lakes, snow-dusted volcanoes, and abundant

Remember that some of the campsites at these locations do not offer food or water so bring sufficient supplies. If you prefer to sleep indoors, you can find plush hotels and resorts in areas such as Bahía Inglesa. There are also plenty of budget options for backpackers. Updated: Apr 30, 2009.

CHAÑARAL

 60m   14,000   52

Chañaral is a good jumping-off point to Parque Nacional Pan de Azúcar, though you can (and it's recommended to) visit the park as part of a day-trip from Copiapó. This tattered town has been hopelessly contaminated with the toxic waste from the immense El Salvador mine. Clean-up efforts have had little effect; the beach is still dirty from the toxic waste and the air is polluted. The Environmental Health Service even considered moving the whole town to escape the mess.

Getting To and Away from Chañaral

Most buses will stop here if you ask the driver. **Tur Bus** has an office on the edge of town on Panamericana Norte. Tel: 56-52-481012. Bus company **Flota Barrios** is located at Merino Jarpa 567. Buses run to Copiapó and stop at towns on the way to Santiago. Updated: Apr 10, 2009.

Services

There is an **ATM** at BCI located at Maipú 319. At Comercio 442, on the west side of town, you'll find **Entel** for long-distance calls. The **post office** is also located on Comercio. Limited **tourist information** can be found at the Municipalidad on the corner of Merino Jarpa and Conchuelas. Updated: May 08, 2009.

Lodging

Accommodation is quite basic in Chañaral. Two options are: **Hostal Los Aromos** (ROOMS: $16 – 26) on a residential street at Los Aromos 7. Single, double and triple rooms are available; **Hotel La Marina** (ROOMS: $8 – 12), on the main street at Merino Jarpa, has rooms with shared bathrooms and chilly showers.

Restaurants

The few restaurants in Chañaral mainly serve traditional Chilean dishes. Try **El Rincón** on Merino Jarpa 567.

PARQUE NACIONAL PAN DE AZÚCAR !

(ENTRANCE: $5) Humboldt penguins are the biggest draw to this 43,754-hectare national park, which has immaculate beaches of fine white sand and steep cliffs rising from the shore. The park is home to a variety of birds, foxes and different types of cactus. The **Conaf center** (where you pay the entrance fee), a small **market** and a **campsite** are all located in the part of the park known as Caleta Pan de Azúcar.

Two kilometers off shore is Isla Pan de Azúcar, home to seals, sea otters, pelicans, plovers and, of course, more than 3,000 Humboldt penguins. Boats offer two-hour trips to give visitors an up-close look at the island for about $8 per person. The best times to go are in the early morning or early evening when the penguins feed. You can also trek 10 kilometers (6.2 mi) north of the village to get a nice view of the coastline from the lookout at Mirador Pan de Azúcar.

Campsites are located on the beaches around the village, and a bit farther south at Playa Piqueros, for approximately $18 per site. There are toilets, water, picnic tables and showers available at these locations. Camping wild in the park is not permitted. A pair of secluded cabins are also available on a beach to the north of the village.

Getting To and Away from Parque Nacional Pan de Azúcar

Chango Turismo (Tel: 56-52-480484) runs two buses daily to Caleta Pan de Azúcar from Chañaral. Buses leave at 8 a.m. and 3 p.m., and return at 10 a.m. and 5 p.m. The company also runs jeep tours to Mirador Pan de Azúcar ($12). Another option is to enlist a ride in a taxi—a good negotiator can usually get the driver to do it for $10 – 15. if you're driving from the north, take the turn marked Las Bombas, located approximately 45 kilometers (28 mi) north of Chañaral. Updated: May 08, 2009.

CALDERA

 40m   14,000   52

Caldera is a typical small beach town. The people are relaxed, the seafood is fresh and life seems to move at a slower pace. The magnificent beaches are what attract most of the visitors, but Caldera boasts some historical, too. Estación de Ferrocarril, the terminus of the first South American railway, was built here in the late 19th century when the city was exporting large amounts of silver. These days, the economy is supported by tourism and by the export of both grapes and copper. Updated: May 08, 2009.

There are plenty of restaurants in town that whip up flavorful seafood. Fish, crab and oysters are local favorites. Reasonable accommodation is also available, though prices drop during the low season. Updated: May 08, 2009.

When to Go

Chileans and tourists alike flock to the beaches of Caldera in January and February, driving up the price of accommodation. If you prefer peace and dramatically lower hotel prices, don't visit during those two months. The weather remains mostly the same during the low season so the only thing you will miss is a little crowd noise. Updated: May 08, 2009.

Getting To and Away From Caldera

Caldera is only a one-hour bus ride from Copiapó, where you will find more frequent service to destinations north and south. **Pullman** (Tel: 56-52-315227) has a bus terminal in Caldera located on the corner of Gallo and Vallejos. **Tur Bus** (Tel: 56-52-316832) operates from Ossa Varas with service to Santiago (and major destinations in between) at: 7:45 a.m., 9:15 a.m., 9 p.m. and 9:15 p.m. They also have a bus going north to Arica (and major destinations in between) at: 11:15 a.m. **Buses Recabarren** runs a frequent service to Copiapó as well. Taxis can take you to Aeropuerto Desierto de Atacama. Updated: Mar 19, 2009.

Getting Around

Most tourists can reach their desired destinations by foot, though Caldera has its fair share of taxis. Public buses and taxis offer quick rides to Bahía Inglesa. Updated: Mar 15, 2009.

Safety

Caldera is a relatively safe and laid-back resort. People who stroll along the beach and streets in the early morning hours rarely encounter a problem. Do be careful of the occasional stray pit bull among the town's roaming dogs. Updated: May 08, 2009.

Services

The **tourism office** is located on the Plaza de Armas but does not keep regular hours. The **post office** is located at Edwards 339 and there is a phone center down the road at Edwards 360. The BCI **bank** on Gana (across from Nueva Miramar) has an ATM. Domo Chango Chile at El Morro 610 has **Internet** access, as well as rooms for rent. Updated: Mar 15, 2009.

Things to See and Do

The magnificent beaches are Caldera's biggest draw. Lounging on the sand is the most popular local activity, that is, if a nap or working on your tan are considered activities. When you've had enough sun, you'll find that the town itself also has a lot to offer.

Estacíon Ferrocarrile

This train station near the beach was originally built in 1850, and has the wear and tear to prove it. This unique piece of architecture was the terminus for South America's first railroad. Updated: May 08, 2009.

Iglesia San Vicente

The Iglesia San Vincente is a brown and cream-colored church with a Gothic tower that looms over the town's main square. Erected in 1862 by English carpenters, the church is one of the more appealing landmarks in Caldera. Updated: May 08, 2009.

Cementerio Laico

Laico was the first non-Catholic cemetery in the city of Caldera. The grounds still feature the elaborate tombs of English, Welsh, German and other European immigrants and a walk through the cemetery provides insight on some of the city's ethnic history. Av. Diego de Almeyda. Updated: May 08, 2009.

Lodging

Caldera has a range of accomodation, but the cheapest and cleanest rooms in town are at Residencial Millaray. Tierra del Sol is a more expensive but comfortable option. Jandy Hotel offers the most amenities. Updated: May 08, 2009.

Residencial Millaray

(ROOMS: $10) Residencial Millaray has simple, clean rooms with shared bathrooms and a comfortable patio for relaxing with a book or a drink. Its location on the plaza is also a plus for those who want to be close to the action. Cousiño 331. Tel: 56-52-315528. Updated: May 08, 2009.

NORTE CHICO

Terra Sol

(ROOMS: $20 – 30) Terra Sol is not the fanciest choice in town, but is a nice mid-range option for those who want to escape budget accommodation. Rooms are comfortable, and private bathrooms are available for a little extra. Breakfast is included in the price. Gallo 370. Tel: 56-52-319885. Updated: May 08, 2009.

Jandy Hotel

(ROOMS: $35, more high season) Jandy is located near the center of town, less than a block from the main square. Rooms have private bathrooms and cable TV and the hotel also offers Internet access, a maid service, bike rental a coffee shop. Gallo 560. Tel: 56-52-316451. Updated: May 08, 2009.

Restaurants

Caldera's seaside location means there is a wealth of delicious options for seafood lovers. Most places also offer international dishes for those not a fan of the diet aquatic. Pirón de Oro has exquisite shellfish; Nuevo Miramar offers one of the best ocean-views in town; and El Plateao has an international flavor. Updated: May 08, 2009.

El Plateao

(ENTREES: $6 – 10) There is someting for almost everyone on the menu at El Plateao. The restaurant serves up sushi, curries and other international cuisine. And the seafood is on par with the better restaurants in Caldera. El Morro 756. Updated: May 08, 2009.

Nuevo Miramar

(ENTREES: $7 – 11) Nuevo Miramar's strength is its romantic location on the beach. The views of the sea are spectacular, while the seafood is acceptable and served in large portions. The atmosphere is also family-friendly. Gana 090. Tel: 52-315381. Updated: May 08, 2009.

Il Pirón di Oro

(ENTREES: $7 – 12) This restaurant specializes in fresh seafood and is arguably the best place to eat in Caldera. The crab dishes are a tasty choice, and the clams and oysters are worth a try, too. Cousiño 218. Updated: May 08, 2009.

AROUND CALDERA
BAHÍA INGLESA

Bahía Inglesa is stunning thanks to a combination of perfect white beaches, clear blue water, and arresting rock formations. The beach is only a short trip south of Caldera; don't forget to bring the camera for a few picture-postcard photos. Updated: May 17, 2009.

Things to See and Do

Windsurfing

The strong winds that sweep across the sea along the coast of Caldera make it one of the prime windsurfing spots in Chile. **Domo Chango Chilean** organizes excursions. El Morro 610, Tel: 56-52-316168. Updated: May 08, 2009.

Santuario de la Naturaleza Granito Orbicular

This sanctuary, located approximately 11 kilometers (6.8 mi) north of town, near Playa Roller, is littered with weird, often absurd granite-core rock formations. Granito Orbicular became a protected area in 1981. Updated: May 08, 2009.

COPIAPÓ

 1,471m 130,990 52

Copiapó's economy is based on mining. The town grew significantly during the 18th-century gold rush, and then again reaped the windfalls of precious metal-mining when silver was discovered at Chañarcillo in 1832.

Now, the city is a nice place to rest between La Serena and Antofagasta, or to use as a base to explore the surrounding area. From here, you can plan an excursion to the beautiful Parque Nacional Nevado Tres Cruces, the highest active volcano in Ojos del Saludo, or to Laguna Verde.

Don't miss Museo Minerológico's impressive collection of glittering minerals. Iglesia Catedral is a majestic church in Plaza Prat and the Locomotion Copiapó at the Escuela de Minas is another fun, touristy attraction. Palacete Viña de Cristo and the Museo Regional de Atacama house a few interesting artifacts. Updated: Apr 30, 2009.

When to Go

Día del Minero (Miner's Day) is celebrated annually on August 10. Two other festivals are noteworthy: one on December 8, the anniversary of the town's founding; and the Fiesta de Candelaria on the first Sunday of February. Updated: Apr 30, 2009.

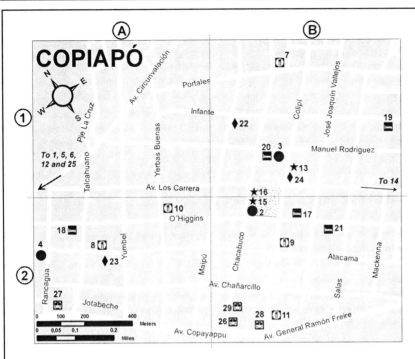

Activities ●

1   Escuela de Minas A1
2   Iglesia Catedral B2
3   Museo Minerológico B1
4   Museo Regional de Atacama A2
5   Palacete Viña de Cristo A1

Airports ✈

6   Aeropuerto Desierto de Atacama A1

Eating 🍴

7   Di Tito B1
8   El Corsario A2
9   Empanadopolis B2
10 Hao-Hwa A2
11 Hotel Miramonti B2

Services ★

12 Conaf Office A1
13 Entel call center B1
14 Hospital San José B1
15 Post Office B2
16 Sernatur office B1

Sleeping 🛏

17 Hotel Diego de Almeida B2
18 Hotel La Casona A2
19 Hotel Montecatini B1
20 Residencial Ben Bow B1
21 Residencial Chacabuco B2

Tours ♦

22 Atacama Chile B1
23 Aventurismo A2
24 Gran Atacama B1

Transportation 🚌

25 Budget Car Rental A1
26 Bus Terminal B2
27 Hertz Car Rental A2
28 Pullman Bus B2
29 Tur Bus B2

Getting To and Away From Copiapó

Copiapó's main **bus terminal** is located three blocks south of Plaza Prat at the corner of Freire and Chacabuco, and has inter-city buses. The terminal for **Tur Bus** is on Chacabuco, with departures to Arica (and all major stops in between) seven times a day. Tur Bus leaves for Santiago (and all major stops in between) around 30 times a day. **Pullman Bus** operates from a terminal at Freire and Colipí. The **Aeropuerto Desierto de Atacama** is 50 kilometers (31 mi) west, so take a taxi from town (about $25) or use the bus ($10). Updated: Apr 30, 2009.

Getting Around

The *colectivos,* or shared taxis, can get you around town for a few pesos. You can also rent a car from **Hertz** (Copayapu 173. Tel: 56-52-213522) or **Budget** (Ramón Freire 050. Tel: 56-52-216272). Updated: May 19, 2009.

Safety

Copiapó does not have too many problems with crime. Be alert and remember to pay attention to suspicious-looking characters, watch for pickpockets and do not flash money around. Use common sense and you should be fine. Updated: Apr 30, 2009.

Services

The helpful **Sernatur** office is located on the northern edge of Plaza Prat at Los Carrera 691, while **Conaf** has an office at Juan Martínez 56 and can provide information on the region's parks. The **post office** is behind the Sernatur and the Entel **call center** is at Colipí 484. There are numerous **banks**, **ATMs**, **Internet** services and **money exchanges** around the plaza. **Hospital San José** is on the corner of Los Carrera and Vicuña. Updated: Mar 12, 2009.

Things to See and Do

Most visitors use Copiapó as a base for other activities, but there are also a few noteworthy places to visit in town.

Museo Regional de Atacama

The museum has displays about the War of the Pacific, the history and development of mining in the region and the area's pre-Columbian inhabitants. The building was originally a Matta family mansion, built in the 1840s. Atacama 98. Open: December – February, Monday – Friday 9 a.m. – 7:30 p.m., Saturday 11 a.m. – 2 p.m. and 4 – 7 p.m., Sunday 11 a.m. – 2 p.m.; March – November, Monday 2 – 5:45 p.m., Tuesday – Friday 9 a.m. – 5:45 p.m., Saturday 10 a.m. – 1 p.m. and 3 – 5:45 p.m., Sunday 10 a.m. – 1 p.m. Updated: Apr 30, 2009.

Museo Minerológico

(ADMISSION: $1) This museum is one of the most interesting places to visit in Copiapó. Founded in 1857 and supported by the Universidad de Atacama, it has a collection of more than 2,000 glittering minerals from around the world, inluding large portions of quartz, marble and malachite. Corner of Rodríguez and Colipí. Tel: 56-52-206606. Monday – Friday 10 a.m. – 1 p.m. and 3:30 – 7 p.m., Saturday 10 a.m. – 1p.m. Closed Sunday. Updated: Apr 30, 2009.

Escuela de Minas

(ADMISSION: $1) The School of Mines is located west of town and is now home to the Universidad de Atacama. Railroad enthusiasts shouldn't miss the attention-grabbing black-and-yellow Locomotion Copiapó housed at the school. Updated: Apr 30, 2009.

Palacete Viña de Cristo

(ADMISSION: free) Although it now belongs to the Universidad de Atacama, this palace once was the premier place to live in Copiapó. It was built in 1860 by Apolinario Soto, who made his fortune as the owner of Tres Puntas silver mine. The mansion features materials imported from Europe and the architecture mixes classical and oriental themes. Open 8 a.m. – 7 p.m.. Closed Saturday and Sunday. Updated: May 04, 2009.

Iglesia Catedral

Iglesia Catedral is perched on the southwest corner of the Plaza Prat. Designed by architect William Rogers, the church has a three-tiered tower and wooden steeple. Updated: Apr 30, 2009.

Tours

There are a number of tour operators in Copiapó that offer adventures to Bahía Inglesa, Ojos del Saldado, Laguna Verde and Nevado Tres Cruces, among others. Remember to obtain permission from the Dirección Nacional de Fronteras y Límites before an ascent of Ojos de Saldado since it is close to the Argentine border. Tour operators can usually help you obtain permission. Updated: Apr 30, 2009.

Aventurismo

Aventurismo is one of the more reliable tour operators in Copiapó. The director, Maximiliano Martínez, is a friendly and knowledge source of information, and makes trips to all the key locations. Atacama 240. Cell: 56-9-5992184, E-mail: ojosdelsalado@aventurismo.cl, URL: www.aventurismo.cl. Updated: May 05, 2009.

Gran Atacama

Gran Atacama has not been around as long as some of the other tour operators in town, but the agency has knowledgeable guides and offers mountain climbing, horseback riding and hiking tours. There are half-day and multi-day options. Colipí 484. Tel: 56-52-219271. Updated: May 05, 2009.

Atacama Chile

Atacama is another reliable tour operator in Copiapó, with friendly guides that make any trip fun. Maipu 580. Tel: 56-52-211191 or 56-9-8722653, E-mail: info@atacamachile.com, URL: www.atacamachile.com. Updated: May 04, 2009.

Lodging

Copiapó is loaded with low-budget accommodation, as well as nice hotels that will appeal to families and business travelers. Hotel La Casona and Hotel Diego de Almeida are a pair of well-kept hotels which cost less than $100 per night; Residencial Ben Bow and Residencial Chacabuco are two good cheap places to sleep; and Hotel Montecatini is a decent mid-range choice with large rooms. Updated: Jul 07, 2009.

Residencial Chacabuco

(ROOMS: $7) Chacabuca is a good budget option for backpackers. The rooms with shared bathrooms are forgettable, but simple and clean. The staff is friendly and the hotel is in a good location. O'Higgins 921. Tel: 56-52-213428. Updated: May 04, 2009.

Residencial Ben Bow

(ROOMS: $7 – 20) Ben Bow is a great option for budget travelers looking for a no-frills place. It is not the most aesthetic building, but the small rooms are relatively clean. Manuel Rodríguez 541. Tel: 56-52-217634. Updated: Jul 07, 2009.

Hotel Montecatini I

(ROOMS: $24 – 45) Montecatini is about as good as it gets for a mid-range option in South America. There is a courtyard, a pool and a nice garden on the premises. The rooms are very well-kept and spacious, with cable TV and private bathrooms. Infante 766. Tel: 56-52-211363. Updated: May 04, 2009.

Hotel La Casona

(ROOMS: $55 – 84) A well-kept place a few blocks from downtown, La Casona is the best mid-range option in Copiapó. The English-speaking owner is quick to make guests feel at home in this old-fashioned house-turned-hotel. All rooms have Internet access, private bathrooms, and phones to make local and international calls. O'Higgins 150. Tel: 56-52-217277, E-mail: reservas@lacasonahotel.cl, URL: www.lacasonahotel.cl. Updated: Jul 07, 2009.

Hotel Diego de Almeida

(ROOMS: $60 – 90) Diego de Almeida is one of the better options in town for those who don't have to count their pennies. It's located on Plaza Prat, and has a pool, sauna, bar and restaurant. Rooms are spacious and well stocked. O'Higgins 760. Tel: 56-52-212075. Updated: May 04, 2009.

Restaurants

Copiapó does not have outstanding restaurants, but it does have numerous places to get your fill at a decent price. Hao-Hwa serves solid Chinese food, Empanadopolis has the best empanadas in town and El Corsario dishes out traditional Chilean meals. Di Tito and Hotel Miramonti offer good Italian fare. Updated: Apr 30, 2009.

Empanadopolis

(MEAL AND SODA: $3) Empanadopolis has some of the cheapest and most enjoyable meals you're likely to find in town. This is where the locals drift for an empanada that's bursting with fillings. Colipí 320. Updated: Apr 30, 2009.

Di Tito

(ENTREES: $4 – 9) Di Tito is another good place for a sit-down meal, especially if you have been in the country for an extended period of time and need a break from traditional Chilean cuisine. The pasta is filling, the pizza tasty, and the prices reasonable. Chacabuco 710. Tel: 56-52-212386. Updated: Apr 30, 2009.

El Corsario

(SET LUNCH: $6) If you have ever wondered whether rabbit tastes like chicken, here is your chance to find out. El Corsario serves this adorable delicacy, as well as other Chilean staples. The *pastel de choclo* is above average. Atacama 245. Tel: 56-52-233659. Updated: Apr 30, 2009.

Hao-Hwa

(MEAL FOR TWO: $10) Hao-Hwa serves some of the best Chinese food north of Santiago. Try the combination plate, piled with enough food for two people. The service is fast and friendly, and they will wrap your meal for take-out if you can't finish. Yerbas Buenas 334. Tel: 56-52-215484. Updated: Apr 30, 2009.

Hotel Miramonti

Do not walk into this hotel-restaurant looking for a cheap dinner. The Italian food is not world-class, but it is filling and will give you a break from empanadas or chicken and fries. Ramón Freire 731, across from the Pullman Bus terminal. Updated: Apr 30, 2009.

NORTE CHICO

AROUND COPIAPÓ
CHAÑARCILLO

When silver was found in Chañarcillo in the 1800s, the population of the area boomed. The ruins of the original mining town are just a short distance from Copiapó. To reach Chañarcillo, take the Panamericana south until kilometer 59 (mi 37), then follow the dirt road east. Updated: May 04, 2009.

PARQUE NACIONAL NEVADO TRES CRUCES

(ENTRANCE: $6) Parque Nacional Nevado Tres Cruces is located east of Copiapó along the international highway to Argentina through Paso de San Francisco. With 60,000 hectares, the park features Andes mountains that reach to about 4,500 meters (14,763 ft) above sea level, as well as wetlands that are home to a variety of wildlife. Flamingos summer here, and other aquatic birds nest in the shallow lagoons. Great herds of *vicuñas* and *guanacos*, both related to the llama, along with the occasional puma, are found here, along with Andean geese, gulls and horned coots. You might also see a condor or two gliding high in the sky.

In the park's 49,000-hectare northern sector, you'll find Laguna Santa Rosa and Salar de Maricunga, the nation's southernmost

Photo by Ricardo Martínez

salt flat. From the lagoon, follow the track north to a Conaf-controlled refuge. There is room to camp and cook and great views of the snow-tipped Volcán Tres Cruces.

A three-hour ride south will bring you to the second sector. Here, at 4,200 meters (13,779 ft) above sea level, is the sprawling, dark-blue Laguna del Negro Francisco. The lake is home to a variety of birds, including flamingos. Awe-inspiring Volcán Copiapó towers over the lake at a height of 6,080 meters (19,948 ft). A refuge and Conaf headquarters are located 4 kilometers (2.5 mi) from the lake. Updated: May 04, 2009.

OJOS DEL SALADO

Though it is not part of Parque Nacional Nevado Tres Cruces, Ojos del Salado is both the highest peak in Chile and the highest active volcano in the world, at 6,893 meters (22,615 ft). The volcano is still intermittantly active, and the last two eruptions occurred in 1937 and 1956.

The ascent of Ojos del Salado is popular and relatively simple, though the final 50 meters (164 ft) are quite technical. The climb takes about a week and should be attempted between October and May. The base of the volcano is a 12-kilometer (7.5 mi) walk from the abandoned police checkpoint on the main road. There are two refuges on the ascent. The first is located at the 5,100-meter (16,732 ft) mark, and the other at 5,700 meters (18,701 ft).

The volcano sits on the Argentine border, so climbers must have written permission from Chile's Dirección de Frontera y Límites (Bandera 52, Santiago. Tel: 56-2-6714110, URL: www.difrol.cl.), which oversees border activities. You can obtain permission online or in person, but you must do it in advance. Copiapó tour operators can arrange a guided trek or ride to the base.

Ojos del Salado is also near the must-see Laguna Verde. At an altitude of 4,500 meters (14,764 ft), the lake's water glows an incredible bright turquoise. There is a campsite near the lake, as well as shallow hot stream where you can swim. Updated: May 04, 2009.

The Huasco Valley Region

The Huasco Valley is a fertile strip of land between La Serena and Copiapó, where locals produce sumptuous olives, delicious wines

NORTE CHICO

and good pisco. The region is also home to profitable but land-stripping mining operations. Updated: Apr 30, 2009.

Huasco was once a small fishing village but expanded thanks to the mining of iron ore and area tourism. Huasco is now known as a good base for exploring the surrounding desert. Just north of Huasco, in the Atacama Desert, is the Llanos de Challe National Park. In September, October and sometimes early November, you may see the rare *desierto florido*, the desert in bloom. The *garra de leon* (lion's paw flower) is a particular highlight of the park and only grows in this unique and isolated location. Updated: Jul 07, 2009.

VALLENAR

 441m   44,000   51

Chilean governor Ambrosio O'Higgins founded Vallenar on January 5, 1789, and promptly named the town "Villa San Ambrosio de Vallenar," after Ballinagh, his hometown in Ireland. Vallenar is now the center of the mining and agricultural industry in the Huasco Province. The city is located near Ruta 5 Norte, and offers easy access to Parque Nacional Llanos de Challe, coastal areas Freirina and Huasco, as well as inner valley locations such as Alto del Carmen, Conay, San Félix and El Tránsito.

Vallenar is also home to the **San Ambrosio**, a church with a copper dome, and the **Huasco Museum** (corner of Ramírez and Brasil, Monday – Friday, 9 a.m. – 1 p.m. and 3 – 6 p.m.). The museum has mineralogical, archaeological, botanical, paleontological, zoological and historical exhibits, including a colonial torture device, a set of clay Inca bottles and photos of the aftermath of Vallenar's 1922 earthquake.

Vallenar has several good accommodation options for travelers: **Hotel Puerto de Vega** (ROOMS: $50 – 70. Ramírez 201. Tel: 56-51-613870, URL: www.puertodevega. cl) is European-themed and conveniently located near the bus terminal; **Residencial Oriental** (ROOMS: $8. Ramírez 201. Tel: 56-51-613870, URL: www.puertodevega.cl) has large, dark, clean rooms, with and without a private bathroom: **Hostal Camino del Rey** (Merced 943. Tel: 56-51-613184) is another solid budget option.

For food, **Il Bocatto** (Prat 750), on the east side of the main square, offers pizzas and other quick meals. **Arriero** (Prat 1061) is a bit pricier than most fast-food options in Vallenar, but the steak is worth the extra money.

The **tourism office** is located on the main square at Plaza 30a (Tel: 56-51-611009). There is nowhere to exchange money in Vallenar, but **banks** and **ATMs** are scattered around the plaza. Updated: Apr 13, 2009.

Getting To and Away From Vallenar

Vallenar's **bus terminal** is located at the corner of Prat and Avenida Matta. The most reliable and popular option is **Tur Bus**, which has a main office adjacent to the main bus terminal. Tur Bus has routes to the capital for approximately $25, as well as to La Serena, Antofagasta, Calama, San Pedro, Arica, and more. Buses leave hourly. The same is true of **Pullman**, which has both a downtown office and one located at Serrano 551 (Tel: 56-51-619587). Updated: Apr 02, 2009.

ALTO DEL CARMEN

Alto del Carmen is a rural community in the Huasco valley, about 45 kilometers (28 mi) east of Vallenar. There are several restaurants and accommodation options here, and the valley is generally used as a starting point to strike out on rubble roads to Conay, Junta Valeriano and El Tránsito. This village also produces pisco at the Planta Pisquera Alto del Carmen. Updated: Apr 02,2009.

PARQUE NACIONAL LLANOS DE CHALLE

(ENTRANCE: $5) Parque Nacional Llanos de Challe is one of the finest places to view the *desierto florido*. The area is also home to the beautiful *garra de león*, a rare deep-red flower (so rare it's in danger of extinction). The desert blooms between late July and September during wetter seasons. Since the bloom is not an annual occurrence, you'll need a little luck on your side to see it.

Travelers will need to arrange private transportation to the park as there is no public access. Camping is available for approximately $15 per site; be sure to bring plenty of food, water and other items because there are none available. You can reach the park via a dirt road that branches east from Panamericana, 17 kilometers (10.5 mi) north of Vallenar. Updated: Apr 13, 2009.

RESERVA NACIONAL PINGÜINO DE HUMBOLDT

(ENTRANCE: $6) The 860-hectare Reserva Nacional Pingüino de Humboldt includes Isla Choros, a nesting place for the Humboldt penguin. Around the island you may also spot bottle-nosed dolphins, sea otters and sea lions.

To see the animals, you'll have to hire a boat ($75 for seven people) at Caleta de Choros. The boats can take you around Isla Choros (though it is not permitted to dock here) or to the white-sand beaches at Isla Damas. Be sure to call Conaf (Tel: 56-09-9016856) to get a weather update because high waves can make boat trips around the islands impossible.

The reserve is located approximately 78 kilometers (48.5 mi) north of La Serena, where a rough gravel road passes through Choros and continues 48 kilometers (29.8 mi) to Caleta de Choros. At Caleta, visitors must pay the admission fee at Conaf's Information Center. It is also possible to camp on Isla Damas near Playa la Poza where a six-person site costs approximately $20 (though you will need to pay for the boat trip there and back). There are toilets, but no food or water available, so remember to bring supplies. Updated: Oct 28, 2008.

LA SERENA

 146m   200,000 51

Most travelers visit the city of La Serena for two reasons: It's an immensely popular summer beach destination for Chilean vacationers, and it serves as the primary hub for exploring the equally popular Elquí Valley (p.258).

The city, which lies about 471 kilometers (293 mi) north of Santiago, was founded in 1544, making it the third oldest city in the country. In its infancy, however, La Serena was almost completely destroyed by fire. Francisco de Aguirre rebuilt the city on the opposite side of the Elquí river, which now divides city into two parts: the *parte baja* (which was burned shortly after it was founded), also known as *Las Companias*,

and the *parte alta*, the area of the city most visited by travelers. The city has a plethora of churches and the stone structures, dating back centuries, which stand in stark contrast to the modern offices that surround them.

Though not a big city, La Serena vibrates with energy and activity during the day. The sunny Plaza de Armas, in the center of town, has benches around a large central fountain, which are a popular place to sit on a nice afternoon. On the plaza's perimeter, you'll find the Iglesia Catedral, and the city's main commercial avenues, Prat and Cordovez.

The main attraction, however, is the beach, which bursts at the seams with tourists from Argentina and Chile during the summer. Along the beach is the Avenida del Mar, a strip of nice restaurants and pricey hotels. As with many of Chile's popular beaches, you'll have to choose between an over-crowded but lively atmosphere in the summer and the much quieter winter. Updated: Sep 22, 2008.

When to Go

During January and February the city comes alive, but the beaches and accommodation options are packed with Chilean tourists. In the winter months, on the other hand, you'll have no problem finding accommodation or touring the surrounding sites, but you'll find much of the city in hibernation. Many stores and restaurants close during the low season, nightlife is nearly non-existent and the beaches are deserted. Your best bet is to visit during the region's spring, when things are gearing up and the summer tourist rush is not yet in full swing. Updated: Oct 28, 2008.

Getting To and Away from La Serena

Pullman and **Tur Bus** both operate out of La Serena (and Coquimbo). Buses are available south to Valparaiso and Santiago and north as far as Iquique. Buses leave every 20 minutes for Ovalle from the main terminal on the corner of Amunátegui & Avenida El Santo.

Buses via Elqui and Sol de Elqui leave frequently for Vicuña and other towns in the valley. You can purchase a tourist pass from La Serena's terminal, which will allow you to get off and on buses as you please. Updated: Oct 28, 2008.

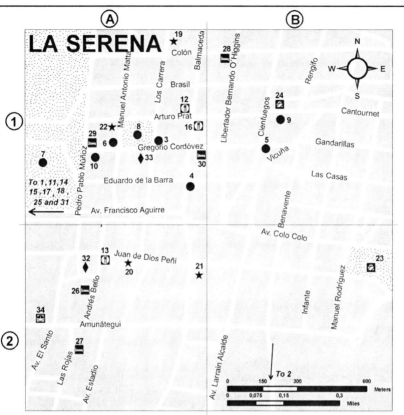

Activities ●

1 Beach A1
2 Cerro Tololo B2
3 Iglesia Catedral A1
4 Iglesia San Francisco A1
5 Museo Arqueológico B1
6 Museo Histórico Casa Gabriel González Videla A1
7 Parque Japonés Kokoro No Niwa A1
8 Plaza de Armas A1
9 San Augustín B1
10 Santo Domingo A1

Eating 🍴

11 Bakulic A1
12 Coffee Express A1
13 El Nuevo Peregrino A2
14 Martín Fierro A1
15 Parrillada Velamar Beach A1
16 Patio Colonial and Beethoven A1
17 Yoko Sushi Bar A1

Nightlife

18 Casino A1

Services ★

19 Lavandería Roma A1
20 Mandamp Laundry A2
21 Regional Hospital A2
22 Sernatur Tourism Office A1

Shopping 🛍

23 Daytime Junk Market B2
24 Mercado La Recova B1

Sleeping 🛏

25 Apart Hotel Stella Mar A1
26 El Punto Hostal A2
27 Hostal Maria Casa A2
28 Hotel El Cid B1
29 Hotel Francisco de Aguirre A1
30 Hotel Londres A1
31 Hotel Playa Campanario A1

Tours ♦

32 Eco Turismo A2
33 Elqui Valley Tour A1

Transportation 🚌

34 Main Bus Terminal A2

NORTE CHICO

Getting Around

In town, you can get around almost entirely on foot. Both the beach and the bus terminal are about a 15-minute walk from the Plaza de Armas. You can also catch a *colectivo* to the Avenida del Mar coastal from either the plaza or the bus terminal. Colectivos make the trip between La Serena and neighboring Coquimbo (p.258), and you can catch a bus either at the terminals or by flagging one down on any of the main streets. Updated: Oct 28, 2008.

Services

Most services in La Serena are clustered around the main square. Calle Cordovez has many **pharmacies** and **banks**.

For **laundry**, Mandamp Laundry (Juan de Dios Peni 363. Tel: 56-52-211 904) offers hotel pick up with two loads or more. The Lavandería Roma is more centrally located at Los Carrera 654.

The city's Sernatur **tourism office** is on Matta 461. Tel: 56-51-225199, E-mail: www. turismoregiondecoquimbo.cl, URL: infocoquimbo@sernatur.cl.

The city's regional **hospital** is on Balmeceda, between Juan de Dios Peni and Amunategui. Updated: Oct 28, 2008.

Things to See and Do

Most people come to La Serena for the beach and the summertime buzz, but there are also a few cultural highlights and sites of interest scattered around the city. The modestly sized city has a whopping 29 churches, some dating back centuries to the times when pirates, like Sir Francis Drake, sacked the town looking for Spanish gold. Most of the churches you'll find to be remarkably well preserved.

The archaeological museum has collected artifacts from across the country and is also a worthwhile visit. There are a large number of craft markets and fairs that pop up along the streets. Although there are several pubs and a new casino on La Serena's Avenida del Mar, if you're looking for top-notch night-life, you should pop over to Coquimbo's Barrio Inglés.

There's no shortage of buses that will take you to many of the valley's places of interest, but a private vehicle will allow you to take advantage of stops along the valley's winding roads. The Embalse Puclaro, for instance,

is a glacially-fed reservoir with a large wind harp that sends eerie harmonic tones echoing through the valley. Updated: Oct 28, 2008.

Plaza de Armas

At the historical heart of La Serena is the Plaza de Armas—a beautifully maintained square anchored by an giant stone fountain. Strolling along the plaza's sidewalks, or people-watching from one of its many benches, is a great way to spend a sunny afternoon.

Many of the town's churches can be found near the plaza. Worth checking out are the neoclassical Iglesia Catedral, built in 1844, and the stone baroque Iglesia San Francisco, on the corner of Balmaceda and de la Barra. On Calle Cordovez is the Renaissance-inspired Santo Domingo, an impressive and historical temple built—and then rebuilt—during the pirate raids that nearly destroyed the city during the 16th and 17th centuries. Updated: Jul 02, 2009.

La Serena Beach

Walk down Avenida Francisco de Aguirre to reach the Avenida del Mar and La Serena's long, popular beach. The beach is not nearly as pristine as others along Chile's coast, but it is an extremely popular destination for Chileans in January and February. Lined with hotels, restaurants and bars, the beach is the center of activity during the summer months, but goes dormant the rest of the year. Updated: Oct 28, 2008.

Parque Japonés Kokoro No Niwa

(ENTRANCE: $1 – 2) La Serena's Japanese Garden is a small but pleasant retreat from the busy plazas and markets just west of the town center. The small waterfalls and carefully landscaped plot, complete with several bridges and pagodas, are intended to settle mind and body. You should note, however, that the tall trees and bushes that line the perimeter can only block out so much of the noise from traffic and construction. Open 10 a.m. – 6 p.m. Closed Monday. Updated: Oct 28, 2008.

Craft Markets

There's a small number of craft markets of varying sizes and quality scattered around the city. The largest market in town, La Recova, is near the Iglesia San Augustín in a two-story covered pavilion with restaurants, unremarkable *artesanias* and tourist information. Far smaller, but far more charming, are the artists' tents set up on the side of the Iglesia Catedral, which sell handicrafts and artisan sweets. There is an interesting daytime junk market on Saturdays in the Plaza de Abastos that is packed with locals sifting through the piles of trash in search of treasures. Updated: Oct 28, 2008.

Museo Arqueológico

La Serena's Museo Arqueológico, a mid-sized museum with archaeological finds from all over Chile, is a solid introduction to the history of the first people to populate the country. An impressive display of Diaguita pottery (some discovered in the small Elqui Valley village of San Isidro) and tools and jewelry from around the country form the majority of the museum's collection. There are also a few shrunken heads and a mummy. But the main attraction is a giant Moai from Easter Island. Information is only in Spanish. Ca. Cordovez. Tel: 56-5-1224 492, E-mail: muarse@entelchile.net. Open, Tuesday – Friday 9:30 a.m. – 3:50 p.m.; Saturday 10 a.m., – 4 p.m.; Sundays and holidays 10 a.m. – 1 p.m. Updated: Jul 07, 2009.

Museo Histórico Casa Gabriel González Videla

This museum is in an adobe house designed by 19th century architect José Viera. The museum is named after the former Chilean president González Videla (1946 – 1952), who was born in La Serena. You can see the results of his urban renewal plan in the neocolonial architecture around the Plaza de Armas. Videla and his family once owned the house, which now belongs to the city. The interior is filled with important historical documents, as well as artifacts from Videla's political and personal life: furniture, photographs and layouts of his architectural plan for La Serena. Head upstairs to view visiting modern art exhibits. Matta 495. Tel: 56-51-217189. Updated: Jul 01, 2009.

Tours

La Serena's many tour operators offer visits to Parque Fray Jorge's cloud forest, penguin watching on Islas Damas, and the Elqui Valley and its observatories. Prices and trip availability vary according to the time of year. Some excursions are not offered at all during the winter, so check with individual agencies for schedules and pricing.

Eco Turismo

Eco Turismo offers comprehensive and comfortable tours of the Elqui Valley, Islas Damas (where you'll find penguins), the cloud forest in Fray Jorge National Park and the Valle del

Encanto. The agency also offers transport to the Mamalluca and Collowara observatories and city tours of La Serena and Coquimbo. Most tours include hotel pick up, a lunch or snack and museum or park entrance fees. Bilingual guides give tours in both Spanish and English, though the explanations in Spanish are often far more in-depth. Andres Bello 937. Tel: (56-51-218970 or 56-9-3464403, E-mail: contacto@eco-turismo.cl or eco-turismo@hotmail.com, URL: www.eco-turismo.cl. Updated: Oct 28, 2008.

Elquí Valley Tour

Elquí Valley Tour is a popular tour operator in La Serena. Many hostels and hotels around town use the company, which requires 24-hour reservations for tours to Vicuña, Islas Damas, the Elquí Valley and the cloud forest in Fray Jorge National Park. The office is on Los Carrera next to the Plaza de Armas. Tel: 56-51-214846, URL: www.elquivalleytour.cl. Updated: Oct 28, 2008.

Lodging

The budget hotels and hostels in La Serena tend to be located closer to the bus station (a 10-minute walk from the city center), while up-market options closer to the center of town. Hotels located on the city's Avenida del Mar tend to be priced higher than those in town, but they provide quick and easy access to La Serena's beaches as well as to beachfront restaurants and bars. Updated: Jul 02, 2009.

Hostal Maria Casa

(ROOMS: $11 – 19) A small, family-run hostel just a few blocks from the main bus terminal, Hostal Maria Casa is a quiet, charming, and inexpensive place to spend the night. The single and double rooms are clean and bright, opening onto a large and sunny central garden, and the Spanish-speaking staff that runs the hostel is eager to converse with travelers. Las Rojas 18. Tel: 56-51-229282, Cell: 56-8-2189984, E-mail: wini1818@hotmail.com, URL: www.hostalmariacasa.cl. Updated: Sep 22, 2008.

El Punto Hostal

(ROOMS: $13 – 60) Hostal El Punto has a great location—halfway between the bus station and the central plaza—and its popularity among backpackers makes it a good place to meet fellow travelers. The hostel is German-run and consists of several small dorms and private rooms, three shared bathrooms and a large outdoor area with tables and lounge chairs. The breakfast, which is included, is very filling. To get there

NORTE CHICO

from the bus terminal, take a right onto Amunétegui St. Take a left at the second corner into Andrés Bello. The hostal will be on your left. Andrés Bello 979. Tel: 56-51-22 84 74, E-mail: info@punto.de, URL: www. hostalelpunto.cl. Updated: Jun 24, 2009

Apart Hotel Stella Mar

(ROOMS: $22 – 48) Located just 300 meters (984 ft) from the ocean, Stella Mar is a good value for those who want beach proximity without the high prices. Backpackers won't find any dorms here, though. The hotel was built to accommodate groups or families, with its selection of apartment-suites—each fully equipped with a kitchenette (microwave, stove and fridge) and WiFi. Guests can relax in the pool or on a padded lounge chair. Large groups (10 or more) can take advantage of Stella Mar's tour packages, which include trips to Valle de Elqui, Punata Choros, and a city tour of La Serena's Plaza de Armas, market and archaeological museum. Av. Cuatro Esquinas 100. Tel: 56-51-210194, E-mail: stellamar@terra.cl, URL: www.stellamar.cl. Updated: Jul 02, 2009.

Hotel del Cid

(ROOMS: $35 – 45) This delightful colonial hotel in the city's center offers simple yet elegantly decorated rooms. Hotel del Cid can accommodate up to 45 guests in its single, double and triple rooms, each with cable TV and private bath. Rates include breakfast and tax. There's a bar and restaurant on-site, as well as laundry service and security boxes. The owners, John and his wife Blanca, are extremely friendly and helpful, as is the rest of the staff. Visa, Mastercard and Express accepted. O'Higgins 138. Tel: 56-51-212692, E-mail: reservas@ hoteldelcid.cl, URL: www.hoteldelcid.cl. Updated: Jul 02, 2009.

Hotel Playa Campanario

(ROOMS: $51 – 110) This beautiful, new hotel is within walking distance of the beach and a good option if you want to enjoy a little privacy while still within the city's center. All rooms come with a private terrace, private bath and central heating (which comes in handy during chilly winter nights). Guests can stay in one of the 41 main rooms or, for a little more privacy, one of the five cozy cabins. The grounds are filled with beautiful gardens, two pools and a playground to entertain the little ones. The biligual staff can help with laundry service and storing luggage. There's a bar and restaurant on-

site, and breakfast is included in the room price. Visa, Mastercard, Express and Diners are accepted. Los Nisperos 668.Tel: 56-51-221482, URL: www.hotelcampanario.cl. Updated: Jul 02, 2009.

Hotel Francisco de Aguirre

(ROOMS: $70 – 95) Hotel Francisco de Aguirre, a grandiose structure located across from the Iglesia Santo Domingo and directly off of the Plaza de Armas, is perhaps the most prestigious of La Serena's accommodation options. The historic three-story building has elegantly decorated rooms, an upscale restaurant, and a host of amenities. Be careful when selecting a room, as construction and traffic on calle Pedro Pablo Muñez can be noisy in the morning. Cordovez 210. Tel: 56-51-222991, E-mail: reserves@fransiscodeaguirre.tie.cl. Updated: Jul 01, 2009.

Hotel Londres

Located on one of La Serena's bustling central avenues, Hotel Londres is close to many of the city's shops and cafes, as well as the Plaza de Armas and several of La Serena's churches and museums. The hotel's amenities are geared toward the business traveler. Rooms—some with private bath and some without—are clean and uncluttered, and the hotel offers several *salones* that guests can rent for business meetings or events. Conact the hotel directly to check prices. Cordovez 550. Tel: 56-51-219066, E-mail: reservas@hotellondres.cl, URL: www.hotellondres.cl. Updated: Jun 24, 2009.

Restaurants

Though it's a big tourist town, pickings are slim when it comes to restaurants in La Serena. You'll mostly find a large selection of Chilean food, especially in the center of town. Balmaceda has some pleasant cafés with outdoor patios, and you'll find a few ethnic restaurants on Prat and O'Higgins.

Your best bet for a good meal is on Avenida del Mar, where you'll find quite a few solid mid-range options like the historic Porotas restaurant, and La Pizza Mia—a popular staple with tasty pizzas, pasta and meats, or Huentalequea, which is open late and offers delicious cheese empanadas and live music. Keep in mind that some restaurants keep irregular hours during the winter, and others close altogether until summer. Updated: Jul 02, 2009.

Mercado La Recova

The street market La Recova, located on the corner of Cienfuegos and Cantournet, is one of the most beautiful of its kind in Chile. The 18th-century neo-colonial market square is surrounded by arches and contains an overwhelming variety of goods. Anything and everything can be found in the stalls that fill the first floor, from pre-Columbian ceramics to stone jewelry and alpaca apparel. The top floor has several small restaurants that serve fresh fish and traditional dishes. It's a great place to grab a bite to eat and watch the people below. Prices are cheaper here than at the seaside restaurants.. Updated: Jul 02, 2009.

Parillada Velamar Beach

(ENTREES: $5 – 8, SPECIALTIES: $5.90 – 11.90) A longtime favorite with both locals and travelers, this beachfront restaurant serves up all kinds of seafood. For $6.90, the *menu del dia* comes with pisco sour, timbal de camarones, salmon, dessert and wine. The fish and seafood menu is massive, and there's a small vegetarian menu, with salad, veggie omelet and fresh fruit. This place is right on the sand, perfect for taking in the sunset—just be sure to come early to reserve a prime spot. Av. del Mar 2300. Tel: 56-51-215461, URL: www.velamarbeach.cl. Updated: Jul 02, 2009.

Yoko Sushi Bar

(PRICE: 10 rolls $6 – 10, tabla (22 rolls) $14.95) This beautiful sushi restaurant is tastefully decorated with Japanese and Chilean influences, and is a good place to try local seafood. In addition to the traditional California rolls and hot rolls, Yoko offers special rolls wrapped in fresh salmon or *palta* (avocado). The drink menu includes sake, bamboo, a sampling of "sours" (pisco, serena, amaretto, mango), cocktails, and a very limited selection of beer and wine. Av. del Mar 5200. Cell: 56-9-8706398, URL: yokosushibar.cl. Updated: Jul 02, 2009.

Bakulic

(MEAL: $30) Founded by Boris Bakulic over 20 years ago, this gorgeous seaside restaurant was rebuilt in 2000 after a tragic fire nearly destroyed it. The restaurant specializes in fresh seafood served with artistic flair. Try the local favorite "Serena sour", which replaces pisco sour's lemon with a papaya, to accompany the delicious *corvina* (seabass) or *congrio a la plancha* (barbequed eel), which comes

with buttered asparagus. There is also a children's menu. Av. del Mar 5700. Tel: 56-51-245715, E-mail: bakulic@adsl.tie.cl. Updated: Jul 02, 2009.

Martín Fierro

(ENTREES: $10 – 20) A mecca for meat-lovers, Martín Fierro offers an impressive 12 different cuts of Argentine beef. Entrees include the signature bacon-wrapped "Martín Fierro filet." They also offer Italian dishes (lasagna, gnocchi, fetuccine) and a sampling of local fish (try the buttered *reineta*). Whatever you order, you can accompany it with one of their many Chilean wines. If you manage to save room for desert, they offer several delectable choices, including tiramisú, and the Alaskan pancake—filled with ice cream and drizzled in chocolate. Martín Fierro can help set up special events for wedding receptions, birthdays and corporate banquets. Cuatro Esquinas and Avenida Pacifico. Tel: 56-51-219002, URL: www.martinfierro.cl. Updated: Jul 02, 2009.

Coffee Express

Coffee Express is the place to go for a coffee and a treat, but don't expect a lot of charm. The coffee is better than most, and there's a selection of inexpensive sandwiches, "artisan" ice creams, and pizzas. The café has a streamlined, international design and is a decent place to have a coffee on a busy afternoon. Balmaceda 391 on the corner with Prat. Tel: 56-32-221673. Updated: Sep 22, 2008.

El Nuevo Peregrino

El Peregrino, one of La Serena's newest restaurants, offers fresh, filling, and healthy meals with a wide selection of vegetarian options and all-natural juices. The décor is bold and colorful, and the prices are reasonable for the quality and quantity of the portions. Live music starts around 11 p.m. on Fridays and Saturdays, though this schedule falters a bit during the winter. Corner of Peni and Andres Bello. Tel: 56-51-483519. E-mail: nuevoperegrino@gmail.com. Updated: Sep 22, 2008.

Patio Colonial and Beethoven Restaurant

Turn down Balmeceda street and in a pleasant little nook you'll find the Patio Colonial. The meandering walkway, reminiscent of a small plaza you might find in Europe or the States, has several restaurants, cafés, teahouses and small shops. The menu at Beethoven Restaurant features various chef's specialties, including fancy salads, risotto and corvina. There is also a happy hour. Ca. Balmaceda 432. Tel: 56-53-218102. Updated: Oct 28, 2008.

AROUND SERENA
CERRO TOLOLO
INTER-AMERICAN OBSERVATORY

(ADMISSION: free) Perched 2,200 meters (7,218 ft) atop a hill 88 kilometers (55 mi) southeast of La Serena lies an impressive cluster of gleeming white domes known as the Observatorio Cerro Tololo. Bought in 1967 by the Association of Universities for Research in Astronomy Incorporation (AURA), this astronomical observatory has five working optical telescopes; at 4.2 meters (13.7 ft), the Southern Astrophysical Research (SOAR) telescope is the largest. A division of the National Optical Astronomy Observatory (NOAO), Cerro Tololo works with the government to to preserve the dark night skies amid population growth.

Although visitors aren't allowed to actually operate the telescopes, it's still fascinating to visit the site and learn about them. Guided two-hour tours are available on Saturdays at 9 a.m. and 1 p.m. They book up fast—especially during the winter—so make reservations several weeks in advance. Tel: 56-51-205200, E-mail: ctiorecp@ctio.noao.edu, URL: www.ctio.noao.edu. Although the tours are listed as free, permits must be purchased at the observatory's offices in La Serena (Casilla 603).

A few things to keep in mind: Cerro Tololo does not provide public transportation, so you will need to set up your own transport (don't forget the return ride). Also, the sale of beverages is not permitted, so they advise you to bring along some water or juice, as the total tour time (including transport) is four hours. To get there from La Serena, head southwest on Route 41. The access road has a large sign with the observatory's blue and yellow emblem. Updated: Jul 03, 2009.

OBSERVATORIO CALLOWARA

(ADMISSION: $2.50 – 3.50) This beautiful, modern observatory just opened in December 2008 and sits atop Cerro Churqui, near the town of Andacollo. Specifically designed for tourists, Callowara has excellent equipment and several observation platforms from which you can soak up the scenery and catch a glimpse of observatories Tololo and Gemini in the distance. There are four telescopes, including a 35.5-centimeter (14-in) Smith-Cassegrain.

Two-hour guided tours are available, starting at 7:30 a.m., 8 a.m. and 10 p.m. during the winter, and 9 a.m., 10:30 a.m. and midnight during the summer. Urmeneta 599, Andacollo. For tickets Tel: 56-51-546494/432964. URL: www.collowara.cl. Updated: Jul 03, 2009.

COQUIMBO

The port town of Coquimbo, dominated by a rather unattractive cross, has been described as the Valparaíso to La Serena's Viña. La Serena has the beach, the polished commercial centers and the historic churches; Coquimbo has a gritty *porteño* feel, an artistic underbelly and fabulous nightlife in **Barrio Inglés**. Like La Serena, Coquimbo is close to the Elguí Valley and receives the bulk of its visitors in the summer.

Coquimbo, like Valparaíso, is a gritty town with an artsy heart and crumbling walls, that, until a few years ago, were in terrible disrepair. The city's salvation has been the bohemian Barrio Inglés, where Victorian-looking mannequins peer down from balconies and live music blares from classy bars and dance venues all night long. Here you'll find local art galleries (a rarity in this region), stylish ethnic restaurants, intriguing open-air markets, and salsatecas.

During the day, head to the port to experience the sights and smells of Coquimbo's **fish market**. At the *marisquerias*, you can sample cheap *paila marina*, a stew full of exotic-looking fresh seafood. On Sundays, there are also two large **open-air markets**, one with piles of fresh produce and the other with cheap flea-market fare.

From the **Coquimbo terminal**, you can take a 30-minute bus ride south along the coast to the captivating beach towns of **Tongoy** and **Guanaqueros**. Updated: Apr 30, 2009.

ELQUÍ VALLEY

the Elquí is a tiny river valley—at places no more than 200 meters wide–that is famous for its pisco crop and poet Gabriela Mistral. Provincial towns dot the valley, such as

NORTE CHICO

Paihuano and Pisco Elquí, which provide adventure tourism excursions in the summer. Cochiguaz is a community of free-thinkers who moved here in the 1960s to live near the earth's magnetic center. In Vicuña, you can take a tour of the country's largest pisco distillery by day and stargaze under spectacularly clear skies at the nearby observatory by night. Updated: Oct 28, 2008.

VICUÑA

 709m   10,000   51

Originally famous as the birthplace of South America's first female Nobel Prize winner, Gabriela Mistral, the town of Vicuña a gateway to the increasingly popular Elquí Valley. Lying about 60 kilometers (37.3 mi) east of La Serena and 500 kilometers (311 mi) from Santiago, Vicuña is a small town with a large square and a surprising number of activities.

There's an educational museum commemorating Gabriela Mistral, several *pisceras* (pisco distilleries) that are open to visitors and astronomical observatories that take advantage of the more than 300 days a year of remarkably clear skies near Vicuña. There are also one-room museums (like the Museo Entomológico e Historia Natural, or the Museo El Solar de los Madariago) scattered around the square.

The main source of revenue in these parts is agriculture: fruits and vegetables like avocado, papaya and, most famously, pisco grapes.

Summers tend to be hot and winters mild, but the strong winds that sweep the valley have led farmers to use protective wind barriers.

Since the town itself is small, there are only a few hotel and hostel options available, but it's not too hard to find accommodations for most price ranges. Cheap restaurants are clustered around the square. Try walking along Gabriela Mistral away from the Bauer Tower for better food options. Updated: Sep 28, 2008.

When to Go

As the weather in the valley is mild year round, there are no bad times to visit Vicuña. Hotels, restaurants and activities are open year-round. Visitors tend to visit Vicuña during the summer, since the pisco crop at this time of year turns the valley a brilliant green, but the views are breathtaking any time. Updated: Oct 28, 2008.

Getting To and Away from Vicuña

The easiest way to get to Vicuña by **bus** is either from La Serena or Coquimbo. Bus companies like **Sol del Elquí** and **Via Elquí** leave frequently from both of these cities. The Vicuña bus terminal is on Prat, between O'Higgins and Avenida las Delicias.

By **car** from La Serena, take the international route Gabriela Mistral, CH-41. Past Vicuña, the route will take you to San Juan, Argentina through the Agua Negra Mountain Pass. The trip from La Serena to Vicuña takes about an hour. Updated: Nov 21, 2008.

Getting Around

Vicuña consists of no more than a few blocks, so it's a short walk to restaurants, museums and the bus station. Updated: Oct 28, 2008

Safety

Vicuña is generally a safe place, with a well-lit and lively main square. Steer clear of dark alleyways and use common sense, particularly at night. Updated: Nov 13, 2008.

Services

Almost all of the services in Vicuña are near the Plaza de Armas. The **tourism office**, in the Bauer Tower on the corner of the main square, is small but well stocked with helpful information.

The **ATMs** at the Banco Estado don't accept Visa cards. For Visa-friendly ATMs, try the pharmacy on Prat near the bus station.

On Calle Chacabuco, there's a **grocery store**, **bank**, several **pharmacies**, as well as a few artisan shops. There are two **Internet** cafés (both called Patricio Andrés Pasten Alfaro) on Orlando Rivera 472 and another on Prat 386. You can rent bikes at Mami Sabina, near the Bauer Tower.

The **hospital** is between Prat and San Martin on Calle Independencia. Updated: Oct 28, 2008.

Things to See and Do

Vicuña is littered with little museums, most notably the Museo Gabriela Mistral. There are several *pisceras* near the town where pisco, the national liquor, is distilled, including Planta

NORTE CHICO

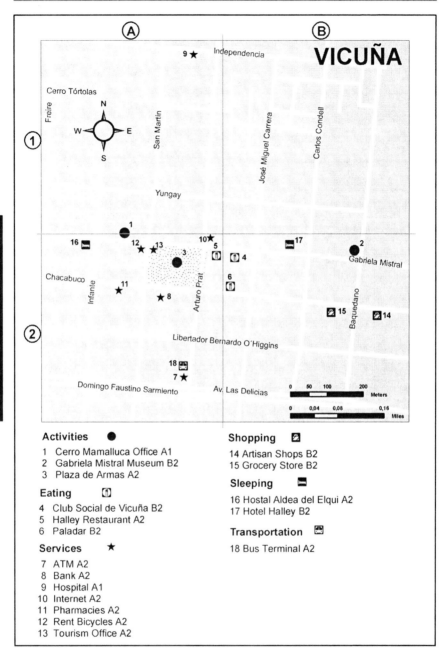

Activities ●
1 Cerro Mamalluca Office A1
2 Gabriela Mistral Museum B2
3 Plaza de Armas A2

Eating 📖
4 Club Social de Vicuña B2
5 Halley Restaurant A2
6 Paladar B2

Services ★
7 ATM A2
8 Bank A2
9 Hospital A1
10 Internet A2
11 Pharmacies A2
12 Rent Bicycles A2
13 Tourism Office A2

Shopping 🗹
14 Artisan Shops B2
15 Grocery Store B2

Sleeping 🛏
16 Hostal Aldea del Elqui A2
17 Hotel Halley B2

Transportation 🚌
18 Bus Terminal A2

Pisco Capel, the largest producer of pisco in the country. These distilleries have tours and tastings year round. The tourist-friendly Mamalluca Observatory is a 20-minute drive from town. Updated: Jul 07, 2009.

Gabriela Mistral Museum

(ENRANCE: $1.50) This small museum, a short walk from Vicuña's Plaza de Armas, is full of educational information (all in Spanish) and memorabilia from the poet's life. Displays in the museum include first editions, photos and statues, various items from Mistral's life, and the official replica of her Nobel Prize medal. Mistral was a profoundly maternal figure and the museum appropriately has a small children's area with interactive displays and local artwork. There is also an audiovisual room with art inspired by the poet. Casilla 50. E-mail: mgmistral@entelchile.net. Open, January – February: Monday – Saturday 10 a.m. – 7 p.m., Sunday 10 a.m. – 6 p.m.; March – December: Monday – Friday 10 a.m. – 5:45 p.m., Saturday 10:30 a.m. – 6 p.m., Sunday and holidays 10 a.m. – 1 p.m. Updated: Oct 28, 2008.

Capel Piscera
(ENTRANCE: $1 – 2) Planta Pisco Capel, the largest Pisco producer in Chile, offers guided tours of its distillery, providing a behind-the-scenes, industrial-scale look at how the country's signature drink is produced, and a chance to purchase the liquor at the end. January – February: Monday – Sunday 10 a.m. – 6 p.m. March – December: Tuesday – Sunday 10 a.m. – 12:30 p.m. and 2:30 – 6 p.m. Updated: Oct 28, 2008.

Mamalluca Observatory Tour
The skies above the Elqui Valley are astoundingly clear almost year round. This makes the valley one of the top spots on the globe for astronomical observation. Mamalluca, just outside of Vicuña, provides visitors with the chance to look at the valley's pristine night sky through some very nice equipment.

Two types of tours are offered: the Basic Astronomy tour, which pairs explanations of astronomical findings with an observation session at the observatory's telescope; and the Andean Cosmovision tour, which teaches the astronomical beliefs of the ancient civilizations to the tune of traditional Andean music. Arrange departures for both tours from the downtown office. Visitors can take their own vehicle, but they must follow in convoy. The shuttle costs $3.
Basic Astronomy: 8:30 p.m., 10:30 p.m., 12:30 a.m., 2:30 a.m.
Andean Cosmovision: 9:15 p.m., 11:15 p.m., 1:15 a.m., 3:15 a.m.
Cerro Mamalluca office: Gabriela Mistral 260. Tel: 56-51-411352, E-mail: reserves@mamalluca.org. Updated: Jul 02, 2009.

Lodging
Vicuña has several decent accommodation options close to the central square. Summer is peak season in Vicuña, so book in advance during

January and February. Prices in the off-season are lower, and some establishments are willing to cut you a deal. Updated: Oct 28, 2008.

Hostal Aldea del Elqui
Hostal Aldea del Elquí is a well-maintained, mid-range hotel one block from Vicuña's main square. The building is a large converted colonial house from 1870. The staff's genuine hospitality and attention to detail make a stay here memorable. The hotel's owner will take time to help you plan your days in the Valley, providing help with bike rentals and tours to nearby atractions. The included breakfast is quite a spread by Chilean standards. Prices vary greatly depending on room and season. Gabriela Mistral N197. Tel: 56-51-543068, E-mail: info@hostalaldeadelelqui.cl, URL: www.hostalaldeadelelqui.cl. Updated: Oct 28, 2008.

Hotel Halley
A tasteful hotel in a restored colonial home, Hotel Halley is luxurious without being showy. Rooms open onto a sunlit central patio. There is an outdoor dining area, as well as an indoor one with a bar. Rooms are pristine and carefully furnished. The outdoor pool is open until late in the evening. The hotel is on one of Vicuña's main streets, close by the Plaza de Armas and near restaurants, shops and services. Gabriela Mistral 542. Tel: 56-51-412070. Updated: Jun 17, 2009.

Restaurants
With the exception of Halley Restaurant, avoid the resto-bars that line the main square, because, although they're cheap, the food is sub-standard. Some of the nicer hotels in town have affiliated restaurants, which offer more expensive but better quality options. It's also worth sticking your head into some of the small bakeries for a snack, since many of them offer surprisingly delicious handmade treats. Updated: Oct 28, 2008.

Club Social de Vicuña
The Club Social offers perhaps the best selection of traditional Chilean food in Vicuña. The atmosphere is especially nice, with several small dining rooms, one of which has a fireplace. There is also a small lounge and a large, open-ceiling dining area in the central outdoor patio. Try the Serena Sour made with pisco and sweetened local papaya juice. Gabriela Mistral 445. Tel: 56-51-412742 / 411853. Updated: Oct 28, 2008.

NORTE CHICO

Halley Restaurant
Halley has a wide selection of above-average Chilean meats, sides and desserts for moderate prices. The dining area is spacious and sunlit during the day with a big-screen TV behind the bar. You can pick up an empanada from the to-go counter on Arturo Prat. This is one of the few places in town where you can get an espresso, if you need a break from Nescafé. Gabriela Mistral 404. Tel: 56-51-411225. Updated: Oct 28, 2008.

Paladar
This tiny bakery is often packed, but the pastries are definitely worth the wait. The real draw is the bakery's selection of empanadas, including several vegetarian options. Come too late in the day and they may be all gone. Patrons of this little bakery say the empanadas are perhaps the best they've ever tasted. Chocabuco 448. Tel: 56-51-412138, E-mail: Paladarelquino@gmail.com. Updated: Oct 28, 2008.

OVALLE

 261m   54,000   53

Ovalle, two hours southeast of La Serena by bus, is relatively untouched by tourism despite its central location amid a handful of tourist destinations. The city was founded in 1821, shortly after Chile won its independence from Spain, and was named after the late Vice President José Tomás Ovalle Bezanilla. Though the valley's more famous northern cousin, the Elqui Valley, is better known for pristine skies and pisco production, the Valle del Limarí (in which Ovalle sits) has some equally impressive, albeit less famous, sites.

Ovalle is a jumping-off point for surrounding sites and activities, and the Municipality of Ovalle is currently working hard to attract more tourists to the region. But accommodation options are still limited, as are eating establishments, though Calle Independencia has dirt-cheap lunches that are surprisingly delicious.

Getting To and Away from Ovalle
Ovalle is 404 kilometers (251 mi) from Santiago, and 30 kilometers (19 mi) east of the Pan-American Highway. There are numerous north-south buses that run many times a day from the city's two bus terminals: **Terminal Media Luna**, at Ariztia Oriente 760,

which has buses to Santiago and other northern destinations; and **Terminal Norte Grande** located at Maestranza 443. There is also private **Transportes Leonor** on Bulnes 11, Monte Patria. Tel: 56-8-3773855, 56-9-9584287, E-mail: transportesleonor@gmail.com / turismo@limariemprende.cl.

If you are **driving**, take the Ruta 5 until the turn off for Ovalle. Updated: Jul 07, 2009.

Getting Around
Visitors should note that during winter, it's nearly impossible to go from Ovalle to popular destinations like Valle del Encanto or Fray Jorge National Park without a private vehicle. For a price, you can hire a chauffeured van from Transportes Leonor, which is based in the Valley.

Lodging
A good budget option is **Jaime's Crazy House**, which also offers free housing if you're willing to teach English while you're there (Tocopilla 92. Tel: 56-53-626761, URL: www.jaimescrazyhouse.com). **Hotel Roxi** is a safe mid-range option with brightly colored rooms, a spacious patio, and shared or private bathrooms (Libertad 155. Tel: 56-53-620080, E-mail: hotelroxi@gmail.com). **Plaza Turismo**, a chic hotel with its own café and prime location on the perimeter of the Plaza de Armas, is comfortable, though expensive. (Victoria 295. Tel: 56-53-662500, E-mail: reserves@plazaturismo.cl, URL: www.plazaturismo.cl).

Restaurants
The Ovalle restaurant scene is quiet, but there are a few nice choices. If you're looking for a nice night out, try nouveau Mexican food at **El Relajo** (Antonio Tirado 177. Tel: 56-53-632441.) For a quirky evening of drinks in a literary, leftist diva bar, head to **El Quijote** (Arauco 294. Tel: 56-53-620501). **Café Haiti** serves very good espresso in a classy mirror-filled room where smoking is allowed (Victoria 307).

AROUND OVALLE
Valle del Encanto
(ADMISSION: $0.20 – 0.55) To call the Valle del Encanto an unconventional archaeological museum would be an understatement. This national monument (19 km/ 11.8 mi west of Ovalle) has some of the most important petroglyphs, pictographs and *piedras tacitas* in Chile, some dating

back more than 4,000 years, with artifacts scattered across a desert valley more than five kilometers (3 mi) wide.

Among the stone carvings are pictographs and petroglyphs of masked faces, hunted animals and human figures. The mysterious *piedras tacitas* (smooth, flat rocks with patterned holes carved into them) have been a recent topic of anthropological discussion. Some scientists believe they were used to prepare food and hallucinogenic powders and others believe they were astronomical maps, filled with water at night to reflect light from the stars.

There are plenty of places in the park to camp or picnic. Many visitors choose to spend a few days hiking and exploring. Stop by the office at the park entrance to get advice about what sites to visit and at what times. The position of the sun determines what pieces are visible, but just before midday is a good time to see the small collection of encased artifacts that park workers have placed on display. URL: www.ovalleencantonativo.cl. Open Monday – Sunday, summer: 8:15 a.m. – 8p.m., winter: 8.15a.m. – 7p.m. Updated: Jul 07, 2009.

Termas de Socos

(ADMISSION: $7 – 18) The hot springs in the tiny town of Socos are out of the way, but popular with families, retirees and travelers. The natural springs have been channeled into small private baths at two neighboring sites: a resort hotel and a nearby campground. The hotel has small rooms connected by an outdoor walkway, a large sitting area full of antiques and archaeological artifacts, and relaxing background music. The camping area is family-friendly, with a swimming pool, playground and picnic area.

The hot springs can be fairly hard to access without your own vehicle, as there are no regular buses that pass nearby. Getting to the small town of Socos takes some maneuvering. Some buses pass through the town on the way to Santiago, but plan your travel arrangements in advance.

Hotel Termas Socos, Panacericana Ruta 5 Norte, Km. 370. Tel: (Santiago) 56-2-363336, (Ovalle) 56-53-1982505. **Camping Termas Socos**, Panacericana Ruta 5 Norte, Km 370. Tel: 56-53-631490, Cell: 56-9-7732016, E-mail: fpcampingsocos@yahoo.es. Updated: Jul 01, 2009.

BARRAZA

The Limarí valley's tiny town of Barraza, one of the oldest in Chile, is ripe with Chilean political and religious history. The town, with an ancient church and small religious museum, is slightly off the main tourist drag. If you visit, stop in at the **Museo Parroquial de Barraza**, located to the right of the **Iglesia de Barraza**, open every day but Monday.

For food, try Barraza's innovative community-based restaurant, **Cabildo Abierto**. This brand-new restaurant is still ironing out some kinks, but its upbeat and hardworking owners serve traditionally prepared Chilean meals cooked in a mud oven. History and archaeology have been incorporated into its décor with petroglyph designs on the walls and a mural in the spacious courtyard depicting the region's legandary ghost stories. Federico Alfonso 380. Cell: 56-9-4255367, E-mail: cabildoabiertobarraza@gmail.com. Updated: Jul 07, 2009.

PARQUE NACIONAL FRAY JORGE

Declared a World Biosphere Reserve by UNESCO in 1977, the nearly 10,000 hectares of Fray Jorge National Park are best known for 400 hectares of dense temperate forest along the pacific coast. This Valdivian forest (named after the Valdivia province in southern Chile where these forests pervade), set high atop the cliffs of the Chilean coast, is watered by coastal mist and very low amounts of annual precipitation, which together create an environment perfect for subtropical plant life. Within this small cloud forest, you'll find cinnamon trees, terabinth shrubs, tepas trees and ferns otherwise exotic to this region. The park has easy walks along the cliffs with raised boardwalks and outlooks. If you want to access the park by car, go in a 4x4.

The best time to visit the park is between October and November when the flora is in full bloom and the weather is ideal for hiking or horseback riding. In the winter, it can be difficult to find transportation to the park, especially from Ovalle. If you don't have private transportation, book a tour with a local company. During most of the year, the park is only open on weekends and holidays. In summer, the park is open Thursday – Sunday; you can enter

NORTE CHICO

families with children—it has several kid-friendly activities, a low-key nightlife, and beaches that are safe for swimming.

The two golden sand beaches in Los Vilos— **La Principal** and **Las Conchas**—are the town's main tourist attractions. Visitors can also take short day trips to surrounding islands and lakes, visit the small aquarium, or take a boat ride around the harbor.

There are plenty of small hotels and cabins in Los Vilos that are close to the beach and reasonably priced. If you're looking for cheaper accommodation, there are also *residenciales*, which tend to be hit-and-miss. The tourism office at the entrance to town has plenty of info on accommodation, so it's a good idea to stop there first before heading into town.

Restaurants serve typical beach-town fare, with fresh, cheap seafood dishes. Many people head to the **Caleta de San Pedro**, where there's a small collection of huts and *marisquerias* selling typical Chilean seafood dishes like *paila marina*, *machas a la parmesana*, and tasty seafood empanadas. Locals recommend the tiny **Crucero del Amor** near the Caleta de San Pedro. Updated: Jul 07, 2009.

When to Go

It rains often in Los Vilos during the summer months of December to February, but that doesn't stop thousands of tourists—about 20,000 a year—from flocking to the beaches in this small town. Semaña Vileña (Vilos Week) takes place in February; in June, Los Vilos celebrates the Fiesta de San Pedro Pescador (Festival of Saint Peter). During the winter months, there's not much to do. Updated: Jul 01, 2009.

Getting To and Away from Los Vilos

Major bus lines (**Tur Bus**, **Pullman**) usually cross Los Vilos on their way from Santiago to other destinations. Buses with more distance to cover (from Arica, for instance), will leave you on the outskirts of town, where you can catch one of the frequent *colectivos* to Avenida Caupolican, the main street in Los Vilos. Ask when you buy your ticket whether the bus stops at the town's main terminal.

Several bus companies operate out of Los Vilos. To get to La Calera, Viña del Mar, or Valparaíso, you'll need to use **Buses Intercomunal** (Avenida Caupolican 692). **Buses Combarbala**, at the same location, sends

the park from 9 a.m. – 4 p.m.; park closes at 6 p.m. E-mail: consulta@conaf.cl, URL: www.conaf.cl. Updated: Jul 10, 2008.

Getting To and Away

On Ruta 5 North, 389 kilometers (241 mi) north of Santiago, turn west (second road toward Fray Jorge) toward the coast. From here, it's 25 kilometers (15.5 mi) to the park, which lies down a long dirt road. The dirt road will bring you to the Visitor Control Center, which has information on entry to the park. Follow the same route to leave the park and return to Ruta 5 for southern and northern destinations. Updated: Jul 01, 2009.

LOS VILOS

 20m   9,500   51

If you are taking a bus from Santiago to Valparaíso, you will pass through the laid-back, friendly beach town of Los Vilos. First declared a minor port in 1855 by President Manuel Montt, the town quickly achieved success through foreign trade and has since been a fruitful maritime community. Most inhabitants work in either the fishing or tourism industries. Los Vilos has also recently become a popular destination for buses to La Calera and Santiago. For other destinations, try **Pullman Buses** (Avenida Caupolican 1111) and **Tur Bus** (Avenida Caupolican 898). Updated: Aug 14, 2008.

Getting Around
The town of Los Vilos can be explored in its entirety on foot. If you need to get to or from the Pan American Highway, there are *colectivos* that pass the Shell station outside of town. Bus companies, such as **Buses Menita,** send *micros* all day long to local destinations like Pichidangui, Quilimari, and Guanguali from the corner of Avenida Caupolican and Calle Rengo. Tel: 56-9-2439438. Updated: Aug 14, 2008.

Safety
Los Vilos is a sleepy beachside town with few dangers. As most of the town's amenities are centrally located, there's little reason to venture farther out. If you're planning to walk to Isla de los Lobos, keep in mind that the paths are filled with trash and are used by day laborers. Updated: Nov 13, 2008.

Services
Nearly every service you'll need in Los Vilos is located on the strip of Caupolican between Calle Elicura and Tegualda. Here you'll find **supermarkets**, **Internet** and **phone** services, **pharmacies**, **money exchange**, **ATMs** and the **bank**.

The Los Vilos **tourism office is** right off the Pan American Highway, a 15-minute walk from town. During the winter, this is the only office in operation (and it's closed on Mondays and Tuesdays), but in summertime a second office opens in the center of town. It's a good idea to stop at one of the offices before making your way into town, as they have a considerable amount of information on places to stay and what to do in the area.

Hospital San Pedro, Arauco 400. Tel: 56-53-541028.
Carabineros (**Police**) de Chile, Tucapel. Tel: 56-53-541068.
Money exchange Chilexpress, Av. Caupolican 686. Updated: Aug 14, 2008.

Things to See and Do
The beaches and nearby islands are what bring most travelers to Los Vilos. **Playa La Principal** and **Las Conchas** are two of the more popular beaches. **Isla de los Huevos** is home to a local seabird colony,

and a few kilometers away there is a seal colony at Isla de los Lobos. Updated: Jul 01, 2009.

Isla de los Lobos
Walking through the hilly pastures on the way to the Isla de los Lobos, you can hear what sounds like the bleeting of sheep in the distance. But it's something far more sinister. It's the *lobos*—well, a colony of approximately 1,500 *lobos marinos* (sea lions) that have confined themselves to a tiny island off the rocky shoreline 5 kilometers (3 mi) south of Los Vilos.

To get there, hire a Jeep in town or hike along the seaside cliffs. Cactuses grow along the shoreline and marine workers bundle *cochayuyo*—an edible type of seaweed that's dried and often sautéed. Be warned, however, if you choose to walk, that parts of the path are littered with trash. The views, on the other hand, are fantastic—rocky shore on one side and distant Andes on the other—and for most of the year you'll have the countryside completely to yourself. It's a good idea to leave early in the day, especially in winter, to avoid being caught in the deserted countryside as darkness falls. From the Plaza de Armas follow Calle Elicura away from town until it becomes a dirt road. Updated: Jul 07, 2009.

Acuario Los Vilos
The small Los Vilos Aquarium, on Avenida Costanera, has a modest display of marine life native to the bay area, including various species of fish, snails and starfish, crabs and algae. The museum's stated purpose is to educate the public about the local marine life so that they'll treat the sea critters with more respect. Although it's a humble display, the museum offers interactive guided activities for kids and periodically hosts special events like the ever-popular shark week. Av. Costanera Salvador Allende 131. Tel: 56-53-541070. Open year-round with hours that vary. Closed Monday. Updated: Oct 28, 2008.

Lodging
The accomodations in Los Vilos tend to reflect the town: small, laid-back and friendly. You won't find any towering Marriotts here, but the relaxed sea-side hotels make up in charm what they lack in glamour.

Hotel Bellavista
Bellavista is an older hotel, with crumbling walls, but bright and clean rooms. The prices are very cheap—especially in the off-season

NORTE CHICO

($8). It's worth paying a little extra for a private bathroom as the shared bathrooms are in a state of disrepair. In the summer, the hotel also has a working restaurant. Bellavista is also located a stone's throw from the beach and from the cheap and delicious seafood restaurants of the Caleta de San Pedro. Av. Rengo 020. Tel: 56-53-541073. Updated: Aug 14, 2008.

American Motel de Turismo

This quiet, mid-range hotel is a ten-minute walk to the beach, which is actually quite far for the tiny beach town. But the private bathrooms, heating, cable TV and WiFi are what draw many travelers. The hotel has comfy, small cabins surrounded by a tall grove of pine trees. There is also covered parking, laundry services and a big breakfast (not included in the price), which you can eat in your room. There are several restaurants nearby and the town's tourism office is across the street. The staff speaks English and German. Casilla 33, just off the Panamerican highway. Tel: 56-53-541163, E-mail: americanmotel-losvilos@gmail.com. Updated: Jun 23, 2009.

Restaurants

Restaurant options are similarly limited in Los Vilos, and the menus skew heavily toward seafood. Take a walk through the Caleta San Pedro fish market that springs up on Sunday mornings for fresh crab. For an easy bite anytime, pop into one of the restaurants near the American Hotel de Turismo.

Restaurant Costanera

Costanera is a tasteful mid-range restaurant, with a mostly seafood menu, long wine list and friendly service. The upstairs dining area has a wall made entirely of windows that overlook the beach and ocean—which is particularly nice at sunset. The daily menu typically a hearty soup with fish for the main course. The restaurant's Celestino—a thick crepe with a dulce de leche filling—is heavenly. Calle Purén 80. Tel: 56-53-541257. Updated: Aug 14, 2008.

Restaurante Roma

Roma, on the city's main drag, is one of the few places in town that doesn't have a primarily seafood menu. The small café serves up yummy pizzas, cheap sandwiches (with vegetarian options), sweets

and a selection of coffees and espresso. The dining area is small and relaxed with local children running in occasionally to buy an ice cream. The restaurant also has WiFi. Av. Caupolicán 712. Tel: 53-542701. Updated: Oct 28, 2008.

!!!!!

The Lake District

The Lake District is Chile's most visited area, and it's easy to see why. Much of the region, which encompasses several huge lakes, forests and white-tipped volcanoes, is protected by national parks and reserves, including the Parque Nacional Vicente Pérez Rosales (p.355), the oldest in the country. With good roads and transportation, the area is a traveler's dream. Despite the fact that thousands of tourists pour into the region each year, hiking trails are plentiful, and you could easily walk for days without ever seeing another person. Kayaking, rafting and climbing are also becoming increasingly

Highlights

Boat down **Valdivia**'s **(p.315)** many rivers—only one facet of this fascinating town. *La Ciudad de Ríos* also has some fine food, including fresh seafood, spätzel, sausages, sauerkraut and crudos.

Scale a perfect cone volcano in the light of dawn, then snowboard back to town. Other adventures awaiting in **Pucón (p.295)** include rafting, fly-fishing and hiking.

Discover riverside hot springs, Southern Chile's best ski runs, volcanoes, smoldering craters and geysers in **Parque Nacional Puyehue (p.338)**.

Explore the endless number of national parks and reserves. Check out **Conguillío (p.286)**, **Alto Bío Bío (p.285)**, **Alerce Andino (p.371)** and many more.

Hot springs – Dozens are located near Pucón, and many others form the Ruta de Termas in the **Siete Lagos Region (p.309)**. Updated: April 16, 2009.

popular as the tourist infrastructure improves, and there are many good bases to choose from. One of the most popular is Pucón, on the shores of Lago Villarrica. It's a laid-back place, with plenty of opportunities for meeting up with other travelers and for some spectacular sporting in the great outdoors.

History

Chile's Lake District contains one of the most important archaeological sites in the Americas. Monte Verde, near Puerto Montt, is the site of a human settlement dating to 14,500 years ago, making it the oldest known human settlement in the Americas, and predating previous settlements by about 1000 years.

The region from Río Bío Bío to Río Cruces and extending into the pampas of modern-day Argentina was also once ruled by the powerful Mapuche-Huilliche nation. Many modern-day villages, like Licán Ray, Curarrehue and Curacautín were founded during the reign of this indigenous nation. The Spaniards arrived in the mid-16th century and created several cities of their own, including Valdivia (1552) and Temuco (1553). These ports were provisioning

stops on the long run around South America. The region was also prized for hardwoods and gold. Colonists were sent inland as far as Lago Puyehue. But the Spaniards could not conquer the Mapuche—supposedly the only indigenous people in the Americas to successfully resist colonization—who rose up against the invaders. By 1605, all the new cities were abandoned. The Europeans fled northward to the Central Valley and south to Chiloé.

Pirates and seafarers also recognized the value of this coast's sheltered coves for restocking provisions and repairing ships. The Dutch occupied Valdivia's ruins in 1643, forcing the Spaniards to recover the city, their "Pearl of the South." A hundred years later, after constructing an elaborate fortress defense system against the Mapuch-Huilliche "internal enemy," Valdivia became a thriving port once again. Osorno was retaken in 1792. The following year the Tratado de las Canoas treaty was signed with the Huilliche. The Spaniards began once more to push inland, looking for the mythical City of Caesars and the very real gold around Puyehue and Ranco Lakes.

The final conquest of the Lake District, though, didn't come until after Chile gained its independence from Spain. The Ley de Colonización (Colonization Law, 1845) encouraged immigration to the region. Thousands of Germans came and found new villages, like Puerto Montt and those around Lago Llanquihue. They also established local industries. The German influence is still strong in the district's architecture and gastronomy. From 1860 to 1881, the Chilean government declared war against the Mapuche with the Pacificación de la Araucania campaign, which ended with the treaty of Cerro Ñielol (Osorno, 1881). The railroad arrived in Osorno in 1895 and finally reached Puerto Montt in 1913, increasing the region's economic importance. A diverse mix of immigrants followed the railroad into the region.

All came to a shattering halt on May 22, 1960, when the largest earthquake in recorded history and the resultant tsunami destroyed the region. Now, almost a half-century later, these cities have recovered most of their glory and are once more playing an important role in Chile's economy. Updated: Jun 22, 2009.

When to Go

The Lake District is a very popular summer destination for Chileans and foreigners alike. From November to March, the entire region hosts a number of activities and promotions to greet

THE LAKE DISTRICT

The Day the Earth Moved

May 22, 1960 is a date few in southern Chile will ever forget: It's the day the largest earthquake in modern history pummeled the region.

Residents of the Lake District had warnings that something catastrophic was afoot. Prior to the quake, four foreshocks larger than magnitude 7.0 on the Richter scale rumbled through the area. The day before, May 21, a 7.9 severely damaged Concepción. On the afternoon of the fateful day, the Earth shuddered in a massive 9.5 tremor, 160 kilometers (100 mi) offshore from Valdivia. First the city crumbled. Then the sea was sucked far back from its beaches before returning as a tsunami towering over 24 meters (80 ft) tall. The wave raced up Río Valdivia and slammed into land, wiping out the city of Valdivia. The massive wave radiated to the northwest as well, striking Hawaii and Japan. All of Southern Chile was affected by the earthquake. Much of Osorno was destroyed, as was over 70 percent of Puerto Montt. Towns as far south as Chiloé and Puerto Aysén were damaged.

Two days later, the tremor triggered an eruption of the Cordón de Caulle volcanic chain in Parque Nacional Puyehue. Highways and railroads were severed. Waterlines and electricity were cut. For more than two months, so little news got through that the rest of Chile was oblivious of the extent of destruction. Through the month of August, the region continued to experience aftershocks of magnitudes up to 7.0.

The final toll of the disaster was staggering. In Chile 1,655 were killed, 3,000 injured and over two million left homeless. Damages amounted to more than half a billion dollars. The tsunami also caused terribly high death tolls and losses in other parts of the world: in Hawaii, 61 dead and $75 million; in Japan, 138 deaths and $50 million; the Philippines, 32 dead and missing; the U.S. west coast had half a million dollars in damages.

For Valdivia, Osorno, Puerto Montt and other towns in southern Chile, this was a benchmark day in their history. Museums in these three cities carry somber photographs of how that catastrophe affected them more than 40 years ago. Updated: Jun 18, 2009.

these visitors. It is also the official season for casting a line for the region's famous trout and salmon. Days are longer and warmer, allowing for trekking through the area's numerable national parks. Summer is also festival time. Villages celebrate their founding days. Frutillar has its world-famous music festival from the end of January through the first week of February.

With fall, hotels, restaurants and the tourism offices shut down in most small villages, but the larger towns continue to offer full services. Ski and snow sport centers at Pucón, Parque Nacional Puyehue, Parque Nacional Vicente Pérez Rosales and others experience a second high season from June to September. In wintry mid-June, We Txipantu, the Mapuche New Year, is an important and highly recommended celebration. Updated: Jun 22, 2009.

Safety

In terms of personal safety, the Lake District does not have many problems. In the larger cities you should take a bit of care at night—the same goes for certain neighborhoods. Outdoor

activities need to be planned with a bit of care. Bring warm and waterproof clothing. Tábano is a species of biting horsefly that plagues the region between December – January. The potentially deadly hanta virus is a serious risk in the area; the disease is carried in rodent excrement. Conaf has pamphlets detailing steps to take to prevent the disease. If you are planning a hike lasting more than one day in a national park, or if you plan to do any mountain or volcano climbing, notify the ranger of your plans. Be aware that ranger stations have only basic first aid posts. They do not have search and rescue capabilities. Updated: Jun 22, 2009.

Border Crossings

In winter, snow can close some of the passes. Check with the carabineros in the nearest town to get an update on road conditions, especially May – September.

PASO PINO HINCHADO

The paved Ruta CH-181 goes to Lonquimay, and after passing through Reserva Nacional Alto Bío Bío, arrives at Paso Pino Hinchado

(1,884 m / 6,123 ft), 70 kilometers (42 mi) away. The Chilean border post is Liucura, 22 kilometers (13.5 mi) from the actual frontier (summer 8 a.m. – 8 p.m., in winter 8 a.m. – 6 p.m.). Pino Hinchado, the Argentine post, is seven kilometers (4.2 mi) from the border (summer 8 a.m. – 8 p.m., winter 8 a.m. – 7 p.m.). In Argentina, the road becomes Argentina Ruta Nacional 22 and heads toward Las Lajas, Argentina, from which you can reach Zapala and Nuequén.

Fuel up in Lonquimay, Chile, or Las Lajas, Argentina. Both towns have *casas de cambio*, lodging and restaurants.

PASO ICALMA

Ruta S-61 passes through a landscape of archaic *araucaría* forests and volcanoes. This route connects Melipueco, the gateway to Parque Nacional Conguillio and the Villarrica and China Muerta National Reserves, with Paso Icalma (1,298 m / 4,219 ft). The road is unpaved. After 54 kilometers (32.5 mi), you will come to the Chilean post Icalma, three kilometers (1.8 mi) from the border (summer 8 a.m. – 8 p.m., winter 8 a.m. – 6 p.m.). After crossing into Argentina, it is 12 kilometers (7.2 mi) to the post at Villa Pehuenia (summer 8 a.m. – 8 p.m., winter 8 a.m. – 7 p.m.). You can reach Zapala and Neuquén from Villa Pehuenia.

To cross at Icalma, you'll need authorization from the Policía Internacional (Victoria: Sotomayor 740, Temuco: Arturo Prat). Snow may close the pass in winter. This border crossing can also be accessed from the north, from Lonquimay to Liucura to Icalma; Icalma is 76 kilometers (46 mi) from Lonquimay. The road to Liucura is paved, but the stretch from Liucura to Icalma is unpaved.

Icalma has a *casa de cambio*. There are many cabins and campgrounds near Icalma and in neighboring Laguna de Icalma and Galletué. Most are only open in the summer.

PASO MAMUIL MALAL

From Pucón, Ruta CH-119 is paved as far as Curarrahue. Then a 37-kilometer (22.5 mi) gravel road will bring you to Paso Mamuil Malal (1,207 m / 3,923 ft). On the Chilean side, the post is called Puesco (summer 8 a.m. – 8 p.m, other seasons 8 a.m. – 6 p.m.). One kilometer (0.6 mi) farther is the Argentine post Tromén (summer 8 a.m. – 8 p.m, other seasons 8 a.m. – 7 p.m.). The gravel highway then becomes Argentina's Ruta Provincial 60.

This crossing is the most direct way to Junín de los Andes (57 km / 34.5 mi) and San Martín de los Andes (98 km / 59 mi).

PASO CARIRRIÑE

From Liquiñe, a poor dirt road heads into the Andes to the 1,215-meter (3,949-ft) pass at Paso Carirriñe. Seven kilometers (4.2 mi) farther you'll come to the Argentine customs. This route enters Parque Nacional Lanín on the other side of the border. The gravel Ruta Provincial 62 will bring you to Junín de los Andes; the paved Ruta Nacional 234 heads southward to San Martín de los Andes. The border on either side is open 8 a.m. – 8 p.m. Paso Carirriñe is closed in winter. This crossing can only be done in a private vehicle, as there is no public transport. Foreigners need authorization from the Policía Internacional in Valdivia (Av. Ramón Picarte 2582). Check with the tourism offices in Valdivia or the carabineros in Liquiñe for current conditions and requirements. Another useful source for information is www.panguipulli.com. Along the Camino Internacional in Liquiñe are 13 hot spring complexes with varying levels of service. Some have lodging. There are also hotels in Liqueñe.

PASO HUA HUM

The land and lake crossing at Paso Hua Hum (sometimes spelled as one word, Huahum) is quite an adventure. Unlike the famous lake crossing from Puerto Varas to Bariloche at Paso Pérez Rosales, farther south, this trip is feasible for budget travelers. The route leads into the heart of Chile's Siete Lagos region. Paso Hua Hum (659 m / 2,142 ft) may be done via public transportation or private car all year round.

Begin your journey at the town of Panguipulli on the northwest corner of Lago Panguipulli. The road is paved as far as Neltume and is unpaved for the last 8 kilometers (4.8 mi) to Puerto Fuy, on the north shore of Lago Pirehueico (Buses Lafit Monday – Saturday 10 a.m., make connections with the ferry; also Monday – Saturday five departures 11:45 a.m. – 4:30 p.m.; Sunday 6:30 p.m., 7:30 p.m.; 2 hours; $5). The bus from Puerto Fuy to Panguipulli leaves at 6 a.m., 7 a.m. and 4 p.m.

The **Transbordador Hua Hum** ferry departs Puerto Fuyand arrives in Puerto Pirehueico (12:30 p.m.; 1.5 hours; foot passenger $3, bicycle $6, motorcycle $8, vehicle $30 – 40 plus insurance), from which it is then 11 kilometers by gravel road to Paso Huahum (take a bus from Argentina or hitch).

THE LAKE DISTRICT

Ciudad de los Césares

Many of the villages the Spaniards founded in Patagonia were created during attempts to find the mythical Ciudad de los Césares, or City of the Caesars, a fabulously rich city made of that precious metal the new-comers lusted after: gold.

The first recorded reference to the Ciudad de los Césares comes from Francisco César, who, along with fourteen other soldiers, had been part of Sebastián Gaboto's expedition of Río de la Plata. César reported that during their three-month sojourn, they had penetrated deep inland to unknown Andean regions and found a city full of jewels and precious metals. Those who read his account presumed he was talking about an Inca city "of the Caesars," or rulers. At the same time, tales began circulating of a city built by Inca Atahualpa's half-brother Pablo Inga who, with untold riches, had escaped Francisco Pizarro's rapacious siege of Cuzco.

The many shipwrecks in the Straits of Magellan gave rise to another version of the story. Simón de Alcazaba captained the 1540 expedition sponsored by the Bishop of Plasencia to secure the Straits for the Spanish. The ship sank in those treacherous waters. Nothing was known of the fate of the 200 people who had survived the wreck until 23 years later, when two of them arrived in Concepción, Chile. Pedro de Oviedo and Antonio de Cobos recounted their adventure and told of a city full of Inca treasure they had discovered.

A third version of the fable came from Spanish colonists who had been forced to flee the Mapuche-Hilliche attacks on Valdivia, Osorno and other settlements toward the end of the 17th century. Some fled inland toward Lago Puyehue, and reported stumbling upon the priceless Ciudad de los Césares.

The search for the City of the Caesars has not ended. Delphos Foundation, a research group, claims the City of the Caesars is three fortresses that the European Knights Templar built in South America to guard their immense wealth. One place under investigation is an abandoned fort at Golfo San Matías near San Antonio Oeste on the Atlantic coast. Another was on the foothills of the Andes and a third on the Pacific coast, near Osorno. Updated: Jun 24, 2009.

From the border, it is 34 kilometers (21 mi) to San Martín de los Andes, by way of Ruta Provincial 48. Reservations are not needed during the low season. Ferries run twice daily December 15 – March 15; reservations are required (Tel: 56-63-31-0435 / 0436, E-mail: reservashuahum@sietelagos.cl, URL: www.panguipulli.cl).

Buses Lafit (Tel: 56-63-311647) also has a direct bus from Panguipulli to San Martín de los Andes (Saturday 10 a.m., $24). From San Martín, Lafit's direct service leaves on Sunday. In summer, this company also operates a ferry across Lago Panguipulli. There is lodging in Puerto Fuy.

PASO CARDENAL ANTONIO SAMORÉ

Paso Cardenal Samoré (1,308 m / 4,251 ft) is the most common border crossing from Chile to Bariloche, Argentina. Begin your trip in Osorno, where the paved Ruta CH-215 passes through Parque Nacional Puyehue to Aduana Pajaritos, the Chilean border post four kilometers (2.4 mi) past the Sector

Anticura ranger station. From there it is 22 kilometers (13.5 mi) to the actual border. After crossing into Argentina, the highway becomes Ruta Nacional 231. It is 43 kilometers (26 mi) to Villa Angostura, the Argentine post located in the midst of Parque Nacional Nahuel Huapi. It is then 70 kilometers (42 mi) to Bariloche. Another route goes north to San Martín de los Andes.

Both border posts are open 8 a.m. – 9 p.m. local time. At the Argentina complex is a *casa de cambio* that exchanges only Argentine and Chilean pesos. Lodging and camping are available in Parque Nacional Puyehue (Anticura and Aguas Calientes Sectors) and in Entre Lagos on Lago Puyehue.

PASO PÉREZ ROSALES

Many visitors dream of sailing in a catamaran across Lago Todos los Santos. The crystal-line waters are edged with evergreen forests and sky-scraping volcanoes. Boats continue through Parque Nacional Vicente Pérez Rosales, on to Argentina's Parque Nacional

Nahuel Pan and finishing up in Bariloche. This is the only way to cross from Chile to Argentina at Paso Pérez Rosales. **Andina del Sud** is the sole provider of this service (Monday – Friday 9 a.m. – 7 p.m., Saturday 9 a.m. – 1 p.m. Varas 437, Puerto Montt. Tel: 56-65-257797, E-mail: agenciapmc@andinadelsud.cl, URL: www.andinadelsud.cl).

The journey involves three boats and three buses. Start in Puerto Montt or Puerto Varas, from which tourists can travel by bus to Petrohué (76 km / 46 mi, 2 hours, altitude: 150 m / 488 ft). Here you will find the main ranger station of Parque Nacional Vicente Pérez Rosales, at the foot of Volcán Osorno. You can then sail a catamaran across Lago Todos los Santos to Puella (1.4 hours, altitude: 150 m / 448 ft). Passengers eat lunch before boarding a bus to Puerto Frías (27 km / 16.5 mi, 2 hours, altitude: 976 m / 3,172 ft). On the way, you will go through immigration procedures at Paso Pérez Rosales.

From Puerto Frías, a ship shuttles tourists across Lago Frías to Puerto Alegre (four nautical miles, 20 min, altitude: 762 m / 2,477 ft). A short bus ride to Puerto Blest is the next leg of the journey (three km / 1.8 mi, 15 minutes, altitude: 756 m / 2,457 ft). From there, a catamaran traverses Lago Nahuel Huapi to Puerto Pañuelo (15 nautical miles, 1.05 hours, altitude: 756 m / 2,457 ft). You have to do the last part of the trip, into Bariloche, by bus (25 km / 15 mi, 30 min, altitude: 760 m / 2,470 ft).

In the fall and winter, you can sign up for tours that last up to two days. . Guests stay at one of the two lodges in Puella: **Hotel Puella** or **Hotel Natura**. The least expensive rooms cost $150. There are no campsites. During the spring and summer months, travelers can choose to do the journey in one day, or overnight in Puella. In any season, trips leave everyday (except January 1 and December 25) at 7:30 a.m. One day expeditions arrive in Bariloche between 8:30 and 9 p.m.; two-day excursions at about 7 p.m. The fare from Puerto Montt to Bariloche is $170. In January and February, the price is $230. Prices do not include meals or hotels. For more information, see www.cruceandino.com, www.crucedelagos.com.ar, www.crucedelagos.cl or www.lakecrossing.cl. You can book with **Andina del Sud** in Puerto Montt. Many travel agencies inside and outside of Chile also make reservations.

PASO VURILOCHE
Die-hard adventurers have a challenge awaiting them in the southern Lakes District: Trekking through Parque Nacional Vicente Pérez Rosales to Paso Vuriloche, the route that had been used by Spanish missionaries. This 40-kilometer (24 mi) track is difficult. The journey can only be done in January and February on horse and the journey lasts five days. Club Andino maintains a refuge along the way. For more information, see: www.clubandino.org/data/i_refugios_tronador_viejo.asp. Updated: Jul 07, 2009.

Things to See and Do
This "Land of Blue Mirrors," named after its many lakes that reflect elegant snowy mountains and native forests, has a number of activities for travelers. Whether you're interested in the great outdoors or history and culture, you will not be disappointed.

The hiking and trekking in Conguillío, Huerquehue, Vicente Pérez Rosales and other national parks is perhaps the biggest draw of the region. Many come to Pucón to climb the active Volcán Villarrica and gaze into its glowing crater. The area is also a fly fisherman's paradise. And winter sport fans will be eager to hit the slopes of the region's premier ski centers, many of which are based on the district's mighty volcanoes. Not only can you go downhill skiing (*esquí alpino*), but you can also ski cross country (*esquí de fondo*) or even try alpine trekking (*esquí randonée*). These activities, along with snowboarding, snowshoeing and ice fishing, make the Lake District an exciting cold-weather destination.

The rich and complex history of Valdivia, Temuco and other cities will hold the attention of history buffs. Reenactors perform in period costumes at the Spanish fortresses near Valdivia. The German influence is also striking throughout the Lake District, in both architecture and gastronomy. The best place to soak in this atmosphere is in Puerto Varas and in the other villages ringing Lago Llanquihue. The Mapuche presence here is also quite strong, so be sure to save time to visit their cultural centers in Temuco, Curarrehue and other neighboring villages. Updated: Jun 22, 2009.

Tours
With lakes, forests, mountains and parks galore, the Lake District has a range of great outdoor activities, like rafting, kayaking,

hiking, horseback riding, fishing and canopy-ing. Excellent transport infrastructure makes independent travel easy and safe, but you can also book day trips for the more technical activities, like whitewater sports or volcano ascents (which require a guide). Because the area is one of the most touristic in Chile, you should have no trouble finding a tour opera-tor in places like Pucón or Puerto Varas. Some tour operators specialize in birdwatching or in water sports, so do not hesitate to shop around for the experts for your dream holiday. A few tour operators will also organize cultural visits to Mapuche villages. A two-day horseback ride in the Cochamó valley can start at $114, a day of canyoning at $64, and an ascent of Volcan Villarica around $70. Updated: Jun 11, 2009.

Lodging

During the warmer months of summer you can find campgrounds and cabins along coun-try roads throughout the Lake District. From November to March, many visitors come to enjoy the region's attractions, and prices rise and lodges fill accordingly. At this time of year, reservations are recommended. In autumn, small town businesses board up for the com-ing winter. Only a few hostels remain open and most campgrounds close. In towns with skiing and other winter activities, winter is another high season, when costs will likewise be higher. All types of lodging are available in the Lake District. Even in out-of-the-way places, you'll find exclusive lodges. For travel-ers on a shoestring, the best bet is camping. Backpacker hostels and hospedajes or family-run inns are also easy on the budget.

TEMUCO

 107m   246,350   45

Temuco lies on the north bank of the Río Cau-tín 670 kilometers (402 miles) south of San-tiago. This city was founded in 1881, after the Spanish signed a peace treaty with the Mapu-che. Prior to that, all this land belonged to the Mapuche nation, who had successfully kept not only Chileans from occupying this region south of the Río Bío Bío, but also fended off the Spaniards and the Inca. Once the wars ended, the Spanish established Fuerte Re-cabarren as the frontier outpost from which they could colonize south-central Chile.

Later the fort grew into the city now known as Temuco — meaning in Mapudungun "sap of the temu" (a medicinal tree). Temuco is the capital of the Región de la Araucanía. The eastern horizon is broken by two loom-ing volcanoes, Villarrica and Llaima.

The center of the city is Plaza Pinto. Here, a statue, Homenaje a la Región de la Araucanía, shows the history of Temuco through various figures: Mapuche leader Ercilla Kallifulifan, a Machi (female religious authority), a Eu-ropean immigrant and a soldier of the Wars of Pacification. You can also find important historical points throughout the city.

Atop Cerro Ñielol is a tree called La Patagua, under whose boughs the armistice between Chile and the Mapuche nation was signed in 1881. After the treaty's signing, the Chileans founded Temuco (February 24, 1881) and European immigration to the region was en-couraged by the central government. Dutch refugees from South Africa's Boer war formed one significant group of newcomers. The Brit-ish were another, leaving landmarks like the Saint Trinity Anglican Church, a clapboard chapel built in 1910 (corner of Mackenna and Lautaro, Plaza Teodoro Schmidt). Germans built their mansions along Avenida Alemán, some of which now house exclusive shops and bistros in the city's Zona Rosa.

Temuco is known as the *Ciudad de los No-bles* for being home to both of Chile's Nobel Prize-winning poets. Gabriela Mistral (Lu-cila Godoy) was headmistress at the Liceo de Niñas in 1920. At that time, she met the young prodigy and future Nobel Prize-winner Neftalí Reyes (aka Pablo Neruda), whose father was a railroad worker. His family home still stands on the 1400 block of Calle Lautaro.

The Museo Feroviario Nacional preserves lo-comotives instrumental in pushing the frontier southward. Temuco was damaged by the 1960 mega-earthquake that struck Valdivia. The Tu-muquense cathedral was destroyed and is now replaced by a new church designed by Geraldo Rendel. It features a wrap-around, second-floor balcony (open daily 9 a.m. – 8 p.m.). Avenida Balmaceda has a horse chestnut-lined median park. At its west end, between Freire and Avenida Preito Norte, is Parque Para la Paz with a monument dedicated to those who disappeared or were openly executed during the 1973 – 1990 Pinochet dictatorship.

Temuco is a major commercial center in the south of Chile. And lumber mills are a main cornerstone of its economy is lumber mills. Several universities are based here, including

THE LAKE DISTRICT

Universidad de la Frontera, Universidad Católica de Temuco, Universidad Autónoma de Chile (ex-Autónoma del Sur) and Universidad Mayor. Temuco serves as a gateway to Conguillio, Tolhuaca, Villarrica and other national parks in the Lakes District, as well as to prime tourist destinations like Pucón. Updated: Jul 06, 2009.

When to Go

Temuco has a temperate climate. The winter months, April through August, are the coldest and rainiest. Temperatures reach only 12 – 15°C (54 – 59°F) during the day and drop to 5°C (41°F) at night. January and February are the hottest months, with days hitting 25°C (77°F). Breezes are frequent. About once a decade Temuco receives a dusting of snow. Some festivities to catch in Temuco include:

February 24: Feria Artesanal de Temuco celebrates the anniversary of the city's founding and draws artisans from all over the country.

June 24: We Xipantu (also known as Nquillatún), meaning "rising of the new sun," is the New Year ceremony of the Mapuche nation.

November: Exposofo is the region's most important agricultural and artisan fair. Updated: Jul 06, 2009.

Getting To and Away From Temuco

BY BUS

The bus terminal, or Rodoviario, is at Vicente Pérez Rosales 01609, about 1.5 kilometers (1 miles) north of the city (Tel: 56-45-225005). It has shops, restaurant, baggage keep, bathrooms and ATM. Most bus companies have ticket windows here, as well as offices in the city, especially on Balmaceda.

To Santiago: Most buses leave 8 p.m. - 2:30 a.m., 8 – 9 hours. **Línea Azul** ($16), **Pullman Bus** (via Los Angeles and Chillán, $44), **JAC** (also 10:15 a.m. plus 7 night buses, $18 – 26), **Nar Bus** (from Balmaceda, 12:20 p.m. and two night, $28), **Tur-Bus** ($40-100). Also **ViaTur**, **Cóndor**, **Cruz del Sur** and others.

To Concepción: 4 hours, $11. **TurBus** (1 a.m., 4:30 a.m., 6:30 a.m.), **ETM** (4:30 p.m.).
To Valdivia: Many buses to Puerto Montt pass through Valdivia, 3 hours $6 – 8. **Pullman Bus** (6:30 a.m., 7 a.m., 5:35 p.m., $8).

To Osorno: Many buses to Puerto Montt pass through Osorno, e.g. **Luna Express**, **NarBus**, **Cruz del Sur**; $10 – 15.

To Puerto Montt: 5 – 6 hours, $11 – 13. **Pullman Bus** (4:15 p.m.), **ETM** (4 p.m.), **TurBus** (6 buses 11 a.m.-4:45 p.m.). Also **NarBus**.

Short-distance buses leave from the Terminal de Buses Rurales, near the Feria Pinto (Av. Pinto 032), except where noted. These include:

To Victoria: 1 hour. **Flota Erbuc** (7:30 a.m., 10 a.m., $2.20), **Bío Bío** (Lautaro 853; every half hour, 6:10 a.m. – 9:30 p.m., $3).

To Curacautín: 1.5 hours. **Erbuc** (6 buses 7:30 a.m. – 6:30 p.m., $2.60), **Bío Bío** (9 buses 7:20 a.m.– 8:30 p.m., $3).

To Malalcahuello crossroads: **Bío Bío** (same bus as Curacautín, $5.20, 2 hours).

To Melipueco: **NarBus** (Balmaceda 953; 6 buses 8 a.m. – 3:30 p.m., 2 hours, $3).
To Lonquimay: Same route as Curacautín, 3.5 hours. **Erbuc** ($5.60), **Bío Bío** ($7.60).

To Villarrica: 1.5 hours. **JAC** (Balmaceda 1005; 8 buses 7:30 a.m. – 6:45 p.m., $3.40), **Buses Villarrica** (Balmaceda 995; every 45 minutes 8 a.m. – 7:30 p.m., $2.60).

To Pucón: **JAC** (departures same as Villarrica, 2 hours, $4.60).

The downtown offices of other companies are: **Cruz del Sur** (Claro Solar 599), **InterSur** (Balmaceda 1372), **TurBus** (Lagos 449).

BY TRAIN

From the train station (Barros Arana 191. Tel: 56-45-233522, URL: www.efe.cl), a rail bus runs to Victoria and points in between (daily 9:30 a.m. and 4:10 p.m., Sunday 8:20 p.m., Monday to Saturday 8:30 p.m., $1.50).

BY AIR

Temuco's Aeropuerto Maquehue is on the far south edge of the city (Camino Maquehue. Tel: 56-45-554800). Depending on the season, **LAN** has three or four flights per day to Santiago (from $92) and once weekly service to Puerto Montt and Balmaceda (Monday – Friday 9 a.m. – 1:30 p.m., 3 p.m. – 6:30 p.m., Saturday 10 a.m. – 1:30 p.m. Bulnes 687). **Skyline** flies twice daily to Santiago (from $70), once daily Monday – Friday to Balmaceda (from $100) and twice daily to

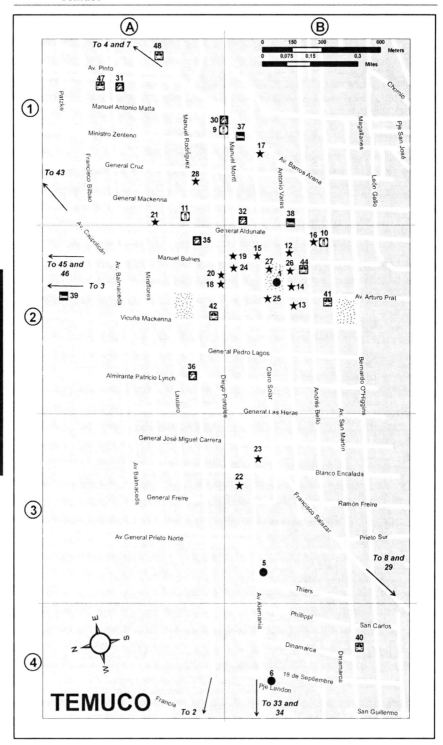

TEMUCO

To 4 and 7
Av. Pinto
Patzke
Manuel Antonio Matta
Ministro Zenteno
Francisco Bilbao
Manuel Rodríguez
General Cruz
General Mackenna
To 43
Av. Caupolicán
General Aldunate
To 45 and 46
To 3
Av. Balmaceda
Miraflores
Manuel Bulnes
Vicuña Mackenna
General Pedro Lagos
Almirante Patricio Lynch
Lautaro
Diego Portales
Claro Solar
General Las Heras
Andrés Bello
Bernardo O'Higgins
Av. San Martín
General José Miguel Carrera
Av. Balmaceda
General Freire
Blanco Encalada
Francisco Salazar
Ramón Freire
Av. General Prieto Norte
Prieto Sur
To 8 and 29
Thiers
Av. Alemania
Phillippi
San Carlos
Dinamarca
Francia
To 2
6
Pje Landon
To 33 and 34
18 de Septiembre
San Guillermo
Manuel Montt
Av. Barros Arana
Antonio Varas
Chomio
Magallanes
León Gallo
Pje San José

THE LAKE DISTRICT

Activities ●

1 Galería de Arte Plaza Anibal Pinto -
   Plaza Pinto B2
2 Milla Ruka A4
3 Monumento Nacional Cerro Ñielo A2
4 Museo Nacional Ferroviario Pablo Neruda A1
5 Museo Regional de la Araucanía B3
6 Sala Exposiciones UCT B4
7 Tren de la Araucania A1

Airports †

8 Aeropuerto Maquehue B3

Eating 🍴

9 La Parrilla de Miguel A1
10 Restaurant El Toltén B2
11 Restaurant Rukayiael Kokav A1

Services ★

12 Afex Casa de Cambio B2
13 ATMs B2
14 Banco de Chile B2
15 Banco de Estado B2
16 BBVA B2
17 Carabineros B1
18 Chilexpress A2
19 Conaf B2
20 Correo Chile A2
21 Farmacia Herbolaria Mapuche A1
22 Hospital Regional B3
23 Lavandería B3
24 Prat. Farmacia Ahumada B2

25 Santander B2
26 Scotiabank B2
27 SERNATUR B2
28 Supermercado Santa Isabel A1

Shopping 🛍

29 Chol Chol B3
30 Donem A1
31 Feria Pinto A1
32 Las Vegas B1
33 Mall Mirage B4
34 Mall Portal Temuco B4
35 Mercado Municipal A2
36 Ski Aventura A2

Sleeping 🛏

37 Hospedaje 525 B1
38 Hotel Aitué B1
39 Panamericana Hotel Temuco A2

Transportation 🚌

40 Automóvil Club de Chile B4
41 Avis B2
42 Budget A2
43 Bus Terminal - Rodoviario A1
44 Hertz B2
45 LAN Office A2
46 Skyline Office A2
47 Terminal de Buses Rurales A1
48 Train Station A1

Puerto Montt (from $72) (Monday – Friday 9 a.m. – 2 p.m., 3 p.m. – 7:30 p.m., Saturday 9:30 a.m. – 1:30 p.m. Bulnes 677. Tel: 56-45-747300). Updated: Jul 06, 2009.

Getting Around

Micros, or city buses, have routes throughout the urban area, passing along Rodríguez and Portales Streets ($0.65). Number 7 from Portales and Bulnes goes to the bus terminal. *Colectivos*, shared taxis, are black and have set routes ($1). Route 11P, which you can catch via Claro Solar, is the one to the bus terminal. Radiotaxis are normal cabs that you can call ahead for or catch at stands on Plaza Pinto (to bus terminal $2.20, to airport $8). The transfer is a private collective minibus with door-to-door service to the airport ($4; Tel: 56-45-386000 / 33-4033).

Several major international car rental companies have offices in downtown Temuco and at the airport: **Avis** (San Martín 755. Tel: 56-45-465280); **Budget** (Mackenna 399. Tel: 56-45-232715) and **Hertz** (Andrés Bello

792. Tel: 56-45-232715). Bicyclists can find parts and repair shops on Lautaro, between Cruz and Matta. Updated: Jul 06, 2009.

Services

TOURISM OFFICES

Sernatur has plenty of information and maps about attractions, lodging and other tourist services in the Araucanía region (Monday – Thursday 9 a.m. – 2 p.m., 3 p.m. – 5:30 p.m.; Friday 9 a.m. – 2 p.m., 3 p.m. – 4:30 p.m. Bulnes 586. Tel: 56-45-211969, Fax: 56-21-5509, E-mail: infoaraucania@sernatur.cl, URL: www.sernatur.cl).

The city maintains a tourism kiosk at the Mercado Municipal, inside the Calle Aldunate entrance (Tuesday – Saturday 9 a.m. – 1 p.m., 3 p.m. – 7 p.m.. Tel: 56-45-973628, URL: www.temucochile.com). **Conaf** (national park office) has excellent topographical maps of trails for all the national parks in the region (Monday – Friday 8:30 a.m. – 5 p.m. Bulnes 931. Tel: 56-45-298100). Other useful organizations are:

THE LAKE DISTRICT

Carabineros (police) (Claro Solar 1284. Tel: 56-45-211604) and **Automóvil Club de Chile** (San Martín 0278. Tel: 56-45-248903).

MONEY

Many money services are near Plaza Pinto. Banks are usually open Monday – Friday 9 a.m. – 2 p.m. and have ATMs that accept MasterCard, Cirrus, Visa and Plus cards:
- **Banco de Chile** (Varas 818)
- **Banco de Estado** (Claro Solar 931) — exchanges U.S. dollars and euros; the ATM accepts only MasterCard and Cirrus
- **BBVA** (Bello 890)
- **Santander** (Prat 620; other ATMs at Prat 724) — exchanges U.S. dollars and euros; ATM: also American Express
- **Scotiabank** (Varas 880)

Afex Casa de Cambio exchanges US dollars, Euros, Sterling Pounds and other currencies, as well as American Express travelers checks (slightly lower rate), and is a **MoneyGram** agent (Monday – Friday 9 a.m. – 6 p.m., Saturday 10 a.m. – 2 p.m. Varas 914. Tel: 56-45-231075). You can find exchange houses around the main plaza. **Chilexpress**, the major Western Union agent, is next to the post office (Monday – Friday 9 a.m. – 7 p.m., Saturday 10 a.m. – 1 p.m. Portales 801).

KEEPING IN TOUCH

Correo Chile, the post office, has its main office downtown (Monday – Friday 9 a.m. – 7 p.m., Saturday 9 a.m. – 1 p.m. Portales 801) and a substation at the Mall Portal Temuco. Internet cafés are located throughout the centro district, with prices ranging from $0.80 to $1.60 per hour; many have Skype. Most open at 10 a.m. and are closed Sunday. A reliable café is **PC Montt** (Monday – Friday 9 a.m. – 11 p.m., Saturday, Sunday 3 p.m. – 9 p.m. Montt 428. $0.80 per hour). Phone centers likewise are common. Prices vary widely, so shop around. One of the cheapest is **Centro de Llamadas**, where local and national calls cost $0.10 per minute and international from $0.20 per minute (Daily 10 a.m. – 9 p.m. Montt 965).

MEDICAL

Temuco's public health facility is **Hospital Regional** (Montt 115. Tel: 56-45-296100). There are several pharmacies on Montt near Prat. **Farmacia Ahumada** is open 24 hours (Bulnes and Montt).

As well as Western medicine, traditional Mapuche healing is accessible in Temuco. Try **Küme Akuleimy-Farmacia Herbolaria Mapuche** (Monday – Friday 9:30 a.m. – 7:45 p.m., Saturday 9:30 a.m. – 2:30 p.m. Aldunate 245. Tel: 56-45-520102, E-mail: fmapuche@gmail.com), which also operates a clinic, **Makewelawen** (Bulnes 352. Tel: 56-45-520888).

LAUNDRY

Lavandería Center charges $5 to wash and dry up to four kilograms (9 lbs) of clothes. It has same-day service (Monday – Saturday 9 a.m. – 7:30 p.m. Montt 250. Tel: 56-45-234436). Updated: Jul 06, 2009

SHOPPING

Temuco is a good place to pick up all you'll need for camping, fly fishing, snow sports and other outdoor activities. The following are good shops to check out:

- Camping: **Donem** (Monday – Friday 10 a.m. – 8 p.m., Saturday 10 a.m. – 7 p.m. Montt 788. Tel: 56-45-273508) has tents, sleeping bags, stoves, gas canisters.

- Fishing: **Olleta Caza y Pesca** (Monday – Friday 9 a.m. – 7:15 p.m., Saturday 10 a.m. – 1:30 p.m. Prat 439). There are also several other shops on Portales, between Cruz and Mackenna. All have excellent stock of rods, reels, flies and spinners.

- Snow sports: **Ski Aventura** (Av. Caupolicán 499. Tel:56-45-741285) sells and rents ski and snowboarding equipment.

You can buy artisan work at the **Mercado Municipal. Wanglen Zome** is a women's collective (Monday – Friday 10 a.m. – 6 p.m., Saturday 10 a.m. – 1 p.m. Aldunate and Claro Solar. Tel: 56-8-9817993). **Chol Chol** is a fair trade organization specializing in traditional Mapuche weaving (Monday – Friday 9 a.m. – 6 p.m. Camino Temuco a Imperial Km. 16. Tel: 56-45-614007, E-mail: info@cholchol.org, URL: www.cholchol.org); the Museo Regional de la Araucanía also sells Chol Chol weavings. Temuco is no stranger to the modern mall, either, as it has two of them: **Mall Portal Temuco** (Av. Alemán 0671) and **Mall Mirage** (Torremolinos 410). Updated: Jul 06, 2009.

Things to See and Do

It's pleasant to stroll through Temuco's Plazas Pinto and Teodoro Schmidt, and along the Avenida Balmaceda to see the various monuments. Another place worthy of a walk is Avenida Alemania, lined with mansions built by the German immigrants. At Cerro Ñielol you can hike on one of several nature trails. The city has two important historical museums, the Museo Regional de la Araucanía and the Museo Nacional Ferroviario Pablo Neruda, as well as several art galleries. Anyone who has never had the chance to ride a steam engine train can do so here, on the Tren de la Araucanía. Updated: Jul 06, 2009.

Monumento Nacional Cerro Ñielol

Cerro Nielol (hills with holes) has several hiking trails through the 89.5 hectares of forest. Founded in 1939 to protect native flora and fauna, its the only one of the country's national monuments located in an urban center. From the park entry (north end of Calle Prat), Sendero Agua Santa (750 m / 2437 ft long) leads to a font of sacred water. Sendero Los Lotos (980 m / 3185 ft) passes waterlily pools, ending at La Patagua, where the Chile-Mapuche peace treaty of 1881 was signed under a tree. Now giant wooden men and women guard this historic space. The Sendero Los Caoihues cuts through a grove of the national flower, which blossoms in fall and

Photo by Tabea Carbonero

winter. Other trails and an interpretive center are also worth exploring. Nationals: Adults $1.40, seniors $0.70, children $0.40. Foreigners: Adults $2, seniors and children $1. Daily 8:30 a.m. - 6 p.m. Updated: Jul 06, 2009.

Museo Regional de la Araucanía

(ADMISSION: Free) The Museo Regional de la Araucania, in a mansion built in 1924, has exhibits on the complex and fascinating history and culture of this region. The museum has information on the Mapuche culture, the wars between that indigenous nation and the Spanish-Chilean invaders, the eventual peace treaty that was signed and the effects of European immigration in the late 19th – early 20th centuries. This museum is a must-visit if you want to understand the Araucanía and its people. Monday – Friday 10 a.m. – 5 p.m., Saturday 11 a.m. – 5 p.m., Sunday 11 a.m. – 2 p.m. Av. Alemania 084. Tel: 56-45-747948. Updated: Jul 06, 2009.

Art Museums

Art aficionados can visit several centers:
• **Galería de Arte Plaza Aníbal Pinto** (Monday – Friday 9 a.m. – 8 p.m., Saturday, Sunday and holidays 10 a.m. – 8 p.m. Plaza Pinto. URL: www.temucochile.cl. Entry: free). Itinerant exhibits.
• **Cultural Aula Magna**, Universidad Católica de Temuco (Monday – Friday 9 a.m. – 1 p.m., 3 p.m. – 5 p.m. Av. Alemania and Theirs. URL: www.uctemuco.cl. Entry: free). Also shows movies in evenings.
• **Sala Exposiciones UCT** (Monday – Friday 10 a.m. – 1 p.m., 3 p.m. – 4:30 p.m. 18 de Septiembre and Av. Alemania. URL: www.uct.cl. Entry: free). Itinerant exhibits. Updated: Jul 06, 2009.

Museo Nacional Ferroviario Pablo Neruda

(ADMISSION: children and students $0.60, senior citizens $1, adults $2) The Museo Nacional Ferroviario Pablo Neruda is both a salute to native son and Nobel-winning poet Pablo Neruda and a museum that attempts to preserve the history of the nation. There are several old train cars on the grounds, as well as a coal storage tower, a native garden and an art gallery, all interspersed with Nerudian verses about the Iron Horse. The real treasure, however, is in the old locomotive shed. Here, in the garages around the round table, are over two dozen US, British and German steam engines (the oldest from 1908), a 1935 Linke Hofmann Werke sleeping car and the Presidential Car, used until 1992.

The museum is open Tuesday through Sunday 9 a.m. – 6 p.m. To get there, walk or take microbus number 1, 4B or 9, or colectivo taxi 20. Av. Barros Arana 0565. Tel: 56-45-

THE LAKE DISTRICT

973940 / 3941, E-mail: museoferroviario@temucochile.com, URL: www.museofer-roviariotemuco.cl. Updated: Jul 06, 2009.

Tren de la Araucanía ❗

(RIDE: Adults $10, children and seniors $6). The black smoke of the 1940 Baldwin Type 80 steam engine puffs into the sky as it chugs through the forests and over the rivers of the Araucanía. Some ride these passenger cars to relive memories of long-ago rail journeys, while others, especially the children, come to take their very first journey by train. The dining car is the highlight of this Tren de la Araucanía, a 1930 Linhke Hofmann Werke wagon of caoba wood lit by brass and crystal fixtures. The Baldwin takes its passengers as far as Victoria, between January – March and August – November. Once a year, the train undertakes a special, longer expedition. The train departs from the Museo Nacional Ferroviario Pablo Neruda, For information about schedules, contact the museum. Av. Barros Arana 0565. Tel: 56-45-973940 / 3941, E-mail: museoferroviario@temucochile.com, URL: www.museoferroviariotemuco.cl. Updated: Jul 06, 2009

Milla Ruka

To get a feel for the Mapuche way of life, you can visit the village of Milla Ruka. Go for a day trip, sample classic Mapuche cuisine and rent a horse to ride to Chol Chol. For a more immersive experience, spend the night with the kin of Millapán. This experience costs $4 ($5 with lunch) or $10 per person for groups (minimum 10, with storytelling, dance and lunch). Room and board is $20 per person. Horseriding is $5 per hour. To get to Milla Ruka by car from Temuco, take Avenida Pedro de Valdivia out of town. At Kilometer 11 (Boyeco), turn right to Conoco Chico. After 8 kilometers (5 mi), turn left onto the Chol Chol-Renaco Pastales road for 350. If you're taking the bus from Balmaceda and Zenteno, take the Panco bus to the Renaco Pastales-Chol Chol crossroads, then walk the rest of the 650 meters (noon and 4 p.m., return 1:15 p.m. and 5 p.m., $3). Tel: 56-9-9950122 / 8-578-6837 (mob.), E-mail: millaruka@hotmail.com, URL: www.millaruka.cl.

Lodging

Temuco has all types of lodging choices, from *hospedajes*, or rooms families rent in their homes, to five-star hotels. Cheaper, though more run-down, hostels are located between the Feria Pinto and the Mercado Municipal markets. Prices rise during the high season (mid-December through February) and for national holidays, like the Fiestas Patrias in mid-September. Reservations are highly recommended at these times.

Hospedaje 525

(ROOMS: $12 – 30) Travelers on a budget can find a room in the home of owners Daniel and Mirta.. The spacious rooms, with polished wood floors and large windows, have basic furnishings with cable TV and closet. Beds have excellent mattresses and plenty of blankets to keep you toasty on chilly nights. The older part of the house has accommodations with common bathrooms; the newer, section with private. The house has a small carport where you can park a car or motorcycle. Zenteno 525. Tel: 56-45-232667. Updated: Jul 06, 2009.

Hotel Aitué

(ROOMS: $72 – 102) Hotel Aitué is located in the heart of Temuco, just two blocks from Plaza Pinto. This unassuming three-star lodging has high-class amenities, like mini-bars, cable TV, hairdryers and in-room WiFi, for a reasonable price. Many touches make this a favorite home-away-from-home to many business travelers. The carpeted rooms are large, and have firm beds. The hotel also has an internet salon that guests can use for free. Central heating keeps Hotel Aitué's residents warm in Temuco's cold, damp winters. Varas 1048. Tel: 56-45-212512 / 1917, E-mail: reserves@hotelaitue.cl, URL: www.hotelaitue.cl. Updated: Jul 06, 2009.

Panamericana Hotel Temuco

(ROOMS: $170 – 238) At the foot of Cerro Ñielol rises the buff-pink Panamericana Hotel, formerly known as Hotel Terra Verde. The 74 rooms are well equipped with extras like sitting areas, WiFi, mini-bars, flat-screen TVs with cable, safe deposit box and glistening white bathrooms. Earth-tone and blue fabrics with innovative designs create a sophisticated, natural atmosphere. Many rooms have a view over the mountain behind. The outdoor pool is open only in summer. The hotel also has a thousand-person convention center. Av. Prat 0220.Tel: 56-45-239999, Fax: 56-45-23-9455, E-mail: reservas@hotelterraverde.cl, URL: www.panamericanahoteles.cl. Updated: Jul 06, 2009.

Restaurants

While in Temuco, try the local specialties, like horse meat, trout, salmon and *cochayuyo*, a type of seaweed. Yerba mate is a

THE LAKE DISTRICT

favorite drink of Temuquenses, and is usually made with herbs and sugar. Vegetarians will be able to find something to eat at many restaurants, though it may be nothing more than a large plate of vegetables. Self-caterers can buy supplies at the **Mercado Municipal** (Alduante and M. Rodríguez) and the cheaper **Feria Pinto** (Pinto, between Lautaro and Balcemeda). **Santa Isabel** (Cruz and M. Rodríguez), is a centrally-located supermarket. **Las Vegas** has a wide selection of dried fruits, nuts, soy "meat" and other stock useful for camping and expeditions (Monday – Friday 9:30 a.m. – 8:30 p.m., Saturday 10 a.m. – 4 p.m. Montt 1024, local 101. Tel: 56-45-213089).

Restaurant El Toltén

(LUNCH SPECIALS: $3.20 – 5.40, À LA CARTE: $6 and up) This is the place to go for good Chilean home cooking at a price that won't break the backpacker's budget. The *colación*, or daily special, comes with salad, main dish with side, and drink. For a small additional cost, a dessert or glass of wine can be added to the meal. El Toltén is very popular with locals. If the front room is full, don't fear: A dozen tables in a back room. À la carte specialties are available in the evenings. Open daily noon to midnight. San Martín 985-A. Tel: 56-45-742904. Updated: Jul 06, 2009.

Restaurant Rukayiael Kokaví

(LUNCH SPECIALS $2.20-3.40, Á LA CARTE FROM $4) Restaurant Rukayiael Kokaví serves up the age-old recipes of the original people of the Araucanía region, the Mapuche. The *desayuno campesino* (peasant breakfast) is traditional katuto bread or *mültxun* (bread with cheese) with toasted-grain coffee, *muzay* (a quinoa drink) or *kinwakao* (quinoa with cocoa). You can also try *yiwin challwa* (fried fish) and *korükoyof* (seaweed cochayuyo soup). Some "import" dishes make it on the menu, like *korüachawal* (chicken stew) and *ilokawella* (horsemeat). This upstairs eatery is warmly decorated with age-burnished wood and Mapuche articles. Open Monday – Saturday 9 a.m. – 9 p.m., Rodríguez 1073. Tel: 56-9-4430671. Updated: Jul 06, 2009.

La Parrilla de Miguel

(DAILY SPECIALS $5.20, Á LA CARTE FROM $6.60) On chilly evenings, a snapping fire warms the polished yet rustic décor of Restaurant La Parrilla de Miguel. The best wines, imported spirits and touches like the cloth napkins let you know you have arrived at one of Temuco's best bistros specializing in grilled meats. *Braseros* for two to four people, with a variety of meats and accompaniments, are a house specialty. Entrées of beef, chicken and salmon are also available and vegetarians have some choices on the menu, including a *tabla* (antipasto plate). You can also enjoy the same grilled meats in the daily lunch special. Open Monday – Saturday 11:30 a.m. – 4 p.m., 7:30 p.m.-midnight. M. Montt 1095. Tel: 56-45-275182 / 46-5210. Updated: Jul 06, 2009.

CURACAUTÍN

 1778m  2,306 45

For the indigenous Mapuche, this valley was Cura Cahuin, "the Meeting Stone," where they rested after the long journeys from one side of the Andes to the other. The zone, rich in *araucaría* trees, was a major place for collecting *piñones* (pine nuts) a staple in the Mapuche diet. In 1882, after Chile signed a peace treaty with the Mapuche, General Gregorio Urrutia Venegas was sent to control the indigenous of the region. He established Fuerte Curacautín on a high mesa with views over the surrounding countryside. Today, this village is simply called Curacautín.

It is easy to get to Curacautín, which is located just northeast of Temuco, on the road to Paso Pino Hinchado on the Argentine border. The shady plaza at the heart of the village, is surrounded by the government buildings, a simple church and various services. In the ex-Gobernación building you'll find the small Museo Histórico. From the village you can see Tolhuaca, Lonquimay and Llaima volcanoes. In March, Curacautinenses celebrate their Raid Turístico, with jaunts to the nearby natural attractions of the village.

What attracts most visitors to Curacautín is the plethora of activities in the countryside. There are two stunning waterfalls: Salto del Indio, a 20-meter (12-ft) cascade through the forest (14 km / 8.5 mi east, come a Manzanar, entry fee), and Salto de Princesa, which is a bit taller, at 25 meters (15 ft); (22 km / 13.5 mi east; free entry).

There are four national parks around Curacautín: Parque Nacional Tolhuca and Reserva Nacional Malleco to the north, Reserva Nacional Malalcahuello-Nalcas to the east, and Parque Nacional Conguillío to the southeast. All the parks provide hiking opportunities for everyone from beginners to the most experienced mountain climbers.

Winter brings a lot of snow to the region, making it a perfect place to go for skiing, snowboarding and other sports. On the southeast slopes of Volcán Lonquimay, 45 kilometers (27 mi) east of Curacautín, is **Centro de Esquí y Montaña Corralco**, an exclusive lodge with hotel, restaurant and skiing facilities (Santiago: Apoquindo 6275, oficina 4. Las Condes. Tel: 56-45-22029325; lodge, from 7 p.m. – midnight: 56-45-21963547 / 3549, E-mail: info@corralco.com, URL: www.corralco.com).

After days hiking or skiing, take a soak in one of the regional hot springs. To the north is **Termas de Tolhuaca**, (at the entrance of Parque Nacional Tolhuaca), which has two pools. A unique feature of this thermal spring is the natural cave with a fumarole where you can inhale sulfur vapors (33 km / 20 mi north, next to PN Tolhuaca; reservations / information in Curacautín: Calama 240. Tel: 56-45-881211).

On the road to the Argentine border, there are two other hot springs. **Termas Malalcahuello**, with a restaurant and hotel, has pools with 47°C (117°F) waters (30 km / 18 mi from Curacautín. Tel: 56-45-17121963541, URL: www.malalcahuello.cl). **Termas Manzanar**'s two pools and 10 private baths that can reach temperatures up to 48°C (118 °F). It also has a hotel and restaurant (18 km / 11 mi east, Camino Internacional. Tel: 56-45-881200, URL: www.termasdemanzanar.cl).

If cool water is what you need after hiking on a summer day, then head to **Balneario Trahuilco** on the banks of Río Blanco. Here you can swim, camp and enjoy various outdoor activities (open December – February, 26 km / 16 mi southeast, toward Parque Nacional Conguillío, entry fee charged).

Getting To and Away From Curacautín

Curacautín is 87 kilometers (54 mi) from Temuco. Two roads pass through town, one by way of Victoria (56 km / 34 mi northwest of Curacautín), and the other by way of Lautaro (54 km / 33 mi southwest). It's 122 kilometers (74.5 mi) from Curacautín to Paso Internacional Pino Hinchado.

From Temuco:
Erbuc (Terminal de Buses Rural, Av. Pinto 032): daily, approximately every two hours 7:30 a.m. – 6:30 p.m., $2.60.
Buses Bío Bío (Lautaro 853): every 1.5 – 2 hours, 7:20 a.m. – 8:30 p.m., $5.
Also **Buses Araucaria** from the Terminal Rodoviario.

From Curacautín:
Buses TurBus (Tel: 56-45-881596) and **InterSur** (Tel: 56-45-881596) both go to Victoria, Ercilla, Collipulli, Santiago (Serrano 101. Tel: 56-45-881596).

Buses Bío Bío (Tel: 56-45-881123): to Lautaro, Temuco, Victoria, Collipullo, Angol, Los Angeles, Concepción; **Erbuc:** to Manzanar, Malalcahuello, Lonquimay, Victoria, Lautaro, Temuco, Captrén; **Araucaria** (Tel: 56-45-881949): to Lautaro, Temuco. All three are located on M. Rodríguez, across from the main plaza.

Buses Staud (located at the Terminal de Buses) goes to Victoria and Malalcahuello. Updated: Jun 22, 2009.

Services

Curacautín has basic services. Across from the plaza is the **Oficina de Turismo** (M. Rodríguez s/n. Tel: 56-45-464858, E-mail: turismocuracautin@yahoo.es). Other information can be found at these websites: www.araucaniandina.com, www.sernatur.cl, www.mcuracautin.cl and www.curacautinchile.cl.

Conaf has an administrative office in town where you can pick up information on the national parks and reserves in the area (Yungay 240. Tel: 56-45-881184, E-mail: laraya@conaf.cl). Check out tour operator **Expediciones Pelehue** (Arturo Prat 790. Tel: 56-45-93765354).

Banco Estado has a MasterCard / Cirrus ATM, and exchanges U.S. dollars and euros (O'Higgins 562). The village also has a **hospital** (Serrano s/n. Tel: 56-45-881225).

On one side of the plaza is a **feria artesanal**, where you can buy sculptures, weavings, wooden utensils and other items made by the Mapuche and other residents of Curacautín.

Lodging

There is a wide selection of lodging options in town and along the Camino Internacional to the Argentine border, toward Lonquimay.

Hotel Turismo: (ROOMS: $10-14) Tarapacá 140. Tel: 56-45-881116, E-mail: hotel-turismocuracautin@gmail.com.

Hospedaje Aliwen: (ROOMS: $20 – 40) Manuel Rodríguez 540. Tel: 56-45-881437.

Hotel del Campo del Bosque Nativo: (ROOMS: $70 – 86) Km 6.8 Camino Curacautín-Tolhuaca. Tel: 56-45-1976148, E-mail: cab.bosquenativo@ctrnet.cl, URL: www.cabanasbosquenativo.cl.

Restaurants
Pick up provisions at the small supermarkets scattered throughout town. There are a couple of eateries you can check out: **Restaurant La Quintrala** (Arica 155. Tel: 56-45-881125); **Restaurant El Gato Negro** (M. Rodríguez 610. Tel: 56-45-881326). Updated: Jun 17, 2009.

LONQUIMAY

 2765m 327 45

The village of Lonquimay, whose name means "The Great Ravine" in the Mapuche's language, lies in a fold of the Andes. The center of town is designed as three concentric ovals (Calles O'Higgins, Carrera Pinto and Portales) with the wooded Plaza de Armas as the "hub." Like the spokes of a wheel, side streets radiate from the inner ring, connecting the circles. The village has a significant Pehuenche indigenous population. Few people live in this hamlet, but the residents still roll out the red carpet for tourists who come to explore Reserva Nacional Malalcahuello-Nalcas and Reserva Nacional Alto Bío Bío, both within a stone's throw from the village.

Lonquimay is also near the Paso Icalma and Paso Pino Hinchado border crossings into Argentina. Because of this strategic position, the first branch of the Chilean portion of the Corredor Bioceánico, a transportation route to connect the Pacific and Atlantic Oceans, passes through the town. Lonquimay was founded January 25, 1897 by Coronel Gregorio Urrutia, as part of Chile's colonization of this region after the peace treaty was signed with the Mapuche. Its original name was Villa Portales, but was later changed to the indigenous name.

Lonquimay's proximity to the Chilean-Argentine border has always made ita strategically important location. In the early 20th century, a trans-Andean rail system from Temuco-Victoria to Bahía Blanca, Argentina, was proposed. The line only made it as far as Lonquimay on the Chilean side, though. Regular rail service ended in 1982. For several decades, the Tren de la Araucanía carried tourists to Lonquimay. As the tracks deteriorated, the service was halted.

One of the last surviving remnants of this line is Túnel de las Raíces, 21 kilometers (12.6 mi) southwest of Lonquimay. This 4.5-kilometer (2.72-mi) long tunnel was built in the 1930s at a great cost, and was Latin America's longest tunnel at the time. The tunnel turned out to be a large miscalculation. The tracks were never extended past Lonquimay and the tunnel was never used. The steam locomotive that powered this line, Engine number 429, a North British 57, is in Temuco's Museo Nacional Ferroviario Pablo Neruda. In recent years, interest in connecting the two neighbors has increased, and studies have been done about possibly building the Ferrocarril Transandino del Sur through Lonquimay.

Come in February to savor Lonquimayino hospitality during Semana del Turismo. This week-long festival has theater, music, cinema and sporting events, culminating in southern Chile's largest goat roast (*asado de chivo*). Goats have a large role in the local economy: **Sociedad Caprina Lonquimay** makes Valle Lonquimay goat cheese (*queso de cabra*) in a variety of flavors (Los Avellanos s/n. Tel: 56-45-892060, URL: www.socapril.cl). **Proyecto Caprino Boer** is working exclusive with the Boer goat breed, known for its meat (Av. Zapala s/n. Tel: 56-45-97849047).

Lonquimay's natural attractions draw many travelers to this small town. **Reserva Nacional Malalcahuello-Nalcas,** to the west, and **Reserva Nacional Alto Bío Bío,** to the east, are just two of the places where you can explore local rivers, lakes and forests. Horseback riding to area sites and indigenous Mapuche-Pehuenche communities, fishing and boating are a few of the activities available. Laguna San Pedro, a mere 2 kilometers (1.2 mi) northeast on the road to Troyo is a great place to go for canoeing, kayaking or fishing (Entry: free). Mountain biking and horseback riding are some of the ways to explore the range of hills covered with old araucaria forest. The views of Llaima, Tolhuaca and Lonquimay Volcanoes are spectacular.

The biggest attraction in the Cordillera, is the **Centro de Esquí Los Arenales**. This 200-hectar winter sport center has two lifts and four downhill ski runs of different grades of difficulty. You can also practice alpine trekking (*esquí randonée*) and cross-country skiing (*esquí de fondo*) here. The resort has araucaria and other native trees, and is populated with foxes, hares and condors. Facilities include cafeteria, restaurant, equipment rental and lessons. (Open July-October. 8 km / 4.8 mi east of Lonquimay in the Cordillera Las Raíces. Information from **Municipalidad de Lonquimay**. Tel: 56-45-464870 or the city's **Oficina de Turismo**. Tel: 56-45-464842).

On the Andean steppe 36 kilometers (22 mi) south are the headwaters of Río Bío Bío. In the forest of araucaria, fescue, spiny cocklebur, calafate, Magellan barberry, Antarctic beech, and coigüe, you can camp, horseback ride or paddle a boat (entrance fee). Toward the Paso de Icalma border crossing into Argentina is Lago Galletué. Visitors go to this deep-blue lake to swim, boat, horseback ride and camp (4 km / 2.4 mi south).

A little further off you'll find Lago Icalma. In summer, Ilcalma is a good place to enjoy the beach, camp, sail and sportfish (75 km / 45 mi south). Both lakes fill up with snow in the wintertime. In 2005, scientists found dinosaur eggs in Lolen, which is nearby. Seven kilometers (4.2 mi) west of Lonquimay is La Cascada , a 30-meter (98-ft) high cascade surrounded by a forest of *coigüe, canelo* (winter's bark), Antarctic beech and *roble*. At the base of the waterfall is a pool where you can swim. Public transportation passes by the turn-off; walk down the 400-meter road to the falls (entry charged).

Getting To and Away From Lonquimay

Lonquimay is 144 kilometers (86.5 mi) east of Temuco. From the Argentine border, the town is 70 kilometers (42 mi) from Paso Pino Hinchado and 76 kilometers (45.6 mi) from Paso Icalma. From Temuco, several companies make the 3.5-hour journey to Lonquimay:

Erbuc: (from Terminal de Buses Rurales, Av. Pinto 032) daily about every 2 hours 7:30 a.m.-6:30 p.m., $5.60)

Bío Bío: (Lautaro 853) approximately each 1.5-2 hours, $7.60. Updated: Jun 17, 2009.

Services
The **Oficina de Turismo** is in the Plaza de Armas (O'Higgins, Plaza de Armas. Tel: 56-45-464842 / 3027) or consult www.araucaniaandina.cl/es/lonquimay or www.turismolonquimay.cl. **Banco Estado** (O'Higgins 1375), **Centro de Llamados y Casa de Cambio Pako** has phone service and changes U.S. dollars and Argentine pesos (Carrera Pinto 101). **Centro de Llamadas CTC** offers national and international phone service and Internet (Condell 199). The town also has a police station and hospital (O'Higgins 1060. Tel: 56-45-557500).

Tours
For tours, check out **Cabalgatas Lanco Patagonia** (Km 104 Ruta Internacional Pino Hinchado. Tel: 56-45-891959 / 9-789-2097), **Circuitos Turísticos Huellas Pehuenche** (Portales 720. Tel: 56-45-96700904), or **Lonkitur** (O'Higgins 1495. Tel: 56-45-892139).

Lodging
Camping Lolen (14 km / 8.7 mi from Lonquimay, Camino Internacional. Tel: 56-45-354144).

Hospedaje Lonquimay: (ROOMS: $12 per person) Carrera Pinto 620. Tel: 56-45-891104, E-mail: chelitahidalgochandia@yahoo.es, URL: www.araucariandina.cl.
Hotel Turismo Lonquimay: (ROOMS: $16 – 50) Caupolicán 925. Tel: 56-45-891087, E-mail: hotel.turismo@gmail.com.

Hostería Donde Juancho: (ROOMS: $20 – 50) O'Higgins 1130. Tel: 56-45-891140, E-mail: dondejuancho@gmail.com, URL: www.dondejuancho.cl.

Restaurants
Restaurant Donde Junacho (O'Higgins 1130. Tel: 56-45-891140).

El Pionero (Colón 840. Tel: 56-45-891044).

Hostería Restaurant Follil Pewenche (Carrera Pinto 110. Tel: 56-45-891110, E-mail: quimque@entelchile.net).
Updated: Jun 17, 2009.

RESERVA NACIONAL ALTO BÍO BÍO

Although it is quite easy to get to Reserva Nacional (RN) Alto Bío Bío, few travelers ever make it here. Founded in 1912, this 33,050-hectare preserve features a canyon gouged by by glaciers and rivers. Many waterways have their headwaters here, which was the reason for the reserve's creation. The Tralilhue, Pino Solo, Liucura and Tue Tue, for example, feed Río Bío Bío. The park is also part of the Reserva de la Biosfera Araucarias (Araucarias Biosphere Reserve), conserving the alto-Andino ecosystem found within the region. RN Alto Bío Bío's temperate climate is typical of the Andean steppe.

Only about 45 percent of RN Alto Bío Bío is covered by forest, primarily of *araucaria* (monkey-puzzle tree), *lenga* (lenga beech), Antarctic beech, *coigüe* and Chilean cedar. Inhabiting this land are *pudú* (Chilean miniature deer), viscacha, *guanaco*, puma, South American grey fox, Patagonian fox, *quique* (lesser grison), a weasel-like animal, and *guiña*. The crested caracara, white-throated hawk, Condor and several species of duck also nest here.

Two legs of the Sendero de Chile pass through RN Alto Bío Bío: Cuelares Grande (Distance: 40 km / 24 mi) and the shorter Cuchares Chico (Distance: 20 km / 12 mi). You can also undertake fishing and horseback riding in the area, or visit one of the indigenous Pehuelche communities within the park. The only brochure-map that **Conaf**, the national park office, has on RN Alto Bío Bío is old and incomplete.

No lodging facilities exist within RN Alto Bío Bío. Camping is allowed only in designated spots. The nearest hostels are in **Liucura**, eight kilometers (4.8 miles) away: **Hostería Pino Hinchado** (Tel: 56-45-197-2034) and **Residencial y Casa de Cambio Pehuén** (Tel: 56-45-197-0065). Otherwise, stay in Lonquimay, 48 kilometers (29 mi) away. Updated: Jun 17, 2009.

Getting To and Away From Reserva Nacional Alto Bío Bío

Reserva Nacional Alto Bío Bío is four kilometers (2.4 mi) north off the Camino Internacional Ruta Ch-181, which leads to the Argentine border. Forty-eight kilometers (29 mi) east of Lonquimay, and just four kilometers (2.4 mi) before Paso Pino Hinchado, buses from Temuco to the Argentine destinations Zapala and Neuquén cross the border at Paso Pino Hinchado. See Getting to and away from Temuco for details. Updated: Jun 17, 2009.

PARQUE NACIONAL TOLHUACA

(ADMISSION: Chilean adults $4, foreigners $6; Chilean senior citizens $2, foreigners $3; Chilean children $0.80, foreigners $3) Parque Nacional (PN) Toluaca is one of Chile's oldest national parks, and was founded in 1935. In Mapudungún, the Mapuche language, Tolhuaca means "cow's forehead."

This reserve protects 6,474 hectares of Andean foothills and, on its Northern edge, the headwaters of the Río Malleco. The landscape was shaped by the ancient activity of Volcán Tolhuaca (2,806 m / 9,120 ft), located to the southeast, between PN Tolhuaca and Reserva Nacional (RN) Malacahuello-Nalcas. Rivers, streams and ravines have carved into the earth here. The park's altitude ranges from 1,000 to 1,821 meters (3,250 – 5,919 ft).

Among many mammal species that live in PN Tolhuaca, you might spot Chilean miniature deer, South American grey fox, Patagonian fox, and Molina's hog-nosed skunk. Nutria is the most common resident, especially in the Laguna Malleco area. Some birds to look out for are the Austral parakeet, Chilean pigeon, Condor and Speckled Teal. Also keep an eye out for the Hortensis butterfly.

PN Tolhuaca has a cold temperate climate. The annual mean temperature is 14°C (57°F). The park receives regular, abundant rains, 2,500 – 3,000 mm (98 –118 in) per year, with a dry period lasting about two months.

Conaf, in Temuco, has a brochure of PN Tolhuaca with a topographical map. Another free bilingual pamphlet-map, titled "Guía Senderos / Araucanía Trails," has GPS coordinates for Tolhuaca and other regional national parks. Check for current road and weather conditions with Conaf or the carabineros. Updated: Jun 16, 2009.

Getting To and Away From Parque Nacional Tolhuaca

From Victoria, a paved road heads eastward 63 kilometers (38 mi), through Inspector Fernández village, to the main entrance of

THE LAKE DISTRICT

Parque Nacional Tolhuaca at Laguna Malleco. Another unpaved route from Curacautín (49 km / 29.5 mi) leads to the caseta de información near Salto La Culebra. Public transportation goes only as far as the villages. To make it the rest of the way to the park, you could try hitchhiking. Otherwise, the only way to get to PN Tolhuaca is in private vehicle or on a tour. Updated: Jun 16, 2009.

Things to See and Do

Hiking Trails

The park has a network of trails to explore:

Sendero Chilpa (*Distance:* 1.5 km / 0.9 mi, *Difficulty:* medium, *Duration:* 1.5 hours). This trail, which begins at the Curacautín road, wanders through araucaria and lenga forest and provides views of the Valle Anino.

Sendero Tolhuaca-Niblinto (distance 12 km / 7.2 mi, *Difficulty:* medium, *Duration:* 4 hours). Accessible from the Laguna Malleco entrance, the trail begins at Prado Mesacura and ends at the administration office of the Reserva Nacional Malleco to the northeast; camping allowed.

Salto Malleco (*Distance:* 1.7 km / 1 mi, *Difficulty:* easy, *Duration:* 1 hour). This path has 13 interpretive stations and leads to Sallto Malleco, a 49-meter (160-ft) high waterfall.

Prados de Mescura (*Distance:* 15 km / 9 mi, *Difficulty:* medium, *Duration:* 3 hours). From the Laguna Malleco entrance, the trail cuts through araucaria forest and glens, to Guardería Prado, west-northwest of Malleco. Features include natural viewpoints and the Río Pichi Malleco. Be sure to bring drinking water.

Lagunillas (*Distance:* 12 km / 7.2 mi, *Difficulty:* medium, *Duration:* 1 day). From the Laguna Malleco entrance, this trail weaves back and forth between PN Tolhuaca and RN Malleco. It reaches an altitude of 1,645 meters (5,346 ft) before arriving at Las Lagunillas, whose crystalline waters are surrounded by araucaria. Condors are common.

La Culebra – Lago Verde (*Distance:* 2.1 km / 1.25 mi *Difficulty:* medium, *Duration:* 1.5 hours). Beginning at the La Culebra entrance near Curacautín, it passes by Salto de la Culebra waterfall, through dense woods and ends at Lago Verde. Along the way are several lookout points over the Laguna Verde and Río Malleco Valleys. There are some short, steep sections.

Laguna Verde (*Distance:* 4 km / 2.4 mi, *Difficulty:* medium, *Duration:* 2 hours). This trail edges the south boundary of the park, from Laguna Malleco to La Culebra. Highlights include a small waterfall, the Colomahuida box canyon and araucaria-lenga forest.After spending a day of hiking on the trails, relax in the **Termas de Tolhuaca**, located just outside the park on the road to Curacautín.

Camping

The park has campsites at the Laguna Malleco entrance and along the Sendero Tolhuaca Niblinto trail. Camping costs $14 for Chileans and $24 for foreigners between January 1 and February 28. The rest of the year, the fee is $8 (Chileans) and $10 (foreigners). No other services exist within the park. You must bring all food and water supplies (or water treatment).

PARQUE NACIONAL CONGUILLIO

Considered one of most beautiful national parks in the Lake District, Parque Nacional (PN) Conguillio has deep valleys and steep hills blanketed with araucaria. Laguna Captrén, with its drowned forest, exudes a mystical ambiance. In other parts of the park, a lunar landscape burned by lava flows astounds visitors. The major culprit in the molding of this landscape was Volcán Lalima (3125 m / 10,157 ft). This volcano erupted 49 times in recent history, the greatest being in 1927 and 1957. It is presently active, with a major eruption in April 2009. The Mapuche's name for this swath of land reflected tranquility: *Kongüjim*, which in Mapudungún means "nestled in the pine nuts," referring to the fruits of the araucaria tree. *Truful-Truful*, one of the sectors of the park, signifies "many falls" in the same language.

Established in 1950, PN Conguillio encompasses 60,832 hectares. The park has a temperate climate. Temperatures range widely, from a summer average of 15°C (59°F) in January to 6°C (45°F) in the winter. The park receives 2,000 – 2,500 millimeters (79 – 99 in) of precipitation per year. Lower altitudes can experience up to one meter (3.25 ft) of snow in winter.

Aside from the extensive forests of *araucaria* (monkey-puzzle tree) on the hilltops, PN Conguillio also has *jovellana*, lenga beech, Antarctic beech, plum-fruited yew, Chilean cedar

THE LAKE DISTRICT

and winter's bark. The park is home to pumas, Patagonian foxes and the South American grey fox. You can see up to 23 species of birds, including the Condor, Magellanic Woodpecker, Ashy-headed Goose, Red-gartered Coot, Neotropic Cormorant and Spectacled Duck.

PN Conguillio is open year-long, so snow sport enthusiasts have the opportunity to ski and snowboard, among other things. You can reach the winter resort of **Los Paraguas** from Guardería Agua las Niñas. The resort has a hostería, restaurant, refuge and ski slopes (Tel: 56-45-562313). The main park administration is located in Sector Arco Iris. This is open only November – June. During the rest of the year, the administration moves to Sector Los Paraguas. In addition, there are four ranger stations: **Truful-Truful** (2 km / 1.2 mi from the park entrance, 12 km / 7.2 mi from Administración Arco Iris and 12 km / 7.2 mi from Melipueco; open all year), **Los Paraguas** (3 km / 1.8 mi from the entrance; open all year), **Caseta Captrén** (11 km / 6.6 mi from the entrance; open November – June) and **Centro de Visitantes** (10 km / 6 mi from Caseta Captrén, 17 km / 10.2 mi from Truful-Truful, 5 km / 3 mi from Administración Arco Iris; open December – March).

The entry fee into the park varies according to where you enter. At Caseta Los Paraguas the cost for Chileans is adults $1, seniors $0.50 and children $0.40; for foreigners $2, seniors and children $1. At the Truful-Truful ranger station, Chileans adults are charged $6, seniors $3 and children $2, and foreigners are charged $8, seniors and children $4.

The Temuco office of Conaf has a topographical map-brochure of PN Conguillio that shows the trails, campsites and other services. The park administration also publishes a bilingual pamphlet-map, titled "Guía Senderos / Araucanía Trails" (free) which has GPS coordinates for Conguillio and other national parks in the region. Check for current road and weather conditions with Conaf or the park police.

Getting To and Away From Parque Nacional Conguillio

Parque Nacional Conguillio is accessible only by private car or by way of a tour from Temuco. The route, through Victoria, Curacautín and Paraguas, ending at the Captrén ranger station, is open all year. Past this point, accessibility depends on the amount of snowfall, though it is usually passable only

November through March. The circuit running from Temuco to Cunco and Melipueco, ending at the Truful ranger station is possible to drive year-round. A paved road passes through the park Captrén ranger station, on the Curacautín side, to Laguna Captrén and Lago Conguillio, then southward to the Truful station and the village of Melipueco. For current weather and road conditions, check with Conaf or park rangers. Public transportation goes only as far as Curacautín (46 km / 28 mi from park) and Melipueco (22 km/14 mi). Check to see if **Buses Erbuc** is operating its occasional service from Curacautín to Guardería Captrén. Otherwise, try hitchhiking. Updated: Jun 22, 2009.

Things to See and Do

PN Conguillio has many trails that wind through its impressive landscape. Whether you are looking for some day hikes or for the greatest challenges Chile's national parks have to offer, you can find them here. Below are a selection of the trails (all times are one way). Because of Volcán Llaima's present activity, check with **Conaf** and the ranger stations within the park to see if any trails or sectors of the park are closed. Some trails require park administration authorization.

For hikers with little experience, PN Conguillio has several interpretive trails:

Cañadón Truful-Truful (*Distance:* 0.8 km / 0.5 mi, *Difficulty:* easy, *Duration:* 45 minutes). The main features of this path are geologic formations (basalt columns and lava flows), and the Truful-Truful waterfalls. This is a good bird watching trail since it takes you through the habitat of the torrent duck.

Las Vertientes (*Distance:* 0.8 km / 0.5 mi, *Difficulty:* easy, *Duration:* 45 minutes). The path passes through a varied forest.

Las Araucarias (*Distance:* 0.8 km / 0.5 mi, *Difficulty:* easy, *Duration:* 45 minutes). Traversing araucaria forest, this track has 13 interpretive stations and leads to the Velo de la Novia waterfall.

Trekkers looking for a bit more of a challenge can set out on one of these trails:

Sierra Nevada (*Distance:* 10 km / 6 mi, *Difficulty:* medium, *Duration:* 3 hours). This loop through the mountains climbs to 2,554 meters (8,300 ft). From the top you can clearly see Volcán Llaima. There are many waterfalls along the way and it is possible to see condors.

THE LAKE DISTRICT

THE LAKE DISTRICT

Los Carpinteros (*Distance:* 8 km / 4.8 mi, *Difficulty:* easy, *Duration:* 2.5 hours). This part of the Sendero de Chile goes through ancient and dense araucaria forest that is nearly 1,800 years old. It is the exclusive habitat of the Black Woodpecker. The Mallín wetlands contain many kinds of waterfowl.

Pastos Blancos (*Distance:* 11 km / 6.6 mi, *Difficulty:* medium, *Duration:* 5 hours). The trail between Lago Conguillio and Volcán Llaima traverses lava flows of the Valle de la Luna, with views of lagunas, lakes and scars of volcanic eruptions.

Tramo de los Escoriales (*Distance:* 20 km / 12 mi, *Difficulty:* medium, *Duration:* 7 hours). This trail connects the Lago Captrén and Truful-Truful ranger stations. You need sturdy boots that are resistant to razor-sharp lava, as well as sun protection and water; park permission is required.

El Contrabandista (*Distance:* 15 km / 9 mi, *Difficulty:* high, *Duration:* 3.5 hours). This trail is part of Sendero de Chile that was originally used by Pehuelche hunters, and later by Chilean-Argentine smugglers. It winds along Río Blanco, Lagos Icalma and Calletue, providing opportunities to visit Pehuelche communities. PN Conguillio also has trails reserved only for those who have expertise in mountain and glacier climbing:

Travesía Río Blanco (*Distance:* 5 km / 3 mi, *Difficulty:* expert, *Duration:* 5 hours). This climb, which climbs to 2,500 meters (8,125 ft), requires experience and mountain climbing equipment.

Travesía Malalcahuello (*Distance:* 10 km / 6 mi, *Difficulty:* expert, duration: 48 hours). This excursion into Sierra Nevada (to 1,600 m/ 5,200 ft altitude), toward Malalcahuello, is only for those who are highly experienced; snow and ice equipment, and authorization from park rangers are needed.

Ruta al Llaima (*Distance:* 8 km / 4.8 mi, *Difficulty:* expert, *Duration:* 8 hours). The first part of this trail, as far as Captrén, is easy. The trek ends at the volcano's crater at 3,125 meters (10,157 ft). Adequate snow and ice climbing equipment, and park authorization are necessary.

Conguillio – Los Paraguas (*Distance:* 9 km / 5.4 mi, *Difficulty:* expert, *Duration:* 10 hours). Only for those with extensive glacier/mountaineering experience, and proper equipment. Park permission is required.

Lodging

The park has camping areas at Laguna Captrén and Lago Conguillio, and cabins (reservations Tel: 56-45-298210, E-mail: ocerda@conaf.cl).

Camping: December 15 – February 28, $30; March 1 – December 14, $20.

Cabins: December 15 – February 28, $90 – 110; March 1 – December 14, $70 – 80.

La Baita Conguillio eco-lodge has cabins on Río Truful with views of Volcán Llaima. Facilities include a restaurant, spa and tours (Tel: 56-45-581253, E-mail: info@labaitaconguilio.cl, URL: www.labaitaconguillio.cl). Hotels, restaurants and other services are also available in Curacautín to the west and Melipueco to the south.

RESERVA NACIONAL MALALCAHUELLO-NALCAS

(ADMISSION: Chilean adults $1, children and seniors $0.50; foreign adults $2, children and seniors $1.) Northwest of Temuco, between Curacautín and Lonquimay, lies the joint nature reserve Reserva Nacional (RN) Malalcahuello-Nalcas. The *Malalcahuello part*, which means "horse corral" in Mapudungún, was established in 1931 and consists of 13,730 hectares.

To the north is Nalca, created in 1967 to protect 13,775 hectares, and named after a native plant with an edible stalk. Volcán Tolhuaca (2,806 m / 9,206 ft) and Volcán Lonquimay (1400 m / 4550 ft) sit on the reserve boundary. The active crater Navidad was formed by an eruption on Christmas Day 1988. The park contains the Nalcas and Lolco Rivers, both tributaries of Río Bío Bío.

RN Malalcahuello-Nalcas summers are warm and dry. Rain and snow come between May and September, with precipitation reaching 2,045 millimeters (81 in) per year. The four winter months, June through September, are icy cold. Temperatures plummet to below freezing and the park usually has two to four meters (6.5 – 13 ft) of snowfall.

In RN Malalcahuello-Nalcas you'll find forests composed of lenga beech, monkey-puzzle tree, Antarctic beech, Chilean rhubarb, and winter's bark, among others. Introduced species such as Douglas-fir and Ponderosa pine also grow here. Fauna include the puma, Patagonian fox, South American grey fox, Chilean miniature deer, kodkod, Molina's hog-nosed skunk and Chilean rock rat. Bird aficionados should get their binoculars out for the Austral Parakeet, Magellanic Woodpecker, Black-chested Buzzard-eagle, White-throated Hawk, Condor, Chilean Flicker, Band-winged Nightjar, Striped Woodpecker and Common Barn Owl.

Getting To and Away From RN Malalcahuello-Nalcas

Reserva Nacional Malalcahuello-Nalcas is 120 kilometers (72 mi) northwest of Temuco. From Temuco, go to Curacautín, and from there to the Camino Internacional. After another 30 kilometers (18 mi), you'll come to the village of Malalcahuello and the turn-off for the national reserve. From Temuco, **Buses Bío Bío** (Temuco: Lautaro 853) passes in front of the national reserve (Approximately every 1.5 – 2 hours, 2 hours, $5.40,). Updated: Jun 17, 2009

Things to See and Do

In the summer, you can trek, hike, horseback ride, fish, mountain bike or climb the volcanoes in the park. Winter sports include downhill skiing and snowboarding at Corralco. In autumn and spring, the amount of snow will dictate the type of activity you can do.If hiking is your favorite activity, head out to the seven trails in the reserve:

Las Araucarias (*Distance:* 1.5 km / 1 mi; *Difficulty:* easy; *Duration:* 1.5 hours). This path leads you through reforested areas of araucaria and other native trees, but you'll see strands of introduced species, as well.

Tres Arroyos (*Distance:* 2.5 km / 1.5 mi; *Difficulty:* medium; *Duration:* 1.5 hours). This hike leads through mixed forests with views of Cordillera de las Raíces and other hills.

El Raleo (*Distance:* 3.5 km/2.1 mi; *Difficulty:* medium; *Duration:* 2 hours). This hike ventures into the Valle Malalcahuello and Río Cautín, and the forest habitat of the chucao bird.

El Coloradito (*Distance:* 30 km / 18 mi; *Difficulty:* medium; *Duration:* 8 hours). This trail reaches an altitude of 1,438 meters (4,674 ft) while traversing different vegetation zones. Fauna include the puma, fox, eagle, condor and other birds.

Laguna Blanca (*Distance:* 40 km / 24 mi; *Difficulty:* difficult; *Duration:* 2 days). A continuation of Sendero Piedra Santa, this trail cuts across lava flows and through araucaria and lenga forest where you'll see lots of fauna and birds, and get some great views of Lonquimay, Llaima and Sierra Nevada volcanoes.

Crater Navidad (*Distance:* 1.5 km / 0.9 mi; *Difficulty:* hard; *Duration:* 2 hours). This trail takes hikers to the geologically active crater, whose last eruption was on December 25, 1988. On cold days it is possible to see the vent steaming.

Cerro Cautín (*Distance:* 4 km / 2.4 mi; *Difficulty:* hard; *Duration:* 3 hours). Climb the cerro to the headwaters of Río Cautín. From the top, you'll have views of Volcán Copahue, Sierra Veluda, Callaqui, as well as Lonquimay and Tolhuaca. The wind and rain erosion have created natural rock sculptures. The Nalcas part of the national reserve has three trails of varying difficulty:

Laguna La Totora (*Distance:* 1 km / 0.6 mi; *Difficulty:* easy; *Duration:* 20 minutes). This trail passes through forests to a lagoon teeming with birdlife: the Ruddy Duck, White-tufted Grebe and Mallard.

Mocho Chico (*Distance:* 8 km / 4.8 mi; *Difficulty:* medium; *Duration:* 3 hours). On the way to the inactive crater Mocho Chico, you can see how vegetation recuperates after a volcanic eruption.

Tolhuaca (*Distance:* 40 km / 24 mi; *Difficulty:* hard; *Duration:* 1 day). This trek to Volcán Tolhuaca covers varied landscape that includes Cajón de Nalcas and virgin forests. Keep your eyes open for condors, pumas, eagles and other birds. Experience and special equipment are essential. Two legs of the Sendero de Chile go through RN Malalcahuello-Nalcas:

Piedra Santa – Laguna Blanca (Distance: 20 km / 12 mi; *Difficulty:* low-medium; *Duration:* 2 days). This trek begins at Laguna Blanca, goes around the base of Volcán Lonquimay, to Malalcahuello.

Cordillera Blanca (*Distance:* 22 km / 13.5 mi; *Difficulty:* medium-hard; *Duration:* 3 days). This trail goes from Malalcahuello village to the Sierra Nevada crossing, and ends at Lago Conguillio in Parque Nacional Conguillio.

The Temuco office of **Conaf** has a topographical map-brochure of RN Malalcahuello-Nalcas that show the trails, campsites and other services. The park administration also publishes a

THE LAKE DISTRICT

bilingual pamphlet-map, titled "Guía Senderos / Araucanía Trails" (free) which has GPS coordinates for Conguillio and other regional national parks. Check for current road and weather conditions with Conaf or the carabineros.

Lodging

There are no established campsites within the reserve. Backcountry camping is allowed on the longer treks, but fires are prohibited (take a camp stove). The ski center, **Centro de Montaña Corralco**, is an exclusive lodge. For current rates for ski lifts, rental and lodging, consult the website (Santiago: Apoquindo 6275, Oficina 4, Las Condes. Tel: 56-2-2029325; lodge, from 5 p.m. – midnight: 56-2-1963547 / 3549, E-mail: info@corralco.com, URL: www.corralco.com).

There are several hostels and restaurants in and around nearby Malalcahuello: **Residencial Los Sauces** (Av. Estación 510. Tel: 56-9-8837880), **Hostería y Cabañas La Casita de Nahuelcura** (Balmaceda 320. Tel: 56-45-1970311, URL: www.hosteriamalalcahuello. cl), **Restaurant Los Pinitos** (Camino Internacional Km 84, entrance to Malalcahuello village. Tel: 56-45-1971464). For more information about Malacahuello pueblo, see www.malalcahuello.cl. Updated: Jun 22, 2009.

MELIPEUCO

 1,505m   1,591   45

Officially, Melipeuco wasn't founded until January 1981. The Mapuche lived on this land they called Melipewco for centuries before. In Mapudungún the name means "the meeting of four waters," and refers to the Peuco, Truful-Truful, Allipen and Sahuelche rivers, which combine here. The village is in the Cordillera area of la Araucanía. It is the closest community to Volcán Llaima, which has recently been erupting. In January, Melipeuco tips its hat to this looming giant with the Feria del Llaima.

Like their ancestors, the indigenous here continue to struggle against the political and economic conquest of the "foreign" settlers. In the 1970s, this was a hotspot for the agrarian reform movement. After the 1973 coup d'etat, a number of activists were arrested, including members of the Mapuche nation. The fight for the preservation of their lands and customs continues today.

The majority of travelers come to Melipeuco for the natural beauty of this landscape. The village serves as a convenient base for visiting national parks and hot springs. A few lesser-known reserves are also nearby. One is Reserva Nacional Villarrica, composed of 60,005 hectares of araucaria and beech forests. Within its boundaries is Nevados de Sollipulli, a dormant volcano (accessable only by 4x4 vehicle; entry: free).

Reserva Nacional China Muerta, 24 kilometers (14.5 mi) northeast, protects 9,727 hectares of araucaria woodlands. Mountain biking is a popular sport here (dirt road to park; Entry: free). Furthermore, Melipueco is the southern access point to Parque Nacional Conguillio (31 km / 19 mi). Within this park are the lakes Verde and Congullío. The emerald waters of Laguna Verde, also called Quililo, are excellent for salmon fishing (pick up a fishing license at Melipeuco's city hall). The native forests surrounding Laguna Conguillio are excellent for birdwatching.

On the way to Parque Nacional Conguillio are the Saltos de Truful-Truful, a two-step waterfall. The first section, near a heap of lava, is 10 meters (32.8 ft) high. The second step is 20 meters (65.6 ft) high. Another spectacular cataract is Salto Carilafquén, a 25 meter (82-ft) high cascade passing through dense vegetation of quila, nalca, beech and mosses.

With so many volcanoes around, it is no surprise that so many hot springs also dot the area. **Termas de Balboa**, aka Moluloc, are rustic pools with 65ºC (149ºF) water (open January – February, 25 km / 15 mi southwest). At the foot of Nevados de Sollipulli, there are not only thermal springs, but also geysers; there are no facilities (open January – March, 23 km / 14 mi southwest by dirt road, 4x4 necessary). At Termas de Huechelepún, crystalline waters bubble next to a wooden hut (open January – March, 25 km / 15 mi southwest).

Getting To and Away From Melipeuco

Melipueco is 92 kilometers (55 mi) southeast of Temuco. The village has a gas station. From Temuco, **NarBus** provides service to Melipeuco with six daily departures 8 a.m. – 3:30 p.m., $32, 2 hours (Terminal de Buses Rurales, Av. Pinto 032).

In Melipueco, there are taxis that shuttle you around town and to local sites. Taxis and pickups run trips out to Parque Nacional Conguillio, charging approximately $15 – 18. Updated: Jun 17, 2009.

Services

Services are virtually nonexistent in Melipeuco. There is no bank. The **Oficina de Información Turística** is open only in the summer (Aguirre Cerda, between Durán and Prat). Other times of the year, consult: www.araucaniandina.com or www.sernatur.cl.

For tours check out **La Bait Conguillio** (Tel: 56-45-416410, E-mail: info@labaitaconguillio.cl, URL: www.labaitaconguillio.cl). There is an artisan market on the plaza.

Lodging

Hospedaje Icalma: (ROOMS: $10 – 13 per person) Aguirre Cerda 729. Tel: 56-9-2808210.

Hostería Hue Telén: (ROOMS: $30 – 40) P. Aguirre Cerda 1. Tel: 56-45-581203, E-mail: pabloparrak1@hotmail.com, URL: www.araucaniandina.cl.

Centro Turístico Los Pioneros: (ROOMS: $24 – 50) 1 kilometer (0.6 mi) from Melipeuco, Camino Internacional Paso Icalma. Tel: 56-45-581002, E-mail: lospionerosmelipeuco@turismoaventura.net, URL: www.araucaniandina.cl. There are also cabins and campsites out of town, especially on the road to Icalma.

Restaurants

There are several restaurants on Aguirre Cerda, including **Pub Restaurant Ruminot** (No. 496. Tel: 56-45-581087), **Restaurant Llaima** (No. 461. Tel: 56-8-5084942), and **Restaurant Juanito** (No. 563). Updated: Jul 07, 2009.

VILLARRICA

 224m   46,700   45

If you're feeling overwhelmed by the hustle and bustle of Pucón, the neighboring town of Villarrica is a nice alternative. Nestled right next to a volcano, the town provides beautiful views in a calm and relaxing setting.

Spending some time in Villarrica, rather than in Pucón, is also more of a cultural experience, as there are many more locals than tourists here. Founded way back in 1552, the town has a fascinating history. Stop by the Museo Histórico Arqueológico to see Mapuche crafts and jewelry.

Although the town may not have all of the amenities for tourists that are available in Pucón, there are plenty of places to stay here. Most lodging options are also less expensive than in more touristy areas. There are a number of pleasant cafés and shops here and, seeing as there's a volcano in plain view, hot springs are nearby. If you get a license, you can also fish in the rivers. Updated: Jun 29, 2009.

When to Go

Villarrica has a humid, temperate climate. The wettest months are in fall and winter (May to July). The drier months are in summer, from December through February. Temperatures average 24 – 28°C (75 – 83 °F). Summertime is when the population of Villarrica swells with tourists seeking outdoor fun and festivals. In January and February, you can catch Jornadas Musicales y Culturales de Villarrica (showcases of the city's varied traditions), Muestra Cultural Mapuche (indigenous artisan works, food, music and storytelling) and the Raid Interlagos (numerous sporting events, including a triathlon). For a complete schedule of the season's events, visit www.villarrica.org. Updated: Dec 18, 2008.

Getting To and Away From Villarrica

All the bus companies in Villarrica are grouped on Bilboa and Anfión Muñoz. **Tur-Bus**, **Jac** and **Pullman Bus** have their own offices. Other outfits leave from a terminal at the corner of Muñoz and Valdivia.

To Santiago: All buses leave 8:30 – 10:30 p.m., 9 – 10 hours. **Jac** (2 buses, $43 – 70), **Pullman** (2 departures, $24 – 28), **TurBus** (6 buses, $20 regular, $90 supercama). Also **Interbus**, **Cóndor**.

To Viña del Mar: **Cóndor** (daily 8:30 p.m., $24).

To Temuco: 1.5 hours. **Jac** (every 20 minutes 6:30 a.m. – 9:30 p.m., $3.40), **Buses Villarrica** (hourly, $2.60).

To Pucón: 30 minutes, $1.40. **Jac** (daily, every 20 minutes 6 a.m. – 9 p.m.), **Vipún Ray** (Monday – Saturday, every 10 minutes 6:30 a.m. – 8:30 p.m.)

To Licán Ray, Coñaripe: $1.40 / $2. **Transporte Coñaripe** (half-hourly 7:30 a.m. – 6:30 p.m.), **Jac** (every 30 – 60 minutes).

To Loncoche: Jac (every 30 – 60 minutes, 7:15 a.m – 9 p.m.).

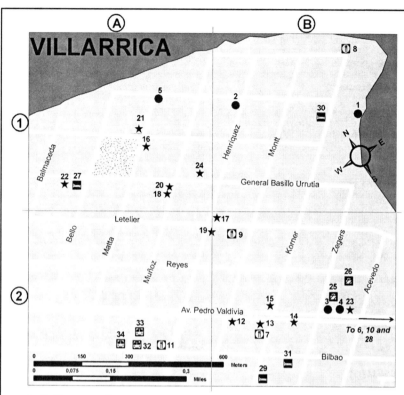

Activities ●

1 Boat Tours B1
2 Cathedral B1
3 Centro Cultural Mapuche B2
4 Museo Arqueológico Municipal B2
5 Museo de Leandro Penchulef A1
6 Parque Natural Dos Rios B2

Eating 🍴

7 Feria Anexo La Artesanal B2
8 Mirador del Lago B1
9 Restauro-Bar The Travellers B2
10 Supermercado Eltit B2
11 Supermercado Unimarc A2

Services ★

12 Banco BCI B2
13 Banco de Chile B2
14 Banco del Estado B2
15 Banco Santander B2
16 Carabineros A1
17 Casas de Cambio B2
18 Chilexpress A1
19 Conaf A2

20 Correos de Chile A1
21 Hospital A1
22 Oficina Cámara de Turismo A1
23 Oficina Municipal de Turismo B2
24 Todo Lavado A1

Shopping 🖼

25 Artesanal Huimpay B2
26 Feria Artesanal B2

Sleeping 🛏

27 Asociación de Hospedaje y Cabañas A1
28 Camping Los Castaños B2
29 Hostal Don Juan B2
30 Hotel Yachting Kiel B1
31 Torre Suiza B2

Transportation 🚍

32 Jac Bus
33 Pullman Bus
34 Tur Bus

To Valdivia, Osorno, Puerto Varas, Puerto Montt: **Jac** (6 departures 8:50 a.m. – 7:10 p.m., $3.20 / $10.80 / $12.20 for both Puertos Varas and Montt).

To Junín and San Martín de los Andes, Argentina: **InterBus** (Monday, Wednesday, Friday, 9:45 a.m., $30).

Note: There is neither air nor train service to Villarrica. You will have to arrive by bus or private vehicle. Updated: Dec 18, 2008.

Getting Around
Three routes of *busetas*, or microbuses, circle the city ($0.60). Another way to get around is by collective taxis, which also have set routes ($0.70) and regular taxis ($2.20, set fare). The only place to rent a bicycle is at **Hostal Torre Suizo**. Lastly, you can stroll the city on foot; just watch out for traffic and only walk during the daytime. Updated: Dec 18, 2008.

Services
TOURISM
For information about what to see and do in Villarrica, drop by the **Oficina Municipal de Turismo** (daily 8:30 a.m. – 1 p.m., 2:30 – 6 p.m. Pedro de Valdivia 1070. Tel: 56-45-20-6619, E-mail: turismo@villarrica.org, URL: www.villarrica.org) or the **Oficina Cámara de Turismo** (daily 9 a.m. – 1 p.m., 3 p.m. – 7 p.m. Urrutia s/n, near the Plaza de Armas. Tel: 56-45-414174, URL: www.turismovillarrica.cl).

The **police station** is also on the Plaza de Armas (Matta 230. Tel: 56-45-411433). **Conaf** dispenses brochures and maps of the area's national parks (Monday – Friday 8:30 a.m. – 5 p.m. Henríquez 430. Tel: 56-45-412379). Fishing licenses for Villarrica or Licán Ray can be obtained from the **Trámite Fácil** office next to the Municipalidad (Anfión Muñoz, half-block from Pedro de Valdivia).

MONEY
All banks in Villarrica are located on the 700-block of Pedro de Valdivia:

• **Banco de Chile**—ATM: MasterCard, Cirrus
• **Santander**—ATM: MasterCard, Cirrus, Visa, Plus
• **BBVA**—ATM: Visa, Plus
• **BCI**—ATM: MasterCard, Cirrus, Visa, Plus
• **Banco del Estado** (Valdivia 957)—ATM: MasterCard, Cirrus

To exchange U.S. dollars or euros, head for **Banco del Estado** or to one of the *casas de cambio* on the 500-block of Henríquez. For Western Union wires, **Chilexpress**, next to the post office, is the local agent (Monday – Friday 9 a.m. – 2 p.m., 3:30 – 7 p.m., Saturday 10 a.m. – 1 p.m. Anfión Muñoz 315. Tel: 56-45-411426).

KEEPING IN TOUCH
Correos de Chile is where to go to send a postcard of this region's stunning lakes and volcanoes (Monday – Friday 9 a.m. – 1 p.m., 2:30 – 6 p.m., Saturday 9 a.m. – 1 p.m. Anfión Muñoz 315). Places where you can access the **Internet** and **phone** are most common on Pedro de Valdivia, especially on the 600 block.

MEDICAL
Villarrica's **hospital** is on the Plaza de Armas (San Martín 460. Tel: 56-45-411169). Most **pharmacies** are on the 400 and 500 blocks of Calle Henríquez.

LAUNDRY
There are several laundromats, including **San José** (Matta 725. Tel: 56-45-411328), **Todo Lavado** (Urrutia 644. Tel: 56-45-414452) and **Villarrica** (Bello 348. Tel: 56-45-412052). Expect to pay $3 and up per kilo for wash and dry.

SHOPPING
Local artisans specialize in all manner of wood crafts, from furniture to kitchen utensils, from games and huge knitting needles. Many of the artisan "malls" only open in the mid-December through February high season. The largest is the **Feria Artesanal**, located behind the municipal tourism information office. **Artesanal Huimpay** is open all year (Zegers, between Valdivia and Reyes). Updated: Dec 18, 2008.

Things to See and Do
Like anywhere in the Lake District, salmon and trout fishing is excellent in Lago Villarrica. Villarrica is graced with three beaches: Playa Pucara and El Pescadito right in town, and Playa Blanca on the other side of the Río Toltén. In summer, boat tours leave from the pier at the north end of Avenida Costanera ($6 per person). Another outdoor activity is to climb Mirador Canela.

In the cultural realm, Villarrica has a Mapuche cultural center and two museums. The Museo Arqueológico Municipal conducts city tours in the summer Monday – Saturday at 10 a.m. The Catedral, built between 1950 and 1958, has two interesting paintings by the Italian artist Giulio di Girdamo (Henríquez and O'Higgins).

Centro Cultural Mapuche—
Wenteche Mapu

(ADMISSION: Free) Wenteche Mapu is a Mapuche cultural center in the heart of Villarrica, where visitors can learn about the customs and religious beliefs of this indigenous nation. In the center of the compound is a *ruka*, or traditional round hut. Center officials occasionally give presentations.The grounds are surrounded by stands where families sell cheese, jams, plants, weavings, carvings and jewelry. After shopping and watching presentations, grab a bite of traditional Mapuche cooking at the eatery in the corner. Daily 10 a.m. – 5 p.m. Valdivia and Zegers. URL: www.villarrica.org. Updated: Dec 18, 2008.

Parque Natural Dos Rios

Zip lines, rafting, fly fishing, trips to the rainforest, tours in restored "citroneta" Citroen 2CVs are just a few of the family-friendly activities offered at the Parque Natural Dos Rios, owned by a German couple, Dagmar and Ralf. Dagmar also offers world-class horseriding lessons in a fully outfitted indoor riding hall (a good way to pass a rainy day) and will introduce the kids to the farm animals, from rabbits to llamas. Accommodation is available in cabins with space for 6 to 8 people, starting at $122 per night. Sector Putue Alto, Casilla 535. Tel: 56-9-4198064, E-mail: info@dosrios.de, URL: www.dosrios.de. Updated: Feb 02, 2009

Villarrica's Museums

Museo de Leandro Penchulef, of the Pontífica Universidad Católica de Chile, has an impressive collection of Mapuche weavings, ceramics, woodcarvings and silver jewelry. Founded with the cooperation of the indigenous community, their customs, culture and beliefs are explained in Spanish and Mapudungun. Guides also discuss the history of Mapuche-Chilean relations. Entrance is free. Monday – Friday 8:30 a.m. – 12:30 p.m., 2:30-6 p.m. Ca. Matta and Av. O'Higgins.

Museo Arqueológico Municipal (Museo Mapuche) (ADMISSION: $0.40) above the public library has several rooms with artifacts from the Mapuche and immigrant populations of Villarrica as well as an interesting collection

of maps. Monday – Saturday 8:30 a.m. – 1 p.m., 3:30 – 6 p.m. Pedro de Valdivia 1050. Tel: 56-8-9693663, E-mail: historicoarqueologico@gmail.com. Updated: Dec 18, 2008.

Mirador Canela

Villarrica's hustling main drag can get to be a bit too much at times, so it can be refreshing to escape to the natural lookout point Mirador Canela. This vantage provides premium views of Volcán Villarrica, the lake and the headwaters of the Río Toltén. The hill gets its name from Villarrica's Brazilian sister city, Canela, in Estado de Grande de Sol. From Calle Valdivia, catch a *colectivo* taxi ($0.70), or walk along Valdivia (20 minutes). Updated: Dec 18, 2008.

Tours

Several agencies in Villarrica offer tours to the local national parks and hot springs, as well as expeditions to climb Volcán Villarrica, fish, horseback ride, whitewater raft and other outdoor activities. Among these are **Politur** (Anfión Muñoz 647. Tel: 56-45-414547, E-mail: turismo@politur.com, URL: www.politur.com) and **Trancura** (Henríquez, Edificio Villarrica Centro. Tel: 56-45-416436, URL: www.trancura.com). Both of these operators also have offices in the neighboring village of Pucón, where prices are lower due to the intense competition of dozens of tour shops. Updated: Dec 18, 2008.

Lodging

Villarrica has hotels that are open all year long; most *hospedajes* (family homestays) and cabins are closed from March to December. The **Asociación de Hospedaje y Cabañas** provides a list of its members' lodging (December – March 10 a.m. – 8 p.m. Urrutia s/n, next to the Oficina Cámara de Turismo). A number of campgrounds and cabins are located on the road from Villarrica to Pucón. The tourism office has a list of them. One that is open year-round is **Camping Los Castaños** (Camino Villarrica-Pucón, Km 1. Tel: 56-45-412330).

Torre Suiza

(ROOMS: $12 – 25)
Housed in a creaky German-style wood house, Torre Suiza is an excellent base for excursions around the Chilean Lake District. The Swiss owners, who bicycled around the world before settling down in Villarica, make every effort to provide the comfort and service an independent traveler might need. The homemade bread, fresh fruit and yogurt make for a delicious breakfast, which is included in the price. There are some rooms with private bathrooms,

as well as several with shared bathroom facilities, including 24 hour hot water. There is also a unisex dormitory and kitchen facilities. Francisco Bilbao 969. Tel: 56-45-411213, E-mail: info@torresuiza.com. Updated: Feb 22, 2009.

Hostal Don Juan

(ROOMS: $14 – 56, CABINS: $36 – 56) Hostal Don Juan is a pleasant surprise. This modern inn has spacious, well-decorated rooms, with shared or private bathroom. The fully equipped kitchen is available for guests' use, as is the free Internet. Out back there are more rooms, log cabins for two to eight people and a nice patio where you can kick back and relax. Everything is immaculately clean. All this, at an incredibly affordable price, makes it a popular rest stop for delegations, though individual travelers are also welcomed. General Körner 770. Tel: 56-45-411833 / 0356, E-mail: reservas@hostaldonjuan.cl, URL: www. hostaldonjuan.cl. Updated: Dec 18, 2008.

Hotel Yachting Kiel

(ROOMS: $36 – 87) Hotel Yachting Kiel is an inn right across from the village's pier (where, yes, the old yacht can be parked) with unobstructed views of Lago Villarrica Lake and Volcán Villarrica. All the guestrooms of this rambling two-story lodge have balconies and incredible views (the front three having the best). Hotel Yachting Kiel provides the creature comforts its distinguished guests seek: private bathrooms with tubs, carpeting, WiFi and heating. The restaurant downstairs specializes in seafood, with fine dishes like coconut breaded shrimp. General Körner 153. Tel: 56-45-411631, E-mail: restkiel@gmail.com, URL: www.restaurantkiel.cl. Updated: Dec 18, 2008.

Restaurants

Villarrica's dining scene mixes both Chilean and international dishes. The *colación*, or daily special, costs $2.60 – 3.20; full lunches are $6 – 8. Local specialties include homemade chocolates, ice cream and cheeses. A farmers market, **Feria Anexo La Artesanal**, sells produce and cheese, and has several empanada stands (Valdivia and Körner). You can pick up groceries at **Supermarket Unimarc** (Alderete and Bilboa). **Supermercado Eltit** is on the road out of town toward Pucón and is a more convenient shop for campers (Saturnino Epulef 1504).

Grapa

(LUNCH SPECIAL: $3, Á LA CARTE: $2 – 3) Grapa—meaning "Gracias Padre" or Thank you, Father—is owned by an Argentine-Chilean couple and is both intimate and bright. An outdoor patio in back provides an au fresco space. Monday to Saturday a lunch menu (salad, main dish) is served noon – 3 p.m. At other times sandwiches are offered. No alcohol is on tap here—only sodas and juices. Open Monday – Saturday 8 a.m. – 11 p.m., Sunday 9 a.m. – 10 p.m. Bilboa 1097. Updated: Dec 18, 2008.

Mirador del Lago

(ENTREES: $10.50 – 15) On a point of land jutting into Lago Villarrica, you might spot a modern wooden building known as Mirador del Lago. This bistro has fantastic views of the lake and the Villarrica and Llaima volcanoes. The ground floor deck and second floor balcony are also good places to observe birds while enjoying a beer or a meal. Mirador del Lago offers mostly steaks, though you'll also find lake-fresh salmon on the menu.. Side dishes cost extra. Open Monday – Saturday noon – 10 p.m., Sunday noon – 4:30 p.m. Prat 880. Tel: 56-6-8474980. Updated: Dec 22, 2008.

Restauro-Bar The Travellers

(ENTREES: $6 – 14) This diner's menu is just as international as its clientele, with Italian, Mexican, Thai and Indian cuisine. There are also Chinese dishes for two. Vegetarians have quite a few entrées they can enjoy. The ambiance is stylish with retro and vanguard music. Only à la carte dishes are available. Open daily 10 a.m. – 3 a.m.; lunch served 1 – 4 p.m., dinner 8 p.m. – midnight. Letelier 753. Tel: 56-45-413617, E-mail: intertravellers@hotmail.com, URL: www.thetravellers. cl. Updated: Jul 08, 2009.

PUCÓN

 220m   21,800   45

The tiny tourist town of Pucón has more to offer than picturesque views—though it has those in spades. It's ground zero for adventure tourism in Chile's northern Patagonia region, attracting Chilean and international visitors interested in everything from fair-weather sports such as rafting, trekking, hiking, horseback riding and fly fishing to cold-weather activities like skiing and snowboarding. The town itself consists largely of a few main roads lined with adventure travel guides, outfitters, a few decent restaurants, hostels, and, on the outskirts, some well-equipped and very comfortable cabins.

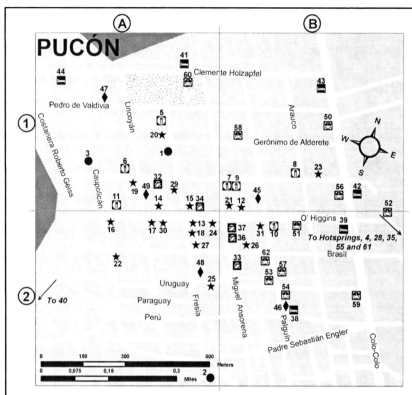

PUCÓN

Activities ●

1 Hiking Experience A1
2 Monasterio Santa Clara A2
3 Museo Mapuche A1

Airports ✝

4 Pucón Airport B2

Eating 🍴

5 Buonatesta A1
6 Madre Tierra A1
7 Restaurant Coronado B1
8 Restaurant !école! B1
9 Ruca Hueney B1
10 Sanguruchos B2
11 Suiza A1

Services ★

12 Ahumada Pharmacy B1
13 Banco Chile A2
14 Banco del Estado A1
15 Banco Santander A1
16 Carabineros (Police) A2
17 Casa de Cambio A2
18 Chilexpress A2
19 Conaf A1
20 Correos Chile (Post Office) A1
21 Cruz Verde Pharmacy B1

22 Cámara de Turismo A2
23 Elena Laundromat B1
24 Galería Artesanal A2
25 Hospital San Francisco A2
26 Magda Laundromat B2
27 Nelly Laundromat A2
28 Pucón Pharmacy B2
29 Relmu Pharmacy A1
30 Sencillito (Casa de Cambios) A2
31 Tourism Office B2

Shopping

32 Alma Verde A1
33 Artesanía El Chucao B2
34 Eltit Supermarket A1
35 Expolibros B2
36 Municipal Market B2
37 Travel Aid B2

Sleeping

38 Backpackers Hostel B2
39 Cabañas Mapulay B2
40 Camping Parque La Poza A2
41 Gran Hotel Pucón A1
42 La Posada del Embrujo B1
43 Paradise Pucón Hostel & Adventure B1
44 Refugio Península A1

THE LAKE DISTRICT

Tours

45 Aguaventura B1
46 Backpackers Adventure B2
47 ITUR A1
48 Language Pucón A2
49 Sol y Nieve A1

Transportation
50 Bicicletería El Pelao B1
51 Centro Sur B2
52 Ciclovía B2

53 Igi Llaima Bus Terminal B2
54 JAC Bus Terminal B2
55 Palguin Bus Depot B2
56 Pucón Rent a Car B1
57 Pullman / Caburga Bus Terminal B2
58 Rent a Car Kilómetro Libre B1
59 San Martín / Centenario Office B2
60 Taxi stands A1
61 Tur Bus Terminal B2
62 Vipuray / Jet Sur Bus Terminal B2

It is possible to walk to almost anywhere, though at night a cheap cab is recommended. Nearby are three major lakes, two national parks and a national reserve, as well as numerous volcanoes. The national parks are filled with several stunningly blue glacial waterfalls and bubbling hot springs, all well worth a tour. The weather can change rapidly here, more often than not from sunny to rainy, so bring appropriate clothing and always have a Plan B in case of inclement weather. It is not uncommon, for instance, for a volcano trek to be canceled at the last minute.

When to Go

The rains in Pucón know no season. They come at any time of the year, though there is less precipitation between October and March. January and February are the driest months. The hottest month is January, with temperatures averaging 12°C (54°F). In July, temperatures drop to 7°C (45°F). In the high season (mid-December through February), prices for lodging, food and other services increase by at least least double.

The biggest event on Pucón's calendar is the Half-Ironman Triathlon in January. A blur of all sorts of other outdoor sporting competitions—from swimming to mountain bike racing on Volcán Villarrica—are hosted in the summer months. Updated: Jan 25, 2009.

Getting To and Away From Pucón

BY BUS

Pucón has no main bus terminal. Most depots are on Palguín, near Uruguay. At this intersection you'll also find a shop and agencia de buses, selling tickets for **Tas-Choapa, Igi Llaima, Condor, Bío Bío, InterSur** and other companies.

Away from the center of town are **TurBus** (Monday – Saturday 9 a.m. – 1 p.m., 3 p.m. – 7 p.m., Sunday and holidays 10 a.m. – 1 p.m.,

4 p.m. – 7 p.m. O'Higgins 910) and **San Martín / Centenario** (Monday – Saturday 10 a.m. – 1 p.m., 4 p.m. – 7 p.m. Colo Colo 612).

To Caburgua: Bus Caburgua (daily 7 a.m., 1:30 p.m., 5:30 p.m., more departures Sundays and holidays, last back 6:30 p.m., 1 hour, $2.80).

To Curarrehue: Vipu Ray (Monday – Saturday every 15 minutes, Sunday half-hourly, $1.40).

To Villarrica: 30 minutes, $1.40. **Vipu Ray** (half-hourly, 6:30 a.m.-8 p.m.), **Jac** (every 10 minutes 6 a.m.-10.15 p.m.).

To Temuco: Jac (every 20 minutes 6 a.m.-10 p.m., 2 hours, $4.40).

To Los Angeles: Jac (daily 8 a.m., 4 hours, $1.40).

To Chillán: Jac (daily 8 a.m., 6 hours, $17.40).

To Santiago: 10-11 hours. TurBus (9:15 a.m., 1 p.m. plus 5 buses 11 a.m. – 5:45 p.m., $22 – 58), **Pullman** (8 p.m., 9 p.m., $24 – 40), **InterSur** (9:45 a.m., $20), **Jac** (8 a.m., 3 buses 8:15 a.m. – 9 p.m., $43 – 70). Also Condor. Some companies continue to Viña del Mar and Valparaíso.

To Puerto Montt: (6 hours, $12 – 14) Many buses stop at Valdivia (3 hours, $6 – 7), Osorno (4 hours, $12), Puerto Varas (5.5 hours, $14): **TurBus** (4 buses 1:45 – 3:45 a.m., 5 buses 11 a.m. – 5:45 p.m.), **Jac** (6:15 a.m., 8:10 a.m., 11:10 a.m., 1:30 p.m., 3:45 p.m.).

To San Martín de los Andes, Argentina: Reserve one day before, 5 – 5.5 hours, $20. **San Martín / Centenario** (Daily 10:30 a.m.), **Igi Llaima** (Monday, Wednesday, Friday 10:15 a.m.).

THE LAKE DISTRICT

BY AIR

Pucón's airfield is five kilometers (3 mi) from the city. It is only open January – February and some long weekend holidays. The next nearest airport with year-round service is 125 kilometers (78 mi) away in Temuco. Both **Lan** and **Skyline** fly into Pucón. Updated: Jan 25, 2009.

Getting Around

Pucón has no public transport system except *colectivo* taxis, which have fixed routes ($0.70). Four private taxi companies run people around town. Catch a cab at a taxi stand or call Radio Taxis (Tel: 56-45-442222 / 2322; to Cuevas Volcánicas with two-hour wait $44, airport transfer to Pucón airfield $10, to Temuco's airport $80. Prices are for up to four passengers).

No international car rental company has offices in Pucón. A half-dozen local agencies fill this market, like **Pucón Rent a Car** (Av. Colo Colo 340. Tel: 56-44-3052, E-mail: info@puconrentacar.cl, URL: www.puconrentacar.cl), **Rent a Car Kilómetro Libre** (Alderete 480. Tel: 56-45-444399, E-mail: kilometrolibre@tie.cl, URL: www.rentacarkilometrolibre.cl) and **Centro Sur** (O'Higgins 575. Tel: 56-45-441303, E-mail: tur.centrosur@gmail.com). You can rent everything from compact cars to 4x4 pickup trucks. Consider road conditions to your destinations when choosing a vehicle. Expect to pay about $35 – 40 per day for a compact, $90 per day for an SUV. Check about insurance and mileage policies. Weekly rates are more economical.

Renting a bike is easy in Pucón. See Mountain Biking for more information. Bikers can find spare parts at **Bicicletería El Pelao**, which also has a repair shop (Colo Colo. Tel: 56-45-449044). Updated: Jan 25, 2009.

Safety

If you are planning climbing or multi-day treks in Villarrica or Huerquehue national park, notify the **Conaf** office in Pucón. Villarrica is one of Chile's most active volcanoes. The municipalidad has a stoplight, the color of which indicates the present danger level of volcanic eruption. Instructions of what to do in case of evacuation are also posted. Signs throughout the town show evacuation routes. Follow officials' instructions. Updated: Jan 26, 2009.

Services

TOURISM

Pucón's municipal tourism office has good information about what to do, how to get around and suggestions for lodging and camping (Daily 8:30 a.m. – 7 p.m. Municipalidad, O'Higgins and Palguín. Tel: 56-45-293003). The **Cámara de Turismo** is another excellent place to go for information (Low season daily 9 a.m. – 1:30 p.m., 4 p.m. – 7 p.m.; High season daily 9 a.m. – 10 p.m. Brasil and Caupolicán. Tel: 56-45-441671, info@puconturismo.cl). Other offices are: **Conaf** (Lincoyán 336. Tel: 56-45-443781), **Carabineros** (O'Higgins s/n. Tel: 56-45-441196, Emergency: 133). Useful websites include: www.puconline.cl, www.interpatagonia.com and www.puconturismo.cl. *Found in Chile* is an English-language tri-monthly publication about what to do and see in the Pucón area and has useful information for travelers. It's free and can be picked up in many shops around town.

MONEY

Most banks are on O'Higgins, unless otherwise noted; hours are Monday – Friday 9 a.m. – 2 p.m:

• **Banco del Estado** (no. 240) — ATM: MasterCard, Cirrus; exchanges U.S. dollars, euros
• **Banco de Chile** (no. 311) — ATM: Visa, Plus
• **Santander** (no. 318) — ATM: MasterCard, Cirrus, Visa, Plus, American Express
• **BCI** (Fresia 174) — ATM: MasterCard, Cirrus, Visa, Plus

All *casas de cambio* likewise are on O'Higgins. All exchange U.S. dollars and euros; some handle other currencies:

• **Sencillito** (Monday – Saturday 11 a.m. – 6:30 p.m. O'Higgins , between Lincoyán and Fresia)
• **Casa de Cambio** (Monday – Saturday 9 a.m. – 10 p.m. O'Higgins 291, Local C)—also changes Argentine peso and other currencies
• **Galería Artesanal** (Monday – Saturday 9 a.m. – 8 p.m. O'Higgins 335c)—also changes travelers checks, Argentine pesos, Brazilian real, pounds sterling and other currencies.

The Western Union agent is **Chilexpress** (Monday – Friday 9 a.m. – 1:30 p.m., 3:30 p.m. – 7 p.m., Saturday 10 a.m. – 1:30 p.m., O'Higgins 524 and Fresia).

MEDICAL

Hospital San Francisco has a German-speaking doctor on staff, as well as several medical personnel who understand English (Uruguay 325. Tel: 56-45-441177). The town follows a *farmacia de turno* system, in which different drugstores are open all night. The list is posted at all pharmacies. **Ahumada** and **Cruz Verde** are on the

THE LAKE DISTRICT

300 and 400 block of O'Higgins. **Relmu** (Fresia 354) and **Pucón** (Camino Internacional 2000) are other providers.

LAUNDRY

Pucón seems to have as many Laundromats as it has tour agencies. They charge a uniform fee of $7 for two to four kilograms of clothes, $10 for five to seven and $14 for eight to 10 kilos. Get the clothes in early enough and they will be ready by the end of the day. Some *lavanderías* are **Nelly** (Monday – Saturday 10 a.m. – 1 p.m., 3 p.m. – 7 p.m. Brasil and Fresia. Tel: 56-45-449001), **Elena** (Monday – Friday 10:30 a.m. – 1 p.m., 4 p.m. – 6 p.m., Saturday 10:30 a.m. – 2 p.m. Urrutia 620) and **Magda** (Monday – Saturday 10 a.m. – 1:30 p.m., 3:30 p.m. – 7:30 p.m. Brasil 420). Updated: Jul 06, 2009.

SHOPPING

Artesanía El Chucao carves stunning wood sculptures of birds (Daily 9:30 a.m. – 8 p.m. Ansorena 565, Local 1. Tel: 56-45-444339, URL: www.chucao.cl). In the same building are many other artisans with stalls exhibiting their wood, wool and other crafts. The **municipal market** is another space almost entirely devoted to the sale of woolens. Elizabeth Poveda creates fine silver and lapis lazuli jewelry, some of Mapuche design (Daily 11 a.m. – 9 p.m. Fresia 295. Tel: 56-45-449530, E-mail: elisjoyas@hotmail.com).

Travel Aid has an excellent selection of road and topographical trekking maps, plus some travel and nature guides. It also sells Argentine car insurance and books tickets for boats deep into Patagonia. The staff speaks English and German (Monday – Saturday 9 a.m. – 8 p.m Ansorena 425, Local 4. Tel: 56-45-444040, E-mail: info@travelaid.cl, URL: www.travelaid.cl). **Expolibros** has a better selection of nature and travel guides, as well as maps, books on local history and works in English (Daily 10 a.m. – 2 p.m., 4 p.m. – 8 p.m. O'Higgins 415, local 3-B. Tel: 56-45-444819).

You can buy or rent fishing tackle from **Alma Verde** (Monday – Saturday 10:45 a.m. – 2 p.m., 4 p.m. – 8 p.m. Urrutia 283. Tel: 56-9-8693016, URL: www.almaverde.cl / www.flyfishingchile.cl). This shop also has classes in fly fishing and organizes expeditions. For stove gas, kayak gear and camping equipment, stop by **Hiking Experience**. It also carries Nautika, Trespass and GoreTex brands (Daily 9 a.m. – 8.30 p.m. Fresia 248, Local 6). Updated: Jan 25, 2009.

Things to See and Do

Pucón is internationally famous for its trekking, volcano climbing, rafting, kayaking, thermal pools and winter sports, as well as birdwatching and fly fishing opportunities. The Mapuche museum and nearby villages can give you a peek into this native culture. A visit to the *cuevas volcánicas* (volcanic caves) will teach you how lava flows (Daily 10 a.m. – 7 p.m. Km 14.5 Camino al Volcán).

Pucón also has sky diving opportunities. One such outfit is **Skydive Pucón** (Aeropuerto Pucón. Tel: 56-9-8200194 / 9360687, E-mail: peter.vermehren@gmail.com, URL: www.skydivepucón.cl). If you're looking for something a bit less stressful, shoot a round at **Mini Golf Alü Antü** (Km 3.5 Camino Internacional, URL: www.minigolfpucon.cl). You can also take leisurely tours around the lake in Vapor Chucao, a 1905 steamship, or in a pedal boat. Updated: Jul 07, 2009.

Monasterio Santa Clara

(ADMISSION: Free) From the far south end of Calle Ansorena, a narrow road passes through a gate, curving to the hill top Monasterio Santa Clara. The plain chapel is dramatically backdropped by Volcán Villarrica. The patio in front provides breathtaking views of the lake and surrounding countryside. Next to the church is a small shop where Capuchin Poor Clare nuns sell their chocolates, cookies, embroidery and other articles. To get there, head south on Calle Ansorena, to the monastery's gate. Monday – Saturday 9 a.m. – noon, 3 p.m – 7 p.m. Updated: Jan 26, 2009.

Museo Mapuche

(ADMISSION: $3) In the lower level of the Hotel Araucaria, you'll find a history of the Mapuche people, native to this Land of Lakes. Once, not too long ago, these lands were their independent nation, fiercely defended against the invading Spaniards and Chileans. In this small museum—a family's private collection, painstakingly gathered over the years—you can learn about the silver jewelry, stone clavas, or staffs of power, wood carving and other crafts that played significant roles in Mapuche culture and society. Caupolicán 243. Tel: 56-45-441963, E-mail: gonzalo@araucarias.cl, URL: www.museomapuche.cl. Updated: Jan 26, 2009.

Circuito Termal

(PRICE: $8 – 16) After a long day of skiing or climbing Volcán Villarrica, a good way to relax strained muscles is to immerse yourself in one of the eight major hot springs near Pucón. Most are open 9 a.m. – 9 p.m., a few until 10 p.m.; Los Pozones is open all night. You can reach the springs by way of a tour or private transportation. There are three on the Camino Internacional to Curarrehue:

• **Menetúe**, with three covered and three open-air pools filled with 28 – 40°C (82 – 104°F) water, a spa, cabins and horseback riding (Km 30. Tel: 56-45-441877, URL: www.menetue.com. Entry: $15).

• **Trancura**, with six pools at 33 – 40°C (91 – 104°F), canopy, tours and cabins (Km 32. Tel: 56-45-441189, URL: www.trancura.com. Entry: $10).

• **San Luis**, with one covered and several open air pools at 36 – 39°C (97 – 102°F), sauna, spa, cabins and restaurant (Km 32. Tel: 56-45-412880, URL: www.termasde-sanluis.cl. Entry $14).

On the unpaved road to Huife, northeast of Pucón, is another trio of springs:

• **Quimey-Co** offers Jacuzzi, sauna and massage along with six pools of 38 – 46°C (100 – 114°F) (Km 30. Tel: 56-45-444091, URL: www.termasquimeyco.com. Entry $10).

• **Huife** is a full-service spa with hotel, massage, restaurant and swimming-pool-style hot springs (28 – 39°C / 84 – 102°F) (Km 33. Tel: 56-45-441222, URL: www.termashuife.cl. Entry: $16).

• **Los Pozones** is a favorite for its natural pools (20 – 45°C / 68 – 113°F) surrounded by forests. It is open all night (Km 36. Tel: 56-45-1972350, URL: www.pozoneshuife-alto.cl. Entry $8 – 10).

The other two hot springs are more difficult to reach. **Liucura**, two kilometers off the road to Caburgua, has two open-air and one roofed pools, as well as three tubs (25 – 28°C / 77 – 82°F). **Río Blanco** is on the far side of Parque Huerquehue. Its three natural pools (35-40°C / 95-104°F) are embraced by emerald forest; lodging in family homes and camping are available (URL: www.miropu-con.cl. Entry: $8). Updated: Jan 26, 2009.

Paddling

(PRICE: $40 – 60, LESSONS: $70 – $110) Take your pick of how you want to traverse the rivers that wind through Pucón's countryside.

Of course, whitewater rafting trips down the Liucura (to Class III rapids) and Trancura (Class III-IV) are a popular option. Kayaking is another way to paddle around Río Liucura or Lago Villarrica. Many tour operators in Pucón rent kayaks and some host classes. Other rafting and kayaking rivers are the Puesco (Class V) Maichín (IV-V) and San Pedro. Purists might object to the ducky—an inflatable kayak that shoots rapids like a raft. But the ultimate insanity (some may declare) is hydrospeeding, or bodyboarding down the tumultuous ríos. Most tour operators offer rafting excursions. Travelers looking for a milder river experience can rent a paddle or rowboat down on Playa La Poza ($6 – 8 half hour, $10 full hour). Vapor Chucao, a 1905 steamship, tours the lake. (Bahía La Poza dock. Tel: 56-45-443386, E-mail: info@vaporchucao.cl, URL: www.va-porchucao.cl. Entry: adults $9, children $5). Updated: Jan 26, 2009.

Horseback Riding

(PRICE: $30 – 70) Leave the hiking boots and kayaks aside to take in the spectacular scenery of Pucón from the saddle, swaying with the rhythm of your horse. This is also a wonderful way to meet the huasos or campesinos and to view the Mapuche indigenous villages of the Pucón region. Some common destinations are Liucura and Quelhue. Traveling by horseback is also a good way to get to some of the more out-of-the-way natural wonders, like Salto El Claro, Cañi Cordillera and Laguna El Espejo. Some stables arrange not only half-day and full-day excursions, but also multi-day explorations of this land's hidden treasures. Try Campo Atilco (Antilco, near Pucón. Tel: 56-9-7139758, E-mail: info@atilco.com, URL: www.antilco.com) or Huepilmalal (Km 27, Camino Pucón-Termas de Huife. Tel: 56-9-6432673, E-mail: info@huepilmalal.cl. Updated: Jul 06, 2009.

Mountain Biking Near Pucón

There are many natural wonders in the countryside around Pucón. Some are only accessible in private vehicle—or by bike. Popular day outings include the waterfalls

Ojos de Caburgua, the Cuevas Volcánicas, a series of cascades on the road to Palguín and the hot springs. You can also visit indigenous villages.

The Ciclovía is the beginning of many journeys. Cycling maps are available from most bike rental shops. The Ciclovía begins on O'Higgins, just east of Calle Colo Colo. Quite a few places lease bikes. Businesses along O'Higgins tend to be more expensive.On average, the cost is $5 per hour, $9 for half day (four hours), $14 for a full day (10 hours). **Pucón Rent a Car** has a biking map on its website. In early December there is a mountain bike race in Pucón; for more information check www.epuwun.cl. Updated: Jul 06, 2009.

Los Ojos del Caburga Waterfalls

Los Ojos del Caburga, a beautiful set of waterfalls that tumbles into a circular pool, 21 kilometers (13 mi) from Pucón, is an easy bike ride. Pick up bikes and a map from one of the tour companies in town and head out through charming villages, over a suspension bridge and into the mountains. The terrain becomes rougher and you will occasionally have to carry your bike over the bumpy bits before arriving at the picturesque pool area, but it is worth the effort and you can reward yourself by picking up a well-earned apple strudel on the way back. Updated: Feb 02, 2009.

Villarrica Volcano

You can only climb Villarica if the active volcano is not on alert. You absolutely need to go with a guide, whose company will lend you the necessary equipment, such as crampons and an ice-axe. The ascent is grueling and often snowy, but you can save yourself some effort by taking a bus to the ski station at the foot of the mountain, before taking a chairlift. From the top of the lift, it is a tough but not technical climb to the summit at 2847 meters (9,340 ft) and you will be rewarded with striking views of the bubbling lava lake in the cone. Updated: Feb 02, 2009.

Reserva Forestal Cañi

The 500-hectare Cañi park, owned by the foundation Lahuén and managed by a community organization, is a sanctuary for the giant conifer Auracaria, or monkey-puzzle tree, one the oldest trees on earth. The Foundation operates the Hostel Ecole, with a very comfortable lounge area, and functions as an informal tour company. A nice trek takes you high up along two lakes to a vantage point with spectacular views over the Villarrica area and to the Argentine border. In the winter, you need to strap on snow shoes to make your way up a very steep hill, through the vast expanse of snow. URL: www.santuariocani.cl. Updated: Jul 07, 2009.

Studying Spanish

ITUR

To really learn about Pucón and the surrounding region, consider enrolling in ITUR's study abroad Spanish language program, which combines academic classes with outdoor adventures and cross-cultural exchanges. Working with the Universidad de la Frontera and the Instituto EuroChileno de Turismo, ITUR offers credited programs in Spanish plus ecology and environmental studies, volcanology, interpretation of cultural heritage, and history

THE LAKE DISTRICT

Photo by Eszter Sára Kóspái

and contemporary studies. Students can also learn how to mountain climb or paddle, with additional first aid and outdoor technique courses. Lincoyán 77. Tel: 56-45-444104, Fax: 56-45-444204, E-mail: myunge@itur.cl. URL: www.itur.cl. Updated: Jul 02, 2009.

Language Pucón
The breadth of outdoor activities may tempt you to stay in Pucón for longer than planned. Language Pucón has special programs to help travelers navigate the road ahead, in one-on-one or group settings. It also arranges homestays. Language Pucón steps beyond the boundaries of Chile's Spanish-based culture, teaching students about Mapuche traditions. Uruguay 306. Tel: 56-45-464062. E-mail: school@languagepucon.com, URL: www.languagepucon.com. Updated: Jan 25, 2009.

Tours
There are tour operators on every block in Picon, where you can arrange to go up the volcano, down the whitewater rivers or out to the hot springs. Avenida O'Higgins is virtually packed with these offices, from one end of the boulevard to the other. Several extend services to skiing, snowboarding and other winter sports. A few agencies, though, have other specialties, like fly fishing and birdwatching tours. With the plethora of tour agencies available, it can be hard to choose; check with several and ask around before settling on one. Updated: Jan 25, 2009.

Backpackers Adventure
Backpackers Adventure is considered by many as one of the better companies for ascending Volcán Villarrica. The guides and assistants are experienced in the ascent, and pay attention to those excursionists who may fall behind. Volcanic and weather conditions permitting, this agency also does night ascents. Backpackers doesn't just do the volcano, however. It also arranges hydrospeeding and rafting trips, horseback rides and canopying. You can, as well, rent a bike. One of Backpackers' most popular outings is the nighttime visit to Los Pozones, to bathe beneath the stars. Backpackers Adventures has special discounts for Israelis. Palguín 695-675. Tel: 56-45-441417, E-mail: info@backpackerspucon.com, URL: www.backpackerspucon.com. Updated: Jan 26, 2009

Sol y Nieve
In the afternoon, people hang out in front of Sol y Nieve, exchanging stories about their day's adventures and preparing for the post-event barbecue. Some have climbed Volcán Villarrica (an excursion for which Sol y Nieve is known). Others have shot the rapids on the Trancura River or gone hydrospeeding on the Liucura. Horseback rides to Calabozos, El Claro or Sierra Madre are also on the agenda. Sol y Nieve also takes their clients out to a choice of local hot springs. Lincoyán 361. Tel: 56-45-444761 / 56-9-9328209. E-mail: info@solynievepucon.cl. URL: www.solynievepucon.cl. Updated: Jan 26, 2009.

Aguaventura
Aguaventura focuses on water in all its forms. This tour operator can take you rafting, ducky-ing, hydrospeeding, kayaking, canoeing or fly fishing on the rushing rivers and still lakes. Aguaventura also leads climbing expeditions up Volcán Villarrica. In the winter season, it has one of Pucón's best selections of skis, snowshoes, snowboards and other equipment for rent. Aguaventura also arranges trips to the hot springs. The company organizes rappelling, canopy, horseback riding and other activities, sells trekking maps and has free Internet. Palguín 336. Tel: 56-45-444246. E-mail: info@aguaventura.com. URL: www.aguaventura.com. Updated: Jan 26, 2009.

Pucón Birding
Birdwatching is a relaxing alternative to Pucón's overload of outdoor adventure sports. The region has four distinct natural habitats—river, lake, forest and mountain— containing some 70 bird species. The ornithologists of Pucón Birding will take you out to spot these endangered, resident and migratory birds. Tel: 56-45-441011 / 9-843-6654, URL: www.puconbirding.cl. Updated: Jan 25, 2009..

Lodging
Pucón is popular with tourists from all walks of life, and hotels fitting all pocketbooks are easy to find. Mid-range inns are clustered around General Urrutia. Most hostels are located south of Avenida O'Higgins. You can find luxary hotels around the Plaza de Armas. Campgrounds are generally open only January – February. The tourism office publishes a complete list of them every December, available at its office or online: www.municipalidadpucon.cl. Most accommodations at least double their prices in the high season.

Camping Parque La Poza
(CAMPING: $5 – 6 per person) Just steps from Playa La Poza is one of the most beautiful campgrounds in the region, Camping Parque La Poza. There are 45 natural sites

with picnic tables, parking space and electricity. The family has grills you can borrow, or you can use the kitchen, complete with a refrigerator, stove and large dining area. The bathhouse has hot water only in the mornings and evenings. Camping La Poza also has a laundry basin. Av. Costanera Roberto Geis 769. Tel: 56-45-444982 / 56-9-5824947, E-mail: campinglapoza@hotmail.com. Updated: Jan 26, 2009.

Paradise Pucón Hostel & Adventure

(ROOMS: $15 per person) A 15-minute walk from the center of town, Paradise Pucón International Hostel is a two-floor lodge surrounded by lush gardens. Double or triple rooms are available (both with private bathrooms), as are dorm beds with shared bathrooms. Amenities include a large living room, a TV and game room, free Internet, a balcony, a dining room, and a volcanic rock fireplace. Outside you'll find a BBQ, dining tables and hammocks.

The hotel offers heating in the winter, as well as hot water 24 hours a day, laundry service, continental or vegetarian breakfast, healthy meals and delicious homemade desserts. Additional services include travel services, bike rental, luggage storage, parking, ski/snowboard equipment rental, and transportation to ski sites or hot springs. Camino Internacional 1865. Tel: 56-45-441601, E-mail: info@paradisepucon.com. URL: www.paradisepucon.com. Updated: Jul 02, 2009.

Backpackers Hostel

(ROOMS: $10 – 20 per person) As well as running a well-respected tour agency, Backpackers also has a popular hostel. It's a comfortable space with the feel of an outdoors lodge. Most rooms have sturdy bunks (which, in the high season, are filled as dorms), though a few have double beds. The accommodations in the main house share clean bathrooms with hot showers. Off the small garden patio are rooms with private bathrooms. The common kitchen is a welcomed relief to the budget traveler's wallet. In the evenings, trevelers hang out in the living room, sharing information and watching TV, keeping warm by the wood stove. Palguín 695. Tel: 56-45-441417, URL: www.backpackerspucon.com. Updated: Jan 26, 2009.

La Posada del Embrujo

(ROOMS: $14 – 27 per person) The owners of this hostel have a unique greeting for all travelers: "May the fire of the volcano, the rain that cleanses, the force of the winds, the shelter of the forest lead you on the path to the warmth of La Posada del Embrujo." Indeed, this inn is as enchanting as the spell implies. A giant dream catcher hangs above the stairwell to the rooms, dispelling nightmares from travel-weary guests. Each room is named after a goddess from different world religions. Pele, named for the Hawaiian volcano goddess, has spectacular views of Volcán Villarrica. The owners speak French and English. Colo Colo 361. Tel: 56-45-443840, E-mail: info@laposadadelembrujo.cl. Updated: Jan 26, 2009.

Refugio Península

(ROOMS: $20 – 30 per person)At the foot of the peninsula, about two blocks from Pucón's main plaza, is Refugio Península. This Hostelling International member is truly a refuge, with large rooms and clean bathrooms. The shady yard has many places to sit and relax, and there are hammocks along the patio decks. In winter, guests gather around the fire in the common room. Refugio Península is close to both La Poza and Grande Beaches. Holzapfel 11. Tel: 56-45-43398, E-mail: alvaro@refugiopeninsula.cl. Updated: Jan 26, 2009.

Cabañas Mapulay

(CABINS: $52 – 155) For travelers looking for a bit of a retreat from those rushing from one high-octane adventure to another, Cabañas Mapulay may be the place to stay. There are 14 cabins for two and four people set in a grassy yard with lots of shade trees. Each has a TV and DVD (the office has a free video library), a completely equipped kitchen and heating. Cabañas Mapulay is located on the corner of the main street in town and the Camino Internacional, not too far from the TurBus station, and is open all year. O'Higgins 755. Tel: 56-45-441948, Fax: 56-45-441914, E-mail: nducras@mapulay.cl, URL: www.mapulay.cl. Updated: Jan 26, 2009.

Gran Hotel Pucón

(ROOMS: $118 – 276) The Gran Hotel Pucón is the grand lady in this town. This stately five-story spa on the shores of Lago Villarrica has pleasant views of the volcano. The rooms along the backside look out to the lake. The rooms are large with wood floors and picture windows. Along the shore is a terraced garden with ivy trellises where you can enjoy a meal, the sunshine or (in season) a few strokes in the heated pool. If you come in winter, you can still get your laps in at the indoor piscina. The bilingual staff is very attentive. Clemente Holzapfel 190. Tel: 600-700-6000, URL: www.granhotelpucon.cl. Updated: Jan 26, 2009.

THE LAKE DISTRICT

Restaurants

Calle Fresia is restaurant row, especially between the main plaza and O'Higgins. Many eateries raise their prices during the high season (mid-December through February). Some culinary delights to keep an eye out for in Pucón are the home-made ice creams, Belgian-style chocolates, cheeses and jams made of local wild fruits. Salmon, trout, *jabalí* (wild boar) and *ciervo* (venison) are popular main dishes.

Small produce shops are common in town. The Mercado municipal is mostly just artisan stands, though there is a good seafood shop inside. Centrally located Supermercado **Eltit** is the largest supermarket in Pucón (Daily 8:30 a.m. – 9 p.m. O'Higgins 336).

Restaurant Coronado

(DAILY SPECIAL: $3.60 and up, Á LA CARTE $2 and up) One of the cheapest places to eat in Pucón is Coronado. This diner serves up Chilean home cooking: beef, chicken, even salmon. A main dish comes with *sopaipillas* (fried bread) and *pebre* (a fresh tomato-onion relish). Vegetarians aren't left out in the cold here. Lasagna, an assortment of sandwiches and other fare will satisfy their appetites. On a warm day, have your meal on the sidewalk patio. Open Monday – Saturday 8 a.m. – 11 p.m., Sunday 8 a.m. – 9 p.m. Urrutia 417.Tel: 56-45-444290. Updated: Jul 07, 2009.

Sanguruchos

(SANDWICHES $2 – 5.60) If you want to delve into the fascinating world of Chilean sandwiches, Sanguruchos is the place to go. This fast-food eatery will show you how this nation has taken the humble sandwich to the extreme. The featured meat (beef, hamburger or hot dog) comes with all the fixings you could ever dream up—and some you would never imagine, like green beans. Vegetarians are graced with an extensive menu, too. Have an order of fries to complete the meal. Sanguruchos' hours are perfect for the late-night munchies. Open daily noon-1 a.m. Palguín 383. Updated: Jan 26, 2009.

Ruca Hueney

(ENTREES: $3 and up) Ruca Hueney is another one of the inexpensive eateries on Urrutia. It has a pleasant sidewalk café in front. The lunch special ($5) is a two-course affair with drink. In the evening, à la carte dishes are served. The menu includes beef, chicken, pork and pasta preparations with a side.

Travelers on a budget could opt for the cheaper *colación*, a more humble plate. The restaurant serves wine, beer and soda. Open daily 10 a.m. – 11 p.m. or midnight. Urrutia 447. Tel: 56-45-442213. Updated: Jan 26, 2009.

Restaurant ¡école!

(ENTREES: $6 and up) Vegetarians can get wonderful healthy meals at iécole! This cozy restaurant prepares delicious international dishes with fresh local produce. Homemade whole-grain bread accompanies most meals. A fine selection of juices, wines and liquors is available, also. Fridays from 8 or 9 p.m. to close, iécole! hosts an open mic for musicians, poets, storytellers and other traveling performers. iécole! is also an International Hosteling inn, a tour agency and a language school. Open daily 8 a.m. – 11 p.m., lunch special ($5) noon – 3:30 p.m., happy hour 6 p.m. – 9 p.m. Urrutia 592. Tel: 56-45-441675 / 3201, URL: www.ecole.cl. Updated: Jul 01, 2009.

Suiza

(ENTREES: $6 – 13) Sometimes you just have to give in to a bit of temptation, and the Suiza is willing to help. This restaurant is mainly known for it's two dozen flavors of artisan ice cream, including chestnut, amaretto and tiramisu. Suiza also bakes all sorts of delightful confections; cookies and cakes in true Swiss fashion. Have a strong espresso or cappuccino with your sweet. If you need something with more substance, Suiza has a three-course menu featuring turkey, lamb and other not-so-common meats, as well as vegetarian options. Monday – Friday 10 a.m. – 9 p.m., Saturday and Sunday 9 a.m. – 9 p.m. O'Higgins 116. Tel: 56-45-441241. Updated: Jan 27, 2009.

Buonatesta

(PIZZAS: $8 and up, PASTAS: $7) Buonatesta is a bit more than a typical Italian restaurant. Yes, the staff prepares pastas. The restaurant also has a menu with half and full pizzas that have natural tomato sauce and a plethora of toppings, such as tons of gooey cheese. Vegetarians will find plenty to eat here, like spinach-ricotta-walnut stuffed ravioli. But what sets Buonatesta apart is the home-brewed beer: red ale, pale ale and a quite excellent stout. The owner has another branch of Buonatesta (Fresia 243) and Focaccia (Monday, Tuesday noon – 4 p.m., 6 p.m. – 11:30 p.m., Wednesday-Sunday noon – 11:30 p.m. Fresia 161. Tel: 56-45-444821, E-mail: focaccia@somoschile.cl) where they serve the same creations. Buonatesta is open

Monday – Friday noon – 3:30 p.m., 6 p.m. – 11:30 p.m., Saturday and Sunday noon – midnight. Fresia 124. Tel: 56-45-444627 / 56-45-441434, E-mail: buonatesta@somoschile.cl. Updated: Jan 27, 2009.

Madre Tierra

(ENTREES: $9 and up) Madre Tierra has both *cocina de montaña* (mountain cooking) and *cultura* (culture). Working with a palette of local fruits, the chef creates fantastic dishes based on native Mapuche and Spanish, German, Croat and other recipes. *Ciervo* (venison), *jabalí* (wild boar), salmon and trout are specialties, as are regional cheeses, sausages and wild fruit liqueurs. In the restaurant, hand-woven table runners grace the hewn-wood and wrought iron tables. The house red wine is a carmenère. Wednesday – Sunday 12:30 p.m. – 4 p.m., 7 p.m. – 11 p.m. Urrutia 199. Tel: 56-45-449005 / 9099. Updated: Jan 27, 2009.

PARQUE NACIONAL VILLARRICA

Most summertime visitors in Pucón have their eyes set on one goal: to climb the snowy cone of Volcán Villarrica and peek into its glowing crater. This active volcano is just one of the wonders within Parque Nacional Villarrica. The 63,000-hectare park was founded in 1940 to protect local mountains, waterways and plant and animal species. Not only can you scale a simmering volcano, but in the warmer months you can trek through the varied landscapes. More sedate activities include fishing, birdwatching, spotting flora and fauna, and photography. In winter, the park is a wonderland for alpine and cross-country skiing, snowshoeing, snowboarding and other cold-weather sports.

When it comes to geologic features, Parque Nacional Villarrica has it all, with glaciers, and active and dormant volcanoes that have scarred the land with lava fields. It has typical Andean mountain terrain with high peaks and steep gorges. The altitude within the park ranges from 600 meters (1,950 ft) to 3,747 meters (12,178 ft). The highest peaks are Quetrupillán, a.k.a El Mocho, with a truncated cone (2,360 m / 7,670 ft), Rucupillán or Villarrica, which is presently active (2,847 m / 9,253 ft) and Lanín, on the Argentine border (3,747 m/12,178 ft). A low chain of hills, Cerro Las Peinetas, is another attractive feature of the park. The protected area is laced with many streams created by glacier and snow melt-off. Major rivers in Parque Nacional Villarrica are Río Trancura and Río Palguín. Lagoons include Laguna de los Patos (also called Laguna Azul), Laguna Avutardas and Lago Quilleihue. Waterfalls like Salto Pichillancahue tumble down the rugged landscape.

Between all these geological highlights are wetlands (*humedales*), which are favorite haunts for all manner of bird life. Those to keep an eye out for are the Magellanic Woodpecker, Red-gartered Coot, Ruddy Duck, Mallard, White-throated Hawk, Andean condor, Black-chested Buzzard-eagle and the Southern Crested Caracara.

Fauna isn't just limited to feathered creatures. Native nutria, South American grey fox, Chilean miniature deer, puma, Molina's hog-nosed skunk and Austral opossum, as well as the introduced wild pig and red deer, make their home in the park. Native flora include the araucaria (monkey-puzzle tree), willow-leafed podocarp and Antarctic beech.

Parque Nacional Villarrica is divided into three sectors. Each has a ranger station, first aid post and camping. Rucupillán, the nearest to Pucón, is the main ranger post. Volcán Villarrica and the Andarivel Base 5 ski center are here. Quetrupillán, the next sector east, is accessible by dirt road from Termas de Palguín. In winter, this part of the park is closed due to heavy snows. The third sector, Puesco, is on the Camino Internacional to Paso Mamuil Mala on the Argentine border. Except for the hotel and restaurant at the ski lodge, no other conveniences can be found within the park. Overnight visitors must camp and bring their own food supplies. Good camping equipment, warm and waterproof clothing and good sun protection are necessary.

In summer (January – March) temperatures reach 20 – 23°C (68 – 73°F), and drop to 9°C (48°F). In winter, the park experiences lows of 4°C (39°F). Rains occur from March to August, reaching 2,500 – 3,500 millimeters (98.4 – 138 in) per year. Snowfall accumulates to 2 meters (6.5 ft), and from May to November, may affect accessibility to some parts of the park, especially Challupén Chinay trail, from the Rucapillán to Quetrupillán ranger stations. Check with the Conaf office in Pucón for conditions (Lincoyán 336. Tel: 56-45-443781).

Entry for foreigners is $6 for adults, $3 for senior citizens and $2 for children; for Chileans, $3 for adults, $1.50 for seniors and $1 for children. The Conaf administration office in Pucón has a free, excellent topographical map of the park with GPS coordinates. More information about the park may be found at: www.parquenacionalvillarrica.blogspot.com. Updated: Jul 08, 2009.

Getting To and Away From Parque Nacional Villarrica

From Temuco, take Ruta 5 to Freire, then turn off for Villarrica and Pucón (120 kilometers / 72 miles, 1 hour). From Temuco, you can also take a bus to Pucón. Even though Parque Nacional Villarrica is close to Pucón, reaching it by public transportation is difficult. Most sectors can only be reached with a private car.

Sector Rucapillán: Follow the road leading out of Pucón, toward the volcano. After 8 kilometers (5 mi) you'll find the ranger station. There is only public transportation to the ski lodge in the winter.

Sector Quetrupillán: This part of the park is accessible only by private vehicle. From Pucón, go to Palguín. From that village, take the Termas de Palguín road to arrive at the Quetrupillán ranger station. (Distance from Pucón: 150 kilometers / 90 miles, 2 hours).

Sector Puesco: This is the easiest sector to reach, whether with your own vehicle or with public transportation. The Camino Internacional to Paso Mamuil Malal passes near the ranger station for this sector. Several of the trails begin off this highway.

For buses from Pucón to the border, see Getting To and Away from Pucón (p. 297). From Currarrehue, buses depart Monday, Wednesday and Friday for Paso Mamuil Malal. From Coñaripe, there's an unpaved road that enters the park through its southern boundary, to the Quetrupillán post (23 kilometers / 14 miles). This road is transitable only in warm weather, with a high-clearance vehicle. Updated: Feb 17, 2009.

Things to See and Do

Hiking

Parque Nacional Villarrica has over a dozen trails leading visitors to explore the deepest recesses of the park, from wetlands to volcanic craters. Some of the routes are easy; others are challenging and require a guide and special equipment. The most accessible trails are (times and distances one way):

El Mirador de los Cráteres (*Distance:* 4 km / 2.4 mi, *Difficulty:* medium, *Duration:* 1.3 hours). The trail begins from the Rucapillán station, traversing lava fields to a lookout point from which you can see volcanoes Villarrica and Llaima, and the lakes Villarrica, Huilipilún and Caburgua; the forest is predominantly beech trees, with birds such as Andean Condor, White-throated Hawk and Magellanic Woodpecker.

Sendero Cráter del Volcán Villarrica. See Climbing Volcán Villarrica (p.307).

Pichillancahue (*Distance:* 3.3 km / 2 mi, *Difficulty:* easy, *Duration:* 1.3 hours). A self-guided path through beech forest, from the Quetrupillán station to glacier Pichillancahue on the east slope of Volcán Villarrica; besides the mighty smoker, you can also spot Choshuenco and Quetrupillán volcanoes.

A host of trails are accessible from the Camino Internacional to Mamuil Malal border crossing:

Sendero Momolluco (*Distance:* 12.5 km / 7.5 mi, *Difficulty:* medium, *Duration:* 6 hours). This route goes along the Momolluco River and the west slope of Volcán Lanín to Lago Verde. You might spot deer.

Sendero Lagos Andonis (*Distance:* 12 km / 7.2 mi, *Difficulty:* medium, *Duration:* 6 hours). This path winds around the base of Volcán Lanín, and Lagunas Huenfuica, Plato and Perdida before ending at Laguna Quilleihue.

Sendero Fauna (*Distance:* 150 m / 500 ft, *Difficulty:* easy, *Duration:* 30 minutes). This trail leads to Laguna Quilleihue, an important nesting and feeding ground for birds.

Parque Nacional Villarrica has three branches of the Sendero de Chile:

Challupén Chinay (*Distance:* 23 km/ 13.8 m, *Difficulty:* medium, *Duration:* 12 hours, 1260-1550 m/4095-5038 ft altitude). This path curves around the base of Volcán Villarrica, from Rucapillán to Quetrupillán ranger stations, through araucaria forests and across Andean plains, with great views of all the volcanoes. You may see wild pigs and deer.

Los Venados (*Distance:* 15 km / 9 mi, *Difficulty:* medium, *Duration:* 10 hours, 1,000 – 1710 m / 3,250 – 5,558 ft altitude). The path begins at the Quetrupillán station and ends at Laguna Azul (also called Laguna de los Patos), where it then connects with the Las Avutardas trail through monkey-puzzle forest.

Tramo Las Avutardas (*Distance:* 17 km / 10.2 mi, *Difficulty:* medium, *Duration:* 12 hours, 950 – 1,650 m/3,088 – 5,363 ft altitude). Winding from Laguna Azul to the Camino Internacional, south of the Puesco ranger station, this trail will lead you past the nesting grounds of the Ashy-headed Goose and Laguna Las Avutardas. This path also visits Azul, Blanca and Las Positas lagoons, and it is possible to see the major volcanoes along this route.

Off these trails are various spurs:

Sendero Colonia Benavides (*Distance:* 4 km / 2.4 mi, *Difficulty:* hard, *Duration:* 1.3 hours). This trail begins outside the south boundary of the park, off the road from Coñaripe. Along the way, the effects of human traffic are evident. It ends in an area with flora and fauna typical of the zone, connecting with the Sendero Los Venados.

Estero Mocho (*Distance:* 4 km / 2.4 mi, *Difficulty:* easy, *Duration:* 1 hour). This is a spur trail off the Sendero Los Venados, beginning about midway between the Quetrupillán station and Laguna Azul. It allows views of several volcanoes and the Valle de Palguín.

Rinconada de Huililco (*Distance:* 10 km / 6 mi, *Difficulty:* medium, *Duration:* 6 hours). Turning off Sendero Las Avutardas, approximately midway between Lagunas Azul and Avutardas, this path approaches ancient volcanic craters. The river is home to otters.

Volcán Quinquilil (*Distance:* 6 km / 3.6 mi, *Difficulty:* hard, *Duration:* 2.3 hours). Another side trail off the Avutardas, midway between Laguna Avutardas and the Puesco ranger station, this path allows extensive views over the volcano and lake-strewn landscape, into Argentina.

Some of the other trails in the park are:

Río Turbio (*Distance:* 4 km / 2.4 mi, *Difficulty:* medium, *Duration:* 2 hours). This goes along the Río Turbio to a lookout, passing lava fields, waterfalls and Volcán Villarrica's glaciers; to the north you can see the double crater of Llaima Volcano.

Los Nevados (*Distance:* 8 km, *Difficulty:* medium, *Duration:* 5 hours). A spur off the Sendero Pichillancahue, leading to the road south of Termas Palguín. It follows along the Chinay and Villarrica creeks and the Cerros los Nevados through beech forests.

Off-trail trekking is discouraged; the risk of doing so is solely the responsibility of the hiker. Updated: Jul 07, 2009.

Climbing Volcán Villarrica

Snow crunches beneath crampons as climbers reach Volcán Villarrica's 200-meter (650-ft) wide crater glowing magenta with simmering lava. It's been a steep five hours up, but the brisk wind and the stunning views of the national park have been worth it. This trek up the stratovolcano is Pucón's most popular draw. The native Mapuche had a different, more fitting name for this mountain: Rucupillán, House of the Spirits (or Demon). For an added adventure, mountaineers can snowboard or ski back to town.

Almost all the tour operators in Pucón offer excursions up Volcán Villarrica. By law, each six-person group must be accompanied by one guide and an assistant. The night before, agencies will give you a go-through, to show you how to suit up for the ascent. Tourists need no special training to climb with a tour; though do be aware the five-kilometer (3-mi) ascent is rated as difficult.

Cost for a tour is $70 – 100; this includes equipment, clothes (gloves, boots, etc.) guide and transportation. A fee is charged for climbing Volcán Villarrica ($10 for Chileans, $14 for foreigners). Check if this is included in the tour's price. Horses can be hired for an additional $10.

If you have verifiable climbing credentials and experience, and have the equipment, you can apply to scale the volcano without a guide. Contact the Conaf office in Temuco or Pucón to make arrangements.

The park service limits the number of climbers. Some tour groups leave at 5 a.m., others at 7 a.m. Climbs may be canceled due to high winds or other adverse weather conditions, or if the volcano's activity increases. Beware of sulfur fumes near the crater. Updated: Jul 07, 2009.

THE LAKE DISTRICT

Skiing

A different type of fun awaits volcano enthusiasts once the yearly snow begins flurrying around the cone of Volcán Villarrica. On the northwest slope of the majestic peak is **Centro de Ski Volcán Villarrica**. The lodge, with cafeteria, bar and restaurant, is at 1,400 meters (4,515 ft) altitude. Facilities include 20 runs for novice to expert skiers and nine lifts. Ski classes are offered. Skis, sleds, snow mobiles and other equipment are available to rent. The ski season is from mid-June through October.

The **Centro de Ski** is 18 kilometers (12 mi) from Pucón by way of a dirt road. If you don't have your own vehicle, you can rent one or book a transfer with the **Enjoy Tour** office at the **Gran Hotel** (Holzapfel 190), or check with local tour agencies, or hire a taxi ($24 one way for up to four passengers) or hitch. In the high season there is public transport ($14 – 16).

It is cheaper to rent equipment in Pucón than at the ski center. **Aguaventura** rents skis, snowshoes and snowboards (Palguín 336. Tel: 56-45-444246, E-mail: info@ remove-this.aguaventura.com, URL: www. aguaventura.com). **Aventur** also rents and sells gear, for both adults and children and offers classes in skiing and snowboarding. Aventur arranges transportation to Centro de Ski, and has a wax and repair workshop (Palguín 383. Tel: 56-45-442796, URL: www. aventurpucon.cl). Updated: Jun 29, 2009.

Lodging

Camping within Parque Nacional Villarrica is principally for those who want to enjoy the many treks there. In the Chinay area of Sector Quetrupillán, six kilometers (3.6 miles) from the ranger station, there are 20 established sites. The Puesco sector has five campsites next to the guardhouse. Sector Quetrupillán-Puesco: January 1 – February 28 ($14 Chileans, $24 foreigners); March 1 – December 31 ($10 Chileans, $16 foreigners). Other established campsites exist on the long trekking routes at Laguna Azul and at Laguna Avutardas. Overnight back-country camping is allowed on the longer trekking routes.

Some rules to observe:
•In populated areas, use previously established campsites to prevent environmental damage.
•Use a camp stove. Do not build a campfire unless absolutely necessary. Be aware of the current forest fire risk (posted at the Conaf office in Pucón and at ranger stations).

•Pack out all trash. Bury human waste and keep waste water away from streams and other potential sources for drinking water.

If you are doing a multi-day trek, first sign in with the Conaf office in Pucón. Also check weather and trail conditions before starting out. Snow can be present from autumn to spring. Weather can change quickly. Updated: Jun 29, 2009.

PARQUE NACIONAL HUERQUEHUE

National park Huerquehue, 35 kilometers (22 mi) from Pucón, offers great hikes along easy trails, even though these are covered with snow most of the year. The eight-kilometer (5 mi) Los Lagos trail heads up a steep switchback path past a refuge cabin and after about two hours arrives at a pristine lake, Lago Toro, surrounded by monkey-puzzle trees (*Araucaria araucana*, a type of pine tree native to Chile and Argentina). The trail then splits and heads toward two other lakes, Lago Verde and Lago Chico, both offering chocolate-box views. You can arrange transport to the entrance of the park with a local tour company which will pick you up later in the day.

The visitor's office, 300 meters (0.2 miles) from the entrance to the park, is open 8 a.m. to 8 p.m. from January to March and the Park Rangers' office from 9 a.m. to 11 p.m., also in the summertime. Updated: Jul 06, 2009.

LICÁN RAY

 207m   2,200   45

From Villarrica, Highway S-95 crosses the land between Lakes Villarrica and Calafquén to Licán Ray (also spelled Licanray). Cattle and sheep pastures, small farms and furniture workshops dot the countryside. Cabins and campgrounds blossom along this road during the summer. On the north shore of Lago Calafquén is Licán Ray, a quiet little village. Or at least it is in the off-season. But come summer, the town swells with vacationers, with the aroma of open-again restaurants and the strains of music festivals floating across the waters. It wasn't always this way, though.

For years the Mapuche community Loncopan was here. In the 1930s, trade by steamship linked the hamlet with others around Lago

Calafquén. Licán Ray was incorporated in 1944. By then it was connected to the outside world by road. In the mid-50s, many left when plans to build a hydroelectric dam at Pullinque were unveiled. According to the plans, the village would be flooded out of existence. Fortunately, those plans were scrapped after the 1960 earthquake. Tourism took hold in the 1960s. The 1971 eruption of Volcán Villarrica created a river of lava that flowed toward the lake, six kilometers (3.6 mi) from Licán Ray, crossing the road to Coñaripe. Looking across Lago Calafquén, to the left, the hardened lava flow. In 1990, a 25-kilometer (15-mi) paved road from Villarrica was finally completed.

Getting To and Away From Licán Ray

Licán Ray is connected by road to Villarrica to the north, Coñaripe to the east and Panguipulli to the south. Public transportation to Licán Ray, however, departs only from Villarrica and Coñaripe. **Jac** buses run the route between Villarrica and Licán Ray daily, every 15 minutes, from 7 a.m. to 9 p.m. ($1.40). Some of these buses continue to Coñaripe ($0.60). To get to Panguipulli, you must first go to Coñaripe. Updated: Dec 27, 2008.

Services

Along Licán Ray's main street, General Urrutia, there is an Internet and phone café, tour operators, restaurants and inns. Urrutia borders the large, shady Plaza de Armas.

Around the public square you'll find the **tourism office** (Urrutia 310. Tel: 56-45-431201), **Iglesia San Francisco**, the **hospital** and the **Jac** bus terminal. Most tourism-oriented businesses are open only in summer. A few restaurants along Urrutia are open year-round, like **The Naños** and **Ulmos de Chiñura**.

Things to See and Do

Licán Ray has a variety of activities for tourists. Between the two beaches, Playa Chica and Playa Grande, is a peninsula. Hiking trails lead to a viewpoint overlooking the lake, 14 islands and the snowy volcanoes. Birdwatching is a popular activity. (The entrance is at the west end of Playa Chica; Entry: $0.60). You can rent rowboats on Playa Chica. From October to March, catamarans go on tours (leaves weekends October – December, daily in summer if there are enough passengers, $4). At the west end of Playa Grande is Arco de Piedra, a natural rock arch. Fishing is also excellent at Licán Ray. (Obtain a permit at the municipality in Villarrica).

Lodging

In the winter, when it rains a lot, camping can be challenging. Many campgrounds are at the north end of Playa Chica. Accommodations open all year are: **Hotel-Restaurant Becker** (Felipe Manquel 105. Tel: 56-45-431553, E-mail: licanbecker@yahoo.es, URL: www. hotelbecker-licanray.com)—two or 2 persons; includes breakfast; **Señora Nadime** (Carimán 25. Tel: 56-45-431093)—$10 per person, including use of kitchen; six-person cabin $36 per day; **Camping El Trebol** (Camino Panguipulli. Tel: 56-9-6849971, E-mail: camping_eltrebol@yahoo.es, URL: www.sernatur.cl). Prices quoted are low season, they climb steeply in the high season. Updated: Dec 27, 2008.

Siete Lagos Region

Deep in the Andean foothills, off the beaten track for most travelers, is a world where mists swirl around crystalline lakes, trout and salmon fishing are excellent, and rushing rivers guarantee jostling rides for the experienced rafters and kayakers. Enchanting villages provide refuge from the rigors of the road. After a day of trekking, hot springs await to soothe tired muscles. This, the Región Siete Lagos, or Seven Lakes Region, encompasses Calafquén, Pellaifa, Pullinque, Neltume, Riñihue and Pirehueico Lakes. Connected by rivers fed by Andean snows, the chain of waterways eventually drains into the Pacific Ocean.

The northern-most lake is Calafquén, upon whose shores are Licán Ray and Coñaripe. A curious thing is that Licán Ray is not considered part of the Seven Lakes area, as it is in the IX Región de la Araucanía and not in X Región de los Ríos. At Coñaripe you'll find the Ruta de Salud, leading to 14 hot springs. The third week of July, Coñaripe hosts a gastronomic fair featuring the *jabalí*, a feral swine introduced from Europe.

An unpaved road goes from Coñaripe (p. 310), wraps around the north shore of Lago Pellaife, and continues to Carirriñe and Liquiñe. Along this route are a number of thermal springs. From Liquiñe a poor road continues to Paso Carirriñe border crossing into Argentina.

To the immediate south of Lago Calafquén are two small lakes, Lago Pullinque, and Lago Panguipulli (p. 311), whose main villages are Panguipulli and Choshuenco. A

THE LAKE DISTRICT

complex system of rivers weave together to connect Lago Panguipulli with Lago Pirehueico. Río Neltume, whose birthplace is Lago Neltume to the east, joins with the Río Fuy from Lago Pirehueico to form the Río Llanquihue. This network of rivers contains some of Chile's best and least-explored rafting country. Nearby is the Reserva Biológico Huilo -Huilo (p.313). On the northern tip of Lago Pirehueico is Puerto Fuy, from which a ferry departs to Puerto Pirehueico near the Argentine border crossing Paso Hua Hum. The Río Enco winds from Lago Panguipulli to the seventh lake of the region, Riñihue.

On the coast there are two small hamlets, Riñimapu and Riñihue. During the off-season, tranquility reigns in the Region of Seven Lakes and its rivers. Lodging and dining services are limited, with better services in Coñaripe, Panguipulli, Choshuenco and the Lago Pirehueico ports, Fuy and Pirehueico. In summer, the pace quickens with the arrival of Chilean tourists on vacation. Cabins, campgrounds and hostels spring to life. Boat tours are offered on many of the lakes. The bilingual website www.sietelagos.cl/web has good information about what's happening in the region. Updated: Jan 21, 2009.

COÑARIPE

 112m   1,420   63

From Licán Ray, a good blacktop road heads 20 kilometers (12 mi) southeast along the north shore of Lago Calafquén to Coñaripe. Dark, ragged bluffs peer from the heavy forest. Occasionally the snowy mass of mighty Villarrica Volcano can be seen.

This road is dotted with small sheep farms. In summer, campgrounds and cabañas bloom along the roadside. Rough black sand beaches trim the teal-blue lake. The route also crosses the lava flow from the 1971 eruption of Volcán Villarrica. Near Coñaripe is the trailhead for the four-kilometer (2.5 mi) leg of the Sendero de Chile.

In Coñaripe, the highway becomes the village's main street, Guido Beck de Ramberga. Major enterprises of the town can be found along this stretch: hotels, restaurants, supermarkets, the lone Internet

and phone courier. Buses also depart from here. The main square is an overgrown green expanse. The municipal Infocentro tourism office, along with the Cámara de Comercio y Turismo Coñaripe, is on the plaza. A rose and fir garden brightens Iglesia Sagrada Familia, a low, angular church shingled in wood.

At the far outskirts of town, an unpaved road heads northeast into Parquer Nacional Villarrica, lined along the way by several hot springs.

Eco Termas Vergara has five pools with 25 – 45°C (77 – 113°F) water that are open year-round. Its **cabins**, though, are open only in summer (Km 14, Camino Los Cajones. Tel: 56-63-21963720 / 3721, E-mail: termasvergara@gmail.com, URL: www.termasvergara.cl.kz.   Entry: $10 – 14).

Two kilometers (1.2 mi) farther are the spectacular **Termas Geométricas**, designed by Chilean architect Germán del Sol. A series of wooden walkways lead to 17 stone pools nestled in the forest (Km 16. Tel: 56-63-22141214, URL: www.termasgeometricas.cl. Entry: $24 – 28). This road cuts across the national park to Pucón, but it is a summer-only road for 4x4 vehicles.

Southeast of Coñaripe are another half-dozen hot springs. These include **Termas Coñaripe** with four pools, hotel, cabañas and a restaurant (Km 15. Tel: 56-45-411111, E-mail: consultas@termasconaripe.cl, URL: www.termasconaripe.cl,   Entry: $14 adults) and **Eco Termas Pellaifa** (Km 16. Tel: 56-45-411973, E-mail: eco-termaspellaifa@hotmail.com), which has a restaurant and cabins.

Next to the tourism **Infocentro** is Calle Tepas. This street goes down to Lago Calafquén. Other hostels (open summer only) are also located here. Before arriving to the lakefront, you'll pass **Feria Campesina Inalafquén Mileiti**, a farmers' and artisan market.

The black sand beach of Lago Calafquén is the perfect place to relax and catch some rays. There is also good trout and salmon fishing. In summer, kayaks, pedal boats and rowboats are available to rent. There are many campgrounds south along the shore. Over a kilometer down the strand is a river. At its mouth is Isla Millahuapi (Isla de Oro), upon which is a permaculture farm. The lakeshore is a perfect place for birdwatching.

In the low season the village is somnolent. It rains quite a bit in winter, making camping challenging. In January and February, full services are available and prices climb.

Getting To and Away From Coñaripe

All transport leaves from Calle Guido Beck de Ramberga.

Terminal de Buses de Panguipulli:
To Panguipulli: Monday – Saturday, 3 to 4 buses daily; Sunday, one in the afternoon.

To Licán Ray / Villarrica: Monday – Saturday 7:50 a.m., 9:20 a.m., 1:45 p.m.; daily 5 p.m., $1 / $2.

Buses for *Liquiñe* depart from Supermercado Coñaripe (Monday – Saturday 5 buses daily, Sunday 7:45 p.m., 1.5 hours, $2).

TurBus, **Jac** and **Inter** share an office:

To Licán Ray / Villarrica: every half hour or hour, 6:45 a.m. – 8:50 p.m., $1 / $2.

To Santiago: daily 8:15 p.m., $42 – 60.

To Termas Geométricas: Colectivo vans leave from the butcher's shop across from Supermercado Coñaripe ($40 - 50 per person round trip). During the summer, cheaper minivans depart on a regular schedule from the main plaza. Updated: Jan 22, 2009.

Services

TOURISM
Municipal Infocentro Tourism Office (Monday – Friday 9 a.m. – 1:30 p.m., 3 p.m. – 6:30 p.m., may be closed in the off-season. Calle Guido Beck de Ramberga, main plaza).

Cámara de Comercio y Turismo Coñaripe (Wednesday – Saturday 10 a.m. – 12:30 p.m., 3 p.m. – 6 p.m., summer only. Calle Guido Beck de Ramberga, main plaza).

Chumay Turismo Aventura (office open in high season. Las Tepas 201. Tel: 56-63-317287, URL: www.lagocalafquen.com).

Offers trekking and hot spring excursions, tours of the Siete Lagos region and Reserva Ecológico Huilo-Huilo, and the Lago Pirehueico crossing into Argentina.

OTHER SERVICES
The **health post** is on Las Tejas; it has emergency services.

Centro de Llamadas Entremaza, next to Porvenir Restaurant on the main drag, provides international calls.

Paquetería Central has slow, expensive Internet (Bamberga 703).

Lodging
Camping Rucahue: Campsites are on a heavily-treed lot near the lakefront; bathhouse (Av. Costanera s/n. Tel: 56-63-317210, E-mail: Griedemann@surnet.cl, URL: www.campingrucahue.cl). $5 per person (low season), $25 per site (January and February).

Hospedaje Calafquén (Guido Beck de Ramberga 761. Tel: 56-63-317301). Rooms $8 per person, cabins for up to five people, with bath and kitchen $30; prices double in summer.

Hotel Elizabeth (Guido Beck de Ramberga 496. Tel: 56-63-317279, E-mail: hotel@hotelelizabeth.cl, URL: www.hotelelizabeth.cl). 1 person $30, 2 persons $44 (high or low season).

Restaurants
There are several dining choices on Guido Beck de Ramberga:

Porvenir Restaurant (No. 661),

Café Restaurante Central (No. 727). These are only open until 8 p.m. in the low season.

Also, **La Terraza Café-Restaurant** (Calle Las Tejas and Costanera). Updated: Jul 02, 2009.

LAGO PANGUIPULLI
From Los Lagos on Ruta 5, a paved secondary road heads northeast 39 kilometers (23.4 mi) to Pangipüyü, the Land of the Spirit of Lions—today called Paguipulli. The lake covers 111 square kilometers (67 sq mi) and is 268 meters (879 ft) deep. On

THE LAKE DISTRICT

the shores of this azure lake are small villages with a much more relaxed feel than Lago Villarrica and other tourist-oriented destinations in the region.

The lake is a paradise for outdoor activities and those looking to get off the beaten trail, with local cuisine that includes *jabalí* (wild boar), *wagyu* (Japanese black cow), *ciervo* (venison), salmon and trout.

Panguipulli town, the principal settlement on Lago Panguipulli, is the governmental seat of the Siete Lagos Region. It is the gateway to the various routes through the area, including the Ruta de Salud, which passes by 14 hot springs.

This village, known as the City of Roses, has a church inspired by Swiss architecture. The lakefront statue, Monumento a los Forjadores y Fundadores de Paguipulli, represents a Mapuche figure, a Capuchin missionary monk and a pioneer. It was mentioned in Spanish chronicles as early as 1776. The town also has a beach and pier.

The other principal town on Lago Panguipulli is **Choshuenco**, on the southeast shore. From this hamlet, tucked into the Andean foothills, you can access Reserva Nacional Mocho-Choshuenco and climb its namesake volcano. The reserve, between Lagos Panguipulli and Riñihue protects over 7,000 hectares of native forest, glens and mountains.

There is good sportfishing at Lago Panguipulli, especially near Choshuenco and on the northwest corner. Trout is the principal catch. The season is November 15 – May 30. The rivers connecting Panguipulli with neighboring lakes are great for rafting.

The Río Enco, which flows at the base of Volcán Mocho-Choshuenco, between Panguipulli and Riñihue Lakes, has Class II and III rapids.

The more challenging river is Río Fuy, uniting Lagos Pirehueico and Panguipulli. This short waterway packs in Class III and IV rapids that whirl around rocks. Tour operators in Panguipulli and Choshuenco arrange fishing, rafting and kayaking adventures.

Plans for a hydroelectric plant are causing concern in the Panguipulli region, for fears of its effects on ecotourism activities,

like rafting, fishing and thermal springs, and on wood extraction, the mainstay of the economy.

Services are limited in both the principal towns on Lago Panguipulli. A larger selection of hotels and restaurants are in the town of Panguipulli. During the summer months (December – February), the area receives many more visitors. In the low season, many hostels, campgrounds and restaurants are closed. Winters are cold and rainy.

Getting To and Away From Lago Panguipulli

You can reach the village of Panguipulli from Valdivia: **Buses Pirehueico** (Monday – Saturday every 45 minutes 6:30 a.m. – 8:30 p.m., Sunday hourly 8 a.m. – 10:30 p.m., 2.5 hours, $5).

Panguipulli village is connected to other villages in the Lake Region:

To Puerto Fuy: for Pirehueico Lake crossing to Argentina, see Lago Pirehueico (p.313).

To Coñaripe: Monday – Saturday, 4-5 buses daily, Sunday 4:25 p.m.

To Liquiñe: Monday – Saturday 3 buses daily, Sunday 4:25 p.m.

Transportation also leaves for Choshuenco. In the summer **Buses La Fit** has a Lago Panguipulli ferry. Updated: Jan 22, 2009.

PANGUIPULLI

 139m   33,300   63

TOURS
Río Fuy Turismo Expediciones (Martínez de Rozas 728. Tel: 56-63-311460, E-mail: contacto@riofuy.cl, URL: www.riofuy.cl) The company has rafting, kayaking, fishing, canopy, snowboarding, trekking, climbing Volcán Mocho-Choshuenco, Sendero del Jabalí and Ruta de Salud tours.

LODGING
Hospedaje Eva Ray (Los Ulmos 62. Tel: 56-63-311483; $12 per person); **Hotel Le Français** (Martínez de Rosas 880. Tel: 56-63-312496; 1 person $52, 2 persons $58 – 68).

RESTAURANTS
On Martínez de Ross there are several eateries, including **Gardylafquén** (No. 722. Tel: 56-63-311887) and Girsol (No. 664. Tel: 56-9-5682927).

CHOSHUENCO

 190m 625 63

TOURS
Rucapillán Expediciones (San Martín 85. Tel: 56-63-318220, E-mail: rafting@ucapillan.cl, URL: www.rucapillan.cl) has rafting, kayaking and trekking.

LODGING
Hostal y Cabañas San Martín (San Martín 74. Tel: 56-63-318290; 1 person $20, 2 persons $32 – 40 per night); **Hostería Ruca-Pillán** (San Martín 85. Tel: 56-63-318220, E-mail: rucapi@telsur.cl, URL: rucapillan.cl; 1 or 2 persons $50).

RESTAURANTS
La Posada (San Martín 335. Tel: 56-63-318213). Updated: Jan 22, 2009.

HUILO-HUILO BIOLOGICAL RESERVE

Fifty-six kilometers (35 mi) from Panguipulli in the Tenth Region, just at the northern edge of Chilean Patagonia, lies the Huilo-Huilo Biological Reserve. The 60,000-hectare Huilo-Huilo is part natural reserve and ecotourism project, and part tourist attraction and housing development (although the lots cover less than one percent of the total project).

The reserve was created in 1999 by the Huilo-Huilo Foundation and declared a UNESCO Biosphere Reserve in 2007. The 250 kilometers (156 mi) of trails through the reserve reveal hundreds of tree and animal species as well as the Fuy, Enco, and Pirihueico Rivers, and numerous springs and lagoons.

The main attractions are the **Huilo-Huilo Falls**, the **hot springs**, the longest zip line system in South America, year-round skiing on the **Mocho Volcano**, and the *Pudu pudu*, which is the world's smallest deer, weighing around 10 kg (22 lbs).

Getting To and Away From Huilo-Huilo Reserve
The main access to Huilo-Huilo Biological Reserve is from Panguipulli along the Huahum Passage, that leads to San Martin de los Andes. The park can be accessed from the road that leaves Temuco and passes through Villarrica, Lican Ray, Coñaripe and Neltume Lake. It is a distance of 170 kilometers (106 mi). By air: arrive at the Choshuenco Airport, 14 kilometers (9 mi) from the reserve or Temuco Airport 190 kilometers (118 mi) Updated: Jun 30, 2009.

Lodging
After a day spent enjoying the flora and fauna of the reserve, spend the night at **Magic Mountain Hotel**, a mountain-shaped building with a waterfall cascading down one side, is one of the most unique accommodations in Chile. Boasting a spa, mini-golf course, hot tubs made out of giant tree trunks, WiFi and a restaurant, this 13-room hotel is a luxurious (albeit pricey) way to spend a night in the forest. Located on Km. 60 Panguipulli International Road, Puerto Fuy. Tel: 56-63-1972651 / 81, E-mail: info@huilohuilo.cl, URL: www.huilohuilo.cl.

An even more expensive option is the **Baobab Hotel**, which requires reservations for a minimum of three days, where rooms cost between $809 – 1722. Created in 2007 in the shape of a tree, and built around a baobab which still stands in the center, the Baobab Hotel has many of the amenities of the Magic Mountain Hotel—sauna, mini golf, hot tubs—but also has an open bar, daily excursions, free entrance to the Huilo-Huilo Waterfalls,

El Puma and La Leona, and the Path of the Spirits as well as transfers to the Temuco Airport. Located next to the Magica Mountain Hotel. Tel: 56-2-3355938 /3344566, E-mail: reservas@huilohuilo.cl, URL: www.huilohuilo.com. Updated: Jul 07, 2009.

LAGO PIREHUEICO

 2,381 m 1,126 63

Lago Pirehueico, the eastern-most lake in the region, was carved into the Andean foothills by glaciers. It is the most pristine

How to Eat a Crudo

One of the many culinary gifts of the German immigrants to the Valdivian menu is the *crudo*, or steak tartar. On a slice of white bread, freshly-ground, super-lean raw beef is spread and generously sprinkled with finely diced onion. How is this open-faced sandwich eaten? Valdivianos first squeeze lemon over the meat. Locals believe this "cooks" the beef. Germans skip this step. Next, prepare the toppings to taste. Add salt and pepper. From the pots, spread on *ají verde* (chopped hot green peppers), *salsa tartar* (an herbed sour cream), *ají rojo* (red chili peppers) and / or mustard. Now you are ready to eat your crudo with a knife and fork. Guten Apetit!

of the Seven Lakes, with near-virgin lenga forest covering its shores, and, occassionally, puma tracks dotting the beach. Unlike its sister, Lago Pirehueico has no road along its shore. There are only two villages on Lago Pirehueico. Puerto Fuy is at the end of a 68-kilometer (36-mi) road from Panguipulli. **Puerto Fuy** (URL: www.puerto-fuy.com) is small, more a respite for those journeying between Chile and Argentina.

The village has more hotels and restaurants than its cousin **Puerto Pirehueico**, 26 kilometers (16 mi) down on the southern tip of the lake. The two hamlets are connected year-round by a vehicle-passenger ferry, providing an inexpensive, alternate lake border crossing. From Puerto Pirehueico, it is eight kilometers (4.8 mi) to Paso Hua Hum, from which it's another 66 kilometers (37 mi) to San Martín de los Andes, Argentina.

The two villages offer few attractions, though some travelers find reason to linger. Summer pastimes include canopying and hiking in the plush evergreen rainforest where Southern *pudu* and wild boar reside. Birdwatching is also fruitful. Keep an eye out for the Slender-billed Parakeet and the Chilean Torrent Duck. Fishing is excellent, not only in Lago Pirehueico, but also in Laguna Caicaén near Puerto Fuy. On the tranquil waters of Laguna Pirehueico, Chile's sixth largest lake, watersport enthusiasts can float in inner tubes or kayak. Puerto Fuy is within easy reach of the rushing torrents of the Río Fuy, the Reserva Biológico Huilo-Huilo and the bewitching Montaña Mágica hotel.

Getting To and Away From Lago Pirehueico

From Panguipulli, **Buses Lafit** has service to Puerto Fuy (Monday – Saturday 10 a.m., making connection with the ferry; also five other departures Monday – Saturday 11:45 a.m. – 4:30 p.m., Sunday 6:30 p.m., 7:30 p.m., 2 hours, $5).

Transbordador (for updated information on fares and schedules, see www.sietelagos.cl). Passenger $3, bicycle $6, motorcycle $8, car $30.

To Puerto Pirehueico: (January – February) 8 a.m., 1 p.m., 6 p.m.; (March) 1 p.m.

To Puerto Fuy : (January – February) 10 a.m., 3 p.m., 8 p.m., (March) 4 p.m.

For details on the Paso Hua Hum border crossing, see Chile-Argentine Border Crossings (p.270). Updated: Jan 23, 2009.

Lodging

Puerto Fuy is your better bet for lodging. It offers a few hotels, as well as camping:

Hospedaje and Restaurant Puerto Fuy (Camino Internacional s/n. Tel: 56-63-1971630; room $5 per person).

Hospedaje y Restaurante San Giovanni (Tel: 56-63-1971562; single $10, double $12 per person, 4-person cabin $50).

Hotel Marina del Fuy (Tel: 56-63-1972426) Also has a restaurant.

Café del Lago (Tel: 56-63-1972398).

Camping is allowed on the beach; other lodging is available in private houses.
Puerto Pirehueico lodging options are quite slim. Private houses rent out rooms.

Cabañas Puerto Pirehueico (Tel: 56-63-322910679 / 8-159-1320, URL: www.piri-hueico.cl) offers completely equipped 6- to 7-person cabins, $150 – 230 (low season), $170 – 250 (high season).

THE LAKE DISTRICT

VALDIVIA

 14m   156,732   63

Of all the cities in the south of Chile, Valdivia is one of the most beautiful and fascinating. The history ranges from original Spanish colonization and Mapuche victories to Spanish reconquest and the deep cultural and economic effects of German immigration. The arts have flourished, as have the sports. Nature reserves drape the banks of the rivers that meet here, in this *Ciudad de los Ríos*.

Valdivia is the capital of the new XIV Región de los Ríos, formed in 2007. The area is aptly named for the many rivers that pass through on their journey from the Andes.

The Cruces, Cau-Cau-Cau, Calle-Calle and others all merge at Valdivia to form the Río Valdivia, which flows down to Bahía de Corral and the Pacific Ocean. This is Chile's most navigable area, with 250 kilometers (150 mi) of rivers, plus the Bahía de Corral to explore in a tour boat or private yacht. Every day sculls ply the Río Valdivia.

Most of Chile's top sport rowers come from Valdivia's three rowing clubs. The river basin is scattered with islands, including Isla Teja (which Valdivia spills onto), Gucamayo, Isla de Rey, Hupi and Mancera.

Spanish fortresses line the banks and isles along the river. These were key in the colonizers' reconquest of the region. The first Valdivia settlement was built 18 kilometers (11 mi) upriver from the Pacific Ocean in 1552 and became their Perla del Sur, the Southern Pearl. It was an important stop for Spanish fleets the rounded the tip of South America, hauling riches from port to port and back to the motherland.

The Spaniards were further delighted by the timber and gold found in the region. But their presence was not welcomed. The indigenous Mapuche who lived in these lands continually attacked the city. Even the Valdiviano's construction of the fortress Fuerte de la Santísima Trinidad in 1602 could not protect them. Two years later, the Mapuche succeeded in driving the invaders out and recuperating their territory. The Spanish colonists fled to the Central Valley or to Chiloé.

Valdivia would have probably become just one more abandoned town that molded in the damp landscape if the Dutch had not stumbled upon the ruins in 1643. This provoked the Spanish crown to recapture the city and claim it once more. Peruvian Viceroy Pedro de Toledo y Leiva, Marquis de Mancera gave the order for Valdivia's reconquista.

In 1645 an elaborate plan moved forward. First, on Isla Mancera where Río Valdivia flows into Bahía de Corral, El Castillo San Pedro de Alcántara de la Isla de Mancera was constructed. Here the future denizens of Valdivia would live until the city was secure from the "internal enemy," the Mapuche-Huilliche. With single-minded determination, the Spaniards built fortresses along both banks of the river and on islands all the way to the sea and up the coast.

Once that area was controlled, their forces moved upstream, conquering land and constructing fortresses, until Valdivia was finally reached and rebuilt. It took over a hundred years, 1760-1779, before the city became Spanish once again.

The ruins of much of the fortress system still exist, making it the second largest in Latin America, after Colombia. Those in Niebla, Corral and Isla Mancera are major attractions. Within the city itself are two tower fortifications: Torreón Los Canelos (Calle Yerbas Buenas and General Lagos) and Torreón del Barro (Av. Arturo Prat Costanera, near Puente Calle Calle).

With the Wars of Independence from Spain, it was imperative to take this stronghold port from which the empire was commanding counterattacks against the rebels. Lord Thomas Cochrane led the Chilean forces to take Valdivia. As the Mapuche controlled all the territory around the city, a land-based attack was not possible. Cochrane chose an amphibious nighttime operation to first take Fuerte Inglés, which quickly fell. The rest of the defense system fell like dominoes, paving the rebels' way to the city. The Spaniards sacked Valdivia before escaping to Osorno and later to Chiloé, Spain's last holding in the region.

Chile's 1845 Colonization Law opened the door for thousands of Germans immigrants. In Valdivia, they established many industries, most notably breweries, set up

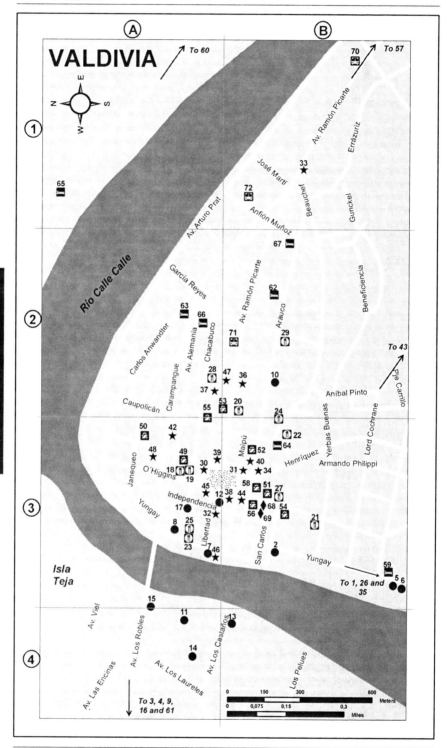

VALDIVIA

To 60

To 57

N E S W

THE LAKE DISTRICT

Río Calle Calle

Av. Arturo Prat

García Reyes

Carlos Anwandter

Av. Alemania

Chacabuco

Caupolicán

Carampangue

Janequeo

O'Higgins

Yungay

Independencia

Libertad

Isla Teja

Av. Viel

Av. Los Robles

Av. Las Encinas

Av. Los Laureles

Av. Los Castaños

Los Pelúes

José Martí

Anfión Muñoz

Av. Ramón Picarte

Beauchef

Errázuriz

Gunckel

Beneficiencia

Arauco

Maipú

Henríquez

Yerbas Buenas

Armando Philippi

Lord Cochrane

Aníbal Pinto

Pje Carillo

San Carlos

Yungay

To 43

To 1, 26 and 35

To 3, 4, 9, 16 and 61

0   150   300   600   Meters

0   0,075   0,15   0,3   Miles

Activities ●

1 Boat Tours B3
2 Centro Cultural El Austral B3
3 Cervecería Kunstmann A4
4 Cine Club UACh A4
5 Club de Remeros Arturo Prat B3
6 Conservatorio de Música B3
7 Corporación Cultural Municipal A3
8 Feria Fluvial A3
9 Jardín Botánico A4
10 Movieland B2
11 Museo de Arte Contemporáneo A4
12 Museo de la Catedral A3
13 Museo Histórico y Antropológico B4
14 Museo R.A. Philippi A4
15 Parque Prochelle A3
16 Parque Saval A4
17 Teatro Municipal Lord Cochrane A3

Eating 🍴

18 Café Haussmann A3
19 Café Las Gringas A3
20 Fuente Valdiviana B2
21 La Última Frontera B3
22 Legado Jazz and Restobar B3
23 Mercado Municipal A3
24 Pub-Restaurant New Orleans B2
25 Restaurant La Estrella A3
26 Restaurant Yang Cheng B3
27 Salón de Té Entrelagos B3
28 Santa Isabel A2
29 Único B2

Services ★

30 Banco de Chile A3
31 Banco Estado B3
32 BBVA A3
33 Carabineros De Chile B1
34 Chilexpress B3
35 Club de Yates B3
36 Comunícate Internet y Centro de
   Llamadas B2
37 Conaf A2
38 Correos Chile B3

39 Farmacia Ahumada A3
40 Farmacias del Dr. Simi B3
41 Hospital Regional B2
42 La Reconquista A3
43 Lavamatic B2
44 Santander B3
45 Scotiabank A3
46 Sernatur A3
47 tecno.cl B2
48 Tourist House A3

Shopping 🛍

49 Alterfluss A3
50 Canela A3
51 Entre Lagos B3
52 Galería Arauco B3
53 Lago Sport B2
54 Librería de Valdivia B3
55 Libros Chiloé A2
56 Nougat B3
57 Pescadores B1
58 Peumayen B3

Sleeping 🛏

59 Albergue Latino B3
60 Camping El Amigo A1
61 Camping Isla Teja A4
62 Hospedaje Valdivia 545 B2
63 Hostal Totem A2
64 Hostal y Cabañas Esmeralda B3
65 Hotel Marina Villa del Río A1
66 Hotel Melillanca A2
67 Residencial Río Calle-Calle B2

Tours ♦

68 Pueblito Expediciones B3
69 Turismo Paraty B3

Transportation 🚌

70 Budget B1
71 Hertz B2
72 Terminal de Buses B1

THE LAKE DISTRICT

a German school and built beautiful mansions. As the territory was taken from Mapuches, the Germans moved into the Lakes District, establishing Puerto Octay, Frutillar and other villages around Lago Llanquihue. Their influence reached into Valdiviano gastronomy too, with spätzel, homemade sausage, sauerkraut and crudos.

This tranquil world was shattered on May 22, 1960, when the largest earthquake in modern history, magnitude 9.5, hit Valdivia. The tsunami that followed wiped the city nearly clean from the land. Little remained. The tidal wave widened the rivers, slicing new channels in the landscape, creating new islands and estuaries.

But the people rebuilt Valdivia, once more as a glorious city on the banks of many rivers. The university, Universidad Austral de Chile on Isla Teja, is a cornerstone of the economy now and assures Valdivianos a full agenda of cultural events. And once more the city is a center of beer brewing. Updated: Jul 01, 2009.

Month	Event
January 16 – 18	Feria de Chocolate
January 29	Expo-Mundo Rural Región de los Ríos
January 29 – February 1	Feria Internacional de Artesanía y de Valdivia
September 17 – 21	Fiesta de las Tradiciones
October 31 – November 2	Expoprimavera
November 28 – 30	Expoarte y Cultura Mapuche
December 12 – 14	Expo comuna

When to Go

People from England and the Pacific Northwest will feel right at home in Valdivia. Winters are cool and rainy. Spring and fall bring spells of hot, sunny days. In summer, though, showers are possible at any moment.

From mid-December through February, Valdivia swells with vacationers. Services increase, prices rise and lodging is scarce.

Getting To and Away From Valdivia

BY BUS

Most long-distance buses leave from Terminal de Buses, which is equipped with bathrooms, showers, shops, restaurants, a call center, Internet access, a tourism information booth, post office, luggage keep and ATM (Anfión Muñoz 360. Tel: 56-63-212212). Bus fares double in the high season.

To Villarrica / Pucón: Jac (4:30 p.m., 5:45 p.m., 8:25 p.m., 3 hours, $6).

To Temuco: 2.5 hours, $5 – 6. **Cruz del Sur** (hourly 6:45 a.m. – 9:30 p.m.), **Jac** (hourly 6:30 a.m. – 8:30 p.m), **NarBus** (8 buses 5:45 a.m.–7 p.m). Also **Inter, TurBus, Pullman**.

To Los Ángeles / Concepción: NarBus (10:45 a.m., 3:15 p.m., 11:15 p.m., 5 hours, $16).

To Santiago: most buses leave 7:30 a.m. – 11:30 p.m., 10 – 12 hours—**Línea Azul** ($18 – 20), **Cruz del Sur** ($34 – 40), **TurBus** ($24 – 40), **Pullman** ($30), **Cóndor** ($22 – 50), **Inter** ($24), **Jac** ($40 – 68).

To Viña del Mar / Valparaíso: some Santiago buses continue to these destinations, e.g. **Cóndor** ($50).

To Osorno: 2 hours, $5 – 11. **Cruz del Sur** (hourly 6:30 a.m.-8:30 p.m.), **TurBus** (9 buses 4:10 a.m. – 5 p.m.). Also **NarBus, Jac**.

To Puerto Varas / Puerto Montt: 3 – 3.5 hours, $8 – 16. Many services are the same as to Osorno. **Jac** (hourly 4:10 .m. – 9:15 p.m.). Also **Cruz del Sur, TurBus, NarBus**.

To Ancud / Castro, Chiloé: Cruz del Sur (half-hourly 6 a.m. – 5 p.m., 6 hours / 7 hours, $15 / $17).

To Quellón, Chiloé: Cruz del Sur (9:45 a.m., 12:45 p.m., 2 p.m., 8.5 hours, $19).

To Panguipulli: Buses Pirehueico (Monday – Saturday every 15 minutes 6:30 a.m. – 8:30 p.m., Sunday 8 a.m. – 10:30 p.m., 2.5 hours, $5).

To Puerto Fuy: by way of Panguipulli.

To Coñaripe: by way of Panguipulli.

To Futrono: 2 hours, $4. **Cordillera Sur** (Monday – Saturday 9 departures 10:30 a.m. – 8:40 p.m., Sunday 2:20 p.m., 7:15 p.m., 8:40 p.m.), **Buses Futrono** (every 1.5 hours 6:45 a.m. – 7:50 p.m.).

To Lago Ranco: Intersur, Jac, Ruta 51.

To Llifén: Cordillera Sur (2:45 p.m., 5 p.m., 7:25 p.m., 2.5 hours, $5).
To Riñahue: Riñahue Sur.

To Argentina: To Junín de los Andes / Neuquén, by way of Temuco: Igi Illaima (Wed, Fri, Sun 11:15 p.m., 14 hours, $36), **San Martín** (Wednesday, Friday, Sunday 7:30 a.m., $34, 12 hours).

To Bariloche, by way of Osorno: San Martín and Andesmar (Mon, Tues, Thurs, Saturday, 8:45 a.m., 7 – 8 hours, $30).

BY AIR

Valdivia's airport is **Aeropuerto Pichoy**, located 32 kilometers (19 mi) north of the city (Ruta 205. Tel: 56-63-272295). **Transfer Aeropuerto** provides transport to the airfield (Tel: 56-63-225533). **LAN** has twice daily flights direct to Santiago (from $100) (Monday – Friday 9 a.m. – 1:30 p.m., 3 p.m. – 6:30 p.m., Saturday 10 a.m. – 1 p.m. Maipú 271. Tel: 56-63-246490 / 600-526-2000, URL: www.lanchile.cl). **Skyline** doesn't fly out of Valdivia, though it does have a ticket office in the city (Monday – Friday 9 a.m. – 1 p.m., 3 p.m. – 6:45 p.m., Saturday 10 a.m. – 1 p.m. Schmidt 303. Tel: 56-63-226280).

BY BOAT

You can also sail into the city. Valdivia's marinas are **Club de Yates** (General Lagos 1445. Tel: 56-63-213028, URL: www.cyv.cl), **Alwoplast** (Camino a Niebla, Km 8. Tel: 56-63-203200, URL: www.alwoplast.cl) and **Cabo Blanco** (Av. España s/n, Las Ánimas. Tel: 56-63-210869). Updated: Jun 18, 2009.

Getting Around

Busetas, or minibuses, have set routes ($0.70), as do colectivo taxis ($1.40). Radio taxis have meters and are cheaper than the cabs you flag down on the street.

International car rental companies operating in Valdivia include: **Avis** (Beaucheff 619. Tel: 56-63-278455), **Hertz** (Picarte 640. Tel: 56-63-218316) and **Budget** (Picarte 1348. Tel: 56-63-340060). Small local companies also lease autos. **Tourist House** (Monday – Saturday 9 a.m. – 7 p.m., extended hours in summer. Calle Henríquez 266. Tel: 56-63-433115, E-mail: info@casadelturista.com, URL: www.casadelturista.com) and **Turismo Los Notros** (Caupolicán 270. Tel: 56-63-211031, E-mail: 1notros@telsur.cl, URL: www.turismolosnotros.cl) rent bicycles. Updated: Jun 09, 2009.

Safety

Care should be taken at night when walking, especially along General Lagos and the neighborhoods east of Riquelme.

Keep to main, well-lit streets or take a taxi. At the bus stations, watch for thieves and *hospedajeras*, peeople offering lodging that may be a scam to set you up for a robbery. It is best to go to the tourism desk at the terminal and ask for the contacts of licensed accommodations. Updated: Jun 18, 2009.

Services

TOURISM

The **municipal tourism office** is on the first floor of the bus terminal (Daily 8 a.m. – 10 p.m. Tel: 56-63-220498, E-mail: turismoterminaldebuses@gmail.com; English spoken). During the summer, branches open in Parque Saval (Isla Teja. Tel: 56-63-220495), and at the north and south entrances into town.

Other tourism offices are **Sernatur** (Monday – Thursday 8:30 a.m. – 5:30 p.m., Friday 8:30 a.m. – 4:30 p.m. Tel: 56-63-239060 / 23-9061, E-mail: infovaldivia@sernatur.cl, URL: www.sernatur.cl; English, German, French spoken) and **Centro de Información Turístico** (CIT) (Monday – Friday 10 a.m. – 4 p.m. Av. Arturo Prat s/n, next to Feria Fluvial. Tel: 56-63-278100; English spoken). Useful websites are: www.valdiviaonline.cl and www.munivaldivia.cl. All offices have extended hours in summer.

Additional services: **Conaf** (national park office) (Monday – Thursday 8:45 a.m. – 5:45 p.m., Friday 8:45 a.m. – 4:45 p.m. Valdes 431. Tel: 56-63-245222, URL: www.conaf.cl), **Carabineros** (police) (Beaucheff 1025. Tel: 56-63-218864 / emergency 133). Consular representatives in town: Austria (Av. España 1000. Tel: 56-63-204021), Germany (Arauco 159. Tel: 56-63-203791).

MONEY

Banks are open for teller transactions Monday – Friday 9 a.m. – 2 p.m. Most are located on or near the Plaza de la República. All ATMs accept MasterCard, Cirrus, Visa and Plus, except where noted:

Banco Estado (Calle Henríquez 562) exchanges U.S. dollars, euros; ATM: MasterCard, Cirrus only.
Banco de Chile (Letelier 300).
Santander (Pérez Rosales 585) exchanges U.S. dollars, euros; ATM: also American Express.
BBVA (Independencia 533).
Scotiabank (O'Higgins 463).
Casas de cambio give lower rates than banks on all exchanges:
Arauco (Monday-Friday 9:30 a.m. – 7 p.m., Saturday 10 a.m. – 2 p.m. Galería Arauco, local 24, corner Arauco and Calle Henríquez) changes U.S. dollars, euros, Argentine pesos; American Express travelers checks.

La Reconquista (Monday – Friday 9 a.m. – 1 p.m., 3 p.m. – 6:30 p.m. Carampangue 325) changes U.S., Canadian and Australian dollars, euros, pounds sterling, Argentine pesos; American Express, Thomas Cook, Visa and other travelers checks; Moneygram agent **Chilexpress** handles Western Union wires (Monday – Friday 9 a.m. – 7 p.m., Saturday 10 a.m. – 1 p.m. Picarte 431).

KEEPING IN TOUCH

Correos Chile is the local post office (Monday – Friday 9 a.m.-7 p.m., Saturday 9 a.m. – 1 p.m. O'Higgins 575). There is a substation at the bus terminal.

Internet cafes are mainly along Picarte and Chacabuco streets. They cost, on average, $0.80 per hour. Most open at 10 a.m. and are closed Sundays. Skype is common, though cafés may not have headsets. **Comunícate Internet y Centro de Llamadas** charges only $0.70 per hour (Monday – Saturday 9:30 a.m. – 10 p.m. Picarte 505).

For cheaper international calls, there is **tecno.cl** across the street, charging $0.20 per minute to the U.S., Canada, the UK and Germany and from $0.25 for other destinations (Monday – Saturday 10 a.m. – 9 p.m., 11 a.m. – 9 p.m. Picarte 500).

MEDICAL

The public health facility is **Hospital Regional** (Ave. Simpson 850. Tel: 56-63-297000). Most pharmacies are located on Avenida Picarte and around the Plaza de la República. **Farmacia Ahumada** is open 24 hours (Picarte 310. Tel: 56-63-257889). **Farmacias del Dr. Simi** is an international discount drugstore (Monday – Saturday 9 a.m. – 9 p.m. Galería Arauco, local 5, Corner Calle Henríquez and Arauco).

LAUNDRY

Laundromats in Valdivia charge per basket load (approximately 5 kg/11 lbs of clothes). **Lavamatic** charges $8 per basket and has same-day service (Monday – Friday 9:30 a.m. – 1 p.m., 3 p.m. – 7 p.m., Saturday 10 a.m – 4:30 p.m. Schmidt 305. Tel: 56-63-211015). Updated: Jul 06, 2009

SHOPPING

All types of outdoor gear, from tents, cook stoves and sleeping bags, to rods, reels and spinners, can be picked up at **Lago Sport** (Monday – Friday 10 a.m. – 1 p.m., 3 p.m. – 8 p.m., Saturday 10 a.m. – 2 p.m.

Picarte, near Caupolicán). Also try **Pescadores** for fishing tackle (Mall Bigger S-6. Tel: 56-63-213038).

Valdivia has many fine chocolatiers, making not only cocoa-based treats, but also *turrones* (nougat candies) and other sweets. Many are at the intersection of Arauco and Pérez Rosales: **Entre Lagos** (Pérez Rosales 622. Tel: 56-63-212047), **Peumayen** (Arauco 241. Tel: 56-63-521840, E-mail: peumayen@gmail.com), **Nougat** (Pérez Rosales 619. Tel: 56-63-246777) and **Alterfluss** (O'Higgins 400-A. Tel: 56-63-244860, E-mail: meister@surnet.cl, URL: www.alterfluss.cl).

More traditional crafts, like woodworking, woolens and ceramics, can be purchased at **Canela** (Monday – Saturday 9 a.m. – 7 p.m. Calle Henríquez 266. Tel: 56-63-433115, E-mail: artesaniacanela@gmail.com) and at the **Mercado Municipal** (Yungay and Chacabuco).

Libros Chiloé has a small selection of travel and nature guides, maps and books in English and German (Monday – Friday 10 a.m. – 2 p.m., 4 p.m. – 8 p.m., Saturday 10 a.m. – 2 p.m., 5 p.m. – 8 p.m. Caupolicán 410. Tel: 56-63-219120 / 224040, E-mail: chiloelibros@surnet.cl).

Librería de Valdivia has a larger selection of literature (including Neruda and Isabel Allende) in English and French, has scant maps and nature guides (Monday – Friday 10 a.m. – 1:30 p.m., 3:30 p.m. – 8 p.m., Saturday 10 a.m. – 2 p.m. Lautaro 177. Tel: 56-63-271810, URL: www.lalibrariadevaldivia.cl). Updated: Jun 18, 2009.

Things to See and Do

Valdivia is full of sights, activities, and explorations. Museums and parks spread through downtown and across Río Valdivia to Isla Teja, boat tours visit natural reserves, isolated villages and historical sites, and the coast and many islands are dotted with colonial fortresses.

The coastal boulevard Avenida Prat is pleasant to stroll along, and Calle Yungay and General Lagos are lined with mansions built by the immigrant German community. Ruins from the 1960 earthquake can still be seen along the northeast bank of Isla Teja and north of the old train station. Most museums, parks and fortresses are closed on Monday in the off-season but have extended hours in summer.

Museums of Valdivia

Valdivia has many museums that cover a broad spectrum of topics. Some are located in the city itself, and others on Isla Teja across the river. Most are closed on Monday.

Museo de la Catedral (Monday – Saturday 10 a.m. – 1 p.m. Independencia 514. Tel: 56-63-232040) In the crypts of Valdivia's cathedral, you'll find a collection of religious art; the cathedral itself is open only for Sunday mass.

Corporación Cultural Municipal (Monday – Friday 9 a.m. – 1 p.m., 3 p.m. – 7 p.m., Saturday 10 a.m. – 1 p.m. Av. Arturo Prat 549, next to Sernatur. Tel: 56-63-219690, E-mail: ccmvald@terra-cl / ccmvald@telsur.cl. Entry: free) has galleries of itinerant exhibits by regional artists.

Centro Cultural El Austral (Tuesday – Sunday 10 a.m. – 1 p.m., 4 p.m. – 7 p.m. Yungay 733. Tel: 56-63-213658, E-mail: ccultural@surnet.cl Entry: free) In a restored German mansion, several rooms exhibit period furnishings and a gallery space.

Museo R.A. Philippi (Tuesday – Saturday 10 a.m. – 6 p.m. Los Laureles s/n, Isla Teja. Tel: 56-63-293723, E-mail: secmuseologica@uach.cl, URL: www.museoaustral.cl. Entry: Adults $3, seniors 2 for 1, children $0.60; joint ticket with Museo Histórico y Antropológico Maurice van de Maele $5)This museum, situated in a 1914 mansion, focuses on natural history.

Museo Histórico y Antropológico Maurice van de Maele (Tuesday – Saturday 10 a.m. – 6 p.m. Los Laureles s/n, Isla Teja. Tel: 56-63-212872, Fax: 56-63-221972, E-mail: secmuseologica@uach.cl, URL: www.museoaustral.cl. Entry: Adults $3, seniors 2 for 1, children $0.60; joint ticket with Museo R.A. Philippi $5) The history and culture of Valdivia, from the original inhabitants, the Mapuche, to the German immigrants.

Museo de Arte Contemporáneo (Tuesday – Sunday 10 a.m. – 1 p.m., 3-7 p.m. Los Laureles s/n, Isla Teja. Tel: 56-63-221968, E-mail: secmuseologica@uach.cl, URL: www.museoaustral.cl. Entry: adults $1.20, students and seniors 2 for 1, children free, free on Sunday) has temporary photography, painting and other fine art exhibits.

Museo de la Cerveza (Daily noon-midnight. Cervecería Kunstmann, Camino a Niebla, Ruta T-350, no. 950. Tel: 56-63-292969, URL: www.lacerveceria.cl. Entry: free) The museum covers the history of beer in Valdivia, with German beer-related postcards, and labels, cans and bottles of beer from around the world.

Steaming into port is the new **Museo Naval Submarino O'Brien**, a floating naval museum that will be docked at a location yet to be decided upon along the river. Updated: Jun 09, 2009.

Performing Arts in Valdivia

Thanks in large part to the Universidad Austral de Chile (UACh), Valdivia has a full slate of musical concerts, dance, cinema and other performance arts throughout the year.

Teatro Municipal Lord Cochrane (Independencia 455. Tel: 56-63-220209) Concerts, dance and other performances.

Conservatorio de Música (General Lagos 1107. Tel: 56-63-221916, Fax: 56-63-213813, E-mail: comusica@uach.cl / extensionmusica@uach.ck, URL: www.uach.cl/conservatorio) Hosts weekly concerts.

Cine Club UACh (Friday 7 p.m., Saturday and Sunday 4 p.m., 7 p.m. Universidad Austral de Chile, Campus Isla Teja s/n. Tel: 56-63-221209, E-mail: cineclub@uach.cl, URL: www.uach.cl/extension/cineclub. Entry: general public $4, students and seniors $2.) Chilean and international films, alternative cinema.

Movieland (Every night. Mall Plaza Los Ríos, Arauco 561. Tel: 56-63-278758) Commercial films in the heart of the city. Updated: Jun 09, 2009.

Feria Fluvial

When the sun rises on Río Valdivia, the merchant stands have already gone up in the Fería Fluvial. Carts of the day's catch are gutted and neatly lined up, mussels and clams clack as they're poured into tubs, and crabs claw vainly upward. Gulls, cormorants and other sea birds hover, circling, overhead, as fishmongers yell out the specials.

Fresh fruits of the sea aren't the only products hawked here. On the other side, bundles

THE LAKE DISTRICT

of cochuyo and strings of dried shell fish hang from crossbeams over sacks of herbs and spices, mounds of fresh-picked produce and buckets of flowers. Av. Arturo Prat s/n, across from the Mercado Municipal. Daily 6 a.m. – 3 p.m. Updated: Jun 09, 2009.

Boat Tours of Valdivia's Rivers

Bahía, Aramo and **Santa María la Blanca** boats do one-hour city tours along the Valdivia and Calle-Calle Rivers pointing out the history of the metropolis and vestiges of the 1960 earthquake. They also navigate around Isla Teja. **Polux** and **Bahía** travel to Punucapa village on the Río Cruces and into the Río Cruces nature reserve.

The Spanish fortresses are on the agenda for **Santa María la Blanca, Santa Sofia** and **Neptuno**. Couples can enjoy a romantic outing on the river with **Góndolas Valdivianas**. All boats leave from Muelle Schuster on Avenida Prat, where their kiosks sell tickets. Some of the companies are: **Santa María la Blanca** (Tel: 56-9-6622670, E-mail: mcaceres@saam.cl; has bilingual guides), **Valdivia Travel / Islote Haverbeck** (Tel: 56-63-227909).

Remeros, or sport rowing boats, are popular in Valdivia. There are several rowing clubs here, including **Club de Remeros Arturo Prat**, which has lessons and rents boats (General Lagos 1089. Tel: 56-63-212581). Canoes and kayaks can be rented from the helipuerto on the riverfront, just west of the **Centro de Información Turística** (CIT). Updated: Jun 09, 2009.

Tours

Many tour agencies offer expeditions to the Spanish fortresses, nature reserves and coastal villages, as well as historical explorations of the city. Some go farther afield, to the volcanoes and hot springs of the Andean region, or to the Seven Lakes region to fish and kayak. Other agencies take visitors on tours by river. Before booking, check whether entry fees and lunch are included in the price of the tour.

Turismo Paraty

Turismo Paraty presents several faces of Valdivia. Three-hour tours teach visitors about the general history of the city or focus specifically on the German colony ($14 per person). Another half-day tour explores the Bosque Valdiviano ($12 per person). Paraty also does full-day trips along the Ruta de los Lagos to Panguipulli and Calafquén, to the hot springs and the coast

($56 – 70 per person). This agency's minimum is two passengers. San Carlos 188. Tel: 56-63-200327, Fax: 56-63-215585, E-mail: paraty@surnet.cl. Updated: Jun 24, 2009.

Ecoturismo Antimahue

The agency creates personalized tours of the coastal forests and beaches, and of the Andean thermal springs and volcanoes. The lakes and waterfalls are also on the itinerary, with both hiking and fishing expeditions available. One all-day tour takes in Parque Oncol, Playa Pilolcura, Curiñanco, Los Molinos, the Spanish fortress at Niebla and Cervecería Kunstmann ($140 for four persons). Tel: 56-63-202577 / 9-8274878, E-mail: pkunstmann@antimahue.com, URL: www.antimahue.com. Updated: Jul 01, 2009.

Pueblito Expediciones

Pueblito Expediciones takes visitors to the waterways of the region in any season. Kayaking is offered on the many rivers and wetlands near Valdivia, on Pirihueico and Riñihue Lakes, and through the Quintupeu-Cahuelmó Fjords. Pueblito also teaches kayaking. Rafting through the Class III and IV rapids of Río San Pedro guarantees to pump the adrenaline. They'll also arrange expeditions to the alerce forests, dunes and sea lion colonies of Reserva Costera Chaihuín. San Carlos 188. Tel: 56-63-245055, E-mail: contacto@pueblitoexpediciones.cl, URL: www.pueblitoexpediciones.cl. Updated: Jun 09, 2009.

Lodging

Valdivia has *hospedajes*, or rooms rented by families, hostels, hotels and even marina hotels for those arriving in their own yacht. From December to March, the summer vacation season, prices increase and rooms are difficult to find. Reservations are recommended at this time of year. Campgrounds and cabins open for the season, also. Check with the municipal tourism office at the bus station and Sernatur for lists of lodging options and prices.

Camping in Valdivia

Valdivia has three campgrounds. The two that are open year-round are both located on Isla Teja. **Fundo Teja Norte** is a small, eight site campground, located near Parque Saval. It has basic facilities and rents horses (Los Lingues s/n. Tel: 56-63-293616; $20 for four people).

Camping Isla Teja offers 60 sites for campers. Its facilities include a mini-market, swimming pool, laundry and sporting courts (Los Cipreses 11 25. Tel: 56-63-213584; $25 for 6

persons).

The third, **Camping El Amigo**, with 12 sites, closes in winter (Bombero Hernández 125. Tel: 56-63-219994; $20 for four persons). Updated: Jun 24, 2009.

Hospedaje Valdivia 545

(ROOMS: $10 – 36 per person) This blue house has rooms for travelers arriving alone or in groups. Bathrooms are shared. The entire inn has recently been refurbished. Behind the house are several totally equipped cabins with two bedrooms, two baths and a kitchen. The continental breakfast, which includes bread, ham, cheese and coffee or tea, is an additional $2. The family has another, shabbier guesthouse at Arauco 869. Valdivia 545. Tel: 56-63-206013. Updated: Jun 09, 2009.

Albergue Latino

(ROOMS: $14 – 36 per person) Just a five-minute walk from the Plaza de la República is a brightly painted old German manor. This is Albergue Latino, a young backpackers' guesthouse on the shore road. Nearby are the Conservatory of Music and other arts departments of the university. Two large dorms share gender-designated baths. There are also private rooms with their own bathrooms.

Albergue Latino has all a budget traveler would want, including free use of the kitchen and Internet, plus a few additional perks, like the international film library and djembe drum jams in the garden. General Lagos 1036. Tel: 56-63-578319 / 229364, E-mail: albergue.latino@gmail.com, URL: albergue-latino.blogspot.com. Updated: Jun 09, 2009.

Residencial Río Calle-Calle

(ROOMS: $16 – 38) Residencial Río Calle-Calle may be a bit expensive for the true budget traveler, but it is well worth the money. This large inn, located just two blocks from Valdivia's bus terminal, offers rooms with either common or private bath. The rooms have nice touches, like desks, cable TVs, reading lamps and gas heaters. In the first-floor hall, breakfast and meals are served. If you like, have a nightcap in the small bar before turning in for the night. Anfión Muñoz 597. Tel: 56-63-213907. Updated: Jun 24, 2009.

Hostal Totem

(ROOMS: $30 – 40) Hostal Totem is an international traveler's choice in the heart of Valdivia. It is located five blocks from the bus terminal and two from the Río Calle-Calle jetty. The señora of this hotel warmly welcomes her guests and willingly discusses the historic photographs of Valdivia that hang throughout the house. Rooms are medium-sized and bright, with private baths and cable TV. The house has central heating. Breakfast is served in a sunny nook. Staff is trilingual, speaking Spanish, English and French. Anwandter 425. Tel: 56-63-292849, E-mail: hostal@turismototem.cl, URL: www.turismototem.cl. Updated: Jun 09, 2009.

Hostal y Cabañas Esmeralda

(ROOMS: $24 – 48, CABINS: $70) At the end of the main street in the bohemian arts neighborhood of Barrio Esmeralda is Hostal y Cabañas Esmeralda. The blue-trimmed white house with a large front porch was built by a German family nearly a century ago. The guest rooms are spacious and beautifully decorated. They each have heating, cable TV and a private bath. At the bottom of the terraced gardens, there are fully equipped cabins. Hostal Esmeralda is in the center of the city, close to attractions and some of the city's finest restaurants. Esmeralda 651. Tel: 56-63-215659, E-mail: hostelesmeralda@chile.com. Updated: Jun 24, 2009.

Hotel Melillanca

(ROOMS: $76 – 105) Hotel Melillanca is a stylish, modern hotel centrally located in Valdivia. Across from one of the city's several pocket parks, this luxury hostel is midway between the bus station and downtown's Plaza de la República. Hotel Melillanca is tastefully furnished, sporting picture windows, wall-to-wall carpeting, oriental throw rugs and flowers. The standard fixtures, like cable TV and private bathrooms are, of course, also provided. After a day of sightseeing, relax in the sauna. Av. Alemania 675. Tel: 56-63-212509, Fax: 56-63-222740, E-mail: reservas@melillanca.cl, URL: www.hotelmelillanca.cl. Updated: Jun 24, 2009.

Hotel Marina Villa del Río

(ROOMS: $100 – 124) Hotel Marina Villa del Río is a top-of-the-line lodging option in Valdivia. Located on the far bank of the Río Calle-Calle in the Los Ánimos section of the city, Villa del Río's rooms have beautiful views of the Avenida Costanera and boats treading the river's waters. As its name implies, this is also a marina from which you can embark on your own explorations of Valdivia's waterways. The hotel has a gym, pool, sauna and Jacuzzi, as well as tennis courts and playgrounds. It isn't all rest and pleasure here, though. Villa del Río also has events and conference rooms. Av. España 1025, Las Ánimas. Tel: 56-63-216292, Fax: 56-63-217851, E-mail: reservas@villadelrio.cl, URL: www.hotelvilladelrio.cl. Updated: Jun 09, 2009.

Restaurants

The influence of the German immigrants is very strong in Valdivia. Microbrews, like Kunstmann, Valbier and Calle-Calle, make delicious drafts that pair nicely with a *crudo* (steak tartar) or homemade sausage with spätzel and *chucrut* (sauerkraut). Just be sure to save room for the rich local chocolates. Being between the ocean and the Andean lakes, Valdivia's cuisine has the best of both worlds. Enjoy deep-water fish and seafood, as well as salmon and trout. Many menus here also include less-common meats like lamb, wild boar and venison.

Inexpensive seafood meals can be found at the homey eateries in the three-story **Mercado Municipal** (Yungay and Chacabuco). The south section of the market has some produce vendors. Better selections are found at the **Feria Fluvial** across the street, or the supermarkets **Unico** (Arauco 697) and **Santa Isabel** (Chacabuco 555). Daily lunch specials run from simple one-plate *colaciónes* (from $3) to three-course meals (from $5). Most diners close on Sunday.

Restaurant La Estrella

(ENTREES: $2.80 – 5.40) Tuck the napkin into your collar and chow down while watching the goings on at the Feria Fluvial and *remeros* slicing upriver. Restaurant La Estrella is one of more than a dozen eateries in the Mercado Municipal, but unlike many of the others, this third-floor diner has excellent views of the riverfront. The fish plates—featuring sierra, conger, corvina and merluza—and seafood dishes like the *paila marina* (seafood stew) are budget priced. Beef and chicken selections are more expensive. All plates come with boiled potatoes and salad. Open daily 9 a.m. – 8 p.m. Mercado Municipal, local 210. Updated: Jun 24, 2009.

Restaurant Yang Cheng

(ENTREES: $4.40 – 13, LUNCH: $4) A calm, elegant atmosphere is what Restaurant Yang Cheng presents to its customers. Its menu has a large range of pork, beef, chicken, duck, seafood and fish dishes. Yang Cheng also has a large selection of vegetarian fare.

Not only Cantonese-style Chinese preparations grace the palate, but also Mongolian, Peking, Sechuan and curries. The daily *menú universitario* has one choice of main dish with chaufan (fried rice) and drink. Open Monday – Saturday noon – 3:30 p.m., 7 p.m. – midnight. General Lagos 1118. Tel: 56-63-224088, E-mail: restaurantyangcheng@gmail.com, URL: www.restaurantyangcheng.cl. Updated: Jun 09, 2009.

La Última Frontera

(ENTREES: $2.40 – 19, LUNCH $5.40) La Última Frontera bills itself as the last frontier of cafés and rock and roll. The maze of rooms in this ancient mansion guarantees that you will find a place to get away for a meal or a drink. The space is done up with original paintings and mobiles. This is a popular place with Valdivia's university students. La Última Frontera serves over three dozen types of sandwiches with many for seafood lovers and vegetarians. There are also *tablas* (antipastos). Besides beers, this café offers juices, coffee and a full bar. It hosts music and literary events. Open Monday – Saturday 10 a.m.-2 a.m. Pérez Rosales 787. Tel: 56-63-235363. Updated: Jun 09, 2009.

Fuente Valdiviana

(ENTREES: $2.60 – 6.40, LUNCH: $5.20) Kunstmann isn't the only bräumeister in town. Fuente Valdiviana serves another of the city's beers, Valbier—and nothing but Valbier—on tap. This amber ale has a deep-honey color with a rich malt flavor subtly accented by hops. Have a mug to accompany the daily lunch special (soup or salad, main dish, dessert). This brew also goes well with a typical Chilean sandwich, hamburger, hot dog or crudo. Fuente Valdiviana has current magazines and newspapers to read while sipping on a stein. Open Monday-Saturday 10 a.m. – 11 p.m. Picarte 418, local 2. Tel: 56-63-432995. Updated: Jun 09, 2009.

Café Haussmann

(ENTREES: from $3) This small café, with only four booths and a counter, is Café Haussmann, locally known for two reasons. One is its steak tartar sandwiches. The other is that it is the only place in town where you can have their house beer on tap. Haussmann's brew is dark amber with a slight malty flavor. This is a creation of a cousin who also sells the bottled product of three types of beer and a bock, at Grassau (the brewery is near Pucón: Camino Freire-Villarrica, Km 7. Tel: 56-45-1974490,

E-mail: info@cervezagrassau.cl, URL: www.cervezagrassau.cl). Open Monday – Saturday 8 a.m. – 9 p.m. O'Higgins 394. Tel: 56-63-213878. Updated: Jun 24, 2009.

Salón de Té Entrelagos

(ENTREES: $4 – 15) Salón de Té Entrelagos is a place to go for an intimate escape. Its small tables are perfect for gathering with friends to have a delectable dessert and coffee. Entrelagos has savory foods, also, like platters of Mexican food, barbecued ribs, seafood and other delights.

Additionally, there are classic sandwiches and some original creations named for Valdivia's islands and rivers. Heavy wood cases around the main room showcase the chocolates and marzipan for which Entrelagos is famous. This café also sells a wide selection of boxed Twinings teas. Open daily 9 a.m. – 10 p.m. Tel: 56-63-218833. Updated: Jun 09, 2009.

Café Las Gringas

(ENTREES: $3 – 13.60, LUNCH: $5.40) Low jazz music wafts through this quarter-circle café called Las Gringas. This is a perfect place to peoplewatch while enjoying breakfast, the lunch special, a sandwich or dessert. Las Gringas prepares a special platter with homemade sausages from the region. But what really makes this place unique is that it sells every microbrew made in Chile. (Try the Volcanes chocolate bock.) Open Monday-Friday 8:15 a.m. – 11:30 p.m., Saturday 10:30 a.m.-1:30 p.m., 7:30 p.m. – 11:30 p.m. O'Higgins 400. Updated: Jun 24, 2009.

Pub-Restaurant New Orleans

(ENTREES: $12 and up) On a corner courtyard on Esmeralda in the chic Barrio Esmeralda, the flavors of ol' Louisiana reportedly have docked in Valdivia port, at the up-scale Restaurant New Orleans. As part of its Cajun and Creole cuisine, this bistro offers fish and seafood, along with chicken, beef and even venison, adorned with sauces like blueberry.

But let's cut to the chase and try the cornerstone of Cajun cooking: seafood gumbo. In a deep bowl, shrimp and large chunks of various unidentifiable sealife sit atop a mound of rice, and the subtle red-pepper heat induces a mild sweat. But, though it's not bad, something is missing from this Valdiviano attempt at Cajun cuisine. Open Monday – Saturday noon-3:30 p.m., 7 p.m. – midnight. Esmeralda 682. Tel: 56-63-218771. Updated: Jun 09, 2009.

Legado Jazz Resto Bar

(ENTREES: $5 and up) The Legado Jazz Resto Bar sits in the artsy Esmeralda neighborhood. Inside of this former home, bare stud walls create intimate seating niches for customers who come to have a shot of Havana Club or other fine Latin American liquor. You can also choose a Chilean wine, an international or regional brew, or a global cocktail. Monday to Friday a daily lunch special is served. Evenings, you can have a tabla, pizza, empanada or other light snack to accompany your drinks. After 11:30 p.m. on Friday and Saturday the heat turns up in Legado with live jazz and blues (cover charge: $2). Open Monday – Saturday noon-3 a.m.. Tel: 56-9-9409893. Updated: Jun 24, 2009.

ISLA TEJA

Valdivia's many rivers weave around a large island, Isla Teja, where German settlers built homes and industries, even a German School. Since the 1960 earthquake and tidal wave, many of the families moved on. Some of their mansions have become museums, like the Museo R.A. Philippi and Museo Histórico y Antropológico Maurice van de Maele. The shattered Anwandter Brewery is now the Museo de Arte Contemporáneo.

Isla Teja is also where the main campus of the Universidad Austral de Chile is located. Its **Jardín Botánico** along the banks of the Cau-Cau River is an enchanting get-away (Daily 8:30 a.m. – 6 p.m. Entry: free). Other parks on the isle are **Parque Prochelle**, which was the garden of the Prochelle Bottcher home (Tuesday – Sunday 8 a.m. – noon, 1 p.m. – 4:30 p.m. Entry: free), **Parque Santa Inés** and **Parque Saval**. Toward the southern point of Isla Teja, you can find ruins from the quake. The road to Niebla and the coast cuts across the island. There is a full range of accommodations on Teja, from camping to yacht clubs, as well as banks, Internet, restaurants and other services. Updated: Jun 22, 2009.

Things to See and Do

Museo de Arte Contemporáneo

(ADMISSION: $1.20, students and seniors 2 for 1, children free) Photos in the reception area of the Museo de Arte Contemporáneo show this building's fate—formerly the Anwandter Brewery—before and after the 1960 mega quake. In a wing that was left standing, the brewery found a new life as a contemporary art museum, hosting temporary exhibits on two levels. Three large gallery spaces have opened in the cavernous building upstairs and below in the cellars. Along the river front there's a glass wall, lending a modern air to the old concrete factory. Tuesday – Sunday 10 a.m. – 1 p.m., 3 p.m. – 7 p.m. Los Laureles s/n, Isla Teja. Tel: 56-63-221968, E-mail: secmuseologica@uach.cl, URL: www.museoaustral.cl. Updated: Jul 01, 2009.

Museo Histórico y Antropológico Mauricio van de Maele

(ADMISSION: $0.60 for children, $3 for adults) On the banks of Río Calle Calle, the former home of the Anwandter brewing family houses the Museo Histórico y Arqueológico Mauricio van de Maele. Named for the museum's founder, the first-floor rooms showcase the furnishings of different periods of Valdivian history, from the Spanish criollo Chileans to the 19th century German immigrants.

The second floor is dedicated to the history and culture of the indigenous peoples of the Lakes district. On display are impressive collections of Mapuche weaving, pottery and silver work. Tuesday – Saturday 10 a.m. - 6 p.m., Los Laureles s/n. Tel: 56-63-212872, Fax: 22-1972, E-mail: secmuseologica@uach.cl, URL: www.museoaustral.cl. Updated: Jun 24, 2009.

Parque Saval

(ADMISSION: $0.20 for children, $0.60 for adults) The grounds of Parque Saval come alive on weekends with families picnicking, strolling and just enjoying the outdoors. This 30-hectare park has two major attractions. Across the water-lily pond that even Monet would find a challenge to paint, islets are scattered like autumn leaves.

On one shore of the lagoon is the Parque de Esculturas Guillermo Ranco Espinosa with more than three dozen wood and metal statues by artists of various countries. From the park's entrance a right-hand road leads to picnic areas. A hiking trail leads to the top of a hill. Tuesday – Sunday 8 a.m. – 8 p.m. Ca. Manuel H. Agüero s/n, past Universidad Austral de Chile, about 3

km (1.8 mi) from the city center. On foot, cross Puente Pedro de Valdivia to Isla Teja and follow Avenida los Robles (the island's main street) to the roundabout at Los Lingues. Updated: Jun 24, 2009.

AROUND VALDIVIA

Up the rivers a bit, you'll come to Punucapa, a small village known for its pilgrimage and brews, and Reserva Natural Río Cruces, a reserve land created from the new brackish ecosystem left behind by the 1960 tsunami. Parque Oncol and the new Parque Nacional Alerce Costero south of Corral are popular destinations for hiking and birdwatching. Be sure to check out the Spanish fortresses studding the banks of the river all the way downstream to the Pacific Ocean. The ones at Niebla, Corral and Isla Mancera are the most popular. These off-the-beaten track towns, though, have a lot to offer travelers, as do the dozens of villages along the coast. From Niebla you can chill at Los Molinos, Curiñanco and other beaches. Near Corral are Amargos and San Carlos, both with colonial forts, Los Liles, Chaihuín and Huiro.

PUNUCAPA

 406m 1,150 63

Up the Río Cruces from Valdivia is the small village of Punucapa, which was originally founded as a Jesuit mission. Every February 2, faithful followers make a pilgrimage both on foot and by boat to the Santuario de la Virgen de la Candelaria, a 19th century wooden church. Punucapa is also famous for its apple sidra, or *chicha de manzana*, a slightly alcoholic drink. The apple liqueur isn't the only thing brewing in this hamlet, though: Cuello Negro, an artisan beer named for the resident black-necked swan, is also made here. Horseback riding and rowing are good ways to enjoy the natural beauty surrounding this hamlet. Punucapa is a popular stop on river tours departing from Valdivia.

Getting To and Away From Punucapa

To get to Punucapa, take the Camino a Niebla. After crossing Puente Cruces, take the turnoff heading north across the peninsula. From that route, another eastward road heads to Punucapa. The easiest way, however, is by boat tour ($8). Updated: Jun 24, 2009.

Things to See and Do

Cervecería Kunstmann and Museo de la Cerveza

(ADMISSION: Free) For a taste of home, German immigrants in Valdivia began brewing their own beer. With the 1960 earthquake, however, all the breweries were destroyed. The industry remained stunted until 1991, when the Kunstmann family pulled out the malt, barley, hops and yeast to once more make beer according to the Reinheitsgebot, or Empèror Konrad II of Hohenstaufen's Edict of Purity (1516).

This history is all explained in the Museo de la Cerveza at Cervecereía Kunstmann. Besides brewing Das Gute Bier, the family also has a restaurant serving German-style food, including spätzel, sauerkraut and mugs of the seven varieties of beer it makes. Large windows behind the bar reveal the brew vats. The restaurant is adorned with beer bottles and cans from around the world and German beer-themed postcards.

To get there, catch a No. 20 bus ($0.80) from in front of Valdivia's Terminal de Bus or along Calle Carampangue. Tell the driver to let you off at Kunstmann, 2.5 km (1.5 miles) after crossing Puente Cruces bridge from Isla Teja. Open daily noon – midnight. Camino a Niebla, Ruta T-350, no. 950. Tel: 56-63-292969, URL: www.lacerveceria.cl. Updated: Jun 24, 2009.

NIEBLA

 3 m   2,736   63

The road west from Valdivia cuts across Isla Teja, then the Puente Cruces bridge, back to the mainland. It passes Cervecería Kunstmann (Km 8) and runs along marshes. Nearing Niebla, cabañas and camping open up in summer. Just before town there is a dock for boats to Corral and Isla Mancera, as well as to various islands. Avenida Lord Cochrane climbs the hill toward the center of Niebla. Playa Chico is below the bluff.

After one kilometer (0.6 mi, 30 min walking) you'll find the Plaza de Armas and the village's most important attraction, Castillo de la Pura y Limpia Concepción de Monfort de Lemus de Niebla, or simply known as **Castillo de**

Niebla (April – October: Tuesday – Sunday 10 a.m. – 5:30 p.m., November – March: Tuesday – Sunday 10 a.m. – 7 p.m. Entry: adults $1.20, university students with ID and seniors $0.60; free on Wednesday). Built in 1671, this fortress was the most powerful in the network of Spanish fortifications guarding Valdivia.

Its 18 cannons protected the mouth of Bahía de Corral. A museum in the former Casa del Castellano details the Spanish fortification strategy and the conquest of Lord Cochrane during the Wars of Independence. In the summer there are historical reenactments at the Castillo. Niebla's largest celebration, Fiesta de La Candelaria, also takes place in the summer, on February 2.

The Muestra Costumbrista de la Costa occurs during the second week of February, and in March and September there are cultural fairs in Niebla and the coastal villages nearby. From the Plaza de Armas, Avenida Cochrane continues past more hostels, to Playa Grande, a broad beach with many restaurants, and Playa de los Enamorados. The road then follows the coast northward to lesser visited pueblitos, like Los Molinos (3.5 km / 2.1 mi) and Curiñanco (25 km / 15 mi), both of which have lodging, camping and restaurants.

For more information about Niebla, visit the **Sernatur** office in Valdivia, or at www.niebla.co.cl. Services in town are very limited. There is no bank. Niebla has many lodging options, especially on the road between the ferry dock and town, as well as on the road to Los Molinos beach.

Getting To and Away From Niebla

Niebla is 17 kilometers (10.2 mi) from Valdivia on Ruta T-350. In Valdivia, catch buseta 20 on Avenida Anwandter in front of the bus terminal, or along Carampangue (daily 8 a.m. – 9 p.m., $0.70). Updated: Jun 24, 2009.

Lodging

Niebla itself has several hostels. **Don Agustín** is open all year. It has eight campsites with potable water, hot showers, electricity and grills (Camino Valdivia-Niebla Km 13. Tel: 56-63-210608; $12 per site). Another option is **Hotel El Castillo** (Duce 750. Tel: 56-63-282061, E-mail: hotelelcastillo@hotmail.com; single $44 – 70, double $58 – 70).

THE LAKE DISTRICT

CORRAL

 282 m   5,463   63

On the south shores of Bahía de Corral is the village of Corral. Here, history and nature are prime attractions, and you'll find ruins of Spanish fortresses and beaches for swimming and fishing. One of the major Spanish forts in town, Castillo San Sebastián de la Cruz, was built in 1645 by orders of Virrey Conde de Castelar and enlarged from 1764 to 1767. Wildflowers now grow on its stone walls. Three guard turrets and a dozen cannons remain on the upper level. On the lower level, several tunnels lead to the beach. A sign designates the maximum height of the May 1960 tidal wave, which reached 10 meters (325 ft). April – October: Tuesday – Sunday 10 a.m. – 5:30 p.m., November – March: Tuesday – Sunday 10 a.m. – 7 p.m. Entry: adults $1.20, university students with ID and seniors $0.60; free on Wednesday.

One of the major Spanish forts in town, Castillo San Sebastián de la Cruz, was built in 1645 by orders of Virrey Conde de Castelar and enlarged from 1764 to 1767. Wildflowers now grow on its stone walls. Three guard turrets and a dozen cannons remain on the upper level. On the lower level, several tunnels lead to the beach. A sign designates the maximum height of the May 1960 tidal wave, which reached 10 meters (325 ft). April – October: Tuesday – Sunday 10 a.m. – 5:30 p.m., November – March: Tuesday – Sunday 10 a.m. – 7 p.m. Entry: adults $1.20, university students with ID and seniors $0.60; free on Wednesday.

From Corral, a road along the coast leads to ruins of an iron mill, a testimony of Chile's industrial revolution. The mill was destroyed in the 1960 quake and tsunami. The road continues to the coastal villages Amargos (2 km / 1.2 mi), San Carlos (5 km / 3 mi), Los Liles (12 km / 7.2 mi, hostels, restaurants), Chaihuín (27 km / 16.2 mi, hostels, camping, restaurants) and Huiro (30 km / 18 mi). There are other Spanish fortresses at Amargos and San Carlos. Near Chaihuín is the newest gem in Chile's national park network, Parque Nacional Alerce Costero, a 20,000-hectare area protecting a coastal alerce forest.

Corral has a basic tourism infrastructure. There is an information kiosk at the dock that is open only in summer. At other times of the year, stop by the **Municipalidad** (Esmeralda s/n. Tel: 56-63-333543, E-mail: turismo_cor-

ral@yahoo.es, URL: www.municipalidadcorral.cl). There is an ATM (MasterCard, Cirrus) at city hall. The town also has Internet, a photo supply shop, grocery stores and restaurants.

In terms of lodging, there is **Hospedaje Mariel** (Tarapacá 36. Tel: 56-63-471290; $10 per person) and **Cabañas Camping El Morrito,** which has 30 sites with potable water, hot showers, aquatic sport equipment for rent, electricity, laundry, mini-market and grills (Ensenada San Juan. Tel: 56-63-219862, E-mail: empresamg@surnet.cl; $28 camping, $80 cabaña for six persons).

ISLA DE MANCERA

Isla de Mandera is in the center of Bahía de Corral at the mouth of the Valdivia River. Previously called Guiguacabín by the indigenous people, this small island played a big role in the Spanish defense systems during the repopulation and holding of Valdivia. Valdivia was abandoned in 1604 following Mapuche attacks against the Spanish invaders.

In 1643, the Dutch occupied the ruins of the city, which drove the Spaniards to reclaim and reoccupy Valdivia in 1645. The first step in the plan was to build El Castillo San Pedro de Alcántara de la Isla de Mancera, on the orders of Peruvian Viceroy Pedro de Toledo y Leiva, Marquis de Mancera. Here the future inhabitants lived for over a century until they were relocated to the new city, between 1760 and 1779.

From the Isla de Mancera dock you can climb the hill to the village's present church, **Capilla de Nuestra Señora de la Candelaria**, constructed in 1910. Across the road are the ruins of the **Castillo**. Within its well-preserved walls are the vegetation-covered ruins of the chapel and other buildings. The site has placards explaining the layout and history of the fort. From the heights it is obvious why this was the lynchpin of the fortress strategy. You can see the mouth of the bay and far upriver. (Winter: 10 a.m. – 1 p.m., 2 p.m. – 6 p.m.; Summer: 11 a.m. – 1 p.m., 2 p.m. – 8 p.m. Entry $1.20).

Follow the path another 20 minutes to the overgrown ruins of the **Plaza Colonial de Isla Mancera** where Valdivia's population-in-exile lived until the city was secure. The road then continues around the base of the hill, to where the gun powder magazines once were, and back to the dock. Today the island is home to fewer than two dozen families, who earn their livelihood from fishing.

When to Go

The big holiday here is the procession of San Pablo and San Pedro, the patron saints of pescadores, to the sea on June 28 and 29. During the summer, there are historic reenactments at the fortress. The Campamentos Musicales de Mancera, a music festival, takes place January 5 – 12. Isla Mancera has only one shop and a few basic eateries. **Camping Canelito**, next to the soccer field, is a campground operated by the municipality of Corral.

Getting To and Away From Isla Mancera

Ferries headed to Corral leave from the dock near Niebla (every 20 minutes 8 a.m. – 8:30 p.m., $1.60). From Corral, the boat leaves for Isla Mancera ($1.20) and continues on to Niebla. Off Ruta 5 south of Valdivia is a 75-kilometer (45-mi) rough road that goes to Corral. Updated: Jun 24, 2009.

LAGO RANCO REGION

The City of Caesars (la Ciudad de Césares) was on the shores of Lago Ranco—or so thought the Valdivia governor don Joaquín de Espinosa Dávalos. In 1777, he sent an expedition in search of the legendary city. The explorers, unable to find a home with the Caesars, founded Llifén instead.

Today the major city on the shores of Lago Ranco is Futrono, "The Place of the Smokes" in Mapudungun (123 kilometers / 74 miles from the region's capital). Surrounded by mountains, this village is the place of traditions and legends. The main reservation of the Mapuche-Huilliche of the area is on Isla Huapi, accessible by boat from Futrono. Here, this indigenous nation maintains its customs. La Piedra de Bruja (the Witch's Stone) is said to bless visitors with a long life. Another mythical place is the Cueva de Weichafe where Mapuche warriors are said to have been protected by the spirits of the cave.

A 124-kilometer (74.5-mi) road, of which only 30 kilometers (18 mi) is paved, runs around Lago Ranco. Heading east on this route is the original settlement of the Lago Ranco region, Llifén. Midway there are several spots of interest, including the Reserva

Natural Mocho-Choshuenco, which is home to the 2,415-meter (7,849-ft) tall Volcán Choshuenco. This park's primary attractions are winter sports and year-round hiking. Between Futrono and Llifén you'll find Cruce Cerrillos, and from there you can take a side road to the Santuario de la Virgen del Lago and the rustic Termas de Cerrillos (15 km / 9 mi northeast).

The port of Llifén is on the far eastern shore of Lago Ranco, 20 kilometers (12 mi) from Futrono. Perhaps what drew the 1777 expedition to stay here were the hot springs located just one kilometer (0.6 mi) from the center of town. The village has many beaches, including Playa Bonita, Puerto Llifén, Piedra Azul, Huequecura and Caunahue. The fine sands of Bonita are accessible only by boat. From Cerro Huequecura there are great views of the lake, islands and the surrounding hills. Rainbow trout fishing is another pastime. Be sure to visit Santuario de Llifén and the Centro Comunitario Artesanal.

From Llifén an unpaved road heads to comuna Maihue on Lago Maihue, with hot springs, fishing and campgrounds. In 1948, poet Pablo Neruda hid out here while going into exile. Various communities around Lago Ranco are developing La Ruta de Neruda, following the footsteps of his flight.

The lake road crosses Río Calcurrupe and Río Nilahue, which has waterfalls upstream. This dirt road swings west through the hamlet of Riñinahue before reaching Lago Ranco. The city has several things to offer the casual visitor.

Parque Municipal Piedra Alfonso Brandt protects 25 hectares of native forest and offers views of the lake and its 13 main islands. Museo Tringlo houses anthropological and archaeological pieces. Lago Ranco's shore has over 10 kilometers (6 mi) of sandy beach. In summer, boats leave from the city's pier for cruises around the lake. The Campeonato Regional de Pesca Deportiva happens the third week of November.

From the town of Lago Ranco the road bends north to the Río Bueno. This river has a stretch of intense Class II and III rapids. Whitewater rafting runs on the coigüe and roble forested banks of this emerald river end at *el tapón* (the stopper), which is full of waves and whirlpools. Expeditions can be arranged with tour operators in Futrono. Balsas take passengers across the stiller

THE LAKE DISTRICT

waters of the mouth of the river. The route then continues northward past Playas San Pedro and Imahue. Four kilometers (2.4 mi) from Futrono, Bahía Coiquea has an expansive white sand beach, camping, a tourist complex and golf course.

Lago Ranco is Chile's third-largest lake. Its surface measures 42,300 hectares. The economy of the region is based on dairy farming. Traditional crafts in wood and wool weaving, along with tourism, are other important aspects of the economy.

When to Go

One of the area's most important celebrations is the Feria Isla Huapi in January and February. In town, travelers can soak up the sun on Playa Galdámez, or check out the Iglesia San Conrado, the Plaza de Armas and the Parque Botánico Futronhue.

Fishing can be an especially rewarding activity on the Ríos Blanco, Caunahue and Hueinahue. The season runs from mid-November to the end of May. Futrono hosts the Rally del Lago Ranco in March and a triathlon in October.

Getting To and Away From Lago Ranco

Travelers can make the journey by taking Ruta 5 Sur out of Valdivia to Los Lagos, where you'll find the 27-kilometer (16-mi), unpaved turnoff for Futrono. Further south on Ruta 5, at Reumén, there is a paved secondary road. A third alternative is to go as far as Río Bueno on Ruta 5, then take a paved road to Lago Ranco (42 km / 25 mi). The Lago Ranco region can easily be reached by bus from Valdivia.

To Futrono: $3.60 – 4, 2 hours—**Cordillera Sur** (Monday – Saturday 9 buses 10:30 a.m. – 8:40 p.m., Sunday 3 buses 2:20 p.m. – 8:40 p.m.), **Buses Futrono** (daily every 1.5 hours 6:45 a.m. – 7:50 p.m.).

To Llifén: Cordillera Sur (Monday – Saturday 2:45 p.m., 7:25 p.m., Sunday 5:45 p.m., $5, 2.5 hours).

To Lago Ranco: Intersur, Jac, Ruta 5. Updated: Jan 23, 2009.

Lodging

Futrono, Llifén and Lago Ranco have plenty of hotels, but most are open only in the summer. Campsites in the Lago Ranco include:

Camping Cuesta de Arena (Cruce Vista Hermosa); **Bahía Coique** (Playa Coique. Tel: 56-63-481264); and **Bahía Las Rosas** (sector Puerto Las Rosas. Tel: 56-63-481615), Maqueo (sector Maqueo).

FUTRONO

 272m   545   63

TOURISM

The tourism office is located in the **Municipalidad** (Balmaceda and O'Higgins. Tel: 56-63-482636, URL: www.turismofutrono.cl).

LODGING

Hostería Futronhue (Balmaceda 90. Tel: 56-63-481265)

Hostería Rosengarden (Km 1.5 Futrono-Llifén. Tel: 56-63-481044; $24 per person)

Cabañas Lahuenco (Km 1, sector Cun-Cun. Tel: 56-63-481326, E-mail: cabañaslahuenco@gmail.com; 1 person $30, 2 people $50 in low season; also has campsites)

RESTAURANTS

Don Floro (Balmaceda 141. Tel: 56-63-481271); **La Guarida** (Padre Leodegario 47. Tel: 56-63-481137); and **La Jungla** (Balmaceda 465. Tel: 56-63-481869).

LLIFÉN

 s/n   2,035   63

SERVICES

The village has a tourism office at the crossroads in the town center, supermarket and other services.

LODGING

Posada del Turista (Tel: 56-63-1971954; $12 per person)

Spa Termas de Llifén (Tel: 56-63-247810, E-mail: reserves@termasllifen.cl, URL: www.termasllifen.cl; $30 per person)

RESTAURANTS

Restaurante Hostería Chollinco (Chollinco km 3. Tel: 56-63-291919, URL: www.hosteriachollinco.cl)

Cocinería Rural Bello Amanecer (Sector Chumpeco s/n. Tel: 56-63-1971941).

THE LAKE DISTRICT

LAGO RANCO

 390m   8,070   63

SERVICES

Lago Ranco has a tourism office in the Municipalidad (Viña del Mar 133. Tel: 56-63-491212, URL: www.lagoranco.cl), food shops, tour operators, Internet, hospital and other services.

LODGING

Hotel Parque Thule (Km 2 Lago Ranco, sector Quillaico. Tel: 56-63-481293. E-mail: hotelth@tripod.com, URL: www.hotelth.tripod.com; $10 per person)

Hospedaje Los Pinos (Valparaíso 537. Tel: 56-63-491329, E-mail: hospedajelospinos@hotmail.com, URL: hospedajelospinos.blogspot.com; $16 per person)

Casona Italiana (Viña del Mar 367. Tel: 56-63-491225; $20 per person)

RESTAURANTS

Phoenix (Viña del Mar 141. Tel: 56-63-491226)

Ruca Ranco (Costanera 1000. Tel: 56-63-491406). Updated: Jan 23, 2009.

OSORNO

 87m   143,028   64

Osorno isn't much to look at, according to some. Admittedly, it isn't as beautiful as Valdivia or full of exciting outdoor sports like Pucón. This city is mostly used as an overnight resting post for travelers just coming over the border from Bariloche, Argentina, before moving on to more fascinating destinations. Nonetheless, Osorno does have a few things of interest—a list that is growing with the construction boom: a new casino on the west bank of the Río Rahue, luxury hotels and other buildings help to improve Osorno's image.

When to Go

Osorno has a rainy, temperate climate. Summer temperatures reach 14ºC (57ºF). Winters, from June to August, are wet and cold, with temperatures averaging only 5ºC (41ºF). Summer is festival time in Osorno. From the end of January to the beginning of March, Osorninos salute their identity with the Fes-tival Nacional de la Leche y la Carne, with gastronomic and artisan fairs, the election of the Milk and Meat Queen, a float parade and concerts. In mid-February, national theater troupes come to perform in the Festival Teatral de Verano. Updated: Feb 09, 2009.

Getting To and Away From Osorno

BY BUS

Terminal de Buses (Errázuriz 1400. Tel: 56-64-234149, URL: www.terminalbususosorno.cl) is where national, international and most regional buses depart. It has phones, restaurants, shops, a tourism information desk, Internet, luggage storage, bathrooms and ATMs (MasterCard, Cirrus, Visa, Plus).

To Valdivia: $5 – 6, 1.5 – 1.75 hours—**Tur-Bus** (10 departures 7:45 a.m. – 10 p.m.), **Jac** (14 buses 9:50 a.m. – midnight), and **Bus Norte** (7:30 p.m., 8:30 p.m.). Also **Buses Pirehueico**.

To Villarrica / Pucón: Jac (10:45 a.m., noon, 2:50 p.m., 6:45 p.m., $11.20 / $12.20, 3.5 / 4 hours).

To Santiago: 12 hours—**Pullman** (9:35 a.m., 10 buses 7:15 – 10:45 p.m., $60), **Tur-Bus** (every half hour 7:45 a.m. – midnight, $50 – 81 depending on service), and **Bus Norte** (14 buses 7:30 – 9:30 p.m., $38 – 72). Also **Buses Fierro, Igi Llaima, Nar Bus**, and **Inter**.

To Valparaíso / Viña del Mar: 14 hours—**Pullman** (9:15 p.m., $52 – 78), **Bus Norte** (8:30 p.m., 9:15 p.m., $54), and **TurBus** (10:30 p.m., $55).

To Puerto Varas / Puerto Montt: Not all services to Puerto Montt pass through Puerto Varas; $3 – 4, 1.5 hours—**Jac** (19 buses 5:30 .m. – 10:40 p.m.), and **Bus Norte** (Puerto Montt only, 5 departures in p.m.). Also **Buses Pirehueico, Fierro, Igi Llaima**.

To Ancud / Castro, Chiloé: **Quillén** (2 p.m., $9 / $11.40, 4 hours / 5 hours).

To Puerto Octay: $2.60 – 3, 1 hour—**Vía Octay** (hourly 7 a.m. – 8 p.m., last back 8 p.m., $2.60, 1 hour). Also, a kiosk on the east end of the bus terminal lot sells tickets for Octay (22 departures 6:50 a.m. – 7:40 p.m., last back 7:40 p.m.).

THE LAKE DISTRICT

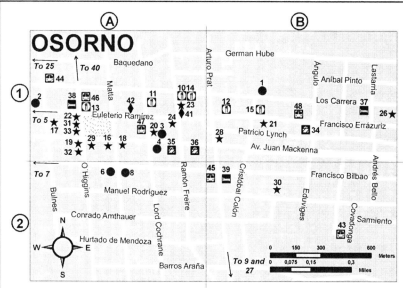

OSORNO

Activities ●
1 Cementario Alemán B1
2 Centro Cine Lido A1
3 Centro Cultural de Osorno A1
4 Centro Cultural Sofía Hott A1
5 Fuerte Reina María Luisa A1
6 Museo Histórico Municipal A2
7 Museo Interactivo de Osorno A2
8 Surazo: Museo de Artes Visuales A2

Airports ✝
9 Aeropuerto Carlos Hott Siebert B2

Eating 🍴
10 Frutas del Patio A1
11 Jano´s Restaurant A1
12 Mercado Municipal B1
13 Restaurant Don Omar A1
14 Restaurante Dalí A1
15 Supermercado Líder B1

Services ★
16 Banco de Chile A1
17 Banco Estado A1
18 BBVA A1
19 BCI A1
20 Cambiotur A1
21 Centro de Llamadas B1
22 Chilexpress A1
23 Ciber Café del Patio A1
24 Comercial Real A1
25 CONAF A1
26 German Consulate B1

27 Hospital Base B2
28 Lavandería Limpec B1
29 Oficina Municipal de Turismo A1
30 Police Station B2
31 Post Office A1
32 Santander A1
33 Sernatur A1

Shopping 🔀
34 Climet B1
35 Librería Clásicos A1
36 Pueblito Artesanal A1

Sleeping 🛏
37 Hospedaje San Diego B1
38 Hotel Lagos del Sur A1
39 Residencial Bilbao B2

Tours ◆
40 Osorno Extremo A1
41 Servitur A1
42 Turismo Frontera A1

Transportation 🚍
43 Auto Express B2
44 Automóvil Club de Chile A1
45 JB Rent a Car B2
46 LAN A1
47 Sky Airlines - Galería Centro A1
48 Terminal de Buses B1

THE LAKE DISTRICT

To Frutillar: Buses Fierro (every half hour 6:30 a.m. – 8:30 p.m., last back 8:30 p.m., $2.60, 1 hour).

To Lago Ranco: Ruta 5 (Monday – Friday 3 a.m., 5 a.m., 7:15 a.m., 6:30 p.m.; Saturday 5 buses 9:30 a.m. – 6:30 p.m., Sunday 4 buses 9:30 a.m. – 5:45 p.m.; $4, 2 hours).

To Panguipulli: Buses Pirehueico (Monday – Saturday 8:10 a.m., plus 5 departures 12:30 – 7 p.m., $9, 4.5 hours).

Osorno is the major hub for travel to Bariloche, crossing at Paso Cardenal Samoné: **Andesmar** (10 a.m., 10:30 a.m., 3 p.m., $28, 5 hours), **Quillén** (4:30 p.m., $24, 5 hours). Also **Tas-Choapa**.

Buses for Aguas Calientes and Entre Lagos leave from the Mercado Municipal (Errázuriz 1300. Tel: 56-64-201237).

To Entre Lagos (from the west end of the market)—every 10 minutes 6:45 a.m. – 9:30 p.m., last back 9:20 p.m., $2.40, 1 hour.

To Aguas Calientes: Expreso Lago Puyehue (9 buses daily 7 a.m. – 7:15 p.m., last return 7 p.m., $4, 1.5 hours). Three of them continue to the Anticura sector of Parque Nacional Puyehue ($9, 2 hours) and to the Chilean customs house near Paso Cardenal Samoné ($10) (10:30 a.m., 3 p.m., 7:15 p.m., minimum 2 passengers).

For destinations on the coast, like Pucatrihue, Bahía Mansa and Maicolpué, head across the Río Riahue to the Feria Libre de Rahue (Chillán 650).

BY TRAIN
Until mid-2007, trains for Puerto Montt and Temuco departed from Osorno. The rail company is awaiting new passenger cars before resuming service. Check the website for the present status (Mackenna 555, URL: www.efe.cl). A long-term private project is the **Tren de los Lagos del Sur del Mundo**, which intends to operate in the future (E-mail: trendeloslagos@yahoo.es, URL: www.steamtrain.cl).

BY AIR
Aeropuerto Carlos Hott Siebert is located at Canal Bajos, south of Osorno (Ruta 215 s/n, Km 7. Tel: 56-64-250540 / 232529). Both national airlines have flights from Temuco:

Lan (Monday – Friday 9 a.m. – 1 p.m., 3 p.m. – 6:30 p.m., Saturday 9:30 a.m. – 1 p.m. Corner of O'higgins and Ramírez)—Santiago (twice daily with a stop in Valdivia, from $160).

Sky Airlines (Monday – Friday 9 a.m. – 1 p.m., Saturday 9:30 a.m. – 1 p.m. Galería Centro Osorno, Cochrane 651)—Santiago (twice daily, from $62). Also Balmaceda / Coyhaique (from $106). Updated: Jul 07, 2009.

Getting Around
Busetas ($0.80) and *colectivo* taxis ($1-1.20) have set routes within the city. The main arteries for both are Bilbao (east-bound) and Los Carrera (west-bound). To get to the airport, take a bus heading to Puyehue and alight at the turnoff; from there it is a 400-meter (1312.3-ft) walk. A cab to the airport costs $8.

Among the local car rental agencies are **JB Rent a Car** (Amthauer 1189. Tel: 56-64-240000) and **Auto Express** (Esmeralda 1603. Tel: 56-64-212788). Updated: Feb 09, 2009.

Safety
Take care around the *mercado municipal* and town parks at night. The Plaza de Armas is patrolled 24 hours a day. Updated: Jul 01, 2009.

Services
TOURISM
Oficina Municipal de Turismo has a kiosk office on the Plaza de Armas (Monday – Friday 8:30 a.m. – 6:30 p.m., weekends and holidays 11 a.m. – 5 p.m. Calle Mackenna. Tel: 56-64-218740, E-mail: turismo@municipalidadosorno.cl). **Sernatur** also has an office but it is understaffed (Monday – Friday 8:30 a.m. – 1 p.m., 2:30 p.m. – 5:30, Edificio Gobernación Provincial, O´Higgins 667. Tel: 56-64-234104 / 7575). Other offices of interest are:

Conaf (national park) (Monday – Friday 9 a.m. – 1 p.m., 2:30 p.m. – 5:30 p.m., Saturday 9 a.m. – 1 p.m., 2:30 p.m. – 4:30 p.m. Martínez de Rosas 430. Tel: 56-64-221301 / 302)

Carabineros (Geise 846. Tel: 56-64-263505, Emergency Tel: 133)—Also has a 24-hour kiosk on the Plaza de Armas.

Automóvil Club de Chile (Bulnes 463. Tel: 56-64-540080 / 85)

Consulado de Alemania (Matta 549, oficina 1108. Tel: 56-64-232151)

MONEY

Most banks are around the Plaza de Armas. They are open Monday – Friday 9 a.m. – 2 p.m. All of the following have ATMs that accept MasterCard, Cirrus, Visa and Plus, except where noted:

Banco Estado (Bulnes 644)—ATM: only MasterCard, Cirrus; exchanges U.S. dollars and euros.
Banco de Chile (Matta 700).
BBVA (Mackenna and Matta).
BCI (Mackenna 801).
Santander (Mackenna 787)—ATM: also American Express; exchanges U.S. dollars and euros.

Casas de cambio have more extensive exchange services:

Turismo Frontera (Monday – Friday 9:30 a.m. – 2 p.m., 3:30 p.m. – 7 p.m., Saturday 9:30 a.m. – 2 p.m. Ramírez 959, Local 12, Galería Cuatro Vientos)—Exchanges only cash U.S. dollars, euros and Argentine pesos.

Comercial Real (Monday – Friday 9:30 a.m. – 1:15 p.m., 3 p.m. – 8 p.m., Saturday 9:30 a.m. – 1:30 p.m., 3 p.m. – 7 p.m. Ramírez 1079. Tel: 56-64-233483)—Exchanges U.S. dollars, euros, sterling pounds, Argentine pesos and other currencies; American Express, Visa, Thomas Cook and other traveler's checks.

Cambiotur (Monday – Friday 9 a.m. – 1 p.m., 3 p.m. – 7 p.m., Saturday 10 a.m. – 1 p.m. Mackenna 680. Tel: 56-64-234846)—U.S. dollars, euro, Argentine pesos and other currencies, and American Express traveler's checks; Money Gram agent.

Chilexpress is the Western Union agent (Monday – Friday 9 a.m. – 7 p.m., Saturday 10 a.m. – 1 p.m. O´Higgins 625).

KEEPING IN TOUCH

Correo Chile will post your letter (Monday – Friday 9 a.m. – 7 p.m., Saturday 9 a.m. – 1 p.m. O'Higgins 607). Internet in Osorno averages $0.60 – 1 per hour; however, the cheaper ones are generally slow. A reliable one is **Cyber Cafe del Patio**, which has Skype and charges $0.80 per hour. It also sells snacks and refreshments (Monday – Saturday 9:30 a.m. – 11:30 p.m.).

On Errázuriz near the bus terminal there are several Internet/phone providers. **Centro de Llamadas** has Internet for $0.80 per hour and international calls from $0.20 per minute (Daily 9 a.m. – 9:30 p.m. Errázuriz 1329).

MEDICAL

Hospital Base is the public health facility (Av. Guillermo Bühler 1765. Tel: 56-64-259200). **Cruz Verde**, **Ahumada** and other pharmacies are on Ramírez, between Calle Cochrane and the Plaza de Armas.

LAUNDRY

Lavandería Limpec is one place to go to get the duds clean before dealing with officialdom at the border. It charges $8.40 per basket (holds four to five kilos / nine to 11 pounds of clothes) and has same-day service (Monday – Friday 8:30 a.m. – 7:30 p.m., Saturday 8:30 a.m. – 1 p.m. Prat 678). Updated: Mar 13, 2009.

SHOPPING

One of the best places to pick up outdoor gear is **Climet**. It has a large selection of fishing tackle, camp stove gas canisters, tents and other items, plus snow sporting equipment. Fishing licenses can be obtained here (Monday – Friday 9 a.m. – 1 p.m., 3 p.m. – 8 p.m., Saturday 10 a.m. – 2 p.m., 3 p.m. – 6 p.m. Angulo 603. Tel: 56-64-233248).

Pueblito Artesanal has almost four dozen artisan shops that sell wood, leather, jewelry, weavings and other crafts (Daily 10 a.m. – 7 p.m. 1100 block of Mackenna, with Freire).

Librería Clásicos carries Spanish and English-language nature guides, as well as road and trekking maps (Monday – Friday 9:30 p.m. – 1 p.m., 3 p.m. – 7:30 p.m., Saturday 10 a.m. – 1:30 p.m. Mackenna 1071. Tel: 56-64-238626). Updated: Mar 13, 2009.

Things to See and Do

Exploring the streets of Osorno unveils many hidden delights of its history. The ruins of the Spanish fortress Fuerte Reina María Luisa are on the banks of the Río Rahue. German influence is seen in the former homes, now mostly restaurants and shops, on Calle Mackenna, and in the Cementerio Alemán. The Plaza de Armas, fronted by the Catedral, is a pleasant place to take a breather. Near the northeast corner of the square is a gift from Nobel Prize-winning poet Gabriela Mistral. A memorial to those who disappeared or were executed during the 1973 – 1989 dictatorship is at Mackenna and Ramírez. The surprises don't end there.

Osorno has the Museo Histórico Municipal, as well as science museums, art museums and several cultural centers.

Museums
While away the time at one of Osorno's many museums while waiting for a bus to your next destination.

Museo Histórico Municipal (Monday – Friday 9:30 a.m. – 5 p.m., Saturday and Sunday 2 p.m. – 6 p.m. Matta 809. Tel: 56-64-238615, E-mail: museosyarchivo@imo.cl, URL: www.osornomuseos.cl. Entry: free)– The history of Osorno, from the original Spanish colony through the 1960 earthquake.

Museo Interactivo de Osorno, MIO (Monday – Thursday 8:45 a.m. – 12:45 p.m., 2:45 p.m. – 5:15 p.m., Friday 8:45 a.m. – 12:45 p.m., 2:45 p.m. – 5:15 p.m., Saturday 2:15 p.m. – 5:45 p.m. Av. Diego Portales 5901. Tel: 56-64-212996, E-mail: mio@municipalidadosorno.cl, URL: www.osornointeractivo.cl. Entry: free)—An interactive science and technology museum in the former train station.

Surazo: Museo de Artes Visuales (Monday – Friday 10:30 a.m. – 1:30 p.m., 3:30 p.m. – 6:30 p.m. Matta 812. Tel: 56-64-313264, E-mail: mavsurazosorno@yahoo.com, URL: www.museosurazo.cl. Entry: by donation)— Art exhibits, film series and music concerts.

Performing Arts
To catch performances or movies, Osorno offers these other venues:

Centro Cultural Sofía Hott (Mackenna 1011)—Art gallery, concerts, literary readings, dance performances and other events.

Centro Cultural de Osorno (Matta 556)— Art exhibits, dance performances, concerts and other cultural fare.

Centro Cine Lido (Ramírez 650. Tel: 56-64-212534, URL: www.centrocinelido.es.tl)—Chilean, Hollywood and international movies. Updated: Feb 10, 2009.

Cemeterio Alemán
(ADMISSION: Free) Latin American cemeteries are a jumble of tombs, one lying virtually atop another. But Cemeterio Alemán is different. Its graves are laid out in precise, straight rows with pathways between. These family plots planted with ivy and roses, backed by sweeping headstones are a window inside the German immigrant community. The stones are inscribed in that language: Hier ruhen sanft (Here they rest in peace), Geliebt, beweint und unvergessen (Beloved, mourned and unforgotten). The oldest grave is that of Herr Justus Schüler, with a metal cross from 1859. A group of other original tombs is in a stone-wall plot near the center of the yard. Mausoleums reflect different styles of German architecture: from neo-Classical and neo-Gothic (all the rage during the Romantic period, when these immigrants came) to Bauhaus. Next to the Lutheran chapel is a blood beech tree from Europe. Daily 9:30 a.m. – 1 p.m., 2 p.m. – 5.30 p.m. Los Carrera, between Colón and Angulo. Updated: Mar 24, 2009.

Fuerte Reina María Luisa
Manuel Olaguer Felui designed this fortress at the bend of the Río Rahue. Originally called Fuerte de San Luis, its name was changed to Fuerte Reina María Luisa to honor the wife of Carlos IV. This fortification was to protect the future citizens who came to rebuild the city in 1794. It served as the residence of Gobernador Ambrosio O'Higgins (1796) and Juan MacKenna (1797 – 1808). After Chile's independence in 1820, Fuerte Reina María Luisa was abandoned. Today all that remains is two towers, a stretch of wall and three cannons. Updated: May 15, 2009.

Tours
Most tour agents in Osorno book air reservations and overseas trips. Very few take visitors on excursions around the city and region. **Osorno Extremo** devotes itself to paintball and canopy adventures (Tel: 56-8-7337984 / 7030715, E-mail: osornoextremo@gmail.com, URL: www.osornoextremo.es.tl). **Servitur** does city tours and day trips to area attractions (Galería Patio Freire, oficina 17. Tel: 56-64-522359 / 73, E-mail: servitur@regionloslagos.cl). Updated: Feb 10, 2009.

Lodging
If you are arriving from Argentina, you may need to spend the night here. However, it's better to continue to your next destination if you can, as Osorno has limited lodging choices. Budget hostels are generally very basic, some bordering on dives. The more decent places are filled with construction workers. Look for hotels that advertise "*habitaciones para vendadores y turistas,*" meaning only travelers are accepted. Between December and late February the city maintains a campground, **Camping Municipal Olegario Mohr**, which has bathrooms and electric-

THE LAKE DISTRICT

ity (off Ruta 5 near Aceso Av. René Soriano; microbus "Universidad"; $18 – 20 per site). In the summer the government also has an **albergue** on Ruta J50; ask at the municipal tourism kiosk on the Plaza de Armas for more information. Updated: Mar 24, 2009.

Hospedaje San Diego

(ROOMS: $12 – 14 per person) This simple white house, surrounded by a gated fence, is a mere two blocks from the bus terminal. You might mistake it for a private home if it weren't for the sign in the window: Hospedaje San Diego. The elderly couple who owns the place, Juana and Héctor, open the door to travelers. The rooms–all upstairs, in two wings off either end of a common sitting area with a wood stove–are spacious and have all the necessities, including a desk. Some get quite stuffy in the summer, though, as their windows face the hall. Everything is kept clean. Los Carrera 1551. Tel: 56-64-237208, E-mail: leonidas@telsur.cl. Updated: Mar 24, 2009.

Residencial Bilbao

(ROOMS: $34 – 48) This bright pink hostel isn't budget, but all the rooms are carpeted and have private baths, telephones, cable TVs and heating. This hotel is geared toward tourists and business travelers with its strategic location in the civic and financial heart of the city. Residencial Bilbao has a larger annex nearer to the bus station (Mackenna 1205. Tel: 56-64-264444), with similar prices. Bilbao 1019. Tel: 56-64-262200, E-mail: reservas@hotelbilbao.cl, URL: www.hotelbalboa.cl. Updated: Mar 24, 2009.

Hotel Lagos del Sur

(ROOMS: $104 – 128) Hotel Lagos del Sur proclaims itself to be "*en el corazón del sur de Chile*"—and it is, as well, in the heart of the city of Osorno. Located just a half-block from the Plaza de Armas, this hostel offers its clients large, well-decorated rooms with private baths and cable TVs. The hotel has all the tourist or businessperson needs, including 24-hour room service. Hotel Lagos del Sur's central heating is a welcomed amenity in Osorno's damp winters. O'Higgins 564. Tel: 56-64-243244, Fax: 56-63-243696, E-mail: hotelagosdelsur@123.cl, URL: www.hotelagosdelsur.cl. Updated: Feb 10, 2009.

Restaurants

Microbrews are a tradition in this region and Osorno is home to Volcanes, which produces several types of beer, including a chocolate bock. For inexpensive dining, ask for a *colación* ($1 – 1.50). The daily menu (a three-course lunch) costs $4 – 8. Pick up food supplies at the **Mercado Muncipal** (Errázuriz 1400), which also has many cheap restaurants, or **Supermercado Líder** (Errázuriz and Colón). Both are close to the bus terminal. **Frutos del Patio** carries dried fruits, nuts, soy products and other foodstuffs suitable for camping or hiking (Monday – Saturday 9 a.m. – 8 p.m. Galería Patio Freire, Local 7. Tel: 56-64-375885, E-mail: frutosdelpatio@vtr.cl). Updated: Feb 10, 2009.

Restaurante Dalí ❗

(ENTREES: $6 – 19, LUNCH: $7) Dalí is an upscale bistro tucked in a corner of Patio Freire's courtyard. This oddly-shaped restaurant is decorated with reproductions of works by namesake artist Salvador Dali. The young chefs add their artistic flair to the novo-Chilean cuisine they create. The menu emphasizes fish and seafood, as well as homemade pastas. Vegetarians can dine here, and weekdays there is a tenedor libre (all-you-can-eat) lunch buffet. Wednesday and Friday nights Dalí's features a seafood buffet. Open Monday – Friday 12:30 p.m. – 3:30 p.m., 7:30 p.m. – midnight. Freire 542, Patio Freire, Local 14. Tel: 56-64-201080, E-mail: dali_angel@surnet.cl / dali_miriam@surnet.cl, URL: www.dalirestaurant.cl. Updated: Mar 24, 2009.

Don Omar

(LUNCH: $3 – 4.60, ENTREES: $3 – 8) Cafe Restaurant Don Omar is a small, popular eatery only a few doors down from Osorno's Plaza de Armas. Its main attraction is its inexpensive daily special. Several daily plates are offered (including a vegetarian option), as just a colación or menu complete (soup or appetizer, main and dessert). Drinks are extra. The pace is hectic here and by the end of the lunch shift, it gets quite haphazard. Come early for better service and the full choice of options. In the evening, the diner is quieter and the waitstaff more rested. Open Monday – Saturday 10 a.m. – midnight. O'Higgins 827. Tel: 56-64-520237 / 20-1354. Updated: Feb 10, 2009.

Jano's Restaurant

ENTREES: $3.50 and up) Jano's Restaurant has it all: 15 types of daily specials, pizzas and all styles of sandwiches. There are boards of grilled meats, canapés or other goodies to share. Jano's also has a variety of non-meat dishes. International and local beers are served, as well as all manner of alcoholic and non-alcoholic drinks. Ser-

vice can be slow on Friday evenings during Happy Hour. Open Monday – Saturday noon – midnight, happy hour begins 4 p.m. Cochrane 547. Updated: Feb 10, 2009.

LAGO PUYEHUE

Lago Puyehue lies in the central part of the Lake District, in one of the most travelled areas of southern Chile. It is the largest body of water between Lago Ranco to the north and Lago Llanquihue to the south. The lake is along Ruta 215, an international highway that connects Osorno to Bariloche by way of the Paso Cardenal Antonio Samoré border crossing. All year long, travelers visit the hot springs or stop to cast a line into the lake's waters for a bit of trout and salmon. In the winter, you can also enjoy skiing at Parque Nacional Puyehue. The Mapuche called this lake Puyehue, which means "place of little fishes" in Mapudungun.

Continuing on Ruta 215 south of Osorno you will see tree-edged pastures, orchards and produce farms. Snowy, cone-shaped Osorno Volcano and the twisted point of Puntiagudo rise on the southeast horizon. At Km 25 of the international route you'll find the Auto Museum Moncopulli with over 80 vintage cars (Tuesday – Sunday 10 a.m. – 6 p.m., daily to 8 p.m. in summer. Tel: 56-64-210744, E-mail: automuseum@moncopulli.cl, URL: www.moncopulli.cl. Entry: adults $4, seniors $3, students $2, children under 10 $1).

Ruta 215 continues eastward, skirting the southern shore of Lago Puyehue. This side of the lake is the more developed, due to its long history. For over 2000 years humans have occupied this area. In 1260 the Mapuche nation crossed the Andes into Central Chile. The Huilliche of the region were displaced southward to the lakes region, including Lago Puyahue. This, in turn, caused the nomadic Poya to move to the Gol Gol River basin and the Puelche to move to the mountains in the south sector of what is now Parque Nacional Puyehue.

On orders of Spanish Governor Pedro de Valdivia, Teniente General Francisco de Villagra was the first white to explore the area, in 1553. The following year, Diego de Ortiz de Gatica was awarded a great expanse of land along the eastern shores of Lago Puyehue. By the 17th century, Spanish fortresses were protecting gold mines near the Termas de Puyehue. You can find vestiges of one fort on Playa Puyehue, near the entrance to the park.

Despite this activity, the region continued to be sparsely settled. In 1804, Juan Mackeena explored the lands around Lago Puyehue. He reported that it was an isolated place with almost no inhabitants, impenetrable mountains and an impassable swamp between Puyehue and Rupanco Lakes. The Reserva Forestal de Puyehue was established in 1914, but later passed into private hands. A rail line was constructed from Entre Lagos to Osorno to ship lumber from Puyehue and Rupanco. Parque Nacional Puyehue was created in 1941, to preserve the remaining virgin forests and natural attractions.

ENTRE LAGOS

Today the only town of note on the shores of Lago Puyehue is Villa Entre Lagos, 46 kilometers (28 mi) from Osorno. Entre Lagos is a cheaper alternative to staying in Parque Nacional Puyehue, with both hostels and camping. Besides being a good base for visiting the national park and hot springs, you can also enjoy fly fishing, horseback riding and water sports.

From Entre Lagos the road continues to be lined with cabañas and camping. Some of the attractions along this route are Golgol and Bahía Futacullín, where the Río Ñilque flows into Lago Puyehue, in front of Isla Fresia. This 400-hectare island in the northeast corner of the lake is covered with native forest, predominantly *pellí* or *roble*. Agencies organize hunting expeditions on Fresia, to bag the introduced species of red deer, fallow deer, mouflon, European roe deer and Bighorn sheep. The boundary for Parque Nacional Puyehue is at the far eastern end of the lake. The turnoff to the Aguas Calientes sector is Km 76, which passes by Termas de Puyehue. The north shore of Lago Puyehue is virtually undeveloped. There is the small village of Mantilhue, with extensive beaches, fishing and water sports.

Getting To and Away From Entre Lagos

From the east end of Osorno's Mercado Municipal, **Expreso Lago Puyehue** leaves for the Aguas Calientes sector of the national park, passing through Entre Lagos (9 buses, 7 a.m. – 7:15 p.m., $3.40, 1.25 hours, last back 7 p.m.). Three of these buses (10:30 a.m., 3 p.m., 7:15 p.m.) continue to the Anticura sector of Parque Nacional Puyehue (minimum $18; if two or more persons $9 each).

Other buses leave for Entre Lagos from the west end of the Mercado Municipal in Osorno (daily every 10 minutes 6:45 a.m. – 9:30 p.m., last back 9:20 p.m., $2.20, 1 hour).

Services

Entre Lagos has a full range of services, including a branch of **Banco Estado** (ATM; U.S. dollar and euro exchange), supermarkets, restaurants, phone call centers, Internet and shops carrying fishing tackle. **Agencia de Viajes e Información** has information about Entre Lagos and the neighboring region (O'Higgins 298. Tel: 56-64-371846, E-mail: agenciapuyehue@gmail.com, URL: www.agenciapuyehue.cl).

Lodging

Hostería y Cabañas Villa Veneto (ROOMS: $12 per person), General Lagos 602. Tel: 56-64-371275; **Hospedajes y Cabañas Miraflores** (ROOMS: $36/single, $50/double), Ramírez 480. Tel: 56-64-371275, E-mail: Olivia.hostalmiraflores@gmail.com.

Along the south shore of the lake, on the Camino Internacional toward Parque Nacional Puyehue, are many campgrounds, including: **No Me Olvides**, Ruta 215, Km 56. Tel: 56-64-371645, E-mail: campnomeolvides@gmail.com); and **Los Copihues**, Km 58, Tel: 56-64-371645, E-mail: camploscopihues@gmail.com). Updated: Feb 18, 2009.

Restaurants

Cafe Entre Lagos, Rodríguez 196. Tel: 56-9-5773093, E-mail: cafeentrelagos@gmail.com); **Restaurant Al Fin el Rancho**, General Lagos 769. Tel: 56-9-0752838, E-mail: restaurantranchopancho@gmail.com).

Things to See and Do

Termas Puyehue

(DAY PASS: $40 – 50 low season, $60 – 70 high, children: $20 – 30 low, $40 – 50 high) Termas Puyuhue, an exclusive hot spring resort, is in a forest clearing on the edge of Parque Nacional Puyuhue. The complex has a broad verandah around the two open-air pools where bathers can sun between dips in the thermal springs. There is also a roofed Olympic-sized basin filled with water between 35 – 36°C (95 – 97°F).

One way to enjoy Termas Puyehue is with a day pass, which includes access to the pools, sauna and gym, plus an open bar and all-you-can-eat lunch buffet. Visitors can also be a guest at the all-inclusive hotel ($300 a night for 2 persons) set in extensive gardens surrounded by native trees.

Services for overnighters include free access to all facilities, horseback riding, bicycles and four meals per day. There is also a cinema, mini-museum and tennis courts. Open 10 a.m. – 6 p.m. From Osorno's Mercado Municipal, Expreso Lago Puyehue passes by the entrance of the hot springs on its way to the national park. Ruta U-485, Km 1. Tel: 600-293-6000, E-mail: reservas@hotelpuyehue.cl, URL: www.puyehue.cl. Updated: Feb 18, 2009

PARQUE NACIONAL PUYEHUE

Parque Nacional (PN) Puyehue is one of Chile's most popular reserves in its national park system, due to the easy accessibility and wide variety of activities. Created in 1941, PN Puyehue protects 107,000 hectares of Andean *precordillera* (foothills) and *cordillera* (range). Altitudes range from 250 meters (813 ft) in the Río Gol Gol valley to the 2236-meter (7267-ft) high Volcán Puyehue. Several legs of the Sendero de Chile cross the Andean plains and wrap around the base of the volcanoes. The Centro de Esquí, on the skirt of Volcán Casablanca, is popular and when you just want to relax, check out the hot springs that bubble and steam at the side of Río Chanleufú. In the Mapuche indigenous language, this little corner of paradise is the Place of Puyes, a freshwater fish: the Puyehue.

Parque Nacional Puyehue's major volcanoes are **Puyehue** (2236 m / 7267 ft), **Casablanca** (1990 m / 6468 ft), **Caldera del Fiucha** (1481 m / 4814 ft) and **El Sarnoso** (1630 m / 5298 ft). El Cordón del Caulle (1793 m / 5828 ft) is a fissure that radiates out from Volcán Puyehue. This is the park's most active volcanic feature and along its length are sulfur and hot springs, as well as geysers. Puyehue also has approximately twenty lakes and lagoons, principally **Lago Constancia** (1290 m / 4193 ft altitude), **Lago Gris** (1080 m / 3510 ft) and **Lago El Paraíso** (990 m / 3218 ft). Major rivers are the Pajaritos, the Gol-Gol and the Chanleufú (Braided River).

More than 700 species of flora grow in these valleys and plains. The best time to catch flowers in bloom is from the end of November to mid-January. In general, PN Puyehue has humid evergreen forest with heavy undergrowth. Although primarily evergreen species–the coigüe, the ulmo, the tepa and the Chilean myrtle–some leaf-changing species, such as the lenga beech, the Antarctic beech, the Chilean fire bush, and the olivillo can be found here. Parque Nacional Puyehue also contains some strains of Patagonian cypress, Guaitecas cypress and, in the Antillanca sector, monkey-puzzle tree. The many ferns add a magical touch to the woodlands. The palmilla reaches almost three meters (10 ft) in height and the transparent filmy fern is the smallest and most fragile. Multitudes of mosses carpet the earth, including the musgo pinito, one of the largest in South America, reaching a height of 70 centimeters (27.6 in).

The fauna of PN Puyehue is equally as rich, and represents a large percentage of the species found in Chile. The area is home to 38 varieties of mammals (27 percent of Chile's total) including the Chilean miniature deer, the kodkod, the Chilean shrew opossum, the austral opossum, the South Andean deer, the lesser grison, the puma and the South American grey fox. Eight introduced animals, like the American mink and the wild boar, are also present. Amphibians represent 35 percent of the variety found in the country, while reptiles and fish also find homes in this humid land. The majority of them are threatened species. Keep an eye out for the Darwin's frog, the short-tail snake and the whitebait.

Parque Nacional Puyehue is an ornithologist's Eden. The 126 types of birds represent 27.3 percent of Chile's known species. Twenty-two are endangered or threatened. Birdwatchers will have the best luck in spotting avian life during the migratory season, October through November. Some birds to train your binoculars on are the condor, the white-throated hawk, the Chilean pigeon, the Magellanic woodpecker, the Franklin's gull, the black-throated huet-huet, the great grebe, the buff-necked ibis, the ringed kingfisher, the Austral thrush, the southern lapwing and several varieties of ducks.

The park is divided into three sectors: **Aguas Calientes, Antillanca** and **Anticura,** each with its own attractions, trails and services. If you are doing the Sendero de Chile, you can camp wherever necessary along the route through the park. The nearest grocery stores are in Entre Lagos, where camp stove fuel (*bencina*) is also sold. There is cheaper lodging in Entre Lagos, 30 kilometers (18 mi) away. On the road between the Camino Internacional and Sector Aguas Calientes is Termas de Puyehue.

Climate

Overall, the park's climate is wet and cool. Most of the park's precipitation falls between May and August, but you need rain clothing throughout the year. Parque Nacional Puyehue has three types of climate zones. The temperate rainy zone receives from 180 to 400 millimeters (7 – 16 in) of precipitation per year. The mountain climate (400 – 1600 m / 1300 – 5200 ft), has snow from winter to spring. In summer (November – March), temperatures reach 14°C (57°F). In winter (June-October) they dip to 5°C (41°F), but you should prepare for below-freezing temperatures. The icy climate is found above 1600 meters (5200 ft). Within this zone is Volcán Casablanca and its Centro de Esquí.

Five to seven meters (192 – 276 in) of precipitation falls annually, and the mean annual temperature is 3.5°C (38°F). Sector Anticura receives an average of 2658 millimeters (105 in) of rain per year, with a mean temperature of 9.8°C (50°F). Aguas Calientes has 3633 millimeters (143 in) of rain and mean temperatures of 8.8°C (48°F).

With each season comes different opportunities for adventure. From spring to fall you can go mountain climbing, bicycling, horseback riding or take a canopy tour. Sport fishing in the Gol-Gol, Chanleufú and Anticura rivers, and the Toro, Paraíso and Puyehue lakes is especially good during these months; however, a license is required. During this warmer time of the year you can also climb the Puyehue and Casablanca Volcanoes, and Cerro Pantojo (previous authorization of and registration with Conaf is required).

Spring and summer are great for camping, picnicking, kayaking and hang gliding, and winter is the season for snow boarding and skiing at one of the most important ski centers in southern Chile. The season runs June 1 – October 30 with Alpine skiing at Antillanca, and cross country at Antillanca, Anticura and Volcán Puyehue. Updated: Jun 22, 2009.

THE LAKE DISTRICT

Getting To and Away From Parque Nacional Puyehue

Parque Nacional Puyehue is on Ruta 215, the international road from Osorno to Bariloche. This is the camino international that leads to Paso Cardenal Antonio Samoré, the principal border crossing in southern Chile. The entire route is paved. At Km 76 is the turn-off for U-485, which goes to Termas de Puyehue and the park's Sector Aguas Calientes (four kilometers / 2.4 miles, paved). Ruta U-485 continues to Antillanca (18 kilometers / miles, narrow gravel). At Km 91 of Ruta 215 is Sector Anticura, 80 kilometers (48 mi) east of Osorno and 30 kilometers (18 mi) east of the village of Entre Lagos.

Expreso Lago Puyehue provides service to Osorno-Aguas Calientes (nine buses daily 7 a.m. – 7:15 p.m., last return 7 p.m., 1.5 hours). Three of them go on to the Anticura sector (10:30 a.m., 3 p.m., 7:15 p.m., minimum two passengers, $9, 2 hours).

A number of companies do the Osorno-Bariloche route, passing by the ranger station at Anticura. See Getting To and Away from Osorno (p.331) for more information on these services. Updated: Jul 06, 2009

Things to See and Do

The Sendero de Chile in Parque Nacional Puyehue

An important part of the Sendero de Chile connects with a trail in Parque Nacional Pérez Rosales, bordering PN Puyehue to the south. The trail covers 75 kilometers (45 mi) and is divided into two legs:

Anticura – Antillanca (*Distance:* 50 km / 30 mi, *Difficulty:* medium to high): This route goes from Sector Anticura, passing through Pampa Frutilla, to the Raihuén crater on Volcán Casablanca in Sector Antillanca. It is open all year, though there are winter restrictions in the highest part. Challenges of this trail include lava fields and snow. There is excellent birdwatching.

Antillanca – Santa Elvira (*Distance:* 25 km / 15 mi, *Difficulty:* medium to high, with some steep 30° slopes): You can begin this trek from Santa Elvira (65 km / 39 mi from Osorno) or from the park administration at Aguas Calientes. Highlights include lagoons, waterfalls, virgin forest, and abundant flora

and fauna, especially birds. From December to March you won't need any special equipment, but you do need good footwear, as you will be walking across lava fields. In other months you will need snow shoes to traverse the volcanoes, or you can sometimes cross country ski the trails (*esquí de fondo, esquí de marcha*). For more details on this trek, see www.senderodechile.cl.

Elvira has lodging and camping, as well as other very basic services. Updated: Jun 22, 2009.

Sector Anticura

Anticura—Rock of the Sun, or Sunned Rock, as the Mapuche called this area—is home to one of PN Puyehue's most potent volcanoes, Puyehue (2236 m / 7267 ft). The most fascinating feature is the Cordón del Caulle volcanic chain, a geological fault with hotspots that ooze lava. The Caulle is the most active volcanic feature of the park, with six eruptions since 1883. Several days after the 1960 earthquake that struck Valdivia, 21 spots lit up simultaneously, their ash appearing as far away as Buenos Aires.

Along the Cordón del Caulle are sulfur (*azufrera*) and hot springs, as well as geysers. Anticura also has the Pampa de Frutillas, a broad plain of wild strawberries, and Lago Costancia, a lake surrounded by mountains near the Argentine border. The ranger station at Sector Anticura has an excellent interpretive center.

The park has a series of trails that enable you to explore the volcanoes, plains and lakes of Sector Anticura:

Salto del Indio (*Distance:* 950 m / 0.5 mi, 30 minutes) and **Salto de la Princesa** (*Distance:* 950 m/0.5 mi, 40 minutes) on the Río Gol Gol, and Salto de Agua on Río Anticura (Distance: 1.2 km/0.75 mi).

Mirador El Puma (*Distance:* 1.4 km / 0.85 mi)—From the ranger station, cross the hanging bridge over Río Anticura, and zigzag up to a mirador with views of Gol-Gol valley, Volcán Puyehue and the Andean plains.

Pampa Frutilla (*Distance:* 20 km / 12 mi, duration: 2 – 3 days)—Along Ruta 215, three kilometers (1.8 mi) past the ranger station toward Aduana Pajaritos is the trailhead, which leads to a high plain covered with wild strawberries. From here you can continue to Pantojo or Volcán Casablanca.

Other trails include **Repucura** (*Distance:* 1.1 km / 0.7 mi, *Duration:* 1 hour), Los Derrumbes (*Distance:* 580 m / 0.35 mi, *Duration:* 45 minutes), **Mirador el Puma** (1.4 km/0.85 mi) and **Pampa del Pudú** (3.5 km/2.1 mi). A leg of the **Sendero de Chile** also begins here, passing through Pampa de Frutillas and Sector Antillanca (*Distance:* 50 km/30 mi, *Difficulty:* medium to high). For more information, see The Sendero de Chile in Parque Nacional Puyehue (p.340) or visit www.senderodechile.cl.

The community living within Sector Anticura operates **Restaurant El Caulle**. Services include restaurant, camping, cabins ($64 double) and an albergue ($9 per person).

You can also find horseback riding, guided hikes to El Caulle, geysers, Volcán Puyehue and fly fishing (Ruta 215, Km 90, E-mail: contacto@elcaulle.com, URL: www.elcaulle.com; in Osorno: Los Carrera 1145, Oficina 15-19. Tel: 56-64-233233). There is a privately run refuge ($14) on Volcán Puyehue. Also at Anticura is **Hostería y Camping Catrue** (eight sites, table, fire pit, water, wood). Updated: Jun 08, 2009.

Sector Antillanca

Antillanca means Jewel of the Sun in Mapudungún. Rising from the Andean plain, is the conical, chunky Volcán Casablanca (1990 meters / 6468 feet). On its slopes is Centro de Ski Antillanca, ranked one of the best ski centers in southern Chile. Operated by the Club Andino de Osorno, this 512-hectare facility has lifts and 17 runs for novice and expert skiers and snowboarders. Equipment rental and ski lessons are available.

All year long, hikers spread across the sector. Sendero Lago Paraíso goes from beyond Control El Toro on Lago Toro to Río Pulefú and Lago Paraíso, then to Cerro Colorado where it joins with the Sendero del Colorado. Other trails are **Río Pulefú, Lago Rupanco, Las Cuevas, Sendero Haique** and **Bertín** (for this, see Sector Aguas Calientes). Two legs of the Sendero de Chile also begin here, one going to Sector Anticura (*Distance:* 50 km / 30 mi, *Difficulty:* medium to high) and to the village of Santa Elvira (25 km / 15 mi, medium to high, with some steep 30° slopes). For more information, see The Sendero de Chile in Parque Nacional Puyehue (p.340) or visit www.senderodechile.cl.

Hotel Antillanca is open all year. The lodge has its own hot springs, restaurant and cafeteria. It also maintains **Club Andino de Osorno** (Oficina Comercial O'Higgins, oficina 1073, Casilla 765. Tel: 56-64-235114 / 2297, E-mail: info@skiantillanca.cl, URL: www.skiantillanca.cl). Updated: Jun 08, 2009.

Sector Aguas Calientes

Sector Aguas Calientes is best-known for its hot springs. It is also the easiest section of the park to reach with public transportation. Rangers lead guided hikes from its interpretive center in January and February. The center also has reliable, bilingual flora and fauna guides for sale (daily 9 a.m. – 1 p.m, 2 p.m. – 6 p.m.). Services include a restaurant, café, picnic area, lodging and camping.

The area is home to two different types of hot springs: covered and open air. You can find the covered pools in the main compound of the sector. To get to the open-air pools, take a path leading down to the banks of Río Chanleufú. There are also individual, private basins available. The waters, which reach a maximum temperature of 74°C (165°F) are rich in sulfates, potassium, sodium, magnesium and other mineral salts. They are said to be good for a host of respiratory, skin and joint ailments. (Daily 8:30 a.m. – 7 p.m. Covered pools: adults $14, children $7; Open pools: adults $6, children $3).

A number of trails wind through the forest to different points of interest. Most are short and easy:

Los Rápidos (*Distance:* 1.25 km / 0.75 mi, *Duration:* 1 hour): After crossing over a hanging bridge near the open air thermal pools, this path continues downstream to the rapids on Río Chanleufú.

El Rocodo (*Distance:* 380 m / 1235 ft, *Duration:* 15 min): A short loop that begins near the picnic area on the other side of the river from the hot springs.

El Pionero (*Distance:* 1.8 km / 1 mi, *Duration:* 1.3 hours): To a mirador behind Aguas Calientes, giving views over Lago Puyehue and Río Chanleufú.

Lago Bertín (*Distance:* 11 km / 6.6 mi, *Duration:* 5 hours): Along the Río Chanleufú, heading into Sector Antillanca to Lago Bertín where there is a rustic refuge for six persons.

THE LAKE DISTRICT

Lago Paraíso (*Distance:* 7 km / 4.2 mi): Beginning from Lago Toro, through evergreen forest to Lago Paraíso.

Another attraction in Sector Aguas Calientes is the **Mallines**, a lagoon with vegetative pillow formations, plus views of Volcán Casablanca with *ciprés de las guaitecas* (on Ruta U 485, 8 km / 4.8 mi from Aguas Calientes). On the road to Antillanca are several other lagoons: **El Espejo** (3.5 km / 2.1 mi from Aguas Calientes), **La Copa** (3.7 km / 2.25 mi) and lakes **El Encanto** (5 km / 3 mi), **Toro Chico** (9 km / 5.4 mi) and Toro (10 km/6 mi).

Both cabins and camping areas are available at Aguas Calientes: **Cabins with kitchenette:** 4-person $140 (high), $96 (low) to 10-person cabins $20 (high), $190 (low) (Tel: 56-64-33170, E-mail: reservas@ termasaguascalientes.com, URL: www.termasaguascalientes.com; in Osorno: **Oficina Comercial Osorno**, Matta 1216. Tel: 56-64-236988; major credit cards accepted).

Camping Chanleufú, past the ranger station, has 34 sites with full services: (low season $20, high season $28). **Camping Los Derrumbes**, at the end of the road, past the park administration building, has 20 more rustic sites (no showers or water, $16).

You can find food at **Restaurant Los Canelos y Quincho** (both very expensive, daily special $12 – 18); which also rents picnic tables ($12) and has a snack shop. Updated: Jul 07, 2009.

LAGO LLANQUIHUE

The crystalline waters of Lago Llanquihue, the country's second largest lake, shine like the five-pointed star of the nation's flag. In the mid-19th century, this area became quite popular with German immigrants. The fertile lands were perfect for raising crops and cattle. The many towns that dot the shores of Lago Llanquihue still retain their Teutonic architecture and cultural traditions. The churches of the region, built by German priests and teachers, are predominantly northern European neo-Romanesque and neo-Gothic in style; the iglesias in Puerto Varas, Frutillar, Puerto Octay, Los Bajos, Playa Maitén and Puerto Fonck are such examples.

But the beauty of the region extends far beyond the man-made elements. *Pachamama* (Mother Earth) created natural wonders long before the arrival of the Germans, or even the indigenous Mapuche-Huilliche people. Ringing the lake are the Osorno (2,652 m / 8,619 ft) and Calbuco Volcanoes (2,015 m / 6,549 ft), and evergreen forests. All this diversity makes Lago Llanquihue one of the most visited lakes in the Lake District.

Reserva Nacional Llanquihue, Parque Nacional Alerce Andino, Monumento Natural Nahuel Ñadi and Parque Nacional Vicente Pérez Rosales protect a large portion of Lago Llanquihue's forests. These parks provide a number of activities for outdoors enthusiasts, including trekking, hiking, horseback riding and mountain climbing. From Puerto Octay, hike around Volcán Osorno to Lago Todos los Santos, or do a three-day mountain bike tour around Lago Llanquihue.

Some of the best fly fishing in the country is here, with brown (*fario*) and rainbow (*arco iris*) trout, and salmon. You can go rafting or canyoning down the rapids of the Petrohué River, which flows between Lagos Petrohué and Llanquihue. For a more relaxed tour, sail from Puerto Varas aboard the Capitán Haase, a motorized, corsair-style 65-foot long boat, or cruise across Lago Todo los Santos into Argentina.

A 186-kilometer (112-mi) circuit around the lake leads you into the many vistas of Lago Llanquihue. From Osorno, Ruta U-55 heads south toward Lago Llaniquihue. Across the rolling land, pine and broad-leaf trees edge fields of alfalfa and pastures of dairy cattle and sheep. Wildflowers blossom alongside the road. After about 50 kilometers (30 mi), you'll arrive at Puerto Octay, on the north point of Lago Llanquihue. This village still retains much of its German character.

From Puerto Octay, the road hugs the north shore, passing through Puerto Fonck, then arriving at Las Cascadas on the eastern shore of Lago Llanquihue (20 km / 12 mi from Puerto Octay). The views of the volcanoes Osorno, Calbuco, Puntiagudo and Tronador (3,460 m / 11,245 ft) are breathtaking. This village makes a good base camp for climbing the peak of Volcán Osorno.

Those who come just to enjoy unblemished nature may soak up the rays on the fine sand beach or hike the trail through the native forests to Laguna Verde. The waterfalls draping the hillside a few kilometers from town are one of the area's main attractions. Las Cascadas is a favorite summer vacation spot. During the low season, the hamlet goes into hibernation.

A narrow gravel road winds southward from Las Cascadas to Ensenada on the southeast corner of lake. Along the way you'll cross a lava flow from the 1835 eruption of Volcán Osorno. Ensenada is the gateway village into Parque Nacional Vicente Pérez Rosales. The big attractions of this park are the **Saltos de Petrohué**, the emerald-colored **Laguna Verde** and the Osorno Volcano with the **Centro de Ski y Montaña Volcán Osorno** (Ensenada - Volcán Osorno, Km 14.3. Tel: 56-65-233445).

From Ensenada, another road heads southeast into the Reserva Nacional Llanquihue, which can be accessed by way of the road to Lago Chapo and Río Blanco village. There, an eight-kilometer (4.8 mi) trail leads to a rustic refuge on the flanks of Volcán Calbuco. A couple of festivals you might want to see while in Ensenada are the *Fiesta de Murta*, focusing on products made of the local myrtle plant (third weekend of April), and the *Fiesta de San Sebastián*, the patron saint (January 20).

The route then heads westward along Lago Llanquihue's southern shore to the most-visited town in this region, Puerto Varas. This village of rose-lined streets is considered one of the most beautiful in Chile. Touring the German architecture, fishing, rafting, boating and canopying are just a few of the adventures you can undertake here. Nearby is Parque Nahuel Ñadi, a 200-hectare nature reserve.

From Puerto Varas, the circuit around the lake begins to swing north. Llanquihue is an agricultural city and home of Cecinas Llanquihue, a sausage maker. Further north is Frutillar, a village renowned for its Bavarian architecture, gardens and annual music festival. Just before returning to Puerto Octay, you come to Quilanto, a hamlet with views of the volcanoes, islands and Península Centinela. For more about the Lago Llanquihue region visit: www.lagollanquihue.cl, www.lagollanquihue.com or www.interpatagonia.com.

Getting To and Away From Lago Llanquihue

You can get to the villages around Lago Llanquihue from Osorno or Puerto Montt. Buses connect Puerto Octay with Las Cascadas and Frutillar. Puerto Varas is the jumping-off point for Ensenada and Parque Nacional Vicente Pérez Rosales.

From Osorno: Osorno's **Terminal de Buses** is at Errázuriz 1400 (Tel: 56-65-234149, URL: www.terminalbusesosorno.cl).

To Puerto Octay: $2.60-3, 1 hour—Vía Octay (hourly 7 a.m. – 8 p.m., last back 8 p.m., $2.60, 1 hour). Also, a kiosk on the east end of the bus terminal lot sells tickets for Octay (22 departures 6:50 a.m. – 7:40 p.m., last back 7:40 p.m.).

To Frutillar: Buses Fierro (half-hourly 6:30 a.m. – 8:30 p.m., last back 8:30 p.m., $2.60, 1 hour).

To Puerto Varas / Puerto Montt: Not all services to Puerto Montt pass through Puerto Varas; $3 – 4, 1.5 hours—Jac (19 buses 5:30 a.m. – 10:40 p.m.), **Bus Norte** (Puerto Montt only, 5 departures in p.m.). Also **Buses Pirehueico**, **Fierro**, and **Igi Llaima**.

From Puerto Montt: The **Terminal de Buses** is at Av. Diego Portales s/n (Tel: 56-65-349011). Micros to villages around Lago Llanquihue leave from Andenes 1-15 every 5 – 15 minutes.
To Puerto Varas: $1.20, 20 minutes.
To Llanquihue: $1.40, 30 minutes.
To Futillar: $1.60, 40 minutes.
To Puerto Octay: go by way of Frutillar; for Ensenada, transfer in Puerto Varas; for las Cascadas, change in Puerto Octay.
Updated: Jun 17, 2009.

AROUND LAGO LLANQUIHUE

LAS CASCADAS

LODGING

Camping Las Cascadas (V. Pérez Rosales s/n. Tel: 56-9-6188333, E-mail: osacacada@hotmail.com): 2 people $8.

La Posada del Colono (Tel: 56-9-7547464, E-mail: laposadadelcolono@hotmail.com, URL: www.laposadadelcolono.cl): 19th-century German house with an archaeological collection, $17 per person.

Hostería Irma (Las Cascadas s/n. Tel: 56-64-396227): $16 per person.

THE LAKE DISTRICT

RESTAURANTS

Restaurant Rio de Lava (Calle Vicente Peres Rosales. Tel: 56-9-88473647)

LLANQUIHUE

Tourism

Corporación Turismo de Llanquihue (Tel: 56-65-242114 / 56-65-242658)

Landschaft (Camino a Totoral, Km 1, Casilla: 158. Tel: 56-65-242658)

Los Ulmos (Casilla 105. Tel: 56-54-338403, Cel: 56-9-6470822)

Keeping in Touch

Cabinas Telefónicas (Baquedano corner M. Bulnes); **Correo** (V. P. Rosales corner O'Higgins)

Shopping

Cecinas Llanquihue (O'Higgins and Matta. Tel: 56-65-242614, URL: www.cecinas-llanquihue.cl): sausages and smoked meats.

Lodging

Camping Baumbach (Camino a Tortoral 2200. Tel: 56-65-242643)

Hospedaje Wiehoff (Errázuriz 154. Tel: 56-9-9596799)

Cabañas Los Encinos (Camino Llanquihue, Tortoral, Km 6. Tel: 56-65-330115)

Restaurants

Baumbach (Camino a Totoral Tel: 56-65-242643)

Las Margaritas (Camino a Totoral, Km 2. Tel: 56-65-242607)

Cervecería Colonos (Km 4. Tel: 56-65-242160). Updated: Jul 07, 2009.

PUERTO OCTAY

 101m   328   64

Visiting the small, picturesque village of Puerto Octay, on the northern-most shore of Lago Llanquihue, is like taking a step back into time to when the German colonists first came. Many of the the port town's farmhouses, surrounded by orchards, are over a century old, and the countryside is dotted with colonial-era mills. Boats leave from the pier, exporting products and taking vacationers on tours around the placid lake. Volcanoes Osorno (2,652 m / 8619 ft) and Puntiagudo (2,190 m / 7118 ft) rise above the eastern horizon.

After the first Mapuche peace treaty was signed in Osorno, Bernardo Philippi and Vicente Pérez Rosales opened the door for immigrants to settle in the Lake District. In 1852 a group of Germans arrived and established Playa Maitén. Two years later on this inlet, others founded Puerto Octay, 9 kilometers (5.4 mi) to the west. This new port on Lago Llanquihue's northern shore soon became the most important on the Puerto Montt-Osorno trade route. Legend says that the village received its name thanks to a group of people who were searching for Cristino Ochs' general store, the only one in the area. Directions, it is told, were given as "*donde Ochs hay*"—or where Ochs is. After the Pan-American Highway was built through the villages along the western shore of the lake, Puerto Octay declined in importance. By the later half of the 20th century, this once bustling port became a sleepy little town.

Puerto Octay is much more relaxed than the more touristy German towns on Lago Llanquihue, like Frutillar and Puerto Varas. Enough of the traditional architecture remains that Octay is designated an Architectural Monument. Strolling around the village, you'll see some stunning examples of buildings in Primitive, Neo-Classic and Chalet styles. From the main plaza you'll see the Iglesia Parroquial (1911), its even older parish house, and the former Escuela de Monjas (1913). The chapel, built in 1867, is one of the oldest structures in town.

Two of the places to learn more about the history of Puerto Octay are on the way to Península Centinela. In the former home of the Niklitschek clan, the Casa de la Cultura Emilio Held Winckler has photos, historical documents and personal articles from the settler families. The center is open December – February: Monday – Saturday 9:30 a.m. – 1 p.m., 3 p.m. – 7 p.m., Sunday 11 a.m. – 1 p.m. (Av. Independencia 591. Tel: 56-64-691490). On the second floor, Museo El Colono has a collection of objects, photographs and machinery illustrating the daily life of the immigrants and the town's history (Daily 10:15 a.m. — 1 p.m., 3 p.m. — 5 p.m. Av. Independencia 591. Tel: 56-64-391266, E-mail: info@museooctay.cl, URL: www.museopuertooctay.cl. Entry: adults $2, seniors $1.40, children to 12 years old free). Also on the way to Península Centinela is Galpón Museo (Camino a Centinela s/n).

Península Centinela is three kilometers (1.8 mi) southwest of Puerto Octay. This five-kilometer (3-mi) long arm of land is fringed by Playa La Baja, a fine-sand beach. You can rent a paddle boat or take a tour of the lake. Part of the Centinela is a nature preserve, laced with hiking trails. At the end of the peninsula is Hotel Centinela, originally a family vacation home, built in 1914. Campsites are also present in this area.

Going north along Lago Llanquihue, you'll come to Playa Maitém (9 km / 5.4 mi). This gently sloping beach surrounded by *maitén* trees is a perfect place to camp, picnic or fish. It was here that the first families settled in 1852. The church was built by Miguel Majevsky. Playa Puerto Fonck, 23 kilometers (14 mi) from Puerto Octay, is even more tranquil. This village has well-preserved colonial buildings, including another Miguel Majevsky church, with a rose-window façade. Puerto Fonck also has an excellent beach where you can rest, picnic and fish.

Puerto Octay forms part of two scenic routes. With local rural and ecotourism providers, explore the mountain landscapes, searching for the mythical City of the Cesares, along the Ruta de los Césares. The Ruta de la Colonización seeks out the cultural and gastronomic legacy of immigrant to Lago Llanquihue. Other possible expeditions from this town include a hike around Volcán Osorno to Lago Todos los Santos, or a three-day mountain bike tour around Lago Llanquihue.

When to Go

The biggest event on Puerto Octay's calendar is Festival El Salmón de Oro. During the first week of February, musicians converge in the municipal stadium to bring these hills alive with music.

Getting To and Away From Puerto Octay

Puerto Octay is approximately 50 kilometers (30 mi) from Osorno, by way of Ruta U-55. With public transportation, you can get to Puerto Octay most easily from Osorno. Buses connect Puerto Octay with Las Cascadas and Frutillar. From Puerto Montt, go first to Frutillar.

From Osorno:
Osorno's **Terminal de Buses** is at Errázuriz 1400 (Tel: 56-64-234149, URL: www.terminalbusususosorno.cl).

To Puerto Octay: $2.60 – 3, 1 hour—**Vía Octay** (hourly 7 a.m. – 8 p.m., last back 8 p.m., $2.60, 1 hour). A kiosk on the east end of the terminal sells tickets for Octay (22 departures 6:50 a.m. – 7:40 p.m.).

To Frutillar: **Buses Fierro** (half-hourly 6:30 a.m. – 8:30 p.m., last back 8:30 p.m., $2.60, 1 hour).

To Puerto Varas / Puerto Montt: Not all services to Puerto Montt pass through Puerto Varas; $3 – 4, 1.5 hours—**Jac** (19 buses 5:30 .m. – 10:40 p.m.), **Bus Norte** (Puerto Montt only, 5 departures in p.m.). Also **Buses Pirehueico, Fierro, Igi Llaima**.

From Puerto Montt:
The **Terminal de Buses** is at Av. Diego Portales s/n (Tel: 56-65-349011). Micros to villages around Lago Llanquihue leave from Andenes 1-15 every five – 15 minutes.

To Futillar: $1.60, 40 minutes.
Updated: Jun 17, 2009.

Services
TOURISM
Municipalidad de Puerto Octay (Esperanza 555. Tel: 56-64-391860, E-mail: turisfomenoctay@surnet.cl, URL: www.puertooctay.cl)—pick up your fishing license here.

MONEY
Banco Estado (P. Montt 345; ATM: MasterCard, Cirrus; exchanges U.S. dollars, euros) **Correo** (Esperanza 555)

MEDICAL
Hospital (P. Montt 601. Tel: 56-64-259258). The town also has Internet, call centers and carabineros post.

SHOPPING
Fábrica Artesanal Longanizas (Sector La Gruta. Tel: 56-9-2651840)

Tours
Bike Way (V.A. O'Connor 867. Tel: 56-64-424202)—bike rental; **Canopy Chile** (camino a Las Cascadas, Km 17. Tel: 56-64-234020, E-mail: contacto@canopychile.cl)

Lodging
Camping El Molino (Costanera Pichi Juan 124. Tel: 56-64-391375)—$20 per site (up to 6 persons)

THE LAKE DISTRICT

Hostería La Baja (Península de Centinela, Km 4. Tel: 56-8-2186897, irisbravo1@hotmail.com)—$13 per person.

Zapato Amarillo (Camino a Osorno, Km 2.5. Tel: 56-64-210787, E-mail: shiela@telsur.cl / info@zapatoamarillo.cl, URL: wwwzapatoamarillo.cl)—dorm $14 per person, single $30, double $24 – 30 per person; use of kitchen, bike rental; speak English, German, Spanish.

Hotel y Marina Centinela (Península de Centinela, Km 4.5. Tel: 56-64-391326, centinela@telsur.cl, URL: www.hotelcentinela.cl)—1 person $118 – 142, 2 persons $124 – 148, suites $180 – 200.

Restaurants

Baviera (Wulf 582. Tel: 56-64-391460); **Pacalú** (P. Montt 713. Tel: 56-64-391450; **Tante Valy** (Km 26. Tel: 56-64-391461) Updated: Jul 01, 2009.

FRUTILLAR

 554m   2,606   65

On the western shore of Lago Llanquihue is one of the Lake District's most popular destinations, Frutillar. Some travelers go there to sail or fish in the lake. Others are drawn to the annual summer music festival, Semanas Musicales de Frutillar, which brings over 400 performers from around the world. Nature lovers can explore the Bosque del Recuerdo and Reserva Experimental Edmundo Winkler.

Flora marvels include the world's most southern groves of *palma chilena*, multitudes of begonia and the copses of *lleuque* (plum-fruited yew) south of the promenade. The biggest attraction for most visitors, though, is the Bavarian architecture, a legacy of early German settlers. The village church is one of the region's best examples of northern European-style churches. The outstanding architecture even extends to the village cemetery, which has the best views of the lake.

Frutillar was just one of the many German settlements on the shores of Lago Llanquihue in the mid-19th century. Founded in 1856, this would become one of the most important ports between Puerto Montt and Osorno. The immigrants built their houses at the base of the hills

inland, reserving the marshy shore for crops. Agricultural industries, especially of cheese, sausage and beer, were a cornerstone of the town's economy. When the railroad arrived in 1907, the Alto Frutillar sector of the city was established around the train station. Local industries, like Cafra (Cooperative Agrícola y Lechera de Frutillar Alto), which makes cheeses, and Lindemann, which produces smoked meats and sausages, still produce here. With the birth of the Semanas Musicales music fest in 1968, Frutillar has become a popular place to spend summer vacations.

Getting To and Away From Frutillar

Paved roads connect Frutillar with Puerto Varas (26 km/16 mi) to the south, and Puerto Octay (25 km/15 mi) and Osorno (70 km/42 mi) to the north. In Alto Frutillar there is a gas station. Public transportation for Frutillar departs from Osorno and Puerto Montt. Many buses travel the Pan-American Highway to other destinations.

From Osorno:
Osorno's **Terminal de Buses** is at Errázuriz 1400 (Tel: 56-65-234149, URL: www.terminalbususosorno.cl). **Buses Fierro** (half-hourly 6:30 a.m. – 8:30 p.m., last back 8:30 p.m., $2.60, 1 hour).

From Puerto Montt:
The **Terminal de Buses** is at Av. Diego Portales s/n (Tel: 56-65-349011). Micros to villages around Lago Llanquihue leave from Andenes 1-15 (every 5 – 15 minutes, $1.60, 40 minutes).

From Frutillar, transportation also leaves for Llanquihue, Puerto Varas, and Puerto Octay. All buses leave from the **Terminal de Buses** in Frutillar Alto (Alessandri s/n. Tel: 56-65-421522). Alto Frutillar is located about four kilometers (2.5 mi) from Frutillar. Colectivos run the two parts of town daily 6 a.m. – midnight. Updated: Jun 17, 2009.

Services

TOURISM
Información Turística (Costanera Philippi, across from the pier. Tel: 56-65-421080) **Secretaría Municipal de Turismo (**Av. Philippi 753. Tel: 56-65-421685) **Corporación Cultural Semanas Musicales** (Av. Philippi 777. Tel: 56-65-421290)

Turismo Tirol (Av. Philippi 615. Tel: 56-65-421900)
Frutitur (Portales 150. Tel: 56-65-421390)
Lagune Club (Camino Los Bajos, Km 3 Tel: 56-65-330033, E-mail: mbertin@laguneclub.com, URL: www.interpatagonia.com/laguneclub)

MONEY
Banco Estado (Philippi 403; ATM: Master-Card, Cirrus; exchanges U.S. dollars, euros)

KEEPING IN TOUCH
Correo (C. Richter 201, local 5, Frutillar Alto). The town also has Internet, call centers and carabineros post. A useful website is www.frutillarsur.cl.

MEDICAL
Hospital (Philippi 753. Tel: 56-65-421261).

SHOPPING
Bauernhaus (Av. Philippi 663. Tel: 56-65-420003)
Artesanías Trayén (V. Pérez Rosales 500. Tel: 56-65-421610)
Artesanías Frutillar (Av. Philippi 539. Tel: 56-65-421539)

Things to See and Do
Frutillar offers a wide range of aquatic sports, including fishing and sailing at the Yacht Club. Sun worshipers bathe on the fine sand beaches. The **Casa de la Oma** is on the road to Tegu_alda. This German colonial mansion, built in 1907, is now home to the Museo de los Colonos. A typical German settlement, composed of five buildings, has been recreated on the garden grounds. The Llavería contains the administrative offices of the site. Further on there is an old flour mill with the original grindstones and mechanisms are on display. **La Casa del Herrero**, the old village smithy, has tools which were used by the new immigrants; **El Campanario**, formerly a coop and grain storehouse, displays horse carriages, butter churns and other agricultural and domestic machinery.

La Casa Patronal or Casona del Campo, built in 1889, is an example of one of the wealthier homes, with a music conservatory and parlors. Tuesday – Sunday 10 a.m. – 2 p.m., 3 p.m. – 6 p.m., extended hours in summer; Entry: adults $2, children $1. Camino a Tegualda, Km 14. Tel: 56-65-421142.
Frutillar has two nature areas, covering 33 hectares; both are run by the Universidad de Chile. The **Bosque del Recuerdo** (Forest of Memories) seeks to preserve native

trees and shrubs of the region. The adjacent **Reserva Experimental Edmundo Winkler** is a botanical garden with panels that explain the plant characteristics and uses. An 800-meter (half-mile) trail runs through the forest (January – March: Daily 9 a.m. – 7 p.m.; March – December Monday – Saturday 9 a.m. – 4 p.m. End of Ca. Caupolicán. Entry: $3, children $1.40).

The majestic and modern **Teatro del Lago** is home to the annual *Semanas Musicales de Frutillar*. For 10 days, from the end of January to the beginning of February, the valleys ring with music from choral groups, symphony orchestras, opera troops and jazz ensembles from around the world. The teatro has an *Escuela de Música*, library, sculpture garden, an artist retreat and campus, an art gallery, sculpture garden and a cine club. The theater hosts concerts and other events throughout the year. The schedule is posted on its website (Av. Philippi 1000. Tel: 56-65-422900, URL: www.teatrodellago.cl).

Lodging
You can find cheap lodging in Alto Frutillar, near the bus station. The high season is from December through February. Lodging is especially difficult to find during the Semanas Musicales music festival. Check out camping at **Los Ciruelillos** (Camino a Punta Larga, Km 1. Tel: 56-65-420163)—$20 per site (up to 6 persons).

Hospedaje Noelia (Av. Philippi 615. Tel: 56-65-421310)—$18 - 22 per person.

Hotel Ayacara (Av. Philippi 1215)—low season $106, high season $150 – 188.

Restaurants
Restaurant Se Cocina (Camino a Totoral, Km 2, Fundo Santa Clara. Tel: 56-9-97577152, E-mail: reservas@secocina.cl, URL: www.secocina.cl); **El Ciervo** (San Martín 64. Tel: 56-65-420185); **Bauernhaus** (Av. Philippi 663. Tel: 56-65-420003). Updated: Jul 07, 2009.

PUERTO VARAS

 88m   34,300   65

Puerto Varas is 20 kilometers (12.4 mi) from the region's capital, Puerto Montt. It is a small, cozy town settled on the southwestern shores of Lake Llanquihue. nick-

THE LAKE DISTRICT

PUERTO VARAS

Activities ●

1 Capitán Haase Settler's Route B1
2 Iglesia Sagrado Corazón de Jesús A2
3 National Park Vicente Peréz Rosales B2
4 Volcano Osorno B2

Eating 🍴

5 Club de Yates B1
6 Focus Restaurant and Pub A2
7 Imperial 605 B2
8 Mediterráneo B1
9 Pim's A2

Nightlife 🍸

10 Apache B2
11 Barómetro A2
12 Casino Puerto Varas B2

Services ★

13 Banco de Chile B2
14 Centro Médico Puerto Varas A1

15 Mistica B1
16 Post Office B2
17 Tourist Office A2
18 Travel Sur B2

Sleeping ▤

19 Cabañas Los Alerces B2
20 Hotel Puelche B2
21 Melié Patagonia A1
22 Solace A2
23 The Guest House A2

Tours ◆

24 Terramotion A1

Transportation ▦

25 Bus Terminal A3
26 Cruz del Sur B2
27 Tas Choapa B1
28 Tur Bus A1

named the City of Rose, Puerto Varas is considered to be one of the prettiest cities in the Chilean Lakes Region. The town is on a hill which offers great views of volcanoes Osorno and Calbuco.

The town was founded in 1854 by Vicente Pérez Rosales, who developed the small port town as a lake navigation center and commercial area. Puerto Varas was made an official port city December 30th, 1927. Puerto Varas tourism sprang into action around 1934, with the building of the first major hotel, now home to the village casino. Soon after the construction of the hotel, the road to the town of Ensenada, 45 kilometers (28 mi) away, was built. The town has grown to a year-round population of 28,000 inhabitants. This number doubles in size during the tourist months (December-March).

Tourism is second only to agriculture as a source of income for the local people. Set at five meters (16 ft) above sea level, Puerto Varas offers tons of different excursions, including sea and lake kayaking, fly fishing, volcano tours, river rafting, horseback riding, and hiking. You can also ski during the winter months on the slopes of Volcano Osorno. For those not so interested in the outdoors, there is a tour of the beautiful, early 1900s homes and churches of the German settlers, as well as museums that explain the history of the area.

Being a major tourist draw, the village is filled with all varieties and qualities of hotels and restaurants. There are multiple four- and five-star accommodations, hostels, and famous houses of the colonial period that have been transformed into hospedajes. It is important to book a hostel or hotel reservation in advance during high season. The restaurants are a diverse, eclectic mix, offering everything from sushi to Mexican food, not to mention the regular Chilean fare.

Puerto Varas is a recommended stop for those traveling in this area of Chile. Although it is quiet during the winter months, it is good place to learn about Chilean culture and people. If you visit during the off season keep in mind that most restaurants are not open on Sundays and some hotels shut down completely. Updated: Jun 16, 2008.

When to Go

Puerto Varas is a summer destination resort. The main high season is from December to early March, with warm and friendly weather,

although don't be surprised to get occasional rain. puerto Varas expands and becomes a festive tourist town during high season, with excursions and activities operational seven days a week. There are also festivals that celebrate the founding of the town in the end of January, as well as music and art festivals in February. Making reservations during these times is a must.

During the off-season from late March to November (March and November have the best weather), the locals are a bit more congenial and there are no lines. There are still enough activities and excursions during this time of year to keep it exciting, but some places do close down or have siesta hours. Be sure to visit the tourism office, located at San Fransisco 431 in the Municipality building, to find out which companies operate during the off season. Updated: Jun 16, 2008.

Getting To and Away From Puerto Varas

BY AIR
There is no airport in Puerto Varas, but you can fly into Osorno or Puerto Montt via **LAN Chile** or **Sky Airlines**. From the airports in the neighboring towns, you can rent a car (recommended as there are many excursions away from Puerto Varas city center), or take a bus or taxi.

BY BUS
Multiple buses from Santiago travel to Puerto Varas. These include **Cruz del Sur** (Tel:56-65-26969325) which leaves from **Los Heroes Terminal**; **Tur Bus** (Tel: 56-65-27787338) which leaves from the **San Borja Terminal**; and the **Tas Choapa** bus line, which departs from the main Santiago bus terminal, city center (Tel: 56-65-27787074 / 56-65-24907561). Schedules and times change often, so contact the bus company ahead of time.

If you fly into Osorno, the major bus is Cruz del Sur, which leaves daily for Puerto Varas during high season—contact them directly for the winter schedule. From the Puerto Montt airport there are taxis available for $20 or minibuses ($1.40).

Check the individual bus companies for exact times of departure. Cruz del Sur has eight departures daily (to Osorno, Valdivia or Tamuco), leaving from the San Francisco 1317 terminal, the office is located at Walker Martinez 230. Tas Choapa and Buses Norte are the most dependable rides for trips to Santiago the Tur Bus. The Tur Bus office is located at San Pedro 210, Tas Choapa at Walker Martinez 227 and Buses Norte at San Pedro 210. If you are traveling to Bariloche, there are three modes of transportation. Tas Choapa has a bus leaving every Monday and Saturday and Cruz del Sur has buses leaving every day during high season. There is also the **Cruce de Lagos** bus and boat combo that is a multiple day trip, traveling to both Argentine and Chilean ports. Check the crossings website for more information, www.crucedelagos.cl. Updated: Jul 01, 2009.

Getting Around

A local blue minibus transit company, **Thaebus**, offers rides throughout town for around $1.40. The terminal is located at the main plaza, off San Fransisco and San José. There are buses to Puerto Montt, Frutillar and Puerto Octay leaving from the main plaza stop as well. Thaebus also travels to Ensenada ($1.50) and Petrohué ($3), leaving from the **Galeria Real** and other stops along Del Salvador street. The bus schedule changes depending on the season, with a constant schedule of departures in the summer and fewer during the winter season. Check with the main tourist office for more information. There is also the occasional taxi. **Travel Sur** (San Pedro 451) offers car rentals within the town. Updated: Jun 13, 2008.

Safety

Puerto Varas is generally a safe place. The military personnel and police walking around town are a great source of information and are eager to help. The locals are also kind and trustworthy when asked for directions. If going beyond the main city center at night, it is advisable to try to blend in with the locals, since they are not accustomed to tourists. Updated: Jun 16, 2008.

Services

TOURISM

The main tourist office is located in the **Municipality building** (San Francisco 431). It is open Monday – Friday, 9 a.m. – 9 p.m. from December – February, and 10 a.m. – 2 p.m. and 4 – 6 p.m. March – November.

MONEY

For money exchange and other banking needs the main bank, **Banco de Chile**, is on the corner of Del Salvador and Santa Rosa. There are also ATMs throughout the city center.

KEEPING IN TOUCH

There are a few Internet cafés sprinkled throughout town. **Mistica** is one of the more dependable cafes, located on San Pedro 201 in front of the Tur Bus office. The **post office** is on the corner of San Pedro and San José.

MEDICAL

Medical services are available at **Centro Médico Puerto Varas** (Walker Martinez 576. Tel: 56-65-2232792, open 24 hours a day).

LAUNDRY

Laundry service is available in any *lavarap*. Most hostels and hotels offer the service as well. Updated: Jun 13, 2008.

Things to See and Do

Puerto Varas has a diverse range of activities, including outdoor adventures such as fly fishing. Whether it is kayaking or mountaineering, skiing or river rafting, canopying or canyoning, you can find it at Puerto Varas. Puerto Varas also has lots of cultural attractions, such as the early 19th-century architecture, museums and antique churches. Updated: Jun 16, 2008.

Iglesia Sagrado Corazón de Jesus

(ADMISSION: Free) This church was built between 1915 and 1918 by Edmundo Niklitschek. It is based on the Marienkirche of the Black Forest in Germany and is built in the neo-romantic style. The light yellow building is made more brilliant by its red details and roof. Locals come in droves on Sundays to partake in mass held in the mornings and evenings. After mass, the serene music from the church service can be heard throughout the center of town. The church is closed when mass is not being held (Tuesday – Friday 8 a.m., Saturday 7 p.m., Sunday 10 a.m., noon, 7 p.m.). Corner of San Fransisco and Verbo Divino. Updated: Jun 13, 2008.

Paseo Patrimonial

Puerto Varas' architecture is heavily influenced by 19th-century German colonization. You can see intricate colonial buildings, built between 1915 and 1930, throughout town. To take a tour of some of the particularly well-preserved homes, stop by the tourism office to pick up a guide map, Paseo Patrimonial, of the ten different sites worth seeing. With the exception of Casa Kuschel, these homes are private. Updated: Jun 13, 2008.

Photo by Andres Amengual

Rafting and Kayaking

White water sports are big in Puerto Varas. There are multiple tour companies that can take you on a leisurely paddle, or on more strenuous escapades. There are also companies, usually set up along the shore of Lake Llanqihue, that will rent individual boats. There are guided sea kayaking ventures in Lake Llanquihue, Lake Todos Los Santos and in the nearby ocean bay of Puerto Octay and the Reloncavi Fjord. The river rafting trips go down class III and IV rapids of the Petrohue and Maullin rivers. Updated: Jun 13, 2008.

Volcano Osorno

Volcano Osorno, elevation 2652 meters (8701 ft), stands on the northeast end of Lake Llanquihue, 51 kilometers (31.7 mi) from Puerto Varas. The mountain looks like a smaller replica of Japanese Mount Fuji with its perfect cone shape. The road has been recently paved and is in great condition, although it is steep in some areas and you should practice caution in snowy conditions.

At 1,200 meters (3937 ft) you will come upon the base of the small ski area, Centro de Ski y Montaña. The ski area ($18) has two new chairlifts that are open year-round as well as a small cafeteria and ski rentals. There is ample terrain for beginner, intermediate and advanced skiers. Exercise caution for the required glacier travel above the lifts.

To get there, follow route 225 51 km toward Ensenada, turn left into national park Vicente Peréz Rosales, then right at KM 5. Tel: 56-65-233445, E-mail: info@volcanosorno.com, URL: www.volcanosorno.com. Updated: Jun 13, 2008.

Capitán Haase Settler's Route Sunset Cruise

(PRICE: $35) Capitán Haase Settler's Route Sunset Cruise is a unique water voyage set on a 65-foot long wooden vessel that has all of the trimmings of a boat from the early 1900s. The boat holds up to 50 passengers and begins its sail around Lake Llanquihue from its private pier. It heads south, past private beaches and houses on the southern shores of the lake. The total package includes a cocktail, music, troll fishing, bilingual guide and, if you're lucky, a great sunset. Tel: 56-65-229300, URL: www.terramotion.cl. Updated: Jun 13, 2008.

Casino Puerto Varas

(COVER: $3) This classy, stylish, modern building is a stone's throw away from the lake. It has over 300 slot machines, roulette, black jack, craps tables, royal 21, bingo, and anything else that you might find at a Las Vegas casino, including a VIP area, two bars and a restaurant (no cover). There is live music most weekends. The casino is, by far, the biggest nightlife draw in the area and tends to have a crowd any night of the week. Daily, 11 a.m. – 6 a.m. Del Salvador 021. Tel: 56-65-492000, Fax: 56-65-492004. Updated: Jun 16, 2008.

Tours

There are lots of tour operators in the area, and many tours are well organized and honest, but be wary when making reservations. Make sure that you are getting exactly what you want for a price that is reasonable. Most companies have guides who speak Spanish, French, German, English and, sometimes, Italian.

Yak Expediciones

Yak Expediciones is a sea kayak, canoe and river rafting tour group with 20 years of experience. The director, Juan Federico Zuazo, has been certified by the British Canoe Union and is very knowledgeable. Yak offers one-day tours on the lakes surrounding Puerto Varas. They also assist with trips to the Patagonia Channels, Reloncavi Fjord and San Rafael Glacier area. Although it is not their specialty, they also assist with treks in the surrounding national parks. Yak Expediciones also teaches a three-day beginners paddling and camping class. Guides speak English. Tel: 56-65-23-44-09, E-mail: info@yakexpediciones.cl, URL: www.yakexpediciones.cl. Updated: Jun 16, 2008.

Terramotion

Terramotion has guided trips for fishing, kayaking, hiking, boating, horseback riding, sailing, river rafting and even a tour of the beef and ham plants of the Puerto Varas area. Although more commercialized than other tour companies, Terramotion guides are thorough and know their area. Prices are on par with other agencies, though guided groups can be larger. San Fransisco 328. Tel: 56-65-229300, Fax: 56-65-229305, E-mail: puertovaras@terramotion.cl, URL: www.terramotion.cl. Updated: Jun 16, 2008.

Lodging

One thing that Puerto Varas has a lot of is accommodations. There is something for every traveler and every wallet. In the high season of January and February, places tend to fill up quickly. Many of the hostels and hospedajes are located in the center of town and do not have much of a view. The hotels a bit outside of the village center, on the lake or hillside, have views of Lake Llanquihue, Volcano Osorno and Volcano Calbuco.

Casa Mawenko

(ROOMS: $12 – 40) Casa Mawenko is an adorable hostel that is perfect for young travelers looking for budget accommodation. The owners, who speak English, have put their heart and soul into the multiple rooms, giving the hostel an artsy, eclectic appeal. Casa Mawenko is more like staying at a good friend's house than a hostel. The owners are very knowledgeable about local happenings and are great at helping direct guests to unknown excursions or good nighttime entertainment. The hostel is on a pedestrian walkway minutes from the city center and is ideal for stumbling home from a night on the town. Smoking is allowed in the common areas. Pasaje Ricke 224. Tel: 56-65-232673, E-mail: casamawenko@gmail.com, URL: www.hostalcasamawenko.blogspot.com. Updated: Jul 07, 2009.

Cabañas Los Alerces

(ROOMS: $70 – 165) Cabañas los Alerces is one of those places that looks nicer on its webpage then it does in reality. The hotel is decorated in a cute, grandma-like fashion, but it has seen better days. The restaurant has a nice ambiance, although you need to cross it to get to the pool, strangely. The hotel, in addition to its single, double and triple rooms, has small cabins, which are good for larger groups.

The staff has the tinge of animosity that comes with working with too many visitors. One of the best attributes of Cabañas los Alerces is its close proximity to the lake shore. Av. Vicente Perez Rosalez 1281. Tel: 56-65-528350, Fax: 56-65-236612, E-mail: reservas@hotellosalerces.cl, URL: www.cabanaslosalerces.cl. Updated: Jul 01, 2008.

Solace

(ROOMS: $80 and up) Solace is a new four-star hotel a five-minute walk from the center of town and lake shore. Trendy, and modern, it has all of the bells and whistles, except for a pool. They offer king- and queen-size beds, a large buffet breakfast (included in the price of the room) and spectacular views of Lake Llanquihue, and Volcanoes Osorno and Calbuco. Imperial 211. Tel: 56-65-364100, E-mail: contacto@solacehotel.cl, URL: www.solacehotel.cl. Updated: Jun 09, 2009.

The Guest House

(ROOMS: $75 – 120) The Guest House, also known as Casa Wetzel, is a cute, inviting hotel with ten rooms, all with private baths. Once a luxurious mansion, constructed in 1926, it was remodeled and transformed into a B&B with modern details. The owners are from the United States and speak perfect English. The location is a five minute

THE LAKE DISTRICT

walk from the city center and beach. There is a large European breakfast included in the room fee. The Guest House offers massages and yoga classes. It also offers private dinner parties for groups of ten or more. O'Higgins 608. Tel: 56-65-231521, Fax: 56-65-232240, E-mail: reservas@vicki-johnson.com, URL: www.vicki-johnson.com/guesthouse. Updated: Jun 16, 2008.

Hotel Puelche

(ROOMS: $127 – 200) Hotel Puelche is set on the hill, not far from the city center. The place is open, bright and welcoming. The rooms are spacious, clean, and a good value. Most of the reception staff speaks English, and is quite helpful with outdoor excursions and tour companies. The restaurant has tasty Chilean food and a warm ambiance, although the dining room staff is a bit stand-offish. The hotel has a nice spa that includes a sauna and massage center. Imperial 695. Tel: 56-65-233600, Fax: 56-65-233350, E-mail: reservas@hotelpuelche.com, URL: www.hotelpuelche.com. Updated: Jun 16, 2008.

Meliá Patagonia

(ROOMS: $160 – 450) Hotel Sol Melia is an over-the-top five-star extravaganza. There are multiple lounge areas, both indoor and outdoor, that have private areas where you can enjoy the view and relax. Some of the seating areas are actual beds covered by fine white linens. There are two restaurants, one specializing in Chilean fare, the other in Mediterranean cuisine. There is also a spa, a pool with two Jacuzzis and a business center. The reception staff is exceptionally cold, but the waiters are quite gracious. Klenner 349. Tel: 56-65-201000, Fax: 56-65-201001, E-mail: reservas.melia.patagonia@solmelia.com, URL: www.es.solmelia.com/hotel/melia-patagonia.htm. Updated: Jun 16, 2008.

Restaurants

Restaurants here are almost as numerous as sleeping accommodations. You can find all types of ambiances, prices and types of food. Puerto Varas does excel in one type of cuisine: Chilean fish and seafood, thanks to its close proximity to both fresh and salt water. Some of the restaurants are more expensive than the exterior would have you think so don't be shy about asking to see the menu before sitting down.

Imperial 605

Imperial 605 was originally called Merlin, a restaurant hailed as one of the best in town for its warm atmosphere and tasty dishes.

The menu is small but the food is fresh and flavorful. The servings are also quite large. It is recommended to make reservations during high season. There are smoking and non-smoking sections. The staff is friendly and helpful about educating guests on interesting places to visit in town. Imperial 605 corner of Tronador. Tel: 56-65-233105. Updated: Jun 16, 2008.

Pim's

This large, rustic restaurant offers a variety of budget food options, particularly Chilean, American and Mexican fare. The bar is huge and offers tons of choices. The interior is decorated with memorabilia that makes the restaurant feel like it could be located anywhere in the United States or Canada. The dining area is very clean and kept warm by a large fireplace. The staff is friendly. Smoking is permitted. San Francisco 712. Tel: 56-65-233998. Updated: Jul 01, 2008.

Focus Restaurant and Pub

Focus is a pasta and BBQ restaurant that looks like a log cabin. Some locals consider it to be the best place in town for grilled meat. Focus also offers typical Chilean dishes. The food is priced extremely well and there are lunch specials. The restaurant is centrally located, providing easy access for those staying in town. The place gets packed during high season. San Francisco 735. Tel: 56-65-235636, E-mail: focus.restaurantpub@gmail.com. Updated: Jul 01, 2009.

Mediterraneo

Mediterraneo specializes in food with a Mediterranean and Chilean flair. The menu includes pasta, fish, salads and soups. The food is fresh and tasty, though the prices are a little high in comparison to other dining experiences of the same caliber. There is also a large wine menu, but not many choices for the beer drinker. The dining area is refreshing and inviting, and has a great view of Lake Llanquihue. Upstairs, a bakery section offers pastries, cakes and coffee. The restaurant has both smoking and non-smoking areas. Santa Rosa 68. Tel: 56-65-237268. Updated: Jun 16, 2008.

Club de Yates

(ENTREES: $10-38) Club de Yates is a romantic, upscale restaurant that serves a gigantic selection of fish and seafood dishes (salmon carpaccio) as well as some chicken (coq au vin), beef (roquefort sauce beef) and pasta choices. The wine list is extensive, although most choices are a bit expensive. The food, on the other hand, is very well priced, especially compared to the surrounding dining options. Built on a pier overlooking the water, Club de Yates has the least obstructed view of Lake Llanquihue in town. It is also one of the only restaurants open on Sunday evenings in the off season. The staff is nice and accommodating. Santa Rosa 161. Tel: 56-65-232000/2383, E-mail: inforeservas@clubdeyates.cl. Updated: Jun 16, 2008.

Apache

Apache is the hotspot for young, adventurous partiers in Puerto Varas. This dingy, ugly cement building attracts teenagers and early 20 year-olds ready to get their groove on. Saturdays usually have a special party, sometimes with live music. Apache offers cheap drink specials and a contest for the best photo of the night uploaded to the website. Smoking is allowed throughout the club. The bar is not located within stumbling distance of the city center, so you will need to get a taxi back. Caupolican 1486. Tel: 56-65-347390, E-mail: puertovaras@apachepub.com, URL: www.apachepub.com/puertovaras. Updated: Jun 17, 2008.

Barómetro

Barómetro is a multi-level bar and dance club for 20 to 30 year-olds. The bar offers some appetizers and drink specials, and there is live music and DJ nights on weekends, usually starting around 10 p.m. Barómetro does host some fairly well-known acts from Santiago from time to time. Smoking is permitted. San Pedro 418. Tel: 56-65-236371, Updated: Jun 16, 2008.

La Playa

For Puerto Varas nightlife located right on the water, go to La Playa. This club has five different locations throughout the country, although none of them have the view that this one does. There is a huge window that looks out over the water as well as an outdoor patio area. This is a lively, fun club that has discounted drinks and live music; only on the weekends though. The doors open around 10 p.m. Vicente Pérez Rosalez 1400. Tel: 56-8-8396577, E-mail: andresassef@laplaya.cl, URL: www.laplaya.cl. Updated: Jun 16, 2008.

ENSENADA

 54m   varies   65

Lying at the foot of Volcán Osorno on the southeastern shore of Lake Llanquihue, Ensenada is little more than a collection of lodges, vacation properties, and modest shops. The town's proximity to Parque Nacional Vicente Pérez Rosale draws anglers, hikers and summer crowds; outside of high season you may have the place to yourself. Puerto Varas lies about 50 kilometers (31 mi) to the west, and Lago Todos los Santos, Laguna Verde and Volcanes Calbuco and Puntiagudo are within striking distance, making Ensenada an excellent base place from which to explore, raft, bike, trek, or soak in hot springs.

Getting To and Away From Ensenada

You can usually reach Ensenada via Puertos Varas or Montt. You can fly into the latter, and into Osorno as well. From there, buses, minibuses and taxis will get you to Puerto Varas—buses run between the town, Ensenada and Petrohué a couple of times a day. If you are driving, Ensenada is just a 20-minute jaunt from Puerto Varas and 1.5 hours from Puerto Montt. Updated: Jul 01, 2009.

Services

Information about the village and services is available at: www.laensenada.cl.

SHOPPING

Conservera Los Alpes (Ruta 225, Km33.5. Tel: 56-65-335354)—smoked salmon and trout.

Río Blanco Mermeladas (Ruta 225 Km 35. Tel: 56-65-335321)—cakes and jams.

Quesos Río Blanco (Ruta 225 Km 36)—cheese

Lavanda de Ensenada (Ruta 225 Km 36.1)—essential oils, soaps

Miel Lückeheide (Ruta 225, Km 43.6. Tel: 56-65-212037)—honey.

Tours

Traypin Adventure (Ruta Internacional 225, Km 42. Tel: 56-8-4101316, URL: www.traypin-adventure.com)—specializes in adventure tourism.

Southern Chile Expeditions (Ruta 225, Km 41. Tel: 56-65-212030)—fly fishing, adventure tourism and rafting.

Terra Sur Ecoaventura (Ruta 225, Km 44. Tel: 56-65-233140)—mountain bikes, horseback riding. Updated: Jun 16, 2008.

THE LAKE DISTRICT

Lodging

For such a small, seasonal town, Ensenada has a vast number of hotels, lodges and campgrounds. In general, rates are priced according to three seasons: low, which lasts from April to September; medium, running the month of March and from September to late December; and high, from year's end to late February.

Rates creep up slightly during the the medium seasons, but expect the price to double between the low season and the high season.

Cabañas Bahia Celeste (Ruta 225, 21 Km. Tel: 56-65-335383, lodge@bahiaceleste.cl, bahiaceleste.cl) has cozy, self-contained lodging for two ($60 per person in low season) to six people ($87). Cabins have lake views and wide wooden decks, plus modern amenities like WiFi, heat, and maid service.

Cabañas & Piscina Rucamalen (Ruta 225, 36 km; Tel: 56-65-335347, reservas@rucamen.cl, www.rucamalen.cl) has private beach-facing cottages, eateries and a heated pool with aquabar. It offers many outdoor activities, including professionally guided multi-day fishing excursions in nearby rivers. Its three-room cabins come with kitchens, cable TVs and central heating. Choose from standard ($77 per person) or superior ($92 per person) accomodation.

Accomodation is also available at **Hospedaje Caryun** (Ruta 225, Km 39.5. Tel: 56-65-212079, URL: www.caryun.cl), **Hospedaje Ensenada** (Ruta 225, Km 43. Tel: 56-65-212050, www.hospedajeensenada.blogspot.com) and **Hotel Borde Lago** (Puerto Varas—Ensenada Km 4. Tel: 56-65-438999, URL: www.bordelago.cl).

Restaurants

Private restaurants are a rarity in Ensenada, but many hotels have establishments on the premises. Midway between Puerto Varas and Ensenada, posh **Club Alemán Molino de Agua** (Ruta 225, Km 21.5. Tel: 56-65-330140) features Chilean and international cuisine. The BBQ at **Las Tranqueras** (Ruta 225, Km 41. Tel: 56-65-212056 / 299092) is a solid bet after a day spent adventuring or relaxing by the lake. Good eats are also available at **Canta Rana** (Ruta 225, Km 42.3. Tel: 56-65-212010) and **Pucará** (Ruta 225, Km 42.5. Tel: 56-65-212018).

PARQUE NACIONAL VICENTE PÉREZ ROSALES

Parque Nacional (PN) Vicente Pérez Rosales touches the eastern shore of Lago Llanquihue and extends to the Argentine border. This is Chile's oldest national park, created in 1926 to protect 253,780 hectares of virgin forest. Within its boundaries are three of southern Chile's most spectacular volcanoes: Puntiagudo (2490 m / 8093 ft), Tronador (3441 m / 1,184 ft) and Osorno (2661 m / 8649 ft), which has a ski center. Travelers can sail to Argentina on Lago Todos los Santos, a giant blue mirror reflecting the forests, mountains and sky. PN Puyehue is on the northern horizon of the park.

The park's altitude ranges from 50 meters (163 ft) on the shores of Lago Llanquihue, to the snowy peak of 3,441-meter-high (11,184 ft-) Volcán Tronador. Río Peulla begins in Tronador's glaciers, and flows into Lago Todos los Santos. Other major rivers include the Negro, Puntiagudo and Chileno. Río Cayutué wends to Laguna Cayutué in the southwest sector of the park. These river valleys, especially those of Río Petrohué and Río Caytué, are some of the park's most beautiful landscapes. Other scenic wonders are Volcán Osorno and its chain of craters, and the Saltos de Petrohué waterfalls. Puntiagudo and Osorno are the youngest mountains, and Picada (1,710 m / 5,558 ft) and Tronador the oldest. The park's volcanic activity creates the Vuriloche, Ralún and El Callao hot springs.

Rosales park has a temperate climate, and is wet year round. The mean annual rainfall ranges from 2,500 millimeters (98.4 in) at Ensenada on Lago Llanquihue, to 4,000 millimeters (157.5 in) at Casapangue, near Paso Pérez Rosales. At higher altitudes, precipitation is in the form of snow. In January, temperatures average 16°C (61°F) and in June, 6.5°C (44°F).

This moist climate creates the perfect environment for the area's humid evergreen forests. The predominant species are winter's bark, lily of the valley tree, Chilean myrtle and Chilean hazel. Patagonian cypress and lenga beech, and Chilean guava grow at higher altitudes. Animals common to these woodlands include the Geoffroy's cat, puma, South American grey fox, Southern river otter and two species of marsupi-

THE LAKE DISTRICT

als: Chilean shrew opossum, and austral opposum. When hiking, keep an eye on the sky for the Condor, Great grebe, Steamer duck, Torrent duck, Ringed kingfisher, Crested caracara, Green-backed Firecrown hummingbird, Magellanic woodpecker, Magellan goose, Red-gartered coot, and Black-chested buzzard-eagle.

PN Vicente Pérez Rosales is divided into six sectors. In the western part: **Ensenada, Saltos de Petrohué** and **Petrohué**. To the north of these are sectores **Volcán Osorno** and **La Picada**. Sector **Peulla** is in the extreme east. There are guarderías (ranger stations) at Saltos de Petrohué, Petrohué, Volcán Osorno and Peulla. At Salto de Petrohué the entry fee is $1.40. Conaf in Puerto Montt (Ochagavá 458. Tel: 56-65-486115) has a pamphlet with a relief map of the park, but it doesn't show any of the trails.

Getting To and Away From PN Vicente Pérez Rosales

Parque Nacional Vicente Pérez Rosales is 64 kilometers (39 miles) from Puerto Varas and 86 kilometers (52 miles) from Puerto Montt. Ruta Internacional 225 heads east to Ensenada and to Petrohué. Most of the road from Puerto Varas is paved. From Ensenada, another paved road goes to Volcán Osorno. From Puerto Montt, go first to Puerto Varas, where buses leave for Ensenada (half-hourly in high season, $4, 1 hour). Ask if the bus will be continuing on to Petrohué. No public transportation covers the 10 kilometers (6 mi) from Ensenada to Volcán Osorno. It is 20 nautical miles across Lago Todos los Santos from Petrohué to Peulla. From Peulla it is 25 kilometers (15 mi) by gravel road to the Argentine border at Paso Pérez Rosales. Updated: Jun 17, 2009.

Things to See and Do

The park is laced with trails that lead from one side of the Andes to the other. The Spanish used a route through the southern section of the modern park in their missionary travels from Chiloé to Nahuelhuapi. Today, visitors have a choice of 16 trails to hike, including multi-day treks and mountain expeditions. The paths fall into three categories: sendero recreativo (recreational trail), sendero educativo or interpretativo (educational or interpretive trail) and sendero de excursión (excursion trail).

Hiking
Recreational Trails:
Saltos del Río Petrohué (*Distance:* 370 m / 1,203 ft, *Difficulty:* easy, *Duration:* 10 min)—Leads to the spectacular waterfalls near the park's western entrance.

Los Enamorados (*Distance:* 600 m / 1,950 ft, *Difficulty:* easy, *Duration:* 30 min)—In Sector Saltos del Río Petrohué.

Laguna Verde (*Distance:* 180 m / 585 ft, *Difficulty:* medium, *Duration:* 20 min)—Another short trail in the western sector, to an emerald-colored lagoon.

Velo de la Novia or Cascada de los Novios (*Distance:* 400 m / 1,300 ft, *Difficulty:* easy, *Duration:* 25 min)—Leads to a cascade from the Sector Peulla ranger station.

Interpretive Trails:
Carilemu (*Distance:* 980 m / 3,185 ft, *Difficulty:* medium, *Duration:* 45 min)—In Sector Saltos del Río Petrohué.

Los Pilleyos (*Distance:* 1.2 km / 1 mi, *Difficulty:* easy, *Duration:* 45 min)—In Sector Ensenada.

Excursion trails:
Note: For security reasons, trekkers doing any of the senderos de excursión must stop into the Conaf office at Secto Petrohué to register and obtain information.

Paso Desolación (*Distance:* 12 km / 7.2 mi, *Difficulty:* medium, *Duration:* 5 – 6 hours round trip)—This trail traverses the eastern slopes of Volcán Osorno, to an altitude of 1,100m (3,608 ft). Views of Volcán Tronador and Lago Todos los Santos.

Rincón del Osorno (*Distance:* 5 km / 3 mi, *Difficulty:* medium, *Duration:* 4 hours round trip)—Beginning in Petrohué, the hike follows the shores of Lago Petrohué.
El Solitario (*Distance:* 6 km / 3.6 mi, *Difficulty:* medium, *Duration:* 2 hours)—This trail begins six kilometers (3.6 mi) down the road to Volcán Osorno and ends one kilometer (0.6 mi) from Saltos del Río Petrohué.

Laguna Margarita (*Distance:* 8 km / 4.8 mi, *Difficulty:* difficult, 8 hours round trip)—From the Peulla ranger station to Laguna Margarita, a small lake surrounded by lenga forest.

Los Alerzales (*Distance:* 3.4 km / 2.1 mi, *Difficulty:* difficult, *Duration:* 4 hours).

El Cayutúe (*Distance:* 25 km / 15 mi, *Difficulty:* medium, *Duration:* 5 hours)— Take the first boat to the trail head on the south bank of Lake Todos los Santos, then hike to Laguna Cuyutúe.

Cerro Rigi (*Distance:* 8 km / 4.8 mi, *Difficulty:* medium, *Duration:* 5.5 hours)—In sector Peulla, near Paso Pérez Rosales.

Paso Vuriloche (*Distance:* 40 km / 24 mi, *Difficulty:* difficult, *Duration:* 5 days on horse)—To the border crossing into Argentina, traveled only January through February. Club Andino maintains a refuge along the way. For more information, see: www.clubandino.org/data/i_refugios_tronador_viejo.asp.

Volcán Osorno (*Distance:* 6 km / 3.6 mi, *Difficulty:* expert, *Duration:* 10 hours—Scale the steep slopes of this stratovolcano.

Termas de Callao (*Distance:* 8 km / 4.8 mi, *Difficulty:* medium, *Duration:* 5 hours) - The journey begins with a launch ride to the north shore of Lago Todos los Santos ($70 one way, whole boat). The path heads to the hot springs, Termas de Callao, where lodging is available. Another trail begins at the mouth of Río Techado.

Other Outdoor Activities
PN Vicente Pérez Rosales offers other adventures for nature seekers. Swimming and trout fishing (November — May) are possible in Sector Ensenada on Lago Llanquihué.

You can also cast your line at Peulla. Rafting and canyoning the white waters of Río Petrohué is guaranteed to get the blood pumping. Kayakers will find a challenge on that river, too, or they can enjoy the tranquil waters of Lago Todos los Santos. Volcán Osorno attracts mountain climbers in warm months, and during the winter skiers and snowboarders head to the 600-hectare Centro de Ski y Montaña Volcán Osorno.

Those seeking to scale Osorno or other peaks must register with Conaf and show their credentials. Finally, given the great diversity of species here, be sure to bring your camera and binoculars.

The park service has a campground at the Petrohué ranger station. The 24 sites have fire pits, tables, parking, potable water and bathrooms ($16 per site per day, for up to five people).

Lodging
There is privately owned lodging in various sectors of the park:

SECTOR PETROHUÉ
Hotel Petrohué (Ruta 225, Km 64. Tel: 56-65-212025, E-mail: reservas@petrohue.cl, URL: www.hotelpetrohue.cl)

SECTOR VOLCÁN OSORNO
Refugio Los Pumas (Camino Ensenada – Volcán Osorno, Km 12)

Centro de Ski y Montaña Volcán Osorno (Camino Ensenada – Volcán Osorno, Km14.3. Tel: 56-65-233445 / 9-76591522 / 9-92623323, URL: www.volcanosorno.com)

Refugio Teski (Camino Ensenada – Volcán Osorno, Km 16)

SECTOR LA PICADA
Refugio Termas El Callao (Valle El Callao. Tel: 56-9-8202337)—privately owned cabaña at the El Callao hot springs.

SECTOR PEULLA
Hotel Peulla (Tel: 56-65-367094, URL: www.hotelpeulla.cl); **Hotel Natura** (Tel: 56-65-367094, URL: www.hotelnatura.cl).

Ensenada village has hotels, restaurants and other services. Camp stove fuel can be bought here and in Ralún. Updated: Jul 07, 2009.

RALÚN

 1,600m   500   65

This town is so tiny that it can easily be missed. Most travelers come here for the hot springs, Termas de Ralún. For a couple of dollars, rowboats take travelers across the river where there are five giant holes of natural spring water. There is also a campground along the river. The lower Petrohue River flows through Ralún, making this a great hidden spot for fly fishing and kayaking. The center of the town doesn't have much more than a church and school, and if you are looking for something other than a campsite to spend the night, you will have better luck in the neighboring town of Puerto Montt. Updated: Jul 02, 2009.

Getting To and Away From Ralún

Ralún is at the end of the paved highway. There is a mini-bus that goes several times a day from Puerto Varas to Ralún. On Ruta 225, there are multiple daily buses that travel the road from Puerto Varas down to Puelo, just let the bus driver know ahead of time that you want to get off at Ralún. Updated: Jul 02, 2009.

COCHAMÓ

 1m 4,636 65

The first Spanish explorers founded what is now Cochamó in 1556, but it did not become a county until 1979, when it declared its independence from Puerto Montt. Bandits Butch Cassidy and the Sundance Kid fled to the Cochamó Valley after the Great Train Robbery in the early 1900s, in an attempt to avoid the posse who had been chasing them throughout South America. Cochamó has some of Patagonia's most amazing mountain valleys, as well as untouched natural land where the local people still live by ancient traditions. With granite walls up to 1,000 meters (3280.8 ft) high, Cochamó is a famous rock climbing destination (To find tours and guides check out www.cochamo.com/climbing). There is also a natural waterslide at the La Junta River and numerous hiking trails through rivers, rock arches and mountain passes. Trail information can be found at www.cochamo.com/trekking.

Getting To and Away From Cochamó

The **Buses Fierro** company leaves from Puerto Montt to Cochamó four times a day, stopping in Puerto Varas. **Buses Río Puelo** also services this route. Once the bus has dropped you off, the road to Cochamó is a 20 kilometer (12 mi) gravel road along the fjord Reloncaví, built in 1986. Its a long dusty four- or five-hour walk unless you can grab a ride with one of the locals. Updated: Jul 02, 2009.

Lodging

Accommodations are limited in the Cochamó Valley, but the **Refugio Cochamó** is a good option ($12-33). To make reservations go to www.cochamo.com/lodging. (The Refugio de-

pends on data satellite service from November to April.) In town, try **Hostal Maura** ($10 per person including breakfast. Tel: 56-9-82439937, E-mail: michel@cochamotours.cl, URL: www.cochamotours.cl). Updated: Jul 02, 2009.

CURARREHUE

This small town of fewer than 6,000 is located near Pucón in the Arucanía Region of Chile. Curarrehue is the last town before the Argentine border. Here you will find Parque Nacional Huerquehue, home to 1,000-year-old trees and Laguna Quillelhue (at the base of Volcán Lanin), as well as hot springs and waterfalls. The vast majority of the population of Curarrehue are Mapuche who are dedicated to agriculture and tourism. Updated: Jun 30, 2009.

PARQUE NACIONAL HUERQUEHUE

(ADMISSION: Chileans – $5 adults, $2.50 seniors, $2 children; foreigners – $8 adults, $4 seniors and children) Parque Nacional (PN) Huerquehue is one of the oldest wildlife areas in Chile. The reserve began in 1912 as Parque Benjamín Vicuña Mackenna and its name was later changed to Colico. Finally, in 1967 this 12,500-hectare protected area came to be known as PN Huerquehue. In Mapudungún, Huerquehue means Place of the Messengers. PN Huerquehue has irregular topography. Its 20 or so lakes, lying within a narrow glacier valley, are connected by a series of trails. Hiking is the most popular activity within the park, but there are also opportunities for cycling, swimming, sport fishing, photography, and wildlife observation. Some of the many species of flowers you'll see are the Inca lily, bush fuchsia, violas and orchids. The woodlands are carpeted with ferns. Mammals you may encounter inleude the South American grey fox, Patagonian fox, Austral opposum, Chilean miniature deer and puma. Bird species include the Chilean pigeon, ashy-headed goose, white-throated hawk, Magellan goose, black-chested buzzard-eagle, condor and Magellanic woodpecker.

Getting To and Away From Parque Nacional Huerquehue

Parque Nacional Huerquehue is 135 kilometers (81 mi) from Temuco, by way of Villarrica and Pucón, on Ruta 119. The roads are all-weather. The main park entrance is 35 kilometers (21 mi) east of Pucón.

THE LAKE DISTRICT

PN Huerquehue makes for a good day trip from Pucón. Buses leave from in front of the **Pullman Bus** station in Pucón, local companies for PN Huerquehue (8:30 a.m., 4 p.m.; return 2 p.m., 5 p.m., $3.20). You can also catch the blue and white buseta from the side of the Pullman office, departing at 9:15 a.m. for Paillaico. This will leave you four kilometers (2.4 mi) from the park. Updated: Jun 24, 2009.

Things to See and Do
Hiking
PN Huerquehue has many trails you can hike, including one several-day trek. All take you on journeys through beautiful landscapes, with excellent views of the lakes and volcanoes.

Autoguiado Ñirrico (*Distance:* 0.8 km / 0.5 mi, *Difficulty:* easy, *Duration:* 30 min)— Seven interpretive stations describe the forest ecosystems and high Andean lake geology.

Los Lagos (*Distance:* 8.8 km / 5.5 mi, *Difficulty:* medium, *Duration:* 3.5 hours)—The trail goes through fern-bedecked maño and coigüe woods, skyscraping araucaria and passes the Nido de Águilas and Trufulco waterfalls. Grand vistas of the Tinquilco and other lakes, Río Pucón and Volcán Villarrica heighten the experience. There is an information center at Nido de Águilas.

Quinchol (*Distance:* 5 km / 3 mi, *Difficulty:* medium, *Duration:* 2 hours)—This hike leads to a pampa of *coirón* (festus) surrounded by araucaria. There are views of Lago Caburgua, Cerro Sebastián and Tinquilco, as well as the Villarrica, Lanín, Quinquilil and Chushuenco volcanoes. Sendero Quinchol connects with the Cerro Sebastián trail.

Cerro San Sebastián (*Distance:* 8 km / 4.8 mi, *Difficulty:* difficult, *Duration:* 5 hours)— On this trek through the araucaria, coigüe and lenga forest you'll be rewarded with great views of volcanoes and lakes. This is also one of few places in the park where you'll see condors.

Los Huerquenes (*Distance:* 20.7 km / 12.5 mi, *Difficulty:* medium, *Duration:* 2 days)—Highlights include thick araucaria and lenga forests, and Laguna las Avutardas. There are camping areas and a refuge along the trail at Renque.

PN Huerquehue has a warm temperate climate with less than four months of dry season. The rains last from May to September.

In total, the park receives up to 2,045 millimeters (81 in) of rain per year. During the winter, the park gets covered in snow. Check with Conaf in Temuco or Pucón about conditions within the park.

Lodging
Two ranger stations guard PN Huerquehue. The main entrance to the park, with the administration office and a guardaparque, is on the shores of Lago Tinquilco, (9 a.m. – 11 p.m. in high season). From January to March the **Centro de Información Ambiental** is open (8 a.m. – 8 p.m.) and rangers lead nature chats and walks. Longer excursions can also be arranged (Chileans $30, foreigners $40). The area also has a picnic area and camping sites, with a ranger's station, an information booth and a first aid station open all year.

There is another ranger station at Renque, with camping areas and a refuge for those who are doing longer treks. Campgrounds are closed in winter (May – September). From January to February the cost is $20 for Chileans and $30 for foreigners. In the other months, Chileans pay $14 and foreigners $20.

Hotel y Cabañas Parque Huerquehue, perched on the shores of Lago Tinquilco, provides horseback riding, fly fishing, trekking and tour services (Tel: 56-65-45441480 / 56-9-37769820. URL: www.parquehuerquehue.cl; two persons $56). **Camping Olga** is in the same area (56-65-45441938, E-mail: campingolga@hotmail.com, URL: www.campingolga.com; two persons and tent $16). Updated: Jun 29, 2009.

PUERTO MONTT
 14m 153,120 65

Puerto Montt has a bounty of attractions, from museums, like Museo Juan Pablo II and Casa del Arte Diego Rivera, to unique religious and secular architecture. Within an hour are some of the region's most spectacular national parks, like Vicente Pérez Rosales and Alerce Andino, as well as Puerto Varas, Frutillar and other villages ringing Lago Llanquihue. Puerto Montt also makes a good point from which to visit small places along the Seno de Reloncaví and Pacific coasts.

Capital of X Región de los Lagos, Puerto Montt is the entrance to Patagonia. It is Chile's link with XI Región General Carlos Ibáñez del Campo (also called Región

THE LAKE DISTRICT

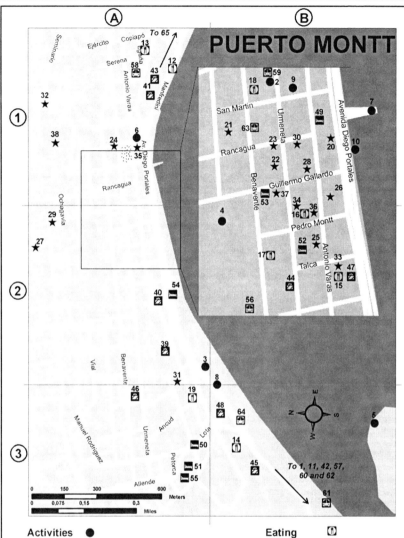

Activities ●

1 Angelmo Market B3
2 Catedral A1
3 Galería de Arte Independiente A2
4 Iglesia de los Jesuitas A2
5 Isla Tenglo B3
6 Monumento a los Colonos Aleman A1
7 Muelle A1
8 Museo Juan Pablo Segundo B2
9 Plaza de Armas A1
10 Sentados frente al mar A1

Airports ✝

11 Aeropuerto El Tepual B3

Eating 🍴

12 Club de Yates A1
13 Degustarte A1
14 Full Fresh Market B3
15 Kalabaza A2
16 Patagonia Deli A2
17 Pizzaria - Café Di Piazza A2
18 Portal del Sur A1
19 Restaurant Don Teo A3

Services ★

20 Afex A1
21 Arco Iris A1
22 Banco de Chile A1
23 Banco del Estado A1
24 BBVA A1
25 BCI A2

Services ★

26 Cambios Boudon A2
27 Carabineros A2
28 Chilexpress A1
29 Conaf A2
30 Correo Chile A1
31 Cyber Fono Market A2
32 Hospital Base de Puerto Montt A1
33 Inter Giro Express A2
34 La Casa del Ciclista Kiefer A2
35 Municipal Tourism Office A1
36 Santander A2
37 Scotiabank A2
38 Sernatur A1

Shopping 🛍

39 Armeria Caza y Pesca Winkler A2
40 Cumbre Sport A2
41 Feria Chilena del Libro A1
42 Latin Star B3
43 Paseo Costanera A1
44 Paseo del Mar A2
45 Pueblitos de Artesanos Melipul B3
46 Rincón Noruego A3
47 Sotavento Libros A2
48 Supermercado Santa Isabel B3

Sleeping ▬

49 Andina del Sud A1
50 Don Tito A3
51 Hostal Pacifico A3
52 Hotel Gamboa A2
53 Hotel O'Grimm A2
54 Hoteles Club Presidente A2
55 Residencia el Taiquino A3

Transportation 🚍

56 Avis A2
57 Empresa Portuaria Puerto Montt B3
58 Hertz & Budget Rent A Car A1
59 LAN A1
60 Naviera Austral & Magallanes Ferries B3
61 Skiffs to Isla Tenglo B3
62 Skorpios Ferries B3
63 Sky Airlines A1
64 Terminal de Buses B3
65 Train Station A1

THE LAKE DISTRICT

de Aysén) and XII Región Magallanes. It is also a strategic transportation hub. Here, the Pan-American Highway seemingly ends, yet with a short ferry ride across the Canal de Chacao, Ruta 5 continues again to Quellón on the southern tip of Chiloé.

The Carretera Austral, Ruta 7, begins in Puerto Montt, winding along the Patagonia coast in strips connected by boat. Ferries depart this port for Chaitén, Puerto Chacabuco, the ice fields of Laguna San Rafael, and Puerto Natales. The southernmost train station is here. Daily flights depart from Aeropuerto El Tepual for destinations in Patagonia and north to Temuco and Santiago. The port is the most important in the south, for transporting both commerce and passengers. Puerto Montt is the departure point for the most exclusive border crossing to Argentina, by way of Lago Todos los Santos.

The city spreads across a narrow coastal plain that then steeply rises up the flanks for those four hills. From Puerto Montt you see the perfect cone of Volcán Osorno (2652 m / 8619 ft), Puntiagudo (2498 m / 8119 ft), and Volcán Calbuco (2015 m / 6549 ft), a squatter-looking mount with streaks of snow.

History

Puerto Montt is a young city, but the area has a long history. Seno de Reloncaví (Reloncaví Sound) was a prehistoric inland sea. Remnants of a petrified forest exist at Playa de Pelluhuín. The oldest remains of a human community ever found in the Americas (dating back 12,500 years ago) are near Puerto Montt. At the end of 1852, German immigrants and Chilotes migrating from Chiloé island arrived at Astilleros de Melipulli (meli—four, pulli—hills). Vicente Pérez Rosales officially founded the city on February 12, 1853, and the name was changed to Puerto Montt, in honor of then-Chilean President Manuel Montt. The area filled with immigrants from Spain, France, Sweden, Denmark, Syria and Palestine.

Like other cities in southern Chile, May 22, 1960, spelled a dramatic change for Puerto Montt. That day's historic earthquake left the city isolated. It had no telephone or telegraph communications. Bridges were destroyed, the Pan-American Highway and railroad lines were cut in several places, and the port was left without electricity and water throughout the autumn. The outside world would eventually learn that 70 percent of Puerto Montt had been destroyed and 80 people had died. Updated: Jul 02, 2009.

When to Go

Puerto Montt has a cool, humid climate. Annual temperatures, which average 10-13°C (50 – 55°F), are highest in January and February (20 – 21°C / 68 – 70°F) and coldest in July (10°C / 43°CF). Rainfall is high, 1,200 – 3,000 millimeters (47-118 in) per year.

When the austral summer arrives, the port swarms with tourists heading for Patagonia. Prices rise and lodging can be difficult to find. Puerto Montt has a bevy of annual music festivals. **The Festival de Jazz** takes place in early November, the Electronic Music fest occurs in December, and the **Festival de la Canción Raíz Folklórica al Mar** (or the Sea Folk Song Festival) happens in early February. Updated: Feb 03, 2009.

Getting To and Away From Puerto Montt

BY BUS

All buses leave from the **Terminal de Buses** (Av. Diego Portales s/n. Tel: 56-65-349011). Services at the depot include phone, money exchange, bathrooms, luggage storage, restaurant and shops.

On the second floor there is an office that provides information about buses and their destinations.

To Hornopirén: **Buses Hornopirén** (2:45 p.m., $7), **TransAustral** (7:50 a.m., 2:30 p.m., 4 p.m., 5 p.m., $7).

To Ancud, Chiloé: **Transchiloé** (8:15 p.m., $7).

To Castro, Chiloé: **Cruz del Sur** (half-hourly 7 a.m. – 9 p.m., $10.60), **Transchiloé** (1:45 p.m., 6:50 p.m., $10). Buses also stop in Ancud.

To Quellón, Chiloé: **Cruz del Sur** (hourly 7 a.m. – 5 p.m., $13), **Transchiloé** (11:20, 3:15 p.m., 4:45 p.m., $12). Buses also stop at Ancud, Castro and Conchi ($10.40 – 11). **Queilen** also services Chiloé Island.

To Punta Arenas: All services go by way of Argentina, 30 hours—**Pullmann Bus** (Wednesday and Saturday 10:45, $50 – 60, semi-cama service), **Queillon** (Monday,

Wednesday, Friday 10:30 a.m., $35, normal clásico service). Also **Turibus**. In January and February book tickets well in advance.

To Osorno: $2.40 – 4, 1.5 hours—**Bus Norte** (9:45 a.m.), **Pullmann** (half-hourly 5:30 – 9:30 p.m.), **Línea Azul** (8:30 p.m.). Also **TurBus, Buses Pirehueico, Fierro, Jac.** Some Santiago-bound buses (e.g. Tur-Bus) also stop in Osorno.

To Valdivia: $8 – 8.60, 3.5 hours—**Tur-Bus** (7:15 a.m., 10:15 a.m., 12:45 p.m., 8:25 p.m.), **Bus Norte** (6:45 a.m.), **Pullmann** (8:25 p.m.), **Línea Azul** (7:45 p.m.).

To Villarrica / Pucón: **Jac** (9 a.m., 10:30 a.m., 1 p.m., 5 p.m., $12.40 / $13.20, 5 – 6 hours).

To Panguipulli: **Bus Pirehueico** (6:30 a.m., 10:50 a.m., 12:40 p.m., 1:45 p.m., 4 p.m., $10, 6 – 7 hours).

To Temuco: 5 hours—**Pullmann** (7:50 a.m., 5:30 p.m., 8:30 p.m.). Also **TurBus, Vía Tur, Jac.**

To Concepción: **Tur Bus** (7 buses 7:15 a.m. – 10:10 p.m., $21-30, 10 hours). Also **Pullmann.** Some buses continue to Los Ángeles.

To Santiago: 13 – 14 hours—**TurBus** (12 buses 8 a.m. – 10:45 p.m., $30 – 46), **Pullman** (hourly 7:30 p.m. – 9:30 p.m., $26), **Línea Azul** (7:45 p.m., 8:30 p.m., $26 – 30). Also **Bus Norte, Cóndor, Vía, NarBus.**

To Valparaíso / Viña del Mar: $33-52, 15 – 16 hours—**TurBus** (8:30 p.m.), **Bus Norte** (7:30 p.m.), **Pullmann** (9:45 a.m.), **Línea Azul** (8:30 p.m.). Also **Cóndor.**

To Bariloche: $24-30, 6 hours—**Andesmar** (8:15 a.m., 1 p.m.), **Vía Bariloche** (3 p.m.), **Buses Norte Nacionales** (8:30 a.m.). In January and February book tickets well in advance.

Micros to villages around Lago Llanquihue leave from Andenes 1 – 15 of the bus terminal every 5 – 15 minutes.

To Puerto Varas: $1.20, 20 minutes.
To Llanquihue: $1.40, 30 minutes.
To Futillar: $1.60, 40 minutes.

For Puerto Octay: go by way of Frutillar; for Ensenada, transfer in Puerto Varas; for las Cascadas, change in Puerto Octay.

Costanera Walking Tour

From the bus terminal, a broad malecón (jetty) hugs the sound's coast. Westward, it ends at the dock for Isla Tenglo boats. Walking east, the promenade passes many places of interest, before arriving in downtown Puerto Montt.

Next to the bus terminal there is an ochre-colored building trimmed in brick. This is the ex-Mercado de la Rampa, now the Museo Histórico Juan Pablo II and public library which hosts literary readings, concerts, movies and other cultural events. On its grounds there are several old steam locomotives, including El Quepo, the first to arrive in the city in 1906. In front of the new Galería de Arte Independiente, Don Quixote rides Rocinante, confronting a giant metal spider straight out of "Wild Wild West." This railroad-shack-cum-gallery exhibits sculptures and other art by young local creators.

Follow the zigzagging wall along the sea. On the beach below, birds feed. Five busts of men instrumental in Chilean and Portomontino history grace tall pedestals. To the south, across the steel-blue waters, snowy mountains rise from the ragged Patagonia coast. Volcán Calbuco looms to the east. A circle of blue slabs, canvasses for graffiti artists, sit on Calle Talcahuano. Next to the slabs there is a skateboard park.

On the scattered green spaces of the malecón, couples rest beneath trees. This grassy expanse is studded with glass huts, below which is a parking lot. Between Calles Pedro Montt and Gallardo, a titanic couple embraces, watching the ocean. This statue, a photo op favorite, is called "Sentados Frente al Mar." On the other side of Avenida Diego Portales is the Bavarian-chalet-styled Hotel Vicente Rosales, with balconies carved by Nicasio García. At the end of Calle San Martín there is a modern covered pier with many benches. Up San Martín is Puerto Montt's Plaza de Armas, also called Plaza Buenaventura Martínez. This was the first public square in Chile to have gardens. Benches in its center have mosaics of native fauna and flora. On the plaza's west side there is a bust of the park's namesake. The Catedral is on the north edge.

Between the costanera park and the Plaza de Armas there is a two-block-long green space. A ground-level fountain is a favorite place for children (and grown-ups) to cool off on hot summer days. Eastward there is a bronze statue, Monumento a los Colonos Alemanes, commemorating the arrival of Germans who founded Puerto Montt. Pichi Juan, accompanied by his dog, points the way to a colonist family.

Across the street is Casa del Arte Diego Rivera, Puerto Montt's art museum and cultural center. It was constructed by the Mexican government in solidarity with the Chilean people after the devastating 1960 earthquake. Opposite Illapel is Puerto Montt's newest mega-shopping center, Mall Costanera, where you can grab a bite to eat and go on a shopping frenzy. Updated: Jan 29, 2009.

Buses for Correntoso, Lago Chapo, Charcas, Arena, Parque Nacional Alerce Andino and other destinations to the southeast of Puerto Montt depart from the West end of the bus terminal.

To Correntoso: Buses JB (Monday – Saturday 7:40 a.m., 4:15 p.m., 5:15 p.m.; daily 12:30 p.m., 8:30 p.m., $2, 45 minutes). Continues to Lago Chapo.

To Chaicas / Caleta la Arena: Fierro, Expresos Austral (every 30 minutes 7:45 a.m. – 7 p.m. $3 / $4, 1.5 hours – 2 hours).

BY TRAIN

Presently passenger service to Osorno and Temuco is suspended, but is projected to begin in the near future. Check the national rail website for updated schedules (Cuarta Terraza s/n, Valle Volcanes. Tel: 56-65-232210, URL: www.efe.cl).

BY BOAT

All types of ships—from cruise liners to private yachts—dock in Puerto Montt. The main port office is **Empresa Portuaria Puerto Montt** (Av. Angelmó 1673. Tel: 56-65-252247, URL: www.empormontt.cl). There are two sets

THE LAKE DISTRICT

of wharves, about a half-kilometer apart. The one closer to Angelmó is where the car and passenger ferries depart (Av. Angelmó 2187). Several of the shipping companies have their offices here. The major boat agencies are:

Skorpios (Av. Angelmó 1660. Tel: 56-65-275646, E-mail: natusk@telsur.cl, URL: www.skorpios.cl)—Skorpio II has special cruises from Puerto Montt to San Rafael and the northern glacial field. See its websites for further information.

Naviera Austral (Av. Angelmó 2187. Tel: 56-65-270430, URL: www.navier-austral.cl)—Operates ferries Alejandrina, Mailén, Don Baldo and Pincoya down the Carretera Austral (Puerto Montt-Chaitén; in summer only, Hornopirén-Ayacara-Chaitén). Between Chaitén and the various Chiloé ports and Quellón, Chiloé-Puerto Chacabuco. Note: The Chaitén-Castro ferry is still suspended due to Volcán Chaitén activity.

Naviera Magallanes / Navimag (Av. Angelmó 2187. Tel: 56-65-432300, URL: www.navimag.cl)—Sails Ferry Evangelistas and Puerto Edén to Puerto Natales, Laguna San Rafael and Puerto Chacabuco. There are discounts for students and seniors. Prices quoted are high season (January – February; November – March for Puerto Natales). Check websites for complete fare information.

To Chaitén: **Naviera Austral** (Monday midnight, Thursday 7 p.m., Saturday 1 a.m., adult $32 – 58.

To Chacabuco: **Navimag** (Thursday 8 p.m.; berth $76 – 82, cabins $216 – 286, lower rates for doubles, triples and quadruples; 24 hours).

To San Rafael: **Navimag** (Saturday 2:30 p.m., berth $1216, cabin $1323 – 1551 single, lower rates for doubles, triples and quadruples, prices round-trip; 5 days).

To Puerto Natales: **Navimag** (Monday 4 p.m.; berth $510, cabin $2100-2470 single, lower rates for doubles, triples and quadruples; 4 days).

To Isla Guar: ($4, 2 hours).
For Isla Guar and other small islands in the sound, boats leave from the Caleta Angelmó market area.

BY AIR
Aeropuerto El Tepual is located northwest of the city (El Tepual Km 13. Tel: 56-65-486200). To arrive at the airport, take Bus ETM from the bus terminal (Monday – Saturday half-hourly 7 a.m. – 9 p.m., Sunday and holidays hourly 8 a.m. – 9 p.m., $3.20, 30 minutes). Airlines have a tendency to come and go in Puerto Montt. The two major national companies reliably connect the city with Santiago, deep Patagonia and other destinations.

Lan (Monday – Friday 9 a.m. – 1 p.m., 3 p.m. – 6:30 p.m., Saturday 9:30 a.m. – 1 p.m. O'Higgins 167) — Santiago (8 – 9 flights daily, from $140), Punta Arenas (2 – 3 daily, from $140), Coyhaique (twice daily, from $140).

Sky Airline (Monday – Friday 9 a.m. – 7 p.m., Saturday 10 a.m. – 1:30 p.m. Benavente 405, local 4. Tel: 56-65-437555, E-mail: ventaspmc@skyairlines.cl)—Santiago (once daily, from $46), Temuco (once daily, from $53), Balmaceda / Coyhaique, from $38). Updated: Jul 01, 2009.

Getting Around
Mini-buses ($0.70) and collective taxis ($0.80) run on set routes. Some regular cabs charge by time, others by distance. All should be metered. For destinations within the city expect to pay $6 – 8 for the whole ride. Radio Taxi Cordillera is one company that does airport transfers (Tel: 56-65-344040). Many car rental companies operate in Puerto Montt, including these international agencies: **Avis** (Benavente 67. Tel: 56-65-253307, E-mail: oficinapmontt@avischile.cl), **Budget** (Varas 162. Tel: 56-65-286277, E-mail: ppomontt@budget.cl), and **Hertz** (Varas 126. Tel: 56-65-259585, URL: www.autorentas.cl).

Avenida Salvador Allende, Avenida Diego Portales and some other streets have bicycle lanes. **La Casa del Ciclista Kiefer** has bike parts (Monday – Friday 9 a.m. – 1 p.m., 3 p.m. – 7 p.m., Saturday 9:30 a.m. – 1 p.m. Pedro Montt 129). Updated: Jul 01, 2009.

Safety
Take care at all hours at the bus terminal and the ports. After dark, avoid Angelmó, the beaches and downtown. Keep to well-lit, populated streets. Be aware of getting ripped off, especially in restaurants where foreigners congregate. Sometimes wait staff upgrade orders, quote wrong prices for items not on the menu or pad bills. Updated: Feb 03, 2009.

Sailing the Southern Seas

The southern seas of Chile are a world apart. Whales, dolphins and toninas leap around any boats plying these waters; penguins and sea lion colonies inhabit the rocky shores; a huge variety of birds soar above ships, seemingly following their journeys through channels and fjords; and ice floes tumble from white mountains, calving into blue bergs. The air is crisp.

How do you get to experience this world? Two major ship lines sail into Chile's southern seas: Naviera Magallanes, more popularly known as **Navimag**, and **Naviera Austral**. They do not compete against each other, though, for the trade on these icy waters. Each has its own routes—and its own personality.

Navimag is the better known company. Its routes, though devoted to carrying cargo to the towns Puerto Chacabuco and Puerto Natales, take the opportunity to make these unforgettable experiences available to tourists. The prices are high, however, making them beyond the economic reach of those ports' inhabitants. (People who live in Puerto Natales fly, as the fare is cheaper.)

The Puerto Natales journey, called Canales Patagónicos, lasts four to five days. Sailing the Kaweskar route, the ferry Evangelistas traverses Canal Moraleda, around Isla Messier, across Golfo de Penas and through Canals Messier and White. It includes a landfall in Puerto Edén, thus providing that village a connection with the outside world, and a pass by of Glaciar Pío XI (south-bound) or Glaciar Amalia (north-bound). Talks, movies and other on-board activities entertain the passengers. Accommodations are in berth (22 bunks per section with shared bathroom) or in one of three classes of cabin. Prices include all meals. This ferry also takes bikes, motorcycles and cars.

A purely tourist excursion is the sail from Puerto Montt to Laguna San Rafael to see the glaciers up-close and to toast the bergs with whiskey on millennium ice. It makes a stop in Puerto Chacabuco to pick up passengers who join the expedition from there. Then, slicing through the frigid waters of Fiordo Aisén and Canal Costa, the ship enters Elefantes Estuary until it approaches the wall of Glaciar San Rafael, the foot of the Campos de Hielo Norte, or Northern Ice Fields. The glacier reflects ice blue in the sunlight. Frosty ice bergs scatter the lagoon. A toast of whiskey on the rocks (in this case, millennium ice) is made to this special place declared a UNESCO Biosphere Reserve in 1979. The crew speaks Spanish and English.

The third route Navimag operates is a normal run between Puerto Montt and Puerto Chacabuco, the gateway into the heart of XI Región de Aysén. It goes directly between the two ports, not stopping at any village along the coasts. The voyage takes 24 hours. The ship also takes vehicles, bikes and motorcycles.

Whereas Navimag is a sleek, thoroughbred shipping company, aiming its passenger services to foreign and moneyed tourists, Naviera Austral is the region's workhorse. It is the most important provider of ferry service from Puerto Montt and Chiloé to the Northern Patagonian villages. On these ships travelers can get to know the common face of Chile. Anyone heading down the Carretera Austral will be taking one of Naviera Austral's ships, whether from Puerto Montt to Chaitén or from Hornopirén to Chaitén (this latter only January to February). On these routes it is possible to see Volcán Chaitén seething on the eastern horizon.

This company's other three routes connect Isla Chiloé with the northern Patagonia mainland. Departing from Quellón on the southern tip of the island, the Don Baldo heads to Chaitén. In January and February another ferry connects Castro and Chaitén. A more fascinating run is the 22-hour Ruta Cordillera journey from Quellón to villages along the coast and fjords: Melinka, Raíl Marín Balmaceda, Santo Domingo, Melimoyu, Puerto Gala (Isla Toto), Puerto Cisnes, Puerto Gaviota (Caleta Amparo), Puerto Aguirre, finally anchoring in Puerto Chacabuco. On this, the Don Baldo pulls into the small villages, delivering

THE LAKE DISTRICT

supplies and dropping passengers off at home. The slower Alejandrina does the trip in 36 hours and has only *butacas*, or seats. The Don Baldo has butacas and berths.

Schedules change throughout the year, with some routes operating only in summer. Boats may be canceled due to weather and sea conditions, especially from May to October.

NAVIMAG

Navimag accepts all credit cards. Special group rates are available; discounts are given for students, minors and seniors, and during the low season. Details on schedules and fares can be obtained at: www.navimag.com. Navimag's offices are:

Santiago (Av. El Bosque Norte 0440, Piso 11, Las Condes. Tel: 56-2-4423120, Fax: 56-2-2035025)

Puerto Montt (Hours: Monday – Friday 9 a.m. – 1 p.m., 2:30 – 6:30 p.m.; Saturday 10 a.m. – 1 p.m. Terminal Transbordadores, Av. Angelmó 2187. Tel: 56-65-432360, Fax: 56-65-276611)

Puerto Chacabuco (Terminal de Transbordadores. Tel: 56-67-351111, Fax: 56-67-351192)

Coyhaique (Paseo Horn 47. Tel: 56-67-233306, Fax: 56-67-233386)

Puerto Natales (Pedro Montt 308. Tel: 56-61-411421, Fax: 56-61-412229)

Punta Arenas (Magallanes 990 Piso 2. Tel: 56-61-200263 / 244400, Fax: 56-61-242003)

NAVIERA AUSTRAL

Naviera Austral's prices remain more constant regardless of the season, though specials are offered in the height of winter. Volcán Chaitén's activity can affect services to Chaitén port. For up-to-date information consult www.navieraustral.cl or drop by one of the company's offices:

Puerto Montt (Av. Angelmó 2187. Tel: 56-65-270430 / 31 / 32, Fax: 56-65-270415, E-mail: contacto@navieraustral.cl).

Quellón, Chiloé (Pedro Montt 457. Tel: 56-65-682207, Fax: 56-65-682601)

Hornopirén (Ingenieros Militares s/n. Tel: 56-7-9681646)

Ayacara (María Mayorga, Ayacara Centro s/n. Tel: 56-7-4751168)

Chaitén (8 a.m. – 9:15 a.m., 10 a.m. – 1 p.m., 3 p.m. – 6 p.m. Av. Concorvado, near Calle Pedro Aguirre Cerda. Tel: 56-9-8750320)

Palena (Sandra Millapinda, José Miguel Carrera 647. Tel: 56-65-741326, 56-9-82951976, E-mail: smillapinda@gmail.com)

Melinka (Elizabeth Ulloa, Av. Costanera s/n. Tel: 56-67-431707, 56-7-6540758)

Puerto Cisnes (Olivia Gómez Goio, Arturo Prat 07. Tel: 56-67-346426 / 8-4482837, E-mail: gomezolivia2@gmail.com)

Puerto Aguirre (Braulio Guaquel Mariman, Balmaceda 350. Tel: 56-67-3-1357, E-mail: brauliojgm@hotmail.com)

Puerto Chacabuco (Terminal de Transbordadores s/n. Tel: 56-67-351493)

Coyhaique (Chaltén Travel, Av. Ogana 1147. Tel: 56-67-246113)

Updated: Jun 24, 2009.

Services

TOURISM

The most convenient place to get information is at the **municipal tourism office** on the southwest corner of the Plaza de Armas (Monday – Friday 9 a.m. – 6 p.m., Saturday 9 a.m. – 2 p.m.; in summer daily 9 a.m. – 9 p.m. Varas 415. Tel: 56-65-223027, Fax: 56-65-261808, E-mail: puertomontt.turismo@gmail.com / turismomontt@puertomonttchile.cl, URL: www.puertomonttchile.cl).

Sernatur, the regional tourism office, is an uphill hike from downtown (Monday – Thursday 8:30 a.m. – 5:30 p.m., Friday 8:30 a.m. – 4:30 p.m. Av. Xº Región 480, edificio anexo, second floor. Tel: 56-65-254580, E-mail: infoloslagos@sernatur.cl, URL: www.sernatur.cl). Other important offices include **Automóvil Club de Chile** (Esmeralda 70. Tel: 56-65-254776 / 350393), **Carabineros** (Gallardo 519, Emergency Tel: 133), and **Conaf** (Monday-Thursday 9 a.m. – 1 p.m., 2 p.m. – 5:45 p.m., Friday 9 a.m. – 1 p.m., 2 p.m. – 4:45 p.m. Ochagavía 464. Tel: 56-65-486102, URL: www.conaf.cl).

Consulates in Puerto Montt:
Argentina (Pedro Montt 160, piso 6. Tel: 56-65-253996)
Germany (Varas 523, office 306. Tel: 56-65-252828)
Italy (Rengifo 916. Tel:56-65-252961)
Poland (O'Higgins 601, dpto. 705. Tel: 56-65-253157)
U.K. (Dione 1030, Lomas de Reloncaví. Tel: 56-65-282676)
Uruguay (Madre Paulina 337. Tel: 56-65-252153)

MONEY

Puerto Montt's banks keep the usual hours (Monday – Friday 9 a.m. – 2 p.m.). ATMs accept MasterCard, Cirrus, Visa and Plus cards, except where noted:

Banco Chile (Urmeneta 464)
Banco del Estado (Urmeneta 444)—ATM: only MasterCard, Cirrus; exchanges U.S. dollars and euros.
BBVA (O'Higgins 156)
BCI (Varas 560)
Santander (Varas 501)—ATM: also American Express.
Scotiabank (Urmeneta 500)—exchanges U.S. dollars and euros.

Exchange bureaus are also located in the center of town. None are open on Sunday. **Afex** (Monday – Friday 8:30 a.m. – 7 p.m., Saturday 10 a.m. – 2 p.m. Av. Portales 516)—all currencies, American Express traveler's checks; MoneyGram agent. Airport office as well.

Cambios Boudon (Monday – Saturday 9 a.m. – 7 p.m. Gallardo 065)—U.S., Australian and Canadian dollars, euros, pound sterling and other currencies; American Express, Citicorp, Thomas Cook and Visa traveler's checks.

Inter Giro Express (Monday – Friday 9 a.m. – 7:30 p.m., Saturday 10 a.m. – 1 p.m. Talca 84, local 7, Mall Paseo Costanera local 107. Tel: 56-65-343683 / 5113909, E-mail puertomontt@interservice.cl, URL: www.crossco.cl9)—U.S. dollars, euros, Argentine pesos, Brazilian real, American Express traveler's checks.

Chilexpress is the Western Union agent (Monday – Friday 9 a.m. – 7 p.m., Saturday 10 a.m. – 1 p.m. Varas 180).

KEEPING IN TOUCH

To post a letter or package, stop by **Correos Chile** (Monday – Friday 9 a.m. – 7 p.m., Saturday 9:30 a.m. – 1 p.m. Rancagua 126).

Internet averages $1.20 – 1.40 per hour. Skype is common; several cafes are open on Sunday. Telephone calls are uniformly expensive, with international service from $0.40 per minute. For both Internet and phone, hunt along Varas. **Ciber Fono Market** is a cheaper option near the bus terminal, charging $0.80 per hour, but it has poor headsets for Skype (Monday – Saturday 9 a.m. – 9 p.m., Sunday noon – 7 p.m. Varas 953).

Biblioteca Regional also has computers for public use (Portales 997. Tel: 56-65-255488).

MEDICAL

Hospital Base de Puerto Montt is the city's main health facility (Semanario s/n. Tel: 56-65-261100). Several pharmacies are on Varas, between Chillán and the Plaza de Armas. They use the de turno system, meaning one of them is open overnight on a rotating basis.

LAUNDRY

Try **Arco Iris**, though at $10 a load, it's another sign you're reaching the end of the "civilized" world (San Martín 232). Updated: Jul 07, 2009.

SHOPPING

The **Feria Artesanal Angelmó** (Av. Diego Portales, blocks 1900-2200, 2 km / 1.2 mi west of Puerto Montt) stretches for three blocks between the main shipping port and the Terminal Transbordador. It offers handcrafted and mass-produced goods, like textiles, wood, leather, lapis lazuli jewelry, shells and kitschy souvenirs. Also on hand are regional jams, chocolates, honey and liqueurs. Another place to purchase artisan wares and observe craftspeople at work is the **Pueblitos de Artesanos de Melipulli** (Av. Portales s/n, across from the bus terminal).

Puerto Montt has two large malls, both located downtown: **Paseo del Mar** (Urmeneta 580) and **Paseo Costanera** (Illapel 10). You can buy gear for fishing, camping and other outdoor sports at somewhat reasonable prices in Puerto Montt: **Armería Caza y Pesca Winkler** (Talcahuano 115. Tel: 56-65-252352), **Cumbre Sport** (Chillán 100. Tel: 56-65-254179) and **Rincón Noruego** (Baquedano 199. Tel: 56-65-511291, E-mail: info@rinconnoruego.com, URL: www.rinconnoruego.com).

Nature and tourism guides, trekking maps and a small selection of English language books are available at **Sotavento Libros** (Monday – Friday 10 a.m. – 1:30 p.m., 3:30 p.m. – 8 p.m., Saturday 10 a.m. – 2 p.m., 5:30 p.m. – 8 p.m. Av. Portales 570. Tel: 56-65-256650, E-mail: sotavento@surnet.cl) and **Feria Chilena del Libro** (Monday – Saturday 10 a.m. – 10 p.m., Sunday and holidays 11 a.m. – 10 p.m. Mall Costanera, local 217. Tel: 56-65-341859). Not too far from the ferry port is **Latin Star**, which has a book exchange, as well as Internet and international calls (Monday – Saturday 9 a.m. – 10 p.m., Sunday and holidays 10 a.m. – 8 p.m. Av. Angelmó 1672. Tel: 56-65-278318). Updated: Feb 03, 2009.

Things to See and Do

Puerto Montt has a few activities to keep its visitors busy while waiting for a ship to sail into Patagonia. If you only have a few hours to spare, walk along the costanera seafront to visit the Museo Histórico Juan Pablo II and the cathedral. You can also walk to the Angelmó market, check out the artisan stalls, pick up supplies for the long boat ride and dine on fresh seafood.

Travelers with a few more days in port may want to skip over to Isla Tenglo, check out the Iglesia de los Jesuitas or the archaeo-logical Museo de Monte Verde. Cultural spaces include the Casa de Arte Diego Rivera, the city's art museum, and the Biblioteca Regional. Near Sernatur is a mirador with a view of the city and sound. Low tide exposes a petrified forest at Playa de Pelluhuín. At Kilometer 12 is Conchales de Piedra Azul, an archaeological site dating from 6300 BC. Modern Piedra Azul village has an old wooden church.

Monte Verde Stone Museum

The museum has a good overview of Puerto Montt's history, from pre-Columbian times to the present, including authentic totems and hunting tools. Luis Mansilla 173, corner Manuel Montt. Tel: 56- 65-292929, Updated: Jan 11, 2007.

Museo Histórico Juan Pablo II

(ADMISSION: $1, seniors $0.60, children $0.40) From the mid-1950s to early 1980s the building was the Mercado de la Rampa, the principal marketplace. With Pope John Paul II's 1987 visit, it was renovated for a mass, then became a museum. Displaying not only articles used by the Pope, the Museo Histórico Juan Pablo II's exhibits trace geologic and human history from the last glacial age to the colonial village Mellipuli and the wave of German immigration in the 19th century. A gallery shows the port in the 1930s and finally the destruction and rebirth of Puerto Montt after the 1960 earthquake. Tuesday – Friday 10 a.m. – 1 p.m., 3:30 p.m. – 6:30 p.m. Portales 997, E-mail: museojp@yahoo.com, URL: www.museohistoricopm.cl. Updated: Jan 29,.2009.

Cathedral

(ADMISSION: Free) This cathedral, built in 1856 by Matias Doggenweiler and August Trauttmann, was inspired by the simple lines of the Parthenon in Athens. The wooden church is topped with a copper cupola. Rectangular blocks of stained glass form the front wall and a brightly painted Christ and host of angels gaze upon those entering the sanctuary. Only ribbed

Doric columns divide the nave from the side aisles, which are decorated with large paintings of Christ's life, while lunette windows illuminate the space. To the left of the square-ended apse is the capilla de San Francisco de Sales, a neo-Gothic-styled chapel covered with murals. The cathedral is one of Puerto Montt's oldest buildings and has also been a theater and, in the 1880s, an army barracks. In 1896, it was reconsecrated as a church dedicated to the Virgin of Mount Carmel. Urmeneta, between San Martin and O'Higgins, Plaza de Armas. Updated: Jan 29, 2009.

Iglesia de los Jesuitas ♪

(ADMISSION: Free) Walking down Gallardo Street, most people just pass by this yellow church. Take a step back, though, and you'll notice Iglesia de los Jesuitas' architecture becomes more interesting. Built in 1872, this hidden treasure of Puerto Montt has somber, neo-Classic lines. It is crowned with an octagonal cupola. Inside, the natural alerce walls are painted with pristine murals. The windows are covered with latticework. The chapel screens have High Gothic touches. Within the campanile's octagonal tower are four bronze bells forged in Austria, rung only on special occasions. There is a bell tower on the knoll behind it. Monday – Friday 7:30 a.m. – 1:30 p.m., 2:30 p.m. – 8 p.m., Saturday 9 a.m. – 1 p.m., 3 p.m. – 7 p.m. Gallardo 269. Updated: Jan 29, 2009.

Isla Tenglo

Where do Puertomontinos go to relax come weekends and holidays? They head right across the narrow channel, Canal de Tenglo, that separates Isla Tenglo from the mainland by only 100 – 150 meters (325 – 488 ft). Its broad dark-grey sand is perfect for sunning or beachcombing. Hike up to the giant cross atop the island's hill. From here there are terrific views of the city, Volcanoes Osorno, Calbuco and Puntigudo and the serrated sierra edging the Patagonia coast. Afterward, enjoy fresh fish and seafood at a simple restaurant before catching the launch at sunset with the Portomosinos returning home. Motorized skiffs shuttle people to Isla Tenglo every five minutes from 6 a.m. to 10 p.m. ($0.60) from the far west end of the Av. Diego Portales costanera park. Updated: Jan 29, 2009.

Angelmó Market

Fishermen anchored their boats in the sheltered waters of the Canal de Tenglo long before Puerto Montt was founded. People come from around the sound and its islands to trade fish, produce and other products in this small cove. This is the closest to a market that Puerto Montt has.

There are two-story, wooden-shingled buildings with restaurants that serve *cancato* and *curanto* (stews of meat or seafood cooked on hot stones). Food isn't the only thing that is hawked here. Artisan stalls line Avenida Angelmó for several blocks before arriving at the market's entrance. To get there from downtown or the bus terminal, walk west on Avenida Diego Portales, which becomes Avenida Angelmó, or take any city micro bus ($0.70) or colectivo taxi ($0.80) whose sign says "Angelmó." Updated: Jan 29, 2009.

Tours

Whether you're looking for a bit of adventure, or a more leisurely tour, Puerto Montt will not disappoint. Outdoor enthusiasts can go hiking or trekking and many tour operators also take visitors rafting or horseback riding in the beautiful countryside. You can also arrange day tours to the lakes or nearby artisan markets.

Eureka Tours

Eureka Tours offers horseback riding, trekking, rafting and cruises. It also helps with car rentals and travel bookings. Tel: 56-65-250412, E-mail: eureka-turismo@entelchile. net, URL: www.chile-travel.com/eureka.htm.

Viajes Express

This outfitter arranges photo safari tours of the national park and volcanoes, summit climbs, trekking, rafting, horseback riding, and car rentals at the airport. Contact Jorge. Tel: 56-65-257137, airport 56-65-263960, URL: www. chile-travel.com/traviweb.htm#outdoor.

Andina del Sud

Andina del Sud can prepare your trip to any corner of the world, make plane reservations and arrange travel for both business and leisure travelers. It can even exchange money. But the reason most vacationers to Chile come to Andina del Sud's office, next door to the municipal tourism office, is to book passage on the Lakes Crossing to Bariloche. For details, see The Lake District—Border Crossings (p.270). Varas 437. Tel: 56-65-257767, E-mail: agenciapmc@andinadelsud.cl, URL: www.andinadelsud.cl. Updated: Jul 01, 2009.

Lodging

Being a port means that Puerto Montt has a wider range of accommodations than other cities. At the bottom are the hotels of mala muerte (bad death) and brothels. Budget lodging with a family atmosphere are located near the bus terminal, along Calles Mira, Lota, V. Pérez Rosales and Ancud. In the high season (mid-December to early-March), national holidays and weekends lodging can be difficult to find. If arriving without reservations, it is best to look after checkout time (noon). There is an official

THE LAKE DISTRICT

lodging kiosk outside Andén (Lane) 11 at the bus station. In summer, several albergues, or dorms, are set up at local schools. Check with the municipal tourism office for listings. On the road to Chinquihue you will find several campgrounds.

Residencial El Taiquino

(ROOMS: $12 – 15 per person) Four blocks from the bus terminal, this simple, well-worn hostel is popular with travelers of all nationalities looking for an inexpensive place to stay in Puerto Montt. El Taiquino offers no-frills private rooms with one bed each—they share common bathrooms. This large, light-yellow house is just a few doors down from a bar, something light sleepers might want to consider before checking in. 114 Perez Rosales. Tel: 56-65-253331, Fax: 65-263363. Updated: Jan 07, 2009.

Don Tito

(ROOMS: $12 – 18 per person) Don Tito and his wife have a pleasant, quiet hostel just two blocks up Avenida Salvador Allende from the bus station. The multi-bed rooms are large, the ones for sole travelers a bit small. A few of the first-floor accommodations are windowless; take a look before choosing. Those rooms with private baths also come with cable TV. Some may find the cushiony foam mattresses to be a minus. Mira 1069. Tel: 56-65-287025. Updated: Jan 29, 2009.

Hotel Gamboa

(ROOMS: $20 – 40) Hotel Gamboa is an old mansion, and upon walking in you are immersed in the Victorian clutter of the small lobby: lace curtains, throws on the chairs and doilies. Gamboa has that musty smell old houses have. Some of the guest rooms have their own baths, but most share common ones. The price makes it a popular hostel. An ordinary breakfast is included. 157 Pedro Montt. Tel: 56-65-252741. Updated: Jul 02, 2009.

Hostal Pacífico

(ROOMS: $32 – 50) Two blocks from the bus station, prim, modern Hostal Pacífico welcomes both business travelers (who receive special rates) and tourists. Rooms vary in size and some have no windows, so check yours out before checking in. All come with private, hot-water baths, WiFi, heating and continental breakfast. If traveling by plane, Pacífico has an airport transfer service (for a charge). Mira 1088. Tel: 56-65-256229, E-mail: info@hostalpacifico.cl, URL: www.hostalpacifico.cl. Updated: Feb 03, 2009.

Hotel O'Grimm

(ROOMS: $80 – 90) Hotel O'Grimm is a hotel for business travelers and tourists in the center of Puerto Montt. In this stately, four-story inn an elevator shuttles guests to nicely decorated rooms with a host of amenities like mini-bars (extra charge on items consumed), in-room safe boxes and cable TV. Some rooms have a sitting area and others have a desk. The family suite has a Jacuzzi. The hostel's heating helps warm its visitors on cold, damp Puertomontino evenings. The carpeting is the one glaring blemish of this hotel. 211 Gallardo. Tel: 56-65-258600, E-mail: hotel@ogrimm.com, URL: www.ogrimm.com. Updated: Jul 01, 2009.

Hoteles Club Presidente

(ROOMS: $110 – 116) Hoteles Club Presidente is the place to stay in Puerto Montt for those travelers wanting all the comforts of home. The well-decorated rooms have uncommon touches, like a separate bathrooms with hair dryers, in-room security boxes and Internet. Additionally, each space has either a sitting or dining area where you can enjoy a meal you make in the kitchenette. The Club Presidente has two parts. The original, with a lobby strewn with antiques, is on Avenida Portales. Behind it, rise nine floors of the newer annex. Some of the rooms have wonderful views of Seno de Reloncaví. Av. Diego Portales 664. Tel: 56-65-251666, Fax: 56-65-251669, E-mail: infocp@presidente.cl, URL: www.presidente.cl. Updated: Feb 03, 2009.

Restaurants

Puertomontino menus feature all types of seafood, in particular *merluza* (hake, similar to cod) and salmon. Many restaurants offer *colaciones* (main dishes) with side, for $2 – 4. A complete three-course lunches (*almuerzo* or *menú ejecutivo*), costs $5 – 8. Beware of dishonest practices by some restaurants, such as up-grading your order or quoting you the wrong price. Most eateries are closed on Sunday.

There are two large supermarkets across from the bus station: **Santa Isabel** (Av. Salvador Allende and Av. Diego Portales) and **Full Fresh Market** (Av. Diego Portales and E. Lillo). Updated: Feb 05, 2009.

Restaurant Don Teo

(ENTREES: $3 – 5.50) Just a few blocks from the bus terminal, Restaurant Don Teo, is an inexpensive, bare-bones diner. The hand-written menus posted on the sun-yellow walls list classic Chilean dishes, like *pollo arvejado* (chicken stewed with peas and carrots), chicken or beef *cazuela* (stew) and salmon. A special plate can be prepared for vegetarians. Restaurant Don Teo is a decent enough place to grab a bite before boarding a long ride. Open Monday – Saturday 10 a.m. – 8 p.m., Sunday 11 a.m. – 9 p.m. Andrés Bello 990. Updated: Jul 07, 2009.

Portal del Sur

(LUNCH: $4) Portal del Sur is a popular place to grab a good, home-cooked meal at an excellent price. Just a hole-in-the-wall eatery with a half-dozen tables crowded into the small space, Portal's only serves lunch (noon – 3 p.m., unless it runs out beforehand), a two-course affair with drink and bread. Don't expect more than one choice on any day. In the evening the señora whips up snacks for the bar clientele. Open Monday – Saturday 10 a.m. – midnight, closed Sunday (unless there's a televised football game). San Martín 167 Tel: 56-65-344496. Updated: Feb 04, 2009.

Degustarte

(ENTREES: $6.40 – 24.60, LUNCH: $4) A taste of art is precisely what you get at Desgustarte. The chefs use local ingredients to create fusion culinary dishes with ethnic flair. Vegetarian fare is a specialty—even soy burgers make it on the menu. Degustarte hangs fine art exhibits on its walls and hosts live jazz concerts and literary readings.

This restaurant has a relaxed atmosphere with shadowbox tables and sofa seating areas. The service is quick and the waitstaff is attentive. Open Monday – Friday noon – 4 p.m., 7 p.m. – 2 a.m., Saturday 6 p.m. – 2 a.m. Live music Friday and Saturday from 11 p.m. Egaña 156. Tel: 56-65-714059. E-mail: elbalconrestobar@gmail.com. Updated: Jul 07, 2009.

Kalabaza

(ENTREES: $4, LUNCH: $5.60) Kalabaza is a small eatery with little for the vegetarian, but much for those wanting to experience the ultimate in Chile's redefinition of fast food. The menu has the whole gamut of sandwiches and some entrées. Tablas are planks of empanadas, kabobs, or an assortment of cheeses and meats to share. Try Kalabaza's pichanga, a plate heaped with French fries, hard-boiled eggs, sausage, cheese, pickles, avocado, tomato and much more. Wash it down with a bottle of microbrew or a mug of Kunstmann on tap. Open Monday – Saturday 9 a.m. – 1 a.m., Saturday and holidays 4 p.m. – 11 p.m. Varas 629. Tel: 56-65-262020, E-mail: kalabaza@surnet.cl. Updated: Feb 05, 2009.

Pizzaría-Cafe DiPiazza

(ENTREES: $4.60, LUNCH: $3.60 – 5) Pizzarría-Cafe DiPiazza prepares 25 types of pizza bedded on *masa pan* (thick) or *masa piedra* (thin) crust. Vegetarians will ogle the varieties made just for them. In addition to these delights, DiPiazza also fixes up all sorts of typical Chilean sandwiches, as well as pastas, gnocchi and ravioli with a choice of six delectable sauces. Of course, lasagna is on the menu, too. The wait service is good, the ambiance relaxed. Open Monday – Friday 9:30 a.m. – 11 p.m., Saturday and Sunday 11 a.m. – 11 p.m. Pedro Montt 181. Tel: 56-65-254174. Updated: Mar 10, 2009.

Patagonia Deli

(ENTREES: $5 – 14.40, LUNCH: $8) This bistro offers typical Chilean hamburgers, hot dogs and Barros Luco, with some interesting twists. The menu also includes pastas, crêpes and empanadas. For a light meal, try the shrimp and cheese pies. Vegetarians will also find something to eat. Double-check your bill. Open Monday – Saturday 9 a.m. – 12:30 a.m. Varas 486. Tel: 56-65-482898, E-mail: patagoniadeli@surnet.cl. Updated: Mar 09, 2009.

Club de Yates Restaurant

(ENTREES: from $11) The murmur of waves washing against the pier leggings of Restaurant Club de Yates fills the dining room of this modern, all-glass bistro. The world-class chefs here create an international menu of over 220 palate-tempting dishes, specializing in seafood. Turf offerings include rabbit, chicken, duck, beef and pork, as well as exotic meats like rhea, pheasant, *jabalí* (wild boar) and goose. The wine list is just as extensive, with over 145 fine vintages to choose from. Open Monday – Saturday noon – 3 p.m., 8 – 11 p.m. Av. Juan Soler Manfredini 2476. Tel: 56-65-263606. E-mail: inforeservas@clubdeyates.cl. URL: www.clubdeyates.cl. Updated: Jan 07, 2009.

PARQUE NACIONAL ALERCE ANDINO

Parque Nacional (PN) Alerce Andino, situated between the Reloncaví Sound and estuary, is a 39,255-hectare park that extends to the south shore of Lago Chapo. Within the park's mountainous territory is a large expanse of virgin alerce forest.

THE LAKE DISTRICT

Patagonian cypress covers 20,000 hectares of the park. Some trees are over 1,000 years old and reach heights of 40 meters (130 ft). Other trees include *tineo, tepa, mañío* and *canelo* (winter's bark). *Coigüe de Chiloé* grows in the mountains in the western part of PN Alerce Andino.

Common animals are Chilean miniature deer, puma, *guiña*, South American grey fox, Molina's hog-nosed skunk, *vizcacha* and Austral opossum. Birds are plentiful. Among the varieties here are the condor, Magellanic woodpecker, black-throated huet-huet, ringed kingfisher, white-throated hawk, mallard, tufted tit-tyrant, Chilean pigeon, and Magellan goose.

This is a land that was carved by glaciers and movements of the Earth's plates. Sheer cliffs fall to deep valleys. The region rises from sea level to Cerro Cuadrada's 1330 meters (4323 ft). On the northern horizon is Volcán Calbuco (2003 m / 6510 ft) in neighboring Reserva Nacional Llanquihue. The largest lake is Lago Chapo, from which Río del Sur flows toward Seno de Reloncaví. There are more than 50 lagoons across the woodlands, including Sargazo, Chaiquenes, Triángulo, Fría, Montaña and Campaña.

The park is divided into four sections, each with its own ranger station. You can reach three of these from the village of Correntoso. Sector Lago Chapo on the lake of the same name on the north edge; Sector Correntoso, the northwestern gateway into the park; and Sector Sargazo. The far southern part of PN Alerce Andino is under the protection of Sector Valle del Río Chaicas, near Lenca. Entry into this national park is $2. A network of trails lead visitors across PN Alerce Andino's undulating landscape.

PN Alerce Andino has a temperate maritime climate, with annual rainfalls of 3,300 – 4,500 millimeters (130 – 177 in). In winter, snow falls above the 700-meter (2275-ft) mark. In July temperatures average 7°C (44°F) and in January 15 – 20°C (59 – 68°F). The best time to visit is November to March, but even during those summer months, warm and rainproof clothing is necessary. Hanta virus is a severe threat in the park. Keep to trails and read the section about Major Health Problems (see p. 56).

Getting To and Away From Parque Nacional Alerce Andino

Ruta V-65 goes from Puerto Montt to Correntoso village, then on to the ranger station at Lago Chapo (46 km / 28 mi). From Correntoso pueblo to Guardería Correntoso it is 2.5 kilometers (1.5 mi). Sector Sargazo is also accessed from this village (10 km / 6 mi). From Puerto Montt, the Carretera Austral (Ruta 7) passes through Lenca (40 km / 24 mi). A rough road, suitable only for 4x4 vehicles, heads to Valle del Río Chaicas and Laguna Chaiquenes (15 km / 9 mi). The ranger station for Sector Valle del Río Chaicas is at Km 17.

Buses for Correntoso, Lago Chapo, Charcas, Arena, Parque Nacional Alerce Andino (and other destinations southeast of Puerto Montt) depart from the west end of that city's bus terminal (Av. Diego Portales s/n. Tel: 56-65-349011).

To Correntoso: **Buses JB** (Monday – Saturday 7:40 a.m., 4:15 p.m., 5:15 p.m.; daily 12:30 p.m., 8:30 p.m., $2, 45 minutes). Continues to Lago Chapo.

To Chaicas / Caleta la Arena: Fierro, **Expresos Austral** (every 30 minutes 7:45 a.m. – 7 p.m. $3 / $4, 1.5 hours – 2 hours). Updated: Jun 17, 2009.

Sector Sargoza

Sargoza (Distance: 10 km / 6 mi, difficulty: medium-hard, duration: 5.5-6 hours) – this trek goes from the ranger station to Laguna Sargoza (2.5 km/1.5 mi, 1 hour) then on to Laguna Fría (8.3 km/5 mi, 4.5 hours).

Rodal Alerce Pequeño (Distance: 2.3 km / 1.4 mi, difficulty: medium, duration: 1.25 hours) – begins at the ranger station.

Aluvión (Distance: 2.6 km / 1.6 mi, difficulty: medium, duration: 1.5 hours) – begins at the ranger station.

Sector Correntoso

Correntoso – Río Pangal (*Distance:* 3.2 km / 2 mi, *Difficulty:* medium, *Duration:* 1.5 – 2 hours)—begins at the ranger station.
Río Pangal – Refugio (*Distance:* 2.1 km / 1.3 mi, *Difficulty:* easy; *Duration:* 45 min – 1 hour).

Mirador Huillifotem (*Distance:* 1 km / 0.6 mi, *Difficulty:* medium-hard, *Duration:* 1 hour)—begins from the ranger station.

Sector Río Chaicas

Chaicas (*Distance:* 8.7 km / 5.25 mi, *Difficulty:* medium, *Duration:* 5 hours).

Saltos Río Chaicas (*Distance:* 3.8 km / 2.3 mi, *Difficulty:* medium, *Duration:* 2 hours).

Laguna Chaiquenes (*Distance:* 5.5 km / 3.3 mi, *Difficulty:* medium, *Duration:* 4 hours.

Laguna Triángulo (*Distance:* 9.5 km / 5.7 mi, *Difficulty:* medium, *Duration:* 6 hours). There is sport fishing for brown and rainbow trout, *farionela* and South American perch, especially on Lago Chapo. Boating tours up Estuario Reloncaví can also be arranged.

Sector Correntoso has five campsites with fire pits. In Sector Río Chaicas, 2.5 kilometers (1.5 mi) from the ranger station, there is another campground with five sites, fire pits, water and bathrooms. The cost for either is $10 per night for up to six people per site. There are basic refuges at Laguna Sargazo, Laguna Fría and Río Pangal ($10). Updated: Jun 17, 2009.

!))))

THE LAKE DISTRICT

CHILOÉ REGION

Chiloé

Just off the coast of the Carretera Austral sits Chiloé, made up of nearly 100 islands, of which only 30 or so are inhabited. Modern development is slowly starting to filter through to the islands from the mainland, but the way of life is still very traditional—people live in houses on stilts on the shore, and there are wooden churches and chapels on every corner.

The main island, Chiloé, is the entry point for most tourists (by boat from Pargua on the mainland). Measuring 200 kilometers by 75 kilometers (124 mi by 47 mi), Chiloé is the second largest island in South America, after Tierra del Fuego.

Parque Nacional de Chiloé, on the west coast, is the reason most people visit (p.388). The

park is very accessible to visitors, with numerous hiking trails meandering through the dense coastal rainforest. Castro, the island's capital, is a good base for exploring the park as it is close by and tours can be easily arranged (p.381). You can also stay at Ancud, a lively little fishing town in the north, which is always bustling with activity and certainly worth a visit (p.376).

All of the inhabited islands can be reached by boat, although some are harder to get to than others. Isla Quinchao and Isla Lemuy are just off the mainland, and easily accessible by bus. You can visit them in a day, but many people choose to stay longer just to chill out and enjoy the slow pace of life. Updated: Dec 04, 2006.

Highlights

Mystical, misty, lushly green, **Chiloé** holds an iconic place in the Chilean national psyche. You can see rolling hills, rocky coastlines, and dusty fishing villages elsewhere, but Chile's largest island is an undeniably pretty place—especially if you're used to Chile's homogenous and homogenizing cities, or have a special interest in delving into the island's unique culture.

No visit to Chiloé is complete without stepping into at least several of the island's centuries-old, wooden, but well preserved **churches**, many of which are certified as World Heritage Sites by UNESCO. Aside from being architecturally beautiful, the churches are culturally significant as the crossroads between Catholicism, imposed by Spanish colonialism, and the rich mythical beliefs that still persist among island residents.

Those in the market for the ultimate in tranquility can hardly go wrong with a stay in **Chonchi (p.388)** or one of Chiloé's other small towns. The island's **national park (p.388)** is a fine place for camping or hiking. Even if your interest in nature is limited, you'll get a kick out of an excursion to the **Pinguinera Puñihuil** penguin reserves near **Ancud (p.378)**. Updated: Jan, 13 2009.

History

Populated first by the Chono, and subsequently by the Huilliche people, Chiloé's indigenous past was met head-on by European colonialism after an indigenous rebellion on the mainland in 1598 caused the Spanish to send settlers to the islands. Chiloé's geographic isolation from the rest of Chile, as well as its notoriously wet weather, dependence on the sea, and particular brand of indigenous-European contact, created a local culture wholly different from the mainland.

Chilotes incorporated Catholicism and native beliefs into a local faith system that had a pre-existent rich and persistent mythology—including magical warlocks and a forest-dwelling gnome who impregnates young virgins. As Chile broke free from the shackles of colonial rule, Spanish leaders took refuge in Chiloé, and it was here that Spain had its last base in all of South America, which it did not abandon until 1826.

Though now linked to the continent by frequent ferries (but still not a bridge, a subject of some controversy), and is visited by many domestic and foreign travelers alike, Chiloé and its more than 155,000 inhabitants still strike visitors with a unique local flavor, that's insular if not exactly isolated. Valparaíso aside, if the main Chilean cities and towns strike you as unimaginative, a visit to Chiloé should be enough to convince you that, if you venture far enough from the country's urban centers, there are indeed strong regional identities within the country that greatly enrich its overall cultural mélange. Updated: Jan 13, 2009.

When to Go

Large numbers of national and foreign visitors depart for Chiloé in January and February, when the weather's clearest, and there's a full calendar of cultural festivals. This influx is most noticeable in tiny Cucao, the gateway to the national park, though in general Chiloé copes well with incomers.

Keep in mind that the months of December and March offer low-season rates, fewer crowds, and decent weather, though if you're intent on limiting your exposure to downpours, you'll want to stick to the high-season months. Unless you have an unnatural affinity for rain and wind, avoid the winter. Updated: Jan 12, 2009.

Safety

In a country already considered one of the safest in Latin America, Chiloé ranks at the top in terms of safety. Crime can happen anywhere, though the vast majority of travelers will be fine by taking common-sense precautions. If anywhere on the island has a reputation among Chilotes for robberies, it's Quellón, though the town is far from what any traveler would consider dangerous, (plus, there's little to draw you there as a tourist in the first place). Updated: Jan 12, 2009.

Things to See and Do

Chiloé has its share of tourist attractions, though much of the island's charm can be found by taking a stroll along the coast, visiting any one of its pleasant small towns, or sitting in a *cocinería* and watching the tide roll in while digging into a steaming bowl of freshly caught seafood.

If you must limit your time in Chiloé to one locale, Castro does a decent job of showing off the island's main charms (in addition to serving as the most central base for exploration). But if relaxation is your aim, you'll be hard-pressed to top the serene, supremely calm vibes of Chonchi. Nature-lovers will enjoy trekking through the national park's varied trails, while those with only a faint appreciation for animal life will find pleasure in touring the island's penguin reserves. Ancud's regional history museum, in addition to the island's wonderful old wood churches, will leave visitors with at least a basic understanding of the unique, mystical aura that separates Chiloé from the rest of the Chile. Updated: Jan 12, 2009.

Tours

You won't have much trouble finding tour operators in Chiloé's cities, especially in Ancud. But you might question as to whether it's worth your money to avail yourself of their services, since most destinations are easy to reach on your own. Most agencies have a fairly standard package of offerings, including outings to the national park, excursions to Chiloé's smaller islands, and a tour of many of the region's most important churches. Prices also tend to be similar, though shop around and you'll discover some mild differences in costs and itineraries– try negotiating the price. Of particular note are some of the special interest tours, usually offered by a particular agency, such as birdwatching or fishing expeditions. You'll do better on tours in the high-season months of January and February, when operators charge lower per person rates.

If you go on only one tour, consider visiting the penguin reserves at Puñihuil, one of the reserve's most popular tours. It's offered by a plethora of agencies—several times daily—from Ancud, and also much less frequently from Castro. Updated: Jan 13, 2009.

Lodging

From basic campsites to luxury hotels with stone massages and flat-screen TVs, one thing *not* in short supply in Chiloé is lodging, and, at least in Castro and Ancud, there are digs to fit any budget.

Most accommodation is in the low- to mid-range, making a stay on the island accessible to travelers of limited means. There's little room for complaint when you can get a warm bed, hot shower, and view of the ocean in a

reasonably comfortable room for $6.50 a night, only two blocks from Castro's downtown plaza. With a glut of options available you'll do well to dust off your negotiation skills; proprietors can often be persuaded to match the rates at other places in town. The cheapest rooms are in *hospedajes*, generally private houses that rent space, usually with a shared bathroom. Ask if breakfast or use of the kitchen is included.

Keep in mind that prices across the island tend to increase 10 to 20 percent in the peak summer months. Updated: Jul 02, 2009.

ANCUD

 114 m   27,292   65

Ancud is the first major population center (if you're arriving in Chiloé from the Puerto Montt area, as most travelers do), and it generally fails to inspire visitors the way that Castro and the rest of the island do.

In fact, with much of its traditional Chilote architecture having been destroyed in a devastating 1960 earthquake—the strongest ever recorded in history and whose effects on Ancud are copiously documented in a photo exhibit in the highly recommended Museo Regional de Ancud (p. 378)—the island's second-largest city lacks the "I'm not on the Chilean mainland anymore" charm that makes Chiloé a preferred destination for visitors. There are no *palafitos* hovering above the coastline, nor is there an impossibly charming 17th-century church (Ancud's church was built in—gasp—1906).

Many tourists are content to get their fill of Ancud from the window of a bus to Castro, or another more idyllic setting elsewhere on the island (of which there are many). If you have time to go further or you simply want to see all of Chiloé, you'll find that Ancud does have redeeming qualities and attractions. The city is a convenient enough base from which at least the basics of Chiloé and its culture (and food) can be enjoyed.

For those keen on exploring the local flora and fauna, Ancud is the main gateway to the Pinguinera Puñihuil, a breeding site for both Humboldt and Magellanic penguins, as well as to the northern access point of Chiloé's national park. Updated: Dec 28, 2008.

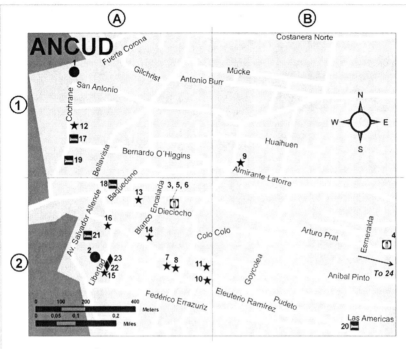

Activities ●

1 Fuerte San Antonio A1
2 Museo Regional Aurelio Bórquez A2

Eating 🍴

3 El Chilotito A2
4 Kuranton B2
5 La Corita A2
6 Restaurant Los Artesanos A2

Services ★

7 BancoEstado A2
8 Cruz Verde Pharmacy A2
9 Hospital de Ancud B1
10 Internet Cafe/Call Center 1 A2
11 Internet Cafe/Call Center 2 A2
12 Internet Café A1
13 Lave Fresh A2

14 Post Office A2
15 Redbanc ATM A2
16 Sernatur A2

Sleeping ▬

17 Alojamiento O´Higgins A1
18 Hospedaje A2
19 Hostal Lluhay A1
20 Hostal San José B2
21 Hotel Polo Sur A2

Tours ◆

22 Chiloé Aventura A2
23 Turismo Pehuen A2

Transportation 🚌

24 Bus Terminal B2

When to Go

Like most of Chiloé, Ancud has a harsh climate. There can be intense rain for weeks at a time with a much-needed reprieve from the rain occuring in December and March.

Summer is the driest time to visit, but it can rain it any season. Don't miss semana Ancuditana (Ancud Week), a festival that takes place in late January to celebrate the islands founding; there is traditional music, dance and food. Updated: Jul 02, 2009.

Getting To and Away From Ancud

Ancud has service to and from all major island destinations. The terminal is inconveniently located (at the corner of Prat and M. Vera), but is only a 20- to 30-minute walk from downtown. Many routes have both larger, more comfortable buses, and also cheaper minibuses that lack bathrooms. Departures to and from the larger Chilote towns are frequent, though generally less so than from Castro's terminal (an exception being Chepu, at the north of Chiloé's national park, which is more easily reached from Ancud).

Transportation to and from the island is available for cities such as Puerto Montt, Osorno, Valdivia, Concepción, Temuco, Punta Arenas, Bariloche and Santiago. Cruz del Sur is the dominant carrier on these routes, and also the most expensive. Queilen Bus is slightly cheaper, and comparable in terms of quality. More destinations are available by first getting to Puerto Montt and buying a connecting ticket from there.

Note that if you are taking the ferry to or from Chiloé, and are willing to brave the wind, you should step outside and watch for penguins and *toninas* (a type of dolphin). Updated: Dec 27, 2008.

Getting Around

Ancud is compact enough that you should have little need for local transport during your stay. The exception is the trip between downtown and the bus terminal (almost a half-hour walk for which you can take a regular taxi or a *colectivo*). Take a taxi at night, when it's unwise to stroll unaccompanied around quiet streets. Major taxi gathering spots are next to the market on Dieciocho and on Pudeto. Updated: Dec 29, 2008.

Safety

Ancud is not a dangerous city. Take normal precautions, such as cabbing it instead of walking alone at night. Note that the Costanera area does tend to attract its share of public drinkers and troublemakers. Updated: Dec 27, 2008.

Services

TOURISM
Sernatur, the government-sponsored tourism information service, has only one Chiloé location on Libertad, next to **Banco de Chile** (open Monday to Thursday, 8:30 to 5:30, and Fridays from 8:30 to 4:30). Tel: 56-65-622800, E-mail: info-chiloe@sernatur.cl.

KEEPING IN TOUCH
You can find internet cafés and call centers on Pudeto 359 and 388; there's also an Internet café at Cochrane 248, which is convenient if you're staying in the part of the city near Fuerte San Antonio. Rates are around $0.75 per hour. The **Post office** is on the corner of Pudeto and Blanco Encalada.

MEDICAL
Hospital de Ancud is located on Latorre 405. Tel: 56-65-622356, URL: www.hospitalancud.cl. **Cruz Verde pharmacy**: Pudeto 298 or Prat 280. Tel: 56-65-626116 or 623000.

MONEY
BancoEstado has a money exchange, Ramirez 229. ATM: Libertad 621 (Redbanc).

LAUNDRY
Lave Fresh offers self-service, but you can also pay them to wash your clothes. Arturo Prat 171. Tel: 56-65-628844, Updated: Dec 29, 2008.

Things to See and Do
The earthquake leveled most buildings of architectural interest in town. Yet Ancud is a worthy place to spend a day or two soaking up coastal views and sampling *curanto*. Don't miss the local historical museum. Ancud is also the jumping-off point for the Pinguinera Puñihuil as well as the northern entrance of Chiloé's national park. Updated: Dec 27, 2008.

Pinguinera Puñihuil
(ENTRANCE: $16) There are other places in Chile to see penguins (further south, and also near La Serena), but the Puñihuil islands, off of Chiloé's west coast, are home to both Magellanic and Humboldt species. A plethora of tour agencies offer several daily outings to Puñihuil, with little (or no) variation in the schedule: a van ride over to the coast, followed by checking out the view from several overlook spots, and then a half-hour boat ride to the islands to see the little critters up close and personal. Tours are $16 per person, though given the competition, there's some wiggle room to negotiate. Updated: Dec 27, 2008.

Museo Regional Aurelio Bórque Canobra (Museo Regional de Ancud)
(ADMISSION: $0.50 children, $1 adults) The Museo Regional de Ancud is small, but holds an impressive collection of artifacts and exhibits, which weave together the islands' history from the indigenous past through the arrival of the Europeans and the 1960 earthquake. Especially interesting are the collections of tools used by the native Chilotes, as well as weapons from the Spanish colonizers, maps from Dutch pirates, and a pictures of the earthquake's aftermath. An enormous blue whale skeleton is displayed outside. Exhibits are labeled in Spanish only. Open 10 a.m. to 7:30 p.m. (Jan – Feb), 10 a.m. to 5:30 p.m.

CHILOÉ

(March – Dec), 10 a.m. to 2 p.m. (Sat – Sun). Closed Mondays March through December. Libertad 370. Tel: 56-65-622002, E-mail: museoancud@surnet.cl, URL:www.dibam.cl/sdm_mr_ancud. Updated: Dec 29, 2008.

Fuerte San Antonio

(ADMISSION: Free) Fuerte San Antonio, the last Spanish foothold in Chile, fell to local forces in 1826. The site could desperately use some explanatory plaques with historical context, since the area is little more than a manicured lawn and a row of cannons. Nonetheless, what's left of the fort still makes for an interesting visit. The juxtaposition of the cannons with the sea and beyond will make a great picture. A small path above the main area will bring you to even better vantage points. Open from 9 a.m. to 8 p.m. Corner of San Antonio and Cochrane. Updated: Dec 29, 2008.

Tours

Turismo Cahuel

Cahuel, run by the same folks who manage the Hostal San José in Ancud, offers the typical slate of Ancud tours (penguin colonies, churches, etc.), at standard prices. The penguin colony tour departs four times daily (10 a.m., 12 p.m., 2 p.m., and 5 p.m.); others are subject to demand. The marathon 12-hour church tour has a four-person minimum. You can find Tourism Cahuel at any of the following locations: Los Cavadas 309, Feria Rural Office 61, Terminal Municipal Office 15, or Las Americas 661. Tel: 56-65-629944, E-mail: hostalsanjose6@hotmail.com. Updated: Dec 27, 2008.

Chiloé Aventura

Chiloé Aventura offers penguin and church tours, with a focus on attentive service and getting people off the beaten path and into Chiloé's serene wilderness. Nine different tours are offered, ranging from trekking and organic farming to bird observation. They also have a golf excursion, and rent bicycles ($3 per hour, or $13 per day). Their prices tend to be somewhat higher than other agencies, though many travelers will be swayed by the breadth of their excursions. Libertad 669. Tel: 56-9-3111285, E-mail: claudiawestermeyer@gmail.com. Updated: Dec 27, 2008.

Lodging

Ancud's accommodations tend to be clustered at the lower end of the price spectrum, with some pricier options in the downtown area. Budget options are most plentiful around the bus terminal and in the residential neighborhood between the city center and the Fuerte San Antonio. The bus terminal is a hike from downtown Ancud, so you'll need to choose which location makes more sense for you, depending on how long you plan on staying in town. Updated: Dec 27, 2008.

Alojamiento O'Higgins

(ROOMS: $10 – 12) In a quiet residential area but close to the main attractions, Alojamiento O'Higgins is a clean, tenderly cared for old house with a quiet, comfortable feel. The furnishings are dated, and the beds may sag a bit in the middle, but visitors will appreciate the sea view from the second-floor commons room, where breakfast is served. Options with both shared and private bathrooms are available. O'Higgins 6. Tel: 56-65-622266. Updated: Dec 27, 2008.

Hostal San José

(Rooms: $10 – 25) Clean, homey, and with a view of Ancud from its hilltop location, Hostal San José is a solid budget option. A 10- or 15-minute walk from downtown in one direction, with the bus terminal in the other, San José is convenient for those who want access to both, though noise does travel between the house's thin walls. Breakfast is included, and visitors also have free use of the kitchen. City ordinances that ban soliciting in the terminal notwithstanding, don't be surprised if you're approached while stepping off the bus. Be sure to bargain for the price. The same goes for the on-site tourism agency (Turismo Cahuel). Las Americas 661. Tel: 56-65-629944, E-mail: hostalsanjose6@hotmail.com. Updated: Dec 29, 2008.

Hostal Lluhay

(ROOMS: $20 – 50) With a welcome sign that has "B&B" translated into some 60 languages, Hostal LLuhay is nothing if not ambitious. The 20 well-appointed rooms, ranging from singles to mini-apartments (all with private bathrooms), are comfortable but unspectacular. Where Hostal Lluhay really shines is in its common areas, filled with plants and a veritable museum of trinkets. There are cheaper options in town, but you'd be hard-pressed to find accommodation with more character. And how many hostels will you find that brew their own beer? WiFi and parking are available, and the owners are happy to help organize excursions. Breakfast is included, but this is a cash only hostel. Lord Cochrane 458, Tel: 56-65-622656, URL: www.hostal-lluhay.cl. Updated: Dec 29, 2008.

CHILOÉ

Hotel Polo Sur

(CABINS: $50 – 65) Polo Sur, a series of large, two-story, fully equipped cabins, is a smart choice for families or other groups looking for apartment-style accommodations in town. The cabins are spacious and brightly decorated (though be careful on the shaky staircases), and receive ample sun pouring in from Ancud's bay, just across the street. The owners also run a restaurant a few doors down by the same name, and manage the cabins from there. Costanera 630, Tel: 56-65-622200. Updated: Dec 27, 2008.

Restaurants

Ancud's culinary scene revolves around local fish and seafood, so much so that you will be hard-pressed to find a restaurant not serving an ocean-based dish–a long search awaits those looking for vegetarian options. There are several fine dining options in the downtown area, although if you're looking for the biggest bang for your buck, head to one of the cocinerías behind the market, where the local catch is served at reasonable prices. Updated: Dec 27, 2008.

El Chilote Mena

(ENTREES: $1 – 4) El Chilote Mena has a tantalizing variety of dishes on its menu, boasting everything from soups, salads and sandwiches to chicken, beef, and seafood, though you may need to go through four or five dishes to find one that is actually available. Prices are reasonable, but portions are not large, and the service can lag. There are separate smoking and non-smoking sections, and a boat-shaped bar where you can enjoy a beer ($2.50). Pudeto 318. Tel: 56-65-625835. Updated: Dec 27, 2008.

La Corita

(PRICES: $1 – 7) Tucked away behind Ancud's market, La Corita is one of several cocinerías that serves up mountains of local seafood at modest prices. There are a few indoor tables, but the bulk of the seating is outside, in a sunny common space shared by the different restaurants. The curanto (enough seafood for two) is a bargain at $6.50. Also sample the array of tasty seafood empanadas, starting at $1.25. Mercado Municipal, 1st floor, local 3. Updated: Dec 27, 2008.

Restaurant Los Artesanos

(DISHES: $8 – 13) Perched on the second floor of Ancud's downtown market, with a cluttered view of the bay, Los Artesanos claims to have "Chiloé's best food." True or not, Los Artesanos is among Ancud's most expensive locales, with its menu of fish, seafood, and various meat dishes. There are two pleasant dining rooms to choose from—aim for a table that overlooks the bay, at least if you can ignore the gas station right outside the window. Menus are translated into English. Mercado Municipal, local 71, 2nd floor. Tel: 56-65-629657, Updated: Dec 27, 2008.

Kuranton

(DISHES: $10) Given the restaurant's name, it is no surprise that Kuranton's specialty is curanto. Serving seafood daily from 11 a.m. to 11 p.m. Kuranton has a pleasant, comfortable vibe, its walls tastefully decorated with local pictures and knickknacks (with several U.S. license plates which are oddly out of place). There also a fireplace for those cold and wet Chiloé evenings. You can eat cheaper elsewhere, though if you're willing to spend a bit more, Kuranton's atmosphere makes for a worthwhile dining experience. Prat 94. Tel: 56-65-623090. Updated: Dec 27, 2008.

El Chilotito

Open on the second floor of the pungent *feria rural* (rural fair, not to be confused with the main market downtown), El Chilotito offers diner-style meals at diner-level prices, including omelets, sandwiches, pastas, and desserts—a welcomed change if you've gone overboard on seafood (though they do have that as well). The pisco sour is a bargain at $1. Smoking is not permitted, and menus are translated into English. Feria Rural, 2nd floor, local 1. Updated: Dec 29, 2008.

QUEMCHI

 16 m   1,668   65

The salmon producing town of Quemchi lacks many of the charms that bring visitors to Chiloé's towns and cities, with its dilapidated plaza (under renovation) and a smallish church that is little more than a chapel. Still, it's a pleasant enough place to take a stroll along the beach. While not overly pretty, the beach offers a certain gripping solitude and silence, punctured only by gulls, and the random passing motorboat. Views of the nearby islands are captivating.

Lodging

If a stay on Quemchi's tranquil coast strikes your fancy, try **Hospedaje La Costanera**, an economical option for groups (Av.

Diego Bahamonde 141, Tel: 56-65-691230). Rates for a three-person cabin start at $30, and include a private bathroom. Slightly cheaper options are available off the coast-line, including at Avenida Pedro Montt 431 (no name or phone number—check for the **Hospedaje Familiar** sign outside), which charges $8 per person.

For a quick bite, head to the small, unnamed fast food joint at Centenario 211. Or try cozy and friendly **Restaurant El Chejo** (Diego Bahamonde 251, Tel: 56-65-691490). The restaurant serves a good range of seafood ($4 – 7) and has outdoor seating with coastal views.

Minibuses make the hour-long trip ($2) from Castro every 60 to 90 minutes weekdays, and less frequently on weekends. There's an ATM next to the town library. Updated: Jan 11, 2009.

TENAÚN

Tenaún is an isolated fishing village on a nice waterfront location across from Isla Mechuque. The local church, simply called "The Church of Tenaún," was built in 1837 and named a World Heritage Site in 2000. The church has severe water damage and is in dire need of repair, but you can still tour the inside or visit a neighboring museum. Updated: Jul 02, 2009.

DALCAHUE

The small town of Dalcahue is the main departure point for ferries leaving for Isla Quinchao. Dalcahue itself is worth more than just a passing glance. In local cocinerías you can watch all women roll empanadas and the Dalcahue church features an unbelievably bright restored painting, representing the mix in Chiloé between traditional and Catholic beliefs.

Minibuses shuttle between Castro and Dalcahue every 15 minutes throughout the day. If you want to stay the night, look for one of the lodging options around the church. Updated: Jul 07, 2009.

ISLA QUINCHAO

Quinchao, five minutes by ferry from Dalcahue, and thus within easy striking distance of Castro, is one of Chiloé's most visited (and largest) islands, though it maintains a virgin,

'even further off the already unbeaten path' feel. The island is populated by farmers and fishermen; the boarding school is filled with students from other school districts. In the town center, look for houses with multi-sided shingles and be sure to visit the Iglesia de Santa María de Loreto (1706) in the Plaza de Armas. Updated: Jul 02, 2009.

CASTRO

 44 m 29,130 65

Both literally and metaphorically, all roads in Chiloé lead to Castro. As Chiloé's largest town, and very much its cultural, geographic, and transportation center, busy Castro gives visitors as good of an introduction to the island as they can get anywhere, and, for many, serves as a base for exploring outlying towns and villages.

The city was founded in 1567, and is Chile's third-oldest. Castro has had a troubled existence. The city was used by Dutch pirates as a short-lived base for conquering the island in 1600. Earthquakes, fires, and, in 1960, a massive tidal wave (an effect of the highly destructive earthquake which hit Chile's south), have ravaged the city but Castro nevertheless retains many vestiges of its past.

A great historical and architectural interest, this is the best place on the island to see the *palafitos*—traditional and, in some cases, run-down houses on a series of wooden stilts. The church (Iglesia San Francisco), though built relatively recently in 1906, charmingly dominates both the cityscape and the downtown plaza.

Castro also has the island's biggest concentration and variety of restaurants. Nowhere else in Chiloé will you have more options for sampling local seafood, nor more choices for branching out when you've had your fill of curanto, salmon and clams. The eateries run the gamut from high-end grills and hip cafés, to Italian restaurants, and even Chinese food.

Castro is also awash in lodging options, which is unsurprising since the city receives the majority of the island's tourists. Budget travelers will find relatively clean, centrally located rooms with comfortable-enough beds and hot showers for $6.50 a night (keep in mind, however, that prices increase in peak

CHILOÉ

months). If you're looking for something up-scale, say a suite overlooking the waterfront, with massage parlor and swimming pool, Castro has that too.

Castro's location, close to Chiloé's geographic center, means that you're never more than a day trip away from any of smaller towns. Transportation across the island is cheap and frequent, making the city a highly convenient base for further explorations.

Castro is bustling, but not jammed with attractions. You could easily see the palafitos and church, enjoy a nice seafood meal, and head to the town's craft market, in less than a day. Still, Castro's easy access to city comforts makes it a nice place to spend a few days, or at least to come back to for a drink and a meal after a long day in the Chiloé countryside. Updated: Jan 13, 2009.

When to Go
The summer months of January and February bring the warmest weather and the least amount of rainfall, but the the number of visitors and local prices both increase. Many hotels charge 10 to 20 percent more in high season. Summer is also the time for most of the area's festivals, which celebrate local foods, crafts, music and folklore. Decent weather, lower prices and fewer crowds can be had just outside the summer months, in December or March, though you may get more rain than you'd like. Updated: Jan 11, 2009.

Getting To and Away From Castro
Castro has the island's most extensive transportation network (though what it doesn't have—despite what the city map might make you believe—is a commercial airport). Departures via minibus to destinations throughout the island are cheap (between $1 and $3) and frequent; some of these same routes to Chiloé's larger towns are also served by bigger, more comfortable buses, though they'll also cost you about 10 to 20 percent more.

Most minibuses depart from the small Rural Terminal (corner of San Martín and Sargento Aldea). For long distances, or for intra-island service on regular-sized buses, head to the terminal behind the church. Both are within easy walking distance from nearly anywhere in town.

Cruz del Sur, which has something close to a monopoly on long-haul travel to and from Chiloé (and even has its own terminal and ferries), has service to major destinations such as Santiago and Concepción (four daily), Temuco (10), Valdivia (seven), Puerto Varas (five), and Puerto Montt via Ancud (25). There's also sporadic service to Bariloche, Argentina (leaving on Thursdays and Sundays), and Punta Arenas (Tuesdays, Thursdays, and Saturdays). Whatever your destination, sit on the driver's side when leaving town for a better view of the palafitos. Updated: Jan 13, 2009.

Getting Around
The sights in compact Castro are easily accessible by foot (except the Modern Art Museum), and part of the town's charm is in just that: walking. If weather or other circumstances require it, the area around the plaza is the place for picking up a bus or taxi—northbound on San Martín, or southbound on O'Higgins. Buses in town are under $1; taxis within town are generally in the $1 to $2 range.

Castro also has a car rental agency, **Salfa Sur** (Gabriela Mistral 499, Tel: 56-65-630414, www.salfasur.cl), though public transit abounds in the area. The independence gained from having your own vehicle won't come cheap—rates start at $33 a day for a two-door hatchback, and increase to $67 for a pick-up truck. You must have a credit card, your passport, driver's license, and be over 21 to rent a car. Updated: Jan 13, 2009.

Photo by Andrés Giordano Valenzuela

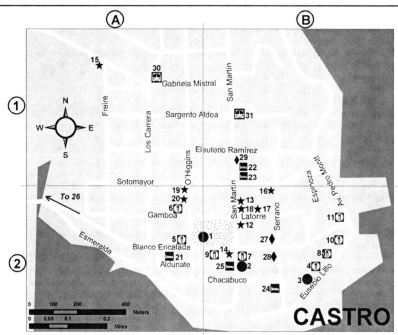

CASTRO

Activities ●
1 Iglesia San Francisco B2
2 Museo Regional de Castro B2
3 Feria Artesanal B2

Eating 🏠
4 Años de Luz B2
5 Café la Bruja del Cuerpo A2
6 Himacar Restaurante A2
7 La Piezza B2
8 "Donde Eladío"Restaurante y
   Fogón B2
9 Ottoschop Café B2
10 Restaurante El Trauco B2
11 Restaurante La Nave B2

Servicios ★
12 Banco del Estado B2
13 Cruz Verde Pharmacy 1 B2
14 Cruz Verde Pharmacy 2 B2
15 Hospital de Castro A1
16 Internet Café 1 B2

17 Internet Café 2 B2
18 Internacional Call Center B2
19 Laundry A2
20 Post Office A2

Sleeping ▣
21 Hostal El Chilote A2
22 Hostal Quelcun B1
23 Hostal Sotomayor B1
24 Hosteria el Castro B2
25 Hotel Esmeraldas B2
26 Palafito Hostal A2

Tours ◆
27 Green Place B2
28 Turismo Pehuén B2
29 Turismo Quelcun B1

Transportation ▣
30 Salfa Sur A1
31 Terminal Rural B1

CHILOÉ

Safety

Castro won't make anyone's list of dangerous cities; the biggest threat you face is from the rain and wind. Some of the side streets leading away from the plaza become quite desolate at night, so avoid walking them alone. Take a taxi or other form of transit. The walking path that runs parallel to Pedro A. Cerda, leading to the overlook sight for the palafitos, is poorly lit and isolated. Updated: Jan 11, 2009.

Services

A mid-sized city, Castro has all the basic services that travelers need.

TOURISM

A helpful tourist information center, smack dab in the plaza, has maps and some small exhibits on local attractions. Bikes and kayaks are available for rental from Green Place (Blanco Encalada 31, Tel: 85160475).

KEEPING IN TOUCH

Internet cafés: Sotomayor 204, Latorre 267, as well as many others. Most charge around $0.75 per hour.
International call center: 289 Latorre. Rates to the U.S. start from $0.20 per minute.
Post office: next to the Regional Government Building on O'Higgins, across from the plaza.

MEDICAL

Pharmacies: as is the case throughout Chile, it's hard to walk down the street without spotting at least one. **Cruz Verde** has two right on the plaza, at San Martín 407, and then on the very next block, at the corner of Blanco and Esmeralda.

The **Hospital de Castro** (Freire 852, Tel: 56-65-632212) can handle most procedures, though more specialized treatments are available in Puerto Montt.

MONEY

BancoEstado (on the plaza, at San Martín 397) will exchange U.S. dollars and euros, though you'll get better rates in Puerto Montt.

LAUNDRY

To enter the laundry place at O'Higgins 438, ring the bell. Updated: Jan 13, 2009.

Things to See and Do

Castro has plenty to offer: the island's best tourist amenities, quirky architecture (the palafitos), and an impressive cathedral. You can easily spend a few days exploring local attractions, including the town market and local museums, before heading out on one of the numerous excursions to the island's more far-flung locales. Updated: Jan 11, 2009.

Museo de Arte Moderno de Chiloé

(ADMISSION: Free) Founded in 1988, and housed inside a series of barns, the Castro art museum (known by its acronym, "MAM") focuses on local and national contemporary works. If the paintings aren't to your liking, you'll also get a nice view of the Castro cityscape from MAM's hilltop location. Unfortunately, this is one part of town not within

walking distance, though a shared taxi along San Martín will drop you off at the door for $1, or take a bus for slightly less (it will leave you about a 10-minute walk from the museum). Call ahead to make sure the museum is open. Pasaje Díaz 181. Tel: 56-65-635454 Updated: Jan 11, 2009.

Museo Regional de Castro

(ADMISSION: Free) Scheduled to be moved to more spacious (and rather unattractive) digs along the waterfront, Castro's free local history museum has a lot crammed into a little space. Pay particular attention to the models of Chiloé's different churches, as well as the exhibit explaining the region's famed *mingas*—the events when neighbors would gather to move entire houses, sometimes across waterways, before celebrating with a party. The museum also has a separate room with exhibits the island's indigenous roots, though in general there's little by way of explanation in the museum. Monday to Saturday 9:30 a.m. to 1 p.m., 3 p.m. to 6:30 p.m., Sunday 9:30 a.m. to 1 p.m. Esmeralda (across from Hotel Esmeralda) Updated: Jan 13, 2009.

Iglesia San Francisco

Near the plaza, its faded yellow and purple-tipped spires dominating the Castro cityscape, Iglesia San Francisco will almost certainly be the first thing to catch your eye when you come in to town. Though not nearly as old as many of the island's churches (it was built in 1906), this is still an architectural treat both outside and the interior (which was finished with bright wood). The perimeter is lined with models of Chiloé's other, more traditional churches. Masses are held daily throughout the year, except on Mondays. Latorre, on the plaza. Updated: Jan 11, 2009.

Feria Artesanal

Though much of Castro's feria artesanal has the same wood trinkets that are offered at every fair in Chile, the main hall has a nice selection of wool socks, scarves, hats and jackets, some of which may serve you well if you haven't prepared adequately for Chiloé's weather. There's also seafood (smoked mussels, anyone?); this is the place in town to stock up on the island's famed liquors, from liquor de oro to chocolate-, coffee-, and raspberry-inspired concoctions, though you'll get better deals in Chonchi Be sure to ask for samples. Don't waste much time in the market's periphery, which is geared

CHILOÉ

more toward locals on the prowl for a pair of jeans or a Bob Marley T-shirt. The market opens around 10 a.m. and closes around 9 p.m. Av. Pedro Montt, along the waterfront (though sometimes it's set up on the town plaza). Updated: Jan 13, 2009.

Palafitos

Chiloé's answer to Venice, the palafitos, are coastal houses perched on wooden stilts. They are an iconic part of the island's architecture, and there's no better place to see them than in Castro. For a nice vantage point, head down Esmeralda, towards the coast. You'll come across a walkway heading out of town (parallel to Pedro A. Cerda) and an overlook point. Stay for a bit and you might see the huge changes in tides that occur over the span of just a few hours. There's also a set of palafitos on the way out of town to the north; when leaving town in that direction via bus, sit on the driver's side to catch a glimpse. Updated: Jan 13, 2009.

Tours

Most of what Castro tour operators have to offer are trips you could easily do on your own, though if you're short on time, and enjoy the background information provided by a guide, touring the national park (standard rate: $15), or visiting Chiloé's most important churches in one day ($15), are adventures to consider. Prices and itineraries tend to be fairly standardized, but be sure to shop around.

You're also better off taking a tour in the high season; some tour operators shut down entirely in off-peak months, and you'll pay higher rates without a critical mass of other travelers joining you on the trip. Updated: Jan 12, 2009.

Turismo Quelcun

Quelcun, run by the folks who own the charming hostel of the same name, has the typical gamut of tours from Castro, including trips to some of Chiloé's smaller islands and to the national park, plus a fishing trip through Chiloé's lakes and rivers. Quelcun also offers a few boat tours. If you contact them ahead of time, they may be able to arrange for guides who speak English, French, or Italian. Their prices are among the most economical when the tours have five or more passengers, though they'll also go with less. San Martín 581. Tel: 56-65-632396, E-mail: quelcun@tel-sur.cl. Updated: Jan 13, 2009.

Turismo Pehuen

With offices in both Castro and Ancud, Turismo Pehuen is a larger operation that focuses on the basics: visiting the penguin reserves (available from Ancud, daily, and from Castro on Thursdays), national park (Wednesdays and Saturdays), and the churches (Tuesdays, Fridays, and Sundays). They also have horseback riding excursions (departing daily), and can organize excursions through Patagonia. Prices tend to be a bit higher than the competition, but they accept U.S. dollars. Blanco 208 (Castro), Libertad 669 (Ancud). URL: www.turismopehuen.cl. Updated: Jan 11, 2009.

Lodging

Budget travelers take heart: you'll be challenged to walk more than a few steps anywhere in Castro without seeing signs for a "hostal" or "hospedaje." Even at the very low end, you can easily snag a place with a warm bed and hot shower, within a few minutes from the plaza, for well under $10. There's also a solid array of mid- and high-range options, though be sure to shop around, as quality can vary widely. As in the rest of Chiloé, prices can climb 15 percent during the high season. Updated: Jan 11, 2009.

Hostal El Chilote

(ROOMS: $10 – 16) Nestled on a quiet side street, yet only a block from the plaza, El Chilote offers economically priced rooms in a comfortable, private house. The building is carpeted, which is atypical at this end of the budget spectrum. Some rooms have a musty, even smoky, smell, so check your room before making a commitment. A basic breakfast is included, as is cable TV; rooms with both private and shared bathrooms are available. Regrettably, the kitchen is off limits. Aldunate 456. Tel: 56-65-635021. Updated: Jan 13, 2009.

Palafito Hostel

(ROOMS: $16 – 40) Stylishly minimalist, and suspended over the water by a grid of wooden poles (hence the name), Palafito Hostel attracts a younger crowd, who are attracted to the lack of TVs and prefer to spend the evening grilling on the deck and watching fishermen haul in their catches. You won't be foregoing all technological comforts entirely if you stay at Palafito as the hotel does have WiFi. With its all-wood interior and spacious common areas, this is a smart choice if you're looking to have the "palafito experience." Breakfast is included and you get free use of the kitchen. Note that it's a 15-minute walk into the main part of town. Ernesto Riquelme 1210. Tel: 56-65-531008, E-mail: palafitohostel@gmail.com, URL: www.palafitohostel.com. Updated: Jan 13, 2009.

Hostal Costa Azul

(ROOMS: $19 – 37) Sunny, spacious and clean, Costa Azul is a solid mid-range option for couples or groups of travelers looking for more than a regular hospedaje. All rooms (none of them singles) have a private bathrooms and cable TVs, and parking is available on-site. The hotel provides breakfast for an extra $3.50, though it's a bit much for bread and coffee (guests do not have use of the kitchen). Rooms with an ocean view typically cost $3.50 extra. Lillo 67. Tel: 56-65-632440, E-mail: costazul@chiloeweb.com. Updated: Jan 13, 2009.

Hostal Quelcun

(ROOMS: $29 – 48) Down a narrow corridor from busy San Martín, Quelcun has tranquility and charm—from the tree-lined courtyard to the carefully chosen local artwork gracing the walls. The husband-and-wife owners, Susana and Juan Carlos, will take good care of you, and you may even get to sample some of Susana's homemade jam for breakfast. WiFi is available throughout, though even if you left your laptop behind, there's a public computer in the lobby.

You could spend less elsewhere, but 10 percent discounts apply to stays of three or more days, 20 percent if you're there for six or more. Dollars are accepted; credit cards are not. San Martín 581. Tel: 56-65-632396, E-mail: quelcun@telsur.cl. Updated: Jan 13, 2009.

Hostería de Castro

(ROOMS: $48 – 96) Don't be fooled by the worn, oddly triangular building—Hostería de Castro packs some serious luxury inside. With a heated swimming pool, spa, and optional stone massages, this is the place to spend some cash and forget about your worries.

The hotel actually has two sections—the older main building, which has 29 well-equipped, if unspectacular and somewhat institutional rooms, and a newer annex with 20 modern, stylish, and more expensive suites, flat-panel TVs and wonderfully large windows for soaking up views of the bay. Such comforts don't come cheap, but if you have the money to spend, this is a good place to use it. Chacabuco 202. Tel: 56-65-632301, URL: www.hosteriadecastro.cl. Updated: Jan 11, 2009.

Photo by Kyle Adams

Hotel Esmeralda

(ROOMS: $50 – 130) Conveniently located a half block from Castro's bustling plaza, Hotel Esmeralda is what you would expect from a business-oriented hotel: a sterile atmosphere and lots of convenient amenities. The building's loud pink exterior notwithstanding, the four-story Hotel Esmeralda is a sober, notably quiet place, and has little of the charm that likely brought you to Castro in the first place.

The hotel does offer a host of services geared toward corporate and other mid- or high-end travelers, including a classy in-house restaurant, WiFi, parking, and a continental breakfast. Ask for a fourth-story room to get a view of downtown Castro. Esmeralda 266. Tel: 56-65-637900, Fax: 56-65-637910, E-mail: hesmeralda@telsur.cl, URL: www.hotelesmeralda.cl. Updated: Dec 27, 2008

Restaurants

Scrumptious, locally caught seafood reigns supreme here. As the island's largest city, Castro also has the most extensive variety of restaurant options, including vegetarian and even Chinese. The two major concentrations of dining establishments can be found around the plaza, and near the market, along the coast. Options abound at different price ranges. For a

CHILOÉ

quick, reasonably accurate way of comparing, ask for the going rate for curanto. Updated: Jan 13, 2009.

La Piazza

(ENTREES: $3.50 – 6.50) A definitive antidote to the deluge of sea creatures of all shapes and sizes that you've probably been consuming since arriving in Chiloé, La Piazza has a full-service Italian menu, including a range of pastas and some 31 kinds of pizza – one of which has mussels as a topping if you're really in the mood for more. The portions are on the small side, and the faux Michelangelo's David on the outside wall, with "El Arte de Hacer Pizzas" (The Art of Making Pizzas) scribbled underneath, does overstate the food's quality, although the prices are agreeable enough ($4 for an individual pizza, $6.50 for a medium; pasta dishes start from $3.50), and there's outdoor seating. Corner of Blanco and Esmeralda. Tel: 56-65-534600. Updated: Jan 13, 2009.

Restaurant La Nave

(ENTREES: $4 – 6.50) La Nave is simple and unpretentious—you don't come here for the faded, burnt-red cement floors—but the restaurant has friendly service and reasonably priced seafood and shellfish dishes. Try tasty platters like the bed of clams topped with melted parmesan cheese ($4). The portions could stand to be larger, though. There's no fixed-price daily lunch menu, and keep in mind that this is a smoking-allowed establishment. Snag a table by the window for a view of the waterfront. Pedro Montt 16. Updated: Jan 13, 2009.

Restaurante El Trauco

(ENTREES: $4 – 8) Across the street from the market, and accordingly somewhat cheaper (there's no waterfront view), El Trauco serves up a decent seafood-laden menu (curanto goes for $7) in casual, family-friendly surroundings. Try the steaming hot paella marina ($4), a hearty fish and seafood stew that will warm your soul after a day braving the wind. El Trauco also shows soccer games on the restaurant's TV, and with beer at $3 a liter, it's a good place to relax (though it has no actual bar). Lillo 31. Tel: 56-65-534572. Updated: Jan 13, 2009.

"Donde Eladio" Restaurante y Fogón

(ENTREES: $5 – 8) Part-regular seafood restaurant, part-*fogón* (a traditional bonfire for grilling meats), and part-meeting space (complete with a projector and seating capacity for 150 people), the mammoth, two-story Donde Eladio is a lot of things, with a formal atmosphere geared toward a middle-aged crowd. With seafood, sandwiches, meat dishes and an extensive wine menu, this is a place to impress without spending as much as the surroundings suggest. Be sure to dress somewhat formally. Lillo 97. Tel: 56-65-631470, URL: www.DondeEladio.cl. Updated: Jan 13, 2009.

Años Luz

(ENTREES: $8 – 13) Años Luz is Castro's version of a trendy, upscale café, featuring a hip, big-city vibe. It is a top spot for enjoying hearty, upmarket cuisine, as well as mixed drinks from their bar, which is a converted boat. Cozy, relaxed, and right on the plaza, Años Luz also regularly has local, live acts. Bring your laptop to avail yourself of the free WiFi. The comforts come at a price; seafood, fish, and meat dinners are expensive, and you could get a full liter of beer elsewhere for the same $2.50 that will buy a mere half-liter here. Still, it's a nice choice if you're looking to dine in style. San Martín 309. Tel: 56-65-532700. Updated: Jan 13, 2009.

Hicamar Restaurante

(ENTREES: $8 – 15) If you want to drop some cash and indulge your red meat fetish, head to Hicamar for a fine selection of grilled cuts and seafood appetizers – and virtually nothing else. Choose from the warm, mood-lit first floor, or the more pedestrian second level, which does, to its credit, have views over the plaza. A grilled plate for two will set you back $13, pisco sours included; individual plates are presented with aesthetic touches. Gamboa 413. Tel: 56-65-532655, E-mail: info@hicamar.cl. Updated: Jan 13, 2009.

Café La Brújula del Cuerpo

Perhaps one of the only restaurants on the island which doesn't have seafood, La Brújula del Cuerpo also distinguishes itself for its reasonably priced burgers and pizzas, a dessert bar, and even two computers with free Internet access. Vegetarians will find some sandwich options on the menu as well; though, in general the food is unlikely to make your "best of Castro." The hopping second-floor bar has pool tables, and is a rowdy place to catch a soccer game. O'Higgins 308. Updated: Jan 13, 2009.

Ottoschop Café

For the full Castro dive bar experience, Ottoschop is your best bet: beer bongs, iffy bathrooms, a menu consisting almost entirely of fried foods, and an almost shocking range of too-loud music (everything from Shakira to Megadeth). Where else in town can you order a two-liter mug of Cristal and a mountain of French fries for under $6 while listening to inebriated locals sing along to "Grease Lightning?" For those with finer tastes, there's also Kunstmann on tap. Blanco 356. Tel: 56-65-636281. Updated: Jan 13, 2009.

CHONCHI !

 45 m   4,589   65

A charming traditional timber town with well-preserved architecture, intoxicatingly tranquil Chonchi is an ideal place to relax. The town has a solid array of attractions, dining and lodging options. Chonchi is also the traditional home of Chiloé's unique *licor de oro* (gold liquor), a brandy-based concoction, which mixes milk, lemon rind and saffron—you have almost certainly never tried anything like it before. It can be had for $4 a bottle at the artisans' market, next to the town's fabulously bright yellow and sky-blue church, which itself is worth a visit.

Chonchi is easy to reach, since minibuses make the half-hour trip to and from Castro every 15 minutes during the day ($1.15).

Lodging

Clean and quiet, **Hospedaje Skorpio** (Irarrázabal 181, Tel: 56-65-671575) has rooms starting at $11, which includes breakfast. Ask for one with a view of the sea. No alcohol is allowed on the premises. Next to the Museo de las Tradiciones Chonchinas, **Hotel Huildin** (Centenario 102, Tel: 56-65-671388, www.hotelhuildin.cl) is also a solid choice, with rooms from $11 in low season (or $14 with breakfast included), to $48 a night for a six-person cabin. All have private bathrooms, and parking is available.

Restaurants

Perched above the water at the end of Chonchi's new central market, **Ballena Azul** offers attractive views and reasonably priced lunch menus and pizzas (try one with a seafood topping for $6.50). The restaurant accepts both U.S. dollars and euros. For cheaper, simpler and faster fare, including empanadas and fried chicken, head to **Picá El Chanchito** (Centenario 211). Updated: Jan 12, 2009.

PARQUE NACIONAL CHILOÉ !

 0 – 859 m   65

Parque Nacional Chiloé is a biologically rich, 43,057-hectare reserve on the western coast of the Island of Chiloé, where sandy beaches and rolling dunes meet thickly forested mountains. The park, which was founded by the Chilean government in 1983, is famous for its short hikes. With minimal effort and planning, you can walk among the twisting, old-growth forests—virtually unchanged since Darwin visited in the HMS Beagle. There you might spy rare and elusive animals, like the Chilote fox and the *pudú* (the world's smallest deer); the vast Pacific beach is among the most beautiful in Chile. With more than 110 different species of birds, El Parque Nacional Chiloé is a birdwatcher's dream.

The park is divided into three major sections: the nothern sector (Chepu), the small island of Metalqui, and the southern sector (Anay). The 7,800-hectare northern sector is best accessed from Ancud, and includes a hiking trail that takes approximately five hours (but is not recommended). Metalqui is a small and rugged island populated by a colony of sea lions. Visitors are not allowed on the island, as the sea lions are protected. The larger southern sector (35,207 hectares) is the park's most accessible and popular area. Hikers can take several footpaths from Cucao, a tiny village at the southern tip of the park. Cucao has bus service to and from Castro. Visitors should be prepared for rain during their trips to the park. The average annual rainfall at Cucao is 2,200 mm, and the weather changes rapidly, so waterproof footwear and a rainjacket are essential. Dry days are the exception here. Updated: Jul 01, 2009.

Getting To and Away From Parque Nacional Chiloé

Cucao, main entry point to the park, has four daily Expresos Interlagos buses to and from Castro—even on holidays and weekends. Buses leave Castro at 9 a.m., 2:30 p.m. and 4 p.m., making the return trip at 10:45 a.m., 1:30 p.m., 4:45 p.m. and 6 p.m. The schedule is posted widely throughout the area, which is fortunate, since buses are the only way in or out of Cucao. One-way tickets cost $3; a round-trip fare is $5. Sporadic bus service is also available from Chonchi.

CHILOÉ

Ancud is the departure point for the Chepu sector, with buses leaving daily at 7 a.m. and 4 p.m. You can also organize transportation, or kayaking, fishing and birdwatching excursions, through Chepu Adventures (Tel: 9-93792481, URL: www.chepuadventures.com). Updated: Jul 08, 2009.

Things to See and Do

Hiking Parque Nacional Chiloé

(ENTRY: $2) Cucao has a number of trail heads to the park. The Sendero Dunas de Cucao is a leisurely 2-kilometer hike through overgrown forests, across an open dune field speckled with low, colorful plants, to a long stretch of sandy beach. Don't plan on swimming here—the water is cold and there are dangerous currents.

The Sendero Interpretivo El Tepual is a kilometer-long trek on winding wooden bridges, through twisting *tepú* trees and over boggy terrain. Backpackers can follow the coastal trail three kilometers north to an Huilliche settlement at Lago Huelde. It's another nine kilometers to a refugio at Río Cole Cole, with a fire pit for cooking. River Anay is another eight kilometers north, with a similar refugio. Note that all refugios are in various states of repair, and it's best to bring a tent or inquire about their condition before leaving Cucao. Updated: Jul 01, 2009.

Lodging

Most of the park accomodations are located in, or just outside of, Cucao. **Cabañas Conaf** (56-65-532502; E-mail: pnchiloe@conaf.cl) offers four six-person cabins equipped with kitchenettes. **Hospedaje El Paraíso** (099-296-5465; Laura Vera, Cucao) has rooms without bathrooms for about $14, and camp sites for about $2. About 200 meters into the park is the **Camping Sector Chanquín** (532-503), with plenty of privacy, hot water, firewood and toilets. Camp sites cost about $4 per person, and a seven-person cabin costs about $50.

A more luxurious stay can be had at **El Fógon de Cucao** (56-99-946-5685), on the shore of Lago Cucao. Camp sites here costs about $6, and rooms in the rustic hostel (without bathrooms) about $20-40. The owners also arrange horseback and kayaking excursions. Camping is allowed anywhere in the park, and does not cost extra. Updated: Jul 01, 2009.

Restaurants

Eateries within the park are a bit limited. **El Arrayán** (Tel: 56-99-219-3565), a small café near the park entrance, is a great place to stop for breakfast before a day of hiking. Meals run from $5 to $7. There is also a restaurant in the hostel **Parador Darwin** (Tel: 56-99-799-9923), where, for $6 to $8, diners can enjoy Chilote cuisine mixed with Hungarian and German recipes. Otherwise, when staying on campgrounds, it's a good idea to stock up on food in one of the markets in Cucao. Updated: Jul 01, 2009.

QUELLÓN

  3 m   13,661   65

Founded in 1905 as a company mill town, gritty, nondescript Quellón can feel like a foreign country compared to Chiloé's other serene, history-filled towns. The city had no road links with the rest of the island until several decades ago, but is now one of the endpoints of the Pan-American Highway, which stretches nearly 48,000 kilometers (30,000 mi) south from Alaska. Quellón a busy port and focal point for the salmon industry, but doesn't have much of interest to travelers.

If you're looking to enter or leave Chiloé from the island's southern extreme, and thus avoid doubling back through Ancud, there is infrequent ferry service from Quellón to Chaitén (starting at $26) and Puerto Chacabuco ($48). Stop by the office of Naviera Austral (Pedro Montt 457, Tel: 682207), or check the schedule online at www.navieraustral.cl. Minibuses cover the almost two hour Castro-Quellón route frequently, leaving every half-hour ($2.25). Updated: Jan 12, 2009.

You'll probably won't want to stay in Quellón, but if you're stuck waiting for a ferry, **Hotel Tierra del Fuego** has cozy, somewhat expensive rooms, starting at $15 for a single with a shared bathroom (Pedro Montt 445, Tel: 56-65-682079). Fully equipped cabins are also available a few doors down, for $40 (Pedro Montt 457, Tel: 56-65-548228). **Hostería Romeo Alfa** (Puerto Montt 554, next to the wharf), offers some decent views and the usual range of seafood dishes ($5 to $7). **Restaurant Los Suizos** (Ladrilleros 399, Tel: 681787) has a surprisingly good value lunch menu ($3.50), and several Swiss dishes, mostly for breakfast.

!!!!!

CHILOÉ

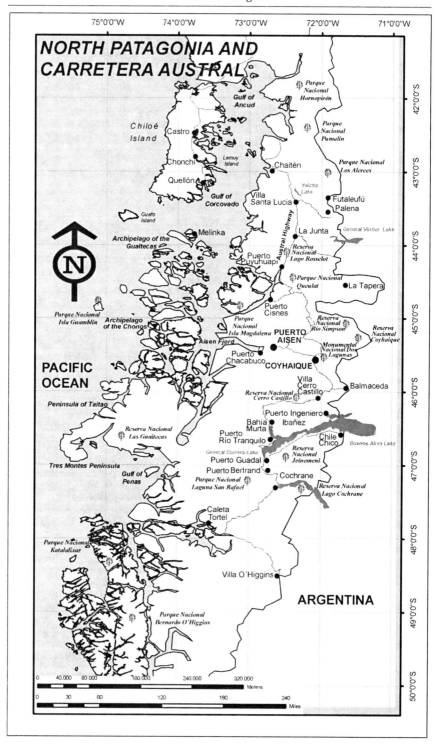

Carretera Austral and Northern Patagonia

Chile's Ruta 7—the Carretera Austral—one of Latin America's most famous highways, begins at Puerto Montt. From spring to fall, travelers mount their motorcycles and bikes to undertake the 1,247-kilometer (775-mile) journey south to Villa O'Higgins.

The Carretera Austral goes through the southern section of Chile's X Región de los Lagos and through the entire length of the XI Región de Aysén. Ferries connect the road between Caleta la Arena and just north of Contao; from Hornopirén to Chaitén; and across Fiordo Mitchell from Puerto Yungay to Río Bravo. You need patience for this journey, but the intense beauty of this virtually untouched part of Chile makes up for the hardships of rain, cold and wind.

Almost half of the region is protected by national parks and reserves. The road is edged with glacier-packed mountains, turquoise rivers and sapphire lakes. It's an outdoor sportsperson's paradise, with hiking, ice climbing, mountain climbing, fly fishing, whitewater rafting and kayaking. You may even encounter some of the country's rarest animals and birds in the pristine temperate rainforests. There are four international lakes spanning the border between Chile and Argentina: Lago Palena (Lago General Vittner in Argentina), Lago General Carrera (Lago Buenos Aires), Lago Cochrane (Lago Pueyrredón) and Lago O'Higgins (Lago San Martín).

The face of the Carretera Austral is changing quickly. During the warm months, crews work to widen the road. It is projected that by 2014 the entire highway as far as Cochrane will be paved. Updated: Jul 10, 2009.

History

For centuries the region was occupied by indigenous nations. The Kaweskar lived along the coast, navigating the channels and fjords in canoes, living off the rich bounty of the sea. The Aónikenk were hunter-gatherers following the migration of *guanaco* and *ñandú* around Lago General Carrera. With Argentine General Roca's Desert Conquest (*Conquista del Desierto*) in 1879, many

Eruption

On May 2, 2008, Volcán Chaitén rumbled to life. The volcano's eruption caused disruptions not only in the lives of locals, but also for tourists, with a number of obstructions along the Carretera Austral. Parts of the route became impassable, ferries stopped running, Parque Pumalín shut down, and Futaleufú and the Chile-Argentine border closed temporarily.

The May 2008 eruption was quite a surprise to all the inhabitants, as this 1,122-meter (3647-ft) tall mountain had been dormant since nearly 7420 BC. The national government called a mandatory evacuation of the village Chaitén (pop: 4, 200) just 10 kilometers (6 mi) southwest of the volcano. By the next afternoon, the ash plume had drifted across both Chile and Argentina, all the way to the Atlantic Ocean. The border town of Futaleufú, 45 kilometers (45 mi) southeast of the volcano, was coated with a foot of fine grey ash.

Lava began flowing down Volcán Chaitén's slopes on May 6. The lava and *lahar* (lava-mud-ash mixture) filled the Chaitén River, which had been diverted by man when the Carretera Austral was built. The river resumed its natural course through the town. Eye witnesses reported that much of the Chaitén village had been buried and swaths of forest near the erupting mountain had been burned.

As the volcano's activity decreased, many residents returned. However, the town was evacuated permanently on February 18, 2009, when a lava dome partially collapsed.

As of February 2010, Chaitén remains in red alert while seismic activity remains high. There is continuing risk of further eruptions, so check with local authorities and www.sernageomin.cl or http://volcanism.wordpress.com/category/volcanoes/chaiten for local conditions before traveling in the area. Updated: Feb 11, 2010.

NORTHERN PATAGONIA

Tehuelche fled to an area that is today known as the Tehuelche region. Shortly after the beginning of the 20th century, however, many of these cultures disappeared.

Soon, white settlers came to claim the land the indigenous peoples had left. First were the powerful Patagonian cattle and sheep companies, like *La Sociedad Nacional de Ganadería y Colonización*. The company created great ranches that spread from Aysén into modern-day Argentina and down to Chile's Magallanes region. In the later part of the 1910s, the Chilean government opened up the region to colonization, offering tracts to pioneers. Many Europeans, especially Germans, carved out villages in these virgins lands. Migrants from Chiloé Island also played a key role in the settling of Northern Patagonia, though little has been recorded of these unsung heroes, whose skills and knowledge led to the success of many new colonies.

For generations, the inhabitants of Northern Patagonia maintained a strong connection with Argentina, importing basic foodstuffs from their neighbors, as well as many cultural customs, traditions and games. However, the arrival of the Carretera Austral in the late 1970s marked the end of that era, and the beginning of the integration of Chile's Northern Patagonia into the country's mainstream. Updated: Jul 10, 2009.

When to Go

The easiest time to visit Chile's Carretera Austral and Northern Patagonia is in the summertime when transportation is more frequent. Various cabañas, campgrounds, lodges and inns open up along the highway. Every village has its *jineteada* (rodeo) and anniversary celebrations, which are much like country fairs, featuring *asados al palo* (meat roasted on an upright spit over a wood fire), traditional games, music, dancing and the election of the festival queen.

The summertime weather is warmer and a bit more stable, though heavy rains can still affect road conditions. Between fall and winter, many places close and transportation is limited, but that shouldn't dissuade travelers from visiting, as the cooler weather allows for excellent skiing and other winter sports. Updated: Jul 10, 2009.

Safety

Personal safety in the Carretera Austral and Northern Patagonia region is not a problem. There is very little theft or other crimes

commited against tourists. If you are driving or bicycling the Carretera Austral, be savvy about gravel road conditions. The highway has many sharp ascents and descents, blind curves and no guard rails. Check your vehicle's oil and tires, carry a spare, and be aware of where gas will be available.

In the realm of natural dangers, be prepared for sudden changes in the weather. Wear raingear and windbreakers. The *tábano*, or biting horsefly, is a menace from mid-December to mid-January. Hantavirus, a potentially fatal disease carried in excrement of rodents, is prevalent throughout the region, so be extra careful with hygiene if you plan to camp. Updated: Jul 10, 2009.

Border Crossings to Argentina
PASO RÍO PUELO
From Puerto Montt take a Hornopirén-bound bus and hop off at the town of Puelo. From here, take a colectivo bus along the Puelo River to the last stop, a few kilometers south of Llanada Grande. This is where the trailhead begins. The Chilean border post is at Lagos de las Rocas. Four kilometers (2.4 mi) before the post is Segundo Corral (a first-aid station, small market and telephone). Several hours beyond Lagos de las Rocas is the Argentine border control at Los Hitos, inside Parque Nacional Río Puelo. Both border posts stamp passports from 8 a.m. – 8 p.m. Campgrounds and wild camping do exist all along the route, but you'll need to speak Spanish fairly well. It is best to do this crossing November – March.

PASO FUTALEUFÚ
Paso Futaleufú, near the Chilean town of the same name, is the most commonly used border crossing on the northern part of the Carretera Austral. The immigration and customs for each country are about 100 meters (325 ft) apart (summer 8 a.m. – 10 p.m., winter 8 a.m.- 8 p.m.). Public transportation from Futaleufú stops at the border to meet buses to Trevelín and Esquel, Argentina (Monday, Friday 9:30 a.m., 6:30 p.m.; in summer also on Wednesdays, $4.70, 2 hr). Alternatively, you can hitchhike from the border into Trevelín, where there are frequent buses (Monday – Friday every 30-60 min, 6:45 a.m. – 11:45 p.m., weekends and holidays hourly 8:15 a.m. – 11:45 p.m., $1, 20 min).

PASO RÍO ENCUENTRO

From Palena, take Calle Pedro Montt east out of town. This becomes Ruta Ch-235, which goes to the border. From the border, it is a 15-minute walk to Carrenleufú, Argentina. The border is open 8 a.m.- 8 p.m. all year long. Although Paso Río Encuentro (near the village of Palena) has immigration and customs services, travelers leaving Chile at this crossing will need a safe-conduct (*salvoconducto*) pass from the local police.

PASO LAS PAMPAS – LAGO VERDE

Paso Las Pampas – Lago Verde is 3 kilometers (1.8 mi) east of Lago Verde and 58 kilometers (35 mi) from La Junta. The nearest town on the Argentine side is Las Pampas. The road between Lago Verde and the pass (Alt: 510 m) is gravel.

There are no customs or immigration officials at this border crossing. You must obtain a safe-conduct pass from the local police (*carabineros*) or from the aduanas office in Coyhaique at least 24 hours in advance. Always check with the police about road and weather conditions if you are traveling between late fall – early spring.

PASO RÍO FRÍAS – APPELEG

A rough gravel road from Villa Amengual goes to La Tapera. From there a dirt track heads to Paso Río Frías. The pass, at 911 meters (2,988 ft) altitude, has no services. You must obtain a safe-conduct pass from the carabineros in Coyhaique. The nearest Argentine village is Villa Appeleg, 56 kilometers (34 mi) east.

PASO COYHAIQUE ALTO

Paso Coyhaique Alto is the route that most Coyhaique – Puerto Montt buses take. It is 50 kilometers (30 mi) due east of Coyhaique on Ruta Internacional Ch-240. Carabineros, customs and immigration posts are open all year 8 a.m. – 8 p.m. The pass is at 795 meters (2,608 ft). The nearest Argentine town of note is Río Mayo on Ruta 40. Near the border is **Camping Fogón del Ingeniero** (Km 7.5, Ruta 240. Tel: 56-67-525697, E-mail: danghff@hotmail.com).

PASO HUEMULES

Paso Huemules (502 m/1,647 ft) is another fully operational border crossing near Coyhaique (54 km/33 mi southeast). It has police, customs and immigration services. It is open all year 8 a.m. – 8 p.m. Follow the Carretera Austral south to the gravel-paved Ruta

Internacional Ch-245 to Balmaceda. The post is five kilometers (3 mi) beyond that town. The closest village in Argentina is Lago Blanco; 108 kilometers (65 mi) further on is Río Guenguel at the junction of Rutas 55 and 40.

PASO INGENIERO IBÁÑEZ – PALLAVICINI

On the north shore of Lago General Carrera is the Paso Ingeniero Ibáñez – Pallavicini. The dirt road Camino X-65 heads 20 kilometers (12 mi) east from Puerto Ibáñez to this pass at 457 meters (1,499 ft). No formal facilities exist here; obtain a safe-conduct permission slip from the carabineros in Puerto Ibáñez.

PASO CHILE CHICO – LOS ANTIGUOS

This is the most commonly used pass in the southern Carretera Austral region. The Chilean facilities at this border crossing, also called Paso Jeínemeni, are three kilometers east of Chile Chico, on the south littoral of Lago General Carrera. Ruta Ch-265 is gravel paved to the border (231 m/757 ft altitude). Five kilometers (3 mi) beyond the border you'll find the Argentine facilities. The Argentine town of Los Antiguos is also nearby. Perito Moreno, on Ruta 40, is 62 kilometers (37 mi) west.

PASO PAMPA ALTA

Seventy-nine kilometers (48 mi) northeast of Coyhaique is Paso Pampa Alta. The nearest Chilean town is Villa Ortega (43 km / 25 mi) and the closest Argentine hamlet is Alto Río Benguer. The dirt and gravel road, Camino Tranversal X-45, crosses the pass at 860 meters (2,821 ft). There are no formal border installations. You must obtain a safe-conduct pass in advance.

PASO ROBALLOS

Paso Roballos (650 m/2132 ft) is 99 kilometers (61 mi) east of Cochrane. Chile's Camino X-63 is gravel to the border. On the Argentine side, Ruta 41 is dirt until it reaches Ruta 40, just north of Bajo Caracoles, near Cueva de las Manos. There are no formal border facilities here. A safe-conduct permission slip is necessary.

PASO RÍO MAYER – RIBERA NORTE

Six kilometers (3.6 mi) north of Villa O'Higgins is a road to Entrada Mayer and the Paso Río Mayer – Ribera Norte. This is the border crossing most locals use to go to Argentina. There is no public transportation and part of the journey must be done on horse. Ruta 81 begins almost 10 kilometers (6 mi) from the pass. Foreigners cannot officially cross here.

NORTHERN PATAGONIA

Padre Antonio Ronchi

One of the most legendary figures of Chile's Aysén region is Padre Antonio Ronchi (born February 3, 1930, Milan, Italy; died December 17, 1997, Santiago de Chile). This Italian priest arrived in Chile in September 1960 with the Madre de la Divina Providencia mission. The following year he was sent to Puerto Cisnes to work with the poor. For over three decades he helped settlements throughout the entire region to create the infrastructure so sorely needed. With his guidance, they built churches, schools, health posts, roads, training centers and radio and TV stations. During the Pinochet dictatorship, his activities came under scrutiny time and again.

His work helped to create economic and social bases for local villages, inspiring projects like the women's artisan cooperative in Puerto Ibáñez and the Maripro radio network. Many villages have statues commemorating him, and in Villa O'Higgins there is a museum honoring his work. The ferry across Fiordo Mitchell, from Puerto Yungay to Río Bravo on the Carretera Austral, is named for him. Many locals fondly remember him and tell tales of his endless journeying on foot, through mud and snows, to help their communities grow. Updated: Jul 07, 2009.

PASO RÍO MOSCO

Heading due south of Villa O'Higgins is Paso Río Mosco. This crossing is little used even by locals, as there are no boats or roads on the other side.

PASO DOS LAGUNAS

This pass, called the most beautiful border crossing in the world, provides the shortest, most direct access to El Chaltén in the neighboring republic. However, it is a trip only for those who have a lot of stamina, deep pockets and patience. Prices are set only for the foreign tourist crowd. The trails can be muddy during the spring thaws. This pass is open October - May, but the best months to do it are January – February when boats from Chile Chico run several times per week.

Weather is always a factor: rains can flood out the Carretera Austral, preventing buses from getting to Villa O'Higgins and high winds can cause changes in the Lago O'Higgins ferry schedule. Check with the Cámara de Turismo in Coyhaique for the up-dated schedule of departures or visit www.villaohiggins.com/hielosur for more information.

The Paso Dos Lagunas journey begins in Villa O'Higgins. From here a seven kilometer (4.2 mi) gravel road leads to Puerto Bahamódez (pickups, January – February: Monday, Wednesday, Saturday; March: Wednesday, Saturday, $3). The boat to Candelaria Mansilla on the opposite shore of Lago O'Higgins, leaves from Bahamodez. (January – February: Monday, Wednesday, Saturday 8 a.m.; March: Wednesday, Saturday 8 a.m.; $80, 2.75 hours; Candelario Mansilla – Puerto Bahamódez same days 5:30 p.m.) .

In Candelario Mansilla you'll find **Hospedaje Rural Candelario Mansilla** (Tel: 56-67-431805, URL: www.casaturismorural.cl, $12 per person).

A steep, two-kilometer (1.2 mi) trail climbs to the Carabineros de Chile, where you get your passport stamped. From here, it's a 20-kilometer (12 mi) trek to Punta Norte on the north shore of Laguna del Desierto. Pack horses are available ($30 - 40). The Gendarmería Argentina, where you get your passport stamped, is at Punta Norte. You can camp for free here, but there are no bathrooms or other facilities. Campfires are allowed.

In the high season, ferries cross Laguna del Desierto to Punta Sur twice a day (2 p.m., 6:30 p.m., $27). Alternatively, you can hike the 12 kilometer (7.2 mi) trail along the east side of the lake. On the south coast is a campsite. There is a bus for the last 37 kilometers (23 mi) to El Chaltén ($24), or you can try hitchhiking or walking the distance.

You should be able to make the crossing in one day if you take all the transportation options. If you are walking around Laguna del Desierto, plan for two days. Bicyclists should also plan for the longer span, as you'll often have to carry your bike. Upon arriving in Villa O'Higgins, reservations for the Lago O'Higgins ferry must be made with **Hielo Sur**, who can also arrange pack horses (Camino Austral Km 1,240, across from airport, Tel: 56-67-431821, E-mail: info@villaohiggins.com, URL: www.villaohiggins.com/hielosur). A complete package costs about $200. High winds can make passage of Lago O'Higgins dangerous. The final go-ahead for ferry service is given by the capitanía of the port, and notice may not be given until 9 p.m. the night before. Updated: Jul 07, 2009.

Things to See and Do

Chile's Northern Patagonia is a magical land with a unique culture and interesting natural formations.. Almost half of the region is protected by national parks and reserves, providing endless opportunities for hiking. The **Sendero de Chile** extends from the north to the south, allowing for days-long adventures away from tourist crowds. There are mountains to climb, glaciers to trek, lakes teeming with trout and roiling rivers to raft or kayak. In summer you can join locals in the celebration of their country fairs and rodeos.

Although most people come during the austral summer months, winter also lures travelers. Quite a few of the parks remain open in winter. You can snowshoe or cross country ski the trails or go on an alpine trek.

At any time of the year, the perfect way to relax after a long day of sightseeing or traveling is to soak in the hot springs that dot the countryside. Updated: Jul 10, 2009.

Tours

National and international tour agencies organize trips to the major attractions, like the glaciers of Parque Nacional Laguna San Rafael or the hot springs at the Termas de Puyuhuapi. Some outfits specialize in whitewater rafting, kayaking or fly fishing.

If you prefer to use local guides to get off the beaten track, two regional organizations can help you do just that. Both have their main offices in Coyhaique. **Casa del Turismo Rural** is the central organization for rural hostels, guides, artisans and other services in the Aysén region (Monday – Friday 10 a.m. – 1 p.m., 2:30 – 7 p.m. Dussen 357, Coyhaique. Tel: 56-67-214031 / 524929, E-mail: contacto@casaturismorural.cl, URL: www. casaturismorural.cl).

The **Escuela de Guías de la Patagonia** trains guides to lead tourists on trekking, skiing, horseback riding, fishing and other expeditions. In addition to this training, students also receive lessons in conservation, geology, biology and other sciences. During the summer months, the Escuela de Guías also offers courses in outdoor skills to foreigners (Casilla 111, Coyhaique. Tel: 56-67-

573096 / 56-7-7591164, E-mail: contacto@escueladeguias.cl, URL: www.escueladeguias.cl). Updated: Jul 10, 2009.

Lodging

In summer, hotels throw open their doors to welcome the tourists to this corner of Chile. Accommodations along the Carretera Austral are either simple affairs or exclusive lodges. All along the highway and into the depths of the countryside are cozy hostels where families serve up hearty breakfasts with home-made goods and invite guests to sit around the woodstove to chat and relax. Along the rivers are first-rate fly-fishing lodges. Other local inns specialize in trekking, ice climbing and horseback riding. Cyclists, trekkers and budget travelers will find many campgrounds along the way. At the end of the season, cabañas begin to close as the locals prepare for the long, dark winter; a few places stay open to receive tourists who come to ski or snowshoe. Updated: Jul 10, 2009.

HORNOPIRÉN

 1,572 m   1,200 65

In the Los Lagos region of Chile, Patagonia's Palena province, is the small town of Hornopirén, (109 km south of Puerto Montt), known by locals as the north gate to the Carretera Austral. The town was originally called Río Negro, but since there are many towns with that name in Chile, the community, la comuna de Hualaihué, decided to rename their home after the nearby volcano. A stratovolcano, Hornopirén lies on the Liquine-Ofqui fault line. The last recorded eruption was in 1835.

Despite the minimal infrastructure there, the town's population increases dramatically during the summer months. Tourists flock there to visit Parque Nacional Hornipirén. There are no banks or ATMs, no pharmacies, nor hospital. There are, however, plenty of places to sleep and eat.

The area is a base for activities such as mountain biking, canoeing, rafting and horseback riding. The 3m-high Río Negro waterfalls, also known as las Cascadas de Doña Tato are nearby. In Hornopirén national park you can trek to glacier fields, volcanoes, the Pinto Concha, Cabro and the Inexplorado lakes. On Isla Llancahue, 50 minutes by boat from town, are indoor and outdoor thermal baths where you can sit and relax.

NORTHERN PATAGONIA

Getting To and Away From Hornopirén

To get to Hornopirén, from Puerto Montt, you have to first take the Carretera Austral and then board a boat from the 'port' of Caleta la Arena, 30 minutes across the Reloncaví estuary, to Caleta Puelche. The town is then 50 minutes along a bumpy road. Check ferry info at: www.navieraustral.cl.

Be aware that the nearby Chaiten volcano erupted in May 2008 (p.391), after being dormant for over 9,000 years. Parts of the Carretera Austral were closed between Chaiten and Hornopirén. The town and its inhabitants were relocated and Chaiten was abandoned. Updated: Jun 10, 2009.

Lodging

Local accomodation includes: **Hotel Hornopirén** (Ca. Ignacio Carrera Pinto 388. Tel: 56-65-217256); **Hostal Catalina** (Av. Ingenieros Militares s/n. Tel: 56-65-217359); **Cabañas Araucaria** (Ca. O'Higgins and Cahuelmo. Tel: 56-65-217320); **Residencial Galicia** (Ca. M. Rodriguez 941. Tel: 56-65-217275) and **Camping Rueda de Agua** (Sector Chaqueihua s/n. Tel: 56-65-217434).

On the islands around Hornopirén are some tourist resorts: **Termas de Llancahue** (Isla Llancahue. Tel: 56-9-6424857) and **Resort Isla Manzano** (Isla Manzano. Tel: 56-65-252299).

PARQUE NACIONAL HORNOPIRÉN

(ADMISSION: Free) Established in 1988, PN Hornopirén protects 48,232 hectares of evergreen forest in an important transition zone. Not only do the Cordilleras Patagónicas del Pacífico begin here, with the landscape sculpted by volcanoes and glaciers, but the park is also the terminus of the Active Volcanic Range (*Cordillera Volcánica Activa*), which includes the Villarrica and Llaima volcanoes.

The area to the south is known as the Volcanic-Glacial Plain, and is home to three majestic cones: Chaitén—which erupted in 2008, after 9,400 years of dormancy; its resting neighbor, Michinmahuida and, across Chaitén Sound, Corcovado. Volcanoes Yates (2,187 m/7,108 ft), Hornopirén (1,572 m/5,109 ft) and Apagoado (1,210 m/3,933 ft) spewed lava during the

Pleistocene Epoch. Approximately 3,000 hectares of *ventisqueros* (hanging glaciers) gleam within the park's boundaries.

This is a rocky, watery landscape covered with Patagonian cypress, Magellan's beech and lenga beech. Four important rivers have headwaters within the park. Río Negro begins its journey from Lago Pinto Concha to Canal Hornopirén. Río Blanco is fed by snowmelts and Lago Inexplorado. The Traidor runs eastward, to join the Río Puelo.

The park has two main hiking trails. The first begins at the ranger station near Chaqueihua Alto and leads to Lago Pinto (difficulty: low-medium, distance: 9.7 kilometers/6 mi, duration: 5 hours one way). The trail is divided into three legs: **Part 1** (2.5 km/1.5 mi) traverse private lands by way of a logging road with steep climbs through a much-eroded landscape. **Part 2** (4.3 km/2.6 mi) also heads through private property. The trail here is more level and is surrounded by evergreen forest. **Part 3** (2.9 km/1.75 mi) enters the national park itself, with a path that gently climbs through pure alerce forest. The Cordillera del Tigre fringes the horizon. The trail ends at the ranger post at Lago Pinto Concha, where there are few services but you're allowed to camp for free.

The second trail, to the south foot of Volcán Yates, is an off-shoot of the above (difficulty: low-medium, distance: 3.65 km/2.2 mi, duration: 1 hour one way). It passes through alerce and lenga woods. The trail offers clear views of Lago Pinto Concha and snowy volcanoes.

When to Go

The best time to hike in Parque Nacional Hornopirén is November to March. Be prepared for mud and low temperatures. Pack food and fuel supplies. Check with Conaf in Río Negro Hornopirén about trail conditions (Bernardo O'Higgins s/n. E-mail: juan.rudolph@conaf.cl). Updated: Jun 10, 2009.

Getting To and Away From Parque Nacional Hornopirén

From Puerto Montt, take the Carretera Austral (Ruta CH-7) south to Caleta La Arena, then cross Estuario Reloncaví to Caleta Puelche and the town of Río Negro Hornopirén (107 kilometers / 64.2 mi). Three bus companies in Puerto Montt provide service to the village: **Buses Hornopirén** (daily 2:45 p.m.), **Transaustral** (daily 7:50 a.m., three departures 2:30-5:30 p.m.) and **Kémel** (daily 8 a.m., three buses 1:30 – 5 p.m.). All charge $7 for the 3.5 hour trip. From Río Negro Hornopirén, the park's Chaqueihua Alto ranger station is 10 kilometers (6 mi) away. Updated: May 29, 2009.

CHAITÉN

 402 m   4,200   65

Chaitén, the capital of the La Palena Province in Chile's Region X Los Lagos, was once a Patagonian transportation hub. The small city was packed with hostels, hotels and restaurants; the markets bustled with fishmongers and artisans; couples strolled the seafront promenade. Tour agencies took visitors on the Futaleufú River, to soak in the hot Termas de Amarillo springs or through the pristine forests of Parque Pumalín. This was the place to embark on a journey down the Carretera Austral or to rest before returning to "civilization" in Chiloé and Puerto Montt. Was. Until May 2, 2008.

The land had been shaking for a few days. Everyone thought the rumbles were coming from Volcán Michinmahuida. But when the volcano blew, everyone—even volcanologists—were surprised to see that it was Cerro Chaitén, a hill that didn't even make it on maps. Chaitén had been dormant for 9,400 years. The government ordered an evacuation of Chaitén, and 7,000 residents left as coarse ash began to fall over the city. The Río Blanco, blocked by ash and lahar (an ash-cinder-mud mixture), broke free of man made restraints and returned to its original course through the center of town. (To view a chronology of Volcán Chaitén's eruption and photos, see: http://geology.com/events/chaiten-volcano).

For three months, ferry services from Chiloé Island and Puerto Montt were suspended. After the ferries began to run again, this southern sliver of Chile was finally reconnected with the rest of the country. Some people began coming back to protect their properties and retrieve belongings. The scene that welcomed them was one of utter devastation. Homes had ash up to their first-floor windows; those near the river were covered to the roof. Inside, the ash was at least 30 centimeters (one foot) deep. Outside was a wasteland of damaged buildings and the twisted wreckage of trucks.

By January 2009, about 100 Chaiteninos had returned, cleaning out their businesses to welcome weary ferry travelers. They reopened hostels and stores, despite the lack of electricity, water and land telephone lines.

Chaitén, though, once more had to be evacuated of townfolk and tourists on February 18, 2009, when one of the volcano's lava domes partially collapsed. The Chilean government officially declared the village off-limits for overnight stays. It later announced Chaitén would be rebuilt near Santa Bárbara to the north. The town of Futaleufú was declared the new capital of Provincia de Palena.

Ferry services continue to bring tourists to this part of Chile's northern Patagonia, but passengers must immediately move on. The nearest lodging is in El Amarillo and Puerto Cárdenas on Lago Yelcho. El Amarillo also has camping, as does Ventisquero Yelcho. Since the initial 2008 eruption, Parque Pumalín has been closed to visitors.

The wood-shingled church on Chaitén's main plaza was not damaged. On the square is an impressive monument to the town's victims of the 1973-1989 dictatorship. The bridge over Río Blanco has the best view of Volcán Chaitén, which looks like something out of The Lord of the Rings. From its ragged slopes billow clouds of steam and ash. It continues to build at astounding rates. Between May 2008 and January 2009 the volcano more than doubled its original height. Volcanologists consider the volcano, only 10 kilometers (6 mi) from town, to be extremely unstable. Volcán Chaitén yet is active, pumping ash clouds into the skies above the Carretera Austral. A third lava dome has formed.

Before embarking on any journey to Chaitén, check with the nearest Carabinero post to see what the present conditions are and to assure ferry services are not disrupted. The latest on the volcano's activity can be scoped out at www.sernageomin.cl (in Spanish) and http://volcanism.wordpress.com/category/volcanoes/chaiten (in English). Updated: Feb 11, 2010.

Getting To and Away From Chaitén

Ruta 7 leads into Chaitén from the south. The last 31 kilometers are paved. You might see ash drifts at the roadside. Carabineros at El Amarillo checkpoint record all visitors entering and leaving the city by highway. Day visitors may come to snap photos, but overnight access is prohibited.

BY BOAT

The seafront road to the port has been partially destroyed. Vehicles should take Diego Portales north to the dock. Naviera Austral has an office on Avenida Concorvado, near Calle Pedro Aguirre Cerda (8 a.m. – 9:15 a.m., 10 a.m. – 1 p.m., 3 – 6 p.m.). Tickets must be purchased at the office. The ferries can transport cars, motorcycles and other vehicles, as well as passengers. For complete fares and updated schedules, see Naviera Austral's website: www.navieraustral.cl.

To Puerto Montt: (direct) Monday 10 a.m., Friday 2 p.m.; (via Ayacara) Wednesday 9 p.m., $41.

To Quellón, Isla Chiloé: Tuesday 10 a.m., $37. The Quellón ferry makes connections with the Ruta Cordillera boat, which goes to Melinka, Puerto Cisnes and Chacabuco along the Carretera Austral south of Chaitén. A stretch of the Carretera Austral between Hornopirén and Chaitén was destroyed. The ferry now departs from Hornopirén, stopping at Ayacara, before docking at Chaitén. This ferry only operates in January and February (southward: Monday, Wednesday, Saturday 9 a.m.; northward Wednesday, Friday, Sunday 10 a.m., $30).

BY BUS

The Chaitén bus schedule is very uncertain. If you ask about departures, the answer is always "When there are boats." Usually, there is at least one bus to Palena, Futaleufú and/or Coyhaique Monday, Tuesday and Friday at 10 a.m. If there are no buses going to your destination, try your luck in Villa Santa Lucía. A common alternative for foreign tourists is to hitchhike (an alternative that V!VA does not endorse). Hiring a driver costs $80 – 100 (negotiable) to Futaleufú or Palena. Updated: Feb 11, 2010.

LAGO YELCHO

Lago Yelcho, a 35-kilometer (21-mile) long sliver of water, sits midway between the coast and the Argentine border. The lake is fed by the Río Futaleufú, which crashes down from the Andes through narrow canyons. Upon reaching the lake, the Futaleufú is calmer, with abundant fishing and boating opportunities. Die-hard kayakers can take a breather on the lake before hitting the rapids of the nascent Río Yelcho to Enseñada Chaitén.

Lago Yelcho is surrounded by virgin forests, and most of its shoreline is uninhabited. On the northwestern tip of the lake is Puerto Cárdenas and the Carretera Austral (Ruta 7); on the southeastern edge, at the crossroads of the Futaleufú–Palena Highways (Rutas 231 and 235), are Puerto Ramírez and Puerto Piedra. Within these hamlets travelers will find a variety of services, from simple hostels to luxury lodges and restaurants.

There are many fishing guides ready to take you out to whirl a fly for fine salmon or trout, and there is ample opportunity for rafting or horseback riding. But Lago Yelcho isn't just about these sports. Visitors can also hike to the glacier Ventisquero Yelcho or soak in the Termas de Amarillo (both near Puerto Cárdenas).

From Chaitén, the first settlement outside of the volcano's red zone is El Amarillo. This is currently the closest place along the Carretera Austral to stay before catching the ferry to Quellón or Puerto Montt. A police checkpoint records all visitors continuing to or departing from Chaitén. El Amarillo village is still only a tiny stop along the Carretera, although its population has grown significantly since the evacuation of Chaitén. Services will undoubtedly improve in the future.

A five-kilometer (3-mi) spur road leads from the carabinero control post up toward the Termas El Amarillo (daily March – December 9 a.m. – 6 p.m., January – February 9 a.m. – 9 p.m. Entry: $6 per person, under six years old, free). These hot springs have long been travelers' favorite spot to soak after completing the journey north on the rigorous Carretera Austral. Termas El Amarillo has several basic, open-air and private pools (50°C/122°F), as well as mud pits. The thermal springs have both campsites and cabañas.

Continuing along the Carretera Austral you'll come to Puerto Cárdenas at Kilometer 45. This small *caserío* (hamlet) is the largest town on the northwestern tip of Lago Yelcho. The fishing here is spectacular. Eleven kilometers (6.6 mi) further down the road, on the west shore of the lake, is a 300-meter (1,000-feet) trail leading to a pool of mineral waters surrounded by burnt-orange clay. At Kilometer 60 of the Southern Highway is the trail head for a six-kilometer (3.6 mile) path along the Río Ventisquero, to the Ventisquero Yelcho, a spectacular glacier. It is a three-hour hike to the ice field (officially free, though current reports indicate locals are now charging an entry fee). There are campsites at the entrance to the Ventisquero.

From the trail head, the Carretera takes a sharp turn south to Villa Santa Lucía, where you can turn toward Puerto Ramirez to Futaleufú and Palena. Puerto Ramírez is on both sides of a bridge spanning the bend of the Río Futaleufú. Five kilometers (3 mi) onward is Puerto Piedra, on the edges of Lago Yelcho.

This is the perfect habitat for brown, rainbow and other trout, as well as for salmon, thus providing adventures for anglers. Besides fly fishing, other outdoor sports include rafting, kayaking and horseback riding. Both settlements have lodging and guide services. Updated: Apr 21, 2009.

Getting To and Away From Lago Yelcho

Puerto Cárdenas is on the Carretera Austral, 46 kilometers (27.5 mi) from Chaitén and 31 kilometers (18.5 mi) from Santa Lucía. Twenty-four kilometers (15 mi) east of Santa Lucía is Puerto Ramírez, the cruce of Ruta 231 to Futaleufú (66 km/40 mi northeast) and Ruta 235 to Palena (60 km/36 mi southeast). The Carretera is paved only between Chaitén and El Amarillo. All other roads are gravel. Gas stations operate in Chaitén, Futaleufú and Palena. The next one south on the Carretera Austral is in La Junta.

There are no direct buses to any of these hamlets. Instead, take a Chaitén-bound vehicle if you want to visit Ventiquero Yelcho, Puerto Cárdenas or El Amarillo. To get to Termas El Amarillo, you'll have to walk the five kilometers up the spur road. For Puerto Piedra or Puerto Ramírez, take any bus heading to Futaleufú or Palena. See Chaitén and Santa Lucía for details on these transport services. Updated: Apr 21, 2009.

Services

Services are limited along the Lago Yelcho circuit. The nearest banks are in Futaleufú and Palena. If arriving by ferry, change money before leaving Puerto Montt or Chiloé. Internet is a rarity, though phone services exist in the larger villages.

Tours

Most tours to Lago Yelcho used to leave from Chaitén. Since that town was evacuated, the only way to go with a guide is with an agency in Palena, or through one of the expensive lodges around the lake. A few local guides also provide services.

In Puerto Ramírez:
El Cruce (Tel: 56-65-264431): fishing.
El Macal (Tel: 56-65-721413): horseback riding, rafting.
El Farellón (Tel: 56-65-741218): boat tours of Lago Yelcho.

In Puerto Piedra:
Lodge Puerto Piedra (Tel: 56-65-731505, URL: www.palenaonline.cl): fishing trips on Lago Yelcho and Río Futaleufú. Updated: Apr 21, 2009.

Lodging

Many hotels and guesthouses in the Lago Yelcho area also have small restaurants.

In El Amarillo:
Residencial Marcella (Tel: 56-65-264442, $16 per person).

Hospedaje Los Mañíos (80 meters before the Termas. Tel: 56-65-731210, $10 – 20).

Termas El Amarillo (Campsite $10 per tent, plus $8 per person; also cabañas).

In Puerto Cárdenas:
Residencial Yelcho (Tel: 56-65-264429).
Cabañas Villa Gesell (Tel: 56-9-8868098, E-mail: contacto@villageselle.com, URL: www.villagesellchile.com, from $100).
Cabaña Yelcho en La Patagonia (7 km/4.2 mi south of Puerto Cárdenas. Tel: 56-65-731337, URL: www.yelcho.cl, cabins from $184, single rooms: $122, doubles: $135, camping: $44).

In Puerto Ramírez:
Camping El Macal (Tel: 56-65-721413).
Hostería El Cruce (Tel: 56-65-264431).
Hostería Verónica (Tel: 54-65-741224, URL: hosteria-veronica.patagoniaverde.com).
Cumbres Nevadas (At the Futaleufú crossroads. Tel: 56-8-2030551 / 56-9-9170088).

In Puerto Piedra:
Lodge Puerto Piedra (Tel: 56-65-731505, URL: www.palenaonline.cl). Updated: Apr 21, 2009.

VILLA SANTA LUCÍA

 614 m   270   65

Villa Santa Lucía is one of the larger settlements between the coast and the Argentine border. Strategically located between Chaitén (81 km/49 mi west), Futaleufú (77 km/46 mi east) and Palena (72 km/43 mi east), Santa Lucía is the crossroads of the Carretera Austral. Most bikers and hitchhikers end their day's journey here. Since the eruption of Volcán Chaitén, the population has doubled.

A long row of buildings lines Calle Los Cerrillos, the street parallel to the Carretera Austral. Near the northern end is a general store where visitors stop to cool off or get directions. Further down this road is the simple village church. One block east is the main square, a large grassy expanse with a playground and a simple wood carving dedicated to the pioneers who settled here. On the east side of the park is a large military base.

Getting To and Away From Villa Santa Lucía

All transportation leaves from Salón de Té Nachito on the plaza. Service is drastically reduced outside of the summertime.

To Chaitén: **Altamirano** (arriving from Futaleufú Monday, Wednesday, Friday, 9:30 a.m., $15).

To Coyhaique: Several companies, including **Don Oscar** (beware of overcharging, daily 10 a.m., 3:30 p.m., $30, 10 hours). These buses pass through La Junta ($6, 2 hours) and Puyuhuapi ($10, 3 hours).

To Futaleufú: Tuesday, Wednesday, Friday 5:30 p.m., $6, 2 hours.

To Palena: Monday, Tuesday, Wednesday, Friday noon, $6, 2 hours. Updated: Jul 01, 2009.

Services

Services are limited in Villa Santa Lucía. Don't waste time searching for a tourism office, bank or post office—there aren't any. A two-computer Internet café and phone center is located a half-block north of the plaza (Monday – Saturday 9 a.m. – 1 p.m., 3 – 9 p.m. Los Coigües. $1.20 per hour). **Salón de Té Nachito** advertises tours to Lago Yelcho and other destinations (Los Avellanos and Los Cípreses).

Lodging

A few new hostels are opening to fill the gap left by the abandonment of Chaitén. The only official hotel is a two-story silver building along the Carretera Austral (Los Cerrillos s/n. $8 per person; unfriendly). Ask around for other lodging options. Costs average $8 – 10 per person. Try the log house advertising

cabañas on the plaza (Los Coigües and Los Sauces), Salón de Té Nachito and Doña Yohanna (Los Cípreses, across from the church). **Minimarket Claudita** allows camping in its backyard, though there is no bathroom (Los Cípresses and Los Sauces; $2 per person). Otherwise, campers can pitch their tents in the field alongside the Carretera Austral.

Restaurants

The only real restaurant in town is Salón de Té Nachito ($6 per meal). Ask around to see if anyone is preparing food. Several general stores have supplies. Two houses sell bread; look for the *pan* (bread) signs outside the house at the south end of Los Cerrillos and the home at the south end of Los Coigües. Updated: Jan 23, 2009.

FUTALEUFÚ

 350 m   2,000   65

Futaleufenses like to say that their land was *pintado por Dios* (painted by God), and it's easy to see why. The village of Futaleufú is snuggled down in a valley ringed by forest-clad mountains, and is watered by the Futaleufú and Espolón Rivers. Its name comes from *Mapudungún* (the Mapuche language) for Big River. Although the village is off the main highway, many come to test their skills on one of the world's best whitewater runs.

History

Futaleufú was a laid-back village until 1985 when a group of rafters and kayakers came in search of virgin rivers. What they found was the Río Futaleufú, a river beyond their wildest dreams. That February, Eric Magneson, Phil De Riemer, Mark Allen and Lars Holbek kayaked the Futa (as the river is respectfully called by those who ride it) all the way to the sea. Two weeks later, Daniel Bolster and Peter Fox tried the same feat in a raft. They had to abandon the twisted wreckage of their craft at the "Terminator" stretch of the river and the legend was born. The Futa is now ranked as one of the world's top three rafting and kayaking rivers.

Futaleufú remains a small village despite the hordes of tourists who descend upon it. Its large Plaza de Armas, with a statue of O'Higgins in the center, is a favorite pecking ground for wandering chickens. On one corner is the Capilla Nuestra Señora del Carmen, a small green, wood-shingled church with a lone bell tower (open for Mass Sunday 7 p.m. Aguirre Cerdo and Rodríguez). It's a village where business owners double, triple, even quadruple up on their duties. The Stihl chainsaw dealer also rents bikes and does laundry. The Buses Altimirano depot is also the post office and a second-hand clothing store. One Internet café also has a money exchange, snack stand, telephone booths and serves as a bus station. Shops close for a few hours during afternoon siesta and most places shut their doors come early evening.

Futaleufú recognizes April 1, 1929 as the day of its founding. The first residents were Chileans who immigrated through Argentina to this valley. Until the spur road off the Carretera Austral reached Futaleufú in 1982, the village was more closely aligned culturally to neighboring Argentina, a mere 10 kilometers (6 mi) away. Futaleufense customs and language reflect these closer ties. "Che" peppers their conversations, they drink maté, play truco cards, and sing and dance to Argentine songs.

In the wake of the eruption of Volcán Chaitén, Futaleufú is changing even more. During the initial blow-up in May 2008, the village received 30 centimeters (one foot) of fine ash. Río Futaleufú's brilliant turquoise color is now more intense, many mountaintop lagoons have filled, and Lago Espolón is silted by the ashes. Many Chaiteninos (from Chaitén) sought refuge here. The greatest adjustment, though, is yet to come. In January 2009, the Chilean government announced that Provincia La Palena's capital will be moved from Chaitén to Futaleufú.

Yet another challenge confronts Futaleufú. The Spanish utility company Endesa has also been granted rights to build dams on Río Futaleufú. The local and international communities are concerned about the effects of this project on the river's eco-system and on tourism. Several groups are working to stop what they see as the destruction of the Futaleufú's unique environment: **Futa Friends** (PO Box 1942, Bozeman, Montana 59771, USA. Tel: 406-586-3460, URL: www.futafriends. org), **Patagonia Chilena Sin Represas**, which has offices in Coyhaique and Cochrane (URL: www.patagoniasinrepresas.cl) and **International Rivers** (URL: www.internationalrivers.org/latin-america/patagonia). Updated: Jun 12, 2009.

When to Go

Futaleufú has four distinct seasons. In summer, temperatures reach 30-40°C (86-100°F) and the air is dry. Winters are cold, dipping to -13°C (9°F), with up to two meters (6.5 feet) of snow.

The village hosts several summer events: **January 23 – 24**: El Rodeo Oficial. Watch local cowboys compete in rodeo events. **Second week of February**: Semana de Futaleufú. Seven days of festivities, with an election of the queen, float parades, tug of war and a closing night concert. **February 20 – 22**: Futafestival. Rafting and kayaking events. **December 24**: Christmas Eve. Midnight mass is celebrated at Capilla Nuestra Señora del Carmen. Updated: Jun 12, 2009.

Getting To and Away From Futaleufú

Highway CH-231 from Puerto Ramírez to Futaleufú is washboard grade, but the road from Futa to the border is paved. Villa Santa Lucía is at the crossroads on the Carretera Austral; buses going to La Junta, Puyuhuapi and Coyhaique pass through there. In the low season, bus service is reduced.

Transport companies are scattered throughout town: **Bus Altimirano** (Balmaced s/n and Prat, Tel: 56-65-721360), **Transporte Lago Espolón** (from Paquetería Para Ti, Aguirre Cerda 505), **Transporte Daniela** (Balmaceda s/n and Prat). Buses **Feryval** and **Cumbres Nevadas** leave from Librería San Sebastián on Prat, across from the Plaza de Armas. **Turismo Futaleufú** and **Transporte Matamala** depart from Centro de Llamadas Ruly (Aguirre Cerda s/n, between Prat and Sargento Aldea, Tel: 56-65-721425).

To Chaitén: **Bus Altimirano** (Friday 6:30 a.m., $10, 3 hours). Alternately, go to Villa Santa Lucía and catch a bus from there or hitchhike. Because of the volcanic activity near Chaitén, bus schedules can change or be canceled. Check with the bus company.

To Palena: **Cumbres Nevadas** (Wednesday 8 a.m., Monday and Friday 3:30 p.m., $5). *To La Junta*: **Bus Altimirano** (Monday, Wednesday, Friday 2 p.m., Friday 6:30 p.m., $15, 3 hours).

To Puyuhuapi/Coyhaique: **Transporte Daniela** (Sunday, Tuesday, Wednesday, Friday 8 a.m., $24 / $40, 5 hours / 9 hours).

To Puerto Montt: 8-10 hours, depending on border procedures; the route is through Argentina. Remember that you will be reentering Chile and will have your bags checked by customs for forbidden fruits and vegetables. **Transporte Lago Espolón** (Thursday 7:45 a.m., $52), **Transporte Matamala** (Tuesday 8:30 a.m., $46), **Altimirano** (Monday, Wednesday 8:30 a.m., $45), **Buses Feryval** (Tuesday 7:30, $48).

To Border: **Turismo Futaleufú** (Monday, Wednesday, Friday 8:45 a.m., 6:45 p.m., $4, 20 minutes).

Futaleufú also has an airfield for emergency and charter flights. Updated: Jun 12, 2009.

Getting Around

Futaleufú is a small town. It has no public transportation system or taxis. **Centro de Llamadas Ruly** rents cars with drivers and sells Argentine car insurance (Aguirre Cerda s/n, between Prat and Sargento Aldea. Tel: 56-65- 721425). The **Stihl** chainsaw agent rents bicycles for $20 per day (daily 9 a.m. – 9 p.m. Aguirre Cerda 537). Updated: May 31, 2009.

Safety

Futaleufú is downwind from Volcán Chaitén, so even though much of the volcanic ash has been removed, lots still remains in the village. Campsites have a whole bedding of it. Travelers with respiratory problems should be prepared. Streams are currently too laden with the fine material for you to be able to drink the water, and attempts to filter it will only damage your pump. In the back country, especially, the ash is still deep. As long as Chaitén Volcano remains active, more ash may drift over the town. If you are heading to Chaitén to catch the ferry to Chiloé or Puerto Montt, check with the carabineros about current dangers or warnings. Updated: Jun 12, 2009.

Services

TOURISM

The **Departamento Turismo Municipal** office is just opposite the Plaza de Armas (summer only, daily 9 a.m. – 9 p.m. O'Higgins 596. Tel: 56-65-721241 / 721370, E-mail: turismo@futaleufu.cl, URL: www.futaleufu.cl). The regional tourism office, **Sernatur**, is another excellent place to get information on Futaleufú and other destinations in the province (Monday – Friday 8:30 a.m. – 1:30 p.m., 2:30 – 6 p.m. Alsea s/n and Carmona. E-mail: infopalena@sernatur.cl). **Conaf** has information on the national parks and reserves (Monday – Friday 8:30 a.m. – 1 p.m., 2 – 5:45 p.m. Mistral s/n and Carmona). The **police** station is next to the municipal tourism office (O'Higgins s/n, Tel: 56-65-721233).

MONEY

Banco del Estado exchanges U.S. dollars and euros. Its ATM accepts only MasterCard and Cirrus cards; some travelers report success in asking for a Visa advance from the inside teller (Monday – Friday 9 a.m. – 2 p.m. O'Higgins and Rodríguez).

Note: In the Carretera Austral region, the only other banks are in Coyhaique and Cochrane. ATMs exist also in Puerto Cisnes and Mañihuales. **Centro de Llamadas Ruly** exchanges U.S. dollars and Argentine pesos (daily 8:30 a.m. – 10 p.m. Aguirre Cerda s/n, between Prat and Sargento Aldea. Tel: 56-65-721425). Other businesses may be willing to exchange or accept non-Chilean currency.

KEEPING IN TOUCH

The **post office** is at the Altimirano bus depot. Although mail is accepted throughout the week, it is picked up only on Thursdays (Monday – Friday 8:30 a.m. – 1 p.m., 2:30 – 5:30 p.m. Balmaced s/n and Prat).

Only a few cybercafés operate in town. **Cyber Lorena** charges $0.80 per hour and has the more reliable computers (Monday – Friday 9:30 a.m. – 1:30 p.m., 4 – 9 p.m. O'Higgins 656). Another Internet provider is **Fonosur** (corner of Rodríguez and Carmona). **Centro de Llamadas Ruly** charges $1 per hour to use its half-dozen computers, which have a tendency to crash. Ruly is also the **Telefónica del Sur** call center (daily 8:30 a.m. – 10 p.m. Aguirre Cerda s/n, between Prat and Sargento Aldea. Tel: 56-65-721425).

MEDICAL

Hospital Futaleufú is the town's only health facility. It has an emergency room (Balmaceda 382. Tel: 56-65-721231). The village has no pharmacy, but you can purchase basic medicines at **Paquetería Para Ti** (Aguirre Cerda 505).

LAUNDRY
Drop your laundry off at the **Stihl** chainsaw dealer, which charges $4 per kilo, with a minimum load of two kilos. The owners can wash knapsacks and sleeping bags, and have same day service (daily 9 a.m. – 9 p.m. Aguirre Cerda 537). For laundry and mending, see **Vicky** (daily 9 a.m. – 10 p.m. Sargento Aldea 273) or **Dervi** (Mistral 393. Tel: 56-65-721469). Updated: Jun 12, 2009.

SHOPPING
An unnamed shop on Sargento Aldea sells locally made wood and wool crafts (Sargento Aldea 273). The restaurants **Sur Andes** also has an artisan store (daily 8:30 a.m. – 10 p.m. Aguirre Cerda 308. Tel: 56-65-721405) and **Martín Pescador** sells artesanía and hand-tied fishing flies (Balmaceda 603. Tel: 56-65-721279). Updated: Jul 02, 2009.

Things to See and Do
Futaleufú is internationally known for its river rafting and kayaking. You can also go hiking or horseback riding to explore the land. While fly fishing is some of the best in the country, especially on Río Espolón, Río Futaleufú and Lago Conconado. Unfortunately, Lago Espolón has been affected by Volcán Chaitén's ash. Pick up your fishing license at the tourism office. Futaleufú will soon have its own Casa de la Cultura on the shores of Laguna Espejo. On Sunday afternoon, catch the action of the five soccer teams. Games begin at 2 p.m. at the field (*cancha*) at Riquelme and Balmaceda. Updated: Jun 12, 2009.

Whitewater Rafting and Kayaking
Experts come from around the world to dip their paddles into Río Futaleufú and to embark on the ride of their lives from the Entrada Rapids through the "Throne Room", the "Infierno" (22 km/14 mi, Class III-IV) and the "Terminator" (7 km/4.2 mi, Class V), which is where the first rafters crashed ashore. The Lower Futa is the most commonly paddled section and features "Corazón", an 8- to 12-kilometer (4.8 to 7.2-mile) rollercoaster stretch. Other rivers, the Azul and Espolón, are used to warm up for the Big One.

Six local companies can arrange rafting and kayaking trips. **Expediciones Chile** only does pre-reserved package deals ($90 per person for a four-hour trip). Río Futaleufú can occasionally be so swollen that even the pros don't feel they can match the river's power. The Upper Futa is the most demanding—especially Infierno —after heavy rains. To learn more about the river, pick up a copy of Tyler Curtis's *Futaleufú White Water: A Paddler's Guide* (www.helipress.com or www.kayaksession.com). Updated: Jun 12, 2009.

Horseback Riding
Horseback riding (*cabalgatas*) is another way to explore the countryside. Some favorite destinations are: Laguna Espejo, Valle de los Reyes, Lago Espolón, Valle del Noroeste and Reserva Nacional Futaleufú. When Volcán Chaitén erupted, most horses were evacuated. Few guides are now offering this diversion, as the fine ash affects the horses and forage is still poor. One guide still saddling up is Fabién Baeza of **Rancho Las Ruedas** (Carmona 337). Updated: Jun 12, 2009.

Hiking
Several day hikes can be done from Futaleufú. The shortest is around Laguna Espejo on the eastside of town. Off this path is another that goes up to Cerro Mirador. Another popular viewpoint is Mirador de la Virgen, a 131-meter (426-ft) knoll southeast of town.

Following Calle Aguirre Cerda west out of the village, you'll find the departure point for other hikes. Just a few kilometers past the bridge is a right-hand trail to Piedra del Águila, the best place to snap a photo of the entire valley (3 hours). Off another side path is Laguna Pinto (3 hours from Futaleufú). The main trail crosses Río del Noroeste, climbing to Lago Noroeste where the fishing is great (5-6 hours). Continue on the main path to reach Lago Las Rozas.

Another adventure from Calle Aguirre Cerda is to take the left branch of the trail, following the Río Espolón to Las Cascadas and Lago Espolón (4 hours). All times are one way. Ask for more information and a map at the Departamento Turismo Municipal office. Overnight treks are not recommended due to the large amount of volcanic ash. Updated: Jun 12, 2009.

Tours

Futaleufú has a half-dozen tour operators that offer not only rafting and kayaking expeditions, but also hiking, horseback riding and fly-fishing adventures. Each year the number of providers grows.

The following are popular:
Austral Excursions (Carrera s/n. Tel: 56-65-721239, E-mail: austral.excursions@hotmail.com).
Fly George Adventures (Aguirre Cerda 645. Tel: 56-65-721478, E-mail: quintin58@hotmail.com)
Futaleufú Explore (O'Higgins 772. Tel: 56-65-721527, URL: www.futaleufuexplore.com).
Patagonia Elements (Prat 497. Tel: 56-65-721514, E-mail: info@patagoniaelements.com, URL: www.patagoniaelements.com).
Zona Sur Rafting and Kayaking (Aguirre Cerda 697. Tel: 56-65-721281, E-mail: andrei.futeulefu@gmail.com).
Expediciones Chile is an exclusive rafting and kayaking tour agent that takes on-line reservations for excursions and has a lodge in Futaleufú: Hotelería Río Grande (US: Expediciones Chile, P.O. Box 752. Tel: Toll Free 1-888-488-9082, 1-208-629-5032; Futaleufú: Gabriela Mistral 296. Tel: 56-65-562639 / 56-65-721386, URL: www.exchile.com). Updated: May 31, 2009.

Lodging

Futaleufú has only a few luxury lodges. Most hostels are homier affairs of generally good quality. Many of the cheaper accommodations do not have locks on the door. With the relocation of Chaitén residents to Futaleufú, more hospedajes and campsites are opening up.

If you plan to camp, be advised that there is still quite a bit of ash on the ground and some campgrounds have been cleared better than others. Campgrounds are open November to March. **Los Coihues** is on the Chaitén road, about 500 meters (quarter mile) from town, on the river ($8 per person; hot shower, free firewood, fire pits, electricity).

Hospedaje Nuevo Estilo

(ROOMS: $10 – 13) Although under new administration, Hospedaje Nuevo Estilo is still called by its old name, Hotel Continental, by many in Futaleufú. This venerable old-timer has been serving travelers for decade with simple, budget-priced rooms, all with shared bathrooms. The singles are fine, but multi-bed accommodations tend to be crowded. Nuevo Estilo has locks on the doors and is an actual hotel, instead of a family-home-cum-inn. Its restaurant serves colaciones at lunchtime and à la carte at dinner. For an extra charge, guests may use the kitchen. Balmaceda 595. Tel: 72-1543, E-mail: nuevoestilofuta@hotmail.com. Updated: Jun 12, 2009.

Cabañas Aguas Blancas

(ROOMS: $60 – 90) Cabañas Aguas Blancas is a small affair: only two cabins for up to five people, near the outskirts if town. Each has a master bedroom on the first floor and another bedroom in the loft. You can have your breakfast on the front porch while watching the sunrise. In cool evenings, curl up for a good read in front of the living room's wood stove. There is also a hot tub in which to relax after a day of shooting the rapids. Cabaña Aguas Blancas is open all year. Hermanas Carrera 702. Tel: 56-65-721335, E-mail: aguasblancas@hotmail.com. Updated: Jul 01, 2009.

Hotel El Barranco

(ROOMS: $70 – 160) Hotel El Barranco is touted as a fishing lodge, but it offers something for all discerning visitors. This inn, completely made of native woods, looks rustic, but is first class. The nine rooms are equipped with two double beds and a trundle bed. The gleaming bathrooms have tree-trunk pedestal basins. El Barranco also has a feature little seen in Chile: a fully handicap-accessible suite. The hotel has a gourmet restaurant with an extensive wine list, and there is also a swimming pool. The tour desk offers not only fishing, but also rafting and kayaking excursions. Price includes breakfast buffet and taxes. O'Higgins 172. Tel: 56-65-721214, E-mail: lodge@elbarrancochile.cl, URL: www.elbarrancochile.cl. Updated: Jun 12, 2009.

Restaurants

Local restaurants close early, between 9 and 10 p.m. Those geared to the foreign tourist crowd are open later. Basic meals are more expensive than in other parts of Chile, with specials costing $7 at lunch and $10 at dinners. Local specialties include *cazuela de gallina* (hen stew) and *asado al palo* (lamb fire-roasted on an upright pole). Delicious desserts are made from *mosqueta* and other regional fruits. The town is building a public market on Carmona, near Laguna Espejo. Neighborhood general stores are common. Updated: May 31, 2009.

Sur Andes

(ENTREES: $6) Vegetarians can count on Sur Andes for tasty veggie dishes. Most of the plates consist of vegetables with rice, though tofu and other soy additions can be special-ordered in advance. There are some meat dishes, but Sur Andes is mostly vegetarian. The chef also makes some wicked desserts of local fruits, as well as *queque de algarroba* (carob cake). Sur Andes also has an adjacent hostel and artisan shop. Open daily 8:30 a.m. – 10 p.m. Pedro Aguirre Cerda 308. Tel: 56-65-721405, URL: www.surandes.com. Updated: Jun 12, 2009.

Cocina Americana

(ENTREES: $7 – 8) Despite what its name may imply to foreigners, Cocina Americana does not specialize in U.S. cuisine. Rather, this home-spun restaurant serves up dishes from Patagonia, both Chilean and Argentine. Portions are much more than you could possibly eat. Meals start with an appetizer of empanadas or pizza before moving on to the main course. Bring a hearty appetite. Open daily noon – 3 p.m., 6 – 11 p.m. Balmaceda 761. Updated: Jun 12, 2009.

Restaurant Martín Pescador

(ENTREES: $8) Each day the menu is different at Martín Pescador. Owner-chef Tatiana creates elegant, novo-Chilean dishes based on seasonal ingredients. This semi-round bistro with large windows and pleasant ambiance is a popular home-away-from-home for foreigner travelers. In evenings visitors share tales of whitewater and fly-fishing adventures. Open daily 5 – 10 p.m. (for food), bar until 1 – 2 a.m. Artisan / fishing shop is open during the day. Balmaceda 603.Tel: 56-65-721279, E-mail: villablancat@hotmail.com / tatianavillablanca@yahoo.com.ar. Updated: Jun 12, 2009.

RESERVA NACIONAL FUTALEUFÚ

(ADMISSION: Free) To the southeast of Futaleufú is the Reserva Nacional Futaleufú, a 12,065-hectare park founded in 1998 to protect the South Andean deer. Besides deer, the reserve is home to the puma, the kodkod, the Molina's hog-nosed skunk and the Patagonian fox. Bird species of note are the Magellanic Woodpecker, the Chilean Flicker, the White-crested Elaenia, the Thorn-tailed Rayadito, the Ringed Kingfisher, the Andean Condor, the Austral Parakeet and the Austral Pygmy Owl.

The park has four main trails:
Veranada Correntoso (distance: 8.5 km/5 mi, duration: 6 hours) leads to a waterfall.
Los Piedreros (5 km/3 mi, 3.5 hours) heads through a Chilean Cedar forest.
La Aguada (4 km/2.4 mi, 3 hours) extends from the Río Chico to the Las Escala Sector of the reserve.
Quila Seca (5.5 km/3.3 mi, 4 hours) winds into lenga forests inhabited by huemul.

There is a ranger station at the end of the Río Chico road and another at the Las Escalas sector, south of Futaleufú. Conaf is improving trails and building several refuges along the principal hiking trails. The work has a scheduled completion date of December 2009. A lot of volcanic ash is still present in the park. Until the refuges are built, overnight stays are not recommended. Stop by the Conaf office in Futaleufú for more information and a map of the park (Monday – Friday 8:30 a.m. – 1:30 p.m., 2:30 p.m. – 6 p.m. Alsea s/n and Carmona. E-mail: infopalena@sernatur.cl).

Bring water, as the streams are not potable due to volcanic ash. The best months to visit the reserve are September – April. The climate is wet and cold, with much snow from early fall to late spring. Wear warm and waterproof clothing. Updated: Jun 12, 2009.

Getting To and Away From Reserva Nacional Futaleufú

Reserva Nacional Futaleufú is 10 kilometers (6 mi) from Futaleufú village. No public transport goes to the reserve. A gravel road passes by the Río Chico sector, and another dirt-gravel one to Las Escalas. For information about arriving to Futaleufú town, see Getting To and Away From Futaleufú (p.401). Updated: Jun 01, 2009.

PALENA

🔺 657 m	👤 1,690	📞 65

Futaleufú may be the rafting capital of Patagonia, but Palena is the center for off-the-beaten-track trekking and horseback riding. Few tourists make it here to experience the magical atmosphere of this village situated 72 kilometers (43 mi) east of Villa Santa Lucía. Alto Palena, as the town is officially called, is the southern-most village in Chile's X Región de los Lagos. Updated: Apr 03, 2009.

NORTHERN PATAGONIA

Getting To and Away From Palena

From Santa Lucía take highway CH-235 45 kilometers (27 mi) east to Puerto Ramírez, the crossroads for Palena-Futaleufú. The road then heads east-southeast to Alto Palena. The village has a Copec gas station (daily 8:30 a.m. – 12:30 p.m., 2:30 p.m. – 6:30 p.m. H. De Mendoza s/n).

Alto Palena has no central bus station, but the following buses run through the town:

To Futaleufú: Cumbres Nevadas (Wednesday 3:30 p.m., Monday and Friday 8 a.m., $5).

To Puerto Montt: **Altamirano** (Tel: 31-4143; by way of Futaleufú, Monday, Wednesday 6 a.m.), **Transaustral** (Tel: 56-65-741319; Monday 6:30 a.m.) Also **Frontera del Sur** (Tel: 56-9-84488837).

To Villa Santa Lucía and Chaitén: Bus **Río Palena** (Tel: 56-65-741280 / 56-65-741319; Monday, Wednesday, Friday 8 a.m.).

The airstrip is only used for charter flights. Updated: Apr 13, 2009.

RESERVA NACIONAL LAGO PALENA

Reserva Nacional Lago Palena, created in 1965, is a 41,380-hectare park composed of Andean foothills ranging from 600 meters (1,950 ft) to 2,024 meters (6,578 ft). The highest peak is Cerro El Serrucho east of Valle Vista Hermosa. The lake for which the park is named, straddles the Argentine border, and is called Lago General Vinttner in the sister republic.

Reserva Nacional Lago Palena is divided into three major sectors: Zancudo, Valle Vista Hermosa sector and Río Corto. The park offers a variety of sporting activities, such as hiking, trekking, horseback riding and fly fishing.

A network of trails wends through the beech forest with Lenga, Magellan's beech and Antarctic beech. From Palena to Lago Verde is a 65-kilometer (39-mile) stretch of the Sendero de Chile. It has two parts. The first part traverses the countryside from Palena to Valle El Azul and is heavily used by locals (27 km/16.2 mi).

The second leg, from Valle El Azul to the boundary between the X Región de los Lagos and XI Región de Aysén (38 km/22.8 mi), is less popular. The trail then continues into the neighboring region of Lago Verde. For complete details see: www.senderodechile.cl. If you are trekking in the park or on the Sendero de Chile, bring a good map and compass. The map provided by Conaf, the national park service, is rudimentary.

The forest flora is principally lenga, with coigüe de Magallanes and ñirre. Mammal inhabitants include the Patagonian fox, the South American grey fox, the puma, the Chilean miniature deer, the nutria, the South Andean deer as well as the non-native wild pig and American mink.

Birdwatchers can look for the Andean Condor, the White-throated Hawk, the Crested Caracara, the Common Barn Owl, the Magellanic Woodpecker, the Caracara, the Magellan Goose, the Ringed Kingfisher, the Black-necked Swan, the Austral Thrush, the Great Grebe and the Neotropic Cormorant, as well as various gulls and hummingbirds. Updated: Apr 22, 2009.

When to Go

The reserve's climate is cold and rainy. Annual precipitation is 900 – 1200 millimeters (35.5 – 47 inches) per year; June is the wettest month. Temperatures range from 4°C to 12 °C (49 – 54 °F). In winter, temperatures dip below freezing. Warm and waterproof clothing is essential due to the park's climatic extremes. Updated: Apr 21, 2009.

Getting To and Away From Reserva Nacional Lago Palena

The reserve is accessible only on horse or by hiking the path. Access is best in summer, when the ranger posts and centro ambiental are open. It is also possible, but difficult, November – December and April– May. Updated: Apr 22, 2009.

Lodging

If you plan to stay overnight in the park, try Refugio Municipal in the Zancudo sector, Refugio Conaf in the Valle Vista Hermosa sector, or campsites (with fire pits, latrines and water) in the Río Corto sector. No food services are available within the park; a gas stove is necessary when backcountry camping, as wood fires pose a hazard. Along the Sendero de Chile are rural hostels and other services. For a list of these, visit: www.palenaonline.cl or www.cuencadelpalena-queulat.cl. Updated: Apr 22, 2009.

NORTHERN PATAGONIA

LA JUNTA

 1,650 m 1,280 67

Seventy kilometers (42 mi) from Santa Lucía is La Junta, *El Pueblo del Encuentro* (The Place of Encounters). La Junta is spanish for "the meeting," and is located where the Rosselot River meets the Río Palena to continue its journey to the sea. Early settlers used to drive their cattle to La Junta to be transported by ship to faraway markets.

For many years, this settlement was just a transitory meeting place. The town was officially founded in 1963, when the government awarded large tracts of land to families who promised to devote themselves to farming. The construction of the Carretera Austral (1976 – 1996) marked a turning point for La Junta. For years La Junta was more strongly aligned economically and culturally with neighboring Argentina, but the Carretera Austral later helped to bring Chilean culture to the town.

Today La Junta serves as a convenient stop for travelers journeying on the Carretera Austral. At the Copec station at the north entrance of town, bicyclists and motorcyclists rest and motorists refuel while hitchhikers wait for another ride.

If you stay for a night or two you can check out the Reserva Nacional Lago Rosselot. This reserve, created in 1983, protects 12,725 hectares of virgin evergreen and lenga forest. It is a cold-climate rainforest, receiving 3,500 millimeters (138 inches) of precipitation per year. Temperatures in January reach 12°C (54°F) and dip to 2°C (36°F) in July.

Most of the Reserva Nacional Lago Rosselot is inaccessible. From La Junta, a steep five-kilometer (3-mile) trail wends to the top of a ridge with tremendous vistas of the Río Palena valley (2 hours). The eastern boundary of the reserve is Lago Rosselot. Trout and salmon fishing in these pure waters is considered to be some of the best in the northern Aysén region.

A 75-kilometer (45-mi) road goes from La Junta to Puerto Raúl Marín Balmaceda on the Pacific coast. In the summer the fishing village has superb fishing and bird watching opportunities. Tourists come to enjoy the white sand beaches, soak in the hot springs and explore the Río Palena's delta. Fishing and birdwatching are superb. Other marine fauna are sighted in season, including sea lions, toninas and whales. Lodging and basic services are available. The village can also be reached by ship from Chiloé.

From La Junta another road heads eastward to Lago Verde (70 km / 142 mi, 1.5 hours). The green lake is in the extreme northeast of the Palena–Queulat river basin. From the village Lago Verde you can go on treks and horseback excursions. Salmon and trout fishing are also good. The Lago Verde–Las Mellizas leg of the Sendero de Chile can be done on foot or on horseback. The trail is 64 kilometers (38.5 mi) long and passes through the Cacique Blanco River Valley. This is a continuation of the Palena–Lago Verde part of the Sendero (for complete details, see: www.senderodechile.cl). Lago Verde pueblo also has camping and hostels. Several guides lead trekking and horseback tours.

February is festival time in La Junta. The second week is La Semana de La Junta, with boating and other competitions. During the last week of February the village holds a rodeo.

Getting To and Away From La Junta

La Junta is on the Carretera Austral, 68 kilometers (41 mi) south of Villa Santa Lucía and 341 kilometers (205 mi) north of Coyhaique. During the summer 2008-09 season, the Chilean government widened the Carretera Austral, with the aim to eventually pave it. South of La Junta the highway is closed from 10 a.m. to 4 p.m. La Junta has mechanic shops and the only gas station between Chaitén and Puyuhuapi.

Bus offices are within a few blocks of the main plaza: **Transportes Altamirano** (Moraleda 13. Tel: 56-67-314143), **Buses Becker** (Portales and Angamos, Tel: 56-67-232167), **Buses Entre Verdes** (Lynch and Varas) and **Buses Queulat** (from Restaurant El Transportista).

To Coyhaique: $20, 7 hours, **Altimirano** (Monday, Wednesday, Friday 6:30 a.m.), **Becker** (Sunady 11 a.m.), **Queulat** (Saturday 2 p.m.)

To Puyuhuapi and Puerto Cisnes: **Entre Verdes** (Monday, Wednesday, Friday 7 a.m., $4 / $8.60, 1 hour / 2.5 hours).
To Lago Verde: **Altimirano** (Tuesday, Thursday, Saturday 5 p.m., $6, 2 hours).

NORTHERN PATAGONIA

To Chaitén: (by way of Santa Lucía, meeting bus from Futaleaufú to the port): Monday, Tuesday, Friday 9:30 a.m., $15, 3 hours; (direct) Queulat (Friday 3 p.m., $16).

To Futaleufú: Altamirano (Wednesday 6 a.m., Thursday 2 p.m., $15, 2.5 hours).
To Puerto Montt (by way of Futaleufú and Argentina): **Altamirano** (Monday, Wednesday 6 a.m., $50, 14 – 15 hours).

To Puerto Raúl Marín Balmaceda: Camping Los Avellanos (summer only, Thursday 8 a.m.). This coastal city is also accessible by way of Naviera Austral's Ruta Cordillera vehicle-passenger ferry that runs between Quellón, Chiloé and Puerto Chacabuco (URL: www.navieraustral.cl).

Other buses pass through on their way north and south. Hitchhiking out of La Junta is a bit difficult. Updated: Jan 23, 2009.

Services
La Junta has most services that travelers need. On the plaza are the **health post** and **tourism office** (summer only, daily 10 a.m. – 1 p.m., 2 – 6 p.m., URL: www.cuencadelpalena-queulat.cl). **Conaf** has information on the Reserva Nacional Lago Rosselot and Parque Nacional Queulat (Monday – Friday 8:30 a.m. – 5:30 p.m. Patricio Lynch s/n, half a block west of the Carretera Austral. Tel: 56-67-314128). La Junta has no bank or pharmacy. The Valle Risopatrón **Copec gas station** is the Chilexpress agent and can change Argentine pesos (daily 8 a.m. – 11 p.m.); also try **Transportes Altimirano**. There is a **post office**, as well as several Internet and phone providers. **Ciber Ruta Austral** has Skype (daily 10 a.m. – 1:30 p.m., 2:30 – 11 p.m. Centro Comercial, 2nd floor, Portales and Lynch).

Lodging
Most hotels are closed in winter. Cheaper hostels are often booked up by road crews. Some families rent rooms in their homes ($10–12).

Camping Los Avellanos is open only in January and February (Carretera Austral, 3 km/1.8 mi north of La Junta. Tel: 56-9-95957815).

Hotel Espacio y Tiempo (Carretera Austral s/n. Tel: 56-67-314141 / 314264, E-mail: espacio@patagoniachile.cl/info@espacioytiempo.cl, URL: www.espacioytiempo.cl, single $75, double $108).

Hostería Copihue (Varas 611. Tel: 56-67-314184, E-mail: ninodelpatagonia@123mail.com / hcopihuepatagon@hotmail.com, $17 per person).

Hospedaje Tía Lety (Varas 596. Tel: 56-9-87635191, $20 per person).

Restaurants
La Junta has few restaurants. Many hostels serve breakfast and some serve other meals as well. **Restaurant El Transportista** (Carretera Austral, across from the Copec gas station) and **Mi Casita de Té** (Carretera Austral and Lynch. Tel: 31-4206) are two good options. There also are several small general stores and bakeries. Updated: Jul 01, 2009.

PUERTO PUYUHUAPI

 5 m   505   67

The Chono indigenous peoples were the first inhabitants of the Puyuhuapi area. In the Chono language, Puyuhuapi means *puyu*, a sweet flower and *huapi*, island.

History
The modern village's story began in the Sudenten German village of Rossbach (today Hranice, Czech Republic). Taking advantage of the Chilean government's offer of land to pioneers, Otto Uebel, Ernesto Ludwig and Walther and Helmut Hopperdietzel made the journey to Patagonia. Their plans to bring more immigrants were interrupted by World War II, but other family members arrived in 1947.

The Germans organized a village where each person was charged with a certain job. Otto Uebel, a chemical engineer, headed up the animal husbandry and farming sections. Walther Hopperdietzel started a carpet factory and opened the first general store. His brother Helmut was the telegraphist, postman and roadwork expert. Ernesto Ludwig, an agronomist, was in charge of building houses and boats, running the sawmill and repairing machinery. Chilotes, or migrants from Chiloé island, were also key in the settling of Puyuhuapi. Most originally came as contract workers, but stayed on as residents.

Puyuhuapi was originally known for boat building, but the demand for wooden boats declined with the introduction of fiberglass crafts. In the 1980s, the local economy became more dependent on fishing. Over-exploitation has forced fishermen to go further asea for conger, manta ray and merluza (hake). Locals have also started farming salmon.

Alfombras de Puyuhuapi still makes rugs, renowned for their fine quality. In summer, the factory gives tours (20 minutes, $10 per group).

Holidays and Festivals

Every February Puyuhuapi has a historical and cultural celebration called Semana Aniversario. Regattas, fishing competitions and diving are some of the activities. During the Encuentro Multicultural, locals serve up Mapuche-Williche gastronomy and German pastries.

Getting To and Away From Puyuhuapi

There is a gas station on the north edge of town, on the other side of the bridge (Calle Aysén, half-block off the highway). During the summer months the Carretera Austral may close for part of the day for roadwork. Contact the tourism office for more information.

Residencial Ventisquero (O'Higgins, between Av. Uebel and Portales, Tel: 56-67-325130) is the bus ticket sales office and ersatz terminal. During the off-season, services are less frequent.

To Coyhaique: $16, 5-6 hours. **Transporte Laguna** (Sunday 10 a.m.), **Daniela** (Sunday, Tuesday, Friday 2 p.m.), **Altamirano** (Monday, Wednesday, Friday 8 a.m.).

To Futaleufú: **Daniela** (Tuesday, Thursday, Saturday 2 p.m., $20, 6-7 hours).

To Puerto Cisnes: **Entre Verdes** (Monday, Wednesday, Friday 8 a.m., $8, 3 hours).

To Lago Verde: **Altamirano** (Tuesday, Thursday, Saturday 4 p.m.).

To La Junta: $5, 3 hours. **Laguna** (Saturday 3 p.m.), **Entre Verdes** (Monday, Wednesday, Friday 7 p.m.), **Altamirano** (Tuesday, Thursday, Saturday 4 p.m.).

To Chaitén: **Queulat** (Monday, Friday 2:30 p.m., $18) or go to Villa Santa Lucía with a Futaleufú-bound bus and wait for another from there. Updated: May 31, 2009.

Services

Puyuhuapi has limited services. During the summer, only the **tourism office** dispenses good information (Monday – Saturday, 10 a.m. – 2 p.m., 4 – 7 p.m. Av. Otto Uebel. URL: www.cuencadelpalena-queulat.cl). The **police** post is also on this same road. Puyuhuapi has no bank or ATM. **Aónikenk** may be able to exchange money (Hamburgo 16).

The **post office** and phone office is at Residencial Ventisquero. Several places have Internet, but can't really be considered cyber cafes since they only have one computer each. ($2 per hour). The **hospital** is on O'Higgins, two blocks from the highway.

SHOPPING

Alfombras de Puyuhuapi (Monday-Friday 9 a.m. – noon, 3:30 – 7 p.m., weekends and holidays 10 a.m. – noon. Ca. Aysén s/n. Tel: 56-67-325131. E-mail: alfombra@puyuhuapi.com).

Comité Adulto Mayor specializes in woolens (Av. Uebel, east of Mistral. Tel: 56-9-76516416).

Artesanías Salas has wood crafts (two blocks north of Avenida Uebel, between the hospital and the church. Tel: 56-67-325238). Updated: Jul 07, 2009.

Things to See and Do

The tourism office has a pamphlet (in English and Spanish) that guides you on a walking tour with explanations of the town's history, architecture and natural beauty. Four of the original German houses remain, all painted golden ochre. The original German cemetery, in an grove of evergreens, is behind Casa Ludwig on the road to Coyhaique. The town also has *casas puyuhuapi* with gambrel roofs.

The Río Pascuahas good fishing holes and is populated with birds such as the Little Blue Heron, the Flying Steamer Duck, the Black-necked Swan and the Ringed Kingfisher. With luck, you may also see toninas and dolphins leaping out of the fjord's waters.

Puyuhuapi is also known for its hot springs at the edge of the sea. **Termas de Ventisquero**, with wood-decked pools and tea room, is the most accessible (summer: daily 9 a.m. – 11 p.m., 6km/3.6 mi south of town off the Carretera Austral. Tel: 56-67-325228, E-mail: termasvp@gmail.com. Entry: adults $24, children $16). Another hot spring, accessible only by boat, is **Termas de Puyuhuapi**. Parque Nacional Queulat, with its extraordinary hanging glacier, is 20 kilometers (12 mi) south of the Puyuhuapi village.

Tours

YR Cabañas has boat tours along the coast (Costanera 177. Tel: 56-9-8748586; $20 for up to four persons, one hour).

Hostería Carretera Austral offers boat tours, trips to Parque Nacional Queulat (Av. Uebel s/n. Tel: 56-67-325119, E-mail: hosteriacarreteraustral@gmail.com).

Lodging

Camping La Sirena has roofed sites (Costanera and Hamburgo. Tel: 56-67-325101; $3 per person).

Residencial Ventisquero (O'Higgins, between Av. Uebel and Portales, Tel: 56-67-325130; $10 per person).

Puyuhuapi Lodge and Spa Termal on Bahía Dorita, accessible only by launch, is the place to go for an ultimate escape from the rigueur of traveling or city life (Santiago: Fidel Oteiza 1921, oficina 1006. Tel: 56-2-2256489, E-mail: info@patagonia-connection.com, URL: www.patagonia-connection.com;, from $184 for one or two persons, special packages available).

Restaurants

You'll find supermarkets along Puyuhuapi's main avenue. Cocinería eateries are cheaper than traditional restaurants. Some hotels have diners.

Aónikenk (Hamburgo 16. Tel: 56-67-325208, E-mail: aonikenkturismo@yahoo.com, URL: www.rutapatagonia.com).

Cocinería Estrella del Sur (Av. Uebel and Mistral. Tel: 56-9-88388470).

Restaurant Rossbach (Aysén, one block from highway. Tel: 56-67-325203).

PARQUE NACIONAL QUEULAT

In the middle of Chile's Northern Patagonia, where the Cordillera Andino Patagónica plunges into the sea and hot springs steam at the edge of Fiordo Queulat, the Spanish believed they would find the mythical *Ciudad de los Césares* (City of the Caesars). This city, founded by the survivors of a Spanish shipwreck, was believed to be a rich place made of gold, silver and diamonds. Only the native Chono, however, recognized the true riches of this magical landscape with lush rainforests and majestic glaciers. They named it *Quenelat*, meaning far away lands or the sound of the waterfalls. Today we call it Parque Nacional Queulat.

Parque Nacional (PN) Queulat was established in 1983 to protect the virgin forest. The park's 154,093 hectares are divided in to three sectors. Sector Angostura is north of Puyuhuapi, on the shores of Lago Risopatrón. South of that village, at Kilometer 200 of the Carretera Austral, is Sector Ventisquero, named after the *ventisquero colgante* or hanging glacier. Further on is Sector Portezuelo. The highest peaks are Alto Nevado (2,225 m/7,232 ft), Overo (2,061 m/6,699 ft) and Ventisquero (1,745 m/5,672 ft). The park has two glacial fields and several major rivers, the most important of which are Queulat, Ventisquero, Bordolí and Pedregoso. The park has a cold temperate coastal rainforest climate. About 3,500 – 4,000 millimeters (138 – 158 inches) of rain falls per year. The eastern part of the park is dryer. Temperatures vary between 4° and 9°C (39° – 48°F).

PN Queulat has a rich biodiversity divided into two ecosystems. The Bosque Patagónicos is composed of lenga beech, Magellan's beech and Chilean holly. The Magellanic woodpecker, the Austral parakeet, the Andean condor, and the Black-throated huet-huet flit through the rainforest. Mammalian denizens include the Chilean miniature deer, the kodkod, the puma, the Southern river otter, the Patagonian fox, and possibly the elusive austral opposum. Two frog species are also found here: the Chilean four-eyed frog and Darwin's frogs. In Fiordo de Queulat you might spot whales, toninas and multitudes of seabirds.

Getting To and Away From Parque Nacional Queulat

Parque Nacional Queulat's Angostura sector is 40 kilometers (24 mi) north of Puerto Puyuhuapi. Other sectors begin 20 kilometers (12 mi) south of Puyuhuapi village (unpaved), or 165 kilometers (99 mi) north of Coyhaique. During the summer months the Carretera Austral may close for parts of the day for roadwork. Consult the tourism offices in the region for updates.

To Sector Angostura: From Puyuhuapi, take any bus heading to La Junta or other northern destination and hop off.

To Sectors Ventisquero and Portazuelo: Any Puyuhuapi-Coyhaique bus will get you there. Sector Ventisquero can be done as a day trip from Puyuhuapi. Updated: Jun 10, 2009.

Things to See and Do

PN Queulat is the perfect place to go sailing, sea kayaking and fishing. The most popular activity, though, is **hiking**. In Sector Angostura, explore **Sendero a Laguna los Pumas** (distance: 2.5 km / 1.5 mi, difficulty: medium – difficult). The trail begins at the Angostura campsite and wends through evergreen forest to Laguna los Pumas, a small lake surrounded by lenga trees.

Sector Ventisquero has three trails:

Sendero al Mirador (distance: 200 m/650 ft, difficulty: easy)—goes to the confluence of Ventisqueros and Desagüe Rivers, where from the lookout point you can see the Ventisquero Colgante.

Sendero a Laguna Témpanos (600 m/1,950 ft, easy)—Crosses Río Ventisqueros over a hanging bridge to Laguna Témpanos, which is fed by the hanging glacier.

Sendero sobre la Morrena (3.2 km/2 mi, medium)—This steep two- to three-hour hike climbs through evergreen forest and over a glacier moraine to a beautiful vantage point of the glacier. Off this is an interpretive trail,

El Aluvión, where visitors can learn about the glacier's dynamics.

In summer, boats sail Laguna Témpanos to the Ventisquero Colgante.

The southernmost part of the park, Sector Portezuelo, has two paths:

Sendero del Padre García (150 m/500 ft, easy)—This trail begins 32 kilometers (19.2 mi) south of Puyuhuapi, on the left side of the Carretera Austral. It goes through dense rainforest to a small waterfall.

Sendero Bosque Encantado (1.7 km/1 mi, medium)—Takes you through evergreen forest to the tree line. There you'll find a

lagoon within a natural rock amphitheater. It is possible to observe the *témpanos* (ice floes), which give birth to the Río Cascada.

Sector Angostura has a ranger station, hiking trails and four (free) campsites (fire pits, potable water, bathhouse with cold-water showers). No entry fee is charged. Sector Ventisquero has a ranger station two kilometers (1.2 mi) off the road, a Centro de Información Ambiental and 10 camp sites (fire pits, potable water, bathhouse with hot-water showers; $10 per person). Entry to this part of the park costs $6. Sector Portezuelo has no services. This part of the park is free. Even though all camp sites have fire pits, Conaf asks that you use a camp stove, to prevent forest fires. Updated: Jun 10, 2009.

PUERTO CISNES

 10 m   5,739   67

Puerto Cisnes is a pretty little village and port of call for the weekly Quellon-Puerto Chacabuco passenger ferry. The village of Puerto Cisnes is filled with colorful boats that bob in the cove's clear water. Mother-of-pearl sands glitter in the momentary sun, leading toward a village backdropped by deep emerald mountains, inspiring the name, *La Perla del Litoral*, or The Pearl of the Coast.

The thin Río San Luís, divides the village into two. The main plaza, with a church, municipal building and public library, is on the far side of the San Luís. The main road is called Avenida Arturo Prat, also called Avenida Costanera. One block inland is Calle Piloto Pardo which, after crossing a pedestrian bridge spanning the San Luís, becomes Calle Gabriela Mistral. At the far end of the bay is the port where the weekly Quellón-Puerto Chacabuco passenger ferry arrives.

History

The Puerto Cisnes area was settled in the 1930s by loggers and fishermen who needed a temporary camp. In the 1950s, people were encouraged to migrate to the town, and Puerto Cisnes was founded on Feb. 11, 1954. The migration included the Italian Catholic missionary order *Obra de Don Guanella* which, over the next decade brought the town's two most venerated characters together: Eugenia Pirzio-Biroli—the many-year mayor responsible for convincing her friend General Augusto Pinochet to construct the highway to her village—and Padre

Antonio Ronchi— who devoted his almost four-decade career to improving the social and economic lives of Ayseninos.

In 1965, Puerto Cisnes became the seat of the regional comuna, which includes Puyuhuapi, La Junta and many other coastal communities. In recent decades, however, Puerto Cisnes' economic base has suffered severe blows. Overfishing has led to salmon farming, but the farms have recently become infected with disease. Farmers have begun raising trout, which earns less than half the price of salmon. Shellfish extraction is at a standstill due to the red tide (*marea roja*), a deadly toxin. The tremendous tourism potential of this village remains untapped.

There are several recommended hiking trails around the village. Paseo Virgen de las Rozas, which begins at the end of Calle Sotomayor, leads to a sanctuary on the slopes of Cerro Leucotón with views of the bay and mountains (10 minutes).

Another trail heads east to Laguna Escondida, a lake surrounded by coigüe, canelo and quila forest. This is one of the best fly-fishing spots. Cerro Gilberto, nine hours north of the city, has spectacular views of the canals, rivers and islands.

Although local fishermen have struggled, fly fishing is a popular sport in the area, particularly at Laguna Escondida, Isla Magdalena and Río Cisnes, the catches being trout and salmon. At sea, anglers can try their luck with austral merluza. A 30-minute journey leads to the *lobería*, a colony of over 100 sea lions. You might also see sea birds and dolphins.

Just off-shore is Isla Magdalena, Chile's second largest island, and home to Parque Nacional Isla Magdalena. Created in 1967, this park has few visitors. It has thick temperate rainforest and Volcán Mentolat (1,660 m/5,395 ft). There is also a natural hot spring on the island.

Fishing permeates every aspect of Cisnense life. Not only is it the mainstay of the local economy, but it also finds its way into the artisan work. Residents specialize in fish skin leather, which is used to make wallets, belts and other items.

Holidays and Festivals

Puerto Cisne has several celebrations each year. The **Festival Costumbrista y Pescado Frito** is at the end of January. This festival showcases crafts, gastronomy and music. **Semana Cisnense** is held during the first week of February and features a marathon, a triathlon, lumbering, a rodeo and *tugar-tugar*—a dance contest of different folk and popular steps. In mid-June is the **Fiesta de San Pedro**, feting the fishermen's patron saint with regattas and a seaside Mass.

When to Go

Puerto Cisnes has rain 320 days per year. Winters are wet, with a cold that seeps into your bones. The tourism season is short, from mid-January through February.

Getting To and Away From Puerto Cisnes

The turn-off from the Carretera Austral for Puerto Cisnes is 256 kilometers (154 mi) south of Chaitén and 197 kilometers (118 mi) north of Coyhaique. The Copec gas station is located in the north part of town (daily 8 a.m. – 11:30 p.m. José M. Caro 37). Puerto Cisnes also has a mechanic and a tire repair shop.

Puerto Cisnes has no main bus terminal. Offices are located in either the south or the north sector of the village. In the south are Terraustral (Piloto Pardo 368. Tel: 56-67-346757) and Don Oscar (Tel: 56-67-346626).

North are Entre Verdes (Paquetería Ángel, Mistral 664) and Taxi Buses Axel (Espiga de Agua shop, Sotomayor and 21 de Mayo. Tel: 56-67-346141).

Buy tickets well in advance, as they sell out, especially for Coyhaique. Ask if the bus can pick you up at your hotel.

To Coyhaique: $14, 4 hours, Terraustral (Monday – Friday 6 a.m., 8 a.m., Saturday 6 a.m., Sunday 10 a.m.), Taxi Buses Axel (Monday – Saturday 6 a.m.), Don Oscar (Monday noon, Friday 3 p.m.).

To Puyuhuapi and La Junta: Entre Verdes (Monday, Wednesday, Friday 4 p.m., $4 / $8.60, 1 hour / 2.5 hours).

Naviera Austral's Ruta Cordillera passenger ferry makes a port of call in Puerto Cisnes. Buy tickets from Olivia Gómez Goio (Prat 07, Tel: 56-67-346426 / 56-8-4482837, E-mail: gomezolivia2@gmail.com).

To the north: Tuesday 8:30 a.m., Thursday 9 p.m., Saturday 1:20 a.m.; butaca seat, non-resident $30 – 57.

To the south: Wednesday 11:40 a.m., Thursday 4:30 p.m., Sunday 11:30 p.m.; butaca seat, non-resident $19-46).The boat also carries vehicles. Consult the website for prices (URL: www.navieraustral.cl). Updated: Jun 12, 2009.

Services

Most services are in the main part of the village, north of Río San Luís. The **tourism office** operates in the public library from mid-January to mid-February (Sotomayor 761). At other times of the year, you can get information at www.cisnes.org. In this part of town you'll find **Internet cafés** (Monday – Saturday 10 a.m. – 1:30 p.m., 3 – 11 p.m. 10 de Julio 331; $1.60 per hour), several call centers, a **post office** (Monday – Friday 9:30 a.m. – 1 p.m., 3 – 6:30 p.m, Saturday 10:30 a.m. – 12:30 p.m Caro, between Mistral and Sotomayor) and a **Western Union/Chilexpress** agent (Mistral 443). There is also a hospital and police office.

South of Río San Luís is a **pharmacy** (Magallanes and Chorrillos) and there's also an **ATM** at the supermarket on the corner of Piloto Pardo and Condell (Monday – Saturday 9 a.m. – 11 p.m., Sunday 10 a.m – 2 p.m, 5 – 10:30 p.m.; MasterCard, Cirrus, Visa, Plus). The clostest monetary facilities north of here are at Futaleufú and Palena, both of which have banks. To the south, there is an ATM at Mañihuales, and Coyhaique has both banks and money exchanges.

Tours

Several guides offer boat and sport fishing trips: **Javier Catalán Alvarado** (Av. Prat s/n. Tel: 56-9-9179487), **Lidia Alda López Arteaga** (Pasaje Las Rosas, Tel: 56-67-346830, E-mail: rodrigoduamante@gmail.com), **Olga Soto Mayorga** (Séptimo de Línea 112. Tel: 56-67-346408, E-mail: tourbellavista@yahoo.es, URL: www.tourbellavista.cl).

Lodging

Many budget and low to mid-range hostels are on Mistral, between 21 de Mayo and Séptimo de Línea, north of Río San Luís.

Cabañas, Camping y Quincho El Salmón (5 km/3 mi before Puerto Cisnes. Tel: 56-8-4413287).

Residencial Santa Teresita (Mistral 910, Tel: 56-67-346820; $10 per person).

Residencial Bella Vista (Séptimo de Línea 112. Tel: 56-67-346408, E-mail: tourbellavista@yahoo.es, URL: www.tourbellavista.cl; $14 per person with breakfast).

Cabañas El Guairao (Costanera 353. Tel: 56-67-346473, E-mail: elguairao@yahoo.com; 1 person $50, 2 persons $60).

On Isla Magdalena, **Blanca Morrás** has a hospedaje and camping (Tel: 56-8-4788674).

Restaurants

Most eating establishments close in the winter, but many hostels prepare meals for their guests. On Aguirre Cerda, between Sotomayor and Mistral, are several fast-food stands. Fish is plentiful, but not other seafood (due to red tide). Minimarkets operate in both parts of town.

Restaurant El Guairao (Costanera 353.Tel: 56-67-346473, E-mail: elguairao@yahoo.com).

Restaurant Panorámico (Steffens and Condell. Tel: 56-67-346908, E-mail: restoranpanoramico@yahoo.es). Updated: Jun 12, 2009.

PUERTO AYSÉN

 5 m 22,360 67

Once upon a time Puerto Aysén was the most important city in this part of the Patagonia. Before being supplanted by Coyhaique in 1974, it was the capital of XI Región General Carlos Ibáñez del Campos. Puerto Aysén (also spelled Aisén) was also the most important southern port, until the river mouth filled with silt and maritime trade moved to Puerto Chacabuco. Today Puerto Aysén is the first large city travelers encounter after arriving by boat to Puerto Chacabuco.

The city is on the banks of the Río Aysén, which is spanned by Puente Presidente Ibáñez. This bridge, built between 1964 and 1966, is now a national monument. Just south of it is the Galería de Artesanos (camino a Puerto Chacabuco and Lago Riesco).

Puerto Aysén has several pleasant parks. You can find many of the town's businesses around the Plaza de Armas. Parque Municipal is on Isla Diaz, just in front of downtown.

Aside from walks around the city, Puerto Aysén also offers a few indoor activities. Stop by the **cathedral** on the Plaza and check out the large, hand-carved altar screen of the Last Supper.

On occasion, the **Cine Municipal** hosts theatrical productions, music concerts, movies and other productions (Calle Esmeralda, Plaza de Armas). The public **library** has a great collection of old photographs (O'Higgins and Sargento Aldea).

If you want to get out of the city, you can head to **Laguna Los Palos**, 10 kilometers (6 mi) north. This lake in a valley of the Andes ranges is a popular place to fish, relax or take a boating tour down the Río Aysén. **Lago Riesco** (25 km/15 mi southeast) has a beach lined with arrayanes (*Myrceugenella apiculata*), a member of the Myrtle family, with stunning fragrant white flowers. In summer, a free *balsa* (small boat) takes passengers to Lago Portales, where you might spot a puma or fox.

When to Go

During the summer you can catch concerts here. Cerro Mirador provides a nice view over the town and river (Latauro, between Carrera and Teniente Merino). If you still feel like stretching your legs, stroll down to Muelle La Balsa, where the fishermen dock.

On the Camino Cementerio, northwest of the center, is the tomb of Padre Antonio Ronchi, the venerated Catholic missionary priest. Across the road is the wharf and Santuario San Pedro where every June 29 the patron saint of fishermen is honored.

Throughout the month of January, locals celebrate the city's founding with fireworks, dances, concerts and other activities. Ciriaco Álvarez, originally of Chonchi descent, was one of the area's pioneer settlers, arriving in the 1880s. Between modern-day Puerto Aysén and Puerto Chacabuco he built a warehouse for goods like cypress wood, which earned him the title *El Rey del Ciprés*, The King of Cypress.

The area consisted of a hodge-podge of houses until 1928, when the hamlet had grown enough to petition the federal government for recognition as a town. Puerto Aysén later became the capital of the XI Región. Puerto Aysen is not as important as it once was, but the town is still a pleasant place to visit.

Getting To and Away From Puerto Aysén

BY TAXI
A taxi to Río Los Palos or Lago Riesco costs about $24 round trip. **Transportes Vilu** (Ibar 671. Tel: 56-67-335050), **Taxis Trapanada** (Pasaje Los Helechos 202. Tel: 56-67-529090).

BY BUS
Only two bus companies stop at Puerto Aysén: **Suray** (Av. Municipal, between Sargento Aldea and Ramírez) and **Sao Paulo** (Serrano, between Sargento Aldea and Carrera).

To Coyhaique: 1 hour—**Suray** (half-hourly Monday – Friday 7 a.m. – 9:20 p.m., Saturday 7:50 a.m. – 9:30 p.m., Sunday 8:55 a.m – 9:30 p.m. $3), **Sao Paulo** (Monday – Friday every 1.5 hours 8:30 a.m. – 8:30 p.m., Saturday every 1.5 – 2 hours 10 a.m.-8 p.m., Sunday and holidays every 2 – 2.5 hours 11 a.m. – 8 p.m., $2.40).

To Puerto Chacabuco: **Suray** (weekdays every 20 minutes, less frequently on weekends, Monday – Friday 7 a.m. – 9:20 p.m., Saturday 8 a.m. – 9:30 p.m, Sunday 9 a.m. – 9:30 p.m., $1.20, 15 – 20 minutes).

BY AIR
Both national carriers have offices in Puerto Aysén: LAN (Sargento Aldea and O'Higgins) and Sky Airlines (Teniente Merino, Plaza de Armas). Flights depart from the airport in Balmaceda, 55 kilometers (33 mi) east of Coyhaique. Updated: Jun 01, 2009.

Services
Puerto Aysén has a full slate of services. **Cámara de Turismo** has information Monday – Friday 9 a.m. – 1 p.m., 3 – 7 p.m.; January – February 9:30 a.m.-10 p.m., Saturday 9 a.m. – 8 p.m., Sunday 9 a.m.-8 p.m. (Teniente Merino 668. Plaza de Armas. Tel: 56-67-332716 / 527425, E-mail: turismoaysen@gmail.com, URL: www.turismoaysen.cl / www.puertoaysen.cl).

Banks are open Monday-Friday 9 a.m. – 2 p.m.: **Banco del Estado** (Carrera and O'Higgins, Plaza de Armas. ATM: MasterCard, Cirrus; exchanges U.S. dollars and euros). The following bank ATMs accept MasterCard, Cirrus, Visa and Plus: **Banco Chile** (Prat and Carrera, Plaza de Armas), **Santander** and **BCI** (both at Sargento Aldea and Prat). There are no casas de cambio. **Chilexpress** is the Western Union agent (Teniente Merino, Plaza de Armas).

Lodging

Camping La Plancha (Camino Lago Los Palos, Km 7. Tel: 56-9-8878572, URL: www. ecoturismolaplancha.cl).

La Posada del Camionero (Sargento Aldea 1860. Tel: 56-67-332548) $14 per person.
Hotel Plaza (O'Higgins 613. Tel: 56-67-332784) has singles with common bathrooms $20, double with private bathrooms $50.
Hotel Caicahues (Michimalonco 660. Tel: 56-67-335680) single $56, double $70.

Restaurants

Restaurant Isla Verde (Teniente Merino 710. Tel: 56-67-334583).
Restaurant Entre Amigos (Sargento Aldea 1033B. Tel: 56-67-333433, URL: www.entreamigos.cl).
Restaurant Munich (Ramírez 1267. Tel: 56-67-333728). Updated: Jun 12, 2009.

PUERTO CHACABUCO

 5 m   1,442   67

Puerto Chacabuco isn't a town as such. The sole purpose of this major port is to fulfill the needs of communities living along the Carretera Austral and the hinterlands of Patagonia. The port is their economic and social lifeline with the rest of Chile. Passenger-car ferries ply the frigid waters to Puerto Montt. Another ferry connects small villages along the coasts and fjords of the region between here and Quellón, Chiloé.

Tourists also come to Puerto Chacabuco to board a streamlined ship or a catamaran to see the glaciers of Laguna San Rafael and sip whiskey on millennium ice. International cruise ships also use Puerto Chacabuco as a port-of-call.

The town has, at its widest, five streets. Near the north entrance of the village is a nondescript church. A few blocks closer to the port is a simple, sprawling public square with a playground and a bust of Guerra del Pacífico naval hero Arturo Prat. Near Puerto Chacabuco is Parque Aikén del Sur, a private nature reserve on the shores of Lago Riesco. There are three interpretive trails through this 300-hectare park, which protects pristine forests. One path leads along a river, another to the lake's shores and a third to Barba del Viejo, a 22-meter (72-ft) high waterfall surrounded by ferns and mosses.

The botanical garden contains 32 species unique to the zone. The interpretive center has interactive exhibits on the natural history and anthropology of the Aysén coastal area (open only in summer 10 a.m .– 8 p.m. Ruta Aysén-Chacabuco Km 10. Tel: 35-1112, URL: www. parqueaiken.cl / www.aikendelsur.cl). Several agencies in Coyhaique offer tours to the park.

Another attraction accessible from Puerto Chacabuco is Termas Maca. A two-and-a-half-hour boat trip takes you to these hot springs on the north shore of Fiordo Aysén.

Getting To and Away From Puerto Chacabuco

Puerto Chacabuco is 14 kilometers (8.5 mi) from Puerto Aysén. In winter, snow may close the Puerto Aysén-Puerto Chacabuco road for a day or two. There is a Copec gas station at the entrance to Puerto Chacabuco.

BY BUS

To Puerto Aysén: **Suray** (Monday – Friday every 20 minutes 7 a.m.– 9:20 p.m., less frequently on Saturday 8 a.m. – 9:30 p.m. and Sunday 9 a.m. – 9:30 p.m., $1.20, 15 – 20 minutes). The bus picks up passengers at the *transbordador* (port) and bus stop pavilions along Avenida O'Higgins.

BY BOAT

Purchase ferry tickets in local offices or on-line. Schedules depend on the season and weather.
Navimag (Only open during embarking day and time of embarkation. Terminal de transbordadores s/n. Tel: 56-67-351111, URL: www.navimag.cl).
Naviera Austral (Terminal de Transbordadores s/n. Tel: 35-1493, E-mail: contacto@naviaeraustral.cl, www.navieraustral.cl).

To Quellón, Chiloé: **Naviera Austral** (Monday 7 p.m., Thursday noon, Friday noon; non-resident seat $72, bunk $76 – 80, car $260). The ferry also makes stops in Puerto Cisnes, Raúl Marín Balmaceda, Melinka and five other ports along the Patagonian Channel.

To Puerto Montt: **Navimag** (every 3 – 5 days, consult website for schedule; bunk $60 – 66, cabins from $80, bicycle $60, car $270, discounts available on passenger fares; 24 hours).

To Laguna San Rafael: **Navimag** (April – August, 1 or 2 departures per month, September – March weekly; berths $285, cabin from $375 round trip, 3 days / 2 nights).

NORTHERN PATAGONIA

Tour agencies in Coyhaique also sell packages to the Laguna's glaciers. For more information, see Getting To and Away From Parque Nacional Laguana San Rafael (p.). Updated: Jun 16, 2009.

Services

Puerto Chacabuco has few services. The carabinero station on Avenida O'Higgins serves as the Centro de Información. The hamlet has an ATM on the main street, a half-block from the plaza (Mastercard, Cirrus, Visa, Plus), a Chilexpress / Western Union agent, phone center and health post.

Lodging

Restaurant-Residencial El Puerto (Av. O'Higgins 80. Tel: 35-1147; $14 per person). **Cabañas Motel** (Ramírez 1173. Tel: 33-3067; $40 for two persons). **Hotel Loberías del Sur** (Carrera 50. Tel: 35-1112, URL: loberiasdelsur.cl; single $250, double $300).

PARQUE NACIONAL LAGUNA SAN RAFAEL

(ADMISSION: foreign adults $6, Chilean adults $5, foreign children $2, Chilean children $1) Parque Nacional (PN) Laguna San Rafael is a must-see destination. Visitors can take a boat through the icy waters of Río Témpanos into Laguna San Rafael, right up to the feet of age-old glaciers in the Northern Ice Field. If you take this trip you might hear the sizzling crunch as the glacier shifts and calves. This national park is the second largest in Chile and is a UNESCO World Biosphere Reserve.

The main *raison d'etre* of PN Laguna San Rafael is to protect the Northern Ice Field (*Campo de Hielo Norte*), a remnant of the last Ice Age. Massive glaciers, like San Quintín, Exploradores, Hualas, Leones, Soler, Steffens and San Rafael, flow from the mountains to the sea.

The national park also has some of the tallest peaks of the Southern Andes, including Monte San Valentín (4,058 m/13,314 ft), Cerro Arenales (3,365 m/11,040 ft), Hyades (2,507 m/8,225 ft) and Tarahua (3,700 m/12,139 ft).

It isn't just about ice fields, though. This 1,742,000-hectare park, created in 1959, has only 440,000 hectares of glaciers. Located between Río Exploradores (north), Río Baker (south) Lago General Carrera (east) and Golfo de Penas (west), much of the park is actually heavily vegetated. Wildlife is bounteous, especially with land and sea birds, and fresh waterfowl like the Black-necked swan, the Andean condor, the Black-throated huet-huet, the Magellanic penguin, and various species of albatrosses, cormorants, ducks and gulls. Land mammals include the Chilean miniature deer, the Patagonian fox, and the South Andean deer. In the sea you'll find the harbor porpoise, sealions, bottlenose dolphins, elephant seals, Chilean dolphins and marine otters.

Precipitation in PN Laguna San Rafael ranges from 5,000 millimeters (197 in) per year in the high-altitude zones and the Campo de Hielo, to 200 millimeters (8 in) in the Río Baker area. At Laguna San Rafael it rains five times more than in Cochrane. Annual temperatures average 9°C (48°F).

Cruise tourists, though, never get to step onto terra firma. Local tours include trekking from the administration at Sector Puntilla del Cisne on the west shore of the lagoon, to the Sector Caiquenes ranger station and then to the foot of the glacier (distance: 5.5 km/3.4 mi, difficulty: medium-difficult, duration: 2 days round trip). The ranger station has five rustic campsites (no hot water, $7 per site).

Along the north boundary of the park is Camino Exploradores—a new road from Puerto Río Tranquilo to Bahía Exploradores—which when completed, is expected to be a shorter and less expensive way to arrive to Laguna San Rafael. Other eastern access points are the Valle Río Leones and Valle Río Soler. At the southern tip of the national park is Ventisquero Steffens and the Ruta Patrimonial Campo de Hielo Norte. Mountain climbers looking for a challenge should head to Monte San Valentín. Updated: Jul 10, 2009.

Getting To and Away From Parque Nacional Laguna San Rafael

Parque Nacional Laguna San Rafael is accessible by not only by sea, but also air and land. Most people visit on a cruise with **Navimag** from Puerto Montt and Puerto Chacabuco (URL: www.navimag. cl. Berths $360, cabins from $500 per person, 2 – 5 days). Catamrans also sail from Puerto Chacabuco: **Patagonia Express** (Tel: Santiago—56-2-2256489, Puyuhuapi—56-67-325103 / 32-5117, Purto

Chacabuco—56-67-351208 / 35-1196, URL: www.patagonia-connection.com) and **Catamaranes del Sur** (Turismo Prado de la Patagonia, 21 de Mayo 417, Coyhaique. Tel: 56-67-234843 / 56-67-213815, Fax: 56-67-213817, E-mail: ventas@turismoprado.cl, URL: www.turismoprado.cl). These companies charge about $350 for a one-day trip. All of the excursions, organized year round, head up the Río Témpanos into Laguna San Rafael, right to the foot of glaciers.

Camino Exploradores is accessible from Puerto Río Tranquilo. For this route, see Bahía Exploradores (p.435). In Río Tranquilo and Puerto Guadal, guides take hikers up the Leones and Soler River Valleys. To get to Glaciar Steffens from Caleta Tortel, make transportation arrangements with the Caleta Tortel municipality. The boat from Caleta Tortel up Fiordo Steffens to the mouth of Río Huemules costs $180 – 220; the boat across Río Huemules costs $60 and horseback rides to the glacier lookout point cost $20.

You can also charter flights over the park from Coyhaique and Puerto Aysén; there is a landing strip at Laguna San Rafael, Sector Caiquenes. Updated: Jul 09, 2009.

RESERVA NACIONAL RÍO SIMPSON

Río Simpson was originally founded as a national park in 1967, but was reclassified in 1999 as a national reserve. The reserve now encompasses 41,620 hectares (101 acres) and has a landscape characterized by gorges and valleys. The highest peaks are the *cerros* (hills) Cordillerano (1,697 m/5,568 ft), Cono Negro (1,594 m/5,230 ft) and La Gloria (1,493 m/4,898 ft). The Río Simpson, classified as the word's fourth best fly-fishing river, runs east-west through the park. Another major waterway is the Río Correntoso, a tributary of the Simpson. Waterfalls lace the cliffs within the reserve, the most notable being Cascada de la Virgen and Velo de la Novia. Both can be seen from the main highway.
RN Río Simpson has a cold temperate maritime climate. It receives precipitation in all seasons, totaling 1,500 – 2,000 millimeters annually (59 – 79 in). The mean temperature is 6°C (43°F), with summer highs reaching 16°C (61°F). This environment is perfect for the reserve's evergreen forests. Common fauna in the reserve are the South Andean deer, the Chilean miniature deer, the puma, the Patagonian fox and the non-native common hare and American mink. Among the bird denizens are the Andean condor, the Black-chested buzzard-eagle, the American kestrel, the Ringed kingfisher and the Austral blackbird.

The main sector, the Sector Administrativo, of RN Río Simpson is on the road between Coyhaique and Puerto Aysén. There is a Environmental Education Center here. Keep an eye out for pudu at Cascada La Virgen. Adjacent to this part of the park is Sector San Sebastián, five kilometers (3 mi) east. Both have trails you can follow along the river to see the waterfalls. Other activities include fishing and horseback riding, and, in winter, snowshoeing and cross-country skiing.

The *Área de Protección Río Claro* on Cerro Huemules, 16 kilometers (10 mi) northwest of Coyhaique, is associated with RN Rio Simpson. The main purpose of this 298-hectare (736-acre) zone is to protect a small population of huemul and condors. It also has a 2.5 kilometer (1.5 mi) interpretive path that connects with the Lago Atravezado leg of the Sendero de Chile (for more information, see www.senderodechile.cl).

Entry into the Administrativo and San Sebastián Sectors is $2 for foreign adults and $1.60 for Chileans. All children are allowed in for free. The Área de Protección Río Claro has a separate entry fee: foreign adults $6, children $2; national adults $3, children $0.60. If you wish to visit this sector, phone the ranger first to arrange a guide (Tel: 56-67-212139). The park is open all year.

San Sebastián has 10 campsites equipped with pavilions, fire pits and bathhouses with hot showers and wash basins ($9 per tent, up to six persons). Outside the park, along the highway, is **Camping Correntoso** (Camino Puerto Aysén—Coyhaique, Río Correntoso. Tel: 56-67-216912, E-mail: pchiblecontreras@gmail.com, URL: www.patagonianueva.com). Updated: Jul 07, 2009.

Getting To and Away From RN Río Simpson

Reserva Nacional Río Simpson is at Km 37 of the Coyhaique—Puerto Aysén road. Buses making the run between the two cities pass by the Administrativo and San

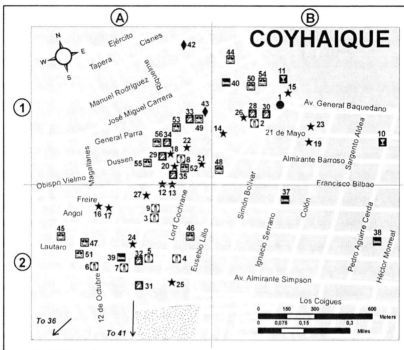

Activities ●

1 Museo Regional de la Patagonia B1

Eating 🍴

2 Café Confluencia B1
3 Frutos Cordillera A2
4 Full Fresh A2
5 Hyper Más A2
6 La Zona A2
7 Restaurant El Túnel A2
8 Restaurant Histórico Ricer A1
9 Varbagón A2

Nightlife ⚑

10 Bar Cervantes B1
11 Bar Chonek B1

Services ★

12 Ahumada Pharmacy A2
13 Banco Chile A2
14 BBVA B1
15 Carabineros B1
16 Casa de Cambio Emperador A2
17 Casa del Turismo Rural A2
18 Chilexpress A1
19 Coalición Ciudana por Aisén
      Reserva de la Vida B1
20 Correo Chile A1
21 Cruz Verde Pharmacy A1
22 Cámara de Turismo A1
23 Cyber Café Innova B1
24 La Oveja A2

25 Lavandería Lavamatic A2
26 Santander B1
27 Servitur kiosk A2

Shopping 🗹

28 Casa Alicia B1
29 Cóndor Explorer A1
30 Feria Artesanos del Ovejero B1
31 Homecenter Sodimac A2
32 La Trucha A2
33 Librería Rincón del Poeta A1
34 Suray A1
35 The North Face A1

Sleeping ▬

36 Cabañas Kooch A2
37 Hospedaje Don Santiago B2
38 Hospedaje Lautaro B2
39 Hospedaje-Cabañas Estefaní A2
40 Hotelera San Rafael B1

Tours ◆

41 Chalten Travel / Naviera Austral A2
42 Expediciones Coyhaique Fly Fishing A1
43 Pura Patagonia A1

Transportation 🚌

44 Acuña Bus Station B1
45 Aero Taxi San Rafael A2
46 Budget Rent-a-Car A2
47 Buses Carretera Austral, Daniela
      and Don Oscar A2

NORTHERN PATAGONIA

Transportation

48 Don Carlos Bus Station B1
49 Hertz A1
50 LAN Office B1
51 Main Bus terminal A2
52 Navimag Office A1

53 Queulat Bus Station A1
54 Rent a Car Traeger B1
55 Sky Airline Office A1
56 Suray Bus Station A1

Sebastián Sectors. See Coyhaique (below) for details. The last bus back to w passes by at about 9 p.m.

A gravel road (4x4 required) goes to Área de Protección Río Claro. Consult Conaf in for instructions on how to get there (Monday – Friday 8:30 a.m. – 1 p.m., 2:30 – 5:30 p.m. Los Coigües s/n. Tel: 56-67-212142). Updated: Jul 07, 2009.

COYHAIQUE

 310 m   42,000   67

Coyhaique is a wayfaring station for travelers following the Carretera Austral. This is the only place along the highway where all services—banks, currency exchange, Internet, gasoline, bicycle parts—are available. It is also a fairly inexpensive place to stay while waiting to fly out of the Balmaceda airport (55 km/33 mi east), or to catch the ferry from Puerto Chacabuco (79 km/48 mi west).

History

The city has long been a resting spot for people traveling through the region. The original inhabitants stayed here to hunt guanaco and rhea (*choique*) with spears, arrows and *boleadoras*, a weapon made of three balls attached to sinew, that was thrown to wrap around the prey's legs.

In the latter half of the 19th century, Mapuche arrived in the zone, fleeing Roca's *Campaña del Desierto*, the ethnic cleansing campaign in Argentina's Patagonia. As a culture, the Aónikenk (also called Tehuelche), disappeared from the region by 1905. By that time, huge livestock farms had begun operations in the Río Coyhaique valley.

In 1906, La Sociedad Industrial de Aisén (then known as Pampa del Corral), a group dedicated to sheep farming, was established, and soon became the most important company in region. Juan Carrasco Noches capitalized on the increasing

number of workers by building the first lodging house in 1926. Soon more settlers came: huasos from the central zone of Chile, Chilotes from Chiloé and gauchos from Argentina.

On October 12, 1929, the village of Baquedano was officially founded. The name was later changed to Coyhaique: "The land of lagoons." Livestock companies began pulling out in the 1930s, but this didn't affect Coyhaique's importance. It continued to be a major city on the Puerto Aysén – Comodoro Rivadavia, Argentina, trade route. In the 1980s, the north leg of the Carretera Austral arrived in the city, with all the expected economic implications.

Today Coyhaique is a pleasant pause in the journey along the Carretera Austral. The city has a series of monuments exhibiting its cultural mix, as well as the strong Argentine influences; mate is faithfully drunk between new and old friends. On the street corners along Avenida Prat and Calle Condell are green stone mosaics of fauna typical of the zone, like trout, huemul (a kind of deer) and bandurria (an ibis-like bird).

Three major nature reserves lie around the city: the Río Simpson and Coyhaique National Reserves and Monumento Natural Dos Lagunas. Puma sightings have increased in the parks in recent years, indicating that the population is rebounding, though no one knows exactly why. The rivers and lakes near Coyhaique teem with fish, making the area an angler's paradise. Updated: Jul 06, 2009.

When to Go

Coyhaique may be called *La Ciudad de Nieve Eterna* (the City of Eternal Snow), but the only snow you'll see in the summer is on distant peaks. Though less wet than its neighbors to the west, Coyhaique still receives 700 millimeters (28 in) of precipitation per year. And yes, in the winter it snows. Winds are strong all year long. In summer, temperatures reach 13 – 15°C (55 – 59°F) and in winter they fall below freezing.

NORTHERN PATAGONIA

There are many festivals between December and March. The end of January to the beginning of February is the **Expo Patagonia**, a fair featuring the region's artisan and agricultural production. The second week of February is the **Semana del Pionero**, a doffing of the hat to Coyhaique's pioneer roots. Entertainment includes horse parades, dances, sharing of mate, literature, conferences and the Festival de Canción Criollo music festival. Updated: Jul 06, 2009.

Getting To and Away From Coyhaique

Schedules for buses, flights and the Barcaza Antonio Ronchi (the ferry across Fiordo Mitchell, from Puerto Yungay to Río Bravo, on the Carretera Austral) are published in the local newspaper.

BY BUS

During the low season (March – November) transportation is cut back. Be prepared to wait several days for a bus down the road. At any time of the year, the Carretera Austral may be closed due to weather conditions.

Coyhaique's main bus terminal (Lautaro and Magallanes) is a small building with bathrooms, a luggage keep (Monday – Saturday 9 a.m. – 5:30 p.m, $2 – 2.50 per bag) and snack stands. Here **Terraustral, Queilon, Sao Paulo, Acuario 13, Altamirano, Patagonia Interlagos, Sabra, Becker** and **Transaustral** have their offices. Across the street is the depot for **Carretera Austral, Daniela** and **Don Oscar** (Lautaro 104. Tel: 56-67-232903). Ask whether the bus will leave from there or the main terminal.

Some companies have their own offices: **Don Carlos** (Subteniente Cruz 63. Tel: 56-67-231981), **Suray** (Prat 265. Tel: 56-67-234088), **Queulat** (General Parra 329. Tel: 56-67-242626) and **Acuña** (Moraleda and Carrera. Tel: 56-67-251579 / 56-9-2173520).

To Puerto Aysén:
Sao Paulo (Monday – Friday every 1.75 hr 7:10 a.m. – 7:20 p.m., Saturday every 1.5 – 2 hr 8:30 a.m. – 6:45 p.m., Sunday and holidays every 1.5 – 2 hr 11:30 a.m. – 6:45 p.m. $2.40). **Suray** (every 30 minutes Monday – Friday 7 a.m. – 9:20 p.m., Saturday 8 a.m. – 9:30 p.m., Sunday 9 a.m. – 9:30 p.m., $3). To continue on to Puerto Chacabuco, transfer in Puerto Aysén.

To Puerto Ibáñez: $8, 1 hour—Acuña (Monday – Wednesday, Friday – Sunday 6:30 a.m.). Also several companies leave from Prat, between Lautaro and Errázuriz (Monday – Friday 6:30 a.m., Saturday 7:30 a.m.). All meet the ferry to Chile Chico.

To Cerro Castillo: Busetas, or microbuses, leave from Prat, between Lautaro and Errázuriz (Monday – Saturday 5 p.m., $7.50 – 8, 1.5 hr).

To Cochrane: All leave at 9:30 a.m., $22, 7 – 8 hours. **Don Carlos** (Monday, Thursday, Saturday), **Sao Paulo** (Tuesday, Thursday, Saturday), **Acuario 13** (Wednesday, Friday, Sunday), **Sabra** (Wednesday, Friday, Saturday). These buses also pass through Cerro Castillo ($9, 1.5 hr), Río Tranquilo ($14, 4 hr), Cruce Guadal ($18, 5.5 hr) and Puerto Bertrand ($20, 6 hr).

To Caleta Tortel: **Sabra** (Wednesday, Saturday).

To Puerto Cisnes: $14, 4 hours—**Becker** (Thursday, Sunday 4:30 p.m.), **Patagonia Interlagos** (Thursday 4 p.m., Sunday 3:30 p.m.), **Terraustral** (Monday – Friday 3 p.m., 5 p.m.; Saturday, Sunday 4 p.m.). **Carretera Austral** (Thursday 4 p.m., Sunday 3:30 p.m.).

To Puyuhuapi: **Carretera Austral** (Monday, Tuesday, Thursday, Saturday 8 a.m., $18, 6 – 7 hr).

To La Junta: **Terraustral** (Monday – Friday 3 p.m., $20).

To Lago Verde: **Altamirano** (Tuesday, Thursday, Saturday 11 a.m., $24, 8 hr).

To Santa Lucía: Carretera Austral (Monday, Tuesday, Thursday, Saturday 8 a.m., $30).

To Chaitén: All leave at 8 a.m.—**Queulat** (Monday – Friday, $34), **Don Oscar** (Tuesday $40), **Daniela** (Monday, Thursday, Saturday, $40). Or go to Santa Lucía and transfer there.

To Futaleufú: All leave at 8 a.m., $40, 12 hours—**Becker** and **Sabra** (Monday – Wednesday, Saturday), **Don Oscar** (Tuesday).

Buses to Chaitén and Futaleufú also pass through Puyuhuapi ($16 – 17), La Junta ($18 – 20) and Villa Santa Lucía ($26).

The following routes go by way of Argentina:
To Puerto Montt / Osorno: 16 hours / 18-20 hours—**Queilón** (Monday – Saturday 5 p.m., $60), **Trans Austral** (Tuesday, Friday 4:45 p.m., $40).

To Ancud / Castro, Chiloé: Queilón (Monday – Saturday 5 p.m., $70).

To Santiago and points between, by way of Osorno: Queilón (Monday – Saturday 5 p.m., $100).

To Comodoro Rivadavia, Argentina. and points between: Trans Austral (Monday, Friday 8 a.m., $40, 10 – 12 hr), reserve well in advance.

BY PLANE
The airport serving Coyhaique is Aeropuerto Balmaceda, 55 kilometers (33 mi) east of the city. Half a dozen agencies provide transfers between Coyhaique and Balmaceda airport, including **T and T Patagonia** (Cochrane 387. Tel: 56-67-256000). Fare costs $8.

LAN (Moraleda 421. URL: www.lan.cl)—Puerto Montt (twice daily, $122 – 145, 1 hr), Santiago (twice daily $122 – 270, 3 hr), Temuco (Sunday).

Sky Airline (Prat and Dussen. Tel: 56-67-240825 / Airport Tel: 56-67-272210, URL: www.skyairline.cl)—Puerto Montt / Santiago (twice daily, $132 / $264), Temuco / Concepción (once daily, $86 – 156 / $100 – 204), Punta Arenas (high season 5 – 6 weekly, low season 3 weekly, $66 – 116).

Don Carlos (Subteniente Cruz 63. Tel: 56-67-231981)—In summer, to Villa O'Higgins (Monday, Thursday 9:30 a.m., $72, 1.3 hr).

Aero Taxi San Rafael (18 de Septiembre 489, Tel: 56-67-573083)—To Melinka and Quellón (Thursday).

BY BOAT
Boats sail from Puerto Chacabuco (79 km/48 mi west) to Laguna San Rafael; regular ferries run to Quellón (Chiloé) and Puerto Montt. Both major companies have offices in Coyhaique: **Naviera Austral** (Chaltén Travel, Av. Ogana 1147. Tel: 56-67-246113, E-mail: info@chaltentravel.cl, URL: www.chaltentravel.cl); **Navimag** (Paseo Horn 47D. Tel: 56-67-233306). Both accept major credit cards. Updated: Jul 06, 2009.

Getting Around
As in other Chilean cities, Coyhaique has micros (city buses, $0.60) and colectivo taxis ($0.80) that run on set routes throughout the urban area. There are also radio (regular) taxis. **Pura Patagonia** rents bikes for $20 per day (Monday – Saturday 9 a.m. – 7 p.m. General Parra 240. Tel: 56-67-246000). **Don Carlos** has a bike repair shop and sells parts (Simpson 231. Tel: 56-67-246713).

It costs more to rent a car in Patagonia than in other parts of Chile. Among the many agencies are **Budget Rent-a-Car** (Errázuriz 454. Tel: 56-67-255171, Fax: 56-67-255172, E-mail: coyhaique@budget.cl, URL: ww.budget.cl), **Hertz** (General Parra 280. Tel: 56-67-245780, URL: www.autorentas.cl) and **Rent a Car Traeger** (Av. Baquedano 457. Tel: 56-67-231648; Aeropuerto Balmaceda. Tel: 56-9-6406412, URL: www.traeger.cl). Updated: Jul 06, 2009.

Services
TOURISM
Two very helpful places to go for information are the **Cámara de Turismo** (Monday – Friday 10 a.m.-2:30 p.m., 3:30 – 7:30 p.m., Saturday and Sunday 11 a.m. – 2 p.m. Plaza de Armas, near Dussen) and **Sernatur** (Monday – Friday 8:30 a.m. – 8 p.m., Saturday and Sunday 10 a.m. – 6 p.m. in high season; Monday – Friday 8:30 a.m. – 5:30 p.m. in low season. Bulnes 35. Tel: 56-67-231752, Fax: 56-67-233949, E-mail: infoaisen@sernatur.cl).

Servitur has a kiosk at the corner of Prat and Freire (Monday – Friday 10 a.m. – 1 p.m., 3:30 – 5:30 p.m.).

Casa del Turismo Rural is the central organization for rural hostels, guides, artisans and other services in the Aysén region (Monday – Friday 10 a.m. – 1 p.m., 2:30 – 7 p.m. Dussen 357. Tel: 56-67-214031 / 56-67-524929, E-mail: contacto@casaturismorural.cl, URL: www.casaturismorural.cl).

For information on the nearby natures reserves, drop by **Conaf** (Monday – Friday 8:30 a.m. – 1 p.m., 2:30 – 5:30 p.m. Los Coigües s/n. Tel: 56-67-212142).

Coalición Ciudana por Aisén Reserva de la Vida works on environmental issues in the region (Horn 47B. Tel: 56-67-573561, URL: www.aisenreservadevida.com). The

NORTHERN PATAGONIA

carabineros handle police, immigration and other matters (Baquedano 534. Tel: 56-67-567071 / emergency 133).

MONEY

Banks are open Monday – Friday, 9 a.m. – 2 p.m. Many are on Calle Condell. All have ATMs that accept MasterCard, Cirrus, Visa and Plus cards, except where noted. **Banco Chile** (Condell 298), **BBVA** (Condell 254), **Santander** (Condell 184) and **Banco del Estado** (Condell and Moraleda) accept MasterCard and Cirrus only. The major supermarkets also have ATMS.

Casas de cambio offer money exchange services, and a few handle money wires: **Austral** (Monday – Friday, 10 a.m. – 1 p.m., 3 – 6:30 p.m., Saturday 10:30 a.m. – 1:30 p.m., 4 – 6 p.m., Sundays and holidays 11 a.m. – 1:30 p.m.).

Paseo Horn (Exchanges U.S. dollars, euros, Argentine pesos).

Cambios Prado (Monday – Friday, 9:30 a.m. – 1 p.m., 3:30 – 7 p.m., Saturday 10 a.m. – 1:30 p.m., 5 – 7 p.m. 21 de Mayo 417): Exchanges U.S. dollars (3 percent less for torn or marked bills), euros and American Express travelers checks; MoneyGram agent.

Casa de Cambio Emperador (Monday – Friday 9 a.m. – 1 p.m., 3 – 9 p.m. Freire 171): Gives poor rates on U.S. dollars, euros, Argentine pesos.

Chilexpress is the Western Union agent in town (Monday – Friday, 9 a.m. – 1:30 p.m., 3-7 p.m., Saturday 10 a.m. – 1 p.m. 21 de Mayo 472).

KEEPING IN TOUCH

Internet cafés are common. Most charge $1.20 per hour, though there are a few cheaper ones, like **Cyber Café Innova** (daily 9:30 a.m. – 11:30 p.m., 21 de Mayo 454; $0.80 per hour) and **La Oveja** (Monday – Friday 10:30 a.m. – 1 p.m., 4 – 9 p.m., Saturday 4 – 9 p.m. Lautaro 294).

Many places have Skype. **Cybermania** has good Internet connection with Skype ($1.20 per hour) and phone booths (national calls $0.20 per minute, international from $0.50 per minute) (daily 10 a.m. – midnight. Prat 563).

If snail mail is more your game, then **Correo Chile** is the place to go (Monday – Friday 9 a.m. – 6:30 p.m., Saturday 10 a.m. – 1 p.m. Cochrane 226, near the Plaza de Armas).

MEDICAL

Coyhaique's public health facility is **Hospital Regional** (Carrera and Dr. Jorge Ibar,.Tel: 56-67-219100). Pharmacies in the city follow the de turno system, meaning one is always open overnight. **Ahumada** and **Cruz Verde** are at the intersection of Prat and Bilbao. Another Cruz Verde branch is inside the Full Fresh supermarket (Cochrane and Lautaro).

LAUNDRY

The señora of **Lavandería Lavamatic** will get your laundry done, for a charge of $10 per basket load, cheaper for fewer clothes (Monday – Saturday 8:30 a.m. – 9:30 p.m. Simpson 417). Updated: Jul 06, 2009.

SHOPPING

There is an artisan market on the Plaza de Armas, between Horn and Dussen. Like a small village of log cabins, these two dozen shops sell jewelry, wood, leather and woolen crafts. Some crafts are of very high quality and originality. Another place to pick up artisan work is the **Feria Artesanos del Ovejero**, next to the Casa de la Cultura (Calle Lillo 23).

Suray has everything for fishing, from flies to waders. It also sells fishing licenses (Monday – Saturday 9 a.m. – 9 p.m. Suray (Prat 265 – 269, Tel: 56-67-234088). **La Trucha** also has a wide selection of fishing gear, plus some camping equipment (Prat 637. Tel: 56-8-407-7645, www.portalcoyhaique.cl/pescaconmosca/tienda.html).

Condor Explorer carries Patagonia-brand clothing, and MSR stove parts and equipment (Dussen 357. Tel: 56-67-573634, E-mail: info@condorexplorer.com). **The North Face** also has a store in Coyhaique (Paseo Horn 47. Tel: 56-67-252096, E-mail: tiendatnfcoyhaique@komax.cl, URL: www.thenorthface.com/sa). The following two shops stock camp stove gas canisters and a wide selection of other camping gear: **Casa Alicia** (Condell 150) and **Homecenter Sodimac** (Av. Ogana 869).

Librería Rincón del Poeta not only has poetry, but also trekking maps of popular destinations in the Chilean and Argentine sections of Patagonia, a sizeable section of used books in English, and nature and travel guides in Spanish and English (Parra 99. Tel: 56-67-241868, E-mail: libro-café@patagoniachile.cl, URL: www.rincondelpoeta.cl). Updated: Jul 06, 2009.

Things to See and Do

Coyhaique has a variety of things to do while hanging out in town, like perusing the Museo Regional or touring the Dolbek brewery. There are also several viewpoints (*miradores*) and monuments. If you want to stretch your legs a bit more, head out to Reserva Nacional Coyhaique, Reserva Nacional Río Simpson or Monumento Natural Dos Lagunas for some hiking, trekking or mountain climbing. On the Simpson and Paloma Rivers, which have Class II-IV rapids, you can raft or kayak. Fishing in the region is also excellent.

Even if you come in winter, you'll still be able to enjoy the outdoors. In the nature reserves, you can cross-country ski or snowshoe. If you prefer downhill skiing, spend the day at Centro de Ski el Fraile, 29 kilometers (17.5 mi) southeast of Coyhaique. Updated: Jul 06, 2009.

Fishing

Snap, plunk. The fly hits the stream glittering in the summer sun. Cold waters flow around the legs of the fisher meditating on the rod, awaiting that slight tug. Soon a brown or rainbow trout, perhaps a salmon will be hooked, its body bending in mid-air, droplets falling back to the river. The *trucha fario* (brown trout) and arco iris (rainbow trout) weigh from up to 20 kilograms (9 lbs). Such a sport is open to novices and pros alike. The best places to cast a line are: Seis Lagunas and Lago Paloma; Lagos Frío, Pollux and Castor (southeast of Coyhaique); Lago Atravesado (west of the city); and Lago Elizalde (southwest). Río Simpson and Río Aysén are also choice spots. Some say Seis Lagunas is the most rewarding place to fish. In Chile, catch and release is practiced.

To get out to any of the lakes, you need to either have your own vehicle or rent one. Various agencies in town arrange fishing tours, like **Expediciones Coyhaique Fly Fishing** (Portales 195. Tel: 56-67-232300, E-mail: german@coyhaiqueflyfishing.com, URL: www.coyhaiqueflyfishing.com. Updated: Jul 06, 2009.

Museo Regional de la Patagonia

(ADMISSION: $1) The Patagonia Museum houses an eclectic collection in two large rooms and several side galleries. Just about everyone in town—you gather from the exhibit cards—has donated some item to the museum. The Museo Regional covers geology and zoology, as well as the culture of the Aónikenk (Tehuelche) nation who once lived in the region. The

history and culture of the settlers is also presented, with an exhibit of a typical Aisén house. A few paintings by local artists adorn the walls. Open Monday – Friday 10 a.m. – 5:30 p.m. Casa de la Cultura, Calle Lillo 23. Tel: 56-67-213174. Updated: Jul 07, 2009.

Monumentos and Miradores

On the west side of Coyhaique, along the Río Simpson and the Avenida Norte-Sur, are several monuments and *miradores* (viewpoints). The first one is Mirador Río Simpson, with vistas over the valley. South on the avenue is the turn-off for Piedra del Indio, a natural rock formation shaped like a native's face. Further south on the bypass are several small parks. In one in particular there are three brightly painted primitive lumber trucks (*carros maderos*). Another displays old printing presses. About a kilometer (0.6 mi) onward is the intersection with the road to Balmaceda. Here you'll find Coyhaique's iconic Monumento al Mate.

On the other side of the city, at Baquedano Lillo, is the Plaza del Pionero. This open-air park displays large carts that have been used for decades to transport goods between Balmaceda, Valle Simpson and Comodoro Rivadavia, Argentina. There are also interesting statues in the park. El Ovejero depicts a man and dog with a herd of sheep. Monumento al Pueblo Migrante Chilote is a salute to the typical family from Chiloé, who were instrumental in the settlement of the region.

To get to the viewpoints and monuments on the west side of the city, begin walking west on Calle Carrera to the bypass, also called Avenida Norte-Sur. A quarter-kilometer (820 ft) south is Mirador Río Simpson. Updated: Jul 07, 2009.

Skiing

Alpine trekking (*esquí randonée*) and cross-country skiing (*esquí de fondo*) are popular sports in Reserva Nacional Coyhaique, Reserva Nacional Río Simpson and Monumento Natural Dos Lagunas.

Centro de Ski El Fraile is 29 kilometers (18 mi) southeast of Coyhaique. Follow Ruta 7 (Carretera Austral) 12 kilometers (7.5 mi) south to the signposted turn. From there it is 17 kilometers (11.6 mi) on a gravel and dirt road to the ski center. Tel: 56-9-6406026, E-mail: contacto@elfraile.cl, URL: www.elfraile.cl. Updated: Jul 07, 2009.

Escuela de Guías de la Patagonia

Escuela de Guías de la Patagonia trains locals as guides in the outdoor tourism industry. Students receive a solid background in conservation, geology, biology and other sciences. Travelers to Coyhaique can hire a guide from the school, or take a course that teaches outdoor skills useful in this Patagonian environment.

From October to April, Escuela de Guías offers three- to five-day classes on trekking, mountain climbing, fly fishing, kayaking, rock climbing, glacier trekking, cross country skiing and other activities. The school also offers a seven-day program in the Cerro Castillo area. Casilla 111, Coyhaique. Tel: 56-67-573096/56-7-7591164, E-mail: contacto@escueladeguias.cl, URL: www.escueladeguias.cl. Updated: Jul 08, 2009.

Tours

Wherever you want to go in and around Coyhaique, whatever you want to do, you'll find a tour operator to help you. Many offer excursions to the national reserves in the area. Others can book a passage on catamarans and ships to the glaciers at Laguna San Rafael. If fishing is your passion, there are guides to take you out to the prime trout spots. If you really want to get off the beaten track, but need a guide for those wild hinterlands, drop by the **Casa del Turismo Rural** which can hook you up with those operating in Aysén's rural zones (see Tourism Offices p. 421). Updated: Jul 06, 2009.

Pura Patagonia

Like most tour operators in town, Pura Patagonia has a full slate of offerings in the Coyhaique region. But one thing that sets Pura Patagonia apart is its city tour. This locally owned agency will not only take you around to see the sites in beautiful downtown Coyhaique and the Reserva Nacional Coyhaique, but they also lead tours of the Dolbek brewery ($30 per person, including entry fees). If you prefer to get out on your own, they also rent bicycles. General Parra 240. Tel: 56-67-246000. Updated: Jul 06, 2009.

Chaltén Travel

Beyond the usual travel agency services, Chaltén Travel has two other specialties. The agency partners with Naviera Austral and sells ferry tickets from Puerto Chacabuco to Quellón, Chiloé, and from Chaitén to Quellón, Puerto Montt and Hornopirén. Another package is a four-day trip from Coyhaique to El Chaltén, Argentina, with stops at various attractions along the way, culminating in a border crossing on horseback to Lago del Desierto (Thursday 8 a.m., $198 for all transportation; does not include lodging or food). Av. Ogana 1147. Tel: 56-67-246113, E-mail: info@chaltentravel.cl, URL: www.chaltentravel.cl. Updated: Jul 06, 2009.

Lodging

Lodging in Coyhaique tends to be fairly basic for a city of its size. The more upscale places are *cabañas* (cabins) and B&Bs located within the city. Inexpensive hostels line the 400 to 600 blocks of Calle Simpson. Some places also have camping. Fishing and other specialty lodges are located outside the city. Updated: Jul 06, 2009.

Hospedaje Don Santiago

(ROOMS: $10 – 24) This large hostel is one of the better deals in Coyhaique, in a quieter part of the city. The rooms are spacious, though few are for the single traveler; most are for couples and large groups. The bathrooms are clean. Although breakfast isn't included in the price and guests can't use the kitchen, a thermos of hot water is available in the morning for you to make your own coffee or tea. Hospedaje Don Santiago is only five blocks from the Plaza de Armas, but with Coyhaique's pentagon grid, it's over 10 blocks from the main bus terminal. Errázuriz 1040. Tel: 56-67-231116 / 56-8-3665419, E-mail: donsantiago2@hotmail.com. Updated: Jul 06, 2009.

Hospedaje Lautaro

(ROOMS: $12) Hospedaje Lautaro is a barebones hostel just two blocks up from Coyhaique's main bus terminal. The main house contains two floors of rooms, a kitchen, and a couple of shared baths. Out in the orchard-shaded garden, tents spring up like multi-colored mushrooms beneath the cherry and plum trees. Along the back of the yard are three more rooms. This hostel is popular with tour groups making the Bariloche-Chaltén trip. The bathrooms have limited hours. Camping $5 per person. Free use of kitchen for room guests; $2 extra for campers. Lautaro 269. Tel: 56-67-238116. Updated: Jul 06, 2009.

Cabañas Kooch

(ROOMS: $14 – 78) Off the road down to Piedra del Indio is Cabañas Kooch, a small operation, with only two cabañas. Each stone and wood cabin has a kitchen, woodstove and cable TV. After dinner in the evening, you can watch the sunsets over the Río Simpson valley. The accommodation is open only from November to March. In the height of summer, though, the cabins are turned into hostels and rented out as dorms. Cabañas are $70-78 per cabin for up to 5 persons; dorms are $14 per person. Camino Piedra el Indio 2. Tel: 56-67-527186, E-mail: koochhostel@ hotmail.com, URL: www.kochhostel.com. Updated: Jul 07, 2009.

Hospedaje-Cabañas Estefaní

(ROOMS: $20) Hospedaje-Cabañas has a bit of an unusual set-up. This inn's cabins, which have up to three bedrooms with single or double accommodations, are rented out per person. The guests within each cabaña, then, share the cabin's bathroom and fully equipped kitchen. Everything is kept clean. Not a bad option for those looking to economize, but don't want to be part of a big hostel scene. Serrano 391. Tel: 56-67-231408. Updated: Jul 06, 2009.

Hotelera San Rafael

(ROOMS: $60 – 82) The flag-topped wall of Hotelera San Rafael surrounds several cabañas, each with a flower and herb garden-edged lawn. These cabins have a kitchenette area with a stove and refrigerator. A newer building houses the larger, more expensive private rooms, much like a standard hotel. All lodgings come with carpeting, heating, cable TV and sanitized bathrooms, and can accommodate one to six people. Price includes breakfast. Moraleda 343. Tel: 56-67-233733, E-mail: csanrafael@patagoniachile.cl, URL: www.hotelerasanrafael.cl. Updated: Jul 07, 2009.

Restaurants

Specialties on Coyhaique menus include trout and salmon from the local rivers, and traditional grilled meats. Ayseninos take great pride in what they produce locally, and many restaurants use regional fruits, meats and other regional delicacies in their dishes. In general, food is a bit more expensive than in the more northern parts of Chile, but you can still find some cheap eats here. If traveling on a budget, look for hostels with common kitchens. Supermarkets open at 9 a.m. and close late. The largest are **Full Fresh** (Cochrane 646) and **Hyper Más** (Lautaro 331). **Frutos Cordillera** stocks a large variety of soy meat, nuts and dried fruits (Monday – Saturday, 10 a.m. – 1:30 p.m., 3:30 – 8:30 p.m. Prat 412). Updated: Jul 06, 2009.

La Zona

(ENTREES: $4) La Zona is a simple corner diner with only six tables. It offers several simple yet filling *colaciones*—or blue plate specials—with a main dish and side. Choose between chicken, pork chops or *pantruca*, a soup with homemade noodles. Drinks, limited to sodas and juices (no beer), are extra. Also on the board are sandwiches, empanadas and breakfast. 12 de Octubre 909. Blue plate special $4. Open daily 10 a.m.– 4:30 p.m., 6:30 p.m.–12:30 a.m. Updated: Jul 07, 2009.

Restaurant El Túnel

(ENTREES: $6 – 10) As you walk by this small corner restaurant, you can see lamb, beef, pork and chicken roasting on the up-right racks and grills through the window. Café Restaurant El Túnel serves good three-course lunch specials, which include a soup or appetizer, a main dish with sides and dessert. Drinks are extra. The à la carte specialties are parrilladas (barbecued meats). Seafood and fish preparations are also on the menu. Open Monday – Saturday 9:30 a.m. – 2 a.m., Sunday noon – 2 a.m. Prat 689. Tel: 56-7-8235822, URL: eltunelparrilladas_coyhaique@hotmail.com. Updated: Jul 07, 2009.

Restaurant Histórico Ricer

(ENTREES: $10 – 15) Restaurant Histórico Ricer doesn't leave a culinary stone unturned. The extensive 17-page menu offers everything from Italian and Arabic foods to grills of Patagonian meats and Austral seafood dishes. While waiting for service (it can be slow), read about Chilean wines in the back section of the menu. While vegetarians have a special chapter in the menu, there are also pizzas and sandwiches. The upstairs dining hall doubles as a museum with photos of pioneers, antiques and other items. Save room for the scrumptious desserts. Paseo Horn 48. Tel: 56-67-216711/56-67-232920, E-mail: restaurant@historicoricer.cl, URL: www.ricer.xteam.cl. Updated: Jul 07, 2009.

Varbagón

(ENTREES: from $6) This bistro bar occupies what was once a railroad passenger car, hence the name, Varbagón. The small diner is popular with young professionals looking for fine, distinctive food at reasonable prices. The restaurant features a main dish of novo-Chilean cuisine with or without meat, dessert and a real espresso to wrap up the session. À la carte offerings include sandwiches, sushi and montados. The air is always filled with jazz music with the occasional live performance. Wifi is also available. Monday – Thursday 10 a.m. – 3:30 p.m., 7 p.m. – midnight; Friday 10 a.m. – 3:30 p.m., 7 p.m. – 2 a.m.; Saturday 9 a.m. – 2 a.m. Freire 327-A. Tel: 56-67-246076, URL: www. varbagon.cl. Updated: Jul 07, 2009.

Café Confluencia

(ENTREES: $7 – 10) Café Confluencia is an artsy bistro for discerning palates. At midday the place fills up for the casero and gourmet lunch dishes. At dinner time, everything is à la carte. Café Confluencia's specialty is *tablas* (antipastos) composed of Latin American and Spanish classics like the *tortilla de patatas* (potato omelet), *ceviche ecuatoriano* (Ecuadorian-style ceviche) and *ajíes rellenos* (stuffed chili peppers). Thursday is theater night (cover: $6). On Friday and Saturday there are free music performances after 11 p.m. Daily special $7.20 – 9.80, à la carte from $7.60. Open Monday – Wednesday 10 a.m. – 11 p.m., Thursday and Friday 10 a.m. – 2 a.m. 21 de Mayo 548. Tel: 56-67-245080. Updated: Jul 07, 2009.

Nightlife

Bar Cervantes

(ENTREES: $4) Bar Cervantes definitely gives anyone venturing inside a real taste of Aysenino life. During the day, it's known as Restaurant Cervantes, serving one of the cheapest meals in town. But come night, this is a working-class bar, where locals drink their beer or wine in two large rooms. The bar is in the back room, complete with a *sapo* game and a multitude of *rayuela* trophies. When the cueca music starts playing, couples get up to dance while the whole crowd claps and sings along. To escape the smoke and noise, you can slip into one of the smaller private rooms. 21 de Mayo 999 and Aguirre Cerda. Lunch served 12:30 – 3 p.m. The bar opens afterward, but the scene gets going after 9 p.m. Updated: Jul 07, 2009.

Bar Chonek

(ADMISSION: $4 – 8) Every town has a rock club, and Coyhaique is no exception. The smoke hangs thick in this red-walled bar plastered with posters of the Ramones, the Beatles, Nirvana and Jimi Hendrix. Friends gather around tables, deep in conversation while a band plays on a small stage. The heat and humidity build as people dance to the pounding rhythms of punk, grunge, garage and rock. Monday – Thursday 10 p.m. – 2 a.m., Friday and Saturday 10 p.m. – 4 .m. Baquedano 484. Updated: Jul 07, 2009.

RESERVA NACIONAL COYHAIQUE

(ADMISSION: foreigners adults $4, children $1; Chileans, adults $1.60, children $0.60) Created in 1948, Reserva Nacional (RN) Coyhaique is one of the oldest nature preserves in the Aysén region. This 2,150-hectare (5,313-acre) reserve on the southern slopes of Cerro Chicao is surrounded by forest, agricultural and cattle lands. Various small rivers flow through the park to the Río Coyhaique. Major bodies of water include the lagoons (lagunas) Verde, Los Mallines, Venus and Los Sapos. In comparison with other parts of the area, the reserve has a relatively dry climate. It receives only 1,100 millimeters (43.5 in) of rain per year. In summer, temperatures average 12.5°C (55°F) and in winter 4.5°C (40°F).

RN Coyhaique has a mixed forest of coigüe, lenga beech, and Antarctic beech trees, and with so many wild strawberries, the reserve could easily be nicknamed Strawberry Fields. Frequently seen fauna include the puma, the Patagonian fox and the Patagonian skunk. Flitting through the forests are the Patagonian Sierra Finch, the Black-chinned Siskin, the Black-chested Buzzard-eagle, the Southern Caracara, the Magellanic Woodpecker, the Austral Parakeet and other birds. Introduced mammal species include the common hare and the American mink. Exotic birds like the House Sparrow, the California Quail and the Common Pheasant can also be found.

The reserve is divided into two sectors: Casa Bruja and Laguna Verde. Sector Casa Bruja has a historical museum and Sector Laguna Verde offers an arboretum featuring the park's major tree species and various hiking trails including:

Los Leñeros (Distance: 2.1 km/1.25 mi, difficulty: medium, duration: 1.5 hr)—From the Laguna Verde ranger post to Casa Bruja.
Los Troperos (1.5 km/1 mi, medium, 1 hr)—An interpretive trail from Laguna Verde to the Las Piedras trailhead; watch the signs, as this is a fragile ecosystem.
Los Carboneros (960 m/0.6 mi, easy – medium, 30 min)—Extends from Laguna Los Mallines to Laguna Venus; walk quietly so you can observe the wildlife.
Los Tejuelos (1.9 km/1.2 mi, medium, 1 hr)—From Laguna Venus to Laguna Los Sapos, through an area frequented by pumas.
El Chucao (2.1 km/1.3 mi, medium, 1.3 hr)—Leads downhill from Laguna Los Sapos to the Laguna Verde ranger station.
Las Piedras (6.64 km/4.2 mi, medium, 3 hr)—Begins at Sendero Tejuelos and extends around Cerro Chucao. Combined with the Los Tejuelos and El Chucao trails, this is a one-day hike.

All trail times given are one way. Many of the trails are continuations of others. In winter, they can be snowshoed or cross-country skied. Conaf has a topographical map of the park, showing the trails and GPS points. This is available at the **Conaf** office in Coyhaique (Monday – Friday 8:30 a.m. – 1 p.m., 2:30 – 5:30 p.m. Los Coigües s/n. Tel: 56-67-212142). At any time of the year, warm clothing and windbreakers are recommended, especially on Sendero Las Piedras. Always carry food and water. RN Coyhaique is open all year, daily 8:30 a.m. – 6 p.m. (except overnight camping).

Both sectors of RN Coyhaique have campgrounds, costing $9 per tent for up to six people. Casa Bruja has five campground sites with bathhouses and showers, two kilometers (1.2 mi) from the ranger station. Laguna Verde has four sites with bathhouses, wash basins and parking. There is also a private campsite at the crossroads before the park entrance ($8). Updated: Jul 07, 2009.

Getting To and Away From Reserva Nacional Coyhaique

You can access the reserve by way of the Coyhaique – Puerto Aysén road, five kilometers (3 mi) north of Coyhaique. Take any north-bound bus to the crossroads ($3), then walk the 3 kilometers (1.8 mi) uphill to the ranger station. All roads within the park are gravel; in winter snow may close the park roads to vehicles. A taxi to the park costs $6 – 8. Updated: Jul 01, 2009.

MONUMENTO NACIONAL DOS LAGUNAS

(ADMISSION: Foreign adults $2, children $1; Chilean adults $1.60, children $0.60) Monumento Natural (MN) Dos Lagunas was established in 1967 as a Parque Nacional de Turismo, and changed to its present status in 1982. This 180-hectare (446-acre) reserve is situated between two lagoons, El Toro and Escondida. These two lagoons are some of the very few in the Aysén Region that have not had species introduced. Surrounded by agricultural and cattle farms, as well as woodlands, MN Dos Lagunas protects a vital nesting ground for birds. It also preserves an important transition from the Cadudifolio forest to the Patagonian steppe. Its climate is similar to that of the city of Coyhaique, although the park's altitude makes for slightly lower temperatures and more snow.

The major flora in MN Dos Lagunas include the Antarctic beech, the Magellan barberry, the wild strawberry, the Yorkshire and many varieties of white and yellow orchids, including the rosey-orange hued *claveles del campo* (Mutisia subulata). Roaming through the woodlands and fields are the Patagonian fox, the Molina's hog-nosed skunk and the big hairy armadillo. In the winter, you can see pumas hunting the common hare. Among the numerous birds are the Magellanic Woodpecker, the Striped Woodpecker, the Chilean Flicker, the Austral Parakeet, the Austral Thrush, the Thorn-tailed Rayadito, the Austral Pygmy Owl and the Caracara. The lagoons are awash with birds, as well. Focus your binoculars on the Red-gartered Coot, the Yellow-billed Pintail, the Great Grebe, the Black-crowned Night Heron, the Buff-necked Ibis, and the Andean Gull.

Although the park has only one entry point, several trails begin from the campground. One is a path to the shores of Laguna El Toro (Distance: 1 km/0.6 mi, difficulty: easy, duration: 20 min). The other is a trail that goes around the base of a hill (2 km/1.2 mi, easy-medium, 1 hr), which then connects with the Sendero Laguna Escondida to a viewpoint at that lagoon (6 km/3.6 mi, medium, 2.5 hr).

The park is open all year 8:30 a.m. – 6 p.m., except for those camping overnight (10 sites, $7 per tent, up to six persons). You must bring water. Take precautions against the hanta virus. Updated: Jul 07, 2009.

Getting To and Away From Monumento Natural Dos Lagunas

Monumento Natural Dos Lagunas is 20 kilometers (12 mi) east of Coyhaique on the Camino Internacional to Coyhaique Alto border crossing into Argentina. The gravel road is in good condition most of the year. The only way to make the trip is with private transportation or by way of a tour. Updated: Jul 07, 2009.

LAGO GENERAL CARRERA

South of Coyhaique, the Carretera Austral skirts a lapis-lazuli-colored lake edged with jade-green forests. This is Lago General Carrera, Chile's largest lake and the second-largest lake in South America, covering over 2,240 square kilometers (865 square mi) between Chile and Argentina, where it is called Lago Buenos Aires.

NORTHERN PATAGONIA

The Campo de Hielo del Norte protects the countryside from strong western winds carrying icy rains, thus creating a cozy microclimate with over 300 days of sun per year.

Around the lake is southern Chile's most productive agricultural land, producing fruit and cool-climate crops. But the earth also brings forth other riches like zinc, copper and gold. In the mid-20th century, mining towns sprung up around Lago General Carrera's shores. Some continue to operate.

Lago General Carrerea's communities are divided into two districts (*comunas*). On the northern rim is the Comuna de Río Ibáñez, whose administrative seat is Puerto Ibáñez, near the Paso Pallavicini border crossing into Argentina. Within this district are the small communities of Levicán (known for its dried fruits), Puerto Avellanos, Cerro Castillo (nestled at the base of a fairy-tale castle mountain), Bahía Murta (with hot springs and fishing) and the old mining communities of Puerto Sánchez and Puerto Cristal (a ghost town that was declared a National Historic Monument in March 2009).

A ferry connects Puerto Ibáñez with Chile Chico on the southern shore of Lago General Carrera. Once every month a boat makes the trip from Chile Chico to Puerto Avellanos, Puerto Cristal and Puerto Sánchez. Chile Chico is just a few kilometers from the Chile Chico–Los Antiguos border post with Argentina.

The Chile Chico district includes Puerto Bertrand (on the shores of Lago Bertrand, famed for its fishing), Río Baker (a rafter's delight), Puerto Guadal (set amid fossil troves), Mallín Grande (where you can fish and horseback ride), Fachinal (a favorite with anglers) and the beaches at Bahía Jara and Puerto Manolo. To the south of Chile Chico is the Reserva Nacional Jeínemeni with abundant wildlife, Lago Verde and the *Cueva de las Manos* (Cave of the Hands), a cave where indigenous peoples left their mark with hand paintings millennia ago.

Jeínemeni's Cave of the Hands isn't the only place the nomadic hunter-gatherers created cave paintings (*pinturas rupestres*). All around Lago General Carrera (or Chelenko, as they called it) are similar sites, especially near Puerto Ibáñez and Cerro Castillo. Archaeologists have found arrowheads, *boleadoras* (throwing weapons) and other stone implements that testify to how these lands became an important ñandú and guanaco hunting ground after the retreat of the glaciers 10,000 years ago. The Tehuelche, fleeing from Argentine General Roca's Conquista del Desierto (1879), left several cemeteries along the shore.

In the 20th century, colonists came from the central and southern regions of Chile, by way of Argentina. Later, Swedes, Finns and other foreigners arrived. Even though a dirt road united the region with Coyhaique, economic and cultural ties were much stronger with neighboring Argentina and remained so until a gravel road was laid in 1952.

Mining used to play a much larger role in the region, especially on the north shore where the Sierra Las Minas contains lead, zinc and copper deposits. In the 1930s, the conflict between colonist landholders and mining companies exploded into the War of Chile Chico. Updated: Jul 07, 2009.

PUERTO IBÁÑEZ

 327 m   757   67

On shores of Lago General Carrera, at the foot of Cerro Pirámide (2,780 m/9,121 ft) is Puerto Ingeniero Ibáñez, the administrative center for Comuna Río Ibáñez and one of the lake's main ports. The heart of the village is the Plaza de Armas, edged with a double row of poplars. In a small park, an Easter Island-style statue stares across the lake's green waters. On the west side of town is a replica of the guanaco and child rock painting found near Cerro Castillo and, to the south, there is a hand-hewn church with an angular bell tower. Next to it is a simple monument to Padre Antonio Ronchi.

The first white settlers came here at the beginning of the 20th century, though its settlement is attributed to 1924. Named for mining engineer Cornelio Ibáñez, the city's coat of arms summarizes it long history. The top band shows a snowy mountain, the middle, an ancient cave painting, and the lower, the village's famous ceramic pots. This is encased in a frame, in whose corners are picks and shovels representing the long mining legacy.

Puerto Ibáñez is an artisan town with almost two dozen workshops. It all started with the Taller Nuestra Señora del Trabajo, established by Padre Ronchi to create jobs and preserve local crafts. In recent years, artisans have struck off on their own. Crafts include leather, wool, homemade jams and porcelain and ceramics using Aónikenk designs.

Like other places around the lake, Puerto Ibáñez is blessed with a microclimate where potatos, peas, corn and other crops grow. Fruit orchards with peaches, cherries and apples are another common feature on this stretch of the shore. Cheese is also widely produced here. These farms (*chacras*) are easy to visit. *Asado de palo* (shishkabob) is a firm tradition, with *cordero* (lamb) and *chivo* (goat) being the preferred meats.

In January and February, a *Sala Museográfica* (museum exhibition) is open in the same building as the **Taller Nuestra Señora del Trabajo** (Ronchi 342). During other times of the year, you can drop in on the artisans and watch them work. Nearby attractions are the Salto del Río Ibáñez waterfall, the Península Levicán, Cerro Pirámide and Lago Lapparent.

A trail in Sendero de Chile network goes between Puerto Ibáñez and Villa Cerro Castillo. Eighteen kilometers (11.2 mi) toward the Paso Pallavicini border crossing into Argentina is Laguna La Pollolla, a favorite haunt for flamingos, ducks, swans and other waterfowl. Scattered around the countryside are petrographs, including the *Cueva de los Guanacos* (Cave of the Guanacos) on Ruta I-16.

Summer is festival time in Puerto Ibáñez. The end of January is the *Copa Integración Chileno-Argentino*, a soccer competition between the two country's teams. The first week of February is the town's anniversary, celebrated with a *jineteada* (rodeo), a beauty pageant, concerts and other events.

Getting To and Away From Puerto Ibáñez

Puerto Ibáñez is 117 kilometers (73 mi, 2 hours) from Coyhaique. Follow the Carretera Austral 86 kilometers (53.5 mi) to where Ruta X-65 turns off for Puerto Ibáñez (31 km/19.5 mi). The entire route is paved. Several places in Puerto Ibáñez sell gasoline by the bottle: **Comercial Las Tres B** (Prat 178. Tel: 56-9-8958934); also at Ronchi 366, Risopatrón 496 and Pasteur 242. There also are several mechanics (*taller mecánico*) and a tire repair shop (*vulcanización*).

Bus and ferry schedules are published in local newspapers. During the low season, services are less frequent. Rain or snow can temporary close the road any time of the year.

BY BUS
To Cerro Castillo: **Minibús San Pablo** (San Salvador 426. Tel: 56-67-423244)— Monday, Wednesday, Friday one morning and one afternoon departure, $1.20.

To Coyhaique: Several companies provide service, leaving daily 7 a.m., 8 a.m. and in conjunction with the ferry ($7 – 8). The main companies are **Minibús Eben Ezer** (Risopatrón 491. Tel: 56-67-423203), **Buses Carolina** (Tel: 56-67-250346) and **Acuña** (Tel: 56-67-251579). They also pick up passengers at their hotels.

BY BOAT
Barcaza El Pinchero to Chile Chico— Tuesday, Wednesday, Friday 10 a.m.; Saturday 11 a.m. The dock is 800 meters (0.5 mi) from town, along Avenida General Carrera. Ticket sales at **Mar del Sur** (Monday – Friday 8:30 a.m. – 1 p.m., 3 – 7 p.m., Saturday 9 a.m. – 2 p.m., Sunday 11 a.m. – 2:30 p.m. Ronchi 166. Tel: 56-67-423309).

To get to Salto del Río Ibáñez (7 km/4.2 mi) and Península Levicán (25 km/15.5 mi), follow Avenida Ronchi north to the signed crossroads past the airfield. Updated: Jul 06, 2009.

Services
Check out the **Tourism Office** (October – March, daily 9 a.m. – 9 p.m, closed April-September. Paseo Comercial, Av. General Carrera 202), or the **Municipalidad** (Soza 161. URL: www.rioibanez.cl) for helpful tourist information.

The town also has a **police** office (General Carrera 1. Tel: 56-67-567089; obtain safe-conduct for Paso Pallavicini here), a **post office** (Ronchi 109) and a **health post** (Acevedo 053. Tel: 56-67-423212). There's free Internet at the **public library** (Ronchi 159).

SHOPPING
Taller Nuestra Señora del Trabajo (Ronchi 342).
Taller Arte Manos (Bolados 161. Tel: 56-67-423268)—ceramics, weavings, porcelain.
Nelida Haro (Chacra 25. Tel: 56-67-423263)—homemade jams (Chacra 2, Camino Aérodomo)—wicker and knives.

NORTHERN PATAGONIA

Tours

Lilian Henríquez Cruz (Tel: 56-8-5327680, E-mail: lijger@hotmail.com)—fly fishing, horseback riding, mountain climbing, rock climbing, skiing.

Lodging

During the road maintenance season (spring – fall) many cheaper hostels are booked by crews, making it difficult to find a room. The following are suitable options:

Camping Municipal (Av. General Carrera, between Risopatrón and Boldas)—$4 per person.
Residencial Ibáñez (Ronchi 04. Tel: 56-67-423227)—$12 – 16 per person.
Shehen Aike (Risopatrón 55. Tel: 56-67-423284 / 09-8527-7681, E-mail: info@aike.ck, URL: www.aike.cl)—$50 per person; Spanish, English, French, German, Italian spoken.

Restaurants

Some hotels serve food. The town has many grocery stores. Here's a few places to try:

Restaurante del Lago (Paseo Comercial, Av. General Carrera 202. Tel: 56-7-6283423, E-mail: zulemantrilla007@hotmail.com).
Restaurante Las Araucarias (Acevedo 247. Tel: 56-8-9840256, E-mail: violeta-milla-06@yahoo.es).
Cafetería Ximena (Ronchi 415. Tel: 56-8-9822284).

VILLA CERRO CASTILLO

 345 m   400   67

Cerro Castillo (2,675 m/8,776 ft) scrapes the sky with its many turret-like peaks. At its foot is the small hamlet of Villa Cerro Castillo. A statue of a pioneer with his dog greets visitors in a grassy park. The main street, Avenida O'Higgins, is lined with restaurants and hostels. At the end of the avenue you'll find the main square and a church. Although officially founded October 29, 1966, Villa Cerro Castillo's big celebration is at the end of January. The *Encuentro Tradiciones Costumbristas* honors the culinary and artisan traditions of the village, with a rodeo, music, dance and asados.

Most travelers come to Villa Cerro Castillo as part of their trekking adventure into Reserva Nacional Cerro Castillo. A section of Sendero de Chile runs from the village to the park, and another heads to Puerto Ibáñez. Travelers with limited time may want to explore the park on horseback.

On the north side of town, Sala Museográfica exhibits photos and belongings of Cerro Castillo's settlers (summer hours: Tuesday – Saturday 11 a.m. – 7 p.m. 0.5 kilometers (0.3 mi) north, 0.4 kilometers (0.25 mi) west of the highway, poorly signposted).

Approximately four kilometers (2.4 mi) south of Cerro Castillo is the turnoff for Ruta I-1, which leads to the archaeological site *Paredón de las Manos*, also known as **Las Manos del Cerro Castillo** (daily 9 a.m. – 9 p.m. Entry: adults $2, seniors $0.80, children free).

Beneath a 35-meter (115-ft) rock overhang are paintings of hands, as well as a reproduction of a guanaco feeding her young. The site is similar to the Cueva de las Manos near Perito Moreno, Argentina. Scientists believe the site was used for rituals between the 8th and 17th centuries.

Before the Paredón is an old two-story schoolhouse that in the future will become a museum. Another painting is La Guanaca on Ruta I-4. Bosque Muerto, a swath of forest killed by ash fallout from Volcán Hudson's eruptions, is twenty-seven kilometers south of town.

Getting To and Away From Villa Cerro Castillo

Villa Cerro Castillo is 95 kilometers (59 mi) south of Coyhaique. North of Cerro Castillo the Carretera Austral is paved; south it is rough gravel. Rain or snow can temporarily close the road at any time of the year.

Gasoline is sold by the bottle at **Provisiones El Forestero** (Los Antiguos 272). There are two mechanics in town. During the low season, bus service is less frequent. All buses stop along Avenida O'Higgins near Café La Querencia.

To Cochrane and points between: daily about 11 a.m., $17 to Cochrane, $11 to Río Tranquilo.

To Coyhaique: daily 2 p.m. and later, $7.

To Puerto Ibáñez: Monday, Wednesday, Friday 9 a.m., $5. Updated: Jul 07, 2009.

Services

Services in Villa Cerro Castillo are very limited. Most businesses in town use the village's public phone as their contact number. There are no money facilities, pharmacy, laundry or post office. However, there is a **tourism office** (open only during the high season, Avenida O'Higgins, 50 m (164 ft) from the highway), **health post** (Calle Los Antiguos) **Internet café** (one computer, $2 per hour) and several phone centers.

SHOPPING

Taller La Amistad—woolen hats, jackets and other wear.
Jorge Aguilar—wood carving.
Eva Llauca—woolen goods.

Tours

El Patagón / Cristián Vidal Sandoval (E-mail: patagoniaindomable@yahoo.es)—horseback riding, fly fishing, rock climbing, and snow excursions.

Expediciones Ruta Más (Carretera Austral 107. E-mail: manuelaguilar1963@hotmail.com)—horseback riding, birdwatching, boating.

Baquedanos de la Patagonia (Bajada Ibáñez. E-mail: baquedanosdepatagonia@yahoo.es)—horseback riding.

Cabalgata Aventura (Tel: 56-67-429200 / 56-67-411610, E-mail: albanio_00@hotmail.com)—The going rate for horseback riding is $10 per tour; a five-hour tour to local sites or the national reserve costs $30 – 40.

Lodging

Most places are basic but cozy; many cheap hostels don't have locks on the doors. In summer, locals offer camping space in their yards, but without bathroom facilities.

Hospedaje El Castillo (O'Higgins 289)—$10 per person, $12 with breakfast.
Teu Shenkenk (O'Higgins 428. E-mail: marsolarave@gmail.com)—$16 per person.
Hospedaje Andreita (Ibáñez del Campo 297)—Room with use of kitchen $8 per person; also has campground with facilities at the end of O'Higgins; $3 per person.

Ten kilometers (6 mi) south of Villa Cerro Castillo on the Carretera Austral is **Camping los Ñires**, which also has a two-bed room (Tel: 56-2-19603818, E-mail: rosachacano@hotmail.com)—$7 per person.

Restaurants

There are several shops along the highway and Avenida O'Higgins:

La Cocina de Sole (in a brightly painted old school bus beside the Carretera Austral).

Villarrica (O'Higgins 574)—also has a hostel costing $12 per person, $14 with breakfast.

Puesto Huemul (Carretera Austral, north of Avenida O'Higgins. Tel: 56-9-2183250, E-Mail: puestohuemul@gmail.com)—fine dining, menu includes *liebre* (hare).

RESERVA NACIONAL CERRO CASTILLO

(ADMISSION: foreign adults $2, children $1; Chilean adults $1.60, children $0.60; four-day trail $6) Reserva Nacional (RN) Cerro Castillo is said to be the next Torres del Paine. Although Conaf and the surrounding communities have been slow on the uptake, savvy travelers have already discovered the beauty of this largely undiscovered park, home to Cerro Castillo (2,675 m/8,776 ft), cragged peaks and chilly blue lagoons.

Founded in 1970, RN Cerro Castillo preserves 179,550 hectares of glacier covered mountains, lagoons and woodlands. To the east, RN Cerro Castillo stretches as far as the Argentine border. Lagos Elizalde, Paloma and Monreal are on the park's north edge. Laguna Chigay is at the park entrance along the Carretera Austral.

RN Cerro Castillo has typical Andean Patagonia forests composed of lenga beech, Antarctic beech, and Chilean fire bush, with Magellan barberry and prickly heath. Devil's strawberry, and some *capachitos* (Calceolaria glandulosa) grow in damp areas. Orchids thrive in dryer areas, and introduced species of pine tree are common.

The reserve has a great diversity of fauna, from Chile's largest animals to its smallest. The South Andean deer, (the *huemul*) is common along the Carretera Austral and herds of guanaco live near the Argentine border. The puma, the Patagonian fox, the Patagonian skunk, the dwarf armadillo, the Geoffroy's cat, and the long-tailed pygmy rice rat are also found within the park. The Condor, the Black-chested Buzzard-eagle, the Austral Parakeet, and the Austral Thrush, are among the many bird species here.

RN Cerro Castillo is divided into five sectors: Laguna Chiguay (where the administrative office is), Las Horquetas, Cerro Castillo, Lago la Paloma and Lago Elizalde. The park is open all year. In winter (May – September), you can ski the trails, though you must have a GPS and radio or cellular phone, and be an expert in snow and ice trekking. Strong snowfalls also occur, often with over two meters (7.5 ft) of accumulation. In spring and fall, conditions are also challenging; heavy rainfall makes the streams run swift and strong, strong winds wrap around the peaks, and snow is possible.

It is essential to have high-quality camping gear at any time of the year. Take precautions against hantavirus. Some trails have loose scree, which becomes very slick and unstable in rain and ice. Also, markers and trails may be difficult to see if hiking at the beginning of the summer.

Trails within RN Cerro Castillo were originally used by settlers in the region. **Sendero Laguna Chiguay**, near the campground in that sector, is a simple path requiring only a few hours to complete. Most hikers come to this national reserve to do the **Valle de la Lima – Villa Cerro Castillo** trek from Chiguay to Campamento Neozelandés at the far side of the great Cerro Castillo mountain (distance: 45 km/28 mi, duration: 3 – 4 days).

This trail goes through Sector Las Horquetas, Valle del Río Turbio, Río La Lima, Portezuelo El Peñón, Estero el Bosque, Laguna Cerro Castillo and Estreo Parada. The beginning and end of the trail are of moderate difficulty; the parts of it deeper into the reserve, however, are more challenging. The trail starts at the Laguna Chiguay ranger station, and heads eastward along a road to Sector Las Horquetas (7.5 km/4.7 mi) and the park boundary (13 km/8.1 mi). Here there are campsites and there's another three-tent site 2.3 kilometers (1.5 mi) on.

From this campground, the land begins to rise and trail conditions become more difficult. If weather conditions allow, you can then do the 6.7-kilometer (4.2 mi) loop around the backside of the massif to Campomento Neozelandés. Then a 16-kilometer (10 mi) trail, part of the Sendero de Chile system, heads to Villa Cerro Castillo. **Sendero de Montaña– Lago Monreal** is in Sector Las Horquetas (distance: 6 km/3.6 mi, difficulty: medium – high, duration: 2 days, round trip).

Conaf has a topographical map with GPS coordinates and official campsites. Businesses in Coyhaique and Villa Cerro Castillo also sell trekking maps. More information can be obtained from the Sendero de Chile website too (www.senderodechile.cl).

There are tour-authorized campsites along the Valle de la Lima-Villa Cerro Castillo route. No wood fires are allowed and you must have a campstove. The ranger station in Sector Laguna Chiguay has a six-tent campground with a bathhouse, hot showers and potable water ($7 per tent).

Getting To and Away From RN Cerro Castillo

From Coyhaique, take any bus heading south and get off at Laguna Chiguay or Las Horquetas ($7). Coming from Puerto Ibáñez or other southern points, take a bus toward Coyhaique and get off at Laguna Chiguay or Las Horquetas. Updated: Jul 08, 2009.

BAHÍA MURTA

 784 m   586 67

Many travelers on the Carretera Austral miss Bahía Murta. But this little village on Lago General Carrera, at the mouth of the Río Murta, has a surprising number of hidden treasures, from abundant sport fishing and trekking, to shrines and hot springs.

The first group of colonists reached this area in 1928. The original village was built near the mouth of the Río Engaño in 1955, but in the 1970s it had to be moved to its present location on the east side of the inlet. Parts of the old town still exist, like the old schoolhouse and the Santuario de Santa Rosa, where every August 30th, a pilgrimage and mass celebrate the feast day of Saint Rosa (3.5 km/2.2 mi south of Cruce Murta). Before the Río Engaño bridge is a track heading west to the Termas El Engaño, natural hot spring pools about seven kilometers (4.2 mi) from the highway (inquire with Tomasa Olivares, who lives at Pasaje 10 de Julio 264, Bahía Murta; entry: $20). Also accessible from this point is Glacier Engaño.

A four-kilometer (2.4 mi) road runs from Cruce Murta to the new village. As it enters town, this road becomes the main street, 5 de Abril. At the end of 5 de Abril is a rocky outcrop with great views of the blue-green lake and snowy mountains. Just 100 meters (328 ft) south of Cruce Murta is the **Museo de Antigüidades**, the local museum, at Residencial Patagonia on the highway. It is open only in the summer.

Bahía Murta has a tradition of cattle raising, which is celebrated with El Gran Rodeo Oficial the second week of January. The second week of February is the town's anniversary celebration. The town is noted for its leather and wool that is dyed with roots and herbs.

Getting To and Away From Bahía Murta

Bahía Murta is 203 kilometers (126 mi) south of Coyhaique. From Cruce Murta, the signposted turn-off on the Carretera Austral, it is four kilometers (2.4 mi) to the village. You can purchase gasoline at the Gato Negro general store. The next gas station south is at Puerto Río Tranquilo. There are two auto and tire repair shops. During the low season, bus service is less frequent. Rain or snow can temporary close the road any time of the year. All buses leave from along 5 de Abril. Departure times are approximate.

To Coyhaique: Wednesday 2 p.m., Sunday 1:30 p.m., $12.
To Cochrane: from **Cruce Murta** on the Carretera Austral.
To Puerto Sánchez: Tuesday, Friday 8 – 8:30 p.m., returns same night, $4.
Updated: Jul 08, 2009.

Services

Basic services include the following: **tourism information** (open only in summer. Calle 5 de Abril s/n), a **post office** (18 de Septiembre 412), a **health office** (5 de Abril 525), **police**, **public telephones** and **Internet** (5 de Abril 297, $2.50 per hour, slow). Most businesses in town, such as hotels and tour operators, use the village's public phone (56-67-419600) as their contact number. For information at other times of the year, check www.rioibanez.cl.

Lodging

Residencial Patagonia (Cruce Murta, Km 190, Carretera Austral. Tel: 56-67-419600)—$10 per person; also has a restaurant.
Hospedaje La Bahía (5 de Abril 653)—$8 per person.
Hostería Lago General Carrera (5 de Abril 314. Tel: 56-67-419600)—$8 per

person. Free camping is allowed on the lake shore, at the end of 5 de Abril. There are windbreaks, but no bathroom facilities.

Restaurants

Asados al palo (shishkabob) is a specialty here. The town is a good place to stock up, as it has many grocery stores. Some hotels also have restaurants.

Restaurant Lago General Carrera (5 de Abril 314).
Restaurant El Record (5 deAbril 297). Updated: Jul 08, 2009.

PUERTO SÁNCHEZ

 215 m 200 📞 67

If you really want to get off the beaten track, then Puerto Sánchez is the place to go. This village is accessible only by a thin road from Bahía Murta, through a mountain range, or by way of a once-monthly ferry from Chile Chico. Puerto Sánchez, on the north shore of Lago General Carrera, has a history of mining. From the 1940s to the mid-80s, zinc and copper were mined here. Settlers arrived around 1930, but the village was named for Eulogio Sánchez, the engineer responsible for mining operations. Today, the three-street by three-street town has an economy based on cattle-raising and artesanía with locally made marmalade, woolens and marble. Tourism is slowly picking up.

From Puerto Sánchez, you can take a boat tour to the Cuevas de Mármol. Sport fishing for trout and salmon will make anglers happy. For fishing or cave tours visit **Luis and Jack Alarcón** (Carmon 11) or **Víctor Soto** (Fritz 1). Visitors can also trek to glacier Ventisquero Müller (Miller) and the headwaters of the Río Müller, Laguna Negra (a small lagoon with great views of Lago General Carrera) or to Cerro Colorado. Sector Mina contains the closed mine. Follow Calle Costanera east for a look at the old wharf.

Be aware that accomodation and dining services are extremely limited. Luis Alarcón of **Turismo Puerto Sánchez** has cabañas and a hospedaje (Tel: 56-2-1960413, E-mail: alarconfidell@yahoo.es, lualo1@hotmail.com). There are no restaurants in town, but there is a general store.Updated: Jul 08, 2009.

Getting To and Away From Puerto Sánchez

During the low season, bus service is less frequent. Rain or snow can temporarily close the road at any time of the year. Calle 12 de Ocubre in Bahía Murta is the beginning of the 26-kilometer (16-mile) road to Puerto Sánchez. There is an auto repair garage in Puerto Sánchez. A bus leaves from Bahía Murta to Puerto Sánchez on Tuesday and Friday 8 – 8:30 p.m., and returns the same night ($4). Updated: Jul 08, 2009.

Services

Services are sparse. Information about what to do can be obtained at posts located at Carmona 12 and Fritz 4. Also, the hamlet has a health post (Fritz s/n), public phone (Fritz 6) and Internet. Most businesses in town, such as hotels and tour operators, use the village's public phone (56-67-411160) as their contact number.

PUERTO RÍO TRANQUILO

 215 m   500   67

Puerto Río Tranquilo on the western shore of Lago General Carrera has become a popular stop on the Carretera Austral circuit. The big draw is its Santurario de la Naturaleza Capilla de Mármol. This natural sanctuary of marble outcroppings was worn by the lake's waves and features caves and two natural rock formations, the *capilla* (chapel) and the *catedral* (cathedral). Condors fly from the cliffs. Tour boats slice the turquoise waters to visit these wonders ($10 per person / $50 per boat, 1.5 hours). Afternoon winds can roughen the lake.

Puerto Río Tranquilo is named for the river at whose mouth it sits, though on earlier maps it is called Puerto Sereno. According to some legends, the first settler to come here in 1929, Pedro Lagos, called it Río Tranquilo. Soon after the Lagos family arrived, others came to set up their homes. During the 1950s the town experienced great growth. In 1955, the village was officially established; the Carretera Austral reached the town in 1987. Río Tranquilo celebrates its anniversary the third week of February.

One block west of the Carretera Austral is the town plaza, which has a grassy knoll in its center. On one corner is the small wooden church with stylistic elements typical of Chiloé

Island. In summer, a Sala Museográfica is open (Godoy 162). Another place where you'll see a preponderance of Chilote architecture is the old cemetery on the southern edge of town. Here the headstones are miniature houses whose "residents" have a beautiful view of the lake. Along the beach is a park, a pleasant place to sit and read, or just watch the sunlight on Lago General Carrera. The fishing on the lake is also quite good.

Construction has begun on a new road to Bahía Exploradores on the north side of Río Tranquilo. This Camino a Exploradores provides access to los Lagos Tranquilo and Bayo, the Glaciares Exploradores and Grosse—a good place to do ice trekking. Further north, at Km 207 (Puente El Belga), is Bosque Arrayanes, or Bosque Encantado, an enchanting, ancient arrayán forest teeming with flora and fauna.

Southwest of Puerto Río Tranquilo is Valle Leones, which leads to Lago Leones and a glacier of the same name. To explore this valley, though, you need to go on tour. You can drive only so far before you have to trek or ride a horse. Further south on the Carretera Austral is a huge swatch of burned woodlands, caused by a forest fire at the beginning of the present century. Along here, too, are great views of Monte San Valentín (4,058 m/13,314 ft), the highest mountain in the Northern Ice Field. Updated: Jul 07, 2009.

Getting To and Away From Puerto Río Tranquilo

Puerto Río Tranquilo is 233 kilometers (145 mi) south of Coyhaique and 97 kilometers (60 mi) north of Cochrane. South of Río Tranquilo the Carretera Austral has some steep climbs and tight curves. An Esso gas station is right on the highway; the town also has mechanic and tire repair shops. During the low season, bus service is less frequent. Rains or snows can temporary close the road at any time of the year. There is no center bus terminal.

Bus depot locations are as follows:
Buses Don Carlos—Hospedaje Silvana (Godoy, between Exploradores and Arrayanes).
Bus Eca—Supermercado El Chino (Godoy 64).
Sao Paulo and Acuario 13—along the Carretera Austral.
Sabra—Donde Kike (Godoy 25).

To Puerto Guadal: **Bus Eca** (Tuesday, Friday 1 p.m., $8).

To Chile Chico: Transportes Ale (Wednesday, Thursday 10:30 a.m., $20).

To Cochrane: 2 hours—**Sao Paulo** and **Acuario 13** (daily 2 p.m., $14), **Sabra** (Monday, Thursday, Saturday 11:30 a.m., $14), **Don Carlos** (Saturday, Monday, Thursday 2:30 p.m., $10).

To Coyhaique: 5 hours—**Sao Paulo** and **Acuario 13** (daily noon, $14), **Don Carlos** (Tuesday, Friday Sunday 11:30 a.m., $13), **Sabra** (Wednesday, Friday, Sunday 11:30 a.m., $14).

To Bahía Exploradores (Km 59): **Mario Reyes** (Tel: 56-8-7423865 / 56-9-8148567) runs a service as far as Km 59 (twice monthly, Wednesday, returns same day, $4.60). For more information, phone him or ask at his pick-up point at Residencial-Provisiones La Paz (Los Exploradores 336). Updated: Jul 07, 2009.

Services
Most businesses in town, such as hotels and tour operators, use the village's public phone (56-67-419500) as their contact number. Puerto Río Tranquilo doesn't have much in the way of services. There is no bank, ATM or money exchange and no pharmacy.

The town does have a tourism information kiosk on the Plaza de Armas (open only in summer; at other times or the year, consult: www.rioibanez.cl), an Internet and phone center (Godoy 51-B, $2.50 per hour), police (El Salto 359), a health station (Flores 137) and a post office. Updated: Jul 07, 2009.

Tours
Many agencies in Puerto Río Tranquilo offer boat tours to the Cuevas, Capilla and Catedral de Mármol. Most are on the Carretera Austral. In the parking lot along the lakefront are two yellow trailers where you can book tours. One of these is Maran Ata (Tel: 56-67-411584), which also arranges boat trips to Puerto Sánchez and Puerto Cristal.

Willy López Pineur organizes tours to the Río Exploradores valley, Capilla de Mármol and the Río Leones valley. Fishing, horseback riding, skiing, kayaking, rafting and mountain climbing trips are also available. Tel: 56-67-419500, E-mail: lopezpineur@yahoo.es.

El Puesto Expediciones leads glacier treks and tours through the Valle Exploradores. Lagos 258. Tel: 56-2-196-4555, E-mail: contacto@elpuesto.cl, URL: www.elpuesto.cl. Updated: Jul 07, 2009.

Lodging
Camping El Pudú: 1 km/0.6 mi south of Puerto Río Tranquilo. Tel: 56-67-573003 / 56-9-8914051, E-mail: aliciaconce@gmail.com, URL: www.puduexpediciones.cl.

Residencial La Paz: shared room $11 per person, camping $5 per person; kitchen. Los Exploradores 336.

Hostal El Puesto: single $90, double $110 with private bath and breakfast. Lagos 258. Tel: 56-2-1964555, E-mail: contacto@elpuesto.cl, URL: www.elpuesto.cl. Updated: Jul 07, 2009.

Restaurants
There are very few sit-down restaurants in Puerto Río Tranquilo. Most eateries serve fast food. Several shops sell groceries. A few options to try:
Snacks Silvana (Carretera Austral).
Donde Kike (Godoy 2).
Hostería Carretera Austral (Carretera Austral 373. Tel: 56-67-419500). Updated: Jul 07, 2009.

BAHÍA EXPLORADORES
Just north of the bridge into Puerto Río Tranquilo begins the new road heading to Bahía Exploradores—a cheaper port from which to take a boat tour to the glaciers of Parque Nacional Laguna San Rafael. Even though the road doesn't yet arrive to that bay, tourists are already enjoying the natural wonders along this developing highway. Fifty-nine kilometers (37 mi) are already completed.

You can hike in along the road, or take transportation in to the Mirador de Glaciar Exploradores at Km 52. Along the way are glimpses of glaciated mountains, and much of the road travels riverside.
The highlights of the route are:

Km 3: The **cemetery** of Familia Berrocal
Km 8: Another **family cemetery** with four weathered tombs. Lago Tranquilo now becomes visible. With the continental divide; waterways begin running westward.
Km 24-25: A **waterfall**.

Km 44: **Hostal Alacaluf.**

Km 46: **Lago Bayo** begins.

Km 50-51: Pieces of ice float in the Lago Bayo's waters, made grey by the Ventisquero Explorador.

Km 52: **Mirador Glaciar Exploradores,** a privately owned access point to Glaciar Exploradores. Travelers come here to trek this river of ice flowing from the heights of Monte San Valentín ($70, includes guide and equipment, minimum 3 persons; 6 hours). If you like, while everyone is trekking, you could just hike the interpretive trail to the mirador (Entry: adults $6, seniors and children $2; 1.5 hours).

A trek through the Camino Exploradores is not a journey to be taken lightly. Be prepared with food and a camp stove, as there are no shops or restaurants along the way. The stream water is pure enough to drink, though after rains, it may be too murky.

Wear warm, rain- and wind-proof clothing. Do not try to climb the glaciers on your own unless you are highly experienced in ice climbing and properly equipped (crampons, pick, etc.). The glacier is crevassed. Whether on your own or on a tour, you will need UVA 400 sunglasses.

For **tours, Orlando Soto S** (Valle Río Exploradores, Tel: 56-67-239221, contact by radio) offers fly fishing, horseback riding, trekking and rock climbing.

Getting To and Away From Bahía Exploradores

One way to travel Camino a Exploradores is with a tour. Some agencies, like **El Puesto Expediciones** (Lagos 258. Tel: 56-2-1964555, E-mail: contacto@elpuesto.cl, URL: www.elpuesto.cl), also take passengers ($20). **Mario Reyes** (Tel: 56-8-7423865 / 56-9-8148567) runs a service as far as Km 59 of the road (twice monthly, Wednesday, returns same day, $4.60). For more information, phone Mario or ask at his pick-up/drop-off point at Residencial-Provisiones La Paz (Los Exploradores 336). During the low season, this service may be less frequent. Rain or snow can temporary close the road any time of the year. You can also trek or bicycle out. Updated: Jul 08, 2009.

Lodging

Hotels are hard to come by. You can camp alongside the road; if you are on private property, ask permission of the landowner first. **Albergue Campo Alacaluf (**Km 44 Camino a Exploradores. Tel: 56-67-419500) offers rooms with a shared ($36 per person) or private bath ($48 per person); prices include breakfast. **Camping** is also available. The staff speak Spanish, German and English. There is also a restaurant. The only **restaurant** on the route is the one at Alacaluf (Km 44). Updated: Jul 08, 2009.

PUERTO BERTRAND

 446 m   270   67

At the southern tip of Lago Bertrand is the hamlet of Puerto Bertrand, which has two sectors. Sector Alto, accessed by Calle Los Manzanos, is where the village church and cheaper lodging are. Downhill, about one kilometer (0.6 mi) further south, is Avenida Costanera, which turns off to downtown Puerto Betrand. The Costanera later becomes the main street, edging upon the lake. Here you'll find the town's only shops, tour operators and several hotels. There is also a small park with a pier midway down the road.

Lago Bertrand's intense blue waters are surrounded by lenga beech forests and, at the east end of the lake, glacier-packed mountains. The lake's waters flow south, first moving swiftly then swirling into rapids as they approach the Río Baker. A bit further south you can stand at a viewpoint and admire the waterfall that is the confluence of the Neff and Baker Rivers.

Lago Bertrand, Lago Plomo and Río Baker are full of brown trout (*trucha fario* or *café*), rainbow trout (*trucha arcoiris*) and Creole perch (*percatrucha*). The season runs from the end of October to mid-April. With Río Baker's Class III rapids, whitewater rafting is growing in popularity. Other summer activities include horseback riding to gaucho camps, hiking along the lake shore, boat rides on Lago Bartrand and Lago Plomo, and taking a rather invigorating dip in the lake. The third week of February marks the town's anniversary. Celebratory festivities include the election of festival queen, games, regattas, fishing competitions and traditional dances. Updated: Jul 08, 2009.

Getting To and Away From Puerto Bertrand

Puerto Bertrand is 25 kilometers (15 mi) south of Puerto Río Tranquilo and 54 kilometers (33 mi) north of Cochrane. No gasoline is available;

the nearest stations are in Puerto Guadal (30 km/18 mi) and Puerto Río Tranquilo, where there is also mechanic and tire repair shop.

During the low season, bus service is less frequent. Puerto Bertrand has no bus depot. You must catch the bus at the Cristo, a large wooden crucifix on the highway near Avenida Costanera. For Cochrane, buses pass by at 3:30 p.m. ($6), for Coyhaique, at 10 a.m. ($16). Updated: Jul 07, 2009.

Services

Services in Puerto Bertrand are limited as the town lacks public Internet, money facilities, pharmacies and post offices. Most businesses in town, such as hotels and tour operators, use the village's public phone as their contact number (Tel: 56-67-419900). For tourism information, stop by the **Comité de la Comunidad**, in front of the wharf (Av. Costanera). Also check www. chilechico.cl. Updated: Jul 06, 2009.

Tours

Baker Patagonia Aventura (Costanera s/n, across from the pier. Tel: 56-67-419900, E-mail: bakerpatagoniaaventura@gmail. com, URL: www.bakerpatagoniaaventura. cl)—short treks, horseback riding, rafting on Río Baker ($34).

Patagonia Adventure Expeditions (Tel: 56-67-411330, E-mail: contacto@adventurepatagonia.com)—three-day treks to the Campo de Hielo.

Norte Turismo Arcadio (Tel: 56-67-411499)—fishing, hiking.

Carmen Alegría (Costanera s/n. Tel: 56-67-419900, E-mail: trural@patagoniachile. cl)—hiking to glaciers, rafting, fishing, horseback riding. Updated: Jul 06, 2009.

Lodging

There are fishing lodges around Puerto Bertrand and along the Río Baker.
Hospedaje Doña Esther (Esparza 8, Sector Alto. Tel: 56-9-9908541)—$10 per person without breakfast, $12 with breakfast; also camping.

Hostería Río Baker (Costanera s/n. Tel: 56-67-419900 / 56-2-1960405, Fax: Santiago 56-2-1960411, E-mail: contactos@greenbakerlodge.cl, URL: www. greenbakerlodge.cl)—$16 per person with breakfast.

Konaiken (6 km / 3.6 mi south of Puerto Bertrand. Tel: 067-41-1598, E-mail: turismo_konaiken@yahoo.es, URL: www.konaiken.blog. com)—cabins ($80 per cabin), restaurant, reiki and other therapies. Updated: Jul 06, 2009.

Restaurants

There are two basic general stores in the village. There are no restaurants, except those at the hotels. Updated: Jul 06, 2009.

PUERTO GUADAL

 215 m 500 67

In the 1930s, a protected bay on the extreme southwest edge of Lago General Carrera became a port for cattle and wool shipping, and the village, known as Puerto Guadal, was quickly established. During the 1960s, a French mining company, Empresa Minera del Plomo, opened mines in the lead-, zinc- and copper-rich mountains. The company pulled out in 1986, and there was little interest in the area until the turn of the century. Modern mining projects did not have sufficient staying power, unfortunately, and most projects were dropped.

The village also used to be a big destination for Argentine tourists, but since Argentina's economic crisis, the number of visitors has dramatically decreased. The village now has a somewhat forlorn look to it.

The avenue in Puerto Guadal is lined with small shops and one-story houses with flower gardens. A few blocks away is the Plaza de Armas. On one corner is a small stucco church. From the plaza, Los Guindos goes toward the lake, then crosses over Eserto El Sapo and follows the shore. Along the way are abstract wooden sculptures. This dirt path passes the old pier and climbs a hill to a lighthouse and mirador with fine views of Lago Genreral Carrera and the surrounding snowy mountains.

On the other side of this inlet is a jut of land with the town's cemetery. On that rocky point is a park with benches, and beyond this mini-peninsula, is another inlet with a beautiful agate beach. In summer, this is a favorite place to swim.

Puerto Guadal, nicknamed *La Perla del Lago* (The Pearl of the Lake), hasn't quite made it onto the foreign tourists' itinerary, which is surprising considering the variety of attractions here. Two kilometers (1.2 mi) away is

NORTHERN PATAGONIA

Mina Escondida, a mine abandoned in 1986. You can still see the installations and machinery left behind.

To the east of town, tumbling through the forest is Cascada Los Maquis, a a 25-meter (82-ft) stepped waterfall. Local guides offer seven-hour horseback expeditions to the tremendous marine fossil field eight kilometers (4.8 mi) to the south.

Puerto Guadal is also convenient for trekking or horseback excursions to Valle Río Leones and the glaciers of Campo de Hielo Norte. Anglers, get your rods out—trout, salmon and smelt (*pejerrey*) are plentiful here. The second week of February is the Aniversario de Puerto Guadal, a week-long salute to local traditions, with horse racing, games and typical foods. Updated: Jul 07, 2009.

Getting To and Away From Puerto Guadal

Puerto Guadal is on Ruta CH-265, 30 kilometers (18 mi) from Puerto Bertrand, 10 kilometers (6 mi) from the Carretera Austral's Cruce Guadal and 115 kilometers (71.5 mi) from Chile Chico. From the Cruce to Guadal is a steep, long climb into the mountains, where the road then descends just as steeply toward Chile Chico. Here, you'll find a gas station (Las Magnolias and Los Notros), mechanic and tire repair shop.

During the low season, bus service is less frequent. Rain or snow can temporarily close the road. Puerto Guadal has no central bus terminal. Bus offices are as follows:

Bus Ale—Centro de Llamadas Fanny (Los Notros 93).
Eca—A small shop on the corner of Los Guindos and Las Magnolias.
Transportes Jarita—Carnicería La Económica (Los Olmos).

To Coyhaique and points between: Bus Eca (Sunday, Wednesday 8:30 a.m., $20).
To Chile Chico: $12, 3 hours—Eca (Tuesday, Friday 7 a.m.), **Jarita** (Wednesday, Friday 6:45 a.m.).

To Cochrane: **Eca** and **Jarita** buses from Chile Chico pass through about 11 a.m. – noon, $13, 4 – 4.5 hours. Updated: Jul 07, 2009.

Services

For tourism information, stop by the Municipalidad (Los Lirios and Los Notros, across from the Plaza de Armas). The village has a phone center, post office (Los Olmos 12), carabineros, and health station (Las Camelias 167. Tel: 56-67-431252). Free Internet is available at the public library (Monday – Friday 9 a.m. – 1 p.m., 2:30 – 6:30 p.m. Las Violets s/n). There are no banks, ATMs or pharmacies.

Tours

Marta Márquez (Los Olmos 541. Tel: 56-67-431218)—horseback riding.

Kalem Guía Regional / Pascual Díaz (Los Alerces, uphill from Los Lirios. Tel: 56-67-431289 / 56-67-431214, E-mail: cabalgasur@hotmail.com).

Patagonia Jet (Tel: 56-67-431263 / 56-9-84401092, E-mail: info@patagoniajet.com, URL: www.patagoniajet.com)—boat and trekking excursions to Campo de Hielo Norte by way of the Leones, Baker and Sur Rivers. Updated: Jul 07, 2009.

Lodging

Camping El Parque (1 km/0.6 mi to Chile Chico. Tel: 56-67-411268).
Hostería Huemules (Las Magnolias 360. Tel: 56-67-431212)—$12 per person.
El Mirador Playa Guadal (Km 2 to Puerto Guadal, Tel: 56-67-431222)—$34 per person. Updated: Jul 07, 2009.

Restaurants

Asados Patagones (Los Olmos 541. Tel: 56-67-431218).
Restoran La Frontera (Los Lirios 399. Tel: 56-67-431234).
There is also a supermarket and several small stores. Updated: Jul 07, 2009.

CHILE CHICO

 215 m   3,757   67

On the southern shores of Lago General Carrera, not too far from the Argentine border, is Chile Chico—Little Chile. The village owes its name to the patriotism its inhabitants declared after *Los Sucesos del Lago Buenos Aires*, otherwise known as *La Guerra de Chile-Chico* (The War of Chile-Chico).

The first pioneers came in 1889. With the establishment of the Oficina de Tierras y Colonización in 1905, the population increased. Come 1918, though, the settlers faced serious problems. Their lands had been given to a mining company, whose officials demanded

---

that the settlers be removed. The residents refused to comply and faced off against the law enforcement officers sent to dislodge them. An armed rebellion ensued, with 50 to 100 deaths. In the end, the settlers won. Afterward, more families began arriving to farm in this warm valley. On May 21, 1929, Chile Chico was officially founded as a city.

The **Mirador Cerro Bandera** (0.5 km/0.3 mi west) is a good place to view the landscape. On the dry side of the verdigris-streaked mountains, the land looks somewhat withered. The lake, dotted with islands, stretches to the north and east, and on the far northwest horizon is Cerro Castillo. Once upon a time, the colonists flew their own banners. Now only a Chilean flag flutters in the strong wind.

A few blocks from the Plaza de Armas is the **Iglesia Nuestra Señora del Carmen** (Portales and Blest Gana). Hidden behind pine trees, this church is a non-descript, modern concrete structure with metal flying buttresses. Down the Avenida O'Higgins is the **Museo de Chile Chico**, displaying fossils, stones, various Aónikenk objects and stuffed fauna (O'Higgins 333). A few blocks east is the **Casa de la Cultura**, which exhibits art and movies (Lautaro and O'Higgins). Anchored next to it is the **Barco Andes**, which plied the blue-green lake from village to village, from 1922 to the 1990s.

One of the nearby attractions is **Puerto Manolo**, a perfect spot for swimming or fishing (1 km/0.6 mi west). Further on is **Bahía Jara**, another beach great for nautical sports (18 km/11 mi). From here you can see the Península Levicán on the other side of the lake. To the east of town is **La Puntilla**, a good place for birdwatching (3 km/1.8 mi).

A bit further, hidden among the farms, is the **Cementerio de Colonos**, the village's original graveyard. **Reserva Nacional Lago Jeínemeni**, 52 kilometers (32.5 mi) to the southeast, is home to the Cueva de las Manos, Lago Jeínemeni and Laguna Verde.

Chile Chico celebrates its anniversary the last week of February. During the third week of September it hosts the Festival Folklore y Domaduras. Neighboring villages also have summer festivities. Bahía Jara has its own *jineteadas* (equestrian displays) with music and rodeos during the fourth week of January.

Getting To and Away From Chile Chico

Chile Chico is on Ruta Ch-265, three kilometers (1.8 mi) from Paso Jeínemeni on the Argentine border, 115 kilometers (71.5 mi) from Puerto Guadal and 125 kilometers (78 mi) from the Carretera Austral (Ruta 7). Between Puerto Guadal and Chile Chico are two major passes through the mountains, Paso Las Llaves and Paso Mallínes. Both have steep ascents and descents with blind curves. Chile Chico has a gas station, mechanic and tire repair. For bike parts, repair or rental, go to **Garnik Bike** (Baquedano 51. Tel: 56-9-9496899, E-mail: ciclismogarnikbike@gmail.com).

During the low season, bus service is less frequent. Buses stop along O'Higgins, near the Telefónica.

BY BUS
To Guadal: **Eca**, **Jarita** (Wednesday, Friday 4 p.m., $12, 3 hr).

To Río Tranquilo: **Nieves del Sur** (Monday 3 p.m., Tuesday and Thursday 5 p.m., $20).

To Cochrane: **Transportes Ale** (Wednesday, Saturday 1 p.m., $26)—passes by Puerto Guadal ($13) and Puerto Bertrand ($20)

To Coyahique: tickets are sold at El Refugio, where the ferry office is (west end of Rodríguez). Buses meet the ferry in Puerto Ibáñez. Buy a ferry ticket first, then a bus ticket. Buses **Carolina**, **Miguel Acuña**, $8.

To Los Antiguos, Argentina: **Transporte Karla, Minibus Jorge Vargas** (daily 9:30 a.m., 2 p.m., 4:30 p.m., $4). Some vans meet the ferry, but charge a higher price. All stop for immigration procedures.

BY BOAT
Mar del Sur (El Refugio, west end of Rodríguez. Tel: 41-1864, E-mail: msur@patagoniachile.cl).

To Puerto Ibáñez: In summer there are departures daily, at other times of the year, only six days per week. Schedules are published in the local newspapers. Passenger $9.25, bicycle $4.35. Reservations should be made in advance for small vehicle $54.50, pick-up $18.50, motorcycle $10.90. Be sure to bring your passport.

NORTHERN PATAGONIA

To Puerto Avellano, Puerto Cristal and Puerto Sánchez: Last Saturday of each month, 1 p.m. The lake can get rough so be prepared for seasickness. Updated: Jul 07, 2009.

Services

Chile Chico offers most services. For tourist information visit the **Tourism office** (summer: daily 8:30 a.m. – 10 p.m., winter: Monday – Friday 9 a.m. – 5 p.m. O'Higgins 333. Tel: 56-67-411359, E-mail: chilechico@iname.com, URL: www.chilechico.cl), or **Conaf** (Blest Gana 121). **Banco del Estado**'s ATM accepts only MasterCard and Cirrus; it exchanges U.S. dollars and euros (100-block of González). Some businesses along O'Higgins exchange Argentine pesos. The town also has a **post office**, **Internet cafés** ($1.60-2 per hour), **police offices** (O'Higgins 506. Tel: 56-67-411313) and **phone** centers. Along the avenue are the **hospital** (No. 331, Tel: 56-67-351388) and several pharmacies.

For shopping, visit: **Artesanías Schuster** (Portales 230)—woodworking; **Taller Artesanal Nazareth** (Ca. O'Higgins and Balmaceda)—wool ponchos, sweaters, hats; **Ferretería Sur** (Ca.O'Higgins 270)—fishing gear.

Tours

Patagonia Challenge (Tel: 56-67-411533 / 56-9-91298967)—rappelling, hiking, excursions to Cueva de las Manos and Bahía Jara.

Agua Hielo Expediciones (Ca. Portales 574, interior. Tel: 56-9-76053580, E-mail: aguahieloexpediciones@gmail.com)—kayak lessons ($20 per 2-3 hour class).

Fernando Georgia Díaz (Ca. O'Higgins 416. Tel: 56-67-411224 / 56-8-5957934, E-mail: fgiorgia@expeditionspatagonia.com / georgiachilechico@hotmail.com, URL: www.expeditionspatagonia.com)—fly fishing, horseback riding, rock climbing, kayaking, rafting, skiing, excursions to Cueva de las Manos.

Lodging

Camping Bahía Jara (Bahía Jara, 18 km/11 mi west of Chile Chico)—$2 per site plus $0.60 per person.
Kon-Aiken (Ca. Burgos 6)—$12 per person with breakfast, camping $4 per person.
Hostería de la Patagonia (Camino Internacional s/n, east end of town. Tel: 56-67-411337, E-mail: hdelapatagonia@gmail.com, URL: www.hosteriadelapatagonia.cl)—$20 per person, camping $5.

Restaurants
Antu Mapu (Ca. O'Higgins 266).
Café-Restaurant El Fogón (Ca. O'Higgins and Burgos).
Lola y Elizabeth (Ca. González 25). Updated: Jul 08, 2009.

RESERVA NACIONAL JEÍNEMENI

(ADMISSION: $2) Reserva Nacional (RN) Lago Jeínemeni—commonly called RN Jeínemeni—was created in 1967. Covering 161,100 hectares that reach all the way to the Argentine border, it is the Región de Aysén's third largest national reserve and the country's fifth largest. Besides conserving a large portion of the Aysén-Patagonia steppe, it also preserves an important archaeological site, La Cueva de las Manos (The Cave of Hands).

The land of RN Lago Jeínemeni is sculpted into sheer mountains and glaciers. Many peaks are over 1,500 meters (4,921 ft). The highest is Cerro Jeínemeni at 2,600 meters (8,530 ft). The largest river is Jeínemeni which flows out of Lago Jeínemeni. Other waterways are the Guisoca, Verde and Amarillo Rivers. Scattered across the steppe are other lakes and lagoons, like the Verde, Guisoca, Ventisquero and Escondida. Precipitation in the reserve varies from 600 millimeters (24 in) in the northeast section to 2,000 millimeters (79 in) at higher altitudes. The average yearly temperature is 4°C (39°F).

The eastern part of RN Lago Jeínemeni is characterized by the Aysén-Patagonia steppe. In the more humid western zone of the reserve is the Aysén Caducifolio forest. Here the dominant flora are the lenga beech, the Antarctic beech, the Magellan barberry and the prickly heath. Birds are abundant. Among those to be seen are the Condor, the Black-chested Buzzard-eagle, the American Kestrel, the Austral Blackbird, the Magellanic Woodpecker, the Austral Parakeet, the Striped Woodpecker, the Austral Thrush, the Black-throated Huet-Huet and the Spectacled Duck. Common mammals include the South Andean deer, the puma, the guanaco the Patagonian skunk, the Geoffroy's Cat, the highland gerbil mouse and the olive grass mouse. Scurrying in the underbrush are the tree lizard and the Chilean four-eyed frog.

The first access point, 25 kilometers (15.5 mi) from Chile Chico is at Sector Piedra Clavada, named after an enigmatic 40-meter

(131 ft) tall free-standing rock polished by the wind and rising out of the pampa. Here is a trail to the archaeological site Cueva de las Manos (not to be confused with a site of the same name near Perito Moreno, Argentina) (distance: 6 km/3.6 mi, difficulty: medium, duration: 1 day round trip). Upon the walls of this cave, the Aónikenk people who once roamed these plains left hundreds of handprints. These cave paintings are estimated to be nearly 7,000 years old.

The road continues southwestward to the main entry into RN Lago Jeínemeni (60 km/36 mi from Chile Chico). On the east shore of Lago Jeínemeni, the ranger station has boating and camping facilities.

From here leave three trails:

La Leona (distance: 20 km/12 mi, difficulty: medium-hard, duration: 2 days)—From Lago Jeínemeni this path follows the Estero San Antonio to Valle Chacabuco, where a new private reserve is being established northeast of Cochrane.

Estero Ventisquero (15 km/9.3 mi, medium – hard, 3 days round trip)—This trail leads to the northwest corner of Lago Verde, up Estero Ventisquero to the glaciers in the deep interior of the reserve.

Lago Verde (5 km/3 mi, medium, 3 hours round trip)—A Hike through an undulating land, from the sapphire-blue Lago Jeínemeni to the emerald-green Lago Verde.

Camping at sites established along Sendero Valle Hermoso on the shores of Lago Jeínemeni costs $5. The only way to arrive to either Sector Piedra Clavada or the administration center is in a private, double-traction vehicle or on tour with a guide. There are no bridges at the main entry to the park and all streams must be forded, so a 4x4 is necessary. Hiring a car in Chile Chico costs about $80 round trip. You'll need to tell the driver when to come back to pick you up. Updated: Jul 08, 2009.

COCHRANE

 165 m   3,800   67

Climb to the top of the hill and you'll get a condors-eye view of the stars of Cochrane spreading out below. The valley is surrounded with mountains. Cochrane is one of the region's fastest-growing cities and is a mandatory stop for journeyers on the Carretera Austral. It's the perfect place to change buses, restock on money and fuel up.

Travelers also spend time here to explore the natural beauty of the surrounding area. Just a few kilometers to the east is the Reserva Nacional Tamango, with endless kilometers of hiking trails meandering through the Andean Patagonian steppe. To the north is the new nature reserve, El Valle Chacabuco. Here, volunteers have been helping scientists restore a vital habitat for the Chilean miniature deer by laying the foundation for a new national park. South of the city you'll find waterfalls and lakes. The trout and salmon fishing is excellent.

You don't have to be an outdoors enthusiast to enjoy Cochrane. The Museo de Cochrane has interesting exhibits. Facing the Plaza de Armas is Parroquia San José Obrero, an unusual octagonal church with a free-standing bell tower. At the corner of Río Colonia and Previske are two salutes to mate, the herbal beverage. One is a wooden sculpture of a hand raising a mate into the sky. The other is a mate-gourd-shaped building used by the Boy and Girl Scouts.

The Cochrane River Valley was discovered in 1899 by explorer Hans Steffens while searching for a pass into Argentina. Much later the river and lake were named after Englishman Lord Thomas Cochrane, a Vice Admiral of the Chilean Navy and a hero of the independence. Like other cities in the region, Cochrane was settled by cattle and sheep farmers that established themselves in these verdant valleys. In the Las Latas area on the shores of Lago Cochrane, a village was built close to the major ranch of the time, Compañía Ganadera Valle Chacabuco (now a nature reserve). The village was later moved to its present location. In 1954, when there were only ten adobe houses, it was officially incorporated. Since the arrival of the Carretera Austral in 1988, the city has grown significantly. Updated: Jul 10, 2009.

When to Go
Rains come every month, with the heaviest falling April – August. October, December and February are the driest. The warmest time of the year is December – February when temperatures reach the low 20s°C (upper 60s°F). Between May and July, highs only reach 5 – 8°C (41 – 46°F) and lows fall to below freezing.

NORTHERN PATAGONIA

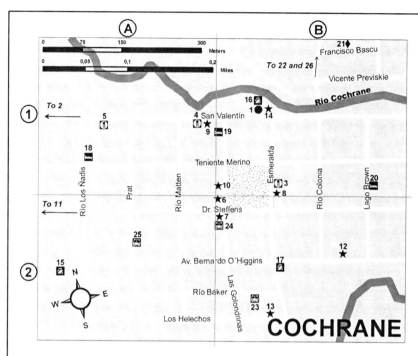

Activities ●

1 Sala Museográfica B1
2 Valle Chacabuco A1

Eating 🍴

3 Café Tamango B1
4 Hervalen A1
5 Restaurant El Fogón A1

Services ★

6 Agrupación Defensores del Espíritu de la Patagonia B2
7 Aguas Patagónicas B2
8 Banco del Estado B1
9 Chilexpress   A1
10 Ciber Centro Cochrane B1
11 Conaf A2
12 Hospital Cochrane B2
13 Lavandería Juanita B2
14 Tourism Office B1

Shopping 🔳

15 Taller Bordados de la Patagonia A2
16 Taller Los Tamangos del Baker B1
17 Teresa Catalán Cuevas B2

Sleeping 🛏

18 Hospedaje La Sureña A1
19 Hotel Wellmann B1
20 Residencial Cero a Cero B1

Tours ♦

21 Kayak B1
22 Oscar Verduga B1

Transportation 🚍

23 Buses Acuario, Aldea, López y Sao Paulo B2
24 Buses Ale B2
25 Buses Don Carlos A2
26 Patagonino Rent a Car B1

Cochrane holds celebrations all year round:
Last week of January: La Ruta del Huemul—A trek from Reserva Nacional Tamango to Valle Chacabuco, home of the future Parque Patagonia.
Mid-February: Festival Costumbrista—rodeo, typical foods and other events.
Second week of March: town anniversary celebration.

August 31 – September 1: Festival de la Escarcha—Frost Festival with traditional Patagonian dances and other cultural displays.
September 18: Día Nacional de la Cueca.
Early November: El Encuentro de Acordeonistas—Encounter of musicians and singers from all over the region.
Early December: El Encuentro de Jineteadas Coraje. Updated: Jul 10, 2009.

NORTHERN PATAGONIA

Getting To and Away From Cochrane

Cochrane is 334 kilometers (208 mi) south of Coyhaique on the Carretera Austral (Ruta 7). The city has two gas stations, a mechanic and tire repair shop.

BY BUS

During the low season, bus service is less frequent. Buy tickets in advance. There is no central bus terminal. The bus offices are sprinkled throughout town:

Don Carlos (Monday – Friday 9 a.m. – 1 p.m., 3 – 7 p.m., Sunday 9 a.m. – noon. Prat 334. Tel: 56-67-522150).
Buses Ale (Monday – Friday 10 a.m. – 11 a.m., 4 – 7 p.m. Las Golondrinas and Steffens. Tel: 56-67-522242).
Buses **Acuario 13**, **Aldea**, **López** and **Sao Paulo** (Monday – Saturday 9 a.m. – 1:30 p.m., 3 – 9 p.m., Sunday 9 a.m. – 1 p.m., 4 – 8 p.m. Río Baker 349. Tel: 56-67-255726 / 56-67-237630).
Sabra (Merino 375. Tel: 56-9-6726390).

To Coyhaique: **Don Carlos, Acuario 13, Sao Paulo, Sabra** (daily 8 a.m. – 9 a.m., $20-22, 7.5 – 8.5 hours)—These buses also stop at Puerto Bertrand ($6), Cruce Guadal ($7), Río Tranquilo ($12), Cruce Murta ($13)and Cerro Castillo ($17).

To Chile Chico: **Transportes Ale** (Wednesday, Saturday 10 a.m., $26, 7 – 8 hours)—Also passes through Puerto Guadal ($13).

To San Lorenzo: **Acuario 13** (Monday, Thursday, $6, 3.5 hours).

To Caleta Tortel: **Aldea** and **López** (daily 9:30 a.m., $12, 4.5 hours).

To Villa O'Higgins: **Don Carlos** (Monday, Tuesday, Friday 8 a.m., $22, 7 – 8 hours).

BY BOAT

Barcaza Padre Antonio Ronchi is the ferry that connects the Carretera Austral between Puerto Yungay and Río Bravo, through Fiordo Mitchell. Check local papers or tourism offices for any change of schedule.

Puerto Yungay – Río Bravo: 10 a.m., noon, 6 p.m.
Río Bravo – Puerto Yungay: 11 a.m., 1 p.m., 7 p.m. Updated: Jul 09, 2009.

Getting Around

Cochrane is so small that it has no city buses or taxis. You can lease an auto from **Patagonino Rent a Car** (Luís Báez 1042. Tel: 56-9-5084051 / 56-8-2510802, E-mail: patagonino@gmail.com). Updated: Jul 09, 2009.

Services

TOURISM

The municipality's **oficina de turismo** is in the same building as the museum (Monday – Friday 8:30 a.m. – 5:30 p.m., in summer also weekends 11 a.m. – 8 p.m. San Valentín 555. Tel: 56-67-522356, E-mail: turismo@cochrane-patagonia.cl, URL: www.cochranepatagonia.cl). For information about Reserva Nacional Tamango and a hiking map, go to **Conaf** (Monday – Friday 8:30 a.m. – 5:30 p.m. Steffens, at the end of Neff. Tel: 56-67-522164, E-mail: piero.caviglia@conaf.cl). **Agrupación Defensores del Espíritu de la Patagonia** is working on regional environmental issues (Las Golondrinas 198. Tel: 56-67-522743). The police station is near the plaza (Esmeralda and Merino).

MONEY

Banco del Estado exchanges U.S. dollars and euros. Its ATM accepts MasterCard and Cirrus; some travelers have said they were successful in getting a cash advance on their Visa card (Monday – Friday 9 a.m. – 2 p.m. Esmeraldsa, between Merino and Steffens, Plaza de Armas). **Chilexpress** is the Western Union agent (Monday– Friday 9:30 a.m. – 12:30 p.m., 3 – 6 p.m., Saturday 10 a.m. – 1 p.m. San Valentín, between Las Golodrinas and Río Maitén). There are no money exchanges.

KEEPING IN TOUCH

When sending a letter from the **post office**, know that the mail goes out only three times per week (Monday – Friday 9:30 a.m. – 1 p.m., 3 – 6 p.m., Saturday 10 a.m. – 1 p.m O'Higgins 650). The only places to go on-line are **Ciber Centro Cochrane** (daily 10 a.m. – 11 p.m. Las Golondrinas, between Merino and Steffens; $1.60 per hour) and the **public library** (San Valentín, next to the museum; 20 minutes free). To place a phone call (national $0.30 per minute, international from $1.70 per minute), head to **Aguas Patagónicas** (Las Golondrinas 399) or **El Encargo** (Merino and Prat).

MEDICAL

The public health facility is **Hospital Cochrane** (O'Higgins 755. Tel: 56-67-261330). **Almacén Farmacéutico Valery** is the only drug store (Río Colonia and San Valentín).

LAUNDRY

Lavandería Juanita does laundry (Los Helechos 336. Tel: 56-7-786-1491). Updated: Jul 10, 2009.

SHOPPING

For such a small town, Cochrane has an impressive number of artisans. For a one-stop shopping excursion, step into the museum / tourism office where **Taller Los Tamangos del Baker** has leather, wood, wool and other crafts for sale (San Valentín 555. Tel: 56-67-522326 / 8-885-5564).

Some individual craftspeople to visit are: **Teresa Catalán Cuevas** (Café Ñirrantal, Av. O'Higgins 650. Tel: 56-67-522604)—jams, liquors and other confections of native fruits.

Taller Bordados de la Patagonia (Av. O'Higgins 157)—embroidery.

For fishing, camping and hardware go to **Melero** (Monday – Saturday 10 a.m. – 1 p.m., 3 – 8 p.m. Las Golondrinas 148). You can obtain a fishing license at the municipality (Esmeralda and Steffens). Updated: Jul 10, 2009.

Things to See and Do

Many travelers who come to Cochrane take a day off to visit the Reserva Nacional Tamango, though there are countless other places where you can explore the wilderness. Laguna Esmeralda , for instance, has excellent swimming, kayaking and fishing (7 km/4.2 mi southeast). Other places to drop a line for trout and salmon are the Cochrane and Baker Rivers and Cochrane Lake. To the south are the waterfalls Salto Valle Castillo (12 km/7.2 mi) and Los Mellizos (10 km/6 mi). From San Lorenzo you can see Laguna Esmeralda, Valle del Río Salto and Campo de Hielo Norte's snowed peaks (30 km/18 mi southwest). A new nature reserve, Valle Chacabuco, sits to the north on the Paso Roballos road. Updated: Jul 09, 2009.

Sala Museográfica

(ADMISSION: Free) Sala Museográfica, also called Museo Cochrane, has more than a few rooms of displays. The first ones give in-depth explanation of the geology and natural history of the Baker River region. Flora and fauna specimens are also highlighted and several galleries are devoted to the pioneers of this land. A small archaeology case shows bone and stone tools from the original inhabitants, the Aónikenk. All explanations are in Spanish. Open Monday – Friday 8:30 a.m. – 5:30 p.m., in summer also weekends 11 a.m. – 8 p.m. San Valentín 555. Tel: 56-67-522356, E-mail: turismo@cochranepatagonia.cl, URL: www.cochranepatagonia.cl. Updated: Jul 10, 2009.

Valle Chacabuco

This former sheep estancia stretches across Valle Chacabuco, from Reserva Nacional Tamango to Reserva Nacional Lago Jeinemeni. Conservación Patagonia, a non-profit organization, is working to protect 173,000 acres of Patagonian steppe in Valle Chacabuco. With the help of biologists, the environment is being restored to its original balance so that the South Andean deer (*huemul*) population can rebound.

Conservacion Patagonica has recently developped a visitors center, hiking trails, campsites and other infrastructure. If you are interested in volunteering in the new park, contact Paula Herrera (E-mail: pherrera@conservacionpatagonica.cl) Km 11 Camino X-63 to Paso Roballos. URL: www.conservacionpatagonica.org. Updated: Jul 10, 2009.

Reserva Nacional Tamango

(ADMISSION: Foreign adults $6, children $3; Chilean adults $2, children $0.60) Reserva Nacional (RN) Tamango, formerly known as RN Lago Cochrane, protects 6,925 hectares of landscape that was carved and polished by retreated glaciers. The main resident is the endangered South Andean deer. The park is also a major bird habitat.

The park has nine trails. Some wind along Río and Lago Cochrane, which define the east edge of the reserve. Others go for the higher ground, to Cerro Tamango (1,722 m/5,650 ft) and Cerro Húngaro (1,214 m/3,983 ft). The river and lake are fine for boating and fishing. There are campsites available. The reserve is open all year. In winter there is a lot of snow and temperatures reach -7ºC (19ºF). Rains are frequent in spring. In summer, temperatures reach 27ºC (81ºF). Conaf has a map with instructions on each of the nine trails. Updated: Jul 10, 2009.

Tours

Tour operators are a scarce commodity in Cochrane. If you'd like to go sport fishing, contact guide **Oscar Verduga** (Calle Luís Báez 840. Tel: 56-67-522526 / 56-9-6724812). **Kayak** gives kayaking lessons, has a repair shop, and organizes river and sea excursions (Bascur 15. Tel: 56-67-522633 / 56-7-6055335, E-mail: rphc@hotmail.com / cayincita@hotmail.com). Updated: Jul 09, 2009.

Lodging

Cochrane has a surprising number of hotels for such a small town. When the summer winds down, many cheaper hostels turn into boarding houses for students. Less expensive lodging can be found east of the plaza. Many of these are family hospedajes with common kitchens. Pricier options are along the blocks west of the Plaza de Armas, especially along Calle Lago Brown. South of Cochrane is Refugio-Camping Ñires, whose English- and German-speaking owners also have a travel library and horses (45 km/28 mi south to Puente Río Barrancosa, then another 9 km down a signposted turn-off. E-mail: lillischindele@yahoo.de). Updated: Jul 10, 2009.

Hospedaje La Sureña

(ROOMS: $4 – 12) Hospedaje La Sureña is a small inn run by a diminutive widow. But the lady of the house is big on welcoming guests to the clean rooms. Most are shared, and there are only a few singles. She also lets travelers pitch a tent in the yard. Beneath the trees are tables where you can eat or catch up on journal writing. All the guests share common bathrooms. The kitchen is open for all to cook in or to sit around the warm wood stove. Rooms $12 per person with breakfast, camping $4. Merino 698. Tel: 56-7-7646669. Updated: Jul 10, 2009.

Residencial Cero a Cero

(ROOMS: $16 – 40) The original part of this rambling inn is an old log house. The rooms are spacious with comfortable beds, TVs and a luxury rarely seen in Southern Chile: their own heaters. Both the common and private bathrooms have plenty of hot water. The included breakfast is a filling affair, with cheeses and meats. The living area is a cozy place to rest after a day of hiking or a long-day's bus journey. Common bathrooms: $16 per person; private bath: single $30, double $40. Lago Brown 464. Tel: 56-67-522158, E-mail: ceroacero@gmail.com. Updated: Jul 10, 2009.

Hotel Wellmann

(ROOMS: $78 – 98) Hotel Wellmann is Cochrane's original hotel, serving travelers for over 40 years. Even these days, it is considered the classiest place to stay. The large rooms are sunny. To keep these spaces cozy and warm, the floors are carpeted and the entire inn has central heating. Although Hotel Wellmann is under renovation, it is still taking guests.

Price includes continental breakfast. Las Golondrinas 565. Tel: 56-67-522171. Updated: Jul 10, 2009.

Restaurants

Cochrane has few restaurants. Most are in hotels, serving the general public during the high season. Food is a bit more expensive here than in other parts of Chile, with daily specials averaging $9. The town has many small grocery stores around. The largest and most complete is **Supermercado Melero** (Monday – Saturday 10 a.m. – 1 p.m., 3 – 8 p.m. Las Golondrinas 148), which also has camp stove fuel. Updated: Jul 09, 2009.

Hervalen

(ENTREES: $1.20 – 8.40) For a quick breakfast on your way to Reserva Nacional Tamango or a light dinner after a day of sightseeing, stop into clean and bright Hervalen. This small, carry-out only snack bar has a wide variety of fast foods, like empanadas, pizza, hot dogs, stuffed potatoes or sandwiches. If your appetite is a bit heftier, order the fried chicken with French fries. Open Monday – Saturday 9:30 a.m. – 2 p.m., 4:30 – 9:30 p.m. San Valentín 466. Tel: 56-9-4877933. Updated: Jul 09, 2009.

Café Tamango

(ENTREES: $3) Set deep in a yard across from the Plaza de Armas is a small white house, home to Café Tamango. The various brightly designed rooms create intimate spaces where you can enjoy a sandwich, pizza or other light meal. On a warm day, the tables on the side patio are a pleasant place to try one of the delicious desserts with an espresso or cappuccino, while leafing through a magazine from the rack. Open Monday – Saturday 10:30 a.m. – 9:30 p.m. Esmeralda 464. Tel: 56-9-1584521. Updated: Jul 10, 2009.

Restaurant El Fogón

(ENTREES: from $10, LUNCH: $9) Of the few eateries in town, Restaurant El Fogón seems to be the most popular. The large portions of home-cooked food may be the reason. The *paila marina* (seafood stew) is chunk-full of fruits of the sea. Salmon prepared with a variety of sauces, including caper, is also on the menu, along with more run-of-the-mill meats. El Fogón also rents rooms for $14 per person with breakfast. Daily 11 a.m. – 4 p.m., 7 – 10:30 p.m. San Valentín 651. Tel: 56-67-522240 / 56-8-2612017. Updated: Jul 10, 2009.

NORTHERN PATAGONIA

CALETA TORTEL

 0–145m 320 67

When the misty clouds part, they reveal a landscape molded into fjords, channels and islands. Across the forested hills streaked with waterfalls are seven kilometers worth (4.2 mi) of boardwalks made from cypress wood. These are the "streets" of a quiet village named Caleta Tortel, declared a Monumento Nacional y Zone Típica in 2001. You can spend hours exploring this maze of boardwalks.

The town is divided into four sectors: Rincón, Centro (Base), Playa Ancha and El Junquillo. All along the way are lookout points, boat docks and stilt houses à la Chilote. Signs identify plant species with local names. Between Sector Rincón and Centro is Plaza Elicura, a wooden square plaza with a wrap-around balcony and benches and brilliant views of the town, hills and sea. Just after Sector Rincón is a lighthouse and mirador with a view down onto the lumber wharves. At the beginning of Sector Centro is the playground Great Britain's Prince William built when he did his gap year here with Raleigh International in 2000.

Caleta Tortel is in the southern zone of the Western Patagonian archipelago on Golfo de Penas, at the mouth of Río Baker. Eighty percent of the Tortel region consists of protected wildlife areas. It is set in the midst of the Campo de Hielo Norte (protected by Parque Nacional Laguna San Rafael) and the Campo de Hielo Sur (protected by Parque Nacional Bernardo O'Higgins). You can visit both of these parks from Caleta Tortel. To the north is Ventisquero Steffens and the Ruta Patrimonial Campo de Hielo Norte, a hike to a viewpoint where you can see the glacier. There is another boat trip that heads south to Ventisquero Jorge Montt, which flows off Campo de Hielo Sur. A project is underway to create a new national marine park that will include Caleta Tortel.

A popular boating excursion from Caleta Tortel goes to the Monumento Histórico Isla de los Muertos ($100–120 per boat). In 1906, Chilotes who worked for the Compañía Explotadora del Baker were buried here. The exact cause of their death is uncertain. Some say it was the result of an epidemic, others that the Compañía exiled them their so it would not have to pay their salaries. You can also hire launches or kayaks to explore the bay, Río Baker, Río Bravo, Lago Quetro and Río Pascua.

Modern Caleta Tortel dates from 1901 when the government gave 100 Chilean and immigrant European families lands in the region. In 1903, Mauricio Braun and other Punta Arenas businessmen founded the Sociedad Nacional de Ganadería y Colonización, later called the Compañía Explotadora del Baker, at Bajo Piragua on the north shore of the Río Baker delta. In what is now Sector Bajo Rincón, locals built a wharf and other installations for the export of the Guaitecas cypress. In 1927, lands were finally transferred to residents. The Compañía's installations burned down in 1932.

Caleta Tortel's economy is yet largely based on timbering cypress. Since becoming connected with the outside world in 2003, crafts and tourism have started playing a larger role. Craftspeople primarily work with wood. The typical wooden hatchets (*hachitas de Madera*) symbolize the resilience and determination of those who colonized this village.

The village's festivities are the Festival de la Canción del Baker the second week of February and the Semana Aniversario with regattas and decorated boat floats (*botes alegóricos*) at the end of May.

Getting To and Away From Caleta Tortel

The turn-off from Carretera Austral is 128 kilometers (79.5 mi) south of Cochrane. From there a road, squeezed between Río Baker and sheer rock cliffs, wends 22 kilometers (13.7 mi) to Caleta Tortel and ends at a parking lot.

Caleta has a vast network of boardwalks. When it rains, the boardwalk is slick. There are a lot of steps, which can be problematic for people with bad knees, ankles or other walking problems. Take this all into consideration when choosing where to stay. Water taxis are also available: from Rincón to Centro the cost is $5, from Rincón to Playa Ancha $10.

BY BUS

Bus service is less frequent during the low season. Rain or snow can temporary close the road at any time of the year. There is no service from Villa O'Higgins to Caleta Tortel, and the Villa-O'Higgins – Cochrane bus does not meet the Cochrane – Caleta Tortel one. All buses leave from the parking lot.

To Cochrane: **Buses Aldea** (Tuesday, Thursday, Saturday 2:30 p.m., Friday 3:30 p.m., $12, 4.5 hours).

To Vagabundo (crossroads with the Carretera Austral, $3).

To Coyhaique: **Don Manuel** (Thursday, Sunday, $38, 10 hours).

If you are coming from the south on a bus, you'll have to walk 22 kilometers to Tortel. Hitchhiking is difficult, as the bus arrives at 3 p.m. To get from Caleta Tortel to Villa O'Higgins, you might be able to make the connection with the Cochrane–Villa O'Higgins bus south, though it will be tight. A bus plies the Caleta Tortel-Puerto Yungay-Lago Quetro route (Thursday 8:30 a.m. $4, same day return, passing by Puerto Yungay at 8 p.m.).

BY BOAT
The tourism office and municipality provide a list of boat service providers for local excursions. Also ask at the municipality about the regular local service to Puerto Edén (in summer: weekly). Updated: Jul 10, 2009.

Services
Most businesses in town, such as hotels and tour operators, use the village's public phone (56-67-211876) as their contact number. The **tourism office** at the portal entrance of the parking lot is open only November – mid-April (daily 10 a.m. – 9 p.m.).

During other times of the year, stop by the **municipality** (Sector Base. Tel: 56-67-211876, E-mail: turismo@municipalidaddetortel.cl, URL: www.municipalidaddetortel.cl). Around the plaza are the public **library** (free Internet), the **phone** center and **post office**. The **Conaf** office and **health post** are in Sector Rincón. There are no banks or pharmacies.

For local crafts, visit:
Agrupación Cultural Entre Hielos (Sector Centro)—wood.
Erika Schoenffendt(Sector Rincón Bajo) —wood, woolens.
María Vargas (Sector Rincón Bajo)—jams.

Tours
Many locals hire boats to do excursions around the bay, to Isla de los Muertos, to Puerto Yungay and up the rivers. The tourism office and municipality provide a list of boat service providers and prices.
Daniel Torres (E-mail: patagontorres@hotmail.com)—kayaking.
Emilia Astorga(Sector El Junquillo, E-Mail: emiliastorge@hotmail.com)—kayaking.

Lodging
Most lodging has shared bathrooms. For free camping, visit Sector El Junquillo on the Río Baker delta. Beware that the delta area has lots of mosquitos.

Hospedaje Hielo Sur (Sector Rincón Bajo. Tel: 56-67-211876)—$10 per person with breakfast.

Hospedaje Brisas del Sur (Sector Playa Ancha. Tel: 56-67-211876)—$17 per person, double with private bathroom $50.

Ecolodge Tortel (Tel: 56-2-1960270, URL: www.ecolodgechile.cl)—double $180 with breakfast.

Restaurants
To ward off the damp chill, Tortelinos drink a lot of mate. Check out **El Mirador** (Sector Base s/n. E-mail: nataysol@hotmail.com). Other restaurants are between the Rincón Bajo and Base Sectors, like **Restaurant Sabores Locales** and **Pub Lady Diana**. Updated: Jul 10, 2009.

VILLA O'HIGGINS

 255 m   500   67

Villa O'Higgins is surrounded by mountains and native forest. In its center is the grassy plaza with the obligatory busts of Chilean heroes. A covered wooden arcade provides shelter from the rain. On Sunday mornings, it's the favorite napping spot for horses.

Villa O'Higgins is a 20th-century town. In 1903 – 1904 the Compañía Ganadera arrived in these parts to establish a massive cattle ranch stretching from the mouth of Río Mayer in Villa O'Higgins south to the coast of Laguna El Río de las Vueltas. When the Chilean government authorized colonization in the region, the Compañía began pulling out. Some workers stayed behind as settlers along with immigrant Europeans. During the 1920s, Chileans also came to build their homes. In 1966, President Eduardo Frei Montalva officially founded Villa O'Higgins.

The area was also part of Padre Antonio Ronchi's circuit in the 1970s and 1980s. One of his projects was the yellow church on the plaza, which now houses the Museo de la Patagonia Padre Antonio Ronchi. Built in 1977, the museum displays the life

NORTHERN PATAGONIA

and work of the hardy folks of this area (If closed, ask at the tourism kiosk or the municipality. Ca. Río Bravo).

The town's economy continues to be based on cattle raising and timber, and in recent years, tourism. Several young artisans are reviving traditional Patagonian craft techniques, like rawhide braiding and woodworking, to create everyday utensils and souvenirs.

Festivities reflect these characteristics of the village:

First week of February: Bandeo de Animales desde Lago O'Higgins a Bahía Bahamóndez—a cattle drive.
Second week of February: El Encuentro Cultural Tropeando pa' no Olvidar—a celebration of Villa O'Higgins' culture and traditions.
September 20: El Aniversario—the town's anniversary celebration with a big BBQ.
Second week of November: El Encuentro Cultural Regional Indígena—a regional meeting of indigenous peoples.
Second week of December: Jineteadas del Mayer—rodeo time!

Although most people come to Villa O'Higgins just to do the border crossing to El Chaltén, the village has its own attractions. Five trekking trails invite visitors out into the wilds. Starting from Cerro Santiago behind the town are three paths: Sendero Cerro Santiago, Sendero Río Mosco and Sendero Cerro Submarino. Sendero Humedales Río Mayer, goes to wetlands frequented by birds. The city has a detailed map for these trails, as well as one for Sendero Altavista, one of two Senderos de Chile in the region. The second trail is the Tramo Ventisquero Chico, which leads from Mansilla Candelario on the far side of Lago O'Higgins to Ventisquero Chico.

The trails are best hiked September – April. The weather changes quickly, so if hiking, take rain and wind-proof clothing, water and high-energy food. Many of these trails may also be done on horseback. Another popular activity is sport fishing. During the summer, Hielo Sur does cruises around Lago O'Higgins to the foot of Glaciar O'Higgins (adults $100, children 8 – 14 $50, children under 8 years free, 11.5 hours).

The end of the Carretera Austral is not Villa O'Higgins. It continues another seven kilometers (4.2 mi) south to Puerto Bahamóndez on Lago O'Higgins. The road is an amazing feat of engineering, with over 90 curves. Here, the great highway finishes its 1,247-kilometer (775-mi) journey from Puerto Montt. The hope is that one day this road will lead further south, passing through Argentina, to Puerto Natales—if engineers can find a way around the glaciers, mountains and numerous lakes.

Getting To and Away From Villa O'Higgins

BY BOAT
The **Barcaza Padre Antonio Ronchi** ferry connects the Carretera Austral between Puerto Yungay and Río Bravo, through Fiordo Mitchell: free, 1 hour. (Puerto Yungay – Río Bravo: 10 a.m., noon, 6 p.m. Río Bravo – Puerto Yungay: 11 a.m., 1 p.m., 7 p.m.). A sign on the north edge of town displays the current hours of this ferry. It also has a hand-carved sign that warns of the difficulty of hitchhiking northward.

Boat **Hielo Sur** runs the Puerto Bahamóndez – Candelario Mansilla ferry, the first leg of the Paso Dos Lagunas border crossing into Argentina (Carretera Austral, across from the airport. Tel: 56-67-431821, E-Mail: hielosur@villaohiggins.com, URL: www.hielosur.com). For complete information, see Carretera Austral and Northern Patagonia Border Crossings – Paso Dos Lagunas (p. 394). Once a week during the summer, this boat brings supplies to the isolated homesteads around the lake, instead of going to Glaciar O'Higgins. In winter, the boat only runs weekly.

BY BUS OR PLANE
Whether you're busing or flying out, **Dan Carlos** is the only act in town (Monday – Friday 9 a.m. – 12:30 p.m., 3 – 6 p.m., Saturday 9 a.m.-noon. Lago O'Higgins, between Río Pascua and Río Mayer). During the low season, bus service is less frequent. Rain or snow can temporary close the road at any time of the year.

Bus To Cochrane (Tuesday, Wednesday, Saturday 8 a.m., $22, 7 – 8 hours).
Plane to Coyhaique: (In summer: Monday, Thursday 1 p.m., $72, 1.3 hr).

There is no service from Villa O'Higgins to Caleta Tortel, and the Villa-O'Higgins – Cochrane bus does not meet the Cochrane – Caleta Tortel one. If you take the bus, you'll have to walk the 22 kilometers (13.7 mi) to Tortel or try hitchhiking, but catching a ride is difficult on this stretch.

To get from Caleta Tortel to Villa O-Higgins, you might be able to make the connection with the Cochrane – Villa O'Higgins bus south, though it will be tight. A bus travels the Lago Quetro – Puerto Yungay – Caleta Tortel route (Puerto Yungay: Thursday 8 p.m., $4).

Pick-up truck to Puerto Bahamóndez (January – February: Monday, Wednesday, Saturday; Early-March: Wednesday, Saturday, $3. This may be paid in U.S. dollars, euros, Argentine pesos or Chilean pesos). Updated: Jul 10, 2009.

Services

During the summer, a **tourism information** kiosk is open on the plaza (Monday – Friday 9 a.m. – 12:30 p.m., 2:30 – 5:30 p.m. Calle O'Higgins). At other times of the year, stop by the **municipality** (Monday – Friday 9 a.m. – 12:30 p.m., 2:30 – 5:30 p.m. Lago Cristie 121. Tel: 56-67-211849, URL: www.villaohiggins.cl). The **Conaf** office is at the end of Río Pascua.

The town also has a **first aid post**, **post office** (Lago Christie and Río Mayer) and **satellite phone**. There is no bank or ATM; for money exchanges, try Hielo Sur. Free **Internet** is available at the public library (Lago Christie and Río Bravo); the town is wired with WiFi, though the connection is unsteady.

There are various crafts shops. Rolando Arratia works in reed and rawhide. Javier Cárdenas and Hugo Alvarado specialize in woodworking. A shop on Lago O'Higgins, between Río Mosco and Rio Bravo, sells fishing gear.

Tours

Hielo Sur (Carretera Austral, across from the airport. Tel: 56-67-431821, E-Mail: hielosur@villaohiggins.com, URL: www.hielosur.com) —Boat excursions to Glaciar O'Higgins and charter trips.

Nelson Henríquez (Tel: 56-67-211849)— Fishing, horseback riding.

Adolfo Guinao (Tel: 56-67-431873)— Horseback riding to local attractions and special excursions on the Ruta Los Colonos (from Villa O'Higgins to Cochrane).

Lodging

North of the airstrip on the main road are several campgrounds.

Hospedaje Carretera Austral (Río Colorado and Lago Salto. Tel: 56-67-431819)— $10 per person.

La Cascada (Lago Salto and Río Mosco. Tel: 56-67-431833)—$12 – 14 per person, kitchen.

Hostería Villa O'Higgins (Lote 5, Predio Angelita. Tel: 56-67-431870)—single $50, double $65.

Restaurants

The town has four basic grocery stores, a butcher shop and a bakery.

Restaurant-Bar Entre Patagones (Carretera Austral s/n, north entrance to town. Tel: 56-67-431810, E-mail: entrepatagones@gmail.com).

Restaurante Campanario (Lago O'Higgins 72).

San Gabriel (O'Higgins and Río Los Ñadis). Updated: Jul 10, 2009.

!!!!!

NORTHERN PATAGONIA

SOUTHERN PATAGONIA

Southern Patagonia, Tierra del Fuego and Antarctica

Icy channels and fjords tear the land, fraying it into thousands of islands. Ragged, glacier-frosted mountains scrape the sky. To the east, the earth relaxes into pampas and steppes. Guanaco and ñandú wade through stiff, golden grasses while flamingos feed in icy lagoons. Wind-sheared trees permanently stoop to one side. In the distance is the frozen continent of Antarctica. Welcome to Southern Patagonia and Tierra del Fuego.

This region is a magnificent land of castle-like, rocky mountains, glistening ice fields and virgin forests. It's the end of the world where ships have long rounded Cape Horn (*El Cabo de Hornos*) and been battered through Drake's Passage and the Straits of Magellan (*Estrecho de Magallanes*).The winds, whistling around

the farthest reaches of the Andes, are notorious for challenging cyclists and hikers. It is a land of 150,000 people, two million sheep, and a half-million penguins.

No road connects Chile's Northern Patagonia with its Southern part. Some day, perhaps, the Carretera Austral will find a way here. In the meantime, the only way to get there by land is to enter Argentina and exit again into Chile. The famous Navimag Canales Patagónicos ferry plows through the icy channels along the Pacific coast, from Puerto Montt to Puerto Natales.

Get ready to join the ranks of the indigenous peoples, explorers and colonizers and strike your claim in this wild land. Updated: Jun 29, 2009.

History

Millennia ago this part of the planet was covered with massive sheets of ice. About 12,000 years ago, the glaciers began receding, gouging the land into lagoons. The waters rose, creating a woven landscape of canals and fjords, embroidered with islands. Around the same time the first humans wandered across the cold Patagonia pampas, following herds of guanaco and milodón to feed their families. These peoples later divided into four nations: the Aónikenk (Tehuelche) who wandered the eastern plains hunting guanaco, the Kaweskar (Alakaluf) who canoed the western channels, the Selk'nam (Ona) who lived on the Tierra del Fuego island and the Yámana (Yaganes), expert mariners who paddled the water passages south of the great island.

European navigators slowly began to explore the Atlantic Ocean further and further south, searching for a way around the world. Piece by piece the complex geography of this land came to be understood. In 1520 Portuguese seaman Ferdinand Magellan, in service to the Spanish crown, discovered the Straits that now bear his name. He died during the voyage around the world, but his crew continued on to become the first to circumnavigate the globe. During a journey to the Far East in 1578, Englishman Sir Francis Drake found his ship blown southward to another "sea" after passing through the Straits. This implied that the land mass south of the Estrecho de Magallanes was an island, and not another continent. The channel south of Tierra del Fuego was then called Drake Passage.

The Dutch East India Company would later come to control this passage through the Straits, forcing competitors to search for an alternate route. Willem Schouten, leaving from the Dutch port Hoorn, sailed out on a search mission. He found another passage, the Strait of Le Maire, and named the islands there Cape Hoorn, later changed to Cape Horn by the British. Robert Fitz Roy, captain of *The Beagle*, explored the intricate tapestry of these shores during two expeditions: from 1826 to 1830 and from 1833 to 1834. Naturalist Charles Darwin was also present on the voyage. Today, the waterway between Tierra del Fuego and Isla Navarino is called Canal Beagle.

Both Chile and Argentina pushed to colonize Patagonia. In the 1870s, Chilotes and European immigrants arrived to establish broad economic empires spanning the region. These were beyond the political control of the distant

Highlights

Parque Nacional Torres del Paine (p.480)—The major goal of most visitors to Chile's Southern Patagonia and Tierra del Fuego is to do the **"W" trek** through the windy wilds of this national park near Puerto Natales.

Navigate the **Patagonian channels and fjords**—Whether a short ride across Seno de Última Esperanza, from **Puerto Natales (p.469)** to **Parque Nacional Bernardo O'Higgins (p.478)** or on the granddaddy of them all, Navimag's **Canales Patagónicos ferry (p.480)** from Puerto Montt to Puerto Natales, this is the way to get up-close to dolphins, sea lions, glaciers and a cornucopia of sea birds.

Penguins—Who could refuse an afternoon with these tuxedoed birds? Catch them at **Monumento Natural Isla de Magdalena (p.468)** in the Strait of Magellan or at the pingüinera at **Seno Otway (p.468)**, both accessible from Punta Arenas.

Parque Nacional Los Glaciares (p.504)—Home to the impressive **Perito Moreno Glacier (p.505)**, this UNESCO World Heritage Site boasts the largest ice caps in the southern hemisphere, outside of Antarctica.

Steam across the **Straits of Magellan** from **Punta Arenas (p.455)** to **Porvenir (p.518)**, where you can enjoy premier birdwatching and trout fishing, chat with a modern-day gold prospector, or trek the Cordillera Darwin.

Ushuaia, Argentina (p.533), is the tourist hub of Tierra del Fuego, and by far the most visited part of the region. Its beautiful setting and proliferation of tourist services make it an excellent base from which you can explore the many nearby attractions.

Visit the world's most southerly town, **Puerto Williams (p.528)**, on Isla Navarino. You can fly there or go by boat. Updated: Jun 10, 2009.

SOUTHERN PATAGONIA

Photo by Jason Halberstadt

capitals of either country. To further consolidate the lands, the indigenous peoples were hunted to near extinction. A few survived in Salesian and Anglican missions.

Three families soon came to possess much of the territory. José Menéndez immigrated from Asturia, Spain and José Nogueira from Portugal. The third was the Braun family from Russia, who settled in Punta Arenas. Don Mauricio Braun expanded his holdings to include millions of hectares of sheep ranches, meat processing plants, mines, the Banco de Chile y Argentina, and interests in telephone, electric, insurance and export-import companies. Shipping between Patagonian ports, from Puerto Deseado, Argentina, to Punta Arenas, was a tri-family enterprise, bolstered by the marriages between them. In 1919, however, employees, having endured peonage-like conditions of these enterprises went on strike. Their protest culminated in the great massacre of 1921, in which untold hundreds of workers died.

Today the Southern Patagonia and Tierra del Fuego is Chile's XII Región de Magallanes, which is divided into four provinces: Última Esperanza (capital: Puerto Natales), Magallanes (capital: Punta Arenas), Tierra del Fuego (capital: Porvenir) and Antarctica. Updated: Jun 10, 2009.

When to Go
From late spring to early fall, especially during the months of December to March, southern Patagonia and Tierra del Fuego are popular destinations for Chilean and foreign tourists. Prices rise and lodging is difficult to come by. Winter (June – August) is a second high season, when people come to enjoy snow sports. At this time of year, only Parque Nacional Torres del Paine and Monumento Natural Cueva del Milodón remain open.

In the summer, the weather is sunny and windy. Daytime temperatures reach 17°

– 20°C (63° – 68°F) and dip to about 5°C (41°F). Daylight lasts up to 18 hours. This is the dryer time of the year, with 10 – 25 millimeters (0.5 – 1 inch) of rain. Winter is less windy. During the day, temperatures only get up to 5° – 8°C (41° – 46°F) for the high and go below freezing for the low. Precipitation, in the form of snow, is an average 25 – 30 millimeters (1 – 1.5 inches). Precipitation varies greatly in the region. Islands west of the Andes receive up to 7,000 millimeters (275 inches) per year, whereas the eastern pampas get only 400 millimeters (16 inches) annually. Updated: Jun 10, 2009.

Safety
For the most part, nature's elements pose the biggest dangers in Chile's Southern Patagonia and Tierra del Fuego. During the summer, winds are strong, making trekking, biking and even driving difficult. If you are riding or driving, traverse the gravel roads with caution. Traction is different than on paved surfaces. Moderate your speed, and beware of flying stones. In winter, tire chains are needed.

At any time of the year the weather can change quickly, with sleet, ice and low temperatures. Always carry warm clothing and water- and windproof clothes. The sun is extremely strong and glares off the glacier and snow. Be sure to use 400 UVA sunglasses and good sunblock.

Another natural hazard is *hanta*, a virus spread in excrement of rodents (see Major Health Problems (p.56). If you are camping, carry chlorine (*cloro*) to clean areas where you plan to eat. Hang food from trees. Updated: Jun 10, 2009.

Border Crossings
Near Puerto Natales are three border crossings (*pasos*). Each provides access to Argentina's Ruta 40:

DOROTEA, CHILE / MINA 1, ARGENTINA
—Located 31 kilometers (18.6 mi) north of Puerto Natales, four kilometers (2.4 mi) south of Río Turbio, Argentina. The turn-off for this crossing from Ruta 9 (the Puerto Natales-Punta Arenas highway) is sign-posted. This is the only paved route, and it is commonly used by buses and other traffic. There are 1.5 kilometers (1 mi) between the border posts. (November 1 – March 31 open 24 hours, April 1 – October 31 8 a.m. – 10 p.m.).

CASAS VIEJAS, CHILE / LAURITA, ARGENTINA

—The turn-off is on Ruta 9, just past that for Paso Dorotea. It is 15 kilometers (9 mi) south of the Argentine village 28 de Noviembre. This is an unpaved road (daily 8 a.m. – 11 p.m.).

RÍO DON GUILLERMO, CHILE / CANCHA CARRERA, ARGENTINA

—Situated 58 kilometers (34.8 mi) north of Puerto Natales on unpaved Ruta 250 and 45 kilometers (27 mi) north of Río Turbio, Argentina (daily 8 a.m. – 10 p.m.).

On the eastern side of Chile are two passes that not only lead into Argentina, but that are also necessary to go through if traveling along Argentina's Ruta 3 from Río Gallegos to Ushuaia.

PASO INTEGRACIÓN AUSTRAL, CHILE / MONTE AYMOND, ARGENTINA—

On Chile Ruta 255, this pass is in Parque Nacional Pali Aike, 67 kilometers (40.2 mi) south of Río Gallegos, Argentina on that country's Ruta 3. Chile Ruta 257 heads to Primera Angostura, where a ferry connects Punta Delgada and Bahía Azul (several ferries daily between 8:30 a.m. and 11:45 p.m., passengers $3.20, those traveling in bus do not pay; car $27.80. For the current schedule, consult the local newspapers or www.tbsa.cl).

PASO SAN SEBASTIÁN

—On the island of Tierra del Fuego, 143 kilometers (85.8 mi) east of Porvenir on Ruta Y-71 and 127 kilometers (76.2 mi) south of Primera Angostura ferry crossing. On the Chilean side, a half-kilometer from the border post, is **Hostería La Frontera** (hotel, camping, restaurant). The distance from the Chilean post to the Argentine is 14 kilometers (8.4 mi), and there is an ACA gas station with hotel and restaurant on the Argentine side. It is then 80 kilometers (48 mi) to Río Grande, Argentina and 303 kilometers (182 mi) to Ushuaia. The road is hard-packed dirt as far as Tolhuin (daily 9 a.m. – 10 p.m.).

Another frontier post, **Paso Río Bellavista**, is in Tierra del Fuego, connecting Porvenir with Argentine Ruta 3 to Ushuaia. Chile Ruta Y-85 leads from Cameron to Pampa Guanaco, from where a rough road heads to the border post.

Fuegian Film

In the wilds of Southern Patagonia grew one of the shoots of Chile's fledgling film industry. Two men played a vital role in this country's early cinematic days: José Bohr of Punta Arenas and Antonio Radonich of Porvenir.

José Bohr was born Yopes Böhr Elzer in Bonn, Germany, in 1901. When he was three years old, his family immigrated to Punta Arenas, Chile. Little has been published about Antonio Radonich, but our story begins with the Radonich family, who opened Tierra del Fuego's first movie house just after the turn of the 20th century, in Porvenir. As a young lad, José Bohr went with his father to view the new phenomenon called moving pictures, an incident Bohr lovingly, humorously recalls in his story "El biografo llega a Porvenir". In 1919 Bohr and Radonich formed Compañia Cinematográfica Magallanes Films, which made *actualidades*, or documentaries of daily life. One of these was "El desarrollo de un pueblo: Magallanes de ayer y de hoy" (1920) made for the 400th anniversary of the discovery of the Magellan Straits. The movie was shot in Porvenir. The two then parted ways. With Estebán Ivanovich, José Bohr founded Patagonian Films in Punta Arenas (1920), and Antonio Radonich became the mogul of Radonich Films.

In 1921, José Bohr moved to Buenos Aires. From there, his career as a film director, screen writer, actor, composer and singer, blossomed. He worked extensively in Mexico and Europe. He died in Oslo, Norway, in 1994. Antonio Radonich eventually disappeared into obscurity. Porvenir's **Museo Provincial Fernando Cordero Rusque** has a case dedicated to the early cinematic work of these pioneers (Monday – Thursday 8 a.m. – 5 p.m., Friday 8 a.m. – 4 p.m., weekends and holidays 10:30 a.m. – 1:30 p.m., 3 – 5 p.m. Zavattaro 402. Tel: 56-61-581800, E-mail: museo@municipalidaddeporvenir.cl / museo@muniporvenir.cl). The house where this whole story began continued to show films until about 1945, and still belongs to the Radonich family. Updated: Jun 10, 2009.

After the border, the road becomes Argentina Ruta b, a dirt track to Río Grande. From there Ruta 3 heads South to Ushuaia (open November – April 15 only). Updated: Jun 10, 2009.

Things to See and Do

The main attractions of the Southern Patagonia and Tierra del Fuego are the national parks and reserves which protect over half of the region. In the north is Parque Nacional Bernardo O'Higgins, home of the Southern Ice Field, the planet's third largest freshwater reserve. Nearby, Parque Nacional Los Glaciares is home to the largest ice caps in the southern hemisphere outside of Antarctica, including the most famous Perito Moreno glacier. In the extreme southeast corner is Parque Nacional Cabo de Hornos. Torres del Paine is the most famous, but other reserves are easier to get to, like Cueva del Milodón, near Puerto Natales; Pali Aike, Magallanes; Laguna Parrillar and Los Pingüinos, near Punta Arenas; and Laguna de los Cisnes, near Porvenir.

But you don't have to go to the parks to see wildlife. The Southern Patagonia and Tierra del Fuego have an amazing amount of wildlife. From the road it is common to see ñandú and guanaco roaming, or flamingos feeding at ponds. Condors soar over the pampa. Taking a boat ride through the channels, you'll see dolphins and whales swimming the frigid channels. Penguins and seabirds are also amazingly abundant.

If history and culture are more to your liking, you won't be disappointed. w has a wide variety of museums, ranging from the mansions of the Braun-Menéndez family to an art gallery. Puerto Natales, Porvenir and even Puerto Williams have small but interesting anthropological and historical exhibit halls. Updated: Jun 10, 2009.

Patagonia Cruises

Besides its wild, windswept flatlands, rugged mountains and virgin forests, Patagonia also has stretches of ice-clad seas, dramatic fjords, pristine coastline dotted with penguin colonies, and islands set in inland seas. One of the best ways to explore the vast portion of Patagonia (inaccessible on foot) is via a cruise ship. There are a variety of boat tours and cruise companies available, which offer itineraries from Puerto Montt to the tip of Chile. Explore the glaciers of La Laguna de San Rafael,

travel up the waterways of Patagonia to Puerto Edén, or sail into Puerto Natales, the gateway to Torres de Paine. A recommended route travels around Cape Horn to Ushuaia, returning to Punta Areas. Tours can be arranged from Puerto Montt, Puerto Natales, Punta Arenas or Ushuaia, or even booked online. Updated: Jul 02, 2009.

Tours

Tour operators are most common in Puerto Natales, El Calafate, El Chaltén, Ushuaia, and Punta Arenas. Those in Puerto Natales, El Calafate, El Chaltén, and Ushuaia focus mainly on adventure tourism, like kayaking, trekking, and climbing in the national parks of Torres del Paine, Los Glaciares, and Tierra del Fuego. Many, though, add Monumento Natural Cueva del Milodón and boat tours through the fjords and glaciers of Parque Nacional Bernardo O'Higgins to their menu of expeditions.

The excursions from Punta Arenas are more extensive due to the city's central location. The nature reserves Laguna Parrillar and Pali Aike are on the bill, as are wildlife expeditions to watch penguins, sea lions and dolphins at Pingüinera Seno Otway, Isla Magdalena and the Straits of Magellan. Operators can arrange tours of the city, Fuerte Bulnes, Faro San Isidro and Cabo Froward. Many agencies also offer trips to the Puerto Natales sites. Excursions to Tierra del Fuego are available and best done from Punta Arenas and Ushuaia. Some guides specialize in treks into the Cordillera Darwin and other wild areas, with fishing expeditions to the Land of Fire's prime spots, or cruises along the Straits of Magellan, through the Beagle Channel, or to Antarctica. You can even book cruises to Cabo de Hornos. Updated: Jul 07, 2009.

Lodging

As Chile and Argentina's most inaccessible region, the Southern Patagonia and Tierra del Fuego is the most expensive, especially regarding lodging. During the warmer months, budget travelers rely on camping to ease their wallets. A cheap alternative for groups is to rent a cabaña together. There are almost no inexpensive, private rooms. Such privacy comes at a price. Most hotels are in the mid- and high-end price range. Boutique inns and B&Bs are becoming more popular, especially in prime destinations. Discerning tourists can find first-class hotels with all the amenities to make their stay to this wild area comfortable.

During the high seasons, especially in summer, prices are higher and reservations are a must. In the lower seasons, some hostels offer discounts. Many inns close during the winter until the warmer weather draws the tourists back down to these cool regions. Updated: May 28, 2009.

CHILEAN PATAGONIA

Magallanes is the part of Chilean Southern Patagonia most tourists visit. The centrally located capital, Punta Arenas, is a convenient hub for getting to Puerto Natales and Parque Nacional Torres del Paine (to the west), Parque Nacional Pali Aike and Seno Otway penguin colony (north), the end of the continent at Cabo Froward and the mythical Tierra del Fuego (east). The north-bound Navimag ferry departs from Puerto Natales for Puerto Montt. Ships steaming to southern horizons, like Isla Navarino and Cabo de Hornos, leave from Punta Arenas. You can also reach the Magallanes region by land routes through Argentina. Updated: May 28, 2009.

PUNTA ARENAS

 54 m   130,000   61

One of the southernmost cities in the world, Punta Arenas sits on the Strait of Magellan, a treacherous channel between the Atlantic and Pacific oceans that passes through the rocky islands of southern Chile and Argentina, between the mainland and the large island of Tierra del Fuego.

The strait was discovered by Ferdinand Magellan in 1520, and has been used ever since as a major trade route by those who'd rather not attempt the more dangerous Drake Passage to the south. Until the construction of the Panama Canal, the Strait of Magellan was the best way to ship goods.

The city of Punta Arenas marks the third attempt to establish a base in the region. The first settlement, in 1584, was led by colorful Spanish historian and explorer Pedro Sarmiento de Gamboa and was named Rey Don Felipe after the king of Spain. The conditions were very harsh, and the 300 original settlers all eventually deserted or perished. By the time British pirate Thomas Cavendish visited the site in 1587, only 18 people were left. Cavendish renamed the site Puerto Hambre, or Port Famine, and it later became a

British naval base. Charles Darwin visited the base during his voyage with the HMS Beagle. Another settlement was sponsored by the Chilean government and was named Fuerte Bulnes, or Fort Bulnes. It, too, was abandoned; a reconstruction is now on the site for interested visitors.

The history of Punta Arenas is a series of boom-and-bust cycles. Punta Arenas was established in 1849 and immediately benefited from the California Gold Rush, as it was often easier to ship supplies around South America than it was to send them overland. When the transcontinental railroad was completed in 1869, traffic through the strait decreased.

The next boom came in the late 1800s, when settlers discovered that sheep thrive in the chilly climate. Wool merchants made vast fortunes; their legacy can still be seen today in their mansions, which line the streets of Punta Arenas. The wool boom fizzled around the time of World War II, but two more booms were waiting in the wings: oil was discovered on the island of Tierra del Fuego and the fishing industry took off. Since the late 1980s, tourism has been a huge industry as well.

There's much to do in Punta Arenas. The city itself is worth a visit. Some of the homes of the old wool barons have been converted

Photo by Luciano Strabel

SOUTHERN PATAGONIA

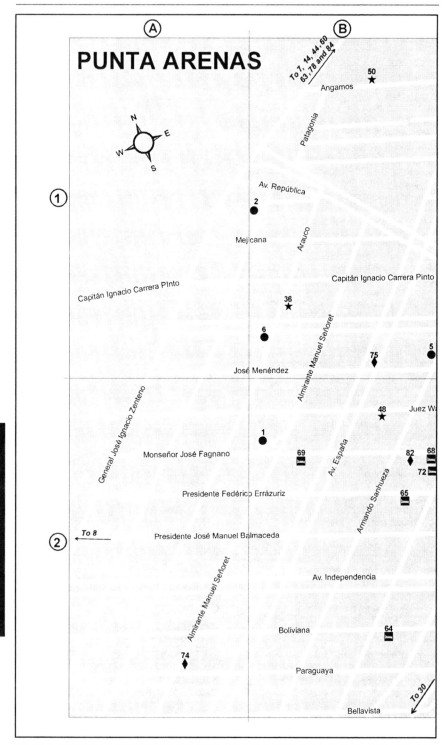

PUNTA ARENAS

To 7, 14, 44, 60
63, 78 and 84

Angamos

50 ★

Patagonia

Av. República

2 ●

Arauco

Mejicana

Capitán Ignacio Carrera Pinto

Capitán Ignacio Carrera Pinto

36 ★

Almirante Manuel Señoret

6 ●

75 ◆

5 ●

José Menéndez

General José Ignacio Zenteno

48 ★

Juez W

1 ●

Monseñor José Fagnano

69 ▪

Av. España

82 ◆

68 ▪

72 ▪

Armando Sanhueza

Presidente Federico Errázuriz

65 ▪

To 8 ←

Presidente José Manuel Balmaceda

Av. Independencia

Almirante Manuel Señoret

Boliviana

64 ▪

74 ◆

Paraguaya

To 30

Bellavista

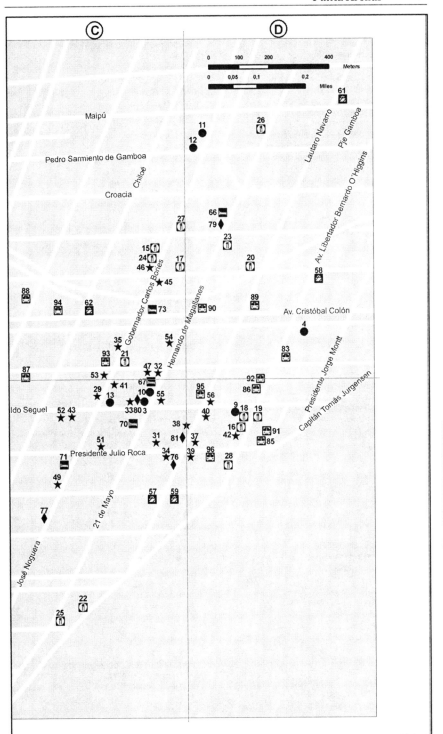

Activities ●

1 Cerro Mirador B2
2 Cervecería Austral B1
3 Cruceros Australis C2
4 Galería Casa Azul D1
5 Mara Patagonia B1
6 Mirador de los Soñadores B1
7 Museo del Recuerdo B1
8 Museo Militar Austral A2
9 Museo Naval y Marítimo D2
10 Museo Regional de Magallanes C2
11 Museo Regional Salesiano
   Maggiorino Borgatello D1
12 Santuario María Auxiliadora D1
13 Sara Braun´s Palace C2

Airports ✝

14 Aeropuerto Presidente Ibáñez del
   Campo B1

Eating ⬦

15 Abu-Gosch C1
16 Brocolino D2
17 El Estribo C1
18 Jekus Pub and Restaurant D2
19 La Luna D2
20 La Marmita Restaurant D1
21 Lomit´s C1
22 Mercado Municipal C2
23 Pachamama D1
24 Restaurant Arco Iris C1
25 Restaurant Remezón C2
26 Restaurante Damiana Elena D1
27 Sabores del Mundo C1
28 Sotito´s D2

Services ★

29 Ahumada C2
30 Argentine Consulate B2
31 Banco de Chile C2
32 Banco Estado C1
33 Banco Estado C2
34 BBVA C2
35 BCI C1
36 Brazilian Consulate B1
37 Cambios Hermandad D2
38 Cambios Opitz C2
39 Cambios Scott D2
40 Cambios Sur D2
41 Chilexpress: Western Union C2
42 Coffee and Travel D2
43 Coffee Net C2
44 CONAF B1
45 Farmacia Cruz Verde C1
46 Farmacias sb C1
47 Futura C1
48 Great Britain Consulate B2
49 Green Internet C2
50 Hospital Regional B1

51 Municipal Tourism Office C2
52 Police C2
53 Post Office C1
54 Public Library C1
55 Santander C2
56 Sernatur D2

Shopping 🛍

57 Alfgal C2
58 Chile Tipico D1
59 Librería Renacer C2
60 Mall El Pionero B1
61 Marcela Alcaíno D1
62 Sports Natura C1
63 Zona Franca B1

Sleeping ▤

64 Amanecer Austral Hostel B2
65 Erratic Rock P.A B2
66 Hospedaje Magallanes D1
67 Hostal Calafate C2
68 Hostal del Rey B2
69 Hostal Oro Fueguino B2
70 Hotel Cabo de Hornos C2
71 Hotel Plaza C2
72 Hotel Restaurant Mercurio B2
73 Hotel Tierra del Fuego C1

Tours ◆

74 Arka Patagonia A2
75 Aventour B1
76 Pali Aike C2
77 Solo Expediciones C2
78 Transbordadora Austral Broom B1
79 Turismo Aonikenk Penguin Tour D1
80 Turismo Comapa C2
81 Turismo Lago Grey C2
82 Turismo Viento Sur B2

Transportation 🚌

83 Aerovías DAP D1
84 Alamo B1
85 Avis D2
86 Budget D2
87 Bus Sur C1
88 Buses Fernández, TuriBus and
   El Pingüino C1
89 Buses Pacheco D1
90 Central de Pasajeros D1
91 EMSA D2
92 Hertz D2
93 LAN C1
94 Pullman C1
95 Queilen Bus, Tecni Austral and
   Buses Ghisoni D2
96 Sky Airline D2

into museums. The most notable is the Palacio Sara Braun, built between 1894 and 1905. Today it houses the elegant if pricey José Nogueira Hotel as well as a museum. Stop in for a coffee or a snack at the restaurant even if you can't afford the hotel itself. There's also the Naval and Maritime museum, showcasing Chilean pilot Luis Pardo Villalón's 1916 rescue of legendary British explorer Ernest Shackleton and his crew at Elephant Island, on the Antarctic peninsula.

Other attractions include the nearby town of Puerto Natales and the Cueva de Milodón, or Ground Sloth Cave, made famous by travel writer Bruce Chatwin in his book, *In Patagonia*.

Punta Arenas is very close to one of the most beautiful vistas in the world: Torres del Paine national park. These majestic mountains are breathtakingly beautiful, and visitors come from around the globe to gaze upon them. Penguin habitats in the nearby Otway inlet are relatively easy to visit, and the Magdalena and Marta islands are home to penguins as well as other marine birds.

You can find a flight from Santiago for less than $100, buses are even cheaper. There are a variety of eating and lodging options in town. Punta Arenas is a good place to consider an all-inclusive tour that includes penguins, Torres del Paine park, and other attractions. Updated: Dec 19, 2007.

When to Go

National Independence Day (September 18) marks the start of the tourism season in Punta Arenas. October brings warmer weather, but more erratic wind and weather conditions. Most tourism services operate normally on all major holidays like Christmas and New Years, although it's always a good idea to inquire beforehand. There are many religious and military holidays celebrated in Punta Arenas, but most do not usually interfere with tourism.

All services like transportation and day tours run normally through mid-April and even into May, but May brings the start of the winter 'off-season' and services slow down. June 29 is the Fiesta de San Pedro y San Pablo, with processions, a special seaside mass, and regattas feting the patron saints of fishermen. At the end of July is the Fiesta de la Patagonia, a winter carnaval with dancing, music and lights through the dark, below-zero streets of Punta Arenas. Updated: Jul 02, 2009.

Getting To and Away From Punta Arenas

Air, bus and boat schedules are published in the local daily newspapers.

BY BUS

Punta Arenas has no central bus station. Several companies share terminals: **Buses Ghisoni** (Tel: 56-61-3422), **Tecni Austral** (Tel: 56-61-3423), **Queilen Bus** (Tel: 56-61-22-2714)—Lautaro Navarro 975; **Buses Fernández** (Tel: 56-61-622-1812), **TuriBus** (Tel: 56-61-227970), **El Pingüino**—Sanhueza 745.

Other companies have their own offices: **Bus Sur** (Menéndez 552. Tel: 56-61-4224), **Pullman** (Av. Colón 568. Tel: 56-61-223359), **Buses Pacheco** (Av. Colón 900. Tel: 56-61-223359). **Central de Pasajeros** sells tickets (with surcharge) for **Tecni Austral**, **Ghisoni** and **TuriBus**, and has a money exchange (Monday – Saturday 9:15 a.m. – 8 p.m., Sunday 10 a.m. – 5 p.m. Av. Colón and Magallanes). During the high season, bus services are more frequent and destinations expanded.

To Puerto Natales: $8, 3 – 3.5 hours—**Buses Fernández** (daily 8 a.m., 9 a.m., five departures 1 p.m. – 8 p.m.), **Bus Sur** (9 a.m., 3 p.m., 7 p..m.).

To Osorno / Puerto Montt / Castro, Chiloé: Same price charged to all three destinations, 27 hours / 28 hours / 33 hours—**Bus Sur** (Monday, Friday 9:30 a.m., $50), **Queilen** (Monday, Friday 9 a.m., $60), **TuriBus** (Tuesday, Thursday, Saturday 9:30 a.m., $40), **Pullman** (Monday, Friday 9 a.m., $50). This route passes through Argentina. Transfer in Osorno for Santiago and other northern destinations.

To Río Grande / Ushuaia, Argentina: $40 / $60, 8 hours / 13 hours—**Tecni Austral** (Tuesday, Thursday, Saturday 8 a.m.), **Pacheco** (Monday, Wednesday, Friday 9 a.m.).

In the high season, **Bus Sur** boards the Punta Delgada-Bahía Azul ferry, connecting the Patagonia mainland with Tierra del Fuego island; the fare is included in the bus ticket.

To Río Gallegos: $14, 4 hours—**Ghisoni** (Monday, Wednesday – Saturday 11 a.m.), **Pacheco** (Tuesday, Friday, Sunday 11:30 a.m.), **El Pingüino** (daily 12:45 p.m.).

SOUTHERN PATAGONIA

BY PLANE

Punta Arenas' Aeropuerto Presidente Ibáñez del Campo is on Ruta 9, 22 kilometers (13 mi) north of the city (Tel: 56-61-219131). **Buses Ghisoni** charges $4 (from the bus station) and $6 (pick-up at your hotel), and taxis are about $10 from the city to the airport ($14 from the airport to the city).

LAN has flights to Puerto Montt and Santiago direct thrice daily, $417 one way. An additional $16 is charged if bought in-office, no charge for on-line purchases (Monday – Friday 9 a.m. – 1 p.m., 3 p.m. – 7 p.m., Saturday 10 a.m. – 1 p.m. Bories 884).

Sky Airline flies once daily Puerto Montt – Santiago ($105 / $160), with a stop Monday and Wednesday in Balmaceda, near Coyhaique ($80) (Monday – Friday 9 a.m. – 7 p.m., Saturday 10 a.m. – 1 p.m. Roca 935. Tel: 56-61-710645, URL: www.skyairline.cl).

Aerovías DAP has flights Monday – Saturday to Porvenir (2 – 3 schedules daily, $76 round trip, 12 minutes) and to Puerto Williams (daily $211 round trip, 1.25 hours, Monday – Friday 8:45 a.m. – 12:45 p.m., 2:30 p.m. – 6:30 p.m., Saturday 9 a.m. – 1 p.m., 3 p.m. – 6 p.m.). O'Higgins 891. Tel: 56-61-6100, URL: www.dap.cl.

BY BOAT

Tres Puentes, four kilometers (2.4 mi) north of downtown, is Punta Arenas' passenger ship port.

Transbordadora Austral Broom is the major ferry company, providing service to various destinations in Chile's Southern Patagonia and Tierra del Fuego. Schedules change, so check the webpage (Monday – Friday 8:30 – 12:15 p.m., 2 p.m. – 6:15 p.m. Av. Bulnes 05075. Tel: 56-61-218100, Fax: 56-61-212186, E-mail: apalma@tabsa.cl, URL: www.tabsa.cl).

To Porvenir: **Ferry Cruz Australis** to Porvenir (all year long, Tuesday – Sunday, passenger $9.80, motorcycle $18, car $63).

To Isla Magdalena: **Barcaza Melinca** (December – February daily 4 p.m, return 9:30 p.m., adults $40, children $20, 1.5 hrs one way). *To Puerto Williams:* Ferry Bahía Azul, Saturday, adult seat $175, adult bunk $210, children 2 – 10 years old 50percent discount, 34 hours.

Punta Delgada-Bahía Azul (connecting the highway between Patagonia and Tierra del Fuego): Several ferries daily between 8:30 a.m. and 11:45 p.m., passengers $3.20 (those traveling in bus do not pay), car $27.80.

Another way to travel from Punta Arenas to Puerto Williams on Isla Navarino is with the Navy's monthly boat. Check at the naval base for further details.

Navimag sails from Puerto Natales to Puerto Montt once a week. It has an office in Punta Arenas where you can reserve passage (Magallanes 990, piso 2. Tel: 56-61-244000, URL: www.navimag.cl).

Cruceros Australis (Santiago office: Av. El Bosque Norte 0440, piso 11. URL: www.australis.com) offers luxury cruises from Punta Arenas to Ushuaia, Argentina, and Cabo de Hornos (October – March, 3 nights / tour days all-inclusive, average fare $1000). Updated: May 21, 2009.

Getting Around

Do not confuse Calle Pedro Montt with Calle Jorge Montt, or Pasaje Bories with Calle Bories.

City buses have numbered routes ($0.55), as do shared taxis (*colectivos*) ($0.65). Colectivos 15 and 20 traverse the downtown-passenger port Tres Puentes route. Taxis are metered. From downtown to the Zona Franca, a three-kilometer (1.8 mi) run, costs about $4.

Bike rental: **Coffee and Travel** (daily 7:30 a.m. – 9:30 p.m. O'Higgins 1069.

Car rental: Many companies offer rentals. Internationally know agencies are: **Alamo** (Bulnes and González. Tel: 56-61-3232), **Budget** (O'Higgins 964. Tel: 56-61-202720), **Avis** (Roca 1044. Tel: 56-61-4381) and **Hertz** (O'Higgins 931. Tel: 56-61-3087). Updated: May 20, 2009.

Safety

Like any big city you always need to use a certain level of common sense when exploring. Thanks to the international attention, business and tourism in Punta Arenas, any traveler can feel comfortable walking the downtown streets, even at night. Bars and night clubs welcome travelers with open arms. It's best not to wander far from the downtown area on foot at night, because of dimly lit and confusing streets. For help, call: **police** at 133, **firefighters** at 132, and **ambulance** at 131. Updated: Jul 01, 2009.

Services

TOURISM

Municipal Tourism Office (low season: Monday – Friday 8 a.m. – 5:30 p.m. Ca. Roca, Plaza de Armas, E-mail: informacionturistica@ puntaareanas.cl, URL: www.puntaareanas.cl). **Sernatur** (Monday – Thursday 8:30 a.m. – 5:30 p.m., Friday 8:30 a.m. – 4:30 p.m. Navarro 999. Tel: 56-61-241330, E-mail: infomagallanes@sernatur.cl). **Conaf** (Monday – Friday 8:30 a.m. – 5:30 p.m. Av. Bulnes 309. Tel: 56-61-238554). **Police:** (Seguel 653. Tel: 56-61-710635 / emergency 133). **Consulates:** Argentina (21 de mayo 1878. Tel: 56-61-261912), Brazil (Arauco 769. Tel: 56-61-241093), Great Britain (Seguel 454. Tel: 56-61-239880), Spain (Ibáñez del Campo 05730. Tel: 56-61-239977).

MONEY

Many financial institutions are on or near Magallanes and Lautaro Navarro. Their hours are usually Monday – Friday 9 a.m. – 2 p.m. Most ATMs accept MasterCard, Cirrus, Visa and Plus cards, except where noted:

BBVA (Roca 899)—ATM: Visa only.
BCI (Bories 837)
Banco de Chile (Roca 864).
Santander (Magallanes 997).
Banco Estado (Magallanes and Montt)—ATM: only MasterCard, Cirrus; also changes U.S. dollars and euros. Branch at Magallanes and Menéndez (Monday – Friday 8 a.m. – 7 p.m., Saturday 9 a.m. – 5 p.m.).

To change currencies or traveler's checks, it is more convenient to go to a *casa de cambio* (exchange house). None are open on Sunday.

Cambios Opitz (Monday – Friday 9 a.m. – 7 p.m., Saturday 9 a.m. – 4 p.m. Lautaro Navarro 1070)—Currencies: US dollar, Euro, Pound Sterling, Argentine peso, Brazilian real. **Cambios Sur** (Monday – Friday 9 a.m. – 7 p.m., Saturday 9:30 a.m. – 2 p.m. Lautaro Navarro 1001)—Travelers checks: American Express, Citi, Visa, Thomas-Cook, MasterCard; Currencies: U.S. dollar, euro, pound sterling, yen, various Latin American currencies. **Cambios Scott** (Monday –Friday 9 a.m. – 7 p.m., Saturday 10 a.m. – 4 p.m. Roca 907)—Currencies: U.S. dollar, euro, pound sterling, yen, Argentine peso. **Cambios Hermandad** (Monday – Saturday 9:30 a.m. – 9:30 p.m. Lautaro Navarro 1099)—Traveler's checks: American Express in various currencies; Currencies: all major world moneys. **Western Union: Chilexpress** (Monday – Friday 9 a.m. – 2 p.m., 3:30 p.m. – 7 p.m., Saturday 10 a.m. – 1 p.m. Bories 911).

KEEPING IN TOUCH

Correos (Monday – Friday 9 a.m. – 6:30 p.m., Saturday 10 a.m. – 1 p.m. Bories and Menéndez).

You can find Internet throughout the city. Most cafes have Skype. Expect to pay $1 – 1.60 per hour. Check out: **Green Internet** (daily 10 a.m. – 11 p.m. Nogueria 1179) or **Coffee Net** (Seguel 670). The public library has free Internet, limited to 20 minutes (Magallanes, between Colón and Menéndez). **Futura** is not only a cyber cafe, but also a phone center; international calls from $0.70 per minute, Internet $1.40 per hour (daily 9 a.m. – 11 p.m. Menéndez 787).

Coffee Net is the newest and nicest Internet cafe in Punta Arenas (just half a block off of the main square) and serves sandwiches, pizzas, desserts and excellent coffee. Open Monday – Saturday 9 a.m. – 10:30 p.m., Sun 2 p.m. – 10:30 p.m. Updated: May 20, 2009.

MEDICAL

Hospital Regional de Punta Arenas (Angamos 180. Tel: 56-61-205000); Pharmacies in Punta Arenas follow the *de turno* system, in which one is assigned to be open in the off-hours. Many drugstores are along Calle Bories: **Farmacia Cruz Verde** (Carrera Pinto and Bories), **Ahumada** (open 24 hours. Bories 950) and **Farmacias sb** (Bories 683). Updated: May 21, 2009.

SHOPPING

For one-stop shopping, spend the day at the **Mall El Pionero** (Av. Eduardo Frei Montalvo, between Ca. Enrique Abello y Manantiales, on the north side of the city). **Andesgear**, located in El Pionero, has the most complete selection of outdoor gear. **ZonAustral Zona Franca** (free-trade zone) is another good spot for comprehensive shopping (Av. Bulnes, Km. 3.5 Norte. Tel: 56-61-216666 / 3311).

Alfgal

This outdoor gear store carries a wide selection of camping, travel and climbing supplies, including tents and sleeping bags, as well as maps and nature guides (Monday – Saturday 10 .m. – 1 p.m., 3 – 8 p.m. Errázuriz 899. Tel: 56-61-240214).

SOUTHERN PATAGONIA

Sports Natura

Sports Natura rents skis and snowboards, and sells camping, trekking and other outdoor sports equipment (Monday – Saturday 10 a.m. – 1 p.m., 3:30 p.m. – 8 p.m. Av. Colón 614-A. Tel: 56-61-247519, E-mail: info@sportnatura.cl, URL: www.sportnatura.cl).

Chile Típico

Chile Típico has a wide range of crafts and souvenirs from Patagonia and the rest of Chile, including of wool, copper, lapis lazuli and wood. Music, books, maps and videos are also available. Monday – Saturday 10 a.m. – 12:30 p.m., 3 p.m. – 8 p.m. Carrera Pinto 1015. Tel: 56-61-225827, E-mail: chiletipico@hotmail.com. Updated: November 27, 2009.

Joyas de Patagonia

Silversmith Marcela Alcaino Mancilla creates and sells jewelry in her workshop using local indigenous motifs. She also gives classes. (Maipú 851. Tel/Fax: 56-61-244244. E-mail: info@joyasdepatagonia.cl, URL: www.joyasdepatagonia.cl. Updated: November 27, 2009.

Librería Renacer

Librería Renacer carries a variety of historical, anthropological and cultural books, nature guides and maps about Patagonia, in Spanish and English. It also has a large selection of works in English and German. Monday – Saturday 10 a.m. – 1 p.m., 3 p.m. – 7 p.m. Errázuriz 914. Tel: 56-61-242537, E-mail: libreriarenacer@hotmail.com. Updated: May 21, 2009.

Things to See and Do

Punta Arenas has many interesting places to explore. The broad boulevards España and Colón have monument parks, such as El Ovejero, and a park filled with statues of characters from Antoine de Saint-Exupéry's *The Little Prince*. Get a good view of the city and the Straits from the several miradores. Punta Arena's wealthy residents left stunning architecture throughout the city. Be sure to check out Sara Braun's Palace (now the Club de la Unión) on the plaza, Cementerio Municipal (with an entrance gate donated by Braun), and the Santuario María Auxiliadora (built 1911-18), a neo-Romanesque church designed by Padre Juan Bernabé (Bulnes and Sarmiento).

There are many nature reserves near the city with abundant wildlife. Check out Reservas Nacionales Magallanes and Laguna Parrillar or Parque Marino Francisco Coloane. You can also visit penguin colonies on Isla Magdalena or at Seno Otway. In winter, many of these nature areas close. With the cold weather, though, Punta Arena offers other activities for the adventurous tourist, like ice skating at Laguna Patinaje and skiing at the Club Andino. South of Punta Arenas are Fuerte Bulnes (a Chilean fortress), Puerto del Hambre and Cabo Froward—the southern-most point of the continent of South America. You can visit these points during a daytrip. Updated: May 25, 2009.

Cruise the Southern Waters

From September through April, Cruceros Australis runs five-day luxury cruises from Punta Arenas to Ushuaia (four days Ushuaia to Punta Arenas) aboard one of three ships: the *M/V Mare Autralis*, *M/V Via Australis*, and, glossy-new for 2010, *M/V Stella Australis*, the biggest of the fleet. All three ships offer gourmet food, an open bar, plush rooms, and a wealth of other amenities.

The 120 or so passengers aboard (210 on the *Stella*) are carried comfortably through the frozen beauty of Southern Patagonia and Tierra del Fuego. The trip goes through the Strait of Magellan and the Beagle Channel, past glaciers, fjords and islets, to Magellenic forest, colonies of penguins and elephant seals, past ice-crusted beaches and finally to Cape Horn, the infamous nautical widow-maker of the pre-Panama Canal world and a stop for Charles Darwin on his 1833 voyage aboard the *HMS Beagle*. At many of these places, zodiacs ferry passengers ashore for hikes and explorations. Prices start at $1,930 low season (Sept, Oct, March, April) and $2,300 high season (Nov. - March). Check website for discounts and special offers. In Punta Arenas, book through Turismo Comapa (Magallanes 990. Tel: 61-710567, Fax: 56-61-225804, URL: www.comapa.com). Av. El Bosque Norte 0440 Floor 11, Santiago. Tel: 56-2-4423115, Fax: 56-2-2035173. URL: www.australis.com.

Museums of Punta Arenas

After the summer high season ends and many tours leave, Punta Arena's various museums remain open. Covering a wide array of topics, some of these museums are considered best in their class in Chile.

Museo Militar Austral (ADMISSION: Free)—Explains the military history of the region, from Fuerte Bulnes to the city's founding. Open daily 9 a.m. – noon, 3 p.m. – 6 p.m. Regimiento Pudeto, Zenteno s/n.

Museo Regional de Magallanes (ADMIS-SION: $2)—Also known as Museo Regional Braun-Menéndez, housed in the family's former mansion which was designed by French architect Antonie Beaulier, this museum displays the social, cultural, economic and political facets of early 20th-century Patagonian life. Open Monday – Saturday 10:30 a.m. – 5 p.m., Sunday and holidays 10:30 a.m. – 2 p.m. Magallanes 940. Tel: 56-61-244216.

Museo Naval y Marítimo (ADMISSION: $2)—Almost 500 years of history of navigating the Straits of Magellan to Antarctica. P. Montt 981. Tel: 56-61-205479.

Museo del Recuerdo (ADMISSION: $2)—A mini historical town displaying machines, carts and other implements from pioneer days, plus a botanical garden. Open Monday – Friday 8 a.m. – 11 a.m., 2 p.m. – 5 p.m., Saturday 9 a.m. – 1:30 p.m. Av. Bulnes 01890. Tel: 56-61-207051.

Galería Casa Azul—Temporary exhibits by students of the Escuela Municipal de Arte; occasional dance and music performances Open Monday – Friday 9 .am. – 1 p.m., 2:30 p.m. -8:30 p.m., Saturday 9 a.m. – 1 p.m. Av. Colón 1027. Tel: 56-61-200674, E-mail: casaazuldelarte@yahoo.es, URL: www.casaazuldelarte.cl. Updated: Jul 01, 2009.

Cervecería Austral—All about making beer at one of the world's southern-most breweries. Open high season only. Patagonia 508.

Museo Regional Salesiano Maggiorino Borgatello (ADMISSION: adults $4, children $1)—Museo Regional Salesiano Maggiorino Borgatello is considered one of the most complete museums on the natural and human history of the Patagonia. The first level has an extensive collection of stuffed birds as part of the fauna halls and a replica of the Cuevas de las Manos (near Perito Moreno, Argentina). On the second level are life-size exhibits illustrating Kaweskar (Alacaluf), Yámana (Yaganes), Selk'nam (Ona) and Aónikenk (Tehuelche) customs, and the Salesian missionary work in the region. On the third story are more displays of indigenous and missionary history, plus some on Antarctica and its exploration. On the fourth floor you can learn all about Patagonian petroleum and other regional industries. The museum also has a print library, photography library and souvenir shop. Tuesday – Sunday 10 a.m. – 12:30 p.m. and 3 p.m – 5:30 p.m. Av.

Bulnes 336. Tel: 56-61-221001, Fax: 56-61-245816, E-mail: musborga@hotmail.com, URL: www.museomaggiorinoborgatello.cl. Updated: Jul 01, 2009.

Miradores
On the highlands of the city are two miradores where you can see the city rolling down to the shores of the Straits and across the Estrecho de Magallanes to the mythical land of Tierra del Fuego. **Mirador de los Soñadores** is a small park on the median of Avenida Colón. The second look-out point, **Cerro Mirador**, is located atop a bluff on Calle Señoret, between Seguel and Fagnano. This terraced plaza gives a less obstructed view of the almost-end of the world. It is located above the commercial port, from where you can watch ships plowing the icy waters toward the horizon. You can easily walk to either of the miradores. Both are about 10 – 15 minutes from downtown. At Cerro Mirador are posts showing the direction and distance to other points around the globe. Updated: May 21, 2009.

Tours
There are many places in downtown Punta Arenas where you can book local tours. Most hotels and hostels can arrange penguin tours, city tours, kayaking or museum visits. But there are also larger, corporate offices that can book flights, multi-day excursions and even packages to Torres del Paine, which is 6 hours, by bus, from Punta Arenas. Most travelers book Torres del Paine related tours in Puerto Natales. More and more tourist activities are opening in Punta Arenas every season and the tourist information office (located in the main plaza) can give you tips on seasonal excursions and the newest local tours. Updated: Jul 01, 2009.

Turismo Comapa
Turismo Comapa, established in 1964, runs some of the best city tours in Punta Arenas, as well as trips to the penguin colonies and more extensive excursions to Torres del Paine, Tierra del Fuego, Cape Horn, Ushuaia, the Falkland Islands and Antarctica. This is also the place to reserve your spot onboard on the Navimag ferry and the luxury cruises of Cruceros Australis. Magallanes 990. Tel: 56-61-710567, Fax: 56-61-225804, URL: www.comapa.com.

Turismo Aonikenk
Founded 1989, Turismo Aonikenk is one of the most trusted tourism agencies in Patagonia. The experienced guides lead the usual

expeditions to Torres del Paine, including treks of the W and Circuit trails, as well as glacier tours, whale watching, and trips to Ushuaia. They also offer a seven-day hike in Dientes de Navarino, and "Cabo Froward," a five-day hike through virgin forest at the absolute southern tip of South America.

Their day trips cover Pali Aike National Park, Fuerte Bulnes, and the penguin colonies at Isla Magdalena and Seno Otway. The penguin half-day tour costs $22, plus $8.50 (entrance) and $1.85 (fee for a private road to access the colony). New fluffy-grey chicks can be seen during the month of December. The staff will also arrange cruises to Antarctica and other sites with Navimag and Cruceros Australis, as well as "self-drive" tours of the region. Guides speak Spanish, English, and German. Turismo Aonikenk operates Hospedaje Magallanes in Punta Arenas. Magallanes 570. Tel: 56-61-228332 / 56-61-228616, Skype: turismo_aonikenk, E-mail: turismo@aonikenk.com, URL: www.aonikenk.com.

Solo Expediciones
Solo Expediciones can take you by boat to visit the penguin colony on Isla Magdalena and the seal colony on Isla Marta for roughly $76. A colony of over 150,000 penguins calls this area home for six months out of the year. There are also no less than 1,700 seals here. The four-hour trip includes bus transfer, boats, and equipment. José Nogueira 1255. URL: www.soloexpediciones.com. Updated: Jul 02, 2009.

Whalesound Tours
Whalesound Tours offers trekking, kayaking and whale watching programs, all mainly focusing on the Strait of Magellan area. You can choose from a variety of day tours, but the most popular programs are the three-day, all-inclusive whale watching tours, the one-day Magellan Strait whale watching helicopter tour and the four-day kayaking program in the Strait. Considered to be scientific, the whale watching programs are serious water expeditions and rarely leave visitors disappointed. Whale tours are all-inclusive and cost $900 per person. Lautaro Navarro 1163, 2°P. Updated: Jul 01, 2009.

Arka Patagonia
Arka Patagonia is an established tour operator, providing a wide variety of popular tours in Punta Arenas and the surrounding region. For those who just have a couple of days, there is a basic tour, which takes in some museums and the Magellan Straits. For those

with a little more time to play, Arka Patagonia has options lasting from three to 14 days, including trekking in Torres Del Paine, visiting glaciers such as the Serrano Glacier and whale watching. A three-day whale watching tour will set you back $700 and the tour is only available from mid-December to mid-May when whales are around. Manuel Señoret 1597. Tel: 56-6-124-8167 / 124-2485, E-mail: info@arkapatagonia.com, URL: www.arkapatagonia.com. Updated: Jan 21, 2008.

Pali Aike
Pali Aike offers a range of tours to suit all tastes, with various opportunities for trekking and horseback riding. For the outdoorsy, they also have trips that combine sailing and walking and Mare Australis cruises. Their three-day whale watching trip costs $900 and takes in other wildlife in the area. Pali Aike can also arrange trips to Antarctica. Lautaro Navarro St. 1125. Tel: 56-6-161-5750 / 51, Fax: 56-6-122-3301, E-mail: turismopaliaike@terra.cl, URL: www.turismopaliaike.com. Updated: Jan 21, 2008.

Turismo Viento Sur
Turismo Viento Sur offers one of the widest range of programs available in this area. Along with the standard hiking trips to Torres Del Paine, and Mare Australis cruises, this company also offers whale watching, kayaking tours, sailing in the Patagonian channels, horseback riding, and more unusually, fly fishing. Fishing enthusiasts can go on four or seven day tours, while those who just want a sample can settle for a one-day trip. Turismo Viento has many one-day trips in and around Punta Arenas and Puerto Natales, for those short on time. A sign of this company's success is that they are now branching out to also provide tours to Easter Island and San Pedro de Atacama. 585 Fagnano St. Tel: 56-61-710840, Fax: 56-61-710840, E-mail: agencia@vientosur.com. URL: www.vientosur.com. Updated: Jan 21, 2008.

Lodging
As one of Patagonia's major cities, Punta Arenas offers all services at any budget level. From luxury hotels, to budget hostels, all can be easily found in the 10-block radius around the center. This same downtown area is full of restaurants, shopping, bus stations and Internet cafes. Most day tours can be organized from any hostel or hotel. Updated: Jul 01, 2009.

Erratic Rock P.A.
(DORM: $15, DOUBLES: $28) This family-owned hostel is just two blocks from the main square. They offer breakfast, WiFi, a

kitchen and a movie room. Errazuuriz 567. Tel: 56-61-221130, URL: www.erraticrock.com. Updated: Jul 01, 2009.

Amanecer Austral Hostel

(ROOMS: $20 – 66) This inn is located in the District Center, a zone south of the city with an enviable tranquility. There are comfortable single or double rooms suitable for families, and separate bathrooms for men and women. Boliviana 533, between Chiloé and Armando Sanhueza. Tel: 56-9-87686689, E-mail: amaneceraustral@hotmail.com. URL: www.amaneceraustral.cl. Updated: Jul 07, 2009.

Hospedaje Magallanes

(ROOMS: $46) Hospedaje Magallanes is run by the Chilean-German tour operator Aonikenk. This guesthouse offers four double rooms that share two bathrooms. In addition to the 10-meter climbing wall in the backyard, you have access to home-made breakfasts, a BBQ and campfire area, free Internet and WiFi. Visitors can also book tours through the in-house travel agency. The owners speak English, German and Spanish. Magallanes 570. Tel: 56-61-228616, E-mail: hospedaje.magallanes@aonikenk.com, URL: www.aonikenk.com. Updated: Jul 02, 2009.

Hotel Restaurant Mercurio

(ROOMS: $47 – 79) The Mercurio has rather dark rooms decorated in an old-fashioned style, but if you can see past that, it may be the place for you. What the hotel lacks in style, it makes up for with its friendly helpful staff and great service. The rooms have cable TV, private bathrooms, hot water and central heating. Some rooms have a tub. The hotel also has Internet service and a safe. Rates include a continental breakfast, but not taxes. Fagnano 595. Tel: 56-61-242300, E-mail: mercurio@chileaustral.com, URL: www.chileaustral.com/mercurio. Updated: Jun 15, 2009.

Hotel Plaza

(ROOMS: $87 – 179) Set on the corner of the Plaza de Armas in a suitably grand-looking building, the Hotel Plaza has a pleasant ambience and comfortable feel. The hotel has 17 warm, carpeted rooms that are decorated in a traditional style. All have private bathrooms, TVs, heating and telephones. The hotel offers Internet, fax services and decent tourist information. There's a cafeteria, and prices include a continental breakfast. José Nogueira 1116. Tel: 56-61-241300, Fax: 56-61-248613, E-mail: hplaza@chileaustral.com, URL: www.hotelplaza.cl. Updated: Jul 07, 2009.

Hotel Tierra del Fuego

(ROOMS: $98 – 140) This luxurious, yet moderately-priced hotel sits on a main corner of downtown Punta Arenas. The hotel runs a cool after-work pub that is directly on the corner of main street and is great for people-watching. Av. Colón 716. Tel: 56-61-226200, E-mail: reservas@puntaarenas.com, URL: www.puntaarenas.com. Updated: Jul 03, 2009.

Hotel Cabo de Hornos

(ROOMS: $110 – 290) Located on the main square, this is Punta Arenas's first hotel. Completely remodeled in 2006, its minimalist stone design and indigenous theme give it a stark, noble feel. Rooms have excellent views over the Strait of Magellan or the central plaza. It's a very professionally run, efficient hotel owned by the Australis group. Plaza Munoz Gamero 1025. Updated: May 07, 2009.

Hostal Oro Fueguino

Oro Fueguino is a colorful, boutique-style hostel located in the historical district of Punta Arenas. Located three blocks uphill from downtown, the hostel overlooks the city and offers great views, especially at night. The hostel has singles, doubles, and group rooms, all with private bathrooms. In addition to all the modern services, Hostal Oro Fueguino has living rooms, day and night time reception, TVs, phones, laundry service, massage parlor and WiFi. Staff speaks English. Fagnano 356. Tel: 56-61-249401. URL: www.orofueguino.cl. Updated: Jul 01, 2009.

Hostal del Rey

Open all year, the Hostal del Rey is family-run and conveniently located just a block and a half from the Plaza de Armas. The snug, cheerily decorated rooms are comfortably furnished and come with both cable TV and private bathrooms with showers and 24-hour hot water. They have singles, doubles, triples and quadruples. This place is popular, in part due to the friendly staff, so you'd be advised to book in advance. Services offered include laundry, baggage storage and fax. They also sell maps. Fagnano 589. Tel: 56-6-1248314 / 56-6-1225877, E-mail: delrey@chileaustral.com, URL: www.chileaustral.com/hdelrey. Updated: Apr 24, 2008.

Hostal Calafate

Hostal Calafate sits right across from the regional museum in the heart of Punta Arenas, just half a block from the Plaza de Armas. Rooms are large and come with cable TV, telephone, heating and either private or shared bathrooms. The hotel houses a great Internet cafe, open 8 a.m – midnight, and for those who bring their laptop with them, there is free WiFi. The hotel has laundry and fax services. It also offers a number of other helpful services including reservations for trips to Torres del Paine, penguin-viewing and other popular destinations. Breakfast is included. Magallanes 922-926. Tel: 56-61-710100 / 241281, E-mail: info@calafate.cl/ hostal@calafate.cl, URL: www.calafate.cl. Updated: Apr 24, 2008.

Restaurants

As can be expected in an ocean-side town, Punta Arena's restaurants serve up a lot of fresh fish and other seafood. Try the *centolla*, or king crab. Exotic meats, like ñandú and guanaco (all farm-raised, as per law) also make the menus. You can find inexpensive daily menus, costing $3 – 5, at restaurants near bus terminals. The women at the **Mercado Municipal** dish up the fruits of the sea and Chilean fare at a reasonable price (Monday – Saturday 9 a.m. – 6 p.m., Sunday 10 a.m. – 2:30 p.m. Lautaro Navarro, near Av. Independencia). **Abu-Gosch**, in the heart of downtown, is an *hipermercado* (super-supermarket) with an ATM (Bories 647). You can buy dried fruits, nuts, flours and other trekking foods at **Pachamama** (Monday – Friday 10 a.m. – 1 p.m., 3 p.m. – 8 p.m., Saturday 10 a.m. – 1:30 p.m. Magallanes 619-A. Tel: 56-61-226171) or **Aysén Envasadora** (Monday – Friday 9:15 a.m. – 12:45 p.m., 2:45 p.m. – 7:30 p.m., Saturday 9:15 a.m. – 1 p.m. Nogueira, between Errázuriz and Balmaceda). Updated: May 20, 2009.

Lomit's

(ENTREES: $4.80 and up) Lomit's is quite the hit with *Puntarenses* and foreigners alike. This eatery serves up typical Chilean sandwiches, like steak, hamburgers, chicken and hotdogs. All are done only as Chileans know how to do them, with a variety of toppings that a Westerner would never think of. If you need a break from touring the city, step in for a coffee, hot chocolate or draft beer. Open daily 9 a.m. – 1 a.m. Menéndez 722. Tel: 56-61-243399. Updated: May 20, 2009.

Restaurante Damiana Elena

(ENTREES: $7) Experience unique, exquisite Chilean cuisine for a bargain price at Damiana Elena, one of Punta Arenas's finest eateries. With antique décor and table settings and an attentive staff, this is a local hotspot where you should arrive before 9 p.m. or make reservations (especially on weekends). Excellent for meats, pastas and seafood, we recommend the salmon with avocado sauce and the salmon ceviche. Open Monday to Saturday from 8 p.m. Magallanes 341. Tel: 56-61-222818. Updated: May 20, 2009.

Restaurante Sabores del Mundo

(LUNCH $7, ENTREES $6 – 14) Commonly called Restaurant Sabores, this is one of Punta Arena's more popular stops for lunch or dinner. The restaurant is known for its generous portions. Its menu specializes in fish (salmon, merluza) and sea foods (king crab, squid, mussels, shrimp and oysters), though it also offers beef and chicken. Lunch specials are a good way to stay on budget, as is the Wednesday all-you-can-eat pasta. Kids menu available, $7. Open Monday – Friday noon – 3 p.m., 8 p.m. – 11 p.m., Saturday and Sunday 8 p.m. – 11 p.m. Mejicana 102, piso 2. Tel: 56-61-221369. Updated: May 21, 2009.

Restaurant Arco Iris

(BUFFET: Monday – Thursday $10, Friday – Sunday $11) Before Restaurant Arco Iris opens its doors, you'll find a line already forming outside the door. This tenedor libre restaurant has become quite the hotspot for locals on account of its all-you-can eat buffet featuring Chilean and Chinese dishes, as well as salad and dessert bars. One drink is included. Be sure to take your plate up to the grill where the parrillero will load you up with lamb, beef, chicken and sausages. Open daily noon – 3 p.m., 8 p.m. – midnight. Bories 671. Tel: 56-61-730060. Updated: May 20, 2009.

El Estribo

(ENTREES: from $10) This restaurant specializes in Patagonia game meats, all raised in captivity, like ñandú (rhea), guanaco, *castor* (beaver) and *caiquén* (goose). If your tastebuds aren't quite ready for such culinary explorations, then settle for more tame meats, like lamb, beef, fish or seafood. Open daily 11:30 a.m. – 3 p.m., 7 p.m. – 11 p.m. Carrera Pinto 762. Tel: 56-61-244714. Updated: May 21, 2009.

Restaurant El Remezón

(ENTREES: $20) Restaurant El Remezón has an exotic menu, which includes lamb, seafood, ñandu, beaver and guanaco. The meals are prepared using the techniques of the region's natives peoples. The chef changes the specials every day based on the best daily and seasonal selections, making this a unique and warm family-run place. Open daily. 21 de Mayo 1469. Tel: 56-61-241029. Updated: Jul 02, 2009.

La Marmita Restaurant

Once the best-known secret in Punta Arenas, Marmita has grown in popularity in the last few years. The chef takes cooking seriously and often comes out to talk to tourists. Marmita is a small and cozy restaurant and has a varied menu; they are famous for their *cangrejo* (crab) and lamb. Veggie meals are available. Open Monday – Saturday 12:30 p.m. – 3 p.m., 6:30 p.m. – 11:30 p.m. Plaza Sampalo 678. Tel: 56-61-222056. Updated: Jul 03, 2009.

Jekus Pub and Restaurant

Jekus Pub is a upscale pub and restaurant that is great for impressing a date or holding a celebration. It's the place to go for some VIP treatment if you're a traveler with a larger budget. Only two blocks downhill from the main plaza, Jekus is a popular haunt for the after work, business crowd, serving a large selection of wine alongside well-prepared meals. Open daily 12:30 p.m. – 4 p.m., 8 p.m. – 12 a.m. O'Higgans 1021. Tel: 56-61-245851. E-mail: jekus.patagonia@gmail.com. Updated: Jul 01, 2009.

La Luna

Just two blocks downhill from the main square, La Luna is eclectic and artistically decorated. This family-run restaurant has a warm and welcoming atmosphere, and the wall of wine bottles and the smell of home-cooked food tend to get folks settled in for a relaxed dining experience. The restaurant has good food and large portions at a decent price. Open 12 p.m. – 3:30 p.m., 7 p.m. – 11:30 p.m. O'Higgans 1017. Tel: 56-61-228555, E-mail: lalunachile@gmail.com. Updated: Jul 01, 2009.

Sotito's

Sotito's is sophisticated and worth a splurge. The menu features both regional and international cuisine, with king crab as a specialty. Patrons can also choose between varied entrees such as eel in margarita sauce and a sea urchin omelette, while strawberries and cream is a highly-rated dessert option. There are plenty of great options for non-fish eaters too. O'Higgins 1138. Tel: 56-61-243565, E-mail: sotitos@chileaustral.com, URL: www.chileaustral.com/sotitos/index.shtml. Updated: Jan 22, 2008.

Brocolino

Another great place to get tasty seafood offerings, Brocolino specializes in French and Italian cuisine, washed down with a good selection of wines. This place is popular with the locals who come to enjoy the delicious king crab, lobster and lamb dishes, among others. If you're not sold on this place yet, meet the chef, who keeps everyone entertained with his antics. 1049 O'Higgins. Tel: 56-61-710.479. Updated: Jan 21, 2008.

V!VA ONLINE REVIEW

BROCOLINO

I love this place! The food is fantastic! I'm a tour leader who regularly brings groups to restaurants and Brocolino always ends up as their favorite!

March 20, 2008

AROUND PUNTA ARENAS

Posada Hostería Río Verde

Posada Hostería Río Verde sits about 60 kilometers (37 mi) northwest of Punta Arenas on an estancia dating to the 1800s. Guests can enjoy the frozen-in-time feel of the lodge by riding horseback over the grounds, learning the ins and outs of sheep and cattle farming, fishing for trout, sailing in the adjacent Skyring Sound, or just relaxing by the fireplace or in the driftwood-decorated pub. For the more adventurous, the Posada offers backcountry treks and guided climbs of Fitz Roy and Paine (which need to be planned well in advance). Tel: 56-61-311131 / 123, URL: www.estanciarioverde.cl. Updated: Jun 30, 2009.

RESERVA NACIONAL MAGALLANES

(ADMISSION: free, except Las Minas sector in the northwest $2) The Magallanes National Reserve is an often overlooked park just fifteen minutes west of downtown Punta Arenas (following Av. Independencia) where nature-lovers can experience some of Patagonia's signature flora and fauna. Created in 1932, the 13,500-hectare (32-acre) reserve is home to coigüe and lenga trees, as well as the gray fox, Culpeo fox, puma and condor.

SOUTHERN PATAGONIA

Two trails, **Las Lengas** (3.6 km/2.23 mi) and **Mirador** (1 km/0.65 mi), provide hiking access and a mountain biking circuit. Camping areas are abundant along the trails. In the winter, skiers can hit the slopes at the Cerro Mirador Ski Center. Updated: Jul 07, 2009.

SENO OTWAY PENGUIN COLONY

(ADMISSION: $8, children free) The large inland sound of Seno Otway, just 65 kilometers (40 mi) north from Punta Arenas, offers visitors a chance to watch the charming 8,000 or so Magellanic penguins (also called Jackass penguins) march from their burrows and dive into the ocean. The viewing platforms offer vistas of the mountains across the sound, and allow visitors to get close enough to see the creatures without disturbing the habitat. You can visit on your own (a taxi from Punta Arenas will cost roughly $50) or arrange a tour, which will take approximately four hours in total and cost about $20. Open from mid-October to the end of March or early April from 8 a.m. – 8 p.m. Updated: Jul 07, 2009.

MAGDALENA ISLAND PENGUIN COLONY

Along with the islet of Marta, the island of Magdalena forms the Monumento Natural Los Pingüinos, the natural habitat of over 100,000 thousand Magellanic penguins and is the site of one of the largest colonies of Southern Chile.

Excursions to the small islands in the middle of the Strait of Magellan, 35 kilometers (22 mi) northeast of Punta Arenas, are an excellent way to observe the little fellows not only on land but also in the water. Tours leave Punta Arenas three times a week during penguin breeding season (November – February) and may pass whales and Southern sea lions. While on Magdalena, visit the solitary Faro Magdalena, a landmark red and white-striped lighthouse that has been casting its light since 1902. The lighthouse has been a national monument since the Chilean navy handed it over to Conaf in 1981, and has exhibits on the local history and navigation of the Strait.

Tours run during the penguin breeding season from November to February. The ferry ride, on the Barcaza Melinka, lasts 1.5 – 2 hours and costs $35 (children pay half price). Contact **Transbordadora Austral Broom** in Punta Arenas for more information. Av. Bulnes 05075. Tel. 56-61-218100, E-mail: correo@tabsa.cl, URL: www.tabsa.cl. Comapa Turismo can also organize tours there, URL: www.comapa.com. Updated: May 25, 2009.

Puerto Hambre (Port Famine)

Though the area around Puerto Hambre (Port Famine) is beautiful, the story of the area is bleak. All that remains of the Spanish outpost of Rey Don Felipe is the ruins of a church, which was originally built in 1584 by Pedro Sarmiento de Gamboa and his 300 Spanish colonists, who arrived in Chile after a long and disastrous voyage from Spain. After settling the outpost, the colonist's only remaining ship was battered and blown to sea in a storm, stranding the colonists in this icy part of the Straits of Magellan. Most either froze or starved to death.

When British captain Thomas Cavendish landed here in 1587, he found just 18 survivors and renamed the area Port Famine. A plaque was added to the site in 1968 after it was declared a National Monument. Tours can be arranged from Punta Arenas to Puerto Hambre and nearby Fuerte Bulnes. Updated: Jul 03, 2009.

Fuerte Bulnes

Approximately 56 kilometers south of Punta Arenas, the original Fuerte Bulnes fort was the first Patagonian settlement in the area. It was built in 1843 by the crew of the *Ancud*, a Chilean vessel sent to the area to claim and occupy the territory. The modern fort, reconstructed 100 years later in 1943, was originally designed as a museum, though the majority of the artifacts have been relocated to museums in Punta Arenas and Santiago. Today, Fuerte Bulnes is a replica of the wooden fort, with a chapel, defense walls and canons. There is no public transport to the fort, but several Punta Arenas agencies take half day tours here. Updated: Jul 07, 2009.

Isla Riesco

Isla Riesco is a 5,110-square-kilometer (3,175-sq. mi) island just a short ferry ride across the Fitz Roy Channel from Río Verde. Though the western portion of the island—protected as the Reserva

Nacional Alacalufes—is nearly impossible to access, the eastern portion has uniquely Patagonian scenery, like its famous wind-contorted trees, as well as a glimpse into *gaucho* (cowboy) culture. The estancia Monte Leon offers lodging and dayhikes (contact **Fundación Yendagaia**: 56-61-22041914; yendegaia@patagonia.com; or monteleon@apn.gov.ar) and the **Fitz Roy Farm Ranch** (www.welcomepatagonia. com) shows guests how gauchos sheer, herd, and wash sheep. Cold temperatures, averaging about 7°C (45°F), and rain are the norm. Updated: Jun 30, 2009.

Río Rubens

Río Rubens is an idyllic trout stream with rolling green shores about halfway between Villa Tehuelches and Puerto Natales. The **Hotel Río Rubens** (Tel: 56-9-6401583; cabins $20 – 75) is a popular stop for cyclists and motorists, known for its down-to-earth atmosphere and hearty meals. Riverside camping is also available. Trout season on the river lasts from November 9th to April 20th. Updated: Jun 30, 2009.

Estancia San Gregorio

Estancia San Gregorio is a relic of the 19th-century Menéndez wool empire in Chilean Patagonia. It consists of a nearly-abandoned compound of yellow buildings lining Ruta 255 about 125 kilometers (78mi) northeast of Punta Arenas. San Gregorio reached its peak between 1910 and 1930 when it produced wool, mutton, hides and tallow.

It is now a national historical monument, and is maintained by a handful of people, including a Menéndez descendent. The corroding skeletons of the British clipper *Ambassador* and the steamer *Amadeo* adorn its beachfront on the Strait of Magellan—a photogenic scene for the apocalypse-minded. Updated: Jun 30, 2009.

PARQUE NACIONAL PALI AIKE

(ADMISSION: $2) Not many travelers make it to the 5,000-hectare Pali Aike National Park, which offers barren beauty and lunar landscapes, just 200 kilometers (124 mi) northeast of Punta Arenas near the Argentine border. The dry Magellanic steppe is mostly covered in basalt, volcanic craters and caves, which provided shelter to inhabitants thousands of years ago.

In the 1930s, an excavation of the Pali Aike Cave uncovered the remains of a prehistoric native horse and giant ground sloth called the milodon (extinct some 11,000 years ago). Human remains, tools and cave paintings were also found. Today the semi-desert vegetation is home to roaming herds of guanacos, in addition to foxes, armadillos, pumas, and waterfowl, which can be spotted from the various hiking trails that lead through the rocky terrain. There is no public transportation to the area; hire a car or book a tour in Punta Arenas. Updated: Jul 03, 2009.

PUERTO NATALES

 3 m   19,000   61

In the last few years Natales has seen a blast of international recognition and is going through a series of big changes. Every season the improvements and growth become more and more noticeable. The town sits under the shadow of the Dorotea mountain range, and is on the shore of the Ultima Esperanza Fjord. Snow-covered mountains and glaciers pouring directly into the fjord can be seen from town. The town still retains a feel of yester-year, which this region of Chile is famous for, yet the new wave of tourism has managed to soften the town around the edges, giving it a fresher, more welcoming atmosphere.

The town was settled mostly by rich European ranchers in 1911 to serve as a port for the export of wool and mutton. As the sheep industry declined during the second half of the 20th century, many residents of Puerto Natales worked in the coal mines of nearby Río Turbio in Argentina. Now, the economy of Puerto Natales is dependent upon tourism, which is expected to increase during the upcoming years as the popularity of trekking and outdoor sports continues to grow worldwide. You can still see evidence of sheep and fishing industries if you look close enough, but the town is mostly about trekking, kayaking, climbing and horseback riding, just to name the biggies.

Since becoming the gateway to Torres del Paine, Puerto Natales has developed quite a solid tourist infrastructure. For its size, the town offers visitors a surprisingly

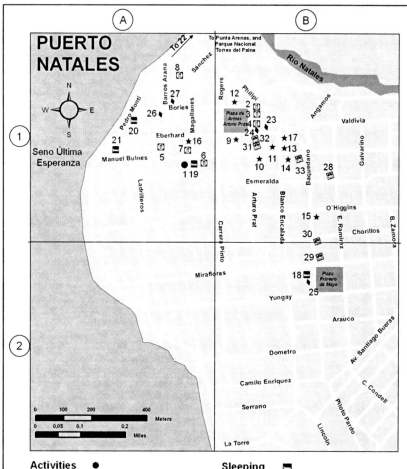

PUERTO NATALES

Activities ●
1 Museo Histórico Municipal A1

Eating 🍴
2 El Living B1
3 Asador Patagónico B1
4 Mesita Grande B1
5 Patagonia Dulce A1
6 Aquaterra A1
7 Chil-e A1
8 Cormorán de las Rocas A1

Services ★
9 Correos de Chile B1
10 Banco de Chile B1
11 Banco Santiago Santander B1
12 Banco Estado B1
13 Central de Llamadas Telefónicas B1
14 Cambios Gasic B1
15 Cyber Café Enyger B1
16 Cambios Sur A1
17 Cambios Mily B1

Sleeping 🛏
18 Erratic Rock B2
19 Aquaterra A1
20 Hotel Indigo A1
21 Hotel CostAustralis A1
22 Weskar Lodge B1

Tours ♦
23 Turismo 21 de Mayo B1
24 Turismo Comapa B1
25 Erratic Rock B2
26 Antares Patagonia A1
27 Indomita Kayak Tours A1

Transportation
28 Buses Fernández B1
29 Bus Sur B2
30 Cootra B1
31 Turismo JBA Patagonia B1
32 Buses Lagoper B1
33 EMSA B1

good variety of restaurants, cafes, hotels and tour companies to choose from, as well as some interesting museums and day-trip options to nearby attractions in wild Patagonia. All types of services and tours for every budget can be found, as long as you have at least one full day in town to plan and shop. Most programs and activities are based around Torres del Paine. Updated: Jul 02, 2009.

When to Go

Puerto Natales' high season runs from October to April. Trekking in Torres del Paine National Park and most other activities are most popular between November and late April. Trekking between November and January (early spring) is a great way to beat the crowd and see the fresh spring growth. February is a busy month, featuring a rodeo competition and a Banff Mountain Film Festival World Tour stop with screenings on the outdoors and extreme sport.

February and March (summer) tend to be the best months in Patagonia with regard to weather. March through April (fall) allow for some cooler and more stable weather patterns. The Big Rock Festival, a live music event, takes place the second week of April. May brings cold temperatures and snowfall. Traveling through Patagonia during late or off-season (May to September) is only recommended for the most seasoned and self-reliant trekkers. Updated: Oct 30, 2009.

Getting To and Away From Puerto Natales

There are three main access points to Puerto Natales. The primary jumping-off point is from Punta Arenas by bus. There are multiple companies that do nothing but drive the three-hour stretch between Punta Arenas and Puerto Natales, multiple times per day between 7 a.m. and 8 p.m. Another access point is via the waterways from the north. There is a weekly departure from Puerto Montt to Puerto Natales on a converted cargo ship, called the Navimag. Up to 300 passengers a week use this ferry to come to Natales.

The third access point is via the Argentine border, from Natales' sister city El Calafate. Daily bus departures run between Natales and Calafate all season. Río Turbio, also near the border, has daily service to Natales as well. There are also regular, less frequent bus trips from Río Gallegos, east of Turbio.

BY BUS
There is no central bus terminal in Puerto Natales. Instead, buses arrive at and depart from each individual company's office.

To Torres del Paine National Park: $15 one-way, $28 return, 2 hours.
Buses Gomez (daily 7:30 a.m. and 2:30 p.m.), Prat 234. Tel: 56-61-411971, URL: www.busesgomez.com.
Turismo JBA Patagonia (daily 7:30 a.m. and 2:30 p.m.), Prat 258. Tel: 56-61-410242.
Buses María José, Arturo Prat 262 and Esmeralda 869. Tel: 56-61-414312.
Buses Lagoper (daily 7:30 a.m. and 2:30 p.m.), Prat 234 A. Tel: 56-61-415700.
Bus-Sur (daily 7:30 a.m. and 2:30 p.m.), Baquedano 668. Tel: 56-61-614224, URL: www.bus-sur.cl.

To Punta Arenas:
Buses Fernàndez ($10, 3 — 3.5 hours, daily 7:15 a.m., 9 a.m., 1 p.m., 2:30 p.m., 5 p.m., 6:30 p.m., 8 p.m.), Ramírez 399. Tel:56-61-411392, URL: www.busesfernandez.com.
Bus-Sur ($8, 3 — 3.5 hours, daily 7 a.m., 10 a.m., 1 p.m., 3 p.m., 7 p.m., 8 p.m.), Baquedano 668. Tel: 56-61-614224, URL: www.bus-sur.cl.
Buses Pacheco ($10, 3 — 3.5 hours, daily 7:30 a.m., 10 a.m., 1:30 p.m., 4 p.m., 7:30 p.m.), Ramirez 224. Tel: 56-61-414800, URL: www.busespacheco.com.

To Río Turbio, Argentina: $8, 1 hour.
Cootra (daily 6:15 a.m.), Baquedano 456. Tel: 56-61-412785.

To El Calafate, Argentina: $21, 5 hours.
Cootra (daily 8:30 a.m.), Baquedano 456. Tel: 56-61-412785.

BY AIR
The nearest airport is a mere 15 minutes (5 km / 3 mi) outside of Puerto Natales, just past Puerto Bories on the way to Parque Nacional Los Glaciares.

Sky Airline doesn't provide service to Puerto Natales, though it has an office on Manuel Bulnes, 692 local 4. Tel: 56-58-410646, URL: www.skyairline.cl. Sky Airline's flights arrive at and depart from the airport in Punta Arenas.

Aerovías DAP has charter flights to El Calafate and Río Gallegos. The office is located in Punta Arenas. URL: www.dap.cl. Updated: Oct 30, 2009.

SOUTHERN PATAGONIA

Photo by Jason Halberstadt

BY BOAT

To Puerto Montt:

Navimag Ferries, Pedro Montt 308. Tel: 56-61-411642, URL: www.navimag.com.

Getting Around

Downtown Puerto Natales (where all services are) is small and easily walkable. The waterfront, downtown, and even nice day hikes can be accomplished on foot with no problem. Taxis are everywhere and usually cost no more than $2 within the city limits. The only other necessary transportation in Puerto Natales is the regular bus that runs daily to Torres del Paine National Park. These tickets can be arranged by almost any hostel or hotel. **Taxi Milodon:** 56-61-410426; **Via Paine:** 56-61-414752. Updated: Mar 17, 2009.

Safety

Puerto Natales is a mellow fishing town made up of working class families. The town sees little action outside of the buses of tourists that flow into it. Almost half of the town's population are kids under the age of 18, and with its remote location and its slow climb to modernization, the kids have little to do, so vandalism and petty crimes do occur. Travelers should stick to the downtown area for late nights out, especially on weekends. Updated: Mar 17, 2009.

Services

TOURISM

CONAF (Tel: 56-61-411438); **police** (Tel: 56-61-41133)

KEEPING IN TOUCH

Post: **Correos de Chile**—Eberhard 429. Tel: 56-61-410202. **Chile Express** (also Western Union agent)—Tomás Rogers 143. Tel: 56-61-411300.

Internet and phone services:
Cyber Cafe Enyger—Chorrillos 701, $0.80 per hour; **The Nethous**—Bulnes 499, $1.60 per hour; **Centro de Llamados**

Telefónica—Blanco Encalada 298. Tel: 56-61-412488; the **Biblioteca Pública**—Phillipi 510, has free Internet (20 – 30 minutes).

MONEY

There are multiple ATMs were you can withdraw Chilean pesos. The are also *casas de cambios* around, where you can change foreign currency.

Banks:
Banco Estado—Bories 492. Tel: 56-61-4411440; **Banco Santander Santiago**—Bulnes 598. Tel: 56-61-411323; **Banco de Chile**—Bulnes 544. Tel: 56-61-413242.

Money exchange:
Cambios Gasic—Bulnes 624. Tel: 56-61-413624; **Cambios Mili**—Blanco Encalada 266. Tel: 56-61-411262; **Cambios Sur**—Eberhard 385. Tel: 56-61-411304.

HEALTH

There is only one main hospital in town and it is not what you would hope for if you were seriously injured far from home. The nearest modern medical facilities are in Punta Arenas, three hours from Natales. Updated: May 06, 2009.

Things to See and Do

Parque Nacional Torres del Paine, considered to be South America's premier national park, is a two- to three-hour ride from Puerto Natales, and is the main tourist draw to the area. With its famous majestic granite pillars and breathtaking landscape, the park is a must-see for extreme adventurists, outdoor enthusiasts, and anyone able to appreciate the wonders of nature. If you have a day or two to spare before embarking into the great outdoors, there are several smaller parks and points of interest worth checking out. The Balmaceda and Serrano glaciers at Parque Nacional Bernardo O'Higgins are only accessible via a three-hour boat ride from Puerto Natales. On the way, you might catch a glimpse of dolphins and sea lions, as well as other sea life. Updated: Mar 16, 2009.

Sea and River Kayaking

Organizing kayaking expeditions is a cinch in Puerto Natales. It is also becoming easier to organize your own tour, and rent kayaks and kayaking equipment. You can paddle from town to Parque Nacional Torres del Paine–where there is exceptional sea kayaking in its fjords and channels–and Parque Nacional Bernardo O'Higgins. Due to O'Higgins remoteness, it is preferable to arrive by boat, then dip your paddle. There is good river kayaking on the Río Serrano as well. Updated: Oct 30, 2009.

Mountain Biking

There are plenty of mountain biking opportunities around Puerto Natales, particularly in Torres del Paine. You can base yourself in Natales and spend days upon days gearing up and down the park's trails, returning to town to give you and your bike a rest. North of Natales you'll come across forest, condor nests, and stunning mountain and lake views. There are excursions on a variety of terrain—paved, gravel and dirt—for every level of rider, and there are also plenty of local tour companies offering mountain bike rentals and guided tours. Updated: Oct 30, 2009.

Ferries and Boat Trips

Puerto Natales is a popular launch point for boats and ferries that head into the icy waters of Southern Chile to explore the fjords, glaciers, channels, majestic mountains, indigenous lake-shore forests, and historic towns of the Patagonia region. Many companies offer chances to sport fish, cross-country trek, visit old cattle estancias, or admire the wildlife at sea lion or cormorant colonies (where hundreds of breeding birds rest on the ice). You can choose from single or multi-day trips to the Glaciers Balmaceda, Serrano, and Amalia, the Fjord of Last Hope, Torres del Paine or Bernardo O'Higgins National Parks. Single-day trips range from $115 to $150. Overnight trips are significantly more expensive, as most boats dock near fancy hosterías that run from $100 – 150 a night. Check out **Navimag Ferries** and **Turismo de Mayo** for up-to-date information about ferry departures and possible excursions. Updated: Jul 07, 2009.

Cueva del Milodón

(ADMISSION: $3) Monumento Nacional Cueva del Milodón is a massive cave where, in 1895, the remains of a three-meter prehistoric ground sloth were discovered. The bones of the slow-moving milodón now reside in London, but a cheesy plastic replica serves as a reminder. The cave became a national monument in 1968 and today is one of the most important archaeological sites in Patagonia. Open 8:30 a.m – 6 p.m. (low season), 8 a.m. – 9 p.m. (high season).

From Puerto Natales, you can either hop on a bus heading to Torres del Paine national park, and ask to be let off at the entrance to the monument, or arrange to see the caves with a tour agency in town (about $5 per person, plus entrance fee). 24 kilometers northeast of Puerto Natales on route 9 northbound. Updated: May 06, 2009.

Horseback Riding Excursions

Located just three kilometers northwest of Puerto Natales in Puerto Bories, Estancia Travel offers "horse riding at the end of the world" packages, ranging from a short two-hour afternoon rides to a ten-day Patagonian adventure. All trips include transfers, a bilingual guide, equipment, and most include meals as well. The trails take you through pristine wilderness: vast pampas, woodland valleys and up steep mountain cliffs. On longer riding expeditions visitors head into Torres del Paine National Park, have open-air barbecues by night, and sleep at working estancias and historic pioneer houses.

Museums in Puerto Natales

If the weather is keeping you from heading out, pass the time sheltered in the various museums of Puerto Natales:

Museo Histórico Municipal
(ADMISSION: Chileans $1, foreigners $2, children to 12 years old free) Excellent bilingual exhibits of the region's history, from the original Kaweskar and Aónikenk indigenous inhabitants to the industrial development by German and English immigrants in the 1930s. Summer: Monday – Friday 8 a.m. – 7 p.m., Saturday 10 a.m. – 1 p.m., 3 p.m. – 7 p.m.; Winter: Monday – Thursday 8 a.m. – 5 p.m., Friday 8 a.m. – 4 p.m. Bulnes 285. Tel: 56-61-4808, E-mail: museonat@123mail.cl / museo@puerto-natales.com.

Museo Salesiano de Fauna Antonio Romanato
(ADMISSION: Donations accepted) An astounding collection of over 100 Patagonian fauna species, plus archaeological artifacts, sea shells and minerals. Monday – Saturday 10 a.m. – 6 p.m. Liceo Salesiano Monseñor José Fagnano, Rossa 1456. Tel: 56-61-411258, E-mail: museo@fagnano.cl.

Museo Histórico e Industrial
(ADMISSION: bilingual tour with guide $7, audio tour $5) The former meat-processing plant of the Sociedad Explotadora Tierra del Fuego was declared a Historical Monument in 1996. Open October 1 – April 30, Tuesday – Sunday 10 a.m. – 8 p.m., bilingual guides

10 a.m. – 6 p.m. Ruta 9, 5 kilometers north of Puerto Natales, Puerto Bories. Tel: 56-61-414328, URL: www.museopuertobories.cl. Updated: May 21, 2009.

Volunteering

Fundación Patagonia

Fundación Patagonia was established in 2004 to connect people to, and encourage the protection of, the Patagonia region—especially Torres del Paine National Park. The foundation achieves these goals with a combination of volunteer opportunities, cultural activities, and international outreach. Perhaps its most well know effort was the joining of Torres del Paine and Yosemite National Park in California as twin national parks. Contact them in advance to find out if there are any opportunities for you to get involved in the management and protection of one of the world's truly great natural treasures. Barros Arana 111. Tel: (56.61) 41 46 11, Fax : (56.61) 41 42 76, E-mail: info@fundacionpatagonia.org, URL: www.fundacionpatagonia.org. Updated: Oct 30, 2009.

Tours

With over 30 different tour operators based in Puerto Natales, there's a range of options, prices, and packages to fulfill your adventure needs, including opportunities for kayaking, trekking, horseback riding, birdwatching, rock and ice-climbing, mountain biking, or in Torres del Paine National Park. Most agencies are on the streets of Eberhard, Baquedano, Blanco Encalada and Arturo Prat, so the best way to compare options is to walk up and talk to the guides themselves. Updated: Mar 16, 2009.

Estancia Travel

Whether you just want to just ride horses, explore the wilderness and see the wildlife, take photographs, or combine horseback riding with a bit of kayaking, Estancia Travel can help you tailor a trip to meet your needs. They offer 10-day excursions into the Patagonian outback, including organically grown meals, local fish and meat, Chilean wine, overnight stays, use of horses, guides, and equipment. Puerto Bories B-13. Tel: 56-61-412221, E-mail: info@estanciatravel.com, URL: estanciatravel.com. Updated: Jul 07, 2009.

Turismo Comapa

Turismo Comapa, established in 1964, is a reliable and experienced agency that operates excursions throughout Southern Patagonia, including city tours and day trips to the penguin colony at Isla Magdalena, as well as more extensive excursions to Torres del Paine, Tierra del Fuego, Cape Horn, Ushuaia, the Falkland Islands and Antarctica. This is also the place to reserve your spot onboard the Navimag ferry (between Puerto Natales and Puerto Montt) or the luxury cruises of Cruceros Australis. Eberhard 555. Tel: 56-61-414300, Fax: 56-61-414361, E-mail: turismocomapa@torresdelpaine.com, URL: www.comapa.com.

Indomita Kayak Tours

Indomita Kayak offers kayaking tours in the nearby fjords and channels of Torres del Paine National Park, Canal de las Montañas, and the Magellan Straits among others. The company's bilingual guides have been exploring Patagonia for more than 10 years, and are all certified as Wilderness First Aid Responders. Kayakers of all levels can choose from two- to 14-day expeditions to observe the flora, fauna and geography that make Patagonia so incredible. Indomita's "Patagonian Mermaids" trip involves a visit to the Francisco Coloane Marine Park, where it's possible to see marine birds, seals and humpback whales. The company also offers a sea kayak school for 3 to 10 days to learn navigation, tide reading, meteorology, rescues, and safety exercises. C. Bories 206. Fax: 56-61-613599, E-mail: info@indomitapatagonia.com, URL: www.indomitapatagonia.com. Updated: Jul 07, 2009.

Erratic Rock

Erratic Rock offers a wide array of adventure tour options in Patagonia. From day trips to penguin colonies, to multiple day excursions to the end of the world, there is something to suit every itinerary, budget, and interest. The most popular tour is to Torres del Paine, and Erratic Rock offers several different packages ranging from simple day trips, to the 15-day "Patagonia Extreme" tour. The professional, friendly guides are passionate about Patagonia, and are eager to answer any questions about the tours. Erratic Rock offers a free information class at 3 p.m. daily, where guides answer questions about trekking in the park. Equipment rentals and customized tours are also available. The tour company runs a hostel of the same name. Baquedano 719. Tel: 56-6-1410355, E-mail: info@erraticrock.com, URL: www.erraticrock.com. Updated: Dec 27, 2007.

Lodging

With the new-found adventure tourism boom in and around the Puerto Natales, you can find all types of lodgings at a variety of comfort levels. Arriving in Puerto Natales by bus, you will notice the new hotels that are starting to fill the skyline along the waterfront. You may be approached by locals offering cheap single beds in their homes and very simple hospedajes.

During high season (Nov — March) it's best to make a reservation for hostels and mid-range B&Bs ahead of time, but finding a bed at one of the luxury hotels isn't as difficult. You can find a budget, no-frills hostel can be found as cheap as $7 per night. For a hostel with park info, Internet and a restaurant serving breakfasts, you'll be paying closer to $15 per night. Numerous hostels, hotels and B&Bs can be found just by walking the downtown streets of Baquedano, Blanco Encalada, Bulnes and Eberhard.

In the low season (May – September) deep discounts on hotels may be negotiated on most hostels. Also call ahead to confirm your hotel is open as some hotels close down for some or all of the low season. It's also extremely cold during the low season. Central heating is optimal, but many hotels use kerosene space heaters. Before you check in, confirm that your room has adequate heating to survive the Patagonian winter! Updated: Oct 30, 2009.

Kaweskar Hostel

(ROOMS: $10 and up) Kaweskar is one of the best budget options in Puerto Natales, with a community kitchen and 24-hour hot water. Kaweskar also offers free baggage storage, rental equipment, tourism information, and bus tickets to both Torres del Paine and Calafate, making this hostal a handy spot to meet other backpackers and get information before heading off to your next destination. Blanco Encalada 754. Tel: 56-61-414553, E-mail: backpackershawashkar@yahoo.es. Updated: Mar 16, 2009.

The Alma Gaucha

(PRICE: $10 – seperate men's and woman's dorms) Live the life of a gaucho in this highly recommended hostel. The friendly owner, Natalino Johnny Callahan, recently moved from a countryside ranch and decorated the hostel with heirlooms. The result is a totally unique, authentic experience at a budget price. If you are lucky, Johnny will offer one of his famous Patagonian asados (BBQ) in his yard, or introduce to the world of the local mate drinking culture. Galvarino 66, Tel: (56.61) 415243, E-mail: almagauchacl@hotmail.com. Updated Oct 30, 2009.

Erratic Rock

(ROOMS: $16 – 36) In geological terms, an erratic rock is a rock that has been carried by a glacier far enough from its source to be deposited in a different environment completely. This definition also aptly describes the owners of this trekker's hostel—two seasoned backpackers, who have succeeded in creating a quality establishment with expert

SOUTHERN PATAGONIA

guide service. The hostel features dorms and private rooms, two living rooms, a DVD collection with over 250 titles, a book exchange, free Internet and WiFi. The hostel also boasts a hearty "trekker's breakfast," which will provide you with the energy necessary to navigate the trails. Most importantly, the friendly staff is eager to provide expert advice and guidance on trekking through nearby Torres del Paine. Equipment rentals are available. Baquedano 719. Tel: 56-6-1410355, E-mail: info@erraticrock.com, URL: www.erraticrock.com. Updated: May 07, 2009.

Erratic Rock 2

(ROOMS: $50) Created specifically with couples in mind, this newer addition to the already successful Erratic Rock allows romantic trekking partners to get some much needed alone time without spending a fortune on a hotel. Only double rooms are available, and all come with cable TV, in-room telephones and private bathrooms. The hostel also offers free bike rentals, and an organic breakfast-in-bed service. There's a cozy lounge and dining room, as well as a kitchen available for guest-use. Tourist information is available, and breakfast and bike rental are included in the price. Benjamin Zamora 732. Tel: 56-6-1414317, E-mail: info@erraticrock.com, URL: www.erraticrock.com. Updated: Apr 24, 2008.

Hotel Martín Gusinde

(ROOMS: $60 – 72) Located near the main square, in front of the casino, Hotel Martín Gusinde is a fair, yet unremarkable choice. The hotel's 28 rooms are clean, come with twin or queen-size beds, and have bathrooms, cable TVs, heating, safes and telephones. The staff is attentive, Internet access is free, and

there's a bar and a restaurant where typical dishes from the area are served, though you may prefer to visit the nearby cafés and eateries. From October to the end of March, room prices more than double. A passable breakfast is included in the price. Carlos Bories 278. Tel: 56-61-412770, E-mail: reservas@hotelmartingusinde.com, URL: www.hotelmartingusinde.com. Updated: November 27, 2009.

The Lady Florence Dixie

(PRICE $76 - 132) Located in the heart of Puerto Natales, the Lady Florence Dixie offers a charming, old-fashioned atmosphere with plenty of modern conveniences. The house was remodeled to keep the vintage charm, while offering central heating, telephone, cable T.V. and fully equipped bathrooms. You might want to consider taking a room in the front of the hotel for a bit extra—the soundproof glass offers stunning views of the mountains, without the city noise invading your room. If you want to save the money, you can still enjoy the lounge on the second floor, which offers comparable views. Manuel Bulnes 655. Tel: (56.61) 411158, Fax: (56.61) 411943, URL: www.hotelflorencedixie.cl/index.html. Updated: Oct 30, 2009.

Aquaterra

(ROOMS: $80 – 110) Aquaterra may not be the fanciest hotel in town, but it is perhaps the friendliest. Aquaterra is run by three transplanted Santiaguinos who fell in love with the cold, windy town of Puerto Natales. It's apparent that much care has gone into the operation of this rustic yet cozy hotel. Rooms are on the smaller side, but are bright and comfortable, and have plush beds with luxurious down comforters. The

Did a unique trek? Got way off the beaten path? Tell others at vivatravelguides.com

hotel has a restaurant and a lounge with a fire-burning stove, perfect for relaxing with a hot cup of coffee or a glass of Chilean wine. A buffet breakfast is included in the price, as well as a welcome drink upon your arrival. The hotel offers massages for $25 per hour, which is well worth the price after completing a punishing trek at Torres del Paine. Av. Bulnes 299. Tel: 56-6-1412239, E-mail: info@aquaterrapatagonia.com, URL: www.aquaterrapatagonia.com. Updated: Mar 17, 2009.

Weskar Lodge

(ROOMS: $98 – 215) Weskar Lodge is a great mid-range hotel for travelers searching for chic, yet rustic surroundings with a stunning view of the waterfront. Since it is a few minutes down the coastline from downtown Puerto Natales, this lodge gives you the feeling of being out in the wild, while still having the conveniences of town nearby. Single, double, triple, and family rooms are available year round. Weskar's in-house restaurant and bar boasts some of the best food in town, served by young and talented local chefs. Huertos Familiares 274-b.Tel: 56-61-414168. URL: www.weskar.cl. Updated: Jul 07, 2009.

Hotel CostAustralis

(ROOMS: $100 – 500) Hotel CostAustralis has great views of the waterfront, only a few blocks from downtown. It offers all the luxury you would expect given the price: clean, friendly, professional services, a restaurant, a bar and all types of rooms, from singles to family rooms. Newly remodeled, the hotel spares no expense on the details. Pedro Montt 262. Tel: 56-6-412000. URL: www.hotelesaustralis.com. Updated: Apr 30, 2009.

Hotel Indigo

(ROOMS: $208 – 350) Hotel Indigo is all about style and design. This luxurious and spacious hotel offers luxuries not normally found in the rustic landscape of Patagonia. A roof-top spa, sauna, massage parlor, restaurant, bar, and large rooms, with amazing views of mountains and glaciers. Bookings should be made online. Ladrilleros 105. Tel: 56-61-413609. URL: www.indigopatagonia.com. Updated: Jul 07, 2009.

Restaurants

You're probably wondering what they eat all the way down here at the end of the Earth. The answer is meat—lots and lots of meat. Magallenic lamb (*cordero magallenico*) is a staple in the region. If you're a conscientious meat eater, you've come to the right place to indulge, as you'll be hard-pressed to find happier, more free-range lamb than around Punta Arenas. Be sure not to miss out on the king crab (*centolla*), another delicious specialty of the region. Most restaurants also serve typical Chilean fare such as *pastel de choclo* (maize pie) and *charquican* (minced meat pie).

Though it's not the easiest place to be vegetarian, most restaurants do offer a couple of veggie options. **El Living** serves 100 percent vegetarian fare, as organic as you can be in this far-flung part of the world, with several options for special diets.

If you're just looking to duck in for a quick bite, most cafe-restaurants serve *churrasco*, a large sandwich, usually consisting of a slab of beef, mayonnaise and whatever else you ask to put on it (tomato, lettuce or avocado, for example). These sandwiches can be made vegetarian. *A lo pobre* means your sandwich will be served with a fried egg and sauteed onions.

Magallenicos are also known for their fondness of sweets. In the center of town, there are several places to stop for a quick chocolate. Be warned that the cappuccinos in this part of the world typically come with a huge dollop of whipped cream, instead of milk. *Submarinos* are basically steaming hot milk with a whole piece of chocolate at the bottom, which melts as you stir and sip your drink. Updated: Jul 07, 2009.

Aquaterra

Located in downtown Puerto Natales, this rustic lodge-style restaurant is warm and has instant appeal. Aquaterra serves up local and international meals with a wide selection of Chilean wines. Meals and finger foods are moderately priced, and the presentation is as classy as it is creative. The drinks are strong and the staff is friendly. This is a great place for a quiet drink on the over stuffed couch next to the wood stove. Bulnes 299. Tel: 56-61-412239, URL: www.aquaterrapatagonia.com. Updated: Apr 29, 2009.

Asador Patagonico

If you want to experience typical Patagonian BBQ, Asador Patagonia is the place to go. Located on the main plaza and always abuzz with customers, Asador has

SOUTHERN PATAGONIA

a comfortable, family-like atmosphere. Patagonian lamb is a favorite; the meat is slow-roasted using wood from fallen trees and seasoned simply—*a la Patagonia*—using only salt. Potatoes and fresh salads are made with local ingredients. Be warned though: Asador is all about the carne, and not much else. Arturo Prat 158. Tel: 56-61-412197 Updated: Mar 17, 2009.

Cormoran de las Rocas

This rounded two-story structure is located atop a small hill close to the water, and offers excellent views of Ultima Esperanza Sound and the snowy mountain ranges beyond it. With professional chefs, an attentive staff, and a killer menu, this classy restaurant might just make you forget you are in rugged Patagonia.

Seafood is definitely their specialty, including king crab, which is typical of the region. Meat dishes are also popular. Most of the fare is meat, but there are wonderful veggie soups and salads. Desserts include a decadent Bailey's custard, tiramisu and calafate cheesecake. The bar upstairs has spectacular views, powerful Pisco sours and a lighter food menu. Miguel Zanchez 72. Tel: 56-61-615131 / 615132, E-mail: contactos@cormorandelasrocas.com, RL: www.cormorandelasrocas.com. Updated: Mar 17, 2009.

Mesita Grande

Mesita Grande basically means "little big table." There are two long tables where hungry trekkers can find a spot to sit. The eatery is a great place to meet other travelers as it mostly caters to backpackers looking for a yummy thin-crust pizza. The owners have a real clay oven where they cook wood-fire grilled pizza, with the dough made to order and rolled out right before your eyes (with all kinds of creative toppings). If you're not in the mood for pizza, Mesita also offers traditional takes on gnocci, lasagna and pastas. Homemade ice creams and dessert pizzas are also available. Arturo Prat 196. Tel: 56-61-411571, E-mail: pizzeria@mesitagrande.cl, URL: www.mesitagrande.cl. Updated: Mar 17, 2009.

Afrigonia

Africa meets Patagonia in this mid-range fusion restaurant. This is the perfect spot to splurge a little on a victory dinner after your trek in Torres del Paine. Delicious curries, fresh tropical ceviche, imaginative veggie and salad combinations as well as Patagonian lamb with African flair

make this restaurant a hit. The desserts here are a must, whether you managed to save room or not. The small restaurant is usually packed, so you may have to be patient waiting for your food. You can share camp stories while you sip some delicious Carmenere wine. Eberhard 343. Tel: 56-61-412232. Updated: Apr 22, 2009.

El Living

El Living is a British-run, friendly little coffee shop. The menu is sure to delight vegetarians and there are even some vegan offerings available. Tasty treats offered include the blue cheese, pear and walnut sandwich, the vegan chickpea patties, burritos and a daily special. Accommodating to the last, the owners can provide options that are wheat-free or gluten free if needed. Wash it all down with a pisco sour or mate. Open from 11 a.m. to 11 p.m. during the summer season. Arturo Prat 156, La Plaza. URL: www.el-living.com. Updated: Apr 24, 2008.

Patagonia Dulce

Patagonia Dulce is a chocolate factory that makes mouth-watering delicacies. The chocolate temptations in the attached cafe come without preservatives or colorants, so enjoy their ice creams or sweets of the day, and don't forget to try the hot chocolate. Barros Arana 233. Tel: 56-6-1415285, URL: www.patagoniadulce.cl. Updated: Apr 24, 2008.

Chill-e

One of the most happening bars in town, Chill-e is a great place to let your hair down. Good vibes, classy cocktails and funky décor all combine to make this place a great night out. Chill-e has some snacks and Mexican food, but is primarily a bar. Manuel Bulnes 343. Updated: Apr 24, 2008.

PARQUE NACIONAL BERNARDO O'HIGGINS

Parque Nacional (PN) Bernardo O'Higgins is the grandest of Chile's national parks. It covers 3,525,091 hectares—an area larger than Belgium. Created in 1969 and expanded in 1985, O'Higgins protects the Southern Ice Field, which covers over 1.1 million hectares. This remnant of the last Ice Age is a UN World Biosphere Reserve. Due to its isolation, PN Bernardo O'Higgins is a land to which few travelers journey. Those who travel on Navimag's Puerto Montt – Puerto Natales ferries glide through the park's channels. Other travelers glimpse slivers of it on trips from Puerto Natales or Villa O'Higgins.

The park extends from the XI Región de Aysén to the XII Región de Magallanes. The administrative office is in Punta Arenas (Monday – Friday 8:30 a.m. – 5:30 p.m. Av. Bulnes 309. Tel: 56-61-238554) with field offices in Puerto Natales (Monday – Friday 8:30 a.m. – 5:30 p.m. Baquedano 847. Tel: 56-61-411843) and Villa O'Higgins (Calle Río Pascua and Río Mayer). The only brochure-map available is of Sector Balmaceda, near Puerto Natales.

To the north of PN Bernardo O'Higgins you'll find PN Laguna San Rafael, which protects the Campo de Hielo Norte, also a UN World Biosphere Reserve. To the west is Reserva Nacional (RN) Katalalixar, preserving a large swath of Pacific coast and islands. RN Alacalufes is on the south edge of O'Higgins. On the east flanks of the park are PN Torres del Paine and Argentina's PN Los Glaciares, home of the Perito Moreno Glacier. PN Bernardo O'Higgins's massive Pío XI is the largest in all of South America. This 64-kilometer (38.4-mi) long tongue of ice licks the waters of Fiordo Eyre. It measures 1,262 square kilometers (487.26 square mi)—the size of the Santiago metropolitan area.

SECTOR BALMACEDA (PUERTO NATALES)

The most easily accessed part of PN Bernardo O'Higgins is Sector Balmaceda, close to Puerto Natales. Boats sail across Seno de Última Esperanza to the foot of Glaciar Balmaceda, then aim for the ranger station at Puerto Toro. During the voyage, keep your eyes open for the black-necked swan, the Coscoroba swan, the Chilean flamingo, the Magellanic penguin, plus various species of gulls, cormorants and ducks, as well as other sea birds. Condors soar overhead.

In the waters around the park, you might spot Commerson's dolphins, South American sea lions and South American fur seals. The port is at the mouth of Laguna Serrano into which Glaciar Serrano flows. An 800-meter (.5 mi) path leads to the glacier. The land, imprinted by past logging, has Magellan's beech, lenga beech, Antarctic beech, Guaitecas cypress and Chilean fire bush. Along the way you can observe birds such as Austral parakeets, Thorn-tailed rayaditos, Rufous-collared sparrows, Black-chinned siskins, Green-backed Firecrown hummingbirds, and Patagonian Sierra-finches.

A less demanding trail, especially designed for visitors with mobility difficulties, leads to a mirador with a view of the glacier. Other activities in this part of the park are kayaking and rappelling. Both activities are limited to the 90 minutes when the tour boat is in the lagoon. Balmaceda Sector has five campsites specifically for those who paddle down the Río Serrano from PN Torres del Paine.

NORTHERN SECTOR (VILLA O'HIGGINS)

You can reach the northern portion of PN Bernardo O'Higgins from Villa O'Higgins at the southern end of the Carretera Austral. There are two trails leading into the north edge of the park: Sendero Altavista and Tramo Ventisquero Chico. Both can be done on foot or on horseback and are open only from November to April. Villa O'Higgins's tourism office has a pamphlet describing the Sendero Altavista hike, which, along with Tramo Ventisquero Chico, is part of the Sendero de Chile trail network (www.senderodechile.cl).

Sendero Altavista is the Tramo (leg) Lago Ciervo of the Sendero de Chile. The sign-posted trailhead begins three kilometers (1.8 mi) west of Villa O'Higgins, off the Carretera Austral, just past Puente Grosse (difficulty: moderate, distance: 16 km/9.6 mi round trip, duration: one day). This trail has views of Lago Ciervo and Río Mayer. It ends at Río and Lago Negro.

Tramo Ventisquero Chico begins at Candelario Mansilla on the other side of Lago O'Higgins. This trail is primarily used by the Chilean Institute of Ice Fields to access a refuge in the Ventisquero Chico sector (difficulty: moderate-hard, distance: 82 km/49.2 mi, duration: 4 days). The trail is divided into two parts: The Candelario Mansilla – Desagüe (mouth) of Lago Chico (24 km/14.4 mi, 4 – 5 hours on horse or 8 hours walking) and Desagüe of Lago Chico-Ventisquero Chico (17 km/10.2 mi, 4 – 5 hours on horse or 7 – 8 hours walking).

The return trip follows the trail from the glacier (ventisquero) back to the mouth of Lago Chico and Candelario Mansilla. Consult with Conaf about conditions before attempting this potentially arduous trek.

SOUTHERN PATAGONIA

Less adventuresome souls can undertake the Excursión Glaciar O'Higgins, a cruise to the foot of Glaciar O'Higgins, to watch it calve into Lago O'Higgins. At three kilometers (1.8 mi) wide and 80 meters (260 feet) high, it is the largest glacier in XI Región de Aysén and the fourth largest in South America. The 11 hour journey, which is done only from December through March, also stops at Candelario Mansilla. Updated: Jun 10, 2009.

Getting To and Away From Parque Nacional Bernardo O'Higgins

Most of Parque Nacional (PN) Bernardo O'Higgins is inaccessible. There are no roads there. From Puerto Natales, tour boats cruise Seno de Última Esperanza to Puerto Toro in Sector Balmaceda (3 hours). You can also kayak down the Río Serrano from PN Torres del Paine to Puerto Toro (2.5 hours).

You can access PN Bernardo O'Higgins from Villa O'Higgins on the north side of the park. Walk from that village to the Sendero Altavista. For Tramo Ventisquero Chico, take the ferry across Lago O'Higgins from Bahía Bahamóndez, seven kilometers (4.2 mi) south of Villa O'Higgins, to Candelario Mansilla ($50 one way). For more information on this or the Excursión Glaciar O'Higgins ($80 – 100), see www.villaohiggins.com/hielosur/index. htm. Both excursions are organized by the operator **Hielo Sur**, based in Villa O'Higgins (E-mail: info@villaohiggins. com. Tel: 56-67-431821).

Navimag's Puerto Montt – Puerto Natales ferry service, **Canales Patagónicos**, passes through the myriad of canals weaving the full length of PN Bernardo O'Higgins (for complete details **see Sailing the Southern Seas (p. 365)**, or visit Navimag's site: www.navimag.com). The boat stops at Puerto Edén, where it is possible to arrange extensive tours into the park. Alternatively, this isolated village can also be reached from Caleta Tortel, whose municipality has a contract for a ferry service. If there is extra space, non-residents are allowed to board. Check with the city hall in Tortel for further information and permission (approximately $25). Updated: Jun 10, 2009.

PARQUE NACIONAL TORRES DEL PAINE

Torres del Paine National Park has the Southern Patagonian Ice Field, one of the largest glaciated areas in the world outside of Antarctica, on one of its borders. Torres del Paine's busy trail system, pricey refugios and an average of 200,000 visitors per year make it feel less remote.

That said, it's extremely popular for a reason. The Torres and Cuernos grace postcards and book covers all over the world and they are a symbol for Chile. "Paine," by the way, means blue, and you will indeed see blues that will blow your mind. Plus, it is possible to get away from the crowds. Try the back end of the circuit, and not just the standard W trek.

To venture even further away from the masses, visit Laguna Azul or Pingo. Even if you don't stray from the well-trodden parts of the park, make sure you check out the icebergs on Lago Grey.

Scientists have traced human settlement in the area to 12,000 years ago. German and British colonists started *estancias* (ranches) in the 1890s. More recently, truckloads of barbed wire fencing have gradually been removed from the park as the land is converted from estancia back to its natural state. National Park Administrator E-mail: jose. linnebrink@conaf.cl; URL: www.p.t.paine. com. Updated: May 06, 2009.

When to Go

The main trekking season in Patagonia is the seven month season between October through late April, although trekking year-round is possible. Trekking between October and November (early spring) is a great way to beat the crowd and see the fresh spring growth.

The summer season (December through March) always tends to have the best months in Patagonia in regards to weather, and trekking this time of year makes river crossings more tolerable. March and April have some cooler and more stable weather patterns. Autumn in Patagonia brings an amazing blast of color, which makes late-season trekking a real treat.

May brings cold temperatures and snowfall. Traveling through Patagonia during the late or off-season is only recommended for the more seasoned and self-reliant

Hotels 🏨

1 Hostería Lago Grey A1
2 Hostería Lago Pehoé B1
3 Hostería Las Torres B1

4 Hostería Mirador del Paine B1
5 Hotel Explora B1

trekkers. The Patagonian winter is not something to be underestimated. Torres del Paine winter night temperatures are as low as -25°C. Updated: Mar 17, 2009.

Getting To and Away From Torres del Paine

The most common way to reach Torres del Paine is by using Puerto Natales, the closest town to the park, as a jumping off point. The majority of visitors fly into Punta Arenas, the nearest airport to the park, and take a three-hour bus ride to Puerto Natales, before heading into Torres del Paine the next day.

BY BUS

From Puerto Natales there are multiple bus services that do nothing more than travel the 2.5 – 3 hours to and from the National Park. These buses run twice daily and will drop you at one of the three stopping points within the

Photo by Dag Olav

park: the entrance at the Laguna Amarga ranger station, the Pudeto catamaran dock on the edge of Lago Pehoé, or the park administration point. The cost of round trip bus tickets to the National Park is between $20 – 25.

There are sometimes more expensive transportation options into the park from Calafate (over the border in Argentina), but services are not consistent.

BY PRIVATE VEHICLE

From Puerto Natales or Punta Arenas, you can also opt to arrange a trip into the park with a private tour company, or rent a car or motorhome to explore on your own, which is significantly more expensive than public transportation, but gives you more freedom to plan your perfect Torres del Paine trip.

EMSA (Roca 1044, Punta Arenas. Tel: 56-61-241182) has a Punta Arenas office and rental desk at the Punta Arenas airport, in addition to an office in Puerto Natales (Bulnes 632. Tel: 56-61-410775) for car and truck rentals.

Andean Roads (E-mail: torlasco@yahoo.com.ar. Tel: 54-911-5422-7623) is one highly reviewed motorhome rental company based in Argentina with a variety of vehicle sizes, ranging from $100 – 200 per day, including

insurance (Argentine pesos, U.S. dollars, and euros are accepted). If you're interested in a motorhome rental, it's important to make reservations well in advance. When heading into the park without a guide, get a good map, and be sure to fill up the gas tank in Puerto Natales. Snow chains are essential in the unpredictable winter months.

BY BOAT

Another (perhaps more exciting and scenic way) to reach the park is by boat, engine-powered catamarans, or human-powered kayaks if you're up for the challenge. There are a variety of catamaran tours that bring visitors from Puerto Natales through Ultimate Esperanza Sound and up Río Serrano to Torres del Paine, passing Glacier Serrano, Glacier Grey, Lago Nordenskjöld and Lago Sarminetö, among other fjords and breathtaking vistas. Most trips depart around 8 a.m. and return to Puerto Natales 10 – 12 hours later, though it's possible to arrange multiple day trips with operators such as **Turismo 21 de Mayo** (Eberhard 560, Puerto Natales. Tel: 56-61-614420) and **Aventour** (Av. España 882, Punta Arenas. Tel: 56-61-241197 / 220174) with stays at *hosterías* on various peninsulas off the fjords. For the more adventurous, sign up for a kayak tour that passes through the same fjords, channels, and rivers into the national park with **Indomita** (C. Bories 206, Puerto Natales. Tel: 56-61-414525). Updated: Jun 29, 2009.

Safety

Torres del Paine National Park has a relatively safe "extreme zone." Trails are well marked, the trail waters are drinkable, there are no poisonous snakes or bugs, transportation is reliable and aside from there not being a proper Search and Rescue in Torres del Paine, all police and park services are ready to help you in case of an emergency. You can find phones and radios at the refugios and hosterias that are scattered throughout the park. The closest hospital (3 hours away in Puerto Natales) has only minimal services. Real hospital facilities are in Punta Arenas, six hours away. There is very little theft. Updated: Mar 17, 2009.

Services

Within the park boundaries of Torres del Paine you can find a variety of services varying from VIP to exclusive to backpacker. Phones and Internet can be used at some of the hosterias and refugios. The hosterias are high-class, whereas refugios are furnished with basic bunks. Trekkers can rent some equipment from the refugios in the park, such as tents, sleeping bags and mattresses. They cost twice as much as in Puerto Natales, but you don't have to lug them between huts. You are not allowed to take this refugio equipment with you to the free campsites (where there are no services), which means if you rent from the refugios, you can only go from refugio to refugio. You can also camp at the refugios with your own equipment without a reservation. The camping option costs roughly $8 per person (not per tent). Hot meals can be purchased at the refugios for about the same price as a restaurant in town. Hot showers can be found at the refugios, as well as water, bathrooms and some store items. Updated: Jul 07, 2009.

Things to See and Do

Aside from the world-class trekking inside the national park, you can explore the landscape by horse, kayaking, by ice climbing or in a boat. Many tour agencies, most of them based in Puerto Natales, can organize programs combining several of these activities. Updated: Jul 02, 2009.

Trekking in Torres del Paine

Featuring spectacular milky lakes and breathtaking mountaintop views, Torres del Paine National Park is Chile's—and possibly South America's—most famous park. Since it was declared an official Biosphere Reserve in 1978, it has attracted adventurers and nature lovers from all over the world who are eager to explore one of the least-spoiled terrains on earth.

And it's no wonder: with its postcard-perfect views, towering granite peaks, majestic mountains, glaciers, waterfalls, babbling streams, lakes, and rivers, Torres del Paine offers unparalleled natural beauty and first-class trekking. More than 100 different bird species, guanacos, foxes, Patagonian deer as well as pumas can be observed in their natural habitat.

What's more, the park is equipped with an excellent infrastructure, making it easy for trekkers of all skill levels (and discomfort thresholds) to plan out their ideal hiking itinerary. Trails and campsites are clearly marked and well-maintained, and there are several restaurants and lodges set up throughout the park.

There are numerous ways to see the park, from simple, brisk day trips, to more ambitious multi-day treks. Popular hiking and trekking circuits include The W, The Circuit, The Valley of the Rio del Francés and others that either wind through the Río Pingo Valley to the base of Torres del Paine or onto Laguna Verde, Laguna Azul and Lago Paine.

Signing up for a trip through an agency is an easy way to hit the trails; you can hire guides from Punta Arenas or Puerto Natales. Most companies will take care of the nitty-gritty details including transport, food and lodging. Larger groups can custom design a trip and contract an agency to take care of the logistical details. When choosing an agency, be sure to focus on its reputation, rather than on prices. If you're averse to guided tours, go-it-your-own trekking is possible with careful planning and foresight.

The weather in Patagonia is unpredictable, and trekkers should be prepared to face harsh winds and bitter cold temperatures at any time of year. Proper gear, including good hiking shoes and a warm sleeping bag, are imperative. The warmest months are from December to March, however, this is also when winds are fiercest. Wintertime is somewhat mild, though days are short and visitors must stay in lodges instead of camping; park access may be limited. Check current weather conditions before heading out. Updated: Jul 02, 2009.

The W Trek

The most highly trekked route in Torres del Paine National Park is called the 'W,' named after a trail system that zig-zags up and down the mountain valleys, from Refugio Grey, on the west side of the park, into Valle Frances, then down and around again, through the Los Cuernos area, up to the Towers and back down. The typical trek takes five to seven days, with five to eight hours of hiking per day. Most notably, the trek boasts many of the park's must-see attractions: Los Torres, Los Cuernos, Valle Frances, Paine Grande, and Glacier Grey. This trail system can be done in a variety of ways, from more rugged camping style treks, to full room and board in refugios (well stocked trail huts) along the trail, where beds, food, and showers await you at the end of each day.

You could also have the best of both worlds: camping in tents, but eating meals in the

SOUTHERN PATAGONIA

The Q Circuit Trek

After the W, there's the Full Circuit, starting with the W, continuing around the backside to Refugio Dickson, up and down over the John Gardner Pass, and back down to Refugio Grey. Fewer folks do the Full Circuit compared to the W, a feeling of accomplishment is undeniable for those who do. It takes 7 – 10 days (depending on the pace and drive) and circumnavigates the park beautifully. But there's more. Another trail is considered to be, by far, the way to claim full bragging rights in Torres del Paine. More than The W. More than the Circuit. Ladies and gentlemen, may we present "the Q."

- **Day 1:** The Administration Center at the south end of the park is where your adventure begins. Most trekkers access the park from the Las Torres area and take the catamaran across Lago Pehoé. If you take public transportation, you will probably arrive around 1 p.m. Check out the visitor's center at the administration center. At this point, your pack will be at its heaviest—day one of what might be a 10-day trip. Trek for two hours and make camp at the free campsite, Las Carrettas.
- **Day 2:** Starting much earlier than the day before, trek up toward Lago Pehoé (approximately 4 hours) then push on another two hours to the free campsite Campamento Italiano at the mouth of spectacular Valle Frances.
- **Day 3:** This morning, leave the tent, extra food, sleeping bag and mat behind. Load your backpack with some food, rain gear, camera, and just a few basics, and head up into Valle Frances without all the extra weight. It's a steep hike, so traveling light is nice. The valley offers natural lookouts, so even if you don't make it to the very end of the valley, you will understand what all the hype is about. Keep an eye on the time and head down to the camp again by around 4 p.m. Then pack up your camp and move on to Refugio Los Cuernos. This is good spot to spend night three.
- **Day 4:** Today, haul your loaded pack all the way around and up to the free campsite Las Torres. This will be a long day, approximately 7 – 9 hours. The signs will direct you to Refugio Chileno, but if you hike one hour further, the Las Torres campsite is free (though Chileno is a beautiful spot and it's tempting to call it a day and camp there). But the following morning you'll want to wake before dawn to try to see the towers in their breathtaking, red morning glow. The early morning trek to the lookout takes at least 45 minutes from Campamento Las Torres, or 1.45 hours from Chileno, though it can take over two hours if you're trying to get there in the pre-dawn darkness.
- **Day 5:** Wake up 1.5 hours before dawn. No matter what time of year it is, it's going to be extremely chilly at this hour. Do not wrap yourself in too many clothes as you will end up sweating by the time you reach the mirador. Only bring your packs loaded with the coats you're not wearing, your sleeping mat and bag, and breakfast. When you reach the top, all of your sweat will have evaporated. Throw on your warm clothes, put down your sleeping mats (so you don't have to sit on an ice cold rock), and crawl into your sleeping bags to experience the towers at dawn. Fire up your stoves and make a hot coffee. After a couple of hours, head back to camp. Pack up and have a nice, downhill trek to the campsite next to Refugio Las Torres. Close the book on the 'W,' repack, maybe buy some things from the little store near Hostería Las Torres to stock up for the back circuit, and call it a day. This is a paid camping area and costs $6.50 per person.
- **Day 6:** Start the back circuit, ideally early and refreshed, as you have an 8 – 10 hour trek to Refugio Dickson. It seems like a huge distance, but the terrain is milder than the 'W'.
- **Day 7:** Progress to Campamento Perros. There is no refugio here, but you still have to pay for camping. It seems like a short day and people tend to think that they could push on further, though it's not recommended.
- **Day 8:** This is the day of the John Gardner Pass. The hardest thing about the pass is the wind. The terrain is manageable, and the view is unmatched. The view of Glacier Grey (and the Patagonian Ice Field on a clear day) is one of the most amazing moments you'll experience in Patagonia, hands down. You'll find two free campsites after coming down off the pass. Staying at the the beautiful and free Campamento Guardes is a nice way to shorten the day, and it offers more views of the glacier from above.
- **Day 9:** If you hurry, you can leave on the mid-day catamaran at 12:30 p.m. If you just want to enjoy the final day at an easier pace, there's a boat at 6:30 p.m. or you can choose to camp a final night. In either case, you just completed the full 'Q'!

Reprinted with permission from Black Sheep Patagonia. Updated: Jul 02, 2009.

Did a unique trek? Got way off the beaten path? Tell others at vivatravelguides.com refugios. There are endless variations you can choose from. Although this trek is growing in popularity, the remote nature, rough trails and strong winds can humble even a seasoned trekker. Updated: Jul 02, 2009.

Ice Hike

Rutas Patagonia guides ice hiking and climbing on Glacier Grey inside Torres del Paine National Park, twice daily. Leaving by boat from Refugio Grey or Hosteria Grey, these half day ice programs cost $140 per person and include climbing equipment. Tel: 56-61-21960761, E-mail: info@rutaspatagonia.com, URL: www.rutaspatagonia.com. Updated: Jun 29, 2009.

Glacier Grey

Glacier Grey is a 270 square kilometers (168 sq. mi) glacier located at the north end of Lago Grey. The easiest way to experience Glacier Grey is aboard the Grey II, which takes travelers from Hosteria Lago Grey, through a field of house-sized chunks of neon blue ice, to the 40-meter-high face of the glacier. The boat departs twice daily, at 8 a.m. and 3 p.m., and operates year-round. Prices vary by season and number of passengers (Tel: 56-61-712100; URL: www.turismolagogrey.com). Alternatively, hikers can follow the Glacier Grey trail, which begins at Refugio Pehoé (by taking a catamaran across Lago Pehoé; $16 one-way) and offers breathtaking views of both Lago Grey and Glacier Grey. For an up-close and unforgettable look at the deep blue crags and caverns, Rutas Patagonia (Tel: 56-61-613874; URL: www.rutaspatagonia.com) straps crampons on your feet to hike on the glacier's surface for about $140. Updated: Jul 01, 2009.

Lago Grey Navigation

This four-hour navigation tour over Lago Grey is a great way to see the 40-meter (131-ft) head wall of ice on Glacier Grey in Torres del Paine National Park. This "sight seeing" tour costs roughly $75 and tickets can be purchased from any of the booking agencies in Puerto Natales or directly from Hosteria Lago Grey's website. The tour can also be used as one way trekker's transportation to the Glacier Grey campsite, instead of trekking the 4 hours from Pehoé. Turismo Lago Grey, Lautaro Navarro 1077, Punta Arenas. URL: www.turismolagogrey.com. Updated: Jun 29, 2009.

Lago Pehoé

Lago Pehoé, though acting as a serene foreground to the jagged Cuernos del Paine, offers little in the way of activities; mostly, it is a starting (or ending) point for various excursions through Torres del Paine National Park. Hikers on the W and Circuit trails will have to cross it via a 45-minute catamaran ride (Read: excellent photo op), as will those doing day hikes to the Glacier Grey trail. Waterfall Salto Grande, which is fed by Lago Nordenskjold and pours into Pehoé, is worthy of a hike. It's within easy reach of the Pudeto catamaran dock. Pehoé is also home to the Hostería Pehoé, the oldest hotel in Torres del Paine. Updated: Jun 29, 2009.

Fly Fishing

The icy turquoise waters of Torres del Paine National Park are home to a variety of fish, including Brown, Steelhead and Rainbow trout, as well as Coho, Chinook, and Atlantic salmon. Sports fishers and anglers need to apply for a license at the National Fishery Department (*Servicio Nacional de Pesca*), on Yungay Street 361 in Puerto Natales. Tel: 56-61-411350, open most days 9 a.m.– 12:30 p.m.and 2:30 to 4:30 p.m.

Just 80 kilometers (50 mi) from Puerto Natales, Lago Toro (Bull Lake) has great year-round fishing, with an abundance of trout that are visible in the crystal waters. At Lago Torro are the headwaters to the Serrano River, which are accessible roughly 168 kilometers (100 mi) from Puerto Natales. Serrano runs to the Bay of Last Hope, ending at the Sound of Ultima Esperanza. The river is full of big Brown and Rainbow trout and Chinook salmon and the best angling is during March and April, though it's possible to fish from November through February.

The muddy waters of Lake Balmaceda, 40 kilometers (25 mi) from Puerto Natales, are home to big trout that often weigh in at up to 9 pounds (4 kg) and can be caught all year long. Flowing from Lake Balmaceda into Almirante Gulf, The Hollemberg River is located 25 kilometers (15 mi) south of Puerto Natales. The best time to catch the Brown and Rainbow trout here is from October through March.

Fly fishing outfitters:
Mara Patagonia—Armando Sanhueza 876, Punta Arenas. Tel: 56-61-710026.

Turismo Comapa—Manuel Bulnes 533, Puerto Natales. Tel: 56-61-414300. Updated: Jun 30, 2009.

SOUTHERN PATAGONIA

Tours

A wide array of tour companies can take you to the Torres del Paine National Park. Tours vary in quality and price, so do a little research beforehand. If you're planning on organizing last minute trips though, Puerto Natales is a good place to do that. There are different types of tours available too, including hiking, trekking and climbing, as well as birdwatching. Updated: Mar 17, 2009.

Vista Paine Horseback Tours

The Vista Paine Horseback Tours company organizes multi-day horseback rides in and around Torres del Paine, with prices starting at $35 (2 hours) to $350 (2 days and nights) for an all inclusive package. English-speaking staff can organize transportation, cabins and custom programs. Tel: 56-9-77318157, E-mail: info@campingchile.com, URL: www.horseridingpatagonia.com. Updated: Jun 29, 2009.

Antares Patagonia

Antares offers trekking and adventure programs in Torres del Paine and surrounding areas, including kayaking, horseback riding and trekking. Multilingual staff and international guides. C. Bories 206, Puerto Natales. URL: www.antarespatagonia.com. Updated: Jun 29, 2009.

Erratic Rock

Erratic Rock offers trekking and climbing tours throughout Argentina and Chile, from backpacker budget programs to VIP tours. Run by climbers, they specialize in expeditions to the North Tower and can help in arranging other Torres del Paine climbing permits. Multilingual staff and international guides. Baquedano 719, Puerto Natales. URL: www.erraticrock.com. Updated: Jun 29, 2009.

Lodging

There are only three options for sleeping inside the National Park: camping (free and paid), *refugios* (trail huts) or *hosterías* (upscale lodge). There is NO wild camping, meaning you may only camp at the designated campsites.

CAMPING

There are two different types of campsites in the park: paid and unpaid. If there is an open and working refugio next to your campsite, then you will have to pay up to $8 per person, not per tent. For this fee you receive all campsite services that the refugios offer, which include water, bathrooms, mini-stores, cooking areas and the option to buy a hot meal. You do not need a reservation for a camping spot anywhere in the park.

You can rent sleeping bags, mats and tents in the refugios—the upside is that you don't have to carry it with you on the trail. The down side is that the gear costs more than twice as much at the refugios than in Puerto Natales, and you can't take the refugio's rental gear away from the refugios to the free campsites (which throws off the groove of a standard trek) and if you rent equipment you still have to pay the camping fee on top of the rental fee.

If there is no refugio next to your campsite, or if the refugio is closed, then camping is free. But there are no services; you must be completely self-sufficient. There is always a creek nearby for water and an outhouse or drop toilet for campers to use. There are no garbage services at the free campsites, but you can dump your trash at the refugios. On the back circuit there are no free campsites, and not always a refugio. Free campsites include: Los Guardes, Italiano, Británico, Japones, Las Torres, Paso, Pingo, and Las Carretas.

REFUGIOS

You can find refugios in various locations on the trail within Torres del Paine National Park. Refugios are private and independently managed. They offer dorm beds (roughly $40), basic hot meals (roughly $18) and paid campsites (roughly $8 per person). Meals can be purchased on the spot, in addition to boxed lunches for hikes, but beds should be reserved in advance to guarantee availability. Normally you need your own sleeping bag, but some refugios offer upgrade options and gear rentals. Contact **Fantastico Sur** (albergue@lastorres.com) or **Vertice** (Tel: 56-61-360361 / 412742, E-mail: ventas@verticepatagonia.cl). Refugio reservations can also be made at info@erraticrock.com.

HOSTERÍAS

The hosterías in the National Park are the more luxurious option for sleeping close to the trail head. Most resemble rustic lodges and have everything you would expect for the price range. Some are directly on the main trail of the 'W', while others are on the perimeter of the park boundries. Updated: Jul 02, 2009.

Hostería Las Torres

(ROOMS: $140 – 450) With the three towers as a backdrop, Hostería Las Torres is the most popular hostería in the National Park. What started as an *estancia* (Patagonian sheep ranch) has a very authentic style and design. With luxurious rooms, a world-class restaurant, spa, information center and more, this famous hotel is worth a visit even if you are not sleeping there. There is also a great place for a victory drink after the trek. Sarmiento 846. Tel: 56-61-363636, E-mail: info@lastorres.com. Updated: Jul 02, 2009.

Lodge Cerro Guido

(ROOMS: $180 and up) Lodge Cerro Guido is located 40 kilometers outside the Laguna Amarga entrance of Torres del Paine National Park. The lodge has a long and interesting history in Patagonia and acts more as a time machine than a hotel. The lodge has a varied menu and bar; they can also arrange excursions to Torres del Paine and horseback tours. Tel: 56-61-21964807, E-mail: bookings@cerroguido.cl. Updated: Jul 02, 2009.

Hostería Mirador Del Payne

(ROOMS: $180 – 265) Mirador del Payne is located by the shore of the Laguna Verde, just outside the National Park. This hostería is part of Estancia El Lazo, a livestock center that dates from the later years of the last century, which allows visitors to experience Chilean ranch life in style. With large, comfortable rooms, a bar, common areas and a large fireplace, this is a great place to relax in an overstuffed sofa with great National Park views out your window. Fagnano 585. Tel: 56-61-226930 E-mail: hosteria@miradordelpayne.com. Updated: Jul 02, 2009.

Hostería Pehoé

(ROOMS: $200 and up) Located on the mirror lakes inside Torres del Paine National Park, Hostería Pehoé is a great mid-range luxury hotel for folks trying to upgrade from the *refugios* (trail huts) while still staying within view of the parks famous granite peaks. The hotel has an in-house bar and restaurant and gives off a crisp and comfortable local feel. Prices listed are for doubles. Turismo Pehoé, 21 de Mayo 1464. Updated: Jun 29, 2009.

Explora: Hotel Salto Chico

(ALL-INCLUSIVE PACKAGES: $2,000 – 12,000) Located inside the national park, Hotel Explora is a five-star, world-famous luxury resort with 30 rooms, and is known not only for its architecture, food and views, but also for its rich and famous clientele. Pampering is the name of the game. A stay at Explora includes trekking tours and transportation into Torres del Paine National Park. U.S. Toll Free Number: 1-866-750-6699. URL: www.explora.com. Updated: Jun 29, 2009.

Hostería Lago Grey

Located at the Southern end of Lago Grey, the hostería offers 30 rooms, in addition to a restaurant, bar, and views of Glacier Grey and the icebergs on the beach below. Navigation tours of Lago Grey depart from the hostería daily. Turismo Lago Grey, Lautaro Navarro 1077. Tel: 56-61-712100, Updated: Jul 02, 2009.

Restaurants

Because Torres del Paine is a National Park, there are limited food options. You can buy hot food in the few refugios, hosterías, and some campgrounds in the park. The refugios also have small stores where you can buy limited dry goods, and prepare three basic hot meals per day for anyone interested. Vegetarian options are also available. Refugio meals cost on average between $10 and $18. All the fancier hotels and hosterías within the park boundaries have in-house restaurants and complete menus, offering everything you would expect from a upscale lodge-style resort. Updated: Jun 29, 2009.

ARGENTINE PATAGONIA

Argentine Patagonia starts in central Argentina and stretches from the Río Colorado to the Straits of Magellan. It is a vast, desolate haven for naturalists with very few inhabitants outside of the coastal cities. The Patagonia Region is filled with unique animals like penguins and elephant seals, along with windswept and barren land, and lakes. From November-May fishing aficionados seek trout, salmon and native species like trahira in rivers and streams in the Andean foothills.

One of the main destinations is the Valdés Peninsula, best reached from the nearby resort of Puerto Madryn. This marine-life preserve for sea elephants, sea lions, Magellanic penguins, whales and much more is a good base while visiting the area. Just south of the Valdés Peninsula, at the Parque Nacional Los Glaciares, is one of Argentina's most popular attractions: the Perito Moreno Glacier. At the base of Mount Fitzroy, this is one of the few places on earth where you can observe an advancing glacier and one of the best areas in Argentina for trekking and climbing. Hike around this UNESCO World Heritage Site or just stare in awe as the tremendous chunks of ice crash into the Canal de los Tempanos.

The Comodoro Rivadavia is nothing more than a passing point for most tourists on their way to the region. This is a shame as there are a few worthwhile sites here including one of Argentina's best museums, the Museo del Petroleo, paid for with money from the oil industry but featuring natural history and cultural exhibitions. In the southwest, find the magnificent Petrified Forest Reserve (Reserva Geológica Bosque Petrificado). Due south are the prehistoric Cuevas de las Manos, with 10,000-year-old paintings of hands, camels, reptiles and other animals.

RÍO TURBIO, ARGENTINA

 352 m 6,650 02902

Long before humans walked on this planet, Río Turbio and the surrounding area was a vast inland sea. This twist of fate is what makes Río Turbio what it is today: Argentina's major coal mining region. After seeing the pristine beauty along Ruta 40 and visiting the virgin wilderness of El Chalten and El Calafate's Parque Nacional Los Glaciares, approaching Río Turbio is quite a shock. The first thing that greets visitors is kilometers of mines and conveyors alongside the highway. Then, before the city itself, come the miners' block housing.

Life in Río Turbio centers on those black carbon seams, which means the city has a somewhat gloomy atmosphere. The streets flow with men who come hoping to find work in the bowels of the earth, and since the announcement of a sixth mine to be opening, the population has swollen by several thousand. It's hard to find room at any of the inns. These are just some of the reasons many travelers pass by Río Turbio on their way from El Calafate to Puerto Natales. The town, though, does have some interesting attractions.

In the mine installations on the east side of Río Turbio is Escuela Museo Minero. It was established in 1978 to teach the village's

students about mining, but tourists are also welcome to learn all about coal, from its ancient geological past through the mining process (Monday - Friday 8 a.m. - noon, 2:30 - 5 p.m. 4 km/2.4 mi east. Entry: free). Not too far away is the turn-off for the Reserva Hidroecológica Vega San José, also known as Dique San José. Located four kilometers (2.4 mi) north of the city, this is a good place to camp, canoe and kayak. Some birds, including flamingos, now reside at this man-made lake.

Traveling south of Río Turbio are more intriguing places. About one kilometer (0.6 mi) away is Bosque de Duendes. A path following the course of a stream wends through a damp forest. Hidden among the trees are over 40 sculptures done by Patagonian woodcarvers. Further south on 40 is a roadside shrine to the folkloric hero Gauchito Gil. Near the Chilean border (4 km/2.4 mi south) is Mina 1, the original mine, which is now a historical site. Also in this district is Centro de Deportes Invernales Valdelen: here you can get your skiing in–both cross-country and alpine. The 500-hectare complex has eight runs, ski lift, hostel, instructors, guides, equipment rental and restaurant. The season runs May - September (Tel.: 42-2708, E-mail: valdelencentrodeesqui@hotmail.com, URL: www.valdelencentrodeski.com.ar).

Andean Condors frequent the Río Turbio area. There are several new viewpoints at Mina 1, Mina 4, and Cerro de la Cruz from which you can watch these majestic birds. On the horizon is the Tren Bioceánico, a 40-kilometer (24 mi) train ride to Puerto Natales, Chile. This line carried cargo and passengers from 1952 to 1997. Service, hopefully, will resume by 2011.

Río Turbio has a few holidays:

October—Feria de Colectividades. The cultures of all the nations who founded this town, including Spain, Italy, Syria, Lebanon, Bolivia and Scotland, are celebrated with food, dances and other shows.

Late August—Fiesta Provincial de la Nieve, a snow festival, with skiing, a triathlon, snow football, folklore and other events.

December 4 – Día del Minero y de Santa Bárbara. Santa Bárbara is the patron saint of miners, and there is a religious procession on this day. This is the only time of the year

SOUTHERN PATAGONIA

women are allowed to enter the mines (bring a helmet and flashlight). At any time of the year, you can visit her chapel, Capilla de Santa Bárbara, which is decorated with flags from the original miners' countries (two blocks east of Plaza San Martín, off Calle San Martín).

December 14 – Aniversario de Río Turbio. This is the city's anniversary fete and includes the Festival de Doma y Folklore, a rodeo and other gaucho events.

History

The history of how all these immigrants came to this valley begins in 1873 when Englishman William Greenwood and Frenchman François Poivre founded a settlement on the banks of a turbulent river. The village Río Turbio was formally founded in 1887. In that same year Teniente Agustín del Castillo discovered coal. During World War II, Santa Cruz Governor Gregores ordered the exploitation of this resource. Since then, the mining industry here has had its cycles. In the 1990s it was privatized, but since the 2004 underground shaft fire which killed 14 workers, the mines are once more operated by state-owned Yacimientos Carboníferos Fiscales (YCF) Río Turbio.

Services

Most services are on Avenida de los Mineros. **The Dirección de Turismo Municipal** is very helpful (Monday – Friday 8 a.m. – 9 p.m., weekends 9 a.m. – 9 p.m. Plazoleta Agustín del Castillo, between Av. de los Mineros and the main plaza, Tel.: 42-1950, Fax: 42-2451, E-mail: turismo@rioturbio.ov.ar, URL: turismo.gov.ar). The **Gendarmería** (immigration police) is at the border (Tel.: 42-1108); **city police** at Castillo near Irigoyen (Tel.: 42-1172).

Banks have ATMs that accept MasterCard, Cirrus, Visa and Plus cards: **Banco Santa Cruz** (Lista, across from tourism office; ATM also accepts American Express); **Banco de la Nación Argentina** (Avenida de los Mineros and Roca; exchanges U.S. dollars, Western Union agent). Many businesses accept Chilean pesos and U.S. dollars, as well as the local currency.

Río Turbio also has a **hospital** (Bolados, between Murallón and Upsala), **post office** (Avenida de los Mineros and Irigoyen) and right next door, **Oyikil**, the phone and Internet ($1.20 per hour, Skype; slow connection)

center. **Keyem Viajes y Turismo** provides tours (Avenida Jorge Newbery 600, Tel.: 02902-42-2591 / (02966)1541-1611).

Lodging

Even though eight hostels operate in Río Turbio, rooms are scarce. Most are solidly booked by migrants coming to work in the mines. The tourism office can help you find a place in a pinch. Free campsites (without services) are at Bosque de los Duendes (1 km/0.6 mi south of town) and at Dique San José (4 km/2.4 mi east).

Albergue Mina 1 (Paraje Mina 1, 4 km/2.4 mi south, near Chilean border, Tel.: 42-24-2498, E-mail: lmartinez@oyikil.com.ar) – shared room $11.

Hotel Yenu (2 de Abril 170, Tel.: 42-1694) -- $23 single, $34 double with breakfast.

Hotel Nazo (Moyano 464, Tel.: 42-1334, Fax.: 42-1800, E-mail: nazo@oyikil.com.ar) – 1 or 2 persons $50 - 56.

Restaurants

Most restaurants in town are rotiserías (chicken joints) or snack stands. At Castillo and Kista is a La Anónima supermarket.

Rotisería El Quincho (Roca and Antartida Argentina, Tel.: 42-1570)

Pizzería Don Pablo (Pellegrini and Sáenz Peña, Tel.: 42-1220)

Restaurante Fond de Cave (Moyano 464, Tel.: 42-1800.

EL CALAFATE, ARGENTINA

 199 m 7,000 54-2962

El Calafate, on the shores of Lake Argentino, is a gateway to the glaciers. About four hours northwest of Río Gallegos, El Calafate is close to some of the world's best big ice, such as the Viedma Glacier, which at 100 meters (328 ft) high and five kilometers (three mi) wide, is the largest in Latin America. Some of the other famous glaciers in the area include: Upsala Glacier, Onelli Glacier, Spegazzini Glacier, Mayo Glacier, Frías Glacier. The Perito Perito Moreno Glacier known as "the eighth wonder of the world," was declared a World Natural Heritage Site by UNESCO in 1981.

SOUTHERN PATAGONIA

Photo by Kyle Adams

The town is named after a wild, thorny bush berry (*Berberis buxifolia*), available in abundance and cooked into many local sweets. The town was originally established as a wool trading outpost in 1927. Although there are only 8,000 residents, El Calafate has a host of craft shops, restaurants and lodging options.

Despite El Calafate's apparent remoteness, its international airport offers direct flights from Buenos Aires and other major Argentine cities. From Buenos Aires flights can run over $500, so start flight-shopping early. Flights from Puerto Natales, Chile, are also available. You can catch a bus to El Calafate from Buenos Aires; you'll have to connect through Río Gallegos. Updated: May 11, 2009.

When to Go

El Calafate has a microclimate created by ice fields to the west, hills to the south and surrounding forests. Its longest day (December 21) has 17 hours of light. The shortest is June 21, when the sun shines for eight hours. Summers are warm but tend to be very windy.

The town is busy and you need to make reservations if you want a room. It is best to book at least a month in advance. Many businesses close after Semana Santa with large end-of-season sales —a shopaholic's dream come true.

In the fall, the poplars turn yellow and the steppe is awash with brilliantly colored foliage. Winds continue to kick up now and again. Come morning, don't be surprised to see the surrounding hills dusted with snow. In the winter the wind is calm with only occasional periods of snow and rain. For more information consult www.elcalafateinvita.com. Updated: Jul 13, 2009.

Getting To and Away From El Calafate

From Ruta 40, paved Ruta 11 arrives to El Calafate. During winter, Ruta 40 may be closed due to ice and snow. In these months, the more common route to El Calafate is Ruta 3 from Río Gallegos. El Calafate has several gas stations, mechanics and tire repair shops (*gomerías*).

BY BUS

All buses in El Calafate leave from a central terminal (Roca 1004). Services include a café, bathrooms and an information desk. All companies have offices here; many are closed 2 – 5 p.m. A few agencies also have downtown branches: **Chalten Travel** (Av. del Libertador 1174.Tel: 54-2902-492212, E-mail: contacto@chaltentravel.com, URL: www.chaltentravel.com) and **Cal-Tur** (Av. del Libertador 1080. Tel: 54-2902-491388, E-mail: caltur@cotecal.com.ar). A long staircase leads down from the bus station to Avenida del Libertador, through the Mercado de Artesanos.

From October to April some companies traverse Ruta 40, making it easier to get to Bariloche and other towns along the route. At other times of the year, the journey requires a transfer at Río Gallegos.

Trips to Puerto San Julián, Puerto Santa Cruz, Puerto Deseado, Comodoro Rivadavia and other destinations along Ruta 3 also require transfer in Río Gallegos; likewise for Buenos Aires, Córdoba and Mendoza, especially in the low season. Buses are less frequent May-September.

To Glaciar Perito Moreno and Parque Nacional Los Glaciares:
Patagonia Ya ($23 round trip, 1.5 hours, depart: 10 a.m., return: 5:15 p.m.)
Taqsa (depart: 9 a.m., return 3:30 p.m.)
Cal-Tur (depart: 9 a.m., return: 4 p.m.)

To El Chaltén:
Chaltén Travel (daily 8 a.m., 6 p.m., $20)
Taqsa (daily 8 p.m., $17), **Cal-Tur** (daily 8 a.m., 6 p.m., $20)

To Río Turbio:
Taqsa (daily noon, $16, 5.5 hours)
Cootra (daily 8:30 a.m., $13, 4 hours).

To Río Gallegos:
Taqsa ($13, 4 hrs., daily 3 a.m, noon, 2 p.m.)
Sportsman (daily 12:30 p.m.).

SOUTHERN PATAGONIA

To Ushuaia:
Sportsman, **Taqsa** (daily 3 a.m., $64, 17 – 17.5 hours; change in Río Gallegos).

To Caleta Olivia:
Taqsa (daily 5:30 p.m., $41, 13.5 hours, transfer in Río Gallegos).

To Comodor Rivadavia:
Sportsman (3 a.m., noon, $43, 16 hours; transfer in Río Gallegos).

To Bariloche:
Chaltén Travel (September – mid-April by way of Ruta 40; in winter by way of Ruta 3 with transfer in Río Gallegos), **Taqsa** (5:30 p.m., $103, 28.5 hours), **Sportsman** (3 a.m., $89, 32 hours).

September to April, **Barivans** has five-day trips to Bariloche via Chile's Carretera Austral ($240 transportation only, Tel: 02944-1564-9834 / 1558-7009, E-mail: info@barivans. com.ar, URL: www.barivans.com.ar).

To Buenos Aires, Argentina:
Pingüino (34 – 38 hours, daily 9 a.m., 8 p.m., $104 – 121), **Sportsman** ($134), **Taqsa** ($124 – 148).

To Puerto Natales, Chile:
Cootra (daily 8:30 a.m., $17, 5 hours), **Zaahj** (Wednesday, Friday, Sunday 8 a.m., $14, 4.5 hours).

To Punta Arenas, Chile:
Pingüino (daily 4 a.m., $23, 9 hours; change in Río Gallegos).

BY AIR
Aeropuerto El Calafate is 23 kilometers (14 mi) east of El Calafate, off Ruta 11 (Tel: 54-2902-491230, E-mail: infoaerocal@cotecal.com.ar). **Ves Patagonia** has shuttle services (Av. del Libertador 1319, local 6. Tel: 54-2902-494355, E-mail: reserves@vespatagonia.com, URL: vespatagonia.com, $8 per person). Taxis charge $20 for the run. There is a $5 departure tax.

Aerolíneas Argentinas (Monday – Friday 9:30 a.m. – 12:30 p.m., 3:30 – 7:30 p.m., Saturday 10 a.m. – 1 p.m. 9 de Julio 57, local 1-2. Tel: 54-2902-492814, E-mail: ftevtas@aerolineas.com.ar, URL: www. aerolineas.com.ar).

To Bariloche: (once daily, from $264, 2 hrs).

To Ushuaia: (once daily, $135, 1 hour).

To Buenos Aires: (thrice daily, $141, 3 – 5 hours).

Lade (Monday – Friday 10 a.m. – 1 p.m., 4 – 7 p.m., Saturday 10 a.m. – noon. Mermoz and Marambio. Tel: 54-2902-491262, E-mail: ladecalafate@cotecal.com.ar, URL: www.lade.com).

To Buenos Aires: (Friday, $123, 10 hours; transfer in Ushuaia).

To Ushuaia: (Thursday, Friday, $104, 1.5 hours).

To Comodoro Rivadavia: (Friday, $66, 1.75 hours).

To Bariloche: (Thursday, $184, 1.5 hours).

To Mar de Plata: (Thursday, $132, 4 hours).

LAN (Monday – Friday 9 a.m. – 1 p.m., 4-8 p.m., Saturday 9 a.m. – 1 p.m., 5 – 8 p.m. Rumbo Sur, 9 de Julio 81, local 2. Tel: 54-2902-492155, E-mail: atofte@lan.com, URL: www.lan.com).

To Buenos Aires: (Wednesday, Friday, Argentines $108 – 143, foreigners from $150). Updated: Jul 13, 2009.

Getting Around

El Calafate has few paved streets, signs and house numbers. Taqsa runs two routes around the city, mainly into the downtown and residential areas. All depart from the bus terminal ($0.60). Remises, or taxis, are metered and expensive. Figure on $3.50 per kilometer (half-mile). There is an initial pick-up fee of $1.

You can also rent a bicycle to get around on your own. Not only does **Patagonia Shop** lease bikes, but it also does wheeled tours to Cuevas del Walicho and other sites (9 de Julio 29. Tel: 54-2902-492767, E-mail: info@ patagoniabikes.com, URL: www.patagoniabikes.com). **HLS Travesías** sells bike parts, too (Buenos Aires 173. Tel: 54-2902-493806, URL: www.travesiasur.com.ar).

Over a dozen agencies rent cars, including: **Avis** (Av. del Libertador 1078. Tel: 54-2902-492877); **Budget** (Friele 2119. Tel: 54-2902-495808); **Dollar Rent a Car** (Av. del Libertador 1341, local 7. Tel: 54-2902-492634). **Hertz** (Av. del Libterador 1822. Tel: 54-2902-493033).

SOUTHERN PATAGONIA

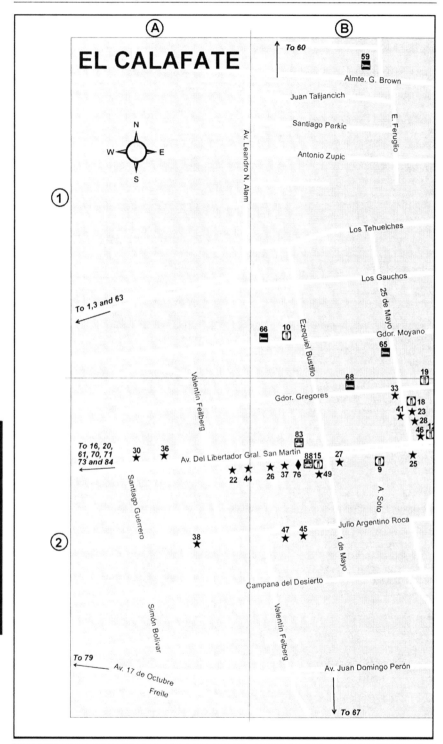

EL CALAFATE

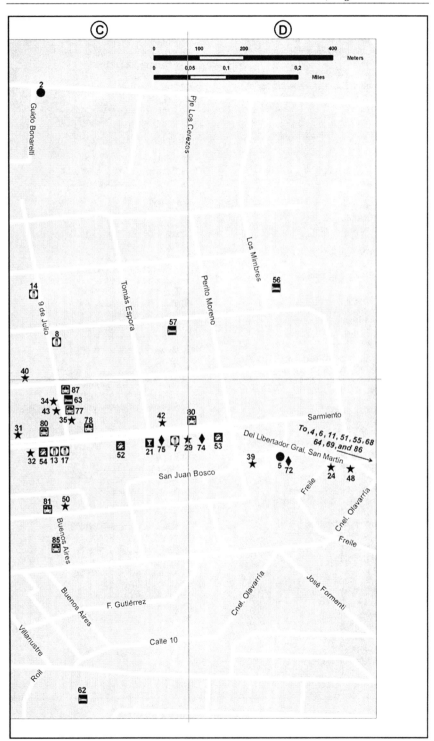

SOUTHERN PATAGONIA

Activities ●

1 Casa Verde A1
2 Centro de Interpretación Histórica C1
3 Mirador A1
4 Museo Regional D2
5 Parroquia Santa Teresita del Niño Jesús D2

Airports ✝

6 Aeropuerto El Calafate D2

Eating 🍴

7 Casimiro Biguá C2
8 El Puesto C1
9 La Cocina B2
10 La Posta B1
11 La Tablita D2
12 La Vaca Atada B2
13 Mi Viejo C2
14 Panadería y Confitería Don Luis C1
15 Pizzería La Lechuza B2
16 Pura Vida A2
17 Rick's Cafe C2
18 Sancho Restaurant B2
19 Tierra Bendita B2

Nightlife ♫

20 Don Diego de la Noche A2
21 Libro y Bar Borges y Álvarez C2

Services ★

22 Abranpampa A2
23 Arroba Ciber Café B2
24 ATM D2
25 Banco de la Nación Argentina B2
26 Banco Patagonia B2
27 Banco Santa Cruz B2
28 Banco Tierra del Fuego B2
29 Casa de Cambios Thaler C2
30 Centro Integral de Comunicaciones A2
31 Ciber Point C2
32 Correo Argentino C2
33 Del Glaciar I B2
34 Del Glaciar II C2
35 El Galpón de Don Emilio C2
36 El Sitio A2
37 Foto Aónikenk B2
38 Hospital Distrital José Formen A2
39 La Barraca D2
40 Lava y Lava C2
41 Lavadero B2
42 Open Calafate C2
43 Patagonia Shop C2
44 Pharmacy Del Cerro A2

45 Pharmacy Don Bosco B2
46 Pharmacy El Calafate B2
47 Pharmacy Minich B2
48 Police D2
49 Secretaría de Turismo de Santa Cruz B2
50 Tourism office (bus station) C2
51 Tourism office (Rosales) D2

Shopping 🛍

52 Boutique del Libro C2
53 Estancia El Tranquilo D2
54 Paseo de los Artesanos C2

Sleeping 🛏

55 Camping Amsa D2
56 Camping El Ovejero D1
57 Camping Jorgito C1
58 Camping Vial D2
59 Casa de Grillos B&B B1
60 Design Suites B1
61 Elan Hotel A2
62 Esplendor El Calafate C2
63 Estancia Cristina office C2
64 Hostal del Glaciar Libertador D2
65 Hotel Kosten Aike B1
66 Hotel Posada Los Álamos B1
67 I Keu Ken Hostel B2
68 Kau Kaleshen Hosteria B2
69 Marco Polo Inn Calafate D2
70 Mirador del Lago Hotel A2
71 Patagonia Queen Hotel Boutique A2

Tours ♦

72 Aventura Andina D2
73 Calafate Fishing A2
74 Hielo y Aventura D2
75 Mil Outdoor Adventure C2
76 Morresi Viajes B2

Transportation

77 Aerolíneas Argentinas C2
78 Avis C2
79 Budget A2
80 Cal-Tur D2
81 Central Bus Terminal C2
82 Chaltén Travel C2
83 Dollar Rent a Car B2
84 Hertz A2
85 HLS Travesías C2
86 Lade D2
87 LAN C2
88 Ves Patagonia Shuttle B2

SOUTHERN PATAGONIA

Travelers frequently team up to rent a vehicle and drive to other parts of Argentina and into Chile. Check with agencies about international rates. Updated: Jul 13, 2009.

Safety

When going out on excursions, remember that the climate can change suddenly. Be sure to have warm and rainproof clothing on hand. Updated: Jul 13, 2009.

Services

TOURISM

The **tourism office** is conveniently located at the bus terminal (Monday – Friday 10 a.m. – 4 p.m., extended hours in summer. Roca 1004. Tel: 54-2902-491090, E-mail: info@elcalafate.gov.ar, URL: www.elcalafate.gov.ar). For travelers arriving by car or bike, the main office is located near the entrance to town (daily 8 a.m. – 8 p.m., extended hours in summer. Coronel Rosales, across from La Tablita).

APN, the national park office, has information about Parque Nacional Los Glaciares, as well as a research library. It sells fishing permits for all of Patagonia. Be sure to say howdy to the bronze, life-size statue of Perito Moreno working at his desk (October – April: daily 8 a.m. – 8 p.m., May – September daily 8 a.m. – 7 p.m. Av. del Libertador 1302. Tel: 54-2902-491005, E-mail: apnglaciares@cotecal.com.ar).

The Secretería de Turismo de Santa Cruz has information about Los Antiguos, Puerto Deseado and other destinations in the province (Monday – Friday 9 a.m. – 4 p.m. 1 de Mayo 50. Tel: 54-2902-492353, E-mail: elcalafate@santacruzpatagonia.gob.ar, URL: www.santacruzpatagonia.gob.ar).

Police (Av. del Libertador 819. Tel: 54-2902-491077 / emergency 101).

Gendarmería Nacional (immigration) (Roca 1640. Tel: 54-2902-491064).

MONEY

Banks are open Monday – Friday 8 a.m. – 1 p.m. Most have Link network ATMs and accept MasterCard, Cirrus, Visa, Plus and American Express cards, except where noted:

Banco Santa Cruz (Av. del Libertador 1285)— also has ATM at Av. del Libertador and Freile.

Banco Tierra del Fuego (25 de Mayo 34) —ATM: only MasterCard, Visa.
Banco de la Nación Argentina (Av. del Libertador 1133)— also exchanges U.S. dollars and euros; Western Union agent.
Banco Patagonia (Av. del Libertador 1355) —ATM: also Diners Club.

Casa de Cambios Thaler exchanges many Western and Latin American currencies, the yen and American Express and other travelers checks in Western currencies (Monday – Friday 10 a.m. – 2 p.m. Av. del Libertador 1242. Tel: 54-2902-493245).

Note: Many businesses add a high surcharge to credit card purchases.

KEEPING IN TOUCH

You can send family and friends post cards of the Eighth Natural Wonder of the World at the post office **Correo Argentino** (Monday – Friday 9 a.m. – 4 p.m., Saturday 9 a.m. – 1 p.m. Av. del Libertador 1133).

Internet is expensive ($3.50 – 4.25 per hour, cheaper for Argentines) and slow in the high season. Most cafes are on the main drag: **Arroba Ciber Cafe** (25 de mayo 560, local 3), **Centro Integral de Comunicaciones** (Av. del Libertador and Leman), **Ciber Point** (Av. del Libertador 1440, local 4). Many locales charge more for use of Skype.

If you prefer making an old-fashioned phone call, use one of these locutorios: **Del Glaciar I** (25 de Mayo 43), **Del Glaciar II** (9 de Julio 57, local 8) or **Open Calafate** (Av. del Libertador 996).

MEDICAL

The regional public health facility is **Hospital Distrital Josçe Formenti** (Roca 1487. Tel: 54-2902-491173). **Pharmacies** are either near the hospital or on the principal avenue: **Don Bosco** (Roca 1350. Tel: 54-2902-492650), **Minich** (Roca 1391. Tel: 54-2902-496180; also Av. del Libertador and Espora. Tel: 54-2902-492180), **Del Cerro** (Av. del Libertador 1337. Tel: 54-2902-491496), **El Calafate** (Av. del Libertador 1190. Tel: 54-2902-491407).

LAUNDRY

Laundry costs $4.50 – 5 per basket load. A few centrally located lavaderos are **Lavadero** (25 de Mayo 43. Tel: 54-2902-492182) and **Lava y Lava** (Gregores 1114. Tel: 54-2902-496566).

SOUTHERN PATAGONIA

PHOTOGRAPHY

Foto Aónikenk cleans cameras and processes film by hand or machine. Its stock includes 35 mm color (ASA 100 – 400), black-and-white and slide film, 110 film, and digital photocards and accessories (Monday – Saturday 10 a.m. – 10 p.m., Sunday 2:20 p.m. Av. del Libertador 1319. Tel: 54-2902-491340). Updated: Jul 13, 2009.

SHOPPING

El Calafate has a variety of artisan crafts, from humble woolens to fine alpaca and jewelry made from stone or silver. Hand-carved *mates* (gourds for drinking yerba mate tea) are also a specialty, as are leather goods. Given the high quality of craftsmanship, most goods are rather expensive. Look for shops all along the main avenue that sell jams, smoked meats, liquors and other homemade products Patagonia is famous for. Clearance time is at the end of the summer, with stores offering large discounts before closing for the winter. Updated: Jul 13, 2009.

Estancia El Tranquilo

Estancia El Tranquilo, once a ranch, turns over 100 years' worth of family recipes into homemade wines, liquors and marmalades. The Helmich family makes two vodkas, Estepvka and Pfeffer, as well as a delicious calafate berry liqueur, Helmich. You can take a tour of the on-site distillery.

The Helmich family also does artisan work, principally out of wool, which can be bought at the shop. Av. del Libertador 935. Tel: 54-2902-494581, E-mail: ahelmich@eltranquilo.com, URL: www.eltranquilo.com.ar. Updated: Jul 13, 2009.

Paseo de los Artesanos

At these artisan stalls, local artisans call out from their colorful stalls, hoping to catch the attention of curious tourists. If you get the chance, you should definitely stop by, as the products offered here will serve you well on your travels throughout the region.

You can get a wool knit hat to keep you warm on a visit to the Perito Moreno Glacier, drink mate from a hand-carved gourd or buy some stone carvings to bring back for friends. 1100 block of Avenida del Libertador, between Mi Viejo restaurant and Correo Argentino. Updated: Jul 13, 2009.

Boutique del Libro

The Boutique del Libro bookshop has a good selection of nature and travel guides, as well as road and trekking maps. It has a large English-language section, including children's literature. Boutique del Libro also carries postcards, calendars and other items to remind you of your visit to this magical land. Av. del Libertador 1033. Tel: 54-2902-491363, E-mail: boutiquedellibro@cotecal.com.ar. Updated: Jul 13, 2009.

Equipment Rental and Sales

If you need to rent or buy camping equipment, check out the following shops:
El Galpón de Don Emilio (9 de Julio 32. Tel: 54-2902-2867, E-mail: elgalpondedonemilio@cotecal.com.ar, URL: www.elgalpondedonemilio.com)—fishing and camping equipment, hiking boots.

Patagonia Shop (9 de Julio 29. Tel: 54-2902-492767, E-mail: info@patagoniabikes.com, URL: www.patagoniabikes.com)—mountain climbing, biking and kayaking equipment rental and sales; also clothing.

La Barraca (Amado 833. Tel: 54-2902-491999, E-mail: labarracacalafate@hotmail.com)—rents clothing, tent, sleeping bag, boot and outdoor gear rentals.

Abranpampa (Av. del Libertador 1341, local 3. Tel: 54-2902-491697, E-mail: abranpampa@cotecal.com.ar)—camping and outdoor adventure clothing rentals and sales. Updated: Jul 13, 2009.

Things to See and Do

Many tourists come here to explore the world's eighth natural wonder, Glaciar Perito Moreno, but El Calafate isn't only about this impressive chunk of ice. You can also wander through museums, or bike to the costanera for birdwatching. Whether you're going on a hike through Bosque Petrificado la Leona, horseback riding through ranches, or fishing at Lago Roca and other area lakes, the options are endless. Updated: Jul 16, 2009.

Reserva Laguna Nímez

Laguna Nímez, a municipal bird reserve, is refuge for over 80 bird species. Look for the Black-necked swan, the Magellan goose, the Long-tailed meadowlark, the caracara and the Magellanic plover, as well as flamingos, ducks, gulls, hawks and herons. It's a true birdwatcher's paradise and a quiet retreat from the bustle of El Calafate. The best time to observe these feathered friends is August to March. The park closes when the lagoon

SOUTHERN PATAGONIA

floods. You can also birdwatch along the coast east of the city and west along Punta Soberana (Daily 9 a.m. – 9 p.m. One km / 0.6 mi from downtown, at the north end of Av. Leonardo N. Alem). Signs in town mark the way to Laguna Nímez. From Avenida del Libertadior, follow Padre Agostini North, crossing the estuary. North of Avenida Brown, Agostini becomes Avenida Alem. Updated: Jul 13, 2009.

Lago Roca and Cerro Cristal

Within the national reserve section of Parque Nacional Los Glaciares is Lago Roca, a thin sliver of a lake known for its fly fishing of brown, grey and rainbow trout. One kilometer (0.6 mi) past Huala campsite is Cerro de los Cristales (1,268 m/4,160 ft), from whose peak you can see Torres del Paine, the various branches of Lago Argentino and Glaciar Perito Moreno.

Trekking and horseback riding can be done from Lago Roca. **Trekking del Glaciar** offers a 10 kilometer (6 mi) excursion in the area, as well trips to Paso Zamora on the Chilean border (Tel: 54-2902-49-8447, E-mail: info@trekkingdelglaciar. com, URL: www.trekkingdelglaciar.com). Updated: Jul 13, 2009.

Pugliesse's Personages

As you stroll around town, drop in to see Fernando Pugliesse's life-size bronze statues of important historical figures. **Iglesia Santa Teresita del Niño Jesús** has one of Padre Manuel González, who ministered to villagers throughout Santa Cruz province, and Alberto María de Agostini, who explored the peaks and glaciers (Av. del Libertador and Olavarria). Perito Moreno, who mapped much of the region, hangs out in the national park office (Av. del Libertador 1302). At Puerto Punta Bandera (where ships debark for the glaciers) is Juan Piñeiro; out at the airport is Comandante Armando Tola, an important figure in Argentine aeronautic history. Updated: Jul 13, 2009.

Horseback Riding

(ENTRY: $30) Companies offer horseback riding trips all year round to Bahía Redonda on Lago Argentino, the Cuevas del Walicho, to the estancias, and even to the Chilean border. Helmets are provided. You will have to sign a waiver form. Two ranches that let you ride like a gaucho are **Alice** (Tel: 54-2902-49-7793) and **Nibepo Aike**

(E-mail: nibepo@speedy.com.ar). Horse center and riding school **El Arriago** can also take you out to enjoy this special land. Av. del Libertador 4315. Tel: 54-2902-493278. Updated: Jul 13, 2009.

Ice Trekking

(TREKS: $95 – 150) If seeing the mega-glacier Perito Moreno isn't enough excitement for you, try a mini-Trekking two-hour excursion across the ice field. If you're up for an even greater challenge, then you can do a trip called the Big Ice. This longer, three-hour trek is offered in the summer only. At this time, visitors can see cerulean-blue lagoons, ice caves and other wonders of Perito Moreno's frozen world. Big Ice is only for people between the ages of 18 and 45. 10 – 65 year olds can do Mini Trekking. The only company authorized by the national park service to do glacier treks is **Hielo y Aventura** (Av. del Libertador 935. Tel: 54-2902-492205, Fax: 54-2902-491053, E-mail: info@hieloyaventura.com). Prices include transportation, a guide and climbing equipment. It does not include entry into the park or food. Updated: Jul 13, 2009.

Boat Trips

Several boats sail from the Magallanes Peninsula to the foot of spectacular ice floes. **Safari Náutico** departs from Bajada los Sombres on the south shore, plows through Brazo Rico and goes up Canal de los Témpanos to the edge of Glaciar Perito Moreno.

Todo Glaciares leaves from Puerto Punta Bandera on the north shore of the peninsula and sails the Brazo Norte to Bahía Onelli, Glaciar Upsala (the largest ice river in the park), and Glaciar Spegazzini (the tallest glacier at 130 meters (400 ft). On the other side of the bay are hiking trails through Andean-Patagonian forests with views of the Onelli, Bolados and Agassiz Glaciers.

Safari Náutico ($31 plus park entry) and **Todos Glaciares** ($96 plus park entry) offer tour guides. Without tour guides the trips cost less: Safari Náutico $10, Todo Glaciares $14. Prices do not include the national park fee.

If you'd like to navigate Lago Argentino in a smaller craft, **Patagonia Shop** rents kayaks and organizes kayaking adventures for all levels of experience (9 de Julio 29. Tel: 54-2902-492767, E-mail: info@patagoniabikes.com, URL: www.patagoniabikes. com). Updated: Jul 13, 2009.

SOUTHERN PATAGONIA

Cuevas de Walichu

(ENTRY: $14) Back in the day, Punta Walichu was a refuge for the ancient peoples who used to wander this valley. In the caves on the point jutting into Lago Argentino, ancestors of the Aónikenk nation left paintings (*pinturas rupestres*) about their lives on these Patagonian plains. The site also has an interpretive center with a small display of fossils, archaeological artifacts and geological information. There are also photos of the last Aónikenk survivors. Not all of the paintings are original. Open daily 9 a.m to 8 p.m. Estancia 25 de Mayo. Tel: 54-2902-497003, E-mail: puntawalichu@cotecal.com.ar, URL: www.puntawalichu.com.ar.

Morresi Viajes has motorized tours to just the Cuevas ($19) or in combination with a city tour ($27); price includes transportation, guide and entry (Av. del Libertador 1341, oficina 14-15. Tel: 54-2902-492075). Updated: Jul 13, 2009.

Bosque Petrificado la Leona

Eons before the Andes rose from the bowels of the earth, the Patagonian steppe was a much warmer land. Dinosaurs roamed through forests of immense trees that covered these environs 65 – 90 million years ago.

Visitors now travel along Lago Viedma's south shore to the foot of Cerro Los Hornos, before embarking on a three-hour hike to the Bosque Petrificado La Leona, 100 kilometers (61 mi) north of El Calafate. There they see fossilized remains, some encased in hardened volcanic ash, others in what was once river mud, that date between 65 and 90 million years ago. E-mail: bosquelaleona@cotecal.com.ar / infolaleona@hotmail.com, URL: www.losglaciares.com/bosquepetrificado.

One way to get to the Bosque Pertificado La Leona is on a tour with **Morresi Viajes** (Av. del Libertador 1341, oficina 14 – 15. Tel: 54-2902-492075, E-mail: morresi@cotecal.com.ar. $70 per person, minimum 2). Nearby **Hotel de Campaña La Leona** has fishing and horseback riding excursions. Updated: Jul 13, 2009.

El Calafate Museums

The city has three museums of interest. It is easy to walk to the Museo Regional and the Centro de Interpretación Histórica Calafate. Visiting Casa Verde requires a little more effort. It sits at the far western end of town,

approximately 3 kilometers (1.8 mi) from the center. No city bus goes that way. A taxi costs $3.70 – 4.30. Updated: Jul 13, 2009.

Museo Regional (Monday – Friday 8 a.m. – 8 p.m., weekends 11 a.m. – 6 p.m. Av. del Libertador 575. Tel: 54-2902-491924, E-mail: cultura@elcalafate.gov.ar. Entry: free)—A small museum with basic paleontological, archaeological and geological exhibits, photos and stuffed animals.

Centro de Interpretación Histórica Calafate (Wednesday – Monday 10 a.m. – 6 p.m. Av. A. Brown and Bonarelli. Tel: 54-2902-492799, E-mail: calafatecentro@yahoo.com.ar. Entry: $5.50)—The museum has a timeline, with artifacts and some photos of the last 14,000 years in the region, from the megafauna of the last Ice Age to the founding of El Calafate. Tours in English; video in six languages.

Casa Verde (October – mid-April daily 4-8 p.m.; mid-April – September irregular hours. Av. Costanera 4212. Tel: 54-2902-498780. Entry: free)—Exhibits are on the flora and birdlife of Bahía Redonda, and there are also interpretive trails. Updated: Jul 13, 2009.

Winter in El Calafate

Summer may be the height of the tourism season, but you can find plenty to do here in the winter. You can navigate to Glaciar Perito Moreno and trek the glaciers, strap on ice skates and glide out to Isla Solitaria, or cut a hole in the ice and fish. Cross-country skiing across the country side is yet another activity. Take a modern sleigh ride through the snow in a 4x4. Updated: Jul 13, 2009.

Tours

There are over 50 tour agencies in El Calafate. Most act as booking agents, arranging your excursion with the companies that are authorized by APN, the national park service. Prices are pretty much the same from one tour operator to another, though if you are on a tight budget, check out several places before deciding. Almost all agencies are on Av. del Libertador. Others specialize in horseback riding, fishing or 4x4 expeditions. Updated: Jul 16, 2009.

Hielo y Aventura

Hielo y Aventura is Parque Nacional Los Glaciares's official purveyor of ice trekking on Perito Moreno Glacier. Whether you choose the two-hour Mini-Trekking or the three-hour Big Ice expedition, Hielo y Aventura can safely lead you on explorations of that icy wonderland. The Mini-Trekking option is available almost all year; Big Ice is only offered in the summer. This company also has a Safari Náutico boat ride from Puerto Bajo de las Sombras to the foot of the Perito Moreno Glacier. Av. del Libertador 935. Tel: 54-2902-492205, Fax: 54-2902-491053, E-mail: info@hieloyaventura.com, URL: www.hieloyaventura.com. Updated: Jul 13, 2009.

Morresi Viajes

Morresi Viajes is the official provider of trips to the cave paintings of Punta Walichu ($19). Cave tours can be combined with a city tour of the various museums and other sites in El Calafate ($27). Morresi also takes tourists out to Bosque Petrificado La Leona ($70) and can arrange tours to the Perito Moreno Glacier ($45), boat rides around the Brazo Sur and Brazo Norte, horseback riding or 4x4 expeditions. Av. del Libertador 1341, oficina 14-15. Tel: 54-2902-492075, E-mail: morresi@cotecal.com.ar. Updated: Jul 13, 2009.

Mil Outdoor Adventure

In the Mil Outdoor Adventure 4x4 Land Rovers and super-buses, you get off the beaten road into the raw countryside. One popular destination is Balcón de El Calafate, through a rock labyrinth (5 daily departures, 3 hours). Ruta de la India Dormida takes you out to fossil fields and unique geological formations like *los sombreros* (the hats) (twice daily, 6 hours). Mil Outdoor Adventure also offers banana-riding through the snow in the winter (twice daily, 4.5 hours). Av. del Libertador 1029. Tel: 54-290249-1437 / 491446, E-mail: info@miloutdoor.com,URL: www.miloutdoor.com. Updated: Jul 13, 2009.

Aventura Andina

Aventura Andina is a one-stop agency for arranging tours. The staff can arrange for you to go to Glaciar Perito Moreno ($17), or Glaciar Upsala and Laguna Onelli on the Todo Glaciares tour ($100). Other adventures are ice trekking ($114), 4x4 rides ($41 – 50), a city tour, the Cuevas de Waliche ($27), and Estancia El Galpón ($44 – 49). Av. del Libertador 761, local 4. Tel: 54-2902-542902 / 491726. Updated: Jul 13, 2009.

Calafate Fishing

Calafate Fishing offers one of the most complete fishing services in El Calafate. Guide Miguel Ángel Almandoz takes anglers out to fly fish for brown and rainbow trout, Chinook salmon and perch. Calafate Fishing can take you to Argentino, Roca, Strobel and Laguna del Desierto or, if you prefer to feel the currents rushing around your waders, to the Santa Cruz, Rico, Bote, Barrancoso, de las Vueltas, Diablo and Caterina Rivers. Av. del Libertador 1826. Tel: 54-2902-496545, E-mail: calafatefishing@cotecal.com.ar, URL: www.calafatefishing.com.ar. Updated: Jul 13, 2009.

Lodging

From basic campgrounds to five-star luxury hotels, there's a lodging option in El Calafate to suit every budget. While many hotels are near Avenida Libertador, smaller inns and hostels have recently popped up on the fringes of town. Prices go up during the high tourist season (generally October to April; the peak is December to February), and visitors may find that good deals are hard to come by during this time. Many hotels only accept cash, and reservations are highly recommended. Updated: Jul 16, 2009.

BUDGET

Camping

For travelers on a budget, camping is an economical option. Campgrounds are open only October to mid-April; none are open in winter. Costs are $4.50 – 6 per person per night. Most are located along the estuary at the east end of town:

Amsa: (Olavarría 65. Tel: 54-2902-492247).
El Ovejero: (Pantín 64. Tel: 54-2902-493422, E-mail: campingelovergero@hotmail.com).
Jorgito: (Moyano 943. Tel: 54-2902-491323).
Vial: (5 de Octubre s/n).

A few campgrounds operate close to Parque Nacional Los Glaciares. There are two sites at Lago Roca (p.554), and **EcoCamp**, in front of Glaciar Perito Moreno, is the ultimate in luxury camping, with real beds inside geodesic-dome tents (E-mail: info@ecocamp-patagonia.com, URL: www.ecocamp-patagonia.com / www.nyca-adventure.com). Updated: Jul 13, 2009.

America del Sur Hostel

(ROOMS: $10 – 40) The first thing you'll notice about Hostal America del Sur is the mountain of hiking boots piled at the door. This place has a shoes-off policy, but the

SOUTHERN PATAGONIA

heated floors will keep your feet toasty warm. The hostel, which is a seven-minute walk from downtown, is a welcoming place for tired trekkers. America del Sur has comfortable, lofty common areas and windows a-plenty, ensuring magnificent views of nearby Lake Argentino. Dorms bed up to four people and come with private bathrooms and lockers. Double rooms are also available, and have private bathrooms. Breakfast is included in the price, and there is a large kitchen for guests to use, as well as a laundry room.

The friendly multilingual staff can assist in arranging tours. The hostel is a 7-minute walk from the bus station. Take a taxi and the hostel will pay the fare when you arrive. From the airport, there is a direct bus. Puerto Deseado 153. Tel: 290-249-3523 / 3525, Fax: 290-249-3523, E-mail: info@americahostel. com.ar,URL: www.americahostel.com.ar. Updated: Dec 19, 2007.

V!VA ONLINE REVIEW

AMERICA DEL SUR HOSTEL

"This place is fantastic! The cleanest hostel I've stayed at yet. The staff is super cool, honest and friendly, they made me feel like family."

November 07, 2007

I Keu Ken Hostel

(ROOMS: $10 – 40) I Keu Ken Hostel is a pleasant inn in a quiet part of town, away from the bustle of the center, with tremendous views of Lago Argentino. The four-bed dorms and private rooms are clean, the bathrooms immaculate and the bilingual staff very helpful. I Keu Ken has everything journeyers need: free Internet, kitchen, lockers, bike rental, book exchange and help arranging tours. Spend evenings playing board games or roasting meats on the fireplace BBQ while enjoying a Patagonian microbrew. Prices include breakfast. Pontoriero 171. Tel: 54-2902-495175, E-mail: ikeuken@cotecal. com.ar, URL: www.patagoniaikeuken.com. ar. Updated: Jul 13, 2009.

Hostal del Glaciar Libertador

(ROOMS: $12 – 50) Hostal del Glaciar Libertador is in a three-story, neo-Gothic-styled house on El Calafate's main street. The hostel has two courtyards: the front one has the reception area and common room, with sitting and writing nooks in the upper level

balconies. The large dorm rooms can accommodate up to four guests and each has its own bathroom and separate vanity area. Upstairs is the fully equipped communal kitchen. The hostel provides a free shuttle to and from both the airport and bus terminal. Av. del Libertador 587. Tel: 54-2902-492492, E-mail: info@glaciar.com, URL: www.glaciar. com. Updated: Jul 13, 2009.

Marco Polo Inn Calafate

(ROOMS: $12 – 77) This Hostelling International affiliate provides a comfortable and fun atmosphere where you can mix and mingle with other travelers: shoot some pool in the common room, have a drink at the bar, or catch up on some TV. Single, double, and triple rooms are available, and there are six- and eight-bed dorms with private bathrooms. The hostel also has a limited number of four- to six-person bungalows, which come complete with individual kitchens and bathrooms. There's a fully equipped communal kitchen, WiFi and maid service. Breakfast is included in the price, and staff can help arrange excursions. The hostel does not accept guests under the ago of 20. Calle 405 No 82 (Calle 405 has now been changed to Esperanza). Tel: 54-2902-493899, E-mail: calafate@marcopoloinn. com.ar. Updated: Apr 28, 2009.

Casa de Grillos B&B

(ROOMS: $20 – 50) Casa de Grillos is ideally located for those looking to "get away from it all" while still enjoying the conveniences of town. Although it is just eight blocks from Avenida del Libertador, the B&B is situated in one of the only wooded areas in the otherwise sparse El Calafate, and is close to Lake Argentino and Lake Nimez. Run by a couple who rents out four spare rooms in their own home, the B&B is small and intimate. Rooms are cozy, and two come with private bathrooms, while the other rooms share a common bathroom. There is also a comfortable common room with a library, TV, and Internet. A complete breakfast is included in the price. Los Condores 1215. Tel: 54-2902-491160, Fax: 54-2902-491160, E-mail: info@casadegrillos. com.ar, URL: www.casadegrillos.com.ar. Updated: Mar 13, 2008.

MID-RANGE

Kau Kaleshen Hostería

(ROOMS: $70) Just steps from the conveniences of the main drag, this inn has modest, yet comfortable and clean, rooms with private bathrooms and individual heating. Rooms are situated around a pretty garden in the back, and in the front is the teahouse, where guests have breakfast. For $6, you can enjoy an afternoon *té completo*—tea service with homemade bread, pastries, and preserves.

The bilingual and very professional staff is a great resource for information on local restaurants, tours, and attractions. Laundry service is available, and the inn is equipped with Internet, a fax, and telephones. Gobernador Gregores 1256. Tel: 029-0-249-1188, Fax: 54-2902-491188, E-mail: kaukaleshen@cotecal.com.ar, URL: www.losglaciares.com/kaukaleshen. Updated: Mar 13, 2008.

HIGH-END

Hotel Posada Los Alamos

(ROOMS: $114 – 419) Hotel Posada Los Alamos has plaid carpeting and old English furniture, and rooms are styled in varying themes and color schemes. There are several luxurious lounges, all with views of the sprawling and well-maintained lawn. The large 144-room hotel, surrounded by the namesake alamo trees, offers guests virtually every amenity they might need, including a restaurant and wine bar, a mini-golf course and tennis court, a large pool and spa, a gym, and even a hair salon. Posada Los Alamos also has a convention center, handicapped facilities, childcare service, and a game room. The hotel is centrally located, and outdoor parking is available. Guatti 1350. Tel: 54-2902-491144, Fax: 54-2902-491186, E-mail: info@posadalosalamos.com, URL: www.posadalosalamos.com. Updated: Apr 28, 2009.

Patagonia Queen Hotel Boutique

(ROOMS: $115 – 218) This boutique hotel has 20 rooms of which 16 are doubles, two are queens and and two are triples with twin beds. All of the rooms, apart from the standards, can be modified. Every room includes heat, cable TV, a mini-fridge, a safe and a Jacuzzi. Guests receive discounts at the following eateries: Casimiro Bigua Trattoria, Casimiro Bigua Casimiro Bigua Parrilla, La Lechuza Pizzas, La Matera Parrilla & Restaurant. Av. Padre Agostini 49. Tel: 54-2902-496701 al 03, E-mail: info@patagoniaqueen.com.ar, URL: www.patagoniaqueen.com.ar. Updated: Jun 16, 2008.

Design Suites

(ROOMS: $125 – 150) Perched on the Nimes peninsula, Design Suites has spectacular panoramic views of Lake Argentino. The emphasis here is on space and style. Common areas are open and bright. The hotel wisely makes use of its prime lakeside location; dramatic floor-to-ceiling windows offer views of the surrounding Patagonian terrain. Rooms feature king-size beds and bathtubs. Amenities include an indoor and outdoor pool, business center, restaurant, bar and lounge. There is also a gym and spa, as well as an art gallery featuring the work of local artists. Design Suites is two kilometers out of town, and provides a half-hourly shuttle service. Calle 94 No. 190. Tel: 54-2902-494525, URL: www.designsuites.com. Updated: Mar 13, 2008.

Esplendor El Calafate

Decorated with contemporary furniture in beiges and browns, dramatic antler chandeliers, large fireplaces, modern art, and wood floors, this boutique hotel is one of the exclusive Fën Hotels. Located in central El Calafate with views of Cerro Calafate and Lago Argentino, Hotel Esplendor El Calafate also has a large event room that can hold up to 170 people, as well as a gift shop with a variety of Argentine fur jackets, vests, and leather bags. Suites have entertainment sets, mini-bars, large stone bathtubs, cozy armchairs and plush king-size beds. Grab a cocktail at the on-site Iglu Bar and then enjoy a trout filet or steak at the Esplendor restaurant. Presidente Peron 1143. Tel: 54-2902-492454 / 54-11-52175700, E-mail: Info@esplendorcalafate.com/reservas@esplendorcalafate.com, URL: www.esplendorcalafate.com. Updated: Apr 24, 2009.

Hotel Kosten Aike

(ROOMS: $201 – 231) What this hotel lacks in charm and character, it makes up for in location. Just a short walk from the restaurants and tourist agencies of the main street, it is one of the biggest hotels in town. Though somewhat conservative in décor, rooms are attractive, comfortable and clean, and come with large private bathrooms. In addition to a restaurant, wine bar, and a fireside lounge, the hotel also features a gym, spa, game room, and a 100-person convention room. The bilingual staff is friendly and helpful, and there is WiFi throughout the hotel. Two handicapped rooms are available. Breakfast is included in the price. Gobernador Moyano 1243. Tel: 54-2902-492424, Fax: 54-2902-491538, E-mail: kostenaike@cotecal.com.ar, URL: www.kostenaike.com.ar. Updated: Mar 13, 2008.

SOUTHERN PATAGONIA

Estancia Cristina

(PACKAGES: $375 – 475) This luxury estancia is in one of the most remote locations in El Calafate, on the northern bank of Lake Argentino. A breathtaking four-hour catamaran ride is the only way to reach this secluded estate. One- and two-day all-inclusive packages are available, and guests can choose from an array of day activities, including trekking, horseback riding, birdwatching, and 4x4 excursions. After a long day of taking in the Patagonian scenery, you can warm your bones in the soaker tub, or simply relax in your spacious and comfortable room. The estancia has an excellent restaurant and bar, a library and Internet, as well as a museum featuring artifacts from the original 20th-century British pioneer owners. Estancia Cristina is the place to splurge in El Calafate. City office: 9 de Julio 69. Tel: 54-2902-491133034, Fax: 54-2902-491293, E-mail: reservations@estancia-cristina.com, URL: www.estanciacristina.com. Updated: Apr 28, 2009.

Restaurants

From simple snack shops to expensive restaurants, there is a wide variety of food options available in El Calafate. Most restaurants are located along the main drag, Avenida Libertador, and tend to be a little pricey. The town is a good place to try typical Patagonian dishes like lamb, trout, and salmon, as well as ice creams, pastries, and jams made from El Calafate's namesake calafate berry. The few grocery stores scattered along the main street are good for stocking up on snacks and packed lunches. Updated: Jul 16, 2009.

BUDGET

El Puesto

(PIZZAS: $2 – 6) This cozy pizza joint specializes in 23 varieties of thin-crust pizza, ensuring that you'll find a topping combo to suit your tastes. Though pizza and pasta dominate the menu, other options like salads and steak, as well as pricier regional dishes, are available too. The food is consistently good, but be warned—this place is tiny, so you may have to wait for a table, especially on busy weekends. You can always avoid the wait by ordering your pie to go. Reservations are highly recommended. Open daily, noon – 3 p.m. and 8 p.m. to midnight. Gobernador Moyano and Av. 9 de Julio. Tel: 54-2902-491620.

Rick's Café

(ENTREES: $4 – 13) Join in the all-you can-eat frenzy at Rick's Café. Long established as the place to go for cheap eats, Rick's Cafe attracts backpackers and others looking for a good meal at a great price. Satiate your meat craving with the Argentine BBQ, which, for about $7, gets you all the steak, mutton, chicken and sausage you can manage. Vegetarians won't go hungry either—there are pasta dishes, as well as a salad bar ($4). The atmosphere is a bit rowdy at times, but is generally festive and cheery. Meats are not of premium quality, but are still worth the price. Av. del Libertador 1105. Tel: 54-2902-492148. Updated: Apr 28, 2009.

V!VA ONLINE REVIEW
RICK'S CAFÉ

> The "eat as much as you want" option from the *parilla* can't be beat for those who want to gorge themselves on good honest meat.
>
> *January 30, 2008*

La Tablita

(ENTREES: $5 – 10) La Tablita is a carnivore's paradise. This very Argentine restaurant serves up massive *parrilladas* (platters of mixed grilled meats), tender filet mignon, lamb, as well as a variety of other meats. For those tired of protein-packed fare, there are a few pasta and other non-meat dishes available. If you have room at the end of your meal, the fruit salad with ice cream is highly recommended. There's also a decent wine list, and the helpful staff will assist you in your wine selection. La Tablita is quite popular and fills up quickly, so reservations are recommended. Open 11 a.m. – 3 p.m., and 7 p.m. – midnight. Wednesday closed for lunch. Coronel Rosales 24. Tel: 54-2902-491065, E-mail: latablita-reservas@cotecal.com.ar, URL: www.interpatagonia.com/latablita. Updated: Apr 28, 2009.

Pura Vida

(ENTREES: $5 – 12) Located a little ways outside of town and overlooking Lake Argentino, Pura Vida is a haven for vegetarians and those craving a change from the usual meat-centric Argentine fare. The restaurant serves up home-style dishes like pumpkin soup and hearty stews, as well as excellent pastas, sandwiches, and shakes. The menu isn't exclusively vegetarian, though, you can also try the regional specialty, *cazuela de cordero*, a

...

lamb and mushroom stew. Service is friendly and relaxed, and the colorful restaurant is a nice place to kick back while enjoying good food. Open Thursday – Tuesday, 7:30 – 11:30 p.m. Av. del Libertador 1876. Tel: 54-2902-493356. Updated: Apr 28, 2009.

Mi Viejo

(ENTREES: $6 – 8) This local favorite specializes in massive portions of grilled lamb that you can see being barbecued at the pit near the restaurant's entrance. Portions here are big: one lamb serves up to seven people, and the $10 parrillada (assortment of mixed meats) feeds three to five people. Other menu options include trout and salmon, or, if you're in the mood for something truly different, pickled hare. Meat cuts here are of excellent quality and are sure to satisfy your carnivorous cravings. Open every day from 11 a.m. – 3 p.m. and 7 p.m. – midnight. Av. del Libertador 1113. Tel: 54-2902-491691, URL: www.calafate.com/miviejo/index.htm. Updated: Apr 28, 2009.

MID-RANGE

Casimiro Biguá

(ENTREES: $6 – 15) This restaurant / wine bar has won the title of El Calafate's most stylish hangout. They have an extensive wine list and regional Patagonian delicacies, with a modern black-and-white décor and sophisticated ambience. The menu changes frequently, but you can usually expect staples like steak, homemade pasta, chicken and seafood, in addition to more elaborate offerings such as salmon in a caper and white wine sauce, and sesame tuna. The Patagonian appetizer platter, comprised of smoked trout and wild boar, as well as an assortment of cheeses, comes highly recommended. Portions here are large, and the waitstaff is friendly and eager to please. WiFi is available throughout the restaurant. Open daily from 10 a.m. – 1 a.m. Av. del Libertador 963. Tel: 54-2902-492590, E-mail: info@casimirobigua.com, URL: www.casimirobigua.com/restaurante.html. Updated: Mar 13, 2008.

La Cocina

(ENTREES: $7 – 9) La Cocina specializes in simple yet satisfying food done well. The menu includes a large selection of homemade pastas and crepes (from classic ham and cheese to steak with pepper and mustard sauce), as well as salads and a variety of simple yet well-prepared meats. The staff remains friendly and enthusiastic even in the midst of lunch and dinner rushes, and the overall atmosphere is warm and inviting. La Cocina is sure to please. Open Tuesday – Sunday, noon – 3:30 p.m. and 7 p.m. – midnight. Av. del Libertador 1245. Tel: 54-2902-491758. Updated: Dec 19, 2007.

Sancho Restaurant

($7 – 13) This family-run restaurant specializes in local food with a Mediterranean twist. The varied menu features dishes like seafood in champagne sauce, trout-stuffed king crab, and spinach gnocchi with pesto. Portions are generous—the half picada appetizer platter easily serves four people—and the food is well prepared. The atmosphere is relaxed and friendly, but service can be slow when it gets busy. Reservations are recommended, especially during the high season. Open daily from 8 p.m. to midnight. 25 de Mayo 80. Tel: 54-2902-492442. Updated: Mar 13, 2008.

La Posta

(ENTREES: $8 – 15) Considered by many to be the best restaurant in town, La Posta, which is part of Los Alamos Hotel, serves up delectable Argentine cuisine with an international flair. Standout dishes include Patagonian lamb with rosehip sauce, king crab-stuffed ravioli, and curried crayfish. Desserts are simply not to be missed. Though upscale and formal, the restaurant has a cozy mountain lodge vibe, and patrons dine by candle light while enjoying top-notch service. A daily breakfast buffet is provided for guests of the hotel. Reservations are recommended, especially during the high season. Open daily from 7 p.m. to midnight. Gobernador Moyano and Bustillo. Tel: 54-2902-491144. Updated: Dec 19, 2007.

Pizzería La Lechuza

Pizzería La Lechuza has over 35 varieties of wood-fired pizza, the most famous of which is the onion with raw ham. If you're not in the mood for pizza, there are also good sandwiches and empanadas on the menu. The restaurant is located across from the National Parks Office. Delivery service is available. Open noon – midnight. Av. del Libertador 1301. Tel: 54-2902-491610, E-mail: lalechuza@corecal.com.ar. Updated: Apr 28, 2009.

HIGH-END

Tierra Bendita

(BUFFET: $12.50) In Spanish, *tenedor libre* means "free fork," and Tierra Bendita has an all-you-can-eat buffet. Here you can find a

SOUTHERN PATAGONIA

typical Argentine parrilla of sausages, beef and Patagonian lamb. But this isn't just a typical buffet; Tierra Bendita also offers Asian dishes. As if that weren't enough, there are also salad and dessert bars. This is the ideal place for eclectic taste buds. Open daily noon – 3 p.m., 7 p.m. – midnight. Gobernador Gregores 1170. Tel: 54-2902-495668. Updated: Jul 13, 2009.

La Vaca Atada

(ENTREES: $15) The two cut-out cows standing outside La Vaca Atada (The Tied Cow) are a landmark in El Calafate, and make this smallish restaurant hard to miss. Popular with both visitors and locals, La Vaca Atada serves up a variety of quality dishes, including homemade pasta, soup, fish, steak, and lamb. The hearty rabbit stew is particularly good. The restaurant is open for lunch and dinner from August until May, and is closed Wednesdays. Av. Libertador 1176. Tel: 54-2902-491227. Updated: Mar 13, 2008.

Panadería y Confitería Don Luís

If you're looking for the richest in baked goods, then Panadería y Confitería Don Luis is the place to go. Located three blocks from the main avenue, Don Luis has all sorts of sweets, including creamy cheesecake, cookies and other desserts. This bakery also prepares salados, or savory goods, like whole-grain breads and foccacio. While Don Luis is not cheap, it will satisfy your craving for something sweet. Open daily 7 a.m.-9 p.m. 9 de Julio 265. Tel: 54-2902-491550, E-mail: donluiscalafate@gmail.com. Updated: Jul 13, 2009.

Nightlife

Don Diego de la Noche

Don Diego de la Noche is one of the best places in El Calafate to spend an evening out. This cafe bar features live music and a dance floor. The bar closes after Semana Santa (Easter week) and re-opens when El Calafate's population swells in the summer. Av. del Libertador 1603. Tel: 54-2902-493270, E-mail: dondiego@cotecal.com.ar. Updated: Jul 13, 2009.

Libro y Bar Borges y Álvarez

Libro y Bar Borges y Álvarez' narrow, glass-walled balcony overlooks El Calafate's main avenue. This is the perfect place to browse for a book or have a coffee or drink. On a sunny day, you can relax at the patio tables below. At night, this is a great place to listen to live music after a day of excursions. Libro-Bar Borges y Álvarez has every type of liquor imaginable, from local microbrews to international whiskies and liquors. Closed Tuesdays. Av. del Libertador 1015. Tel: 54-2902-491464, E-mail: peladex@cotecal.com.ar. Updated: Jul 13, 2009.

PARQUE NACIONAL LOS GLACIARES, ARGENTINA

Parque Nacional Los Glaciares has some of the largest ice caps in the southern hemisphere outside of Antarctica. This protected area was created in 1937 to preserve the 724,000 hectares of rugged Argentine wilderness in the province of Santa Cruz. In 1981, UNESCO made the park a World Heritage Site.

The 35 kilometer wide Perito Moreno Glacier is one of the most popular stops since it's easy to get close to the moving, groaning ice mass. There are another 200 small glaciers and 47 large glaciers within the park—including Upsala, the largest glacier in South America—all of which are astonishing, but more difficult to access. The national park borders Chile's Parque Nacional Laguna San Rafael and Parque Nacional Bernardo O'Higgins, which also both protect the ice fields.

Mt. Fitz Roy and Cerro Torre are two other park highlights—offering breathtaking views, exhilarating hikes and immensely challenging, technical climbs.

The park also has beech forests, dry Patagonian prairieland, mountain lakes and rivers formed by glacial melt, including Lago Argentino and Lago Viedma. Both lakes offer great trout and salmon fishing, and flow into the Atlantic Ocean via the Río Santa Cruz. At Lago Viedma, you can go ice trekking or take tours to the base of the Viedma Glacier.

In the Fitz Roy region, visit some of the old pioneer estancias near Lago Argentino and El Chaltén. There are several old haciendas in the region: near Perito Moreno is Los Notros, near El Calafate is Estancia Cristina, and right outside of El Chaltén are Hosteria El Pilar and La Quinta.

During the winter, temperatures average 0.6°C (33.08°F) with heavy snowfall. Visitors come for the great skiing, ice skating, and photography, but many roads and businesses close up shop. The summer season (November — March), with temperatures averaging 13.4°C (56.12°F), is definitely the most popular time to visit the park.

During December and January, national and international tourists flock to the park, making these the most crowded months.

There are four access points to the park, two of which are free (Lago Roca and the sector near El Chaltén). At the other two, (both by El Calafate) international visitors have to pay a $30 entrance fee. Updated: May 05, 2009.

PERITO MORENO GLACIER

When it snows high in the Patagonian Andes, the snow does not melt—rather, it accumulates, forming the massive Southern Patagonian Ice Field, a glacier system that straddles Argentina and Chile.

The enormous pressure of tons and tons of snow and ice compresses the existing ice and gives it a distinctive bluish tint. Under such great pressure, the ice actually flows, inching out of the Andes and into the valleys where it melts, forming lakes and rivers. The Perito Moreno Glacier is one of 48 such outlets for the South Patagonian Ice Field.

Once every few years, the glacier plugs up Lago Argentino, cutting off the Brazo Rico arm of the lake. The water level of Brazo Rico side can rise up to 30 meters before pressure causes the forward edge of the glacier to shatter into a torrent of ice, water and debris. The last such occurrence was in 2004.

Great chunks of ice crack off the face of the glacier every few minutes and tumble into the lake with a roar. These hunks of ice, which can weigh several tons, form slowly melting icebergs. There are observation platforms where you can watch this process; many visitors also take tour boats into the lake. The boats keep a respectful distance—you never know when a hunk of ice is going to break off—but the views are spectacular.

A basic hike on the glacier costs about $60 – 70 per person. Glacier hiking is dangerous and a guide is absolutely essential. Entry into the national park is $17 for foreigners and $5.50 for Argentines. Tours cost $32 – 40 (includes guide and transport; does not include park entry). A cheaper transportation alternative is to take a bus to the park ($23 round trip, 1.5 hours each way; **Patagonia Ya** 10 a.m., return 5:15 p.m.; **Taqsa** 9 a.m., return 3:30 p.m.; **Cal-Tur** daily 9 a.m., return 4 p.m.). Updated: Jul 13, 2009.

EL CHALTÉN, ARGENTINA

 160 m   500   54-2962

The wild and windy town of El Chaltén was built in 1985 at the confluence of the Río de las Vueltas and Río Fitz Roy to support the growing numbers of tourists in the area who wanted to explore the famous Fitz Roy mountains. Argentina also worked on developing the town. In 1994, an international ruling council declared that Argentina indeed owned the land.

The saw-tooth mountain range provides a dramatic backdrop for the town, which includes two of the toughest challenges for mountain climbers: Cerro Fitz Roy and Cerro el Torre. El Chaltén is the indigenous Tehuelche (Aónikenk) name for Fitz Roy, which in their language means "Smoking Mountain."

El Chaltén has grown significantly since its founding, though there are still only 500 or so year-round residents. Located just north of Los Glaciares National Park, this small village has earned the title of Argentina's national trekking capital, and now thousands of international outdoor enthusiasts come every year to summit Cerro Fitz Roy. The majority of visitors arrive between January and March.

With plenty of hostels, restaurants, and outdoor supplies shops, El Chaltén is a good base for climbers looking to set out on multiple-day guided excursions into the National Park or on simple day trips into the nearby foothills. The town has basic tourist services from October until April or May, after which El Chaltén tends to shut down for the harsh winter season.

The village church, Nuestra Señora de la Patagonia, is a small, yellow, tin chapel with a beautiful stained glass portrait of the Virgin (Los Andeles, between Avenida Güemes and McLoed). Another chapel of interest is the Toni Egger Gedankkapelle, to commemorate climbers who have lost their lives on the peaks. Updated: Jul 16, 2009.

SOUTHERN PATAGONIA

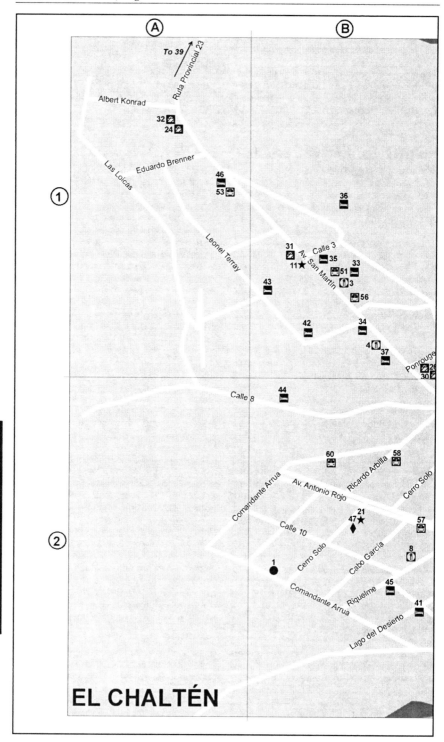

SOUTHERN PATAGONIA

EL CHALTÉN

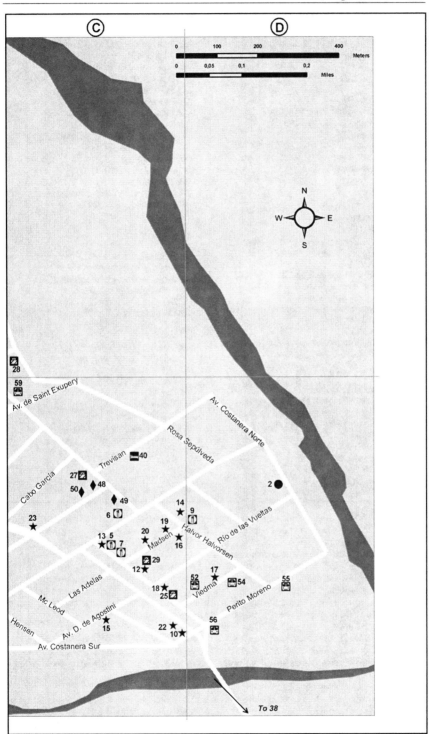

Activities ●

1   Biblioteca Popular Mujer Pionera B2
2   Tony Egger Gedankkapelle D2

Eating ⬚

3   Boccato B1
4   La Cervecería Brew Pub and Resto B1
5   Panadería Lo de Haydée C2
6   Pangaea C2
7   Restaurant Aónikenk Chaltén C2
8   Rotisseria Isadoro Quemeiquipan B2
9   The Shelter D2

Services ★

10   Banco Santa Cruz C2
11   Boulevard II B1
12   ChalteNet C2
13   Chaltén Travel servicio de Internet C2
14   Farmacia El Cerro C2
15   Health Center C2
16   Gendarmeria Nacional C2
17   Javier D2
18   Locutorio Boulevard C2
19   Police / Fire Department C2
20   Post Office C2
21   Sheuen B2
22   Tourist Information Office C2
23   Wash & Go C2

Shopping ▣

24   Cacao Theobroma A1
25   Camping Center C2
26   Chaltén Art Cueros B1
27   El Huemul Sabores de Patagonia C2
28   Eolia C1
29   Marco Polo C2
30   Tempano B1
31   Topa Topa B1
32   Viento Oeste A1

Sleeping ▤

33   Albergue Hostel Pioneros del Valle B1
34   Albergue Patagonia B1
35   Albergue y Camping Lago del
     Desierto B1
36   El Refugio Campground B1
37   El Relincho B1
38   Estancia La Quinta D2
39   Hostería El Pilar A1
40   Hostería Posada Lunajuim C2
41   Hosteria Thiamalú B2
42   Kalenshen B1
43   Lo de Tomy B1
44   Los Cerros B2
45   Nothofagus Bed and Breakfast B2
46   Rancho Grande Hostel and
     Restaurante A1

Tours ♦

47   Fierita Cabalgatas B2
48   FitzRoy Expediciones C2
49   Mountaineering Patagonia C2
50   Patagonia Aventura C2

Transportation ▦

51   Cal-Tur B1
52   Chaltén Móvil D2
53   Chaltén Travel A1
54   Las Lengas D2
55   Mata Negra D2
56   new bus terminal D2
57   Taqsa B2
58   Tere Torres B2
59   Trans Patagonia Servicios C2
60   Vía Chaltén B2

When to Go

January – March are summer months in Patagonia, with an average temperature of 13.3°C (56°F). During these warm, clear months, El Chaltén fills up with both vacationing Argentines and international climbers. El Chaltén is extremely crowded during the summer, so book accommodation well in advance (even a month ahead). In the winter (June – August), El Chaltén is also a popular destination for cross-country skiers, though the weather is extremely cold during these months, and can make regional travel difficult. In the off-season, businesses cut their hours and take an extended lunch break. During the winter, most places close, except the essential ones. The majority of businesses re-open in time for the town's founding celebration (Oct 12), and remain open until Semana Santa in mid-April.

The low season is October – November, March – April (with the exception of Semana Santa). The high Season is December – February, Semana Santa; winter: May – September.

Fiestas and Holidays

To celebrate El Chaltén's founding on October 12, the town erupts with live music, dancing, and BBQs.

El Día Nacional de Trekking is celebrated on February 4, and the Fiesta Nacional de Trekking takes place during the first week

SOUTHERN PATAGONIA

in February. Both festivals have a variety of outdoor events: rock climbing, running marathons, bouldering, mountain biking and horseback riding. Each day concludes with a lively night-time music festival.

On November 10, El Chaltén also pays tribute its gaucho heritage on the national Día de la Tradición, the day on which José Hernández, author of the legendary cowboy story, Martín Fierro, was born. Updated: Apr 22, 2009.

Getting To and Away From El Chaltén

BY BUS

The majority of visitors reach El Chaltén by bus from El Calafate. The trip takes approximately 3.5 to 4 hours, and the bus usually stops for a 20-minute break halfway along Route 40. A roundtrip ticket between El Calafate and El Chaltén is roughly $38, a one-way ticket costs approximately $20.

In the high season, buses from El Calafate to El Chaltén run everyday at 7:30 a.m., 8:00 a.m., 1 p.m., and 6:30 p.m. There is an additional 6 a.m. bus on even days of the month. In winter, snow can close roads, especially to Lago del Desierto and Piedra Buena. The only way to reach El Chaltén during the cold months is by way of El Calafate and Río Gallegos. A new bus terminal, due to open in time for the 2009 – 2010 high season, is being built at Avenida Güemes and P. Moreno, at the entrance to town.

Cal-Tur (Daily 7 a.m. – 10 p.m. Av. San Martín 451. Tel: 54-2962-493079)—to El Calafate.

Chaltén Travel (Av. San Martín 724. Tel: 54-2962-493005)—October – mid-April: El Calafate-Bariloche and points between via Ruta 40; mid-April – September: El Calafate only.

Las Lengas (Daily 9 a.m. – 9 p.m. De Viedma 95. Tel: 54-2962-493023)—Piedra Buena, Hostería El Pilar / Río Eléctrico, Lago del Desierto; driver Raúl is very knowledgeable about the history and nature of the region.

Taqsa (Monday – Friday 10 a.m. – 1 p.m., 5:30 – 8 p.m.; Saturday, Sunday 11 a.m. – 1 p.m., 5:30 – 8 p.m. Av. Antonio Rojo 88. Tel: 54-2962-493294).

Trans Patagonia Servicios (TPS) (Daily 11:30 a.m. – 2:30 p.m., 7:30 p.m. – midnight.

Av. San Martín 229, local 3. Tel: 54-2962-493356)—Tres Lagos, Piedra Buena, Río Gallegos.

To Hostería El Pilar / Río Eléctrico: **Las Lengas** (summer: 7 a.m., 8:30 a.m., 3 p.m.; winter: noon, $11.50 / $16. By remis $23 – 25).

To Lago del Desierto: **Las Lengas** (summer: 8:30 a.m., 3 p.m.; winter: noon with 2-hour wait, $23). **Remis** ($57 – 69).

To Bahía Túnel (Lago Viedma): **Remis** ($23-26).

To Piedra Buena: **Las Lengas** (October – April or May: daily 5:30 a.m., $32), **TPS** (October – May: Tuesday, Thursday, Saturday; less frequent in winter 5 a.m., $28, 4.5 hours).

To Río Gallegos: **TPS** (October – May: Monday – Saturday 5 a.m., less frequent in winter, $28, 5 hours).

To Bariloche and other northern points: **Taqsa** (11 p.m., $86, 32 hours; to Perito Moreno $40, Los Antiguos $43, Esquel $73, El Bolsón $83), **Chaltén Travel** (October – mid-April only, $55). October – mid-April many busses take Ruta 40; the rest of the year, via Ruta 3.

To El Calafate: **Chaltén Travel** (daily 8 a.m., 6 p.m., $20, 3.5 hours), **Cal-Tur** (daily 8 a.m., 6 p.m., $20, 3.5 hours).

BY CAR OR BIKE

Highway **RP-23**, a paved road off **RN-40**, leads to El Chaltén. It continues north to Lago del Desierto. The following roads lead to El Chaltén: **Ruta 40** (paved from Tres Lagos south to El Calafate, except for a six-kilometer stretch near of Río Leonas; can close in winter); **Ruta 5** (from Río Gallegos, paved); and **Ruta 288** (from Piedra Buena, gravel; can close in winter). Updated: Apr 23, 2009.

SOUTHERN PATAGONIA

BY PLANE

Aeropuerto Internacional El Calafate is the nearest airport, and offers daily flights from Buenos Aires, with less frequent flights from other Argentine cities. After arriving in Calfate, the quickest way to travel to El Chaltén is by bus.

Getting Around

No car rental agencies operate in El Chaltén. **Albergue Patagonia** rents mountain bikes for a minimum of two hours ($9; 4 hours; $14; 6 hours, $20; all day $28. Av. San Martín 376. Tel: 54-2962-493019).

Remis (taxis) only operate 5 a.m. – midnight. Fares within the city cost $2.50 – 3.50. Some of the providers are **Chaltén Móvil** (Viedma 58. Tel: 54-2962-493061, **Mata Negra** (P. Moreno 195. Tel: 54-2962-493256), **Tere Torres** (Arbilla 40. Tel: 54-2962-493202) and **Vía Chálten** (Arrua 314. Tel: 54-2962-493175). Updated: Jul 16, 2009.

Safety

El Chaltén has no real problems with crime. If you plan to hike in Parque Nacional Los Glaciares, be aware of the weather conditions. Some hostels and businesses post the forecast for the next day. Also check with the park service to see which trails may be closed. Take warm clothing and rain gear with you. If conditions begin to change for the worse, head back. It's always a good idea to carry high-energy snacks and water with you. Updated: Jul 16, 2009.

Services

With the recent influx of visitors, El Chaltén has developed a fairly strong infrastructure that caters to hikers and climbers, with several shops where you can rent or buy outdoor gear (along Av. San Martin, one of two central streets). There is still no mobile phone service in the area, and most businesses don't have addresses.

Most buses coming into town stop by the Los Glaciares National Park Information Office for a short presentation in English and Spanish about the national park (Tel: 54-2962-02962 / 54-2962-493004). At the office, you can get up-to-date reports on hiking trails and campsites, acquire fishing permits, or register your expedition.

TOURISM

Tourist Information Office (October – April: Daily 8 a.m. - 9 p.m. / May

– September: Monday – Friday 8 a.m. – 4 p.m. Av. Guemes 21. Tel: 54-2962-02962 / 493011, E-mail: comfomelChalten@yahoo. com, URL: www.elchalten.com).

APN (National Park office) (October – March: Daily 9 a.m. – 6 p.m. / April – September: Daily 10 a.m. – 5 p.m.)—Staff speaks English; during high season there are volunteers who speak other languages. APN accepts summer volunteers. Basic Spanish is necessary. For more information, contact voluntariosglaciares@apn.gov.ar.

Immigration (Madsen 66. Tel: 54-2962-493140).

Police / Fire department (Av. San Martín 14, Tel: 54-2962-02962 / 54-2962-493003)—Dial 101.

MONEY

Banco Santa Cruz (P. Moreno and Av. Güemes, near tourism office)—ATM only: Accepts MasterCard, Cirrus, Visa, Plus, American Express; some travelers report their cards being rejected, or that the machine was out of money. Few businesses accept credit cards, and those that do add a high surcharge.

KEEPING IN TOUCH

Internet is expensive and slow (especially if quite a few people are online at the same time). Rates run at $3 – 3.50 per hour for foreigners. The only café with Skype is **ChalteNet** (Av. Güemes 77).

Other providers include: **Chaltén Travel servicio de Internet** (Av. Güemes 127); and **Locutorio Boulevard** (Av. Güemes 127) with the latter being the cheaper option.

For phone services visit Locutorios **Boulevard** (Av. Güemes 127), **Boulevard II** (Av. San Martín 624) or **Javier** (De Viedma 52).

Post Office (Monday – Friday 9 a.m. – 4 p.m., Saturday 9 a.m. – 1 p.m. Madsen s/n, between Av. Güemes and Halvorsen).

MEDICAL

Dial 107 to reach the **hospital**. For a doctor's consultation ($4.50), contact **Puesto Sanitario** (Av. de Agostini 70. Tel: 54-2962-02962 / 493033). There is a pharmacy on Río de las Vueltas, **Farmacia El Cerro** (Río de las Vueltas y Halvorsen 41. Tel: 54-2962-493253).

What's In a Name?

El Chaltén has an eye-catching mountain range, with a jagged set of peaks on the horizon. Two spires are especially noticeable: Cerro Torre and Cerro FitzRoy. Each peak around El Chaltén has a name and history.

Cordón de las Adelas (2,825 m/9,268 ft)—named for the mother of Alfred Kölliker, the man who led the first exhaustive expedition of the Campo de Hielo in 1915.

Cerro Torre (3,102 m/10,177 ft)—Francisco "Perito" Moreno named this peak, likening it to a tower.

Aguja Egger (2,900 m/9,514 ft)—named in memory of Tony Egger, who died during an attempt to summit Cerro Torre in 1959.

Aguja Standhardt (2,800 m/9,186 ft)—named for the German photographer who lived in the area and photographed the region until his death in the 1960s.

Techado Negro (2,152 m/7,060 ft)—Louis Lliboutry baptized the mountain in honor of its shape and color.

Aguja Saint Exupéry (2,558 m/8,392 ft)—honors Antoine de Saint-Exupéry who, besides being the author of *Le Petit Prince,* flew over the Andes, establishing the first postal connection between Buenos Aires and Punta Arenas; Saint-Exupéry also served as director of Aéropostale Argentina 1929 – 1931.

Aguja Rafael Suárez (2,482 m/8,143 ft)—also called Innominata, this peak is named for a young Argentine climber who disappeared during the ascent of Cerro Adela in 1974.

Cerro Fitz Roy (3,405 m/11,171 ft)—the Aónikenk called it Chaltén, the mountain that smokes, but Perito Moreno baptized it in honor of Robert Fitz Roy, captain of The HMS Beagle.

Aguja Poincenot (3,002 m/9,849 ft)—memorializes Jacques Poincenot, a member of the 1952 expedition that made the first successful ascent of FitzRoy, but who could not taste the victory as he died while fording the Río Fitz Roy.

Aguja Val Biois (2,492 m/8,176 ft)—Bruno de Dona named the peak for a valley in his home Italian province Belluno.

Agujas Guillaumet (2,579 m/8,461 ft) and **Mermoz** (2,732 m/8,963 ft)—Lliboutry named these twin peaks to honor French Aéropostale pilots Henri Guillaumet and Jean Mermoz who, with Saint-Exupéry, flew on the first regular airmail route between Buenos Aires and Punta Arenas

Now that you have been introduced to these peaks, if any of them are beckoning you to climb them, you must obtain permission from APN. Updated: Jul 16, 2009.

LAUNDRY

Sheuen (Cerro Solo 117. Tel: 54-2962-493222). **Wash & Go** (Av. Rojo and Riquelme). Updated: Jul 16, 2009.

SHOPPING

Many specialty shops close in the winter or have reduced hours. At the beginning and end of the high season (October – November; March – April), businesses close during the lunch hour.

Marco Polo sells naturalist and travel guides, as well as hiking and road maps. It also has music and English-language sections (Madsen 12. E-mail: marcopolo_chalten@yahoo.com.ar). Many other businesses also sell maps.

Local artisan goods are of high quality, but are expensive. Locals work in leather and wood, as well as sheep, guanaco and llama wool. A stroll along Avenidas Güemes and San Martín will take you past all of the shops. A few worth checking out are **Topa Topa**, which has items made of wood and wool, as well as photographs (Av. San Martín 664. Tel: 54-2962-493163); **Manos** (Mercado Artesanal Nativo Originario y Solidaridad) which carries mostly hand-woven and knitted woolens (Av. San Martín 320, local 3, Paseo Tierra de Vientos. E-mail: e.vogliotti@gmail.com); and **Chaltén Art Cueros**, which specializes in fine leathers (Av. San Martín 249. Tel: 54-2962-493138).

Like many places in the Argentine Patagonia, El Chaltén has chocolaterías and ice cream parlors. Jams made of *sauco* (elderberry), *calafate* (Magellan barberry),

On a Rainy Day

Whether the weather is keeping you from hitting the trails, or an injury has rained on your parade, El Chaltén's community offers a few activities to fill the hours: **APN**, the national park service, has an interpretive center at its headquarters. One room covers the natural and human history of Parque Nacional Los Glaciares. A second room provides an in-depth history of the park's two challenging peaks, El Torre and Fitz Roy, and has an exhibit showing the ins and outs of mountain climbing. Documentaries in a variety of languages are shown daily at 2 p.m (TP-23, at the village entry).

The tourism office also has a small exhibit with mainly geologic and archaeological artifacts (Avenida Guemes 21). **Biblioteca Popular Mujer Pionera** has free art and photographic exhibits, Sunday movies, literary readings and other activities, as well as a library (Comandante Arrua, between Arbilla and Cerro Soto). **Tony Egger Gedankkapelle** is a memorial chapel dedicated to Tony Egger and other climbers who have died on those rock spires (Costanera Norte and Río de las Vueltas). Updated: Jul 16, 2009.

grosella (currant), *mosqueta* (rose hip) and other local fruits are popular. **El Huemul Sabores de Patagonia** carries cured meats, sausages, marmalades, wines, pastas and other regional products (Av. Güemes 123). **Cacao Theobroma** serves up chocolates, ice cream, shakes and hot cocoa (Av. San Martín 890, Tel: 54-2962-493093). Updated: Jul 16, 2009.

OUTDOOR GEAR RENTAL AND SALES

During the summer, El Chaltén has many shops that specialize in camping and mountaineering gear. Most close at the end of the season, but a few remain open during the winter. Most carry a selection of new and used goods.

Viento Oeste (Av. San Martín 898. Tel: 54-2962-493200): Rents all sorts of gear, including snowshoes and skis. It also sells outdoors clothing, gas canisters, climbing gear, trekking maps, guides, music and miscellaneous souvenirs.

Eolia (Pasaje Fonrouge 45. Tel: 54-2962-493066): Has hiking boots and snow shoes. Eolia also rents four-season tents, sleeping bags and all cooking gear. It also sells and recycles gas stove cartridges. Eolia is affiliated with the tour operator Serac Ski and Andismo.

Camping Center (Av. San Martín 56. Tel: 54-2962-493264)—Affliated with Patagonia Adventure and Fitz Roy Expediciones, this shop has full rental and sales services; closed in the off-season.

Tempano (Av. San Martín 275. Tel: 54-2962-493318)—Sells good quality mountaineering equipment. Closed in the off-season. Updated: Jul 16, 2009.

Things to See and Do

El Chaltén bills itself as the National Trekking Capital—and for good reason. This northern part of Parque Nacional Los Glaciares has many trails that wind around the mountains to lagoons and lakes. Wildlife and birds are plentiful. The park doesn't charge en entry fee and you can hike most trails without a guide. Climbing the Torre and Viedma Glaciers, horseback riding and kayaking down the Río de las Vueltas are just a few of the possible activities. Many climbers aspire to climb Cerros Torre and Fitz Roy, considered two of the world's most difficult peaks. Updated: Jul 15, 2009.

Hiking in El Chaltén !

El Chaltén has many hiking trails that weave around the base of the two giant massifs, Torre and FitzRoy. There are three main circuits, each with its own set of trails. The first trail head is near the APN office, and goes to Mirador de las Águilas, Mirador de los Cóndores, Pliegue del Tumbado and Laguna Toro.

The Fitz Roy circuit includes the hikes to Laguna Capri, Laguna de los Tres, Piedras Blancas, Poincenot and Río Blanco. The Cerro Torre zone has trails to the Mirador del Torre, Laguna Torre and Mirador Maestri. Other trails include Chorrillo del Salto and Piedra del Fraile. At Lago del Desierto there are treks to Glaciar Huemul, Punta Norte and Lago O'Higgins. The Cañadón del Río de las Vueltas trail is now closed.

In the winter, you can cross-country ski or snow shoe along some of these trails, like

Laguna Capri. You can also climb Chorrillo del Salto. A guide is especially recommended at this time of year.

The weather can change at any moment, so bring warm and rainproof clothing. A windbreaker is essential, especially in summer. Carry high-energy food and water (though the stream water is potable). Use sturdy footwear. Carry all trash out.

If camping, bring a rain-resistant tent and a camp stove. No wood fires are allowed. In the park, there are free sites at Laguna Capri, Poincenot, De Agostini and Laguna Toro. Only climbers are allowed to use Campamento Río Blanco. At Piedra del Fraile and Lago del Desierto, there are private campgrounds, but you have to pay a fee.

In the spring and fall, check with APN about hiking conditions, in the event that foul weather has closed trails. Registration with APN is required for all climbing excursions, and hikes to the Laguna de los Tres, Laguna Piedras Blancas and Laguna Toro or into any part of the park where there are no marked trails. In winter, any excursion in the park must be registered with the park service. Search and rescue is done by the APN, Club Andino and trained volunteers from the village. There is no helicopter; the nearest hospital with triage is in El Calafate.

Lago Toro Hike
The trail to Lago Toro (not to be confused with Laguna Torre) makes for a long, but relatively easy, hike. Starting at the sign-posted trailhead on the grounds of the national park headquarters, the path hugs the Río Tunel valley before crossing some hills and then descending into a forest. The Campamento Lago Toro is in the woods, and you will have to spend the night there, but you can continue on to the lake itself.

Piedra del Fraile Hike
Piedra del Fraile is a gigantic boulder that sits on private land in the Río Electrico valley. To get to the site, you must start at the Puente del Río Electrico, a low bridge accessible by public transportation from El Chaltén. The path, which can be difficult to follow at times, winds through the forest toward Cerro Electrico before veering off in the direction of the river and the boulder. You can do the trail as a daytrip, or you could stay at Refugio los Troncos, a private campsite located beneath Piedra del Fraile.

Hike to Chorrillo del Salto
One of the easiest hikes in Los Glaciares National Park, this trail leads to the pretty Chorrillo del Salto waterfall. The path is well marked and leaves from Route 23, the road toward Lago del Desierto, about five kilometers beyond El Chaltén. The path cuts through the forests near the Río de las Vueltas before arriving at the 20-meter waterfall. The round-trip hike can be done in a couple of hours.

Laguna Torre Hike
Hikers hoping to get a perfect view of Cerro Torre should set off for Laguna Torre, a glacial lake at the foot of the mountain. The lake is a reasonable turn-around point for a day hike out of El Chaltén, and you can reach it via an interesting, but not overly taxing, nine-kilometer trail. The trailhead on Calle Riquelme is marked with a sign, and, after leaving town, the path goes through the Río Fitz Roy valley. At the end of the trail, you will have to ascend a small moraine and some sand dunes, but it is the view of Cerro Torre, rather than the climb, that is likely to take your breath away.

Laguna de los Tres Hike
Laguna de los Tres is the terminus of a rewarding 20-kilometer, two-day hike in Los Glaciares National Park. The trail starts at the northern end of Avenida San Martín, next to the sign for the Sendero Fitz Roy. The path then climbs through a boulder-strewn forest until it reaches Campamaneto Poincenot, where many trekkers choose to spend the night. You could also push on if it's early enough in the day, and stop at Poincenot on the return leg. After leaving Poincenot, you must walk across a bridge over the Río Blanco, before climbing a steep moraine to Laguna de los Tres, where, across the glacier-blue water, you'll have a perfect view of Mount Fitz Roy.

Lago del Desierto
To get to Lago del Desierto start on the south shore of Punta Sur. The hike takes you through virgin lenga forest to a lagoon and Glaciar Huemul (distance: 2 km/1.2 mi, difficulty: medium, duration: 2 hours round-trip). There are panoramic views of the lake and Fitz Roy's south wall. A ferry traverses the steely waters of Lago del Desierto from Punta Sur to Punta Norte in the north. Fitz Roy, Cerro Vespignani and glaciers frame the landscape. Near the Gendarmería Nacional post there is a short, self-guided trail to Mirador Centinela.

SOUTHERN PATAGONIA

Lago Viedma

Cruise through this lake's icy waters to the foot of Argentina's largest glacier, Glaciar Viedma, towering 40 meters (131 ft) above the water. On the northern horizon, you'll be able to see Cerro Huemul and the other needle-like peaks of the southern Andes.

Patagonia Aventura provides transfers to the lake ($14), runs cruises on the Lago Viedma boat (daily, $28, 2.5 hours), and offers ice trekking tours ($85 – 100, 6 – 9 hours). San Martín 56. Tel: 54-2962-436424, E-mail: info@patagonia-aventura.com.ar,URL: www.patagonia-aventura.com.ar). Updated: Jul 16, 2009.

Horseback Riding

Explore the ragged landscape surrounding El Chaltén the way the pioneers did it: on horseback. The most popular trail leads to Cerro Fitz Roy, the most famous mountain on this northern side of Parque Nacional Los Glaciares. The half-day journey takes riders to the base of the mountain, through untouched forests mottled with celestite-colored lakelets. The Valle del Río de las Vueltas is a three-hour route following the course of the river. Other excursions can also be arranged.

Only two companies offer horseback riding: **El Relincho** (Av. San Martín 505. Tel: 54-2962-493007) and **Fierita Cabalgatas** (Cerro Solo 141. Tel: 54-2962-493203). A three-hour excursion costs approximately $43 per person. Updated: Jul 16, 2009.

Kayaking and Canoeing

The only companies that have kayaking and canoeing excursions are **Patagonia Aventura** (San Martín 56. Tel: 54-2962-436424, E-mail: info@patagonia-aventura.com.ar, URL: www.patagonia-aventura.com.ar) and **FitzRoy Expediciones** (Av. San Martín, Tel: 54-2962-493017, E-mail: info@fitzroyexpediciones.com.ar, URL: www.fitzroyexpediciones.com.ar). Updated: Jul 16, 2009.

Ice Trekking

To climb Glacier Viedma, the largest ice floe in Argentina, you first have to take a boat across Lake Viedma. There are two trails you can take across the glacier: the six-hour **Viedma Glacier track**, which visits ice caves, and the nine-hour **Viedma Pro**, which includes more intensive ice climbing. The most challenging of regularly offered ice treks in Parque Nacional Los Glaciares is the mythical **Cerro Torre**, which can be done on a one-day tour,

or one-to-two-night expeditions. You can also arrange treks across Glaciar Huemul at Lago del Desierto or Cerro FitzRoy. The best time to go trekking is October to April. You don't need experience, but you do have to be in good physical condition, especially for the Cerro Torre climb.

A number of companies offer climbing trips: **Cerro Torre—Fitz Roy Expediciones** (Av. San Martín. Tel: 54-2962-493017, E-mail: info@fitzroyexpediciones.com.ar, URL: www.fitzroyexpediciones.com.ar).

Mountaineering Patagonia (Av. San Martín 16. Tel: 54-2962-493194, URL: www.mountaineeringpatagonia.com).

Glaciar Viedma: Patagonia Aventura (San Martín 56. Tel: 54-2962-436424, E-mail: info@patagonia-aventura.com.ar, URL: www.patagonia-aventura.com.ar).

Winter Sports

Come winter, snow blankets the Río de las Vueltas valley. It's time to break out the skis (both cross country and alpine) and hit the trails into Parque Nacional Los Glaciares. You can snowshoe to Chorrillo del Salto where you can practice ice climbing. You can also ice skate on the frozen lagoons. The solitude and muted silence of this landscape is unforgettable. Winter is also an ideal time of the year to observe wildlife.

One of the few tour operators offering winter excursions is **Mountaineering Patagonia** (Av. San Martín 16. Tel: 54-2962-493194, URL: www.mountaineeringpatagonia.com). Check with the national park office about conditions in the park. Heavy snow may close some trails. You must officially register your snowshoe or ski trek with the APN office. Snow will make markers impossible to see. Do not camp unless you have a proper four-weather tent and other appropriate gear. Several gear rental shops have skis and snowshoes. Updated: Jul 16, 2009.

Miradores Los Cóndores and Las Águilas

Both trails begin at the park office. The main trail passes through the compound toward the trail head to the left. The path then rises steadily and near the top of the hill, the trail forks. The left route heads up to **Mirador de los Cóndores** (distance: 1 km / 0.6 mi, difficulty: easy, duration: 40 minutes). This cliff-top viewpoint is close to condor nests and offers great views of the city, the Río de las Vueltas and the mountain ranges.

The right fork is the new **Mirador de las Águilas** trail (distance: 2 km/01.2 mi, difficulty: easy, duration: 1 hour). This path cuts across flat brushland dotted with clusters of trees. It ends at a point where you can sit and take in the view south of El Chaltén. Cerro Huemel is to the right and Bahía Túnel and Lago Viedma are straight ahead in the distance. Updated: Jul 16, 2009.

Tours

When throngs of tourists arrive in El Chaltén in the warm months between October and April, the town buzzes with tour operators. Popular trips include treks to the glaciers, boat tours of the lake or adventures on horseback. Some load up the vans to take travelers on a five-day run up to Bariloche. Others prepare hikers for the trek to Villa O'Higgins, by way of Lago del Desierto. Most operators close after Semana Santa. Few stay open during the winter. If you need a guide at this time of year, inquire at the tourism office or APN. Updated: Jul 16, 2009.

Patagonia Aventura

Patagonia Aventura can take you across Lago del Desierto to begin the Paso Dos Lagunas trek to Chile, on Lago Viedma or on a trek across Glaciar Viedma and—if you're daring enough—trek across it. The Viedma excursions come in three sizes: *Viedma Light* (a 2.5-hour boat ride), *Viedma Trek* (a six-hour outing to climb the glacier) and the *Viedma Pro* (a nine-hour trek and ice climbing expedition on the glacier). San Martín 56. Tel: 54-2962-436424, E-mail: info@patagonia-aventura.com.ar, URL: www.patagonia-aventura.com.ar. Updated: Jul 16, 2009.

Fitz Roy Expediciones

Since 1985, Fitz Roy Expediciones has been leading visitors to explore this corner of Parque Nacional Los Glaciares. Its biggest expedition is ice trekking on Cerro Torre, which can be done as a one-day outing or an all-inclusive one-to-two-night expedition. All of these treks leave from Campamento Thorwood near Laguna Torre, a two-hour (10 km/6 mi) hike from the glacier. Fitz Roy also offers kayaking trips on the Río de las Vueltas, Lago del Desierto or Río La Leona. Many of this agency's packages include accommodation in its lodge on Río de las Vueltas, 20 kilometers

(12 mi) north of El Chaltén. Fitz Roy Expediciones also has two-day courses in rock and ice climbing. Av. San Martín. Tel: 54-2962-493017, E-mail: info@fitzroyexpediciones.com.ar, URL: www.fitzroyexpediciones.com.ar. Updated: Jul 16, 2009.

Mountaineering Patagonia

The professional mountain guides at Mountaineering Patagonia take travelers glacier trekking and mountain climbing. They also do multi-day treks across the Campo de Hielo and the Huemul Circuit. Mountaineering Patagonia also has a rock and ice climbing school with half- and full-day courses. In winter, they lead ski outings on Cerro Vespignani, snowshoeing trips to Laguna Capri and other one-day treks. Ask about custom packages.Av. San Martín 16. Tel: 54-2962-493194, E-mail: info@mountaineeringpatagonia.com, URL: www.mountaineeringpatagonia.com. Updated: Jul 16, 2009.

Lodging

El Chaltén has a broad range of lodging options, from campgrounds to comfortable resorts. Many hostels are geared to budget travelers, and four of them are Hostelling International members. In the summer high season, prices rise and reservations are highly recommended. After Semana Santa (Easter Week), many hotels and cabins close. Although an increasing number have been staying open to cater to tourists in the winter. Ask about winter season discounts.

Note: APN's two free campgrounds, Campamento Confluencia at the east entrance of town, and Campamento Madsen, at the north end, are now permanently closed. Updated: Jul 15, 2009.

BUDGET

El Refugio Campground

(CAMPING: $5.50) El Refugio is a private campground within walking distance of El Chaltén. Located next to the De Las Vueltas River, this spot has grassy areas, trees, and views of the mountains. Hot showers and BBQ pits are provided. Calle 3 s/n. Tel: 54-2962-493221. Updated: May 11, 2009.

El Relincho

(CAMPING: $5.70) El Relincho is a family-owned campground and cabin complex in the city. The wooded sites have fire pits, bathhouses with 24-hour hot water, and laundry basins. The reception/common area is a great place to seek refuge on dank days. There's a playground for the kids. Each four-to-six-person cabin has a fully equipped kitchen, private bathroom, linens, towels and cleaning service. El Relincho also has stables and can organize horseback rides through the Río de las Vueltas valley. Av. San Martín 505. Tel: 54-2962-493007, URL: www.elchalten.com/elrelincho/imprimir.php. Updated: Jul 16, 2009.

Albergue y Camping Lago del Desierto

(CAMPING: $5.70, DORMS: $10) Albergue y Camping Lago del Desierto is a good option for shoestring travelers. This large house has four-bed dorms with shared bathrooms and six-bed dorms with private facilities. Travelers on a tighter budget can pitch their tents in the side yard and use the shared bathrooms. Small, twisted trees act as windbreaks. Guests can use the inside kitchen or the BBQ grills outside. Closed May - September. Lago del Desierto 152. Tel: 54-2962-493245. Updated: Jul 16, 2009.

Albergue Patagonia

(ROOMS: $11.50 – 14.50) Albergue Patagonia is a comfortable and clean hostel on the main drag, that caters to travelers and backpackers on a budget. The hostel has a fully equipped kitchen and dining area for guests, hot showers, a library, a book exchange, a reading loft, mountain bike rentals, and breakfast. The owners have lived in El Chaltén for years, and can give you advice about trekking and climbing activities. Rooms for three to six people are available with private or shared bathrooms. Lockers are available, but you have to bring your own lock. Av. San Martín 376. Tel: 54-2962-493019, URL: www.elchalten.com/patagonia/index.php. Updated: May 07, 2009.

Rancho Grande Hostel

(DORMS: $13, ROOMS: $37 – 45) Rancho Grande is one of the largest backpackers' hostel in El Chaltén. The front room is the restaurant-bar and, on the second level, there is a seating area with Internet for guests. Dorm rooms are worn and spare, but have bunk beds and built-in locker nooks. The common kitchen is small and basic. There are free movies every night, which are open to the general public as well. Rancho Grande is a Hostelling International member and is associated with Chaltén Travel. Av. San Martín 724. Tel: 49-3005, E-mail: ranchogrande@chaltentravel.com, URL: www.ranchograndehostel.com. Updated: Jul 16, 2009.

Albergue Hostel Pioneros del Valle

(DORM: $14.30) Pioneros del Valle is a new, gleaming backpacker hostel. This medium-sized albergue has six-bed dorms with private baths and lockers to safely stow away knapsacks. The kitchen/dining area is large and sunny. The common area has cable TV and free Internet. Hostel Pioneros del Valle is located right behind the Cal-Tur bus company office with which it is affiliated. In the low season, look for bus-and-accommodation specials. Av. San Martín 451. Tel: 54-2962-493079, E-mail: calturchalten@elchalten.net.ar, URL: www.guiachalten.com.ar/pioneros7index.htm. Updated: Jul 16, 2009.

MID-RANGE

Nothofagus Bed and Breakfast

(ROOMS: $28 – 70) The Nothafagus B&B, named after a native Patagonian tree, had just three rooms when it opened in 2001, but owners Eva and Gerardo recently expanded their cute eco-friendly home to accommodate more guests. The B&B now has seven rooms, four of them with shared bathrooms. Some rooms have a distinct log cabin feel with big blankets and wooden ceilings. Wake up refreshed to hot coffee, breads, and cake, and a view of the impressive Mt. Fitz Roy peaking over the hillside. Credit cards are not accepted. Prices include breakfast. Calle 10 no. 40. Tel: 54-2962-493087, E-mail: contacto@nothofagusbb.com.ar, URL: www.nothofagusbb.com.ar/en. Updated: Apr 23, 2009.

Hostería Thiamalú

(ROOMS: $37 – 52) Hostería Thiamalú is a small, family-run inn. Its five rooms are spacious and well-decorated. There are double, triple, and quadruple accommodations. Some have bunks. All rooms come with private bathroom with modern fixtures and 24-hour hot water. Individual heaters allow you to keep the rooms toasty. In the common sitting room, guests may share their hiking tales. During the winter months, Thiamalú provides meals for its guests. Lago del Desierto 99. Tel: 54-2962-493136, E-mail: info@thiamalu.com.ar, URL: www.thiamalu.com.ar. Updated: Jul 16, 2009.

HIGH-END

Kalenshen

(ROOMS: $100 – 140, CABINS: $225) The Kalenshen complex offers 17 rooms and six little cottages. The cottages house two to four people, and have mini-kitchens and outdoor BBQs. The hotel has handmade wood furniture, giving the place a rustic feel. Kalenshen's biggest claim to fame is its heated indoor pool—the only one in El Chaltén—though there is also an on-site restaurant, a gym, Internet. The staff can arrange tours and excursions. Terray 30. Tel: 54-2962-493108, E-mail: kalenshen@yahoo.com.ar, URL: www.kalenshen.com.ar/english. Updated: Apr 23, 2009.

Hosteria El Pilar

(ROOMS: $108 – $125) El Pilar is an estancia-style country house with ten simple yet comfortable rooms in the Chaltén countryside. As it is a secluded spot located near many trailheads, the hosteria has become popular with trekking groups looking for a quiet place to rest after a long day in the mountains. Curl up on a couch in front of the fireplace, take in the views of Mt. Fitz Roy and Aguja Poincenot, and enjoy the international and local cuisine in the restaurant. Camino a Lago del Desierto, Ruta 23. Tel: 54-2962-493002, E-mail: info@hosteriaelpilar.com.ar, URL: www.hosteriaelpilar.com.ar. Updated: Apr 23, 2009.

Estancia La Quinta

(ROOMS: $120 – 220) Estancia La Quinta is an old converted ranch house nestled against the foothills of Fitz Roy and Cerro Torre. The hotel, owned by the grand-daughter of the original pioneering family, retains its historic charm, but has been renovated with a fresh coat of soft yellow paint, and is surrounded by a lovely flower garden. While not fancy, the rooms are comfortable. La Quinta also has library with over 1,000 books on a variety of Patagonia themes. Open October – April. RP-23, south of El Chaltén (9301). Tel: 54-2962-493012, E-mail: info@estancialaquinta.com.ar, URL: www.estancialaquinta.com.ar/index.htm. Updated: Apr 29, 2009.

Hosteria Posada Lunajuim

(ROOMS: $121 – 178) The large restaurant-lounge area of the Posada Lunajuim is a comfortable spot to rest, read, or grab a drink and dinner. The thirty rooms feature the owner's personal art collection, and the beds all have cozy Egyptian cotton blankets and feather quilts. The hosteria can help to arrange hiking and sailing excursions. Prices include tax and breakfast. Trevisan 45. Tel: 54-2962-493047, E-mail: info@posadalunajuim.com.ar, URL: www.posadalunajuim.com.ar. Updated: Apr 23, 2009.

Los Cerros

(ROOMS: $218 – 473) The owners of Los Notros—a luxury lodge that overlooks the Perito Moreno glacier—have recently set up shop in El Chaltén, opening the most extravagant hotel in town with multi-night all-inclusive packages. Los Cerros is sleek yet cozy, with panoramic views of the river valley and mountainous peaks. The rooms are comfortable and rustically decorated. There is a TV room downstairs and WiFi is available. The on-site restaurant offers gourmet Patagonian cuisine, such as lamb, hare stew, fish, and wild game, paired with fine Argentine wines. The hotel can also arrange local excursions with a Los Glaciares National Park ranger, including horseback riding, half- or full-day hikes, sailing, ice walks and glacier treks. All-inclusive packages range from $816 to $3,280 per person for two to four nights. Calle 8 s/n. Tel: 54-2962-493182, E-mail: info@experiencepatagonia.com, URL: www.experiencepatagonia.com/en/lc_en. Updated: Apr 23, 2009.

Lo de Tomy

(HOUSE: $350, APARTMENTS: $30 – 80) Lo de Tomy rents a large, fully furnished house with a kitchen (includes help from a maid and cook), dining and living rooms, and three bedrooms with room for up to six people. You can also rent apartments, with single or double beds. All rentals have satellite TV, fireplaces, room service, Jacuzzis and WiFi. A lamb dinner is available for $25 per person. Discounts are available for long-term stays. Lionel Terray 140, Av. San Martin 480. Tel: 54-2962-493254, URL: lodetomy.com.ar. Updated: May 07, 2009.

Restaurants

There is an impressive array of restaurants open in the summer, from simple snack shops to bistros, most places feature typical Argentine fare, like milanesas, pastas, pizzas, parrillas and empanadas. Things to keep an eye out for include Patagonian lamb and trout. Shops also sell locally made products, like native-fruit marmalades, chocolates, sausages and cured meats. Most restaurants open only October – April. Updated: Jul 16, 2009.

Restaurant Aónikenk Chaltén

(ENTREES: $5.70) Restaurant Aónikenk Chaltén has homemade pastas prepared with interesting fillings like ricotta with nuts and sweet pepper with eggplant. Sauces are extra. Various types of milanesas are also on the menu, including one made of soy "steak." The specialties of the house, though, are lentils made with *chorizo* (sausage) and *polenta con osobuco* (grits with beef shanks). The thick steaks served are big enough to cover the plate. Fresh bread with delicious spreads, like blue cheese, accompanies each meal. Av. Güemes 23. Tel: 54-2962-493070. Updated: Jul 16, 2009.

La Cervecería Brew Pub and Resto

(ENTREES: $6.80) At La Cervecería Brew Pub and Resto you can try bräumeister Blanca's pilsner and bock beers made in-house. La Cervecería offers home-made pastas. The raviolis have unusual fillings, like the mediterraneo (eggplant, mozzarella, black olives and tomatoes), trout, salmon with mushrooms and lamb. The eatery has ten types of pizzas. Vegetarians will have no problem finding something to eat here. This small restaurant is comfortable and rustic and the bar has tractor-seat stools. Av. San Martín 320. Tel: 54-2962-493109. Updated: Jul 16, 2009.

Restaurant Rancho Grande

(LUNCH: $8.50) Restaurant Rancho Grande is popular with everyone, from tourists to locals. The service is fast and the restaurant has hamburgers and *milanesas* (breaded cutlets). Pastas come with an assortment of sauces. An order of French fries is big enough for two. During the week, there is a lunch special. For drinks, Rancho Grande has sodas, beers and wines. Av. San Martín 724. Tel: 54-2962-493005, E-mail: ranchogrande@chaltentravel.com, URL: www.ranchograndehostel.com. Updated: Jul 16, 2009.

Pangaea

(ENTREES: $10) Pastas are the bistro's specialty, with stuffed varieties like sorrentino de cordero. Unlike in other diners in El Chaltén, sauces are included in the price here. Beef, chicken milanesas and trout are also on the menu, and sides cost extra. For a lighter meal, try a roquefort and lamb empanada, or another type of savory pie. Pangaea also has vegetarian dishes. Lago del Desierto 330. Tel: 54-2962-493084.Updated: Jul 16, 2009.

Panadería Lo de Haydée

Panadería Lo de Haydée on El Chaltén's main street, has savory white and whole-grain breads, six different flavors of empanadas served hot out of the oven and a selection of quiches. For those with a sweet tooth, there are *facturas*, the delicious Danish pastries common in Argentina, as well as cakes, pies and other delights. Open daily 8 a.m. – 10 p.m. Av. Güemes 15. Tel: 54-2962-493272. Updated: Jul 16, 2009.

Rotissería Isadoro Quemeiquipan

Rotissería Isadoro Quemeiquipan is one of the cheapest places to eat in El Chaltén. The eatery has only two tables and several benches, but that doesn't stop budget travelers from stopping by to watch a movie from Juan's video library while he's in the kitchen preparing orders. The restaurant specializes in pizza, empanadas, milanesa sandwiches and other typical Argentine quick bites. Rotissería Isadoro Quemeiquipan is open well into the fall, but closes in the winter. Riquelme 142. Tel: 54-2962-493284. Updated: Jul 16, 2009.

The Shelter

The Shelter doesn't have much on the menu, just pizza and empanadas, but Locals say these are the best pizzas in town. All are baked in a brick oven. A cornucopia of toppings is available, guaranteeing meat eaters and vegetarians alike a fine and filling meal. The empanadas are just as good. Halvorsen 65. Tel: 54-2962-493259. Updated: Jul 16, 2009.

Boccato

Boccato is yet another one of El Chaltén's fast-food carry-out joints. The selection here includes *tortas* (calzones, or stuffed pizzas), milanesas, sandwiches and empanadas. You can get pizza by the pie or slice. Boccato also has something not seen on many menus: *super panchos*, or giant hot dogs.

It's a convenient place to pick up some food for a bus ride to Tres Lagos, Piedra Buena or Río Gallegos. Boccato is also the TPS (Trans Patagonia Services) depot. Av. San Martín 229, local 3. Tel: 54-2962-493356. Updated: Jul 16, 2009.

CHILEAN TIERRA DEL FUEGO

PORVENIR

45m	6,400	61

Rainbows frequently paint the sky above the Cordón de Boquerón hills in western Tierra del Fuego. The mythical gold at the end of the rainbow drew many, especially Croats and Chilotes (Chiloé Island natives) to this cold, rainy land. In 1879, Chilean Navy Lieutenant Ramón Serrano Montaner, while exploring the coast and land of Tierra del Fuego, discovered gold in the rivers. The news quickly spread. By 1887 over 200 prospectors were panning the waters, gathering dust and nuggets.

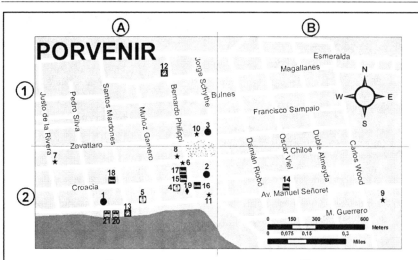

Activities ●

1 Casa de Miguel Radonich A2
2 Iglesia San Francisco de Sales A2
3 Museo Provincial Fernando Cordero A1

Eating 🍴

4 Club Croata A2
5 Restaurant de Turismo Patagonia A2

Services ★

6 Banco del Estado A2
7 Carabineros A2
8 Correos A2
9 Hospital Dr. Shamorro B2
10 Oficina de Turismo A1
11 Supermercado Paulina A2

Shopping 🎁

12 Artesanía Kore A1
13 Teresa Muñoz Araya A2

Sleeping 🛏

14 Hostal El Chispa B2
15 Hotel Central A2
16 Residencial Dalmacia A2
17 Hotel y Restaurante Rosas A2
18 Hosteria y Restaurante Yendegaia A2

Tours ◆

19 Cordillera Darwin Expediciones A2

Transportation 🚌

20 Aerovías DAP A2
21 Transbordador Austral Broom A2

To accomodate the rush, newcomers founded Porvenir on the eastern shores of the Straits of Magellan. Porvenir, which means future, reflected the bright hopes of all those involved in those feverish times. By the end of the 19th century, however, the rivers seemed played out. People either decided to settle down or move on to more golden pastures. That is until 1903 when some Californians arrived. They thought that the special dredging equipment used by the 49ers in their own state could help extract more gold out of the Cordón de Boquerón.

The fever peaked again between 1906 and 1908. But the high cost of transporting the machinery to and across the wind-swept, cold Land of Fires could not be paid off by the meager finds.

Some hardy souls yet battle the elements out in those lone hills, searching for a fist-full of gold dust or a nugget to make their futures brighter. The town's economy is now based on fish processing and tourism. Some journeyers come to traverse the Ruta de Oro, see the abandoned dredges and talk with modern-day prospectors. Others visit the many estancias—some of which are still working.

Some visitors come to fish in the Río Cordón, while others are drawn to the trekking in the Cordillera Darwin, Parque Nacional Alberto de Agostini or other reserves. Birdwatching at Laguna Nacional Laguna de los Cines is the pot at the end of the rainbow for many others.

It isn't easy getting out into the wild here—and you should book a tour unless you have your own car or bike. In the warmer summer months, adventuresome, well-equipped visitors can walk the island's dirt roads.

SOUTHERN PATAGONIA

With its simple pleasures and interesting history, the city of Porvenir is a popular escape for Puntarenses. Visitors come to walk along the costanera and to see flamingos, swans and other birds that rest in the bay. Boat tours into Bahía de Porvenir offer the chance to watch dolphins playing in the frigid waters.

The town's Croatian and Chilote founders left their unique imprints on both the town's architecture, and their culinary artistry. For a lesson on the indigenous, mining and colonization history of Tierra del Fuego, spend an hour in the local musem. For an extended visit into the wilds, or just to soak in the small-town atmosphere, Porvenir is a destination worth hopping on the ferry for. Updated: May 22, 2009.

When to Go

Tourism services are in full swing during the summer months from October to April when days are longer and warmer, though winds are strong and it may rain at any moment.

Once the summer is over, the weather begins to wear the cold cloak of winter, and tourism-dependent businesses close. But flamingos and swans still visit Porvenir's sheltered bay. Porvenir has a full calendar of events. Its six-part car racing is only one of the hot competitions here. Updated: May 22, 2009.

Month	Event
January	31—The largest asado (BBQ) in Tierra del Fuego
February	6-7—Fiesta Costumbrista, paying tribute to Porvenir's rich ethnic history, and the René Schneider auto circuit race
March/ April	Semana Santa car race
May	21—International regatta in Bahía de Porvenir
June	19-20—Aniversario de Porvenir, celebrating the town's founding, with another car race

Month	Event
August	13-15—Yet another auto carrera, this time in honor of the *Hermandad Chileno-Argentina*, Chilean-Argentine Brotherhood
September	17-19—Patagonia basketball tournament, regattas on Porvenir Bay and equestrian competitions
October	9-10—Porvenir's fifth auto race of the year 12—International Nautical Festival
November	14-16 — Raid Náutico Internacional, a 170-kilometer (102-mile) float on the Río Grande
December	4-5—The final auto racing competition of the year 12-13—Regional Rodeo Championship

Getting To and Away From Porvenir

BY LAND

Although there are roads from Porvenir to other parts of Tierra del Fuego, including to Ushuaia, Argentina, little public transportation exists. The only bus service is to Cerro Sombrero (Monday, Wednesday, Friday 5 p.m., $7, 1.5 hours), but there are few buses to other destinations. For any other destinations, you will have to go back to Punta Arenas.

If you have your own car or bike, you can cross into Argentina at Paso San Sebastián (all year) or Paso Bellavista (November – April 15). In Porvenir you'll find a Copec gas station, mechanics and a tire repair shop.

Transbordador Austral Broom (URL: www.tabsa.cl) and **Aerovías DAP** (www.aeroviasdap.cl) share an office. Monday – Saturday 9 a.m. – 1 p.m., 3 – 5 p.m. Av. Señoret and Santos Mardones.

BY PLANE

Aeropuerto de Porvenir is 5 kilometers (3 mi) northwest of the city. **DAP** provides transportation there ($3). **Aerovías DAP**

SOUTHERN PATAGONIA

has flights Monday – Saturday Punta Arenas – Porvenir (2 – 3 schedules daily, $76 round trip, 12 minutes).

BY BOAT

The main way to get to Porvenir is by ferry from Punta Arenas. The port is at Bahía Chilota, 5 kilometers (3 mi) from town. **Transbordadora Austral Broom** runs the ferry Cruz Australis Punta Arenas-Porvenir (all year long, Tuesday – Sunday, passenger $9.80, motorcycle $18, car $63). You can purchase tickets at Restaurant Pingüino, to the right of the loading dock. Schedules change, so check the webpage (www.tabsa. cl). Updated: May 22, 2009.

Getting Around

The town is small enough to get around on foot. To get to the ferry port at Bahía Chilota, catch a *combi* (minibus) from the plaza about an hour before the boat's scheduled departure ($1.60) or share a cab ($6 per vehicle) from the plaza or the taxi stand on Phillipi, near Señoret.

There is no public transport to sites outside Porvenir. Hiring a driver costs at least $250 per vehicle. **Hotel Rosas** has a car rental agency (Tel: 56-61-580088). Updated: May 22, 2009.

Safety

Porvenir is a safe town. If driving into the interior of the island, be sure to carry an extra tire, gas and other necessities. In fall and spring the weather is unpredictable, so be sure to prepare for cold and wet conditions if camping, hiking or biking at these times. Updated: May 22, 2009.

Services

TOURISM

Oficina de Turismo, located in the museum, has a variety of brochures about the town (ask for the one on historical architecture) and the island. Open Monday – Thursday 8 a.m. – 5 p.m., Friday 8 a.m. – 4 p.m., weekends and holidays 10:30 a.m. – 1:30 p.m., 3 p.m. – 5 p.m. Zavattaro 402. Tel: 56-61-581800, E-mail: museo@municipalidad-deporvenir.cl / museo@muniporvenir.cl. The **carabineros** (immigration and police) are on Chiloé 880 and Justo de la Rivera. Tel: 56-61-761171.

MONEY

Banco Estado has an ATM that accepts MasterCard and Cirrus, and exchanges U.S. dollars and euros (Monday – Friday 9 a.m. – 1 p.m. Phillipi, between Croacia and Chiloé). **Supermercado Paulina** changes money (Señoret 346), as do other businesses, like the call center on Phillipi.

KEEPING IN TOUCH

Correos: Monday – Friday 9 a.m. – 1 p.m., 3 – 6 p.m. Chiloé and Phillipi. An unnamed **phone** center has both international call service ($1 per minute) and Internet ($1.60 per hour). Open daily 10:30 a.m. – 1 p.m., 4:30 p.m. – 8:30 p.m. Phillipi 277. The **public library** provides a half-hour free Internet. Monday – Saturday 8 a.m. – 7 p.m. Muñoz Gamero and Zavatarro.

MEDICAL

Hospital Dr. Shamorro (Señoret and Wood. Tel: 56-61-580034). Porvenir has no pharmacies, except for the one at the hospital.

SHOPPING

On Avenida Señoret, along the coast, is a pod of buildings that forms the local crafts market. **Agrupación de Artesanos Haalchin** is a collective of artisans crafting Selk'nam dolls, wood carvings and masks, among other items (Tuesday – Sunday 11:15 a.m. – 4:30 p.m. Tel: 56-61-581271).

Next door **Teresa Muñoz Araya** sells jackets, sweaters, hats and other knitted wear. All are made from natural-color wool from Tierra del Fuego (Monday – Saturday noon – 6 p.m. Home workshop: Los Cisnes 0429). **Artesanía Kore** is the home workshop of Gastón Pérez who makes masks and replicas of Selk'nam utilitarian ware out of lenga and whale bone (corner Magallanes and Phillipi, Av. Señoret s/n and Santos Mardones). Updated: Jul 02, 2009.

Things to See and Do

Porvenir has enough simple treasures so that you'll want to spend at least an afternoon in this quiet, bayside town. The village has distinctive Fuegian architecture, reflecting the predominant influence of the Croatian and Chilote immigrant population. A walk along the costanera makes for a pleasant outing, as it brings natural and human history together. A visit to **Museo Provincial Fernando Cordero Rusque** is also high on the list. If you have an extra day to spare, walk out to **Monumental Natural Laguna de los Cisnes** for some prime birdwatching, or take a boat tour of Bahía de Porvenir to see dolphins.

SOUTHERN PATAGONIA

Rounding the Horn

In 1929, a 24-year-old Irving McClure Johnson went aboard the Peking with a motion-picture camera and the brave, stubborn, half-suicidal goal of rounding Cape Horn. The amateur filmmaker and explorer from Maine—depicted in home footage climbing telephone poles and wrestling friends in preparation for his Jack London life at sea—climbed, camera-in-hand, high into the ship's rigging while the Peking pitched and shook through nearly fatal Patagonian storms. He could've easily been killed, the ship wrecked, sunk, never heard from again. But he survived—and got some amazing footage. This will probably not be your experience aboard one of the cruise ships of Cruceros Austral, which operates three and four-day luxury cruises through these same adventurous waters between Punta Arenas and Ushuaia.

Since its discovery in 1578, more than 800 ships have been lost attempting to round the Horn. The winds at these latitudes (56° south) can literally blow around the world without encountering land, building to frightening strength. This has earned the lower latitudes nicknames like "the roaring forties," "the furious fifties," and "the screaming sixties." Waves in this region, fed by the winds and rolling likewise free of interruption, become shortened and heightened as they hit the shallow waters near Cape Horn, making them all the more dangerous to early sailing ships. The much-feared "rogue waves" here can tower to 30 meters (100 ft). And then, of course, there's the freezing temperatures and ice to deal with. But the tragic history of the region is somehow part of its magnetism, and the tour guides aboard one of the three pocket cruisers—the M/V Mare Australis, M/V Via Australis and the newly-unveiled M/V Stella Australis—don't let you forget it.

Aboard a Cruceros Australis cruise ship, passengers can soak up this history and thrilling scenery more or less free of its dangers. The 120-passenger Mare, 140-passenger Via, and 210-passenger Stella cradle guests in plush cabins with gourmet meals, an open bar and a library, among other amenities. Prices for the shorter cruise from Ushuaia to Punta Arenas start at $1,050 low season (Sept, Oct, March, April) and $1,330 high season (Nov. - March). For the four-day trip in the other direction, prices start at $1,930 low season and $2,300 high season. Check the website for discounts and special offers. The cruise, which runs between September and April, passes through the Strait of Magellan and the Beagle Channel, places named for some of the world's greatest explorations: the Flat Earth-shattering circumnavigation by Ferdinand Magellan in 1519, and the 1831 voyage of the HMS Beagle that eventually carried Charles Darwin to the Galapagos Islands.

Ships stop frequently to shuttle passengers ashore in zodiacs so they can explore damp Magellanic forests, approach towering blue glaciers, observe colonies of Magellanic Penguins and elephant seals, and hike around the 425-meter (1,394-ft) rock promontory of Cape Horn, the absolute southernmost point in the world short of Antarctica. The guides on these expeditions are knowledgeable and eager to share, possessing a bit of the zeal, or lunacy, of Irving Johnson and other sailors who have risked their lives in these seas simply to say They Did It. This is the draw of Cruceros Australis, after all: to peer safely into the world of daring and exploration, into an icy-bearded past when reckless men fought against the cruelest nature had to offer; to sit comfortably on deck amid the glaciers and wind and say, "Those guys must have been insane."

Porvenir also serves as a convenient base for touring the surrounding countryside, such as around the Circuito Histórico Cultural, the Ruta de Oro, or Petróleo. Longer expeditions can be arranged from here, like fishing at Lago Blanco, Río Cordón and other great trout holes. Visitors can also try trekking in the Cordillera Darwin, Parque Nacional Alberto de Agostini and other reserves. Updated: May 25, 2009.

Monumento Nacional de los Cisnes

Just five kilometers (3 mi) north of Porvenir is Monumento Nacional de los Cisnes, a 25-hectare reserve. This lagoon is an important spot for aquatic and shore birds, such as the Chilean flamingo and the black-necked swan for which it is named, and the rare Magellanic plover, whose population here is one of the largest in the world. The lagoon's islets are important nesting grounds for the Coscoroba Swan, Imperial Shag, Black-faced Ibis, Chilean Skua, Kelp Gull, Flying Steamer Duck and Black-necked Swan. In all, you can see over 40 dozen types of water and land birds here.

To get there, take the road heading to Bahía Azul. Or head to the cemetery, toward the airfield (3 km/1.8 mi). Just before the Laguna Chica farm is a footpath that will give you direct access to the lagoon. The path goes through private property. On the way, along the stream beds, you can spot other species not found at the lake, like the Sedge Wren and the White-tufted Grebe. Updated: Jul 07, 2009.

Circuito Histórico Cultural

The Circuito Histórico Cultural is a journey through the many facets of Feugian history, from ancient indigenous sites to modern-day gold prospectors.

The road departs Porvenir toward Cordón Baquedano. At this mountain range's highest point, 500 meters (1,625 ft), you can view the Straits of Magellan. The road winds past abandoned gold dredges from the early-20th century explorations and the sod huts of *pirquineros*, where you can see today's gold hunters yet panning the streams for the precious metal.

The road comes out to the international Ruta Y-71, which leads to the ruins of Puerto Nuevo, the port that served Estancia Caleta Josefina. Just past Puerto Nuevo is the estancia and Onaisín, where several buildings and the community cemetery remain.

At kilometer 110 on this road is the Marazzi site, excavated by French archaeologist Annette Laming-Emperaire in 1965. This location was used over 9,000 years ago by the original inhabitants of the land. The only way to follow the Circuito Histórico Cultural is by way of tour or in private car or bike. A hired car from Porvenir would start at $200.

The circuit as far as Marazzi is 115 kilometers (69 mi) and takes about 5 hours. If you are driving, be sure you leave with a full tank of gas. There is a gas station on the Argentine side of the border at Paso San Sebastián. If you continue along Ruta Y-71 to Paso San Sebastián on the Argentine border, you can visit Estancia Sebastián and its cemetery. Twenty kilometers (12 mi) southwest of San Sebastián is the 10,280 – 11,800 year old Tres Arroyos archaeological site. Updated: May 29, 2009.

Onaisín and Estancia Caleta Josefina

Onaisín was the town associated with Estancia Caleta Josefina and was therefore part of its extensive holdings, which also included Pueblo Nuevo. The estancia was founded by the Sociedad Explotadora de Tierra del Fuego as a sheep ranch in 1893. Caleta Josefina was one of the most successful ranches in Tierra del Fuego. Its first administrator was New Zealander Alexander A. Cameron.

Today, all that remain are the health post and a large *galpón* (storehouse), probably the oldest in the region. At the far edge of Onaisín, on the left side of the road, is the estancia's cemetery, locally also called the *cementerio inglés*, English cemetery. The graveyard was declared a national monument in 1976.

The only way to visit Onaisín and Estancia Caleta Josefina is on tour or with your own means of transportation (car or bike). A hired car from Porvenir would cost at least $200. From Porvenir take Ruta Y-71 along Bahía Inútil, toward Paso Fronteriz. Updated: May 29, 2009.

Lago Blanco

Arguably, the best trout fishing in the world, is in Tierra del Fuego. On the south side of the island there is a 5,000-hectare lake and typical Fuegian forest. This is Lago Blanco, where beavers build their homes, myriad types of waterfowl rest and wild horses roam. The landscape is dominated by mountains. You can kayak the crystalline waters; this is also a fly fisher's paradise, with brown and rainbow trout weighing 2 – 14 kilograms (4.5 – 31 lbs).

The only way to get to Lago Blanco is on tour or with private transportation (car or bike). If driving, be sure you leave with a full tank of gas. Follow Ruta Y-71 along Bahía Inútil to Km 103, then right 47 kilometers (28.2 mi) to the village of Camerón, from where it is another 74 kilometers (44.5 mi).

The best time to catch trucha cafe (also called *trucha marrón*, brown trout) is February – March; *trucha arcoiris* (rainbow trout) fishing is best June – July. In the center of

SOUTHERN PATAGONIA

the lake is Isla Victoria, where the *Club de Pesca y Caza de Cerro Sombrero* (Fishing and Hunting Club of Cerro Sombrero) has a lodge. Camping is also possible around the lake. Updated: Jun 10, 2009.

Museo Provincial Fernando Cordero Rusque

(ADMISSION: adults $1, children free) Museo Provincial Fernando Cordero Rusque is an impressive village museum. It has a half-dozen galleries that cover the history of Tierra del Fuego. Stuffed fauna—especially of birds and the skeleton of a marine elephant—are one surprise here. A section on modern history covers the exploration of the Straits of Magellan, the Salesian missionary work (including the instruments of the Isla Dawson indigenous children's band), gold exploitation and Porvenir's immigrant founders. Other rooms focus on the Selk'nam people who once wandered these lands. Treasures include archaeological remains, an explanation of the Hain initiation ceremony, and a naturally mummified body dating from 1424 AD, found on Isla Tres Magotes. On the grounds is Tierra del Fuego's first astronomic observatory and other relics. Open Monday – Thursday 8 a.m. – 5 p.m., Friday 8 a.m., weekends and holidays 10:30 a.m., 3 p.m. Zavattaro 402. Tel: 56-61-581800, E-mail: museo@municipalidad-deporvenir.cl / museo@muniporvenir.cl. Updated: May 29, 2009.

Costanera Walk

Walking along the coastal road can help you uncover a bit about the natural and human history of Porvenir. The old wharf at the entrance to town is a favorite hangout for gulls, cormorants and other seabirds. Strolling up Avenida Señoret, you will find several of the village's first buildings. On the right, at the foot of Calle Justo de la Rivera, is Vicente Camelio's house (1930s), the first mechanic's garage in Porvenir and now the Club Volantes de Porvenir. On the corner of Señoret and Silva, to the left, is one of the oldest edifices, home of Miguel Radonich and Tierra del Fuego's first cinema (1900-05). On the beach is a cluster of artisan shops. Along the seashore you'll also find a wooden sculpture of a Selk'nam hunter, carved by Richard Yasic Israel (1999). The Selk'nam called Bahía de Porvenir "*Karkanke*," meaning Low Waters. Across the avenue is the Club Croata, built by Simón Cvitanic (1926).

As the road begins to curve with the bay, the Paseo de las Américas begins. In Parque Croata (formerly Parque Yugoslavia) is a white, globe-shaped monument erected in 1983 to honor the people who came to this promised land. On the sea side of the boulevard are Plazas de las Banderas and de Recuerdo with an odd assortment of old carts, trucks, ship parts and other implements of the early 20th century. Just south of the obelisk, on the left side of Santa María, is the house of the Mariano Mimica Mimica family, who were some of Porvenir's most important citizens. The house dates to 1920.

Avenida Santa María continues along the coast of Bahía de Porvenir. The stretch called Laguna de los Croatas (Laguna de los Yugoslavos) is frequented all year long by waterfowl. In winter its possible to spot the Chilean Flamingo and the Black-necked Swan. Also keep an eye out for dolphins.

A signposted road out of town will take you to the top of Cerro Mirador, from where you can view the town, the Straits of Magellan and the Cordillera Darwin. The main dirt road hugs the side of the bay to the lone Casa de Piedra, built at the end of the 19th century by Natalio Foretic and used to process lime.

Cerro Mirador is a 20–30 minute walk, one way, from town. Casa de Piedra, (2 km/1.2 mi) is an hour one way. Updated: Jun 10, 2009.

Porvenir's Historical Architecture

Porvenir has good examples of Fuegian architecture. Croatians and Chilotes colonized this bay and created the style. A few of the buildings date from between 1900 and 1905, though most are from the 1920s and '30s, when sheep farming was bringing in a lot of money for certain residents. Several buildings have now found a new life as hotels. Some of the more noteworthy edifices are as follows:

Iglesia San Francisco de Sales (1900-05)—The design of the original village church was inspired by Monseñor Fagnano, who founded the parish in 1898 (Ca. Croacia, between Phillipi and Schythe).

Casa de Miguel Radonich (1900-05)—One of Chile's pioneering filmmaker families operated Tierra del Fuego's first movie house, until 1945, from their house. (Av. Señoret and Calle Silva).

Club Croata (1926)—Built by Simón Cvitanic, this is the social center for the descendants of Croatian immigrants and one of Porvenir's finest restaurants (Av. Señoret, between Gamero and Phillipi).

Casa de Piedra (late 19th century)—This is Porvenir's oldest edifice. It was here that owner Natalio Foretic made lime (*cal*) that was used in building construction in this town and in Punta Arenas (far side of bay, 2 km/1.2 mi southwest of Porvenir).

Ask for the historical architecture brochure-map at the tourism office. Updated: Jun 10, 2009.

Tours
Only one tour agency operates in Porvenir, and only during the high season: **Agencia de Viajes Cordillera Darwin**. The agency has trips on the Ruta de Oro, into Cordón Baquedano, to estancias and other destinations. Av. Señoret and Phillipi.

At Bahía Chilota you'll find **Cordillera Darwin Expediciones**, which in addition to the tour agency, organizes fishing trips to Río Cóndor, treks in Parque Nacional Alberto de Agostini and dolphin-watching in Bahía de Porvenir Bahia. Chilota s/n. Tel. / Fax: 56-61-580167, Cel: 56-9-8886380, E-mail: gerencia@cordilleradarwin.com / expediciones@cordilleradarwin.com, URL: www.cordilleradarwin.com.

Tour operators in Punta Arenas also offer trips to Porvenir. Updated: May 25, 2009.

Lodging
Even though Porvenir has a dozen hotels, lodging can be hard to find. In the summer months, tourists fill rooms soon after the ferry arrives. Advance reservations are highly recommended. Once autumn comes, cheaper options are occupied by workers.

If you are visiting between the autumn to spring, expect to pay a bit more for a room. Some families rent rooms in their homes. Check with the tourism office for more information on lodging options, or where camping is allowed. Updated: May 29, 2009.

Residencial Dalmacia
(ROOMS: $10 per person) The majestic chalet that used to be the home of the Vincente Mimica family is now Residencial Dalmacia. This hostel has large rooms and those on the back side of the house have commanding views of Bahía de Porvenir. Residencial Dalmacia is often booked solid by work crews, especially outside the summer holidays, so call ahead. Croacia 469. Tel: 56-61-580008. E-mail: angelacardenas1945@hotmail.com. Updated: Jun 10, 2009.

Hostal El Chispa
(ROOMS: $14 per person) Once upon a time El Chispa was the house that Nicolás Sieckovic built. It later was home for many decades to the first *Compañía de Bomberos* (fire department). Since the beginning of the millennium, the hostel has played host to tourists. From autumn to spring, it is frequently occupied by work crews. El Chispa also has an inexpensive restaurant. Señoret and Viel. Tel: 56-61-580054. Updated: Jun 10, 2009.

Hotel Central
(ROOMS: $26 – 48) Hotel Central is one of Porvenir's most established hostels. Widower Don Pedro continues with the tradition that he and his wife established many years ago. On the outside, the inn is rather plain-looking, but inside you find the warmth of a family home. The rooms are a bit small, but comfortable and warm. Each comes with its own bathroom (with tub) and cable TV. The simple breakfast is served in the dining room downstairs. Phillipi 298. Tel: 56-61-580077. Updated: Jun 10, 2009.

Hostería Yendegaia
(ROOMS: $30 – 50) Yendegaia is another one of Porvenir's historic houses— this one being the mansion of Croatian immigrant Doimo Tafra Popovic. The house was built in 1926, and has since become an inn. Owner Vicente Couve, son of the famed Chilean nature photographer Enrique Couve, has seven spacious rooms which are warmly decorated, the beds draped with down comforters. Each room has its own large, private bath. Vicente is a wealth of information about Patagonian and Fuegian lore. Hostería Yendegaia also has a good restaurant. Croacia 702. Tel: 56-61-581919. E-mail: info@hosteriayendegaia.com. Updated: May 29, 2009.

Hotel Rosas
(ROOMS: $36 – 48) The front façade of Hotel Rosas makes it seem just like another run-of-the-mill hostel, but it is Porvenir's largest and most complete hotel. Each room is spacious and simply decorated, with private bathrooms, 24-hour hot water, cable TV and other amenities. The owner is very knowledgeable about the attractions

SOUTHERN PATAGONIA

in and around Porvenir, can arrange tours and rents cars. The adjacent restaurant is also very popular. Phillipi 296. Tel: 56-61-580088. E-mail: hotelrosas@chile.com. Updated: Jun 10, 2009.

Restaurants

The restaurant scene in Porvenir is quite sparse. Some of the best places to eat are in the town's hotels. Few independent bistros exist. Seafood is a big item on the menus, at surprisingly inexpensive prices. Be sure to try *centolla*, or Southern king crab. Many places offer daily specials on weekdays, which are generally more expensive than on the mainland. Several small general stores sell provisions. Updated: Jun 10, 2009.

Club Croata

(ENTREES: from $4.40) Club Croata is the meeting place for Porvenir's Croatian community, though anyone is welcomed to partake of the delicious food. Constructed by Simón Cvitanic in 1926, this center has a comfortable, homey feeling with bay views. No daily special is served here, all is à la carte. *Plato de fondo* (entrée) portions are generous enough for two people to share, and *entrada* (appetizer) portions make for a nice light meal. Try the house specialties, such as *lengua* (tongue) or the truly exquisite *Triología Austral*, crêpes stuffed with shellfish, oysters and king crab. Open Tuesday – Sunday 11 a.m. – 3 p.m., 7 p.m. – 10:30 p.m. Señoret 542. Tel: 56-61-580053. Updated: Jun 10, 2009.

Restaurant de Turismo Patagonia

(ENTREES: $8) Restaurant de Turismo Patagonia has the simple, understated elegance of a small village restaurant. Pull up a folding chair at one of the wooden tables with woven cloths and prepare to enjoy traditional Chilean dishes. Seafood and fish are big on the menu, but so are beef and chicken. The "dessert" is the view of Bahía de Porvenir. Open daily noon – 2 p.m., 7 p.m. – 9 p.m. Señoret 688. Updated: Jun 10, 2009.

Restaurant, Hostería Yendegaia

(DAILY SPECIAL: $10, ENTREES from $8) Hostería Yendegaia not only does a first-class job of providing lodging for travelers coming to Porvenir, but also in feeding them. The soups and main dishes have light, delicate flavors. The house wine is of good quality and served in a full goblet. A three-course special is offered daily. The dining experience is made even more pleasant by the light and warmth of the dining hall, and Vicente's exemplary service. Open noon – 3 p.m., 8 p.m. – 10:30 p.m. Croacia 702. Tel: 56-61-581919. E-mail: info@hosteriayendegaia.com. Updated: May 26, 2009.

Restaurant, Hotel Rosas

(SET LUNCH: $8.60, ENTREES from $8) Hotel Rosas restaurant is a popular place to eat for both locals and tourists alike. Its menu features typical Chilean surf and turf culinary fare. On weekdays a three-course (appetizer or soup, main dish, dessert) luncheon special is served; the drinks are extra. In the evening only à la carte dishes are offered. Open daily noon – 2:30 p.m., 7 p.m. – 11 p.m. Phillipi 296. Tel: 56-61-580088. E-mail: hotelrosas@chile.com. Updated: May 25, 2009.

NAVARINO ISLAND

 172 m   2,000   54-2901

Isla Navarino is a small island in the Beagle Channel, off Tierra Del Fuego, and is home to the southernmost city in the world, Puerto Williams (in spite of Ushaia's competing claims to that title). Founded in 1953 as a naval base, Puerto Williams still has an obvious military presence. Every year the island has 8,000 visitors, but 6,000 of them come on the cruise ships, usually only for the day. Isla Navarino is a still a wild place.

It is divided by the Dientes de Navarino mountain range into northern and southern regions. The southern half of the island is very exposed to the strong Antarctic winds and is a boggy, muddy, swampy area. The northern part is more sheltered. Isla Navarino is also a very pristine and remote area where you can encounter snowfall even in summer; it's a real paradise for trekking. Updated: Jul 02, 2009.

Getting To and Away From Navarino Island

Whether by air or sea, just getting to Isla Navarino is part of the adventure.

BY PLANE

The Patagonian airline **DAP** flies a 20-odd seat Twin Otter seaplane from Punta Arenas to Puerto Williams daily in the summer. The flight over Tierra del Fuego and the Strait of Magellan, which lasts 1.25 hours, is incredibly scenic, and oddly enough, the least expensive option, costing around $211 round-trip. The airport in Puerto Williams is five kilometers (3 mi) northwest of the town (Tel: 56-61-621109). A DAP representative is available in Centro Comercial. Note that flights fill up very quickly. DAP in Punta Arenas: O'Higgins 891. Tel: 56-61-616100, E-mail: ventas@aeroviasdap.cl, URL: www.aeroviasdap.cl.

BY BOAT
Punta Arenas-based **Transbordadora Austral Broom** (URL: www.tabsa.cl) operates a weekly passenger ferry to Puerto Williams, a 36-hour trip through the Straits of Magellan and along the Beagle Channel. Though the accommodation and services are spartan, the passing scenery of hanging glaciers and mountains truly convey an end-of-the-world sensation. At the end of each month the ferry continues on to Puerto Toro, a small settlement with no services, yet even further south than Puerto Williams. The ferry returns the same day. In Puerto Williams, ask in the Centro Comercial for availability and schedules. Tickets cost $175 – 210, children pay half price.

Another way to travel from Punta Arenas to Puerto Williams on Isla Navarino is with the Navy's monthly boat. Check at the naval base for further details.

Ushuaia Boating in Ushuaia, Argentina, has regular zodiac service to Isla Navarino October – March or April. The trajectory leads from Ushuaia to Puerto Navarino (40 minutes, immigration), followed by a minibus to Puerto Williams (daily, one way $130, round trip $240) (in Ushuaia: **Muelle Turístico**, E-mail: ushuaiaboating@argentin.com). Inquire at **Hostal Coiron** (Ricardo Maragano 168) in Puerto Williams.

From Ushuaia, you can also check at the **Muelle Club Nautico** and try to hitch a ride on a private yacht to Isla Navarino or the other South Atlantic Islands. Very few boats travel between the two ports from June to August. Updated: Jul 07, 2009.

Trekking the Dientes Circuit
The Isla Navarino Dientes Circuit, the southernmost trekking opportunity in the world, is miles beyond any ordinary trekking experience. For the serious hiker, the five-day Dientes Circuit is a chance to experience unique terrain at what is literally the last scrap of land before the legendary Cape Horn and Antarctic Sea. The route winds through broken mountains and landscapes that come from the floor of the ocean and offer unparalleled views stretching as far as Cape Horn.

Because of the difficulty of the route and the distance of Isla Navarino from the beaten path, the Dientes Circuit receives a fraction of Chile's annual trekking visitors. The route was developed in the early 1990s and marked with the Chilean numbered trail marker system in early 2001, but it is still far from a well-marked path. The 38 trail points are spread over 53 kilometers, with four significant passes to cross and a maze of beaver ponds and dams to negotiate in the valleys between.

To trek the Dientes, you need to be self-reliant and capable at route finding, as there is a good chance you will not see another soul on the circuit. You should not underestimate the weather. Strong winds sweep up from the white continent and make the passes, especially the final one, Paso Virginia, very dangerous. Blasts of wind strong enough to knock a heavily loaded trekker from their feet are not uncommon and come without warning. Also, there are no refugios on the route and there is no entrance fee to pay. You are only required to check in with the carabineros in Puerto Williams.

The trailhead is three kilometers away from the village. It is strongly advised to follow the route from Puerto Williams, as the markers are only painted on one side. Since the markers are *cairns* (rock piles), individual trail markers are often difficult to distinguish from their surroundings without the red signage painted on them.

The Dientes Circuit is broken into five stages, each stage requiring about five hours to complete. With the long daylight hours of the southern hemisphere summer, some might be tempted to combine two stages into one day.

While it is possible to do the circuit in four days, it would involve a day where you have to climb two passes, or a very long final day, descending from the nearly 900-meter Paso Virginia back to sea level, over a distance of 23 kilometers. The route markers end more than 300 meters above sea level, looking down on Bahia Virginia, and from there, you must negotiate the cow pastures and calafate bushes to the coastal road, then hike the final 8 kilometers of pavement back to Puerto Williams. Passing trucks will often stop for trekkers on the final stretch. Otherwise, it's about a two-hour walk back to Puerto Williams. Updated: Jun 15, 2009.

SOUTHERN PATAGONIA

PUERTO WILLIAMS

 172 m  2,000   54-2901

If you are looking for the end of the world, Puerto Williams is the place. The largest settlement on Isla Navarino and the only one with services, Puerto Williams is the most austral town in the world, less than 1,000 kilometers from Antarctica (Ushuaia, 60 km to the west, on the Northern shore of the Beagle Channel, can, semantically speaking, claim to be the southernmost "city").

The nomadic Yaghan people populated the region as far back as 7,500 years ago, but today's Puerto Williams is a by-product of Chile's anxious desire to protect its Antarctic claim from Argentine intrusion. Despite the visible military presence—the town's real estate is dominated by white military housing and administrative buildings—this capital of Chile's Antarctic province has grown since its founding in 1953 to include a core of permanent residents supported by fishing, services, public service and tourism.

Even in the high season the number of tourists is limited—if you arrive between May and October you will likely be the only tourist in town—and the place retains a charm and innocence you would expect from such isolation. If you are arriving by boat, locals will send for immigration and customs officials when you arrive, with handshakes and smiles.

Cows and horses wander the streets, locals sell empanadas (try **Jacqueline's Place**, 216 Piloto Pardo. 4:30 – 12 p.m. Monday – Friday), and the one plumber, **Patricio**, does triple duty as fisherman and trekking guide (gabydayca@ hotmail.com, trekking from 50,000 pesos per day). Expat adventurers, Antarctic explorers, circumnavigating sailors, and hardened fisherman mingle at the **Micalvi Yacht club**, fashioned out of a half-sunken old ship that doubles as a colorful dive bar (Seno Lauta Costanera s/n. Tel. 56-61-620042, open after 9 p.m.; in winter, check notices on the door as it may be closed).

The stunning cloudscapes of the epic Southern sky, the snowy mountains lining the Beagle Channel, and the ominous peaks known as Dientes de Navarino surround Puerto Williams and give it what is arguably the most impressive natural scenery in the Southern Americas. The island's wilderness attracts intrepid trekkers who come to do the four- to five-day, 53-kilometer Dientes de Navarino Circuit and the

7-day, 41-kilometer Lago Windhond Circuit. The trailheads are easily accessible by continuing along the road past the Altar of the Virgin, at the Western edge of town. Both require a high level of fitness, trekking experience, and complete supply of food for the duration of the trip. Because they are infrequently traveled, those fortunate and fit enough to complete them cite the Navarino circuits as a more rewarding alternative to the famed Torres del Paine circuit. **Denny at Fuegia** (Patrullero Ortiz 049. Tel: 56-61-621251), who has worked with the Chilean government to map the island, has the most intimate knowledge of the trails and conditions.

Less experienced hikers have plenty of options as well, including the Cerro Bandera (altitude 610 m, accessible via the beginning of the Dientes Circuit), which offers breathtaking views of the Beagle Channel and the Dientes, the Cascada Las Bronces waterfall (trailhead 2 km west of town), and the guided trails of the ecoreserve Parque Omora (3 km west of town).

The trekking season lasts from December to April and varies with snowfall (ask at Fuegia for conditions), but hikes to Cerro Bandera, Cascada Los Bronces, and Parque Omora are possible year-round.

The **Museo Martin Gusinde**, recently remodeled, has a wonderful collection of artifacts related to the island's natural and cultural history. It was named after a priest and anthropologist who worked with the Onas and Yagan Indians. (Corner of Aragay and Gusinde. Tel: 56-61-621043, open summer 9 a.m. – 1 p.m., 2:30 p.m. – 7 p.m. and winter 8 a.m. – 1 p.m., 2:30 p.m. – 6 p.m., Sat and Sun 2:30 p.m. – 6:30 p.m., admission free).

Just east of town you will find **Villa Ukika**, home to 50 of the last 70 remaining descendents of the Yaghan people. Among the town's residents is an 81-year-old woman who is the single direct descendant of pure Yaghan ancestry. **Kipa-Akar** is a museum/shop in the village displaying Yaghan crafts.

The king crab season runs from July to November and is big business for the local fishermen. If you happen to be in town during that time, you owe it to yourself to visit the docks and watch as boats unload hundreds of kilos worth of the gigantic red crustaceans. Every restaurant in town serves centolla, but try the informal restaurant run by Pati at Residencial Pusaki for special homemade delights.

SOUTHERN PATAGONIA

Services

The town has new services popping up every year, but is still far from being able to handle a wave of tourism. Internet cafes, restaurants, hostels and hotels can all be found, but at an above average cost compared to the rest of Chile. Backpacker hostels are also more expensive here, often costing the same as mid-range hotels in other parts. Hotel Lakutaia boasts the luxury top-spot on Navarino Island, catering to the five-star crowd, although this is not what you would expect from this little village.

Banco de Chile has a location in front of the naval grocery store on Yelcho Street with counter service and an ATM (closed from 1 a.m. to 6 a.m.) that accepts Visa, Mastercard and Cirrus.

A community **Health Center** is located at corner of Evout and Canal Murray. The **post office** is in Centro Commercial off of Usphashun, open 9:30 a.m. – 1 p.m. and 4 p.m. – 7 p.m., Saturaday until noon. Internet is available in the Centro Comercial, $2.75 per 30 minutes; **Supermarkets Simon y Simon** and **Temuco** are across from each other on Piloto Pardo, next to Residencial Pusaki.

Tours

Fuegia & Co. (Patrullero Ortiz #049. Tel: 56-61-621251, E-mail: fuegia@usa.net); **Turismo Shila** (Centro Comercial. Tel: 56-61-621745, URL: www.turismoshila.cl) Updated: Jul 07, 2009.

Lodging

Residencial Pusaki ($18.45 per night low season, shared room and bathroom; Piloto Pardo 222. Tel: 56-61-621116).
Hostal Akainij ($24 low season, $30 high, single with private bath; Austral 22. Tel: 56-61-1621173).
Lodge Lakutaia ($250, Seno Lauts. Tel: 56-61-621733, E-mail: www.lakutaia.cl).

Restaurants

Cabo de Hornos (Ricardo Maragaño 146)—serves beaver and king crab.
Dientes de Navarino (Centro Comercial Sur 14. Tel: 56-61-9621074)—specializes in fish.
Patagonia (Yelcho 230. Tel: 56-61-621075)—dishes out king crab, beaver, rabbit and other interesting meats.

To liven up your evenings, head off to **Camblor** (Patricio Capedeville 41. Tel: 56-61-621033) for the occasional karaoke or dance night. Updated: Jul 07, 2009.

ARGENTINE TIERRA DEL FUEGO

RÍO GRANDE, ARGENTINA

 0m   55,300   54-2964

Few travelers stop in Río Grande. In summer, bicyclists and motorcyclists break for the night here. In winter, Punta Arenas-Ushuaia buses have a lay-over, and some journeyers decide to rest before heading down the road. Otherwise, not many visitors come—but they are missing out. The city is set in the *Reserva para Aves Playeras Costa Atlántica* (Atlantic Coast Shore Bird Reserve) and is filled with migratory birds during the summer. Some of the species that come are the Red Knot, Sanderling, Hudsonian Godwit, Whimbrel and Numenius phaenopus. There are several prime birdwatching spots along the seafront: the boat-shaped Observatorio de Aves Playeras (Elcano, between Belgrano and Thorne), the stretch of beach at Beauvoir and Vernet, and Punta Popper, at the mouth of the Río Grande river (3.5 km/2 mi east; remis $6 one way).

You can trace the history of Río Grande in the town's various museums, monuments and historical sites. For millennia, the Selk'nam (Ona) indigenous people lived here. Casa Cultural del Pueblo Indígena Rafaela Ishton has photos, scale models of dwellings (kawi), masks and paintings of this culture. The cultural center also strives to preserve the nation's language and traditions (Monday – Friday 9 a.m. – noon, 2 p.m. – 5 p.m. Ameghino and Piedrabuena. Entry: free).

Residents established massive local sheep farms in the late 19th and early 20th centuries. One of the largest meat-processing plants was set up in 1903 by Alejandro Menéndez Behety to ship frozen mutton to England and other European markets. What remains of the installations are on the south bank of Río Grande river (follow Pacheco across the river, then Alambrador to Portolán. Entry: free).

Along Santa Fe in the center of the city, Paseo Crucero General Belgrano is a walk that has monuments to the fallen of the Falklands War. It is named for the ship sunk by British forces. At the sea end of the Paseo are monuments to the Argentine armed forces. On the east end of town **Centro de Ex Combatientes**

Malvinas Argentinas has photos and other displays memorializing the Falklands War (Monday – Friday 9 a.m. – 4 p.m. Lasserre 678. Tel: 54-2964-43788. Entry: free).

Río Grande's history comes together at the **Museo Municipal Virginia Choquintel**. This museum covers human history as well as the region's flora and fauna, petroleum exploitation and other industries (Monday – Friday 9 a.m. – 5 p.m., Saturday 3 p.m. – 7 p.m. Alberdi 555. Tel: 54-2964-430647. Entry: free).

You can organize day excursions out to former estancias. Many are now lodges, with day programs for horseback riding, birdwatching and fishing. The lakes and rivers around Río Grande teem with trout and other fish. The fishing season is November – March, with catch-and-release continuing until the end of April. Another outing to make from Río Grande is to **Misión Salesiana**, which has a historic church and museum.

Most of the festivals celebrated in Río Grande deal with the great outdoors:

2nd week of March— Exposición Rural y Comercial de Tierra del Fuego (state fair).

2nd week of April—La Vuelta Tierra del Fuego— motocross race.

Mid-August—Carrera de la Humanidad —Argentine-Chilean auto race.

1st – 2nd week of November—Ride Internacional de Tierra del Fuego—canoe and kayaking from Argentina to Chile.

1st – 2nd week of December—Fiesta Provincial de la Pesca de Róbalo—the dates of this sea fishing competition depend on the tides; also Rally de los Lagos, a mountain bike competition around the region's lake.

Getting To and Away From Río Grande

BY LAND
Río Grande is on Argentina's Ruta 3, 81 kilometers (48.6 mi, paved) southeast of the San Sebastián border crossing with Chile and 222 kilometers (133 mi, partially paved) north of Ushuaia. The city has several gas stations, auto mechanics and tire repair shops. CR Motos has motorcycle parts and repair shops (Espora 969. Tel: 54-2964-434101). Four places have

bicycle parts and can make repairs, including **Everest** (Estrada 526. Tel: 54-2964-434101) and **Rueda a Rueda** (Antártida Argentina 726. Tel: 54-2964-420751).

Four city bus, *colectivo*, routes run in the urban area ($0.60). *Remises* are shared taxis that run on fixed routes; fares depend on the destination. Taxis are the most expensive form of transportation. Car rental agencies include **Avis** (Aeropuerto. Tel: 54-2964 -15455001), **Budget** (San Martín 1095. Tel: 54-2964-427164) and **Hertz** (San Martín 236. Tel: 54-2964-426534; also at airport).

Río Grande's bus terminal has a restaurant, Internet and bathrooms (Finocchio and Obligado). All bus companies have offices here and all buses depart from the terminal. Some also have offices in the city: **Líder** (P. Moreno 635. Tel: 54-2964-420003), **Montiel** (25 de Mayo 712. Tel: 54-2964-420997) and **Tecni Austral** (Roca 157. Tel: 54-2901-431408/412). There are more departures and destinations during the summer high season.

To Tolhuin / Ushuaia: 1.5 / 3 hours, $10 / $ 17—**Montiel** (Monday – Saturday approximately every 2 hours 6 a.m. – 9 p.m., Sunday and holidays every 2 – 3 hours 9:30 a.m. – 9 p.m.), **Líder** (Monday – Saturday every 2-2.5 hours 6 a.m. – 8:30 p.m., Sunday and holidays 6 departures 8:30 a.m. – 8:30 p.m.).

To Río Gallegos: 8 hours, $34—**Tecni Austral** (daily 8:30 a.m.), **Marga / Taqsa** (daily 8:15 a.m.).

For other destinations in Argentina, transfer at Río Gallegos.

To Punta Arenas, Chile: 8 hours, $33 – **Tecni Austral** (Monday, Wednesday, Friday 8:30 a.m.), **Pacheco** (Tuesday, Thursday, Saturday 10 a.m.).

BY AIR
Rio Grande's airport is approximately five kilometers (3 mi) from town (Ruta Provincial 5. Tel: 54-2964-420699). Colectivo city bus **Línea A** passes by ($0.60). A *remis* costs $6.

Aerolíneas Argentinas (Monday – Friday 9 a.m. – 12:30 p.m., 3 p.m. – 7 p.m., Saturday 9:30 a.m. – noon).

—*To Buenos Aires*: daily, 3.25 hours, $142). **LADE** (Monday – Friday 9 a.m. – 3 p.m. Lasserre 429. Tel: 54-2964-422968).

—*To Río Gallegos*: Monday – Thursday, $48, 50 minutes.
—*To El Calafate*: Thursday, $71.

—*To Mar de Plata:* Thursday, $122.

—*To Bariloche:* Thursday, $200.

—*To Comodoro Rivadavia:* Monday – Thursday, $98.

Cedma (Monday – Friday 10 a.m. – 1 p.m., 3-7 p.m. 25 de Mayo 714. Tel: 54-2964-434364).

—*To Río Gallegos:* Monday, Wednesday, Friday. Updated: Jul 28, 2009.

Services

TOURISM
Centro Municipal de Información Turística (Monday – Friday 9 a.m. – 5 p.m. Rosales 350, Plaza Altamirante Brown. Tel: 54-2964-431324, E-mail: turismo@riogrande.gov.ar, URL: www.riogrande.gov.ar).

Automóvil Club Argentino (A.C.A.) (9 de Julio 655. Tel: 54-2964-430820, URL: www.aca.org.ar).

Immigration (Beauvoir 23. Tel: 54-61-421924).

Provincial Police (Belgrano 750. Tel: emergency 101).

Chilean Consulate (Fagnano 1167. Tel: 54-2964-430523).

You can obtain fishing licenses at **Asociación Club de Pesca con Mosca** (Montilia 140. Tel: 54-2964-421268). For fishing gear visit: **Angler's Adventure** (Rosales 644), **Tolkeyen** (Blegrano 511) or **Fly Shop** (Rosales 796).

Tents, camp stove gas and other camping supplies are available at **Everest** (Estrada 52, San Martín 170) and **Scandanavian-Vraie General Store** (Espora 687).

MONEY
Banks are all located in the 100 and 200 blocks of San Martín and are open Monday – Friday 10 a.m. – 3 p.m. All have ATMs that accept MasterCard, Cirrus, Visa and Plus:

Banco Francés BBVA (San Martín No. 175), HBSC (No. 194).
Patagonia-Sudameris (No. 145).
Tierra del Fuego (No. 193).
Banco de la Nación Argentina (San Martín 219) also exchanges American dollars and euros.

Casa de Cambio Thaler exchanges U.S. dollars, euros and other major Western currencies, some South American currencies and yen, as well as American Express travelers checks (Monday – Friday 10 a.m. – 3 p.m. Espora 631. Tel: 54-2964-421154).

KEEPING IN TOUCH
Internet and phone services are common, though Skype is non-existent. **Correos Argentinos** is the main mail service (Monday - Friday 9 a.m. – 12:30 p.m., 3 p.m. – 6 p.m., Saturday 9 a.m. – 12:30 p.m.).

MEDICAL
Most pharmacies are near **Hospital Regional** (Ameghino 755. Tel: 54-2964-422086, emergency 107) and there are two on San Martín.

SHOPPING
Río Grande artisans work mainly in wood, leather or pottery:
Paseo de los Artesanos (weekends and holidays 2 – 8 p.m. Fagnano and Rosales).
Cerámica Krenn (Alberdi 569. Tel: 54-2964-421122, E-mail: ceramicakrenn@speedy.com.ar).
Nanica (Moyano 439. Tel: 54-2964-426376).

Tours
Most travel agencies in Río Grande only book tickets. None do tours, though several can make reservations for visits to the surrounding estancias. One is **Shlek'nam Viajes** (Belgrano 1122. Tel: 54-2964-426180, E-mail: shelknam@netcobbs.com.ar).

Lodging
Hotels are typically more expensive in Río Grande than in Ushuaia, so it pays to do some comparison shopping.

The **Club Náutico** has camping November – March (800 m / 0.5 mi south on Ruta 3; $4.30).

Hostel Argentino (San Martín 64. Tel: 54-2964-420969, E-mail: hostealargentino@gmail.com)—$14.30 –17.20 per person.

SOUTHERN PATAGONIA

El Puesto (Juan Bautista Thorne 345. Tel: 56-02964-420923, E-mail: bybelpuesto@yahoo.com.ar)—single $28.69, double $40.

Hotel Ibarra (Rosales 357. Tel: 54-2964-0071, E-mail: hotelibarra@netcombbs.com.ar, URL: www.federicoibarrahotel.com.ar)—single $78, double $94.

Estancias

Families in Argentina's Tierra del Fuego have turned their sheep farming estancias into B&B lodges with tourist activities such as fishing, horseback riding, birdwatching, and photographic safaris. The most interesting ranches are located near Río Grande. The following are worth a visit:

B&B Estancia Rolito (Ruta Complimentaria 21, ex A, 88 km / 53 mi from Río Grande. Tel: 54-02901-492007, E-mail: rolitotdf@hotmail.com / info@turismodelcampo.com.ar)

B&B Estancia San Pablo (Ruta Complimentaria 21, ex A, 132 km / 79 mi from Río Grande. Tel: 54-2964-15610630, E-mail: cabosanpablo@infovia.com.ar / cabosanpablo@uolsinectis.com.ar)

B&B Estancia El Rodeo (Ruta Complimentaria 12, ex E, 53 km / 32 mi from Río Grande. Tel: 54-2964-426354, E-mail: elrodeo@netcombbs.com.ar / goodalla@netcombbs.com.ar)

Hostería Posada del Guanaco Estancia Despedida (Ruta Complimentaria 8, ex Ruta B, Km 35. Tel: 54-2964-420041, E-mail: despedida@infovia.com.ar, URL: www.estanciadespedida.com.ar).

Hostería Estancia Tepi (Ruta Complimetaria 21, ex A, 80 km / 48 mi from Río Grande. Tel: 54-2964-427245, E-mail: loredid@hotmail.com

The only way to get out to one of the estancias is in private car; you can rent a vehicle or hire a driver in Río Grande. There are no tours.

Several agencies, including Shlek'nam Viajes (Belgrano 1122), can reserve your visit to a ranch. The tourism office (Rosales 350, Plaza Altamirante Brown. Tel: 54-2964-431324) has a complete list of estancias and booking agencies to consult. Updated: Jul 20, 2009.

Restaurants

Confitería Roca (Espora 643. Tel: 54-2964-425471)

Nistro Resto-Bar (12 de Octubre 602. Tel: 54-2964-15619023)

Parrilla Los Troncos (Islas Malvinas 998. Tel: 54-2964-433982). Updated: Jul 28, 2009.

TOLHUIN, ARGENTINA

 14m 2,000 54-2901

Founded in 1972, Tolhuin is an ideal off-the-beaten-path destination whose charm lies in its small-town feel and breathtaking natural surroundings. Due to its location in the heart of Tierra del Fuego, the town was called Tolhuin, which in Selk'nam means "heart."

This small lake-side town is a welcome relief from the monotony of sheep ranches that dominate the rolling hills and plains of northern Tierra del Fuego. Located between the Strait of Magellan and the Beagle Channel, Tolhuin offers rugged mountain scenery without Ushuaia's tourists, as well as one of the best-known bakeries in the region, La Unión Panadería.

From here it is two hours by car to either of Tierra del Fuego's cities, Río Grande in the north, or Ushuaia in the south. Most visitors are Argentine truckers en route to other places, or residents of La Isla (Tierra del Fuego). In fact, the town is well removed from the tourist circuit, and its few dirt-road streets are lined by low houses and wood cabins.

Tolhuin gives the visitor a chance to experience one of the southernmost regions of the world, without feeling like just another tourist. Here, in what E. Lucas Bridges deemed "the Uttermost Part of the Earth," the sun no longer rises in the east and sets in the west, but hovers longingly in the north. At night, the stars of the Southern Hemisphere emerge luminous in the obsidian skies, and the Southern Cross wordlessly points the way to Antarctica. The raw power of the gale-force winds of Tierra del Fuego that howl in from the South Pacific cannot be exaggerated, penetrating clothing, bending trees, and swaying signposts.

The unbroken white of the southern Andean Cordillera spreads from west to east here, just south of Tolhuin, and morphs

SOUTHERN PATAGONIA

into geologically young, sharp white peaks. To the north of the Cordillera lies wonderfully Tolkien-esque forests of lenga and beech, which come to a dead end at sheer vertical cliffs that drop off precipitously into the shimmering aqua waters of the 100-kilometer long Lago Fagnano, which shares a border with Chile.

Travelers come for the fishing in Fagnano's glacial waters and hiking or horseback riding into the marvelous and (mostly) uninhabited surrounding mountains. Of course, empanadas and cappuccinos at **La Unión** must top off any visit; the bakery is known for its delicious European-style pastries, inexpensive Argentine delicacies—such as the lamb empanadas—and coffees. Tolhuin is the perfect destination for those looking to experience the mountains and scenery of southern Tierra del Fuego without the tourist traps of other towns.

The tiny Tolhuin **tourist office** can provide information about local tours and activities (Av. de los Shelknam 80. Tel: 54-2964-492-380, 492-125). To fully immerse yourself in the beauty of the Tierra del Fuego wilderness, camp at **Hain Campgrounds** for less than $3 per person, with sheltered grassy sites right on Lake Fagnano, bathrooms and hot showers (Tel: 54-2964-603606). No tent? Try **La Posada de los Ramires** (Av. de los Shelknam 411) or **Hostería Kaikén** (On Ruta Nacional 3, Km 2942). Updated: May 07, 2009.

Getting To and Away From Tolhuin

BY BUS

Buses and minivans travel daily from Rio Grande to Ushuaia via the National Route 3, stopping at the Panaderia La Unión in Tolhuin. It's roughly 132 kilometers from Río Grande to Tolhuin, and another 108 kilometers further south from Tolhuin to Ushuaia.

During the high season, more companies provide service to and from Tolhin. Buses are more frequent and fares higher. From autumn to spring, weather can affect travel.

To Ushuaia: $10,1.5 – 1.75 hours—**Montiel** (every 2 hours, Monday – Saturday 7:30 a.m. – 10:30 p.m., Sunday and holidays every 2 – 3 hours 11 a.m. – 10:45 p.m.), **Líder** (every 2 hours, daily 7:30 a.m. – 8 p.m.).

To Río Grande: $10, 1.5 – 1.75 hours—**Montiel** (every 2 hours, Monday – Saturday 7:30 a.m. – 10:30 p.m., Sunday and holidays every 2 – 3 hours 11 a.m. – 10:45 p.m.), **Líder** (every 2 hours, daily 7:30 a.m. – 8 p.m.).

For services to El Calafate, Río Gallegos and other Argentina destinations, and to Puntas Arenas, Chile, transfer in Río Grande.

BY PLANE

The closest international airport is **Malvinas Argentinas** in Ushuaia (Tel: 54-02901-431232), though there are domestic flights into Rio Grande (Tel: 54-2964-42-1612).

The following commercial airlines operate flights to Ushuaia:

LADE (Tel: 54-0810-810-LADE (5233), E-mail: lade@lade.com.ar, URL: www.lade.com.ar)
Aerolíneas Argentinas. (Tel: 54-0810-222-VOLAR (86527))
LAN (Tel: 54-0810-9999-526). Updated: May 18, 2009.

USHUAIA, ARGENTINA

It's hard to imagine a more dramatic setting for the world's southernmost city: precipitous snow-capped mountains jutting 1,500 meters out of the Beagle Channel and vast expanses of unexplored nature.

The beautiful landscapes and plethora of outdoor activities have attracted a rapidly increasing stream of international travelers, many of whom use Ushuaia as the launching point for a cruise to Antarctica. Since it is only 1,000 kilometers (670 mi) from the white continent, over 90 percent of the world's cruises to Antarctica begin in Ushuaia.

The area's first human inhabitants were the Yamana, also called Yaghan or Fuegians by the English. Ushuaia is named for the word the Yamana used for the area. There is possibly one surviving Yamana woman; the last surviving Yamana man died in 1993. "At some future period, not very distant as measured by centuries, the civilized races of man will almost certainly exterminate, and replace the savage races throughout the world," said Charles Darwin. He entered what is now known as the Beagle Channel in 1832.

SOUTHERN PATAGONIA

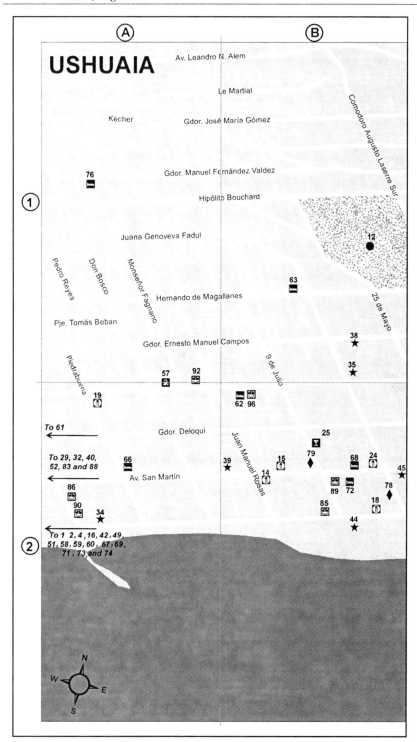

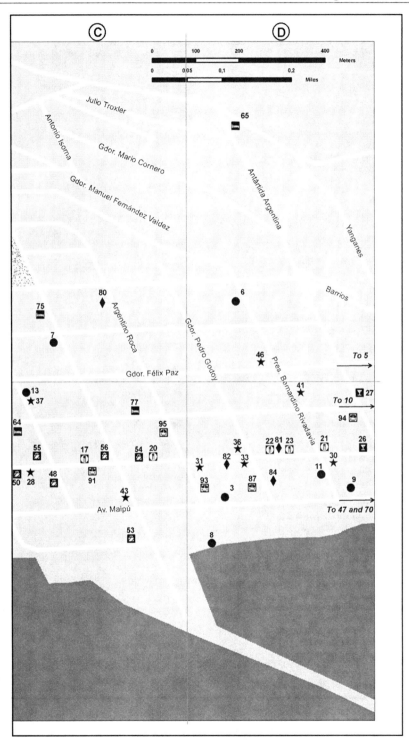

SOUTHERN PATAGONIA

Activities ●

1 Alliance Française / Alianza Francesa A2
2 Antigua Casa Bebán A2
3 Antigua Casa de Gobierno D2
4 Casa de la Cultura A2
5 Cine Packewaia D1
6 Inti Main D1
7 Micro Cine C1
8 Muelle Turístico D2
9 Museo del Fin del Mundo D2
10 Museo Marítimo y del Presidio D2
11 Museo Yámana D2
12 Parque Yatana B1
13 Ushuaia Biking C2

Eating ⬆

14 Arco Iris B2
15 Bodegon Fueguino B2
16 Chez Manu A2
17 Chocolatería y Confitería Laguna Negra C2
18 El Almacén - Ramos General B2
19 El Bambú A2
20 El Griego C2
21 La Rueda Parrilla D2
22 Parrilla La Estancia D2
23 Rancho Argentino D2
24 Tante Sara Resto-Bar B2

Nightlife ⬛

25 Dublin Irish Pub B2
26 Invisible Pub D2
27 Kaitek D2

Services ★

28 Andina Farmacia C2
29 APN - Parque Nacional Tierra de
    Fuego A2
30 Banco de la Nación Argentina D2
31 Banco de Tierra del Fuego D2
32 Banco del Sol A2
33 Banco Patagonia D2
34 Clean and Point A2
35 Club Andino Ushuaia B1
36 Correo Argentino D2
37 DHL C2
38 Digital Sur B1
39 Farmacia Salk B2
40 Farmacia San Martin A2
41 Finis Terrae D2
42 Hospital Regional Ushuaia A2
43 Instituto Fueguino de Turismo C2
44 OCA B2
45 Secretaría de Turismo B2
46 Soles del Milenio D1

Shopping ◧

47 Beagle D2
48 Boutique del Libro Travel Book C2

49 Cape Horn A2
50 Compañía de Guías de Patagonia C2
51 Hain A2
52 La Anónima A2
53 Paseo Artesanal Enriqueta
    Gastelumendi C2
54 Timberland C2
55 Wind Fly C2
56 World's End C2
57 Z A2

Sleeping ▭

58 Camping La Pista del Andino A2
59 Camping Municipal A2
60 Cumbres del Martial A2
61 El Jardín A2
62 Freestyle Backpackers Hostel B2
63 Hostal del Bosque B1
64 Hostel Cruz del Sur C2
65 Hostel Patagonia País D1
66 Hostel Yakush A2
67 Hosteria Bella Vista A2
68 Hotel Cesar B2
69 Hotel Del Glaciar A2
70 Kawi Yoppen D2
71 Las Hayas Resort Hotel A2
72 Lennox Hotel B2
73 Los Cauquenes A2
74 Los Yámanas A2
75 Posada Feguino C1
76 Tango B&B A1
77 Tierra Mistica Cabañas C2

Tours ♦

78 All Patagonia Viajes y Turismo B2
79 Canal Fun & Nature B2
80 Cecilia Di Matteo C1
81 Comapa Turismo D2
82 Rumbo Sur D2
83 Tolkeyen Patagonia Turismo A2
84 Ushuaia Outdoors D2

Transportation ▦

85 Aerolíneas Argentinas B2
86 Alamo A2
87 Budget D2
88 Buses Pancheco A2
89 Cinco Estrellas B2
90 Dollar A2
91 Lade C2
92 Líder A1
93 Marga and Taqsa D2
94 Montiel D2
95 Tecni Austral C2
96 Turismo Ushuaia B2

First settled by the Argentine government as a penal colony in 1902, the city has experienced an economic and population boom in the last few decades that has converted the city into a melting pot for Argentines and others from neighboring countries. Few of the 64,000 inhabitants were actually born in Ushuaia or other parts of Tierra del Fuego as most came from afar to benefit from the higher wages. Currently, the economy is fueled by government jobs and subsidies, port activities such as trade and fishing, petroleum and, of course, the rapidly growing tourism industry.

Prison labor built a railway that now conveys tourists on the apocalyptically named End of the World Train (*Tren del Fin del Mundo*). The town is a major tourist attraction, offering tours of the area through the Tierra del Fuego National Park and ending at a beacon made famous by Jules Verne in his novel, *The Lighthouse at the End of the World*.

The Parque Nacional Tierra del Fuego (to the west of the city), Mount Martial and the Andean range (to the north and to the east), and the Beagle Channel (to the south) envelop the city. The ski resort Cerro Castor provides world-class powder and uncrowded slopes that attract families and Europe's top national ski teams alike. Summer activities include horseback riding, hiking, and mountain climbing inside Tierra del Fuego National Park, itself home to such natural wonders as Lakes Escondido, Fagnano and the Martial Glacier.

The coastal city has many marvelous views; its *Bahia Encerrada* (Closed Bay) surrenders to the cold each year in order to become a natural skating rink. The city has a historical old town and the Presidio and Maritime Museum, formerly the old jail where Argentina's most hardened criminals where sent, and who are now represented by wax replicas of themselves. As its name indicates, it is also a maritime museum, featuring historic miniatures of Argentine naval vessels. Ushuaia's tax-free status also makes it a great place to shop, especially for imported goods.

The boom in travel means the city has numerous hotels, hostels, lodges and B&Bs that charge a premium for the privilege of staying at the end of the world. Diversity and quality of restaurants is lagging behind hotel infrastructure. Updated: May 18, 2009.

When to Go

The warmest months in Ushuaia are October through April, averaging 46°F (7.7°C). These months don't usually see much snowfall, making it a good time to visit if you're interested in hiking, trekking, mountain-biking, fishing or boating on the Beagle Channel.

May through September are the coldest months, with temperatures averaging 36°F (2.2°C), though it's still possible to enjoy skiing, canoeing and fishing. Come autumn, the forests near Ushuaia turn brilliant shades of red, orange and yellow.

Due to Ushuaia's location near the Southern Pole, in the summer month of January, there is often sunlight for 17 to 18 hours and the city fills up with tourists. In the coldest winter month of July, there is typically daylight for just seven or eight hours.

Besides outdoor activities, Ushuaia hosts a significant list of cultural events, holidays, and fiestas. In April and May, the annual Festival de Ushaia includes two weeks of daily classical music concerts by international philharmonic orchestras, quartets, and chamber groups and operas performing in the Las Hayas Resort Hotel.

In June, the National Celebration of the Longest Night welcomes the beginning of the winter season in Ushuaia with a grand city-wide celebration, including ski tours, the Marcha de Antorchas (Torch Parade), and a closing party in town hall featuring live music and a fireworks show. Other local events include the International Mountain Film Festival, the Ushuaia Sled Dog Race, the Snow Sculptors National Meeting, the End of the World Rally, and the "Ushuaia a Fuego Lento," a gastronomic festival held in August. Updated: May 08, 2009.

Getting To and Away From Ushuaia

Transportation schedules change with the season, with more services offered during the summer.

BY BUS

Ushuaia has a central bus station at Maipú and Fudal, across from the YPF gas station. However, only **Tecni Austral**, **Marga**, **Taqsa** and short-distance buses leave from there. Individual ticket offices are in the downtown area:

Tecni Austral (Tolkar travel agency, Roca 157. Tel: 54-2901-431408, E-mail: tolkarturismo@infovia.com.ar).
Líder (Gobernador Paz 921. Tel: 54-2901-436421, E-mail: liderush@speedy.com.ar).
Buses Pacheco (Tolkeyén travel agency, San Martín 1267. Tel: 54-2901-437073).
Marga and Taqsa (Godoy 41. Tel: 54-2901 435453).
Montiel (Deloqui 110. Tel: 54-2901 421366). During high season, prices are higher and services more frequent. For up-to-date information, visit: www.e-ushuaia.com.

To Tolhuin / Río Grande: 1.5 / 3.5 hours, $10 / $17. **Líder** (every 2 hours 6 a.m. – 8:30 p.m.), **Montiel** (every 2 hours 6 a.m. – 9 p.m.).

To Río Gallegos: Taqsa, Tecni Austral (daily 5 a.m., 12 - 12.5 hours, $51).

To El Calafate: daily 5 a.m. with connection in Río Gallegos, 19 hours. **Taqsa** ($64).

To Punta Arenas / Puerto Natales, Chile: Tecni Austral (Monday, Wednesday, Friday 5 a.m., 12 / 15 hours, $50 / $67; for Puerto Natales, change in Punta Arenas).

Several companies service nearer destinations, departing from the depot on Maipú. Prices are round trip.

To Estación Tren del Fin del Mundo: 9 a.m., return 5 p.m., $8.50

To Parque Nacional Tierra del Fuego: high season half-hourly 9 a.m. – 3 p.m., last return 7 p.m.; low season hourly 9 a.m. – 1 p.m., last return 5 p.m., $13. When the national park is free in the winter, bus fare is $14.

To Glaciar Martial: 10 a.m., return 4 p.m., $5.75.

To Lagos Escondido and Fagnano: 10 a.m., 2 p.m.; return 2 p.m., 6 p.m., $32

To ski centers: 9 a.m., 10 a.m., 1 p.m.; return 2 p.m., 6 p.m., $11.50 Also to Estancia Harberton in high season.

BY PLANE
Aeropuerto Internacional Malvinas Argentinas is located approximately four kilometers (2.4 mi) from downtown. Among its services are ATMs and a tourist information desk. The airport tax is an additional $7.

Aerolíneas Argentinas (Monday – Friday 9:30 a.m. – 5 p.m., Saturday 9:30 a.m. – noon. Maipú and 9 de Julio. Tel: 54-2901-436338; airport: daily 10:30 a.m. – 2:30 p.m., 6:30 - 9:30 p.m. Tel: 54-2901-437265).

To El Calafate (high season 3 – 4 daily, low season 1 daily, $107).
To Río Gallegos (1 daily, $62).
To Buenos Aires (high season daily, low season 3 weekly, $112 – 148).

In the high season, Aerolíneas Argentinas also offers service to **Trelew**.

Lade (Monday – Friday 9 a.m. – 3 p.m. San Martín 542, local 5. Tel: 54-2901-421123, E-mail: ushuaia@lade.com.ar).

To Río Grande (twice weekly, $21).
To Rio Gallegos (thrice weekly, $60).
To El Calafate (twice weekly, $104).
To Bariloche (1 weekly, $200).
To Comodoro Rivadavia (thrice weekly, $107).
To Mar de Plata (twice weekly, $124).
To Aeroparque Buenos Aires (twice weekly $144).

LAN Chile (airport: 54-2901-424244). **Rumbo Sur travel agency** handles ticket sales in Ushuaia (Monday – Friday 9 a.m. – 8 p.m., Saturday 9 a.m. – 1 p.m., 5 p.m. – 8 p.m. San Martín 350. Tel: 54-2901-421139, E-mail: informes@rumbosur.com.ar).

To Buenos Aires (high season daily, low season 4 weekly, $155 one way. Round trip is cheaper).

BY BOAT
Ushuaia Boating in Ushuaia, Argentina, has regular service to Isla Navarino October – March or April. The first leg is a boat from Ushuaia to Puerto Navarino (40 minutes, immigration), followed by a minibus to Puerto Williams (daily, one way $130, round trip $240) (in Ushuaia: **Muelle Turístico**, E-mail: ushuaiaboating@argentin.com). From Ushuaia, you can also check at the **Muelle AFASyN** and try to hitch a ride on a private yacht to Isla Navarino or the other South Atlantic Islands. **Cruceros Australis** (www.australis.com) has luxury Ushuaia – Cabo de Hornos – Punta Arenas cruises (October – March, three-night / four-day all inclusive, $1000). Its agent in Ushuaia is **Tolkar** (Roca 157. Tel: 54-2901-431408, E-mail: tolkarturismo@infovia.com.ar).

Ushuaia is also the hopping-off point for trips to Antarctica. Agencies such as **Turismo Ushuaia** (Gobernador Paz 865. Tel: 54-2901-436003, E-mail: ushuaiaturismo@speedy.com.ar), have last-minute tickets, sometimes at discount. Shop around. Tickets for the Navimag ship from Puerto Natales to Puerto Montt, Chile are sold by **Comapa Viajes y Turismo** (Monday – Friday 9 a.m. – 1 p.m., 3:30 p.m. – 7:30 p.m., Saturday 9 a.m. – 1 p.m. San Martín 245. Tel: 54-2901-430727, E-mail: comapaush@speedy.com.ar, URL: www.comapa.com). Updated: Jul 21, 2009.

Getting Around

When renting a car, check about mileage costs and insurance. Inquire about the possibility of taking the vehicle into Chile.

Alamo (Belgrano 96. Tel: 54-2901-431131, E-mail: ushuaia@alamoargentina.com.ar).

Budget (Gobernador Godoy 45, piso 1, oficina 102. Tel: 54-2901-437373, E-mail: Ushuaia@budgetargentina.com).

Dollar (Belgrano 58. Tel: 54-2901-437203, E-mail: Ushuaia@dollar.com.ar).

Avis (Aeropuerto Internacional de Ushuaia, local 8. Tel: 54-290143-3323, E-mail: avisushuaia@infovia.com.ar)—possible to take rented car into Chile.

Cinco Estrellas (San Martín 788, Local 50. Tel: 54-2901-43-6709, E-mail: cincoestrentacar@yahoo.com.ar)—can rent to El Calafate and Chile.

Crossing Patagonia Rent a Car (Maipú 857. Tel: 54-2901-432607, e-mail: info@crossingpatagonia.com, URL: www.crossingpatagonia.com)—can drop car off in another city.

Hertz (San Martín 245. Tel: 54-2901-432098, E-mail: hertzushuaia@infovia.com.ar)—can drive to Chile. Updated: Jul 21, 2009.

Safety

In general, there are no security problems Ushuaia. Nonetheless, take common-sense measures against thievery. The weather is unpredictable—even in summer. When going hiking or on other outings, bring raingear and warm clothing. Protect yourself from the sun (glasses, sunblock), particularly in summer when sunlight lasts almost 18 hours. The ozone layer is thin here. Outbreaks of *marea roja* (red tide, a deadly nerve toxin) may affect shellfish. Be aware of any official warnings.

When choosing lodging, guides or other services, use only licensed professionals to avoid rip-offs. Direct any complaints to the tourism office. Updated: Jul 21, 2009.

Services

During the summer high season, more services are offered and hours are extended. You can get End of the World stamps in your passport at any of the city tourism offices or at the museums.

Photo by Dag Olav

SOUTHERN PATAGONIA

Beers at the End of the World

Here at the End of the World, three *cervecerías* brew beers. Try them at the local bars, or pick up an assortment of them at souvenir and local shops and host your own tasting party with other travelers. **Beagle** is the most common; it makes three kinds of cervezas: Indian Pale Ale, Fueguian Ale and Fueguian Stout. Many travelers consider this to be the best Ushuaian beer. (daily 8 a.m. – 6 p.m. Soberanía Nacional 2723. Tel: 54-2901-434624, URL: www.cervezabeagle.com.ar).

Cape Horn makes a *negra* (stout), *rubia* (pilsen) and *tostada* (red ale) with glacial water and Patagonian-grown hops. The stout rates as the better beer. (P. Lawrence 894. E-mail: cervezacapehorn@speedy.com.ar).The most difficult to find is **Hain**. It's an interesting brew—not only for its concoctions, but also the descriptions. It also makes three types: *k'terrnen* (pale ale), *shoort* (dark, "representing intrepid men and strength") and *mataan* (smoked), an intriguing concoction made with malt smoked over lenga wood (8 a.m. – 6 p.m. Fueguia Basket 686. Tel: 54-2901-604702, www.cervezahain.com.ar). Updated: Jul 20, 2009.

TOURISM

The **Secretaría de Tourism** (city tourism office) is in the former Biblioteca Popular Sarmiento (Monday – Friday 8 a.m. – 10 p.m., weekends and holidays 9 a.m. – 8 p.m. San Martín 674. Tel: 54-2901-424550 / 43-2001, Fax: 54-2901-432000, E-mail: muniush@speedy.com.ar, URL: www.e-ushuaia.com). There are also branch offices at the **Muelle Turístico** (Monday – Friday 9 a.m. – 7 p.m., weekends and holidays 9 a.m. – 6 p.m.) and the airport.

APN – Parque Nacional Tierra del Fuego (national park office) (Monday – Friday 9 a.m. – 4 p.m. San Martín 1395. URL: parquesnacionales.gov.ar). If coming in the ice and snow season, check here if the road to the park is open.

Club Andino Ushuaia (Monday – Friday 9 a.m. – 1 p.m., 3 p.m. – 8 p.m. Fadul 50. Tel: 54-2901-422335, URL: www.clubandinoushuaia.com.ar).

The **Instituto Fueguino de Turismo** has an Antarctica tourism office in Ushuaia (Av. Maipú 505. Tel: 54-2901-421423 / 3340, E-mail: anartida@tierradelfuego.org.ar, URL: www.tierradelfuego.org.ar).

Policia Provincial (Deloqui 492. Tel: 54-2901-421773 / emergency 101).

Consulates:
Chile (Jainen 50. Tel: 54-2901-430909); Finland (Gobernador Paz 1569. Tel: 54-2901-423240); **France** (O. Andrade 563. Tel: 54-2901-430025); **Italy** (de la Pradera 1889, Barrio Casas del Sur. Tel: 54-2901-440406); **Spain** (Oficina Río Claro Seguros, 25 de Mayo 260, floor 1. Tel: 54-2901-430864).

MONEY

During the summer, some banks extend their services to include money exchange for foreigners. Most money facilities are on San Martín or Maipú. Services are also available at the airport. All banks have ATMs that accept MasterCard, Cirrus, Visa, Plus, Diners Club and American Express, with 24-hour access. Bank hours are open 10 a.m. – 3 p.m. Commission is charged on travelers checks and credit card transactions.

Banco de Tierra del Fuego (in high season, also open on weekends. San Martín and Roca). In high season, exchanges U.S. dollars, euros, travelers checks.
Banco de la Nación Argentina (San Martín 190). Exchanges U.S. dollars, euros; Western Union agent.
Banco Patagonia (Godoy and San Martín).
Banco del Sol (San Martín and Patagonia). Exchanges U.S. dollars, euros.
Casa de Cambio Thaler exchanges many Western and Latin American currencies and yen, as well as American Express, MasterCard and Visa travelers checks in major currencies (at lower rate) (Monday – Friday 10 a.m. – 3 p.m. San Martín 209. Tel: 54-2901-421911).
Pago Fácil is another Western Union agent in Ushuaia (Monday – Saturday 10 a.m. – 1 p.m., 4 p.m. – 9 p.m. Perón Norte 158. Tel: 54-2901-444521).

KEEPING IN TOUCH

Send your "End of the World" postcard to family and friends at **Correo Argentino**. Packages weighing over a kilogram need to pass through the customs department of the post office (Monday – Friday 10 a.m., Saturday 9 a.m. – 1 p.m. San Martín 309). Other courier services are **OCA** (Monday – Friday 9 a.m. – 6 p.m., Saturday 9 a.m. – 12:30 p.m. Maipú 790) and **DHL** (Monday – Friday 9 a.m. – 1:30 p.m., 3 p.m. – 6 p.m. 25 de Mayo 260, ground floor, office 5. Tel: 54-2901-430894).

There are a number of Internet cafes along San Martín and Gobernador Paz. In general, Internet is expensive in Ushuaia, costing up to $3 per hour. At peak times it is slow. Skype is common. A cheaper option is an unnamed Internet shop that charges $1.70 per hour (Monday – Saturday 10 a.m. – midnight, Sunday 1 p.m. – midnight Gobernador Paz and 25 de Mayo).

Telephone booths are located all through the city, including one at Rivadavia and Paz (Monday-Saturday 9 a.m. – 10 p.m., Sunday and holidays 10 a.m. – 2 p.m.). International rates are from $0.25 per minute.

MEDICAL
Hospital Regional Ushuaia provides medical assistance to the city (Maipú and 12 de Octubre. Tel: 54-2901-421439 / emergency 107). Several pharmacies are located along San Martín, including **Andina Farmacia** (San Martín 638), **Farmacia Salk** (San Martín 931) and **Farmacia San Martín** (San Martín 1241). They follow the *de turno* system in which one is appointed to be open overnight. Schedules and addresses are published in the daily papers and posted in drugstore windows. Most pharmacies are open Monday – Friday 9 a.m. – 10 p.m., Saturday 10 a.m. – 8 p.m.

LAUNDRY
Soles del Milenio has same-day service if you drop off your bundle in the morning (Monday – Saturday 10 a.m. – 6 p.m. Gobernador Paz 219. Tel: 54-2901-424108. Wash $3, wash and dry $6 per basket). **Clean and Point** does clothing and heavy items like sleeping bags; it has same-day service (Monday – Friday 9 a.m. – 12:30 p.m., 3:30 p.m. – 8 p.m., Saturday 9 a.m. – 1 p.m. Maipú 1163. Tel: 54-2901-424477. Wash, dry, fold $11.50 per bag).

CAMERA
Several photo shops are located on San Martín. One is **Foto Eduardo's**, which has a large selection of cameras and accessories, stocks 35 mm (100, 200, 400 ISO) and 110 film, and does film processing (Monday – Friday 9:30 a.m., Saturday 10 a.m. – 9 p.m.).

For camera repairs, try **Digital Sur** (Gobernador Campos 664. Tel: 54-2901-434867). Updated: Jul 21, 2009.

SHOPPING
Stores have extended hours during the summer high season. Take advantage of sales here during the low season. Because Ushuaia is a tax-free zone, prices are lower on many items. Souvenir shops along San Martín display items to help you recall your visit to the end of the world, from clothing and jewelry to chocolates and local-fruit jams. Sculptures made of semi-precious stones are a specialty in this town.

Paseo Artesanal Enriqueta Gastelumendi is an indoor artisan market. Over three dozen local artisans crafting wood, stone, leather and other materials have stalls and workshops here (high season: daily 10 a.m. – 8 p.m., low season weekends 10 a.m. – 1 p.m., 4 p.m. – 8 p.m. Maipú and Lasserre).

La Anónima has a super large branch carrying electronics, clothes and other items (about 2 km/1.2 mi east of downtown, on the Costanera). Updated: Jul 21, 2009.

World's End
Of all the souvenir shops along San Martín, World's End is one that stands heads and shoulders above the rest. This store has high-quality t-shirts, fleeces and other clothing with designs reflecting the natural beauty of Tierra del Fuego and Antarctica. It also has a nice selection of postcards, posters and calendars. There are penguins and other stuffed wildlife toys, as well. World's End has another store a few blocks away at San Martín 702 (Tel: 54-2901-422665). Open Monday – Saturday 10 a.m. – 1 p.m., 4 p.m. – 9 p.m. San Martín 505. Tel: 54-2901-422971, E-mail: administracion@findelmundoshop.com.ar. Updated: Jul 21, 2009.

Boutique del Libro Travel Bookstore
Boutique del Libro Travel Bookstore has an extensive selection of books about Tierra del Fuego and Antarctica. Anything you might want to know about these lands, their natural or human history, or the indigenous cultures, can be found here. Besides Spanish, Boutique del Libro also has books in English, German, Portuguese and other languages. This shop has just about every guidebook on the market. Children aren't

SOUTHERN PATAGONIA

left out here, either. A large selection will fulfill the curiosity of any age. Boutique del Libro also carries trekking and road maps, videos, postcards and posters. Open Monday – Saturday 10 a.m. – 1 p.m., 4 p.m. – 8 p.m. 25 de Mayo 62. Tel: 54-2901-432117, E-mail: boutiqueantartida@speedy.com.ar. Updated: Jul 21, 2009.

Outdoor Gear Rental and Sales

Compañía de Guías de Patagonia rents camping equipment, as well as hiking and climbing gear and sells trekking maps (Monday – Friday 9 a.m. – noon. San Martín 654. Tel: 54-2901-437753, URL: www.companiadeguias.com.ar). **Rentush** rents camping equipment, with free delivery (Tel: 54-02901-15459847, URL: www.rentush.com). **Wind Fly** (25 de Mayo 155. Tel: 54-2901-431713, URL: www.windflyushuaia.com.ar) rents snowboards, skis and winter clothing, and also carries a selection of fishing and camping supplies.

There are several outdoor clothing stores along San Martin, such as **Timberland** (Monday – Friday 9:30 a.m. – noon, 4 p.m. – 8:30 p.m., Saturday 9:30 a.m. – noon, 4 p.m. – 8 p.m. San Martín 477) and **Z**, which has skiing, snowboarding and other winter sport gear (Monday – Friday 4 p.m. – 9 p.m., Saturday 10:30 a.m. – 1 p.m., 5 p.m. – 9 p.m. Gobernador Paz 953). Updated: Jul 21, 2009.

Things to See and Do

Claiming to be the "southernmost city in the world" (which it is, aside from tiny Puerto Williams a bit further south in Chile), Ushuaia is perhaps worth visiting just so you can claim to have been here. But for the many people who make their way here by air or by boat, Ushuaia is also a stopping-off point for cruises into the Beagle Channel or to the Falkland Islands.There are plenty of activities to warrant a long stay, from skiing to organized trips to Antarctica.

Several travel agencies offer day and night tours of Ushuaia on mountain bike, as an alternative to the typical tour. You can also wheel out on your own to the ranches, Tierra del Fuego National Park and other attractions. The advantage of going solo is that you can stop whenever you want to snap photos or just to enjoy the scenery. Bring a picnic lunch.

Some hostels rent bicycles to their guests (average $10 – 15 per day). If you prefer to

go on tour, **Ushuaia Biking** has city and other excursions on bike (Monday – Friday 9 a.m. – 7 p.m., Saturday 9 a.m. – 4 p.m. Gador Viajes, 25 de Mayo 260, 3rd floor. Tel: 54-2901-431572, E-mail: grush@gadorviajes.com.ar). Other tour operators offering outings are **Canal** (Monday – Friday 10 a.m. – 7 p.m., Saturday 4 p.m. – 8 p.m. 9 de Julio 118, local 1. Tel: 54-2901-437395, E-mail: info@canalfun.com, URL: www.canalfun.com) and **Cecilia Di Matteo** (Monday – Friday 9 a.m. – noon. Roca 467. Tel: 54-2901-436514, E-mail: info@ceciliadimatteo.com.ar, URL: www.ceciliadimatteo.com.ar). Updated: Jul 22, 2009.

Boating on the Beagle Channel

Way down at the bottom of the South American continent, the Beagle Channel is a treacherous strait that flows for 240 kilometers (150 mi) out into the Antarctic Ocean between Chile and Argentina. The channel is named after Darwin's ship, the *HMS Beagle*, which navigated the icy waters of the Tierra del Fuego region between 1826 and 1830. A trip through the Beagle Channel to visit nearby islands, or across it to the southernmost habitation in Chile's Puerto Williams, is an unforgettable journey.

Ushuaia's yacht harbor, the biggest port on the channel, is an exciting place to visit as the boats are moored inside and the sailors around them are certain to have some stories to tell, many having made the ambitious journey across the Atlantic and a good number either planning to go to Antarctica or buzzing from their recent visit to the icy continent at the bottom of the world. If you are lucky, you can catch the lift of a lifetime with them over the choppy waters between the mountainous and glacier-fed deep south.

The Channel offers beautiful views of Ushuaia and the surrounding snow-capped mountains, along with a chance to experience the tranquility of the wild surroundings.

Tough weather conditions are sometimes not worth risking, but even on the calmest of days this area is windy. The waves rise up to four feet even when it is "flat."

Many companies offer boat tours of the Channel, visiting a sea-lion colony at Los Lobos, sea birds (mostly cormorant colonies) at Isla de Pájaros, Isla Martillo penguin colony, Estancia Harberton, Parque Nacional Tierra del Fuego, Bridges island, and the Les Eclaireus lighthouse.

Current low season prices are $39 – 43; during the high season, prices are slightly higher and longer trips are offered. In addition, boats charge a boarding tax (*tasa de embarque*) of $1.75 per person is charged. All tour operators have offices at the **Muelle Turístico** on the wharf (on Maipú between Lasserre and Roca). Among these operators are:

Montave Barracuda (Tel: 54-2901-437066)—offers a three-hour trip for up to 70 people to see the sea lion and cormorant colonies, and the lighthouse.

Tres Marías Excursiones (Tel: 54-2901-421897)—has an eight-person boat leaving twice daily to see the same sights. Due to its small size, the boat gets closer to the islands, and stops to see a rock-cormorant colony on the Isla "H" in the Islas Bridges natural reserve.

Patagonia Adventure Explorer (Tel: 54-2901-15465842)—has 18-person boats leaving at 9: 30 a.m. and 3 p.m. to see Los Lobos and Isla Bridges.

All Patagonia Viajes y Turismo (Juana Fadul 48. Tel: 54-2901-433622)—works with visitors to create unique itineraries visiting various locations in the Channel. Updated: May 21, 2009.

Ski Resort Cerro Castor

Located 26 kilometers from Ushuaia, the ski resort of Cerro Castor offers perhaps the longest and most consistent ski season in South America. The season lasts from the 9th of July until the 16th of October. It has the reputation of being one of Argentina's premiere spots for all things winter.

With unbeatable snow conditions, and a geographic location much less drastic than some of the other northern Andean resorts in Chile and northern Argentina, where winds and temperatures can be brutal, Cerro Castor is the ideal spot for a South American ski trip.

Ski Resort Cerro Castor offers 23 trails and 24 kilometers of slope. The resort uses state of the art snowmaking and snow leveling technology, and during the off season, takes special care to ensure that the slopes are prepared to their optimum condition before ski season begins.

At Cerro Castor it is possible to rent skis of all shapes and sizes: junior skis, snowboards, snowblades, ski fox, snowshoes and Nordic skis. Cerro Castro also provides private and group ski, snowboard and snowblade lessons.

There is frequent transport from Ushuaia to Ski Resort Cerro Castor and back, making it easy to lodge in Ushuaia if you should choose to do so. Several bus companies depart from the parking lot across from the YPF gas station, Maipú & Fadul, to the ski center—hourly in the low season, half-hourly in the high season from 9 a.m. – 1 p.m. $11.50 round trip. Remise or taxis cost about $7.50 one way. Ruta 3 – Km 26. Tel: 54-290-499301, E-mail: contacto@cerrocastor.com, URL: www.cerrocastor.com. Updated: May 18, 2009.

"El Tren del Fin del Mundo"

The "Train to the End of the World" was originally constructed as a train to move prisoners who were logging the Tierra del Fuego region to provide wood for the population in Argentina's interior. It then became the first train to be used for tourist purposes in Latin America. Today it is an elegantly decorated and heated steam locomotive that gives the passenger unbeatable panoramic views of the Tierra del Fuego region as it traverses the 14 kilometers between its "Fin del Mundo" and "Del Parque" Stations. The round trip journey lasts two hours and 15 minutes. There are three to seven daily departures from the "Fin del Mundo" Station (Ruta 3 Km 3042, Ushuaia, 8 km outside town).

This is the perfect way to see the breathtaking landscape of the Tierra del Fuego region, and learn its history as you carve through its mountains along the Pipo River. You need to pay the National Park entry fee is paid before boarding the train at the Fin del Mundo station. Updated: May 18, 2009.

Estancia Harberton

Located 85 kilometers east of Ushuaia, the Estancia Harberton, which was founded in 1886, is the oldest in Tierra del Fuego and the oldest house on the Argentinean part of the island. It sits on a narrow peninsula overlooking the Beagle Channel. The founder, local pioneer and missionary Thomas Bridges, was given the land by the Argentine government in recognition of his work with the indigenous population. The original farmhouse was manufactured in England by Thomas Bridges's father in law, shipped

SOUTHERN PATAGONIA

to Argentina, and then assembled where it stands today. The Estancia Harberton has remained in the Bridges family to this day, and is now partly owned and fully managed by Thomas Bridges's great grandson.

Although sheep farming was the purpose of the estancia at its founding, today it is its history that attracts people there. Day guests can go on guided tours in English or Spanish through its grounds, buildings, cemetery and botanical garden. Tourists wanting to sleep the night have the option of staying in the renovated cookhouse or the shepherds' house ($60 – 80). Another option, if you aquire special permission in advance, is to camp on its grounds.

Other interesting sights nearby the Estancia Harberton are: the Museo Acatushún de Aves y Mamíferos Marinos Australes, a museum dedicated to the area's many marine birds and mammals; and the Magellanic penguin rookeries at Isla Martillo. Estancia Harberton is most easily reached via tours operating out of Ushuaia, some of which come by boat. Open from 10 a.m. to 7 p.m. Closed Christmas, New Years and Easter. To get there head 85 kilometers east of Ushuia, via Ruta 3. Tel: 54-02901-422742, E-mail: estanciaharberton@tierradelfuego.org.ar. Updated: Dec 19, 2007.

Glaciar Martial

(ADMISSION: Free) Glaciar Martial is one of the most popular outings in Ushuaia. Just seven kilometers (4.2 mi) from town, this glacier flows down the side of the mountain of the same name. A chairlift (*aerosilla*) takes you halfway up Cerro Martial to a trail leading to the edge of the glacier (distance: 5.9 km/3.5 mi, difficulty: intermediate-difficult, duration: 3 hours round trip). At the entrance is another trail that bypasses the aerosilla and connects with the main trail. Off this is an unnamed path going into the pure lenga forest (20 min). Other paths wind eastward off the main trail. Sendero del Filo goes to a viewpoint with a panoramic view of the city and Beagle Channel (15 min). Connecting this trail with the chairlift is a trail called the Sendero del Bosque (15 min).

Glaciar Martial is seven kilometers (4.2 mi) from Ushuaia. You can find the trailhead at the Paseo de las Rosas in front of the old cemetery. The lift costs $10 for foreigners, $5.70 for Argentines, $5 for residents; children up to 9 years old ride for free. Open from 9:30 a.m. – 6:30 p.m.

In spring and fall the chairlift is closed for a month or so for maintenance. The tourism office has a map of the Glaciar Martial trails. Only part of the main trail is marked, so the mountain part of the trail is best done with a guide. In the ice and snow season, it is important to check with the tourism office about conditions.

In winter, snow and ice make travel to the glacier very tough, and sometimes impossible. Do not walk on the glacier itself without a guide, as it is crevassed. In winter you can snowboard and ski on the run at the **Centro de Montaña Glaciar Martial**. Updated: Jul 21, 2009.

Hikes around Ushuaia

Aside from the hikes in Parque Nacional Tierra del Fuego and to Glaciar Martial, there are several other trails you can explore:

Old Prisoners' Trail (distance: 5.1 km/3.2 mi, difficulty: low, duration: 2.25 hours one way). This was the trail used by inmates at the local prison to quarry stone and to log. It follows the original rail line. The first track starts in front of the hospital (Maipú and 12 de Octubre), crosses Buena Esperanza stream and Calle Aónikenk to Avenida Alem (1.9 km/1.2 mi). The second leg then follows the embankment of the old railroad (3.2 km/2 mi). Some of the original lenga wood ties are still in place. At kilometer 3.5, take the right fork. The forest ends at kilometer 3.7, and the trail passes a waterfall (km 4.4) before ending at a viewpoint.

Cerro del Medio Trail (6.4 km/4 mi, intermediate-high, 3 hours one way). Originally a path used for logging, the Cerro del Medio trail begins at Plaza 25 de Mayo near the waterfront, up Calle Lasserre to Magallanes, then left passing Parque Yatana to Avenida Alem and left to Calle Rodríguez (1.3 km/0.8 mi). The second leg begins at the wooden bridge on Calle Rodríguez (3.3 km/2 mi). It wends through treeless slopes that present a good view of Ushuaia and Canal Beagle. At kilometer 2.9, you find the old woodcutters' trail; turn right, and at kilometer 3.4, turn left. At Chorrillo del Este stream (km 3.8) the trail becomes steep until the treeline (km 4.6). The third part of this trail follows the stream to Laguna Margot (km 5.7) and Cerro del Medio ridge (km 6.4, steep) where the views of Tierra del Fuego are incredible.

To get there, take city bus Línea B which passes by the trailhead of the second leg of The Old Prisoners' Trail ($0.50). The tourism office has a self-guiding pamphlet of these and Glaciar Martial trails.

Travel agents in town can arrange longer treks in Tierra del Fuego. **Compañía de Guías de Patagonia** does a seven-day trek across the island, from Lago Yehuin to Ushuaia (Monday – Friday 9 a.m. – noon. San Martín 628. Tel: 54-2901-437753, URL: www.companiadeguias.com.ar). Updated: Jul 21, 2009.

Museo Marítimo y del Presidio

(ADMISSION: General $12, students with ID $8.50, family ticket $17; discounts for Mercosur and Argentine citizens. Ticket good for two entries within 48 hours, ask to have it date-stamped). For almost a half-century the hallways of the old prison housed Argentina's criminals and political prisoners. Now the five-spoke penitentiary is not one museum, but six. The Museo Marítimo exhibits a historical collection of regional maps dating back to the 16th century, along with scale models of the ships that explored the Land of Fire's channels and Antarctica. Museo del Presidio explains life in Argentina's most notorious prison.

The upstairs annex is a prison and police museum. To get a taste of what the jail was like, pavilion 1 has been kept in its original state. The Antarctica Museum graces the upper floor of another spoke. Two art collections are also housed here: a contemporary gallery and Argentina's only maritime art collection.

The museum is in the naval base on Yaganes at the east end of Gobernador Paz. Open daily 10 a.m. – 8 p.m.; guided tours 11:30 a.m., 4:30 p.m., 6:30 p.m. All explanations are in Spanish and English. In the summer high season there are special tours in which visitors dress up as prisoners (Spanish only; Monday, Wednesday, Friday 8:15 – 9:30 p.m. Reservations: 54-2901-436321. Entry: $17). Yaganes and Gobernador Paz. Tel: 54-2901-437481, E-mail: info@museomaritimo.com, URL: www.museomaritimo.com. Updated: Jul 21, 2009.

Other Museums

For a break from the outdoors, get inside one of Ushuaia's impressive other museums. Note that museums have extended hours in the high season:

Museo del Fin del Mundo was built as the private residence of Governor Manual Fernández and later served as the Banco de la Nación Argentina. It's now home to a museum that has good Spanish/English explanations of regional history, shipwrecks, indigenous nations and an excellent collection of stuffed birds. Open Monday - Saturday, noon - 7 p.m., guided tours 2 p.m., 5 p.m. Maipú 173. Tel: 42-1863, Fax: 54-2901-421201, E-mail: museo@tierradelfuego.org.ar, URL: tierradelfuego.org.ar/museo. Entry: $6).

Antigua Casa de Gobierno, in the former governor's house and legislature, has interesting exhibits on the shipwreck of the Monte Cervantes, Fueguian maps and old photos of the city. Open Monday – Saturday noon – 7 p.m., guided tours 2 p.m., 5 p.m. Maipú 465. Tel: 54-2901-422551. Entry: included in the Museo del Fin del Mundo ticket.

Museo Yámana covers the history and culture of the indigenous Yámana nation that once lived along the Beagle Channel's coasts. Open daily, noon – 7 p.m. Rivadavia 56. Tel: 54-2901-422874, E-mail: mundoyamana@infovia.com.ar. Entry: $4.25. Updated: Jul 23, 2009.

Ushuaia Culture

Aside from the museums in the city, Ushuaia has cultural centers where performances and visual arts are showcased. The main tourism office posts the week's events.

Casa de la Cultura has galleries showing temporary art exhibits and hosts the Cine Club (Monday evenings, free), dance performances, music concerts, and conferences. Av. Malvinas and 12 de Octubre, in back of the sports compound.

Antigua Casa Bebán houses itinerant art and historical displays, and lectures on art and history. Open Monday – Friday, 10 a.m. – 6 p.m., weekends and holidays, noon – 6 p.m. Maipú and Plüschow. Entry: free.

Cine Packewaia plays current and classic movies. Naval base, Yaganes and Gobernador Paz. Entry: Monday $2.50, Tuesday – Sunday $3 – 3.75.

Inti Main presents a number of courses, shows movies on Thursday night (9 p.m., Entry: $3 – 5 including beer and snack), and hosts art exhibits and other cultural events.

SOUTHERN PATAGONIA

Open Monday – Saturday, 11 a.m. – 9:30 p.m. Rivadavia 451. Tel: 54-2901-432916, E-mail: inti_main@yahoo.com.ar.

Alliance Française / Alianza Francesa presents art exhibits, French films and talks. Kayen 152. Tel: 54-2901-424974, E-mail: aftdf@hotmail.com, URL: aftdf.org.ar.

Micro Cine has a regular, free movie double-feature on Friday nights, plus occasional showings on other nights. Lasserre 74. Updated: Jul 22, 2009.

Winter Sports in Ushuaia

Most tourists come to Ushuaia when the summer days are long, but there's plenty of action for snow bums when the weather turns cold. Outside the city there are 10 winter centers (*centros invernales*) that offer just about every snow sport you can imagine. Besides skiing (downhill and cross-country), you can snowboard, ice skate or snowmobile. For something different, try snowshoeing or dog sledding. Some of the centers nearest to Ushuaia are:

Laguna del Diablo—ice skating and ice hockey; skate rental. Calles Alem and Las Lajas, Costa de la Laguna.

Glaciar Martial—downhill skiing, lift, snowboarding, canopy; clothing rental. 7 kilometers (4.2 mi) from city. Tel: 54-2901-1551-2204 / 1551-030.

Winter centers on Ruta 3:

Valle de Lobos—snowshoeing, dog sledding, night skiing. 18 kilometers (11 mi). Tel: 54-2901-1561-2319 / 0-8006, URL: www.gatocuruchet.com.ar.

Tierra Mayor—cross-country skiing, ice skating, snowshoeing, snowmobiling, sledding, ice climbing, dog sledding, night skiing; rents sports clothing. 21 kilometers (13 mi). Tel: 54-2901-1561-9245, URL: www.nunatakadventure.com.

Las Cotorras—cross-country skiing, snowshoeing, dog sledding, sledding; clothing rental. 25 kilometers (15.5 mi). Tel: 54-2901-1553-0048.

Cerro Castor—downhill skiing, snowboarding, ski lift, snowshoeing. 27 kilometers (17 mi). Tel: 54-2901-499303, URL: www.cerrocastor.com.

The season officially starts the second week of June and runs into September. Every year Ushuaia participates in the national circuit of rugby x-treme and hosts an international dog-sledding competition.

The tourism office keeps an updated list of the winter centers' services all throughout the snow season. Some winter sports centers rent equipment and have instructors. Many also have restaurants. Updated: Jul 28, 2009.

Parque Yatana

(ADMISSION: Argentines $3, foreigners $6, children under 12 free) Parque Yatana is the last stand of native forest left in Ushuaia. The forest, whose name in Yaghan means "weave," is a space for the indigenous to practice their crafts, which are shown at the art center in the park and along the hiking trails. Every year this community passes the longest night (June 20 – 21) with songs, drumming, storytelling and other activities. Artist Mónica Alvarado has her own website: www.monicaalvarado.com.ar. The art center also has classes. Open Tuesday – Saturday 3 p.m. – 8 p.m. 25 de Mayo y Magallanes. Tel: 54-2901-425212. Updated: Jul 22, 2009.

Studying Spanish

Finis Terrae

Finis Terrae Spanish School offers lesson packages in a private or group setting for one to three weeks, including activities such as sightseeing, short treks, birdwatching, and a visit to the anthropological museum. There are also packages that include a homestay with a local family. Rivadavia 263. Tel: 54-2901-433871, E-mail: info@spanishpatagonia.com, URL: www.spanishpatagonia.com. Updated: May 08, 2009.

AIE Spanish School

Argentina Idioma Español offers two-week Spanish classes, either private, or with a small group (or a combination of the two), including two excursions per week. Courses include all the necessary materials, including Spanish book, orientation package, meals, and a certification upon completion of the course. E-mail: info@patagoniaspanish.com, URL: www.patagoniaspanish.com. Updated: May 08, 2009.

Tours

Ushuaia certainly does not suffer from a lack of tour operators. There are dozens of companies in town offering to take visitors biking in Tierra del Fuego National Park, cruising along the Beagle Channel, or trekking across glaciers. The tour operators are, for the most part, quite professional and nearly all of them have bilingual guides who greatly enhance the experience. Many tour operators are also able to arrange boat, train and plane tickets, and they can further help set up more extravagant trips, like cruises to Antarctica. Updated: May 13, 2009.

Ushuaia Outdoors

Locally run Ushuaia Outdoors offers treks of varying difficulty, taking in mountains and glaciers. One special trip is a hike through the ice caves at the Alvear Glacier. There are also opportunities for travelers to raft, kayak or canoe on the region's waterways. Ushuaia Outdoors does not offer many nautical excursions, but it can arrange a trip through the Beagle Channel. Gob. Godoy 51. Tel: 54-2901-424498, E-mail: info@ushuaiaoutdoors.com.ar, URL: www.ushuaiaoutdoors.com.ar. Updated: May 06, 2009.

Antarctica Travels

If Ushuaia is not cold enough, remote enough or far enough south for you, talk to Alicia Petiet. An expert in organizing trips to Antarctica, she can set up a once-in-a-lifetime trip for you. Itineraries vary depending on the vessel and the ice conditions, but you can count on spending several days exploring the Antarctic Peninsula. The prices are steep, but there aren't many other ways to get to Antarctica, short of becoming a research scientist. Tel: 54-2901-15512589, E-mail: alicia@antarcticatravels.com, URL: www.antarcticatravels.com/index.html. Updated: May 06, 2009.

Tolkeyen Patagonia Turismo

Tolkeyen has nearly 20 years of experience in running tours, and it is a rather slick operation. The company does not offer as many tours as its competitors, and its land excursions, mostly bus-based trips to the national park and Lago Fagnano, are especially limited in scope. Its nautical offerings are more varied, however, and include trips to penguin and sea lion colonies, as well as to the Harberton Ranch. Tolkeyen can also set up flights, cruises and hotel reservations for you. Av. de los Ñires 2205 (9410). Tel: 54-2901-445955, E-mail: reservas@tolkeyenpatagonia.com, URL: www.tolkeyenpatagonia.com. Updated: May 06, 2009.

Rumbo Sur

Rumbo Sur, the oldest tour operator in Ushuaia, opened its door to travelers in 1971. Today, it offers visitors a wide array of trips. In addition to the usual hiking and biking trips in the wilderness around Ushuaia, Rumbo Sur runs fly-fishing trips on Lake Fagnano and multi-day bird watching expeditions around Tierra del Fuego. The truly hearty can travel by sailboat around Patagonia or to Antarctica. Rumbo Sur can also help with cruise and ferry passages, Antarctic expeditions and tickets for El Tren del Fin de Mundo. San Martín 350. Tel: 54-2901-422275/422441/421139, E-mail: informes@rumbosur.com.ar, URL: www.rumbosur.com.ar. Updated: May 12, 2009.

Comapa Turismo

Comapa is a large tour operator with offices in both Argentinean and Chilean Patagonia. The company books passages on Navimag ferries around Tierra del Fuego and Cruceros Australis ships running between Ushuaia and Punta Arenas.

For those travelers with a bank account to match their sense of adventure, Comapa can also arrange trips, by air or by sea, to Antarctica. It also runs day hikes around Ushuaia and pricier, multi-day backpacking trips. San Martín 245. Tel: 54-2901-430727, URL: www.comapa.com/index-en.html. Updated: May 05, 2009.

Canal Fun & Nature

Canal, one of the better-known tour operators in Ushuaia, targets the young and active with its adventurous trips. Travelers can choose to hike and bike in the national park or on Gable Island, canoe and kayak in the Beagle Chanel, or ski at Cerro Castor.

Most of Canal's excursions are day trips, but multi-day kayaking expeditions are also available. The company's guides are also willing to help you come up with custom trips and can even arrange team-building activities for your company or organization. 9 de Julio 118. Tel: 54-2901-437395, URL: www.canalfun.com. Updated: May 05, 2009.

Lodging

From funky backpackers' hostels to low-key family lodges and luxury resorts with spas and golf courses, Ushuaia has accommodation for nearly every traveler—though it does tend to be a bit pricey. During high season in January and February, it's essential to reserve

SOUTHERN PATAGONIA

in advance. In the winter, many hotels close for the season; those that stay open typically offer slightly reduced rates. Check with the local tourism office for a list of year-round accommodations (Tel: 54-2901-432000 / Calling from outside of Tierra del Fuego: 0800-333-1476). In warmer months, camping is available at **La Pista del Andino in Club Andino**, Ushuaia's ski area; at Kawi Yoppen on Ruta Nacional kilometer 3; and at **Camping Municipal**, 10 kilometers west of town toward Tierra del Fuego National Park. Updated: Jul 21, 2009.

BUDGET

Camping

If your budget is more limited, camping will help ease the pocketbook. Campgrounds are open in summer only.

Kawi Yoppen has sites with fire pits, and, in case of poor weather, refuges. Adults $3, minors $1.50, plus $1.50 per tent (camping or refuge). Ruta 3, kilometer 3030. Tel: 54-2901-15496747, E-mail: kawiyoppen@speedy.com.ar, URL: www.kawiyoppen.com.ar.

Camping Municipal has sites and firepits. Ruta 3, 8 km / 4.8 mi from Ushuaia.

Camping La Pista del Andino has a common kitchen, fire pits, tables and motorhome pads. Adults $5.50, children under 12 $2.75; electric hook-up for motor homes $2.50 extra; tent rental $6 – 10. City bus Línea C passes by ($0.50). Alem 2873, at west end of the city. Tel: 54-2901-435890, E-mail: lapistadelandino@infovia.com.ar, URL: www.lapistadelandino.com.ar. There are also free and pay campsites in Parque Nacional Tierra del Fuego. Updated: Jul 22, 2009.

Hostel Cruz del Sur

(ROOMS: $9.50 and up) Located in the center of town, this colorful hostel is warm and welcoming for sociable backpackers on a budget. Walls are lined with travel memorabilia—maps, photos, postcards—and upstairs you'll find cozy common areas with cable TV, a library, and a kitchen to make yourself at home. The nearby dorm rooms, however, are sometimes a bit noisier. There is free Internet access, and WiFi is available in most areas of the hostel. The owner, Lucca, speaks Spanish, Italian, and English, and often organizes group tours and events for his guests. Basic breakfast makings are provided, you just have to make your own tea

and toast your own bread. Deloquí 636. Tel: 54-2901-434099, URL: www.xdelsur.com.ar. Updated: May 08, 2009.

Hostel Patagonia País

(ROOMS: $13, breakfast included) Located on the northern edge of downtown, Hostel Patagonia País is close to many of Ushuaia's services and attractions. Ramón and his family give a warm welcome to travelers and are ready to help them explore the region. Four-, six- and eight-person dorms are kept immaculately clean, though the mattresses are a bit thin. Guests trade tales in the fully equipped kitchen. The hostel could use a few more bathrooms and some spaces for guests to get away from the bustle. There are discounts for MiniHostel members and in the low season. Av. Alem 152. Tel: 54-2901-431886, E-mail: ushuaiasur01@speedy.com.ar / patagoniaushuaia@hotmail.com, URL: www.hostel-patagoniapais.com. Updated: Jul 23, 2009.

Hostel Yakush

(ROOMS: $13.50 – 15) Yakush is run by an extremely friendly Ushuaian local, who has created a spotless and bright hostel with big windows overlooking the main drag. Yakush offers big rooms with bunks and double beds, a comfortable, funky lounge with futons, and an exchange library, tourist information, Internet and musical instruments. The common areas close at 11 p.m., making Yakush a nice laid-back spot to catch up on sleep. The typical Argentine medialunas and yerba mate or coffee are provided for breakfast. Prices include breakfast, tax, and a half hour of Internet use. Piedrabuena 118 (on the corner of San Martín). Tel: 54-2901-435807, E-mail: yakush@speedy.com.ar, URL: hostelyakush.com.ar/homeenglish.htm. Updated: May 08, 2009.

Freestyle Backpackers Hostel

(ROOMS: $14 – 16) Just three blocks from the bay, Freestyle is a new luxury hostel with clean lines, wooden floors, and comfy leather couches in the common areas. Choose bunk beds in shared rooms with private or shared bathrooms. A fully equipped kitchen with large stoves and marble countertops, an outdoor grill, and a dining room are available for guest use. Breakfast is included, and there are public telephones, computers and Internet access, a large living/game room with a pool table, TV and DVD player, in addition to laundry services and tourist info. Gobernador Paz 866. Tel: 54-2901-432874, E-mail: info@ushuaiafreestyle.com, URL: www.ushuaia-freestyle.com. Updated: May 08, 2009.

El Jardín

This youth hostel in downtown Ushuaia appeals to adventurous, backpacking types. The rooms and bathrooms are shared, but the prices include breakfast, kitchen facilities—and let's not leave out the panoramic view of both the Beagle Channel and the Martial Glacier. The well-named El Jardín has a 600-square-meter indoor garden, in addition to an artificial climbing wall, ping pong, a BBQ and medical assistance—in case of any unexpected frostbite or whatnot. Gob. Paz 1486. Tel: 54-2901-442044, E-mail: eljardinhostel@gmail.com, URL: www.tierradelfuego.org.ar/albergueeljardin. Updated: May 08, 2009.

MID-RANGE

Hotel Cesar

(ROOMS: $40-70 per person) This hotel, about four blocks from the port, looks like it would be the perfect design for a gingerbread house. On the inside it has what you need to stay warm and cozy away from the witchy cold. It has been around for more than 20 years, is open all year round, and provides amenities like a book and video library, baggage storage, laundry/valet service and a restaurant that serves international and typical local dishes. Av. San Martín 753. Tel: 54-2901-421460, Fax: 54-2901-432721, E-mail: hotelcesarhostal@speedy.com.ar /cesarhostal@infovia.com.ar, URL: www.hotelcesarhostal.com.ar. Updated: Mar 27, 2009.

Hostal del Bosque

(ROOMS: $50 – 80) Clean, comfortable, and convenient, this hotel offers basic, fairly priced accommodation. The spacious two-room suites, which can house up to four people, are somewhat bland in décor, but come with large bathrooms, living areas, and basic kitchenettes. A limited number of one and three-room suites are also available.

The hostel's welcoming on-site restaurant serves fixed-price meals and good complimentary breakfasts. Only a three-minute walk from downtown. Room and laundry service are available. Breakfast is included. Rates increase from October to March. Magallanes 709. Tel: 54-2901-430777 / 0803, E-mail: reservas@hostaldelbosque.com.ar, URL: www.hostaldelbosque.com.ar. Updated: Mar 13, 2008.

Tango B&B

(ROOMs: from $60) Tango B&B offers daily room service in an excellent location, seven blocks away from the main street. There are private bathrooms with warm and drinkable water available 24 hours per day. The B&B also has free Internet, a safe box at the front desk, parking and a live tango show for free! Valdez 950. Tel: 54-2901-422895, Fax: 54-2901-422895, E-mail: tangobyb@speedy.com.ar, URL: www.tangobyb.com.ar. Updated: Jun 22, 2009.

Tierra Mistica Cabañas

(ROOMS: $85 – 162) These comfortable cabins accommodate one to six people, and are equipped with all the necessities. Cabins are nicely decorated with crafts and regional pictures. There are private bathrooms, with plenty of hot water. Gobernador Deloqui 429. Tel: 54-2901-423092, Fax: 54-2901-423092, E-mail: tierramistica@infovia.com.ar, URL: www.tierramisticaush.com.ar. Updated: May 08, 2009.

HIGH-END

Posada Fueguina

(ROOMS: $96 – 197) Posada Fueguina, conveniently located three blocks from downtown, offers spacious single to quadruple rooms with nice views of the Beagle Channel. Or, if you're in the mood for something a little more rustic (but still comfortable), you can stay in one of the charming wood cabins, which can accommodate up to five people. All habitations are spotless and well-maintained, and come with Jacuzzis and mini-fridges. There's a restaurant, bar, and lounge, as well as free Internet and tourist information. Handicapped equipped rooms are available. Closed May – Sept. Lasserre 438. Tel: 54-2901-423467, Fax: 54-2901-424758, E-mail: info@posadafueguina.com.ar, URL: www.posadafueguina.com.ar. Updated: Mar 13, 2008.

Hosteria Bella Vista

(ROOMS: $108 – 472) For those looking for a quiet spot away from the city, the Bella Vista is just five kilometers from Ushuaia's downtown and four kilometers from the Malvinas International Airport. There are great views of the Beagle Channel. The hotel has 10 private rooms (of these, two are triples and eight are doubles). There is a roomy breakfast/dinner area, two living rooms, a playground and parking area. The hotel operates a no-smoking policy.

The traditional breakfast is served complete with tasty bread and algae from the Beagle Channel. Other services offered include: cable TV, telephones, mini-bar,

SOUTHERN PATAGONIA

general transportation. Cabo de Hornos 4018. Tel: 54-2901-445976, Fax: 54-2901-443510, E-mail: info@hosteriabellavista.com, URL: www.hosteriabellavista.com. Updated: Nov 16, 2006.

Lennox Hotel

(ROOMS: $132 – 165) Just steps from the hustle and bustle of Avenida San Martín, stylish Hotel Lennox is the hippest place to sleep in Ushuaia. The lobby and communal areas of the hotel, which feature floor lighting and ground-to-ceiling mirrors, are modern and elegant. The rooms themselves are small and rather ordinary, but mini-bars in the bathrooms come in handy for warming up on cold Ushuaia days. The walls are a bit thin; request a room overlooking the bay, and away from the noisy street. The view overlooking Beagle Channel from the third-floor dining room is extraordinary; get up early at least once to watch the breathtaking sunrise over your morning coffee. The staff is professional and extremely friendly, and breakfast is included in the price. Rates nearly double during high season (October – March). San Martín 776. Tel: 54-2901-436430, Fax: 54-2901-436430, E-mail: info@lennoxhotel.com.ar, URL: www.lennoxhotel.com.ar. Updated: Mar 13, 2008.

Hotel Del Glaciar

(ROOMS: low season, $159 – 259) This luxury hotel looks like a long, large, Swiss Motel Six, but it offers a relaxed and warm fancy-shmancy atmosphere that includes the Restaurant Temaukel, which has specialty dishes like black sea bass or Patagonian lamb. Or order food to your room and enjoy king crab while taking in the view of the Beagle Channel or the Martial Glacier. Ask the concierge to arrange a Siberian husky-drawn sleigh ride. Av. Luis Fernando Martial 2355. Tel: 54-2901-430640, Fax: 54-2901-430636, E-mail: delglaciar@speedy.com.ar, resrvas@hoteldelglaciar.com, URL: www.hoteldelglaciar.com. Updated: May 08, 2009.

Cumbres del Martial

(ROOMS: $175 – 270, $36 extra for children under 12) Situated at the base of Martial Glacier and tucked away in a tranquil forest on the bank of stream Buena Esperanza, this charming inn offers guests an intimate luxury experience in a peaceful Patagonian setting. Four swanky wood cabins, each one named for a different variety of Argentine wine, come complete with all the basic necessities, as well as romantic extras like a fireplace and private Jacuzzi.

The six standard rooms (named after Argentine sweets; there's a dulce de leche room, among others), have private balconies and comfortable king-size beds. The inn has a spa and clubhouse, a comfy guest lounge with a bar and free Internet, and a teahouse. Cumbres del Martial is a great retreat for honeymooners and other hopeless romantics. Luis F. Martial 3560, 7 km from Ushuaia. Tel: 54-29014-24779, Fax: 54-29-0-142-4779, E-mail: info@cumbresdelmartial.com.ar, URL: www.cumbresdelmartial.com.ar. Updated: Mar 13, 2008.

Los Yámanas

(ROOMS: $206 – 307) Call ahead to reserve —only two of the 41 rooms are suites and the rest are standard. All the rooms have views of the Beagle Channel. To fit the surroundings, the rooms have a rustic look and come with modern conveniences like satellite TV, mini-bars, safes, free WiFi, breakfast buffet and access to the spa and workout center. Don't miss one of the hotel's canoe floats. Costa de los Yámanas 2850. Tel: 54-2901-445960, Fax: 54-2901-443216, E-mail: reservaslosyamanas@arnet.com.ar, URL: www.hotelyamanas.com.ar. Updated: May 08, 2009.

Los Cauquenes

(ROOMS: $187 – 568) The creators of this luxury resort seem to have thought of everything that a guest could want. Get a suite with a wooden deck that has a view of the Beagle Channel. After visiting their complete fitness center, indulge in any of the various spa treatments—like the Caviar Mask—and finish off in a Jacuzzi, where you can also soak in the views. The resort also aims to please the palette; check out the Restaurant Reinamora and the wine bar for regional and international cuisine. In addition, the resort has a shuttle with a set schedule that stops at important points around the city, like the supermarket and the Maritime Museum. Calle Reinamora 3462. Barrio Bahía Cauquén. Tel: 54-2901-441300, Fax: 54 2901-441301, E-mail: eventos@loscauquenesushuaia.com.ar, URL: www.loscauquenes.com. Updated: May 12, 2009.

Las Hayas Resort Hotel

(ROOMS: $270 – 320) Las Hayas Resort Hotel offers elegant accommodations, stunning views, and a variety of amenities. The hotel boasts one of the only swimming pools in Ushuaia (heated and indoors, of course), a gym, spa, indoor squash courts, a business center and conference rooms. Guests are also entitled to automatic membership at the local golf club during their stay. There are two on-site restaurants: formal Luis Marshal, considered one of the best in the area, and a more casual restaurant, where guests dine in a charming indoor garden. Rooms are spacious and quiet, and are very heavily decorated (perhaps a little overdone) with upholstered walls, tapestries and sweeping curtains. The hotel offers a shuttle service to town during summer months. Buffet breakfast is included. Av. Luis Fernando Martial 1650, , 3 km out of town on the road to Glacier Martial. Tel: 54-2901-430710, Fax: 54-2901-430719, E-mail: lashayashotelushuaia@fibertel.com.ar, URL: www.lashayashotel.com. Updated: Mar 13, 2008.

Finisterris Lodge Relax
(ROOMS: $345 – 450) The lodge provides personal cabins with five fully equipped rooms that include a bathroom with a double Jacuzzi, kitchen/dining room and a private spa area. Plus, let's not forget the unforgettable views. Enjoy diving, sailing, aerial tours, fishing or golfing, then return to your private cabin and relax in your own private spa with a sauna, alternating pressure shower and steam bath. In addition, guests have the opportunity to indulge in the personal services of the resident private chef and sommelier. Tel: 54-2901-616125, E-mail: info@finisterris.com, URL: www.finisterris.com. Updated: May 08, 2009.

Restaurants
Visitors to Ushuaia expecting the same old meat-and-more-meat fare of Argentina are in for a surprise. With a bay fed by Antarctic waters, the city and the surrounding region boast a wealth of delicious seafood, not to mention a local delicacy, Patagonian lamb (head toward San Martín and Maipú). For those uninterested in a change of diet, *parrilladas* and pizza joints abound. Updated: Jul 16, 2009.

Rancho Argentino (San Martin 237. Tel: 54-2901-430100)—From Fuegian lamb to beef and baked empanadas. Updated: Jan 16, 2007.

Bodegon Fueguino (San Martin 859. Tel: 54-2901-431972). Updated: Jan 16, 2007.

Chocolatería y Confitería Laguna Negra
(SNACKS: $1.50 – $3.70) When you need a break, stop in at Chocolatería y Confitería Laguna Negra. Its shelves are stocked with homemade chocolates, jams, honeys and beer. Follow the smell of roasting coffee to the back of the shop where a small cafe serves drinks, sandwiches and desserts. Try the *Torta Laguna Negra*, made of chocolate, figs and cognac. Monday – Saturday 9 a.m. – 9 p.m. San Martín 513. Tel: 54-2901-431144, E-mail: info@lagunanegra.com.ar. Updated: Jul 21, 2009.

El Griego
(SET LUNCH: $5, ENTREES from $5.50) The staff welcome diners with a smile to this old tin house, handing them a bilingual menu with strange English translations. Monday through Friday there is a lunch special (main dish only, with side and bread) and on weekends homemade pasta specials. The menu also offers typical Argentine dishes like milanesas with various presentations, but has few vegetarian choices. Open Monday – Saturday 8 a.m. – 10 p.m., Sunday 10 a.m. – 10 p.m. San Martín 471. Tel: 54-2901-424185. Updated: Jul 20, 2009.

Tante Sara Resto-Bar
(ENTREES: $5.40 – 8) Tante Sara is a hopping bistro on Ushuaia's main street. It has an extensive wine and cocktail list, and a variety of coffees, straight up or with liqueurs. Make your stomach happy with the desserts, appetizers and meals served here. In the words of owner Aunt Sara: "Disfruta, es el fin del mundo" (*Enjoy, it's the end of the world*). Service can be slow. Tante Sara also has a bakery and candy shop at San Martín 175. San Martín 701. Tel: 54-2901-433521, URL: www.tantesara.com. Updated: Jul 22, 2009.

El Bambú !
(PRICE PER KILO: $6.30) Vegetarians—and anyone looking for a break from the Argentine carnivorous diet—should hit up El Bambú. The only meat served is soy-based. This family-run restaurant has dozens of dishes from Italy, China and other corners of the world. Food is sold by the kilogram. Monday – Friday 11 a.m. – 5 p.m., 7 p.m. – 9:30 p.m. Piedrabuena 276. Tel: 54-2901-437028. Updated: Jul 21, 2009.

Parilla La Estancia
(BUFFET: $17, ENTREES from $8.50) Parrilla La Estancia is a long-time favorite among less budget-conscious travelers and locals. Every day for lunch and dinner you can choose from the delectable salads and hot dishes presented in the tenedor libre buffet, which includes grilled lamb, beef and other meats. For a more standard meal, select one of the dozens of à la carte plates. A bottle of wine from the lengthy wine list is a perfect

SOUTHERN PATAGONIA

touch to any meal. Open daily noon – 2:30 p.m., 7 p.m. – 11:30 p.m. San Martín 253. Tel: 54-2901-431421, E-mail: laestanciaushu@hotmail.com. Updated: Jul 21, 2009.

Chez Manu

(ENTREES: $10 – 18) Chez Manu is perched above the city. Its dining room windows give unparalleled views of the bay below. The owners of Chez Manu are French, so the menu is a French take on Fuegian cuisine. Enjoy their lamb, fresh catch of the day or ratatouille. Chez Manu offers an extensive list of wines that you can enjoy while marveling at the views. Luis Martial 2135. Tel: 54-2901-432253, URL: www.tierradelfuego.org.ar/chezmanu. Updated: Mar 13, 2008.

Arco Iris

(BUFFET: $11) In the crowded tenedor libre (all-you-can-eat) market along San Martín, Arco Iris stands apart. Not only does East meet West here, with a balance of Argentine parrilla and Chinese-style entrées, but it is also the least expensive. The buffet includes salads, appetizers and hot dishes. Of the over 40 offerings, only a few are seafood and vegetarian. To top the food fest off there is a dessert and ice cream bar. Open daily noon – 3 p.m., 8 p.m. – midnight. San Martín 96. Tel: 54-2901-431306. Updated: Jul 20, 2009.

El Almacén – Ramos General !

(LUNCH: $11) Since 1906, the Salomón family, originally from Syria-Lebanon, has had a Ramos Generales (general store) at this address. El Almacén still sells a few things, but is now a museum preserving the memory of those long-gone times and products. (Check out the bathroom "signs"). It is also a comfy place to kick back for a snack and drink.

Its bar has locally brewed beers, a wine bar and French liqueurs. Coffees come from all over Latin America. Accompany your drink with a panini, sandwich, cheese & cold cut platter or a French pastry. On Friday and Saturday nights are special events with music and storytelling. Open daily 9 a.m. – midnight. Maipú 737-739. Tel: 5-2901-421317, URL: www.ramosgeneralesushuaia.com. Updated: Jul 14, 2009.

La Rueda Parrilla

(BUFFET: $15) Like parrilla restaurants all along San Martín, upright racks of lamb roast over a fire pit in the front window of La Rueda. This isn't your typical barbecue joint, though. La Rueda is an all-you-can-eat buffet that includes grilled lamb, beef and sausages, as well as over 50 hot and cold dishes, and seafood. Save some room for the dessert bar, too. La Rueda also sells a whole roasted chicken with fries (takeout only $7). Open Tuesday – Sunday noon – 2:30 p.m., 7:30 p.m. – 11 p.m. San Martín 193. Tel: 54-2901-436540, E-mail: parrillalarueda@yahoo.com.ar. Updated: Jul 20, 2009.

NIGHTLIFE

Dublin Irish Pub

Irish travelers will tell you there's an Irish pub wherever you go in the world. Even here in Ushuaia there's one. But is Dublin Irish Pub really an Irish pub? Well, it does have Guinness stout and the emerald spot of Eire, though it lacks the Celtic music. Popular with travelers, it's a great place to swap travel tales and have a pint. 9 de Julio 168. Tel: 54-2901-430744. Updated: Jul 20, 2009.

Kaitek

(COVER: $4.50) One of Ushuaia's most happening scenes is Kaitek Lounge Bar. Even though it is open during the week, Friday and Saturday is the time to come. On these nights DJs spin pop hits from the 80s and 90s. Watch for the Rastamax nights when the focus is on reggae, funk and soul music. Kaitek has local and international beers, a full bar and cocktails, plus tapas and tablas (boards) decked with Patagonian meats and cheeses. Open 8 p.m. – 3:30 a.m. Antártida Argentina 239. Tel: 54-2901-431723, E-mail: info.kaitek@speedy.com.ar. Updated: Jul 28, 2009.

Invisible Pub !

(SNACKS: from $4) Invisible Pub is quickly gaining popularity for its Tuesday night tango lessons (7 p.m.) and Wednesday night live jazz jam sessions, which begin at 11 p.m. but really get grooving at 1 a.m. Thursday is the night to practice all your tango moves. All of this is just a warm-up for the weekends, when rock, ska and reggae shake the walls. There is no cover or drink minimum. Invisible Pub has international beers as well as all three local brews. It is also open during the day, offering breakfasts and light meals. Open daily 8 a.m. – 4 a.m. San Martín 19. Tel: 54-2901-435255, E-mail: invisiblepub@hotmail.com, URL: www.invisiblepub.com.ar. Updated: Jul 28, 2009.

SOUTHERN PATAGONIA

PARQUE NACIONAL TIERRA DEL FUEGO, ARGENTINA

The night Ferdinand Magellan sailed through the Straits that would one day bear his name, he saw the fires of the Selk'nam peoples along the shores. For this reason, he called the land *"Tierra de los Fuegos"*—The Land of the Fires. Few travelers make it to this end of the Earth. The main island is shaped like a massive jig-saw puzzle piece with a long, westward tail ridged by the Cordillera Darwin. It is the largest isle of the archipelago, mostly protected by the Alberto de Agostini and Cabo de Hornos National Parks. Across the Beagle Channel from Tierra del Fuego Island is Isla Navarino, home of the world's southern-most town, Puerto Williams.

The area that is today known as the Tierra del Fuego National Park was home to Yamana tribes some 10,000 years ago, who lived in beach-side huts and built lenga canoes from the nearby forests. It's still possible to see overgrown, grassy mounds of mussel shells near the shoreline, indicating previous Yamana settlement areas.

Created in 1960, Parque Nacional Tierra del Fuego is the only national park in Argentina with a coastline. At 63,000 hectares, it is massive in size, stretching from the west of Ushuaia to the Chilean border, and north to Lago Fagnano. Only a small portion (2,000 hectares) of the park is open to the public, where camping, hiking and fishing can be done. The rest of Tierra del Fuego National Park is restricted and preserved for scientific purposes.

This part of Patagonia is made up of a mix of peaks and valleys with rivers, thick forests and glacial lakes in the picturesque landscape. Inside the park is a network of hiking paths that are quite easy to navigate, and lead you to the coastline, and through dense forests and mountains.

It's possible to fish for trout inside the park, but a license is required from the park administration office in Ushuaia (Av. San Martín 1395. Tel: 2901-421-315, E-mail: tierradelfuego@apn.gov.ar, Monday – Friday 9am – 3pm). They can also provide maps and hiking trails in the park, or you can pick them up at the park entrance.

Getting To and Away From PN Tierra del Fuego

Tierra del Fuego National Park is a short trip 12 kilometers (7.5 mi) west of Ushuaia on Ruta Nacional 3, and can be reached via "El Tren del Fin del Mundo," or by bus or bike.

Buses and minivans that drive to and from the park leave from the parking lot across from the YPF gas station, Maipú & Fadu. Several companies depart hourly in the low season, half-hourly in the high season 9 a.m. – 1 p.m., last return 5 p.m., $14.50 round trip. You can also go on tour. Ask at your hostel if they have an agent that takes people to the park (from $11.50 round trip). If you're so inclined, you can reach the National Park by bicycle. The ride usually takes about an hour from Ushuaia. However, the trails inside the park are not bike-accessible, so you'll have to lock it up and explore by foot once you arrive. Updated: May 18, 2009.

Wildlife

The wildlife in Tierra del Fuego National Park is varied and easy to spot. Roughly 90 species of birds are found in the park. Even in its best attempts to avoid you, the Black-browed Albatross, at over two meters, is tough to miss. Other birds include the Andean Condor, the Magellanic Oystercatcher, the Upland Goose, the Orange-billed Steamer Duck, the Thorn-tailed Rayadito and the Magellanic Woodpecker. There are 20 species of mammals within the park; the most common are the otter, beaver, rabbit, and the red and silver fox. Visit some of the biggest beaver dam systems in the park by walking 400 meters up the Los Castores stream.

Hiking

The **Sendera Costera** (Coastal Path) is a recommended three to four hour, well-marked walk, stretching from one beautiful Tierra del Fuego bay to another. Starting at Bahía Ensenada, the path meanders along the rocky shore and beech forests, with great views of the Beagle Channel and nearby islands.

The path briefly joins the Ruta Nacional 3 to cross the wide Río Lapataia, passes a small campground, and takes you inland to Bahía Lapataia, with views across the channel to Isla Navarino. From the Lago Roca campground, **Senda Hito XXIV** is a four-kilometer (2.5 mi) roundtrip walk through dense forests and around the tranquil pebble shores of Lake Roca to Hito XXIV (Guidepost 24), the

SOUTHERN PATAGONIA

marked border of Argentina and Chile. Walk up to it, take a picture, but don't cross! It's illegal—and regularly patrolled.

Lodging

Though there are no hotels or lodges within the national park, there are several free campgrounds that offer potable water, but no services. Camping Ensenada and Río Pipo aren't far from the park entrance, and on the islands in Río Lapataia are three campgrounds: Las Bandurrias, Laguna Verde and Los Cauquenes. Camping Lago Roca is the only paying campground in the park, nine kilometers (5.6 mi) from the entrance, offering hot showers and a small yet pricey grocery store and confitería selling snacks and sweets.

ANTARCTICA

With its massive icebergs, jagged mountain ranges, and vast expanses of empty polar planes, Antarctica presents some of the most awe-inspiring landscape on the planet. While it is the coldest, driest, windiest, most uninhabitable continent on earth, such extreme conditions provide for dreamlike vistas and an undisturbed frozen wonderland populated by only the most adaptable creatures. It is the largest remaining wilderness, spanning 13.6 million square kilometers around the South Pole and is covered with a sheet of ice four kilometers deep at its thinnest. While icy terrain and bone-chilling temperatures make it inhospitable to most, a wide variety of penguins, seals, whales, seabirds, and a small handful of brave humans call Antarctica home.

Antarctica has maintained a special mystique since before its existence was even confirmed. Long before anyone set eyes on the continent, Pythagoras and Aristotle postulated that the earth would topple over if there weren't a substantial land mass at the bottom of the globe to balance the northern continents. Though never sighting land, James Cook became the first to cross the Antarctic Circle in 1773. It wasn't until 1820 that Russian explorer Fabian von Bellingshausen became the first known person to see the lands of the Antarctic, stirring curiosity and prompting expeditions from many European nations.

Though several countries have since made territorial claims over areas of the region, no single nation has definitive control over any part, as determined by the Antarctic Treaty of 1961. Today Antarctica is host to international scientific research sites with several nations sharing curiosity and increasing concerns about the future of the region.

Antarctica is not easy to access and relatively few make the journey, adding to its austere beauty and allure. Adventurous travelers will find endless untouched lands of otherworldly landscapes marked by glacial deserts, luminous carved icebergs, and towering mountain peaks. Whether exploring by boat or by aircraft, a trip to Antarctica is bound to be a magical, unmatched experience.

The **Antarctic Peninsula** has jagged mountaintops and glaciers and offers some of the best wildlife-viewing opportunities on the continent. Visit the **Lemaire Channel, Hope Bay, Paradise Bay** and **Wiencke Island** historical sites and museums.

The historically rich **Falkland Islands**, made up of over 700 islands, are not considered sub-Antarctic, but are still a common stop for tourists. Travelers can enjoy wildlife viewing, trekking, horseback riding, fishing and scuba diving. Wildlife zealots should not miss a visit to **Sea Lion Island**.

Two mountain ranges outline the narrow landscape of the **South Georgia Islands** creating a breathtaking view. In spite of its dark whaling and sealing history, which nearly drove the animals into extinction, wildlife now flourishes. Witnessing the animals in such impressive numbers is an experience not to be missed.

The **South Shetland Islands** are worth visiting as well. View the remains of the Endurance, ship wreckage from the famous journey of Ernest Shackleton at Elephant Island. Visit **King George Island**, one of the most populated locations in Antarctica. **Livington Island** is an important historic site with a museum set up by scientists and researchers. A favorite destination is **Deception Island** where travelers can see the ghostly remains of whaling stations as well as take advantage of the rare opportunity to take a dip in the Antarctic Ocean. The warm waters are heated by the island's volcanic activity.

Depending on your itinerary, opportunities for kayaking, on-shore camping and scuba diving are available as well.

Wildlife

The ecosystem in Antarctica is a very delicate balance of land, air and marine species each playing vital roles, and each highly dependent upon the other. The health of this ecosystem is considered key in understanding the effects of global warming. In the past 50 years, the minimum temperature has risen almost 3°C (37°F).

Land species are very sparse, especially flora. Plants are limited to lichens, mosses, algas, mushrooms and two flowering plants. A few types of insects and mites are also present.

More diversity can be found in the seas around Antarctica. The entire ecosystem web rests upon on small crustaceans—the krill, which forms the main diet for birds, sea lions and whales. It is the foundation of the Antarctic food chain.

Two classes of mammals are present. Penniped (fin-footed) species include: the Crabeater seal, the Fur seal, the Elephant seal, the Weddell seal, the Leopard seal and the Ross seal. Cetaceans are not permanent residents. They come only in summer. Their ranks include: Blue whales, Fin whales, Sei whales, Dwarf whales, Humpback whales, Black Right whales, Sperm whales and Killer whale.

Birds form the largest fauna group, with penguins representing 90 percent of the avifauna. Of the 17 species worldwide, seven are found here: Emperor, King, Macaroni, Rockhopper, Adelie, Gentoo, Chinstrap.

Migratory birds, arriving during those warm austral months, include various species of albatrosses, petrels, cormorants, gulls, skuas and Snowy Sheathbills.

Scientists at the Antarctic research station of 40 nations are working on base lines of the flora and fauna populations, to understand not only global warming, but also the effects of tourism on the environment there. Despite international conventions, the fishing industry is beginning to impact the Antarctic region. A future danger lies in the tremendous mineral, petroleum and natural reserves that Antarctica is believed to have. A proposal has been presented to prohibit any such exploration for 50 years. Updated: Jul 22, 2009.

When to Go

Tours go to Antarctica from the beginning of October to the end of March. In October only one ship, an ice cutter, runs the route. In the growing hours of light in November, the penguins beginning arriving, courting and laying eggs. By December, the hatchlings have emerged. In January and February, you'll see a carpet of penguins, with the young now almost the size of their parents. Other animals are also numerous in these months.

These summer months have temperatures ranging from -5°C to 5°C (23 – 41°F). Don't expect to see the Aurora Australis, as the days are too long. The best time of the year to see Southern Lights are March – September. Updated: Jul 22, 2009.

Getting To and Away From Antarctica

Since the late 1950s, tourist have been embarking on the journey to Antarctica. In those days, only the most wealthy could afford to take the pioneering trips. From 1965 on, more ships began traversing the turbulent waters to the Antarctic Peninsula to experience this unique world. Every year, the number of trips grows, with now approximately 30 ships offering services there. Ninety percent of the tours depart form Ushuaia, only 1,000 kilometers (610 mi) from the Great White Continent. A handful depart from Punta Arenas, 1,168 kilometers (701 mi) away. International cruises also breeze past the coastline. These days, two types of excursions leave: cruise ships and expeditions.

Both types of excursions can follow one of three traditional routes from Ushuaia. The Classic Antarctic (*Clásico Antártico*) goes around the South Shetland Islands and Elephant Island to the eastern side of the peninsula near Base Esperanza and Isla Paulet and turns northward at Cerro Nevado. It then edges the coast as far as Base Brown just north of the Antarctic Circle, then returns to Ushuaia. This trip usually lasts about 10 days. The Classic Antarctica across the Polar Circle (*Cruzando el Circulo Polar Antártico*) heads to the South Shetland Islands, then heads directly to the west coast of the peninsula, following it below the Antarctic Circle. On the north swing, it skirts the islands along the west coast on the ship's return to port. This excursion lasts approximately two weeks.

The longest trip, lasting up to three weeks, is the Falklands – South Georgian Islands

SOUTHERN PATAGONIA

– Antarctic Peninsula route. It does not go as far south along the Antarctic Peninsula's west coast as the other two routes do.

All ships and their detailed itineraries are posted before the tour season begins on the Instituto Fueguino de Turismo—Oficina Antartica website. Children under 10 are not allowed to go. Very few companies accept children passengers at all. Most ships have some sort of medical personnel aboard. When you buy an excursion, you will have to sign a contract with the company declaring you have no health problems or diseases.

The cost of a tour to Antarctica depends on many factors, such as size of cabins, whether you have a private or shared bathroom, how luxurious the food is, the number of professional naturalist guides aboard, whether it does landings and a myriad of other factors. Costs are high, ranging from $5,000 to $30,000. Add to this $200 – 400 in port fees (*tazas de embarque*). An extra $1,500 can mean a world of difference in the quality of service and experience. Single rooms are very expensive.

CRUISE SHIPS
Cruise ships (*cruceros*) hold 250 – 500 passengers, offer many comforts not seen on the smaller ships, as well as naturalist programs. You will be able to see much of the marine wildlife, like whales and sea lions, and the tremendous ice fields and bergs. However, these cruises are not allowed to do landings.

EXPEDITIONS
Expeditions (*expediciones*) are generally smaller boats with a focus on providing an educational experience. These have onboard geologists, marine biologists and other natural scientists, as well as professional photographers who can help you capture this magical world on film. Because there are fewer passengers, most of these do landings by zodiac boat at approved spots on the peninsula and islands. Quarters, however, are more cramped and amenities are pared to the bare necessities.

Tours
Budget travelers come to Ushuaia hoping to get a last-minute deal at a bargain price. However, these are becoming harder and harder to come by. Many companies prefer to sell online in advance. With a bit of determination, you may get a boat for $2,500 – 3,000. Be patient, as you might have to wait a while before your

ship comes in. As soon as you get into Ushuaia, hit all the tour agencies possible. Everyone has lists of last-minute deals for different ships. The recommended ones are as follows:

Canal (9 de Julio 118, local 1. Tel: 54-2901-437345, Fax: 54-2901-435777, E-mail: info@canalfun.com, URL: www.canalfun.com).
Rumbo Sur (San Martín 350. Tel: 54-2901-421139, Fax: 54-2901-430699, E-mail: informes@rumbosur.com.ar, URL: www.rumbosur.com.ar).
Alicia Petiet (Tel: 54-2901-155-12589, E-mail: Alicia@antarcticatravels.com, URL: www.antarcticatravels.com).

Ushuaia Turismo works exclusively with the boats **Ushuaia** and **Antarctic Dreams**, the only ones with Spanish-speaking as well as English-speaking staff (Gobernador Paz 865. Tel: 54-2901-1561-6969, Fax: 54-2901-436003, E-mail: ushuaiaturismo@speedy.com.ar, www.ushuaiaturismoevt.com.ar).

If you prefer to reserve your trip in advance, some international companies to consult about cruises or expeditions are:

Polar Cruises (Tel: 1-888-484-2244, URL: www.polarcruises.com).
Adventure Life (1655 S 3rd St. W, Ste 1, Missoula MT, 59801, USA. Tel: 1-406-541-2677, Toll free: 800-344-6118, Fax: 1-406-541-2676, URL: www.adventure-life.com).
Quark Expeditions (47 Water Street, Norwalk, CT, 06854, USA. Tel: 1-203-803-2888, Fax: 1-203-857-0427, Toll free: 1-866-961-2961, URL: www.quarkexpeditions.com).
GAP Adventures (19 Charlotte Street, Toronto, Ontario M5V 2H5, Canada. URL: www.gapadventures.com) You can also reach Antarctica in your own private boat.

Besides a tour, another way you can get to Antarctica is with a job. The research stations hire not only for scientific positions, but also auxiliary staff. Applicants must pass stringent physical and psychological examinations. Updated: Jul 22, 2009.

Useful Websites
Instituto Fueguino de Turismo—Oficina Antartica (Av. Maipú 505, Ushuaia. Tel: 54-2901-42-1423, E-mail: antartida@tierradelfuego.org.ar, URL: www.tierradelfuego.org.ar/antartida).

Instituto Antártico Argentino (URL: www.dna.gov.ar).

Instituto Anártico Chileno (Plaza Muñoz Gamero 1055, Punta Arenas. Tel: 56-61-298100, URL: www.inch.cl).

US Antarctic Program (URL: www.usap.gov).

British Antarctic Survey (URL: www.antarctica.ac.uk).

International Association of de Antarctica Tour Operators (URL: www.iaato.org). **International Polar Year** (URL: www.ipy.org).

Greenpeace Antarctica Campaign (URL: www.greenpeace.org/international/campaigns/climate-change/impacts/global_melting/arctic_antarctic). Updated: Jul 20, 2009.

Packing List

As accommodations tend to be quite cramped on most ships, especially on expeditions, it is best to pack lightly. Bring only what is essential.

• gloves: wool, plus a waterproof pair
• socks: wool or polypropylene
• knee-high rubber boots
• wind and water-repellant parka
• waterproof pants
• sweater (wool or polartec)
• scarf
• hat
• sunglasses
• sunscreen (polarized lenses)
• day pack
• camera, plus extra digital card or film, and batteries
• seasickness remedy
• any special medicine you might need

It is best to dress in many thin layers, instead of a few bulky ones. Layering creates air pockets that keep you warmer, and can be peeled off or put on as to suit your comfort level, thus preventing sweating. Only cruise ships will have a shop where you can buy chocolates and other comfort foods. Check to see if drinks (e.g. soda) are included in the price of the excursion and/or if it is available on board. Also ask if beer, wine and other liquors are allowed. If you are on a cruise, you may need formal clothes too. Updated: Jul 22, 2009.

}}}}}

Pacific Islands

Chile's offshore assets are as alluring as the mainland. Each year, thousands of tourists make the five-hour plane journey to Easter Island, now one of the most popular travel destinations for overseas visitors. Thousands of miles from the mainland, the island is famous for its *Moai* sculptures and ancient cultural celebrations.

Although much closer to the mainland than Easter Island, the Juan Fernández Archipelago has never attracted as many visitors. The islands are beautiful and well worth the effort to get there. The road less traveled doesn't get much more remote than this. Updated: Jul 07, 2009.

THE JUAN FERNÁNDEZ ARCHIPELAGO

Just 670 kilometers west of Chile's mainland lie three tiny inactive volcanic islands that make up the Archipelago Juan Fernández. These islands are not nearly as famous as Chile's Easter Island, but in the 1960s, officials took the drastic step of renaming two of the islands in hopes of attracting more tourists.

The largest island, Masatierra, became Isla Robinson Crusoe, and Isla Masafuera is now known as Alejandro Selkirk. In 1704, Scottish sailor Alexander Selkirk was marooned on one of islands for four years, and his story became the basis for Daniel Defoe's 1917 classic novel, *Robinson Crusoe*. The smallest island, just over 500 hectares, kept its name of Isla Santa Clara. The only inhabited island in the archipelago is Robinson Crusoe, where most visitors stay.

With the exception of the small airfield and the 600-inhabitant fishing village of San Juan Bautista on Isla Robinson Crusoe, the three islands are almost completely uninhabited national park lands. Due to the quantity of endemic flora and fauna, the area is also a UNESCO World Biosphere Reserve. The maritime climate and high humidity have create a unique ecosystem, and the warm, clear waters are full of big, delicious lobsters.

The islands offer great birdwatching, fishing and hiking opportunities, as well as some of the best scuba diving in the country. From the village, you can walk up to the Mirador Alejandro Selkirk, the lookout point from where Selkirk scoured the horizon for ships. The hike to the lookout is a nice three-kilometer

Highlights

Accompany a local islander on a **lobster fishing trip**, and then pull up a chair for dinner at the pier in **San Juan Bautista (p.561)** to sample a delicious meal of fresh *perol de langosta* (lobster casserole).

Explore the seven **Cuevas de los Patriotas (Caves of the Patriots) (p.561)**, where 42 Chilean soldiers were exiled and forced to take shelter after their defeat in the 1814 Battle of Rancagua with Spain.

Hike the green hillsides to **Mirador de Selkirk (p.561)** to get sweeping vistas of what Richard Henry Dana called "the most romantic spot of earth that my eyes had ever seen," in his 1830s nautical story, *Two Years before the Mast*.

Dive off the rocks and go for a sublime swim at **El Palillo (p.561)**.

Navigate through the lush forests on a hunt for a glimpse of the **red hummingbird** and other exotic species. Updated: Jul 02, 2009.

trip through forest, which takes an hour and a half in total. Playa Arenal, the island's only sandy beach, is a lovely place to hang out for a couple of days. The beach has crystal-clear waters, which are great for swimming.

Due to the limited number of visitors, there is little to no tourist infrastructure. There are no banks or ATMS anywhere on the archipelago, so be sure to bring sufficient cash for your visit. Updated: Jul 02, 2009.

History

Spanish navigator Juan Fernández discovered the archipelago in 1574 en route to Valparaíso. Over the years, the islands have been used as a stop-off point and hideout for various explorers, pirates, and hunters seeking either refuge or the valuable pelts of the local fur seals. No permanent residents lived in the area until 1750 when the Spanish founded San Juan Bautista on the island then known as Masatierra (now Robinson Crusoe).

The most famous island inhabitant was Scotsman Alexander Selkirk, who, after quarreling

PACIFIC ISLANDS

with the captain of his ship, the Cinque Ports, insisted on being put ashore here in 1704. Selkirk managed to survive on the desert island for four years in utter isolation, wearing the hides and eating the meat of goats that had been introduced to the archipelago by the Spaniards. It wasn't until 1708 that Selkirk spotted the ships that were to be his saving grace—the Duke and Duchess, navigated by British Commander Woodes Rogers and privateer William Dampier. They took Selkirk home to Scotland. Years later, Selkirk's adventures inspired Daniel Defoe's epic novel, *Robinson Crusoe*, though the location of Defoe's story was changed to the Caribbean.

After the wars of independence between Chile and Spain, 42 Chilean political prisoners were exiled to the archipelago for several years after their defeat in 1814. For several years, they took shelter in caves that are today known as the Caves of the Patriots.

In 1915, just over 100 years later, the islands were the site of the historic WWI confrontation between the British navy and a German cruiser, the Dresden. The Germans scuttled their own vessel in Bahía Cumberland before the British had the chance to sink it. Updated: Jul 03, 2009.

Geography and Climate

Robinson Crusoe, Santa Clara and Alejandro Selkirk, collectively known as the Juan Fernández Archipelago, are rugged and mountainous. The islands are volcanic in origin, part of a submarine mountain range that emerges out of, the Pacific Ocean. The highest point of the range is Cerro de los Inocentes, a 1,319 m (4,327-foor) peak on Isla Alejandro Selkirk. The concentrated, uneven topography of the islands lends to erratic rainfall. There is far more precipitation at high altitudes, though rain increases everywhere during the winter months. The areas of the islands with elevations above 1,640 feet (500 m) experience rainfall almost daily, while lower parts of Robinson Crusoe and Santa Clara are as dry as the Atacama Desert.

Island temperatures range from 3 to 34°C (37.5 – 93°F), with the cooler temperatures at the higher elevations. The mean temperature of 15°C, however, is a result of the cold Humboldt Current that runs northwestward along the coast, from the south of Chile to the north of Peru. As the islands are far west of the mainland, they escape some of the upwelling of subantarctic waters, and enjoy a Mediterranean-esque climate, with chilly, wet winters, and warm, dry summers. The climate also depends on the seasonal fluctuations of El Niño. Updated: Jul 02, 2009.

Wildlife

The Juan Fernández Islands are home to a remarkable number of species of flora and fauna, which is why the archipelago was named a national park in 1935, a biosphere reserve in 1977, and nominated for a World Heritage listing in 1995. The islands are home to three major flora communities—the evergreen rainforest, the evergreen heath (dwarf-shrub habitat) and the herbaceous steppe—and are said to have 16 endemic genres of plants and almost 130 endemic plant species, including cinnamon trees, "the apple tree of Juan Fernández", chonta palm trees, and small orange trees.

The only native mammal is the Juan Fernández fur seal. There are almost 9,000 on the archipelago's territory, though the species was facing extinction just a century ago. Sadly, the Juan Fernández hummingbird has known a reverse slide in numbers; there are only 250 of the beautiful red (male) and green (female) birds left, and extinction is a serious threat. Other birds native to the islands are the Juan Fernández firecrown and the Masafuera Rayadito. The elephant seal also lives on the islands.

As there is an abundance of plant life here not found anywhere else on earth, the wildlife is closely monitored. Only 10 percent of the islands is still natural vegetation. Forty-six percent of the flora has suffered from land erosion. Introduced animals such as goats, rats, dogs, cats and rabbits have destroyed a significant amount of vegetation. To fight this decline, in the mid-1990s the Chilean government created a $2.5 million restoration program. This project works to restore native trees, ferns, and fruit-bearing bushes, while also protecting the some 800 birds that inhabit the islands in the summer (numbers drop to 440 for the winter season), and the archipelago's dependent land and sea animals. Updated: Jul 03, 2009.

When to Go

Try to plan your trip around the rainy season, which falls from October to February. The leeward (western) side of Robinson Crusoe is generally dry, even in winter months. Festival days are: June 29th—the celebration of San Pedro, the patron saint of fishermen—and

PACIFIC ISLANDS

November 22nd—the commemoration of the day in 1574 when the archipelago was discovered by Juan Fernández. This later celebration includes a 13-kilometer boat race from Bahía Cumberland to Punta de Isla. Updated: Jul 02, 2009.

Getting To and Away from the Juan Fernández Archipelago

BY PLANE

There is only limited transportation to the remote archipelago. Several small private charters based in Santiago offer round-trip flights. Most fly from either Los Cerrillos (ULC) or Tobalaba in Santiago and touch down at La Punta, the tiny airport on Isla Robinson Crusoe. From there passengers can take a scenic ferry ride (1.5 hours) to San Juan Bautista—the island's main town. Flight times vary, but expect to be in the air anywhere from 2.5 to 3.5 hours, depending on weather conditions.

Flights run daily during the high season (winter), then gradually decrease in frequency. If you visit during the low season, be sure to check the flight schedule beforehand. The region's erratic weather greatly impacts flight times, so it's best to have a flexible schedule that can accommodate delays. Keep in mind that these are very small planes, with space for 10 or fewer passengers. Pack lightly, as most limit luggage allowance to 10 kilograms (22 lbs.).

ATA (Aerotransportes Araucanía Ltda.) has upscale, and therefore expensive, flights to the archipelago. ATA also has a flight school and an air ambulance. Flights to the islands are just under two hours and include lunch on-board. The company has a 4x4 to help transport you and your luggage to Bahía El Padre. ATA also has vehicles for luggage transfers to anywhere on the island. Av. Larrain 7941, Hangar 3, Aerodromo Tobalaba.Tel: 56-2-2750363 / 37185 / 5209, URL: www.aerolineasata.cl.

LASSA, also flys from Santiago Tobalaba to the islands. Tel: 56-2-2735209 Fax: 56-2-2734309, E-mail: lassa@terra.cl.

BY BOAT

Naviera del Sur has the only boat service to Robinson Crusoe Island, leaving from Valparaíso. This private company caters mostly to locals who get dibs on the seats. Your best chance at booking this boat is to reserve at least one month in advance. Round trips cost $180, and each way takes anywhere from 36 to 48 hours, depending on the climate and sea conditions. This trip is also made by the Chilean Navy who sometimes take on passengers during their provisioning trips to the island. Blanco 1623, Oficina 602. Tel: 56-32-594304, URL: www.navieradelsur.cl. Updated: Jul 03, 2009.

Getting Around

After arriving at San Juan, you can explore its various islands both by foot and by boat taxis for transport. Transport to the other islands can be arranged at San Juan Bautista. Although it's possible to travel independently, more and more areas are restricting access to guided tours only. Therefore, your best bet is to book through a tour operator that can arrange transportation, lodging and guided tours. Updated: Jul 03, 2009.

V!VA Update: Chile's **Ministry of Public Works** (MOP) is currently working on a proposal that would lay out a 12-km (7.5-mile) roadway through Robinson Crusoe, eliminating the current hour-long boat trip (or four-hour walk) necessary to get from the island's airstrip to its main settlement, San Juan Bautista. Although this would undoubtedly ease access around the island, the road would destroy the long, but scenic, hike through arid desert and patches of rainforest. The roadway would also take away from both the mystique of the remote location, and the diversity of the flora and fauna species—untouched by humans, the two main reasons visitors go to the islands in the first place. For more information about this road project, visit MOP's website (www.mop.cl).

SAFETY

As it is such a small community, in addition to being fairly difficult to get to, the islands are all quite safe. You shouldn't have issues with theft or violence, but still be on guard and practice sound travel habits. Always keep an eye on your belongings and don't carry too much cash—or at least don't flash it around if you do have large amounts on you (remember there are no banks or ATMs on the island)!

Be most cautious while on self-guided hikes. Bring a map, plenty of water and let someone know (a friend, or perhaps your hostel owner) if you're taking off alone. It's easy to arrange a guided hike through a travel agency; consider this option if you are less experienced. Updated: Jul 02, 2009.

SAN JUAN BAUTISTA

 5 – 30 m 598   32

The tiny, dusty town of San Juan Bautista (Saint John the Baptist) has the distinction of being the only populated area on historic Robinson Crusoe Island. San Juan Bautista and the airport are also the five percent of land not contained in San Juan Fernández National Park. This fishing village's economy is based on the sale and trade of spiny lobsters (also called Juan Fernández lobster or langosta). The lobsters are really no more than expensive crayfish (selling at $20 a pop)! Tourism is also becoming an arriving force in the local economy.

San Juan Bautista was founded in 1750 when the Spanish sent 200 colonists to the island as a deterrent both to pirates and to the British (who had also sent military personnel to check out the area). Twenty years later, Fuerte Santa Barbara was constructed by Spanish engineer José Antonio Birt. The fort is now a national monument, complete with cannon and tall stone walls. Damaged by earthquakes in 1822 and 1835, the fortress was finally reconstructed in 1974. Fuerte Santa Barbara is accessible from Mirador de Selkirk via the plaza along Subida El Castillo.

Continue further south of Fuerte Santa Barbara and you will find a group of seven caves known as the Cuevas de los Patriotas, where 42 Chileans were exiled after being defeated in battle.

Spanish colonists as well as survivors of the doomed German cruiser Dresden, were eventually laid to rest in San Juan's cemetery, (near the lighthouse, in the north part of Bahia Cumberland).

As a nod to marooned Alexander Selkirk (who later became the model for Robinson Crusoe in Daniel Defoe's famous novel) there are plaques at the top of the Mirador de Selkirk, where every day for four years Selkirk would climb 550 meters to look for ships on the horizon.

Although the days of Alexander Selkirk are long gone, the island is still quite isolated from the modern world. You might be surprised, then, to discover that the infrastructure of San Juan Bautista is surprisingly up-to-date. The town has a satellite Internet connection, several vehicles and cable TV. There is a post office (Correo de Chile) on the south side of the plaza, but money exchanges and ATMs are difficult to find. Remember to bring small bills to the island, as many vendors are not able to break large denominations. Conaf has a kiosk near the plaza with brochures, maps and information about both the local village and surrounding national park. For great swimming and diving, head to the rocks at El Palillo, at the southern end of the town's coastal road. There is a variety of food and accommodation options available, even though the island has no more than a few hundred visitors per year.

As the hostels and hotels can be a bit pricey, many opt to camp while staying in San Juan. For a cheap, no-frills night, try **Camping Los Cañones**, which has a decent location and cold showers (Tel: 56-32-751050). **Hostal Villa Green** is a solid option, offering breakfast along with half and full board (Tel: 56-32-751044). A bit more expensive is the **Hosteria Aldea Daniel Defoe**, also offering half and full board (Tel: 56-32-751075). Most of the hostels and hotels in town also serve food. Not surprisingly, spiny lobster and other seafood dishes are the local speciality. Bear in mind that many places require a day's notice when ordering lobster. Near the plaza try **The Nocturno** for fish empanadas and other seafood dishes (Tel: 56-32-751113). For something lighter but still close by, **El Remo** serves sandwiches and salads and is open late (Tel: 56-32-751030). When dining out with more than two people, its always helpful to call ahead. Updated: Jul 06, 2009.

EASTER ISLAND

In the Pacific Ocean, thousands of miles from the Chilean mainland, is Easter Island, famous for its wondrous Moai sculptures and ancient cultural celebrations. The island was named by the first European expedition to set foot there, led by Dutchman Roggeveen, who spotted the island on Easter Sunday of 1722. Rapa Nui, its name in the local tongue, means belly button of the world.

The island has awe-inspiring volcanoes, stone quarries and sacred sites. The world-famous enigmatic sculptures, the Moai, are the reason most people visit the island, and they never disappoint.

Armed with a well-planned itinerary, you can see most of the island in four days, though you'll want to stay longer to take advantage

PACIFIC ISLANDS

of all the hiking, biking, diving or surfing opportunities. There are many hotels and places to stay on the island, but those looking for a quiet retreat would do well to choose a hotel away from the center of the capital city, Hanga Roa, where the noisy nightclubs can make for a sleepless night. Updated: May 22, 2009.

History

Of pre-European history of Rapa Nui, nothing written exists, but many of the icons, artifacts, statues and Moais have been re-erected or restored. Archaeologists believe that Rapa Nui was first discovered and populated by sea farers from Polynesia in the 4th century A.D. According to local legend, Rapa Nui was discovered by King Hotu Matua, who dreamt of the island. The king set sail from the Polynesian Island of Marae-Renga in search of the island from his dream. After several days at sea, he and his followers they came to Easter Island, and King Hotu Matua quickly recognized the beautiful beach of Anakena.

Most native islanders call the island Rapa Nui; another name by which the islanders refer to Rapa Nui is *Te Pito o Te Henua*, which also means "the navel of the world." Given that the closest neighbor to the island is Pitcairn Island, 2,250 kilometers (1,398 miles) away, the name makes sense.

In 1770, Rapa Nui was visited by the Spanish sailor Felipe Gonzalez, who mapped the island and claimed it for King Carlos III of Spain. But the islanders remained unaware that they had a new king. Four years after Gonzalez, Captain Cook briefly anchored off Rapa Nui to try and get provisions for his crew. He didn't find much in terms of food and continued on in his search to find a southern trade route.

In 1805, the crew of an American schooner abducted two dozen Rapa Nui locals to serve as slaves. The 24 captured islanders were taken to help hunt for seals. When, after three days at sea, they were allowed on deck, they all leapt overboard to swim home and drowned. Between 1862 and 1864, Peruvian slave traders raided the island, taking about 3,000 people as slaves and shipping them to mainland Peru to work in guano mines or estates. The Peruvians were persuaded to repatriate the slaves in 1864, but most died on the voyage home. The sixteen who survived the voyage infected native islanders with tuberculosis and smallpox, further reducing the population.

The slave raids of the 1860s and the enforced population transfers of the 1870s had a crushing impact on Rapa Nui. The island's population dwindled to about 100 people, shattering the local culture. Despite hundreds of books and thousands of papers on the "mysteries" of Rapa Nui, these destructive European incursions of the 19th century, which nearly wiped out Rapa Nui's civilization, have been largely ignored by historians.

In the late 1860s the French plantation empire of Jean-Baptiste Onésime Dutrou-Bornier bought huge tracts of land on Rapa Nui. Dutrou forced the islanders to work in miserable conditions and for little pay. In 1877 the islanders rose up in revolt, killing Dutrou and his family, and effectively ending his tyranny. In the years following Dutrou's death, Chile bought up nearly the entire island, leaving only the town of Hanga Roa in the possession of the islanders. The island has been under Chilean government since Sep. 9, 1888, when Chile annexed Rapa Nui.

Initially, Chile took no real interest in Rapa Nui and leased the island to the English wool trading company, Williamson Balfour. The activities of Williamson Balfour caused soil erosion and damaged the island's fragile ecosystem. In 1953 the wool trading company's lease was revoked and island management was assumed by the Chilean government. It wasn't until 1964 that the islanders had a say in how their island was run and were allowed to leave the island. In the same year, islanders were given full citizenship of Chile and were consequently allowed to vote. Nowadays, the islanders enjoy freedom and a democracy equal to most developed civilizations. Both Spanish and the Rap Nui language are taught in schools. Islanders do not consider themselves 100 percent Chilean, and their connections to Polynesia can be clearly seen in their features, clothing and beliefs. Updated: Jun 19, 2009.

Traditions

Islanders consider themselves and their culture to be more Polynesian than Latin. Their hospitality is second to none.

However, as with many isolated societies, islanders have their skeletons in the closet. Until recently, the islanders harbored a dark side to their culture. It used to be an accepted part of the culture for the father to be the

Photo by Dag Olav

PACIFIC ISLANDS

first man to have sex with his daughter. In the last 10-20 years many women have come forward to speak out against this practice. The local police have begun to prosecute offenders under Chilean law, but in some parts of the island, the practice continues. Updated: Jun 03, 2008.

Politics

As a province and commune of Chile, Easter Island is administratively attached to the country's V Region, that of Valparaíso. Sharing political power over the island (plus the inhabited islets of Salas y Gómez 380 km away) are the provincial governor appointed by the President of the Republic, and a six-person municipal council. Following years of demands for greater autonomy by the Rapa Nui community, the constitutional reform of 2007 granted Easter Island the status of "special territory," a status change which has yet to come into force. Updated: May 21, 2009.

Population

Roughly 4,000 people live on Rapa Nui year-round. Of these more than 65 percent are native islanders, the remainder being of European or Castizo origin. Since the island is governed by Chile, many islanders travel to the mainland for healthcare or to study and work. Most of those who stay on Rapa Nui depend on tourism for a living. Updated: Jun 15, 2009.

Economy

From an economy based on the cultivation of sweet potato, chicken raising, sheep ranching and coastal fishing, the island has shifted to a cash economy based on tourism. Since the opening of the Mataveri airport in the 1960s, Rapa Nui has had a steady influx of visitors. An average of 40,000 visitors—ten times the local population—come every year. While most jobs are related either directly or indirectly to tourism, a small portion of islanders also are employed in the central government. Updated: May 22, 2009.

Geography

Rapa Nui is a tiny volcanic island with an area of 163 square kilometers (63 sq mi), and is barely twice the size of Manhattan. It emerged from the Pacific Ocean after the eruptions of its three now inactive volcanoes: Poike (370 meters high with a crater 150 meters in diameter), Rano Kau (300 meters high with a 1,600-meter wide crater and fresh water lagoon) and Terevaka (the island's highest point at 511 meters).

Several patches of eucalyptus and other mixed forests dot the island, but for the most part, the undulating hills are covered in grassland. The island can be hot and humid in summer, and cooler than you might expect in winter.

The island has one good beach, Anakena, which you should avoid on windy days as sudden sand storms can occur. If it is raining, the ascent to Rano Kau can be difficult on the mud roads. If you have little 4x4 driving experience, try to visit the volcano and park on drier days. Updated: Jun 19, 2009.

Wildlife

The island has many animals that Westerners will recognize: semi-wild horses, rabbits, and herds of cattle. Before the arrival of the Europeans no mammals lived here and the only native fauna were seabirds such as pelicans, terns, sea swallows, frigate birds and albatross. Seagulls, such as the San Felix Gull and the San Ambrosio Gull are island scavengers. Two reptiles, Lepidodactylus lugubris and Ablepharus boutoui poecilopleurus, also live on the island. Below the waterline, scuba divers will discover 160 endemic species of fish. For land lovers, a walk along the craggy shoreline will reveal small snails whose shells the locals use to make necklaces.

Estimates put the total number of plant species on the island at 150, with 45 considered indigenous, including three endemic species of grass. The exact nature of the island flora is uncertain and many authorities disagree on the identification and classification of some of the plants. Amazingly, recent studies of fossils indicate that prior to the arrival of the first Polynesians, the island had a much greater array of trees, shrubs, ferns, and grasses. The long-extinct Jubaea palm is thought to have been the principal wood used to transport the immense stone statues. Updated: Jun 19, 2009.

When to Go

The island has a sub-tropical climate and the tourist season lasts year round. If you're visiting Chile in January or February, plan your trip to the island to coincide with the festival of *Tapati Rapa Nui*. The two-week event is a celebration of the islanders' ancient culture, and features singing, dancing and feasting.

Another one of the year's highlights takes place during the last two weeks of January: The Rapa Nui Olympics. The most famous event is the race to get an egg and become the *Orongo* (The Bird Man of Rapa Nui). The movie "Rapa Nui," shown in the Hanga Roa cinema, depicts how these kings were once chosen. Young men have to climb a steep cliff, dive down into shark-invested waters of the Pacific and swim to a rocky, offshore island. Here, they must obtain an egg from a seabird's nest and return safely to the cliff top with the egg intact. The first to return with his egg is Bird Man for the next year. See the box on the next page for more information.

The Easter Island marathon (which includes a half-marathon and 10km race) takes place in early June. If you are traveling from North America, you can book the trip through the specialized operator, Marathon Tours & Travel (www.marathontours.com). Updated: Jul 07, 2009.

Health

The must-not-forget for visitors to Easter Island is insect repellent. Ironically, it was an infected tourist who brought dengue fever to the island. You will need to take precautions against the Aedes Aegypti mosquito, so use a repellent with a 25-35 percent concentration of DEET on any exposed skin to avoid bites. The island's mosquito hotspot is the town center, where a dip in the land enables both man and mosquito to shelter from the Pacific winds. Aedes Aegypti mosquitoes can carry yellow fever although this disease is not currently present on the island. Scorpions and black widow spiders live on the island, so look out when walking through long grass, especially on the northern coast. Bites are not usually fatal but can be very painful. Updated: Jun 19, 2009.

Getting To and Away From Easter Island

Apart from Chilean military charters, the only airline flying to Rapa Nui is LAN Chile. There is a daily flight departing Santiago around 8:30 a.m. every day except Monday. A round trip costs in the vicinity of $500. The airplane continues on from Rapa Nui to Tahiti on Wednesdays and Sundays, stopping on the island when returning to Santiago on Mondays and Thursdays. Flying from Santiago to Rapa Nui and vice versa is considered an internal flight so you are not subject to international passport clearance. However, if you are flying from Tahiti into Chile, you very strict customs rules apply and you are forbidden from bringing in vegetal or animal products. Updated: Jun 19, 2009.

The Bird Man Cult

Islanders once had their own unique religion, the Bird Man Cult of Orongo or *Tangata Manu*, which was practiced until the 1860s. The cult members worshipped three principal deities: *Make-Make*, the overlord, the creator and the god of fertility; *Hawa-Tuu-Take*, the deity of eggs; and *Via Ho*, the wife of Hawa-Tuu-Take. The cult is thought to be the source of feuds in the 1800s during which many Moai leaders were toppled.

According to ancient tradition, each year a competition would be held in honor of Hawa-Tuu-Take. Legend says that competitors were revealed in dreams by *Ivi-Attuas*—individuals with the gift of prophecy. Selected candidates would then choose a *Hopu* to represent them in the perilous competition. Each Hopu supposedly had to climb down and dive off a cliff face on the Rano Kau volcano, before swimming to a rocky island through shark-infested waters to find a Sooty Tern egg. The competition was extremely dangerous and many Hopu died from falling off the cliff, drowning or being eaten by sharks.

The first Hopu to return with an intact Sooty Tern's egg and present it to their candidate would be the winner. Once a winner was declared a fire would be lit on the landward rim of the volcano Rano Krau, its position denoting whether the new Tangata Manu was from the west or the east of the island. The Tangata Manu would become the leader for that year, with exclusive rights to collect that season's wild bird's eggs and fledglings for his clan.

The cult worship on the island, along with its practices, was suppressed by Christian missionaries in the 1860s. Today Orongo village ceremonies are only practiced at the annual games held during the summer. Updated: Jun 24, 2009.

PACIFIC ISLANDS

Getting Around

The best way to get around the island is on foot: you take in a lot more of the land than you do driving. Just head off in a different direction from Hanga Roa each day. For those with limited time, the most efficient way to reach the sites is by 4x4. ATVs, motorbikes and bicycles can also be hired for a day. Do be careful though, since the roads are unevenly surfaced and horses and cattle tend to wander across without warning. It is possible to go pony trekking, too. Updated: Jun 19, 2009.

Safety

Crime is virtually non-existent on the island. Still, it is best not tempt anyone by leaving your bags unattended or your car doors unlocked. Also, in the interest of preservation and personal safety, avoid touching any of the unique statues or climbing on the stone platforms and mounds (ahus). Islanders take the idea of honoring their ancestors very seriously, and touching the statues is considered disrespectful. When heading out for the day, take gear for all types of weather. Since Easter Island is a tiny piece of land in the middle of the Pacific Ocean, storms blow in very quickly. There are very few trees to provide shade, so you'll need sunblock and a hat. Do not forget to carry enough water on the more strenuous walks, as there are very few places to get fresh water outside of the main town. Updated: Jun 24, 2009.

Things to See and Do

Year-round activities on Easter Island include scuba diving and tuna fishing. For a more cultural experience, check out the weekly shows like *Kari Kari*, the national folkloric ballet where audience participation is part of the extravaganza. There is a small cinema in Hanga Roa, but don't get too excited because they only screen one film: "Rapa Nui."

The biggest attractions on Easter Island are the monolithic Moai sculptures. An area called Ahu Tongariki features what is considered to be the most complete and impressive groupings of sculptures on the island. If you don't have much time to explore, this is the one place you shouldn't miss. Another particularly picturesque spot on the island is the village of Orongo, on the slopes of an extinct volcano. Orongo is a good place to kick back for a few days or to base yourself for visits around the island. Updated: Jun 03, 2008.

Hiking

Rapa Nui offers a number of interesting day hikes and places to have a picnic. There are three main routes from Hanga Roa to different parts of the island. They are easy to find and frequented by the locals, too. To hike independently, pick up a trail map from Sernatur (Av. Policarpo Toro, open 8:30 a.m. – 6 p.m., closed weekends). Scenic routes include the coast to Anakena (5 hours) and the climb to Mauna Terevaka (3 hours). If you'd rather join a tour, Toki Tour (Av. Pont, Tel: 56-32-2551026, URL: www.tokitour.cl) offers full- and half-day excursions ($60-100). Whichever option you choose, wear good walking boots, sunscreen and carry a flashlight for exploring caves. Updated: Aug 30, 2009.

Bicycling Rapa Nui

Biking is an excellent way to discover the island and bikes can be rented at numerous outlets along Av. Atamu Tekena in Hanga Roa. Make Make (Av. Atamu Tekena, URL: www.makemakerapanui.com, open 9 a.m. – 1 p.m. and 4 p.m. – 8 p.m.) has the best selection and offers half and full day rentals ($8/10). They also provide maps showing major roads and tracks. All roads are bike friendly, but be on your guard for potholes and wandering animals. Popular routes go between Hanga Roa and Anakena (2-3 hours), Tangarika (3 hours) and Rano Kau (2 hours uphill). Updated: Aug 30, 2009.

Horseback riding

All hiking routes can also be done on horseback. Highly recommended are **Cabalgatas Pantu** (located in Hotel Pikera Uri, Tel: 56-32-2100577, URL: www.rapanuiturismopantu.cl). They cater to groups only (mininmum 3 people), have well-kept horses and run full and half-day tours all around the island ($55-100). They also have a two-day option with overnight camping ($400). Individuals can hire horses and book similar tours at the equally recommended **Uri Tahai** (Tel: 56-32-2551499). They don't have an office, so phone for reservations.

Diving / Snorkelling

Once you've conquered the land-based activities, there's a vast underwater world for you to explore. **Mike Rapu Diving Centre** (Av. Te Pito o Te Henua, Tel: 56-32-2551055, www.mikerapu.cl) dive four times daily to the south-west of the island (US$60-70) and rent high quality and modern equipment (included in the price). They also run night dives ($90) and PADI courses. For those who prefer their action on the surface, snorkelling equipment can be rented at the same place from US$10 per half day. Updated: Aug 30, 2009.

Surfing

If you fancy donning your wetsuit and hitting the surf, **Make Make** (Av. Atamu Tekena, www.makemakerapanui.com, open 9 a.m. – 1 p.m. and 4 p.m. – 8 p.m.) is the best option. Two-hour lessons start at $60, while experts can hire boards for $30-40 per half day with or without wetsuit. Waves are good all year round, but true thrill seekers might find them a little tame. The rocky coast means surfing is only possible off Hanga Pea.

Tours

A host of operators—many based in Hanga Roa on Easter Island itself—offer tours either by foot, horseback or from the comfort of a 4x4 vehicle. Packages range from simple day outings to longer five to seven day trips that include visits to the most spectacular archaeological sites, like the Orongo ceremonial village ruins or the Moai (the statues). Prices determine the level of luxury; tours tend to be in the high range, especially since they do not usually include airfare, which can cost $500 – 800 from Santiago. If booked locally, a simple four-day tour with transportation, meals, accommodation, bilingual guide and entrance to the national park starts at $285 per person; a seven-day tour should be in the $800 – $900 range. Tour operators based on the mainland also offer trips, but these tend to be a lot more expensive unless you are with a large group. If you prefer to organize your own trip, tour operators can arrange your car rentals, transfers and hotel reservations. Updated: Jul 07, 2009.

HANGA ROA

Easter Island's capital and only urban center, Hanga Roa, lies in a low area on the western coast. The town of 3,500+ inhabitants is a pleasure to walk around. The town's car speed limit is as low as 30 kilometers per hour, creating a slow pace in the area. The center of Hanga Roa, though planted with trees and shrubs, still has a windswept feeling.

Two sizeable craft markets and many small shops around town offer a range of local souvenirs. Café and restaurant menus vary, though a budget favorite seems to be tuna empanadas. Food on the island is pricey though, with average dishes costing $12.

Two local supermarkets offer a good alternative, though prices still reflect the island's remoteness. There is a good selection of hotels in the center of town, but if you want to relax and have a quieter stay on the island choose a place to the north of Hanga Roa. Updated: Jul 07, 2009.

Getting Around

As the airport is quite close to the city, most hotels and tour agencies offer shuttle services back and forth. Within the city, you can reach most places on foot. Cars, bicycles, motorbikes and scooters can also be rented easily through hotels, tour agencies and rental stations. The roads in Hanga Roa are paved, but many outside the city are not.

Rent-a-Car Insular offers regular cars ($45 – $65 per day), 4x4s and bicycles. A 4x4 is the best option to explore the island's poor roads, especially if it has been raining. Av. Atamu Tekena s/n. Updated: Jun 19, 2009.

Services

In general, services on the island are up to three times more expensive than on the mainland.

TOURISM

The tourism office, Sernatur, is open 8:30 a.m. – 6 p.m., closed weekends. Av. Policarpo Toro.

MONEY

The only bank is **Banco Estado** (open 8 a.m. to 1 p.m.), where you can change money or traveler's checks. Banco Estado has an ATM compatible only with Mastercard, and does not do Visa cash advances over the counter. Opposite the beach, **Banco Santander** has an ATM that accepts Visa, but doesn't always work. The gas station near the airport also has an ATM. There is a **Casa de Cambio** opposite Feria Artesanal that allows cash withdrawals with a Visa card, but they charge a staggering 15 percent tax service. Updated: Jul 06, 2009.

Photo by Dag Olav

PACIFIC ISLANDS

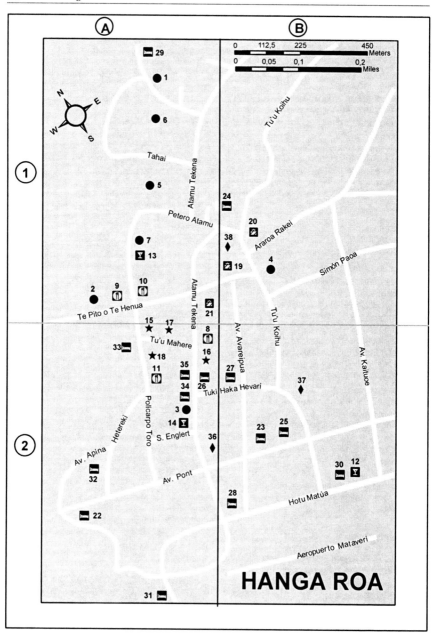

HANGA ROA

KEEPING IN TOUCH

You can send your postcards at the **Correos de Chile** (post office), which is by the radio station and the municipal buildings, between the church and the quay. Besides in cybercafés, Internet is available in most hotels in Hanga Roa.

MEDICAL

Only one hospital covers all of the island's medical needs. It is in the eastern suburbs of Hanga Roa. There are pharmacies, but if you are on medication, it is best to take it with you, as medicine is very expensive to buy on the island.

PACIFIC ISLANDS

Activities

1	Cabalgatas Pantu A1
2	Mike Rapu Diving Centre A1
3	Make Make A2
4	Iglesia Hanga Roa B1
5	Cementerio Hanga Roa A1
6	Museum Sebastián Englert A1
7	Kari Kari A1

Eating 🍴

8	Té Moana A2
9	La Taverne Du Pecheur A 1
10	Merahi Ra'a A1
11	Kana Nehe Nehe A2

Nightlife ▼

12	Discoteque Piriti B2
13	Tomoko Discoteque A1
14	Aloha Pub-Restaurant A2

Services ★

15	Sernatur (Tourism Office) A2
16	Rent a Card Insular A2
17	Banco Estado A2
18	Banco Santander A2

Shopping

19	Kiani B1
20	Mercado Artesenal B1
21	Et Cetera A1

Sleeping 🛏

22	Camping Mihinoa A2
23	Hostelling Internacional Kona Tau B2
24	Residencial Petero Atamu B1
25	Villa Tiki B2
26	Hotel/Restaurant Orongo A2
27	Residencial Chez Erika B2
28	Residencial Miru B2
29	Hostal Akapu A1
30	Hotel Manutara B2
31	Hotel Lorana A2
32	Residencial Ana Rapu A2
33	Bar-Restaurant Pea A2
34	Restaurant Hetu'u A2
35	Kaimana Inn A2

Tours ◆

36	Toki Tour A2
37	Rapa Nui B2
38	Aku Aku Turismo B1

LAUNDRY
Most hotels and guesthouses offer a laundry service for a small charge.

SHOPPING
Easter Island lacks fine boutiques, but there is a treasure chest of souvenir shops to explore. Most are concentrated along Av. Atamu Tekena and Av. Te Pito o Te Henua. For replica Moai, don your haggling hat and head to **Mercado Artesanal** (Monday – Saturday, 9:30 – 7 p.m., Sun: 8 a.m. – 2 p.m., Calle Tu´u Koihu). You'll find them in all shapes and sizes. Just remember that whatever you buy, you have to lug home.

To expand your wardrobe, try **Kiani** (Av. Te Pito o Te Henua) which sells traditional Polynesian clothes in every colour and pattern imaginable. Alternatively, choose your own fabric and have something custom-made in one to three days.

For something more intellectual, brush up on your Rapa Nui history, at **Et Cetera** (Av. Te Pito o Te Henua) which has an extensive collection of English and Spanish books. Some are a bit tattered: the owners will tell you they're historical relics, but what better way to while away those post sunset evenings? Updated: Jul 07, 2009.

Things to See and Do
Hanga Roa is the gateway to the rest of the island, with plenty of agencies and guides concentrated in a relatively small area. While you're in town, check out Hanga Roa's selection of shows, exhibits and museums within the city.

Museum Sebastián Englert
(ADMISSION: $2) This fascinating museum is partially the work of Father Sebastián Englert. He spent 30 years on the island (from 1935 onward) collecting artifacts. When he died in 1969 his collection became the property of the

state; scientific surveys throughout the 1960s greatly added to the museum's collection. A bonus is the art gallery which exhibits the work of local artists. There is also a reasonably priced café. Open weekdays 9:30 a.m. – 5:30 p.m.; weekends 9:30 a.m. – 12:30 p.m. Sector Tahai s/n. Tel: 56-32-2551020, E-mail: mapse@mapse.cl, URL: www.museorapanui.cl. Updated: Jul 07, 2009.

Kari Kari
(ADMISSION: $20) The folkloric traditional ballet, Kari Kari, is the pride of Easter Island. This spectacular dance is guaranteed to bring out the Polynesian in you, as the dancers twirl and stomp in their grass skirts to the sound of traditional instruments. Tickets are pricey, but worth it. Get there early for a guaranteed entry and good seats; because this is a popular performance. Open until 10 p.m. Av. Policarpo Toro s/n. URL: karikari.bizland.com. Updated: Jul 07, 2009.

Iglesia Hanga Roa
(ADMISSION: Free) The island's Catholic Church overlooks Hanga Roa from a small hill on the Northern side of town. Inside, intricate wood carvings combine Rapa Nui culture and Christian ceremony. There's also a particularly cool Sunday morning service in the Rapa Nui language. Everyone's invited and it has been known to get quite lively. Tu'u Koihu. Services on Saturday at 9 a.m. and Sunday at 9 a.m. And 11: a.m. Open until 8 p.m. Updated: Aug 30, 2009.

Cementerio Hanga Roa
(ADMISSION: Free) Often overlooked, the cemetery is definitely worth visiting during a coastal wander. Islanders believed in death the soul is returned to the ocean. Accordingly, graves face inland, so that grieving relatives can gaze over the Pacific to view their loved ones. Gravestones are small and traditional, with a mass of wooden crosses dotting the site. Some graves are unmarked, although the cemetery was still accepting burials until recently. Av. Policarpo Toro. Updated: Aug 30, 2009.

Tours
Sign up for a tour if you want to explore with the proper equipment and an experienced guide. The following are a few of the island's best operators:

Aku Aku Toursimo offers open or private multi-day tours, including a family package, which include airport transfer, accommodation and meals. Tours are on foot or on horseback. Tu'u Koihu s/n, Box 32. Tel: 56-32-2100770, Fax: 56-2-6332491, URL: www.akuakuturismo.cl.

Rapa Nui Travel divides their tours into traditional and adventure options. While traditional tours visit beaches, archaeological sites, museums, cultural shows, churches and the great crater lake, adventure tours take guests trekking, horseback riding, scuba diving, snorkeling or boating. Tu'u Koihu s/n. Tel: 56-32-2100548, E-mail: rntravel@entel-chile.net , URL: www.rapanuitravel.com.

Toki Tour can arrange for guests to stay in a hotel, bungalow or at a campground. They also offer fishing, sunrise and sunset tours, city tours, horseback riding, cultural shows, diving, islet tours, motorbiking and mountain biking. Avenida Pont con Atamu Tekena s/n. Tel: 56-32-2551026 / 56-32-2551295, E-mail: info@tokitour.cl, URL: www.tokitour.cl. Updated: Jul 08, 2009.

Lodging
When you first book a room, ask what is included in the room rate, as hotels tend to offer full board and guesthouses only B&B. Others include laundry service. If you want a quieter vacation, avoid the center of Hanga Roa. Anakena beach has the island's only campground. You should carry all the food and water you'll need as there are no shops outside of Hanga Roa. Some of the guest houses may allow you to set up your tent on their lawn for a fee.

Camping Mihinoa
(ROOMS: US$14-55, CAMPSITES: US$10 per person) Mihinoa is an excellent budget option just south of town and the prime location for sunset lovers. The "no shoes inside" rule means the spacious rooms are always spotless. Facilities are basic and hot water only comes on at either end of the day, but you'll be out Moai-spotting most of the time anyway. The owners speak English, Spanish and French and provide 24-hour kitchen access and WiFi. Breakfast not included. Av. Pont, Tel: 56-32-2551593, URL: www.mihinoa.com. Updated: Aug 30, 2009.

Residencial Miru
(ROOMS: $15) Located 5 minutes from the town center, the quiet Residencial Miru offers simple, tidy single and double rooms, all with comfy beds and private bathrooms. There is a common room as well as a kitchen

that guests can use. The owner, Sandra will be happy to point you to all the services that you may need in town. Av. Atamu Takena s/n. Tel: 100-365. Updated: Jun 19, 2009.

Hostelling Internacional Kona Tau

(ROOMS: US$20-65. Discounts for HI cardholders) Exactly what you'd expect from an HI hostel, with bright, airy rooms, large chillout space and welcoming atmosphere. All rooms have a private bathroom and open onto a terrace where you can enjoy great views of Rano Aroi and the centre of the island. The non-central location can feel isolated, but the friendly owner can help organise cultural and nocturnal activities. Avareipua, Tel: 56-32-2100321. Updated: Aug 30, 2009.

Residencial Petero Atamu

(ROOMS: US$20 per bed, CHALETS: US$100) At the end of a dirt road, the location isn't the prettiest, but Petero Atamu provides decent budget accommodation. Of the six rooms, four have private baths, while all are spacious and cheery, even the eight-bed dorms. Groups should also consider one of the two self-contained chalets, which include single and double beds, washing machine and kitchen. The owner is fluent in the local language. Av. Petero Atamu, Tel: 56-32-2551735. Updated: Aug 30, 2009.

Residencial Ana Rapu

(ROOMS: $35 – $140) Ana Rapu offers rooms, cabins or campsites. Compared to most places on the island, the prices here are pretty low. The rooms are nothing special, but you get what you pay for. The Residencial also offers car, motorcycle or bike rentals, Internet, laundry services, horseback riding and boat trips. Av. Apina s/n. Tel: 56-32-2100540, E-mail: info@anarapu.cl, URL: www.anarapu.cl. Updated: July 10, 2009.

Hostal Akapu

(ROOMS: $46 – $110) Right by the sea, Hostal Akapu has both individual rooms and entire bungalows with private bathrooms and hot water. The bungalows are definitely the better option, with great ocean views and open terraces. Neither the bungalows nor the individual rooms are particularly spacious, but they're a good place to relax and take in the sea air. A communal TV, an open kitchen and WiFi are also included. Sector Tahai s/n. Tel: 56-32-21009, E-mail: info@hostalakapurapanui.cl, URL: www.hostalakapurapanui.cl. Updated: Jul 08, 2009.

Hotel Orongo

(ROOMS: US$50-80) Quite simply the best mid-range accommodation on the island. All eight rooms, single and double, are large with nice wood furniture. The private bathrooms are modern, while the central garden, although a little on the wild side, helps further the illusion that you've made it to the middle of nowhere. There's also an excellent craft shop and restaurant on-site. Rooms go quickly, so book early. Av. Atamu Tekena, Tel: 56-32-2100294, URL: www.hotelorongo.com. Updated: Aug 30, 2009.

Residencial Chez Erika

(ROOMS: US$50-75) Although not in the same league as the other mid-range hotels, Chez Erika is still a good bright and breezy option. Colourful walls are the theme, although that might be a ploy to hide the fact that some rooms are a little past their sell-by date. To be safe, ask to see several selection. Internet and breakfast included. Av. Tuki Haka Hevari, Tel: 56-32-2100474. Updated: Aug 30, 2009.

Villa Tiki

(ROOMS US$70-90) All six double and triple rooms are enormous with huge windows through which light floods in. If you want to be fussy, some rooms are slightly better than others, so ask for one overlooking the garden. The breakfast, including freshly squeezed fruit juice, will have you delaying your sightseeing as you're made to feel like one of the family. Av. Pont, Tel: 56-32-2100327. Updated: Aug 30, 2009.

Hotel Iorana

(ROOMS: $100 – $200) One of the most luxurious accommodation options on the island, this hotel has the feel of a resort, with tennis courts, swimming pools and beautiful views. The food alone and the impressive breakfast spread in particular is worth the high price. Rooms are clean and comfortable with large private bathrooms. Ana Magaro s/n. Tel: 56-32-2100608, Fax: 56-32-2100312, E-mail: ioranahotel@entelchile.net, URL www.ioranahotel.cl. Updated: July 10, 2009.

Hotel Manutara

(ROOMS: $115 – $200) Hotel Manutara has a friendly, welcoming staff ready to assist you with all your travel needs. The grounds are beautiful, with pleasant gardens and lots of flowers, and the rooms are relatively large and very clean. For those looking to relax there are swimming pools, a massage parlor and a coffee shop.

PACIFIC ISLANDS

Tours, excursions and car rentals can easily be arranged. Hotu Matua s/n. Tel: 56-32-2551501/2551502/2551503, Fax: 56-32-2100768, E-mail: manutarahotel@entelchile.net, www.hotelmanutara.cl. Updated: July 10, 2009.

Restaurants

The general level of service in local eateries is good, but prices are much higher here than on the mainland. Menus at most restaurants and cafés are printed in Spanish, English and Japanese. The cuisine is seafood-oriented, tuna is a local specialty.

Merahi Ra'a

(ENTREES: $8 – $14) Merahi Ra'a has fresh, tasty fish dishes. The ambiance is nothing to write home about, but there is a small terrace that overlooks the harbor. Try the delicious tuna ceviche or the grilled tuna with salad and fries. Av. Te Pinto o Te Henua s/n. Tel: 56-32-2551125. Updated: Jul 08, 2009.

Bar-Restaurant Pea

(ENTREES: $12-14) Sumptuous food, a backdrop of lapping waves and a sunset which paints the sky red, this place has it all. The décor is charmingly simple, the dishes, mouth watering. For fish lovers, the tuna ceviche is exquisite. Be careful not to run up a huge bar tab as you while away the hours admiring the perfect view. Av. Policarpo Toro, Tel: 56-32-2100382. Updated: Aug 30, 2009.

Restaurant Hetu'u

(ENTREES: $12-16) Occupying a prime spot at the centre of the Atamu Tekena, Restaurant Hetu'u offers prompt service, good atmosphere and tasty dishes on an extensive menu. The shrimp gets rave reviews, but there's also a number of good vegetarian options. Either way, the desserts will have you licking your lips. Av. Atamu Tekena. Updated: Sep 22, 2009.

Te Moana

(ENTREES: $12 – $28) Te Moana has a small patio, charming island décor, and a tranquil atmosphere. Most dishes consist of fish with a side of vegetables and potatoes. The grilled fish, the surf-and-turf platter and the sweet coconut ceviche served on the half shell are definitely worth a try. In typical island fashion the service can be a bit slow, but the food is reasonably priced. Av. Atamu Tekena s/n. Tel: 32-2-551578. Updated: Jul 08, 2009.

Kona Nehe Nehe

(ENTREES: $14 – $17) The biggest appeal of this restaurant/café is that it serves non-seafood dishes like lasagna and pasta, and is a safe haven for vegetarians. The dining area is spacious and well decorated with a nice view of the ocean. Av. Policarpo Toro s/n. Tel: 56-32-2551677. Updated: Jul 08, 2009.

La Taverne du Pêcheur

(ENTREES $15 – 25) This French restaurant serves dishes made with fresh, tasty ingredients. It's no surprise that seafood is the specialty, with a menu offering mussels, oysters, shrimp, crab, sea urchin, and the local favorite, *rape rape* (a small lobster). If seafood's not your cup of tea, try the roquefort beef and fresh vegetables. La Taverne is a little more expensive than other local restaurants, but the portions are huge, the wine is exquisite and the desserts are to die for. The service is sometimes slow, though. Av. Te Pito o Te Henua s/n. Tel: 32-210-0619. Updated: Jul 08, 2009.

Restaurant Orongo

(ENTREES: $15-40) Next to the hotel of the same name, Orongo is a restaurant in its own right. Like everywhere else, fish and steak form the backbone of the menu, but you can't do much better for the price. The speciality, Polynesian buffet featuring six different types of local fish is to die for. Theoretically it's for two, but you won't want to share. Av. Atamu Tekena, Tel: 56-32-2100294, URL: www.hotelorongo.com. Updated: Aug 30, 2009.

Kaimana Inn

(ENTREES: $15-60) If the smell of the food wafting out of the front door isn't enough to tempt you inside, then either your nose is on the blink or they're closed. As well as the usual fish and meat, they do a mean line in pizzas. For an extra $40, you can be wined and dined to the backdrop of traditional Rapa Nui singing and dancing (Mondays, Wednesdays and Fridays 9 p.m. start). Call ahead for reservations. Av. Atamu Tekena, Tel: 56-32-255740, URL: www.kaimanainn.com. Updated: Aug 30, 2009.

Nightlife

Discotheque Piriti

(ADMISSION: $6. Only men pay before 1 a.m.) The island's hotspot is the place to go if you want to chat up other travelers. It looks shabby on the outside, but inside it simmers with a fusion of Euro-American pop and Latin American tunes. The action doesn't properly get going until 1 a.m., so if you arrive before then, you might find yourself sat in a corner on your own. Drinks are expensive. Av. Hotu Matu'a. Updated: Aug 30, 2009.

Toroko discotheque

(ADMISSION: $6. Only men pay before 1 a.m.) From the outside, Toroko looks even more dilapidated than Piriti, nevertheless, it's the place to go if you want to get down and dance up a storm with the locals. All the action is squeezed into a room the size of a tennis court, so wild dancers will literally be bouncing off the walls. The music is a mixture of Rapa Nui, Polynesian and Chilean classics. You'll be lonely if you arrive much before 1 a.m. Av. Policarpo Toro. Updated: Aug 30, 2009.

Aloha Pub-Restaurant

(NO COVER CHARGE) For something a little more mellow, head to Aloha, with its cozy atmosphere and laid-back beats. There's a good selection of bottled beers and a massive cocktail list. At the end of the night, if all the drinking has given you the munchies, try one of Aloha's specialty steaks, which, in spite of being huge, won't break your budget. Av. Atamu Tekena, Tel: 56-32-2551383. Open until 1 a.m. Updated: Oct 12, 2009.

RAPA NUI NATIONAL PARK

Once you take a step outside the boundaries of Hanga Roa you are in Rapa Nui National Park, which is also a World Heritage Site. There are virtually no services in the park, no hotels, no restaurants, not even toilets! The exception is a kiosk at Anakena Beach. There is a Conaf cabin atop Rano Kau at Orongo and park rangers are available to provide information. You should take everything you need with you for your trip, including a bag for trash.

Without a doubt the highlights are, well... everything! There's a lot to marvel at here: the Moai, the ceremonial platforms they stand on, the petrogylphs, the magnetic rock, the bird man cave paintings, the volcanoes and their lava tubes and the deep blue Pacific Ocean. You'll be amazed by the sheer sense of isolation you get as you stand on top of a volcano in the middle of the ocean. Updated: Jul 07, 2009.

Things to See and Do
Moais

Around 95 percent of the Moai statues found on the island are crafted from the volcanic rock found around Rano Raraku. Within the crater of this volcano is a beautiful lake, which was formed by the activity of the Terevaka volcano. Around the area are some four hundred or so Moai, all in different stages of creation.

All but one group of Moai face inland with their backs to the sea. The only Moai facing seaward are at Ahu Akivi, where seven Moai stand in a line gazing out across the Pacific Ocean. Archaeologists have determined that the Moai were built from 1000-1500 AD, though some Ahu (the platform on which the Moai stand) are dated earlier than this.

Most of the Moai inhabit the coastal areas of the island and are easily accessible. Among the most famous Moai line-ups are the 15 Ahu Tongariki, the sea-gazing seven of Ahu Akivi and the Ahu Nau Nau who are prepared for the sun at Anakena beach in their red *Pukao* (hats). Every Moai are photogenic, so take extra film or memory cards and snap away.

You should plan to spend a day at the Moai manufacturing sites of Rano Raraku on the slopes of Volcano Terevaka, where the Moai sprout from the ground in various stages of fabrication. A few Moai are still crowned with their cylindrical, red, volcanic Pukao, which were quarried from the volcanic cinder cone Puna Pau near Hanga Roa. Most Moai have not only lost their hats, but other finer features as well, including fingers, eyes and other smaller pieces. This occurred during the years of long-ear and short-ear inter-clan wars of the 1800s. The only existing Moai with carvings down its back is in the British Museum in London, England, but you can buy a postcard of it on the island.

At Poukura Bay are the remains of Ahu Hanga Poukura. This Ahu was decimated during the wars, and the Moai's red Pukao are scattered among the fallen Moai. Along the coast at Ahu Hanga Tee, eight fallen Moai serve as a reminder of the clan clashes of the 1800s. The Moai lie strewn like giant chess pieces and have lain there for over 200 years. Remember that although they look neglected, there are large fines for standing or walking on the Ahu, Moai, petroglyphs, or any artifact or piece of heritage on the island.

PACIFIC ISLANDS

Of the 313 known Ahu sites around the island, Moai reportedly once stood on 125 of them. Many Ahu platforms remain partially overgrown or hidden from sight, so be careful where you walk. Some of the Ahu platforms have been used for burials, but this was not their original function. With only theories about why they were created, we can really only marvel at them and speculate about their origin and purpose.

Although most Ahu platforms are without Moai heads, the bases can be worth visiting for a glimpse of the craftsmanship of the stone masonry. Beautiful basalt blocks lined up and placed with perfection form the base at Ahu Vinapu and at Ahu Huri a Murenga, north of Ahu Vinapu.

Petroglyphs
Many petrogylphs can be found in the enclosed national park area atop volcano Rano Kau. The entrance fee to the area of $10 per person may seem expensive, but it is the only time you have to pay to enter a national park area on the island.

Stone Dwellings
The crater of the Rano Kau volcano is spectacular, with its patchwork of reed beds scattered across the lagoon. The crater is almost perfectly round with a lower lip on the ocean side where lava once flowed out. Here, on the top of the volcano, you'll find the remains of 56 *hare paenga* (houses) that were once the village of Orongo.

Hare paenga are boat-shaped, windowless, low stone dwellings, typically up to six meters long, with very low entrances, which means you'll have to crawl in order to enter. Many are just ruins, but some have been restored. One hare paenga has part of its roof removed to display its construction and interior.

You can find good examples of hare paenga at Ahu Te Peu, although for some of the dwellings there are only outlines of stone left. Just north of Hanga Roa is Ahu Tahai, there is a complex of three Ahu: Ahu Kote Riku on the northern side, Ahu Tahai in the center and Ahu Vai Uri to the south. The site also has stone dwellings.

Rapa Nui has its own writing system, *rongorongo*, that is as unique as the island's culture. You can spot rongorongo among the island's petroglyphs. There is the mass of petroglyphs at the village of Orongo, but you can find these drawings on stone across the island. Many are hidden away on the eastern Poike peninsula. You'll need to walk around to the eastern face of volcano Poike and enter a cave in order to see them.

Around the island, you will find small round stone towers called *Pipi Horeko*, which mark the borders of clan territories. According to legend, Hotu, the first king of Rapa Nui, divided his land the following way: Tu'u Maheke, the firstborn son of Hotu, inherited the land between Anakena and Maunga Tea-Tea (maunga meaning hill). Miru, the second child, received the lands between Anakena and Hanga Roa.

Marama, the third, inherited the lands between Anakena and Rano Raraku. Raa, his fourth child, settled to the northwest of Maunga Tea-Tea. Koro Orongo, his fifth, decided to live between Akahanga and Rano Raraku. Hotu Iti, the sixth, was given the eastern part of the island. Tupahotu and Ngaure, Hotus youngest children were left with the remaining parts of the island, Rano Kau and the Hanga Roa areas.

Navel of the World
The famed magnetic rock, the navel of the world, can be found on the northern coast, between Anakena and Poike. It is a large, smooth, round stone with four smaller stones around it and is surrounded by a low stone wall. Placing a compass on the rock causes its needle to spin. The wall around the rock can be a welcome shelter from the relentless Pacific winds, but also hides the rock, so keep a look out for it.

Caves
It's worth noting that many features of Rapa Nui are hidden from view. If you can't find what you are looking for, ask a local; few signs exist and you can walk right by the things without ever seeing them. The entrance of AnaKaharga (*ana* meaning cave), a small space with two windows, is a good example of this. The cave is so well concealed that it was once used by women to hide from slave raiders. You can walk right by the depression in the ground, which leads to the three-foot high and two-foot wide entrance of this spectacular lava tube cave.

Take a flashlight, because Dos Ventanas (Two Windows) cave, is completely dark on the inside. If you want to reach the ventanas—two openings in the cliff face some 50 meters or more above the sea—you have to crawl on hands and knees through an old lava tube. You might get a few scrapes, but the experience and the view from the cave are well worth the effort.

Several of the lava tubes and caves on the island extend for several kilometers. These caves, although possible to explore, require extensive preparation and equipment. One of these, Ana Te Pahu, north of Hanga Roa, is a beautiful example of how those on Rapa Nui once lived. A part of the cave has been divided into individual living areas with stone walls. A section where the roof collapsed was turned into a sunken garden by ancient cave dwellers, and is now a small, lush banana tree forest.

Ana Kai Tangata has surprisingly well-preserved red and white cave paintings of birds that are similar to the symbols in the Rongorongo writing. The birdman cult members of Orongo are responsible for these paintings. To get to the cave, which is located on the coast near the airport, you'll need to descend a cliff face stairway of abrasive volcanic rock that can be slippery when wet.

In Ana O Keke, also known as the cave of the virgins, which is on the northern side of the Poike peninsula, you'll find a series of good petroglyphs. Walk further around the peninsula and you'll come to Ana Hue Neru, a large coastal cave. Updated: Jul 07, 2009.

)))))

Chilean Flora & Fauna Species

FLORA

Common Name - Chile	Taxonomic Name	English Name
alerce	*Fitzroya cupressoides*	Patagonian cypress, Chilean false larch
araucaria, pehuén	*Araucaria araucana*	monkey puzzle tree
avellano	*Gevuina avellana*	Chilean hazel
cadillo	*Acaena splendens*	-----
calafate	*Berberis buxifolia*	Magellan barberry
canelo	*Drimys winteri*	winter's bark
canelo andino, canelo enano	*Drimys andina (Reiche) R.A. Rodr. & Quez.*	-----
chaura	*Pernettya mucronata*	Chilean wintergreen
chilco	*Fuchsia magellanica*	bush fuchsia
chungungo	*Pinus ponderosa*	Ponderosa pine
ciervo rojo (introduced species)		
ciprés de la cordillera	*Austurocedrus chilensis*	Chilean cedar
ciprés de las guaitecas, guaitecas	*Pilgerodendron uviferum*	Guaitecas cypress
coigüe, coihue	*Nothofagus dombeyi or donbeyi*	-----
coigüe de Chiloé	*Nothofagus nitida*	-----
coigüe de Magallanes	*Nothofagus betuloides*	Magellan's beech
hualo	*Nothofagus glauca*	Southern beech
guindo santo	*Eucryphia glutinosa*	Chilean eucryphia
laurel	*Laurelia sempervirens*	Chilean laurel, Chilean sassafras
leña de piedra	*Azorella incisa*	-----
lenga, ñire	*Nothofagus pumilio*	lenga beech
llareta	*Azorella incisa*	-----
lleuque	*Prumnopitys andina*	plum-fruited yew
luma	*Amomyrtus luma*	Chilean myrtle
maitén	*Maitenus boaria*	maiten
mañío de hoja larga	*Podocarpus salignus*	willow-leafed podocarp
mañío de hojas cortas	*Saxegothaea conspicua*	Prince Albert's yew

Common Name - Chile	Taxonomic Name	English Name
maño macho	*Podocarpus nubigenus*	Chilean podocarp
neneo	*Mulinum spinosum*	-----
ñire, ñirre	*Nothofagus Antarctica*	Antarctic beech
notro, ciruelillo	*Embothrium coccineum*	Chilean fire bush
olivillo, palo muerto	*Aextoxicon punctatum*	-----
orquídea de flor dorada	*Chloraea alpina*	yellow dog orchid
peumo	*Peumus boldus*	boldo
pico de loro	*Chloraea magellanica*	Magellan's orchid
pino oregón (introduced species)	*Pseudotzuga menziessi*	Pseudotzuga menziessi
pino ponderosa (introduced species)	*Pinus ponderosa*	Ponderosa pine
quillay	*Quillaja saponaria*	soap bark tree
radal enano	*Orites myrtoidea*	Chilean myrtle
raulí	*Nothofagus alpina*	-----
roble	*Nothofagus oblicua*	-----
sauco del diablo	*Pseudopanax laetevirens*	-----
tepa	*Laurelia philippiana*	-----
tiaca, triaca	*Caldcluvia paniculata*	-----
tineo, palo santo	*Weinmannia trichosperma*	-----
notro, ciruelillo	*Embothrium coccineum*	-----
trevo, palo santo, palo blanco	*Dasyphylum diacantoides*	-----
ulmo	*Eucryphia cordifolia*	-----

FAUNA: MAMMALS, REPTILES & AMPHIBIANS, BIRDS

chingue patagónico, chingue de la Patagonia	*Conepatus humboldti*	Patagonian skunk
comadrejita trompuda, zorrino	*Orites myrtoidea*	Chilean myrtle
coipo	*Nothofagus alpina*	-----
culpeo, zorro culpeo, zorro colorado	*Nothofagus oblicua*	-----
gato de geofroy	*Pseudopanax laetevirens*	-----
guanaco	*Laurelia philippiana*	-----
huemul	*Caldcluvia paniculata*	-----
Jabalí (introduced species)	*Weinmannia trichosperma*	-----

Common Name - Chile	Taxonomic Name	English Name
liebre (introduced species)	*Embothrium coccineum*	-----
monito del monte	*Dasyphylum diacantoides*	-----
piche	*Eucryphia cordifolia*	-----
pudú	*Pudu pudu*	Chilean miniature deer
puma	*Puma concolor*	puma, mountain lion, cougar
ratita de pie sedoso	*Eligmodontia typus*	highland gerbil mouse
Ratón colilargo	*Oligoryzomys longicaudatus*	long-tailed pygmy rice rat
ratoncito oliváceo	*Abrothrix olivaceus*	olive grass mouse
visón (introduced species)	*Mustela vison*	American mink
vizcacha austral	*Lagidium wolfshonni*	Wolffsohn's viscacha
zorro chilla	*Psuedolopex griseus*	South American grey fox
	Liolaemus zullyi	Type of lizard or tree iguana
sapito de cuatro ojos	*Pleurodema thaul*	Chilean four-eyed frog
sapito de Darwin	*Rhynoderma Darwin*	Darwin's frogs
Águila	*Geranoetus melanoleucus*	Black-chested Buzzard-eagle, Grey Buzzard-eagle
Aguilucho, pueco	*Buteo albigula*	White-throated Hawk
Bandurria	*Theristicus caudatus*	Buff-necked Ibis
Cachaña	*Enicognathus ferrugineus*	Austral Parakeet
Carancho	*Polyborus plancus*	Striped Woodpecker
Carpinterito	*Picoides lignarius*	Striped Woodpecker
Carpintero Negro, Carpintero Grande	*Campephilus magellanicus*	Magellanic Woodpecker
Cernícalo	*Falco sparverius*	American Kestrel
Chucao	*Scelorchilus rubecula*	Chucao
Chuncho	*Glaucidium nanum*	Austral Pygmy Owl
Cisnes de Cuello Negro	*Cignus melancoriphus*	Black-necked Swan
Cometocino	*Phrygilus patagonicus*	Patagonian Sierra Finch
Comorán	*Phalacrocorax olivaceus*	Neotropic Cormorant
Condor	*Vultur gryphus*	Andean condor

Common Name - Chile	Taxonomic Name	English Name
Fiofío	*Elaenia albiceps*	White-crested Elaenia
Gallina Ciego	*Caprimulgus longirostris*	Band-winged Nightjar
Gaviota andina	*Larus serranus*	Andean Gull
Huala	*Podiceps major*	Great Grebe
Huairavo, Garza Bruja	*Nycticorax nycticorax*	Black-crowned Night Heron
Huet-Huet, Hued-hued	*Polyborus plancus*	Black-crowned Night Heron
Jilguero	*Carduelis barbatus*	Black-chinned Siskin
Loica	*Sturnella loyca*	Long Tailed Meadowlark
MartínPescador	*Ceryle torquata*	Ringed Kingfisher
Pato Anteojillo	*Anas specularis*	Spectacled Duck
Pato Corta-corriente	*Merganetta armata*	Torrent Duck
Pato Jergón	*Anas georgica*	Yellow-billed Pintail
Pato Rana Pico Ancha	*Oxyura jamaicensis*	Ruddy Duck
Pato Real	*Anas platyrhynchos*	Mallard
Picaflor chico	*Sepanoides galeritus*	Green-backed Firecrown Hummingbird
Pitío	*Colaptes pitius*	Chilean Flicker
Queltehue	*Vanellus chilensis*	Southern Lapwing
Rayadito, Tintica	*Aphrastura spinicauda*	Thorn-tailed Rayadito
Remolinera	*Cinclodes patagonicus*	Dark-bellied Cinclodes
Tagua	*Fulica armillata*	Red-gartered Coot
Tiuque	*Milvago chimango*	Caracara
Torcaza	*Patagioenas (Columba) araucana*	Chilean Pigeon
Tordo	*Curaeus curaeus*	Austral Blackbird
Tucúquere	*Bubo virgianianus*	Great Horned Owl
Zorzal	*Turdua falklandii*	Austral Thrush

For more information on flora and fauna species in Chile see:
- www.iucnredlist.org
- www.gochile.cl/eng/Guide/ChileFloraFauna/Fauna.asp
- www.chileflora.com/Florachilena/FloraEnglish/EPlantdbase.htm

Environmental Tips for Travelers

By Nicola Robinson, Nicola Mears and Heather Ducharme, Río Muchacho Organic Farm

While traveling in a foreign country, it is important to minimize your impact. Here are some tips you should keep in mind while on your trip. Some of this advice may be more difficult to take on board while traveling than it would be to incorporate into your daily lives at home. However, even if you only put into practice three or four of the suggestions, on the road or at home, it will certainly help reduce your impact on the planet.

Garbage

• Carry a water bottle and always check if there is somewhere to fill it up at your hotel / restaurant—most hotels and restaurants have purified water in 20-litre bottles called *botellones*. These places usually also sell water in small bottles and might be reluctant to begin with as they think they are losing a sale. Of course you will need to pay for the refill also. If you have to buy bottles, buy the biggest you can and just refill from there, especially if you plan to be in the same place for a while.

• Purify your own water to avoid creating garbage.

• Try to avoid excessive wrapping and plastic bags which are all too readily dished out for each small purchase. If you can, explain to the shop keeper why you want to give the bag back. If you shop in a local market, take your own bag or have them place everything in one large plastic bag instead of numerous small ones.

• Use a digital camera instead of film. The process of developing film can produce a lot of waste, and unwanted photos are non recyclable and often end up in the trash.

• Use a reusable container for soap so you can use your own instead of the small hotel soaps, which come individually wrapped. If you use hotel soap, use one and take the remainder with you—it will just be thrown out.

• Avoid using excessive cosmetic products such as hairspray, mousse, aftershave and perfume, or try to find effective environmentally-friendly alternatives such as biodegradable shampoos and crystal deodorants, which last longer (most containers for these products are non recyclable). Avoid using disposable products such as plastic razors and single-use contact lenses.

• Try to use rechargeable batteries or eliminate use of batteries entirely. For example, use a wind-up or solar torch or radio.

• Use recycled paper for letters home, trip diaries and toilet paper.

• Buy in bulk if you are traveling in a large group to reduce packaging.

• Recycle whatever you can in the country you are traveling. Some products that can not be recycled in the host country can be recycled in your home countries (such as batteries), so please take them home if possible.

Food and health

• Avoid eating foods that you know are from endangered or threatened species (research these before you come to the country). Buy and eat locally grown and locally processed foods wherever possible, rather than food shipped from long distances, which use more energy and packaging.

• Consider using alternative natural medical products for common travelers' illnesses. This may be healthier for you and keeps you from leaving behind pharmaceuticals in the local water and soil (this is becoming a detectable problem in first world countries, thought to affect aquatic organisms like fish and frogs).

Nature, Flora and fauna

• Avoid buying souvenirs of local fauna. Many stores sell cases of bright colored butterflies, spiders and insects which are caught by the hundreds in the Amazon. The sales people will tell you that they are not caught but that they raise them—it is not true!

• Avoid buying souvenirs that are made with endangered species or species that have to be killed to be made into a craft. Support crafts made from renewable resources.

• Don't collect insects, flora and fauna without a permit. Leave them for everyone to enjoy.

• When walking, stay on the trails and close gates behind you.

Camping and Water

• Use toilets where they exist. If there are no toilets, bury human waste in a hole 20 centimeters deep. Human waste should be buried at least 50 meters from water sources.

• Use biodegradable soaps and detergents.

• Don't wash shampoo and detergent off directly in rivers, but rather as far away as you can (4 meters minimum).

• Avoid making fires.

• Use a T-shirt when swimming instead of sunscreen, as it's harmful to marine life.

Transport

• Use public transport instead of private (e.g. bus instead of rental car) when possible to reduce fossil fuel use. Share rental cars and taxis with others. If possible, walk or use a bicycle. It not only helps the planet, but it keeps you in shape as well!

Electricity

• Lights, fans, TVs, radios, or computers: If you are not using it, turn it off!

Packing lists

(* indicates something that might not be available in Chile)

GENERAL PACKING LIST:

There are a number of items that every traveler should consider bringing to Chile as follows:

□ **Medicines and prescriptions** (Very important. Bringing all relevant medical info and medicines may well save you a lot of grief in Chile)
□ **Photocopies of passport** and other relevant ID documents
□ Paperback novels (sometimes you'll be sitting on buses, in airports, or somewhere else for a long time. It is possible to find and /or exchange books in several places in Colombia, but don't count on much selection if you don't read Spanish)
□ Voltage converter and plug adapter
□ A good camera (see photography section)
□ Water bottle (bottled water is readily available in Chile, but you may want your own bottle)
□ Sunglasses
□ Motion sickness medicine
□ Lip balm
□ *Tampons (difficult to find outside the major cities)
□ Sun hat
□ Condoms and other contraceptives
□ *Foot powder
□ Antacid tablets, such as Rolaids
□ Mild painkillers such as aspirin or ibuprofen
□ *GPS device (especially for hikers)
□ Watch with alarm clock
□ Diarrhea medicine (i.e. Imodium)
□ Warm clothes (The highlands are cooler than you think)

BACKPACKER PACKING LIST:

□ All of the above, plus:
□ Rain poncho
□ Plastic bags
□ *Swiss army knife/Leatherman
□ Toilet paper
□ *Antibacterial hand gel
□ Small padlock

Additional Items

□ _____
□ _____
□ _____
□ _____
□ _____
□ _____
□ _____
□ _____

ANTI-PACKING LIST: THINGS NOT TO BRING TO CHILE

- ✗ Expensive jewelry. Just leave it home.
- ✗ Nice watch or sunglasses. Bring a cheap one you can afford to lose.
- ✗ Go through your wallet: what won't you need? Leave your drivers' license (unless you're planning on driving), business cards, video-club membership cards, 7-11 coffee club card, social security card and anything else you won't need at home. The only thing in your wallet you'll want is a student ID, and if you lose your wallet you'll be grateful you left the rest at home.
- ✗ Illegal drugs. You didn't need us to tell you that, did you?
- ✗ Stickers and little toys for kids. Some tourists like to hand them out, which means the children pester every foreigner they see.
- ✗ Really nice clothes or shoes, unless you're planning on going to a special event or dining out a lot.

APPENDIX

Useful Spanish Phrases

Conversational

Hello	Hola
Good morning	Buenos días
Good afternoon	Buenas tardes
Good evening	Buenas noches
Yes	Sí
No	No
Please	Por favor
Thank you	Gracias
It was nothing	De nada
Excuse me	Permiso
See you later	Hasta luego
Bye	Chao
Cool	Bacán
How are you (formal)	¿Cómo está?
" " (informal)	¿Qué tal?
I don't understand	No entiendo.
Do you speak English?	¿Habla inglés?
I don't speak Spanish.	No hablo español.
I'm from England	Soy de Inglaterra
" " the USA	Soy de los Estados Unidos.

Health/Emergency

Call....	¡Llame a...!
an ambulance	una ambulancia
a doctor	un médico
the police	la policía
It's an emergency.	Es una emergencia.
I'm sick	Estoy enfermo/a
I need a doctor	Necesito un médico.
Where's the hospital?	¿Dónde está el hospital?
I'm allergic to...	Soy alérgico/a a
antibiotics	los antibióticos.
penicillin	penicilina
peanuts	maní
shellfish	los mariscos
milk	leche
eggs	huevos
wheat	trigo

Getting Around

Where is...?	¿Dónde está...?
the bus station	la estación de bus?
a bank	un banco
an ATM	un cajero automático
the bathroom	el baño
Where does the bus leave from?	¿De dónde sale el bus/colectivo?
Left, right, straight	Izquierda, derecha, directo.
One city block	Una cuadra
Ticket	Boleto

Accommodation

Where is a hotel?	¿Donde hay un hotel?
I want a room.	Quiero una habitación.
Single / Double / Marriage	Simple / Doble / Matrimonial
How much does it cost per night?	¿Cuanto cuesta por una noche?
Does that include breakfast?	¿Incluye el desayuno?
Does that include taxes?	¿Incluye los impuestos?
Is there 24-hour hot water?	¿Hay agua caliente veinticuatro horas al día?

INDEX

INDEX

INDEX

Get these other guidebooks before your trip!

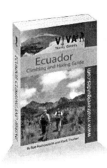